Collins *Gem*

Latin
Dictionary

Latin ▸ English English ▸ Latin

Collins Gem

An Imprint of HarperCollinsPublishers

first published in this edition 1957
second edition 1996

© William Collins Sons & Co. Ltd. 1957
© HarperCollins Publishers 1996

latest reprint 2001

ISBN 0-00-470763-X

Professor D A Kidd
Canterbury University

Editor
Joyce Littlejohn

editorial staff
Ian Brookes
Denis Bruce, Michael D Igoe

A catalogue record for this book is
available from the British Library

Typeset by Tradespools Ltd, Frome, Somerset

*Printed and bound in Great Britain by
Omnia Books Ltd, Glasgow, G64*

CONTENTS

INTRODUCTION

Whether you are learning Latin for the first time or wish to "brush up" what you learned some time ago, this dictionary is designed to help you understand Latin and to express yourself in Latin, if you so wish.

HOW TO USE THE DICTIONARY

Headword

This is shown in **bold type**. On the Latin-English side all long vowels are shown by placing a ‾ above them. Latin nouns show the genitive singular form in bold. Latin verbs show the first person singular of the present indicative as the headword, followed by the infinitive, the first person singular of the perfect indicative and usually the past participle, all in bold type:

elegīa, -ae
elementum, -ī
ēlevō, āre
ēmātūrēscō, -ēscere, -uī

Part of Speech

Next comes the part of speech (noun, verb, adjective etc), shown in *italics*. Part of speech abbreviations used in the dictionary are shown in the abbreviations list (*p vii*). Where a word has more than one part of speech, each new part of speech is preceded by a black lozenge (♦). If a Latin headword is a preposition, the case taken by the preposition comes immediately after the part of speech, in *italics* and in brackets.

era, -ae *f*
ticklish *adj*
thunder *n* tonitrus *m* ♦ *vi* tonare, intonare.
ērgā *prep* (*with acc*) towards; against.

iv

Meanings

Where a word or a part of speech has only one meaning, the translation comes immediately after the part of speech. However, many words have more than one meaning. Where the context is likely to show which translation is correct, variations in meaning are simply separated by a semi-colon. But usually there will also be an "indicator" in *italics* and in brackets. Some meanings relate to specific subject areas, for example religion, politics, military matters etc – these indicators are in small italic capitals.

ēnsiger, -ī *adj* with his sword.
toy *n* crepundia *ntpl* ♦ *vi* ludere.
toll collector *n* exactor *m*; portitor *m*.
eō, -īre, īvī and **iī, itum** *vi* to go; (*MIL*) to march; (*time*) to pass; (*event*) to proceed, turn out.

Translations

Most words can be translated directly. On the English-Latin side, translations of nouns include the gender of the Latin noun in *italics*. However, sometimes a phrase is needed to show how a word is used, but in some cases a direct translation of a phrase would be meaningless: the symbol ~ in front of a translation shows that the translation is natural English, but does not mean word for word what the Latin means. Sometimes, even an approximate translation would not be very helpful (for place names, for example) – in these cases, an explanation in *italics* is given instead. In other cases, the user will need more information than simply the translation; in these cases, "indicators" are included in the translation(s), giving, for instance, the case required by a Latin verb or preposition or further details about a place or person.

thumb *n* pollex *m*; **have under one's ~** in potestate sua habere.
elephantomacha, -ae *m fighter mounted on an elephant.*

v

Erymanthus, -i *m* mountain range in Arcadia (*where Hercules killed the bear*).

thwart *vt* obstare (*dat*), officere (*dat*).

Pronunciation

Since Latin pronunciation is regular, once the basic rules have been learned (*see pp xi–xiii*), the dictionary does not show phonetic transcriptions against each headword, but does show all long vowels.

Other Information

The dictionary also includes:

- a basic grammar section
- information about life in Roman times:
  – how numbers and dates were calculated and expressed – geographical names – key events in Roman history – (*important historical and mythological characters and events are listed within the body of the main text*).
- a section on Latin poetry and scansion

ABBREVIATIONS

abl	ablative	**m**	masculine
acc	accusative	**MATH**	mathematics
adj	adjective	**MED**	medicine
adv	adverb	**MIL**	military
AGR	agriculture	**mod**	modern
ARCH	architecture	**n**	noun
art	article	**NAUT**	nautical
ASTRO	astronomy	**neg**	negative
AUG	augury	**nom**	nominative
CIRCS	circumstances	**nt**	neuter
COMM	business	**num**	numeral
compar	comparative	**occ**	occasionally
conj	conjunction	**p**	participle
cpd	compound	**pass**	passive
dat	dative	**perf**	perfect
defec	defective	**perh**	perhaps
ECCL	ecclesiastical	**pers**	person
esp	especially	**PHILOS**	philosophy
excl	exclamatory	**pl**	plural
f	feminine	**POL**	politics
fig	figurative	**ppa**	perfect participle active
fut	future		
gen	genitive	**ppp**	perfect participle passive
GEOG	geography		
GRAM	grammar	**prep**	preposition
imperf	imperfect	**pres**	present
impers	impersonal	**pron**	pronoun
impv	imperative	**prop**	properly
indecl	indeclinable	**PROV**	proverb
indic	indicative	**relat**	relative
inf	informal	**RHET**	rhetoric
infin	infinitive	**sg**	singular
interj	interjection	**sim**	similarly
interrog	interrogative	**subj**	subjunctive
LIT	literature	**superl**	superlative
loc	locative	**THEAT**	theatre

UNIV	university	voc	vocative
usu	usually	vt	transitive verb
vi	intransitive verb		

LATIN ABBREVIATIONS

A.	Aulus; (*vote: against a bill*) antīquō; (*verdict*) absolvō.	Mam.	Mamericus.
		n.	nepōs.
		non.	Nōnās, Nōnīs.
a.d.	ante diem.	Num.	Numerius.
a.u.c.	annō urbis conditae.	P.	Pūblius.
C	centum.	P.C.	Patrēs cōnscrīptī.
C.	Gāius; (*verdict*) condemnō.	P.M.	Pontifex Māximus.
		P.P.	Pater Patriae.
Cn.	Gnaius.	Pr.	Praetōr(ēs).
D	quīngentī.	P.R.	Populus Rōmānus.
D.	Decimus; (*before dates in letters*) dabam.	R.	Rōmānus.
		R.P.	Rēs pūblica.
		Q.	Quaestor; Quīntus.
D.D.	dōnō decit.	S.	Sextus.
D.D.D.	dat, dicat, dēdicat.	S.C.	Senātus cōnsultum.
D.O.M.	Deō Optimō Māximō.	s.d.	salūtem dīcit.
		Ser.	Servius.
f.	fīlius.	Sex.	Sextus.
HS	sēstertiī, sēstertia.	Sp.	Spurius.
Id.	Īdus, Īdibus.	s.p.d.	salūtem plūrinam dīcit
Imp.	Imperator.		
I.O.M.	Iovī Optimō Māximō.	S.P.Q.R.	Senātus Populusque Rōmānus.
K.	Kaesō.	T.	Titus.
Kal.	Kalendas, Kalendīs.	Ti.	Tiberius.
L	quīnquāgintā.	Tr.	Tribūnus.
L.	Lūcius.	T.P.	Tribūnicia potestās.
M	mīlle.	V	quīnque.
M.	Marcus.	X	decem.
M'.	Manius.		

LATIN ALPHABET

The Latin alphabet is the one which has been almost universally adopted by the modern languages of Europe and America. In the Classical period it had 23 letters, namely the English alphabet without letters **j**, **v** and **w**.

Letter v

The symbol **v** was the capital form of the letter **u**, but in a later age the small **v** came into use to represent the consonantal **u**, and as it is commonly so employed in modern editions of Latin authors, it has been retained as a distinct letter in this dictionary for convenience.

Letter j

The symbol **j** came to be used as the consonantal **i**, and is found in older editions of the Classics, but as it has been almost entirely discarded in modern texts, it is not used in this dictionary, and words found spelt with a **j** must therefore be looked up under **i**.

Letters w, y, z

The letter **w** may be seen in the Latinized forms of some modern names, *e.g.* **Westmonasterium**, Westminster. The letters **y** and **z** occur only in words of Greek origin.

ORTHOGRAPHY

Many Latin words which begin with a prefix can be spelled in two ways. The prefix can retain its original spelling, or it can be assimilated, changing a letter depending on the letter which follows it. Compare the following:

ad before **g, l, r** and **p**:

adpropinquare	appropinquare
adgredi	aggredi
adloquor	alloquor
adrogans	arrogans

ad is also often assimilated before **f** and **n**:

adfectus	affectus
adnexus	annexus

and **ad** is often shortened to **a** before **sc**:

adscendere	ascendere

in changes to **il** before **l**, to **im** before **m** or **p** and to **ir** before **r**.

con becomes **cor** when followed by another **r** and **col** when followed by **l**.

We have provided cross-references in the text to draw your attention to the alternative forms of words. Thus, although **arrogantia** does not appear in the Latin-English section, the cross-reference at **arr-** will point you to the entry for **adrogantia**, where the translation is given.

PRONUNCIATION

The ancient pronunciation of Latin has been established with a fair degree of certainty from the evidence of ancient authorities and inscriptions and inferences from the modern Romance languages. It is not possible, of course, to recapture the precise nuances of Classical Latin speech, but what follows is now generally accepted and generally understood as a reasonably accurate guide to the sounds of Latin as spoken by educated Romans during the two centuries from Cicero to Quintilian.

ACCENT

The Latin accent in the Classical period was a weak stress, perhaps with an element of pitch in it. It falls, as in English, on the second last syllable of the word, if that syllable is long, and on the third last syllable if the second last is short. Disyllabic words take the accent on the first syllable, unless they have already lost a final syllable, *e.g.* illíc(e).

Inflected words are commonly learned with the accent wrongly placed on the last syllable, for convenience in memorizing the inflexions. But it is advisable to get the accent as well as the ending right.

The correct accent of other words can easily be found by noting carefully the quantity of the second last syllable and then accenting the word as in English, according to the rule given above. Thus fuḗrunt is accented on the second last syllable because the **e** is long, whereas **fúerant** is accented on the third last, because the **e** is short.

VOWELS

Vowels are pure and should not be diphthongized as in certain sounds of Southern English. They may be long or short. Throughout this Dictionary all vowels known or believed by the best authorities to be long are marked with a line above them; those unmarked are either known to be short or of uncertain quantity.

Short		Long	
agricolā	rat	rāmus	rather
hedera	pen	avē	pay
itaque	kin	cīvis	keen
favor	rob	ampliō	robe
nebula	full	lūna	fool

y is a Greek sound and is pronounced (both short and long) as u in French *ie* rue.

DIPHTHONGS

aestas	try	
audiō	town	
hei	payee	
meus	ay-oo	with the accent on first sound
moecha	toy	
tuitus	Louis	

CONSONANTS

balneae	baby	
abstēmius	apse	
subtractus	apt	
castra	car	
chorda	sepulchre	
interdo	dog	
cōnflō	fortune	
ingredior	go	
habeō	hand	(but faintly)
iaceo	yes	(consonantal i = j)
Kalendae	oak	
congelō	let	

xii

co<u>m</u>es	<u>m</u>an	(*final m was hardly sounded and may have simply nasalized the preceding vowel*)
pā<u>n</u>is	<u>n</u>o	
pa<u>ng</u>o	fi<u>ng</u>er	
stu<u>p</u>eō	a<u>p</u>t	
ra<u>ph</u>anus	<u>p</u>ill	
exse<u>qu</u>or	<u>qu</u>ite	
su<u>pr</u>ēmus	<u>br</u>ae	(*Scottish*)
mā<u>gnus</u>	<u>s</u>ister	(*never as in rose*)
lae<u>t</u>us	s<u>t</u>op	
<u>th</u>eātrum	<u>t</u>ake	
<u>v</u>apor	<u>w</u>in	
	(*and consonantal u*)	
de<u>x</u>tra	si<u>x</u>	(*ks, not gs*)
<u>z</u>ōna	<u>z</u>ero	

Double consonants lengthen the sound of the consonant.

LATIN – ENGLISH

A

ā *prep (with abl)* from; after; since; by, in respect of; **ab epistulīs,** ā **manū** secretary; **ab hāc parte** on this side; **ab integrō** afresh; ā **nōbīs** on our side; ā **tergō** in the rear; **copiōsus ab frūmentō** rich in corn; **usque ab** ever since.

ā *interj* ah!

ab *prep see* ā.

abāctus *ppp of* abigō.

abacus, -ī *m* tray; sideboard; gaming board; panel; counting table.

abaliēnō, -āre, -āvī, -ātum *vt* to dispose of; to remove, estrange.

Abantiadēs *m* Acrisius *or* Perseus.

Abās, -antis *m* a king of Argos.

abavus, -ī *m* great-great-grandfather.

abbās, -ātis *m* abbot.

abbātia *f* abbey.

abbātissa *f* abbess.

Abdēra, -ōrum *or* **ae** *ntpl or fs a* town in Thrace.

Abdērītānus *adj see n.*

Abdērītēs *m* Democritus *or* Protagoras.

abdicātiō, -ōnis *f* disowning, abdication.

abdicō, -āre, -āvī, -ātum *vt* to disown; to resign; **sē ~** abdicate.

abdīcō, -icere, -īxī, -ictum *vt* (AUG) to be unfavourable to.

abditus *ppp of* abdō.

abdō, -ere, -idī, -itum *vt* to hide; to remove.

abdōmen, -inis *nt* paunch, belly; gluttony.

abdūcō, -ūcere, -ūxī, -uctum *vt* to

lead away, take away; to seduce.

abductus *ppp of* abdūcō.

abecedārium, -īī *nt* alphabet.

abēgī *perf of* abigō.

abeō, -īre, -īī, -itum *vi* to go away, depart; to pass away; to be changed; to retire (*from an office*); **sīc ~** turn out like this.

abequitō, -āre, -āvī, -ātum *vi* to ride away.

aberrātiō, -ōnis *f* relief (*from trouble*).

aberrō, -āre, -āvī, -ātum *vi* to stray; to deviate; to have respite.

abfore *fut infin of* absum.

abfuī *perf of* absum.

abfutūrus *fut p of* absum.

abhinc *adv* since, ago.

abhorreō, -ēre, -uī *vi* to shrink from; to differ; to be inconsistent.

abiciō, -icere, -iēcī, -iectum *vt* to throw away, throw down; to abandon, degrade.

abiectus *ppp of* abiciō ◆ *adj* despondent; contemptible.

ablēgnus *adj* of fir.

abiēns, -euntis *pres p of* abeō.

abiēs, -etis *f* fir; ship.

abigō, -igere, -ēgī, -āctum *vt* to drive away.

abitus, -ūs *m* departure; exit.

abiūdicō, -āre, -āvī, -ātum *vt* to take away (*by judicial award*).

abiūnctus *ppp of* abiungō.

abiungō, -ungere, -ūnxī, -ūnctum *vt* to unyoke; to detach.

abiūrō, -āre, -āvī, -ātum *vt* to deny on oath.

ablātus *ppp of* auferō.

The present infinitive verb endings are as follows: -āre = 1st; -ēre = 2nd; -ere = 3rd and -īre = 4th. See sections on irregular verbs and noun declensions.

ablēgātiō, **-ōnis** f sending away.

ablēgō, **-āre**, **-āvī**, **-ātum** vt to send out of the way.

abligurriō, **-īre**, **-īvī**, **-ītum** vt to spend extravagantly.

ablocō, **-āre**, **-āvī**, **-ātum** vt to let (a house).

ablūdō, **-dere**, **-sī**, **-sum** vi to be unlike.

abluō, **-uere**, **-uī**, **-ūtum** vt to wash clean; to remove.

abnegō, **-āre**, **-āvī**, **-ātum** vt to refuse.

abnepōs, **-ōtis** m great-great-grandson.

abneptis f great-great-granddaughter.

abnoctō, **-āre** vi to stay out all night.

abnōrmis adj unorthodox.

abnuō, **-uere**, **-uī**, **-ūtum** vt to refuse; to deny.

aboleō, **-ēre**, **-ēvī**, **-itum** vt to abolish.

abolēscō, **-ēscere**, **-ēvī** vi to vanish.

abolitiō, **-ōnis** f cancelling.

abolla, **-ae** f greatcoat.

abōminātus adj accursed.

abōminor, **-ārī**, **-ātus** vt to deprecate; to detest.

Aborīginēs, **-um** mpl original inhabitants.

aborior, **-īrī**, **-tus** vi to miscarry.

abortiō, **-ōnis** f miscarriage.

abortīvus adj born prematurely.

abortus, **-ūs** m miscarriage.

abrādō, **-dere**, **-sī**, **-sum** vt to scrape off, shave.

abrāsus ppp of **abrādō**.

abreptus ppp of **abripiō**.

abripiō, **-ipere**, **-ipuī**, **-eptum** vt to drag away, carry off.

abrogātiō, **-ōnis** f repeal.

abrogō, **-āre**, **-āvī**, **-ātum** vt to annul.

abrotonum, **-ī** nt southernwood.

abrumpō, **-umpere**, **-ūpī**, **-uptum** vt to break off.

abruptus ppp of **abrumpō** ♦ adj steep; abrupt, disconnected.

abs etc see **ā**.

abscēdō, **-ēdere**, **-essī**, **-essum** vi to depart, withdraw; to cease.

abscīdō, **-dere**, **-dī**, **-sum** vt to cut off.

abscindō, **-ndere**, **-dī**, **-ssum** vt to tear off, cut off.

abscissus ppp of **abscindō**.

abscīsus ppp of **abscīdō** ♦ adj steep; abrupt.

abscondō, **-ere**, **-ī** and **idī**, **-itum** vt to conceal; to leave behind.

absēns, **-entis** pres p of **absum** ♦ adj absent.

absentia, **-ae** f absence.

absiliō, **-īre**, **-īī** and **uī** vi to spring away.

absimilis adj unlike.

absinthium, **-ī** and **iī** nt wormwood.

absis, **-īdis** f vault; (ECCL) chancel.

absistō, **-istere**, **-titī** vi to come away; to desist.

absolūtē adv fully, unrestrictedly.

absolūtiō, **-ōnis** f acquittal; perfection.

absolūtus ppp of **absolvō** ♦ adj complete; (RHET) unqualified.

absolvō, **-vere**, **-vī**, **-ūtum** vt to release, set free; (law) to acquit; to bring to completion, finish off; to pay off, discharge.

absonus adj unmusical; incongruous; **~ ab** not in keeping with.

absorbeō, **-bēre**, **-buī**, **-ptum** vt to swallow up; to monopolize.

absp- etc see **asp-**.

absque prep (with abl) without, but for.

abstēmius adj temperate.

abstergeō, **-gēre**, **-sī**, **-sum** vt to wipe away; (fig) to banish.

absterreō, **-ēre**, **-uī**, **-itum** vt to

scare away, deter.

abstinēns, -entis adj continent.

abstinenter adv with restraint.

abstinentia, -ae f restraint, self-control; fasting.

abstineō, -inēre, -inuī, -entum vt to withhold, keep off ♦ vi to abstain, refrain; **sē ~** refrain.

abstitī perf of **absistō**.

abstō, -āre vi to stand aloof.

abstractus ppp of **abstrahō**.

abstrahō, -here, -xī, -ctum vt to drag away, remove; to divert.

abstrūdō, -dere, -sī, -sum vt to conceal.

abstrūsus ppp of **abstrūdō** ♦ adj deep, abstruse; reserved.

abstulī perf of **auferō**.

absum, abesse, āfuī vi to be away, absent, distant; to keep clear of; to be different; to be missing, fail to assist; **tantum abest ut** so far from; **haud multum āfuit quīn** I was (they were etc) within an ace of.

absūmō, -ere, -psī, -ptum vt to consume; to ruin, kill; (time) to spend.

absurdē adv out of tune; absurdly.

absurdus adj unmusical; senseless, absurd.

Absyrtus, -ī m brother of Medea.

abundāns, -antis adj overflowing; abundant; rich; abounding in.

abundanter adv copiously.

abundantia, -ae f abundance, plenty; wealth.

abundē adv abundantly, more than enough.

abundō, -āre, -āvī, -ātum vi to overflow; to abound, be rich in.

abūsiō, -ōnis f (RHET) catachresis.

abusque prep (with abl) all the way from.

abūtor, -tī, -sus vi (with abl) to use

up; to misuse.

Abȳdēnus adj see n.

Abȳdos, Abȳdus, -ī m a town on Dardanelles.

ac etc see **atque**.

Acadēmīa, -ae f Plato's Academy at Athens; Plato's philosophy; Cicero's villa.

Acadēmica ntpl Cicero's book on the Academic philosophy.

Acadēmus, -ī m an Athenian hero.

acalanthis, -dis f thistlefinch.

acanthus, -ī m bear's-breech.

Acarnānes, -um mpl the Acarnanians.

Acarnānia, -iae f a district of N.W. Greece.

Acarnānicus adj see n.

Acca Lārentia, -ae, -ae f Roman goddess.

accēdō, -ēdere, -essī, -essum vi to come, go to, approach; to attack; to be added; to agree with; (duty) to take up; **ad rem pūblicam ~** to enter politics; **prope ~ ad** to resemble; **~ēdit quod, hūc ~ēdit ut** moreover.

accelerō, -āre, -āvī, -ātum vt, vi to hasten.

accendō, -endere, -endī, -ēnsum vt to set on fire, light; to illuminate; (fig) to inflame, incite.

accēnseō, -ēre, -uī, -um vt to assign.

accēnsī mpl (MIL) supernumeraries.

accēnsus ppp of **accendō** and **accēnseō**.

accēnsus, -ī m officer attending a magistrate.

accentus, -ūs m accent.

accēpī perf of **accipiō**.

acceptiō, -ōnis f receiving.

acceptum nt credit side (of ledger); **in ~ referre** place to one's credit.

The present infinitive verb endings are as follows: -āre = 1st; -ēre = 2nd; -ere = 3rd and -īre = 4th. See sections on irregular verbs and noun declensions.

acceptus ppp of **accipiō** ♦ adj acceptable.

accersō etc see **accessō**.

accessiō, **-ōnis** f coming, visiting; attack; increase, addition.

accessus, **-ūs** m approach, visit; flood tide; admittance, entrance.

Acciānus adj see **Accius**.

accidō, **-dere**, **-dī**, **-sum** vt to fell, cut into; to eat up, impair.

accidō, **-ere**, **-ī** vi to fall (at, on); (senses) to strike; (usu misfortune) to befall, happen.

accingō, **-gere**, **-xī**, **-ctum** vt to gird on, arm; (fig) to make ready.

acciō, **-īre**, **-īvī**, **-ītum** vt to summon; to procure.

accipiō, **-ipere**, **-ēpī**, **-eptum** vt to take, receive, accept; (guest) to treat; (information) to hear; to interpret, take as; to suffer; to approve.

accipiter, **-ris** m hawk.

accisus ppp of **accidō**.

accītus ppp of **acciō**.

accītus, **-ūs** m summons.

Accius, **-ī** m Roman tragic poet.

acclāmātiō, **-ōnis** f shout (of approval or disapproval).

acclāmō, **-āre**, **-āvī**, **-ātum** vi to cry out against; to hail.

acclārō, **-āre**, **-āvī**, **-ātum** vt to make known.

acclīnātus adj sloping.

acclīnis adj leaning against; inclined.

acclīnō, **-āre**, **-āvī**, **-ātum** vt to lean against; **sē ~** incline towards.

acclīvis adj uphill.

acclīvitās, **-ātis** f gradient.

accola, **-ae** m neighbour.

accolō, **-olere**, **-oluī**, **-ultum** vt to live near.

accommodātē adv suitably.

accommodātiō, **-ōnis** f fitting together; compliance.

accommodātus adj suited.

accommodō, **-āre**, **-āvī**, **-ātum** vt to fit, put on; to adjust, adapt, bring to; to apply; **sē ~** devote oneself.

accommodus adj suitable.

accrēdō, **-ere**, **-idī**, **-itum** vi to believe.

accrēscō, **-ēscere**, **-ēvī**, **-ētum** vi to increase, be added.

accrētiō, **-ōnis** f increasing.

accubitiō, **-ōnis** f reclining (at meals).

accubō, **-āre** vi to lie near; to recline (at meals).

accumbō, **-mbere**, **-buī**, **-bitum** vi to recline at table; **in sinū ~** sit next to.

accumulātē adv copiously.

accumulō, **-āre**, **-āvī**, **-ātum** vt to pile up, amass; to load.

accūrātē adv painstakingly.

accūrātiō, **-ōnis** f exactness.

accūrātus adj studied.

accūrō, **-āre**, **-āvī**, **-ātum** vt to attend to.

accurrō, **-rrere**, **-currī** and **rrī**, **-rsum** vi to hurry to.

accursus, **-ūs** m hurrying.

accūsābilis adj reprehensible.

accūsātiō, **-ōnis** f accusation.

accūsātor, **-ōris** m accuser, prosecutor.

accūsātōriē adv like an accuser.

accūsātōrius adj of the accuser.

accūsō, **-āre**, **-āvī**, **-ātum** vt to accuse, prosecute; to reproach; **ambitūs ~** prosecute for bribery.

acer, **-is** nt maple.

ācer, **-ris** adj sharp; (sensation) keen, pungent; (emotion) violent; (mind) shrewd; (conduct) eager, brave; hasty, fierce; (circumstances) severe.

acerbē adv see **acerbus**.

acerbitās, **-ātis** f bitterness; (fig) harshness, severity; sorrow.

acerbō, **-āre**, **-āvī**, **-ātum** vt to

aggravate.

acerbus adj bitter, sour; harsh; (fig) premature; (person) rough, morose, violent; (things) troublesome, sad.

acernus adj of maple.

acerra, -ae f incense box.

acervātim adv in heaps.

acervō, -āre, -āvī, -ātum vt to pile up.

acervus, -ī m heap.

acēscō, -ere, acuī vt to turn sour.

Acestēs, -ae m a mythical Sicilian.

acētum, -ī nt vinegar; (fig) wit.

Achaemenēs, -is m first Persian king, type of Oriental wealth.

Achaeus adj Greek.

Achāia, -ae f a district in W. Greece; Greece; Roman province.

Achāicus adj see n.

Achātēs, -ae m companion of Aeneas.

Achelōius adj see n.

Achelōus, -ī m river in N.W. Greece; river god.

Acherōn, -ontis m river in Hades.

Acherūsius adj see Acherōn.

Achillēs, -is m Greek epic hero.

Achillēus adj see n.

Achīvus adj Greek.

Acīdālia, -ae f Venus.

Acīdalius adj see n.

acidus adj sour, tart; (fig) disagreeable.

aciēs, -ēī f sharp edge or point; (eye) sight, keen glance, pupil; (mind) power, apprehension; (MIL) line of troops, battle order, army, battle; (fig) debate; **prīma ~** van; **novissima ~** rearguard.

acinacēs, -is m scimitar.

acinum, -ī nt berry, grape; fruit seed.

acinus, -ī m berry, grape; fruit seed.

acipēnser, -eris m sturgeon.

acipēnsis, -is m sturgeon.

aclys, -dis f javelin.

aconītum, -ī nt monkshood; poison.

acor, -ōris m sour taste.

acquiēscō, -ēscere, -ēvī, -ētum vi to rest, die; to find pleasure (in); to acquiesce.

acquīrō, -rere, -sīvī, -sītum vt to get in addition, acquire.

Acragās, -antis m 300 Agrigentum.

acrātophorum, -ī nt wine jar.

acrēdula, -ae f a bird (unidentified).

acriculus adj peevish.

acrimōnia, -ae f pungent taste; (speech, action) briskness, go.

Acrisiōniadēs, -ae m Perseus.

Acrisius, -ī m father of Danae.

acriter adv see acer.

acroāma, -tis nt entertainment, entertainer.

acroāsis, -is f public lecture.

Acroceraunia, -ōrum ntpl a promontory in N.W. Greece.

Acrocorinthus, -ī f fortress of Corinth.

acta, -ae f beach.

ācta, -ōrum ntpl public records, proceedings; **~ diurna, ~ pūblica** daily gazette.

Actaeus adj Athenian.

āctiō, -ōnis f action, doing; official duties, negotiations; (law) action, suit, indictment, pleading, case, trial; (RHET) delivery; (drama) plot; **~ grātiārum** expression of thanks, **~ōnem intendere, īnstituere** bring an action.

āctitō, -āre, -āvī, -ātum vt to plead, act often.

Actium, -ī and iī nt a town in N.W. Greece; Augustus's great victory.

Actius, -iacus adj see n.

āctivus adj of action, practical.

The present infinitive verb endings are as follows: **-āre** = 1st; **-ēre** = 2nd; **-ere** = 3rd and **-īre** = 4th. *See sections on irregular verbs and noun declensions.*

āctor, -ōris m driver, performer; (*law*) plaintiff, pleader; (*COMM*) agent; (*RHET*) orator; (*drama*) actor; ~ **pūblicus** manager of public property; ~ **summārum** cashier.

āctuāria f pinnace.

āctuāriolum, -ī nt small barge.

āctuārius adj fast (ship).

āctuōsē adv actively.

āctuōsus adj very active.

āctus ppp of **agō**.

āctus, -ūs m moving, driving; right of way for cattle or vehicles; performance; (*drama*) playing a part, recital, act of a play.

āctūtum adv immediately.

acuī perf of **acēscō**; perf of **acuō**.

acula, -ae f small stream.

aculeātus adj prickly; (*words*) stinging; quibbling.

aculeus, -ī m sting, prickle barb; (*fig*) sting.

acūmen, -inis nt point, sting; (*fig*) shrewdness, ingenuity; trickery.

acuō, -uere, -uī, -ūtum vt to sharpen; to exercise; (*the mind*) to stimulate; to rouse (to action).

acus, -ūs f needle, pin; **acū pingere** embroider; **rem acū tangere** ≈ hit the nail on the head.

acūtē adv see **acūtus**.

acūtulus adj rather subtle.

acūtus adj sharp, pointed; (*senses*) keen; (*sound*) high-pitched; severe; intelligent.

ad prep (with acc) to, towards, against; near, at; until; (*num*) about; with regard to, according to; for the purpose of, for; compared with; besides; **ad Castoris** to the temple of Castor; **ad dextram** on the right; **ad hōc** besides; **ad locum** on the spot; **ad manum** at hand; **ad rem** to the point; **ad summam** in short; **ad tempus** in time; **ad ūnum omnes** all without exception; **ad urbem**

esse wait outside the city gates; **ad verbum** literally; **nīl ad** nothing to do with; **usque ad** right up to.

adāctiō, -ōnis f enforcing.

adāctus ppp of **adigō**.

adāctus, -ūs m snapping (*of teeth*).

adaequē adv equally.

adaequō, -āre, -āvī, -ātum vt to make equal, level; to equal, match ♦ vi to be equal.

adamantēus, adamantinus adj see **adamās**.

adamās, -antis m adamant, steel; diamond.

adamō, -āre, -āvī, -ātum vt to fall in love with.

adaperiō, -īre, -uī, -tum vt to throw open.

adapertilis adj openable.

adaquō, -āre, -āvī, -ātum vt (*plants, animals*) to water.

adaquor vi to fetch water.

adauctus, -ūs m growing.

adaugeō, -gēre, -xī, -ctum vt to aggravate; (*sacrifice*) to consecrate.

adaugēscō, -ere vi to grow bigger.

adbibō, -ere, -ī vt to drink; (*fig*) to drink in.

adbītō, -ere vi to come near.

adc- etc see **acc-**.

addecet, -ēre vt it becomes.

addēnseō, -ēre vt to close (ranks).

addīcō, -īcere, -īxī, -ictum vi (*AUG*) to be favourable ♦ vt (*law*) to award; (*auction*) to knock down; (*fig*) to sacrifice, devote.

addictiō, -ōnis f award (*at law*).

addictus ppp of **addīcō** ♦ m bondsman.

addiscō, -scere, -dicī vt to learn more.

additāmentum, -ī nt increase.

additus ppp of **addō**.

addō, -ere, -idī, -itum vt to add, put to, bring to; to impart; to increase; **~ gradum** quicken pace; **~e quod** besides.

addoceō, -ēre, -uī, -tum *vt* to teach new.

addubitō, -āre, -āvī, -ātum *vi* to be in doubt ♦ *vt* to question.

addūcō, -ūcere, -ūxī, -uctum *vt* to take, bring to; to draw together, pull taut, wrinkle; (*fig*) to induce; (*pass*) to be led to believe.

adductus *ppp of* **addūcō** ♦ *adj* contracted; (*fig*) severe.

adedō, -edere, -ēdī, -ēsum *vt* to begin to eat; to eat up; to use up; to wear away.

adēmī *perf of* **adimō**.

ademptiō, -ōnis *f* taking away.

ademptus *ppp of* **adimō**.

adeō, -īre, -iī, -itum *vt, vi* to go to, approach; to address; to undertake, submit to, enter upon.

adeō *adv* so; (*after pron*) just; (*after conj, adv, adj: for emphasis*) indeed, very; (*adding an explanation*) for, in fact, thus; or rather; **~ nōn ... ut** so far from; **atque ~, sīve ~** or rather; **usque ~** so far, so long, so much.

adeps, -ipis *m/f* fat; corpulence.

adeptiō, -ōnis *f* attainment.

adeptus *ppa of* **adipīscor**.

adequitō, -āre, -āvī, -ātum *vi* to ride up (to).

adesdum come here!

adesse *infin of* **adsum**.

adēsus *ppp of* **adedō**.

adfābilis *adj* easy to talk to.

adfābilitās, -ātis *f* courtesy.

adfabrē *adv* ingeniously.

adfatim *adv* to one's satisfaction, enough, ad nauseam.

adfātur, -rī, -tus *vt* (*defec*) to speak to.

adfātus *ppa of* **adfātur**.

adfātus, -ūs *m* speaking to.

adfectātiō, -ōnis *f* aspiring; (*RHET*) affectation.

adfectātus *adj* (*RHET*) studied.

adfectiō, -ōnis *f* frame of mind, mood; disposition; goodwill; (*ASTRO*) relative position.

adfectō, -āre, -āvī, -ātum *vt* to aspire to, aim at; to try to win over; to try to make pretence of; **viam ~ ad** try to get to.

adfectus *ppp of* **adficiō** ♦ *adj* affected with, experienced (*abl*); (*person*) disposed; (*things*) weakened; (*undertakings*) well-advanced.

adfectus, -ūs *m* disposition, mood; fondness; (*pl*) loved ones.

adferō, adferre, attulī, adlātum *and* **allātum** *vt* to bring, carry to; to bring to bear, use against; to bring news; (*explanation*) to bring forward; to contribute (*something useful*).

adficiō, -icere, -ēcī, -ectum *vt* to affect; to endow, afflict with (*abl*); **exsiliō ~** banish; **honōre ~** honour; *also used with other nouns to express the corresponding verbs*.

adfictus *ppp of* **adfingō**.

adfigō, -gere, -xī, -xum *vt* to fasten, attach; to impress (*on the mind*).

adfingō, -ngere, -nxī, -ctum *vt* to make, form (*as part of*); to invent.

adfinis, -is *m/f* neighbour; relation (*by marriage*) ♦ *adj* neighbouring; associated with (*dat or gen*).

adfinitās, -ātis *f* relationship (*by marriage*).

adfirmātē *adv* with assurance.

adfirmātiō, -ōnis *f* declaration.

adfirmō, -āre, -āvī, -ātum *vt* to declare; to confirm.

adfixus *ppp of* **adfigō**.

adflātus, -ūs *m* breath, exhalation.

The present infinitive verb endings are as follows: -āre = 1st; -ēre = 2nd; -ere = 3rd and -īre = 4th. See sections on irregular verbs and noun declensions.

(fig) inspiration.

adfleō, **-ēre** *vi* to weep (at).

adflīctātiō, **-ōnis** *f* suffering.

adflīctō, **-āre**, **-āvī**, **-ātum** *vt* to harass, distress.

adflīctor, **-ōris** *m* destroyer.

adflīctus *ppp of* **adflīgō** ♦ *adj* distressed, ruined; dejected; depraved.

adflīgō, **-īgere**, **-īxī**, **-īctum** *vt* to dash against, throw down; *(fig)* to impair, crush.

adflō, **-āre**, **-āvī**, **-ātum** *vt*, *vi* to blow on, breathe upon.

adfluēns, **-entis** *adj* rich (in).

adfluenter *adv* copiously.

adfluentia, **-ae** *f* abundance.

adfluō, **-ere**, **-xī**, **-xum** *vi* to flow; *(fig)* to flock in, abound in.

adfore *fut infin of* **adsum**.

adforem *imperf subj of* **adsum**.

adfuī *perf of* **adsum**.

adfulgeō, **-gēre**, **-sī** *vi* to shine on; to appear.

adfundō, **-undere**, **-ūdī**, **-ūsum** *vt* to pour in; to rush (troops) to.

adfūsus *adj* prostrate.

adfutūrus *fut p of* **adsum**.

adgemō, **-ere** *vi* to groan at.

adglomerō, **-āre** *vt* to add on.

adglūtinō, **-āre** *vt* to stick on.

adgravēscō, **-ere** *vi* to become worse.

adgravō, **-āre**, **-āvī**, **-ātum** *vt* to aggravate.

adgredior, **-dī**, **-ssus** *vt* to approach, accost; to attack; *(a task)* to undertake, take up.

adgregō, **-āre**, **-āvī**, **-ātum** *vt* to add, attach.

adgressiō, **-ōnis** *f* introductory remarks.

adgressus *ppa of* **adgredior**.

adhaereō, **-rēre**, **-sī**, **-sum** *vi* to stick to; *(fig)* to cling to, keep close to.

adhaerēscō, **-ere** *vi* to stick to or in; *(speech)* to falter.

adhaesiō, **-ōnis** *f* clinging.

adhaesus, **-ūs** *m* adhering.

adhibeō, **-ēre**, **-uī**, **-itum** *vt* to bring, put, add; to summon, consult, treat; to use, apply *(for some purpose)*.

adhinniō, **-īre**, **-īvī**, **-ītum** *vi* to neigh to; *(fig)* to go into raptures over.

adhortātiō, **-ōnis** *f* exhortation.

adhortātor, **-ōris** *m* encourager.

adhortor, **-ārī**, **-ātus** *vt* to encourage, urge.

adhūc *adv* so far; as yet, till now; still; ~ **nōn** not yet.

adiaceō, **-ēre**, **-uī** *vi* to lie near, border on.

adiciō, **-icere**, **-iēcī**, **-iectum** *vt* to throw to; to add; to turn (mind, eyes) towards.

adiectiō, **-ōnis** *f* addition.

adiectus *ppp of* **adiciō**.

adiectus, **-ūs** *m* bringing close.

adigō, **-igere**, **-ēgī**, **-āctum** *vt* to drive (to); to compel; **iūs iūrandum** ~ put on oath; **in verba** ~ force to owe allegiance.

adimō, **-imere**, **-ēmī**, **-emptum** *vt* to take away (from *dat*).

adipātum *nt* pastry.

adipātus *adj* fatty; *(fig)* florid.

adipiscor, **-ipiscī**, **-eptus** *vt* to overtake; to attain, acquire.

aditus, **-ūs** *m* approach, access *(to a person)*; entrance; *(fig)* avenue.

adiūdicō, **-āre**, **-āvī**, **-ātum** *vt* to award (in arbitration); to ascribe.

adiūmentum, **-ī** *nt* aid, means of support.

adiūncta *ntpl* collateral circumstances.

adiūnctiō, **-ōnis** *f* uniting; addition; *(RHET)* proviso; repetition.

adiūnctus *ppp of* **adiungō** ♦ *adj* connected.

adiungō, -ungere, -ūnxī, -ūnctum
vt to yoke; to attach; (suspicion etc)
to direct; (remark) to add.

adiūrō, -āre, -āvī, -ātum vt, vi to
swear, swear by.

adiūtō, -āre, -āvī, -ātum vt to help.

adiūtor, -ōris m helper; (MIL)
adjutant; (POL) official; (THEAT)
supporting cast.

adiūtrīx, -rīcis f see adiūtor.

adiūtus ppp of adiuvō.

adiuvō, -uvāre, -ūvī, -ūtum vt to
help; to encourage.

adj- etc see adi-.

adlābor, -bī, -psus vi to fall, move
towards, come to.

adlabōrō, -āre, -āvī, -ātum vi to
work hard; to improve by taking
trouble.

adlacrimō, -āre, -āvī, -ātum vi to
shed tears.

adlāpsus ppa of adlābor.

adlāpsus, -ūs m stealthy
approach.

adlātrō, -āre, -āvī, -ātum vt to bark
at; (fig) to revile.

adlātus ppp of adferō.

adlaudō, -āre, -āvī, -ātum vt to
praise highly.

adlectō, -āre, -āvī, -ātum vt to
entice.

adlēctus ppp of adlegō.

adlectus ppp of adliciō.

adlēgātī mpl deputies.

adlēgātiō, -ōnis f mission.

adlēgō, -āre, -āvī, -ātum vt to
despatch, commission; to
mention.

adlegō, -egere, -ēgī, -ēctum vt to
elect.

adlevāmentum, -ī nt relief.

adlevātiō, -ōnis f easing.

adlevō, -āre, -āvī, -ātum vt to lift
up; to comfort; to weaken.

adliciō, -icere, -exī, -ectum vt to

attract.

adlīdō, -dere, -sī, -sum vt to dash
(against); (fig) to hurt.

adligō, -āre, -āvī, -ātum vt to tie
up, bandage; (fig) to bind, lay
under an obligation.

adlinō, -inere, -ēvī, -itum vt to
smear; (fig) to attach.

adlīsus ppp of adlīdō.

adlocūtiō, -ōnis f address;
comforting words.

adlocūtus ppa of adloquor.

adloquium, -ī and **iī** nt talk,
encouragement.

adloquor, -quī, -cūtus vt to speak
to, address.

adlūdiō, -āre, -āvī, -ātum vi to play
(with).

adlūdō, -dere, -sī, -sum vi to joke,
play.

adluō, -ere, -ī vt to wash.

adluviēs, -ēī f pool left by flood water.

adluviō, -ōnis f alluvial land.

admātūrō, -āre, -āvī, -ātum vt to
hurry on.

admētior, -tīrī, -nsus vt to
measure out.

adminiculor, -ārī, -ātus vt to prop.

adminiculum, -ī nt (AGR) stake; (fig)
support.

administer, -rī m assistant.

administrātiō, -ōnis f services;
management.

administrātor, -ōris m manager.

administrō, -āre, -āvī, -ātum vt to
manage, govern.

admīrābilis adj wonderful,
surprising.

admīrābilitās, -ātis f
wonderfulness.

admīrābiliter adv admirably;
paradoxically.

admīrātiō, -ōnis f wonder,
surprise, admiration.

admīror, -ārī, -ātus vt to wonder

at, admire; to be surprised at.

admīsceō, -scēre, -scuī, -xtum vt to mix in with, add to; (fig) to involve; **sē ~** interfere.

admissārius, -ī and **iī** m stallion.

admissum, -ī nt crime.

admittō, -ittere, -īsī, -issum vt to let in, admit; to set at a gallop; to allow; to commit (a crime); **equō ~issō** charging.

admixtiō, -ōnis f admixture.

admixtus ppp of **admisceō**.

admoderātē adv suitably.

admoderor, -ārī, -ātus vt to restrain.

admodum adv very, quite; fully; yes; (with neg) at all.

admoneō, -ēre, -uī, -itum vt to remind, suggest, advise, warn.

admonitiō, -ōnis f reminder, suggestion, admonition.

admonitor, -ōris m admonisher (male).

admonitrīx, -rīcis f admonisher (female).

admonitū at the suggestion, instance.

admordeō, -dēre, -sum vt to bite into; (fig) to cheat.

admorsus ppp of **admordeō**.

admōtiō, -ōnis f applying.

admōtus ppp of **admoveō**.

admoveō, -ovēre, -ōvī, -ōtum vt to move, bring up, apply; to lend (an ear), direct (the mind).

admurmurātiō, -ōnis f murmuring.

admurmurō, -āre, -āvī, -ātum vi to murmur (of a crowd approving or disapproving).

admutilō, -āre, -āvī, -ātum vt to clip close; (fig) to cheat.

adnectō, -ctere, -xuī, -xum vt to connect, tie.

adnexus, -ūs m connection.

adnīsus ppp of **adnītor**.

adnītor, -tī, -sus and **-xus** vi to lean on; to exert oneself.

adnīxus ppp of **adnītor**.

adnō, -āre vt, vi to swim to.

adnotō, -āre, -āvī, -ātum vt to comment on.

adnumerō, -āre, -āvī, -ātum vt to pay out; to reckon along with.

adnuō, -uere, -uī, -ūtum vi to nod; to assent, promise; to indicate.

adoleō, -olēre, -oluī, -ultum vt to burn; to pile with gifts.

adolēscen- etc see **adulēscen-**.

adolēscō, -ēscere, -ēvī vi to grow up, increase; to burn.

Adōnis, -is and **idis** m a beautiful youth loved by Venus.

adopertus adj covered.

adoptātiō, -ōnis f adopting.

adoptiō, -ōnis f adoption.

adoptīvus adj by adoption.

adoptō, -āre, -āvī, -ātum vt to choose; to adopt.

ador, -ōris and **oris** nt spelt.

adōreus adj see n.

adōrea f glory.

adorior, -īrī, -tus vt to accost; to attack; to set about.

adōrnō, -āre, -āvī, -ātum vt to get ready.

adōrō, -āre, -āvī, -ātum vt to entreat; to worship, revere.

adortus ppa of **adorior**.

adp- etc see **app-**.

adrādō, -dere, -sī, -sum vt to shave close.

Adrastus, -ī m a king of Argos.

adrāsus ppp of **adrādō**.

adrēctus ppp of **adrigō ♦** adj steep.

adrēpō, -ere, -sī, -tum vi to creep, steal into.

adreptus ppp of **adripiō**.

Adria etc see **Hadria** etc.

adrīdeō, -dēre, -sī, -sum vt, vi to laugh, smile at; to please.

adrigō, -igere, -ēxī, -ēctum vt to raise; (fig) to rouse.

adripiō, -ipere, -ipuī, -eptum vt to seize; to appropriate; to take hold of; to learn quickly; (law) to arrest; to satirize.

adrōdō, -dere, -sī, -sum vt to gnaw, nibble at.

adrogāns, -antis adj arrogant, insolent.

adroganter adv see **adrogāns**.

adrogantia, -ae f arrogance, presumption, haughtiness.

adrogātiō, -ōnis f adoption.

adrogō, -āre, -āvī, -ātum vt to ask; to associate; to claim, assume; (fig) to award.

adsc- etc see **asc-**.

adsecla etc see **adsecula**.

adsectātiō, -ōnis f attendance.

adsectātor, -ōris m follower.

adsector, -ārī, -ātus vt to attend on, follow (esp a candidate).

adsecula, -ae m follower (derogatory).

adsēdī perf of **adsideō**; perf of **adsīdō**.

adsēnsiō, -ōnis f assent, applause; (PHILOS) acceptance of the evidence of the senses.

adsēnsor, -ōris m one in agreement.

adsēnsus ppa of **adsentior**.

adsēnsus, -ūs m assent, approval; echo; (PHILOS) acceptance of the evidence of the senses.

adsentātiō, -ōnis f flattery.

adseptātiuncula f trivial compliments.

adsentātor, -ōris m flatterer (male).

adsentātōriē adv ingratiatingly.

adsentātrīx, -rīcis f flatterer (female).

adsentiō, -entīre, -ēnsī, -ēnsum -entior, -entīrī, -ēnsus vi to agree, approve.

adsentor, -ārī, -ātus vi to agree, flatter.

adsequor, -quī, -cūtus vt to overtake; to attain; to grasp (by understanding).

adserō, -ere, -uī, -tum vt (law) to declare free (usu with manū), liberate (a slave); to lay claim to; appropriate; ~ **in servitūtem** claim as a slave.

adserō, -erere, -ēvī, -itum vt to plant near.

adsertiō, -ōnis f declaration of status.

adsertor, -ōris m champion.

adserviō, -īre vi to assist.

adservō, -āre, -āvī, -ātum vt to watch carefully; to keep, preserve.

adsessiō, -ōnis f sitting beside.

adsessor, -ōris m counsellor.

adsessus, -ūs m sitting beside.

adsevēranter adv emphatically.

adsevērātiō, -ōnis f assertion; earnestness.

adsevērō, -āre, -āvī, -ātum vt to do in earnest; to assert strongly.

adsideō, -idēre, -ēdī, -essum vi to sit by; to attend, assist; to besiege; to resemble.

adsīdō, -idere, -ēdī vi to sit down.

adsiduē adv continually.

adsiduitās, -ātis f constant attendance; continuance; frequent recurrence.

adsiduō adv continually.

adsiduus adj constantly in attendance, busy; continual, incessant.

adsiduus, -ī m taxpayer.

adsignātiō, -ōnis f allotment (of land).

adsignō, -āre, -āvī, -ātum vt to allot (esp land); to assign; to impute, attribute; to consign.

The present infinitive verb endings are as follows: -āre = 1st; -ēre = 2nd; -ere = 3rd and -īre = 4th. See sections on irregular verbs and noun declensions.

adsiliō, -īlīre, -iluī, -ultum vi to leap at or on to.

adsimilis adj like.

adsimiliter adv similarly.

adsimulātus adj similar; counterfeit.

adsimulō, -āre, -āvī, -ātum vt, vi to compare; to pretend, imitate.

adsistō, -istere, -titī vi to stand (by); to defend.

adsitus ppp of **adserō**.

adsoleō, -ēre vi to be usual.

adsonō, -āre vi to respond.

adsp- etc see **asp-**.

adsternō, -ere vt to prostrate.

adstipulātor, -ōris m supporter.

adstipulor, -ārī, -ātus vi to agree with.

adstitī perf of **adsistō**; perf of **adstō**.

adstō, -āre, -itī vi to stand near, stand up; to assist.

adstrepō, -ere vi to roar.

adstrictē adv concisely.

adstrictus ppp of **adstringō** ♦ adj tight, narrow; concise; stingy.

adstringō, -ngere, -nxī, -ctum vt to draw close, tighten; to bind, oblige; to abridge.

adstruō, -ere, -xī, -ctum vt to build on; to add.

adstupeō, -ēre vi to be astonished.

adsuēfaciō, -acere, -ēcī, -actum vt to accustom, train.

adsuēscō, -scere, -vī, -tum vi to accustom, train.

adsuētūdō, -inis f habit.

adsuētus ppp of **adsuēscō** ♦ adj customary.

adsultō, -āre, -āvī, -ātum vi to jump; to attack.

adsultus, -ūs m attack.

adsum, -esse, -fuī vi to be present; to support, assist (esp at law); to come; to appear before (a tribunal); **animō** ~ pay attention; **iam aderō** I'll be back soon.

adsūmō, -ere, -psī, -ptum vt to take for oneself, receive; to take also.

adsūmptiō, -ōnis f taking up; (logic) minor premise.

adsūmptīvus adj (law) which takes its defence from extraneous circumstances.

adsūmptum, -ī nt epithet.

adsūmptus ppp of **adsūmō**.

adsuō, -ere vt to sew on.

adsurgō, -gere, -rēxī, -rēctum vi to rise, stand up; to swell, increase.

adt- etc see **att-**.

adulātiō, -ōnis f (dogs) fawning; servility.

adulātor, -ōris m sycophant.

adulātōrius adj flattering.

adulēscēns, -entis m/f young man or woman (usu from 15 to 30 years).

adulēscentia, -ae f youth (age 15 to 30).

adulēscentula, -ae f girl.

adulēscentulus, -ī m quite a young man.

adulō, -āre, -āvī, -ātum; adulor, -ārī, -ātus vt, vi to fawn upon, flatter, kowtow.

adulter, -ī m, -a, -ae f adulterer, adulteress ♦ adj adulterous.

adulterīnus adj forged.

adulterium, -ī and **iī** nt adultery.

adulterō, -āre, -āvī, -ātum vt, vi to commit adultery; to falsify.

adultus ppp of **adolēscō** ♦ adj adult, mature.

adumbrātim adv in outline.

adumbrātiō, -ōnis f sketch; semblance.

adumbrātus adj false.

adumbrō, -āre, -āvī, -ātum vt to sketch; to represent, copy.

aduncitās, -ātis f curvature.

aduncus adj hooked, curved.

adurgeō, -ēre vt to pursue closely.

adūrō, -rere, -ssī, -stum vt to burn; to freeze; (fig) to fire.

adusque prep (with acc) right up to
♦ adv entirely.

adūstus ppp of **adūrō** ♦ adj brown.

advecticius adj imported.

advectō, -āre vt to carry
frequently.

advectus ppp of **advehō**.

advectus, -ūs m bringing.

advehō, -here, -xī, -ctum vt to
carry, convey; (pass) to ride.

advēlō, -āre vt to crown.

advena, -ae m/f stranger ♦ adj
foreign.

adveniō, -enīre, -ēnī, -entum vi to
arrive, come.

adventicius adj foreign,
extraneous; unearned.

adventō, -āre, -āvī, -ātum vi to
come nearer and nearer, advance
rapidly.

adventor, -ōris m visitor.

adventus, -ūs m arrival, approach.

adversāria ntpl daybook.

adversārius, -ī and iī m opponent
♦ adj opposing.

adversātrīx, -īcis f antagonist.

adversiō, -ōnis f turning (the
attention).

adversor, -ārī, -ātus vi to oppose,
resist.

adversum, -ī nt opposite,
misfortune ♦ prep (+ acc) towards,
against ♦ adv to meet.

adversus ppp of **advertō** ♦ adj
opposite, in front; hostile; ~ō
flūmine upstream; ~ae rēs
misfortune ♦ prep (+ acc) towards,
against ♦ adv to meet.

advertō, -tere, -tī, -sum vt to turn,
direct towards; to call attention;
animum ~ notice, perceive; (with
ad) to attend to; (with **in**) to punish.

advesperāscit, -scere, -vit vi it is
getting dark.

advigilō, -āre vi to keep watch.

advocātiō, -ōnis f legal assistance,
counsel.

advocātus, -ī m supporter in a
lawsuit; advocate, counsel.

advocō, -āre, -āvī, -ātum vt to
summon; (law) to call in the
assistance of.

advolō, -āre, -āvī, -ātum vi to fly
to, swoop down upon.

advolvō, -vere, -vī, -ūtum vt to roll
to; to prostrate.

adytum • eluge adver-.

adytum, -ī nt sanctuary.

Aeacidēs, -idae m Achilles;
Pyrrhus.

Aeacus, -ī m father of Peleus, and
judge of the dead.

Aeaea, -ae f Circe's island.

Aeaeus adj of Circe.

aedēs, -is f temple; (pl) house.

aedicula, -ae f shrine; small house,
room.

aedificātiō, -ōnis f building.

aedificātiuncula, -ae f little house.

aedificātor, -ōris m builder.

aedificium, -ī and iī nt building.

aediflcō, -āre, -āvī, -ātum vt to
build, construct.

aedīlicius adj aedile's ♦ m
ex-aedile.

aedīlis, -is m aedile.

aedīlitās, -ātis f aedileship.

aedis, -is see **aedēs**.

aeditumus, aedituus, -ī m temple-
keeper.

Aeduī, -ōrum mpl a tribe of central
Gaul.

Aeētēs, -ae m father of Medea.

Aegaeus adj Aegean ♦ nt Aegean
Sea.

Aegātēs, -um fpl islands off Sicily.

aeger, -rī adj ill, sick; sorrowful;
weak.

Aegīna, -ae f a Greek island.

Aegīnēta, -ae m inhabitant of Aegina.

*The present infinitive verb endings are as follows: -āre = 1st; -ēre = 2nd; -ere = 3rd and
-īre = 4th. See sections on irregular verbs and noun declensions.*

aegis, -dis f shield of Jupiter or
Athena, aegis.
Aegisthus, -ī m paramour of
Clytemnestra.
aegocerōs, -ōtis m Capricorn.
aegrē adv painfully; with
displeasure; with difficulty;
hardly; **~ ferre** be annoyed.
aegrēscō, -ere vi to become ill; to
be aggravated.
aegrimōnia, -ae f distress of mind.
aegritūdō, -inis f sickness;
sorrow.
aegror, -ōris m illness.
aegrōtātiō, -ōnis f illness, disease.
aegrōtō, -āre, -āvī, -ātum vi to be
ill.
aegrōtus adj ill, sick.
Aegyptius adj see n.
Aegyptus, -ī f Egypt ♦ m brother of
Danaus.
aelinos, -ī m dirge.
Aemiliānus adj esp Scipio, destroyer
of Carthage.
Aemilius, -ī Roman family name; **Via
~ia** road in N. Italy.
aemulātiō, -ōnis f rivalry (good or
bad); jealousy.
aemulātor, -ōris m zealous
imitator.
aemulor, -ārī, -ātus vt to rival,
copy; to be jealous.
aemulus, -ī m rival ♦ adj rivalling;
jealous.
Aeneadēs, -ae m Trojan; Roman.
Aenēās, -ae m Trojan leader and hero
of Virgil's epic.
Aenēis, -idis and **idos** f Aeneid.
Aenēius adj see n.
aēneus adj of bronze.
aenigma, -tis nt riddle, mystery.
aēnum, -ī nt bronze vessel.
aēnus adj of bronze.
Aeolēs, -um mpl the Aeolians.
Aeolia f Lipari Island.
Aeolidēs m a descendant of Aeolus.
Aeolis, -idis f Aeolia (N.W. of Asia
Minor).
Aeolis, -idis f daughter of Aeolus.
Aeolius adj see n.
Aeolus, -ī m king of the winds.
aequābilis adj equal; consistent,
even; impartial.
aequābilitās, -ātis f uniformity;
impartiality.
aequābiliter adv uniformly.
aequaevus adj of the same age.
aequālis adj equal, like; of the
same age, contemporary;
uniform.
aequālitās, -ātis f evenness; (in
politics, age) equality, similarity.
aequāliter adv evenly.
aequanimitās, -ātis f goodwill;
calmness.
aequātiō, -ōnis f equal
distribution.
aequē adv equally; just as (with **ac,
atque, et, quam**); justly.
Aequī, -ōrum mpl a people of central
Italy.
Aequicus, Aequiculus adj see n.
Aequimaelium, -ī and **iī** nt an open
space in Rome.
aequinoctiālis adj see n.
aequinoctium, -ī and **iī** nt equinox.
aequiperābilis adj comparable.
aequiperō, -āre, -āvī, -ātum vt to
compare; to equal.
aequitās, -ātis f uniformity; fair
dealing, equity; calmness of
mind.
aequō, -āre, -āvī, -ātum vt to make
equal, level; to compare; to equal;
solō ~ raze to the ground.
aequor, -is nt a level surface, sea.
aequoreus adj of the sea.
aequum, -ī nt plain; justice.
aequus, -ī adj level, equal;
favourable, friendly, fair, just;
calm; **~ō animō** patiently; **~ō
Marte** without deciding the issue;
~um est it is reasonable; **ex ~ō**
equally.

āēr, āēris m air, weather; mist.

aerāria f mine.

aerārium nt treasury.

aerārius adj of bronze; of money ♦ m a citizen of the lowest class at Rome; **tribūnī ~ī** paymasters; a wealthy middle class at Rome.

aerātus adj of bronze.

aereus adj of copper or bronze.

aerifer, -ī adj carrying cymbals.

aeripēs, -edis adj bronze-footed.

āerius adj of the air; lofty.

aerūgō, -inis f rust; (fig) envy, avarice.

aerumna, -ae f trouble, hardship.

aerumnōsus adj wretched.

aes, aeris nt copper, bronze; money; (pl) objects made of copper or bronze (esp statues, instruments, vessels; soldiers' pay); **~ aliēnum** debt; **~ circumforāneum** borrowed money; **~ grave** Roman coin, as.

Aeschylus, -ī m Greek tragic poet.

Aesculāpius, -ī m god of medicine.

aesculētum, -ī nt oak forest.

aesculous adj see **aesculus**.

aesculus, -ī f durmast oak.

Aesōn, -onis m father of Jason.

Aesonidēs, -ae m Jason.

Aesōpius adj see n.

Aesōpus, -ī m Greek writer of fables.

aestās, -ātis f summer.

aestifer, -ī adj heat-bringing.

aestimātiō, -ōnis f valuation, assessment; **lītis ~** assessment of damages.

aestimātor, -ōris m valuer.

aestimō, -āre, -āvī, -ātum vt to value, estimate the value of; **māgnī ~** think highly of.

aestīva, -ōrum ntpl summer camp, campaign.

aestīvus adj summer.

aestuārium, -ī and **iī** nt tidal

waters, estuary.

aestuō, -āre, -āvī, -ātum vi to boil, burn; (movement) to heave, toss; (fig) to be excited; to waver.

aestuōsus adj very hot; agitated.

aestus, -ūs m heat; surge of the sea; tide; (fig) passion; hesitation.

aetās, -ātis f age, life; time.

aetātem adv for life.

aetātula, -ae f tender age.

aeternitās, -ātis f eternity.

aeternō, -āre vt to immortalize.

aeternus adj eternal, immortal; lasting; **in ~um** for ever.

aethēr, -eris m sky, heaven; air.

aetherius adj ethereal, heavenly; of air.

Aethiops, -is adj Ethiopian; (fig) stupid.

aethra, -ae f sky.

Aetna, -ae f Etna (in Sicily).

Aetnaeus, Aetnēnsis adj see n.

Aetōlia, -iae f a district of N. Greece.

Aetōlus, -icus adj see n.

aevitās, -ātis old form of **aetās**.

aevum, -ī nt age, lifetime; eternity; **in ~** for ever.

Afer, -rī adj African.

āfore fut infin of **absum**.

Āfrānius, -ī m Latin comic poet.

Āfrica, -ae f Roman province (now Tunisia).

Āfricānae fpl panthers.

Āfricānus adj name of two Scipios.

Āfricus adj African ♦ m south-west wind.

āfuī, āfutūrus perf, fut p of **absum**.

Agamemnōn, -onis m leader of Greeks against Troy.

Agamemnonius adj see n.

Aganippē, -ēs f a spring on Helicon.

agāsō, -ōnis m ostler, footman.

age, agedum come on!, well then.

agellus, -ī m plot of land.

Agēnōr, -oris m father of Europa.

The present infinitive verb endings are as follows: -āre = 1st; -ēre = 2nd; -ere = 3rd and -īre = 4th. See sections on irregular verbs and noun declensions.

Agēnoreus *adj see n.*
Agēnoridēs, -ae *m* Cadmus; Perseus.
agēns, -entis *adj* (*RHET*) effective.
ager, -rī *m* land, field; countryside; territory.
agg- *etc see* **adg-**.
agger, -is *m* rampart; mound, embankment, any built-up mass.
aggerō, -āre, -āvī, -ātum *vt* to pile up; to increase.
aggerō, -rere, -ssī, -stum *vt* to carry, bring.
aggestus, -ūs *m* accumulation.
agilis *adj* mobile; nimble, busy.
agilitās, -ātis *f* mobility.
agitābilis *adj* light.
agitātiō, -ōnis *f* movement, activity.
agitātor, -ōris *m* driver, charioteer.
agitō, -āre, -āvī, -ātum *vt* (*animals*) to drive; to move, chase, agitate; (*fig*) to excite (*to action*); to persecute, ridicule; to keep (*a ceremony*) ♦ *vi* to live; to deliberate.
agmen, -inis *nt* forward movement, procession, train; army on the march; **~ claudere** bring up the rear; **novissimum ~** rearguard; **primum ~** van.
agna, -ae *f* ewe lamb; lamb (*flesh*).
agnāscor, -scī, -tus *vi* to be born after.
agnātus, -ī *m* relation (*by blood on father's side*).
agnellus, -ī *m* little lamb.
agnīnus *adj* of lamb.
agnitiō, -ōnis *f* recognition, knowledge.
agnitus *ppp of* **agnōscō**.
agnōmen, -inis *nt* an extra surname (*eg Africanus*).
agnōscō, -ōscere, -ōvī, -itum *vt* to recognize; to acknowledge, allow; to understand.

agnus, -ī *m* lamb.
agō, agere, ēgī, āctum *vt* to drive, lead; to plunder; to push forward, put forth; (*fig*) to move, rouse, persecute; to do, act, perform; (*time*) to pass, spend; (*undertakings*) to manage, wage; (*public speaking*) to plead, discuss; to negotiate, treat; (*THEAT*) to play, act the part of; **~ cum populō** address the people; **age** come on!, well then; **age age** all right!; **āctum est dē** it is all up with; **aliud ~** not attend; **animam ~** expire; **annum quartum ~** be three years old; **causam ~** plead a cause; **hōc age** pay attention; **id ~ ut** aim at; **lēge ~** go to law; **nīl agis** it's no use; **quid agis?** how are you?; **rēs agitur** interests are at stake; **sē ~** go, come.
agrāriī *mpl* the land reform party.
agrārius *adj* of public land; **lēx ~a** a land law.
agrestis *adj* rustic; boorish, wild, barbarous ♦ *m* countryman.
agricola, -ae *m* countryman, farmer.
Agricola, -ae *m* a Roman governor of Britain; his biography by Tacitus.
Agrigentīnus *adj see n.*
Agrigentum, -ī *nt* a town in Sicily.
agripeta, -ae *m* landgrabber.
Agrippa, -ae *m* Roman surname (*esp Augustus's minister*).
Agrippīna, -ae *f* mother of Nero; **Colōnia ~a** *or* **~ēnsis** Cologne.
Agyīeus, -eī *and* **eos** *m* Apollo.
āh *interj* ah! (*in sorrow or joy*).
aha *interj* expressing reproof or laughter.
ahēn- *etc see* **aēn-**.
Āiāx, -ācis *m* Ajax (*name of two Greek heroes at Troy*).
āiō *vt* (*defec*) to say, speak; **ain tū?/ain vērō?** really?; **quid ais?** I say!

āla, -ae f wing; armpit; (MIL) wing of army.

alabaster, -rī m perfume box.

alacer, -ris adj brisk, cheerful.

alacritās, -ātis f promptness, liveliness; joy, rapture.

alapa, -ae f slap on the face; a slave's freedom.

ālāriī mpl allied troops.

ālārius adj (MIL) on the wing.

ālātus adj winged.

alauda, -ae f lark; name of a legion of Caesar's.

alāzōn, -onis m braggart.

Alba Longa, -ae, -ae f a Latin town (precursor of Rome).

Albānus adj Alban; **Lacus ~, Mōns ~** lake and mountain near Alba Longa.

albātus adj dressed in white.

albeō, -ēre vi to be white; to dawn.

albēscō, -ere vi to become white; to dawn.

albicō, -āre vi to be white.

albidus adj white.

Albiōn, -ōnis f ancient name for Britain.

albitūdo, -inis f whiteness.

Albula, -ae f old name for the Tiber.

albulus adj whitish.

album, -ī nt white; records.

Albunea, -ae f a spring at Tibur; a sulphur spring near Alban Lake.

albus adj white, bright.

Alcaeus, -ī m Greek lyric poet.

alcēdō, -inis f kingfisher.

alcēdōnia mpl halcyon days.

alcēs, -is f elk.

Alcibiadēs, -is m brilliant Athenian politician.

Alcidēs, -ae m Hercules.

Alcinous, -ī m king of Phaeacians in the Odyssey.

ālea, -ae f gambling, dice; (fig) chance, hazard; **iacta ~ est** the die is cast; **in ~am dare** to risk.

āleātor, -ōris m gambler.

āleātōrius adj in gambling.

ālec etc see **allec**.

āleō, -ōnis m gambler.

āles, -itis adj winged; swift ♦ m/f bird; omen.

alēscō, -ere vi to grow up.

Alexander, -rī m a Greek name; Paris (prince of Troy); Alexander the Great (king of Macedon).

Alexandrēa (later **-ia**), **-ēae** f Alexandria in Egypt

algeō, -gēre, -sī vi to feel cold; (fig) to be neglected.

algēscō, -ere vi to catch cold.

Algidus, -ī m mountain in Latium.

algidus adj cold.

algor, -ōris m cold.

algū abl sg m with cold.

aliā adv in another way.

aliās adv at another time; at one time ... at another.

alibī adv elsewhere; otherwise; in one place ... in another.

alicubī adv somewhere.

alicunde adv from somewhere.

alīd old form of aliud.

aliēnātiō, -ōnis f transfer; estrangement.

aliēnigena, -ae m foreigner.

aliēnigenus adj foreign; heterogeneous.

aliēnō, -āre, -āvī, -ātum vt to transfer (property by sale); to alienate, estrange; (mind) to derange.

aliēnus adj of another, of others; alien, strange; (with abl or ab) unsuited to, different from; hostile ♦ m stranger.

āliger, -ī adj winged.

alimentārius adj about food.

alimentum, -ī nt nourishment, food; obligation of children to

The present infinitive verb endings are as follows: -āre = 1st; -ēre = 2nd; -ere = 3rd and -īre = 4th. See sections on irregular verbs and noun declensions

parents; (*fig*) support.

alimōnium, -ī *and* **iī** *nt* nourishment.

aliō *adv* in another direction, elsewhere; one way ... another way.

aliōquī, aliōquin *adv* otherwise, else; besides.

aliōrsum *adv* in another direction; differently.

ālipēs, -edis *adj* wing-footed; fleet.

aliptēs, -ae *m* sports trainer.

aliquā *adv* some way or other.

aliquam *adv*: ~ **diū** for sometime; ~ **multī** a considerable number.

aliquandō *adv* sometime, ever; sometimes; once, for once; now at last.

aliquantisper *adv* for a time.

aliquantō *adv* (*with comp*) somewhat.

aliquantulum *nt* a very little ♦ *adv* somewhat.

aliquantulus *adj* quite small.

aliquantum *adj* a good deal ♦ *adv* somewhat.

aliquantus *adj* considerable.

aliquātenus *adv* to some extent.

aliquī, -qua, -quod *adj* some, any; some other.

aliquid *adv* at all.

aliquis, -quid *pron* somebody, something; someone *or* something important.

aliquō *adv* to some place, somewhere else.

aliquot *adj* (*indecl*) some.

aliquotiēns *adv* several times.

aliter *adv* otherwise, differently; in one way ... in another.

alitus *ppp of* **alō**.

ālium, -ī *and* **iī** *nt* garlic.

aliunde *adv* from somewhere else.

alius, alia, aliud *adj* other, another; different; alius ... alius some ... others; **alius ex aliō** one after the other; **in alia omnia īre** oppose a

measure; **nihil aliud quam** only.

all- *etc see* **adl-**.

allēc, -is *nt* fish pickle.

allex, -icis *m* big toe.

Allia, -ae *f* tributary of the Tiber (*scene of a great Roman defeat*).

Alliēnsis *adj see* **Allia**.

Allobrogēs, -um *mpl* a people of S.E. Gaul.

Allobrogicus *adj see n.*

almus *adj* nourishing; kindly.

alnus, -ī *f* alder.

alō, -ere, uī, -tum *and* **itum** *vt* to nourish, rear; to increase, promote.

Alpēs, -ium *fpl* Alps.

Alphēus, -ī *m* river of Olympia in S.W. Greece.

Alpīnus *adj see n.*

alsī *perf of* **algeō.**

alsius, alsus *adj* cold.

altāria, -ium *ntpl* altars, altar; altar top.

altē *adv* on high, from above; deep; from afar.

alter, -īus *adj* the one, the other (*of two*); second, the next; fellow man; different; ~ **ego**, ~ **idem** a second self; **-um tantum** twice as much; **ūnus et ~** one or two.

altercātiō, -ōnis *f* dispute, debate.

altercor, -ārī, -ātus *vi* to wrangle, dispute; to cross-examine.

alternīs *adv* alternately.

alternō, -āre, -āvī, -ātum *vt* to do by turns, alternate.

alternus *adj* one after the other, alternate; elegiac (*verses*).

alteruter, -īusutrīus *adj* one or the other.

altilis *adj* fat (*esp fowls*).

altisonus *adj* sounding on high.

altitonāns, -antis *adj* thundering on high.

altitūdō, -inis *f* height, depth; (*fig*) sublimity, (*mind*) secrecy.

altivolāns, -antis *adj* soaring on

high.

altor, -ōris m foster father.

altrīnsecus adv on the other side.

altrīx, -īcis f nourisher, foster mother.

altum, -ī nt heaven; sea (usu out of sight of land); **ex ~ō repetītus** far-fetched.

altus adj high, deep; (fig) noble; profound.

ālūcinor, -ārī, -ātus vi to talk wildly; (mind) to wander.

aluī perf of **alō**.

alumnus, -ī m/f foster child; pupil.

alūta, -ae f soft leather; shoe, purse, face patch.

alveārium, -ī and liī nt beehive.

alveolus, -ī m basin.

alveus, -eī m hollow; trough; (ship) hold; bath tub; riverbed.

alvus, -ī f bowels; womb; stomach.

amābilis adj lovely, lovable.

amābilitās, -ātis f charm.

amābiliter adv see **amābilis**.

Amalthēa, -ae f nymph or she-goat; **cornū -ae** horn of plenty.

Amalthēum, -ī nt Atticus's library.

āmandātiō f sending away.

āmandō, -āre, -āvī, -ātum vt to send away.

amāns, -antis adj fond ♦ m lover.

amanter adv affectionately.

āmanuēnsis, -is m secretary.

amāracinum, -inī nt marjoram ointment.

amāracum, -ī nt, **amāracus, -ī** m/f, sweet marjoram.

amārē adv see **amārus**.

amāritiēs, -ēī f, **amāritūdō, -inis** f, **amāror, -ōris** m bitterness.

amārus adj bitter; (fig) sad; ill-natured.

amāsius, -ī and **iī** m lover.

Amathūs, -ūntis f town in Cyprus.

Amathūsia f Venus.

amātiō, -ōnis f lovemaking.

amātor, -ōris m lover, paramour.

amātorculus m poor lover.

amātoriē adv amorously.

amātōrius adj of love, erotic.

amātrīx, -rīcis f mistress.

Amāzōn, -onis f Amazon, warrior woman.

Amāzonides fpl Amazons.

Amāzonius adj see n.

ambāctus, -ī m vassal.

ambāgēs, -is f windings; (speech) circumlocution, quibbling; enigma.

ambedō, -edere, -ēdī, -ēsum vt to consume.

ambēsus ppp of **ambedō**.

ambigō, -ere vt, vi to wander about; to be in doubt; to argue; to wrangle.

ambiguē adv doubtfully.

ambiguitās, -ātis f ambiguity.

ambiguus adj changeable, doubtful, unreliable; ambiguous.

ambiō, -īre, -iī, -ītum vt to go round, encircle; (POL) to canvass for votes; (fig) to court (for a favour).

ambitiō, -ōnis f canvassing for votes; currying favour; ambition.

ambitiōsē adv ostentatiously.

ambitiōsus adj winding; ostentatious, ambitious.

ambitus ppp of **ambiō**.

ambitus, -ūs m circuit, circumference; circumlocution; canvassing, bribery; **lēx de ~ū** a law against bribery.

ambō, ambae, ambō num both, two.

Ambracia, -ae f district of N.W. Greece.

Ambraciēnsis, -us adj see n.

ambrosia, -ae f food of the gods.

ambrosius adj divine.

The present infinitive verb endings are as follows: **-āre** = 1st; **-ēre** = 2nd; **-ere** = 3rd and **-īre** = 4th. See sections on irregular verbs and noun declensions.

ambūbāia, -ae f Syrian flute-girl.

ambulācrum, -ī nt avenue.

ambulātiō, -ōnis f walk, walking; walk (place).

ambulātiuncula f short walk.

ambulō, -āre, -āvī, -ātum vi to walk, go; to travel.

ambūrō, -rere, -ssī, -stum vt to burn up; to make frostbitten; (fig) to ruin.

ambūstus ppp of **ambūrō**.

amellus, -ī m Michaelmas daisy.

āmēns, -entis adj mad, frantic; stupid.

āmentia, -ae f madness; stupidity.

āmentum, -ī nt strap (for throwing javelin).

ames, -itis m fowler's pole.

amfr- etc see **anfr-**.

amīca, -ae f friend; mistress.

amiciō, -īre, -tus vt to clothe, cover.

amīciter, -ē adv see **amīcus**.

amīcitia, -ae f friendship; alliance.

amictus ppp of **amiciō**.

amictus, -ūs m (manner of) dress; clothing.

amiculum, -ī nt cloak.

amīculus, -ī m dear friend.

amīcus, -ī m friend ♦ adj friendly, fond.

āmissiō, -ōnis f loss.

āmissus ppp of **āmittō**.

amita, -ae f aunt (on father's side).

āmittō, -ittere, -īsī, -issum vt to let go, lose.

Ammōn, -is m Egyptian god identified with Jupiter.

Ammōniacus adj see n.

amnicola, -ae m/f sth growing by a river.

amniculus m brook.

amnicus adj see n.

amnis, -is m river.

amō, -āre, -āvī, -ātum vt to love, like; (colloq) to be obliged to; **ita mē dī ament!** ≈ bless my soul!;

amābō please!

amoenitās, -ātis f delightfulness (esp of scenery).

amoenus adj delightful.

āmōlior, -īrī, -ītus vt to remove.

amōmum, -ī nt cardamom.

amor, -ōris m love; (fig) strong desire; term of endearment; Cupid; (pl) love affairs.

āmōtiō, -ōnis f removal.

āmōtus ppp of **āmoveō**.

āmoveō, -ovēre, -ōvī, -ōtum vt to remove; to banish.

amphibolia, -ae f ambiguity.

Amphīōn, -onis m musician and builder of Thebes.

Amphīonius adj see n.

amphitheātrum, -ī nt amphitheatre.

Amphitrītē, -ēs f sea goddess; the sea.

Amphitryō, -ōnis m husband of Alcmena.

Amphitryōniadēs m Hercules.

amphora, -ae f a two-handled jar; liquid measure; (NAUT) measure of tonnage.

Amphrȳsius adj of Apollo.

Amphrȳsus, -ī m river in Thessaly.

ample adv see **amplus**.

amplector, -ctī, -xus vt to embrace, encircle; (mind) to grasp; (speech) to deal with; (fig) to cherish.

amplexor, -ārī, -ātus vt to embrace, love.

amplexus ppa of **amplector**.

amplexus, -ūs m embrace, encircling.

amplificātiō, -ōnis f enlargement; (RHET) a passage elaborated for effect.

amplificē adv splendidly.

amplificō, -āre, -āvī, -ātum vt to increase, enlarge; (RHET) to enlarge upon.

amplio, -āre, -āvī, -ātum vt to enlarge; (law) to adjourn.

ampliter *adv see* **amplūs**.

amplitūdō, -inis *f* size; (*fig*) distinction; (*RHET*) fullness.

amplius *adv* more (*esp amount or number*), further, longer; ~ **ducentī** more than 200; ~ **nōn petere** take no further legal action; ~ **prōnūntiāre** adjourn a case.

amplūs *adj* large, spacious; great, abundant; powerful, splendid, eminent; (*sup*) distinguished.

ampulla, -ae *f* a two-handled flask; (*fig*) high-flown language.

ampullārius, -ārī *m* flask-maker.

ampullor, -ārī *vi* to use high-flown language.

amputātiō, -ōnis *f* pruning.

amputātus *adj* (*RHET*) disconnected.

amputō, -āre, -āvī, -ātum *vt* to cut off, prune; (*fig*) to lop off.

Amūlius, -ī *m* king of Alba Longa, grand-uncle of Romulus.

amurca, -ae *f* lees of olive oil.

amussitātus *adj* nicely adjusted.

Amyclae, -ārum *fpl* town in S Greece.

Amyclaeus *adj see n.*

amygdalum, -ī *nt* almond.

amystis, -dis *f* emptying a cup at a draught.

an *conj* or; perhaps; (*with single question*) surely not; **haud sciō** ~ I feel sure.

Anacreōn, -ontis *m* Greek lyric poet.

anadēma, -tis *nt* headband.

anagnōstēs, -ae *m* reader.

anapaestum, -ī *nt* poem in anapaests.

anapaestus *adj*: ~ **pēs** anapaest.

anas, -tis *f* duck.

anaticula *f* duckling.

anatīnus *adj see n.*

anatocismus, -ī *m* compound

interest.

Anaxagorās, -ae *m* early Greek philosopher.

Anaximander, -rī *m* early Greek philosopher.

anceps, -ipitis *adj* two-headed; double; wavering, doubtful; dangerous ♦ *nt* danger.

Anchīsēs, -ae *m* father of Aeneas.

Anchīsēus *adj* Aeneas.

Anchīsiadēs *m* Aeneas.

ancīle, -is *nt* oval shield (*esp one said to have fallen from heaven in Numa's reign*).

ancilla, -ae *f* servant.

ancillāris, -ārī *adj* of a young servant.

ancillula *f* young servant.

ancīsus *adj* cut round.

ancora, -ae *f* anchor.

ancorārius *adj see n.*

ancorāle, -is *nt* cable.

Ancus Marcius, -ī, -ī *m* 4th king of Rome.

Ancȳra, -ae *f* Ankara (capital of Galatia).

andabata, -ae *m* blindfold gladiator.

Andrius *adj see* **Andros**.

androgynē, -ēs *f* hermaphrodite.

androgynus, -ī *m* hermaphrodite.

Andromachē, -ēs *f* wife of Hector.

Andromeda, -ae *f* wife of Perseus; a constellation.

Andronicus, -ī *m* Livius (earliest Latin poet).

Andros (-us), -ī *m* Aegean island.

ānellus, -ī *m* little ring.

anēthum, -ī *nt* fennel.

ānfrāctus, -ūs *m* bend, orbit; roundabout way; (*words*) digression, prolixity.

angelus, -ī *m* angel.

angina, -ae *f* quinsy.

angiportum, -ī *nt* alley.

angiportus, -ūs *m* alley.

The present infinitive verb endings are as follows: -āre = 1st; -ēre = 2nd; -ere = 3rd and -īre = 4th. See sections on irregular verbs and noun declensions.

angō, -ere vt to throttle; (fig) to distress, torment.

angor, -ōris m suffocation; (fig) anguish, torment.

anguicomus adj with snakes for hair.

anguiculus, -ī m small snake.

anguifer, -ī adj snake-carrying.

anguigena, -ae m one born of serpents; Theban.

anguīlla, -ae f eel.

anguimanus adj with a trunk.

anguipēs, -edis adj serpent-footed.

anguis, -is m/f snake, serpent; (constellation) Draco.

Anguitenēns, -entis m Ophiuchus.

angulātus adj angular.

angulus, -ī m angle, corner; out-of-the-way place; **ad parēs ~ōs** at right angles.

angustē adv close, within narrow limits; concisely.

angustiae, -ārum fpl defile, strait; (time) shortness; (means) want; (CIRCS) difficulty; (mind) narrowness; (words) subtleties.

angusticlāvius adj wearing a narrow purple stripe.

angustō, -āre vt to make narrow.

angustum, -ī nt narrowness; danger.

angustus adj narrow, close; (time) short; (means) scanty; (mind) mean; (argument) subtle; (CIRCS) difficult.

anhēlitus, -ūs m panting; breath, exhalation.

anhēlō, -āre, -āvī, -ātum vi to breathe hard, pant; to exhale.

anhēlus adj panting.

anicula, -ae f poor old woman.

Aniēnsis, Aniēnus adj of the river Anio.

Aniēnus m Anio.

anīlis adj of an old woman.

anīlitās, -tātis f old age.

anīliter adv like an old woman.

anima, -ae f wind, air; breath; life; soul, mind; ghost, spirit; **~am agere, efflāre** expire; **~am comprimere** hold one's breath.

animadversiō, -ōnis f observation; censure, punishment.

animadversor, -ōris m observer.

animadvertō, -tere, -tī, -sum vt to pay attention to, notice; to realise; to censure, punish; **~ in** punish.

animal, -ālis nt animal; living creature.

animālis adj of air; animate.

animāns, -antis m/f/nt living creature; animal.

animātiō, -ōnis f being.

animātus adj disposed, in a certain frame of mind; courageous.

animō, -āre, -āvī, -ātum vt to animate; to give a certain temperament to.

animōsē adv boldly, eagerly.

animōsus adj airy; lifelike; courageous, proud.

animula, -ae f little soul.

animulus, -ī m darling.

animus, -ī m mind, soul; consciousness; reason, thought, opinion, imagination; heart, feelings, disposition; courage, spirit, pride, passion; will, purpose; term of endearment; **~ī** in mind, in heart; **~ī causā** for amusement; **~ō fingere** imagine; **~ō male est** I am fainting; **~ō esse** be patient, calm; **bonō ~ō esse** take courage; be well-disposed; **ex ~ō** sincerely; **ex ~ō effluere** be forgotten; **in ~ō habēre** purpose; **meō ~ō** in my opinion.

Aniō, -ēnis m tributary of the Tiber.

Anna Perenna, -ae, -ae f Roman popular goddess.

annālēs, -ium mpl annals, chronicle.

annālis adj of a year; **lēx ~** law prescribing ages for public offices.

anne etc see **an**.

anniculus adj a year old.

anniversārius adj annual.

annōn or not.

annōna, -ae f year's produce; grain; price of corn; the market.

annōsus adj aged.

annōtīnus adj last year's.

annus, -ī m year; **~ māgnus** astronomical great year; **~ solidus** a full year.

annuus adj a year's; annual.

anquīrō, -rere, -sīvī, -sītum vt to search for; to make inquiries; (law) to institute an inquiry (dē) or prosecution (abl or gen).

ānsa, -ae f handle; (fig) opportunity.

ānsātus adj with a handle; (comedy) with arms akimbo.

ānser, -is m goose.

ānserīnus adj see n.

ante prep (with acc) before (in time, place, comparison) ♦ adv (place) in front; (time) before.

anteā adv before, formerly.

antecapiō, -apere, -ēpī, -eptum vt to take beforehand, anticipate.

antecēdō, -ēdere, -essī, -essum vt to precede; to surpass.

antecellō, -ere vi to excel, be superior.

anteceptus ppp of **antecapiō**.

antecessiō, -ōnis f preceding; antecedent cause.

antecessor, -ōris m forerunner.

antecursor, -ōris m forerunner, pioneer.

anteeō, -īre, -īī vi to precede, surpass.

anteferō, -ferre, -tulī, -lātum vt to carry before; to prefer; to

anticipate.

antefīxus adj attached (in front)
♦ ntpl ornaments on roofs of buildings.

antegredior, -dī, -ssus vt to precede.

antehabeō, -ēre vt to prefer.

antehāc adv formerly, previously.

antelātus ppp of **anteferō**.

antelūcānus adj before dawn.

antemerīdiānus adj before noon.

antemittō, -ittere, -īsī, -issum vt to send on in front.

antenna, -ae f yardarm.

antepīlānī, -ōrum mpl (MIL) the front ranks.

antepōnō, -ōnere, -osuī, -ositum vt to set before; to prefer.

antequam conj before.

Anterōs, -ōtis m avenger of slighted love.

antēs, -ium mpl rows.

antesignānus, -ī m (MIL) leader; (pl) defenders of the standards.

antestō, antistō, -āre, -ētī vi to excel, distinguish oneself.

antestor, ōrī, -ātus vi to call a witness.

anteveniō, -enīre, -ēnī, -entum vt, vi to anticipate; to surpass.

antevertō, -tere, -tī, -sum vt to precede; to anticipate; to prefer.

anticipātiō, -ōnis f foreknowledge.

anticipō, -āre, -āvī, -ātum vt to take before, anticipate.

anticus adj in front.

Antigonē, -ēs f daughter of Oedipus.

Antigonus, -ī m name of Macedonian kings.

Antiochēnsis adj see n.

Antiochīa, -īae f Antioch (capital of Syria).

Antiochus, -ī m name of kings of Syria.

The present Infinitive verb endings are as follows: **-āre** = 1st; **-ēre** = 2nd; **-ere** = 3rd and **-īre** = 4th. See sections on irregular verbs and noun declensions.

antīquārius, -ī and **iī** *m* antiquary.

antīquē *adv* in the old style.

antīquitās, -ātis *f* antiquity, the ancients; integrity.

antīquitus *adv* long ago, from ancient times.

antīquō, -āre, -āvī, -ātum *vt* to vote against (a bill).

antīquus *adj* ancient, former, old; good old-fashioned, honest, illustrious; **antīquior** more important; **antīquissimus** most important.

antistēs, -itis *m/f* high priest, chief priestess; (*fig*) master (*in any art*).

Antisthenēs, -is and **ae** *m* founder of Cynic philosophy.

antistita, -ae *f* chief priestess.

antistō *etc see* **antestō.**

antitheton, -ī *nt* (*RHET*) antithesis.

Antōnīnus, -ī *m* name of Roman emperors (*esp Pius and Marcus Aurelius*).

Antōnius, -ī *m* Roman name (*esp the famous orator, and Mark Antony*).

antrum, -ī *nt* cave, hollow.

ānulārius, -ī *m* ringmaker.

ānulātus *adj* with rings on.

ānulus, -ī *m* ring; equestrian rank.

ānus, -ī *m* rectum; ring.

anus, -ūs *f* old woman ♦ *adj* old.

ānxiē *adv see* **ānxius.**

ānxietās, -ātis *f* anxiety, trouble (*of the mind*).

ānxifer, -ī *adj* disquieting.

ānxitūdō, -inis *f* anxiety.

ānxius *adj* (*mind*) troubled, disquieting.

Āones, -um *adj* Boeotian.

Āonia *f* part of Boeotia.

Āonius *adj* of Boeotia, of Helicon.

Aornos, -ī *m* lake Avernus.

apage *interj* away with!, go away!

apēliōtēs, -ae *m* east wind.

Apellēs, -is *m* Greek painter.

aper, -rī *m* boar.

aperiō, -īre, -uī, -tum *vt* to

uncover, disclose, open; (*country*) to open up; (*fig*) to unfold, explain, reveal.

apertē *adv* clearly, openly.

apertum, -ī *nt* open space; **in ~ō esse** be well known; be easy.

apertus *ppp of* **aperiō** ♦ *adj* open, exposed; clear, manifest; (*person*) frank.

aperuī *perf of* **aperiō.**

apex, -icis *m* summit; crown, priest's cap; (*fig*) crown.

aphractus, -ī *f* a long open boat.

apiārius, -ī and **iī** *m* beekeeper.

Apīcius, -ī *m* Roman epicure.

apicula, -ae *f* little bee.

apis, -is *f* bee.

apīscor, -iscī, -tus *vt* to catch, get, attain.

apium, -ī and **iī** *nt* celery.

aplustre, -is *nt* decorated stern of a ship.

apoclētī, -ōrum *mpl* committee of the Aetolian League.

apodytērium, -ī and **iī** *nt* dressing room.

Apollināris, -ineus *adj:* **lūdī ~ināres** Roman games in July.

Apollō, -inis *m* Greek god of music, archery, prophecy, flocks and herds, and often identified with the sun.

apologus, -ī *m* narrative, fable.

apophorēta, -ōrum *ntpl* presents for guests to take home.

apoproēgmena, -ōrum *ntpl* (*PHILOS*) what is rejected.

apostolicus *adj see* **n.**

apostolus, -ī *m* (*ECCL*) apostle.

apothēca, -ae *f* storehouse, wine store.

apparātē *adv see* **apparātus.**

apparātiō, -ōnis *f* preparation.

apparātus *adj* ready, well-supplied, sumptuous.

apparātus, -ūs *m* preparation; equipment, munitions; pomp, ostentation.

appāreō, -ēre, -uī, -itum vi to come in sight, appear; to be seen, show oneself; to wait upon (an official); ~et it is obvious.

appāritiō, -ōnis f service; domestic servants.

appāritor, -ōris m attendant.

apparō, -āre, -āvī, -ātum vt to prepare, provide.

appellātiō, -ōnis f accosting; appeal; title; pronunciation.

appellātor, -ōris m appellant.

appellitātus adj usually called.

appellō, -āre, -āvī, -ātum vt to speak to; to appeal to; (for money) to dun; (law) to sue; to call, name; to pronounce.

appellō, -ellere, -ulī, -ulsum vt to drive, bring (to); (NAUT) to bring to land.

appendicula, -ae f small addition.

appendix, -icis f supplement.

appendō, -endere, -endī, -ensum vt to weigh, pay.

appetēns, -entis adj eager; greedy.

appetenter adv see **appetēns**.

appetentia, -ae f craving.

appetītiō, -ōnis f grasping, craving.

appetītus ppp of **appetō**.

appetītus, -ūs m craving; natural desire (as opposed to reason).

appetō, -ere, -īvī, -ītum vt to grasp, try to get at; to attack; to desire ♦ vi to approach.

appingō, -ere vt to paint (in); (colloq) to write more.

Appius, -ī m Roman first name; **Via ~ia** main road from Rome to Capua and Brundisium.

applaudō, -dere, -sī, -sum vt to strike, clap ♦ vi to applaud.

applicātiō, -ōnis f applying (of the mind); **iūs ~ōnis** the right of a patron

to inherit a client's effects.

applicātus and **itus** ppp of **applicō**.

applicō, -āre, -āvī and **uī**, -ātum and **itum** vt to attach, place close (to); (NAUT) to steer, bring to land; **sē**, **animum** ~ devote self, attention (to).

applōrō, -āre vt to deplore.

appōnō, -ōnere, -osuī, -ositum vt to put (to, beside); (meal) to serve; to add, appoint; to reckon.

apporrectus adj stretched nearby.

apportō, -āre, -āvī, -ātum vt to bring, carry (to).

apposcō, -ere vt to demand also.

appositē adv suitably.

appositus ppp of **appōnō** ♦ adj situated near; (fig) bordering on; suitable.

apposuī perf of **appōnō**.

appōtus adj drunk.

apprecor, -ārī, -ātus vt to pray to.

apprehendō, -endere, -endī, -ēnsum vt to take hold of; (MIL) to occupy; (argument) to bring forward.

apprīmē adv especially.

apprīmō, -imere, -essī, -essum vt to press close.

approbātiō, -ōnis f acquiescence; proof.

approbātor, -ōris m approve.

approbē adv very well.

approbō, -āre, -āvī, -ātum vt to approve; to prove; to perform to someone's satisfaction.

apprōmittō, -ere vt to promise also.

approperō, -āre, -āvī, -ātum vt to hasten ♦ vi to hurry up.

appropinquātiō, -ōnis f approach.

appropinquō, -āre, -āvī, -ātum vi to approach.

appugnō, -āre vt to attack.

appulsus ppp of **appellō**.

The present infinitive verb endings are as follows: -āre = 1st; -ēre = 2nd; -ere = 3rd and -īre = 4th. See sections on irregular verbs and noun declensions.

appulsus, -ūs m landing; approach.

aprīcātiō, -ōnis f basking.

aprīcor, -ārī vi to bask.

aprīcus adj sunny; basking; in ~um prōferre bring to light.

Aprīlis adj April, of April.

aprūgnus adj of the wild boar.

aps- etc see **abs-**.

aptē adv closely; suitably, rightly.

aptō, -āre, -āvī, -ātum vt to fit, put on; (fig) to adapt; to prepare, equip.

aptus adj attached, joined together, fitted (with); suitable.

apud prep (with acc) **1.** (with persons) beside, by, with, at the house of, among, in the time of; (speaking) in the presence of, to; (judgment) in the opinion of; (influence) with; (faith) in; (authors) in. **2.** (with places) near, at, in; **est ~ mē** I have; **sum ~ mē** I am in my senses.

Āpūlia, -iae f district of S.E. Italy.

Āpūlus adj see n.

aput prep see **apud**.

aqua, -ae f water; **~ mihī haeret** I am in a fix; **~ intercus** dropsy; **~m adspergere** revive; **~m praebēre** entertain; **~m et terram petere** demand submission; **~ā et ignī interdīcere** outlaw.

aquae fpl medicinal waters, spa.

aquaeductus, -ūs m aqueduct; right of leading water.

aquāliculus m belly.

aquālis, -is m/f washbasin.

aquārius adj of water ♦ m water carrier, water inspector; a constellation.

aquāticus adj aquatic; humid.

aquātilis adj aquatic.

aquātiō, -ōnis f fetching water; watering place.

aquātor, -ōris m water carrier.

aquila, -ae f eagle; standard of a legion; (ARCH) gable; a constellation; **~ae senectūs** a vigorous old age.

Aquileia, -ae f town in N. Italy.

Aquileiēnsis adj see n.

aquilifer, -ī m chief standard-bearer.

aquilīnus adj eagle's.

aquilō, -ōnis m north wind; north.

aquilōnius adj northerly.

aquilus adj swarthy.

Aquīnās, ātis adj see n.

Aquīnum, -ī nt town in Latium.

Aquītānia, -iae f district of S.W. Gaul.

Aquītānus adj see n.

aquor, -ārī, -ātus vi to fetch water.

aquōsus adj humid, rainy.

aquula, -ae f little stream.

āra, -ae f altar; (fig) refuge; a constellation; **~ae et focī** hearth and home.

arabarchēs, -ae m customs officer in Egypt.

Arabia, -iae f Arabia.

Arabicē adv with all the perfumes of Arabia.

Arabicus, Arabicius, Arabus adj see n.

Arachnē, -s f Lydian woman changed into a spider.

arānea, -ae f spider; cobweb.

arāneola, f, -olus m small spider.

arāneōsus adj full of spiders' webs.

arāneum, -ī nt spider's web.

arāneus, -i m spider ♦ adj of spiders.

Arar, -is m river Saône.

Arātēus adj see **Arātus**.

arātiō, -ōnis f ploughing, farming; arable land.

arātiuncula f small plot.

arātor, -ōris m ploughman, farmer; (pl) cultivators of public land.

arātrum, -ī nt plough.

Arātus, -ī m Greek astronomical poet.

Araxēs, -is m river in Armenia.

arbiter, -rī *m* witness; arbiter, judge, umpire; controller; ~ **bibendī** president of a drinking party.

arbitra, -ae *f* witness.

arbitrāriō *adv* with some uncertainty.

arbitrārius *adj* uncertain.

arbitrātus, -ūs *m* decision; meō ~ū in my judgment.

arbitrium, -ī and -ī *nt* decision (of an arbitrator); judgment; mastery, control.

arbitror, -ārī, -ātus *vt, vi* to be a witness of; to testify; to think, suppose.

arbor, (arbōs), -oris *f* tree; ship, mast, oar; ~ **īnfēlīx** gallows.

arboreus *adj* of trees, like a tree.

arbustum, -ī *nt* plantation, orchard; (*pl*) trees.

arbustus *adj* wooded.

arbuteus *adj* of the strawberry tree.

arbutum, -ī *nt* fruit of strawberry tree.

arbutus, -ī *f* strawberry tree.

arca, -ae *f* box; moneybox, purse; coffin; prison cell; **ex ~ā absolvere** pay cash.

Arcadēs, um *mpl* Arcadians.

Arcadia, -iae *f* district of S. Greece.

Arcadicus, -ius *adj see* **Arcadia**.

arcānō *adv* privately.

arcānum, -ī *nt* secret, mystery.

arcānus *adj* secret, able to keep secrets.

arceō, -ēre, -uī, -tum *vt* to enclose; to keep off, prevent.

accessitū *abl sg m* at the summons.

arcessītus *ppp of* **arcessō ♦** *adj* far-fetched.

arcessō, -ere, -īvī, -ītum *vt* to send for, fetch; (*law*) to summon, accuse; (*fig*) to derive.

archetypus, -ī *m* original.

Archilochus, -ī *m* Greek iambic and elegiac poet.

archimagīrus, -i *m* chief cook.

Archimēdēs, -is *m* famous mathematician of Syracuse.

archipīrāta, -ae *m* pirate chief.

architectōn, -onis *m* master builder; master in cunning.

architector, -ārī, -ātus *vt* to construct; (*fig*) to devise.

architectūra, -ae *f* architecture.

architectus, -ī *m* architect; (*fig*) author.

archōn, -ontis *m* Athenian magistrate.

Archytās, -ae *m* Pythagorean philosopher of Tarentum.

arcitenēns, -entis *adj* holding a bow ♦ *m* Apollo.

Arctophylax, -cis *m* (constellation) Bootes.

arctos, -ī *f* Great Bear, Little Bear; north, north wind; night.

Arctūrus, -ī *m* brightest star in Boötes.

arctus *etc see* **artus** *etc*

arcuī *perf of* **arceō**.

arcula, -ae *f* casket; (*RHET*) ornament.

arcuō, -āre, -āvī, -ātum *vt* to curve.

arcus, -ūs *m* bow; rainbow; arch, curve; (*MATH*) arc.

ardea, -ae *f* heron.

Ardea, -ae *f* town in Latium.

ardeliō, -ōnis *m* busybody.

ārdēns, -entis *adj* hot, glowing, fiery; (*fig*) eager, ardent.

ārdenter *adv* passionately.

ārdeō, -dēre, -sī, -sum *vi* to be on fire, burn, shine; (*fig*) to be fired, burn.

ārdēscō, -ere *vi* to catch fire, gleam; (*fig*) to become inflamed,

The present infinitive verb endings are as follows: -āre = 1st; -ēre = 2nd; -ere = 3rd and -īre = 4th. See sections on irregular verbs and noun declensions.

wax hotter.

ārdor, -ōris m heat, brightness; (fig) ardour, passion.

arduum, -ī nt steep slope; difficulty.

arduus adj steep, high; difficult, troublesome.

ārea, -ae f vacant site, open space, playground; threshing-floor; (fig) scope (for effort).

ārefaciō, -acere, -ēcī, -actum vt to dry.

arēna etc see **harēna**.

ārēns, -entis adj arid; thirsty.

āreō, -ēre vi to be dry.

āreola, -ae f small open space.

Arēopagītēs m member of the court.

Arēopagus, -ī m Mars' Hill in Athens; a criminal court.

Arēs, -is m Greek god of war.

ārēscō, -ere vi to dry, dry up.

Arestoridēs, -ae m Argus.

aretālogus, -ī m braggart.

Arethūsa, -ae f spring near Syracuse.

Arethūsis adj Syracusan.

Argēī, -ōrum mpl sacred places in Rome; effigies thrown annually into the Tiber.

argentāria, -ae f bank, banking; silver mine.

argentārius adj of silver, of money ♦ m banker.

argentātus adj silver-plated; backed with money.

argenteus adj of silver, adorned with silver; silvery (in colour); of the silver age.

argentum, -ī nt silver, silver plate; money.

Argēus, -īvus, -olicus adj Argive; Greek.

Argīlētānus adj see n.

Argīlētum, -ī nt part of Rome (noted for bookshops).

argilla, -ae f clay.

Argō, -ūs f Jason's ship.

Argolis, -olidis f district about Argos.

Argonautae, -ārum mpl Argonauts.

Argonauticus adj see n.

Argos nt, **-ī, -ōrum** mpl town in S.E. Greece.

Argōus adj see **Argō**.

argūmentātiō, -ōnis f adducing proofs.

argūmentor, -ārī, -ātus vt, vi to prove, adduce as proof; to conclude.

argūmentum, -ī nt evidence, proof; (lit) subject matter, theme, plot (of a play); (art) subject, motif.

arguō, -uere, -uī, -ūtum vt to prove, make known; to accuse, blame, denounce.

Argus, -ī m monster with many eyes.

argūtē adv subtly.

argūtiae, -ārum fpl nimbleness, liveliness; wit, subtlety, slyness.

argūtor, -ārī, -ātus vi to chatter.

argūtulus adj rather subtle.

argūtus adj (sight) clear, distinct, graceful; (sound) clear, melodious, noisy; (mind) acute, witty, sly.

argyraspis, -dis adj silver-shielded.

Ariadna, -ae f daughter of Minos of Crete.

Ariadnaeus adj see n.

āridulus adj rather dry.

āridum, -ī nt dry land.

āridus adj dry, withered; meagre; (style) flat.

ariēs, -etis m ram; 1st sign of Zodiac; battering ram; beam used as a breakwater.

arietō, -āre vt, vi to butt, strike hard.

Ariōn, -onis m early Greek poet and musician.

Ariōnius adj see n.

arista, -ae f ear of corn.

Aristaeus, -ī m legendary founder of

beekeeping.
Aristarchus, -ī *m Alexandrian scholar; a severe critic.*
Aristidēs, -is *m Athenian statesman noted for integrity.*
Aristippēus *adj see n.*
Aristippus, -ī *m Greek hedonist philosopher.*
aristolochia, -ae *f birthwort.*
Aristophanēs, -is *m Greek comic poet.*
Aristophanēus *and* **ius** *adj see n.*
Aristotelēs, -is *m Aristotle (founder of Peripatetic school of philosophy).*
Aristotelēus, *and* **ius** *adj see n.*
arithmētica, -ōrum *ntpl* arithmetic.
āritūdō, -inis *f* dryness.
Ariūsius *adj of Ariusia in Chios.*
arma, -ōrum *ntpl* armour, shield; arms, weapons *(of close combat only);* warfare, troops; *(fig)* defence, protection; implements, ship's gear.
armāmenta, -ōrum *ntpl* implements, ship's gear.
armāmentārium, -ī *and* **iī** *nt* arsenal.
armāriolum, -ī *nt* small chest.
armārium, -ī *and* **iī** *nt* chest, safe.
armātū *m abl* armour; **gravi ~** with heavy-armed troops.
armātūra, -ae *f* armour, equipment; **levis ~** light-armed troops.
armātus *adj* armed.
Armenia, -ae *f* Armenia.
Armeniaca, -acae *f* apricot tree.
Armeniacum, -acī *nt* apricot.
Armenius *adj see Armenia.*
armentālis *adj* of the herd.
armentārius, -ī *and* **iī** *m* cattle herd.
armentum, -ī *nt* cattle *(for*

ploughing),* herd *(cattle etc).*
armifer, -ī *adj* armed.
armiger, -ī *m* armour-bearer ♦ *adj* armed; productive of warriors.
armilla, -ae *f* bracelet.
armillātus *adj* wearing a bracelet.
armipotēns, -entis *adj* strong in battle.
armisonus *adj* resounding with arms.
armō, -āre, -āvī, -ātum *vt* to arm, equip; to rouse to arms *(against).*
armus, -ī *m* shoulder *(esp of animals).*
Arniēnsis *adj see Arnus.*
Arnus, -ī *m* river Arno.
arō, -āre, -āvī, -ātum *vt* to plough, cultivate; to live by farming; *(fig: sea, brow)* to furrow.
Arpīnās, -ātis *adj see n.*
Arpīnum, -ī *nt* town in Latium *(birthplace of Cicero).*
arquātus *adj* jaundiced.
arr- *etc see* **adr-.**
arrabō, -ōnis *m* earnest money.
ars, artis *f* skill *(in any craft);* the art *(of any profession);* science, theory; handbook; work of art; moral quality, virtue; artifice, fraud.
ārsī *perf of* **ārdeō.**
ārsus *ppp of* **ārdeō.**
artē *adv* closely, soundly, briefly.
artēria, -ae *f* windpipe; artery.
artēria, -ōrum *ntpl* trachea.
arthrīticus *adj* gouty.
articulātim *adv* joint by joint; *(speech)* distinctly.
articulō, -āre, -āvī, -ātum *vt* to articulate.
articulōsus *adj* minutely subdivided.
articulus, -ī *m* joint, knuckle; limb; *(words)* clause; *(time)* point, turning point; **in ipsō ~ō temporis** in the nick of time.

The present infinitive verb endings are as follows: **-āre** = 1st; **-ēre** = 2nd; **-ere** = 3rd and **-īre** = 4th. *See sections on irregular verbs and noun declensions.*

artifex, -icis *m* artist, craftsman, master; (*fig*) maker, author ♦ *adj* ingenious, artistic, artificial.

artificiōsē *adv* skilfully.

artificiōsus *adj* ingenious, artistic, artificial.

artificium, -ī and iī *nt* skill, workmanship; art, craft; theory, rule of an art; ingenuity, cunning.

artō, -āre *vt* to compress, curtail.

artolaganus, -ī *m* kind of cake.

artopta, -ae *m* baker; baking tin.

artus *adj* close, narrow, tight; (*sleep*) deep; (*fig*) strict, straitened.

artus, -ūs *m* joint; (*pl*) limbs, body; (*fig*) strength.

ārula, -ae *f* small altar.

arundō *etc see* **harundō** *etc.*

arvīna, -ae *f* grease.

arvum, -ī *nt* field; land, country, plain.

arvus *adj* ploughed.

arx, arcis *f* fortress, castle; height, summit; (*fig*) bulwark, stronghold; **arcem facere ē cloācā** make a mountain out of a molehill.

ās, assis *m* (*weight*) pound; (*coin*) bronze unit, of low value; (*inheritance*) the whole (*subdivided into 12 parts*); **ad assem** to the last farthing; **hērēs ex asse** sole heir.

Ascānius, -ī *m* son of Aeneas.

ascendō, -endere, -endī, -ēnsum *vt, vi* to go up, climb, embark; (*fig*) to rise.

ascēnsiō, -ōnis *f* ascent; (*fig*) sublimity.

ascēnsus, -ūs *m* ascent, rising; way up.

ascia, -ae *f* axe; mason's trowel.

asciō, -īre *vt* to admit.

ascīscō, -iscere, -īvī, -ītum *vt* to receive with approval; to admit (*to some kind of association*); to appropriate, adopt (*esp customs*); to arrogate to oneself.

ascītus *adj* acquired, alien.

Ascra, -ae *f* birthplace of Hesiod in Boeotia.

Ascraeus *adj* of Ascra; of Hesiod; of Helicon.

ascrībō, -bere, -psī, -ptum *vt* to add (*in writing*); to attribute, ascribe; to apply (*an illustration*); to enrol, include.

ascrīpticius *adj* enrolled.

ascrīptiō, -ōnis *f* addition (*in writing*).

ascrīptīvus *adj* (*MIL*) supernumerary.

ascrīptor, -ōris *m* supporter.

ascrīptus *ppp of* **ascrībō.**

asella, -ae *f* young ass.

asellus, -ī *m* young ass.

Āsia, -ae *f* Roman province; Asia Minor; Asia.

asīlus, -ī *m* gad fly.

asinus, -ī *m* ass; fool.

Āsis, -dis *f* Asia.

Āsius (Āsiānus, Āsiāticus) *adj see* n.

Āsōpus, -ī *m* river in Boeotia.

asōtus, -ī *m* libertine.

asparagus, -ī *m* asparagus.

aspargō *etc see* **aspergō.**

aspectābilis *adj* visible.

aspectō, -āre *vt* to look at, gaze at; to pay heed to; (*places*) to face.

aspectus *ppp of* **aspiciō.**

aspectus, -ūs *m* look, sight; glance, sense of sight; aspect, appearance.

aspellō, -ere *vt* to drive away.

asper, -ī *adj* rough; (*taste*) bitter; (*sound*) harsh; (*weather*) severe; (*style*) rugged; (*person*) violent, exasperated, unkind, austere; (*animal*) savage; (*CIRCS*) difficult.

asperē *adv see adj.*

aspergō, -gere, -sī, -sum *vt* to scatter, sprinkle; to bespatter, besprinkle; **aquam ~** revive.

aspergō, -inis *f* sprinkling; spray.

asperitās, -ātis f roughness, unevenness, harshness, severity; (fig) ruggedness, fierceness; trouble, difficulty.

aspernātiō, -ōnis f disdain.

aspernor, -ārī, -ātus vt to reject, disdain.

asperō, -āre, -āvī, -ātum vt to roughen, sharpen; to exasperate.

aspersiō, -ōnis f sprinkling.

aspersus ppp of **aspergō**.

aspiciō, -icere, -exī, -ectum vt to catch sight of, look at; (places) to face; (fig) to examine, consider.

aspīrātiō, -ōnis f breathing (on); evaporation; pronouncing with an aspirate.

aspīrō, -āre, -āvī, -ātum vi to breathe, blow; to favour; to aspire, attain (to) ♦ vt to blow, instil.

aspis, -dis f asp.

asportātiō, -ōnis f removal.

asportō, -āre vt to carry off.

aspreta, -ōrum ntpl rough country.

ass- etc see **ads-**.

Assaracus, -ī m Trojan ancestor of Aeneas.

asser, -is m pole, stake.

assula, -ae f splinter.

assulātim adv in splinters.

assum, -ī nt roast; (pl) sweating-bath.

assus adj roasted.

Assyria, -ae f country in W. Asia.

Assyrius adj Assyrian; oriental.

ast conj (laws) and then; (vows) then; (strong contrast) and yet.

ast- etc see **adst-**.

Actraea, -ae f goddess of Justice.

Astraeus, -ī m father of winds; **~ī frātrēs** the winds.

astrologia, -ae f astronomy.

astrologus, -ī m astronomer; astrologer.

astrum, -ī nt star, heavenly body, constellation; a great height; heaven, immortality, glory.

astu nt (indecl) city (esp Athens).

astus, -ūs m cleverness, cunning.

astūtē adv cleverly.

astūtia, -ae f slyness, cunning.

astūtus adj artful, sly.

Astyanax, -ctis m son of Hector and Andromache.

asȳlum, -ī nt sanctuary.

asymbolus adj with no contribution.

at conj (adversative) but, on the other hand; (objecting) but it may be said; (limiting) at least, but at least; (continuing) then, thereupon; (transitional) now; (with passionate appeals) but with; look now!; **~ enim** yes, but; **~ tamen** nevertheless.

Atābulus, -ī m sirocco.

atat interj (expressing fright, pain, surprise) oh!

atavus, -ī m great-great-great-grandfather; ancestor.

Atella, -ae f Oscan town in Campania.

Ātellānicus, Ātellānius adj see n.

Ātellānus adj: **fābula ~āna** kind of comic show popular in Rome.

āter, -rī adj black, dark; gloomy, dismal; malicious; **diēs ~rī** unlucky days.

Athamantēus adj see **Athamās**.

Athamantiadēs m Palaemon.

Athamantis f Helle.

Athamās, -antis m king of Thessaly (who went mad).

Athēnae, -ārum fpl Athens.

Athēnaeus, -iēnsis adj see n.

atheos, -ī m atheist.

athlēta, -ae m wrestler, athlete.

athlēticē adv athletically.

Athos (dat -ō, acc -ō, -on, -ōnem) m mount Athos in Macedonia.

Atlanticus adj: **mare ~anticum**

The present infinitive verb endings are as follows: -āre = 1st; -ēre = 2nd; -ere = 3rd and -īre = 4th. See sections on irregular verbs and noun declensions.

Atlantic Ocean.

Atlantiadēs m Mercury.

Atlantis f lost Atlantic island; a Pleiad.

Atlās, -antis m giant supporting the sky; Atlas mountains.

atomus, -ī f atom.

atque (before consonants **ac**) conj (connecting words) and, and in fact; (connecting clauses) and then, and so, and yet; (in comparison) as, than, to, from; ~ **adeō** and that too; or rather; ~ **nōn** and not rather; ~ **sī** as if; **alius** ~ different from; **contrā** ~ opposite to; **idem** ~ same as; **plūs** ~ more than.

atquī conj (adversative) and yet, nevertheless, yes but; (confirming) by all means; (minor premise) now; ~ **sī** if now.

ātrāmentum, -ī nt ink; blacking.

ātrātus adj in mourning.

Atreus, -eī m son of Pelops (king of Argos).

Atrīdēs m Agamemnon; Meneleaus.

ātriēnsis, -is m steward, major-domo.

ātriolum, -ī nt anteroom.

ātrium, -ī and **iī** nt hall, open central room in Roman house; forecourt of a temple; hall (in other buildings).

atrōcitās, -ātis f hideousness; (mind) brutality; (PHILOS) severity.

atrōciter adv savagely.

Atropos, -ī f one of the Fates.

atrōx, -ōcis adj hideous, dreadful; fierce, brutal, unyielding.

attāctus ppp of **attingō**.

attāctus, -ūs m contact.

attagēn, -is m heathcock.

Attalica ntpl garments of woven gold.

Attalicus adj of Attalus; of Pergamum; ornamented with gold cloth.

Attalus, -ī m king of Pergamum

(who bequeathed his kingdom to Rome).

attamen conj nevertheless.

attat etc see **atat**.

attegia, -ae f hut.

attemperātē adv opportunely.

attemptō etc see **attentō**.

attendō, -dere, -dī, -tum vt to direct (the attention); to attend to, notice.

attenē adv carefully.

attentiō, -ōnis f attentiveness.

attentō, -āre, -āvī, -ātum vt to test, try; (loyalty) to tamper with; to attack.

attentus ppp of **attendō** ♦ adj attentive, intent; businesslike, careful (esp about money).

attentus ppp of **attineō**.

attenuātē adv simply.

attenuātus adj weak; (style) brief; refined; plain.

attenuō, -āre, -āvī, -ātum vt to weaken, reduce; to diminish; to humble.

atterō, -erere, -rīvī, -rītum vt to rub; to wear away; (fig) to impair, exhaust.

attestor, -ārī, -ātus vt to confirm.

attexō, -ere, -uī, -tum vt to weave on; (fig) to add on.

Atthis, -dis f Attica.

Attiānus adj see **Attius**.

Attica, -ae f district of Greece about Athens.

Atticē adv in the Athenian manner.

Atticissō vi to speak in the Athenian manner.

Atticus adj Attic, Athenian; (RHET) of a plain and direct style.

attigī perf of **attingō**.

attigō see **attingō**.

attineō, -inēre, -inuī, -entum vt to hold fast, detain; to guard; to reach for ♦ vi to concern, pertain, be of importance, avail.

attingō, -ingere, -igī, -āctum vt to

touch; to strike, assault; to arrive at; to border on; to affect; to mention; to undertake; to concern, resemble.

Attis, -dis *m* Phrygian priest of Cybele.

Attius, -ī *m* Latin tragic poet.

attollō, -ere *vt* to lift up, erect; (*fig*) to exalt, extol.

attondeō, -ondēre, -ondī, -ōnsum vt to shear, prune, crop; (*fig*) to diminish; (*comedy*) to fleece.

attonitus *adj* thunderstruck, terrified, astonished; inspired.

attonō, -āre, -uī, -itum *vt* to stupefy.

attōnsus *ppp of* **attondeō**.

attorqueō, -ēre *vt* to hurl upwards.

attractus *ppp of* **attrahō**.

attrahō, -here, -xī, -ctum *vt* to drag by force, attract; (*fig*) to draw, incite.

attrectō, -āre *vt* to touch, handle; to appropriate.

attrepidō, -āre *vi* to hobble along.

attribuō, -uere, -uī, -ūtum *vt* to assign, bestow; to add; to impute, attribute; to lay as a tax.

attribūtiō, -ōnis *f* (*money*) assignment; (*GRAM*) predicate.

attribūtum, -ī *nt* (*GRAM*) predicate.

attribūtus *ppp of* **attribuō** ♦ *adj* subject.

attrītus *ppp of* **atterō** ♦ *adj* worn, bruised; (*fig*) impudent.

attulī *perf of* **adferō**.

au *interj* (*expressing pain, surprise*) oh!

auceps, -upis *m* fowler; (*fig*) eavesdropper; a pedantic critic.

auctārium, -ī *and* **iī** *nt* extra.

auctificus *adj* increasing.

auctiō, -ōnis *f* increase; auction sale.

auctiōnārius *adj* auction; **tabulae**

~ae catalogues.

auctiōnor, -ārī, -ātus *vi* to hold an auction.

auctitō, -āre *vt* to greatly increase.

auctō, -āre *vt* to increase.

auctor, -ōris *m/f* **1.** (*originator: of families*) progenitor; (: *of buildings*) founder; (: *of deeds*) doer. **2.** (*composer: of writings*) author, historian; (: *of knowledge*) investigator, teacher; (: *of news*) informant. **3.** (*instigator: of action*) adviser; (: *of measures*) promoter; (: *of laws*) proposer, supporter; ratifier. **4.** (*person of influence: in public life*) leader; (: *of conduct*) model; (: *of guarantees*) witness, bail; (: *of property*) seller; (: *of women and minors*) guardian; (: *of others' welfare*) champion; **mē ~ōre** at my suggestion.

auctōrāmentum, -ī *nt* contract; wages.

auctōrātus *adj* bound (*by a pledge*); hired out (*for wages*).

auctōritās, -ātis *f* **1.** source; lead, responsibility. **2.** judgment; opinion; advice; support; bidding, guidance; (*of senate*) decree; (*of people*) will. **3.** power; (*person*) influence, authority, prestige; (*things*) importance, worth; (*conduct*) example; (*knowledge*) warrant, document, authority; (*property*) right of possession.

autumn- *etc see* **autumn-**.

auctus *ppp of* **augeō** ♦ *adj* enlarged, great.

auctus, -ūs *m* growth, increase.

aucupium, -ī *and* **iī** *nt* fowling; birds caught; (*fig*) hunting (after), quibbling.

aucupō, -āre *vt* to watch for.

aucupor, -ārī, -ātus *vi* to go fowling ♦ *vt* to chase; (*fig*) to try

---

The present infinitive verb endings are as follows: **-āre** = 1st; **-ēre** = 2nd; **-ere** = 3rd and **-īre** = 4th. *See sections on irregular verbs and noun declensions.*

to catch.

audācia, -ae f daring, courage; audacity, impudence; (pl) deeds of daring.

audācter, audāciter adv see **audāx**.

audāx, -ācis adj bold, daring; rash, audacious; proud.

audēns, -entis adj bold, brave.

audenter adv see **audēns**.

audentia, -ae f boldness, courage.

audeō, -dēre, -sus vt, vi to dare, venture; to be brave.

audiēns, -entis m hearer ♦ adj obedient.

audientia, -ae f hearing; **~m facere** gain a hearing.

audiō, -īre, -īvī and -iī, -ītum vt to hear; to learn, be told; to be called; to listen, attend to, study under (a teacher); to examine a case; to agree with; to obey, heed; **bene/male ~** have a good/bad reputation.

audītiō, -ōnis f listening; hearsay, news.

audītor, -ōris m hearer; pupil.

audītōrium, -ī and iī nt lecture room, law court; audience.

audītus, -ūs m (sense of) hearing; a hearing; rumour.

auferō, auferre, abstulī, ablātum vt to take away, carry away; to mislead, lead into a digression; to take by force, steal; to win, obtain (as the result of effort); **aufer** away with!

Aufidus, -ō m river in Apulia.

aufugiō, -ugere, -ūgī vi to run away ♦ vt to flee from.

Augēās, -ae m king of Elis (whose stables Hercules cleaned).

augeō, -gēre, -xī, -ctum vt to increase; to enrich, bless (with); to praise, worship ♦ vi to increase.

augēscō, -ere vi to begin to grow, increase.

augmen, -inis nt growth.

augur, -is m/f augur; prophet, interpreter.

augurāle, -is nt part of camp where auspices were taken.

augurālis adj augur's.

augurātiō, -ōnis f soothsaying.

augurātō adv after taking auspices.

augurātus, -ūs m office of augur.

augurium, -ī and iī nt augury; an omen; prophecy, interpretation; presentiment.

augurius adj of augurs.

augurō, -āre vt, vi to take auguries; to consecrate by auguries; to forebode.

auguror, -ārī, -ātus vt, vi to take auguries; to foretell by omens; to predict, conjecture.

Augusta, -ae f title of the emperor's wife, mother, daughter or sister.

Augustālis adj of Augustus; **lūdī ~ēs** games in October; **praefectus ~is** governor of Egypt; **sodālēs ~ēs** priests of deified Augustus.

augustē adv see **augustus**.

augustus adj venerable, august, majestic.

Augustus, -ī m title given to C Octavius, first Roman emperor, and so to his successors ♦ adj imperial; (month) August, of August.

aula, -ae f courtyard of a Greek house; hall of a Roman house; palace, royal court; courtiers; royal power.

aula etc see **olla**.

aulaeum, -ī nt embroidered hangings, canopy, covering; (THEAT) curtain.

aulicī, -ōrum mpl courtiers.

aulicus adj of the court.

Aulis, -idis and **is** f port in Boeotia from which the Greeks sailed for Troy.

auloedus, -ī m singer accompanied by flute.

aura, -ae f breath of air, breeze, wind; air, upper world; vapour, odour, sound, gleam; (*fig*) winds (*of public favour*), breeze (*of prosperity*), air (*of freedom*), daylight (*of publicity*).

aurāria, -ae f gold mine.

aurārius adj of gold.

aurātus adj gilt, ornamented with gold; gold.

Aurēlius, -ī m Roman name; lēx ~ia law on the composition of juries; via ~ia main road running NW from Rome

aureolus adj gold; beautiful, splendid.

aureus adj gold, golden; gilded; (*fig*) beautiful splendid ♦ m gold coin.

aurichalcum, -ī nt a precious metal

auricomus adj golden-leaved.

auricula, -ae f the external ear; ear.

aurifer, -ī adj gold-producing.

aurifex, -icis m goldsmith.

aurīga, -ae m charioteer, driver; groom; helmsman; a constellation.

aurigēnā, -ae adj gold-begotten.

auriger, -ī adj gilded.

aurigō, -āre vi to compete in the chariot race.

auris, -is f ear; (*RHET*) judgment; (*AGR*) earthboard (*of a plough*); ad ~em admonēre whisper; in utramvis ~em dormīre sleep soundly.

aurītulus, -ī m "Long-Ears".

aurītus adj long-eared; attentive.

aurōra, -ae f dawn, morning; goddess of dawn; the East.

aurum, -ī nt gold; gold plate, jewellery, bit, fleece *etc*; money; lustre; the Golden Age.

auscultātiō, -ōnis f obedience.

auscultātor, -ōris m listener.

auscultō, -āre, -āvī, -ātum vt to listen to; to overhear ♦ vi (*of servants*) to wait at the door; to obey.

ausim subj of **audeō**.

Ausones, -um mpl indigenous people of central Italy.

Ausonia f Italy.

Ausonidae mpl Italians.

Ausonius, -is adj Italian

auspex, -icis m augur, soothsayer; patron, commander; witness of a marriage contract.

auspicātō adv after taking auspices; at a lucky moment.

auspicātus adj consecrated; auspicious, lucky.

auspicium, -ī and **iī** nt augury, auspices; right of taking auspices; power, command; omen; ~ facere give a sign.

auspicō, -āre vi to take the auspices.

auspicor, -ārī, -ātus vi to take the auspices; to make a beginning ♦ vt to begin, enter upon.

auster, -rī m south wind; south.

austērē adv see **austērus**.

austēritās, -ātis f severity.

austērus adj severe, serious; gloomy, irksome.

austrālis adj southern.

austrīnus adj from the south.

ausum, -ī nt enterprise.

ausus ppa of **audeō**.

aut conj or; either ... or; or else or at least, or rather.

autem conj (*adversative*) but, on the other hand; (*in transitions, parentheses*) moreover, now, and; (*in dialogue*) indeed.

authepsa, -ae f stove.

autographus adj written with his

The present infinitive verb endings are as follows: **-āre** *= 1st;* **-ēre** *= 2nd;* **-ere** *= 3rd and* **-īre** *= 4th. See sections on irregular verbs and noun declensions.*

own hand.
Autolycus, -ī m a robber.
automaton, -ī nt automaton.
automatus adj spontaneous.
Automedōn, -ontis m a charioteer.
autumnālis adj autumn, autumnal.
autumnus, -ī m autumn ♦ adj autumnal.
autumō, -āre vt to assert.
auxī perf of **augeō.**
auxilia, -iōrum ntpl auxiliary troops; military force.
auxiliāris adj helping, auxiliary; of the auxiliaries ♦ mpl auxiliary troops.
auxiliārius adj helping; auxiliary.
auxiliātor, -ōris m helper.
auxilior, -ūs m aid.
auxilior, -ārī, -ātus vi to aid, support.
auxilium, -ī and **iī** nt help, assistance.
avārē, avāriter adv see **avārus.**
avāritia, -ae f greed, selfishness.
avāritiēs, -ēī f avarice.
avārus adj greedy, covetous; eager.
avē, avēte, avētō impv hail!, farewell!
āvehō, -here, -xī, -ctum vt to carry away; (pass) to ride away.
āvellō, -ellere, -ellī and **ulsī (-olsī), -ulsum (-olsum)** vt to pull away, tear off; to take away (by force), remove.
avēna, -ae f oats; (music) reed, shepherd's pipe.
Aventīnum, -ī nt Aventine hill.
Aventīnus, -ī m Aventine hill in Rome ♦ adj of Aventine.
avēns, -entis adj eager.
aveō, -ēre vt to desire, long for.
Avernālis adj of lake Avernus.
Avernus, -ī m lake near Cumae (said to be an entrance to the lower world); the lower world ♦ adj birdless; of Avernus; infernal.

āverruncō, -āre vt to avert.
āversābilis adj abominable.
āversor, -ārī, -ātus vi to turn away ♦ vt to repulse, decline.
āversor, -ōris m embezzler.
āversum, -ī nt back.
āversus ppp of **āvertō** ♦ adj in the rear, behind, backwards; hostile, averse.
āvertō, -tere, -tī, -sum vt to turn aside, avert; to divert; to embezzle; to estrange ♦ vi to withdraw.
avia, -ae f grandmother.
avia, -ōrum ntpl wilderness.
aviārium, -ī nt aviary, haunt of birds.
aviārius adj of birds.
avidē adv see **avidus.**
aviditās, -ātis f eagerness, longing; avarice.
avidus adj eager, covetous; avaricious, greedy; hungry; vast.
avis, -is f bird; omen; ~ **alba** a rarity.
avītus adj of a grandfather; ancestral.
avius adj out of the way, lonely, untrodden; wandering, astray.
āvocāmentum, -ī nt relaxation.
āvocātiō, -ōnis f diversion.
āvocō, -āre vt to call off; to divert, distract; to amuse.
āvolō, -āre vi to fly away, hurry away; to depart, vanish.
āvolsus, avulsus ppp of **āvellō.**
avunculus, -ī m uncle (on mother's side); ~ **magnus** great-uncle.
avus, -ī m grandfather; ancestor.
Axenus, -ī m Black Sea.
axicia, axitia, -ae f scissors.
āxilla -ae f armpit.
axis, -is m axle, chariot; axis, pole, sky, clime; plank.
azȳmus adj unleavened.

B

babae interj (expressing wonder or joy) oho!

Babylōn, -ōnis f ancient city on the Euphrates.

Babylōnia f the country under Babylon.

Babylōnicus, -ōniēnsis adj see n.

Babylōnius adj Babylonian; Chaldaean, versed in astrology.

bāca, -ae f berry; olive; fruit; pearl.

bācātus adj of pearls.

bacca etc see **bāca**.

baccar, -is nt cyclamen.

Baccha, -ae f Bacchante.

Bacchānal, -ālis nt place consecrated to Bacchus; (pl) festival of Bacchus.

bacchātiō, -ōnis f revel.

Bacchēus, -ious, -ius adj see n.

Bacchiadae, -ārum mpl kings of Corinth (founders of Syracuse).

bacchor, -ārī, -ātus vi to celebrate the festival of Bacchus; to revel, rave; to rage.

Bacchus, -ī m god of wine, vegetation, poetry, and religious ecstasy; vine, wine.

bācifer, -ī adj olive-bearing.

bacillum, -ī nt stick, lictor's staff.

Bactra, -ōrum ntpl capital of Bactria in central Asia (now Balkh).

Bactriāna f Bactria.

Bactriānus and **ius** adj Bactrian.

baculum, -ī nt, **-us, -ī** m stick, staff.

Baetica f Roman province (now Andalusia).

Baeticus adj see **Baetis**.

Baetis, -is m river in Spain (now Guadalquivir).

Bagrada, -ae m river in Africa (now Mejerdah).

Bāiae, -ārum fpl Roman spa on Bay of Naples.

Bāiānus adj see n.

bāiulō, -āre vt to carry (something heavy).

bāiulus, -ī m porter.

bālaena, -ae f whale.

balanus, -ī f balsam (from an Arabian nut); a shellfish.

balatrō, -ōnis m jester.

bālātus, -ūs m bleating.

balbus adj stammering.

balbūtiō, -īre vt, vi to stammer, speak indistinctly; (fig) to speak obscurely.

Baliārēs, -ium fpl Balearic islands.

Baliāris, Baliāricus adj see n.

balineum etc see **balneum** etc.

ballista, -ae f (MIL) catapult for shooting stones and other missiles; (fig) weapon.

ballistārium, -ī and **iī** nt catapult.

balneae, -ārum fpl bath, baths.

balneāria, -orum ntpl bathroom.

balneārius adj of the baths.

balneātor, -ōris m bath superintendent.

balneolum, -ī nt small bath.

balneum, -ī nt bath.

bālō, -āre vi to bleat.

balsamum, -ī nt balsam, balsam tree.

baltea, -ōrum ntpl belt (esp swordbelt; woman's girdle; strapping).

balteus, -ī m belt (esp swordbelt; woman's girdle; strapping).

Bandusia, -ae f spring near Horace's birthplace.

baptisma, -tis nt baptism.

baptizō, -āre vt (ECCL) to baptize.

barathrum, -ī nt abyss; the lower world; (fig) a greedy person.

barba, -ae f beard.

barbarē adv in a foreign language, in Latin; in an uncivilized way;

The present infinitive verb endings are as follows: **-āre** = 1st; **-ēre** = 2nd; **-ere** = 3rd and **-īre** = 4th. See sections on irregular verbs and noun declensions.

roughly, cruelly.

barbaria, -ae, -ēs acc, and **em** f a foreign country (outside Greece or Italy); (words) barbarism; (manners) rudeness, stupidity.

barbaricus adj foreign, outlandish; Italian.

barbarus adj foreign, barbarous; (to a Greek) Italian; rude, uncivilized; savage, barbarous ♦ m foreigner, barbarian.

barbātulus adj with a little beard.

barbātus adj bearded, adult; ancient (Romans); of philosophers.

barbiger, -ī adj bearded.

barbitos (acc -on) m lyre, lute.

barbula, -ae f little beard.

Barcās, -ae m ancestor of Hannibal.

Barcinus adj see n.

bardus adj dull, stupid.

bardus, -ī m Gallic minstrel.

bārō, -ōnis m dunce.

barrus, -ī m elephant.

bascauda, -ae f basket (for the table).

bāsiātiō, -ōnis f kiss.

basilica, -ae f public building used as exchange and law court.

basilicē adv royally, in magnificent style.

basilicum, -ī nt regal robe.

basilicus adj royal, magnificent ♦ m highest throw at dice.

bāsiō, -āre vt to kiss.

basis, -is f pedestal, base.

bāsium, -ī and **iī** nt kiss.

Bassareus, -eī m Bacchus.

Batāvī, -ōrum mpl people of Batavia (now Holland).

batillum, -ī nt firepan.

Battiadēs, -ae m Callimachus.

bātuō, -ere, -ī vt to beat.

baubor, -ārī vi (of dogs) to howl.

Baucis, -idis f wife of Philemon.

beātē adv see **beātus**.

beātitās, -ātis f happiness.

beātitūdō, -inis f happiness.

beātulus, -ī m the blessed man.

beātus adj happy; prosperous, well-off; rich, abundant.

Bēdriacēnsis adj see n.

Bēdriācum, -ī nt village in N. Italy.

Belgae, -ārum mpl people of N. Gaul (now Belgium).

Bēlīdēs, -īdae m Danaus, Aegyptus, Lynceus.

Bēlides, -um fpl Danaids.

bellāria, -ōrum ntpl dessert, confectionery.

bellātor, -ōris m warrior, fighter ♦ adj warlike.

bellātōrius adj aggressive.

bellātrix, -icis f warrioress ♦ adj warlike.

bellē adv well, nicely; ~ habēre be well (in health).

Bellerophōn, -ontis m slayer of Chimaera, rider of Pegasus.

Bellerophontēus adj see n.

bellicōsus adj warlike.

bellicus adj of war, military; ~um canere give the signal for marching or attack.

belliger, -ī adj martial.

belligerō, -āre, -āvī, -ātum vi to wage war.

bellipotēns, -entis adj strong in war.

bellō, -āre, -āvī, -ātum vi to fight, wage war.

Bellōna, -ae f goddess of war.

bellor, -ārī vi to fight.

bellulus adj pretty.

bellum, -ī nt war, warfare; battle; ~ gerere wage war; ~ī in war.

bellus adj pretty, handsome; pleasant, nice.

bēlua, -ae f beast, monster (esp large and fierce); any animal; (fig) brute; ~ Gaetula India elephant.

bēluātus adj embroidered with animals.

bēluōsus adj full of monsters.

Bēlus, -ī *m* Baal; an oriental king.
Bēnācus, -ī *m* lake in N. Italy (*now* Garda).
bene *adv* (*compar* **melius,** *superl* **optimē**) well; correctly; profitably; very ♦ *interj* bravo!, good!; ~ **dīcere** speak well; speak well of, praise; ~ **emere** buy cheap; ~ **est tibi** you are well off; ~ **tācēre do well;** do good to; ~ **facis** thank you; **rem ~ gērere be** successful; ~ **sē habēre** have a good time; ~ **habet** all is well, it's all right; ~ **merērī dē** do a service to; ~ **partum** honestly acquired; ~ **tē** ! your health!; ~ **vēndere** sell at a high price; ~ **vīvere** live a happy life.
benedīcō, -īcere, -īxī, -ictum *vt* to speak well of, praise; (*ECCL*) to bless.
benedictiō, -ōnis *f* (*ECCL*) blessing.
beneficentia, -ae *f* kindness.
beneficiāriī, -ōrum *mpl* privileged soldiers.
beneficium, -ī *and* **iī** *nt* benefit, favour; (*POL, MIL*) promotion; -**ō tuō** thanks to you.
beneficus *adj* generous, obliging.
Beneventānus adj see n.
Beneventum, -ī *nt* town in S. Italy (*now* Benevento).
benevolē *adv see* **benevolus**.
benevolēns, -entis *adj* kind-hearted.
benevolentia, -ae *f* goodwill, friendliness.
benevolus *adj* kindly, friendly; (*of* servants) devoted.
benīgnē *adv* willingly, courteously; generously; (*colloq*) no thank you; ~ **facere** do a favour.
benīgnitās, -ātis *f* kindness, liberality, bounty.

benīgnus *adj* kind, friendly; favourable; liberal, lavish; fruitful, bounteous.
beō, -āre, -āvī, -ātum *vt* to gladden, bless, enrich.
Berecyntia *f* Cybele.
Berecyntius *adj* of Berecyntus; of Cybele.
Berecyntus, -ī *m* mountain in Phrygia sacred to Cybele.
Berenīcē, -ēs *f* a queen of Egypt; **comā ~ēs** a constellation.
bēryllus, -ī *m* beryl.
bēs, bessis *m* two-thirds of the as; two-thirds.
bēstia, -ae *f* beast; wild animal for the arena.
bēstiārius *adj* of beasts ♦ *m* beast fighter in the arena.
bēstiola, -ae *f* small animal.
bēta, -ae *f* beet.
bēta *nt indecl* Greek letter beta.
bibī *perf of* **bibō**.
bibliopōla, -ae *m* bookseller.
bibliothēca, -ae, -ē, -ēs *f* library.
bibō, -ere, -ī *vt* to drink; to live on the banks of (a river); to drink in, absorb; (*fig*) to listen attentively, be imbued; ~ **aquas** be drowned; **Graecō mōre ~** drink to one's health.
bibulus *adj* fond of drink, thirsty; (*things*) thirsty.
Bibulus, -ī *m* consul with Caesar in 59 BC.
biceps, -ipitis *adj* two-headed.
biclīnium, -ī *and* **iī** *nt* dining couch for two.
bicolor, -ōris *adj* two-coloured.
bicorniger, -ī *adj* two-horned.
bicornis *adj* two-horned, two-pronged; (*rivers*) two-mouthed.
bicorpor, -is *adj* two-bodied.
bidēns, -entis *adj* with two teeth or prongs ♦ *m* hoe ♦ *f* sheep (*or other*

*The present infinitive verb endings are as follows: -***āre** *= 1st; -***ēre** *= 2nd; -***ere** *= 3rd and* -**īre** *= 4th. See sections on irregular verbs and noun declensions.*

sacrificial animal).

bidental, -ālis nt a place struck by lightning.

biduum, -ī nt two days.

biennium -ī and iī nt two years.

bifāriam adv in two parts, twice.

bifer, -ī adj flowering twice a year.

bifidus adj split in two.

biforis adj double-doored; double.

biformātus, biformis adj with two forms.

bifrōns, -ontis adj two-headed.

bifurcus adj two-pronged, forked.

bigae, -ārum fpl chariot and pair.

bigātus adj stamped with a chariot and pair.

biiugī, -ōrum mpl two horses yoked abreast; chariot with two horses.

biiugis, biiugus adj yoked.

bilībra, -ae f two pounds.

bilībris adj holding two pounds.

bilinguis adj double-tongued; bilingual; deceitful.

bilis, -is f bile, gall; (fig) anger, displeasure; ~ **ātra, nigra** melancholy; madness.

bilīx, -īcis adj double-stranded.

bilūstris adj ten years.

bimaris adj between two seas.

bimarītus, -ī m bigamist.

bimāter, -ris adj having two mothers.

bimembris adj half man, half beast; (pl) Centaurs.

bimēstris adj of two months, two months old.

bimulus adj only two years old.

bīmus adj two years old, for two years.

bīnī, binae, bīna num two each, two by two; a pair; (with pl nouns having a meaning) two.

binoctium, -ī and iī nt two nights.

binōminis adj with two names.

Biōn, -ōnis m satirical philosopher.

Biōnēus adj satirical.

bipalmis adj two spans long.

bipartītō adv in two parts, in two directions.

bipartītus adj divided in two.

bipatēns, -entis adj double-opening.

bipedālis adj two feet long broad or thick.

bipennifer, -ī adj wielding a battle-axe.

bipennis adj two-edged ♦ f battle-axe.

bipertītō etc see **bipartītō**.

bipēs, -edis adj two-footed ♦ m biped.

birēmis adj two-oared; with two banks of oars ♦ f two-oared skiff; galley with two banks of oars.

bis adv twice, double; ~ **ad eundem** make the same mistake twice; ~ **diē, in diē** twice a day; ~ **tantō, tantum** twice as much; ~ **terque** frequently; ~ **terve** seldom.

bissextus, -ī m intercalary day after 24th Feb.

Bistones, -um mpl people of Thrace.

Bistonis f Thracian woman, Bacchante.

Bistonius adj Thracian.

bisulcilingua, -ae adj fork-tongued, deceitful.

bisulcus adj cloven.

Bīthynia, -iae f province of Asia Minor.

Bīthynicus, Bīthynius, -us adj see **Bīthynia**.

bītō, -ere vi to go.

bitūmen, -inis nt bitumen, a kind of pitch.

bitūmineus adj see **bitūmen**.

bivium nt two ways.

bivius adj two-way.

blaesus adj lisping, indistinct.

blandē adv see **blandus**.

blandidicus adj fair-spoken.

blandiloquentia, -ae f attractive language.

blandiloquus, -entulus *adj* fair-
spoken.

blandīmentum, -ī *nt* compliment,
allurement.

blandior, -īrī, -ītus *vi* to coax,
caress; to flatter, pay
compliments; (*things*) to please,
entice.

blanditia, -ae *f* caress, flattery;
charm, allurement.

blandītim *adv* caressingly.

blandus *adj* smooth-tongued,
flattering, fawning; charming,
winsome.

blaterō, -āre *vi* to babble.

blatiō, -īre *vt* to babble.

blatta, -ae *f* cockroach.

blennus, -ī *m* idiot.

bliteus *adj* silly.

blitum, -ī *nt* kind of spinach.

boārius *adj* of cattle; **forum ~um**
cattle market in Rome.

Bodotria, -ae *f* Firth of Forth.

Boeōtarchēs *m* chief magistrate of
Boeotia.

Boeōtia, -iae *f* district of central
Greece.

Boeōtius, -us *adj see n.*

boiae, -ārum *fpl* collar.

Boiī, -ōrum *mpl* people of S.E. Gaul.

Boiohaemī, -ōrum *mpl*
Bohemians.

bōlētus, -ī *m* mushroom.

holus, -ī *m* (*dice*) throw; (*net*) cast;
(*fig*) haul, piece of good luck;
titbit.

bombus, -ī *m* booming, humming,
buzzing.

bombȳcinus *adj* of silk.

bombyx, -ȳcis *m* silkworm; silk.

Bona Dea, -ae, -ae *f* goddess
worshipped by women.

bonitās, -ātis *f* goodness; honesty,
integrity; kindness, affability.

Bonōnia, -ae *f* town in N. Italy

(*now* Bologna).

Bonōniēnsis *adj see n.*

bonum, -ī *nt* a moral good;
advantage, blessing; (*pl*)
property; **cuī ~ō ?** who was the
gainer?

bonus *adj* (*compar* **melior,** *superl*
optimus) good; kind; brave; loyal;
beneficial; lucky ♦ *mpl* upper
class party, conservatives; **-a
aetās** prime of life; **-ō animō** of
good cheer; well-disposed; **-ae
artēs** integrity; culture, liberal
education; **-a dicta** witticisms; **-a
fidēs** good faith; **-ī mōrēs**
morality; **-ī nummī** genuine
money; **-a pars** large part;
conservative party; **-ae rēs**
comforts, luxuries; prosperity;
morality; **-ā veniā** with kind
permission; **-a verba** words of
good omen; well-chosen diction;
-a vōx loud voice.

boō, -āre *vi* to cry aloud.

Boōtēs, -ae *nt* constellation
containing Arcturus.

Boreās, -ae *m* north wind; north.

Boreus *adj see n.*

Borysthenēs, -is *m* river Dnieper.

Borysthenidae *mpl* dwellers near the
Dnieper.

Borysthenius *adj see* **Borys-
thenīdae.**

hōs, bovis *m/f* ox, cow; kind of
turbot; **~ Lūca** elephant; **bovī
clitellās impōnere** = put a round
peg in a square hole.

Bosporānus *adj see n.*

Bosporius *adj:* **~ Cimmerius** *strait
from Sea of Azov to Black Sea.*

Bosporus, -ī *m* strait from Black Sea
to Sea of Marmora.

Boudicca, -ae *f* British queen
(*falsely called Boadicea*).

bovārius *etc see* **boārius.**

The present infinitive verb endings are as follows: **-āre** = 1st; **-ēre** = 2nd; **-ere** = 3rd and
-īre = 4th. *See sections on irregular verbs and noun declensions.*

Bovillae, -ārum *fpl* ancient Latin town.

Bovillānus *adj see n.*

bovillus *adj* of oxen.

brācae, -ārum *fpl* trousers.

brācātus *adj* trousered; barbarian (*esp of tribes beyond the Alps*).

bracchiālis *adj* of the arm.

bracchiolum, -ī *nt* dainty arm.

bracchium, -ī and iī *nt* arm, forearm; (*shellfish*) claw; (*tree*) branch; (*sea*) arm; (*NAUT*) yardarm; (*MIL*) outwork, mole; **levī, mollī bracchiō** casually.

bractea *etc see* **brattea.**

brassica, -ae *f* cabbage.

brattea, -ae *f* gold leaf.

bratteola, -ae *f* very fine gold leaf.

Brennus, -ī *m* Gallic chief who defeated the Romans.

brevī *adv* shortly, soon; briefly, in a few words.

brevia, -ium *ntpl* shoals.

breviārium, -ī and iī *nt* summary, statistical survey, official report.

breviculus *adj* shortish.

breviloquēns, -ēntis *adj* brief.

brevis *adj* short, small, shallow; brief, short-lived; concise.

brevitās, -ātis *f* shortness, smallness; brevity, conciseness.

breviter *adv* concisely.

Brigantēs, -um *mpl* British tribe in N. England.

Briganticus *adj see n.*

Brīsēis, -idos *f* captive of Achilles.

Britannia, -iae *f* Britain; the British Isles.

Britannicus *m* son of emperor Claudius.

Britannus, -icus *adj see n.*

Bromius, -ī and iī *m* Bacchus.

brūma, -ae *f* winter solstice, midwinter; winter.

brūmālis *adj* of the winter solstice; wintry; **~ flexus** tropic of Capricorn.

Brundisīnus *adj see n.*

Brundisium, -ī and iī *nt* port in S.E. Italy (*now* Brindisi).

Bruttiī, -ōrum *mpl* people of the toe of Italy.

Bruttius *adj see n.*

brūtus *adj* heavy, unwieldy; stupid, irrational.

Brūtus, -ī *m* liberator of Rome from kings; murderer of Caesar.

bubile, -is *nt* stall.

būbo, -ōnis *m/f* owl.

būbula, -ae *f* beef.

bubulcitor, -ārī *vi* to drive oxen.

bubulcus, -ī *m* ploughman.

būbulus *adj* of cattle.

būcaeda, -ae *m* flogged slave.

bucca, -ae *f* cheek; mouth; ranter.

buccō, -ōnis *m* babbler.

buccula, -ae *f* visor.

bucculentus *adj* fat-cheeked.

būcerus *adj* horned.

būcina, -ae *f* shepherd's horn; military trumpet; night watch.

būcinātor, -ōris *m* trumpeter.

būcolica, -ōrum *ntpl* pastoral poetry.

būcula, -ae *f* young cow.

būfō, -ōnis *m* toad.

bulbus, -ī *m* bulb; onion.

būlē, -es *f* Greek senate.

būleuta *m* senator.

būleutērium *nt* senate house.

bulla, -ae *f* bubble; knob, stud; gold charm worn round the neck by children of noblemen.

bullātus *adj* wearing the bulla; still a child.

būmastus, -ī *f* kind of vine.

būris, -is *m* plough-beam.

Burrus *old form of* Pyrrhus.

Busīris, -idis *m* Egyptian king killed by Hercules.

bustirapus, -ī *m* graverobber.

bustuārius *adj* at a funeral.

bustum, -ī *nt* funeral place; tomb, grave.

buxifer, **-ī** *adj* famed for its box trees.

buxum, **-ī** *nt* boxwood; flute, top, comb, tablet.

buxus, **-ī** *f* box tree; flute.

Byzantium, **-ī** and **iī** *nt* city on Bosporus (*later Constantinople, now Istanbul*).

Byzantius *adj see* n.

C

caballīnus *adj* horse's.

caballus, **-ī** *m* horse.

cacātus *adj* impure.

cachinnātiō, **-ōnis** *f* loud laughter.

cachinnō, **-āre** *vi* to laugh, guffaw.

cachinnō, **-ōnis** *m* scoffer.

cachinnus, **-ī** *m* laugh, derisive laughter; (*waves*) splashing.

cacō, **-āre** *vi* to evacuate the bowels.

cacoēthes, **-is** *nt* (*fig*) itch.

cacula, **-ae** *m* soldier's slave.

cacūmen, **-inis** *nt* extremity, point, summit, treetop; (*fig*) height, limit.

cacūminō, **-āre** *vt* to make pointed.

Cācus, **-ī** *m* giant robber, son of Vulcan.

cadāver, **-is** *nt* corpse, carcass.

cadāverōsus *adj* ghastly.

Cadmēa, **-ēae** *f* fortress of Thebes.

Cadmēis, **-ēidis** *f* Agave, Ino; Semele.

Cadmēus, **(-ēius)** *adj* of Cadmus; Theban.

Cadmus, **-ī** *m* founder of Thebes.

cadō, **-ere**, **cecidī**, **cāsum** *vi* to fall; to droop, die, be killed; (*ASTRO*) to set; (*dice*) to be thrown; (*events*) to happen, turn out; (*money*) to be due; (*strength, speech, courage*) to diminish, cease, fail; (*wind, rage*) to subside; (*words*) to end; ~ in subside; (*words*) to end; ~ in

suit, agree with; come under; ~ sub be exposed to; **animīs** ~ be disheartened; **causā** ~ lose one's case.

cādūceātor, **-ōris** *m* officer with flag of truce.

cādūceus, **-ī** *m* herald's staff; Mercury's wand.

cādūcifer, **-ī** *adj* with herald's staff.

cadūcus *adj* falling, fallen; (*fig*) perishable, fleeting, vain; (*law*) without an heir ♦ *nt* property without an heir.

Cadurcī, **-ōrum** *mpl* Gallic tribe.

Cadurcum, **-ī** *nt* linen coverlet.

cadus, **-ī** *m* jar, flask (*esp for wine*); urn.

caecigenus *adj* born blind.

Caeciliānus *adj see* n.

Caecilius, **-ī** *m* Roman name (*esp early Latin comic poet*).

caecitās, **-ātis** *f* blindness.

caecō, **-āre**, **-āvī**, **-ātum** *vt* to blind; to make obscure.

Caecubum, **-ī** *nt* choice wine from the *Ager Caecubus* in S. Latium.

caecus *adj* blind; invisible, secret; dark, obscure; (*fig*) aimless, unknown, uncertain; **appāret** ~ō ♦ it's as clear as daylight; **domus** ~a a house with no windows; ~ā diē **emere** buy on credit; ~um corpus the back.

caedēs, **-is** *f* murder, massacre; gore; the slain.

caedō, **-ere**, **cecīdī**, **caesum** *vt* to cut; to strike, to kill, cut to pieces; (*animals*) to sacrifice.

caelāmen, **-inis** *nt* engraved work.

caelātor, **-ōris** *m* engraver.

caelātūra, **-ae** *f* engraving in bas-relief.

caelebs, **-ibis** *adj* unmarried (bachelor *or* widower); (*trees*) with no vine trained on.

caeles, -itis adj celestial ♦ mpl the gods.

caelestis, -is adj of the sky, heavenly; divine; glorious ♦ mpl the gods ♦ ntpl the heavenly bodies.

Caeliānus adj see n.

caelibātus, -ūs m celibacy.

caelicola, -ae m god.

caelifer, -ī adj supporting the sky.

Caelius, -ī m Roman name; Roman hill.

caelō, -āre, -āvī, -ātum vt to engrave (in relief on metals), carve (on wood); (fig) to compose.

caelum, -ī nt engraver's chisel.

caelum, -ī nt sky, heaven; air, climate, weather; (fig) height of success, glory; **~um ac terrās miscēre** create chaos; **ad ~um ferre** extol; **dē ~ō dēlāpsus** a messiah; **dē ~ō servāre** watch for omens; **dē ~ō tangī** be struck by lightning; **digitō ~um attingere** ≈ be in the seventh heaven; **in ~ō esse** be overjoyed.

caementum, -ī nt quarrystone, rubble.

caenōsus adj muddy.

caenum, -ī nt mud, filth.

caepa, -ae f, **caepe, -is** nt onion.

Caere nt indecl (gen -itis, abl -ēte) f ancient Etruscan town.

Caeres, -itis and **ētis** adj; **-ite cērā dignī** like the disfranchised masses.

caerimōnia, -ae f sanctity; veneration (for gods); religious usage, ritual.

caeruleus, caerulus adj blue, dark blue, dark green, dusky ♦ ntpl the sea.

Caesar, -is m Julius (great Roman soldier, statesman, author); Augustus; the emperor.

Caesareus, and **iānus,** and **īnus** adj see n.

caesariātus adj bushy-haired.

caesariēs, -ēī f hair.

caesicius adj bluish.

caesim adv with the edge of the sword; (RHET) in short clauses.

caesius adj bluish grey, blue-eyed.

caespes, -itis m sod, turf; mass of roots.

caestus, -ūs m boxing glove.

caesus ppp of **caedō.**

caetra, -ae f targe.

caetrātus adj armed with a targe.

Caicus, -ī m river in Asia Minor.

Cāiēta, -ae; -ē, -ēs f town in Latium.

Cāius etc see **Gaius.**

Calaber, -rī adj Calabrian.

Calabria f S.E. peninsula of Italy.

Calamis, -idis m Greek sculptor.

calamister, -rī m, **-rum, -rī** nt curling iron; (RHET) flourish.

calamistrātus adj curled; foppish.

calamitās, -ātis f disaster; (MIL) defeat; (AGR) damage, failure.

calamitōsē adv see **calamitōsus.**

calamitōsus adj disastrous, ruinous; blighted, unfortunate.

calamus, -ī m reed; stalk; pen, pipe, arrow, fishing rod.

calathiscus, -ī m small basket.

calathus, -ī m wicker basket; bowl, cup.

calātor, -ōris m servant.

calcāneum, -ī nt heel.

calcar, -āris nt spur.

calceāmentum, -ī nt shoe.

calceātus ppp shod.

calceolārius, -ī and **iī** m shoemaker.

calceolus, -ī m small shoe.

calceus, -ī m shoe.

Calchās, -antis m Greek prophet at Troy.

calcitrō, -āre vi to kick; (fig) to resist.

calcō, -āre, -āvī, -ātum vt to tread, trample on; (fig) to spurn.

calculus, -ī m pebble, stone;

draughtsman, counting stone, reckoning, voting stone; **~um redūcere** take back a move; **~ōs subdūcere** compute; **ad ~ōs vocāre** subject to a reckoning.

caldārius *adj* with warm water.

caldus *etc see* **calidus.**

Calēdonia, -ae *f* the Scottish Highlands.

Calēdonius *adj see n.*

calefaciō, (calfaciō), fācere, -fēcī, -factum *vt* to warm, heat; (*fig*) to provoke, excite.

calefactō, -āre *vt* to warm.

Calendae *see* **Kalendae.**

Calēnus *adj* of Cales ♦ *nt* wine of Cales.

caleō, -ēre *vi* to be warm, be hot, glow; (*mind*) to be inflamed; (*things*) to be pursued with enthusiasm; to be fresh.

Calēs, -ium *fpl* town in Campania.

calēscō, -ere, -uī *vi* to get hot; (*fig*) to become inflamed.

calidē *adv* promptly.

calidus *adj* warm, hot; (*fig*) fiery, eager; hasty; prompt ♦ *f* warm water ♦ *nt* warm drink.

caliendrum, -ī *nt* headdress of hair.

caliga, -ae *f* soldier's boot.

caligātus *adj* heavily shod.

cālīginōsus *adj* misty, obscure.

cālīgō, -inis *f* mist, fog; dimness, darkness; (*mind*) obtuseness; (*CIRCS*) trouble.

cālīgō, -āre *vi* to be misty, be dim; to cause dizziness.

Calīgula, -ae *m* emperor Gaius.

calix, -cis *m* wine cup; cooking pot.

calleō, -ēre *vi* to be thick-skinned; (*fig*) to be unfeeling; to be wise, be skilful ♦ *vt* to know, understand.

callidē *adv see* **callidus.**

calliditās, -ātis *f* skill; cunning.

callidus *adj* skilful, clever; crafty.

Callimachus, -ī *m* Greek poet of Alexandria.

Calliopē, -ēs, and **ēa, -ēae** *f* Muse of epic poetry.

callis, -is *m* footpath, mountain track; pass; hill pastures.

Callistō, -ūs *f* daughter of Lycaon; (*constellation*) Great Bear.

callōsus *adj* hard-skinned; solid.

callum, -ī *nt* hard or thick skin; firm flesh; (*fig*) callousness.

calō, -āre, -āvī, -ātum *vt* to convoke.

cālō, -ōnis *m* soldier's servant; drudge.

calor, -ōris *m* warmth, heat; (*fig*) passion, love.

Calpē, -ēs *f* Rock of Gibraltar.

Calpurniānus *adj see n.*

Calpurnius, -ī *m* Roman name.

caltha, -ae *f* marigold.

calthula, -ae *f* yellow dress.

caluī *perf of* **calēscō.**

calumnia, -ae *f* chicanery, sharp practice; subterfuge; misrepresentation; (*law*) dishonest accusation, blackmail; being convicted of malicious prosecution; **~am iūrāre** swear that an action is brought in good faith.

calumniātor, -ōris *m* legal trickster, slanderer.

calumnior, -ārī, -ātus *vt* to misrepresent, slander; (*law*) to bring an action in bad faith; **sē** ~ deprecate oneself.

calva, -ae *f* bald head.

calvitium, -ī *and* **iī** *nt* baldness.

calvor, -ārī *vt* to deceive.

calvus *adj* bald.

calx, -cis *f* heel; foot; **~ce petere, ferīre** kick; **adversus stimulum ~cēs** = kicking against the pricks.

The present infinitive verb endings are as follows: -āre = 1st; -ēre = 2nd; -ere = 3rd and -īre = 4th. See sections on irregular verbs and noun declensions.

calx, -cis f pebble; lime, chalk; finishing line, end; **ad carcerēs ā ~ce revocārī** have to begin all over again.

Calydōn, -ōnis f town in Aetolia.

Calydōnis adj Calydonian.

Calydōnius f Deianira; **~ōnius amnis** Achelous; **~ hērōs** Meleager; **~ōnia rēgna** Daunia in S. Italy.

Calypsō, -ūs (acc -ō) f nymph who detained Ulysses in Ogygia.

camēlīnus adj camel's.

camella, -ae f wine cup.

camēlus, -ī m camel.

Camēna, -ae f Muse; poetry.

camera, -ae f arched roof.

Camerīnum, -ī nt town in Umbria.

Camers, -tis, and **Camers, -tis** adj of Camerinum.

Camillus, -ī m Roman hero (who saved Rome from the Gauls).

camīnus, -ī m furnace, fire; forge; **oleum addere ~ō** ≈ add fuel to the flames.

cammarus, -ī m lobster.

Campānia, -iae f district of W. Italy.

Campānicus, and **ius**, and **us** adj Campanian, Capuan.

campē, -ēs f evasion.

campester, -ris adj of the plain; of the Campus Martius ♦ nt loincloth ♦ ntpl level ground.

campus, -ī m plain; sports field; any level surface; (fig) theatre, arena (of action, debate); **~ Martius** level ground by the Tiber (used for assemblies, sports, military drills).

Camulodūnum, -ī nt town of Trinobantes (now Colchester).

camur, -ī adj crooked.

canālis, -is m pipe, conduit, canal.

cancellī, -ōrum mpl grating, enclosure; barrier (in public places), bar of law court.

cancer, -rī m crab; (constellation) Cancer; south, tropical heat; (MED) cancer.

candefaciō, -ere vt to make dazzlingly white.

candēla, -ae f taper, tallow candle; waxed cord; **~am appōnere valvīs** set the house on fire.

candēlābrum, -ī nt candlestick, chandelier, lampstand.

candēns, -entis adj dazzling white; white-hot.

candeō, -ēre vi to shine, be white; to be white-hot.

candēscō, -ere vi to become white; to grow white-hot.

candidātōrius adj of a candidate.

candidātus adj dressed in white ♦ m candidate for office.

candidē adv in white; sincerely.

candidulus adj pretty white.

candidus adj white, bright; radiant, beautiful; clothed in white; (style) clear; (mind) candid, frank; (CIRCS) happy; **~ā sententiā** acquittal.

candor, -ōris m whiteness, brightness, beauty; (fig) brilliance, sincerity.

cānēns, -entis adj white.

cāneō, -ēre, -uī vi to be grey, be white.

cānēscō, -ere vi to grow white; to grow old.

canīcula, -ae f bitch; Dog Star, Sirius.

canīnus adj dog's, canine; snarling, spiteful; **~ littera** letter R.

canis, -is m/f dog, bitch; (fig) shameless or angry person; hanger-on; (dice) lowest throw; (ASTRO) Canis Major, Canis Minor; (myth) Cerberus.

canistrum, -ī nt wicker basket.

cānitiēs, -ēī f greyness; grey hair; old age.

canna, -ae f reed; pipe; gondola.

cannabis, -is f hemp.

Cannae, -ārum fpl village in Apulia (scene of great Roman defeat by Hannibal).

Cannēnsis adj see n.

canō, canere, cecinī vt, vi to sing; to play; to sing about, recite, celebrate; to prophesy; (MIL) to sound; (birds) to sing, crow.

canor, -ōris m song, tune, sound.

canōrus adj musical, melodious; singsong ♦ nt melodiousness.

Cantaber, -rī m Cantabrian.

Cantabria, -riae f district of N. Spain.

Cantabricus adj see n.

cantāmen, -inis nt charm.

cantharis, -idis f beetle; Spanish fly.

cantharus, -ī m tankard.

canthērīnus adj of a horse.

canthērius, -ī and **iī** m gelding.

canticum, -ī nt aria in Latin comedy; song.

cantilēna, -ae f old song, gossip; **~am eandem canere** keep harping on the same theme.

cantiō, -ōnis f song; charm.

cantitō, -āre, -āvī, -ātum vt to sing or play often.

Cantium, -ī and **iī** nt Kent.

cantiunculae, -ārum fpl fascinating strains.

cantō, -āre, -āvī, -ātum vt, vi to sing; to play; to sing about, recite, celebrate; to proclaim, harp on; to use magic spells; to sound; to drawl.

cantor, -ōris m, **-rīx, -rīcis** f singer, musician, poet; actor.

cantus, -ūs m singing, playing, music; prophecy; magic spell.

cānus adj white, grey, hoary; old ♦ mpl grey hairs.

Canusīnus adj see n.

Canusium, -ī nt town in Apulia (famous for wool).

capācitās, -ātis f spaciousness.

capāx, -ācis adj capable of holding, spacious, roomy; capable, able, fit.

capēdō, -inis f sacrificial dish.

capēduncula f small dish.

capella, -ae f she-goat; (ASTRO) bright star in Auriga.

Capēna, -ae f old Etruscan town.

Capēnās, -us adj: **Porta ~** a Roman gate leading to the Via Appia.

caper, -rī m goat, odour of the armpits.

caperrō, -āre vi to wrinkle.

capessō, -ere, -īvī, -ītum vt to seize, take hold of, try to reach, make for; to take in hand, engage in; **rem pūblicam ~** go in for politics.

capillātus adj long-haired; ancient.

capillus, -ī m hair (of head or beard); a hair.

capiō, oro, cēpī, captum vt to take, seize; to catch, capture; (MIL) to occupy, take prisoner; (NAUT) to make, reach (a goal); (fig) to captivate, charm, cheat; (pass) to be maimed, lose the use of; to choose; (appearance) to assume; (habit) to cultivate; (duty) to undertake; (ideas) to conceive, form; (feeling) to experience; (harm) to suffer; to receive, get, inherit; to contain, hold; (fig) to bear; (mind) to grasp; **cōnsilium ~** come to a decision; **impetum ~** gather momentum; **initium ~** start; **oculō capī** lose an eye; **mente captus** insane; **cupidō eum cēpit** he felt a desire.

capis, -dis f sacrificial bowl with one handle.

capistrātus adj haltered.

capistrum, -ī nt halter, muzzle.

capital, -ālis nt capital crime.

---

*The present infinitive verb endings are as follows: -**āre** = 1st; -**ēre** = 2nd; -**ere** = 3rd and -**īre** = 4th. See sections on irregular verbs and noun declensions.*

capitālis adj mortal, deadly, dangerous; (law) capital; important, excellent.

capitō, -ōnis m bighead.

Capitōlīnus adj of the Capitol; of Jupiter.

Capitōlium, -ī nt Roman hill with temple of Jupiter.

capitulātim adv summarily.

capitulum, -ī nt small head; person, creature.

Cappadocia, -ae f country of Asia Minor.

capra, -ae f she-goat; odour of armpits; (ASTRO) Capella.

caprea, -ae f roe.

Capreae, -ārum fpl island of Capri.

capreolus, -ī m roebuck; (pl) crossbeams.

Capricornus, -ī m (constellation) Capricorn (associated with midwinter).

caprificus, -ī f wild fig tree.

caprigenus adj of goats.

caprimulgus, -ī m goatherd, rustic.

caprīnus adj of goats.

capripēs, -edis adj goat-footed.

capsa, -ae f box (esp for papyrus rolls).

capsō archaic fut of **capiō.**

capsula, -ae f small box; **dē ~ā tōtus** ≈ out of a bandbox.

Capta, -ae f Minerva.

captātiō, -ōnis f catching at.

captātor, -ōris m one who courts; legacy hunter.

captiō, -ōnis f fraud; disadvantage; (argument) fallacy, sophism.

captiōsē adv see **captiōsus.**

captiōsus adj deceptive; dangerous; captious.

captiuncula, -ae f quibble.

captīvitās, -ātis f captivity; capture.

captīvus adj captive, captured; of

captives ♦ m/f prisoner of war.

captō, -āre, -āvī, -ātum vt to try to catch, chase; to try to win, court, watch for; to deceive, trap.

captus ppp of **capiō** ♦ m prisoner.

captus, -ūs m grasp, notion.

Capua, -ae f chief town of Campania.

capulāris adj due for a coffin.

capulus, -ī m coffin; handle, hilt.

caput, -itis nt head; top, extremity; (rivers) source; (more rarely) mouth; person, individual; life; civil rights; (person) chief, leader; (towns) capital; (money) principal; (writing) substance, chapter; principle, main point, the great thing; **~ cēnae** main dish; **~itis accūsāre** charge with a capital offence; **~itis damnāre** condemn to death; **~itis dēminūtiō** loss of political rights; **~itis poena** capital punishment; **~ita cōnferre** confer in secret; **in ~ita** per head; **suprā ~ut esse** to be imminent.

Cār, -is m Carian.

carbaseus adj linen, canvas.

carbasus, -ī f (pl -a, -ōrum nt) Spanish flax, fine linen; garment, sail, curtain.

carbō, -ōnis m charcoal, embers.

carbōnārius, -ī and **iī** m charcoal burner.

carbunculus, -ī m small coal; precious stone.

carcer, -is m prison; jailbird; barrier, starting place (for races); **ad ~ēs ā calce revocārī** have to begin all over again.

carcerārius adj of a prison.

carchēsium, -ī and **iī** nt drinking cup; (NAUT) masthead.

cardiacus, -ī m dyspeptic.

cardō, -inis m hinge; (ASTRO) pole, axis, cardinal point; (fig) juncture, critical moment.

carduus, -ī m thistle.

cārē adv see **cārus.**

cārectum, -ī nt sedge.

cāreō, -ēre, -uī vi (with abl) to be free from, not have, be without; to abstain from, be absent from; to want, miss.

cārex, -icis f sedge.

Cāria, -ae f district of S.W. Asia Minor.

Cāricus adj Carian ♦ f dried fig.

cariēs (acc -em, abl -ē) f dry rot.

carīna, -ae f keel; ship.

Carīnae, -ārum fpl district of Rome.

carīnārius, -ī and iī m dyer of yellow.

cariōsus adj crumbling; (fig) withered.

cāris, -idis f kind of crab.

cāritas, -ātis f dearness, high price; esteem, affection.

carmen, -inis nt song, tune; poem, poetry, verse; prophecy; (in law, religion) formula; moral text.

Carmentālis adj see n.

Carmentis, -is, and a, -ae f prophetess, mother of Evander.

carnārium, -ī and iī nt fleshhook; larder.

Carneadēs, -is m Greek philosopher (founder of the New Academy).

Carneadēus adj see n.

carnifex, -icis m executioner, hangman; scoundrel; murderer.

carnificīna, -ae f execution, torture; ~am facere be an executioner.

carnificō, -āre vt to behead, mutilate.

carō, -nis f flesh.

cārō, -ere vt to card.

Carpathius adj see n.

Carpathus, -ī f island between Crete and Rhodes.

carpatina, -ae f leather shoe.

carpentum, -ī nt two-wheeled coach.

carpō, -ere, -sī, -tum vt to pick, pluck, gather; to tear off; to browse, graze on; (wool) to card; (fig) to enjoy, snatch; to carp at, slander; to weaken, wear down; to divide up; (journey) to go, travel.

carptim adv in parts; at different points; at different times.

carptor, -ōris m carver.

carptus ppp of carpō.

carrus, -ī m waggon.

Carthāginiēnsis adj see n.

Carthāgō, -inis f Carthage (near Tunis); ~ Nova town in Spain (now Cartagena).

caruncula, -ae f piece of flesh.

cārus adj dear, costly; dear, beloved.

Carystēus adj see n.

Carystos, -ī f town in Euboea (famous for marble).

casa, -ae f cottage, hut.

cascus adj old.

cāseolus, -ī m small cheese.

cāseus, -ī m cheese.

casia, -ae f cinnamon; spurge laurel.

Caspius adj Caspian.

Cassandra, -ae f Trojan princess and prophetess, doomed never to be believed.

cassēs, -ium mpl net, snare; spider's web.

Cassiānus adj see n.

cassida, -ae f helmet.

Cassiepēa, -ae, Cassiopē, -ēs f mother of Andromeda; a constellation.

cassis, -idis f helmet.

Cassius, -ī m Roman family name.

cassō, -āre vi to shake.

cassus adj empty; devoid of, without (abl); vain, useless; ~ lūmine dead; in -um in vain.

The present infinitive verb endings are as follows: -āre = 1st; -ēre = 2nd; -ere = 3rd and -īre = 4th. See sections on irregular verbs and noun declensions.

Castalia, -ae f spring on Parnassus, (*sacred to Apollo and the Muses*).

Castalides, -dum fpl Muses.

Castalius, -s adj see n.

castanea, -ae f chestnut tree; chestnut.

castē adv see castus.

castellānus adj of a fortress ♦ mpl garrison.

castellātim adv in different fortresses.

castellum, -ī nt fortress, castle; (*fig*) defence, refuge.

castēria, -ae f rowers' quarters.

castīgābilis adj punishable.

castīgātiō, -ōnis f correction, reproof.

castīgātor, -ōris m reprover.

castīgātus adj small, slender.

castīgō, -āre, -āvī, -ātum vt to correct, punish; to reprove; to restrain.

castimōnia, -ae f purity, morality; chastity, abstinence.

castitās, -ātis f chastity.

castor, -oris m beaver.

Castor, -oris m twin brother of Pollux (*patron of sailors*); star in Gemini.

castoreum, -ī nt odorous secretion of the beaver.

castra, -ōrum ntpl camp; day's march; army life; (*fig*) party, sect; ~ movēre strike camp; ~ mūnīre construct a camp; ~ pōnere pitch camp; bīna ~ two camps.

castrēnsis adj of the camp, military.

castrō, -āre vt to castrate; (*fig*) to weaken.

castrum, -ī nt fort.

castus adj clean, pure, chaste, innocent; holy, pious.

cāsū adv by chance.

casula, -ae f little cottage.

cāsus, -ūs m fall, downfall; event, chance, accident; misfortune, death; opportunity; (*time*) end; (*GRAM*) case.

Catadūpa, -ōrum ntpl Nile cataract near Syene.

catagraphus adj painted.

Catamītus, -ī m Ganymede.

cataphractēs, -ae m coat of mail.

cataphractus adj wearing mail.

cataplus, -ī m ship arriving.

catapulta, -ae f (*MIL*) catapult; (*fig*) missile.

catapultārius adj thrown by catapult.

cataracta, -ae f waterfall; sluice; drawbridge.

catasta, -ae f stage, scaffold.

catē adv see catus.

catēia, -ae f javelin.

catella, -ae f small chain.

catellus, -ī m puppy.

catēna, -ae f chain; fetter; (*fig*) bond, restraint; series.

catēnātus adj chained, fettered.

caterva, -ae f crowd, band; flock; (*MIL*) troop, body; (*THEAT*) company.

catervātim adv in companies.

cathedra, -ae f armchair, sedan chair; teacher's chair.

catholicus adj (*ECCL*) orthodox, universal.

Catilīna, -ae m Catiline (*conspirator suppressed by Cicero*).

Catilīnārius adj see n.

catīllō, -āre vt to lick a plate.

catīllus, -ī m small dish.

catīnus, -ī m dish, pot.

Catō, -ōnis m famous censor and author, idealised as the pattern of an ancient Roman; famous Stoic and republican leader against Caesar.

Catōniānus adj see n.

Catōnīnī mpl Cato's supporters.

catōnium, -ī and **iī** nt the lower world.

Catulliānus adj see n.

Catullus, -ī m Latin lyric poet.

catulus, -ī *m* puppy; cub, young of other animals.

catus *adj* clever; wise; sly, cunning.

Caucasius *adj see n.*

Caucasus, -ī *m* Caucasus mountains.

cauda, -ae *f* tail; **~am iactāre** fawn; **~am trahere** be made a fool of.

caudeus *adj* wooden.

caudex, -icis *m* trunk; block of wood; book, ledger, *(fig)* blockhead.

caudicālis *adj* of woodcutting.

Caudīnus *adj see n.*

Caudium, -ī *nt Samnite town.*

caulae, -ārum *fpl* opening; sheepfold.

caulis, -is *m* stalk; cabbage.

Cauneus *adj* Caunian.

Caunus, -ī *f town in Caria* ♦ *fpl* dried figs.

caupō, -ōnis *m* shopkeeper, innkeeper.

caupōna, -ae *f* shop, inn.

caupōnius *adj see n.*

caupōnor, -ārī *vt* to trade in.

caupōnula, -ae *f* tavern.

Caurus, -ī *m* north-west wind.

causa, -ae *f* cause, reason; purpose, sake; excuse, pretext; connection, case, position; *(law)* case, suit; *(POL)* cause, party; *(RHET)* subject matter; **~am agere, ōrāre** plead a case; **~am dēfendere** speak for the defence; **~am dīcere** defend oneself; **~ā** for the sake of; **cum ~ā** with good reason; **quā dē ~ā** for this reason; **in ~ā esse** be responsible; **per ~am** under the pretext.

causārius *adj (MIL)* unfit for service.

causia, -ae *f* Macedonian hat.

causidicus, -ī *m* advocate.

causificor, -ārī *vi* to make a pretext.

causor, -ārī, -ātus *vt, vi* to pretend, make an excuse of.

caussa *etc see* **causa.**

causula, -ae *f* petty lawsuit; slight cause.

cautē *adv* carefully, cautiously; with security.

cautēla, -ae *f* caution.

cautēs, -is *f* rock, crag.

cautim *adv* warily.

cautiō, -ōnis *f* caution, wariness; *(law)* security, bond, bail; **mihi ~ est** I must take care; **mea ~ est** I must see to it.

cautor, -ōris *m* wary person; surety.

cautus *ppp of* **caveō** ♦ *adj* wary, provident; safe, secure.

cavaedium, -ī *and* **iī** *nt* inner court of a house.

cavea, -ae *f* cage, stall, coop, hive; *(THEAT)* auditorium; theatre; **prima ~** upper class seats; **ultima ~** lower class seats.

caveō, -ēre, cāvī, cautum *vt* to beware of, guard against ♦ *vi* (with **ab** *or* **abl**) to be on one's guard against; *(with dat)* to look after; *(with* **nē**) to take care that ... not; *(with* **ut**) to take good care that; *(with subj or inf)* to take care not to, do not; *(law)* to stipulate, decree; *(COMM)* to get a guarantee, give a guarantee, stand security; **cavē!** look out!

caverna, -ae *f* hollow, cave, vault; *(NAUT)* hold.

cavilla, -ae *f* jeering.

cavillātiō, -ōnis *f* jeering, banter; sophistry.

cavillātor, -ōris *m* scoffer.

The present infinitive verb endings are as follows: -āre = 1st; -ēre = 2nd; -ere = 3rd and -īre = 4th. See sections on irregular verbs and noun declensions.

cavillor, -ārī, -ātus vt to scoff at
♦ vi to jeer, scoff; to quibble.

cavō, -āre, -āvī, -ātum vt to hollow,
excavate.

cavus adj hollow, concave,
vaulted; (river) deep-channelled
♦ nt cavity, hole.

Caystros, -us, -ī m river in Lydia
(famous for swans).

-ce demonstrative particle appended to
pronouns and adverbs.

Cēa, -ae f Aegean island (birthplace
of Simonides).

cecidī perf of **cadō**.

cecidī perf of **caedō**.

cecinī perf of **canō**.

Cecropidēs, -idae m Theseus;
Athenian.

Cecropis, -idis f Aglauros; Procne;
Philomela; Athenian, Attic.

Cecropius adj Athenian ♦ f
Athens.

Cecrops, -is m ancient king of Athens.

cēdō, -ere, cessī, cessum vi to go,
walk; to depart, withdraw,
retreat; to pass away, die; (events)
to turn out; to be changed (into);
to accrue (to); to yield, be inferior
(to) ♦ vt to give up, concede,
allow; ~ **bonīs, possessiōne** make
over property (to); ~ **forō** go
bankrupt; ~ **locō** leave one's post;
~ **memoriā** be forgotten.

cedo (pl **cette**) impv give me, bring
here; tell me; let me; look at!

cedrus, -ī f cedar, perfumed
juniper; cedar oil.

Celaenō, -ūs f a Harpy; a Pleiad.

cēlāta ntpl secrets.

celeber, -ris adj crowded,
populous; honoured, famous;
repeated.

celebrātiō, -ōnis f throng;
celebration.

celebrātus adj full, much used;
festive; famous.

celebritās, -ātis f crowd;

celebration; fame.

celebrō, -āre, -āvī, -ātum vt to
crowd, frequent; to repeat,
practise; to celebrate, keep (a
festival); to advertise, glorify.

celer, -is adj quick, swift, fast;
hasty.

Celerēs, -um mpl royal bodyguard.

celeripēs, -edis adj swift-footed.

celeritās, -ātis f speed, quickness.

celeriter adv see **celer**.

celerō, -āre vt to quicken ♦ vi to
make haste.

cella, -ae f granary, stall, cell;
garret, hut, small room;
sanctuary of a temple.

cellārius adj of the storeroom ♦ m
steward.

cellula, -ae f little room.

cēlō, -āre, -āvī, -ātum vt to hide,
conceal, keep secret; **id mē ~at** he
keeps me in the dark about it.

celōx, -ōcis adj swift ♦ f fast ship,
yacht.

celsus adj high, lofty; (fig) great,
eminent; haughty.

Celtae, -ārum mpl Celts (esp of
central Gaul) ♦ nt the Celtic nation.

Celtibērī, -ōrum mpl people of
central Spain.

Celtibēria, -iae f Central Spain.

Celtibēricus adj see n.

Celticus adj Celtic.

cēna, -ae f dinner (the principal
Roman meal); **inter ~am** at table.

cēnāculum, -ī nt dining-room;
upper room, garret.

cēnāticus adj of dinner.

cēnātiō, -ōnis f dining-room.

cēnātus ppa having dined, after
dinner ♦ ppp spent in feasting.

Cenchreae, -ārum fpl harbour of
Corinth.

cēnitō, -āre vi to be accustomed to
dine.

cēnō, -āre, -āvī, -ātum vi to dine
♦ vt to eat, dine on.

cēnseō, -ēre, -uī, -um vt (census) to assess, rate, take a census, make a property return; (fig) to estimate, appreciate, celebrate; (senate or other body) to decree, resolve; (member) to express an opinion, move, vote; to advise; to judge, think, suppose, consider; **cēnsuī ~endō** for census purposes.

cēnsiō, -ōnis f punishment; expression of opinion.

cēnsor, -ōris m censor; (fig) severe judge, critic.

cēnsōrius adj of the censors, to be dealt with by the censors; (fig) severe; **homō ~** an ex-censor.

cēnsūra, -ae f censorship; criticism.

cēnsus ppp of **cēnseō; capite ~ī** the poorest class of Roman citizens.

cēnsus, -ūs m register of Roman citizens and their property, census; registered property; wealth; **~um agere, habēre** hold a census; **sine ~ū** poor.

centaurēum, -ī nt centaury.

Centaurēus adj see n.

Centaurus, -ī m Centaur, half man half horse.

centēnī, -um num a hundred each, a hundred.

centēsimus adj hundredth ♦ f hundredth part; (interest) 1 per cent monthly (12 per cent per annum).

centiceps adj hundred-headed.

centiēns, -ēs adv a hundred times.

centimanus adj hundred-handed.

centō, -ōnis m patchwork; **~ōnēs sarcīre** = tell tall stories.

centum num a hundred.

centumgeminus adj hundred-fold.

centumplex adj hundred-fold.

centumpondium, -ī and **iī** nt a hundred pounds.

centumvirālis adj of the centumvirī.

centumvirī, -ōrum mpl a bench of judges who heard special civil cases in Rome.

centunculus, -ī m piece of patchwork, saddlecloth.

centuria, -ae f (MIL) company; (POL) century (a division of the Roman people according to property).

centuriātim adv by companies, by centuries.

centuriātus adj divided by centuries; **comitia ~a** assembly which voted by centuries.

centuriātus, -ūs m division into centuries; rank of centurion.

centuriō, -āre, -āvī, -ātum vt (MIL) to assign to companies; (POL) to divide by centuries.

centuriō, -ōnis m (MIL) captain, centurion.

centussis, -is m a hundred asses.

cēnula, -ae f little dinner.

Ceōs, acc -ō see **Cea.**

Cēpheis f Andromeda.

Cēphēius adj of Cepheus.

Cēphēus adj Ethiopian.

Cēpheus -eī (acc -ea) m king of Ethiopia (father of Andromeda).

Cēphisis adj see n.

Cēphisius m Narcissus.

Cēphisus, -ī m river in central Greece.

cēpī perf of **capiō.**

cēra, -ae f wax; honey cells; writing tablet, notebook; seal; portrait of an ancestor; **prīma ~** first page.

Cerāmīcus, -ī m Athenian cemetery.

cērārium, -ī and **iī** nt seal-duty.

cerastēs, -ae m a horned serpent.

cerasus, -ī f cherry tree; cherry.

cērātus adj waxed.

Ceraunia, -ōrum nt, **Ceraunī** m mountains in Epirus.

The present infinitive verb endings are as follows: -āre = 1st; -ēre = 2nd; -ere = 3rd and -īre = 4th. See sections on irregular verbs and noun declensions.

Cerbereus adj see n.

Cerberus, -ī m three-headed watchdog of Hades.

cercopithēcus, -ī m monkey.

cercūrus, -ī m Cyprian type of ship.

cerdō, -ōnis m tradesman.

Cereālia, -ium ntpl festival of Ceres.

Cereālis adj of Ceres; of corn, of meal.

cerebrōsus adj hot-headed.

cerebrum, -ī nt brain; understanding; quick temper.

Cerēs, -eris f goddess of agriculture; (fig) grain, bread.

cēreus adj waxen; wax-coloured; (fig) supple, easily led ♦ m taper.

cēriāria, -ae f taper maker.

cērina, -ōrum ntpl wax-coloured clothes.

cērintha, -ae f honeywort.

cernō, -ere, -crēvī, crētum vt to see, discern; to understand, perceive; to decide, determine; (law) to decide to take up (an inheritance).

cernuus adj face downwards.

cērōma, -atis nt wrestlers' ointment.

cērōmaticus adj smeared with wax ointment.

cerrītus adj crazy.

certāmen, -inis nt contest, match; battle, combat; (fig) struggle, rivalry.

certātim adv emulously.

certātiō, -ōnis f contest; debate; rivalry.

certē adv assuredly, of course; at least.

certō adv certainly, really.

certō, -āre, -āvī, -ātum vi to contend, compete; (MIL) to fight it out; (law) to dispute; (with inf) to try hard.

certus adj determined, fixed, definite; reliable, unerring; sure, certain; mihi ~um est I have

made up my mind; ~um scīre, prō ~ō habēre know for certain, be sure; ~iōrem facere inform.

cērula, -ae f piece of wax; ~ miniāta red pencil.

cērussa, -ae f white lead.

cērussātus adj painted with white lead.

cerva, -ae f hind, deer.

cervīcal, -ālis nt pillow.

cervīcula, -ae f slender neck.

cervīnus adj deer's.

cervīx, -īcis f neck; in ~īcibus esse be a burden (to), threaten.

cervus, -ī m stag, deer; (MIL) palisade.

cessātiō, -ōnis f delaying, inactivity, idleness.

cessātor, -ōris m idler.

cessī perf of cēdō.

cessiō, -ōnis f giving up.

cessō, -āre, -āvī, -ātum vi to be remiss, stop; to loiter, delay; to be idle, rest, do nothing; (land) to lie fallow; to err.

cestrosphendonē, -ēs f (MIL) engine for shooting stones.

cestus, -ī m girdle (esp of Venus).

cētārium, -ī and **iī** nt fishpond.

cētārius, -ī and **iī** m fishmonger.

cētera adv in other respects.

cēterī, -ōrum adj the rest, the others; (sg) the rest of.

cēterōquī, -n adv otherwise.

cēterum adv for the rest, otherwise; but for all that; besides.

Cethēgus, -ī m a conspirator with Catiline.

cētr- etc see caetr-.

cette etc see cedo.

cētus, -ī m (-ē ntpl) sea monster, whale.

ceu adv just as, as if.

Cēus adj see Cēa.

Cēÿx, -ÿcis m husband of Alcyone, changed to a kingfisher.

Chalcidēnsis, (-discus) adj see n.

Chalcis, -dis f chief town of Euboea.

Chaldaeī, -aeōrum mpl Chaldeans; astrologers.

Chaldāicus adj see n.

chalybēius adj of steel.

Chalybes, -um mpl a people of Pontus (famous as ironworkers).

chalybs, -is m steel.

Chāones, -um mpl a people of Epirus.

Chāonia, -iae f Epirus.

Chāonius, -is adj see n.

Chaos (abl -ō) nt empty space, the lower world, chaos.

chara, -ae f an unidentified vegetable.

charistia, -ōrum ntpl a Roman family festival.

Charites, -um fpl the Graces.

Charōn, -ontis m Charon (ferryman of Hades).

charta, -ae f sheet of papyrus, paper; writing.

chartula, -ae f piece of paper.

Charybdis, -is f monster personifying a whirlpool in the Straits of Messina; (fig) peril.

Chatti, -ōrum mpl a people of central Germany.

Chelae, -ārum fpl (ASTRO) the Claws (of Scorpio); Libra.

chelydrus, -ī m watersnake.

chelys (acc -yn) f tortoise; lyre.

cheragra, -ae f gout in the hands.

Cherronēsus, Chersonēsus, -ī f Gallipoli peninsula; Crimea.

chiliarchus, -ī m officer in charge of 1000 men; chancellor of Persia.

Chimaera, -ae f fire-breathing monster formed of lion, goat and serpent.

Chimaeriferus adj birthplace of Chimaera.

Chios, -ī f Aegean island (famous for wine).

Chīus adj Chian ♦ nt Chian wine; Chian cloth.

chīrographum, -ī nt handwriting; document.

Chīrōn, -ōnis m a learned Centaur (tutor of heroes).

chīronomos, -ī m/f, **chīronomōn, -untis** m mime actor.

chīrūrgia, -ae f surgery; (fig) violent measures.

chlamydātus adj wearing a military cloak.

chlamys, -dis f Greek military cloak.

Choerilus, -ī m inferior Greek poet.

chorāgium, -ī and **iī** nt producing of a chorus.

chorāgus, -ī m one who finances a chorus.

choraulēs, -ae m flute-player (accompanying a chorus).

chorda, -ae f string (of an instrument); rope.

chorēa, -ae f dance.

chorēus, -ī m trochee.

chorus, -ī m choral dance; chorus, choir of singers or dancers; band, troop.

Christiānismus, -ī m Christianity.

Christiānus adj Christian.

Christus, -ī m Christ.

Chrȳsēis, -ēidis f daughter of Chryses.

Chrȳsēs, -ae m priest of Apollo in the Iliad.

Chrȳsippēus adj see n.

Chrȳsippus, -ī m Stoic philosopher.

chrysolithos, -ī m/f topaz.

chrȳsos, -ī m gold.

cibārius adj food (in cpds); common ♦ ntpl rations.

cibātus, -ūs m food.

cibōrium, -ī and **iī** nt kind of drinking cup.

*The present infinitive verb endings are as follows: -**āre** = 1st; -**ēre** = 2nd; -**ere** = 3rd and -**īre** = 4th. See sections on irregular verbs and noun declensions.*

cibus, -ī m food, fodder, nourishment.

cicāda, -ae f cicada, cricket.

cicātrīcōsus adj scarred.

cicātrīx, -īcis f scar; (plants) mark of an incision.

ciccus, -ī m pomegranate pip.

cicer, -is nt chickpea.

Cicerō, -ōnis m great Roman orator and author.

Cicerōniānus adj see n.

cichorēum, -ī nt chicory.

Cicōnes, -um mpl people of Thrace.

cicōnia, -ae f stork.

cicur, -is adj tame.

cicūta, -ae f hemlock; pipe.

cieō, ciēre, cīvī, citum vt to move, stir, rouse; to call, invoke; (fig) to give rise to, produce; **calcem ~** make a move (in chess).

Cilicia, -ae f country in S. Asia Minor (famous for piracy).

Ciliciēnsis, (-us) adj see n.

Cilix, -cis, -ssa adj Cilician ♦ nt goats' hair garment.

Cimbrī, -ōrum mpl people of N. Germany.

Cimbricus adj see n.

cīmex, -icis m bug.

Cimmeriī, -ōrum mpl people of the Crimea; mythical race in caves near Cumae.

Cimmerius adj see n.

cinaedus adj lewd.

cinaedus, -ī m sodomite; lewd dancer.

cincinnātus adj with curled hair.

Cincinnātus, -ī m ancient Roman dictator.

cincinnus, -ī m curled hair; (fig) rhetorical ornament.

Cincius, -ī m Roman tribune; Roman historian.

cincticulus, -ī m small girdle.

cinctus ppp of **cingō**.

cinctus, -ūs m girding; **~ Gabīnus** a ceremonial style of wearing the toga.

cinctūtus adj girded.

cinefactus adj reduced to ashes.

cinerārius, -ī and iī m hair curler.

cingō, -gere, -xī, -ctum vt to surround, enclose; to gird, crown; (MIL) to besiege, fortify; to cover, escort; **ferrum ~or** I put on my sword.

cingula, -ae f girth (of animals).

cingulum, -ī nt belt.

cingulus, -ī m zone.

ciniflō, -ōnis m hair curler.

cinis, -eris m ashes; (fig) ruin.

Cinna, -ae m colleague of Marius; poet friend of Catullus.

cinnamōmum, cinnamum, -ī nt cinnamon.

cinxī perf of **cingō**.

Cinyphius adj of the Cinyps, river of N. Africa; African.

Cinyrās, -ae m father of Adonis.

Cinyrēius adj see n.

cippus, -ī m tombstone; (pl) palisade.

circā adv around, round about ♦ prep (with acc) (place) round, in the vicinity of, in; (time, number) about; with regard to.

Circaeus adj see **Circē**.

circamoerium, -ī and iī nt space on both sides of a wall.

Circē, -ēs and ae f goddess with magic powers living in Aeaea.

circēnsēs, -ium mpl the games.

circēnsis adj of the Circus.

circinō, -āre vt to circle through.

circinus, -ī m pair of compasses.

circiter adv (time, number) about ♦ prep (with acc) about, near.

circueō, circumeō, -īre, -īvī and iī, -itum vt, vi to go round, surround; (MIL) to encircle; to visit, go round canvassing; to deceive.

circuitiō, -ōnis f (MIL) rounds; (speech) evasiveness.

circuitus ppp of **circueō**.

circuitus, -ūs m revolution; way

round, circuit; (*RHET*) period,
periphrasis.
circulātor, -ōris *m* pedlar.
circulor, -ārī *vi* to collect in
crowds.
circulus, -ī *m* circle; orbit; ring;
social group.
circum *adv* round about ♦ *prep*
(*with acc*) round, about; near; ~
insulās mittere send to the islands
round about.
circumagō, -agere, -ēgī, -āctum *vt*
to turn, move in a circle, wheel;
(*pass: time*) to pass; (: *mind*) to be
swayed.
circumarō, -āre *vt* to plough round.
circumcaesūra, -ae *f* outline.
circumcīdō, -dere, -dī, -sum *vt* to
cut round, trim; to cut down,
abridge.
circumcircā *adv* all round.
circumcīsus *ppp of* **circumcīdō**
♦ *adj* precipitous.
circumclūdō, -dere, -sī, -sum *vt* to
shut in, hem in.
circumcolō, -ere *vt* to live round
about.
circumcursō, -āre *vi* to run about.
circumdō, -āre, -edī, -atum *vt* to
put round; to surround, enclose.
circumdūcō, -ūcere, -ūxī, -uctum
vt to lead round, draw round; to
cheat; (*speech*) to prolong, drawl.
circumductus *ppp of* **circumdūcō**
circumeō *etc see* **circueō**.
circumequitō, -āre *vt* to ride
round.
circumferō, -ferre, -tulī, -lātum *vt*
to carry round, pass round; to
spread, broadcast; to purify;
(*pass*) to revolve.
circumflectō, -ctere, -xī, -xum *vt*
to wheel round.
circumflō, -āre *vt* (*fig*) to buffet.
circumfluō, -ere, -xī *vt*, *vi* to flow

round; (*fig*) to overflow, abound.
circumfluus *adj* flowing round;
surrounded (by water).
circumforāneus *adj* itinerant;
(*money*) borrowed.
**circumfundō, -undere, -ūdī,
-ūsum** *vt* to pour round,
surround; (*fig*) to crowd round,
overwhelm; (*pass*) to flow round.
circumgemō, -ere *vt* to growl
round.
circumgestō, -āre *vt* to carry
about.
circumgredior, -dī, -ssus *vt*, *vi* to
make an encircling move,
surround.
circumiaceō, -ēre *vi* to be
adjacent.
circumiciō, -icere, -iēcī, -iectum
vt to throw round, put round; to
surround.
circumiecta *ntpl* neighbourhood.
circumiectus *adj* surrounding.
circumiectus, -ūs *m* enclosure;
embrace.
circumit- *etc see* **circuit-**.
circumitiō, -ōnis *f see* **circuitiō**.
circumitus, -ūs *m see* **circuitus**.
circumlātus *ppp of* **circumferō**.
circumligō, -āre, -āvī, -ātum *vt* to
tie to, bind round.
circumlinō, -ere, -tum *vt* to smear
all over, bedaub.
circumluō, -ere *vt* to wash.
circumluviō, -ōnis *f* alluvial land.
circummittō, -ittere, -īsī, -issum
vt to send round.
**circummoeniō (circummūniō),
-īre, -īvī, -ītum** *vt* to fortify.
circummūnītiō, -ōnis *f* investing.
circumpadānus *adj* of the Po
valley.
circumpendeō, -ēre *vi* to hang
round.
circumplaudō, -ere *vt* to applaud

on all sides.

circumplector, -ctī, -xus *vt* to embrace, surround.

circumplicō, -āre, -āvī, -ātum *vt* to wind round.

circumpōnō, -pōnere, -posuī, -positum *vt* to put round.

circumpōtātiō, -ōnis *f* passing drinks round.

circumrētiō, -īre, -īvī, -ītum *vt* to ensnare.

circumrōdō, -rosī, -rodere *vt* to nibble round about; (*fig*) to slander.

circumsaepiō, -īre, -sī, -tum *vt* to fence round.

circumscindō, -ere *vt* to strip.

circumscrībō, -bere, -psī, -ptum *vt* to draw a line round; to mark the limits of; to restrict, circumscribe; to set aside; to defraud.

circumscrīptē *adv* in periods.

circumscrīptiō, -ōnis *f* circle, contour; fraud; (*RHET*) period.

circumscrīptor, -ōris *m* defrauder.

circumscrīptus *ppp of* **circumscrībō** ♦ *adj* restricted; (*RHET*) periodic.

circumsecō, -āre *vt* to cut round.

circumsedeō, -edēre, -ēdī, -essum *vt* to blockade, beset.

circumsēpiō *etc see* **circumsaepiō**.

circumsessiō, -ōnis *f* siege.

circumsessus *ppp of* **circumsedeō**.

circumsīdō, -ere *vt* to besiege.

circumsiliō, -īre *vi* to hop about; (*fig*) to be rampant.

circumsistō, -sistere, -stetī *vt* surround.

circumsonō, -āre *vi* to resound on all sides ♦ *vt* to fill with sound.

circumsonus, -ī *adj* noisy.

circumspectātrīx, -īcis *f* spy.

circumspectiō, -ōnis *f* caution.

circumspectō, -āre *vt, vi* to look all round, search anxiously, be on the lookout.

circumspectus *ppp of* **circumspiciō** ♦ *adj* carefully considered, cautious.

circumspectus, -ūs *m* consideration; view.

circumspiciō, -icere, -exī, -ectum *vi* to look all round; to be careful ♦ *vt* to survey; (*fig*) to consider, search for.

circumstantēs, -antium *mpl* bystanders.

circumstetī *perf of* **circumsistō**; *perf of* **circumstō**.

circumstō, -āre, -etī *vt, vi* to stand round; to besiege; (*fig*) to encompass.

circumstrepō, -ere *vt* to make a clamour round.

circumsurgēns, -entis *pres p* rising on all sides.

circumtentus *adj* covered tightly.

circumterō, -ere *vt* to crowd round.

circumtextus *adj* embroidered round the edge.

circumtonō, -āre, -uī *vt* to thunder about.

circumvādō, -dere, -sī *vt* to assail on all sides.

circumvagus *adj* encircling.

circumvallō, -āre, -āvī, -ātum *vt* to blockade, beset.

circumvectiō, -ōnis *f* carrying about; (*sun*) revolution.

circumvector, -ārī *vi* to travel round, cruise round; (*fig*) describe.

circumvehor, -hī, -ctus *vi, vi* to ride round, sail round; (*fig*) to describe.

circumvēlō, -āre *vt* to envelop.

circumveniō, -enīre, -ēnī, -entum *vt* to surround, beset; to oppress; to cheat.

circumvertō, circumvortō, -ere *vt* to turn round.

circumvestiō, -īre *vt* to envelop.

circumvinciō, **-īre** vt to lash about.

circumvīsō, **-ere** vi to look at all round.

circumvolitō, **-āre**, **-āvī**, **-ātum** vt, vi to fly round; to hover around.

circumvolō, **-āre** vt to fly round.

circumvolvō, **-vere** vt to roll round.

circus, **-ī** m circle; the Circus Maximus (famous Roman racecourse); a racecourse.

Cīrrha, **-ae** f town near Delphi (sacred to Apollo).

Cirrhaeus adj see n.

cirrus, **-ī** m curl of hair; fringe.

cis prep (with acc) on this side of; (time) within.

Cisalpīnus adj on the Italian side of the Alps, Cisalpine.

cisium, **-ī** and **iī** nt two-wheeled carriage.

Cissēis, **-dis** f Hecuba.

cista, **-ae** f box, casket; ballot box.

cistella, **-ae** f small box.

cistellātrīx, **-īcis** f keeper of the moneybox.

cistellula, **-ae** f little box.

cisterna, **-ae** f reservoir.

cistophorus, **-ī** m an Asiatic coin.

cistula, **-ae** f little box.

citātus adj quick, impetuous.

citerior (sup **-imus**) adj on this side, nearer.

Cithaerōn, **-ōnis** m mountain range between Attica and Boeotia.

cithara, **-ae** f lute.

citharista, **-ae** m, **citharistria**, **-ae** f lute player.

citharizō, **-āre** vi to play the lute.

citharoedus, **-ī** m a singer who accompanies himself on the lute.

citimus adj nearest.

citō (com **-ius**, sup **-issimē**) adv quickly, soon; non ~ not easily.

citō, **-āre**, **-āvī**, **-ātum** vt to set in motion, rouse; to call (by name); appeal to, cite, mention.

citrā adv on this side, this way, not so far ♦ prep (with acc) on this side of, short of; (time) before, since; apart from; ~ quam before.

citreus adj of citrus wood.

citrō adv hither, this way; **ultrō ~que** to and fro.

citrus, **-ī** f citrus tree; citron tree.

citus ppp of cieō ♦ adj quick.

cīvicus adj civic, civil; **corōna ~a** civic crown for saving a citizen's life in war.

cīvīlis adj of citizens, civil; political, civilian; courteous, democratic; **iūs ~e** civil rights, Civil Law; code of legal procedure.

cīvīlitās, **-ātis** f politics; politeness.

cīvīliter adv like citizens; courteously.

cīvis, **-is** m/f citizen, fellow citizen.

cīvitās, **-ātis** f citizenship; community state; city; **~āte dōnāre** naturalize.

clādēs, **-is** f damage, disaster, ruin; defeat; (flg) scourge, dare **~em** make havoc.

clam adv secretly; unknown ♦ prep (with acc) unknown to; ~ **mē** habēre keep from me.

clāmātor, **-ōris** m bawler.

clāmitātiō, **-ōnis** f bawling.

clāmitō, **-āre**, **-āvī**, **-ātum** vt, vi to bawl, screech, cry out.

clāmō, **-āre**, **-āvī**, **-ātum** vt, vi to shout, cry out; to call upon, proclaim.

clāmor, **-ōris** m shout, cry; acclamation.

clāmōsus adj noisy.

clanculum adv secretly ♦ prep (with acc) unknown to.

clandestīnō adv see clandestīnus.

The present infinitive verb endings are as follows: -āre = 1st; -ēre = 2nd; -ere = 3rd and -īre = 4th. See sections on irregular verbs and noun declensions.

clandestīnus adj secret.

clangor, -ōris m clang, noise.

clārē adv brightly, loudly, clearly, with distinction.

clāreō, -ēre vi to be bright, be clear; to be evident; to be renowned.

clārēscō, -ere, clāruī vi to brighten, sound clear; to become obvious; to become famous.

clārigātiō, -ōnis f formal ultimatum to an enemy; fine for trespass.

clārigō, -āre vi to deliver a formal ultimatum.

clārisonus adj loud and clear.

clāritās, -ātis f distinctness; (RHET) lucidity; celebrity.

clāritūdō, -inis f brightness; (fig) distinction.

Clarius adj of Claros ♦ m Apollo.

clārō, -āre vt to illuminate; to explain; to make famous.

Claros, -ī f town in Ionia (famous for worship of Apollo).

clārus adj (sight) bright; (sound) loud; (mind) clear; (person) distinguished; **~ intonāre** thunder from a clear sky; **vir ~issimus** a courtesy title for eminent men.

classiārius adj naval ♦ mpl marines.

classicula, -ae f flotilla.

classicum, -ī nt battle-signal; trumpet.

classicus adj of the first class; naval ♦ mpl marines.

classis, -is f a political class; army; fleet.

clāthrī, -ōrum mpl cage.

clāthrātus adj barred.

clātrī, -ōrum mpl see **clāthrī**.

claudeō, -ēre vi to limp; (fig) to be defective.

claudicātiō, -ōnis f limping.

claudicō, -āre vi to be lame; to waver, be defective.

Claudius, -ī m patrician family name (esp Appius Claudius Caecus, famous censor); the Emperor Claudius.

Claudius, -iānus, -iālis adj see n.

claudō, -dere, -sī, -sum vt to shut, close; to cut off, block; to conclude; to imprison, confine, blockade; **agmen ~** bring up the rear.

claudō, -ere etc see **claudeō**.

claudus adj lame, crippled; (verse) elegiac; (fig) wavering.

clausī perf of **claudō**.

claustra, -ōrum ntpl bar, bolt, lock; barrier, barricade, dam.

clausula, -ae f conclusion; (RHET) ending of a period.

clausum, -ī nt enclosure.

clausus ppp of **claudō**.

clāva, -ae f club, knotty branch; (MIL) foil.

clāvārium, -ī and iī nt money for buying shoe nails.

clāvātor, -ōris m cudgel-bearer.

clāvicula, -ae f vine tendril.

clāviger, -ī m (Hercules) club bearer; (Janus) key-bearer.

clāvis, -is f key.

clāvus, -ī m nail; tiller, rudder; purple stripe on the tunic (broad for senators, narrow for equites); **~um annī movēre** reckon the beginning of the year.

Cleanthēs, -is m Stoic philosopher.

clēmēns, -entis adj mild, gentle, merciful; (weather, water) mild, calm.

clēmenter adv gently, indulgently; gradually.

clēmentia, -ae f mildness, forbearance, mercy.

Cleopatra, -ae f queen of Egypt.

clepō, -ere, -sī, -tum vt to steal.

clepsydra, -ae f waterclock (used for timing speakers); **~am dare** give leave to speak; **~am petere** ask leave to speak.

clepta, -ae *m* thief.

cliēns, -entis *m* client, dependant; follower; vassal-state.

clienta, -ae *f* client.

clientēla, -ae *f* clientship, protection; clients.

clientulus, -ī *m* insignificant client.

clīnāmen, -inis *nt* swerve.

clīnātus *adj* inclined.

Clīō, -ūs *f Muse of history.*

clipeātus *adj* armed with a shield.

clipeus, -ī *m*, **-um, -ī** *nt* round bronze shield; disc; medallion on a metal base.

clitellae, -ārum *fpl* packsaddle, attribute of an ass.

clitellārius *adj* carrying packsaddles.

Clitumnus, -ī *m river in Umbria.*

clīvōsus *adj* hilly.

clīvus, -ī *m* slope, hill; **~ sacer** *part of the Via Sacra.*

cloāca, -ae *f* sewer, drain.

Cloācīna, -ae *f Venus.*

Clōdius, -ī *m Roman plebeian name (esp the tribune, enemy of Cicero).*

Cloēlia, -ae *f Roman girl hostage (who escaped by swimming the Tiber).*

Clōthō *(acc* **-ō** *) f one of the Fates.*

clueō, -ēre, -eor, -ērī *vi* to be called, be famed.

clūnis, -is *m/f* buttock.

clūrīnus *adj* of apes.

Clūsīnus *adj see n.*

Clūsium, -ī *nt old Etruscan town (now Chiusi).*

Clūsius, -ī *m Janus.*

Clytaemnēstra, -ae *f wife of Agamemnon (whom she murdered).*

Cnidius *adj see n.*

Cnidus, -ī *f town in Caria (famous for worship of Venus).*

coacervātiō, -ōnis *f* accumulation.

coacervō, -āre *vt* to heap, accumulate.

coacēscō, -ēscere, -uī *vi* to become sour.

coāctō, -āre *vt* to force.

coāctor, -ōris *m* collector (of money).

coāctōrēs agminis rearguard.

coāctum, -ī *nt* thick coverlet.

coāctus *adj* forced.

coāctus, -ūs *m* compulsion.

coāctus *ppp of* **cōgō.**

coāctus, -ūs *m* compulsion.

coaedificō, -āre, -ātum *vt* to build on.

coaequō, -āre, -āvī, -ātum *vt* to make equal, bring down to the same level.

coagmentātiō, -ōnis *f* combination.

coagmentō, -āre, -āvī, -ātum *vt* to glue, join together.

coagmentum, -ī *nt* joining, joint.

coāgulum, -ī *nt* rennet.

coalēscō, -ēscere, -uī, -itum *vi* to grow together; *(fig)* to agree together; to flourish.

coangustō, -āre *vt* to restrict.

coarct- *etc see* **coart-**

coarguō, -ere, -ī *vt* to convict, prove conclusively.

coartātiō, -ōnis *f* crowding together.

coartō, -āre, -āvī, -ātum *vt* to compress, abridge.

coccineus, coccinus *adj* scarlet.

coccum, -ī *nt* scarlet.

cochlea, coclea, -ae *f* snail.

cocleāre, -is *nt* spoon.

cocles, -itis *m* man blind in one eye; *surname of Horatius who defended the bridge.*

coctilis *adj* baked; of bricks.

coctus *ppp of* **coquō ♦** *adj (fig)* well considered.

The present infinitive verb endings are as follows: **-āre** *= 1st;* **-ēre** *= 2nd;* **-ere** *= 3rd and* **-īre** *= 4th. See sections on irregular verbs and noun declensions.*

cocus etc see **coquus**.

Cōcȳtius adj see n.

Cōcȳtos, -us, -ī m river in the lower world.

cōda etc see **cauda**.

cōdex etc see **caudex**.

cōdicillī, -ōrum mpl letter, note, petition; codicil.

Codrus, -ī m last king of Athens.

coēgī perf of **cōgō**.

coel- etc see **cael-**.

coemō, -emere, -ēmī, -emptum vt to buy up.

coemptiō, -ōnis f a form of Roman marriage; mock sale of an estate.

coemptiōnālis adj used in a mock sale; worthless.

coen- etc see **caen-** or **cēn-**.

coeō, -īre, -īvī and **iī, -itum** vi to meet, assemble; to encounter; to combine, mate; (wounds) to close; to agree, conspire ♦ vt: ~ **societātem** make a compact.

coepiō, -ere, -ī, -tum vt, vi to begin (esp in perf tenses); **rēs agī ~tae sunt** things began to be done; **coepisse** to have begun.

coeptō, -āre, -āvī, -ātum vt, vi to begin, attempt.

coeptum, -ī nt beginning, undertaking.

coeptus ppp of **coepiō**.

coeptus, -ūs m beginning.

coepulōnus, -ī m fellow-banqueter.

coerātor etc see **cūrātor**.

coerceō, -ēre, -uī, -itum vt to enclose; to confine, repress; (fig) to control, check, correct.

coercitiō, -ōnis f coercion, punishment.

coetus, coitus, -ūs m meeting, joining together; assembly, crowd.

cōgitātē adv deliberately.

cōgitātiō, -ōnis f thought, reflection; idea, plan; faculty of thought, imagination.

cōgitātus adj deliberate ♦ ntpl ideas.

cōgitō, -āre, -āvī, -ātum vt, vi to think, ponder, imagine; to feel disposed; to plan, intend.

cognātiō, -ōnis f relationship (by blood); kin, family; (fig) affinity, resemblance.

cognātus, -ī m, **-a, -ae** f relation ♦ adj related; (fig) connected, similar.

cognitiō, -ōnis f acquiring of knowledge, knowledge; idea, notion; (law) judicial inquiry; (comedy) recognition.

cognitor, -ōris m (law) attorney; witness of a person's identity; (fig) defender.

cognitus adj acknowledged.

cognitus ppp of **cognōscō**.

cognōmen, -inis nt surname; name.

cognōmentum, -ī nt surname, name.

cognōminis adj with the same name.

cognōminō, -āre, -āvī, -ātum vt to give a surname to; **verba ~āta** synonyms.

cognōscō, -ōscere, -ōvī, -itum vt to get to know, learn, understand; to know, recognize, identify; (law) to investigate; (MIL) to reconnoitre.

cōgō, -ere, coēgī, coāctum vt to collect, gather together; (liquids) to thicken, curdle; to contract, confine; to compel, force; to infer; **agmen ~** bring up the rear; **senātum ~** call a meeting of the senate.

cohaerentia, -ae f coherence.

cohaereō, -rēre, -sī, -sum vi to stick together, cohere; to cling to; (fig) to be consistent, harmonize; to agree, be consistent with.

cohaerēscō, -ere vi to stick together.

cohaesus ppp of **cohaereō.**

cohērēs, -ēdis m/f co-heir.

cohibeō, -ēre, -uī, -itum vt to hold together, encircle; to hinder, stop; (fig) to restrain, repress.

cohonestō, -āre vt to do honour to.

cohorrēscō, -ēscere, -uī vi to shudder all over.

cohors, -tis f courtyard; (MIL) cohort (about 600 men); retinue (esp of the praetor in a province); (fig) company.

cohortātiō, -ōnis f encouragement.

cohorticula, -ae f small cohort.

cohortor, -ārī, -ātus vt to encourage, urge.

coitiō, -ōnis f encounter; conspiracy.

coitus etc see **coetus.**

colaphus, -ī m blow with the fist, box.

Colchis, -idis f Medea's country (at the E. end of the Black Sea).

Colchis, -us, -icus adj Colchian.

cōleus etc see **culleus.**

cōlis etc see **caulis.**

collabāscō, -ere vi to waver also.

collabefactō, -āre vt to shake violently.

collabefīō, -fierī, factus vi to be destroyed.

collābor, -bī, -psus vi to fall in ruin, collapse.

collacerātus adj torn to pieces.

collacrimātiō, -ōnis f weeping.

collactea, -ae f foster-sister.

collāpsus ppa of **collābor.**

collāre, -is nt neckband.

Collātia, -iae f ancient town near Rome ♦ m husband of Lucretia.

Collātīnus adj of Collatia.

collātiō, -ōnis f bringing together,

combination; (money) contribution; (RHET) comparison; (PHILOS) analogy.

collātor, -ōris m contributor.

collātus ppp of **cōnferō.**

collaudātiō, -ōnis f praise.

collaudō, -āre, -āvī, -ātum vt to praise highly.

collaxō, -āre vt to make porous.

collēcta, -ae f money contribution.

collēcticius adj hastily gathered.

collēctiō, -ōnis f gathering up; (RHET) recapitulation.

collēctus ppp of **colligō.**

collēctus, -ūs m accumulation.

collēga, -ae m colleague, associate.

collēgī perf of **colligō.**

collēgium, -ī and iī nt association in office; college, guild (of magistrates, etc).

collībertus, -ī m fellow freedman.

collibet, collubet, -uit and **itum est** vi it pleases.

collīdō, -dere, -sī, -sum vt to beat together, strike, bruise; (fig) to bring into conflict.

colligātiō, -ōnis f connection.

colligō, -āre, -āvī, -ātum vt to fasten, tie up; (fig) to combine; to restrain, check.

colligō, -igere, -ēgī, -ēctum vt to gather, collect; to compress, draw together; to check; (fig) to acquire; to think about; to infer, conclude; **animum, mentem ~** recover, rally; **sē ~** crouch; recover one's courage; **vāsa ~** (MIL) pack up.

Collīna Porta gate in N.E. of Rome.

collīneō, -āre vt, vi to aim straight.

collinō, -inere, -ēvī, -itum vt to besmear; (fig) to deface.

colliquefactus adj dissolved.

collis, -is m hill, slope.

*The present infinitive verb endings are as follows: -**āre** = 1st; -**ēre** = 2nd; -**ere** = 3rd and -**īre** = 4th. See sections on irregular verbs and noun declensions.*

collīsi *perf of* collīdō.

collīsus *ppp of* collīdō.

collītus *ppp of* collinō.

collocātiō, -ōnis *f* arrangement; giving in marriage.

collocō, -āre, -āvī, -ātum *vt* to place, station, arrange; to give in marriage; *(money)* to invest; *(fig)* to establish; to occupy, employ.

collocuplētō, -āre, -āvī *vt* to enrich.

collocūtiō, -ōnis *f* conversation.

colloquium, -ī *and* **iī** *nt* conversation, conference.

colloquor, -quī, -cūtus *vi* to converse, hold a conference ♦ *vt* to talk to.

collubet *etc see* collibet.

collūceō, -ēre *vi* to shine brightly; *(fig)* to be resplendent.

collūdō, -dere, -sī, -sum *vi* to play together *or* with; to practise collusion.

collum, -ī *nt* neck; **~ torquēre, obtorquēre, obstringere** arrest.

colluō, -uere, -uī, -ūtum *vt* to rinse, moisten.

collus *etc see* collum.

collūsiō, -ōnis *f* secret understanding.

collūsor, -ōris *m* playmate, fellow gambler.

collūstrō, -āre, -āvī, -ātum *vt* to light up; to survey.

colluviō, -ōnis, -ēs, -em, -ē *f* sweepings, filth; *(fig)* dregs, rabble.

collybus, -ī *m* money exchange, rate of exchange.

collȳra, -ae *f* vermicelli.

collȳricus *adj see* n.

collȳrium, -ī *and* **iī** *nt* eye lotion.

colō, -ere, -uī, cultum *vt* (AGR) to cultivate, work; *(place)* to live in; *(human affairs)* to cherish, protect, adorn; *(qualities, pursuits)* to cultivate, practise; *(gods)* to

worship; *(men)* to honour, court; **vītam ~** live.

colocāsia, -ae *f, -a, -ōrum* *ntpl* Egyptian bean, caladium.

colōna, -ae *f* country-woman.

colōnia, -ae *f* settlement, colony; settlers.

colōnicus *adj* colonial.

colōnus, -ī *m* crofter, farmer; settler, colonist.

color (colōs), -ōris *m* colour; complexion; beauty, lustre; *(fig)* outward show; *(RHET)* style, tone; colourful excuse; **~ōrem mūtāre** blush, go pale; **homō nullius -ōris** an unknown person.

colōrātus *adj* healthily tanned.

colōrō, -āre, -āvī, -ātum *vt* to colour, tan; *(fig)* to give a colour to.

colossus, -ī *m* gigantic statue *(esp that of Apollo at Rhodes)*.

colostra, colustra, -ae *f* beestings.

coluber, -rī *m* snake.

colubra, -ae *f* snake.

colubrifer, -ī *adj* snaky.

colubrīnus *adj* wily.

coluī *perf of* colō.

cōlum, -ī *nt* strainer.

columba, -ae *f* dove, pigeon.

columbar, -āris *nt* kind of collar.

columbārium, -ī *and* **iī** *nt* dovecote.

columbīnus *adj* pigeon's ♦ *m* little pigeon.

columbus, -ī *m* dove, cock-pigeon.

columella, -ae *f* small pillar.

columen, -inis *nt* height, summit; pillar; *(fig)* chief; prop.

columna, -ae *f* column, pillar; *a pillory in the Forum Romanum*; waterspout.

columnārium, -ī *and* **iī** *nt* pillar tax.

columnārius, -ī *m* criminal.

columnātus *adj* pillared.

colurnus *adj* made of hazel.

colus, -ī *and* **ūs** *f (occ m)* distaff.

cōlȳphia, -ōrum *ntpl* food of athletes.

coma, -ae *f* hair (*of the head*); foliage.

comāns, -antis *adj* hairy, plumed; leafy.

cōmarchus, -ī *m* burgomaster.

comātus *adj* long-haired; leafy; **Gallia ~** Transalpine Gaul.

combibō, -ere, -ī *vt* to drink to the full, absorb.

combibō, -ōnis *m* fellow drinker.

combūrō, -rere, -ssī, -stum *vt* to burn up; (*fig*) to ruin.

combūstus *ppp of* **combūrō**.

comedō, -ēsse, -ēdī, -ēsum *and* **-ēstum** *vt* to eat up, devour; (*fig*) to waste, squander; **sē ~** pine away.

Cōmēnsis *adj see* **Cōmum**.

comes, -itis *m/f* companion, partner; attendant, follower; one of a magistrate's or emperor's retinue; (*medieval title*) count.

comēs, comēst *pres tense of* **comedō**.

comēstus, comēsus *ppp of* **comedō**.

comētēs, -ae *m* comet.

cōmicē *adv* in the manner of comedy.

cōmicus, -ī *m* comedy actor, comedy writer ♦ *adj* of comedy, comic.

cōmis *adj* courteous, friendly.

cōmissābundus *adj* carousing.

cōmissātiō, -ōnis *f* Bacchanalian revel.

cōmissātor, -ōris *m* reveller.

cōmissor, -ārī, -ātus *vi* to carouse, make merry.

cōmitās, -ātis *f* kindness, affability.

comitātus, -ūs *m* escort, retinue; company.

cōmiter *adv see* **cōmis**.

comitia, -iōrum *ntpl* assembly for the election of magistrates and other business (*esp the ~* *centuriāta*); elections.

comitiālis *adj* of the elections; **~ morbus** epilepsy.

comitiātus, -ūs *m* assembly at the elections.

comitium, -ī *and* **iī** *nt* place of assembly.

comitō, -āre, -āvī, -ātum *vt* to accompany.

comitor, -ārī, -ātus *vt, vi* to attend, follow.

commaculō, -āre, -āvī, -ātum *vt* to stain, defile.

commanipulāris, -is *m* soldier in the same company.

commeātus, -ūs *m* passage; leave, furlough; convoy (of troops or goods); (MIL) lines of communication, provisions, supplies.

commeditor, -ārī *vt* to practise.

commeminī, -isse *vt, vi* to remember perfectly.

commemorābilis *adj* memorable.

commemorātiō, -ōnis *f* recollection, recounting.

commemorō, -āre, -āvī, -ātum *vt* to recall, remind; to mention, relate.

commendābilis *adj* praiseworthy.

commendāticius *adj* of recommendation or introduction.

commendātiō, -ōnis *f* recommendation; worth, excellence.

commendātor, -ōris *m* commender (*male*).

commendātrīx, -rīcis *f* commender (*female*).

commendātus *adj* approved, valued.

The present infinitive verb endings are as follows: -āre = 1st; -ēre = 2nd; -ere = 3rd and -īre = 4th. See sections on irregular verbs and noun declensions.

commendō, **-āre**, **-āvī**, **-ātum** vt to entrust, commit, commend (to one's care or charge); to recommend, set off to advantage.

commēnsus ppa of **commētior**.

commentāriolum, **-ī** nt short treatise.

commentārius, **-ī** and **iī** m, **-ium**, **-ī** and **iī** nt notebook; commentary, memoir; (law) brief.

commentātiō, **-ōnis** f studying, meditation.

commenticius adj fictitious, imaginary; false.

commentor, **-ārī**, **-ātus** vt, vi to study, think over, prepare carefully; to invent, compose, write.

commentor, **-ōris** m inventor.

commentum, **-ī** nt invention, fiction; contrivance.

commentus ppa of **comminīscor** ♦ adj feigned, fictitious.

commeō, **-āre** vi to pass to and fro; to go or come often.

commercium, **-ī** and **iī** nt trade, commerce; right to trade; dealings, communication.

commercor, **-ārī**, **-ātus** vt to buy up.

commereō, **-ēre**, **-uī**, **-itum**; **-eor**, **-ērī**, **-itus** vt to deserve; to be guilty of.

commētior, **-tīrī**, **-nsus** vt to measure.

commētō, **-āre** vi to go often.

commictus ppp of **commingō**.

commigrō, **-āre**, **-āvī**, **-ātum** vi to remove, migrate.

commīlitium, **-ī** and **iī** nt service together.

commīlitō, **-ōnis** m fellow soldier.

comminātiō, **-ōnis** f threat.

commingō, **-ingere**, **-īnxī**, **-īctum** vt to pollute.

comminīscor, **-ī**, **commentus** vt to devise, contrive.

comminor, **-ārī**, **-ātus** vt to threaten.

comminuō, **-uere**, **-uī**, **-ūtum** vt to break up, smash; to diminish; to impair.

comminus adv hand to hand; near at hand.

commisceō, **-scēre**, **-scuī**, **-xtum** vt to mix together, join together.

commiserātiō, **-ōnis** f (RHET) passage intended to arouse pity.

commiserēscō, **-ere** vt to pity.

commiseror, **-ārī** vt to bewail ♦ vi (RHET) to try to excite pity.

commissiō, **-ōnis** f start (of a contest).

commissum, **-ī** nt enterprise; offence, crime; secret.

commissūra, **-ae** f joint, connection.

commissus ppp of **committō**.

committō, **-ittere**, **-īsī**, **-issum** vt to join, connect, bring together; to begin, undertake; (battle) to join, engage in; (offence) to commit, be guilty of; (punishment) to incur, forfeit; to entrust, trust; **sē urbī ~** venture into the city.

commixtus ppp of **commisceō**.

commodē adv properly, well; aptly, opportunely; pleasantly.

commoditās, **-ātis** f convenience, ease, fitness; advantage; (person) kindliness; (RHET) apt expression.

commodō, **-āre**, **-āvī**, **-ātum** vt to adjust, adapt; to give, lend, oblige with; (with dat) to oblige.

commodulē, **-um** adv conveniently.

commodum, **-ī** nt convenience; advantage, interest; pay, salary; loan; **~ō tuō** at your leisure; **~a vītae** the good things of life.

commodum adv opportunely; just.

commodus adj proper, fit, full; suitable, easy, opportune; (person) pleasant, obliging.

commōlior, -īrī vt to set in motion.

commonefaciō, -facere, -fēcī, -factum vt to remind, recall.

commoneō, -ēre, -uī, -itum vt to remind, impress upon.

commōnstrō, -āre vt to point out.

commorātiō, -ōnis f delay, residence; (RHET) dwelling (on a topic).

commoror, -ārī, -ātus vi to sojourn, wait; (RHET) to dwell ♦ vt to detain.

commōtiō, -ōnis f excitement.

commōtiuncula f slight indisposition.

commōtus ppp of **commoveō** ♦ adj excited, emotional.

commoveō, -ovēre, -ōvī, -ōtum vt to set in motion, move, dislodge, agitate; (mind) to unsettle, shake, excite, move, affect; (emotions) to stir up, provoke.

commūne, -is nt common property; state; in **~e** for a common end; equally; in general.

commūnicātiō, -ōnis f imparting; (RHET) making the audience appear to take part in the discussion.

commūnicō, -āre, -āvī, -ātum vt to share (by giving or receiving); to impart, communicate; **sēnsilic cum** make common cause with.

commūniō, -īre, -īvī and iī, -ītum vt to build (a fortification), to fortify, strengthen.

commūniō, -ōnis f sharing in common, communion.

commūnis adj common, general, universal; (person) affable, democratic; **~ia loca** public places; **~ēs locī** general topics; **~is sēnsus** popular sentiment; **aliquid ~e habēre** have something in common.

commūnitās, -ātis f fellowship; sense of fellowship; affability.

commūniter adv in common, jointly.

commūnītiō, -ōnis f preparing the way.

commurmuror, -ārī, -ātus vi to mutter to oneself.

commūtābilis adj changeable.

commūtātiō, -iōnis f change.

commūtātus, -ūs m change.

commūtō, -āre, -āvī, -ātum vt to change, exchange, interchange.

cōmō, -ere, -psī, -ptum vt to arrange, dress, adorn.

cōmoedia, -ae f comedy.

cōmoedicē adv as in comedy.

cōmoedus, -ī m comic actor.

comōsus adj shaggy.

compāctiō, -ōnis f joining together.

compāctus ppp of **compingō**.

compāgēs, -is, -ō, -inis f joint, structure, framework.

compār, -aris m/f comrade, husband, wife ♦ adj equal.

comparābilis adj comparable.

comparātē adv by bringing in a comparison.

comparātiō, -ōnis f comparison; (ASTRO) relative positions; agreement; preparation, procuring.

comparātīvus adj based on comparison.

compāreō, -ēre vi to be visible; to be present, be realised.

comparō, -āre, -āvī, -ātum vt to couple together, match; to compare; (POL) to agree (about respective duties); to prepare, provide; (custom) to establish; to procure, purchase, get.

compāscō, -ere vt to put (cattle) to graze in common.

The present infinitive verb endings are as follows: -āre = 1st; -ēre = 2nd; -ere = 3rd and and -īre = 4th. See sections on irregular verbs and noun declensions.

compāscuus adj for common pasture.

compeciscor, -īscī, -tus vi to come to an agreement.

compectum, -tī nt agreement.

compediō, -īre, -ītum vt to fetter.

compēgī perf of **compingō**.

compellātiō, -ōnis f reprimand.

compellō, -āre, -āvī, -ātum vt to call, address; to reproach; (law) to arraign.

compellō, -ellere, -ulī, -ulsum vt to drive, bring together, concentrate; to impel, compel.

compendiārius adj short.

compendium, -ī and **iī** nt saving; abbreviating; short cut; ~ī **facere** save; abridge; ~ī **fierī** be brief.

compēnsātiō, -ōnis f (fig) compromise.

compēnsō, -āre, -āvī, -ātum vt to balance (against), make up for.

compercō, -cere, -sī vt, vi to save; to refrain.

comperendinātiō, -iōnis f adjournment for two days.

comperendinātus, -ūs m adjournment for two days.

comperendinō, -āre vt to adjourn for two days.

comperiō, -īre, -ī, -tum (occ **-ior**) vt to find out, learn; ~**tus** detected; found guilty; ~**tum habēre** know for certain.

compēs, -edis f fetter, bond.

compēscō, -ere, -uī vt to check, suppress.

competītor, -ōris m, **-rīx, -rīcis** f rival candidate.

competō, -ere, -īvī and **iī, -ītum** vi to coincide, agree; to be capable.

compīlātiō, -ōnis f plundering; compilation.

compīlō, -āre, -āvī, -ātum vt to pillage.

compingō, -ingere, -ēgī, -āctum vt to put together, compose; to

lock up, hide away.

compitālia, -ium and **iōrum** ntpl festival in honour of the Lares Compitales.

compitālicius adj of the Compitalia.

compitālis adj of crossroads.

compitum, -ī nt crossroads.

complaceō, -ēre, -uī and **itus sum** vi to please (someone else) as well, please very much.

complānō, -āre vt to level, raze to the ground.

complector, -ctī, -xus vt to embrace, clasp; to enclose; (speech, writing) to deal with, comprise; (mind) to grasp, comprehend; to honour, be fond of.

complēmentum, -ī nt complement.

compleō, -ēre, -ēvī, -ētum vt to fill, fill up; (MIL) to man, make up the complement of; (time, promise, duty) to complete, fulfil, finish.

complētus adj perfect.

complexiō, -ōnis f combination; (RHET) period; (logic) conclusion of an argument; dilemma.

complexus, -ūs m embrace; (fig) affection, close combat; (speech) connection.

complicō, -āre vt to fold up.

complōrātiō, -iōnis f, **-us, -ūs** m loud lamentation.

complōrō, -āre, -āvī, -ātum vt to mourn for.

complūrēs, -ium adj several, very many.

complūriēns adv several times.

complūsculī, -ōrum adj quite a few.

compluvium, -ī and **iī** nt roof opening in a Roman house.

compōnō, -ōnere, -osuī, -ositum vt to put together, join; to compose, construct; to compare, contrast; to match, oppose; to put away, store up, stow; (*dead*) to lay out, inter; to allay, quieten, reconcile; to adjust, settle, arrange; to devise, prepare ♦ *vi* to make peace.

comportō, -āre *vt* to collect, bring in.

compos, -tis *adj* in control, in possession; sharing; **vōtī ~** having got one's wish.

compositē *adv* properly, in a polished manner.

compositiō, -ōnis *f* compounding, system; (*words*) arrangement; reconciliation; matching (of fighters).

compositor, -ōris *m* arranger.

compositūra, -ae *f* connection.

compositus *ppp of* **compōnō** ♦ *adj* orderly, regular; adapted, assumed, ready; calm, sedate; (*words*) compound; **compositō, ex compositō** as agreed.

compōtātiō, -ōnis *f* drinking party.

compōtiō, -īre *vt* to put in possession (of).

compōtor, -ōris *m*, **-rīx, -rīcis** *f* fellow drinker.

comprānsor, -ōris *m* fellow guest.

comprecātiō, -ōnis *f* public supplication.

comprecor, -ārī, -ātus *vt, vi* to pray to, to pray for.

comprehendō (comprendō), -endere, -endī, -ēnsum *vt* to grasp, catch; to seize, arrest, catch in the act; (*words*) to comprise, recount; (*thought*) to grasp, comprehend; to hold in affection; **numerō ~** count.

comprehēnsibilis *adj* conceivable.

comprehēnsiō, -ōnis *f* grasping, seizing; perception, idea; (*RHET*)

period.

comprehēnsus, comprēnsus *ppp of* **comprehendō**.

comprendō *etc see* **comprehendō**.

compressī *perf of* **comprimō**.

compressiō, -ōnis *f* embrace; (*RHET*) compression.

compressus *ppp of* **comprimō**.

compressus, -ūs *m* compression, embrace.

comprimō, -imere, -essī, -essum *vt* to squeeze, compress; to check, restrain; to suppress, withhold; **animam ~** hold one's breath; **~essis manibus** with hands folded, idle.

comprobātiō, -ōnis *f* approval.

comprobator, -ōris *m* approver.

comprobō, -āre, -āvī, -ātum *vt* to prove, make good; to approve.

comprōmissum, -ī *nt* mutual agreement to abide by an arbitrator's decision.

comprōmittō, -ittere, -īsī, -issum *vt* to undertake to abide by an arbitrator's decision.

compsī *perf of* **cōmō**.

cōmptus *ppp of* **cōmō** ♦ *adj* elegant.

cōmptus, -ūs *m* coiffure; union.

compulī *perf of* **compellō**.

compulsus *ppp of* **compellō**.

compungō, -ungere, -ūnxī, -ūnctum *vt* to prick, sting, tattoo.

computō, āre, āvī, ātum *vt* to reckon, number.

Cōmum, -ī *nt* (*also* **Novum Cōmum**) town in N. Italy (*now* Como).

cōnāmen, -inis *nt* effort; support.

cōnāta, -ōrum *ntpl* undertaking, venture.

cōnātus, -ūs *m* effort; endeavour; inclination, impulse.

concaedēs, -ium *fpl* barricade of felled trees.

The present infinitive verb endings are as follows: -āre = 1st; -ēre = 2nd; -ere = 3rd and -īre = 4th. See sections on irregular verbs and noun declensions.

concalefaciō, -facere, -fēcī, -factum vt to warm well.

concaleō, -ēre vi to be hot.

concalēscō, -ēscere, -uī vi to become hot, glow.

concallēscō, -ēscere, -uī vi to become shrewd; to become unfeeling.

concastīgō, -āre vt to punish severely.

concavō, -āre vt to curve.

concavus adj hollow; vaulted, bent.

concēdō, -ēdere, -essī, -essum vi to withdraw, depart; to disappear, pass away, pass; to yield, submit, give precedence, comply ♦ vt to give up, cede; to grant, allow; to pardon, overlook.

concelebrō, -āre, -āvī, -ātum vt to frequent, fill, enliven; (study) to pursue eagerly; to celebrate; to make known.

concēnātiō, -ōnis f dining together.

concentiō, -ōnis f chorus.

concenturiō, -āre vt to marshal.

concentus, -ūs m chorus, concert; (fig) concord, harmony.

conceptiō, -ōnis f conception; drawing up legal formulae.

conceptīvus adj (holidays) movable.

conceptus ppp of **concipiō**.

conceptus, -ūs m conception.

concerpō, -ere, -sī, -tum vt to tear up; (fig) to abuse.

concertātiō, -ōnis f controversy.

concertātor, -ōris m rival.

concertātōrius adj controversial.

concertō, -āre, -āvī, -ātum vi to fight; to dispute.

concessiō, -ōnis f grant, permission; (law) pleading guilty and asking indulgence.

concessō, -āre vi to stop, loiter.

concessus ppp of **concēdō**.

concessus, -ūs m permission.

concha, -ae f mussel, oyster, murex; mussel shell, oyster shell, pearl; purple dye; trumpet, perfume dish.

conchis, -is f kind of bean.

conchīta, -ae m catcher of shellfish.

conchȳliātus adj purple.

conchȳlium, -ī and **iī** nt shellfish, oyster, murex; purple.

concīdō, -ere, -ī vi to fall, collapse; to subside, fail, perish.

concīdō, -dere, -dī, -sum vt to cut up, cut to pieces, kill; (fig) to ruin, strike down; (RHET) to dismember, enfeeble.

conciēō, -iēre, -īvī, -itum; conciō, -īre, -ītum vt to rouse, assemble; to stir up, shake; (fig) to rouse, provoke.

conciliābulum, -ī nt place for public gatherings.

conciliātiō, -ōnis f union; winning over (friends, hearers); (PHILOS) inclination.

conciliātor, -ōris m promoter.

conciliātrix, -īcis m, **-īcula, -ae** f promoter, matchmaker.

conciliātus, -ūs m combination.

conciliātus adj beloved; favourable.

conciliō, -āre, -āvī, -ātum vt to unite; to win over, reconcile; to procure, purchase, bring about; to promote.

concilium, -ī and **iī** nt gathering, meeting; council; (things) union.

concinnē adv see **concinnus**.

concinnitās, -ātis, -ūdō, -ūdinis f (RHET) rhythmical style.

concinnō, -āre, -āvī, -ātum vt to arrange; to bring about, produce; (with adj) to make.

concinnus adj symmetrical, beautiful; (style) polished, rhythmical; (person) elegant, courteous; (*things*) suited, pleasing.

concinō, -ere, -uī *vi* to sing, play, sound together; (*fig*) to agree, harmonize ♦ *vt* to sing about, celebrate, prophesy.

conciō *etc see* **conciēō**.

concio- *etc see* **contio-**.

concipiō, -ipere, -ēpī, -eptum *vt* to take to oneself, absorb; (*women*) to conceive; (*senses*) to perceive; (*mind*) to conceive, imagine, understand; (*feelings, acts*) to harbour, foster, commit; (*words*) to draw up, intimate formally.

concīsiō, -ōnis *f* breaking up into short clauses.

concīsus *ppp of* **concīdō** ♦ *adj* broken up, concise.

concitātē *adv see* **concitātus**.

concitātiō, -ōnis *f* acceleration; (*mind*) excitement, passion; riot.

concitātor, -ōris *m* agitator.

concitātus *ppp of* **concitō** ♦ *adj* fast; excited.

concitō, -āre, -āvī, -ātum *vt* to move rapidly, bestir, hurl, to urge, rouse, impel; to stir up, occasion.

concitor, -ōris *m* instigator.

concitus, concītus *ppp of* **conciēō**; *ppp of* **concitō**.

conclāmātiō, -ōnis *f* great shout.

conclāmitō, -āre *vi* to keep on shouting.

conclāmō, -āre, -āvī, -ātum *vt, vi* to shout, cry out; to call to help; (*MIL*) to give the signal; (*dead*) to call by name in mourning; **vāsa ~** give the order to pack up; **~ātum est** it's all over.

conclāve, -is *nt* room.

conclūdō, -dere, -sī, -sum *vt* to shut up, enclose; to include, comprise; to end, conclude, round

off (*esp with a rhythmical cadence*); (*PHILOS*) to infer, demonstrate.

conclūsē *adv* with rhythmical cadences.

conclūsiō, -ōnis *f* (*MIL*) blockade; end, conclusion; (*RHET*) period, peroration; (*logic*) conclusion.

conclūsiuncula, -ae *f* quibble.

conclūsum, -ī *nt* logical conclusion.

conclūsus *ppp of* **conclūdō**.

concolor, -ōris *adj* of the same colour.

concoquō, -quere, -xī, -ctum *vt* to boil down; to digest; (*fig*) to put up with, stomach; (*thought*) to consider well, concoct.

concordia, -ae *f* friendship, concord, union; *goddess of* Concord.

concorditer *adv* amicably.

concordō, -āre *vi* to agree, be in harmony.

concors, -dis *adj* concordant, united, harmonious.

concrēbrēscō, -ēscere, -uī *vi* to gather strength.

concrēdō, -ere, -idī, -itum *vt* to entrust.

concremō, -āre, -āvī, -ātum *vt* to burn.

concrepō, -āre, -uī, -itum *vi* to rattle, creak, clash, snap (*fingers*) ♦ *vt* to beat.

concrēscō, -scere, -vī, -tum *vi* to harden, curdle, congeal, clot; to grow, take shape.

concrētiō, -ōnis *f* condensing; matter.

concrētum, -ī *nt* solid matter, hard frost.

concrētus *ppa of* **concrēscō** ♦ *adj* hard, thick, stiff, congealed; compounded.

The present infinitive verb endings are as follows: -āre = 1st; -ēre = 2nd; -ere = 3rd and -īre = 4th. *See sections on irregular verbs and noun declensions.*

concrīminor, -ārī, -ātus *vi* to bring a complaint.

concruciō, -āre *vt* to torture.

concubīna, -ae *f* (female) concubine.

concubīnātus, -ūs *m* concubinage.

concubīnus, -ī *m* (male) concubine.

concubitus, -ūs *m* reclining together (at table); sexual union.

concubius *adj*: **~iā nocte** during the first sleep ♦ *nt* the time of the first sleep.

conculcō, -āre *vt* to trample under foot, treat with contempt.

concumbō, -mbere, -buī, -bitum *vi* to lie together, lie with.

concupīscō, -īscere, -īvī, -ītum *vt* to covet, long for, aspire to.

concūrō, -āre *vt* to take care of.

concurrō, -rere, -rī, -sum *vi* to flock together, rush in; (*things*) to clash, meet; (*MIL*) to join battle, charge; (*events*) to happen at the same time, concur.

concursātiō, -ōnis *f* running together, rushing about; (*MIL*) skirmishing; (*dreams*) coherent design.

concursātor, -ōris *m* skirmisher.

concursiō, -ōnis *f* meeting, concourse; (*RHET*) repetition for emphasis.

concursō, -āre *vi* to collide; to rush about, travel about; (*MIL*) to skirmish ♦ *vt* to visit, go from place to place.

concursus, -ūs *m* concourse, gathering, collision; uproar; (*fig*) combination; (*MIL*) assault, charge.

concussī *perf of* **concutiō.**

concussus *ppp of* **concutiō.**

concussus, -ūs *m* shaking.

concutiō, -tere, -ssī, -ssum *vt* to strike, shake, shatter; (*weapons*) to hurl; (*power*) to disturb, impair; (*person*) to agitate, alarm; (*self*) to

search, examine; to rouse.

condālium, -ī *and* **iī** *nt* slave's ring.

condecet, -ēre *vt impers* it becomes.

condecorō, -āre *vt* to enhance.

condemnātor, -ōris *m* accuser.

condemnō, -āre, -āvī, -ātum *vt* to condemn, sentence; to urge the conviction of; to blame, censure; **ambitūs ~** convict of bribery; **capitis ~** condemn to death; **vōtī ~ātus** obliged to fulfil a vow.

condēnsō, -āre, -eō, -ēre *vt* to compress, move close together.

condēnsus *adj* very dense, close, thick.

condiciō, -ōnis *f* arrangement, condition, terms; marriage contract, match; situation, position, circumstances; manner, mode; **eā ~ōne ut** on condition that; **sub ~ōne** conditionally; **his ~ōnibus** on these terms; **vītae ~** way of life.

condīcō, -īcere, -īxī, -ictum *vt, vi* to talk over, agree upon, promise; **ad cēnam ~** have a dinner engagement.

condidī *perf of* **condō.**

condignē *adv see* **condignus.**

condignus *adj* very worthy.

condīmentum, -ī *nt* spice, seasoning.

condiō, -īre, -īvī, -ītum *vt* to pickle, preserve, embalm; to season; (*fig*) to give zest to, temper.

condiscipulus, -ī *m* school-fellow.

condiscō, -scere, -dicī *vt* to learn thoroughly, learn by heart.

conditiō *etc see* **condiciō.**

conditiō, -ōnis *f* preserving, seasoning.

conditor, -ōris *m* founder, author, composer.

conditōrium, -ī *and* **iī** *nt* coffin, urn, tomb.

condītus *adj* savoury; (*fig*)

polished.

conditus ppp of **condō**.

conditus ppp of **condiō**.

condō, -ere, -idī, -itum vt 1. (build, found: arts) to make, compose, write; (: institutions) to establish 2. (put away for keeping, store up: fruit) to preserve; (: person) to imprison; (: dead) to bury; (: memory) to lay up; (: time) to pass, bring to a close 0. (put out of sight, conceal: eyes) to close; (: sword) to sheathe, plunge; (: troops) to place in ambush.

condocefaciō, -ere vt to train.

condoceō, -ēre, -uī, -tum vt to train.

condolēscō, -ēscere, -uī vi to begin to ache, feel very sore.

condōnātiō, -ōnis f giving away.

condōnō, -āre, -āvī, -ātum vt to give, present, deliver up; (debt) to remit; (offence) to pardon, let off.

condormiscō, -iscere, -īvī vi to fall fast asleep.

condūcibilis adj expedient.

condūcō, -ūcere, -ūxī, -uctum vt to bring together, assemble, connect; to hire, rent, borrow; (public work) to undertake, get the contract for; (taxes) to farm ♦ vi to be of use, profit.

conductī, -ōrum mpl hirelings, mercenaries.

conducticius adj hired.

conductiō, -ōnis f hiring, farming.

conductor, -ōris m hirer, tenant; contractor.

conductum, -ī nt anything hired or rented.

conductus ppp of **condūcō**.

conduplicō, -āre vt to double.

condūrō, -āre vt to make very hard.

condus, -ī m steward.

cōnectō, -ctere, -xuī, -xum vt to tie, fasten, link, join; (logic) to state a conclusion.

cōnexum, -ī nt logical inference.

cōnexus ppp of **cōnectō** ♦ adj connected; (time) following.

cōnexus, -ūs m combination.

cōnfābulor, -ārī, -ātus vi to talk (to), discuss.

cōnfarreātiō, -ōnis f the most solemn of Roman marriage ceremonies.

cōnfarreō, -āre, -ātum vi to marry by confarreatio.

cōnfātālis adj bound by the same destiny.

cōnfēcī perf of **cōnficiō**.

cōnfectiō, -ōnis f making, completion; (food) chewing.

cōnfector, -ōris m maker, finisher; destroyer.

cōnfectus ppp of **cōnficiō**.

cōnferciō, -cire, -tum vt to stuff, cram, pack closely.

cōnferō, -ferre, -tulī, -lātum vt to gather together, collect; to contribute; to confer, talk over; (MIL) to oppose, engage in battle; to compare; (words) to condense, to direct, transfer; to transform (into), turn (to); to devote, bestow, to ascribe, assign, impute; (time) to postpone, capite ~ put heads together, confer; gradum ~ cum walk beside; sē ~ go, turn (to); sermōnēs ~ converse; signa ~ join battle.

cōnfertim adv in close order.

cōnfertus ppp of **cōnferciō** ♦ adj crowded, full; (MIL) in close order.

cōnfervēscō, -vēscere, -buī vi to boil up, grow hot.

cōnfessiō, -ōnis f acknowledgement, confession.

cōnfessus ppa of **cōnfiteor** ♦ adj

The present infinitive verb endings are as follows: -āre = 1st; -ēre = 2nd; -ere = 3rd and -īre = 4th. See sections on irregular verbs and noun declensions.

acknowledged, certain; **in ~ō esse/in ~um venīre** be generally admitted.

cōnfestim *adv* immediately.

cōnficiō, -icere, -ēcī, -ectum *vt* to make, effect, complete, accomplish; to get together, procure; to wear out, exhaust, consume, destroy; (*COMM*) to settle; (*space*) to travel; (*time*) to pass, complete; (*PHILOS*) to be an active cause; (*logic*) to deduce; (*pass*) it follows.

cōnfictiō, -ōnis *f* fabrication.

cōnfictus *ppp of* **cōnfingō**.

cōnfidēns, -entis *pres p of* **cōnfīdō** ♦ *adj* self-confident, bold, presumptuous.

cōnfidenter *adv* fearlessly, insolently.

cōnfidentia, -ae *f* confidence, self-confidence; impudence.

cōnfidentiloquus *adj* outspoken.

cōnfīdō, -dere, -sus sum *vi* to trust, rely, be sure; **sibi ~** be confident.

cōnfīgō, -gere, -xī, -xum *vt* to fasten together; to pierce, shoot; (*fig*) to paralyse.

cōnfingō, -ingere, -inxī, -ictum *vt* to make, invent, pretend.

cōnfīnis *adj* adjoining; (*fig*) akin.

cōnfīnium, -ī *nt* common boundary; (*pl*) neighbours; (*fig*) close connection, borderland between.

cōnfiō, -fierī *occ pass of* **cōnficiō**.

cōnfirmātiō, -ōnis *f* establishing; (*person*) encouragement; (*fact*) verifying; (*RHET*) adducing of proofs.

cōnfirmātor, -ōris *m* guarantor (*of money*).

cōnfirmātus *adj* resolute; proved, certain.

cōnfirmō, -āre, -āvī, -ātum *vt* to strengthen, reinforce; (*decree*) to

confirm, ratify; (*mind*) to encourage; (*fact*) to corroborate, prove, assert; **sē ~** recover; take courage.

cōnfiscō, -āre *vt* to keep in a chest; to confiscate.

cōnfisiō, -ōnis *f* assurance.

cōnfisus *ppa of* **cōnfīdō**.

cōnfiteor, -itērī, -essus *vt, vi* to confess, acknowledge; to reveal.

cōnfixus *ppp of* **cōnfīgō**.

cōnflagrō, -āre, -āvī, -ātum *vi* to burn, be ablaze.

cōnflictiō, -ōnis *f* conflict.

cōnflictō, -āre, -āvī, -ātum *vt* to strike down, contend (with); (*pass*) to fight, be harassed, be afflicted.

cōnflictus, -ūs *m* striking together.

cōnflīgō, -gere, -xī, -ctum *vt* to dash together; (*fig*) to contrast ♦ *vi* to fight, come into conflict.

cōnflō, -āre, -āvī, -ātum *vt* to ignite; (*passion*) to inflame; to melt down; (*fig*) to produce, procure, occasion.

cōnfluēns, -entis, -entēs, -entium *m* confluence of two rivers.

cōnfluō, -ere, -xī *vi* to flow together; (*fig*) to flock together, pour in.

cōnfodiō, -odere, -ōdī, -ossum *vt* to dig; to stab.

cōnfore *fut infin of* **cōnsum**.

cōnfōrmātiō, -ōnis *f* shape, form; (*words*) arrangement; (*voice*) expression; (*mind*) idea; (*RHET*) figure.

cōnfōrmō, -āre, -āvī, -ātum *vt* to shape, fashion.

cōnfossus *ppp of* **cōnfodiō** ♦ *adj* full of holes.

cōnfrāctus *ppp of* **cōnfringō**.

cōnfragōsus *adj* broken, rough; (*fig*) hard.

cōnfrēgī *perf of* **cōnfringō**.

cōnfremō, -ere, -uī *vi* to murmur
aloud.

cōnfricō, -āre *vt* to rub well.

cōnfringō, -ingere, -ēgī, -āctum *vt*
to break in pieces, wreck; (*fig*) to
ruin.

cōnfugiō, -ugere, -ūgī *vi* to flee for
help (to), take refuge (with); (*fig*)
to have recourse (to).

cōnfugium, -ī and iī *nt* refuge.

cōnfundō, -undere, -ūdī, -ūsum *vt*
to mix, mingle, join; to mix up,
confuse, throw into disorder;
(*mind*) to perplex, bewilder; to
diffuse, spread over.

cōnfūsē *adv* confusedly.

cōnfūsiō, -ōnis *f* combination;
confusion, disorder; ōris ~ going
red in the face.

cōnfūsus *ppp of* cōnfundō ♦ *adj*
confused, disorderly, troubled.

cōnfūtō, -āre, -āvī, -ātum *vt* to
keep from boiling over; to
repress; to silence, confute.

congelō, -āre, -āvī, -ātum *vt* to
freeze, harden ♦ *vi* to freeze over,
grow numb

congeminō, -āre, -āvī, -ātum *vt* to
double.

congemō, -ere, -uī *vi* to groan,
sigh ♦ *vt* to lament.

conger, -rī *m* sea eel.

congeriēs, -ēī *f* heap, mass,
accumulation.

congerō, -rere, -ssī, -stum *vt* to
collect, accumulate, build;
(*missiles*) to shower; (*speech*) to
comprise; (*fig*) to heap (upon),
ascribe.

congerō, -ōnis *m* thief.

congerrō, -ōnis *m* companion in
revelry.

congestīcius *adj* piled up.

congestus *ppp of* congerō.

congestus, -ūs *m* accumulating;

congiālis *adj* holding a congius.

congiārium, -ī and iī *nt* gift of food
to the people, gratuity to the
army.

congius, -ī and iī *m* Roman liquid
measure (*about 6 pints*).

conglaciō, -āre *vi* to freeze up.

conglīscō, -ere *vi* to blaze up.

conglobātiō, -ōnis *f* mustering.

conglobō, -āre, -āvī, -ātum *vt* to
make round; to mass together.

conglomerō, -āre *vt* to roll up

conglūtinātiō, -ōnis *f* gluing,
cementing; (*fig*) combination.

conglūtinō, -āre, -āvī, -ātum *vt* to
glue, cement, (*fig*) to join, weld
together; to contrive.

congraecō, -āre *vt* to squander on
luxury.

congrātulor, -ārī, -ātus *vi* to
congratulate.

congredior, -dī, -ssus *vt*, *vi* to
meet, accost; to contend, fight.

congregābilis *adj* gregarious.

congregātiō, -ōnis *f* union,
society.

congregō, -āre, -āvī, -ātum *vt* to
collect, assemble, unite.

congressiō, -ōnis *f* meeting,
conference.

congressus *ppa of* congredior.

congressus, -ūs *m* meeting,
association, union; encounter,
fight.

congruēns, -entis *adj* suitable,
consistent, proper; harmonious.

congruenter *adv* in conformity.

congruō, -ere, -ī *vi* to coincide; to
correspond, suit; to agree,
sympathize.

congruus *adj* agreeable.

coniciō, -icere, -iēcī, -iectum *vt* to
throw together; to throw, hurl; to
put, fling, drive, direct; to infer;

*The present infinitive verb endings are as follows: -āre = 1st; -ēre = 2nd; -ere = 3rd and
-īre = 4th. See sections on irregular verbs and noun declensions.*

conjecture; (*augury*) to interpret;
sē ~ rush, fly; devote oneself.
coniectiō, -ōnis f throwing,
conjecture, interpretation.
coniectō, -āre vt to infer,
conjecture, guess.
coniector, -ōris m (male)
interpreter, diviner.
coniectrīx, -rīcis f (female)
interpreter, diviner.
coniectūra, -ae f inference,
conjecture, guess; interpretation.
coniectūrālis adj (*RHET*) involving a
question of fact.
coniectus ppp of **coniciō**.
coniectus, -ūs m heap, mass,
concourse; throwing, throw,
range; (*eyes, mind*) turning,
directing.
cōnifer, cōniger, -ī adj cone-
bearing.
cōnītor, -tī, -sus and **xus** vi to lean
on; to strive, struggle on; to
labour.
coniugālis adj of marriage,
conjugal.
coniugātiō, -ōnis f etymological
relationship.
coniugātor, -ōris m uniter.
coniugiālis adj marriage- (*in cpds*).
coniugium, -ī and **iī** nt union,
marriage; husband, wife.
coniugō, -āre vt to form (*a
friendship*); **~āta verba** words
related etymologically.
coniūnctē adv jointly; on familiar
terms; (*logic*) hypothetically.
coniūnctim adv together, jointly.
coniūnctiō, -ōnis f union,
connection, association; (*minds*)
sympathy, affinity; (*GRAM*)
conjunction.
coniūnctum, -ī nt (*RHET*)
connection; (*PHILOS*) inherent
property (*of a body*).
coniūnctus ppp of **coniungō ✦** adj
near; connected, agreeing,

conforming; related, friendly,
intimate.
**coniungō, -ūngere, -ūnxī,
-ūnctum** vt to yoke, join together,
connect; (*war*) to join forces in; to
unite in love, marriage,
friendship; to continue without a
break.
coniūnx, -ugis m/f consort, wife,
husband, bride.
coniūrātī, -ōrum mpl conspirators.
coniūrātiō, -ōnis f conspiracy,
plot; alliance.
coniūrātus adj (*MIL*) after taking
the oath.
coniūrō, -āre, -āvī, -ātum vi to
take an oath; to conspire, plot.
coniux etc see **coniūnx**.
cōnīveō, -vēre, -vī and **xī** vi to shut
the eyes, blink; (*fig*) to be asleep;
to connive at.
conj- etc see **coni-**.
conl- etc see **coll-**.
conm- etc see **comm-**.
conn- etc see **cōn-**.
Conōn, -is m Athenian commander;
Greek astronomer.
cōnōpēum (-eum), -ēī nt mosquito
net.
cōnor, -ārī, -ātus vt to try, attempt,
venture.
conp- etc see **comp-**.
conquassātiō, -ōnis f severe
shaking.
conquassō, -āre, -ātum vt to
shake, upset, shatter.
conqueror, -rī, -stus vt, vi to
complain bitterly of, bewail.
conquestiō, -ōnis f complaining;
(*RHET*) appeal to pity.
conquestus ppa of **conqueror**.
conquestus, -ūs m outcry.
conquiēscō, -scere, -vī, -tum vi to
rest, take a respite; (*fig*) to be at
peace, find recreation; (*things*) to
stop, be quiet.
conquinīscō, -ere vi to cower,

squat, stoop down.

conquīrō, -rere, -sīvī, -sītum *vt* to search for, collect.

conquīsītē *adv* carefully.

conquīsītiō, -ōnis *f* search; (*MIL*) levy.

conquīsītor, -ōris *m* recruiting officer; (*THEATRE*) claqueur.

conquīsītus *ppp of* **conquīrō ♦** *adj* select, costly.

cōnr- *etc see* **corr-**.

cōnsaepiō, -īre, sī, -tum *vt* to enclose, fence round.

cōnsaeptum, -tī *nt* enclosure.

cōnsalūtātiō, -ōnis *f* mutual greeting.

cōnsalūtō, -āre, -āvī, -ātum *vt* to greet, hail.

cōnsānēscō, -ēscere, -uī *vi* to heal up.

cōnsanguineus *adj* brother, sister, kindred ♦ *mpl* relations.

cōnsanguinitās, -ātis *f* relationship.

cōnscelerātus *adj* wicked.

cōnscelerō, -āre, -āvī, -ātum *vt* to disgrace.

cōnscendō, -endere, -endī, -ēnsum *vt, vi* to climb, mount, embark.

cōnscēnsiō, -ōnis *f* embarkation.

cōnscēnsus *ppp of* **cōnscendo**.

cōnscientia, -ae *f* joint knowledge, being in the know; (*sense of*) consciousness; moral sense, conscience, guilty conscience.

cōnscindō, -ndere, -dī, -ssum *vt* to tear to pieces; (*fig*) to abuse.

cōnsciō, -īre *vt* to be conscious of guilt.

cōnscīscō, -scere, -vī *and* **iī, -ītum** *vt* to decide on publicly; to inflict on oneself; **mortem (sibi) ~** commit suicide.

cōnscissus *ppp of* **cōnscindō**.

cōnscītus *ppp of* **cōnscīscō**.

cōnscius *adj* sharing knowledge, privy, in the know; aware, conscious (of); conscious of guilt ♦ *m/f* confederate, confidant.

cōnscreor, -ārī *vi* to clear the throat.

cōnscrībō, -bere, -psī, -ptum *vt* to enlist, enrol; to write, compose, draw up, prescribe.

cōnscrīptiō, -ōnis *f* document, draft.

cōnscrīptus *ppp of* **cōnscrībō; patrēs ~ī** *patrician and elected plebeian members*; senators.

cōnsecō, -āre, -uī, -tum *vt* to cut up.

cōnsecrātiō, -ōnis *f* consecration, deification.

cōnsecrō, -āre, -āvī, -ātum *vt* to dedicate, consecrate, deify; (*fig*) to devote; to immortalise; **caput ~** doom to death.

cōnsectārius *adj* logical, consequent ♦ *ntpl* inferences.

cōnsectātiō, -ōnis *f* pursuit.

cōnsectātrīx, -īcis *f* (*fig*) follower.

cōnsectiō, -ōnis *f* cutting up.

cōnsector, -ārī, -ātus *vt* to follow, go after, try to gain; to emulate, imitate; to pursue, chase.

cōnseoūtiō, -ōnis *f* (*PHILOS*) consequences, effect; (*RHET*) sequence.

cōnsēdī *perf of* **cōnsīdō**.

cōnsenēscō, -ēscere, -uī *vi* to grow old, grow old together; (*fig*) to fade, pine, decay, become obsolete.

cōnsēnsiō, -ōnis *f* agreement, accord; conspiracy, plot.

cōnsēnsū *adv* unanimously.

cōnsēnsus *ppp of* **cōnsentiō**.

cōnsēnsus, -ūs *m* agreement, concord; conspiracy; (*PHILOS*)

The present infinitive verb endings are as follows: -āre = 1st; -ēre = 2nd; -ere = 3rd and -īre = 4th. *See sections on Irregular verbs and noun declensions.*

common sensation; (*fig*) harmony.

cōnsentāneus *adj* agreeing, in keeping with; **~um est** it is reasonable.

cōnsentiō, -entīre, -ēnsī, -ēnsum *vi* to agree, determine together; to plot, conspire; (*PHILOS*) to have common sensations; (*fig*) to harmonize, suit, be consistent (with); **bellum ~** vote for war.

cōnsequēns, -entis *pres p of* **cōnsequor ♦** *adj* coherent, reasonable; logical, consequent **♦** *nt* consequence.

cōnsequor, -quī, -cūtus *vt* to follow, pursue; to overtake, reach; (*time*) to come after; (*example*) to follow, copy; (*effect*) to result, be the consequence of; (*aim*) to attain, get; (*mind*) to grasp, learn; (*events*) to happen to, come to; (*standard*) to equal, come up to; (*speech*) to do justice to.

cōnserō, -erere, -ēvī, -itum *vt* to sow, plant; (*ground*) to sow with, plant with; (*fig*) to cover, fill.

cōnserō, -ere, -uī, -tum *vt* to join, string together, twine; (*MIL*) to join battle; **manum/manūs ~** engage in close combat; **ex iūre manum ~** lay claim to (*in an action for possession*).

cōnsertē *adv* connectedly.

cōnsertus *ppp of* **cōnserō**.

cōnserva, -ae *f* fellow slave.

cōnservātiō, -ōnis *f* preserving.

cōnservātor, -ōris *m* preserver.

cōnservītium, -ī *and* **iī** *nt* being fellow slaves.

cōnservō, -āre, -āvī, -ātum *vt* to preserve, save, keep.

cōnservus, -ī *m* fellow slave.

cōnsessor, -ōris *m* companion at table, fellow spectator; (*law*) assessor.

cōnsessus, -ūs *m* assembly; (*law*) court.

cōnsēvī *perf of* **cōnserō**.

cōnsīderātē *adv* cautiously, deliberately.

cōnsīderātiō, -ōnis *f* contemplation.

cōnsīderātus *adj* (*person*) circumspect; (*things*) well-considered.

cōnsīderō, -āre, -āvī, -ātum *vt* to look at, inspect; to consider, contemplate.

cōnsīdō, -īdere, -ēdī, -essum *vi* to sit down, take seats; (*courts*) to be in session; (*MIL*) to take up a position; (*residence*) to settle; (*places*) to subside, sink; (*fig*) to sink, settle down, subside.

cōnsignō, -āre, -āvī, -ātum *vt* to seal, sign; to attest, vouch for; to record, register.

cōnsilēscō, -ere *vi* to calm down.

cōnsiliārius, -ī *and* **iī** *m* adviser, counsellor; spokesman **♦** *adj* counselling.

cōnsiliātor, -ōris *m* counsellor.

cōnsilior, -ārī, -ātus *vi* to consult; (*with dat*) to advise.

cōnsilium, -ī *and* **iī** *nt* deliberation, consultation; deliberating body, council; decision, purpose; plan, measure, stratagem; advice, counsel; judgement, insight, wisdom; **-ium capere, inīre** come to a decision, resolve; **-ī esse** be an open question; **-iō** intentionally; **eō ~iō ut** with the intention of; **prīvātō ~iō** for one's own purposes.

cōnsimilis *adj* just like.

cōnsipiō, -ere *vi* to be in one's senses.

cōnsistō, -istere, -titī *vi* to stand, rest, take up a position; to consist (of), depend (on); to exist, be; (*fig*) to stand firm, endure; (*liquid*) to solidify, freeze; to stop, pause, halt, come to rest; (*fig*) to come to

a standstill, come to an end.
cōnsitiō, -ōnis f sowing, planting.
cōnsitor, -ōris m sower, planter.
cōnsitus ppp of **cōnserō**.
cōnsōbrīnus, -ī m, **-a, -ae** f cousin.
cōnsociātiō, -ōnis f society.
cōnsociō, -āre, -āvī, -ātum vt to
share, associate, unite.
cōnsōlābilis adj consolable.
cōnsōlātiō, -ōnis f comfort,
encouragement, consolation.
cōnsōlātor, -ōris m comforter.
cōnsōlātōrius adj of consolation.
cōnsōlor, -ārī, -ātus vt to console,
comfort, reassure; (things) to
relieve, mitigate.
cōnsomniō, -āre vt to dream
about.
cōnsonō, -āre, -uī vi to resound;
(fig) to accord.
cōnsonus adj concordant; (fig)
suitable.
cōnsōpiō, -īre, -ītum vt to put to
sleep.
cōnsors, -tis adj sharing in
common; (things) shared in
common ♦ m/f partner, colleague.
cōnsortiō, -ōnis f partnership,
fellowship.
cōnsortium, -ī and **iī** nt society,
participation.
cōnspectus ppp of **cōnspiciō** ♦ adj
visible; conspicuous.
cōnspectus, -ūs m look, view,
sight; appearing on the scene;
(fig) mental picture, survey; in
-um venīre come in sight, come
near.
cōnspergō, -gere, -sī, -sum vt to
besprinkle; (fig) to sprinkle.
cōnspiciendus adj noteworthy,
distinguished.
cōnspiciō, -icere, -exī, -ectum vt
to observe, catch sight of; to look
at (esp with admiration);

contemplate; (pass) to attract
attention, be conspicuous, be
notorious; (mind) to see, perceive.
cōnspicor, -ārī, -ātus vt to
observe, see, catch sight of.
cōnspicuus adj visible;
conspicuous, distinguished.
cōnspīrātiō, -ōnis f concord,
unanimity; plotting, conspiracy.
cōnspīrō, -āre, -āvī, -ātum vi to
agree, unite; to plot, conspire;
(music) to sound together.
cōnsponsor, -ōris m co-guarantor.
cōnspuō, -ere vt to spit upon.
cōnspurcō, -āre vt to pollute.
cōnspūtō, -āre vt to spit upon (with
contempt).
cōnstabiliō, -īre, -īvī, -ītum vt to
establish.
cōnstāns, -antis pres p of **cōnstō**
♦ adj steady, stable, constant;
consistent; faithful, steadfast.
cōnstanter adv steadily, firmly,
calmly; consistently.
cōnstantia, -ae f steadiness,
firmness, consistency, harmony;
self-possession, constancy.
cōnsternātiō, -ōnis f disorder,
tumult; (horses) stampede; (mind)
dismay, alarm.
cōnsternō, -ernere, -rāvī, -rātum
vt to spread, cover, thatch, pave;
-rāta nāvis decked ship
cōnsternō, -āre, -āvī, -ātum vt to
startle, stampede; to alarm, throw
into confusion.
cōnstīpō, -āre vt to crowd
together.
cōnstitī perf of **cōnstō**.
cōnstituō, -uere, -uī, -ūtum vt to
put, place, set down; (MIL) to
station, post, halt; to establish,
build, create; to settle, arrange,
organize; to appoint, determine,
fix; to resolve, decide; **bene**

*The present infinitive verb endings are as follows: -āre = 1st; -ēre = 2nd; -ere = 3rd and
-īre = 4th. See sections on irregular verbs and noun declensions.*

~**ūtum corpus** a good constitution.
cōnstitūtiō, -ōnis f state,
condition; regulation, decree;
definition, point at issue.
cōnstitūtum, -ūtī nt agreement.
cōnstō, -āre, -itī, -āium vi to stand
together; to agree, correspond,
tally; to stand firm, remain
constant; to exist, be; to consist
(of), be composed (of); (*facts*) to be
established, be well-known;
(*comm*) to cost; **sibi** ~ be
consistent; **inter omnēs** ~**at** it is
common knowledge; **mihi** ~**at** I
am determined; **ratiō** ~**at** the
account is correct.
cōnstrātum, -ī nt flooring, deck.
cōnstrātus ppp of **cōnsternō**.
cōnstringō, -ingere, -inxī, -ictum
vt to tie up, bind, fetter; (*fig*) to
restrain, restrict; (*speech*) to
compress, condense.
cōnstructiō, -ōnis f building up;
(*words*) arrangement, sequence.
cōnstruō, -ere, -xī, -ctum vt to
heap up; to build, construct.
cōnstuprātor, -ōris m debaucher.
cōnstuprō, -āre vt to debauch,
rape.
cōnsuādeō, -ēre vi to advise
strongly.
Cōnsuālia, -ium ntpl festival of
Consus.
cōnsuāsor, -ōris m earnest
adviser.
cōnsūdō, -āre vi to sweat
profusely.
**cōnsuēfaciō, -facere, -fēcī,
-factum** vt to accustom.
cōnsuēscō, -scere, -vī, -tum vt to
accustom, inure ♦ vi to get
accustomed; to cohabit (with);
(*perf tenses*) to be accustomed, be
in the habit of.
cōnsuētūdō, -inis f custom, habit;
familiarity, social intercourse;
love affair; (*language*) usage,

idiom; ~**ine/ex** ~**ine** as usual;
epistulārum ~ correspondence.
cōnsuētus ppp of **cōnsuēscō** ♦ adj
customary, usual.
cōnsuēvī perf of **cōnsuēscō**.
consul, -is m consul; ~ **dēsignātus**
consul elect; ~ **ōrdinārius** regular
consul; ~ **suffectus** successor to a
consul who has died during his term of
office; ~ **iterum/tertium** consul for
the second/third time; ~**em creāre,
dīcere, facere** elect to the
consulship; **L. Domitiō App.
Claudiō** ~**ibus** in the year 54 B.C.
cōnsulāris adj consular, consul's;
of consular rank ♦ m ex-consul.
cōnsulāriter adv in a manner
worthy of a consul.
cōnsulātus, -ūs m consulship;
~**um petere** stand for the
consulship.
cōnsulō, -ere, -uī, -tum vi to
deliberate, take thought; (*with dat*)
to look after, consult the interests
of; (*with dē or in*) to take
measures against, pass sentence
on ♦ vt to consult, ask advice of;
to consider; to advise
(something); to decide; **bonī/
optimī** ~ take in good part, be
satisfied with.
cōnsultātiō, -ōnis f deliberation;
inquiry; case.
cōnsultē adv deliberately.
cōnsultō adv deliberately.
cōnsultō, -āre, -āvī, -ātum vt, vi to
deliberate, reflect; to consult;
(*with dat*) to consult the interests
of.
cōnsultor, -ōris m counsellor;
consulter, client.
cōnsultrīx, -īcis f protectress.
cōnsultum, -ī nt decree (esp of the
Senate); consultation; response
(*from an oracle*).
cōnsultus ppp of **cōnsulō** ♦ adj
considered; experienced, skilled

♦ *m* lawyer; **iūris ~us** lawyer.
cōnsuluī *perf of* **cōnsulō**.
(**cōnsum**) **futūrum, fore** *vi* to be all right.
cōnsummātus *adj* perfect.
cōnsummō, -āre *vt* to sum up; to complete, perfect.
cōnsūmō, -ere, -psī, -ptum *vt* to consume, use up, eat up; to waste, squander; to exhaust, destroy, kill; to spend, devote.
cōnsūmplō, -ōnis *f* wasting.
cōnsūmptor, -ōris *m* destroyer.
cōnsūmptus *ppp of* **cōnsūmō**.
cōnsuō, -uere, -uī, -ūtum *vt* to sew up; (*fig*) to contrive.
cōnsurgō, -gere, -rēxī, -rēctum *vi* to rise, stand up; to be roused (to); to spring up, start.
cōnsurrēctiō, -ōnis *f* standing up.
Cōnsus, -ī *m* ancient Roman god (*connected with harvest*).
cōnsusurrō, -āre *vi* to whisper together.
cōnsūtus *ppp of* **cōnsuō**.
contābefaciō, -ere *vt* to wear out.
contābēscō, -ēscere, -uī *vi* to waste away.
contabulātiō, -ōnis *f* flooring, storey.
contabulō, -āre, -āvī, -ātum *vt* to board over, build in storeys.
contāctus *ppp of* **contingō**.
contāctus, -ūs *m* touch, contact; contagion, infection.
contāgēs, -is *f* contact, touch.
contāgiō, -ōnis *f*, **contāgium, -ī** *and* **iī** *nt* contact; contagion, infection; (*fig*) contamination, bad example.
contāminātus *adj* impure, vicious.
contāminō, -āre, -āvī, -ātum *vt* to defile; (*fig*) to mar, spoil.
contechnor, -ārī, -ātus *vi* to think out plots.

contegō, -egere, -ēxī, -ēctum *vt* to cover up, cover over; to protect; to hide.
contemerō, -āre *vt* to defile.
contemnō, -nere, -psī, -ptum *vt* to think light of, have no fear of, despise, defy; to disparage.
contemplātiō, -ōnis *f* contemplation, surveying.
contemplātor, -ōris *m* observer.
contemplātus, -ūs *m* contemplation.
contemplō, -āre, -āvī, -ātum; -or, -ārī, -ātus *vt* to look at, observe, contemplate.
contempsī *perf of* **contemnō**.
contemptim *adv* contemptuously, slightingly.
contemptiō, -ōnis *f* disregard, scorn, despising.
contemptor, -ōris *m* (male) despiser, defiler.
contemptrīx, -rīcis *f* (female) despiser, defiler.
contemptus *ppp of* **contemnō** ♦ *adj* contemptible.
contemptus, -ūs *m* despising, scorn; being slighted; **-uī esse** be despised.
contendō, -dere, -dī, -tum *vt* to stretch, draw, tighten; (*instrument*) to tune; (*effort*) to strain, exert; (*argument*) to assert, maintain; (*comparison*) to compare, contrast; (*source*) to direct ♦ *vi* to exert oneself, strive; to hurry; to journey, march; to contend, compete, fight; to entreat, solicit.
contentē *adv* (*from* **contendō**) earnestly, intensely.
contentē *adv* (*from* **contineō**) closely.
contentiō, -ōnis *f* straining, effort; striving (after); struggle, competition, dispute; comparison.

The present infinitive verb endings are as follows: **-āre** = 1st; **-ēre** = 2nd; **-ere** = 3rd and **-īre** = 4th. *See sections on irregular verbs and noun declensions.*

contrast, antithesis.

contentus *ppp of* **contendō** ♦ *adj* strained, tense; (*fig*) intent.

contentus *ppp of* **contineō** ♦ *adj* content, satisfied.

conterminus *adj* bordering, neighbouring.

conterō, -erere, -rīvī, -rītum *vt* to grind, crumble; to wear out, waste; (*time*) to spend, pass; (*fig*) to obliterate.

conterreō, -ēre, -uī, -itum *vt* to terrify.

contestātus *adj* proved.

contestor, -ārī, -ātus *vt* to call to witness; **lītem ~** open a lawsuit by calling witnesses.

contexō, -ere, -uī, -tum *vt* to weave, interweave; to devise, construct; (*recital*) to continue.

contextē *adv* in a connected fashion.

contextus *adj* connected.

contextus, -ūs *m* connection, coherence.

conticēscō (-īscō), -ēscere, -uī *vi* to become quiet, fall silent; (*fig*) to cease, abate.

contigī *perf of* **contingō**

contignātiō, -ōnis *f* floor, storey.

contignō, -āre *vt* to floor.

contiguus *adj* adjoining, near; within reach.

continēns, -entis *pres p of* **contineō** ♦ *adj* bordering, adjacent; unbroken, continuous; (*time*) successive, continual, uninterrupted; (*person*) temperate, continent ♦ *nt* mainland, continent; essential point (*in an argument*).

continenter *adv* (*place*) in a row; (*time*) continuously; (*person*) temperately.

continentia, -ae *f* moderation, self-control.

contineō, -inēre, -inuī, -entum *vt*

to hold, keep together; to confine, enclose; to contain, include, comprise; (*pass*) to consist of, rest on; to control, check, repress.

contingō, -ingere, -igī, -āctum *vt* to touch, take hold of, partake of; to be near, border on; to reach, come to; to contaminate; (*mind*) to touch, affect, concern ♦ *vi* to happen, succeed.

contingō, -ere *vt* to moisten, smear.

continuātiō, -ōnis *f* unbroken, succession, series; (*RHET*) period.

continuī *perf of* **contineō**

continuō *adv* immediately, without delay; (*argument*) necessarily.

continuō, -āre, -āvī, -ātum *vt* to join together, make continuous; to continue without a break; **verba ~** form a sentence.

continuus *adj* joined (to); continuous, successive, uninterrupted; **~ā nocte** the following night; **trīduum ~um** three days running.

cōntiō, -ōnis *f* public meeting; speech, address; rostrum; **~ōnem habēre** hold a meeting; deliver an address; **prō ~ōne** in public.

cōntiōnābundus *adj* delivering a harangue, playing the demagogue.

cōntiōnālis *adj* suitable for a public meeting, demagogic.

cōntiōnārius *adj* fond of public meetings.

cōntiōnātor, -ōris *m* demagogue.

cōntiōnor, -ārī, -ātus *vi* to address a public meeting, harangue; to declare in public; to come to a meeting.

cōntiuncula, -ae *f* short speech.

contorqueō, -quēre, -sī, -tum *vt* to twist, turn; (*weapons*) to throw, brandish; (*words*) to deliver forcibly.

contortē adv intricately.

contortiō, -ōnis f intricacy.

contortor, -ōris m perverter.

contortulus adj somewhat complicated.

contortuplicātus adj very complicated.

contortus ppp of **contorqueō** ♦ adj vehement; intricate.

contrā adv (place) opposite, face to face; (speech) in reply; (action) to fight, in opposition, against someone; (result, with **esse**) adverse, unsuccessful; (comparison) the contrary, conversely, differently; (argument) on the contrary, on the other hand; ~ **atque, quam** contrary to what, otherwise than ♦ prep (with acc) facing, opposite to; against; contrary to, in violation of.

contractiō, -ōnis f contracting; shortening; despondency.

contractiuncula, -ae f slight despondency.

contractus ppp of **contrahō** ♦ adj contracted, narrow; short; in seclusion.

contrādīcō, -dīcere, -dīxī, -dictum (usu two words) vt, vi to oppose, object; (law) to be counsel for the other side

contrādictiō, -ōnis f objection.

contrahō, -here, -xī, -ctum vt to draw together, assemble; to bring about, achieve; (comm) to contract, make a bargain; to shorten, narrow; to limit, depress; (blame) to incur; (brow) to wrinkle; (sail) to shorten; (sky) to overcast.

contrāriē adv differently.

contrārius adj opposite, from opposite; contrary; hostile,

harmful ♦ nt opposite, reverse; **ex ~ō** on the contrary.

contrectābiliter adv so as to be felt.

contrectātiō, -ōnis f touching.

contrectō, -āre, -āvī, -ātum vt to touch, handle; (fig) to consider.

contremīscō, -īscere, -uī vi to tremble all over; (fig) to waver ♦ vt to be afraid of.

contremō, -ere vi to quake.

contribuō, -uere, -uī, -ūtum vt to bring together, join, incorporate.

contristō, -āre, -āvī, -ātum vt to sadden, darken, cloud.

contrītus ppp of **conterō** ♦ adj trite, well-worn.

contrōversia, -ae f dispute, argument, debate, controversy.

contrōversiōsus adj much disputed.

contrōversus adj disputed, questionable.

contrucīdō, -āre, -āvī, -ātum vt to massacre.

contrūdō, -dere, -sī, -sum vt to crowd together.

contrunco, -āre vt to hack to pieces.

contrūsus ppp of **contrūdō**.

contubernālis, -is m/f tent companion; junior officer serving with a general; (fig) companion, mate.

contubernium, -ī and **iī** nt service in the same tent, mess; service as junior officer with a general; common tent; slaves' home.

contueor, -ērī, -itus vt to look at, consider, observe.

contuitus, -ūs m observing, view

contulī perf of **cōnferō**.

contumācia, -ae f obstinacy, defiance.

contumāciter adv see **contumāx**.

The present infinitive verb endings are as follows: -āre = 1st; -ēre = 2nd; -ere = 3rd and -īre = 4th. See sections on irregular verbs and noun declensions.

contumāx, -ācis *adj* stubborn, insolent, pig-headed.

contumēlia, -ae *f* (*verbal*) insult, libel, invective; (*physical*) assault, ill-treatment.

contumēliōsē *adv* insolently.

contumēliōsus *adj* insulting, outrageous.

contumulō, -āre *vt* to bury.

contundō, -undere, -udī, -ūsum *vt* to pound, beat, bruise; (*fig*) to suppress, destroy.

contuor *etc see* **contueor.**

conturbātiō, -ōnis *f* confusion, mental disorder.

conturbātus *adj* distracted, diseased.

conturbō, -āre, -āvī, -ātum *vt* to throw into confusion; (*mind*) to derange, disquiet; (*money*) to embarrass.

contus, -ī *m* pole.

contūsus *ppp of* **contundō.**

contūtus *see* **contuitus.**

cōnūbiālis *adj* conjugal.

cōnūbium, -ī *and* **iī** *nt* marriage; **iūs ~ī** right of intermarriage.

cōnus, -ī *m* cone; (*helmet*) apex.

convador, -ārī, -ātus *vt* (*law*) to bind over.

convalēscō, -ēscere, -uī *vi* to recover, get better; (*fig*) to grow stronger, improve.

convallis, -is *f* valley with hills on all sides.

convāsō, -āre *vt* to pack up.

convectō, -āre *vt* to bring home.

convector, -ōris *m* fellow passenger.

convehō, -here, -xī, -ctum *vt* to bring in, carry.

convellō, -ellere, -ellī, -ulsum *and* **olsum** *vt* to wrench, tear away; to break up; (*fig*) to destroy, overthrow; **signa ~** decamp.

convena, -ae *adj* meeting.

convenae, -ārum *m/f* crowd of strangers, refugees.

conveniēns, -entis *pres p of* **conveniō ♦** *adj* harmonious, consistent; fit, appropriate.

convenienter *adv* in conformity (with), consistently; aptly.

convenientia, -ae *f* conformity, harmony.

conveniō, -enīre, -ēnī, -entum *vi* to meet, assemble; (*events*) to combine, coincide; (*person*) to agree, harmonize; (*things*) to fit, suit; (*impers*) to be suitable, be proper ♦ *vt* to speak to, interview.

conventīcium, -ī *and* **iī** *nt* payment for attendance at assemblies.

conventīcius *adj* visiting regularly.

conventiculum, -ī *nt* gathering; meeting place.

conventiō, -ōnis *f* agreement.

conventum, -ī *nt* agreement.

conventus *ppp of* **conveniō.**

conventus, -ūs *m* meeting; (*law*) local assizes; (*COMM*) corporation; agreement; **~ūs agere** hold the assizes.

converrō, -rere, -rī, -sum *vt* to sweep up, brush together; (*comedy*) to give a good beating to.

conversātiō, -ōnis *f* associating (with).

conversiō, -ōnis *f* revolution, cycle; change over; (*RHET*) well-rounded period; verbal repetition at end of clauses.

conversō, -āre *vt* to turn round.

conversus *ppp of* **converrō;** *ppp of* **convertō.**

convertō, -tere, -tī, -sum *vt* to turn round, turn back; (*MIL*) to wheel; to turn, direct; to change, transform; (*writings*) to translate ♦ *vi* to return, turn, change.

convestiō, -īre, -īvī, -ītum *vt* to clothe, encompass.

convexus *adj* vaulted; rounded;

hollow; sloping ♦ nt vault, hollow.

convīciātor, -ōris m slanderer.

convīcior, -ārī, -ātus vt to revile.

convīcium, -ī and **iī** nt loud noise, outcry; invective; abuse; reproof, protest.

convictiō, -ōnis f companionship.

convictor, -ōris m familiar friend.

convictus ppp of **convincō**.

convīctus, -ūs m community life, intercourse; entertainment.

convincō, -incere, -īcī, -ictum vt to refute, convict, prove wrong; to prove, demonstrate.

convīsō, -ere vt to search, examine; to pervade.

convitium see **convīcium**.

convīva, -ae m/f guest.

convīvālis adj festive, convivial.

convīvātor, -ōris m host.

convīvium, -ī and **iī** nt banquet, entertainment; guests.

convīvor, -ārī, -ātus vi to feast together, carouse.

convocātiō, -ōnis f assembling.

convocō, -āre, -āvī, -ātum vt to call a meeting of, muster.

convolnerō see **convulnerō**.

convolō, -āre, -āvī, -ātum vi to flock together.

convolsus see **convulsus**.

convolvō, -vere, -vī, -ūtum vt to roll up, coil up; to intertwine.

convomō, -ere vt to vomit over.

convorrō see **converrō**.

convortō see **convertō**.

convulnerō, -āre vt to wound seriously.

convulsus ppp of **convellō**.

cooperiō, -īre, -uī, -tum vt to cover over, overwhelm.

cooptātiō, -ōnis f electing, nominating (of new members).

coopto, -āre, -āvī, -ātum vt to elect (as a colleague).

coorior, -īrī, -tus vi to rise, appear; to break out, begin.

coortus, -ūs m originating.

cōpa, -ae f barmaid.

cophinus, -ī m basket.

cōpia, -ae f abundance, plenty; number; resources, wealth, prosperity; (MIL, usu pl) troops, force; (words, thought) richness, fulness, store; (action) opportunity, facility, means, access; **prō eā** according to one's resources, as good as possible considering.

cōpiolae, -ārum fpl small force.

cōpiōsē adv abundantly, fully, at great length.

cōpiōsus adj abounding, rich, plentiful; (speech) eloquent, fluent.

cōpis adj rich.

cōpula, -ae f rope, leash, grapnel; (fig) bond.

cōpulātiō, -ōnis f coupling, union.

cōpulātus adj connected, binding.

cōpulō, -āre, -āvī, -ātum vt to couple, join; (fig) to unite, associate.

coqua, -ae f cook.

coquīnō, -āre vi to be a cook.

coquīnus adj of cooking.

coquō, -quere, -xī, -ctum vt to cook, boil, bake; to parch, burn; (fruit) to ripen; (stomach) to digest; (thought) to plan, concoct; (care) to disquiet, disturb.

coquus (cocus), -ī m cook.

cor, cordis nt heart; (feeling) heart, soul; (thought) mind, judgement; **cordī esse** please, be agreeable.

cōram adv in one's presence; in person ♦ prep (with abl) in the presence of, before.

corbis, -is m/f basket.

corbīta, -ae f slow boat.

The present infinitive verb endings are as follows: -āre = 1st; -ēre = 2nd; -ere = 3rd and -īre = 4th. See sections on irregular verbs and noun declensions.

corbula, -ae f little basket.

corculum, -ī nt dear heart.

Corcÿra, -ae f island off W. coast of Greece (now Corfu).

Corcÿraeus adj see n.

cordātē adv see **cordātus**.

cordātus adj wise.

cordolium, -ī and **iī** nt sorrow.

Corfiniēnsis adj see n.

Corfinium, -ī nt town in central Italy.

coriandrum, -ī nt coriander.

Corinthiacus, -iēnsis, -ius adj: ~ium aes Corinthian brass (an alloy of gold, silver and copper).

Corinthus, -ī f Corinth.

corium (corius m) **-ī** and **iī** nt hide, skin; leather, strap.

Cornēlia, -iae f mother of the Gracchi.

Cornēliānus, -ius adj: lēgēs ~iae Sulla's laws.

Cornēlius, -ī m famous Roman family name (esp Scipios, Gracchi, Sulla).

corneolus adj horny.

corneus adj of horn.

corneus adj of the cornel tree, of cornel wood.

cornicen, -inis m horn-blower.

cornicula, -ae f little crow.

corniculārius, -ī and **iī** m adjutant.

corniculum, -ī nt a horn-shaped decoration.

corniger, -ī adj horned.

cornipēs, -edis adj horn-footed.

cornīx, -īcis f crow.

cornū, -ūs, -um, -ī nt horn; anything horn-shaped; (army) wing; (bay) arm; (book) roller-end; (bow) tip; (helmet) crest-socket; (land) tongue, spit; (lyre) arm; (moon) horn; (place) side; (river) branch; (yardarm) point; anything made of horn: bow, funnel, lantern; (music) horn; (oil) cruet; anything like horn; beak, hoof, wart; (fig) strength, courage; ~ cōpiae Amalthea's horn, symbol of plenty.

cornum, -ī nt cornelian cherry.

cornum see **cornū**.

cornus, -ī f cornelian cherry tree; javelin.

corōlla, -ae f small garland.

corōllārium, -ī and **iī** nt garland for actors; present, gratuity.

corōna, -ae f garland, crown; (ASTRO) Corona Borealis; (people) gathering, bystanders; (MIL) cordon of besiegers or defenders; **sub ~ā vēndere, vēnīre** sell, be sold as slaves.

Corōnaeus, -ēus, -ēnsis adj see **Corōnēa**.

corōnārium aurum gold collected in the provinces for a victorious general.

Corōnēa, -ēae f town in central Greece.

corōnō, -āre, -āvī, -ātum vt to put a garland on, crown; to encircle.

corporeus adj corporeal; of flesh.

corpulentus adj corpulent.

corpus, -oris nt body; substance, flesh; corpse; trunk, torso; person, individual; (fig) structure, corporation, body politic.

corpusculum, -ī nt particle; term of endearment.

corrādō, -dere, -sī, -sum vt to scrape together, procure.

corrēctiō, -ōnis f amending, improving.

corrēctor, -ōris m reformer, critic.

corrēctus ppp of **corrigō**.

corrēpō, -ere, -sī vi to creep, slink, cower.

correptē adv briefly.

correptus ppp of **corripiō**.

corrīdeō, -ēre vi to laugh aloud.

corrigia, -ae f shoelace.

corrigō, -igere, -ēxī, -ēctum vt to make straight; to put right, improve, correct.

corripiō, -ipere, -ipuī, -eptum vt to seize, carry off, get along quickly;

(*speech*) to reprove, reproach, accuse; (*passion*) to seize upon, attack; (*time, words*) to cut short; **sē gradum, viam ~** hasten, rush.

corrōborō, -āre, -āvī, -ātum *vt* to make strong, invigorate.

corrōdō, -dere, -sī, -sum *vt* to nibble away.

corrogō, -āre *vt* to gather by requesting.

corrūgō, -āre *vt* to wrinkle.

corrumpō, -umpere, -upī, -uptum *vt* to break up, ruin, waste; to mar, adulterate, falsify; (*person*) to corrupt, seduce, bribe.

corruō, -ere, -ī *vi* to fall, collapse ♦ *vt* to overthrow, heap up.

corruptē *adv* perversely; in a lax manner.

corruptēla, -ae *f* corruption, bribery; seducer.

corruptiō, -ōnis *f* bribing, seducing; corrupt state.

corruptor, -ōris *m*, **-rīx, -rīcis** *f* corrupter, seducer.

corruptus *ppp of* **corrumpō** ♦ *adj* spoiled, corrupt, bad.

Corsus *adj* Corsican.

cortex, -icis *m/f* bark, rind; cork.

cortīna, -ae *f* kettle, cauldron; tripod of Apollo; (*fig*) vault, circle.

corulus, -ī *f* hazel.

Cōrus *see* **Caurus**.

coruscō, -āre *vt* to butt; to shake, brandish ♦ *vi* to flutter, flash, quiver.

coruscus *adj* tremulous, oscillating; shimmering, glittering.

corvus, -ī *m* raven; (*MIL*) grapnel.

Corybantēs, -ium *mpl* priests of Cybele.

Corybantius *adj see* n.

cōrycus, -ī *m* punchball.

corylētum, -ī *nt* hazel copse.

corylus, -ī *f* hazel.

corymbifer *m* Bacchus.

corymbus, -ī *m* cluster (*esp of ivy berries*).

coryphaeus, -ī *m* leader.

cōrytos, -us, -ī *m* quiver.

cōs *f* hard rock, flint; grindstone.

Cōs, Coī *f* Aegean island (*famous for wine and weaving*) ♦ *nt* Coan wine ♦ *ntpl* Coan clothes.

cosmēta, -ae *m* master of the wardrobe.

costa, -ae *f* rib; side, wall.

costum, -ī *nt* an aromatic plant, perfume.

cothurnātus *adj* buskined, tragic.

cothurnus, -ī *m* buskin, hunting boot; tragedy; elevated style.

cotīd- *see* **cottīd-**.

cōtis *f see* **cōs**.

cottabus, -ī *m* game of throwing drops of wine.

cottana, -ōrum *ntpl* Syrian figs.

cottīdiānō *adv* daily.

cottīdiānus *adj* daily; everyday, ordinary.

cottīdiē *adv* every day, daily.

coturnīx, -īcis *f* quail.

Cotyttia, -ōrum *ntpl festival of Thracian goddess Cotytto.*

Cōus *adj* Coan.

covīnārius, -ī and **iī** *m* chariot fighter.

covinnus, -ī *m* war chariot; coach.

coxa, -ae, coxendīx, -īcis *f* hip.

coxī *perf of* **coquō**.

crābrō, -ōnis *m* hornet.

crambē, -ēs *f* cabbage; **~ repetīta** stale repetitions.

Crantor, -oris *m Greek Academic philosopher.*

crāpula, -ae *f* intoxication, hangover.

crāpulārius *adj* for intoxication.

crās *adv* tomorrow.

The present infinitive verb endings are as follows: **-āre** = 1st; **-ēre** = 2nd; **-ere** = 3rd and **-īre** = 4th. *See sections on irregular verbs and noun declensions.*

crassē *adv* grossly, dimly.

Crassiānus *adj see* **Crassus**.

crassitūdō, -inis *f* thickness, density.

crassus *adj* thick, gross, dense; *(fig)* dull, stupid.

Crassus, -ī *m famous orator; wealthy politician, triumvir with Caesar and Pompey.*

crāstinum, -ī *nt* the morrow.

crāstinus *adj* of tomorrow; **diē ~ī** tomorrow.

crātēr, -is *m*, **-a, -ae** *f* bowl *(esp for mixing wine and water)*; crater; a constellation.

crātis, -is *f* wickerwork, hurdle; *(AGR)* harrow; *(MIL)* faggots for lining trenches; *(shield)* ribs; *(fig)* frame, joints.

creātiō, -ōnis *f* election.

creātor, -ōris *m*, **-rīx, -rīcis** *f* creator, father, mother.

creātus *m (with abl)* son of.

crēber, -rī *adj* dense, thick, crowded; numerous, frequent; *(fig)* prolific, abundant.

crēbrēscō, -ēscere, -uī *vi* to increase, become frequent.

crēbritās, -ātis *f* frequency.

crēbrō *adv* repeatedly.

crēdibilis *adj* credible.

crēdibiliter *adv see* **crēdibilis**.

crēditor, -ōris *m* creditor.

crēditum, -ītī *nt* loan.

crēdō, -ere, -idī, -itum *vt, vi* to entrust, lend; to trust, have confidence in; to believe; to think, suppose; **~erēs** one would have thought.

crēdulitās, -ātis *f* credulity.

crēdulus *adj* credulous, trusting.

cremō, -āre, -āvī, -ātum *vt* to burn, cremate.

Cremōna, -ae *f town in N. Italy.*

Cremōnēnsis *adj see* **n**.

cremor, -ōris *m* juice, broth.

creō, -āre, -āvī, -ātum *vt* to create,

produce, beget; to elect (to an office); to cause, occasion.

creper, -ī *adj* dark; doubtful.

crepida, -ae *f* sandal; **nē sūtor suprā ~am ≈** let the cobbler stick to his last.

crepidātus *adj* wearing sandals.

crepidō, -inis *f* pedestal, base; bank, pier, dam.

crepidula, -ae *f* small sandal.

crepitācillum, -ī *nt* rattle.

crepitō, -āre *vi* to rattle, chatter, rustle, creak.

crepitus, -ūs *m* rattling, chattering, rustling, creaking.

crepō, -āre, -uī, -itum *vi* to rattle, creak, snap (fingers) ♦ *vt* to make rattle, clap; to chatter about.

crepundia, -ōrum *ntpl* rattle, babies' toys.

crepusculum, -ī *nt* twilight, dusk; darkness.

Crēs, -ētis *m* Cretan.

crēscō, -scere, -vī, -tum *vi* to arise, appear, be born; to grow up, thrive, increase, multiply; to prosper, be promoted, rise in the world.

Crēsius *adj* Cretan.

Crēssa, -ae *f* Cretan.

Crēta, -ae *f* Crete.

crēta, -ae *f* chalk; good mark.

Crētaeus *and* **-icus** *and* **is, -idis** *adj see* **n**.

crētātus *adj* chalked; dressed in white.

Crētē *see* **Crēta**.

crēteus *adj* of chalk, of clay.

crētiō, -ōnis *f* declaration of accepting an inheritance.

crētōsus *adj* chalky, clayey.

crētula, -ae *f* white clay for sealing.

crētus *ppp of* **cernō** ♦ *ppa of* **crēscō** ♦ *adj* descended, born.

Creūsa, -ae *f wife of Jason; wife of Aeneas.*

crēvī *perf of* **cernō**; *perf of* **crēscō**.

crībrum, -ī *nt* sieve.

crīmen, -inis *nt* accusation, charge, reproach; guilt, crime; cause of offence; **esse in ~ine** stand accused.

crīmīnātiō, -ōnis *nf* complaint, slander.

crīminator, -ōris *m* accuser.

crīminō, -āre *vt* to accuse.

crīminor, -ārī, -ātus *dep* to accuse, impeach; (*things*) to complain of, charge with.

crīminōsē *adv* accusingly, slanderously.

crīminōsus *adj* reproachful, slanderous.

crīnālis *adj* for the hair, hair- (*in cpds*) ♦ *nt* hairpin.

crīnis, -is *m* hair; (*comet*) tail.

crīnītus *adj* long-haired; crested; **stēlla ~a** comet.

crīspāns, -antis *adj* wrinkled.

crīspō, -āre *vt* to curl, swing, wave.

crīspus *adj* curled; curly-headed; wrinkled; tremulous.

crista, -ae *f* cockscomb, crest; plume.

cristātus *adj* crested, plumed.

criticus, -ī *m* critic.

croceus *adj* of saffron, yellow.

crocinus *adj* yellow ♦ *nt* saffron oil.

crōciō, -īre *vi* to croak.

crocodīlus, -ī *m* crocodile.

crocotārius *adj* of saffron clothes.

crocotula, -ae *f* saffron dress.

crocus, -ī *m*, **-um, -ī** *nt* saffron; yellow.

Croesus, -ī *m* king of Lydia (*famed for wealth*).

crotalistria, -ae *f* castanet dancer.

crotalum, -ī *nt* rattle, castanet.

cruciābilitās, -ātis *f* torment.

cruciāmentum, -ī *nt* torture.

cruciātus, -ūs *m* torture; instrument of torture; (*fig*) ruin, misfortune.

cruciō, -āre, -āvī, -ātum *vt* to torture; to torment.

crūdēlis *adj* hard-hearted, cruel.

crūdēlitās, -ātis *f* cruelty, severity.

crūdēliter *adv see* **crūdēlis**.

crūdēscō, -escere, -uī *vi* to grow violent, grow worse.

crūdītās, -ātis *f* indigestion.

crūdus *adj* bleeding; (*food*) raw, undigested; (*person*) dyspeptic; (*leather*) rawhide; (*fruit*) unripe; (*age*) immature, fresh; (*voice*) hoarse; (*fig*) unfeeling, cruel, merciless.

cruentō, -āre *vt* to stain with blood, wound.

cruentus *adj* bloody, gory; bloodthirsty, cruel; blood-red.

crumēna, -ae *f* purse; money.

crumilla, -ae *f* purse.

cruor, -ōris *m* blood; bloodshed.

cruppellāriī, -ōrum *mpl* mail-clad fighters.

crūrifragius, -ī *and* **iī** *m* one whose legs have been broken.

crūs, -ūris *nt* leg, shin.

crūsta, -ae *f* hard surface, crust; stucco, embossed or inlaid work.

crūstulum, -ī *nt* small pastry.

crūstum, -ī *nt* pastry.

crux, -ucis *f* gallows, cross; (*fig*) torment; **abī in malam ~cem** = go and be hanged!

crypta, -ae *f* underground passage, grotto.

cryptoporticus, -ūs *f* covered walk.

crystallinus *adj* of crystal ♦ *ntpl* crystal vases.

crystallum, -ī *nt*, **-us, -ī** *m* crystal.

cubiculāris, cubiculārius *adj* of the

The present infinitive verb endings are as follows: -āre = 1st; -ēre = 2nd; -ere = 3rd and -īre = 4th. See sections on irregular verbs and noun declensions.

bedroom ♦ *m* valet de chambre.
cubiculum, -ī *nt* bedroom.
cubīle, -is *nt* bed, couch; (*animals*) lair, nest; (*fig*) den.
cubital, -ālis *nt* cushion.
cubitālis *adj* a cubit long.
cubitō, -āre *vi* to lie (in bed).
cubitum, -ī *nt* elbow; cubit.
cubitus, -ūs *m* lying in bed.
cubō, -āre, -uī, -itum *vi* to lie in bed; to recline at table; (*places*) to lie on a slope.
cucullus, -ī *m* hood, cowl.
cucūlus, -ī *m* cuckoo.
cucumis, -eris *m* cucumber.
cucurbita, -ae *f* gourd; cupping glass.
cucurrī *perf of* **currō**.
cūdō, -ere *vt* to beat, thresh; (*metal*) to forge; (*money*) to coin.
cūiās, -tis *pron* of what country?, of what town?
cuicuimodī (*gen of* **quisquis** *and* **modus**) of whatever kind, whatever like.
cūius *pron* (*interrog*) whose?; (*rel*) whose.
culcita, -ae *f* mattress, pillow; eyepatch.
cūleus *see* **culleus.**
culex, -icis *m/f* gnat.
culīna, -ae *f* kitchen; food.
culleus, cūleus, -ī *m* leather bag for holding liquids; *a fluid measure.*
culmen, -inis *nt* stalk; top, roof, summit; (*fig*) height, acme.
culmus, -ī *m* stalk, straw.
culpa, -ae *f* blame, fault; mischief; **in ~ā sum, mea ~a est** I am at fault *or* to blame.
culpātus *adj* blameworthy.
culpitō, -āre *vt* to find fault with.
culpō, -āre, -āvī, -ātum *vt* to blame, reproach.
cultē *adv* in a refined manner.
cultellus, -ī *m* small knife.
culter, -rī *m* knife, razor.

cultiō, -ōnis *f* cultivation.
cultor, -ōris *m* cultivator, planter, farmer; inhabitant; supporter, upholder; worshipper.
cultrīx, -īcis *f* inhabitant; (*fig*) nurse, fosterer.
cultūra, -ae *f* cultivation, agriculture; (*mind*) care, culture; (*person*) courting.
cultus *ppp of* **colō** ♦ *adj* cultivated; (*dress*) well-dressed; (*mind*) polished, cultured ♦ *ntpl* cultivated land.
cultus, -ūs *m* cultivation, care; (*mind*) training, culture; (*dress*) style, attire; (*way of life*) refinement, civilization; (*gods*) worship; (*men*) honouring.
culullus, -ī *m* goblet.
cūlus, -ī *m* buttocks.
cum *prep* (*with abl*) with; (*denoting accompaniment, resulting circumstance, means, dealings, comparison, possession*); ~ **decimō** tenfold; ~ **eō quod, ut** with the proviso that; ~ **prīmīs** especially; ~ **māgnā calamitāte cīvitātis** to the great misfortune of the community; ~ **periculō suō** at one's own peril.
cum *conj* (*time*) when, whenever, while, as, after, since; (*cause*) since, as, seeing that; (*concession*) although; (*condition*) if; (*contrast*) while, whereas; **multī annī sunt ~ in aere meō est** for many years now he has been in my debt; **aliquot sunt annī ~ vōs dēlēgī** it is now some years since I chose you; ~ **māximē** just when; just then, just now; ~ **prīmum** as soon as; ~ **... tum** not only ... but also; both ... and.
Cūmae, -ārum *fpl* town near Naples (*famous for its Sibyl*).
Cūmaeānum, -āni *nt Cicero's Cumaean residence.*

Cūmaeus, -ānus adj see n.

cumba, cymba, -ae f boat, skiff.

cumera, -ae f grain chest.

cumīnum, -ī nt cumin.

cumque (quomque) adv -ever, -soever; at any time.

cumulātē adv fully, abundantly.

cumulātus adj increased; complete.

cumulō, -āre, -āvī, -ātum vt to heap up; to amass, increase; to fill up, overload; (fig) to fill, overwhelm, crown, complete.

cumulus, -ī m heap, mass; crowning addition, summit.

cūnābula, -ōrum ntpl cradle.

cūnae, -ārum fpl cradle.

cunctābundus adj hesitant, dilatory.

cunctāns, -antis adj dilatory, reluctant; sluggish, tough.

cunctanter adv slowly.

cunctātiō, -ōnis f delaying, hesitation.

cunctātor, -ōris m loiterer; one given to cautious tactics (esp Q Fabius Maximus).

cunctor, -ārī, -ātus vi to linger, delay, hesitate; to move slowly.

cūnctus adj the whole of; (pl) all together, all.

cuneātim adv in the form of a wedge.

cuneātus adj wedge-shaped.

cuneus, -ī m wedge; (MIL) wedge-shaped formation of troops; (THEATRE) block of seats.

cunīculus, -ī m rabbit; underground passage; (MIL) mine.

cunque see **cumque**.

cūpa, -ae f vat, tun.

cupidē adv eagerly, passionately.

Cupīdineus adj see **Cupīdō**.

cupiditās, -ātis f desire, eagerness, enthusiasm; passion;

lust; avarice, greed; ambition; partisanship.

cupīdō, -inis f desire, eagerness; passion, lust; greed.

Cupīdō, -inis m Cupid (son of Venus).

cupidus adj desirous, eager; fond, loving; passionate, lustful; greedy, ambitious; partial.

cupiēns, -entis pres p of **cupiō** ♦ adj eager, desirous.

cupienter adv see **cupiēns**.

cupiō, -ere, -īvī and **iī, -ītum** vt to wish, desire, long for; (with dat) to wish well.

cupītor, -ōris m desirer.

cupītus ppp of **cupiō**.

cuppēdia, -ae f fondness for delicacies.

cuppēdia, -ōrum ntpl delicacies.

cuppēdinārius, -ī m confectioner.

cuppēdō, -inis f longing, passion.

cuppes, -dis adj fond of delicacies.

cupressētum, -ī nt cypress grove.

cupresseus adj of cypress wood.

cupressifer, -ī adj cypress-bearing.

cupressus, -ī f cypress.

cūr adv why?; (indirect) why, the reason for.

cūra, -ae f care, trouble, pains (bestowed); anxiety, concern, sorrow (felt); attention (to), charge (of), concern (for); (MED) treatment, cure; (writing) work; (law) trusteeship; (poet) love; (person) mistress, guardian; ~ **est** I am anxious; ~ **esse** be attended to, looked after.

cūrābilis adj troublesome.

cūralium, -ī and **iī** nt red coral.

cūrātē adv carefully.

cūrātiō, -ōnis f charge, management; office; treatment, healing.

cūrātor, -ōris m manager, overseer; (law) guardian.

The present infinitive verb endings are as follows: -āre = 1st; -ēre = 2nd; -ere = 3rd and -īre = 4th. See sections on irregular verbs and noun declensions.

cūrātūra, -ae f dieting.
cūrātus adj cared for; earnest, anxious.
curculiō, -ōnis m weevil.
curculiunculus, -ī m little weevil.
Curēnsis adj see n.
Curēs, -ium mpl ancient Sabine town.
Cūrētēs, -um mpl attendants of Jupiter in Crete.
Cūrētis, -idis adj Cretan.
cūria, -ae f earliest division of the Roman people; meeting-place of a curia; senate house; senate.
cūriālis, -is m member of a curia.
cūriātim adv by curiae.
cūriātus adj of the curiae; comitia ~a earliest Roman assembly.
cūriō, -ōnis m president of a curia; ~ māximus head of all the curiae.
cūriō, -ōnis adj emaciated.
cūriōsē adv carefully, inquisitively.
cūriōsitās, -ātis f curiosity.
cūriōsus adj careful, thoughtful, painstaking; inquiring, inquisitive, officious; careworn.
curis, -ītis f spear.
cūrō, -āre, -āvī, -ātum vt to take care of, attend to; to bother about; (with gerundive) to get something done; (with inf) to take the trouble; (with ut) to see to it that; (public life) to be in charge of, administer; (MED) to treat, cure; (money) to pay, settle up; aliud ~ā never mind; corpus/cutem~ take it easy; prōdigia ~ avert portents.
curriculum, -ī nt running, race; course, lap; (fig) career; ~ō at full speed.
currō, -ere, cucurrī, cursum vi to run; to hasten, fly ♦ vt to run through, traverse; ~entem incitāre ≈ spur a willing horse.
currus, -ūs m car, chariot; triumph; team of horses; plough-wheels.

cursim adv quickly, at the double.
cursitō, -āre vi to run about, fly hither and thither.
cursō, -āre vi to run about.
cursor, -ōris m runner, racer; courier.
cursūra, -ae f running.
cursus, -ūs m running, speed; passage, journey; course, direction; (things) movement, flow; (fig) rapidity, flow, progress; ~ honōrum succession of magistracies; ~ rērum course of events; ~um tenēre keep on one's course; ~ū at a run; māgnō ~ū at full speed.
curtō, -āre vt to shorten.
curtus adj short, broken off; incomplete.
curūlis adj official, curule; aedīlis ~ patrician, aediile; sella ~ magistrates' chair; equī ~ horses provided for the games by the state.
curvāmen, -inis nt bend.
curvātūra, -ae f curve.
curvō, -āre, -āvī, -ātum vt to curve, bend, arch; (fig) to move.
curvus adj bent, curved, crooked; (person) aged; (fig) wrong.
cuspis, -dis f point; spear, javelin, trident, sting.
custōdēla, -ae f care, guard.
custōdia, -ae f watch, guard, care; (person) sentry, guard; (place) sentry's post, guardhouse; custody, confinement, prison; lībera ~ confinement in one's own house.
custōdiō, -īre, -īvī and iī, -ītum vt to guard, defend; to hold in custody, keep watch on; to keep, preserve, observe.
custōs, -ōdis m/f guard, body-guard, protector, protectress; jailer, warder; (MIL) sentry, spy; container.
cutícula, -ae f skin.

cutis, -is f skin; **~em cūrāre** ≈ take it easy.

cyathissō, -āre vi to serve wine.

cyathus, -ī m wine ladle; (*measure*) one-twelfth of a pint.

cybaea, -ae f kind of merchant ship.

Cybēbē, Cybelē, -ēs f Phrygian mother-goddess, Magna Mater.

Cybelēius adj see n.

Cyclades, -um fpl group of Aegean islands.

cyclas, -adis f formal dress with a border.

cyclicus adj of the traditional epic stories.

Cyclōpius adj see n.

Cyclops, -is m one-eyed giant (*esp Polyphemus*).

cycnēus adj of a swan, swan's.

cycnus, -ī m swan.

Cydōnius adj Cretan ♦ ntpl quinces.

cygnus see **cycnus**.

cylindrus, -ī m cylinder; roller.

Cyllēnē, -ēs and **ae** f mountain in Arcadia.

Cyllēnius, -is, -ius adj see n.

Cyllēnius, -ī m Mercury.

cymba see **cumba**.

cymbalum, -ī nt cymbal.

cymbium, -ī and **iī** nt cup.

Cynicē adv like the Cynics.

Cynicus, -ī m a Cynic philosopher (*esp Diogenes*) ♦ adj Cynic.

cynocephalus, -ī m dog-headed ape.

Cynosūra, -ae f constellation of Ursa Minor.

Cynosūris, -idis adj see n.

Cynthia, -iae f Diana.

Cynthius, -ī m Apollo.

Cynthus, -ī m hill in Delos (*birthplace of Apollo and Diana*).

cyparissus, -ī f cypress.

Cypris, -idis f Venus.

Cyprius adj Cyprian; copper.

Cyprus, -ī f island of Cyprus (*famed for its copper and the worship of Venus*).

Cyrēnaeī, -aicī mpl followers of Aristippus.

Cyrēnaeus, -aicus, -ēnsis adj see n.

Cyrēnē, -ēs f, **-ae, -ārum** fpl town and province of N. Africa.

Cyrnēus adj Corsican.

Cyrus, -ī m Persian king.

Cytaeis, -idis f Medea.

Cythēra, -ae f island S. of Greece (*famed for its worship of Venus*).

Cytherēa, -ae and **ēia, -ēiae** and **-ēis, -ēidis** f Venus.

Cythereus, Cythēriacus adj Cytherean; of Venus.

cytisus, -ī m/f cytisus (*a kind of clover*).

Cyzicēnus adj see **Cyzicum**.

Cyzicum, -ī nt, **-us, -os, -ī** f town on Sea of Marmora.

D

Dācī, -ōrum mpl Dacians, a people on the lower Danube.

Dācia, -iae f the country of the Dācī (*now Romania*).

Dācicus, -icī m gold coin of Domitian's reign.

dactylicus adj dactylic.

dactylus, -ī m dactyl.

Daedalēus adj see n.

daedalus adj artistic, skilful in creating; skilfully made, variegated.

Daedalus, -ī m mythical Athenian craftsman and inventor.

Dalmatae, -ārum mpl Dalmatians (*a people on the East coast of the Adriatic*).

Dalmatia, -iae f Dalmatia.

The present infinitive verb endings are as follows: **-āre** = 1st: **-ēre** = 2nd; **-ere** = 3rd and **-īre** = 4th. *See sections on irregular verbs and noun declensions.*

Dalmaticus adj see n.

dāma, -ae f deer; venison.

Damascēnus adj see n.

Damascus, -ī f Damascus.

damma f see **dama**.

damnātiō, -ōnis f condemnation.

damnātōrius adj condemnatory.

damnātus adj criminal; miserable.

damnificus adj pernicious.

damnō, -āre, -āvī, -ātum vt to condemn, sentence; to procure the conviction of; (heirs) to oblige; to censure; **capitis/capite ~** condemn to death; **māiestātis, dē māiestāte ~** condemn for treason; **vōtī ~** oblige to fulfil a vow.

damnōsē adv ruinously.

damnōsus adj harmful, ruinous; spendthrift; wronged.

damnum, -ī nt loss, harm, damage; (law) fine, damages; **~ facere** suffer loss.

Danaē, -ēs f mother of Perseus.

Danaēius adj see n.

Danaī, -ōrum and **um** mpl the Greeks.

Danaïdes, -idum fpl daughters of Danaus.

Danaus, -ī m king of Argos and father of 50 daughters.

Danaus adj Greek.

danista, -ae m moneylender.

danisticus adj moneylending.

danō see **dō**.

Dānuvius, -ī m upper Danube.

Daphnē, -ēs f nymph changed into a laurel tree.

Daphnis, -idis (acc -im and -in) m mythical Sicilian shepherd.

dapinō, -āre vt to serve (food).

daps, dapis f religious feast; meal, banquet.

dapsilis adj sumptuous, abundant.

Dardania, -iae f Troy.

Dardanidēs, -idae m Trojan (esp Aeneas).

Dardanus, -ī m son of Jupiter and ancestor of Trojan kings.

Dardanus, -ius, -is, -idis adj Trojan.

Darēus, -ī m Persian king.

datārius adj to give away.

datātim adv passing from one to the other.

datiō, -ōnis f right to give away; (laws) making.

datō, -āre vt to be in the habit of giving.

dator, -ōris m giver; (sport) bowler.

Daulias, -adis adj see n.

Daulis, -dis f town in central Greece (noted for the story of Procne and Philomela).

Daunias, -iadis f Apulia.

Daunius adj Rutulian; Italian.

Daunus, -ī m legendary king of Apulia (ancestor of Turnus).

dē prep (with abl: movement) down from, from; (origin) from, of, out of; (time) immediately after, in; (thought, talk, action) about, concerning; (reason) for, because of; (imitation) after, in accordance with; **~ industriā** on purpose; **~ integrō** afresh; **~ nocte** during the night; **diem ~ diē** from day to day.

dea, -ae f goddess.

dealbō, -āre vt to whitewash, plaster.

deambulātiō, -ōnis f walk.

deambulō, -āre, -āvī, -ātum vi to go for a walk.

deamō, -āre, -āvī, -ātum vt to be in love with; to be much obliged to.

dearmātus adj disarmed.

deartuō, -āre, -āvī, -ātum vt to dismember, ruin.

deasciō, -āre vt to smooth with an axe; (fig) to cheat.

dēbacchor, -ārī, -ātus vi to rage furiously.

dēbellātor, -ōris m conqueror.

dēbellō, -āre, -āvī, -ātum vi to bring a war to an end ♦ vt to subdue; to fight out.

dēbeō, -ēre, -uī, -itum vt to owe; (with inf) to be bound, ought, should, must; to have to thank for, be indebted for; (pass) to be destined.

dēbilis adj frail, weak, crippled.

dēbilitās, -ātis f weakness, infirmity.

dēbilitātiō, -ōnis f weakening.

dēbilitō, -āre, -āvī, -ātum vt to cripple, disable; (fig) to paralyse, unnerve.

dēbitiō, -ōnis f owing.

dēbitor, -ōris m debtor.

dēbitum, -ī nt debt.

dēblaterō, -āre vt to blab.

dēcantō, -āre, -āvī, -ātum vt to keep on repeating ♦ vi to stop singing.

dēcēdō, -ēdere, -essī, -essum vi to withdraw, depart; to retire from a province (after term of office); to abate, cease, die; (rights) to give up, forgo; (fig) to go wrong, swerve (from duty); **dē viā** ~ get out of the way.

decem num ten.

December, -ris adj of December ♦ m December.

decempeda, -ae f ten-foot rule.

decempedātor, -ōris m surveyor.

decemplex, -icis adj tenfold.

decemprimī, -ōrum mpl civic chiefs of Italian towns.

decemscalmus adj ten-oared.

decemvirālis adj of the decemviri.

decemvirātus, -ūs m office of decemvir.

decemvirī, -ōrum and **um** mpl commission of ten men (for public or religious duties).

decennis adj ten years'.

decēns, -entis adj seemly, proper; comely, handsome.

decenter adv with propriety.

decentia, -ae f comeliness.

dēceptus ppp of **dēcipiō**.

dēcernō, -ernere, -rēvī, -rētum vt to decide, determine; to decree; to fight it out, decide the issue.

dēcerpō, -ere, -sī, -tum vt to pluck off, gather; (fig) to derive, enjoy.

dēcertātiō, -ōnis f deciding the issue.

dēcertō, -āre, -āvī, -ātum vi to fight it out, decide the issue.

dēcessiō, -ōnis f departure; retirement (from a province); deduction, disappearance.

dēcessor, -ōris m retiring magistrate.

dēcessus, -ūs m retirement (from a province); death; (tide) ebbing.

decet, -ēre, -uīt vt, vi it becomes, suits; it is right, proper.

dēcidō, -ere, -ī vi to fall down, fall off; to die; (fig) to fail, come down.

dēcīdō, -dere, -dī, -sum vt to cut off; to settle, put an end to.

deciēns, deciēs adv ten times.

decimus, decumus adj tenth; cum ~ō tenfold; **-um** for the tenth time.

dēcipiō, -ipere, -ēpī, -eptum vt to ensnare; to deceive, beguile, disappoint.

dēcīsiō, -ōnis f settlement.

dēcīsus ppp of **dēcīdō**.

Decius, -ī m Roman plebeian name (esp P Decius Mus, father and son, who devoted their lives in battle).

Decius, -iānus adj see n.

dēclāmātiō, -ōnis f loud talking; rhetorical exercise on a given theme.

dēclāmātor, -ōris m apprentice in public speaking.

The present infinitive verb endings are as follows: **-āre** = 1st; **-ēre** = 2nd; **-ere** = 3rd and **-īre** = 4th. *See sections on irregular verbs and noun declensions.*

dēclāmātōrius adj rhetorical.

dēclāmitō, -āre vi to practise rhetoric; to bluster ♦ vt to practise pleading.

dēclāmō, -āre, -āvī, -ātum vi to practise public speaking, declaim; to bluster.

dēclārātiō, -ōnis f expression, making known.

dēclārō, -āre, -āvī, -ātum vt to make known; to proclaim, announce, reveal, express, demonstrate.

dēclīnātiō, -ōnis f swerving; avoidance; (RHET) digression; (GRAM) inflection.

dēclīnō, -āre, -āvī, -ātum vt to turn aside, deflect; (eyes) to close; to evade, shun ♦ vi to turn aside, swerve; to digress.

dēclīve nt slope, decline.

dēclīvis adj sloping, steep, downhill.

dēclīvitās, -ātis f sloping ground.

dēcocta, -ae f a cold drink.

dēcoctor, -ōris m bankrupt.

dēcoctus ppp of **dēcoquō** ♦ adj (style) ripe, elaborated.

dēcōlō, -āre vi to run out; (fig) to fail.

dēcolor, -ōris adj discoloured, faded; ~ aetās a degenerate age.

dēcolōrātiō, -ōnis f discolouring.

dēcolōrō, -āre, -āvī, -ātum vt to discolour, deface.

dēcoquō, -quere, -xī, -ctum vt to boil down; to cook ♦ vi to go bankrupt.

decor, -ōris m comeliness, ornament, beauty.

decorē adv becomingly, beautifully.

decorō, -āre, -āvī, -ātum vt to adorn, embellish; (fig) to distinguish, honour.

decōrum, -ī nt propriety.

decōrus adj becoming, proper;

beautiful, noble; adorned.

dēcrepitus adj decrepit.

dēcrēscō, -scere, -vī, -tum vi to decrease, wane, wear away; to disappear.

dēcrētum, -ī nt decree, resolution; (PHILOS) doctrine.

dēcrētus ppp of **dēcernō**.

dēcrēvī perf of **dēcernō**; perf of **dēcrēscō**.

decuma, -ae f tithe; provincial land tax; largess.

decumāna, -ae f wife of a tithe-collector.

decumānus adj paying tithes; (MIL) of the 10th cohort or legion ♦ m collector of tithes; **~ī, -ōrum** mpl men of the 10th legion; **porta ~a** main gate of a Roman camp.

decumātēs, -ium adj pl subject to tithes.

dēcumbō, -mbere, -buī vi to lie down; to recline at table; to fall (in fight).

decumus see **decimus**.

decuria, -ae f group of ten; panel of judges; social club.

decuriātiō, -ōnis f, **decuriātus, -ūs** m dividing into decuriae.

decuriō, -āre, -āvī, -ātum vt to divide into decuriae or groups.

decuriō, -ōnis m head of a decuria; (MIL) cavalry officer; senator of a provincial town or colony.

dēcurrō, -rrere, -currī and **rrī, -rsum** vt, vi to run down, hurry, flow, sail down; to traverse; (MIL) to parade, charge; (time) to pass through; (fig) to have recourse to.

dēcursiō, -ōnis f military manoeuvre.

dēcursus ppp of **dēcurrō**.

dēcursus, -ūs m descent, downrush; (MIL) manoeuvre, attack; (time) career.

dēcurtātus adj mutilated.

decus, -oris nt ornament, glory,

beauty; honour, virtue; (*pl*) heroic deeds.

dēcussō, -āre *vt* to divide crosswise.

dēcutiō, -tere, -ssī, -ssum *vt* to strike down, shake off.

dēdecet, -ēre, -uit *vt* it is unbecoming to, is a disgrace to.

dēdecorō, -āre *vt* to disgrace.

dēdecorus *adj* dishonourable.

dēdecus, -oris *nt* disgrace, shame; vice, crime.

dēdī *perf of* **dō**.

dēdicātiō, -ōnis *f* consecration.

dēdicō, -āre, -āvī, -ātum *vt* to consecrate, dedicate; to declare (property in a census return).

dēdidī *perf of* **dēdō**.

dēdignor, -ārī, -ātus *vt* to scorn, reject.

dēdiscō, -scere, -dicī *vt* to unlearn, forget.

dēditīcius, -ī and **iī** *m* one who has capitulated.

dēditiō, -ōnis *f* surrender, capitulation.

dēditus *ppp of* **dēdō ♦** *adj* addicted, devoted; **-ā operā** intentionally.

dēdō, -ere, -idī, -itum *vt* to give up, yield, surrender; to devote.

dēdoceō, -ēre *vt* to teach not to.

dēdoloō, -āre, -uī *vi* to cease grieving.

dēdūcō, -ūcere, -ūxī, -uctum *vt* to bring down, lead away, deflect; (*MIL*) to lead, withdraw; (*bride*) to bring home; (*colony*) to settle; (*hair*) to comb out; (*important person*) to escort; (*law*) to evict, bring to trial; (*money*) to subtract; (*sail*) to unfurl; (*ship*) to launch; (*thread*) to spin out; (*writing*) to compose; (*fig*) to bring, reduce, divert, derive.

dēductiō, -ōnis *f* leading off;

settling a colony; reduction; eviction; inference.

dēductor, -ōris *m* escort.

dēductus *ppp of* **dēdūcō ♦** *adj* finely spun.

deerrō, -āre, -āvī, -ātum *vi* to go astray.

deesse *infin of* **dēsum**.

dēfaecō, -āre, -āvī, -ātum *vt* to clean; (*fig*) to make clear, set at ease.

dēfatīgātiō, -ōnis *f* tiring out; weariness.

dēfatīgō, -āre, -āvī, -ātum *vt* to tire out, exhaust.

dēfatīscor *etc see* **dēfetīscor**.

dēfectiō, -ōnis *f* desertion; failure, faintness; (*ASTRO*) eclipse.

dēfector, -ōris *m* deserter, rebel.

dēfectus *ppp of* **dēficiō ♦** *adj* weak, failing.

dēfectus, -ūs *m* failure; eclipse.

dēfendō, -dere, -dī, -sum *vt* to avert, repel; to defend, protect; (*law*) to speak in defence, urge, maintain; (*THEATRE*) to play (a part); **crīmen ~** answer an accusation.

dēfēnsiō, -ōnis *f* defence, speech in defence.

dēfēnsitō, -āre *vt* to defend often.

dēfēnsō, -āre *vt* to defend.

dēfēnsor, -ōris *m* averter, defender, protector, guard.

dēferō, -ferre, -tulī, -lātum *vt* to bring down, bring, carry; to bear away; (*power, honour*) to offer, confer; (*information*) to report; (*law*) to inform against, indict; to recommend (for public services); **ad cōnsilium ~** take into consideration.

dēfervēscō, -vēscere, -vī and **buī** *vi* to cool down, calm down.

dēfessus *adj* tired, exhausted.

The present infinitive verb endings are as follows: **-āre** = 1st; **-ēre** = 2nd; **-ere** = 3rd and **-īre** = 4th. *See sections on irregular verbs and noun declensions.*

dēfetīgō *etc see* **dēfatīgō**.

dēfetīscor, -tīscī, -ssus *vi* to grow weary.

dēficiō, -icere, -ēcī, -ectum *vt, vi* to desert, forsake, fail; to be lacking, run short, cease; (ASTRO) to be eclipsed; **animō ~** lose heart.

dēfīgō, -gere, -xī, -xum *vt* to fix firmly; to drive in, thrust; (*eyes, mind*) to concentrate; (*fig*) to stupefy, astound; (*magic*) to bewitch.

dēfingō, -ere *vt* to make, portray.

dēfīniō, -īre, -īvī, -ītum *vt* to mark the limit of, limit; to define, prescribe; to restrict; to terminate.

dēfīnītē *adv* precisely.

dēfīnītiō, -ōnis *f* limiting, prescribing, definition.

dēfīnītīvus *adj* explanatory.

dēfīnītus *adj* precise.

dēfīō, -ierī *vi* to fail.

dēflagrātiō, -ōnis *f* conflagration.

dēflagrō, -āre, -āvī, -ātum *vi* to be burned down, perish; to cool down, abate ♦ *vt* to burn down.

dēflectō, -ctere, -xī, -xum *vt* to bend down, turn aside; (*fig*) to pervert ♦ *vi* to turn aside, deviate.

dēfleō, -ēre, -ēvī, -ētum *vt* to lament bitterly, bewail ♦ *vi* to weep bitterly.

dēflexus *ppp of* **dēflectō**.

dēflōrēscō, -ēscere, -uī *vi* to shed blooms; (*fig*) to fade.

dēfluō, -ere, -xī, -xum *vi* to flow down, float down; to fall, drop, droop; (*fig*) to come from, be derived; to flow past; (*fig*) to pass away, fail.

dēfodiō, -odere, -ōdī, -ossum *vt* to dig, dig out; to bury; (*fig*) to hide away.

dēfore *fut infin of* **dēsum**.

dēfōrmis *adj* misshapen, disfigured, ugly; shapeless; (*fig*) disgraceful, disgusting.

dēfōrmitās, -ātis *f* deformity, hideousness; baseness.

dēfōrmō, -āre, -āvī, -ātum *vt* to form, sketch; to deform, disfigure; to describe; to mar, disgrace.

dēfossus *ppp of* **dēfodiō**.

dēfraudō, -āre *vt* to cheat, defraud; **genium ~** deny oneself.

dēfrēnātus *adj* unbridled.

dēfricō, -āre, -uī, -ātum *and* **tum** *vt* to rub down; (*fig*) to satirize.

dēfringō, -ingere, -ēgī, -āctum *vt* to break off, break down.

dēfrūdō *etc see* **dēfraudō**.

dēfrutum, -ī *nt* new wine boiled down.

dēfugiō, -ugere, -ūgī *vt* to run away from, shirk ♦ *vi* to flee.

dēfuī *perf of* **dēsum**.

dēfūnctus *ppa of* **dēfungor** ♦ *adj* discharged; dead.

dēfundō, -undere, -ūdī, -ūsum *vt* to pour out.

dēfungor, -ungī, -ūnctus *vi* (*with abl*) to discharge, have done with; to die.

dēfutūrus *fut p of* **dēsum**.

dēgener, -is *adj* degenerate, unworthy, base.

dēgenerātum, -ātī *nt* degenerate character.

dēgenerō, -āre, -āvī, -ātum *vi* to degenerate, deteriorate ♦ *vt* to disgrace.

dēgerō, -ere *vt* to carry off.

dēgō, -ere, -ī *vt* (*time*) to pass, spend; (*war*) wage ♦ *vi* to live.

dēgrandinat it is hailing heavily.

dēgravō, -āre *vt* to weigh down, overpower.

dēgredior, -dī, -ssus *vi* to march down, descend, dismount.

dēgrunniō, -īre *vi* to grunt hard.

dēgustō, -āre *vt* to taste, touch; (*fig*) to try, experience.

dehinc adv from here; from now, henceforth; then, next.

dehīscō, -ere vi to gape, yawn.

dehonestāmentum, -ī nt disfigurement.

dehonestō, -āre vt to disgrace.

dehortor, -ārī, -ātus vt to dissuade, discourage.

Dēianīra, -ae f wife of Hercules.

dēiciō, -icere, -iēcī, -iectum vt to throw down, hurl, fell; to overthrow, kill; (eyes) to lower, avert; (law) to evict; (MIL) to dislodge; (ship) to drive off its course; (hopes, honours) to foil, disappoint.

dēiectiō, -ōnis f eviction.

dēiectus ppp of **dēiciō** ♦ adj low-lying; disheartened.

dēiectus, -ūs m felling; steep slope.

dēierō, -āre, -āvī, -ātum vi to swear solemnly.

dein etc see **deinde**.

deinceps adv successively, in order.

deinde, dein adv from there, next; then, thereafter; next in order.

Dēiotarus, -ī m king of Galatia (defended by Cicero).

Dēiphobus, -ī m son of Priam (second husband of Helen).

dēiungō, -ere vt to sever.

dēiuvō, -āre vt to fail to help.

dej- etc see **dei-**.

dēlābor, bī, -psus vi to fall down, fly down, sink; (fig) to come down, fall into.

dēlacerō, -āre vt to tear to pieces.

dēlāmentor, -ārī vt to mourn bitterly for.

dēlāpsus ppa of **dēlābor**.

dēlassō, -āre vt to tire out.

dēlātiō, -ōnis f accusing, informing.

dēlātor, -ōris m informer, denouncer.

dēlectābilis adj enjoyable.

dēlectāmentum, -ī nt amusement.

dēlectātiō, -ōnis f delight.

dēlectō, -āre vt to charm, delight, amuse.

dēlectus ppp of **dēligō**.

dēlectus, -ūs m choice; see also **dīlectus**.

dēlēgātiō, -ōnis f assignment.

dēlēgī perf of **dēligō**.

dēlēgō, -āre, -āvī, -ātum vt to assign, transfer, make over; to ascribe.

dēlēnificus adj charming.

dēlēnimentum, -ī nt solace, allurement.

dēlēniō, -īre, -īvī, -ītum vt to soothe, solace; to seduce, win over.

dēlēnītor, -ōris m cajoler.

dēleō, -ēre, -ēvī, -ētum vt to destroy, annihilate; to efface, blot out.

Dēlia, -ae f Diana.

Dēliacus adj of Delos.

dēlīberābundus adj deliberating.

dēlīberātiō, -ōnis f deliberating, consideration.

dēlīberātivus adj deliberative.

dēlīberātor, -ōris m consulter.

dēlīberātus adj determined.

dēlīberō, -āre, -āvī, -ātum vt, vi to consider, deliberate, consult; to resolve, determine; **~ārī potest** it is in doubt.

dēlībō, -āre, -āvī, -ātum vt to taste, sip; to pick, gather; to detract from, mar.

dēlibrō, -āre vt to strip the bark off.

dēlibuō, -uere, -uī, -ūtum vt to smear, steep.

dēlicātē adv luxuriously.

The present infinitive verb endings are as follows: **-āre** = 1st; **-ēre** = 2nd; **-ere** = 3rd and **-īre** = 4th. *See sections on irregular verbs and noun declensions.*

dēlicātus *adj* delightful; tender, soft; voluptuous, spoiled, effeminate; fastidious.

dēliciae, -ārum *fpl* delight, pleasure; whimsicalities, sport; (*person*) sweetheart, darling.

dēliciolae, -ārum *fpl* darling.

dēlicium, -ī *and* **iī** *nt* favourite.

dēlicō, -āre *vt* to explain.

dēlictum, -ī *nt* offence, wrong.

dēlicuus *adj* lacking.

dēligō, -igere, -ēgī, -ēctum *vt* to select, gather; to set aside.

dēligō, -āre, -āvī, -ātum *vt* to tie up, make fast.

dēlingō, -ere *vt* to have a lick of.

dēlīni- *etc see* **dēlēni-**.

dēlinquō, -inquere, -īquī, -ictum *vi* to fail, offend, do wrong.

dēliquēscō, -quēscere, -cuī *vi* to melt away; (*fig*) to pine away.

dēliquiō, -ōnis *f* lack.

dēlīrāmentum, -ī *nt* nonsense.

dēlīrātiō, -ōnis *f* dotage.

dēlīrō, -āre *vi* to be crazy, drivel.

dēlīrus *adj* crazy.

dēlitēscō, -ēscere, -uī *vi* to hide away, lurk; (*fig*) to skulk, take shelter under.

dēlītigō, -āre *vi* to scold.

Dēlius, -iacus *adj see n.*

Delmatae *see* **Dalmatae**.

Dēlos, -ī *f* sacred Aegean island (*birthplace of Apollo and Diana*).

Delphī, -ōrum *mpl* town in central Greece (*famous for its oracle of Apollo*); the Delphians.

Delphicus *adj see n.*

delphīnus, -ī *and* **delphīn, -is** *m* dolphin.

Deltōton, -ī *nt* (*constellation*) Triangulum.

dēlubrum, -ī *nt* sanctuary, temple.

dēluctō, -āre, -or, -ārī *vi* to wrestle.

dēlūdificō, -āre *vt* to make fun of.

dēlūdō, -dere, -sī, -sum *vt* to dupe, delude.

dēlumbis *adj* feeble.

dēlumbō, -āre *vt* to enervate.

dēmadēscō, -ēscere, -uī *vi* to be drenched.

dēmandō, -āre *vt* to entrust, commit.

dēmarchus, -ī *m* demarch (*chief of a village in Attica*).

dēmēns, -entis *adj* mad, foolish.

dēmēnsum, -ī *nt* ration.

dēmēnsus *ppa of* **dēmētior**.

dēmenter *adv see* **dēmēns**.

dēmentia, -ae *f* madness, folly.

dēmentiō, -īre *vi* to rave.

dēmereō, -ēre, -uī, -itum, -eor, -ērī *vt* to earn, deserve; to do a service to.

dēmergō, -gere, -sī, -sum *vt* to submerge, plunge, sink; (*fig*) to overwhelm.

dēmessus *ppp of* **dēmetō**.

dēmētior, -tīrī, -nsus *vt* to measure out.

dēmetō, -tere, -ssuī, -ssum *vt* to reap, harvest; to cut off.

dēmigrātiō, -ōnis *f* emigration.

dēmigrō, -āre *vi* to move, emigrate.

dēminuō, -uere, -uī, -ūtum *vt* to make smaller, lessen, detract from; **capite ~** deprive of citizenship.

dēminūtiō, -ōnis *f* decrease, lessening; (*law*) right to transfer property; **capitis ~** loss of political rights.

dēmīror, -ārī, -ātus *vt* to marvel at, wonder.

dēmisse *adv* modestly, meanly.

dēmissīcius *adj* flowing.

dēmissiō, -ōnis *f* letting down; (*fig*) dejection.

dēmissus *ppp of* **dēmittō** ♦ *adj* low-lying; drooping; humble, unassuming; dejected; (*origin*) descended.

dēmītigō, -āre *vt* to make milder.

dēmittō, -ittere, -īsī, -issum vt to let down, lower, sink; to send down, plunge; (*beard*) to grow; (*ship*) to bring to land; (*troops*) to move down; (*fig*) to cast down, dishearten, reduce, impress; **sē ~** stoop; descend; be disheartened.

dēmiūrgus, -ī m chief magistrate in a Greek state.

dēmō, -ere, -psī, -ptum vt to take away, subtract.

Dēmocritus, -ius, -ēus adj see n.

Dēmocritus, -ī m Greek philosopher (author of the atomic theory).

dēmōlior, -īrī vt to pull down, destroy.

dēmōlītiō, -ōnis f pulling down.

dēmōnstrātiō, -ōnis f pointing out, explanation.

dēmōnstrātīvus adj (*RHET*) for display.

dēmōnstrātor, -ōris m indicator.

dēmōnstrō, -āre, -āvī, -ātum vt to point out; to explain, represent, prove.

dēmorior, -ī, -tuus vi to die, pass away ♦ vt to be in love with.

dēmoror, -ārī, -ātus vi to wait ♦ vt to detain, delay.

dēmortuus ppa of **dēmorior**.

Dēmosthenēs, -is m greatest Athenian orator.

dēmoveō, -ovēre, -ōvī, -ōtum vt to remove, turn aside, dislodge.

dempsī perf of **dēmō**.

dēmptus ppp of **dēmō**.

dēmūgītus adj filled with lowing.

dēmulceō, -cēre, -sī vt to stroke.

dēmum adv (*time*) at last, not till; (*emphasis*) just, precisely; **ibi ~** just there; **modo ~** only now; **nunc ~** now at last; **post ~** not till after; **tum ~** only then.

dēmurmurō, -āre vt to mumble

through.

dēmūtātiō, -ōnis f change.

dēmūtō, -āre vt to change, make worse ♦ vi to change one's mind.

dēnārius, -ī and iī m Roman silver coin.

dēnārrō, -āre vt to relate fully.

dēnāsō, -āre vt to take the nose off.

dēnatō, -āre vi to swim down.

dēnegō, -āre, -āvī, -ātum vt to deny, refuse, reject ♦ vi to say no.

dēnī, -ōrum adj ten each, in tens; ten; tenth.

dēnicālis adj for purifying after a death

dēnique adv at last, finally; (*enumerating*) lastly, next, (*summing up*) in short, briefly; (*emphasis*) just, precisely.

dēnōminō, -āre vt to designate.

dēnormō, -āre vt to make irregular.

dēnotō, -āre, -āvī, -ātum vt to point out, specify; to observe.

dēns, dentis m tooth; ivory; prong, fluke.

dēnsē adv repeatedly.

dēnsō, -āre, -āvī, -ātum, dēnseō, -ēre, -ī vt to thicken; (*ranks*) to close.

dēnsus adj thick, dense, close; frequent; (*style*) concise.

dentālia, -ium ntpl ploughbeam.

dentātus adj toothed; (*paper*) polished.

dentiō, -īre vi to cut one's teeth; (*teeth*) to grow.

dēnūbō, -bere, -psī, -ptum vi to marry, marry beneath one.

dēnūdō, -āre, -āvī, -ātum vt to bare, strip; (*fig*) to disclose.

dēnūntiātiō, -ōnis f intimation, warning.

dēnūntiō, -āre, -āvī, -ātum vt to intimate, give notice of, declare;

*The present infinitive verb endings are as follows: -**āre** = 1st; -**ēre** = 2nd; -**ere** = 3rd and -**īre** = 4th. See sections on irregular verbs and noun declensions.*

to threaten, warn; (*law*) to summon as witness.

dēnuō *adv* afresh, again, once more.

deonerō, -āre *vt* to unload.

deorsum, deorsus *adv* downwards.

deōsculor, -ārī *vt* to kiss warmly.

dēpaciscor *etc see* **dēpeciscor**.

dēpactus *adj* driven in firmly.

dēpāscō, -scere, -vī, -stum, -scor, -scī *vt* to feed on, eat up; (*fig*) to devour, destroy, prune away.

dēpeciscor, -īscī, -tus *vt* to bargain for, agree about.

dēpectō, -ctere, -xum *vt* to comb; (*comedy*) to flog.

dēpectus *ppa of* **dēpeciscor**.

dēpecūlātor, -ōris *m* embezzler.

dēpecūlor, -ārī, -ātus *vt* to plunder.

dēpellō, -ellere, -ulī, -ulsum *vt* to expel, remove, cast down; (*MIL*) to dislodge; (*infants*) to wean; (*fig*) to deter, avert.

dēpendeō, -ēre *vi* to hang down, hang from; to depend on; to be derived.

dēpendō, -endere, -endī, -ēnsum *vt* to weigh, pay up.

dēperdō, -ere, -idī, -itum *vt* to lose completely, destroy, ruin.

dēpereō, -īre, -iī *vi* to perish, be completely destroyed; to be undone ♦ *vt* to be hopelessly in love with.

dēpexus *ppp of* **dēpectō**.

dēpingō, -ingere, -inxī, -ictum *vt* to paint; (*fig*) to portray, describe.

dēplangō, -gere, -xī *vt* to bewail frantically.

dēplexus *adj* grasping.

dēplōrābundus *adj* weeping bitterly.

dēplōrō, -āre, -āvī, -ātum *vi* to weep bitterly ♦ *vt* to bewail bitterly, mourn; to despair of.

dēpluit, -ere *vi* to rain down.

dēpōnō, -ōnere, -osuī, -ositum *vt* to lay down; to set aside, put away, get rid of; to wager; to deposit, entrust, commit to the care of; (*fig*) to give up.

dēpopulātiō, -ōnis *f* ravaging.

dēpopulātor, -ōris *m* marauder.

dēpopulor, -ārī, -ātus; -ō, -āre *vt* to ravage, devastate; (*fig*) to waste, destroy.

dēportō, -āre, -āvī, -ātum *vt* to carry down, carry off; to bring home (from a province); (*law*) to banish for life; (*fig*) to win.

dēposcō, -scere, -poscī *vt* to demand, require, claim.

dēpositum, -ī *nt* trust, deposit.

dēpositus *ppp of* **dēpōnō** ♦ *adj* dying, dead, despaired of.

dēprāvātē *adv* perversely.

dēprāvātiō, -ōnis *f* distorting.

dēprāvō, -āre, -āvī, -ātum *vt* to distort; (*fig*) to pervert, corrupt.

dēprecābundus *adj* imploring.

dēprecātiō, -ōnis *f* averting by prayer; imprecation, invocation; plea for indulgence.

dēprecātor, -ōris *m* intercessor.

dēprecor, -ārī, -ātus *vt* to avert (by prayer); to deprecate, intercede for.

dēprehendō, dēprendō, -endere, -endī, -ēnsum *vt* to catch, intercept; to overtake, surprise; to catch in the act, detect; (*fig*) to perceive, discover.

dēprehēnsiō, -ōnis *f* detection.

dēprehēnsus, dēprēnsus *ppp of* **dēprehendō**.

dēpressī *perf of* **dēprimō**.

dēpressus *ppp of* **dēprimō** ♦ *adj* low.

dēprimō, -imere, -essī, -essum *vt* to press down, weigh down; to dig deep; (*ship*) to sink; (*fig*) to suppress, keep down.

dēproelior, **-ārī** *vi* to fight it out.

dēprōmō, **-ere**, **psī**, **-ptum** *vt* to fetch, bring out, produce.

dēproperō, **-āre** *vi* to hurry up ♦ *vt* to hurry and make.

depsō, **-ere** *vt* to knead.

dēpudet, **-ēre**, **-uit** *v impers* not to be ashamed.

dēpugis *adj* thin-buttocked.

dēpugnō, **-āre**, **-āvī**, **-ātum** *vi* to fight it out, fight hard.

dēpulī *perf of* dēpellō.

dēpulsiō, **-ōnis** *f* averting; defence.

dēpulsō, **-āre** *vt* to push out of the way.

dēpulsor, **-ōris** *m* repeller.

dēpulsus *ppp of* dēpellō.

dēpurgō, **-āre** *vt* to clean.

dēputō, **-āre** *vt* to prune; to consider, reckon.

dēpȳgis *etc see* dēpugis.

dēque *adv* down.

dērēctā, **-ē**, **-ō** *adv* straight.

dērēctus *ppp of* dērigō ♦ *adj* straight, upright, at right angles; straightforward.

dērelictiō, **-ōnis** *f* disregarding.

dērelinquō, **-inquere**, **-īquī**, **-ictum** *vt* to abandon, forsake.

dērepente *adv* suddenly.

dērēpō, **-ere** *vi* to creep down.

dēreptus *ppp of* dēripiō.

dērīdeō, **-dēre**, **-sī**, **-sum** *vt* to laugh at, deride.

dērīdiculum, **-ī** *nt* mockery, absurdity; object of derision.

dērīdiculus *adj* laughable.

dērigēscō, **-ēscere**, **-uī** *vi* to stiffen, curdle.

dērigō, **-igere**, **-ēxī**, **-ēctum** *vt* to turn, aim, direct; (*fig*) to regulate.

dēripiō, **-ipere**, **-ipuī**, **-eptum** *vt* to tear off, pull down.

dērīsor, **-ōris** *m* scoffer.

dērīsus *ppp of* dērīdeō.

dērīsus, **-ūs** *m* scorn, derision.

dērīvātiō, **-ōnis** *f* diverting.

dērīvō, **-āre**, **-āvī**, **-ātum** *vt* to lead off, draw off.

dērogō, **-āre** *vt* (*law*) to propose to amend; (*fig*) to detract from.

dērōsus *adj* gnawed away.

dēruncinō, **-āre** *vt* to plane off; (*comedy*) to cheat.

dēruō, **-ere**, **-ī** *vt* to demolish.

dēruptus *adj* steep ♦ *ntpl* precipice.

dēsaeviō, **-īre** *vi* to rage furiously; to cease raging.

dēscendō, **-endere**, **-endī**, **-ēnsum** *vi* to come down, go down, descend, dismount; (*MIL*) to march down; (*things*) to fall, sink, penetrate; (*fig*) to stoop (to), lower oneself.

dēscēnsiō, **-ōnis** *f* going down.

dēscēnsus, **-ūs** *m* way down.

dēscīscō, **-īscere**, **-īvī** *and* **iī**, **-ītum** *vi* to desert, revolt; to deviate, part company.

dēscrībō, **-bere**, **-psī**, **-ptum** *vt* to copy out; to draw, sketch; to describe; *see also* dīscrībō.

dēscriptiō, **-ōnis** *f* copy; drawing, diagram; description.

dēscrīptus *ppp of* dēscrībō; *see also* dīscriptus.

dēsecō, **-āre**, **-uī**, **-tum** *vt* to cut off.

dēserō, **-ere**, **-uī**, **-tum** *vt* to desert, abandon, forsake; (*bail*) to forfeit.

dēsertor, **-ōris** *m* deserter.

dēsertus *ppp of* dēserō ♦ *adj* desert, uninhabited ♦ *ntpl* deserts.

dēserviō, **-īre** *vi* to be a slave (to), serve.

dēses, **-idis** *adj* idle, inactive.

dēsiccō, **-āre** *vt* to dry, drain.

The present infinitive verb endings are as follows: -āre = 1st; -ēre = 2nd; -ere = 3rd and -īre = 4th. See sections on irregular verbs and noun declensions.

dēsideō

104 dēsubitō

dēsideō, -idēre, -ēdī vi to sit idle.

dēsīderābilis adj desirable.

dēsīderātiō, -ōnis f missing.

dēsīderium, -ī and **iī** nt longing, sense of loss; want; petition; **mē ~ tenet urbis** I miss Rome.

dēsīderō, -āre, -āvī, -ātum vt to feel the want of, miss; to long for, desire; (casualties) to lose.

dēsidia, -ae f idleness, apathy.

dēsidiōsē adv idly.

dēsidiōsus adj lazy, idle; relaxing.

dēsīdō, -īdere, -ēdī vi to sink, settle down; (fig) to deteriorate.

dēsignātiō, -ōnis f specifying; election (of magistrates).

dēsignātor etc see **dissignātor**.

dēsignātus adj elect.

dēsignō, -āre, -āvī, -ātum vt to trace out; to indicate, define; (POL) to elect; (art) to depict.

dēsiī perf of **dēsinō**.

dēsiliō, -īre, -uī, -ultum vi to jump down, alight.

dēsinō, -nere, -ī vt to leave off, abandon ♦ vi to stop, desist; to end (in).

dēsipiēns, -ientis adj silly.

dēsipientia, -ae f folly.

dēsipiō, -ere vi to be stupid, play the fool.

dēsistō, -istere, -titī, -titum vi to stop, leave off, desist.

dēsitus ppp of **dēsinō**.

dēsōlō, -āre, -āvī, -ātum vt to leave desolate, abandon.

dēspectō, -āre vt to look down on, command a view of; to despise.

dēspectus ppp of **dēspiciō** ♦ adj contemptible.

dēspectus, -ūs m view, prospect.

dēspēranter adv despairingly.

dēspērātiō, -ōnis f despair.

dēspērātus adj despaired of, hopeless; desperate, reckless.

dēspērō, -āre, -āvī, -ātum vt, vi to despair, give up hope of.

dēspexī perf of **dēspiciō**.

dēspicātiō, -ōnis f contempt.

dēspicātus adj despised, contemptible.

dēspicātus, -ūs m contempt.

dēspicientia, -ae f contempt.

dēspiciō, -icere, -exī, -ectum vt to look down on; to despise ♦ vi to look down.

dēspoliātor, -ōris m robber.

dēspoliō, -āre vt to rob, plunder.

dēspondeō, -ondēre, -ondī and **opondī, -ōnsum** vt to pledge, promise; to betroth; to devote; to give up, despair of; **animum ~** despair.

dēspūmō, -āre vt to skim off.

dēspuō, -ere vi to spit on the ground ♦ vt to reject.

dēsquāmō, -āre vt to scale, peel.

dēstillō, -āre vi to drop down ♦ vt to distil.

dēstimulō, -āre vt to run through.

dēstinātiō, -ōnis f resolution, appointment.

dēstinātus adj fixed, decided.

dēstinō, -āre, -āvī, -ātum vt to make fast; to appoint, determine, resolve; (archery) to aim at; (fig) to intend to buy ♦ nt mark; intention; **~ātum est mihi** I have decided.

dēstitī perf of **dēsistō**.

dēstituō, -uere, -uī, -ūtum vt to set apart, place; to forsake, leave in the lurch.

dēstitūtiō, -ōnis f defaulting.

dēstitūtus ppp of **dēstituō**.

dēstrictus ppp of **dēstringō** ♦ adj severe.

dēstringō, -ingere, -inxī, -ictum vt (leaves) to strip; (body) to rub down; (sword) to draw; to graze, skim; (fig) to censure.

dēstruō, -ere, -xī, -ctum vt to demolish; to destroy.

dēsubitō adv all of a sudden.

dēsūdāscō, -ere vi to sweat all over.

dēsūdō, -āre vi to exert oneself.

dēsuēfactus adj unaccustomed.

dēsuētūdō, -inis f disuse.

dēsuētus adj unaccustomed, unused.

dēsultor, -ōris m circus rider; (fig) fickle lover.

dēsultūra, -ae f jumping down.

dēsum, deesse, -fuī vi to be missing, fail, fall in one's duty.

dēsūmō, -ere, -psī, -ptum vt to select.

dēsuper adv from above.

dēsurgō, -ere vi to rise.

dētegō, -egere, -ēxī, -ēctum vt to uncover, disclose; (fig) to reveal, detect.

dētendō, -endere, -ēnsum vt (tent) to strike.

dētentus ppp of **dētineō**.

dētergō, -gere, -sī, -sum vt to wipe away, clear away; to clean; to break off.

dēterior, -ōris adj lower; inferior, worse.

dēterius adv worse.

dēterminātiō, -ōnis f boundary, end.

dēterminō, -āre, -āvī, -ātum vt to bound, limit; to settle.

dēterō, -erere, -rīvī, -rītum vt to rub, wear away; (style) to polish; (fig) to weaken.

dēterreō, -ēre, -uī, -itum vt to frighten away; to deter, discourage, prevent.

dētersus ppp of **dētergeō**.

dētestābilis adj abominable.

dētestātiō, -ōnis f execration, curse; averting.

dētestor, -ārī, -ātus vt to invoke, invoke against; to curse, execrate; to avert, deprecate.

dētexō, -ere, -uī, -tum vt to weave, finish weaving; (comedy) to steal; (fig) to describe.

dētineō, -inēre, -inuī, -entum vt to hold back, detain; to keep occupied.

dētondeō, -ondēre, -ondī, -ōnsum vt to shear off, strip.

dētonō, -āre, -uī vi to cease thundering.

dētorqueō, -quēre, -sī, -tum vt to turn aside, direct; to distort, misrepresent.

dētractātiō, -ōnis f declining.

dētractātor, -ōris m disparager.

dētractiō, -ōnis f removal, departure.

dētractō etc see **dētrectō**.

dētractus ppp of **dētrahō**.

dētrahō, -here, -xī, -ctum vt to draw off, take away, pull down; to withdraw, force to leave; to detract, disparage.

dētrectō, -āre, -āvī, -ātum vt to decline, shirk; to detract from, disparage.

dētrīmentōsus adj harmful.

dētrīmentum, -ī nt loss, harm; (MIL) defeat; ~ **capere** suffer harm.

dētrītus ppp of **dēterō**.

dētrūdō, -dere, -sī, -sum vt to push down, thrust away; to dislodge, evict; to postpone; (fig) to force.

dētruncō, -āre, -āvī, -ātum vt to cut off, behead, mutilate.

dētrūsus ppp of **dētrūdō**.

dēturbō, -āre, -āvī, -ātum vt to dash down, pull down; (fig) to cast down, deprive.

Deucaliōn, -ōnis m son of Prometheus (survivor of the Flood).

Deucaliōnēus adj see **Deucaliōn**.

deūnx, -cis m eleven twelfths.

deūrō, -rere, -ssī, -stum vt to burn up; to frost.

*The present infinitive verb endings are as follows: -**āre** = 1st; -**ēre** = 2nd; -**ere** = 3rd and -**īre** = 4th. See sections on irregular verbs and noun declensions.*

deus, -ī (*voc* **deus**, *pl* **dī, deos, deum, dīs**) *m* god; **dī** **melior̄a**! Heaven forbid!; **dī tē ament**! bless you!

deūstus *ppp of* **deūrō**.

deūtor, -ī *vi* to maltreat.

dēvastō, -āre *vt* to lay waste.

dēvehō, -here, -xī, -ctum *vt* to carry down, convey; (*pass*) to ride down, sail down.

dēvellō, -ellere, -ellī *and* **olsī, -ulsum** *vt* to pluck, pull out.

dēvēlō, -āre *vt* to unveil.

dēveneror, -ārī *vt* to worship; to avert by prayers.

dēveniō, -enīre, -ēnī, -entum *vi* to come, reach, fall into.

dēverberō, -āre, -āvī, -ātum *vt* to thrash soundly.

dēversor, -ārī *vi* to lodge, stay (as guest).

dēversor, -ōris *m* guest.

dēversōriolum, -ī *nt* small lodging.

dēversōrium, -ī *and* **iī** *nt* inn, lodging.

dēversōrius *adj* for lodging.

dēverticulum, -ī *nt* by-road, by-pass; digression; lodging place; (*fig*) refuge.

dēvertō, -tere, -tī, -sum *vi* to turn aside, put up; to have recourse to; to digress.

dēvertor, -tī, versus *vi see* **dēvertō**.

dēvexus *adj* sloping, going down, steep.

dēvinciō, -cīre, -xī, -ctum *vt* to tie up; (*fig*) to bind, lay under an obligation.

dēvincō, -incere, -īcī, -ictum *vt* to defeat completely, win the day.

dēvītātiō, -ōnis *f* avoiding.

dēvītō, -āre *vt* to avoid.

dēvius *adj* out of the way, devious; (*person*) solitary, wandering off the beaten track; (*fig*) inconstant.

dēvocō, -āre, -āvī, -ātum *vt* to call down, fetch; to entice away.

dēvolō, -āre *vi* to fly down.

dēvolvō, -vere, -vī, -ūtum *vt* to roll down, fall; (*wool*) to spin off.

dēvorō, -āre, -āvī, -ātum *vt* to swallow, gulp down; to engulf, devour; (*money*) to squander; (*tears*) to repress; (*trouble*) to endure patiently.

dēvors-, dēvort- *see* **dēvers-, dēvert-.**

dēvortia, -ōrum *ntpl* byways.

dēvōtiō, -ōnis *f* devoting; (*magic*) spell.

dēvōtō, -āre *vt* to bewitch.

dēvōtus *ppp of* **dēvoveō ♦** *adj* faithful; accursed.

dēvoveō, -ovēre, -ōvī, -ōtum *vt* to devote, vow, dedicate; to give up; to curse; to bewitch.

dēvulsus *ppp of* **dēvellō.**

dextella, -ae *f* little right hand.

dexter, -erī *and* **rī** *adj* right, right-hand; handy, skilful; favourable.

dexteritās, -ātis *f* adroitness.

dextra *f* right hand, right-hand side; hand; pledge of friendship.

dextrā *prep* (*with acc*) on the right of.

dextrē (*compar* **-erius**) *adv* adroitly.

dextrōrsum, -rsus, -vorsum *adv* to the right.

dī *pl of* **deus.**

diabathrārius, -ī *and* **iī** *m* slipper maker.

diabolus, -ī *m* devil.

diāconus, -ī *m* (*ECCL*) deacon.

diadēma, -tis *nt* royal headband, diadem.

diaeta, -ae *f* diet; living room.

dialectica, -ae, -ē, -ēs *f* dialectic, logic ♦ *ntpl* logical questions.

dialecticē *adv* dialectically.

dialecticus *adj* dialectical ♦ *m* logician.

Diālis *adj* of Jupiter ♦ *m* high priest of Jupiter.

dialogus, -ī *m* dialogue, conversation.

Diāna, -ae f virgin goddess of hunting (also identified with the moon and Hecate, and patroness of childbirth).

Diānius adj of Diana ♦ nt sanctuary of Diana.

diāria, -ōrum ntpl daily allowance of food or pay.

dibaphus, -ī f Roman state robe.

dica, -ae f lawsuit.

dicācitās, ātis f raillery, repartee.

dicāculus adj pert.

dicātiō, -ōnis f declaration of citizenship.

dicāx, -ācis adj witty, smart.

dichorēus, -ī m double trochee.

diciō, -ōnis f power, sway, authority.

dicis causā for the sake of appearance.

dicō, -āre, -āvī, -ātum vt to dedicate, consecrate; to deify; to devote, give over.

dīcō, -cere, -xī, dictum vt to say, tell; to mention, mean, call, name; to pronounce; (RHET) to speak, deliver; (law) to plead; (poetry) to describe, celebrate; (official) to appoint; (time, place) to settle, fix ♦ vi to speak (in public); **causam ~** plead; **iūs ~** deliver judgment; **sententiam ~** vote; **~cō** namely; **~xī** I have finished; **dictum factum** no sooner said than done.

dicrotum, -ī nt bireme.

Dictaeus adj Cretan.

dictamnus, -ī f dittany (a kind of wild marjoram).

dictāta, -ōrum ntpl lessons, rules.

dictātor, -ōris m dictator.

dictātōrius adj dictator's.

dictātūra, -ae f dictatorship.

Dictē, -ēs f mountain in Crete (where Jupiter was brought up).

dictiō, -ōnis f speaking, declaring;

style, expression, oratory; (oracle) response.

dictitō, -āre vt to keep saying, assert; to plead often.

dictō, -āre, -āvī, -ātum vt to say repeatedly; to dictate; to compose.

dictum, -ī nt saying, word; proverb; bon mot, witticism; command.

dictus ppp of dīcō.

Dictynna, -ae f Britomartis; Diana.

Dictynnaeus adj see n.

dīdicī perf of discō.

dīdō, -ere, -idī, -itum vt to distribute, broadcast.

Dīdō, -ūs and **-ōnis** (acc -ō) f Queen of Carthage.

dīdūcō, -ūcere, -ūxī, -uctum vt to separate, split, open up; (MIL) to disperse; (fig) to part, divide.

diēcula, -ae f one little day.

diērēctus adj crucified; **abī ~** go and be hanged.

diēs, -ēī m/f day; set day (usu fem); a day's journey; (fig) time; **~ meus** my birthday; **~em dīcere** impeach; **~em obīre** die; **~em dē ~ē, ~em ex ~ē** from day to day; **in ~em** to a later day; for today; **in ~ēs** daily.

Diēspiter, -ris m Jupiter.

diffāmō, -āre, -āvī, -ātum vt to divulge; to malign.

differentia, -ae f difference, diversity; species.

differitās, -ātis f difference.

differō, -erre, distulī, dīlātum vt to disperse; to divulge, publish; (fig) to distract, disquiet; (time) to put off, delay ♦ vi to differ, be distinguished.

differtus adj stuffed, crammed.

difficilis, -e adj difficult; (person)

The present infinitive verb endings are as follows: -āre = 1st; -ēre = 2nd; -ere = 3rd and -īre = 4th. See sections on irregular verbs and noun declensions.

awkward, surly.

difficiliter *adv* with difficulty.

difficultās, -ātis *f* difficulty, distress, hardship; surliness.

difficulter *adv* with difficulty.

diffīdēns, -entis *adj* nervous.

diffīdenter *adv* without confidence.

diffīdentia, -ae *f* mistrust, diffidence.

diffīdō, -dere, -sus *vi* to distrust, despair.

diffindō, -ndere, -dī, -ssum *vt* to split, open up; (*fig*) to break off.

diffingō, -ere *vt* to remake.

diffissus *ppp of* **diffindō**.

diffissus *ppa of* **diffindō**.

diffiteor, -ērī *vi* to disown.

diffluēns, -entis *adj* (*RHET*) loose.

diffluō, -ere *vi* to flow away; to melt away; (*fig*) to wallow.

diffringō, -ere *vt* to shatter.

diffugiō, -ugere, -ūgī *vi* to disperse, disappear.

diffugium, -ī *and* **iī** *nt* dispersion.

diffundītō, -āre *vt* to pour out, waste.

diffundō, -undere, -ūdī, -ūsum *vt* to pour off; to spread, diffuse; to cheer, gladden.

diffūsē *adv* expansively.

diffūsilis *adj* diffusive.

diffūsus *ppp of* **diffundō** ♦ *adj* spreading; (*writing*) loose.

Dīgentia, -ae *f* tributary of the Anio (*near Horace's villa*).

dīgerō, -rere, -ssī, -stum *vt* to divide, distribute; to arrange, set out; to interpret.

dīgestiō, -ōnis *f* (*RHET*) enumeration.

dīgestus *ppp of* **dīgerō**.

digitulus, -ī *m* little finger.

digitus, -ī *m* finger; toe; inch; (*pl*) skill in counting; **~um porrigere, prōferre** take the slightest trouble; **~um trānsversum nōn discēdere** not swerve a finger's

breadth; **attingere caelum ~ō** reach the height of happiness; **licērī ~ō** bid at an auction; **mōnstrārī ~ō** be a celebrity; **extrēmī, summī ~ī** the fingertips; **concrepāre ~is** snap the fingers.

digladior, -ārī *vi* to fight fiercely.

dignātiō, -ōnis *f* honour, dignity.

dignē *adv see* **dignus**.

dignitās, -ātis *f* worth, worthiness; dignity, rank, position; political office.

dignō, -āre *vt* to think worthy.

dignor, -ārī *vt* to think worthy; to deign.

dignōscō, -ere *vt* to distinguish.

dignus *adj* worth, worthy; (*things*) fitting, proper.

dīgredior, -dī, -ssus *vi* to separate, part; to deviate, digress.

dīgressiō, -ōnis *f* parting; deviation, digression.

dīgressus *ppa of* **dīgredior**.

dīgressus, -ūs *m* parting.

dīiūdicātiō, -ōnis *f* decision.

dīiūdicō, -āre *vt* to decide; to discriminate.

dīiun- *etc see* **disiun-**.

dīlābor, -bī, -psus *vi* to dissolve, disintegrate; to flow away; (*troops*) to disperse; (*fig*) to decay, vanish.

dīlacerō, -āre *vt* to tear to pieces.

dīlāminō, -āre *vt* to split in two.

dīlaniō, -āre, -āvī, -ātum *vt* to tear to shreds.

dīlapidō, -āre *vt* to demolish.

dīlāpsus *ppa of* **dīlābor**.

dīlargior, -īrī *vt* to give away liberally.

dīlātiō, -ōnis *f* putting off, adjournment.

dīlātō, -āre, -āvī, -ātum *vt* to expand; (*pronunciation*) to broaden.

dīlātor, -ōris *m* procrastinator.

dīlātus *ppp of* **differō**.

dīlaudō, -āre vt to praise extravagantly.

dīlēctus ppp of **dīligō ♦** adj beloved.

dīlēctus, -ūs m selection, picking; (MIL) levy; **~um habēre** hold a levy, recruit.

dīlēxī perf of **dīligō**.

dīligēns, -entis adj painstaking, conscientious, attentive (to); thrifty.

dīligenter adv see **dīligēns**.

dīligentia, -ae f carefulness, attentiveness; thrift.

dīligō, -igere, -ēxī, -ēctum vt to prize especially, esteem, love.

dīlōricō, -āre vt to tear open.

dīlūceō, -ēre vi to be evident.

dīlūcēscit, -cēscere, -xit vi to dawn, begin to grow light.

dīlūcidē adv see **dīlūcidus**.

dīlūcidus adj clear, distinct.

dīlūculum, -ī nt dawn.

dīlūdium, -ī and **iī** nt interval.

dīluō, -uere, -uī, -ūtum vt to wash away, dissolve, dilute; to explain; (fig) to weaken, do away with.

dīluviēs, -iēī f, **-ium, -ī** and **iī** nt flood, deluge.

dīluviō, -āre vt to inundate.

dīmānō, -āre vi to spread abroad.

dīmēnsiō, -ōnis f measuring.

dīmēnsus adj measured.

dīmētior, -tīrī, -nsus vt to measure out.

dīmētō, -āro, -or, -ārī vt to mark out.

dīmicātiō, -ōnis f fighting, struggle.

dīmicō, -āre, -āvī, -ātum vi to fight, struggle, contend.

dīmidiātus adj half, halved.

dīmidius adj half **♦** nt half.

dīmissiō, -ōnis f sending away; discharging.

dīmissus ppp of **dīmittō**.

dīmittō, -ittere, -īsī, -issum vt to send away, send round; to let go, lay down; (meeting) to dismiss; (MIL) to disband, detach; (fig) to abandon, forsake.

dīminuō, -ere vt to dash to pieces.

dīmoveō, -ovēre, -ōvī, -ōtum vt to part, separate; to disperse; to entice away.

Dindymēnē, -ēnēs f Cybele.

Dindymus, -ī m mountain in Mysia (sacred to Cybele).

dīnōscō see **dignōscō**.

dīnumerātiō, -ōnis f reckoning up.

dīnumerō, -āre vt to count, reckon up; to pay out.

diōbolāris adj costing two obols.

dioecēsis, -is f district; (ECCL) diocese.

dioecētēs, -ae m treasurer.

Diogenēs, -is m famous Cynic philosopher; a Stoic philosopher.

Diomēdēs, -is m Greek hero at the Trojan War.

Diomēdēus adj see n.

Diōnaeus adj see **Diōnē**.

Diōnē, -ēs and **a, -ae** f mother of Venus; Venus.

Dionȳsius, -ī m tyrant of Syracuse.

Dionȳsus, -ī m Bacchus; **-ia, -iōrum** ntpl Greek festival of Bacchus.

diōta, -ae f a two-handled wine jar.

diplōma, -tis nt letter of recommendation.

Dipylon, -ī nt Athenian gate.

Dircaeus adj Boeotian.

Dircē, -ēs f famous spring in Boeotia.

dīrēctus ppp of **dīrigō ♦** adj straight; straightforward, simple; see also **dērēctus**.

dīrēmī perf of **dirimō**.

diremptus ppp of **dirimō**.

The present infinitive verb endings are as follows: -āre = 1st; -ēre = 2nd; -ere = 3rd and -īre = 4th. See sections on irregular verbs and noun declensions.

diremptus 110 **discrepātiō**

diremptus, -ūs m separation.
direptiō, -ōnis f plundering.
direptor, -ōris m plunderer.
direptus ppp of **dīripiō**.
dīrexi perf of **dīrigō**.
diribeō, -ēre vt to sort out (votes taken from ballot-boxes).
dīribitiō, -ōnis f sorting.
dīribitor, -ōris m ballot-sorter.
dīrigō, -igere, -ēxī, -ēctum vt to put in line, arrange; see also **dērigō**.
dirimō, -imere, -ēmī, -emptum vt to part, divide; to interrupt, break off; to put an end to.
dīripiō, -ipere, -ipuī, -eptum vt to tear in pieces; to plunder, ravage; to seize; (fig) to distract.
dīritās, -ātis f mischief, cruelty.
dirumpō, disrumpō, -umpere, -ūpī, -uptum vt to burst, break in pieces; (fig) to break off; (pass) to burst (with passion).
dīruō, -ere, -ī, -tum vt to demolish; to scatter; **aere ~tus** having one's pay stopped.
diruptus ppp of **dīrumpō**.
dīrus adj ominous, fearful; (pers) dread, terrible ♦ fpl bad luck; the Furies ♦ ntpl terrors.
dīrutus ppp of **dīruō** ♦ adj bankrupt.
dīs, dītis adj rich.
Dīs, Dītis m Pluto.
discēdō, -ēdere, -ēssī, -essum vi to go away, depart; to part, disperse; (MIL) to march away; (result of battle) to come off; (POL) to go over (to a different policy); to pass away, disappear; to leave out of consideration; **ab signis ~** break the ranks; **victor ~** come off best.
disceptātiō, -ōnis f discussion, debate.
disceptātor, -ōris m, **-rīx, -rīcis** f arbitrator.

disceptō, -āre vt to debate, discuss; (law) to decide.
discernō, -ernere, -rēvī, -rētum vt to divide, separate; to distinguish between.
discerpō, -ere, -sī, -tum vt to tear apart, disperse; (fig) to revile.
discessiō, -ōnis f separation, departure; (senate) division.
discessus, -ūs m parting; departure; marching away.
discidium, -ī and **iī** nt disintegration; separation, divorce; discord.
discīdō, -ere vt to cut in pieces.
discīnctus ppp of **discingō** ♦ adj ungirt; negligent; dissolute.
discindō, -ndere, -dī, -ssum vt to tear up, cut open.
discingō, -gere, -xī, -ctum vt to ungird.
disciplīna, -ae f teaching, instruction; learning, science, school, system; training, discipline; habits.
discipulus, -ī m, **-a, -ae** f pupil, apprentice.
discissus ppp of **discindō**.
disclūdō, -dere, -sī, -sum vt to keep apart, separate out.
discō, -ere, didicī vt to learn, be taught, be told.
discolor, -ōris adj of a different colour; variegated; different.
discondūcit it is not worthwhile.
disconveniō, -īre vi to disagree, be inconsistent.
discordābilis adj disagreeing.
discordia, -ae f discord, disagreement.
discordiōsus adj seditious.
discordō, -āre vi to disagree, quarrel; to be unlike.
discors, -dis adj discordant, at variance; inconsistent.
discrepantia, -ae f disagreement.
discrepātiō, -ōnis f dispute.

discrepitō, -āre *vi* to be quite different.

discrepō, -āre, -uī *vi* to be out of tune; to disagree, differ; to be disputed.

discrētus *ppp of* **discernō**.

discrībō, -bere, -psī, -ptum *vt* to distribute, apportion, classify.

discrīmen, -inis *nt* interval, dividing line, distinction, difference; turning point, critical moment; crisis, danger.

discrīminō, -āre *vt* to divide.

discrīptē *adv* in good order.

discrīptiō, -ōnis *f* apportioning, distributing.

discrīptus *ppp of* **discrībō** ♦ *adj* secluded; well-arranged.

discruciō, -āre *vt* to torture; (*fig*) to torment, trouble.

discumbō, -mbere, -buī, -bitum *vi* to recline at table; to go to bed.

discupiō, -ere *vi* to long.

discurrō, -rrere, -currī *and* **rrī, -rsum** *vi* to run about, run different ways.

discursus, -ūs *m* running hither and thither.

discus, -ī *m* quoit.

discussus *ppp of* **discutiō**.

discutiō, -tere, -ssī, -ssum *vt* to dash to pieces, smash; to scatter; to dispel.

disertē, -im *adv* distinctly; eloquently.

disertus *adj* fluent, eloquent; explicit.

disiciō, -icere, -iēcī, -iectum *vt* to scatter, cast asunder; to break up, destroy; (*MIL*) to rout.

disiectō, -āre *vt* to toss about.

disiectus *ppp of* **disiciō**.

disiectus, -ūs *m* scattering.

disiūnctiō, -ōnis *f* separation, differing; (*logic*) statement of alternatives; (*RHET*) a sequence of short co-ordinate clauses.

disiūnctius *adv* rather in the manner of a dilemma.

disiūnctus *ppp of* **disiungō** ♦ *adj* distinct, distant, removed; (*speech*) disjointed; (*logic*) opposite.

disiungō, -ungere, -ūnxī, -ūnctum *vt* to unyoke; to separate, remove.

dispālēscō, -ere *vi* to be noised abroad.

dispandō, -andere, ānsum *and* **-essum** *vt* to spread out.

dispar, -aris *adj* unlike, unequal.

disparilis *adj* dissimilar.

disparō, -āre, -āvī, -ātum *vt* to segregate.

dispart- *etc see* **dispert-**.

dispectus *ppp of* **dispiciō**.

dispellō, -ellere, -ulī, -ulsum *vt* to scatter, dispel.

dispendium, -ī *and* **iī** *nt* expense, loss.

dispennō *etc see* **dispandō**.

dispēnsātiō, -ōnis *f* management, stewardship.

dispēnsātor, -ōris *m* steward, treasurer.

dispēnsō, -āre, -āvī, -ātum *vi* to weigh out, pay out; to manage, distribute; (*fig*) to regulate.

dispercutiō, -ere *vt* to dash out.

disperdō, -ere, -idī, -itum *vt* to ruin, squander.

dispereō, -īre, -iī *vi* to go to ruin, be undone.

dispergō, -gere, -sī, -sum *vt* to disperse, spread over, space out.

dispersē *adv* here and there.

dispersus *ppp of* **dispergō**.

dispertiō, -īre, -īvī, -ītum; -ior, -īrī *vt* to apportion, distribute.

dispertītiō, -ōnis *f* division.

dispessus *ppp of* **dispandō**.

The present infinitive verb endings are as follows: **-āre** = 1st; **-ēre** = 2nd; **-ere** = 3rd and **-īre** = 4th. *See sections on irregular verbs and noun declensions.*

dispiciō, -icere, -exī, -ectum vt to
see clearly, see through; to
distinguish, discern; (fig) to
consider.

displiceō, -ēre vi (with dat) to
displease; **sibi ~** be in a bad
humour.

displōdō, -dere, -sum vt to burst
with a crash.

dispōnō, -ōnere, -osuī, -ositum vt
to set out, arrange; (MIL) to station.

disposītē adv methodically.

disposītiō, -ōnis f arrangement.

disposītūra, -ae f arrangement.

disposītus ppp of **dispōnō** ♦ adj
orderly.

disposītus, -ūs m arranging.

dispudet, -ēre, -uit v impers to be
very ashamed.

dispulsus ppp of **dispellō**.

disputātiō, -ōnis f argument.

disputātor, -ōris m debater.

disputō, -āre, -āvī, -ātum vt to
calculate; to examine, discuss.

disquīrō, -ere vt to investigate.

disquīsītiō, -ōnis f inquiry.

disrumpō etc see **dīrumpō**.

dissaepiō, -īre, -sī, -tum vt to
fence off, separate off.

dissaeptum, -ī nt partition.

dissāvior, -ārī vi to kiss
passionately.

dissēdī perf of **dissideō**.

dissēminō, -āre vt to sow,
broadcast.

dissēnsiō, -ōnis f disagreement,
conflict.

dissēnsus, -ūs m dissension.

dissentāneus adj contrary.

dissentiō, -entīre, -ēnsī, -ēnsum
vi to disagree, differ; to be unlike,
be inconsistent.

dissēp- etc see **dissaep-**.

disserēnō, -āre vi to clear up.

disserō, -erere, -ēvī, -itum vt to
sow, plant at intervals.

disserō, -ere, -uī, -tum vt to set out

in order, arrange; to examine,
discuss.

disserpō, -ere vi to spread
imperceptibly.

dissertō, -āre vt to discuss, dispute.

dissideō, -idēre, -ēdī, -essum vi to
be distant; to disagree, quarrel; to
differ, be unlike, be uneven.

dissignātiō, -ōnis f arrangement.

dissignātor, -ōris m master of
ceremonies; undertaker.

dissignō, -āre vi to arrange,
regulate; see also **dēsignō**.

dissiliō, -īre, -uī vi to fly apart,
break up.

dissimilis adj unlike, different.

dissimiliter adv differently.

dissimilitūdō, -inis f unlikeness.

dissimulanter adv secretly.

dissimulantia, -ae f dissembling.

dissimulātiō, -ōnis f disguising,
dissembling; Socratic irony.

dissimulātor, -ōris m dissembler.

dissimulō, -āre, -āvī, -ātum vt to
dissemble, conceal, pretend that
. . . not, ignore.

dissipābilis adj diffusible.

dissipātiō, -ōnis f scattering,
dispersing.

dissipō, dissupō, -āre, -āvī, -ātum
vt to scatter, disperse; to spread,
broadcast; to squander, destroy;
(MIL) to put to flight.

dissitus ppp of **disserō**.

dissociābilis adj disuniting;
incompatible.

dissociātiō, -ōnis f separation.

dissociō, -āre, -āvī, -ātum vt to
disunite, estrange.

dissolūbilis adj dissoluble.

dissolūtē adv loosely, negligently.

dissolūtiō, -ōnis f breaking up,
destruction; looseness; (law)
refutation; (person) weakness.

dissolūtum, -ī nt asyndeton.

dissolūtus ppp of **dissolvō** ♦ adj

loose; lax, careless; licentious.
dissolvō, -vere, -vī, -ūtum vt to
unloose, dissolve; to destroy,
abolish; to refute; to pay up,
discharge (debt); to free, release.
dissonus adj discordant, jarring,
disagreeing, different.
dissors, -tis adj not shared.
dissuādeō, -dēre, -sī, -sum vt to
advise against, oppose.
dissuāsiō, -ōnis f advising against.
dissuāsor, -ōris m opposer.
dissultō, -āre vi to fly asunder.
dissuō, -ere vt to undo, open up.
dissupō etc see **dissipō**.
distaedet, -ēre v Impers to weary,
disgust.
distantia, -ae f diversity.
distendō (-nō), -dere, -dī, -tum vt
to stretch out, swell.
distentus ppp of **distendō** ♦ adj full
♦ ppp of **distineō** ♦ adj busy.
disterminō, -āre vt to divide, limit.
distichon, -ī nt couplet.
distinctē adv distinctly, lucidly.
distinctiō, -ōnis f differentiating,
difference; (GRAM) punctuation;
(RHET) distinction between words.
distinctus ppp of **distinguō** ♦ adj
separate, distinct; ornamented,
set off; lucid.
distinctus, -ūs m difference.
distineō, -inēre, -inuī, -entum vt
to keep apart, divide; to distract;
to detain, occupy; to prevent.
distinguō, -guere, -xī, -ctum vt to
divide, distinguish, discriminate;
to punctuate; to adorn, set off.
distō, -āre vi to be apart, be
distant; to be different.
distorqueō, -quēre, -sī, -tum vt to
twist, distort.
distortiō, -ōnis f contortion.
distortus ppp of **distorqueō** ♦ adj
deformed.

distractiō, -ōnis f parting,
variance.
distractus ppp of **distrahō** ♦ adj
separate.
distrahō, -here, -xī, -ctum vt to
tear apart, separate, estrange; to
sell piecemeal, retail; (mind) to
distract, perplex; **aciem** ~ break
up a formation; **controversiās** ~
end a dispute; **vōcēs** ~ leave a
hiatus.
distribuō, -uere, -uī, -ūtum vt to
distribute, divide.
distribūtē adv methodically.
distribūtiō, -ōnis f distribution,
division.
districtus ppp of **distringō** ♦ adj
busy, occupied; perplexed;
severe.
distringō, -ngere, -nxī, -ctum vt to
draw apart; to engage, distract;
(MIL) to create a diversion against.
distruncō, -āre vt to cut in two.
distulī perf of **differō**.
disturbō, -āre, -āvī, -ātum vt to
throw into confusion; to
demolish; to frustrate, ruin.
dītēscō, -ere vi to grow rich
dithyrambicus adj dithyrambic.
dithyrambus, -ī m dithyramb.
dītiae, -ārum fpl wealth.
ditiō etc see **diciō**.
dītō, -āre vt to enrich.
diū (comp **diūtius**, sup **diūtissimē**)
adv long, a long time; long ago; by
day.
diurnum, -ī nt day-book; ācta ~a
Roman daily gazette.
diurnus adj daily, for a day; by
day, day- (in cpds).
dius adj divine, noble.
diūtinē adv long.
diūtinus adj long, lasting.
diūtissimē, -ius etc see **diū**.
diūturnitās, -ātis f long time, long

*The present infinitive verb endings are as follows: -āre = 1st; -ēre = 2nd; -ere = 3rd and
-īre = 4th. See sections on irregular verbs and noun declensions.*

duration.

diūturnus adj long, lasting.

dīva, -ae f goddess.

dīvāricō, -āre vt to spread.

dīvellō, -ellere, -ellī, -ulsum vt to
tear apart, tear in pieces; (fig) to
tear away, separate, estrange.

dīvendō, -ere, -itum vt to sell in
lots.

dīverberō, -āre vt to divide, cleave.

dīverbium, -ī and **iī** nt (comedy)
passage in dialogue.

dīversē adv in different directions,
variously.

dīversitās, -ātis f contradiction,
disagreement, difference.

dīversus, dīvorsus ppp of **dīvertō**
♦ adj in different directions,
apart; different; remote;
opposite, conflicting; hostile
♦ mpl individuals.

dīvertō, -tere, -tī, -sum vi to turn
away; differ.

dīves, -itis adj rich.

dīvexō, -āre vt to pillage.

dīvidia, -ae f worry, concern.

dīvidō, -idere, -īsī, -īsum vt to
divide, break open; to distribute,
apportion; to separate, keep
apart; to distinguish; (jewel) to set
off; **sententiam** ~ take the vote
separately on the parts of a motion.

dīviduus adj divisible; divided.

dīvīnātiō, -ōnis f foreseeing the
future, divination; (law) inquiry to
select the most suitable
prosecutor.

dīvīnē adv by divine influence;
prophetically; admirably.

dīvīnitās, -ātis f divinity;
divination; divine quality.

dīvīnitus adv from heaven, by
divine influence; excellently.

dīvīnō, -āre, -āvī, -ātum vt to
foresee, prophesy.

dīvīnus adj divine, of the gods;
prophetic; superhuman, excellent

♦ m soothsayer ♦ nt sacrifice;
oath; **rēs ~a** religious service,
sacrifice; **~a hūmānaque** all
things in heaven and earth; **~ī
crēdere** believe on oath.

dīvīsī perf of **dīvidō**.

dīvīsiō, -ōnis f division;
distribution.

dīvīsor, -ōris m distributor;
bribery agent.

dīvīsus ppp of **dīvidō** ♦ adj
separate.

dīvīsus, -ūs m division.

dīvitiae, -ārum fpl wealth; (fig)
richness.

dīvor- etc see **dīver-**.

dīvortium, -ī and **iī** nt separation;
divorce (by consent); road fork,
watershed.

dīvulgātus adj widespread.

dīvulgō, -āre, -āvī, -ātum vt to
publish, make public.

dīvulsus ppp of **dīvellō**.

dīvum, -ī nt sky; **sub ~ō** in the open
air.

dīvus adj divine; deified ♦ m god.

dīxī perf of **dīcō**.

dō, dare, dedī, datum vt to give; to
permit, grant; to put, bring,
cause, make; to give up, devote;
to tell; to impute; **fābulam** ~
produce a play; **in fugam** ~ to put to
flight; **litterās** ~ post a letter;
manūs ~ surrender; **nōmen** ~
enlist; **operam** ~ take pains, do
one's best; **poenās** ~ pay the
penalty; **vēla** ~ set sail; **verba** ~
cheat.

doceō, -ēre, -uī, -tum vt to teach;
to inform, tell; **fābulam** ~ produce
a play.

dochmius, -ī and **iī** m dochmiac
foot.

docilis adj easily trained, docile.

docilitās, -ātis f aptness for being
taught.

doctē adv skilfully, cleverly.

doctor, -ōris *m* teacher, instructor.

doctrīna, -ae *f* instruction, education, learning; science.

doctus *ppp of* **doceō ♦** *adj* learned, skilled; cunning, clever.

documentum, -ī *nt* lesson, example, proof.

Dōdōna, -ae *f* town in Epirus *(famous for its oracle of Jupiter)*.

Dōdōnaeus, -is, -idis *adj, see* **Dōdōna.**

dōdrāns, -antis *m* three-fourths.

dogma, -tis *nt* philosophical doctrine.

dolābra, -ae *f* pickaxe.

dolēns, -entis *pres p of* **doleo ♦** *adj* painful.

dolenter *adv* sorrowfully.

doleō, -ēre, -uī, -itum *vt, vi* to be in pain, be sore; to grieve, lament, be sorry (for); to pain; **cuī ~et meminit** = once bitten, twice shy.

dōliāris *adj* tubby.

dōliolum, -ī *nt* small cask.

dōlium, -ī *and* **iī** *nt* large wine jar.

dolō, -āre, -āvī, -ātum *vt* to hew, shape with an axe.

dolō, -ōnis *m* pike; sting; fore-topsail.

Dolopes, -um *mpl* people of Thessaly.

Dolopia, -iae *f* the country of the people of Thessaly.

dolor, -ōris *m* pain, pang; sorrow, trouble; indignation, resentment; *(RHET)* pathos.

dolōsē *adv see* **dolōsus.**

dolōsus *adj* deceitful, crafty.

dolus, -ī *m* deceit, guile, trick; **~ malus** wilful fraud.

domābilis *adj* tameable.

domesticus *adj* domestic, household; personal, private; of one's own country, internal **♦** *mpl*

members of a household; **bellum ~** civil war.

domī *adv* at home.

domicilium, -ī *and* **iī** *nt* dwelling.

domina, -ae *f* mistress, lady of the house; wife, mistress; *(fig)* lady.

domināns, -antis *pres p of* **dominor ♦** *adj (words)* literal **♦** *m* tyrant.

dominātiō, -ōnis *f* mastery, tyranny.

dominātor, -ōris *m* lord.

dominātrix, -rīcis *f* queen.

dominātus, -ūs *m* mastery, sovereignty.

dominicus *adj (ECCL)* the Lord's.

dominium, -ī *and* **iī** *nt* absolute ownership; feast.

dominor, -ārī, -ātus *vi* to rule, be master; *(fig)* to lord it.

dominus, -ī *m* master, lord, owner; host; despot; *(ECCL)* the Lord.

Domitiānus *m* Roman Emperor.

Domitius, -ī *m* Roman plebeian name *(esp with surname Ahenobarbus)*.

domitō, -āre *vt* to break in.

domitor, -ōris *m*, **-rīx, -rīcis** *f* tamer; conqueror.

domitus *ppp of* **domō.**

domō, -āre, -uī, -itum *vt* to tame, break in; to conquer.

domus, -ūs *and* **ī** *f* house *(esp in town)*; home, native place; family; *(PHILOS)* sect; **~ī** at home; in peace; **~ī habēre** have of one's own, have plenty of; **~um** home(wards); **~ō** from home.

dōnābilis *adj* deserving a present.

dōnārium, -ī *and* **iī** *nt* offering; altar, temple.

dōnātiō, -ōnis *f* presenting.

dōnātīvum, -ī *nt* largess, gratuity.

dōnec (dōnicum, dōnique) *conj*

The present infinitive verb endings are as follows: -āre = 1st; -ēre = 2nd; -ere = 3rd and -īre = 4th. See sections on irregular verbs and noun declensions.

until; while, as long as.
dōnō, -āre, -āvī, -ātum vt to
present, bestow; to remit,
condone (for another's sake); (fig)
to sacrifice.
dōnum, -ī nt gift; offering.
dorcas, -dis f gazelle.
Dōrēs, -um mpl Dorians (mostly the
Greeks of the Peloponnese).
Dōricus adj Dorian; Greek.
Dōris, -dis f a sea nymph; the sea.
dormiō, -īre, -īvī, -ītum vi to sleep,
be asleep.
dormītātor, -ōris m dreamer.
dormītō, -āre vi to be drowsy, nod.
dorsum, -ī nt back; mountain
ridge.
dōs, dōtis f dowry; (fig) gift,
talent.
Dossēnus, -ī m hunchback, clown.
dōtālis adj dowry (in cpds), dotal.
dōtātus adj richly endowed.
dōtō, -āre vt to endow.
drachma (drachuma), -ae f a Greek
silver coin.
dracō, -ōnis m serpent, dragon;
(ASTRO) Draco.
dracōnigena, -ae adj sprung from
dragon's teeth.
drāpeta, -ae m runaway slave.
Drepanum, -ī, -a, -ōrum nt town in
W. Sicily.
dromas, -dis m dromedary.
dromos, -ī m racecourse at Sparta.
Druidēs, -um, -ae, -ārum mpl
Druids.
Drūsiānus adj see **Drūsus**.
Drūsus, -ī m Roman surname (esp
famous commander in Germany under
Augustus).
Dryades, -um fpl woodnymphs,
Dryads.
Dryopes, -um mpl a people of Epirus.
dubiē adv doubtfully.
dubitābilis adj doubtful.
dubitanter adv doubtingly,
hesitatingly.

dubitātiō, -ōnis f wavering,
uncertainty, doubting; hesitancy,
irresolution; (RHET) misgiving.
dubitō, -āre, -āvī, -ātum vt, vi to
waver, be in doubt, wonder,
doubt; to hesitate, stop to think.
dubium nt doubt.
dubius adj wavering, uncertain;
doubtful, indecisive; precarious;
irresolute ♦ nt doubt; **in ~um
vocāre** call in question; **in ~um
venīre** be called in question; **sine
~ō, haud ~ē** undoubtedly.
ducēnī, -ōrum adj 200 each.
ducentēsima, -ae f one-half per
cent.
ducentī, -ōrum num two hundred.
ducentiēs, -iēns adv 200 times.
dūcō, -cere, -xī, ductum vt to lead,
guide, bring, take; to draw, draw
out; to reckon, consider; (breath) to
inhale; (ceremony) to conduct;
(changed aspect) to take on,
receive; (dance) to perform;
(drink) to quaff; (metal) to shape,
beat out; (mind) to attract, induce,
deceive; (oars) to pull; (origin) to
derive, trace; (time) to prolong,
put off, pass; (udders) to milk;
(wool) to spin; (a work) to
construct, compose, make; (COMM)
to calculate; **īlia ~** become
broken-winded; **in numerō
hostium ~** regard as an enemy; **ōs
~ make faces; parvī ~** think little
of; **ratiōnem ~** have regard for;
uxōrem ~ marry.
ductim adv in streams.
ductitō, -āre vt to lead on, deceive;
to marry.
ductō, -āre vt to lead, draw; to take
home; to cheat.
ductor, -ōris m leader,
commander; guide, pilot.
ductus ppp of **dūcō**.
ductus, -ūs m drawing, drawing

off; form; command, generalship.

dūdum *adv* a little while ago, just now; for long; **haud ~** not long ago; **iam ~ adsum** I have been here a long time; **quam ~** how long.

duellum *etc see* **bellum.**

Duillius, -ī *m* consul who defeated the Carthaginians at sea.

duim *pres subj of* **dō.**

dulce, -iter *adv see* **dulcis.**

dulcēdō, -inis *f* sweetness; pleasantness, charm.

dulcēscō, -ere *vi* to become sweet.

dulciculus *adj* rather sweet.

dulcifer, -ī *adj* sweet.

dulcis *adj* sweet; pleasant, lovely; kind, dear.

dulcitūdō, -inis *f* sweetness.

dūlicē *adv* like a slave.

Dūlichium, -ī *nt* island in the Ionian Sea near Ithaca.

Dūlichius *adj* of Dulichium; of Ulysses.

dum *conj* while, as long as; provided that, if only; until *♦ adv* (*enclitic*) now, a moment; (*with neg*) yet.

dūmētum, -ī *nt* thicket, thornbushes.

dummodo *conj* provided that.

dūmōsus *adj* thorny.

dumtaxat *adv* at least; only, merely.

dūmus, -ī *m* thornbush.

duo, duae, duo *num* two.

duodeciēns, -ēs *adv* twelve times.

duodecim *num* twelve.

duodecimus *adj* twelfth.

duodēnī, -ōrum *adj* twelve each, in dozens.

duodēquadrāgēsimus *adj* thirty-eighth.

duodēquadrāgintā *num* thirty-eight.

duodēquīnquāgēsimus *adj* forty-eighth.

duodētrīciēns *adv* twenty-eight times.

duodētrīgintā *num* twenty-eight.

duodēvīcēnī *adj* eighteen each.

duodēvīcēsimus *adj* twenty-second.

duodēvīgintī *num* eighteen.

duoetvīcēsimānī, -ānōrum *mpl* soldiers of the 22nd legion.

duoetvīcēsimus *adj* twenty-second.

duovirī, duumvirī, -ōrum *mpl* a board of two men; colonial magistrates; **~ nāvālēs** naval commissioners (for supply and repair); **~ sacrōrum** keepers of the Sibylline Books.

duplex, -icis *adj* double, twofold; both; (*person*) false.

duplicārius, -ī *and* **iī** *m* soldier receiving double pay.

dupliciter *adv* doubly, on two accounts.

duplicō, -āre, -āvī, -ātum *vt* to double, increase; to bend.

duplus *adj* double, twice as much *♦ nt* double *♦ f* double the price.

dupondius, -ī *and* **iī** *m* coin worth two asses.

dūrābilis *adj* lasting.

dūrāmen, -inis *nt* hardness.

dūrateus *adj* wooden.

dūrē, -iter *adv* stiffly; hardily; harshly, roughly.

dūrēscō, -ēscere, -uī *vi* to harden.

dūritās, -ātis *f* harshness.

dūritia, -ae, -ēs, -em *f* hardness; hardiness; severity; want of feeling.

dūrō, -āre, -āvī, -ātum *vt* to harden, stiffen; to make hardy, inure; (*mind*) to dull *♦ vi* to harden; to be patient, endure; to hold out, last; (*mind*) to be steeled.

dūruī *perf of* **dūrēscō.**

The present infinitive verb endings are as follows: -āre = 1st; -ēre = 2nd; -ere = 3rd and -īre = 4th. See sections on irregular verbs and noun declensions.

dūrus adj hard, harsh, rough; hardy, tough; rude, uncultured; (*character*) severe, unfeeling, impudent, miserly; (*CIRCS*) hard, cruel.

duumvirī etc see **duovirī**.

dux, ducis m leader, guide; chief, head; (*MIL*) commander, general.

dūxī perf of **dūcō**.

Dymantis, -antidis f Hecuba.

Dymās, -antis m father of Hecuba.

dynamis, -is f plenty.

dynastēs, -ae m ruler, prince.

Dyrrhachīnus adj see n.

Dyrrhachium (Dyrrhachium), -ī nt Adriatic port (*now* Durazzo).

E

ē prep see **ex**.

ea f pron she, it ♦ adj see **is**.

eā adv there, that way.

eādem adv the same way; at the same time.

eadem f adj see **idem**.

eaīdem, eapse f of **ipse**.

eapse f of **ipse**.

eātenus adv so far.

ebenus etc see **hebenus**.

ēbibō, -ere, -ī vt to drink up, drain; to squander; to absorb.

ēblandior, -īrī vt to coax out, obtain by flattery; **~ītus** obtained by flattery.

Eborācum, -ī nt York.

ēbrietās, ātis f drunkenness.

ēbriolus adj tipsy.

ēbriōsitās, -ātis f addiction to drink.

ēbriōsus adj drunkard; (*berry*) juicy.

ēbrius adj drunk; full; (*fig*) intoxicated.

ēbulliō, -īre vi to bubble up ♦ vt to brag about.

ebulus, -ī m, **-um, -ī** nt danewort, dwarf elder.

ebur, -is nt ivory; ivory work.

Eburācum, -ī nt York.

eburātus adj inlaid with ivory.

eburneolus adj of ivory.

eburneus, eburnus adj of ivory; ivory-white.

ēcastor interj by Castor!

ecce adv look!, here is!, there is!; lo and behold!; **~a, ~am, ~illam, ~istam** here she is!; **~um, ~illum** here he is!; **~ōs, ~ās** here they are!

eccerē interj there now!

eccheuma, -tis nt pouring out.

ecclēsia, -ae f a Greek assembly; (*ECCL*) congregation, church.

eccum etc see **ecce**.

ecdicus, -ī m civic lawyer.

ecf- see **eff-**.

echidna, -ae f viper; **~ Lernaea** hydra.

echīnus, -ī m sea-urchin; hedgehog; a rinsing bowl.

Echīōn, -onis m Theban hero.

Echīonidēs m Pentheus.

Echīonius adj Theban.

Ēchō, -us f wood nymph; echo.

ecloga, -ae f selection; eclogue.

ecquandō adv ever.

ecquī, -ae, -od adj interrog any.

ecquid, -ī adv whether.

ecquis, -id pron interrog anyone, anything.

ecquō adv anywhere.

eculeus, -ī m foal; rack.

edācitās, -ātis f gluttony.

edāx, -ācis adj gluttonous; (*fig*) devouring, carking.

ēdentō, -āre vt to knock the teeth out of.

ēdentulus adj toothless; old.

edepol interj by Pollux, indeed.

ēdī perf of **edō**.

ēdīcō, -īcere, -īxī, -ictum vt to declare; to decree, publish an edict.

ēdictiō, -ōnis f decree.

ēdictō, -āre vt to proclaim.

ēdictum, -ī nt proclamation, edict (esp a praetor's).

ēdidī perf of **ēdō**.

ēdiscō, -ere, ēdidicī vt to learn well, learn by heart.

ēdisserō, -ere, -uī, -tum vt to explain in detail.

ēdissertō, -āre vt to explain fully.

ēditīcius adj chosen by the plaintiff.

ēditiō, -ōnis f publishing, edition; statement; (law) designation of a suit.

ēditus ppp of **ēdō** ♦ adj high; descended ♦ nt height; order.

edō, edere and **ēsse, ēdī, ēsum** vt to eat; (fig) to devour.

ēdō, -ere, -idī, -itum vt to put forth, discharge; to emit; to give birth to, produce; (speech) to declare, relate, utter; (action) to cause, perform; (book) to publish; (POL) to promulgate; **lūdōs ~** put on a show; **tribūs ~** nominate tribes of jurors.

ēdoceō, -ēre, -uī, -ctum vt to instruct clearly, teach thoroughly.

ēdomō, -āre, -uī, -itum vt to conquer, overcome.

Ēdōnus adj Thracian.

ēdormiō, -īre vi to have a good sleep ♦ vt to sleep off.

ēdormīscō, -ere vt to sleep off.

ēducātiō, -ōnis f bringing up, rearing.

ēducātor, -ōris m foster father, tutor.

ēducātrīx, -īcis f nurse.

ēducō, -āre, -āvī, -ātum vt to bring up, rear, train; to produce.

ēdūcō, -ūcere, -ūxī, -uctum vt to draw out, bring away; to raise up, erect; (law) to summon; (MIL) to

lead out, march out; (ship) to put to sea; (young) to hatch, rear, train.

edūlis adj edible.

ēdūrō, -āre vi to last out.

ēdūrus adj very hard.

effarciō etc see **efferciō**.

effātus ppa of **effor** ♦ adj solemnly pronounced, declared ♦ nt axiom; (pl) predictions.

effectiō, -ōnis f performing; efficient cause.

effector, -ōris m, **-rīx, -rīcis** f producer, author.

effectus ppp of **efficiō**.

effectus, -ūs m completion, performance; effect.

effēmināte adv see **effēminātus**.

effēminātus adj effeminate.

effēminō, -āre, -āvī, -ātum vt to make a woman of; to enervate.

efferātus adj savage.

efferciō, -cīre, -tum vt to cram full.

efferitās, -ātis f wildness.

efferō, -āre, -āvī, -ātum vt to make wild; (fig) to exasperate.

efferō (ecferō), -re, extulī, ēlātum vt to bring out, carry out; to lift up, raise; (dead) to carry to the grave; (emotion) to transport; (honour) to exalt; (news) to spread abroad; (soil) to produce; (trouble) to endure to the end; **sē ~** rise; be conceited.

effertus ppp of **efferciō** ♦ adj full, bulging.

efferus adj savage.

effervēscō, -vēscere, -buī vi to boil over; (fig) to rage.

effervō, -ere vi to boil up.

effētus adj exhausted.

efficācitās, -ātis f power.

efficāciter adv effectually.

efficāx, -ācis adj capable, effective.

The present indicative verb endings are as follows: -āre = 1st; -ēre = 2nd; -ere = 3rd and -īre = 4th. See sections on irregular verbs and noun declensions.

efficiēns, -entis *pres p of* efficiō
♦ *adj* effective, efficient.
efficienter *adv* efficiently.
efficientia, -ae *f* power, efficacy.
efficiō, -icere, -ēcī, -ectum *vt* to
make, accomplish; to cause, bring
about; (*numbers*) to amount to;
(*soil*) to yield; (*theory*) to make out,
try to prove.
effictus *ppp of* effingō.
effigiēs, -ēī, -a, -ae *f* likeness,
copy; ghost; portrait, statue; (*fig*)
image, ideal.
effingō, -ngere, -nxī, -ctum *vt* to
form, fashion; to portray,
represent; to wipe clean; to
fondle.
efflāgitātiō, -ōnis *f* urgent
demand.
efflāgitātus, -ūs *m* urgent request.
efflāgitō, -āre *vt* to demand
urgently.
efflictim *adv* desperately.
efflictō, -āre *vt* to strike dead.
effligō, -gere, -xī, -ctum *vt* to
exterminate.
efflō, -āre, -āvī, -ātum *vt* to
breathe out, blow out ♦ *vi* to
billow out; **animam ~** expire.
efflōrēscō, -ēscere, -uī *vi* to
blossom forth.
effluō, -ere, -xī *vi* to run out, issue,
emanate; (*fig*) to pass away,
vanish; (*rumour*) to get known; **ex
animō ~** become forgotten.
effluvium, -ī *and* **iī** *nt* outlet.
effodiō, -odere, -ōdī, -ossum *vt* to
dig up; (*eyes*) to gouge out; (*house*)
to ransack.
effor, -ārī, -ātus *vt* to speak, utter;
(*augury*) to ordain; (*logic*) to state a
proposition.
effossus *ppp of* effodiō.
effrēnātē *adv see* effrēnātus.
effrēnātiō, -ōnis *f* impetuousness.
effrēnātus *adj* unbridled, violent,
unruly.

effrēnus *adj* unbridled.
effringō, -ingere, -ēgī, -āctum *vt*
to break open, smash.
effugiō, -ugere, -ūgī *vi* to run
away, escape ♦ *vt* to flee from,
escape; to escape the notice of.
effugium, -ī *and* **iī** *nt* flight,
escape; means of escape.
effulgeō, -gēre, -sī *vi* to shine out,
blaze.
effultus *adj* supported.
effundō, -undere, -ūdī, -ūsum *vt*
to pour forth, pour out; (*crops*) to
produce in abundance; (*missiles*)
to shoot; (*rider*) to throw; (*speech*)
to give vent to; (*effort*) to waste;
(*money*) to squander; (*reins*) to let
go; **sē ~, ~undī** rush out; indulge
(in).
effūsē *adv* far and wide; lavishly,
extravagantly.
effūsiō, -ōnis *f* pouring out,
rushing out; profusion,
extravagance; exuberance.
effūsus *ppp of* effundō ♦ *adj* vast,
extensive; loose, straggling;
lavish, extravagant.
effūtiō, -īre *vt* to blab, chatter.
ēgelidus *adj* mild, cool.
egēns, -entis *pres p of* egeō ♦ *adj*
needy.
egēnus *adj* destitute.
egeō, -ēre, -uī *vi* to be in want;
(*with abl or gen*) to need, want.
Ēgeria, -ae *f* nymph who taught
Numa.
ēgerō, -rere, -ssī, -stum *vt* to carry
out; to discharge, emit.
egestās, -ātis *f* want, poverty.
ēgestus *ppp of* ēgerō.
ēgī *perf of* agō.
ego *pron* I; **~met** I (*emphatic*).
ēgredior, -dī, -ssus *vi* to go out,
come out; to go up, climb; (*MIL*) to
march out; (*NAUT*) to disembark,
put to sea; (*speech*) to digress ♦ *vt*
to go beyond, quit; (*fig*) to

overstep, surpass.

ēgregiē adv uncommonly well, singularly.

ēgregius adj outstanding, surpassing; distinguished, illustrious.

ēgressus ppa of **ēgredior**.

ēgressus, -ūs m departure; way out; digression; (NAUT) landing; (river) mouth.

eguī perf of **egeō**.

ēgurgitō, -āre vt to lavish.

ehem interj (expressing surprise) ha!, so!

ēheu interj (expressing pain) alas!

eho interj (expressing rebuke) look here!

eī dat of **is**.

ei interj (expressing alarm) oh!

eia interj (expressing delight, playful remonstrance, encouragement) aha!, come now!, come on!

ēiaculor, -ārī vt to shoot out.

ēiciō, -icere, -iēcī, -iectum vt to throw out, drive out, put out; (joint) to dislocate; (mind) to banish; (NAUT) to bring to land, run aground, wreck; (rider) to throw; (speech) to utter; (THEAT) to hiss off; **sē** ~ rush out, break out.

ēiectāmenta, -ōrum ntpl refuse.

ēiectiō, -ōnis f banishment.

ēiectō, -āre vt to throw up.

ēiectus ppp of **ēiciō ♦** adj shipwrecked.

ēiectus, -ūs m emitting.

ēierō, ēiūrō, -āre vt to abjure, reject on oath, forswear; (office) to resign; **bonam cōpiam** ~ declare oneself bankrupt.

ēiulātiō, -ōnis f, **ēiulātus, -ūs** m wailing.

ēiulō, -āre vi to wail, lament.

ēius pron his, her, its; **~modi** such.

ej- etc see **ei-**.

ēlābor, -bī, -psus vi to glide away, slip off; to escape, get off; to pass away.

ēlabōrātus adj studied.

ēlabōrō, -āre, -āvī, -ātum vi to exert oneself, take great pains ♦ vt to work out, elaborate.

ēlāmentābilis adj very mournful.

ēlanguēscō, -ēscere, -ī vi to grow faint; to relax.

ēlapsus ppa of **ēlābor**.

ēlātē adv proudly.

ēlātiō, -ōnis f ecstasy, exaltation.

ēlātrō, -āre vt to bark out.

ēlātus ppp of **efferō ♦** adj high; exalted.

ēlavō, -avāre, -avī, -autum and **ōtum** vt to wash clean; (comedy) to rob.

Elea, -ae f town in S. Italy (birthplace of Parmenides).

Eleātēs, -āticus adj see n.

ēlecebra, -ae f snare.

ēlectē adv choicely.

ēlectilis adj choice.

ēlectiō, -ōnis f choice, option.

ēlectō, -āre vt to coax out.

ēlectō, -āre vt to select.

Ēlectra, -ae f a Pleiad (daughter of Atlas; sister of Orestes).

ēlectrum, -ī nt amber; an alloy of gold and silver.

ēlectus ppp of **ēligō ♦** adj select, choice.

ēlōtus, -ūs m choice.

ēlegāns, -antis adj tasteful, refined, elegant; fastidious; (things) fine, choice.

ēleganter adv with good taste.

ēlegantia, -ae f taste, finesse, elegance; fastidiousness.

ēlēgī perf of **ēligō**.

elegī, -ōrum mpl elegiac verses.

elegīa, -ae f elegy.

Eleleides, -eidum fpl Bacchantes.

The present infinitive verb endings are as follows: -are = 1st; -ēre = 2nd; -ere = 3rd and -īre = 4th. See sections on irregular verbs and noun declensions.

Eleleus, -eī m Bacchus.
elementum, -ī nt element; (pl) first principles, rudiments; beginnings; letters (of alphabet).
elenchus, -ī m a pear-shaped pearl.
elephantomacha, -ae m fighter mounted on an elephant.
elephantus, -ī, elephās, -antis m elephant; ivory.
Ēlēus, -ius, -ias adj Elean; Olympian.
Eleusīn, -is f Eleusis (Attic town famous for its mysteries of Demeter).
Eleusīus adj see **Eleusīn**.
eleutheria, -ae f liberty.
ēlevō, -āre vt to lift, raise; to alleviate; to make light of, lessen, disparage.
ēliciō, -ere, -uī, -itum vt to lure out, draw out; (god) to call down; (spirit) to conjure up; (fig) to elicit, draw.
ēlīdō, -dere, -sī, -sum vt to dash out, squeeze out; to drive out; to crush, destroy.
ēligō, -igere, -ēgī, -ēctum vt to pick, pluck out; to choose.
ēlīminō, -āre vt to carry outside.
ēlīmō, -āre vt to file; (fig) to perfect.
ēlinguis adj speechless; not eloquent.
ēlinguō, -āre vt to tear the tongue out of.
Ēlis, -idis f district and town in W. Peloponnese (famous for Olympia).
Elissa, -ae f Dido.
ēlīsus ppp of **ēlīdō**.
ēlixus adj boiled.
elleborōsus adj quite mad.
elleborus, -ī m, **-um, -ī** nt hellebore.
ellum, ellam there he (she) is!
ēlocō, -āre vt to lease, farm out.
ēlocūtiō, -ōnis f delivery, style.
ēlocūtus ppa of **ēloquor**.
ēlogium, -ī and **iī** nt short saying;

inscription; (will) clause.
ēloquēns, -entis adj eloquent.
ēloquenter adv see adj.
ēloquentia, -ae f eloquence.
ēloquium, -ī and **iī** nt eloquence.
ēloquor, -quī, -cūtus vt, vi to speak out, speak eloquently.
ēlūceō, -cēre, -xī vi to shine out, glitter.
ēluctor, -ārī, -ātus vi to struggle, force a way out ♦ vt to struggle out of, surmount.
ēlūcubrō, -āre, -or, -ārī, -ātus vt to compose by lamplight.
ēlūdificor, -ārī, -ātus vt to cheat, play up.
ēlūdō, -dere, -sī, -sum vt to parry, ward off, foil; to win off at play; to outplay, outmanoeuvre; to cheat, make fun of ♦ vi to finish one's sport.
ēlūgeō, -gēre, -xī vt to mourn for.
ēlumbis adj feeble.
ēluō, -uere, -uī, -ūtum vt to wash clean; (money) to squander; (fig) to wash away, get rid of.
ēlūsus ppp of **ēlūdō**.
ēlūtus ppp of **ēluō** ♦ adj insipid.
ēluviēs, -em f discharge; overflowing.
ēluviō, -ōnis f deluge.
Elysium, -ī nt Elysium.
Elysius adj Elysian.
em interj there you are!
ēmancipātiō, -ōnis f giving a son his independence; conveyance of property.
ēmancipō, -āre vt to declare independent; to transfer, give up, sell.
ēmānō, -āre, -āvī, -ātum vt to flow out; to spring (from); (news) to leak out, become known.
Ēmathia, -ae f district of Macedonia; Macedonia, Thessaly.
Ēmathius adj Macedonian, Pharsalian; **~des, ~dum** fpl

Muses.

ēmātūrēscō, -ēscere, -uī *vi* to soften.

emāx, -ācis *adj* fond of buying.

emblēma, -tis *nt* inlaid work, mosaic.

embolium, -ī *and* **iī** *nt* interlude.

ēmendābilis *adj* corrigible.

ēmendātē *adv see* **emendātor.**

ēmendātiō, -ōnis *f* correction.

ēmendātor, -ōris *m,* **-rīx, -rīcis** *f* corrector.

ēmendātus *adj* faultless.

ēmendō, -āre, -āvī, -ātum *vt* to correct, improve.

ēmēnsus *ppa of* **ēmētior ♦** *adj* traversed.

ēmentior, -īrī, -ītus *vi* to tell lies **♦** *vt* to pretend, fabricate; **-ītus** pretended.

ēmercor, -ārī *vt* to purchase.

ēmereō, -ēre, -uī, -itum *-eor, -ērī* *vt* to earn fully, deserve; to lay under an obligation; to complete one's term of service.

ēmergō, -gere, -sī, -sum *vt* to raise out; (*fig*) to extricate **♦** *vi* to rise, come up, emerge; (*fig*) to get clear, extricate oneself; (*impers*) it becomes evident.

ēmeritus *ppa of* **ēmereor ♦** *adj* superannuated, worn-out **♦** *m* veteran.

ēmersus *ppp of* **ēmergō.**

emetica, -ae *f* emetic.

ēmētior, -tīrī, -nsus *vi* to measure out; to traverse, pass over; (*time*) to live through; (*fig*) to impart.

ēmetō, -ere *vt* to harvest.

ēmī *perf of* **emō.**

ēmicō, -āre, -uī, -ātum *vi* to dart out, dash out, flash out; (*fig*) to shine.

ēmigrō, -āre, -āvī, -ātum *vi* to remove, depart.

ēminēns, -entis *pres p of* **ēmineō ♦** *adj* high, projecting; (*fig*) distinguished, eminent.

ēminentia, -ae *f* prominence; (*painting*) light.

ēmineō, -ēre, -uī *vi* to stand out, project; to be prominent, be conspicuous, distinguish oneself.

ēminor, -ārī *vi* to threaten.

ēminus *adv* at *or* from a distance.

ēmīror, -ārī *vt* to marvel at.

ēmissārium, -ī *and* **iī** *nt* outlet.

ēmissārius, -ī *and* **iī** *m* scout.

ēmissicius *adj* prying.

ēmissiō, -ōnis *f* letting go, discharge.

ēmissus *ppp of* **ēmittō.**

ēmissus, -ūs *m* emission.

ēmittō, -ittere, -īsī, -issum *vt* to send out, let out; to let go, let slip; (*missile*) to discharge; (*person*) to release, free; (*sound*) to utter; (*writing*) to publish.

emō, -ere, ēmī, emptum *vt* to buy, procure; to win over; **bene ~** buy cheap; **male ~** buy dear; **in diem ~** buy on credit.

ēmoderor, -ārī *vt* to give expression to.

ēmodulor, -ārī *vt* to sing through.

ēmolior, -īrī *vt* to accomplish.

ēmolliō, -īre, -iī, -ītum *vt* to soften; to mollify; to enervate.

ēmolumentum, -ī *nt* profit, advantage.

ēmoneō, -ēre *vt* to strongly advise.

ēmorior, -ī, -tuus *vi* to die; (*fig*) to pass away.

ēmortuālis *adj* of death.

ēmoveō, -ovēre, -ōvī, -ōtum *vt* to remove, drive away.

Empedoclēs, -is *m* Sicilian philosopher.

Empedoclēus *adj see* n.

The present infinitive verb endings are as follows: **-āre** = 1st; **-ēre** = 2nd; **-ere** = 3rd and **-īre** = 4th. *See sections on irregular verbs and noun declensions.*

empīricus, -ī *m* empirical doctor.

emporium, -ī and **iī** *nt* market, market town.

emptiō, -ōnis *f* buying; a purchase.

emptitō, -āre *vt* to often buy.

emptor, -ōris *m* purchaser.

emptus *ppp of* **emō.**

ēmulgeō, -ēre *vt* to drain.

ēmunctus *ppp of* **ēmungō ♦** *adj* discriminating.

ēmungō, -gere, -xī, -ctum *vt* to blow the nose of; (*comedy*) to cheat.

ēmūniō, -īre, -īvī, -ītum *vt* to strengthen, secure; to build up; to make roads through.

ēn *interj* (*drawing attention*) look!, see!; (*excited question*) really, indeed; (*command*) come now!

ēnārrābilis *adj* describable.

ēnārrō, -āre, -āvī, -ātum *vt* to describe in detail.

ēnāscor, -scī, -tus *vi* to sprout, grow.

ēnatō, -āre *vi* to swim ashore; (*fig*) to escape.

ēnātus *ppa of* **ēnāscor.**

ēnāvigō, -āre *vi* to sail clear, clear ♦ *vt* to sail over.

Enceladus, -ī *m* giant under Etna.

endromis, -dis *f* sports wrap.

Endymiōn, -ōnis *m* a beautiful youth loved by the Moon, and doomed to lasting sleep.

ēnecō, -āre, -uī and **āvī, -tum** and **ātum** *vt* to kill; to wear out; to torment.

ēnervātus *adj* limp.

ēnervis *adj* enfeebled.

ēnervō, -āre, -āvī, -ātum *vt* to weaken, unman.

ēnicō *etc see* **ēnecō.**

enim *conj* (*affirming*) yes, truly, in fact; (*explaining*) for, for instance, of course; **at ~** but it will be objected; **quid ~** well?; **sed ~** but

actually.

enimvērō *conj* certainly, yes indeed.

Enīpeus, -eī *m* river in Thessaly.

ēnisus *ppa of* **ēnītor.**

ēniteō, -ēre, -uī *vi* to shine, brighten up; (*fig*) to be brilliant, distinguish oneself.

ēnitēscō, -ēscere, -uī *vi* to shine, be brilliant.

ēnītor, -tī, -sus and **xus** *vi* to struggle up, climb; to strive, make a great effort ♦ *vt* to give birth to; to climb.

ēnixē *adv* earnestly.

ēnīxus *ppa of* **ēnītor ♦** *adj* strenuous.

Enniānus *adj* see n.

Ennius, -ī *m* greatest of the early Latin poets.

Ennosigaeus, -ī *m* Earthshaker, Neptune.

ēnō, -āre, -āvī *vi* to swim out, swim ashore; to fly away.

ēnōdātē *adv* lucidly.

ēnōdātiō, -ōnis *f* unravelling.

ēnōdis *adj* free from knots; plain.

ēnōdō, -āre, -āvī, -ātum *vt* to elucidate.

ēnōrmis *adj* irregular; immense.

ēnōtēscō, -ēscere, -uī *vi* to get known.

ēnotō, -āre *vt* to make a note of.

ēnsiculus, -ī *m* little sword.

ēnsiger, -ī *adj* with his sword.

ēnsis, -is *m* sword.

enthymēma, -tis *nt* argument.

ēnūbō, -bere, -psī *vi* to marry out of one's station; to marry and go away.

ēnucleātē *adv* plainly.

ēnucleātus *adj* (*style*) straight-forward; (*votes*) honest.

ēnucleō, -āre *vt* to elucidate.

ēnumerātiō, -ōnis *f* enumeration; (*RHET*) recapitulation.

ēnumerō, -āre *vt* to count up; to

pay out; to relate.

ēnūntiātiō, -ōnis f proposition.

ēnūntiātum, -ī nt proposition.

ēnūntiō, -āre vt to disclose, report; to express; to pronounce.

ēnūptiō, -ōnis f marrying out of one's station.

ēnūtriō, -īre vt to feed, bring up.

eō, īre, īvī and **iī, -itum** vi to go; (MIL) to march; (time) to pass; (event) to proceed, turn out: **in alia omnia ~** vote against a bill; **in sententiam ~** support a motion; **sic eat** so may he fare!; **ī** (mocking) go on!

eō adv (place) thither, there; (purpose) with a view to; (degree) so far, to such a pitch; (time) so long; (cause) on that account, for the reason; (with compar) the; **accēdit eō** besides; **rēs erat eō locī** such was the state of affairs; **eō magis** all the more.

eōdem adv to the same place, purpose or person; **~ locī** in the same place.

Ēōs f dawn ♦ m morning star; Oriental.

Ēous adj at dawn, eastern.

Ēpamīnōndās, -ae m Theban general.

ēpāstus adj eaten up.

ephēbus, -ī m youth (18 to 20).

ephēmeris, -idis f diary.

Ephesius adj see n.

Ephesus, -ī f Ionian town in Asia Minor.

ephippiātus adj riding a saddled horse.

ephippium, -ī and **iī** nt saddle.

ephorus, -ī m a Spartan magistrate, ephor.

Ephyra, -ae, -ē, -ēs f Corinth.

Ephyrēius adj see Ephyra.

Epicharmus, -ī m Greek philosopher

and comic poet.

epichysis, -is f kind of jug.

epicōpus adj rowing.

Epicūrēus, epicus adj epic.

Epicūrus, -ī m famous Greek philosopher.

Epidaurius adj see n.

Epidaurus, -ī f town in E. Peloponnese.

epidicticus adj (RHET) for display.

epigramma, -tis nt inscription; epigram.

epilogus, -ī m peroration.

epimēnia, -ōrum ntpl a month's rations.

Epimēthis, -dis f Pyrrha (daughter of Epimetheus).

epirēdium, -ī and **iī** nt trace.

Ēpīrōtēs, -ōtae m native of Epirus.

Ēpīrōticus, -ēnsis adj see n.

Ēpīrus, -os, -ī f district of N.W. Greece.

episcopus, -ī m bishop.

epistolium, -ī and **iī** nt short note.

epistula, -ae f letter; **ab ~īs** secretary.

epitaphium, -ī and **iī** nt funeral oration.

epithēca, -ae f addition.

epitoma, -ae, -ē, -ēs f abridgement.

epityrum, -ī nt olive salad.

epops, -is m hoopoe.

epos (pl -ē) nt epic.

ēpōtō, -āre, -āvī, -um vt to drink up, drain, to waste in drink; to absorb.

epulae, -ārum fpl dishes; feast, banquet.

epulāris adj at a banquet.

epulō, -ōnis m guest at a feast; priest in charge of religious banquets.

epulor, -ārī, -ātus vi to be at a feast ♦ vt to feast on.

The present infinitive verb endings are as follows: -āre = 1st; -ēre = 2nd; -ere = 3rd and -īre = 4th. *See sections on irregular verbs and noun declensions.*

epulum, **-ī** *nt* banquet.

equa, **-ae** *f* mare.

eques, **-itis** *m* horseman, trooper; (*pl*) cavalry; knight, member of the equestrian order.

equester, **-ris** *adj* equestrian; cavalry- (*in cpds*).

equidem *adv* (*affirming*) indeed, of course, for my part; (*concessive*) to be sure.

equīnus *adj* horse's.

equīria, **-ōrum** *ntpl* horseraces.

equitātus, **-ūs** *m* cavalry.

equitō, **-āre** *vi* to ride.

equuleus *etc see* **eculeus**.

equulus, **-ī** *m* colt.

equus, **-ī** *m* horse; (ASTRO) Pegasus; ~ **bipēs** seahorse; ~**ō merēre** serve in the cavalry; ~**is virīsque** with might and main.

era, **-ae** *f* mistress (of the house); (*goddess*) Lady.

ērādīcō, **-āre** *vt* to root out, destroy.

ērādō, **-dere**, **-sī**, **-sum** *vt* to erase, obliterate.

Eratō *f* Muse of lyric poetry.

Eratosthenēs, **-is** *m* famous Alexandrian geographer.

Erebēus *adj see* **n.**

Erebus, **-ī** *m* god of darkness; the lower world.

Erechtheus, **-eī** *m* legendary king of Athens.

Erechthēus *adj see* **n.**

Erechthīdae *mpl* Athenians

Erechthis, **-idis** *f* Orithyia; Procris.

ērēctus *ppp of* **ērigō ♦** *adj* upright, lofty; noble, haughty; alert, tense; resolute.

ērēpō, **-ere**, **-sī** *vi* to creep out, clamber up **♦** *vt* to crawl over, climb.

ēreptiō, **-ōnis** *f* seizure, robbery.

ēreptor, **-ōris** *m* robber.

ēreptus *ppp of* **ēripiō**.

ergā *prep* (*with acc*) towards;

against.

ergastulum, **-ī** *nt* prison (*esp for slaves*); (*pl*) convicts.

ergō *adv* therefore, consequently; (*questions, commands*) then, so; (*resuming*) well then; (*with gen*) for the sake of, because of.

Erichthonius, **-ī** *m* a king of Troy; a king of Athens **♦** *adj* Trojan; Athenian.

ēricius, **-ī** *and* **iī** *m* hedgehog; (MIL) beam with iron spikes.

Ēridanus, **-ī** *m* mythical name of river Po.

erifuga, **-ae** *m* runaway slave.

ērigō, **-igere**, **-ēxī**, **-ēctum** *vt* to make upright, raise up, erect; to excite; to encourage.

Ērigonē, **-ēs** *f* (*constellation*) Virgo.

Ērigonēius *adj see* **n.**

erīlis *adj* the master's, the mistress's.

Erīnȳs, **-yos** *f* Fury; (*fig*) curse, frenzy.

Eriphȳla, **-ae** *f* mother of Alcmaeon (*who killed her*).

ēripiō, **-ipere**, **-ipuī**, **-eptum** *vt* to tear away, pull away, take by force; to rob; to rescue; **sē ~** escape.

ērogātiō, **-ōnis** *f* paying out.

ērogitō, **-āre** *vt* to enquire.

ērogō, **-āre**, **-āvī**, **-ātum** *vt* to pay out, expend; to bequeath.

errābundus *adj* wandering.

errāticus *adj* roving, shifting.

errātiō, **-ōnis** *f* wandering, roving.

errātum, **-ī** *nt* mistake, error.

errātus, **-ūs** *m* wandering.

errō, **-āre**, **-āvī**, **-ātum** *vi* to wander, stray, lose one's way; to waver; to make a mistake, err **♦** *vt* to traverse; **stēllae ~antēs** planets.

errō, **-ōnis** *m* vagabond.

error, **-ōris** *m* wandering; meander, maze; uncertainty;

error, mistake, delusion; deception.

ērubēscō, -ēscere, -uī vi to blush; to feel ashamed ♦ vt to blush for, be ashamed of; to respect.

ērūca, -ae f colewort.

ēructō, -āre vt to belch, vomit; to talk drunkenly about; to throw up.

ērudiō, -īre, -iī, -ītum vt to educate, instruct.

erudite adv learnedly.

ērudītiō, -ōnis f education, instruction; learning, knowledge.

ērudītulus adj somewhat skilled.

ērudītus ppp of ērudiō ♦ adj learned, educated, accomplished.

ērumpō, -umpere, -ūpī, -uptum to break open; to make break out ♦ vi to burst out, break through; to end (in).

ēruō, -ere, -ī, -tum vt to uproot, tear out; to demolish, destroy; to elicit, draw out; to rescue.

ēruptiō, -ōnis f eruption; (MIL) sally.

ēruptus ppp of ērumpō.

erus, -ī m master (of the house); owner.

ērutus ppp of ēruō.

ervum, -ī nt vetch.

Erycīnus adj of Eryx; of Venus; Sicilian ♦ f Venus.

Erymanthius, -is adj see n.

Erymanthus and **ī** m mountain range in Arcadia, (where Hercules killed the bear).

Eryx, -cis m town and mountain in the extreme W. of Sicily.

esca, -ae f food, tit-bits; bait.

escārius adj of food; of bait ♦ ntpl dishes.

ēscendō, -endere, -endī, -ēnsum vi to climb up, go up ♦ vt to mount.

ēscēnsiō, -ōnis f raid (from the

coast); disembarkation.

esculentus adj edible, tasty.

Esquiliae, -iārum fpl Esquiline hill in Rome.

Esquilīnus adj Esquiline ♦ f Esquiline gate.

essedārius, -ī and **iī** m chariot fighter.

essedum, -ī nt war chariot.

essitō, -āre vt to usually eat.

ēst pres of edō.

estrīx, -īcis f glutton.

ēsuriālis adj of hunger.

ēsuriō, -īre, -ītum vi to be hungry ♦ vt to hunger for.

ēsurītiō, -ōnis f hunger.

ēsus ppp of edō.

et conj and; (repeated) both … and; (adding emphasis) in fact, yes; (comparing) as, than ♦ adv also, too; even.

etenim conj (adding an explanation) and as a matter of fact, in fact.

etēsiae, -ārum fpl Etesian winds.

etēsius adj see n.

ēthologus, -ī m mimic.

etiam adv also, besides; (emphatic) even, actually; (affirming) yes, certainly; (indignant) really!; (time) still, as yet; again; ~ atque ~ again and again; ~ cavēs! do be careful!; nihil ~ nothing at all.

etiamdum adv still, as yet.

etiamnum, etiamnunc adv still, till now, till then; besides.

etiamsī conj even if, although.

etiamtum, etiamtunc adv till then, still.

Etrūria, -ae f district of Italy north of Rome.

Etruscus adj Etruscan.

etsī conj even if, though; and yet.

etymologia, -ae f etymology.

eu interj well done!, bravo!

Euan m Bacchus.

The present infinitive verb endings are as follows: -āre = 1st; -ēre = 2nd; -ere = 3rd and -īre = 4th. See sections on irregular verbs and noun declensions.

Euander and **rus, -rī** m Evander (*ancient king on the site of Rome*).

Euandrius adj see n.

euax interj hurrah!

Euboea, -oeae f Greek island.

Euboicus adj Euboean.

euge, eugepae interj bravo!, cheers!

Euhan m Bacchus.

euhāns, -antis adj shouting the Bacchic cry.

Euhias f Bacchante.

Euhius, -ī m Bacchus.

euhoe interj ecstatic cry of Bacchic revellers.

Euius, -ī m Bacchus.

Eumenides, -um fpl Furies.

eunūchus, -ī m eunuch.

Euphrātēs, -is m river Euphrates.

Eupolis, -dis m Athenian comic poet.

Euripidēs, -is m Athenian tragic poet.

Euripidēus adj see n.

Euripus, -ī m strait between Euboea and mainland; a channel, conduit.

Eurōpa, -ae and **ē, -ēs** f mythical princess of Tyre (*who was carried by a bull to Crete*); continent of Europe.

Eurōpaeus adj see n.

Eurōtās, -ae m river of Sparta.

Eurōus adj eastern.

Eurus, -ī m east wind; south-east wind.

Eurydicē, -ēs f wife of Orpheus.

Eurystheus, -eī m king of Mycenae (*who imposed the labours on Hercules*).

euschēmē adv gracefully.

Euterpē, -ēs f Muse of music.

Euxīnus m the Black (Sea).

ēvādō, -dere, -sī, -sum vi to come out; to climb up; to escape; to turn out, result, come true ♦ vt to pass, mount; to escape from.

ēvagor, -ārī, -ātus vi (MIL) to manoeuvre; (fig) to spread ♦ vt to stray beyond.

ēvalēscō, -ēscere, -uī vi to grow, increase; to be able; to come into vogue.

Ēvander etc see Euander.

ēvānēscō, -ēscere, -uī vi to vanish, die away, lose effect.

ēvangelium, -ī and **iī** nt (ECCL) Gospel.

ēvānidus adj vanishing.

ēvāsī perf of ēvādō.

ēvastō, -āre vt to devastate.

ēvehō, -here, -xī, -ctum vt to carry out; to raise up, exalt; to spread abroad; (pass) to ride, sail, move out.

ēvellō, -ellere, -ellī, -ulsum vt to tear out, pull out; to eradicate.

ēveniō, -enīre, -ēnī, -entum vi to come out; to turn out, result; to come to pass, happen, befall.

ēventum, -ī nt result, issue; occurrence, event; fortune, experience.

ēventus, -ūs m result, issue; success; fortune, fate.

ēverberō, -āre vt to beat violently.

ēverriculum, -ī nt dragnet.

ēverrō, -rere, -rī, -sum vt to sweep out, clean out.

ēversiō, -ōnis f overthrow, destruction.

ēversor, -ōris m destroyer.

ēversus ppp of ēverrō; ppp of ēvertō.

ēvertō, -tere, -tī, -sum vt to turn out, eject; to turn up, overturn; to overthrow, ruin, destroy.

ēvestīgātus adj tracked down.

ēvictus ppp of ēvincō.

ēvidēns, -entis adj visible, plain, evident.

ēvidenter adv see evidēns.

ēvidentia, -ae f distinctness.

ēvigilō, -āre, -āvī, -ātum vi to be wide awake ♦ vt to compose carefully.

ēvīlēscō, -ere vi to become

worthless.

ēvinciō, -cīre, -xī, -ctum vt to
garland, crown.

ēvinco, -incere, -īcī, -ictum vt to
overcome, conquer; to prevail
over; to prove.

ēvirō, -āre vt to castrate.

ēviscerō, -āre vt to disembowel,
tear to pieces.

ēvītābilis adj avoidable.

ēvītō, -āre, -āvī, -ātum vt to avoid,
clear.

ēvocātī, -ōrum mpl veteran
volunteers.

ēvocātor, -ōris m enlister.

ēvocō, -āre, -āvī, -ātum vt to call
out, summon; to challenge; to call
up; to call forth, evoke.

ēvolō, -āre, -āvī, -ātum vi to fly
out, fly away; to rush out; (fig) to
rise, soar.

ēvolūtiō, -ōnis f unrolling (a
book).

ēvolvō, -vere, -vī, -ūtum vt to roll
out, roll along; to unroll, unfold;
(book) to open, read; (fig) to
disclose, unravel, disentangle.

ēvomō, -ere, -uī, -itum vt to vomit
up, disgorge.

ēvulgō, -āre, -āvī, -ātum vt to
divulge, make public.

ēvulsiō, -ōnis f pulling out.

ēvulsus ppp of **ēvellō**.

ex, ē prep (with abl) (place) out of,
from, down from; (person) from;
(time) after, immediately after,
since; (change) from being;
(source, material) of; (cause) by
reason of, through; (conformity) in
accordance with; **ex itinere** on the
march; **ex parte** in part; **ex quō**
since; **ex rē, ex ūsū** for the good
of; **ē rē pūblicā** constitutionally;
ex sententiā to one's liking; **aliud
ex aliō** one thing after another;

ūnus ex one of.

exacerbō, -āre vt to exasperate.

exāctiō, -ōnis f expulsion;
supervision; tax; (debts) calling
in.

exāctor, -ōris m expeller;
superintendent; tax collector.

exāctus ppp of **exigō** ♦ adj precise,
exact.

exacuō, -uere, -uī, -ūtum vt to
sharpen; (fig) to quicken, inflame.

exadversus, -um adv, prep (with
acc) right opposite.

exaedificātiō, -ōnis f construction.

exaedificō, -āre vt to build up; to
finish the building of.

exaequātiō, -ōnis f levelling.

exaequō, -āre, -āvī, -ātum vt to
level out; to compensate; to put on
an equal footing; to equal.

exaestuō, -āre vi to boil up.

exaggerātiō, -ōnis f exaltation.

exaggerō, -āre, -āvī, -ātum vt to
pile up; (fig) to heighten, enhance.

exagitātor, -ōris m critic.

exagitō, -āre, -āvī, -ātum vt to
disturb, harass; to scold, censure;
to excite, incite.

exagōga, -ae f export.

exalbēscō, -ēscere, -uī vi to turn
quite pale.

exāmen, -inis nt swarm, crowd;
tongue of a balance; examining.

exāminō, -āre, -āvī, -ātum vt to
weigh; to consider, test.

examussim adv exactly, perfectly.

exanclō, -āre vt to drain; to endure
to the end.

exanimālis adj dead; deadly.

exanimātiō, -ōnis f panic.

exanimis adj lifeless, breathless;
terrified.

exanimō, -āre, -āvī, -ātum vt to
wind; to kill; to terrify, agitate;
(pass) to be out of breath.

---

*The present infinitive verb endings are as follows: -āre = 1st; -ēre = 2nd; -ere = 3rd and
-īre = 4th. See sections on irregular verbs and noun declensions.*

exanimus see **exanimis.**

exārdēscō, -dēscere, -sī, -sum vi
to catch fire, blaze up; (fig) to be
inflamed, break out.

exārēscō, -ēscere, -uī vi to dry,
dry up.

exarmō, -āre vt to disarm.

exarō, -āre, -āvī, -ātum vt to
plough up; to cultivate, produce;
(brow) to furrow; (writing) to pen.

exārsī perf of **exārdēscō.**

exasciātus adj hewn out.

exasperō, -āre, -āvī, -ātum vt to
roughen; (fig) to provoke.

exauctōrō, -āre, -āvī, -ātum vt
(MIL) to discharge, release; to
cashier.

exaudiō, -īre, -īvī, -ītum vt to hear
clearly; to listen to; to obey.

exaugeō, -ēre vt to increase.

exaugurātiō, -ōnis f desecrating.

exaugurō, -āre vt to desecrate.

exauspicō, -āre vi to take an omen.

exbibō etc see **ēbibō.**

excaecō, -āre vt to blind; (river) to
block up.

excandēscentia, -ae f growing
anger.

excandēscō, -ēscere, -uī vi to
burn, be inflamed.

excantō, -āre vt to charm out,
spirit away.

excarnificō, -āre vt to tear to
pieces.

excavō, -āre vt to hollow out.

excēdō, -ēdere, -essī, -essum vi to
go out, go away; to die, disappear;
to advance, proceed (to); to
digress ♦ vt to leave; to overstep,
exceed.

excellēns, -entis pres p of **excellō**
♦ adj outstanding, excellent.

excellenter adv see **excellēns.**

excellentia, -ae f superiority,
excellence.

excellō, -ere vi to be eminent,
excel.

excelsē adv loftily.

excelsitās, -ātis f loftiness.

excelsum, -ī nt height.

excelsus adj high, elevated;
eminent, illustrious.

exceptiō, -ōnis f exception,
restriction; (law) objection.

exceptō, -āre vt to catch, take out.

exceptus ppp of **excipiō.**

excernō, -ernere, -rēvī, -rētum vt
to sift out, separate.

excerpō, -ere, -sī, -tum vt to take
out; to select, copy out extracts;
to leave out, omit.

excessus, -ūs m departure, death.

excetra, -ae f snake.

excidiō, -ōnis f destruction.

excidium, -ī and **iī** nt overthrow,
destruction.

excidō, -ere, -ī vi to fall out, fall;
(speech) to slip out, escape;
(memory) to get forgotten, escape;
(person) to fail, lose; (things) to
disappear, be lost.

excīdō, -dere, -dī, -sum vt to cut
off, hew out, fell; to raze; (fig) to
banish.

excieō vt see **exciō.**

exciō, -īre, -īvī and **iī, -ītum** and
ītum vt to call out, rouse,
summon; to occasion, produce; to
excite.

excipiō, -ipere, -ēpī, -eptum vt to
take out, remove; to exempt,
make an exception of, mention
specifically; to take up, catch,
intercept, overhear; to receive,
welcome, entertain; to come next
to, follow after, succeed.

excīsiō, -ōnis f destroying.

excīsus ppp of **excīdō.**

excitātus adj loud, strong.

excitō, -āre, -āvī, -ātum vt to
rouse, wake up, summon; to raise,
build; to call on (to stand up); (fig)
to encourage, revive, excite.

excitus, excītus ppp of **exciō.**

exclāmātiō, -ōnis f exclamation.
exclāmō, -āre, -āvī, -ātum vi to cry out, shout ♦ vt to exclaim, call.
exclūdō, -dere, -sī, -sum vt to shut out, exclude; to shut off, keep off; (egg) to hatch out; (eye) to knock out; (fig) to prevent, except.
exclūsiō, -ōnis f shutting out.
exclūsus ppp of exclūdō.
excoctus ppp of excoquō.
excōgitātiō, -ōnis f thinking out, devising.
excōgitō, -āre, -āvī, -ātum vt to think out, contrive.
excolō, -olere, -oluī, -ultum vt to work carefully; to perfect, refine.
excoquō, -quere, -xī, -ctum vt to boil away; to remove with heat, make with heat; to dry up.
excors, -dis adj senseless, stupid.
excrēmentum, -ī nt excretion.
excreō etc see exscreō.
excrēscō, -scere, -vī, -tum vi to grow, rise up.
excrētus ppp of excernō.
excruciō, -āre, -āvī, -ātum vt to torture, torment.
excubiae, -ārum fpl keeping guard, watch; sentry.
excubitor, -ōris m sentry.
excubō, -āre, -uī, -itum vi to sleep out of doors; to keep watch; (fig) to be on the alert.
excūdō, -dere, -dī, -sum vt to strike out, hammer out; (egg) to hatch; (fig) to make, compose.
exculcō, -āre vt to beat, tramp down.
excultus ppp of excolō.
excurrō, -rrere, -currī and **rrī, -rsum** vi to run out, hurry out; to make an excursion, (MIL) to make a sortie; (place) to extend, project; (fig) to expand.

excursiō, -ōnis f raid, sortie; (gesture) stepping forward; (fig) outset.
excursor, -ōris m scout.
excursus, -ūs m excursion, raid, charge.
excūsābilis adj excusable.
excūsātē adv excusably.
excūsātiō, -ōnis f excuse, plea.
excūsō, -āre, -āvī, -ātum vt to excuse; to apologize for; to plead as an excuse.
excussus ppp of excutiō.
excūsus ppp of excūdō.
excutiō, -tere, -ssī, -ssum vt to shake out, shake off; to knock out, drive out, cast off; (fig) to discard, banish; to examine, inspect.
exdorsuō, -āre vt to fillet.
exec- etc see exsec-.
exedō, -ēsse, -ēdī, -ēsum vt to eat up; to wear away, destroy; (feelings) to prey on.
exedra, -ae f hall, lecture room.
exedrium, -ī and **iī** nt sitting room.
exēmī perf of eximō.
exemplar, -āris nt copy; likeness; model, ideal.
exemplārēs mpl copies.
exemplum, -ī nt copy; example, sample, precedent, pattern; purport, nature; warning, object lesson; ~ **dare** set an example; ~**ī causā, gratiā** for instance.
exemptus ppp of eximō.
exenterō, -āre vt (comedy) to empty, clean out; to torture.
exeō, -īre, -iī, -itum vi to go out, leave; to come out, issue; (MIL) to march out; (time) to expire; to spring up, rise ♦ vt to pass beyond; to avoid; ~ **ex potestāte** lose control.
exeq- etc see exseq-.
exerceō, -ēre, -uī, -itum vt to keep

*The present infinitive verb endings are as follows: -**āre** = 1st; -**ēre** = 2nd; -**ere** = 3rd and -**īre** = 4th. See sections on irregular verbs and noun declensions.*

busy, supervise; (*ground*) to work, cultivate; (*MIL*) to drill, exercise; (*mind*) to engage, employ; (*occupation*) to practise, follow, carry on; (*trouble*) to worry, harass; **sē ~** practise, exercise.

exercitātiō, -ōnis f practice, exercise, experience.

exercitātus adj practised, trained, versed; troubled.

exercitium, -ī and **iī** nt exercising.

exercitō, -āre vt to exercise.

exercitor, -ōris m trainer.

exercitus ppp of **exerceō** ♦ adj disciplined; troubled; troublesome.

exercitus, -ūs m army (*esp the infantry*); assembly; troop, flock; exercise.

exerō etc see **exserō**.

exēsor, -ōris m corroder.

exēsus ppp of **exedō**.

exhālātiō, -ōnis f vapour.

exhālō, -āre vt to exhale, breathe out ♦ vi to steam; to expire.

exhauriō, -rīre, -sī, -stum vt to drain off; to empty; to take away, remove; (*fig*) to exhaust, finish; (*trouble*) to undergo, endure to the end.

exhērēdō, -āre vt to disinherit.

exhērēs, -ēdis adj disinherited.

exhibeō, -ere, -uī, -itum vt to hold out, produce (in public); to display, show; to cause, occasion.

exhilarātus adj delighted.

exhorrēscō, -ēscere, -uī vi to be terrified ♦ vt to be terrified at.

exhortātiō, -ōnis f encouragement.

exhortor, -ārī, -ātus vt to encourage.

exigō, -igere, -ēgī, -āctum vt to drive out, thrust; (*payment*) to exact, enforce; to demand, claim; (*goods*) to dispose of; (*time*) to pass, complete; (*work*) to finish;

(*news*) to ascertain; to test, examine, consider.

exiguē adv briefly, slightly, hardly.

exiguitās, -ātis f smallness, meagreness.

exiguus adj small, short, meagre ♦ nt a little bit.

exiliō etc see **exsiliō**.

exīlis adj thin, small, meagre; poor; (*style*) flat, insipid.

exīlitās, -ātis f thinness, meagreness.

exīliter adv feebly.

exilium etc see **exsilium**.

exim see **exinde**.

eximiē adv exceptionally.

eximius adj exempt; select; distinguished, exceptional.

eximō, -imere, -ēmī, -emptum vt to take out, remove; to release, free; to exempt; (*time*) to waste; (*fig*) to banish.

exin see **exinde**.

exināniō, -īre, -iī, -ītum vt to empty; to pillage.

exinde adv (*place*) from there, next; (*time*) then, thereafter, next; (*measure*) accordingly.

existimātiō, -ōnis f opinion, judgment; reputation, character; (*money*) credit.

existimātor, -ōris m judge, critic.

existimō, -āre, -āvī, -ātum vt to value, estimate, judge, think, consider.

existō etc see **exsistō**.

existumō vt see **existimō**.

exitiābilis adj deadly, fatal.

exitiālis adj deadly.

exitiōsus adj pernicious, fatal.

exitium, -ī and **iī** nt destruction, ruin.

exitus, -ūs m departure; way out, outlet; conclusion, end; death; outcome, result.

exlēx, -ēgis adj above the law, lawless.

exoculō, -āre vt to knock the eyes out of.

exodium, -ī and iī nt afterpiece.

exolēscō, -scere, -vī, -tum vi to decay, become obsolete.

exolētus adj full-grown.

exonerō, -āre, -āvī, -ātum vt to unload, discharge; (fig) to relieve, exonerate.

exoptātus adj welcome.

exoptō, -are, -āvī, -ātum vt to long for, desire.

exōrābilis adj sympathetic.

exōrātor, -ōris m successful pleader.

exōrdior, -dīrī, -sus vt to lay the warp; to begin.

exōrdium, -ī and iī nt beginning; (RHET) introductory section.

exorior, -īrī, -tus vi to spring up, come out, rise; to arise, appear, start.

exōrnātiō, -ōnis f embellishment.

exōrnātor, -ōris m embellisher.

exōrnō, -āre, -āvī, -ātum vt to equip, fit out; to embellish, adorn.

exōrō, -āre, -āvī, -ātum vt to prevail upon, persuade; to obtain, win by entreaty.

exōrsus ppa of exōrdior ♦ adj begun ♦ ntpl preamble.

exōrsus, -ūs m beginning.

exortus ppa of exorior

exortus, -ūs m rising; east.

exos, -ossis adj boneless.

exōsculor, -ārī, -ātus vt to kiss fondly.

exossō, -āre vt to bone.

exōstra, -ae f stage mechanism; (fig) public.

exōsus adj detesting.

exōticus adj foreign.

expallēscō, -ēscere, -uī vi to turn pale, be afraid.

expalpō, -āre vt to coax out.

expandō, -ere vt to unfold.

expatrō, -āre vt to squander.

expavēscō, -ere, **expāvī** vi to be terrified ♦ vt to dread.

expect- etc see **exspect-**.

expediō, -īre, -īvī and iī, -ītum vt to free, extricate, disentangle; to prepare, clear (for action); to put right, settle; to explain, relate; (impers) it is useful, expedient.

expedītē adv readily, freely.

expedītiō, -ōnis f (MIL) expedition, enterprise.

expedītus ppp of expediō ♦ adj light-armed; ready, prompt; at hand ♦ m light-armed soldier; in -ō esse, habēre be, have in readiness.

expellō, -ellere, -ulī, -ulsum vt to drive away, eject, expel; to remove, repudiate.

expendō, -endere, -endī, -ēnsum vt to weigh out; to pay out; (penalty) to suffer; (mind) to ponder, consider, judge.

expēnsum, -ī nt payment, expenditure.

expergēfaciō, -facere, -fēcī, -factum vt to rouse, excite.

expergīscor, -gīscī, -rēctus vi to wake up; to bestir oneself.

expergō, -ere, -ī, -itum vt to awaken.

experiēns, -entis pres p of experior ♦ adj enterprising.

experientia, -ae f experiment; endeavour; experience, practice.

experīmentum, -ī nt proof, test; experience.

experior, -īrī, -tus vt to test, make trial of; to attempt, experience; (law) to go to law; (perf tenses) to know from experience.

experrēctus ppa of expergīscor.

expers, -tis adj having no part in,

not sharing; free from, without.

expertus *ppa of* **experior ♦** *adj*
proved, tried; experienced.

expetessō, -ere *vt* to desire.

expetō, -ere, -īvī *and* **iī, -ītum** *vt* to
aim at, tend towards; to desire,
covet; to attack; to demand,
require **♦** *vi* to befall, happen.

expiātiō, -ōnis *f* atonement.

expictus *ppp of* **expingō**.

expilātiō, -ōnis *f* pillaging.

expilātor, -ōris *m* plunderer.

expilō, -āre, -āvī, -ātum *vt* to rob,
plunder.

expingō, -ingere, -inxī, -ictum *vt*
to portray.

expiō, -āre, -āvī, -ātum *vt* to
purify; to atone for, make amends
for; to avert (evil).

expirō *etc see* **exspirō**.

expiscor, -ārī, -ātus *vt* to try to find
out, ferret out.

explānātē *adv see* **explānātus**.

explānātiō, -ōnis *f* explanation.

explānātor, -ōris *m* interpreter.

explānātus *adj* distinct.

explānō, -āre, -āvī, -ātum *vt* to
state clearly, explain; to
pronounce clearly.

explaudō *etc see* **explōdō**.

explēmentum, -ī *nt* filling.

expleō, -ēre, -ēvī, -ētum *vt* to fill
up; to complete; (*desire*) to satisfy,
appease; (*duty*) to perform,
discharge; (*loss*) to make good;
(*time*) to fulfil, complete.

explētiō, -ōnis *f* satisfying.

explētus *ppp of* **expleō ♦** *adj*
complete.

explicātē *adv* plainly.

explicātiō, -ōnis *f* uncoiling;
expounding, analyzing.

explicātor, -ōris *m*, **-rīx, -rīcis** *f*
expounder.

explicātus *adj* spread out; plain,
clear.

explicātus, -ūs *m* explanation.

explicitus *adj* easy.

explicō, -āre, -āvī *and* **uī, -ātum**
and **itum** *vt* to unfold, undo,
spread out; (*book*) to open; (*MIL*) to
deploy, extend; (*difficulty*) to put in
order, settle; (*speech*) to develop,
explain; to set free.

explōdō, -dere, -sī, -sum *vt* to hiss
off, drive away; (*fig*) to reject.

explōrātē *adv* with certainty.

explōrātiō, -ōnis *f* spying.

explōrātor, -ōris *m* spy, scout.

explōrātus *adj* certain, sure.

explōrō, -āre, -āvī, -ātum *vt* to
investigate, reconnoitre; to
ascertain; to put to the test.

explōsī *perf of* **explōdō**.

explōsiō, -ōnis *f* driving off (the
stage).

explōsus *ppp of* **explōdō**.

expoliō, -īre, -īvī, -ītum *vt* to
smooth off, polish; (*fig*) to refine,
embellish.

expolītiō, -ōnis *f* smoothing off;
polish, finish.

expōnō, -ōnere, -osuī, -ositum *vt*
to set out, put out; (*child*) to
expose; (*NAUT*) to disembark;
(*money*) to offer; (*fig*) to set forth,
expose, display; (*speech*) to
explain, expound.

exporrigō, -igere, -exī, -ectum *vt*
to extend, smooth out.

exportātiō, -ōnis *f* exporting.

exportō, -āre, -āvī, -ātum *vt* to
carry out, export.

exposcō, -ere, expoposcī *vt* to
implore, pray for; to demand.

expositīcius *adj* foundling.

expositiō, -ōnis *f* narration,
explanation.

expositus *ppp of* **expōnō ♦** *adj*
open, affable; vulgar.

expostulātiō, -ōnis *f* complaint

expostulō, -āre, -āvī, -ātum *vt* to
demand urgently; to complain of,
expostulate.

expōtus *ppp of* **ēpōtō**.

expressus *ppp of* **exprimō ♦** *adj* distinct, prominent.

exprimō, -imere, -essī, -essum *vt* to squeeze out, force out; to press up; *(fig)* to extort, wrest; *(art)* to mould, model; *(words)* to imitate, portray, translate, pronounce.

exprobrātiō, -ōnis *f* reproach.

exprobrō, -āre, -āvī, -ātum *vt* to reproach, cast up.

exprōmō, -ere, -psī, -ptum *vt* to bring out, fetch out; *(acts)* to exhibit, practise; *(feelings)* to give vent to; *(speech)* to disclose, state.

expugnābilis *adj* capable of being taken by storm.

expugnācior, -ōris *adj* more effective.

expugnātiō, -ōnis *f* storming, assault.

expugnātor, -ōris *m* stormer.

expugnō, -āre, -āvī, -ātum *vt* to storm, reduce; to conquer; *(fig)* to overcome, extort.

expulī *perf of* **expellō**.

expulsiō, -ōnis *f* expulsion.

expulsor, -ōris *m* expeller.

expulsus *ppp of* **expellō**.

expultrix, -icis *f* expeller.

expungō, -ungere, -ūnxī, ūnctum *vt* to prick out, cancel.

expūrgātiō, -ōnis *f* excuse.

expūrgō, -āre *vt* to purify; to justify.

exputō, -āre *vt* to consider, comprehend.

exquīrō, -rere, -sīvī, -sītum *vt* to search out, investigate; to inquire; to devise.

exquīsītē *adv* with particular care.

exquīsītus *ppp of* **exquīrō ♦** *adj* well thought out, choice.

exsaeviō, -īre *vi* to cease raging.

exsanguis *adj* bloodless, pale;

feeble.

exsarciō, -cīre, -tum *vt* to repair.

exsatiō, -āre *vt* to satiate, satisfy.

exsaturābilis *adj* appeasable.

exsaturō, -āre *vt* to satiate.

exsce- *etc see* **esce-**.

exscindō, -ndere, -dī, -ssum *vt* to extirpate.

exscreō, -āre *vt* to cough up.

exscrībō, -bere, -psī, -ptum *vt* to copy out; to note down.

exsculpō, -ere, -sī, -tum *vt* to carve out; to erase; *(fig)* to extort.

exsecō, -āre, -uī, -tum *vt* to cut out; to castrate.

exsecrābilis *adj* cursing, deadly.

exsecrātiō, -ōnis *f* curse; solemn oath.

exsecrātus *adj* accursed.

exsecror, -ārī, -ātus *vt* to curse; to take an oath.

exsectiō, -ōnis *f* cutting out.

exsecūtiō, -ōnis *f* management; discussion.

exsecūtus *ppa of* **exsequor**.

exsequiae, -ārum *fpl* funeral, funeral rites.

exsequiālis *adj* funeral.

exsequor, -quī, -cūtus *vt* to follow, pursue; to follow to the grave; *(duty)* to carry out, accomplish; *(speech)* to describe, relate; *(suffering)* to undergo; *(wrong)* to avenge, punish.

exserciō *vt see* **exsarciō**.

exserō, -ere, -uī, -tum *vt* to put out, stretch out; to reveal.

exsertō, -āre *vt* to stretch out repeatedly.

exsertus *ppp of* **exserō ♦** *adj* protruding.

exsibilō, -āre *vt* to hiss off.

exsiccātus *adj (style)* uninteresting.

exsiccō, -āre, -āvī, -ātum *vt* to dry

The present infinitive verb endings are as follows: **-āre** = 1st; **-ēre** = 2nd; **-ere** = 3rd and **-īre** = 4th. *See sections on irregular verbs and noun declensions.*

up; to drain.

exsicō *etc see* **exsecō.**

exsignō, -āre *vt* to write down in detail.

exsiliō, -īre, -uī *vi* to jump up, spring out; to start.

exsilium, -ī *and* **iī** *nt* banishment, exile; retreat.

exsistō, -istere, -titī, -titum *vi* to emerge, appear; to arise, spring (from); to be, exist.

exsolvō, -vere, -vī, -ūtum *vt* to undo, loosen, open; to release, free; to get rid of, throw off; (*debt, promise*) to discharge, fulfil, pay up; (*words*) to explain.

exsomnis *adj* sleepless, watchful.

exsorbeō, -ēre, -uī *vt* to suck, drain; to devour, endure.

exsors, -tis *adj* chosen, special; free from.

exspargō *etc see* **exspergō.**

exspatior, -ārī, -ātus *vi* to go off the course.

exspectābilis *adj* to be expected.

exspectātiō, -ōnis *f* waiting, expectation.

exspectātus *adj* looked for, welcome.

exspectō, -āre, -āvī, -ātum *vt* to wait for, till; to see; to expect; to hope for, dread; to require.

exspergō, -gere, -sum *vt* to scatter; to diffuse.

exspēs *adj* despairing.

exspīrātiō, -ōnis *f* exhalation.

exspīrō, -āre, -āvī, -ātum *vt* to breathe out, exhale; to emit ♦ *vi* to rush out; to expire, come to an end.

exsplendēscō, -ere *vi* to shine.

exspoliō, -āre *vt* to pillage.

exspuō, -uere, -uī, -ūtum *vt* to spit out, eject; (*fig*) to banish.

exsternō, -āre *vt* to terrify.

exstillō, -āre *vi* to drip.

exstimulātor, -ōris *m* instigator.

exstimulō, -āre *vt* to goad on; to excite.

exstinctiō, -ōnis *f* annihilation.

exstinctor, -ōris *m* extinguisher; destroyer.

exstinguō, -guere, -xī, -ctum *vt* to put out, extinguish; to kill, destroy, abolish.

exstirpō, -āre *vt* to root out, eradicate.

exstitī *perf of* **exsistō.**

exstō, -āre *vi* to stand out, project; to be conspicuous, be visible; to be extant, exist, be.

exstructiō, -ōnis *f* erection.

exstruō, -ere, -xī, -ctum *vt* to heap up; to build up, construct.

exsūdō, -āre *vi* to come out in sweat ♦ *vt* (*fig*) to toil through.

exsūgō, -gere, -xī, -ctum *vt* to suck out.

exsul, -is *m/f* exile.

exsulō, -āre, -āvī, -ātum *vi* to be an exile.

exsultātiō, -ōnis *f* great rejoicing.

exsultim *adv* friskily.

exsultō, -āre, -āvī, -ātum *vi* to jump up, prance; (*fig*) to exult, run riot, boast; (*speech*) to range at will.

exsuperābilis *adj* superable.

exsuperantia, -ae *f* superiority.

exsuperō, -āre, -āvī, -ātum *vi* to mount up; to gain the upper hand, excel ♦ *vt* to go over; to surpass; to overpower.

exsurdō, -āre *vt* to deafen; (*fig*) to dull.

exsurgō, -gere, -rēxī, -rēctum *vi* to rise, stand up; to recover.

exsuscitō, -āre *vt* to wake up; (*fire*) to fan; (*mind*) to excite.

exta, -ōrum *ntpl* internal organs.

extābēscō, -ēscere, -uī *vi* to waste away; to vanish.

extāris *adj* sacrificial.

extemplō *adv* immediately, on the

spur of the moment; **quom ~ as
soon as.**

extemporālis *adj* extempore.

extempulō *see* **extemplō.**

extendō, -dere, -dī, -tum *and*
extēnsum *vt* to stretch out,
spread, extend; to enlarge,
increase; (*time*) to prolong; **sē ~
exert oneself; īre per ~tum fūnem**
walk the tightrope.

extēnsus *ppp of* **extendō.**

extentō, -āre *vt* to strain, exert.

extentus *ppp of* **extendō** ♦ *adj*
broad.

extenuātiō, -ōnis *f* (RHET)
diminution.

extenuō, -āre, -āvī, -ātum *vt* to
thin out, rarefy; to diminish,
weaken.

exter *adj* from outside; foreign.

exterebrō, -āre *vt* to bore out; to
extort.

extergeō, -gēre, -sī, -sum *vt* to
wipe off, clean; to plunder.

exterior, -ōris *adj* outer, exterior.

exterius *adv* on the outside.

exterminō, -āre *vt* to drive out,
banish; (*fig*) to put aside.

externus *adj* outward, external;
foreign, strange.

exterō, -erere, -rīvī, -rītum *vt* to
rub out, wear away.

exterreō, -ēre, -uī, -itum *vt* to
frighten.

extersus *ppp of* **extergeō.**

exterus *see* **exter.**

extexō, -ere *vt* to unweave; (*fig*) to
cheat.

extimēscō, -ēscere, -uī *vi* to be
very frightened ♦ *vt* to be very
afraid of.

extimus *adj* outermost, farthest.

extin- *etc see* **exstin-**

extispex, -icis *m* diviner.

extollō, -ere *vt* to lift up, raise; (*fig*)

to exalt, beautify; (*time*) to defer.

extorqueō, -quēre, -sī, -tum *vt* to
wrench out, wrest; to dislocate;
(*fig*) to obtain by force, extort.

extorris, -e *adj* banished, in exile.

extortor, -ōris *m* extorter.

extortus *ppp of* **extorqueō.**

extrā *adv* outside; **~ quam** except
that, unless ♦ *prep* (*with acc*)
outside, beyond; free from;
except.

extrahō, -here, -xī, -ctum *vt* to
draw out, pull out; to extricate,
rescue; to remove; (*time*) to
prolong, waste.

extrāneus, -ī *m* stranger ♦ *adj*
external, foreign.

extraōrdinārius *adj* special,
unusual.

extrārius *adj* external; unrelated
♦ *m* stranger.

extrēmitās, -ātis *f* extremity, end.

extrēmum, -ī *nt* end; **ad ~** at last.

extrēmum *adv* for the last time.

extrēmus *adj* outermost, extreme;
last; utmost, greatest, meanest.

extrīcō, -āre, -āvī, -ātum *vt* to
disentangle, extricate; to clear
up.

extrīnsecus *adv* from outside,
from abroad; on the outside.

extrītus *ppp of* **exterō.**

extrūdō, -dere, -sī, -sum *vt* to
drive out; to keep out; (*sale*) to
push.

extulī *perf of* **efferō.**

extumeō, -ēre *vi* to swell up.

extundō, -undere, -udī, -ūsum *vt*
to beat out, hammer out; (*comedy*)
to extort; (*fig*) to form, compose.

exturbō, -āre, -āvī, -ātum *vt* to
drive out, throw out, knock out;
(*wife*) to put away; (*fig*) to banish,
disturb.

exūberō *vi* to abound.

*The present infinitive verb endings are as follows: -āre = 1st; -ēre = 2nd; -ere = 3rd and
-īre = 4th. See sections on irregular verbs and noun declensions.*

exul *etc see* **exsul.**

exulcerō, -āre, -āvī, -ātum *vt* to aggravate.

exululō, -āre *vi* to howl wildly ♦ *vt* to invoke with cries.

exūnctus *ppp of* **exungō.**

exundō, -āre *vi* to overflow; to be washed up.

exungō, -ere *vt* to anoint liberally.

exuō, -uere, -uī, -ūtum *vt* to draw out, put off; to lay aside; to strip.

exūrō, -rere, -ssī, -stum *vt* to burn up; to dry up; to burn out; (*fig*) to inflame.

exūstiō, -ōnis *f* conflagration.

exūtus *ppp of* **exuō.**

exuviae, -ārum *fpl* clothing, arms; hide; spoils.

F

faba, -ae *f* bean.

fabālis *adj* bean- (*in cpds*).

fābella, -ae *f* short story, fable; play.

faber, -rī *m* craftsman (*in metal, stone, wood*), tradesman, smith; (*MIL*) artisan; ~ **ferrārius** blacksmith; ~ **tignārius** carpenter ♦ *adj* skilful.

Fabius, -ī *m* Roman family name (*esp Q F Maximus Cunctator, dictator against Hannibal*).

Fabius, -iānus *adj see* n.

fabrē *adv* skilfully.

fabrēfaciō, -facere, -fēcī, -factum *vt* to make, build, forge.

fabrica, -ae *f* art, trade; work of art; workshop; (*comedy*) trick.

fabricātiō, -ōnis *f* structure.

fabricator, -ōris *m* artificer.

Fabricius, -ī *m* Roman family name (*esp C F Luscinus, incorruptible commander against Pyrrhus*).

Fabricius, -iānus *adj see* n.

fabricō, -āre; -or, -ārī, -ātus *vt* to make, build, forge.

fabrīlis *adj* artificer's ♦ *ntpl* tools.

fābula, -ae *f* story; common talk; play, drama; fable; ~**ae**! nonsense!; **lupus in ~ā** ≈ talk of the devil!

fābulor, -ārī, -ātus *vi* to talk, converse ♦ *vt* to say, invent.

fābulōsus *adj* legendary.

facessō, -ere, -īvī, -ītum *vt* to perform, carry out; to cause (trouble) ♦ *vi* to go away, retire.

facētē *adv* humorously; brilliantly.

facētiae, -ārum *fpl* wit, clever talk, humour.

facētus *adj* witty, humorous; fine, genteel, elegant.

faciēs, -ēī *f* form, shape; face, looks; appearance, aspect, character.

facile *adv* easily; unquestionably; readily; pleasantly.

facilis *adj* easy; well-suited; ready, quick; (*person*) good-natured, approachable; (*fortune*) prosperous.

facilitās, -ātis *f* ease, readiness; (*speech*) fluency; (*person*) good nature, affability.

facinorōsus *adj* criminal.

facinus, -oris *nt* deed, action; crime.

faciō, -ere, fēcī, factum (*imp* **fac**, *pass* **fīō**) *vt* to make, create, compose, cause; to do, perform; (*profession*) to practise; (*property*) to put under; (*value*) to regard, think of; (*words*) to represent, pretend, suppose ♦ *vi* to do, act; (*religion*) to offer sacrifice; (*with* **ad** *or* **dat**) to be of use; **cōpiam ~** afford an opportunity; **damnum ~** suffer loss; **metum ~** excite fear; **proelium ~** join battle; **rem ~** make money; **verba ~** talk; **māgnī ~** think highly of; **quid tibi faciam?** how am I to answer you?; **quid tē faciam?** what am I to do

with you?; **fac sciam** let me know;
fac potuisse suppose one could
have.

factiō, -ōnis f making, doing;
group, party, faction (*esp in politics
and chariot racing*).

factiōsus *adj* factious,
oligarchical.

factitō, -āre, -āvi, -ātum *vt* to keep
making or doing; to practise; to
declare (to be).

factor, -ōris m (*sport*) batsman.

factum, -ī nt deed, exploit.

factus *ppp of* **faciō**.

facula, -ae f little torch.

facultās, -ātis f means,
opportunity; ability; abundance,
supply, resources.

fācundē *adv see* **fācundus**.

fācundia, -ae f eloquence.

fācundus *adj* fluent, eloquent.

faeceus *adj* impure.

faecula, -ae f wine lees.

faenebris *adj* of usury.

faenerātiō, -ōnis f usury.

faenerātō *adv* with interest.

faenerātor, -ōris m moneylender.

faenerō, -āre; -or, -ārī, -ātus *vt* to
lend at interest; to ruin with
usury; (*fig*) to trade in.

faenīlia, -um *ntpl* hayloft.

faenum, -ī nt hay; **~ habet in cornū**
he is dangerous.

faenus, -oris nt interest; capital
lent at interest; (*fig*) profit,
advantage.

faenusculum, -ī nt a little interest.

Faesulae, -ārum *fpl* town in
Etruria (*now Fiesole*).

Faesulānus *adj see n.*

faex, faecis f sediment, lees; brine
(of pickles); (*fig*) dregs.

fāgineus, fāginus *adj* of beech.

fāgus, -ī f beech.

fala, -ae f siege tower, used in

assaults; (*Circus*) pillar.

falārica, -ae f a missile, firebrand.

falcārius, -ī *and* **iī** m sicklemaker.

falcātus *adj* scythed; sickle-
shaped.

falcifer, -ī *adj* scythe-carrying.

Falernus *adj* Falernian (*of a district
in N. Campania famous for its wine*)
♦ *nt* Falernian wine.

Faliscī, -ōrum *mpl* a people of S.E.
Etruria (*with chief town Falerii*).

Faliscus *adj see n.*

fallācia, -ae f trick, deception.

fallāciter *adv see* **fallāx**.

fallāx, -ācis *adj* deceitful,
deceptive.

fallō, -lere, fefellī, -sum *vt* to
deceive, cheat, beguile; to
disappoint, fail, betray; (*promise*)
to break; to escape the notice of,
be unknown to; (*pass*) to be
mistaken; **mē ~lit** I am mistaken;
I do not know.

falsē *adv* wrongly, by mistake;
fraudulently.

falsidicus *adj* lying.

falsificus *adj* deceiving.

falsiiūrius *adj* perjurious.

falsiloquus *adj* lying.

falsiparēns, -entis *adj* with a
pretended father.

falsō *adv see* **falsē**.

falsus *ppp of* **fallō** ♦ *adj* false,
mistaken; deceitful; forged,
falsified; sham, fictitious ♦ *nt*
falsehood, error.

falx, falcis f sickle, scythe; pruning
hook; (*MIL*) siege hook.

fāma, -ae f talk, rumour, tradition;
public opinion; reputation, fame;
infamy.

fāmēlicus *adj* hungry.

famēs, -is f hunger; famine; (*fig*)
greed; (*RHET*) poverty of
expression.

fāmigerātiō, -ōnis f rumour.

fāmigerātor, -ōris m telltale.

familia, -ae f domestics, slaves of a household; family property, estate; family, house; school, sect; **pater ~ās** master of a household; **~am dūcere** be head of a sect, company *etc.*

familiāris adj domestic, household, family; intimate, friendly; (*entrails*) relating to the sacrificer ♦ m servant; friend.

familiāritās, -ātis f intimacy, friendship.

familiāriter adv on friendly terms.

fāmōsus adj celebrated; infamous; slanderous.

famula, -ae f maidservant, handmaid.

famulāris adj of servants.

famulātus, -ūs m slavery.

famulor, -ārī vi to serve.

famulus, -ī m servant, attendant ♦ adj serviceable.

fānāticus adj inspired; frantic, frenzied.

fandī gerund of **for.**

fandum, -ī nt right.

fānum, -ī nt sanctuary temple.

fār, farris nt spelt; corn; meal.

farciō, -cīre, -sī, -tum vt to stuff, fill full.

farīna, -ae f meal, flour.

farrāgō, -inis f mash, hotch-potch; medley.

farrātus adj of corn; filled with corn.

farsī perf of **farciō.**

fartem, -im f acc filling; mincemeat.

fartor, -ōris m fattener, poulterer.

fartus ppp of **farciō.**

fās nt divine law; right; **~ est** it is lawful, possible.

fascia, -ae f band, bandage; streak of cloud.

fasciculus, -ī m bundle, packet.

fascinō, -āre vt to bewitch, (*esp with the evil eye*).

fascinum, -ī nt, **-us, -ī** m charm.

fasciola, -ae f small bandage.

fascis, -is m bundle, faggot; soldier's pack, burden; (*pl*) rods and axe carried before the highest magistrates; high office (*esp the consulship*).

fassus ppa of **fateor.**

fāstī, -ōrum mpl register of days for legal and public business; calendar; registers of magistrates and other public records.

fastīdiō, -īre, -iī, -ītum vt to loathe, dislike, despise ♦ vi to feel squeamish, be disgusted; to be disdainful.

fastīdiōsē adv squeamishly; disdainfully.

fastīdiōsus adj squeamish, disgusted; fastidious, nice; disagreeable.

fastīdium, -ī and **iī** nt squeamishness, distaste; disgust, aversion; disdain, pride.

fastīgātē adv in a sloping position.

fastīgātus adj sloping up or down.

fastīgium, -ī and **iī** nt gable, pediment; slope; height, depth; top, summit; (*fig*) highest degree; acme, dignity; (*speech*) main headings.

fāstus adj lawful for public business.

fastus, -ūs m disdain, pride.

Fāta ntpl the Fates.

fātālis adj fateful, destined; fatal, deadly.

fātāliter adv by fate.

fateor, -tērī, -ssus vt to confess, acknowledge; to reveal, bear witness to.

fāticanus, -inus adj prophetic.

fātidicus adj prophetic ♦ m prophet.

fātifer, -ī adj deadly.
fatigātiō, -ōnis f weariness.
fatīgō, -āre, -āvī, -ātum vt to tire, exhaust; to worry, importune; to wear down, torment.
fātiloqua, -ae f prophetess.
fatīscō, -ere; -or, -ī vi to crack, split; (fig) to become exhausted.
fatuitās, -ātis f silliness.
fātum, -ī nt divine word, oracle; fate, destiny; divine will; misfortune, doom, death; **~ō obīre** die a natural death.
fātur, fātus 3rd pers, ppa of **for**.
fatuus adj silly; unwieldy ♦ m fool.
faucēs, -ium fpl throat; pass, narrow channel, chasm; (fig) jaws.
Faunus, -ī m father of Latinus (god of forests and herdsmen, identified with Pan); (pl) woodland spirits, Fauns.
faustē adv see **faustus**.
faustitās, -ātis f good fortune, fertility.
faustus adj auspicious, lucky.
fautor, -ōris m supporter, patron.
fautrīx, -īcis f protectress.
favea, -ae f pet slave.
faveō, -ēre, fāvī, fautum vi (with dat) to favour, befriend, support; **~ linguīs** keep silence.
favilla, -ae f embers, ashes; (fig) spark.
favitor etc see **fautor**.
Favōnius, -ī m west wind, zephyr.
favor, -ōris m favour, support; applause.
favōrābilis adj in favour; pleasing.
favus, -ī m honeycomb.
fax, facis f torch, wedding torch, funeral torch; marriage, death; (ASTRO) meteor; (fig) flame, fire, instigator; guide; **facem praeferre** act as guide.
faxim, faxō old subj and fut of **faciō**.

febrīcula, -ae f slight fever.
febris, -is f fever.
Februārius, -ī m February ♦ adj of February.
februum, -ī nt purification; **Februa** pl festival of purification in February.
fēcī perf of **faciō**.
fēcunditās, -ātis f fertility; (style) exuberance.
fēcundō, -āre vt to fertilise.
fēcundus adj fertile, fruitful; fertilising; (fig) abundant, rich, prolific.
fefellī perf of **fallō**.
fel, fellis nt gall bladder, bile; poison; (fig) animosity.
fēlēs, -is f cat.
fēlīcitās, -ātis f happiness, good luck.
fēlīciter adv abundantly; favourably; happily.
fēlīx, -īcis adj fruitful; auspicious, favourable; fortunate, successful.
fēmella, -ae f girl.
fēmina, -ae f female, woman.
fēmineus adj woman's, of women; unmanly.
femur, -oris and inis nt thigh.
fēn- etc see **faen-**.
fenestra, -ae f window; (fig) loophole.
fera, -ae f wild beast.
ferācius adv more fruitfully.
fērālis adj funereal; of the Feralia, deadly ♦ ntpl festival of the dead in February.
ferāx, -ācis adj fruitful, productive.
ferbuī perf of **ferveō**.
ferculum, -ī nt litter, barrow; dish, course.
ferē adv almost, nearly, about; quite, just; usually, generally, as a rule; (with neg) hardly; **nihil ~** hardly anything.

The present infinitive verb endings are as follows: -āre = 1st; -ēre = 2nd; -ere = 3rd and -īre = 4th. See sections on irregular verbs and noun declensions.

ferentārius, -ī *and* **iī** m a light-
armed soldier.

Feretrius, -ī m *an epithet of Jupiter.*

feretrum, -ī nt bier.

fēriae, -ārum fpl festival, holidays;
(*fig*) peace, rest.

fēriātus adj on holiday, idle.

ferīnus adj of wild beasts ♦ f game.

feriō, -īre vt to strike, hit; to kill,
sacrifice; (*comedy*) to cheat;
foedus ~ conclude a treaty.

feritās, -ātis f wildness, savagery.

fermē *see* **ferē.**

fermentum, -ī nt yeast; beer; (*fig*)
passion, vexation.

ferō, ferre, tulī, lātum vt to carry,
bring, bear; to bring forth,
produce; to move, stir, raise; to
carry off, sweep away, plunder;
(*pass*) to rush, hurry, fly, flow,
drift; (*road*) to lead; (*trouble*) to
endure, suffer, sustain; (*feelings*)
to exhibit, show; (*speech*) to talk
about, give out, celebrate;
(*bookkeeping*) to enter; (*CIRCS*) to
allow, require; **sē ~** rush, move;
profess to be, boast; **condiciōnem,
lēgem ~** propose terms, a law;
iūdicem ~ sue; **sententiam,
suffrāgium ~** vote; **signa ~** march;
attack; **aegrē, graviter ~** be
annoyed at; **laudibus ~** extol; **in
oculīs ~** be very fond of; **prae sē ~**
show, declare; **fertur, ferunt** it is
said, they say; **ut mea fert opiniō**
in my opinion.

ferōcia, -ae f courage; spirit,
pride, presumption.

ferōcitās, -ātis f high spirits,
aggressiveness; presumption.

ferōciter adv bravely; insolently.

Fērōnia, -ae f old Italian goddess.

ferōx, -ōcis adj warlike, spirited,
daring; proud, insolent.

ferrāmentum, -ī nt tool, implement.

ferrārius adj of iron; **faber ~**

blacksmith ♦ f iron-mine, iron-
works.

ferrātus adj ironclad, ironshod
♦ mpl men in armour.

ferreus adj of iron, iron; (*fig*) hard,
cruel; strong, unyielding.

ferrūgineus adj rust-coloured,
dark.

ferrūgō, -inis f rust; dark colour;
gloom.

ferrum, -ī nt iron; sword; any iron
implement; force of arms; **~ et
ignis** devastation.

fertilis adj fertile, productive;
fertilising.

fertilitās, -ātis f fertility.

ferula, -ae f fennel; staff, rod.

ferus adj wild; uncivilised, cruel
♦ m beast.

fervēfaciō, -ere, -tum vt to boil.

fervēns, -entis pres p of **ferveō**
♦ adj hot; raging; (*fig*) impetuous,
furious.

ferventer adv hotly.

ferveō, -vēre, -buī vi to boil, burn;
(*fig*) to rage, bustle, be agitated.

fervēscō, -ere vi to boil up, grow
hot.

fervidus adj hot, raging; (*fig*) fiery,
violent.

fervō, -vere, -vī vi *see* **ferveō.**

fervor, -ōris m seething; heat; (*fig*)
ardour, passion.

Fescenninus adj Fescennine (*a kind
of ribald song, perhaps from
Fescennium in Etruria*).

fessus adj tired, worn out.

fēstīnanter adv hastily.

fēstīnātiō, -ōnis f haste, hurry.

fēstīnō, -āre vi to hurry, be quick
♦ vt to hasten, accelerate.

fēstīnus adj hasty, quick.

fēstīvē adv gaily; humorously.

fēstīvitās, -ātis f gaiety,
merriment; humour, fun.

fēstīvus adj gay, jolly; delightful;
(*speech*) humorous.

festūca, -ae f rod (*with which slaves were manumitted*).

festus adj festal, on holiday ♦ nt holiday; feast.

fētiālis, -is m priest who carried out the ritual in making war and peace.

fētūra, -ae f breeding; brood.

fētus adj pregnant; newly delivered; (*fig*) productive, full of.

fētus, -ūs m breeding, bearing, producing; brood, young; fruit, produce; (*fig*) production.

fiber, -rī m beaver.

fibra, -ae f fibre; section of lung or liver; entrails.

fibula, -ae f clasp, brooch; clamp.

ficēdula, -ae f fig pecker.

fictē adv falsely.

fictilis adj clay, earthen ♦ nt jar; clay figure.

fictor, -ōris m sculptor; maker, inventor.

fictrīx, -īcis f maker.

fictūra, -ae f shaping, invention.

fictus ppp of **fingō** ♦ adj false, fictitious ♦ nt falsehood.

ficulnus adj of the fig tree.

fīcus, -ī and **ūs** f fig tree; fig.

fidēle adv faithfully, surely, firmly.

fidēlia, -ae f pot, pail; **de eādem ~ā duōs parietēs dealbāre** = kill two birds with one stone.

fidēlis adj faithful, loyal; trustworthy, sure.

fidēlitās, -ātis f faithfulness, loyalty.

fidēliter adv faithfully, surely, firmly.

Fidēnae, -ārum fpl ancient Latin town.

Fidēnās, -ātis adj see n.

fīdēns, -entis pres p of **fīdō** ♦ adj bold, resolute.

fīdenter adv see **fīdens**.

fīdentia, -ae f self-confidence.

fidēs, -eī f trust, faith, belief; trustworthiness, honour, loyalty, truth; promise, assurance, word; guarantee, safe-conduct, protection; (*comm*) credit; (*law*) good faith; (*~ mala* dishonesty; **rēs ~que** entire resources; **~em facere** convince; **~em servāre ergā** keep faith with; **dī vostram ~em!** for Heaven's sake!; **ex fidē bonā** in good faith.

fidēs, -is f (*usu pl*) stringed instrument, lyre, lute; (*astro*) Lyra.

fīdī perf of **findō**.

fidicen, -inis m musician; lyric poet.

fidicina, -ae f music girl.

fidicula, -ae f small lute.

Fidius, -ī m an epithet of Jupiter.

fīdō, -dere, -sus vi (*with dat or abl*) to trust, rely on.

fidūcia, -ae f confidence, assurance; self-confidence; (*law*) trust, security.

fidūciārius adj to be held in trust.

fīdus adj trusty, reliable; sure, safe.

fīgō, -gere, -xī, -xum vt to fix, fasten, attach; to drive in, pierce; (*speech*) to taunt.

figulāris adj a potter's.

figulus, -ī m potter; builder.

figūra, -ae f shape, form; nature, kind; phantom; (*rhet*) figure of speech.

figūrō, -āre vt to form, shape.

fīlātim adv thread by thread.

fīlia, -ae f daughter.

fīlicātus adj with fern patterns.

fīliola, -ae f little daughter.

fīliolus, -ī m little son.

fīlius, -ī and **iī** m son; **terrae ~** a nobody.

filix, -cis f fern.

The present infinitive verb endings are as follows: -āre = 1st; -ēre = 2nd; -ere = 3rd and -īre = 4th. See sections on irregular verbs and noun declensions.

filum, **-ī** *nt* thread; band of wool, fillet; string, shred, wick; contour, shape; (*speech*) texture, quality.

fimbriae, **-ārum** *fpl* fringe, end.

fimus, **-ī** *m* dung; dirt.

findō, **-ndere**, **-dī**, **-ssum** *vt* to split, divide; to burst.

fingō, **-ere**, **finxī**, **fictum** *vt* to form, shape, make; to mould, model; to dress, arrange; to train; (*mind, speech*) to imagine, suppose, represent, sketch; to invent, fabricate; **vultum ~** compose the features.

finiō, **-īre**, **-īvī**, **-ītum** *vt* to bound, limit; to restrain; to prescribe, define, determine; to end, finish, complete ♦ *vi* to finish, die.

fīnis, **-is** *m* (*occ f*) boundary, border; (*pl*) territory; bound, limit; end; death; highest point, summit; aim, purpose; **~ bonōrum** the chief good; **quem ad ~em?** how long?; **~e genūs** up to the knee.

fīnītē *adv* within limits.

fīnitimus *adj* neighbouring, adjoining; akin, like ♦ *mpl* neighbours.

fīnītor, **-ōris** *m* surveyor.

fīnitumus *adj see* **fīnitimus**.

fīnītus *ppp of* **fīniō** ♦ *adj* (*RHET*) well-rounded.

fīnxī *perf of* **fingō**.

fīō, **fierī**, **factus** *vi* to become, arise; to be made, be done; to happen; **quī fit ut?** how is it that?; **ut fit** as usually happens; **quid mē fīet?** what will become of me?

firmāmen, **-inis** *nt* support.

firmāmentum, **-ī** *nt* support, strengthening; (*fig*) mainstay.

firmātor, **-ōris** *m* establisher.

firmē *adv* powerfully, steadily.

firmitās, **-ātis** *f* firmness, strength; steadfastness, stamina.

firmiter *adv see* **firmē**.

firmitūdō, **-inis** *f* strength, stability.

firmō, **-āre**, **-āvī**, **-ātum** *vt* to strengthen, support, fortify; (*mind*) to encourage, steady; (*fact*) to confirm, prove, assert.

firmus *adj* strong, stable, firm; (*fig*) powerful, constant, sure, true.

fiscella, **-ae** *f* wicker basket.

fiscina, **-ae** *f* wicker basket.

fiscus, **-ī** *m* purse, moneybox; public exchequer; imperial treasury, the emperor's privy purse.

fissilis *adj* easy to split.

fissiō, **-ōnis** *f* dividing.

fissum, **-ī** *nt* slit, fissure.

fissus *ppp of* **findō**.

fistūca, **-ae** *f* rammer.

fistula, **-ae** *f* pipe, tube; panpipes; (*MED*) ulcer.

fistulātor, **-ōris** *m* panpipe player.

fīsus *ppa of* **fīdō**.

fīxī *perf of* **fīgō**.

fīxus *ppp of* **fīgō** ♦ *adj* fixed, fast, permanent.

flābellifera, **-ae** *f* fanbearer.

flābellum, **-ī** *nt* fan.

flābilis *adj* airy.

flābra, **-ōrum** *ntpl* blasts, gusts; wind.

flacceō, **-ēre** *vi* to flag, lose heart.

flaccēscō, **-ere** *vi* to flag, droop.

flaccidus *adj* flabby, feeble.

flaccus *adj* flap-eared.

Flaccus, **-ī** *m* surname of Horace.

flagellō, **-āre** *vt* to whip, lash.

flagellum, **-ī** *nt* whip, lash; strap, thong; (*vine*) shoot; (*polyp*) arm; (*feelings*) sting.

flāgitātiō, **-ōnis** *f* demand.

flāgitātor, **-ōris** *m* demander, dun.

flāgitiōsē *adv* infamously.

flāgitiōsus *adj* disgraceful, profligate.

flāgitium, **-ī** and **iī** *nt* offence, disgrace, shame; scoundrel.

flāgitō, -āre, -āvī, -ātum vt to demand, importune, dun; (law) to summon.

flagrāns, -antis pres p of **flagrō ♦** adj hot, blazing; brilliant; passionate.

flagranter adv passionately.

flagrantia, -ae f blazing; (fig) shame.

flagrō, -āre vi to blaze, burn, be on fire; (feelings) to be excited, be inflamed; (ill-will) to be the victim of.

flagrum, -ī nt whip, lash.

flāmen, -inis m priest of a particular deity.

flāmen, -inis nt blast, gale, wind.

flāminica, -ae f wife of a priest.

Flāminīnus, -ī m Roman surname (esp the conqueror of Philip V of Macedon).

flāminium, -ī and **iī** nt priesthood.

Flāminius, -ī m Roman family name (esp the consul defeated by Hannibal).

Flāminius, -iānus adj; **Via -ia** road from Rome N.E. to Ariminum.

flamma, -ae f flame, fire; torch, star; fiery colour, (fig) passion; danger, disaster.

flammeolum, -ī nt bridal veil.

flammēscō, -ere vi to become fiery.

flammeus adj fiery, blazing; flame-coloured **♦** nt bridal veil.

flammifer, -ī adj fiery.

flammō, -āre, -āvī, -ātum vi to blaze **♦** vt to set on fire, burn; (fig) to inflame, incense.

flammula, -ae f little flame.

flātus, -ūs m blowing, breath; breeze; (fig) arrogance.

flāvēns, -entis adj yellow, golden.

flāvēscō, -ere vi to turn yellow.

Flāviānus adj see n.

Flāvius, -ī m Roman family name

(esp the emperors Vespasian, Titus and Domitian).

flāvus adj yellow, golden.

flēbilis adj lamentable; tearful, mournful.

flēbiliter adv see **flēbilis**.

flectō, -ctere, -xī, -xum vt to bend, turn; to turn aside, wheel; (promontory) to round; (mind) to direct, persuade, dissuade **♦** vi to turn, march.

fleō, -ēre, -ēvī, -ētum vi to weep, cry **♦** vt to lament, mourn for.

flētus, -ūs m weeping, tears.

flexanimus adj moving.

flexī perf of **flectō**.

flexibilis adj pliant, flexible; fickle.

flexilis adj pliant.

flexiloquus adj ambiguous.

flexiō, -ōnis f bending, winding; (voice) modulation.

flexipēs, -edis adj twining.

flexuōsus adj tortuous.

flexūra, -ae f bending.

flexus ppp of **flectō ♦** adj winding.

flexus, -ūs m winding, bending; change.

flīctus, -ūs m collision.

flō, -āre, -āvī, -ātum vt, vi to blow; (money) to coin.

floccus, -ī m bit of wool, triviality; **-ī nōn faciō** ≈ I don't care a straw for.

Flōra, -ae f goddess of flowers.

Flōrālis adj see n.

flōrēns, -entis pres p of **flōreō ♦** adj in bloom, bright; prosperous, flourishing.

flōreō, -ēre, -uī vi to blossom, flower; (age) to be in one's prime; (wine) to froth; (fig) to flourish, prosper; (places) to be gay with.

flōrēscō, -ere vi to begin to flower; to grow prosperous.

flōreus adj of flowers, flowery.

flōridulus adj pretty, little.

flōridus adj of flowers, flowery; fresh, pretty; (style) florid, ornate.

flōrifer, -ī adj flowery.

flōrilegus adj flower-sipping.

flōrus adj beautiful.

flōs, -ōris m flower, blossom; (wine) bouquet; (age) prime, heyday; (youth) downy beard, youthful innocence; (fig) crown, glory; (speech) ornament.

flōsculus, -ī m little flower; (fig) pride, ornament.

flūctifragus adj surging.

flūctuātiō, -ōnis f wavering.

flūctuō, -āre vi to toss, wave; (fig) to rage, swell, waver.

flūctuōsus adj stormy.

flūctus, -ūs m wave; flowing, flood; (fig) disturbance; ~ūs (pl) in simpulō ≈ a storm in a teacup.

fluēns, -entis pres p of fluō ♦ adj lax, loose, enervated; (speech) fluent.

fluenta, -ōrum ntpl stream, flood.

fluenter adv in a flowing manner.

fluentisonus adj wave-echoing.

fluidus adj flowing, fluid; lax, soft; relaxing.

fluitō, -āre vi to flow, float about; to wave, flap, move unsteadily; (fig) to waver.

flūmen, -inis nt stream, river; (fig) flood, flow, fluency; adversō ~ine upstream; secundō ~ine downstream.

flūmineus adj river- (in cpds).

fluō, -ere, -xī, -xum vi to flow; to overflow, drip; (fig) to fall in, fall away, vanish; (speech) to run evenly; (CIRCS) to proceed, tend.

flūtō etc see **fluitō**.

fluviālis adj river- (in cpds).

fluviātilis adj river- (in cpds).

flūvidus etc see **fluidus**.

fluvius, -ī and **iī** m river, stream.

fluxī perf of **fluō**.

fluxus adj flowing, loose, leaky; (person) lax, dissolute; (thing) frail, fleeting, unreliable.

fōcāle, -is nt scarf.

foculus, -ī m stove, fire.

focus, -ī m hearth, fireplace; pyre, altar; (fig) home.

fodicō, -āre vt to nudge, jog.

fodiō, -ere, fōdī, fossum vt to dig; to prick, stab; (fig) to goad.

foedē adv see **foedus**.

foederātus adj confederated.

foedifragus adj perfidious.

foedītās, -ātis f foulness, hideousness.

foedō, -āre, -āvī, -ātum vt to mar, disfigure; to disgrace, sully.

foedus adj foul, hideous, revolting; vile, disgraceful.

foedus, -eris nt treaty, league; agreement, compact; law.

foen- etc see **faen-**.

foeteō, -ēre vi to stink.

foetidus adj stinking.

foetor, -ōris m stench.

foetu- etc see **fētu-**.

foliātum, -ī nt nard oil.

folium, -ī and **iī** nt leaf.

folliculus, -ī m small bag; eggshell.

follis, -is m bellows; punchball; purse.

fōmentum, -ī nt poultice, bandage; (fig) alleviation.

fōmes, -itis m tinder, kindling.

fōns, fontis m spring, source; water; (fig) origin, fountainhead.

fontānus adj spring- (in cpds).

fonticulus, -ī m little spring.

for, fārī, fātus vt, vi to speak, utter.

forābilis adj penetrable.

forāmen, -inis nt hole, opening.

forās adv out, outside.

forceps, -ipis m/f tongs, forceps.

forda, -ae f cow in calf.

fore, forem fut infin, imperf subj of **sum**.

forēnsis adj public, forensic; of the

marketplace.

foris, -is f (usu pl) door; (fig) opening, entrance.

foris adv out of doors, outside, abroad; from outside, from abroad; ~ **cēnāre** dine out.

fōrma, -ae f form, shape, appearance; mould, stamp, last; (person) beauty; (fig) idea, nature, kind.

fōrmāmentum, -ī nt shape.

fōrmātūra, -ae f shaping.

Formiae, -ārum fpl town in S. Latium.

Formiānus adj of Formiae ♦ nt villa at Formiae.

formīca, -ae f ant.

formīcinus adj crawling.

formīdābilis adj terrifying.

formīdō, -āre, -āvī, -ātum vt, vi to fear, be terrified.

formīdō, -inis f terror, awe, horror; scarecrow.

formīdolōsē adv see **formīdolōsus**.

formīdolōsus adj fearful, terrifying; afraid.

fōrmō, -āre, -āvī, -ātum vt to shape, fashion, form.

fōrmōsitās, -ātis f beauty.

fōrmōsus adj beautiful, handsome.

fōrmula, -ae f rule, regulation; (law) procedure, formula; (PHILOS) principle.

fornācula, -ae f small oven.

fornāx, -ācis f furnace, oven, kiln.

fornicātus adj arched.

fornix, -icis m arch, vault; brothel.

forō, -āre vt to pierce.

Foroiūliēnsis adj see **Forum Iuli**.

fors, fortis f chance, luck ♦ adv perchance; ~**te** by chance, as it happened; perhaps; nē ~**te** in case; sī ~**te** if perhaps; in the hope that.

forsan, forsit, forsitan adv

perhaps.

fortasse, -is adv perhaps, possibly; (irony) very likely.

forticulus adj quite brave.

fortis adj strong, sturdy; brave, manly, resolute.

fortiter adv vigorously; bravely.

fortitūdō, -inis f courage, resolution; strength.

fortuītō adv by chance.

fortuītus adj casual, accidental.

fortūna, -ae f chance, luck, fortune; good luck, success; misfortune; circumstances, lot; (pl) possessions; ~**ae fīlius** Fortune's favourite; ~**am habēre** be successful.

fortūnātē adv see **fortūnātus**.

fortūnātus adj happy, lucky; well off, rich, blessed.

fortūnō, -āre vt to bless, prosper.

forulī, -ōrum mpl bookcase.

forum, -ī nt public place, market; market town; Roman Forum between the Palatine and Capitol; public affairs, law courts, business; ~ **boārium** cattle market; ~ **olitōrium** vegetable market; ~ **piscātōrium** fish market; ~ **agere** hold an assize; ~ **attingere** enter public life; **cēdere ~ō** go bankrupt; **utī ~ō** take advantage of a situation.

Forum Iūlī colony in S. Gaul (now Fréjus).

forus, -ī m gangway; block of seats; (bees) cell frame.

fossa, -ae f ditch, trench.

fossiō, -ōnis f digging.

fossor, -ōris m digger.

fossus ppp of **fodiō**.

fōtus ppp of **foveō**.

fovea, -ae f pit, pitfall.

foveō, -ēre, fōvī, fōtum vt to warm, keep warm; (MED) to

The present infinitive verb endings are as follows: -āre = 1st; -ēre = 2nd; -ere = 3rd and -īre = 4th. See sections on irregular verbs and noun declensions.

frāctus 148 **frīgeō**

foment; to fondle, keep; *(fig)* to cherish, love, foster, pamper, encourage; **castra ~** remain in camp.

frāctus *ppp of* **frangō** ♦ *adj* weak, faint.

frāga, -ōrum *ntpl* strawberries.

fragilis *adj* brittle, fragile; frail, fleeting.

fragilitās, -ātis *f* frailness.

fragmen, -inis *nt (pl)* fragments, ruins, wreck.

fragmentum, -ī *nt* fragment, remnant.

fragor, -ōris *m* crash, din; disintegration.

fragōsus *adj* crashing, roaring, breakable; rough.

frāgrāns, -antis *adj* fragrant.

framea, -ae *f* German spear.

frangō, -angere, -ēgī, -āctum *vt* to break, shatter, wreck; to crush, grind; *(fig)* to break down, weaken, humble; *(emotion)* to touch, move; **cervicem ~** strangle.

frāter, -ris *m* brother; cousin; *(fig)* friend, ally.

frāterculus, -ī *m* brother.

frāternē *adv* like a brother.

frāternitās, -ātis *f* brotherhood.

frāternus *adj* brotherly, a brother's, fraternal.

frātricīda, -ae *m* fratricide.

fraudātiō, -ōnis *f* deceit, fraud.

fraudātor, -ōris *m* swindler.

fraudō, -āre, -āvī, -ātum *vt* to cheat, defraud; to steal, cancel.

fraudulentus *adj* deceitful, fraudulent.

fraus, -audis *f* deceit, fraud; delusion, error; offence, wrong; injury, damage; **lēgī ~dem facere** evade the law; **in ~dem incidere** be disappointed; **sine ~de** without harm.

fraxineus, fraxinus *adj* of ash.

fraxinus, -ī *f* ash tree; ashen spear.

Fregellae, -ārum *fpl town in S. Latium.*

Fregellānus *adj see* n.

frēgī *perf of* **frangō**.

fremebundus *adj* roaring.

fremitus, -ūs *m* roaring, snorting, noise.

fremō, -ere, -uī, -itum *vi* to roar, snort, grumble ♦ *vt* to shout for, complain.

fremor, -ōris *m* murmuring.

frendō, -ere *vi* to gnash the teeth.

frēnō, -āre, -āvī, -ātum *vt* to bridle; *(fig)* to curb, restrain.

frēnum, -ī *nt (pl* -a, -ōrum *nt,* -ī, -ōrum *m)* bridle, bit; *(fig)* curb, check; **~ōs dare** give vent to; **~um mordēre** ≈ take the bit between one's teeth.

frequēns, -entis *adj* crowded, numerous, populous; regular, repeated, frequent; **~ senātus** a crowded meeting of the senate.

frequentātiō, -ōnis *f* accumulation.

frequenter *adv* in large numbers; repeatedly, often.

frequentia, -ae *f* full attendance, throng, crowd.

frequentō, -āre, -āvī, -ātum *vt* to crowd, populate; to visit repeatedly, frequent; to repeat; *(festival)* to celebrate, keep.

fretēnsis *adj* of the Straits of Messina.

fretum, -ī *nt* strait; sea; *(fig)* violence; **~ Siciliēnse** Straits of Messina.

fretus, -ūs *m* strait.

frētus *adj* relying, confident.

fricō, -āre, -uī, -tum *vt* to rub, rub down.

frictus *ppp of* **frīgō**.

frīgefactō, -āre *vt* to cool.

frīgeō, -ēre *vi* to be cold; *(fig)* to be lifeless, flag; to be coldly received, fall flat.

frīgerāns *adj* cooling.

frīgēscō, -ere *vi* to grow cold; to become inactive.

frīgida, -ae *f* cold water.

frīgidē *adv* feebly.

frīgidulus *adj* rather cold, faint.

frīgidus *adj* cold, cool; chilling; (*fig*) dull, torpid; (*words*) flat, uninteresting.

frīgō, -gere, -xī, -ctum *vt* to roast, fry.

frīgus, -oris *nt* cold; cold weather, winter; death; (*fig*) dullness, inactivity; coldness, indifference.

friguttiō, -īre *vi* to stammer.

friō, -āre *vt* to crumble.

fritillus, -ī *m* dice box.

frīvolus *adj* empty, paltry.

frīxī *perf of* frīgō.

frondātor, -ōris *m* vinedresser, pruner.

frondeō, -ēre *vi* to be in leaf.

frondēscō, -ere *vi* to become leafy, shoot.

frondeus *adj* leafy.

frondifer, -ī *adj* leafy.

frondōsus *adj* leafy.

frōns, -ondis *f* leaf, foliage; garland of leaves.

frōns, -ontis *f* forehead, brow; front, facade; (*fig*) look, appearance, exterior; **~ontem contrahere** frown; **ā ~onte** in front; **in ~onte** in breadth.

frontālia, -um *ntpl* frontlet.

frontō, -ōnis *m* a broad-browed man.

frūctuārius *adj* productive; paid for out of produce.

frūctuōsus *adj* productive, profitable.

frūctus *ppa of* fruor.

frūctus, -ūs *m* enjoyment; revenue, income; produce, fruit; (*fig*) consequence, reward; **~uī**

esse be an asset (to); **~um percipere** reap the fruits (of).

frūgālis *adj* thrifty, worthy.

frūgālitās, -ātis *f* thriftiness, restraint.

frūgāliter *adv* temperately.

frūgēs *etc see* frūx.

frūgī *adj* (*indecl*) frugal, temperate, honest; useful.

frūgifer, -ī *adj* fruitful, fertile.

frūgiferēns, -entis *adj* fruitful.

frūgilegus *adj* food-gatherering.

frūgiparus *adj* fruitful.

frūmentārius *adj* of corn, corn- (*in cpds*) ♦ *m* corn dealer; **lēx ~a** law about the distribution of corn; **rēs ~a** commissariat.

frūmentātiō, -ōnis *f* foraging.

frūmentātor, -ōris *m* corn merchant, forager.

frūmentor, -ārī, -ātus *vi* to go foraging.

frūmentum, -ī *nt* corn, grain, (*pl*) crops.

frūniscor, -ī *vt* to enjoy.

fruor, -uī, -ūctus *vt, vi* (*usu with abl*) to enjoy, enjoy the company of; (*law*) to have the use and enjoyment of.

frūstillātim *adv* in little bits.

frūstrā *adv* in vain, for nothing; groundlessly; in error; **~ esse** be deceived; **~ habēre** foil.

frūstrāmen, -inis *nt* deception.

frūstrātiō, -ōnis *f* deception, frustration.

frūstrō, -āre; -or, -ārī, -ātus *vt* to deceive, trick.

frūstulentus *adj* full of crumbs.

frūstum, -ī *nt* bit, scrap.

frutex, -icis *m* bush, shrub; (*comedy*) blockhead.

fruticētum, -ī *nt* thicket.

fruticor, -ārī *vi* to sprout.

fruticōsus *adj* bushy.

The present infinitive verb endings are as follows: **-āre** = 1st; **-ēre** = 2nd; **-ere** = 3rd and **-īre** = 4th. *See sections on irregular verbs and noun declensions.*

frūx, -ūgis f, **-ūgēs, -ūgum** fruits of the earth, produce; (fig) reward, success; virtue; **sē ad ~ūgem bonam recipere** reform.

fuam old pres subj of **sum**.

fūcātus adj counterfeit, artificial.

fūcō, -āre, -āvī, -ātum vt to paint, dye (esp red).

fūcōsus adj spurious.

fūcus, -ī m red dye, rouge; bee glue; (fig) deceit, pretence.

fūcus, -ī m drone.

fūdī perf of **fundō**.

fuga, -ae f flight, rout; banishment; speed, swift passing; refuge; (fig) avoidance, escape; **~am facere, in ~am dare** put to flight.

fugācius adv more timidly.

fugāx, -ācis adj timorous, shy, fugitive; swift, transient; (with gen) avoiding.

fūgī perf of **fugiō**.

fugiēns, -entis pres p of **fugiō ♦** adj fleeting, dying; averse (to).

fugiō, -ere, fūgī, -itum vi to flee, run away, escape; to go into exile; (fig) to vanish, pass swiftly ♦ vt to flee from, escape from; to shun, avoid; (fig) to escape, escape notice of; **~e quaerere** do not ask; **mē ~it** I do not notice or know.

fugitīvus, -ī m runaway slave, truant, deserter ♦ adj fugitive.

fugitō, -āre vt to flee from, shun.

fugō, -āre, -āvī, -ātum vt to put to flight; to banish; to rebuff.

fulcīmen, -inis nt support.

fulciō, -cīre, -sī, -tum vt to prop, support; to strengthen, secure; (fig) to sustain, bolster up.

fulcrum, -ī nt bedpost; couch.

fulgeō, -gēre, -sī vi to flash, lighten; to shine; (fig) to be illustrious.

fulgidus adj flashing.

fulgō etc see **fulgeō**.

fulgor, -ōris m lightning; flash, brightness; (fig) splendour.

fulgur, -is nt lightning; thunderbolt; splendour.

fulgurālis adj on lightning as an omen.

fulgurātor, -ōris m interpreter of lightning.

fulgurītus adj struck by lightning.

fulgurō, -āre vi to lighten.

fulica, -ae f coot.

fūlīgō, -inis f soot; black paint.

fulix, -cis f see **fulica**.

fullō, -ōnis m fuller.

fullōnius adj fuller's.

fulmen, -inis nt thunderbolt; (fig) disaster.

fulmenta, -ae f heel of a shoe.

fulmineus adj of lightning; deadly.

fulminō, -āre vi to lighten; (fig) to threaten.

fulsī perf of **fulciō**; perf of **fulgeō**.

fultūra, -ae f support.

fultus ppp of **fulciō**.

Fulvia, -iae f wife of M. Antony.

Fulvius, -ī m Roman family name.

fulvus adj yellow, tawny, dun.

fūmeus adj smoking.

fūmidus adj smoky, smoking.

fūmifer, -ī adj smoking.

fūmificō, -āre vi to burn incense.

fūmificus adj steaming.

fūmō, -āre vi to smoke, steam.

fūmōsus adj smoky, smoked.

fūmus, -ī m smoke, steam.

fūnāle, -is nt cord; wax torch; chandelier.

fūnambulus, -ī m tightrope walker.

fūnctiō, -ōnis f performance.

fūnctus ppa of **fungor**.

fūnda, -ae f sling; dragnet.

fundāmen, -inis nt foundation.

fundāmentum, -ī nt foundation; **~a agere, iacere** lay the foundations.

Fundānus adj see **Fundī**.

fundātor, -ōris m founder.

Fundī, -ōrum mpl coast town in Latium.

funditō, -āre vt to sling.

funditor, -ōris m slinger.

funditus adv utterly, completely; at the bottom.

fundō, -āre, -āvī, -ātum vt to found; to secure; (fig) to establish, make secure.

fundō, -ere, fūdī, fūsum vt to pour, shed, spill; (metal) to cast; (solids) to hurl, scatter, shower; (MIL) to rout; (crops) to produce in abundance; (speech) to utter; (fig) to spread, extend.

fundus, -ī m bottom; farm, estate; (law) authorizer.

fūnebris adj funeral- (in cpds); murderous.

fūnerātus adj killed.

fūnereus adj funeral- (in cpds); fatal.

fūnestō, -āre vt to pollute with murder, desecrate.

fūnestus adj deadly, fatal; sorrowful, in mourning.

fungīnus adj of a mushroom.

fungor, -gī, fūnctus vt, vi (usu with abl) to perform, discharge, do; to be acted on.

fungus, -ī m mushroom, fungus; (candle) clot on the wick.

fūniculus, -ī m cord.

fūnis, -is m rope, rigging; **~em dūcere** be the master.

fūnus, -eris nt funeral; death; corpse; ruin, destruction.

fūr, fūris m thief; slave.

fūrācissimē adv most thievishly.

fūrāx, -ācis adj thieving.

furca, -ae f fork; fork-shaped pole; pillory.

furcifer, -ī m gallows rogue.

furcilla, -ae f little fork.

furcillō, -āre vt to prop up.

furcula, -ae f forked prop; **~ae Caudīnae** Pass of Caudium.

furenter adv furiously.

furfur, -is m bran; scurf.

Furia, -ae f Fury, avenging spirit; madness, frenzy, rage.

furiālis adj of the Furies; frantic, fearful; infuriating.

furiāliter adv madly.

furibundus adj mad, frenzied.

furiō, -āre, -āvī, -ātum vt to madden.

furiōsē adv in a frenzy.

furiōsus adj mad, frantic.

furnus, -ī m oven.

furō, -ere vi to rave, rage, be mad, be crazy.

furor, -ārī, -ātus vt to steal; to pillage; to impersonate.

furor, -ōris m madness, frenzy, passion.

fūrtificus adj thievish.

fūrtim adv by stealth, secretly.

fūrtīvē adv secretly.

fūrtīvus adj stolen; secret, furtive.

fūrtō adv secretly.

fūrtum, -ī nt theft, robbery; (pl) stolen goods; (fig) trick, intrigue.

fūrunculus, -ī m pilferer.

furvus adj black, dark.

fuscina, -ae f trident.

fuscō, -āre vt to blacken.

fuscus adj dark, swarthy; (voice) husky, muffled.

fūsē adv diffusely.

fūsilis adj molten, softened.

fūsiō, -ōnis f outpouring.

fūstis, -is m stick, club, cudgel; (MIL) beating to death.

fūstuārium, -ī and lī nt beating to death.

fūsus ppp of **fundō** ♦ adj broad, diffuse; copious.

fūsus, -ī m spindle.

The present infinitive verb endings are as follows: -āre = 1st; -ēre = 2nd; -ere = 3rd and -īre = 4th. See sections on irregular verbs and noun declensions.

futtile 152 **gelidus**

futtile *adv* in vain.
futtilis, -is *adj* brittle; worthless.
futtilitās, -ātis *f* futility.
futūrum, -ī *nt* future.
futūrus *fut p of* **sum ♦** *adj* future, coming.

G

Gabiī, -iōrum *mpl* ancient town in Latium.
Gabīnius, -ī *m* Roman family name (*esp Aulus, tribune 67 B.C.*).
Gabīnius, -iānus *adj*: **lēx ~ia** *law giving Pompey command against the pirates.*
Gabīnus *adj see* **Gabiī.**
Gādēs, -ium *fpl* town in Spain (now Cadiz).
Gāditānus *adj see n.*
gaesum, -ī *nt* Gallic javelin.
Gaetūlī, -ōrum *mpl* African people N of Sahara.
Gaetūlus, -icus *adj* Gaetulian; African.
Gāius, -ī *m* Roman praenomen (*esp emperor Caligula*).
Gāius, -ia *m/f* (*wedding ceremony*) bridegroom, bride.
Galatae, -ārum *mpl* Galatians of Asia Minor.
Galatia, -iae *f* Galatia.
Galba, -ae *m* Roman surname (*esp emperor 68–9*).
galbaneus *adj* of galbanum, a Syrian plant.
galbinus *adj* greenish-yellow ♦ *ntpl* pale green clothes.
galea, -ae *f* helmet.
galeātus *adj* helmeted.
galērītus *adj* rustic.
galērum, -ī *nt*, **-us, -ī** *m* leather hood, cap; wig.
galla, -ae *f* oak apple.
Gallī, -ōrum *mpl* Gauls (*people of what is now France and N. Italy*).
Gallia, -iae *f* Gaul.

Gallicānus *adj* of Italian Gaul.
Gallicus *adj* Gallic ♦ *f* a Gallic shoe.
gallīna, -ae *f* hen; **~ae albae fīlius** fortune's favourite.
gallīnāceus *adj* of poultry.
gallīnārius, -ī *and* **iī** *m* poultry farmer.
Gallograecī, -ōrum *mpl* Galatians.
Gallograecia, -iae *f* Galatia.
gallus, -ī *m* cock.
Gallus, -ī *m* Gaul; Roman surname (*esp the lyric poet; priest of Cybele*).
ganea, -ae *f* low eating house.
ganeō, -ōnis *m* profligate.
ganeum, -ī *nt* low eating house.
Gangaridae, -ārum *mpl* a people on the Ganges.
Gangēs, -is *m* river Ganges.
Gangēticus *adj see n.*
gannïō, -īre *vi* to yelp; (*fig*) to grumble.
gannītus, -ūs *m* yelping.
Ganymēdēs, -is *m* Ganymede, (*cup bearer in Olympus*).
Garamantes, -um *mpl* N. African tribe.
Garamantis, -idis *adj see n.*
Gargānus, -ī *m* mountain in E. Italy.
garriō, -īre *vi* to chatter.
garrulitās, -ātis *f* chattering.
garrulus *adj* talkative, babbling.
garum, -ī *nt* fish sauce.
Garumna, -ae *f* river Garonne.
gaudeō, -ēre, gāvīsus *vt, vi* to rejoice, be pleased, delight (in); in **sē, in sinū ~** be secretly pleased.
gaudium, -ī *and* **iī** *nt* joy, delight, enjoyment.
gaulus, -ī *m* bucket.
gausape, -is *nt, -a, -ōrum* *pl* a woollen cloth, frieze.
gāvīsus *ppa of* **gaudeō.**
gāza, -ae *f* treasure, riches.
gelidē *adv* feebly.
gelidus *adj* cold, frosty; stiff, numb; chilling ♦ *f* cold water.

gelō, -āre vt to freeze.

Gelōnī, -ōrum mpl Scythian tribe (now Ukraine).

gelū, -ūs nt frost, cold; chill.

gemebundus adj groaning.

gemellipara, -ae f mother of twins.

gemellus adj twin, double; alike ♦ m twin.

geminātiō, -ōnis f doubling.

geminō, -āre, -āvī, -ātum vt to double, bring together; to repeat ♦ vi to be double.

geminus adj twin, double, both; similar ♦ mpl twins (esp Castor and Pollux).

gemitus, -ūs m groan, sigh; moaning sound.

gemma, -ae f bud, precious stone, jewel; jewelled cup, signet.

gemmātus adj bejewelled.

gemmeus adj jewelled; sparkling.

gemmifer, -ī adj gem-producing.

gemmō, -āre vi to bud, sprout; to sparkle.

gemō, -ere, -uī, -itum vi to sigh, groan, moan ♦ vt to bewail.

Gemōniae, -ārum fpl steps in Rome on which bodies of criminals were thrown.

genae, -ārum fpl cheeks; eyes, eye sockets.

geneālogus, -ī m genealogist.

gener, -ī m son-in-law.

generālis adj of the species; universal.

generāliter adv generally.

generāscō, -ere vi to be produced.

generātim adv by species, in classes; in general.

generātor, -ōris m producer.

generō, -āre, -āvī, -ātum vt to breed, procreate.

generōsus adj high-born, noble; well-stocked; generous,

chivalrous; (things) noble, honourable.

genesis, -is f birth; horoscope.

genethliacon, -ī nt birthday poem.

genetīvus adj native, inborn.

genetrīx, -īcis f mother.

geniālis adj nuptial; joyful, genial.

geniāliter adv merrily.

geniculātus adj jointed.

genista, -ae f broom.

genitābilis adj productive.

genitālis adj fruitful, generative; of birth.

genitāliter adv fruitfully.

genitor, -ōris m father, creator.

genitus ppp of **gignō**.

genius, -ī and **iī** m guardian spirit; enjoyment, inclination; talent; **~iō indulgēre** enjoy oneself.

gēns, gentis f clan, family, stock, race; tribe, people, nation; descendant; (pl) foreign peoples; **minimē gentium** by no means, **ubi gentium** where in the world.

genticus adj national.

gentīlicius adj family.

gentīlis adj family, hereditary; national ♦ m kinsman.

gentīlitās, -ātis f clan relationship.

genū, -ūs nt knee.

genuālia, -um ntpl garters.

genuī perf of **gignō**.

genuīnus adj natural.

genuīnus adj of the cheek ♦ mpl back teeth.

genus, -eris nt birth, descent, noble birth, descendant, race; kind, class, species, respect, way; (logic) genus, general term; **id ~ of** that kind; **in omnī ~ere** in all respects.

geōgraphia, -ae f geography.

geōmetrēs, -ae m geometer.

geōmetria, -ae f geometry.

geōmetricus adj geometrical

The present infinitive verb endings are as follows: -āre = 1st; -ēre = 2nd; -ere = 3rd and -īre = 4th. See sections on irregular verbs and noun declensions.

♦ *ntpl* geometry.
germānē *adv* sincerely.
Germānī, -ōrum *mpl* Germans.
Germānia, -iae *f* Germany.
Germānicus *adj, m cognomen of Nero Claudius Drusus and his son.*
germānitās, -ātis *f* brotherhood, sisterhood; relation of sister colonies.
germānus *adj* of the same parents, full (brother, sister); genuine, true ♦ *m* full brother ♦ *f* full sister.
germen, -inis *nt* bud, shoot; embryo; (*fig*) germ.
gerō, -rere, -ssī, -stum *vt* to carry, wear; to bring; (*plants*) to bear, produce; (*feelings*) to entertain, show; (*activity*) to conduct, manage, administer, wage; (*time*) spend; **mōrem** ~ comply, humour; **persōnam** ~ play a part; **sē** ~ behave; **sē medium** ~ be neutral; **prae sē** ~ exhibit; **rēs ~stae** exploits.
gerō, -ōnis *nt* carrier.
gerrae, -ārum *fpl* trifles, nonsense.
gerrō, -ōnis *m* idler.
gerulus, -ī *m* carrier.
Gēryōn, -onis *m mythical three-bodied king killed by Hercules.*
gessī *perf of* gerō.
gestāmen, -inis *nt* arms, ornaments, burden; litter, carriage.
gestiō, -ōnis *f* performance.
gestiō, -īre *vi* to jump for joy, be excited; to be very eager.
gestitō, -āre *vt* to always wear or carry.
gestō, -āre *vt* to carry about, usually wear; to fondle; to blab; (*pass*) to go for a ride, drive, sail.
gestor, -ōris *m* telltale.
gestus *ppp of* gerō.
gestus, -ūs *m* posture, gesture; gesticulation.

Getae, -ārum *mpl Thracian tribe on the lower Danube.*
Geticus *adj Getan, Thracian.*
gibbus, -ī *m* hump.
Gigantēs, -um *mpl Giants, sons of Earth.*
Gigantēus *adj see n.*
gignō, -ere, genuī, genitum *vt* to beget, bear, produce; to cause.
gilvus *adj* pale yellow, dun.
gingīva, -ae *f* gum.
glaber, -rī *adj* smooth, bald ♦ *m* favourite slave.
glaciālis *adj* icy.
glaciēs, -ēī *f* ice.
glaciō, -āre *vt* to freeze.
gladiātor, -ōris *m* gladiator; (*pl*) gladiatorial show.
gladiātōrius *adj* of gladiators ♦ *nt* gladiators' pay.
gladiātūra, -ae *f* gladiator's profession.
gladius, -ī *and* **iī** *m* sword; (*fig*) murder, death; **~ium stringere** draw the sword; **suō sibi ~iō iugulāre** ≈ beat at his own game.
glaeba, -ae *f* sod, clod of earth; soil; lump.
glaebula, -ae *f* small lump; small holding.
glaesum *etc see* glēsum.
glandifer, -ī *adj* acorn-bearing.
glandium, -ī *and* **iī** *nt* glandule (*in meat*).
glāns, -andis *f* acorn, nut; bullet.
glārea, -ae *f* gravel.
glāreōsus *adj* gravelly.
glaucūma, -ae *f* cataract; **~am ob oculōs obicere** ≈ throw dust in the eyes of.
glaucus *adj* bluish grey.
glēba *etc see* glaeba.
glēsum, -ī *nt* amber.
glīs, -īris *m* dormouse.
glīscō, -ere *vi* to grow, swell, blaze up.
globōsus *adj* spherical.

globus, -ī *m* ball, sphere; (*MIL*)
troop; mass, crowd, cluster.

glōmerāmen, -inis *nt* bell.

glomerō, -āre, -āvī, -ātum *vt* to
form into a ball, gather,
accumulate.

glomus, -eris *nt* ball of thread,
clue.

glōria, -ae *f* glory, fame; ambition,
pride, boasting; (*pl*) glorious
deeds.

glōriātiō, -ōnis *f* boasting.

glōriola, -ae *f* a little glory.

glōrior, -ārī, -ātus *vt, vi* to boast,
pride oneself.

glōriōsē *adv see* **glōriōsus.**

glōriōsus *adj* famous, glorious,
boastful.

glūten, -inis *nt* glue.

glūtinātor, -ōris *m* bookbinder.

gluttiō, -īre *vt* to gulp down.

gnāruris, gnārus *adj* knowing,
expert; known.

gnātus *see* **nātus.**

gnāvus *see* **nāvus.**

Gnōsius *and* **lacus** *and* **ias** *adj* of
Cnossos, Cretan.

Gnōsis, -idis *f* Ariadne.

Gnōsus, -ī *f* Cnossos (*ancient capital
of Crete*) ♦ *f* Ariadne.

gōbiō, -ōnis, gōblus, -ī *and* **iī** *m*
gudgeon.

Gorgiās, -ae *m* Sicilian sophist and
teacher of rhetoric.

Gorgō, -ōnis *f* mythical monster
capable of turning men to stone,
Medusa.

Gorgoneus *adj*: **equus ~** Pegasus;
lacus ~ Hippocrene.

Gortȳna, -ae *f* Cretan town.

Gortȳnius, -iacus *adj* Gortynian,
Cretan.

gōrȳtos, -ī *m* quiver.

grabātus, -ī *m* camp bed, low
couch.

Gracchānus *adj see* **n.**

Gracchus, -ī *m* Roman surname
(*esp the famous tribunes Tiberius and
Gaius*).

gracilis *adj* slender, slight, meagre,
poor; (*style*) plain.

gracilitās, -ātis *f* slimness,
leanness; (*style*) simplicity.

grāculus, -ī *m* jackdaw.

gradātim *adv* step by step,
gradually.

gradātiō, -ōnis *f* (*RHET*) climax.

gradior, -adī, -essus *vi* to step,
walk.

Grādīvus, -ī *m* Mars.

gradus, -ūs *m* step, pace; stage,
step towards; firm stand, position,
standing; (*pl*) stair, steps; (*hair*)
braid; (*MATH*) degree; (*fig*) degree,
rank; **citātō, plēnō ~ū** at the
double; **suspēnsō ~ū** on tiptoe; **dē
~ū dēicī** be disconcerted.

Graecē *adv* in Greek.

Graecia, -iae *f* Greece; **Māgna ~** S.
Italy.

graecissō, -āre *vi* to ape the
Greeks.

graecor, -ārī *vi* to live like Greeks.

Graeculus *adj* (*contemptuous*)
Greek.

Graecus *adj* Greek.

Grāiugena, -ae *m* a Greek.

Grāius *adj* Greek.

grallātor, -ōris *m* stiltwalker.

grāmen, -inis *nt* grass; herb.

grāmineus *adj* grassy; of cane.

grammaticus *adj* literary,
grammatical ♦ *m* teacher of
literature and language ♦ *f/ntpl*
grammar, literature, philology.

grānāria, -ōrum *ntpl* granary.

grandaevus *adj* aged, very old.

grandēscō, -ere *vi* to grow.

grandiculus *adj* quite big.

grandifer, -ī *adj* productive.

*The present infinitive verb endings are as follows: -āre = 1st; -ēre = 2nd; -ere = 3rd and
-īre = 4th. See sections on irregular verbs and noun declensions.*

grandiloquus, -ī m grand speaker; boaster.

grandinat, -āre vi it hails.

grandis adj large, great, tall; old; strong; (style) grand, sublime; ~ **nātū** old.

granditās, -ātis f grandeur.

grandō, -inis f hail.

grānifer, -ī adj grain-carrying.

grānum, -ī nt seed, grain.

graphicē adv nicely.

graphicus adj fine, masterly.

graphium, -ī and **iī** nt stilus, pen.

grassātor, -ōris m vagabond; robber, footpad.

grassor, -ārī, -ātus vi to walk about, prowl, loiter; (action) to proceed; (fig) to attack, rage against.

grātē adv with pleasure; gratefully.

grātēs fpl thanks.

grātia, -ae f charm, grace; favour, influence, regard, friendship; kindness, service; gratitude, thanks; **~am facere** excuse; **~am referre** return a favour; **in ~am redīre cum** be reconciled to; **~ās agere** thank; **~ās habēre** feel grateful; **~ā** (with gen) for the sake of; **eā ~ā** on that account; **~īs** for nothing.

Grātiae, -ārum fpl the three Graces.

grātificātiō, -ōnis f obligingness.

grātificor, -ārī vi to do a favour, oblige ♦ vt to make a present of.

gratiīs, grātīs adv for nothing.

grātiōsus adj in favour, popular; obliging.

grātor, -ārī, -ātus vi to rejoice, congratulate.

grātuītō adv for nothing.

grātuītus adj free, gratuitous.

grātulābundus adj congratulating.

grātulātiō, -ōnis f rejoicing; congratulation; public thanksgiving.

grātulor, -ārī, -ātus vt, vi to congratulate; to give thanks.

grātus adj pleasing, welcome, dear; grateful, thankful; (acts) deserving thanks; **~um facere** do a favour.

gravātē adv reluctantly, grudgingly.

gravātim adv unwillingly.

gravēdinōsus adj liable to colds.

gravēdō, -inis f cold in the head.

graveolēns, -entis adj strong-smelling.

gravēscō, -ere vi to become heavy; to grow worse.

graviditās, -ātis f pregnancy.

gravidō, -āre vt to impregnate.

gravidus adj pregnant; loaded, full.

gravis adj heavy; loaded, pregnant; (smell) strong, offensive; (sound) deep, bass; (body) sick; (food) indigestible; (fig) oppressive, painful, severe; important, influential, dignified.

gravitās, -ātis f weight, severity, sickness; importance, dignity, seriousness; **annōnae ~** high price of corn.

graviter adv heavily; strongly, deeply; severely, seriously, violently; gravely, with dignity; **~ ferre** be vexed at.

gravō, -āre vt to load, weigh down; to oppress, aggravate.

gravor, -ārī vt, vi to feel annoyed, object to, disdain.

gregālis adj of the herd, common ♦ m comrade.

gregārius adj common; (MIL) private.

gregātim adv in crowds.

gremium, -ī nt bosom, lap.

gressus ppa of gradior.

gressus, -ūs m step; course.

grex, -egis m flock, herd; company, troop.

grunniō, -īre *vi* to grunt.
grunnītus, -ūs *m* grunting.
grūs, -uis *f* crane.
grȳps, -ypis *m* griffin.
gubernāclum (gubernāculum), -ī
nt rudder, tiller; helm,
government.
gubernātiō, -ōnis *f* steering,
management.
gubernātor, -ōris *m* steersman,
pilot, governor.
gubernātrix, -īcis *f* directress.
gubernō, -āre, -āvī, -ātum *vt* to
steer, pilot; to manage, govern.
gula, -ae *f* gullet, throat; gluttony,
palate.
gulōsus *adj* dainty.
gurges, -itis *m* abyss, deep water,
flood; (*person*) spendthrift.
gurgulliō, -ōnis *f* gullet, windpipe.
gurgustium, -ī and **iī** *nt* hovel,
shack.
gustātus, -ūs *m* sense of taste;
flavour.
gustō, -āre, -āvī, -ātum *vt* to taste;
to have a snack; (*fig*) to enjoy,
overhear; *prīmīs labrīs ~* have a
superficial knowledge of.
gustus, -ūs *m* tasting; preliminary
dish.
gutta, -ae *f* drop; spot, speck.
guttātim *adv* drop by drop.
guttur, -is *nt* throat, gluttony.
gūtus, -ī *m* flask.
Gyās, -ae *m* giant with a hundred
arms.
Gȳgaeus *adj see n.*
Gȳgēs, -is and **ae** *m* king of Lydia
(*famed for his magic ring*).
gymnasiarchus, -ī *m* master of a
gymnasium.
gymnasium, -ī and **iī** *nt* sports
ground, school.
gymnasticus *adj* gymnastic.
gymnicus *adj* gymnastic.

gynaecēum, -ēī and **īum, -īī** *nt*
women's quarters.
gypsātus *adj* coated with plaster.
gypsum, -ī *nt* plaster of Paris; a
plaster figure.
gȳrus, -ī *m* circle, coil, ring;
course.

H

ha *interj* (*expressing joy or laughter*)
hurrah!, ha hā!
habēna, -ae *f* strap; (*pl*) reins; (*fig*)
control; *~ās dare, immittere* allow
to run freely.
habeō, -ēre, -uī, -itum *vt* to have,
hold; to keep, contain, possess;
(*fact*) to know; (*with infin*) to be in a
position to; (*person*) to treat, regard, consider; (*action*) to make,
hold, carry out ♦ *vi* to have possessions; *ōrātiōnem ~* make a speech;
in animō ~ intend; *prō certō ~* be
sure; *sē ~* find oneself, be; *sibi,*
sēcum ~ keep to oneself; (*fight*) *~et*
a hit!; *bene ~et* it is well; *sic ~et*
so it is; *sīo ~ētō* be sure of this.
habilis *adj* manageable, handy;
suitable, nimble, expert.
habilitās, -ātis *f* aptitude.
habitābills *adj* habitable.
habitātiō, -ōnis *f* dwelling, house.
habitātor, -ōris *m* tenant,
inhabitant.
habitō, -āre, -āvī, -ātum *vt* to
inhabit ♦ *vi* to live, dwell; to
remain, be always (in).
habitūdō, -inis *f* condition.
habitus *ppp of* **habeō** ♦ *adj* stout; in
a humour.
habitus, -ūs *m* condition,
appearance; dress; character,
quality; disposition, feeling.
hāc *adv* this way.
hāctenus *adv* thus far, so far; till

The present infinitive verb endings are as follows: -āre = 1st; -ēre = 2nd; -ere = 3rd and
-īre = 4th. See sections on irregular verbs and noun declensions.

now.

Hadria, -ae f town in N. Italy; Adriatic Sea.

Hadriānus, -ānī m emperor Hadrian.

Hadriāticus and **acus** adj of emperor Hadrian.

haedilia, -ae f little kid.

haedīnus adj kid's.

haedulus, -ī m little kid.

haedus, -ī m kid; (ASTRO, usu pl) the Kids (a cluster in Auriga).

Haemonia, -ae f Thessaly.

Haemonius adj Thessalian.

Haemus, -ī m mountain range in Thrace.

haereō, -rēre, -sī, -sum vi to cling, stick, be attached; (nearness) to stay close, hang on; (continuance) to linger, remain (at); (stoppage) to stick fast, come to a standstill, be at a loss.

haerēscō, -ere vi to adhere.

haeresis, -is f sect.

haesī perf of **haereō**.

haesitantia, -ae f stammering.

haesitātiō, -ōnis f stammering; indecision.

haesitō, -āre vi to get stuck; to stammer; to hesitate, be uncertain.

hahae, hahahae see **ha**.

hālitus, -ūs m breath, vapour.

hallex, -icis m big toe.

hallūc- see **ālūc-**.

hālō, -āre vi to be fragrant ♦ vt to exhale.

hāluc etc see **ālūc**.

halyaeetos, -ī m osprey.

hama, -ae f water bucket.

Hamādryas, -adis f woodnymph.

hāmātilis adj with hooks.

hāmātus adj hooked.

Hamilcar, -is m father of Hannibal.

hāmus, -ī m hook; talons.

Hannibal, -is m famous Carthaginian general in 2nd Punic War.

hara, -ae f stye, pen.

harēna, -ae f sand; desert, seashore; arena (in the amphitheatre).

harēnōsus adj sandy.

hariola, -ae f, **hariolus, -ī** m soothsayer.

hariolor, -ārī vi to prophesy; to talk nonsense.

harmonia, -ae f concord, melody; (fig) harmony.

harpagō, -āre vt to steal.

harpagō, -ōnis m grappling hook; (person) robber.

harpē, -ēs f scimitar.

Harpȳiae, -ārum fpl Harpies (mythical monsters, half woman, half bird).

harundifer, -ī adj reed-crowned.

harundineus adj reedy.

harundinōsus adj abounding in reeds.

harundō, -inis f reed, cane; fishing rod; shaft, arrow; (fowling) limed twig; (music) pipe, flute; (toy) hobbyhorse; (weaving) comb; (writing) pen.

haruspex, -icis m diviner (from entrails); prophet.

haruspica, -ae f soothsayer.

haruspicīnus adj of divination by entrails ♦ f art of such divination.

haruspicium, -ī and **iī** nt divination.

Hasdrubal, -is m brother of Hannibal.

hasta, -ae f spear, pike; sign of an auction sale; **sub ~ā vēndere** put up for auction.

hastātus adj armed with a spear ♦ mpl first line of Roman army in battle; **primus ~** 1st company of hastati.

hastīle, -is nt shaft, spear, javelin; vine prop.

hau, haud adv not, not at all.

hauddum adv not yet.

haudquāquam adv not at all, not

by any means.

haurió, -rīre, -sī, -stum vt to draw, draw off, derive; to drain, empty, exhaust; to take in, drink, swallow, devour.

haustus ppp of **haurió**.

haustus, -ūs m drawing (water); drinking; drink, draught.

haut etc see **haud**.

hebdomas, -dis f week.

Hēbē, -ēs f goddess of youth (cup bearer to the gods).

hebenus, -ī f ebony.

hebeó, -ēre vi to be blunt, dull, sluggish.

hebes, -tis adj blunt, dull, sluggish; obtuse, stupid.

hebescó, -ere vi to grow dim or dull.

hebetó, -āre vt to blunt, dull, dim.

Hebrus, -ī m Thracian river (now Maritza).

Hecatē, -ēs f goddess of magic (and often identified with Diana).

Hecatēius, -ēis adj see n.

hecatombē, -ēs f hecatomb.

Hector, -is m son of Priam (chief warrior of the Trojans against the Greeks).

Hectoreus adj of Hector; Trojan.

Hecuba, -ae and **ē, -ēs** f wife of Priam.

hedera, -ae f ivy.

hederiger, -ī adj wearing ivy.

hederósus adj covered with ivy.

hēdychrum, -ī nt a cosmetic perfume.

hei, heia etc see **ei, eia**.

Helena, -ae and **ē, -ēs** f Helen (wife of Menelaus, abducted by Paris).

Helenus, -ī m son of Priam (with prophetic powers).

Hēliades, -um fpl daughters of the Sun (changed to poplars or alders, and their tears to amber).

Helicē, -ēs f the Great Bear.

Helicón, -ōnis m mountain in Greece sacred to Apollo and the Muses.

Helicóniades, -um fpl the Muses.

Helicónius adj see **Helicón**.

Hellas, -dis f Greece.

Hellē, -ēs f mythical Greek princess (carried by the golden-fleeced ram, and drowned in the Hellespont).

Hellēspontius, -iacus adj see n.

Hellēspontus, -ī m Hellespont (now Dardanelles).

helluó, -ōnis m glutton.

helluor, -ārī vi to be a glutton.

helvella, -ae f a savoury herb.

Helvētiī, -ōrum mpl people of E. Gaul (now Switzerland).

Helvētius, -cus adj see n.

hem interj (expressing surprise) eh?, well well!

hēmerodromus, -ī m express courier.

hēmicillus, -ī m mule.

hēmicyclium, -ī and **iī** nt semicircle with seats.

hēmīna, -ae f half a pint.

hendecasyllabī, -ōrum mpl hendecasyllabics, verses of eleven syllables.

hepteris, -is f ship with seven banks of oars.

hera etc see **era**.

Hēra, -ae f Greek goddess identified with Juno.

Hēraclītus, -ī m early Greek philosopher.

Hēraea, -aeórum ntpl festival of Hera.

herba, -ae f blade, young plant; grass, herb, weed.

herbēscó, -ere vi to grow into blades.

herbeus adj grass-green.

herbidus adj grassy.

The present infinitive verb endings are as follows: **-āre** = 1st; **-ēre** = 2nd; **-ere** = 3rd and **-īre** = 4th. See sections on irregular verbs and noun declensions.

herbifer, -ī adj grassy.

herbōsus adj grassy, made of turf; made of herbs.

herbula, -ae f little herb.

herciscō, -ere vt to divide an inheritance.

hercle interj by Hercules!

herctum, -ī nt inheritance.

Hercule interj by Hercules!

Herculēs, -is and **ī** m mythical Greek hero, later deified.

Herculeus adj: **arbor ~** poplar; **urbs ~** Herculaneum.

here etc see **herī**.

hērēditārius adj inherited; about an inheritance.

hērēditās, -ātis f inheritance; **~ sine sacris** a gift without awkward obligations.

hērēdium, -ī and **iī** nt inherited estate.

hērēs, -ēdis m/f heir, heiress; (fig) master, successor.

herī adv yesterday.

herīlis etc see **erīlis**.

Hermēs, -ae m Greek god identified with Mercury; Hermes pillar.

Hernicī, -ōrum mpl people of central Italy.

Hernicus adj see n.

Hērodotus, -ī m first Greek historian.

hērōicus adj heroic, epic.

hērōina, -ae f demigoddess.

hērōis, -dis f demigoddess.

hērōs, -is m demigod, hero.

hērōus adj heroic, epic.

herus etc see **erus**.

Hēsiodēus, -īus adj see n.

Hēsiodus, -ī m Hesiod (Greek didactic poet).

Hesperia, -iae f Italy; Spain.

Hesperides, -idum fpl keepers of a garden in the far West.

Hesperius, -is adj western.

Hesperus, -ī m evening star.

hesternus adj of yesterday.

heu interj (expressing dismay or pain)

oh!, alas!

heus interj (calling attention) ho!, hallo!

hexameter, -rī m hexameter verse.

hexēris, -is f ship with six banks of oars.

hiātus, -ūs m opening, abyss; open mouth, gaping; (GRAM) hiatus.

Hibēres, -um mpl Spaniards.

Hibēria, -iae f Spain.

hiberna, -ōrum ntpl winter quarters.

hibernācula, -ōrum ntpl winter tents.

Hibernia, -ae f Ireland.

hibernō, -āre vi to winter, remain in winter quarters.

hibernus adj winter, wintry.

Hibērus, -icus adj Spanish.

Hibērus, -ī m river Ebro.

hibiscum, -ī nt marsh mallow.

hibrida, hybrida, -ae m/f mongrel, half-breed.

hic, haec, hōc pron, adj this; he, she, it; my, the latter, the present; **hic homō** I; **hōc magis** the more; **hōc est** that is.

hic adv here; herein; (time) at this point.

hīce, haece, hōce emphatic forms of **hic, haec, hōc**.

hīcine, haecine, hōcine emphatic forms of **hic, haec, hōc**.

hiemālis adj winter, stormy.

hiemō, -āre vi to pass the winter; to be wintry, stormy.

hiems, (hiemps), -is f winter; stormy weather, cold.

Hierōnymus, -ī m Jerome.

Hierosolyma, -ōrum ntpl Jerusalem.

Hierosolymārius adj see n.

hietō, -āre vi to yawn.

hilare adv see **hilaris**.

hilaris adj cheerful, merry.

hilaritās, -ātis f cheerfulness.

hilaritūdō, -inis f merriment.

hilarō, -āre vt to cheer, gladden.

hilarulus adj a gay little thing.

hilarus etc see **hilaris**.

hillae, -ārum fpl smoked sausage.

Hilōtae, -ārum mpl Helots (of Sparta).

hīlum, -ī nt something, a whit.

hinc adv from here, hence; on this side, from this source, for this reason; (time) henceforth.

hinniō, -īre vi to neigh.

hinnītus, -ūs m neighing.

hinnuleus, -ī m fawn.

hiō, -āre vi to be open, gape, yawn; (speech) to be disconnected, leave a hiatus ♦ vt to sing.

hippagōgī, -ōrum fpl cavalry transports.

hippocentaurus, -ī m centaur.

hippodromos, -ī m racecourse.

Hippolytus, -ī m son of Theseus (slandered by stepmother Phaedra).

hippomanes, -is nt mare's fluid; membrane on foal's forehead.

Hippōnactēus adj of Hipponax ♦ m iambic verse used by Hipponax.

Hippōnax, -ctis m Greek satirist.

hipppotoxotae, -ārum mpl mounted archers.

hīra, -ae f the empty gut.

hircīnus adj of a goat.

hircōsus adj goatish.

hircus, -ī m he-goat; goatish smell.

hirnea, -ae f jug.

hirq- etc see **hirc-**.

hirsūtus adj shaggy, bristly; uncouth.

hirtus adj hairy, shaggy; rude.

hirūdō, -inis f leech.

hirundininus adj swallows'.

hirundō, -inis f swallow.

hīscō, -ere vi to gape; to open the mouth ♦ vt to utter.

Hispānia, -iae f Spain.

Hispāniēnsis, -us adj Spanish.

hispidus adj hairy, rough.

Hister, -rī m lower Danube.

historia, -ae f history, inquiry; story.

historicus adj historical ♦ m historian.

histricus adj of the stage.

histriō, -ōnis m actor.

histriōnālis adj of an actor.

histriōnia, -ae f acting.

hiulcē adv with hiatus.

hiulcō, -āre vt to split open.

hiulcus adj gaping, open; (speech) with hiatus.

hodiē adv today; nowadays; now; up to the present.

hodiernus adj today's.

holitor, -ōris m market gardener.

holitōrius adj for market gardeners.

holus, -eris nt vegetables.

holusculum, -ī nt small cabbage.

Homēricus adj see n.

Homērus, -ī m Greek epic poet, Homer.

homicīda, -ae m killer, murderer.

homicīdium, -ī and **iī** nt murder.

homō, -inis m/f human being, man; (pl) people, the world; (derogatory) fellow, creature; **inter -inēs esse** be alive; see the world.

homullus, -ī, homunciō, -ōnis, homunculus, -ī m little man, poor creature, mortal

honestās, -ātis f good character; honourable reputation; sense of honour, integrity; (things) beauty.

honestē adv decently, virtuously.

honestō, -āre vt to honour, dignify, embellish.

honestus adj honoured, respectable; honourable, virtuous; (appearance) handsome

---

The present infinitive verb endings are as follows: **-āre** = 1st; **-ēre** = 2nd; **-ere** = 3rd and **-īre** = 4th. *See sections on irregular verbs and noun declensions.*

♦ *m* gentleman ♦ *nt* virtue, good;
beauty.

honor, -ōris *m* honour, esteem;
public office, position,
preferment; award, tribute,
offering; ornament, beauty; **-ōris
causā** out of respect; for the sake
of; **~ōrem praefārī** apologize for a
remark.

honōrābilis *adj* a mark of respect.

honōrārius *adj* done out of respect,
honorary.

honōrātē *adv* honourably.

honōrātus *adj* esteemed,
distinguished; in high office;
complimentary.

honōrificē *adv* in complimentary
terms.

honōrificus *adj* complimentary.

honōrō, -āre, -āvī, -ātum *vt* to do
honour to, embellish.

honōrus *adj* complimentary.

honōs *etc see* **honor**.

hōra, -ae *f* hour; time, season; (*pl*)
clock; **in -ās** hourly; **in ~am
vīvere** ≈ live from hand to mouth.

hōraeum, -ī *nt* pickle.

Horātius, -ī *m* Roman family name
(*esp the defender of Rome against
Porsenna*); the lyric poet Horace.

Horātius *adj see n.*

hordeum, -ī *nt* barley.

horia, -ae *f* fishing smack.

hōrnō *adv* this year.

hōrnōtinus *adj* this year's.

hōrnus *adj* this year's.

hōrologium, -ī *and* **iī** *nt* clock.

horrendus *adj* fearful, terrible;
awesome.

horrēns, -entis *pres p of* **horreō**
♦ *adj* bristling, shaggy.

horreō, -ēre, -uī *vi* to stand stiff,
bristle; to shiver, shudder,
tremble ♦ *vt* to dread; to be
afraid, be amazed.

horrēscō, -ere *vi* to stand on end,
become rough; to begin to quake;

to start, be terrified ♦ *vt* to dread.

horreum, -ī *nt* barn, granary,
store.

horribilis *adj* terrifying; amazing.

horridē *adv see* **horridus**.

horridulus *adj* protruding a little;
unkempt; (*fig*) uncouth.

horridus *adj* bristling, shaggy,
rough, rugged; shivering;
(*manners*) rude, uncouth;
frightening.

horrifer, -ī *adj* chilling; terrifying.

horrificē *adv* in awesome manner.

horrificō, -āre *vt* to ruffle; to
terrify.

horrificus *adj* terrifying.

horrisonus *adj* dread-sounding.

horror, -ōris *m* bristling;
shivering, ague; terror, fright,
awe, a terror.

hōrsum *adv* this way.

hortāmen, -inis *nt* encouragement.

hortāmentum, -ī *nt*
encouragement.

hortātiō, -ōnis *f* harangue,
encouragement.

hortātor, -ōris *m* encourager.

hortātus, -ūs *m* encouragement.

Hortēnsius, -ī *m* Roman family
name (*esp an orator in Cicero's time*).

hortor, -ārī, -ātus *vt* to urge,
encourage, exhort, harangue.

hortulus, -ī *m* little garden.

hortus, -ī *m* garden; (*pl*) park.

hospes, -itis *m*, **hospita, -ae** *f* host,
hostess; guest, friend; stranger,
foreigner ♦ *adj* strange.

hospitālis *adj* host's, guest's;
hospitable.

hospitālitās, -ātis *f* hospitality.

hospitāliter *adv* hospitably.

hospitium, -ī *and* **iī** *nt* hospitality,
friendship; lodging, inn.

hostia, -ae *f* victim, sacrifice.

hostiātus *adj* provided with
victims.

hosticus *adj* hostile; strange ♦ *nt* enemy territory.

hostīlis *adj* of the enemy, hostile.

hostīliter *adv* in hostile manner.

hostīmentum, -ī *nt* recompense.

hostiō, -īre *vt* to requite.

hostis, -is *m/f* enemy.

hūc *adv* hither, here; to this, to such a pitch; ~ **illūc** hither and thither.

hui *interj* (*expressing surprise*) ho!, my word!

hūiusmodī such.

hūmānē, -iter *adv* humanly; gently, politely.

hūmānitās, -ātis *f* human nature, mankind; humanity, kindness, courtesy; culture, refinement.

hūmānitus *adv* in accordance with human nature; kindly.

hūmānus *adj* human, humane, kind, courteous; cultured, refined, well-educated; ~**ō māior** superhuman.

humātiō, -ōnis *f* burying.

hūme-, hūmi- *see* **ūme-, ūmi-**.

humilis *adj* low, low-lying, shallow; (*condition*) lowly, humble, poor; (*language*) commonplace; (*mind*) mean, base.

humilitās, -ātis *f* low position, smallness, shallowness; lowliness, insignificance; meanness, baseness.

humiliter *adv* meanly, humbly.

humō, -āre, -āvī, -ātum *vt* to bury.

humus, -ī *f* earth, ground; land; **~ī** on the ground.

hyacinthinus *adj* of the hyacinthus.

hyacinthus, -ī *m* iris, lily.

Hyades, -um *fpl* Hyads (*a group of stars in Taurus*).

hyaena, -ae *f* hyena.

hyalus, -ī *m* glass.

Hybla, -ae *f* mountain in Sicily (*famous for bees*).

Hyblaeus *adj see* n.

hybrida *etc see* **hibrida**.

Hydaspēs, -is *m* tributary of river Indus (*now Jelum*).

Hydra, -ae *f* hydra (*a mythical dragon with seven heads*).

hydraulus, -ī *m* water organ.

hydria, -ae *f* ewer.

Hydrochous, -ī *m* Aquarius.

hydrōpicus *adj* suffering from dropsy.

hydrōps, -is *m* dropsy.

hydrus, -ī *m* serpent.

Hylās, -ae *m* a youth loved by Hercules.

Hymēn, -enis, Hymenaeus, -ī *m* god of marriage; wedding song; wedding.

Hymettius *adj see* n.

Hymettus, -ī *m* mountain near Athens (*famous for honey and marble*).

Hypanis, -is *m* river of Sarmatia (*now Bug*).

Hyperboreī, -ōrum *mpl* fabulous people in the far North.

Hyperboreus *adj see* n.

Hyperīōn, -onis *m* father of the Sun; the Sun.

hypodidasculus, -ī *m* assistant teacher.

hypomnēma, -tis *nt* memorandum.

Hyrcānī, -ōrum *mpl* people on the Caspian Sea.

Hyrcānus *adj* Hyrcanian.

I

Iacchus, -ī *m* Bacchus; wine

iaceō, -ēre, -uī *vi* to lie; to be ill, lie dead; (*places*) to be situated, be flat or low-lying, be in ruins;

The present infinitive verb endings are as follows: **-āre** = 1st; **-ēre** = 2nd; **-ere** = 3rd and **-īre** = 4th. *See sections on irregular verbs and noun declensions.*

(*dress*) to hang loose; (*fig*) to be inactive, be downhearted; (*things*) to be dormant, neglected, despised.

iaciō, -ere, iēcī, iactum *vt* to throw; to lay, build; (*seed*) to sow; (*speech*) to cast, let fall, mention.

iactāns, -antis *pres p of* iactō ♦ *adj* boastful.

iactanter *adv* ostentatiously.

iactantia, -ae *f* boasting, ostentation.

iactātiō, -ōnis *f* tossing, gesticulation; boasting, ostentation; ~ **populāris** publicity.

iactātus, -ūs *m* waving.

iactitō, -āre *vt* to mention, bandy.

iactō, -āre, -āvī, -ātum *vt* to throw, scatter; to shake, toss about; (*mind*) to disquiet; (*ideas*) to consider, discuss, mention; (*speech*) to boast of; **sē ~** waver, fluctuate; to behave ostentatiously; to be officious.

iactūra, -ae *f* throwing overboard; loss, sacrifice.

iactus *ppp of* iaciō.

iactus, -ūs *m* throwing, throw; **intrā tēlī iactum** within spear's range.

iacuī *perf of* iaceō.

iaculābilis *adj* missile.

iaculātor, -ōris *m* thrower, shooter; light-armed soldier.

iaculātrīx, -īcis *f* huntress.

iaculor, -ārī, -ātus *vt* to throw, hurl, shoot; to throw the javelin; to shoot at, hit; (*fig*) to aim at, attack.

iaculum, -ī *nt* javelin; fishing net.

iāien- *etc see* iēn-.

iam *adv* (*past*) already, by then; (*present*) now, already; (*future*) directly, very soon; (*emphasis*) indeed, precisely; (*inference*) therefore, then surely; (*transition*) moreover, next; **iam dūdum** for a

long time, long ago; immediately; **iam iam** right now, any moment now; **non ~** no longer; **iam ... iam** at one time ... at another; **iam nunc** just now; **iam prīdem** long ago, for a long time; **iam tum** even at that time; **si iam** supposing for the purpose of argument.

iambēus *adj* iambic.

iambus, -ī *m* iambic foot; iambic poetry.

lānālis *adj see* lānus.

lāniculum, -ī *nt* Roman hill across the Tiber.

iānitor, -ōris *m* doorkeeper, porter.

iānua, -ae *f* door; entrance; (*fig*) key.

lānuārius *adj of* January ♦ *m* January.

lānus, -ī *m* god of gateways and beginnings; archway, arcade.

lapetīonidēs, -ae *m* Atlas.

lapetus, -ī *m* a Titan (*father of Atlas and Prometheus*).

lāpyx, -gis *adj* Iapygian; Apulian ♦ *m* west-north-west wind from Apulia.

lāsōn, -onis *m* Jason (*leader of Argonauts, husband of Medea*).

lāsonius *adj see* n.

iaspis, -dis *f* jasper.

lbēr- *etc see* Hibēr-.

ibi *adv* there; then; in this, at it.

ibīdem *adv* in the same place; at that very moment.

ibis, -is *and* **idis** *f* ibis.

lcarium, -ī *nt* Icarian Sea.

lcarius *adj see* n.

lcarus, -ī *m* son of Daedalus (*drowned in the Aegean*).

īcō, -ere, -ī, ictum *vt* to strike; **foedus ~** make a treaty.

ictericus *adj* jaundiced.

ictis, -dis *f* weasel.

ictus *ppp of* īcō.

ictus, -ūs *m* stroke, blow; wound; *(metre)* beat.

Īda, -ae; -ē, -ēs *f* mountain in Crete; mountain near Troy.

Īdaeus *adj* Cretan; Trojan.

idcircō *adv* for that reason; for the purpose.

īdem, eadem, idem *pron* the same; also, likewise.

identidem *adv* repeatedly, again and again.

ideō *adv* therefore, for this reason, that is why.

idiōta, -ae *m* ignorant person, layman.

īdōlon, -ī *nt* apparition.

idōneē *adv see* **idōneus**.

idōneus *adj* fit, proper, suitable, sufficient.

Īdūs, -uum *fpl* Ides *(the 15th March, May, July, October, the 13th of other months)*.

iēci *perf of* **iaciō**.

iecur, -oris *and* **inoris** *nt* liver; *(fig)* passion.

iecusculum, -ī *nt* small liver.

iēiūniōsus *adj* hungry.

iēiūnitās, -ātis *f* fasting; *(fig)* meagreness.

iēiūnium, -ī *and* **iī** *nt* fast; hunger; leanness.

iēiūnus *adj* fasting, hungry; *(things)* barren, poor, meagre; *(style)* feeble.

ientāculum, -ī *nt* breakfast.

igitur *adv* therefore, then, so.

ignārus *adj* ignorant, unaware; unknown.

ignāvē, -iter *adv* without energy.

ignāvia, -ae *f* idleness, laziness; cowardice.

ignāvus *adj* idle, lazy, listless; cowardly; relaxing.

ignēscō, -ere *vi* to take fire, burn.

igneus *adj* burning, fiery.

igniculus, -ī *m* spark; *(fig)* fire, vehemence.

ignifer, -ī *adj* fiery.

ignigena, -ae *m* the fireborn (Bacchus).

ignipēs, -edis *adj* fiery-footed.

ignipotēns, -entis *adj* fire-working (Vulcan).

ignis, -is *m* fire, a fire; firebrand, lightning; brightness, redness; *(fig)* passion, love.

ignōbilis *adj* unknown, obscure; low-born.

ignōbilitās, -ātis *f* obscurity; low birth.

ignōminia, -ae *f* dishonour, disgrace.

ignōminiōsus *adj* *(person)* degraded, disgraced; *(things)* shameful.

ignōrābilis *adj* unknown.

ignōrantia, -ae *f* ignorance.

ignōrātiō, -ōnis *f* ignorance.

ignōrō, -āre, -āvī, -ātum *vt* to not know, be unacquainted with; to disregard.

ignōscō, -scere, -vī, -tum *vt, vi* to forgive, pardon.

ignōtus *adj* unknown; low-born; ignorant.

īlex, -icis *f* holm oak.

īlia, -um *ntpl* groin; entrails; — **dūcere** become broken-winded.

Īlia, -ae *f* mother of Romulus and Remus.

Īliadēs, -adae *m* son of Ilia; Trojan.

Īlias, -dis *f* the Iliad; a Trojan woman.

īlicet *adv* it's all over, let us go; immediately.

īlicō *adv* on the spot; instantly.

īlignus *adj* of holm oak.

Īlīthyia, -ae *f* Greek goddess of childbirth.

Īlium, -on, -ī *nt*, **-os, -ī** *f* Troy.

The present infinitive verb endings are as follows: -āre = 1st; -ēre = 2nd; -ere = 3rd and -īre = 4th. See sections on irregular verbs and noun declensions.

Īlius, -acus adj Trojan.

illā adv that way.

illābefactus adj unbroken.

illābor, -bī, -psus vi to flow into, fall down.

illāborō, -āre vi to work (at).

illāc adv that way.

illacessītus adj unprovoked.

illacrimābilis adj unwept; inexorable.

illacrimō, -āre; -or, -ārī vi to weep over, lament; to weep.

illaesus adj unhurt.

illaetābilis adj cheerless.

illāpsus ppa of illābor.

illaqueō, -āre vt to ensnare.

illātus ppp of īnferō.

illaudātus adj wicked.

ille, -a, -ud pron and adj that, that one; he, she, it; the famous; the former, the other; **ex ~ō** since then.

illecebra, -ae f attraction, lure, bait, decoy bird.

illecebrōsus adj seductive.

illectus ppp of illiciō.

illēctus adj unread.

illepidē adv see illepidus.

illepidus adj inelegant, churlish.

illex, -icis m/f lure.

illēx, -ēgis adj lawless.

illexī perf of illiciō.

illībātus adj unimpaired.

illīberālis adj ungenerous, mean, disobliging.

illīberālitās, -ātis f meanness.

illīberāliter adv see illīberālis.

illic, -aec, -ūc pron he, she, it; that.

illīc adv there, yonder; in that matter.

illiciō, -icere, -exī, -ectum vt to seduce, decoy, mislead.

illicitātor, -ōris m sham bidder (at an auction).

illicitus adj unlawful.

illīdō, -dere, -sī, -sum vt to strike, dash against.

illigō, -āre, -āvī, -ātum vt to fasten on, attach; to connect; to impede, encumber, oblige.

illim adv from there.

illīmis adj clear.

illinc adv from there; on that side.

illinō, -inere, -ēvī, -itum vt to smear over, cover, bedaub.

illiquefactus adj melted.

illīsī perf of illīdō.

illīsus ppp of illīdō.

illitterātus adj uneducated, uncultured.

illitus ppp of illinō.

illō adv (to) there; to that end.

illōtus adj dirty.

illūc adv (to) there; to that; to him/her.

illūceō, -ēre vi to blaze.

illūcēscō, -cēscere, -xī vi to become light, dawn.

illūdō, -dere, -sī, -sum vt, vi to play, amuse oneself; to abuse; to jeer at, ridicule.

illūminātē adv luminously.

illūminō, -āre, -āvī, -ātum vt to light up; to enlighten; to embellish.

illūsiō, -ōnis f irony.

illūstris adj bright, clear; distinct, manifest; distinguished, illustrious.

illūstrō, -āre, -āvī, -ātum vt to illuminate; to make clear, explain; to make famous.

illūsus ppp of illūdō.

illuviēs, -ēī f dirt, filth; floods.

Illyria, -ae f, **-cum, -cī** nt Illyria.

Illyricus, -us adj see Illyricum.

Illyriī, -ōrum mpl people E. of the Adriatic.

Ilva, -ae f Italian island (now Elba).

imāginārius adj fancied.

imāginātiō, -ōnis f fancy.

imāginor, -ārī vt to picture to oneself.

imāgō, -inis f likeness, picture,

statue; portrait of ancestor;
apparition, ghost; echo, mental
picture, idea; (*fig*) semblance,
mere shadow; (*RHET*) comparison.
imbēcillē *adv* faintly.
imbēcillitās, -ātis *f* weakness,
helplessness.
imbēcillus *adj* weak, frail;
helpless.
imbellis *adj* non-combatant;
peaceful; cowardly.
imber, -ris *m* rain, heavy shower;
water; (*fig*) stream, shower.
imberbis, imberbus *adj* beardless.
imbibō, -ere, -ī *vt* (*mind*) to
conceive; to resolve.
imbrex, -icis *f* tile.
imbricus *adj* rainy.
imbrifer, -ī *adj* rainy.
imbuō, -uere, -uī, -ūtum *vt* to wet,
steep, dip; (*fig*) to taint, fill; to
inspire, accustom, train, to begin,
be the first to explore.
imitābilis *adj* imitable.
imitāmen, -inis *nt* imitation;
likeness.
imitāmenta, -ōrum *ntpl* pretence.
imitātiō, -ōnis *f* imitation.
imitātor, -ōris *m*, **-rīx, -rīcis** *f*
imitator.
imitātus *adj* copied.
imitor, -ārī, -ātus *vt* to copy,
portray; to imitate, act like.
immadēscō, -ēscere, -uī *vi* to
become wet.
immāne *adv* savagely.
immānis *adj* enormous, vast;
monstrous, savage, frightful.
immānitās, -ātis *f* vastness,
savageness, barbarism.
immānsuētus *adj* wild.
immātūritās, -ātis *f* over-
eagerness.
immātūrus *adj* untimely.
immedicābilis *adj* incurable.

immemor, -is *adj* unmindful,
forgetful, negligent.
immemorābilis *adj* indescribable,
not worth mentioning.
immemorātus *adj* hitherto untold.
immēnsitās, -ātis *f* immensity.
immēnsum, -ī *nt* infinity, vast
extent ♦ *adv* exceedingly.
immēnsus *adj* immeasurable,
vast, unending.
immerēns, -entis *adj* undeserving.
immergō, -gere, -sī, -sum *vt* to
plunge, immerse.
immeritō *adv* unjustly.
immeritus *adj* undeserving,
innocent; undeserved.
immersābilis *adj* never
foundering.
immersus *ppp of* **immergō**.
immētātus *adj* unmeasured.
immigrō, -āre, -āvī, -ātum *vi* to
move (into).
immineō, -ēre, -uī *vi* to overhang,
project; to be near, adjoin,
impend; to threaten, be a menace
to; to long for, grasp at.
imminuō, -uere, -uī, -ūtum *vt* to
lessen, shorten; to impair; to
encroach on, ruin.
imminūtiō, -ōnis *f* mutilation;
(*RHET*) understatement.
immisceō, -scēre, -scuī, -xtum *vt*
to intermingle, blend; **sē ~** join,
meddle with.
immiserābilis *adj* unpitied.
immisericorditer *adv*
unmercifully.
immisericors, -dis *adj* pitiless.
immissiō, -ōnis *f* letting grow.
immissus *ppp of* **immittō**.
immītis *adj* unripe; sour,
inexorable.
immittō, -ittere, -īsī, -issum *vt* to
let in, put in; to graft on; to let go,
let loose, let grow; to launch,

*The present infinitive verb endings are as follows: -āre = 1st; -ēre = 2nd; -ere = 3rd and
-īre = 4th. See sections on irregular verbs and noun declensions.*

throw; to incite, set on.
immīxtus *ppp of* **immisceō**.
immo *adv* (*correcting preceding words*) no, yes; on the contrary, or rather; ~ **sī** ah, if only.
immōbilis *adj* motionless; immovable.
immoderātē *adv* extravagantly.
immoderātiō, -ōnis *f* excess.
immoderātus *adj* limitless; excessive, unbridled.
immodestē *adv* extravagantly.
immodestia, -ae *f* license.
immodestus *adj* immoderate.
immodicē *adv see* **immodicus**.
immodicus *adj* excessive, extravagant, unruly.
immodulātus *adj* unrhythmical.
immolātiō, -ōnis *f* sacrifice.
immolātor, -ōris *m* sacrificer.
immōlītus *adj* erected.
immolō, -āre, -āvī, -ātum *vt* to sacrifice; to slay.
immorior, -ī, -tuus *vi* to die upon; to waste away.
immorsus *adj* bitten; (*fig*) stimulated.
immortālis *adj* immortal, everlasting.
immortālitās, -ātis *f* immortality; lasting fame.
immortāliter *adv* infinitely.
immōtus *adj* motionless, unmoved, immovable.
immūgiō, -īre, -īī *vi* to roar (in).
immulgeō, -ēre *vt* to milk.
immundus *adj* unclean, dirty.
immūniō, -īre, -īvī *vt* to strengthen.
immūnis *adj* with no public obligations, untaxed, free from office; exempt, free (from).
immūnitās, -ātis *f* exemption, immunity, privilege.
immūnītus *adj* undefended; (*roads*) unmetalled.
immurmurō, -āre *vi* to murmur

(at).
immūtābilis *adj* unalterable.
immūtābilitās, -ātis *f* immutability.
immūtātiō, -ōnis *f* exchange; (*RHET*) metonymy.
immūtātus *adj* unchanged.
immūtō, -āre, -āvī, -ātum *vt* to change; (*words*) to substitute by metonymy.
impācātus *adj* aggressive.
impāctus *ppp of* **impingō**.
impār, -aris *adj* unequal, uneven, unlike; no match for, inferior; (*metre*) elegiac.
imparātus *adj* unprepared, unprovided.
impariter *adv* unequally.
impāstus *adj* hungry.
impatiēns, -entis *adj* unable to endure, impatient.
impatienter *adv* intolerably.
impatientia, -ae *f* want of endurance.
impavidē *adv see* **impavidus**.
impavidus *adj* fearless, undaunted.
impedīmentum, -ī *nt* hindrance, obstacle; (*pl*) baggage, luggage, supply train.
impediō, -īre, -īvī *and* **iī, -ītum** *vt* to hinder, entangle; to encircle; (*fig*) to embarrass, obstruct, prevent.
impedītiō, -ōnis *f* obstruction.
impedītus *adj* (*MIL*) hampered with baggage, in difficulties; (*place*) difficult, impassable; (*mind*) busy, obsessed.
impēgī *perf of* **impingō**.
impellō, -ellere, -ulī, -ulsum *vt* to strike, drive; to set in motion, impel, shoot; to incite, urge on; (*fig*) to overthrow, ruin.
impendeō, -ēre *vi* to overhang; to be imminent, threaten.
impendiō *adv* very much.

impendium, -ī and **iī** nt expense, outlay; interest on a loan.

impendō, -endere, -endī, -ēnsum vt to weigh out, pay out, spend; (fig) to devote.

impenetrābilis adj impenetrable.

impēnsa, -ae f expense, outlay.

impēnsē adv very much; carefully.

impēnsus ppp of **impendō** ♦ adj (cost) high, dear; (fig) great, earnest.

imperātor, -ōris m commander-in-chief, general; emperor; chief, master.

imperātōrius adj of a general; imperial.

imperātum, -ī nt order.

imperceptus adj unknown.

impercussus adj noiseless.

imperditus adj not slain.

imperfectus adj unfinished, imperfect.

imperfōssus adj not stabbed.

imperiōsus adj powerful, imperial; tyrannical.

imperītē adv awkwardly.

imperītia, -ae f inexperience.

imperītō, -āre vt, vi to rule, command.

imperītus adj inexperienced, ignorant.

imperium, -ī and **iī** nt command, order; mastery, sovereignty, power; military command, supreme authority; empire; (pl) those in command, the authorities.

impermissus adj unlawful.

imperō, -āre, -āvī, -ātum vt, vi to order, command; to requisition, demand; to rule, govern, control; to be emperor.

imperterritus adj undaunted.

impertiō, -īre, -īvī and **iī, -ītum** vt

to share, communicate, impart.

imperturbātus adj unruffled.

impervius adj impassable.

impetibilis adj intolerable.

impetis (gen), **-e** (abl) m force; extent.

impetrābilis adj attainable; successful.

impetrātiō, -ōnis f favour.

impetriō, -īre vt to succeed with the auspices.

impetrō, -āre, -āvī, -ātum vt to achieve; to obtain, secure (a request).

impetus, -ūs m attack, onset; charge; rapid motion, rush; (mind) impulse, passion.

impexus adj unkempt.

impiē adv wickedly.

impietās, -ātis f impiety, disloyalty, unfilial conduct.

impiger, -rī adj active, energetic.

impigrō adv see adj.

impigritās, -ātis f energy.

impingō, -ingere, -ēgī, -āctum vt to dash, force against; to force upon; (fig) to bring against, drive.

impiō, -āre vt to make sinful.

impius adj (to gods) impious; (to parents) undutiful; (to country) disloyal; wicked, unscrupulous.

implācābilis adj implacable.

implācābiliter adv see adj.

implācātus adj unappeased.

implacidus adj savage.

impleō, -ēre, -ēvī, -ētum vt to fill; to satisfy; (time, number) to make up, complete; (duty) to discharge, fulfil.

implexus adj entwined; involved.

implicātiō, -ōnis f entanglement.

implicātus adj complicated, confused.

implicitē adv intricately.

implicō, The present infinitive verb endings are as follows: **-āre** = 1st; **-ēre** = 2nd; **-ere** = 3rd and **-īre** = 4th. See sections on irregular verbs and noun declensions.

and **itum** *vt* to entwine, enfold,
clasp; (*fig*) to entangle, involve; to
connect closely, join.

implōrātiō, -ōnis *f* beseeching.

implōrō, -āre, -āvī, -ātum *vt* to
invoke, entreat, appeal to.

implūmis *adj* unfledged.

impluō, -ere *vi* to rain upon.

impluvium, -ī *and* **iī** *nt* roof-opening
of the Roman atrium; rain basin in the
atrium.

impolītē *adv* without ornament.

impolītus *adj* unpolished,
inelegant.

impollūtus *adj* unstained.

impōnō, -ōnere, -osuī, -ositum *vt*
to put in, lay on, place; to embark;
(*fig*) to impose, inflict, assign; to
put in charge; (*tax*) to impose;
(*with dat*) to impose upon, cheat.

importō, -āre, -āvī, -ātum *vt* to
bring in, import; (*fig*) to bring
upon, introduce.

importūnē *adv see adj.*

importūnitās, -ātis *f* insolence, ill
nature.

importūnus *adj* unsuitable;
troublesome; ill-natured, uncivil,
bullying.

importuōsus *adj* without a
harbour.

impos, -tis *adj* not master (of).

impositus, impostus *ppp of*
impōnō.

impotēns, -entis *adj* powerless,
weak; with no control over;
headstrong, violent.

impotenter *adv* weakly; violently.

impotentia, -ae *f* poverty; want of
self-control, violence.

impraesentiārum *adv* at present.

imprānsus *adj* fasting, without
breakfast.

imprecor, -ārī *vt* to invoke.

impressiō, -ōnis *f* (MIL) thrust,
raid; (*mind*) impression; (*speech*)
emphasis; (*rhythm*) beat.

impressus *ppp of* **imprimō.**

imprīmis *adv* especially.

imprimō, -imere, -essī, -essum *vt*
to press upon, impress, imprint,
stamp.

improbātiō, -ōnis *f* blame.

improbē *adv* badly, wrongly;
persistently.

improbitās, -ātis *f* badness,
dishonesty.

improbō, -āre, -āvī, -ātum *vt* to
disapprove, condemn, reject.

improbulus *adj* a little
presumptuous.

improbus *adj* bad, inferior (in
quality); wicked, perverse, cruel;
unruly, persistent, rebellious.

imprōcērus *adj* undersized.

imprōdictus *adj* not postponed.

imprōmptus *adj* unready, slow.

improperātus *adj* lingering.

improsper, -ī *adj* unsuccessful.

improsperē *adv* unfortunately.

imprōvidē *adv see adj.*

imprōvidus *adj* unforeseeing,
thoughtless.

imprōvīsus *adj* unexpected; **~ō, de
~ō, ex ~ō** unexpectedly.

imprūdēns, -entis *adj*
unforeseeing, not expecting;
ignorant, unaware.

imprūdenter *adv* thoughtlessly,
unawares.

imprūdentia, -ae *f*
thoughtlessness; ignorance;
aimlessness.

impūbēs, -eris *and* **is** *adj* youthful;
chaste.

impudēns, -entis *adj* shameless,
impudent.

impudenter *adv see adj.*

impudentia, -ae *f* impudence.

impudīcitia, -ae *f* lewdness.

impudīcus *adj* shameless;
immodest.

impugnātiō, -ōnis *f* assault.

impugnō, -āre, -āvī, -ātum *vt* to

attack; (fig) to oppose, impugn.

impulī perf of **impellō**.

impulsiō, -ōnis f pressure; (mind) impulse.

impulsor, -ōris m instigator.

impulsus ppp of **impellō**.

impulsus, -ūs m push, pressure, impulse; (fig) instigation.

impūne adv safely, with impunity.

impūnitās, -ātis f impunity.

impūnītē adv with impunity.

impūnitus adj unpunished.

impūrātus adj vile.

impūrē adv see adj.

impūritās, -ātis f uncleanness.

impūrus adj unclean; infamous, vile.

imputātus adj unpruned.

imputō, -āre, -āvī, -ātum vt to put to one's account; to ascribe, credit, impute.

īmulus adj little tip of.

īmus adj lowest, deepest, bottom of; last.

in prep (with abl) in, on, at; among; in the case of; (time) during, (with acc) into, on to, to, towards; against; (time) for, till; (purpose) for; ~ **armīs** under arms; ~ **equō** on horseback; ~ **eō esse ut** be in the position of; be on the point of; ~ **hōrās** hourly; ~ **modum** in the manner of; ~ **rem** of use; ~ **ūniversum** in general.

inaccessus adj unapproachable.

inacēscō, -ere vi to turn sour.

Īnachidēs, -idae m Perseus; Epaphus.

Īnachis, -idis f Io.

Īnachius adj of Inachus, Argive, Greek.

Īnachus, -ī m first king of Argos.

inadsuētus adj unaccustomed.

inadūstus adj unsinged.

inaedificō, -āre, -āvī, -ātum vt to

build on, erect; to wall up, block up.

inaequābilis adj uneven.

inaequālis adj uneven; unequal; capricious.

inaequāliter adv see adj.

inaequātus adj unequal.

inaequō, -āre vt to level up.

inaestimābilis adj incalculable; invaluable; valueless.

inaestuō, -āre vi to rage in.

inamābilis adj hateful.

inamārēscō, -ere vi to become bitter.

inambitiōsus adj unambitious.

inambulātiō, -ōnis f walking about.

inambulō, -āre vi to walk up and down.

inamoenus adj disagreeable.

inanimus adj lifeless, inanimate.

ināniō, -īre vt to make empty.

inānis adj empty, void; poor, unsubstantial; useless, worthless, vain, idle ♦ nt (PHILOS) space; (fig) vanity.

inānitās, -ātis f empty space; inanity.

ināniter adv idly, vainly.

inarātus adj fallow.

inārdēscō, -dēscere, -sī vi to be kindled, flare up.

inass- etc see **inads-**.

inattenuātus adj undiminished.

inaudāx, -ācis adj timorous.

inaudiō, -īre vt to hear of, learn.

inaudītus adj unheard of, unusual; without a hearing.

inaugurātō adv after taking the auspices.

inaugurō, -āre vi to take auspices ♦ vt to consecrate, inaugurate.

inaurēs, -ium fpl earrings.

inaurō, -āre, -āvī, -ātum vt to gild, (fig) to enrich.

The present infinitive verb endings are as follows: **-āre** = 1st; **-ēre** = 2nd; **-ere** = 3rd and **-īre** = 4th. *See sections on irregular verbs and noun declensions.*

inauspicātō *adv* without taking the auspices.

inauspicātus *adj* done without auspices.

inausus *adj* unattempted.

incaeduus *adj* uncut.

incalēscō, -ēscere, -uī *vi* to grow hot; (*fig*) to warm, glow.

incalfaciō, -ere *vt* to heat.

incallidē *adv* unskilfully.

incallidus *adj* stupid, simple.

incandēscō, -ēscere, -uī *vi* to become hot; to turn white.

incānēscō, -ēscere, -uī *vi* to grow grey.

incantātus *adj* enchanted.

incānus *adj* grey.

incassum *adv* in vain.

incastīgātus *adj* unrebuked.

incautē *adv* negligently.

incautus *adj* careless, heedless; unforeseen, unguarded.

incēdō, -ēdere, -essī, -essum *vi* to walk, parade, march; (MIL) to advance; (*feelings*) to come upon.

incelebrātus *adj* not made known.

incēnātus *adj* supperless.

incendiārius, -ī and **iī** *m* incendiary.

incendium, -ī and **iī** *nt* fire, conflagration; heat; (*fig*) fire, vehemence, passion.

incendō, -ere, -ī, incēnsum *vt* to set fire to, burn; to light, brighten; (*fig*) to inflame, rouse, incense.

incēnsiō, -ōnis *f* burning.

incēnsus *ppp of* incendō.

incēnsus *adj* not registered.

incēpī *perf of* incipiō.

inceptiō, -ōnis *f* undertaking.

inceptō, -āre *vt* to begin, attempt.

inceptor, -ōris *m* originator.

inceptum, -ī *nt* beginning, undertaking, attempt.

inceptus *ppp of* incipiō.

incērō, -āre *vt* to cover with wax.

incertō *adv* not for certain.

incertus *adj* uncertain, doubtful, unsteady ♦ *nt* uncertainty.

incessō, -ere, -īvī *vt* to attack; (*fig*) to assail.

incessus, -ūs *m* gait, pace, tramp; invasion; approach.

incestē *adv* see *adj*.

incestō, -āre *vt* to pollute, dishonour.

incestus *adj* sinful; unchaste, incestuous ♦ *nt* incest.

incestus, -ūs *m* incest.

incho- *etc see* incoh-.

incidō, -idere, -dī, -āsum *vi* to fall upon, fall into; to meet, fall in with, come across; to befall, occur, happen; in mentem ~ occur to one.

incīdō, -dere, -dī, -sum *vt* to cut open; to cut up; to engrave, inscribe; to interrupt, cut short.

incīle, -is *nt* ditch.

incīlō, -āre *vt* to rebuke.

incingō, -gere, -xī, -ctum *vt* to gird, wreathe; to surround.

incinō, -ere *vt* to sing, play.

incipiō, -ipere, -ēpī, -eptum *vt, vi* to begin.

incipissō, -ere *vt* to begin.

incīsē *adv* in short clauses.

incīsim *adv* in short clauses.

incīsiō, -ōnis *f* clause.

incīsum, -ī *nt* clause.

incīsus *ppp of* incīdō.

incitāmentum, -ī *nt* incentive.

incitātē *adv* impetuously.

incitātiō, -ōnis *f* inciting; rapidity.

incitātus *ppp of* incitō ♦ *adj* swift, rapid; equō ~ō at a gallop.

incitō, -āre, -āvī, -ātum *vt* to urge on, rush; to rouse, encourage, excite; to inspire; to increase; sē ~ rush; currentem ~ ≈ spur a willing horse.

incitus *adj* swift.

incitus *adj* immovable; ad ~ās, ~ā redigere to bring to a standstill.

inclāmō, -āre vt, vi to call out, cry out to; to scold, abuse.

inclārēscō, -ēscere, -uī vi to become famous.

inclēmēns, -entis adj severe.

inclēmenter adv harshly.

inclēmentia, -ae f severity.

inclīnātiō, -ōnis f leaning, slope; (*fig*) tendency, inclination, bias; (*CIRCS*) change; (*voice*) modulation.

inclīnātus adj inclined, prone; falling; (*voice*) deep.

inclīnō, -āre, -āvī, -ātum vt to bend, turn; to turn back; (*fig*) to incline, direct, transfer; to change ♦ vi to bend, sink; (*MIL*) to give way; (*fig*) to change, deteriorate; to incline, tend, turn in favour.

inclitus etc see **inclutus**.

inclūdō, -dere, -sī, -sum vt to shut in, keep in, enclose; to obstruct, block; (*fig*) to include; (*time*) to close, end.

inclūsiō, -ōnis f imprisonment.

inclūsus ppp of **inclūdō**.

inclutus adj famous, glorious.

incoctus ppp of **incoquō**.

incoctus adj uncooked, raw.

incōgitābilis adj thoughtless.

incōgitāns, -antis adj thoughtless.

incōgitantia, -ae f thoughtlessness.

incōgitō, -āre vt to contrive.

incognitus adj unknown, unrecognised; (*law*) untried.

incohātus adj unfinished.

incohō, -āre, -āvī, -ātum vt to begin, start.

incola, -ae f inhabitant, resident.

incolō, -ere, -uī vt to live in, inhabit ♦ vi to live, reside.

incolumis adj safe and sound, unharmed.

incolumitās, -ātis f safety.

incomitātus adj unaccompanied.

incommendātus adj unprotected.

incommodē adv inconveniently, unfortunately.

incommoditās, -ātis f inconvenience, disadvantage.

incommodō, -āre vi to be inconvenient, annoy.

incommodum, -ī nt inconvenience, disadvantage, misfortune.

incommodus adj inconvenient, troublesome.

incommūtābilis adj unchangeable.

incompertus adj unknown.

incompositē adv see adj.

incompositus adj in disorder, irregular.

incomptus adj undressed, inelegant.

inconcessus adj forbidden.

inconciliō, -āre vt to win over (by guile); to trick, inveigle, embarrass.

inconcinnus adj inartistic, awkward.

inconcussus adj unshaken, stable.

inconditē adv confusedly.

inconditus adj undisciplined, not organised; (*language*) artless.

inconsīderātē adv see adj.

inconsīderātus adj thoughtless, ill-advised.

inconsōlābilis adj incurable.

inconstāns, -antis adj fickle, inconsistent.

inconstanter adv inconsistently.

inconstantia, -ae f fickleness, inconsistency.

inconsultē adv indiscreetly.

inconsultū without consulting.

inconsultus adj indiscreet, ill-advised; unanswered; not consulted.

incōnsūmptus adj unconsumed.

The present infinitive verb endings are as follows: -āre = 1st; -ēre = 2nd; -ere = 3rd and -īre = 4th. See sections on irregular verbs and noun declensions.

incontāminātus adj untainted.

incontentus adj untuned.

incontinēns, -entis adj intemperate.

incontinenter adv without self-control.

incontinentia, -ae f lack of self-control.

inconveniēns, -entis adj ill-matched.

incoquō, -quere, -xī, -ctum vt to boil; to dye.

incorrēctus adj unrevised.

incorruptē adv justly.

incorruptus adj unspoiled; uncorrupted, genuine.

incrēbrēscō, incrēbēscō, -ēscere, -uī vi to increase, grow, spread.

incrēdibilis adj incredible, extraordinary.

incrēdibiliter adv see adj.

incrēdulus adj incredulous.

incrēmentum, -ī nt growth, increase; addition; offspring.

increpitō, -āre vt to rebuke; to challenge.

increpō, -āre, -uī, -itum vi to make a noise, sound; (news) to be noised abroad ♦ vt to cause to make a noise; to exclaim against, rebuke.

incrēscō, -scere, -vī vi to grow in, increase.

incrētus adj sifted in.

incruentātus adj unstained with blood.

incruentus adj bloodless, without bloodshed.

incrūstō, -āre vt to encrust.

incubō, -āre, -uī, -itum vi to lie in or on; (fig) to brood over.

incubuī perf of **incubō**; perf of **incumbō**.

inculcō, -āre, -āvī, -ātum vt to force in; to force upon, impress on.

inculpātus adj blameless.

incultē adv uncouthly.

incultus adj uncultivated; (fig) neglected, uneducated, rude.

incultus, -ūs m neglect; squalor.

incumbō, -mbere, -buī, -bitum vi to lean, recline on; to fall upon, throw oneself upon; to oppress, lie heavily upon; (fig) to devote attention to, take pains with; to incline.

incūnābula, -ōrum ntpl swaddling clothes; (fig) cradle, infancy, birthplace, origin.

incūrātus adj neglected.

incūria, -ae f negligence.

incūriōsē adv carelessly.

incūriōsus adj careless, indifferent.

incurrō, -rrere, -rrī and **curri, -rsum** vi to run into, rush, attack; to invade; to meet with, get involved in; (events) to occur, coincide.

incursiō, -ōnis f attack; invasion, raid; collision.

incursō, -āre vt, vi to run into, assault; to frequently invade; (fig) to meet, strike.

incursus, -ūs m assault, striking; (mind) impulse.

incurvō, -āre vt to bend, crook.

incurvus adj bent, crooked.

incūs, -ūdis f anvil.

incūsātiō, -ōnis f blaming.

incūsō, -āre, -āvī, -ātum vt to find fault with, accuse.

incussī perf of **incutiō**.

incussus ppp of **incutiō**.

incussus, -ūs m shock.

incustōdītus adj unguarded, unconcealed.

incūsus adj forged.

incutiō, -tere, -ssī, -ssum vt to strike, dash against; to throw; (fig) to strike into, inspire with.

indāgātiō, -ōnis f search.

indāgātor, -ōris m explorer.

indāgātrīx, -rīcis f female

explorer.

indāgō, -āre vt to track down; (fig) to trace, investigate.

indāgō, -inis f (hunt) drive, encirclement.

indaudiō etc see **inaudiō**.

inde adv from there, from that, from them; on that side; from then, ever since; after that, then.

indēbitus adj not due.

indēclīnātus adj constant.

indecor, -is adj dishonourable, a disgrace.

indecōrē adv indecently.

indecorō, -āre vt to disgrace.

indecōrus adj unbecoming, unsightly.

indēfēnsus adj undefended.

indēfessus adj unwearied, tireless.

indēflētus adj unwept.

indēiectus adj undemolished.

indēlēbilis adj imperishable.

indēlībātus adj unimpaired.

indemnātus adj unconvicted.

indēplōrātus adj unlamented.

indēprēnsus adj undetected.

indeptus ppa of **indipīscor**.

indēsertus adj unforsaken.

indēstrictus adj unscathed.

indētōnsus adj unshorn.

indēvītātus adj unerring.

index, -icis m forefinger; witness, informer; (book, art) title, inscription; (stone) touchstone; (fig) indication, pointer, sign.

India, -iae f India.

indicātiō, -ōnis f value.

indicente mē without my telling.

indicium, -ī and **iī** nt information, evidence; reward for information; indication, sign, proof; ~ profitērī, offerre ≈ turn King's evidence; ~ postulāre, dare ask, grant permission to give evidence.

indicō, -āre, -āvī, -ātum vt to point out; to disclose, betray; to give information, give evidence; to put a price on.

indīcō, -īcere, -īxī, -ictum vt to declare, proclaim, appoint.

indictus ppp of **indīcō**.

indictus adj not said, unsung; **causā ~ā** without a hearing.

Indicus adj see n.

indidem adv from the same place or thing.

indidī perf of **indō**.

indifferēns, -entis adj neither good nor bad.

indigena, -ae m native ♦ adj native.

indigēns, -entis adj needy.

indigentia, -ae f need; craving.

indigeō, -ēre, -uī vi (with abl) to need, want, require; to crave.

indiges, -etis m national deity.

indigestus adj confused.

indignābundus adj enraged.

indignāns, -antis adj indignant.

indignātiō, -ōnis f indignation.

indignē adv unworthily; indignantly.

indignitās, -ātis f unworthiness, enormity; insulting treatment; indignation.

indignor, -ārī, -ātus vt to be displeased with, be angry at.

indignus adj unworthy, undeserving; shameful, severe; undeserved.

indigus adj in want.

indīligēns, -entis adj careless.

indīligenter adv see adj.

indīligentia, -ae f carelessness.

indipīscor, -ī, indeptus vt to obtain, get, reach.

indireptus adj unplundered.

indiscrētus adj closely connected, indiscriminate, indistinguishable.

The present infinitive verb endings are as follows: **-āre** = 1st; **-ēre** = 2nd; **-ere** = 3rd and **-īre** = 4th. *See sections on irregular verbs and noun declensions.*

indisertē adv without eloquence.
indisertus adj not eloquent.
indispositus adj disorderly.
indissolūbilis adj imperishable.
indistinctus adj confused, obscure.
inditus ppp of **indō**.
indīviduus adj indivisible,
  inseparable ♦ nt atom.
indō, -ere, -idī, -itum vt to put in or
  on; to introduce; to impart,
  impose.
indocilis adj difficult to teach, hard
  to learn; untaught.
indoctē adv unskilfully.
indoctus adj untrained, illiterate,
  ignorant.
indolentia, -ae f freedom from
  pain.
indolēs, -is f nature, character,
  talents.
indolēscō, -ēscere, -uī vi to feel
  sorry.
indomitus adj untamed, wild;
  ungovernable.
indormiō, -īre vi to sleep on; to be
  careless.
indōtātus adj with no dowry;
  unhonoured; (fig) unadorned.
indubitō, -āre vi to begin to doubt.
indubius adj undoubted.
indūcō, -ūcere, -ūxī, -uctum vt to
  bring in, lead on; to introduce; to
  overlay, cover over; (fig) to move,
  persuade, seduce; (book-keeping)
  to enter; (dress) to put on; (public
  show) to exhibit; (writing) to erase;
  animum, in animum ~ determine,
  imagine.
inductiō, -ōnis f leading, bringing
  on; (mind) purpose, intention;
  (logic) induction.
inductus ppp of **indūcō**.
indugredior etc see **ingredior**.
induī perf of **induō**.
indulgēns, -entis pres p of **indulgeō**
  ♦ adj indulgent, kind.
indulgenter adv indulgently.

indulgentia, -ae f indulgence,
  gentleness.
indulgeō, -gēre, -sī vi (with dat) to
  be kind to, indulge, give way to; to
  indulge in ♦ vt to concede; **sibi ~**
  take liberties.
induō, -uere, -uī, -ūtum vt (dress)
  to put on; (fig) to assume,
  entangle.
indup- etc see **imp-**.
indūrēscō, -ēscere, -uī vi to
  harden.
indūrō, -āre vt to harden.
Indus, -ī m Indian; Ethiopian;
  mahout.
Indus adj see n.
industria, -ae f diligence; **dē, ex ~ā**
  on purpose.
industriē adv see **industrius**.
industrius adj diligent,
  painstaking.
indūtiae, -ārum fpl truce,
  armistice.
indūtus ppp of **induō**.
indūtus, -us m wearing.
induviae, -ārum fpl clothes.
indūxī perf of **indūcō**.
inēbriō, -āre vt to intoxicate; (fig)
  to saturate.
inedia, -ae f starvation.
inēditus adj unpublished.
inēlegāns, -antis adj tasteless.
inēleganter adv without taste.
inēluctābilis adj inescapable.
inēmorior, -ī vi to die in.
inēmptus adj unpurchased.
inēnārrābilis adj indescribable.
inēnōdābilis adj inexplicable.
ineō, -īre, -īvī and iī, -itum vi to go
  in, come in; to begin ♦ vt to enter;
  to begin, enter upon, form,
  undertake; **cōnsilium ~** form a
  plan; **grātiam ~** win favour;
  numerum ~ enumerate; **ratiōnem
  ~** calculate, consider, contrive;
  suffrāgium ~ vote; **viam ~** find out
  a way.

ineptē adv see adj.

ineptia, -ae f stupidity; (pl) nonsense.

ineptiō, -īre vi to play the fool.

ineptus adj unsuitable; silly, tactless, absurd.

inermis, inermus adj unarmed, defenceless; harmless.

inorrāns, -antis adj fixed.

inerrō, -āre vi to wander about in.

iners, -tis adj unskilful; inactive, indolent, timid; insipid.

inertia, -ae f lack of skill; idleness, laziness.

inērudītus adj uneducated.

inescō, -āre vt to entice, deceive.

inēvectus adj mounted.

inēvītābilis adj inescapable.

inexcītus adj peaceful.

inexcūsābilis adj with no excuse.

inexercitātus adj untrained.

inexhaustus adj unexhausted.

inexōrābilis adj inexorable; (things) severe.

inexperrēctus adj unawakened.

inexpertus adj inexperienced; untried.

inexpiābilis adj inexpiable; implacable.

inexplēbilis adj insatiable.

inexplētus adj incessant.

inexplicābilis adj inexplicable; impracticable, unending.

inexplōrātō adv without making a reconnaissance.

inexplōrātus adj unreconnoitred.

inexpugnābilis adj impregnable, safe.

inexspectātus adj unexpected.

inexstīnctus adj unextinguished; insatiable, imperishable.

inexsuperābilis adj insurmountable.

inextrīcābilis adj inextricable.

īnfabrē adv unskilfully.

īnfabricātus adj unfashioned.

īnfacētus adj not witty, crude.

īnfācundus adj ineloquent.

īnfāmia, -ae f disgrace, scandal.

īnfāmis adj infamous, disreputable.

īnfāmō, -āre, -āvī, -ātum vt to disgrace, bring into disrepute.

īnfandus adj unspeakable, atrocious.

īnfāns, -antis adj mute, speechless; young, infant; tongue-tied; childish ♦ m/f infant, child.

īnfantia, -ae f inability to speak; infancy; lack of eloquence.

īnfatuō, -āre vt to make a fool of.

īnfaustus adj unlucky.

īnfector, -ōris m dyer.

īnfectus ppp of **īnficiō**.

īnfectus adj undone, unfinished; rē ~ā without achieving one's purpose.

īnfēcunditās, -ātis f infertility.

īnfēcundus adj unfruitful.

īnfēlīcitās, -ātis f misfortune.

īnfēlīciter adv see adj.

īnfēlīcō, -āre vt to make unhappy.

īnfēlīx, -īcis adj unfruitful; unhappy, unlucky.

īnfēnsē adv aggressively.

īnfēnsō, -āre vt to make dangerous, make hostile.

īnfēnsus adj hostile, dangerous.

īnferciō, -īre vt to cram in.

īnferiae, -ārum fpl offerings to the dead.

īnferior, -ōris compar of **īnferus**.

īnferius compar of **īnfrā**.

īnfernē adv below.

īnfernus adj beneath; of the lower world, infernal ♦ mpl the shades ♦ ntpl the lower world.

īnferō, -re, intulī, illātum vt to carry in, bring to, put on; to move forward; (*fig*) to introduce, cause; (*book-keeping*) to enter; (*logic*) to infer; **bellum** ~ make war (on); **pedem** ~ advance; **sē** ~ repair, rush, strut about; **signa** ~ attack, charge.

inferus (*compar* **-ior**, *superl* **infimus**) *adj* lower, below ♦ *mpl* the dead, the lower world ♦ *compar* lower; later; inferior ♦ *superl* lowest, bottom of; meanest, humblest.

infervēscō, -vēscere, -buī *vi* to boil.

infestē *adv* aggressively.

infestō, -āre *vt* to attack.

infestus *adj* unsafe; dangerous, aggressive.

inficet- *see* **infacet-**.

inficiō, -icere, -ēcī, -ectum *vt* to dip, dye, discolour; to taint, infect; (*fig*) to instruct, corrupt, poison.

infidēlis *adj* faithless.

infidēlitās, -ātis *f* disloyalty.

infidēliter *adv* treacherously.

infidus *adj* unsafe, treacherous.

infigō, -gere, -xī, -xum *vt* to thrust, drive in; (*fig*) to impress, imprint.

infimus *superl of* **inferus**.

infindō, -ere *vt* to cut into, plough.

infinitās, -ātis *f* boundless extent, infinity.

infinitē *adv* without end.

infinitiō, -ōnis *f* infinity.

infinitus *adj* boundless, endless, infinite; indefinite.

infirmātiō, -ōnis *f* invalidating, refuting.

infirmē *adv* feebly.

infirmitās, -ātis *f* weakness; infirmity, sickness.

infirmō, -āre *vt* to weaken; to invalidate, refute.

infirmus *adj* weak, indisposed; weak-minded; (*things*) trivial.

infit *vi* (*defec*) begins.

infitiālis *adj* negative.

infitiās eō deny.

infitiātiō, -ōnis *f* denial.

infitiātor, -ōris *m* denier (of a debt).

infitior, -ārī, -ātus *vt* to deny, repudiate.

infixus *ppp of* **infigō**.

inflammātiō, -ōnis *f* (*fig*) exciting.

inflammō, -āre, -āvī, -ātum *vt* to set on fire, light; (*fig*) to inflame, rouse.

inflātē *adv* pompously.

inflātiō, -ōnis *f* flatulence.

inflātus, -ūs *m* blow; inspiration ♦ *adj* blown up, swollen; (*fig*) puffed up, conceited; (*style*) turgid.

inflectō, -ctere, -xī, -xum *vt* to bend, curve; to change; (*voice*) to modulate; (*fig*) to affect, move.

inflētus *adj* unwept.

inflexiō, -ōnis *f* bending.

inflexus *ppp of* **inflectō**.

infligō, -gere, -xī, -ctum *vt* to dash against, strike; to inflict.

inflō, -āre, -āvī, -ātum *vt* to blow, inflate; (*fig*) to inspire, puff up.

influō, -ere, -xī, -xum *vi* to flow in; (*fig*) to stream, pour in.

infodiō, -odere, -ōdī, -ossum *vt* to dig in, bury.

informātiō, -ōnis *f* sketch, idea.

informis *adj* shapeless; hideous.

informō, -āre, -āvī, -ātum *vt* to shape, fashion; to sketch; to educate.

infortūnātus *adj* unfortunate.

infortūnium, -ī *and* **iī** *nt* misfortune.

infossus *ppp of* **infodiō**.

infrā (*compar* **inferius**) *adv* underneath, below ♦ *compar* lower down ♦ *prep* (*with acc*) below, beneath, under; later than.

infrāctiō, -ōnis *f* weakening.

infrāctus *ppp of* **infringō**.

infragilis *adj* strong.

īnfremō, -ere, -uī vi to growl.

īnfrēnātus ppp of īnfrēnō.

īnfrēnātus adj without a bridle.

īnfrendō, -ere vi to gnash.

īnfrēnis, -us adj unbridled.

īnfrēnō, -āre, -āvī, -ātum vt to put a bridle on, harness; (fig) to curb.

īnfrequēns, -entis adj not crowded, infrequent; badly attended.

īnfrequentia, -ae f small number; emptiness.

īnfringō, -ingere, -ēgī, -āctum vt to break, bruise; (fig) to weaken, break down, exhaust.

īnfrōns, -ondis adj leafless.

īnfucātus adj showy.

īnfula, -ae f woollen band, fillet, badge of honour.

īnfumus etc see īnfimus.

īnfundō, -undere, -ūdī, -ūsum vt to pour in or on; to serve; (fig) to spread.

īnfuscō, -āre vt to darken; to spoil, tarnish.

īnfūsus ppp of īnfundō.

ingeminō, -āre vt to redouble ♦ vi to be redoubled.

ingemīscō, -īscere, -uī vi to groan, sigh ♦ vt to sigh over.

ingemō, -ere, -uī vt, vi to sigh for, mourn.

ingenerō, -āre, -āvī, -ātum vt to engender, produce, create.

ingeniātus adj with a natural talent.

ingeniōsē adv cleverly.

ingeniōsus adj talented, clever; (things) naturally suited.

ingenitus ppp of ingignō ♦ adj inborn, natural.

ingenium, -ī and iī nt nature; (disposition) bent, character; (intellect) ability, talent, genius; (person) genius.

ingēns, -entis adj huge, mighty, great.

ingenuē adv liberally, frankly.

ingenuitās, -ātis f noble birth, noble character.

ingenuus adj native, innate; free-born; noble, frank; delicate.

ingerō, -rere, -ssī, -stum vt to carry in; to heap on; to throw, hurl; (fig) to press, obtrude.

ingignō, -ignere, -enuī, -enitum vt to engender, implant.

inglōrius adj inglorious.

ingluviēs, -ēī f maw; gluttony.

ingrātē adv unwillingly; ungratefully.

ingrātiīs, ingrātis adv against one's will.

ingrātus adj disagreeable, unwelcome; ungrateful, thankless.

ingravēscō, -ere vi to grow heavy, become worse, increase.

ingravō, -āre vt to weigh heavily on; to aggravate.

ingredior, -dī, -ssus vt, vi to go in, enter; to walk, march; to enter upon, engage in; to commence, begin to speak.

ingressiō, -ōnis f entrance; beginning; pace.

ingressus, -ūs m entrance; (MIL) inroad; beginning; walking, gait.

ingruō, -ere, -ī vi to fall upon, assail.

inguen, -inis nt groin.

ingurgitō, -āre vt to pour in; sē ~ gorge oneself; (fig) to be absorbed in.

ingustātus adj untasted.

inhabilis adj unwieldy, awkward; unfit.

inhabitābilis adj uninhabitable.

inhabitō, -āre vt to inhabit.

inhaereō, -rēre, -sī, -sum vi to

The present infinitive verb endings are as follows: -āre = 1st; -ēre = 2nd; -ere = 3rd and -īre = 4th. See sections on irregular verbs and noun declensions.

stick in, cling to; to adhere, be closely connected with; to be always in.

inhaerēscō, -ere vi to take hold, cling fast.

inhālō, -āre vt to breathe on.

inhibeō, -ēre, -uī, -itum vt to check, restrain, use, practise; **~rēmis/nāvem** back water.

inhibitiō, -ōnis f backing water.

inhiō, -āre vi to gape ♦ vt to gape at, covet.

inhonestē adv see adj.

inhonestō, -āre vt to dishonour.

inhonestus adj dishonourable, inglorious; ugly.

inhonōrātus adj unhonoured; unrewarded.

inhonōrus adj defaced.

inhorreō, -ēre, -uī vt to stand erect, bristle.

inhorrēscō, -ēscere, -uī vi to bristle up; to shiver, shudder, tremble.

inhospitālis adj inhospitable.

inhospitālitās, -ātis f inhospitality.

inhospitus adj inhospitable.

inhūmānē adv savagely; uncivilly.

inhūmānitās, -ātis f barbarity; discourtesy, churlishness, meanness.

inhūmāniter adv = **inhūmānē**.

inhūmānus adj savage, brutal; ill-bred, uncivil, uncultured.

inhumātus adj unburied.

inibi adv there, therein; about to happen.

īniciō, -icere, -iēcī, -iectum vt to throw into, put on; (fig) to inspire, cause; (speech) to hint, mention; **manum ~** take possession.

iniectus, -ūs m putting in, throwing over.

inimīcē adv hostilely.

inimīcitia, -ae f enmity.

inimīcō, -āre vt to make enemies.

inimīcus adj unfriendly, hostile; injurious ♦ m/f enemy; **~issimum** greatest enemy.

iniquē adv unequally, unjustly.

inīquitās, -ātis f unevenness; difficulty; injustice, unfair demands.

inīquus adj unequal, uneven; adverse, unfavourable, injurious; unfair, unjust; excessive; impatient, discontented ♦ m enemy.

initiō, -āre vt to initiate.

initium, -ī and **iī** nt beginning; (pl) elements, first principles; holy rites, mysteries.

initus ppp of **ineō**.

initus, -ūs m approach; beginning.

iniūcundē adv see adj.

iniūcunditās, -ātis f unpleasantness.

iniūcundus adj unpleasant.

iniungō, -ungere, -ūnxī, -ūnctum vt to join, attach; (fig) to impose, inflict.

iniūrātus adj unsworn.

iniūria, -ae f wrong, injury, injustice; insult, outrage; severity, revenge; unjust possession; **~ā** unjustly.

iniūriōsē adv wrongfully.

iniūriōsus adj unjust, wrongful; harmful.

iniūrius adj wrong, unjust.

iniūssū without orders (from).

iniūssus adj unbidden.

iniūstē adv see adj.

iniūstitia, -ae f injustice, severity.

iniūstus adj unjust, wrong; excessive, severe.

inl- etc see **ill-**.

inm- etc see **imm-**.

innābilis adj that none may swim.

innāscor, -scī, -tus vi to be born in, grow up in.

innatō, -āre vt to swim in, float on; to swim, flow into.

innātus *ppa of* **innāscor ♦** *adj* innate, natural.

innāvigābilis *adj* unnavigable.

innectō, -ctere, -xuī, -xum *vt* to tie, fasten together, entwine; *(fig)* to connect; to contrive.

innītor, -tī, -xus *and* **sus** *vi* to rest, lean on; to depend.

innō, -āre *vi* to swim in, float on, sail on.

innocēns, -entis *adj* harmless, innocent; upright, unselfish.

innocenter *adv* blamelessly.

innocentia, -ae *f* innocence; integrity, unselfishness.

innocuē *adv* innocently.

innocuus *adj* harmless; innocent; unharmed.

innōtēscō, -ēscere, -uī *vi* to become known.

innovō, -āre *vt* to renew; **sē ~** return.

innoxius *adj* harmless, safe; innocent; unharmed.

innuba, -ae *adj* unmarried.

innūbilus *adj* cloudless.

innūbō, -bere, -psī *vi* to marry into.

innumerābilis *adj* countless.

innumerābilitās, -ātis *f* countless number.

innumerābiliter *adv* innumerably.

innumerālis *adj* numberless.

innumerus *adj* countless.

innuō, -ere, -ī *vi* to give a nod.

innūpta, -ae *adj* unmarried.

Īnō, -ūs *f* daughter of Cadmus.

inoblītus *adj* unforgetful.

inobrutus *adj* not overwhelmed.

inobservābilis *adj* unnoticed.

inobservātus *adj* unobserved.

inoffēnsus *adj* without hindrance, uninterrupted.

inofficiōsus *adj* irresponsible; disobliging.

inolēns, -entis *adj* odourless.

inolēscō, -scere, -vī *vi* to grow in.

inōminātus *adj* inauspicious.

inopia, -ae *f* want, scarcity, poverty, helplessness.

inopīnāns, -antis *adj* unaware.

inopīnātō *adv* unexpectedly.

inopīnātus *adj* unexpected; off one's guard.

inopīnus *adj* unexpected.

inopiōsus *adj* in want.

inops, -is *adj* destitute, poor, in need (of); helpless, weak, (*speech*) poor in ideas.

inōrātus *adj* unpleaded.

inōrdinātus *adj* disordered, irregular.

inōrnātus *adj* unadorned, plain; uncelebrated.

īnous *adj* see **n**.

inp- *etc see* **imp-**.

inquam *vt* (*defec*) to say; (*emphatic*) I repeat, maintain.

inquiēs, -ētis *adj* restless.

inquiētō, -āre *vt* to unsettle, make difficult.

inquiētus *adj* restless, unsettled.

inquilīnus, -ī *m* inhabitant, tenant.

inquinātē *adv* filthily.

inquinātus *adj* filthy, impure.

inquinō, āre, -āvī, -ātum *vt* to defile, stain, contaminate.

inquīrō, -rere, -sīvī, -sītum *vt* to search for, inquire into; (*law*) to collect evidence.

inquīsītiō, -ōnis *f* searching, inquiry; (*law*) inquisition.

inquīsītor, -ōris *m* searcher, spy; investigator.

inquīsītus *ppp of* **inquīrō**.

inquīsītus *adj* not investigated.

inr- *etc see* **irr-**.

īnsalūtātus *adj* ungreeted.

īnsānābilis *adj* incurable.

īnsānē *adv* madly.

The present infinitive verb endings are as follows: -āre = 1st; -ēre = 2nd; -ere = 3rd and -īre = 4th. See sections on irregular verbs and noun declensions.

īnsānia, -ae f madness; folly, mania, poetic rapture.

īnsāniō, -īre, -īvī, -ītum vi to be mad, rave; to rage; to be inspired.

īnsānitās, -ātis f unhealthiness.

īnsānum adv (slang) frightfully.

īnsānus adj mad; frantic, furious; outrageous.

īnsatiābilis adj insatiable; never cloying.

īnsatiābiliter adv see adj.

īnsatietās, -ātis f insatiateness.

īnsaturābilis adj insatiable.

īnsaturābiliter adv see adj.

īnscendō, -endere, -endī, -ēnsum vt, vi to climb up, mount, embark.

īnscēnsiō, -ōnis f going on board.

īnscēnsus ppp of **īnscendō**.

īnsciēns, -entis adj unaware; stupid.

īnscienter adv ignorantly.

īnscientia, -ae f ignorance, inexperience; neglect.

īnscītē adv clumsily.

īnscītia, -ae f ignorance, stupidity, inattention.

īnscītus adj ignorant, stupid.

īnscius adj unaware, ignorant.

īnscrībō, -bere, -psī, -ptum vt to write on, inscribe; to ascribe, assign; (book) to entitle; (for sale) to advertise.

īnscrīptiō, -ōnis f inscribing, title.

īnscrīptus ppp of **īnscrībō**.

īnsculpō, -ere, -sī, -tum vt to carve in, engrave on.

īnsectātiō, -ōnis f hot pursuit; (words) abusing, persecution.

īnsectātor, -ōris m persecutor.

īnsector, -ārī, -ātus; -ō, -āre vt to pursue, attack, criticise.

īnsectus adj notched.

īnsedābiliter adv incessantly.

īnsēdī perf of **īnsīdō**.

īnsenēscō, -ēscere, -uī vi to grow old in.

īnsēnsilis adj imperceptible.

īnsepultus adj unburied.

īnsequēns, -entis pres p of **īnsequor** ♦ adj the following.

īnsequor, -quī, -cūtus vt to follow, pursue hotly; to proceed; (time) to come after, come next; (fig) to attack, persecute.

īnserō, -erere, -ēvī, -itum vt to graft; (fig) to implant.

īnserō, -ere, -uī, -tum vt to let in, insert; to introduce, mingle, involve.

īnsertō, -āre vt to put in.

īnsertus ppp of **īnserō**.

īnserviō, -īre, -īī, -ītum vt, vi to be a slave (to); to be devoted, submissive (to).

īnsessus ppp of **īnsīdō**.

īnsībilō, -āre vi to whistle in.

īnsīdeō, -ēre vi to sit on or in; to remain fixed ♦ vt to hold, occupy.

īnsidiae, -ārum fpl ambush; (fig) trap, trickery.

īnsidiātor, -ōris nt soldier in ambush; (fig) waylayer, plotter.

īnsidior, -ārī, -ātus vi to lie in ambush; (with dat) to lie in wait for, plot against.

īnsidiōsē adv insidiously.

īnsidiōsus adj artful, treacherous.

īnsīdō, -idere, -ēdī, -essum vi to settle on; (fig) to become fixed, rooted in ♦ vt to occupy.

īnsigne, -is nt distinguishing mark, badge, decoration; (pl) insignia, honours; (speech) purple passages.

īnsigniō, -īre vt to distinguish.

īnsignis adj distinguished, conspicuous.

īnsignītē adv remarkably.

īnsigniter adv markedly.

īnsilia, -um ntpl treadle (of a loom).

īnsiliō, -īre, -uī vi to jump into or onto.

īnsimulātiō, -ōnis f accusation.

īnsimulō, -āre, -āvī, -ātum vt to

charge, accuse, allege (esp falsely).

īnsincērus adj adulterated.

īnsinuātiō, -ōnis f ingratiating.

īnsinuō, -āre, -āvī, -ātum vt to bring in, introduce stealthily ♦ vi to creep in, worm one's way in, penetrate; **sē ~** ingratiate oneself; to make one's way into.

īnsipiēns, -entis adj senseless, foolish.

īnsipienter adv foolishly.

īnsipientia, -ae f folly.

īnsistō, -istere, -titī vi to stand on, step on; to stand firm, halt, pause; to tread on the heels, press on, pursue; to enter upon, apply oneself to, begin; to persist, continue.

īnsitiō, -ōnis f grafting; grafting time.

īnsitīvus adj grafted; (fig) spurious.

īnsitor, -ōris m grafter.

īnsitus ppp of **īnserō** ♦ adj innate; incorporated.

īnsociābilis adj incompatible.

īnsōlābiliter adv unconsolably.

īnsolēns, -entis adj unusual, unaccustomed; excessive, extravagant, insolent.

īnsolenter adv unusually; immoderately, insolently.

īnsolentia, -ae f inexperience, novelty, strangeness; excess, insolence.

īnsolēscō, -ere vi to become insolent, elated.

īnsolidus adj soft.

īnsolitus adj unaccustomed, unusual.

īnsomnia, -ae f sleeplessness.

īnsomnis adj sleepless.

īnsomnium, -ī nt dream.

īnsonō, -āre, -uī vi to resound, sound; to make a noise.

īnsōns, -ontis adj innocent; harmless.

īnsōpītus adj sleepless.

īnspectō, -āre vt to look at.

īnspectus ppp of **īnspiciō**.

īnspērāns, -antis adj not expecting.

īnspērātus adj unexpected; **-ō, ex ~ō** unexpectedly.

īnspergō, -gere, -sī, -sum vt to sprinkle on.

īnspiciō, -icere, -exī, -ectum vt to look into; to examine, inspect; (MIL) to review; (mind) to consider, get to know.

īnspīcō, -āre vt to sharpen.

īnspīrō, -āre, -āvī, -ātum vt, vi to blow on, breathe into.

īnspoliātus adj unpillaged.

īnspūtō, -āre vt to spit on.

īnstābilis adj unsteady, not firm; (fig) inconstant.

īnstāns, -antis pres p of **īnstō** ♦ adj present; urgent, threatening.

īnstanter adv vehemently.

īnstantia, -ae f presence; vehemence.

īnstar nt (indecl) likeness, appearance; as good as, worth.

īnstaurātiō, -ōnis f renewal.

īnstaurātīvus adj renewed.

īnstaurō, -āre, -āvī, -ātum vt to renew, restore; to celebrate; to require.

īnsternō, -ernere, -rāvī, -rātum vt to spread over, cover.

īnstīgātor, -ōris m instigator.

īnstīgātrīx, -rīcis f female instigator.

īnstīgō, -āre vt to goad, incite, instigate.

īnstillō, -āre vt to drop on, instil.

īnstimulātor, -ōris m instigator.

īnstimulō, -āre vt to urge on.

īnstinctor, -ōris m instigator.

The present infinitive verb endings are as follows: -āre = 1st; -ēre = 2nd; -ere = 3rd and -īre = 4th. See sections on irregular verbs and noun declensions.

īnstinctus adj incited, inspired.

īnstinctus, -ūs m impulse, inspiration.

īnstipulor, -ārī, -ātus vi to bargain for.

īnstita, -ae f flounce of a lady's tunic.

īnstitī perf of **īnsistō**.

īnstitiō, -ōnis f stopping.

īnstitor, -ōris m pedlar.

īnstituō, -uere, -uī, -ūtum vt to set, implant; to set up, establish, build, appoint; to marshal, arrange, organize; to teach, educate; to undertake, resolve on.

īnstitūtiō, -ōnis f custom; arrangement; education; (pl) principles of education.

īnstitūtum, -ī nt way of life, tradition, law; stipulation, agreement; purpose; (pl) principles.

īnstō, -āre, -itī vi to stand on or in; to be close, be hard on the heels of, pursue; (events) to approach, impend; (fig) to press on, work hard at; (speech) to insist, urge.

īnstrātus ppp of **īnsternō**.

īnstrēnuus adj languid, slow.

īnstrepō, -ere vi to creak.

īnstructiō, -ōnis f building; setting out.

īnstructius adv in better style.

īnstructor, -ōris m preparer.

īnstructus ppp of **īnstruō** ♦ adj provided, equipped; prepared, versed.

īnstructus, -ūs m equipment.

īnstrūmentum, -ī nt tool, instrument; equipment, furniture, stock; (fig) means, provision; dress, embellishment.

īnstruō, -ere, -xī, -ctum vt to erect, build up; (MIL) to marshal, array; to equip, provide, prepare; (fig) to teach, train.

īnsuāsum, -ī nt a dark colour.

īnsuāvis adj disagreeable.

īnsūdō, -āre vi to perspire on.

īnsuēfactus adj accustomed.

īnsuēscō, -scere, -vī, -tum vt to train, accustom ♦ vi to become accustomed.

īnsuētus ppp of **īnsuēscō**.

īnsuētus adj unaccustomed, unused; unusual.

īnsula, -ae f island; block of houses.

īnsulānus, -ī m islander.

īnsulsē adv see adj.

īnsulsitās, -ātis f lack of taste, absurdity.

īnsulsus adj tasteless, absurd, dull.

īnsultō, -āre, vt, vi to jump on, leap in; (fig) to exult, taunt, insult.

īnsultūra, -ae f jumping on.

īnsum, īnesse, īnfuī vi to be in or on; to belong to.

īnsūmō, -ere, -psī, -ptum vt to spend, devote.

īnsuō, -uere, -uī, -ūtum vt to sew in, sew up in.

īnsuper adv above, on top; besides, over and above; (prep with abl) besides.

īnsuperābilis adj unconquerable, impassable.

īnsurgō, -gere, -rēxī, -rēctum vi to stand up, rise to; to rise, grow, swell; to rise against.

īnsusurrō, -āre vt, vi to whisper.

īnsūtus ppp of **īnsuō**.

intābēscō, -ēscere, -uī vi to melt away, waste away.

intāctilis adj intangible.

intāctus adj untouched, intact; untried; undefiled, chaste.

intāminātus adj unsullied.

intēctus ppp of **integō**.

intēctus adj uncovered, unclad; frank.

integellus adj fairly whole or pure.

integer, -rī adj whole, complete, unimpaired, intact; sound, fresh, new; (*mind*) unbiassed, free; (*character*) virtuous, pure, upright; (*decision*) undecided, open; in ~rum **restituere** restore to a former state; **ab, dē, ex ~rō** afresh; ~**rum est mihi** I am at liberty (to).

integō, -egere, -ēxī, -ēctum *vt* to cover over; to protect.

Integrāscō, -ere *vi* to begin all over again.

integrātiō, -ōnis *f* renewing.

integrē *adv* entirely; honestly; correctly.

integritās, -ātis *f* completeness, soundness; integrity, honesty; (*language*) correctness.

integrō, -āre *vt* to renew, replenish, repair; (*mind*) to refresh.

Integumentum, -ī *nt* cover, covering, shelter.

intellēctus *ppp of* **intellegō**.

intellēctus, -ūs *m* understanding; (*word*) meaning.

intellegēns, -entis *pres p of* **intellegō ♦** *adj* intelligent, a connoisseur.

intellegenter *adv* intelligently.

intellegentia, -ae *f* discernment, understanding; taste.

intellegō, -egere, -ēxī, -ēctum *vt* to understand, perceive, realize; to be a connoisseur.

intemerātus *adj* pure, undefiled.

intemperāns, -antis *adj* immoderate, extravagant; incontinent.

intemperanter *adv* extravagantly.

intemperantia, -ae *f* excess, extravagance; arrogance.

intemperātē *adv* dissolutely.

intemperātus *adj* excessive.

intemperiae, -ārum *fpl* inclemency; madness.

intemperiēs, -ēī *f* inclemency, storm; (*fig*) fury.

intempestīvē *adv* inopportunely.

intempestīvus *adj* unseasonable, untimely.

intempestus *adj* (*night*) the dead of; unhealthy.

intemptātus *adj* untried.

intendō, -dere, -dī, -tum *vt* to stretch out, strain, spread; (*weapon*) to aim; (*tent*) to pitch; (*attention, course*) to direct, turn; (*fact*) to increase, exaggerate; (*speech*) to maintain; (*trouble*) to threaten ♦ *vi* to make for, intend; **animō ~** purpose; **sē ~** exert oneself.

intentē *adv* strictly.

intentiō, -ōnis *f* straining, tension; (*mind*) exertion, attention; (*law*) accusation.

intentō, -āre *vt* to stretch out, aim; (*fig*) to threaten with, attack.

intentus *ppp of* **intendō ♦** *adj* taut; attentive, intent; strict; (*speech*) vigorous.

intentus, -ūs *m* stretching out.

intepeō, -ēre *vi* to be warm.

intepēscō, -ēscere, -uī *vi* to be warmed.

inter *prep* (*with acc*) between; among, during, in the course of; in spite of; ~ **haec** meanwhile; ~ **manūs** within reach; ~ **nōs** confidentially; ~ **sē** mutually, one another; ~ **sīcāriōs** in the murder court; ~ **viam** on the way.

interāmenta, -ōrum *ntpl* ship's timbers.

interaptus *adj* joined together.

interārēscō, -ere *vi* to wither away.

interbibō, -ere *vi* to drink up.

interbītō, -ere *vi* to fall through.

intercalāris *adj* intercalary.

The present infinitive verb endings are as follows: **-āre** = 1st; **-ēre** = 2nd; **-ere** = 3rd and **-īre** = 4th. *See sections on irregular verbs and noun declensions.*

intercalārius *adj* intercalary.

intercalō, -āre *vt* to intercalate.

intercapēdō, -inis *f* interruption, respite.

intercēdō, -ēdere, -ēssī, -ēssum *vi* to come between, intervene; to occur; to become surety; to interfere, obstruct; (*tribune*) to protest, veto.

interceptiō, -ōnis *f* taking away.

interceptor, -ōris *m* embezzler.

interceptus *ppp of* **intercipiō**.

intercessiō, -ōnis *f* (*law*) becoming surety; (*tribune*) veto.

intercessor, -ōris *m* mediator, surety; interposer of the veto; obstructor.

intercidō, -ere, -ī *vi* to fall short; to happen in the meantime; to get lost, become obsolete, be forgotten.

intercīdō, -dere, -dī, -sum *vt* to cut through, sever.

intercinō, -ere *vt* to sing between.

intercipiō, -ipere, -ēpi, -eptum *vt* to intercept; to embezzle, steal; to cut off, obstruct.

intercīsē *adv* piecemeal.

intercīsus *ppp of* **intercīdō**.

interclūdō, -dere, -sī, -sum *vt* to cut off, block, shut off, prevent; **animam ~** suffocate.

interclūsiō, -ōnis *f* stoppage.

interclūsus *ppp of* **interclūdō**.

intercolumnium, -ī *and* **iī** *nt* space between two pillars.

intercurrō, -ere *vi* to mingle with; to intercede; to hurry in the meantime.

intercursō, -āre *vi* to crisscross; to attack between the lines.

intercursus, -ūs *m* intervention.

intercus, -tis *adj*: **aqua ~** dropsy.

interdīcō, -īcere, -īxī, -ictum *vt, vi* to forbid, interdict; (*praetor*) to make a provisional order; **aquā et igni ~** banish.

interdictiō, -ōnis *f* prohibiting, banishment.

interdictum, -ī *nt* prohibition; provisional order (by a praetor).

interdiū *adv* by day.

interdō, -are *vt* to make at intervals; to distribute; **nōn ~uim** I wouldn't care.

interductus, -ūs *m* punctuation.

interdum *adv* now and then, occasionally.

intereā *adv* meanwhile, in the meantime; nevertheless.

interēmī *perf of* **interimō**.

interemptus *ppp of* **interimō**.

intereō, -īre, -iī, -itum *vi* to be lost, perish, die.

interequitō, -āre *vt, vi* to ride between.

interesse *infin of* **intersum**.

interfātiō, -ōnis *f* interruption.

interfātur, -ārī, -ātus *vi* to interrupt.

interfectiō, -ōnis *f* killing.

interfector, -ōris *m* murderer.

interfectrīx, -rīcis *f* murderess.

interfectus *ppp of* **interficiō**.

interficiō, -icere, -ēcī, -ectum *vt* to kill, destroy.

interfīō, -ierī *vi* to pass away.

interfluō, -ere, -xī *vt, vi* to flow between.

interfodiō, -ere *vt* to pierce.

interfugiō, -ere *vi* to flee among.

interfuī *perf of* **intersum**.

interfulgeō, -ēre *vi* to shine amongst.

interfūsus *ppp* lying between; marked here and there.

interiaceō, -ēre *vi* to lie between.

interibi *adv* in the meantime.

intericiō, -icere, -iēcī, -iectum *vt* to put amongst or between; interpose, mingle; **annō ~iectō** after a year.

interiectus, -ūs *m* coming in between; interval.

interiī *perf of* **intereō**.

interim *adv* meanwhile, in the meantime; sometimes; all the same.

interimō, -imere, -ēmī, -emptum *vt* to abolish, destroy, kill.

interior, -ōris *adj* inner, interior; nearer, on the near side; secret, private; more intimate, more profound.

interitiō, -ōnis *f* ruin.

interitus, -ūs *m* destruction, ruin, death.

interiūnctus *adj* joined together.

interius *adv* inwardly; too short.

interlābor, -ī *vi* to glide between.

interlegō, -ere *vt* to pick here and there.

interlinō, -inere, -ēvī, -itum *vt* to smear in parts; to erase here and there.

interloquor, -quī, -cūtus *vi* to interrupt.

interlūceō, -cēre, -xī *vi* to shine through, be clearly seen.

interlūnia, -ōrum *ntpl* new moon.

interluō, -ere *vt* to wash, flow between.

intermēnstruus *adj* of the new moon ♦ *nt* new moon.

interminātus *ppa of* **interminor** ♦ *adj* forbidden.

interminātus *adj* endless.

interminor, -ārī, -ātus *vi* to threaten; to forbid threateningly.

intermisceō, -scēre, -scuī, -xtum *vt* to mix, intermingle.

intermissiō, -ōnis *f* interruption.

intermittō, -ittere, -īsī, -issum *vt* to break off; to interrupt; to omit, neglect, to allow to elapse ♦ *vi* to cease, pause.

intermixtus *ppp of* **intermisceō**.

intermorior, -ī, -tuus *vi* to die suddenly.

intermortuus *adj* falling unconscious.

intermundia, -ōrum *ntpl* space between worlds.

intermūrālis *adj* between two walls.

internātus *adj* growing among.

internecīnus *adj* murderous, of extermination.

interneciō, -ōnis *f* massacre, extermination.

internecīvus *adj* = **internecīnus**.

internectō, -ere *vt* to enclasp.

internōdia, -ōrum *ntpl* space between joints.

internōscō, -scere, -vī, -tum *vt* to distinguish between.

internūntia, -iae *f* messenger, mediator, go-between.

internūntiō, -āre *vi* to exchange messages.

internūntius, -ī *and* **iī** *m* messenger, mediator, go-between.

internus *adj* internal, civil ♦ *ntpl* domestic affairs.

interō, -erere, -rīvī, -rītum *vt* to rub in; (*fig*) to concoct.

interpellātiō, -ōnis *f* interruption.

interpellātor, -ōris *m* interrupter.

interpellō, -āre, -āvī, -ātum *vt* to interrupt; to disturb, obstruct.

interpolis *adj* made up.

interpolō, -āre *vt* to renovate, do up; (*writing*) to falsify.

interpōnō, -ōnere, -osuī, -ositum *vt* to put between *or* amongst, insert; (*time*) to allow to elapse; (*person*) to introduce, admit; (*pretext etc*) to put forward, interpose; **fidem ~** pledge one's word; **sē ~** interfere, become involved.

interpositiō, -ōnis *f* introduction.

interpositus *ppp of* **interpōnō**.

The present infinitive verb endings are as follows: -āre = 1st; -ēre = 2nd; -ere = 3rd and -īre = 4th. See sections on irregular verbs and noun declensions.

interpositus, -ūs m obstruction.

interpres, -tis m/f agent, negotiator; interpreter, explainer, translator.

interpretātiō, -ōnis f interpretation, exposition, meaning.

interpretātus adj translated.

interpretor, -ārī, -ātus vt to interpret, explain, translate, understand.

interprimō, -imere, -essī, -essum vt to squeeze.

interpūnctiō, -ōnis f punctuation.

interpūnctus adj well-divided
♦ ntpl punctuation.

interquiēscō, -scere, -vī vi to rest awhile.

interrēgnum, -ī nt regency, interregnum; interval between consuls.

interrēx, -ēgis m regent; deputy consul.

interritus adj undaunted, unafraid.

interrogātiō, -ōnis f question; (law) cross-examination; (logic) syllogism.

interrogātiuncula, -ae f short argument.

interrogō, -āre, -āvī, -ātum vt to ask, put a question; (law) to cross-examine, bring to trial.

interrupte adv interruptedly.

interrumpō, -umpere, -ūpī, -uptum vt to break up, sever; (fig) to break off, interrupt.

intersaepiō, -īre, -sī, -tum vt to shut off, close.

interscindō, -ndere, -dī, -ssum vt to cut off, break down.

interserō, -erere, -ēvī, -itum vt to plant at intervals.

interserō, -ere, -uī, -tum vt to interpose.

intersitus ppp of **interserō**.

interspīrātiō, -ōnis f pause for breath.

interstinguō, -guere, -ctum vt to mark, spot; to extinguish.

interstringō, -ere vt to strangle.

intersum, -esse, -fuī vi to be between; to be amongst; be present at; (time) to elapse; **~est** there is a difference; it is of importance, it concerns, it matters; **meā ~est** it is important for me.

intertextus adj interwoven.

intertrahō, -here, -xī vt to take away.

intertrīmentum, -ī nt wastage; loss, damage.

interturbātiō, -ōnis f confusion.

intervallum, -ī nt space, distance, interval; (time) pause, interval, respite; difference.

intervellō, -ere vt to pluck out; to tear apart.

interveniō, -enīre, -ēnī, -entum vi to come on the scene, intervene; to interfere (with), interrupt; to happen, occur.

interventor, -ōris m intruder.

interventus, -ūs m appearance, intervention; occurrence.

intervertō, -tere, -tī, -sum vt to embezzle; to rob, cheat.

intervīsō, -ere, -ī, -um vt to have a look at, look and see; to visit occasionally.

intervolitō, -āre vi to fly about, amongst.

intervomō, -ere vt to throw up (amongst).

intervortō vt see **intervertō**.

intestābilis adj infamous, wicked.

intestātō adv without making a will.

intestātus adj intestate; not convicted by witnesses.

intestīnus adj internal ♦ nt and ntpl internals, entrails.

intexō, -ere, -uī, -tum vt to inweave, embroider, interlace.

intibum, -ī *nt* endive.

intimē *adv* most intimately, cordially.

intimus *adj* innermost; deepest; secret; intimate ♦ *m* most intimate friend.

intingō (intinguō), -gere, -xī, -ctum *vt* to dip in.

intolerābilis *adj* unbearable; irresistible.

intolerandus *adj* intolerable.

intolerāns, -antis *adj* impatient; unbearable.

intoleranter *adv* excessively.

intolerantia, -ae *f* insolence.

intonō, -āre, -uī, -ātum *vi* to thunder, thunder out.

intōnsus *adj* unshorn, unshaven; long-haired, bearded; uncouth.

intorqueō, -quēre, -sī, -tum *vt* to twist, wrap round; to hurl at.

intortus *ppp of* **intorqueō** ♦ *adj* twisted, curled; confused.

intrā *adv* inside, within ♦ *prep (with acc)* inside, within; (*time*) within, during; (*amount*) less than, within the limits of.

intrābilis *adj* navigable.

intractābilis *adj* formidable.

intractātus *adj* not broken in; unattempted.

intremīscō, -īscere, -uī *vi* to begin to shake.

intremō, -ere *vi* to tremble.

intrepidē *adv see adj.*

intrepidus *adj* calm, brave; undisturbed.

intrīcō, -āre *vt* to entangle.

intrīnsecus *adv* on the inside.

intrītus *adj* not worn out.

intrīvī *perf of* **interō**.

intrō *adv* inside, in.

intrō, -āre, -āvī, -ātum *vt, vi* to go in, enter; to penetrate.

intrōdūcō, -ūcere, -ūxī, -uctum *vt*

to bring in, introduce, escort in; to institute.

intrōductiō, -ōnis *f* bringing in.

intrōeō, -īre, -iī, -itum *vi* to go into, enter.

intrōferō, -ferre, -tulī, -lātum *vt* to carry inside.

intrōgredior, -dī, -ssus *vi* to step inside.

introitus, -ūs *m* entrance; beginning.

intrōlātus *ppp of* **intrōferō**.

intrōmittō, -ittere, -īsī, -issus *vt* to let in, admit.

intrōrsum, intrōrsus *adv* inwards, inside.

intrōrumpō, -ere *vi* to break into.

intrōspectō, -āre *vt* to look in at.

intrōspiciō, -icere, -exī, -ectum *vt* to look inside; to look at, examine.

intubum *etc see* **intibum**.

intueor, -ērī, -itus *vt* to look at, watch; to contemplate, consider; to admire.

intumēscō, -ēscere, -uī *vi* to begin to swell, rise; to increase; to become angry.

intumulātus *adj* unburied.

intuor *etc see* **intueor**.

inturbidus *adj* undisturbed; quiet.

intus *adv* inside, within, in; from within.

intūtus *adj* unsafe; unguarded.

inula, -ae *f* elecampane.

inultus *adj* unavenged; unpunished.

inumbrō, -āre *vt* to shade; to cover.

inundō, -āre, -āvī, -ātum *vt, vi* to overflow, flood.

inunguō, -unguere, -ūnxī, -ūnctum *vt* to anoint.

inurbānē *adv see adj.*

inurbānus *adj* rustic, unmannerly, unpolished.

The present infinitive verb endings are as follows: -āre = 1st; -ēre = 2nd; -ere = 3rd and -īre = 4th. See sections on irregular verbs and noun declensions.

inurgeō, -ēre *vi* to push, butt.

inūrō, -rere, -ssī, -stum *vt* to brand; (*fig*) to brand, inflict.

inūsitātē *adv* strangely.

inūsitātus *adj* unusual, extraordinary.

inūstus *ppp of* **inūrō**.

inūtilis *adj* useless; harmful.

inūtilitās, -ātis *f* uselessness, harmfulness.

inūtiliter *adv* unprofitably.

invādō, -dere, -sī, -sum *vt, vi* to get in, make one's way in; to enter upon; to fall upon, attack, invade; to seize, take possession of.

invalēscō, -ēscere, -uī *vi* to grow stronger.

invalidus *adj* weak; inadequate.

invāsī *perf of* **invādō**.

invectiō, -ōnis *f* importing; invective.

invectus *ppp of* **invehō**.

invehō, -here, -xī, -ctum *vt* to carry in, bring in; **sē ~** attack.

invehor, -hī, -ctus *vi* to ride, drive, sail in *or* into, enter; to attack; to inveigh against.

invēndibilis *adj* unsaleable.

inveniō, -enīre, -ēnī, -entum *vt* to find, come upon; to find out, discover; to invent, contrive; to win, get.

inventiō, -ōnis *f* invention; (*RHET*) compiling the subject-matter.

inventor, -ōris *m* inventor, discoverer.

inventrīx, -rīcis *f* inventor, discoverer.

inventus *ppp of* **inveniō** ♦ *nt* invention, discovery.

invenustus *adj* unattractive; unlucky in love.

inverēcundus *adj* immodest, shameless.

invergō, -ere *vt* to pour upon.

inversiō, -ōnis *f* transposition; irony.

inversus *ppp of* **invertō** ♦ *adj* upside down, inside out; perverted.

invertō, -tere, -tī, -sum *vt* to turn over, invert; to change, pervert.

invesperāscit, -ere *vi* it is dusk.

investigātiō, -ōnis *f* search.

investigātor, -ōris *m* investigator.

investīgō, -āre, -āvī, -ātum *vt* to follow the trail of; (*fig*) to track down, find out.

inveterāscō, -scere, -vī *vi* to grow old (in); to become established, fixed, inveterate; to grow obsolete.

inveterātiō, -ōnis *f* chronic illness.

inveterātus *adj* of long standing, inveterate.

invexī *perf of* **invehō**.

invicem *adv* in turns, alternately; mutually, each other.

invictus *adj* unbeaten; unconquerable.

invidentia, -ae *f* envy.

invideō, -idēre, -īdī, -īsum *vt, vi* to cast an evil eye on; (*with dat*) to envy, grudge; to begrudge.

invidia, -ae *f* envy, jealousy, ill-will; unpopularity.

invidiōsē *adv* spitefully.

invidiōsus *adj* envious, spiteful; enviable; invidious, hateful.

invidus *adj* envious, jealous, hostile.

invigilō, -āre *vi* to be awake over; to watch over, be intent on.

inviolābilis *adj* invulnerable; inviolable.

inviolātē *adv* inviolately.

inviolātus *adj* unhurt; inviolable.

invīsitātus *adj* unseen, unknown, strange.

invīsō, -ere, -ī, -um *vt* to go and see, visit, have a look at; to inspect.

invīsus *adj* hateful, detested; hostile.

invīsus adj unseen.

invītāmentum, -ī nt attraction, inducement.

invītātiō, -ōnis f invitation; entertainment.

invītātus, -ūs m invitation.

invītē adv unwillingly.

invītō, -āre, -āvī, -ātum vt to invite; to treat, entertain; to summon; to attract, induce.

invītus adj against one's will, reluctant.

invius adj trackless, impassable; inaccessible.

invocātus ppp of **invocō**.

invocātus adj unbidden, uninvited.

invocō, -āre, -āvī, -ātum vt to call upon, invoke; to appeal to; to call.

involātus, -ūs m flight.

involitō, -āre vi to play upon.

involō, -āre vi to fly at, pounce on, attack.

involūcre, -is nt napkin.

involūcrum, -ī nt covering, case.

involūtus ppp of **involvō** ♦ adj complicated.

involvō, -vere, -vī, -ūtum vt to roll on; to wrap up, envelop, entangle.

involvolus, -ī m caterpillar.

invulnerātus adj unwounded.

iō interj (joy) hurrah!; (pain) oh!; (calling) ho there!

Ioannes, -is m John.

iocātiō, -ōnis f joke.

iocor, -ārī, -ātus vt, vi to joke, jest.

iocōsē adv jestingly.

iocōsus adj humorous, playful.

ioculāris adj laughable, funny ♦ ntpl jokes.

ioculārius adj ludicrous.

ioculātor, -ōris m jester.

ioculor, -ārī vi to joke.

ioculus, -ī m a bit of fun.

iocus, -ī m (pl -a, -ōrum nt) joke, jest; extrā ~um seriously; per

~um for fun.

Iōnes, -um mpl Ionians.

Iōnia, -iae f Ionia, coastal district of Asia Minor.

Iōnium, -ī nt Ionian Sea, W. of Greece.

Iōnius, -icus adj Ionian.

iōta nt (indecl) Greek letter I.

Iovis gen of **Iuppiter**.

Īphianassa, -ae f Iphigenia.

Īphigenīa, -ae f daughter of Agamemnon (who sacrificed her at Aulis to Diana).

ipse, -a, -um, -īus pron self, himself etc; in person, for one's own part, of one's own accord, by oneself; just, precisely; very; the master, the host.

ipsissimus his very own self; **nunc ~um** right now.

īra, -ae f anger, rage; object of indignation.

īrācundē adv angrily.

īrācundia, -ae f irascibility, quick temper; rage, resentment.

īrācundus adj irascible, choleric, resentful.

īrāscor, -ī vi to be angry, get furious.

īrātē adv see adj.

īrātus adj angry, furious.

īre infin of **eō**.

Īris, -dis (acc -m) f messenger of the gods; the rainbow.

īrōnīa, -ae f irony.

irrāsus adj unshaven.

irraucēscō, -cēscere, -sī vi to become hoarse.

irredivīvus adj irreparable.

irrelīgātus adj not tied.

irreligiōsē adv see adj.

irreligiōsus adj impious.

irremeābilis adj from which there is no returning.

irreparābilis adj irretrievable.

irrepertus adj undiscovered.

irrēpō, -ere, -sī *vi* to steal into, insinuate oneself into.

irreprehēnsus *adj* blameless.

irrequiētus *adj* restless.

irresectus *adj* unpared.

irresolūtus *adj* not slackened.

irrētiō, -īre, -iī, -ītum *vt* to ensnare, entangle.

irretortus *adj* not turned back.

irreverentia, -ae *f* disrespect.

irrevocābilis *adj* irrevocable; implacable.

irrevocātus *adj* without an encore.

irrīdeō, -dēre, -sī, -sum *vi* to laugh, joke ♦ *vt* to laugh at, ridicule.

irrīdiculē *adv* unwittily.

irrīdiculum, -ī *nt* laughing stock.

irrigātiō, -ōnis *f* irrigation.

irrigō, -āre, -āvī, -ātum *vt* to water, irrigate; to inundate; (*fig*) to shed over, flood, refresh.

irriguus *adj* well-watered, swampy; refreshing.

irrīsiō, -ōnis *f* ridicule, mockery.

irrīsor, -ōris *m* scoffer.

irrīsus *ppp of* irrīdeō.

irrīsus, -ūs *m* derision.

irrītābilis *adj* excitable.

irrītāmen, -inis *nt* excitement, provocation.

irrītātiō, -ōnis *f* incitement, irritation.

irrītō, -āre, -āvī, -ātum *vt* to provoke, incite, enrage.

irrītus *adj* invalid, null and void; useless, vain, ineffective; (*person*) unsuccessful; **ad –um cadere** come to nothing.

irrogātiō, -ōnis *f* imposing.

irrogō, -āre *vt* to propose (a measure) against; to impose.

irrōrō, -āre *vt* to bedew.

irrumpō, -umpere, -ūpī, -uptum *vt, vi* to rush in, break in; to intrude, invade.

irruō, -ere, -ī *vi* to force a way in, rush in, attack; (*speech*) to make a blunder.

irruptiō, -ōnis *f* invasion, raid.

irruptus *ppp of* irrumpō.

irruptus *adj* unbroken.

is, ea, id *pron* he, she, it; this, that, the; such; **nōn is sum quī** I am not the man to; **id** (*with vi*) for this reason; **id quod** what; **ad id** hitherto; for the purpose; besides; **in eō est** it has come to this; one is on the point of; it depends on this.

Ismara, -ōrum *ntpl*, **-us, -ī** *m Mt Ismarus in Thrace.*

Ismarius *adj* Thracian.

Īsocratēs, -is *m Athenian orator and teacher of rhetoric.*

iste, -a, -ud, -īus *pron* that of yours, (*law*) your client, the plaintiff, the defendant; (*contemptuous*) the fellow; that, such.

Isthmius *adj, ntpl* the Isthmian Games.

Isthmus (-os), -ī *m Isthmus of Corinth.*

istic, -aec, -uc *and* **oc** *pron* that of yours, that.

istīc *adv* there; in this, on this occasion.

istinc *adv* from there; of that.

istīusmodī such, of that kind.

istō, istōc *adv* to you, there, yonder.

istōrsum *adv* in that direction.

istūc *adv* (to) there, to that.

ita *adv* thus, so; as follows; yes; accordingly; **itane?** really?; **nōn ita** not so very; **ita ut** just as; **ita ... ut** so, to such an extent that; on condition that; only in so far as; **ita ... ut nōn** without; **ut ... ita** just as ... so; although ... nevertheless.

Ītalī, -ōrum *mpl* Italians.

Ītalia, -iae *f* Italy.

Ītalicus, -is, -us *adj* Italian.

itaque *conj* and so, therefore,

accordingly.

item *adv* likewise, also.

iter, -ineris *nt* way, journey, march; a day's journey or march; route, road, passage; (*fig*) way, course; ~ **mihi est** I have to go to; ~ **dare** grant a right of way; ~ **facere** to journey, march, travel; **ex, in ~inere** on the way, on the march; **māgnis ~ineribus** by forced marches.

iterātiō, -ōnis *f* repetition.

iterō, -āre, -āvī, -ātum *vt* to repeat, renew; to plough again.

iterum *adv* again, a second time; ~ **atque** ~ repeatedly.

Ithaca, -ae; -ē, -ēs *f* island W. of Greece (*home of Ulysses*).

Ithacēnsis, -us *adj* Ithacan.

Ithacus, -ī *m* Ulysses.

itidem *adv* in the same way, similarly.

itiō, -ōnis *f* going.

itō, -āre *vi* to go.

itus, -ūs *m* going, movement, departure.

iuba, -ae *f* mane; crest.

Iuba, -ae *m* king of Numidia (*supporter of Pompey*).

iubar, -is *nt* brightness, light.

iubātus *adj* crested.

iubeō, -ēre, -ssī, -ssum *vt* to order, command, tell; (*greeting*) to bid; (*MED*) to prescribe; (*POL*) to decree, ratify, appoint.

iūcundē *adv* agreeably.

iūcunditās, -ātis *f* delight, enjoyment.

iūcundus *adj* delightful, pleasing.

Iūdaea, -ae *f* Judaea, Palestine.

Iūdaeus, -ī *m* Jew.

Iūdaeus, Iūdaïcus *adj* Jewish.

iūdex, -icis *m* judge; (*pl*) panel of jurors; (*fig*) critic.

iūdicātiō, -ōnis *f* judicial inquiry;

opinion.

iūdicātum, -ī *nt* judgment, precedent.

iūdicātus, -ūs *m* office of judge.

iūdiciālis *adj* judicial, forensic.

iūdiciārius *adj* judiciary.

iūdicium, -ī and **iī** *nt* trial; court of justice; sentence; judgment, opinion; discernment, taste, tact; **in ~ vocāre, -ō accessere** sue, summon.

iūdicō, -āre, -āvī, -ātum *vt* to judge, examine, sentence, condemn; to form an opinion of, decide; to declare.

iugālis *adj* yoked together; nuptial.

iugātiō, -ōnis *f* training (*of a vine*).

iūgerum, -ī *nt* a land measure (*240 x 120 feet*).

iūgis *adj* perpetual, never-failing.

iūglāns, -andis *f* walnut tree.

iugō, -āre, -āvī, -ātum *vt* to couple, marry.

iugōsus *adj* hilly.

Iugulae, -ārum *fpl* Orion's Belt.

iugulō, -āre, -āvī, -ātum *vt* to cut the throat of, kill, murder.

iugulus, -ī *m*, **-um, -ī** *nt* throat.

iugum, -ī *nt* (*animals*) yoke, collar; pair, team; (*MIL*) yoke of subjugation; (*mountain*) ridge, height, summit; (*ASTRO*) Libra; (*loom*) crossbeam; (*ship*) thwart; (*fig*) yoke, bond.

Iugurtha, -ae *m* king of Numidia (*rebel against Rome*).

Iugurthinus *adj* see n.

Iūleus *adj* of Iulus; of Caesar; of July.

Iūlius, -ī *m* Roman family name (*esp Caesar*); (*month*) July.

Iūlius, -iānus *adj* see n.

Iūlus, -ī *m* son of Aeneas, Ascanius.

iūmentum, -ī *nt* beast of burden, packhorse.

The present infinitive verb endings are as follows: -**āre** = 1st; -**ēre** = 2nd; -**ere** = 3rd and -**īre** = 4th. *See sections on irregular verbs and noun declensions.*

iunceus adj of rushes; slender.

iuncōsus adj rushy.

iūnctiō, -ōnis f union.

iūnctūra, -ae f joint; combination; relationship.

iūnctus ppp of **iungō** ♦ adj connected, attached.

iuncus, -ī m rush.

iungō, -gere, iūnxī, iūnctum vt to join together, unite; to yoke, harness; to mate; (river) to span, bridge; (fig) to bring together, connect, associate; (agreement) to make; (words) to compound.

iūnior, -ōris adj younger.

iūniperus, -ī f juniper.

Iūnius, -ī m Roman family name; (month) June.

Iūnius adj of June.

Iūnō, -ōnis f Roman goddess wife of Jupiter, patroness of women and marriage.

Iūnōnālis adj see n.

Iūnōnicola, -ae m worshipper of Juno.

Iūnōnigena, -ae m Vulcan.

Iūnōnius adj = **Iūnōnālis**.

Iuppiter, Iovis m Jupiter (king of the gods, god of sky and weather); ~ **Stygius** Pluto; **sub love** in the open air.

iūrātor, -ōris m sworn judge.

iūreconsultus etc see **iūrisconsultus.**

iūreiūrō, -āre vi to swear.

iūreperitus etc see **iūrisperitus.**

iūrgium, -ī and **iī** nt quarrel, brawl.

iūrgō, -āre vi to quarrel, squabble ♦ vt to scold.

iūridiciālis adj of law, juridical.

iūrisconsultus, -ī m lawyer.

iūrisdictiō, -ōnis f administration of justice; authority.

iūrisperītus adj versed in the law.

iūrō, -āre, -āvī, -ātum vi, vt to swear, take an oath; to conspire; **in nōmen** ~ swear allegiance to; **in**

verba ~ take a prescribed form of oath; **~ātus** having sworn, under oath.

iūs, iūris nt broth, soup.

iūs, iūris nt law, right, justice; law court; jurisdiction, authority; ~ **gentium** international law; ~ **pūblicum** constitutional law; **summum** ~ the strict letter of the law; ~ **dīcere** administer justice; **suī iūris** independent; **iūre** rightly, justly.

iūsiūrandum, iūrisiūrandī nt oath.

iussī perf of **iubeō.**

iussū abl m by order.

iussus ppp of **iubeō** ♦ nt order, command, prescription.

iūstē adv justly, rightly.

iūstificus adj just dealing.

iūstitia, -ae f justice, uprightness, fairness.

iūstitium, -ī and **iī** nt cessation of legal business.

iūstus adj just, fair; lawful, right; regular, proper ♦ nt right ♦ ntpl rights; formalities, obsequies.

iūtus ppp of **iuvō.**

iuvenālis adj youthful ♦ ntpl youthful games.

Iuvenālis, -is m Juvenal (Roman satirist).

iuvenāliter adv vigorously, impetuously.

iuvenca, -ae f heifer; girl.

iuvencus, -ī m bullock; young man ♦ adj young.

iuvenēscō, -ēscere, -uī vi to grow up; to grow young again.

iuvenīlis adj youthful.

iuvenīliter adv see adj.

iuvenis adj young ♦ m/f young man or woman (20-45 years), man, warrior.

iuvenor, -ārī vi to behave indiscreetly.

iuventa, -ae f youth.

iuventās, -ātis f youth.

iuventūs, -ūtis f youth, manhood; men, soldiers.

iuvō, -āre, iūvī, iūtum vt to help, be of use to; to please, delight; **~at mē** I am glad.

iuxtā adv near by, close; alike, just the same ♦ prep (with acc) close to, hard by; next to; very like, next door to; **~ ac, cum, quam** just the same as.

iuxtim adv near; equally.

īvī perf of eō.

Ixīon, -onis m Lapith king (bound to a revolving wheel in Tartarus).

Ixīoneus adj see n.

Ixīonidae, -ārum mpl Centaurs.

Ixīonidēs, -ae m Pirithous.

J

J see I.

K

Kalendae, -ārum fpl Kalends, first day of each month.

Karthāgō see **Carthāgō**.

L

labāscō, -ere vi to totter, waver.

lābēcula, -ae f aspersion.

labefaciō, -facere, -fēcī, -factum (pass -fīō, -fierī) vt to shake; (fig) to weaken, ruin.

labefactō, -āre, -āvī, -ātum vt to shake; (fig) to weaken, destroy.

labellum, -ī nt lip.

lābellum, -ī nt small basin.

Laberius, -ī m Roman family name (esp a writer of mimes).

lābēs, -is f sinking, fall; ruin, destruction.

lābēs, -is f spot, blemish; disgrace, stigma; (person) blot.

labia, -iae f lip.

Labiēnus, -ī m Roman surname (esp Caesar's officer who went over to Pompey).

labiōsus adj large-lipped.

labium, -ī and **iī** nt lip.

labō, -āre vi to totter, be unsteady, give way; to waver, hesitate, collapse.

lābor, -bī, -psus vi to slide, glide; to sink, fall; to slip away, pass away; (fig) to fade, decline, perish; to be disappointed, make a mistake.

labor (-ōs), -ōris m effort, exertion, labour; work, task; hardship, suffering, distress; (ASTRO) eclipse.

labōrifer, -ī adj sore afflicted.

labōriōsē adv laboriously, with difficulty.

labōriōsus adj troublesome, difficult; industrious.

labōrō, -āre, -āvī, -ātum vi to work, toil, take pains; to suffer, be troubled (with), be in distress; to be anxious, worried ♦ vt to work out, make, produce.

labōs etc see **labor**.

labrum, -ī nt lip; edge, rim; **primīs ~īs gustāre** acquire a smattering of.

lābrum, -ī nt tub, vat; bath.

lābrusca, -ae f wild vine.

lābruscum, -ī nt wild grape.

labyrinthēus adj labyrinthine.

labyrinthus, -ī m labyrinth, maze (esp that of Cnossos in Crete).

lac, lactis nt milk.

Lacaena, -ae f Spartan woman ♦ adj Spartan.

Lacedaemōn (-ō), -onis (acc -ona) f Sparta.

Lacedaemonius adj Spartan.

lacer, -ī adj torn, mangled.

The present infinitive verb endings are as follows: -āre = 1st; -ēre = 2nd; -ere = 3rd and -īre = 4th. See sections on irregular verbs and noun declensions.

lacerated; tearing.

lacerātiō, -ōnis f tearing.

lacerna, -ae f cloak (worn in cold weather).

lacernātus adj cloaked.

lacerō, -āre, -āvī, -ātum vt to tear, lacerate, mangle; (ship) to wreck; (speech) to slander, abuse; (feeling) to torture, distress; (goods, time) to waste, destroy.

lacerta, -ae f lizard; a seafish.

lacertōsus adj brawny.

lacertus, -ī m upper arm, arm; (pl) brawn, muscle.

lacertus, -ī m lizard; a sea fish.

lacessō, -ere, -īvī and iī, -ītum vt to strike, provoke, challenge; (fig) to incite, exasperate.

Lachesis, -is f one of the Fates.

lacinia, -ae f flap, corner (of dress).

Lacinium, -ī nt promontory in S. Italy, with a temple of Juno.

Lacinius adj see n.

Lacō (-ōn), -ōnis m Spartan; Spartan dog.

Lacōnicus adj Spartan ♦ nt sweating bath.

lacrima, -ae f tear; (plant) gumdrop.

lacrimābilis adj mournful.

lacrimābundus adj bursting into tears.

lacrimō, -āre, -āvī, -ātum vt, vi to weep, weep for.

lacrimōsus adj tearful; lamentable.

lacrimula, -ae f tear, crocodile tear.

lacrum- etc see **lacrim-**.

lactāns, -antis adj giving milk; sucking.

lactātiō, -ōnis f allurement.

lactēns, -entis adj sucking; milky, juicy.

lacteolus adj milk-white.

lactēs, -ium fpl guts, small intestines.

lactēscō, -ere vi to turn to milk.

lacteus adj milky, milk-white.

lactō, -āre vi to dupe, wheedle.

lactūca, -ae f lettuce.

lacūna, -ae f hole, pit; pool, pond; (fig) deficiency.

lacūnar, -āris nt panel ceiling.

lacūnō, -āre vt to panel.

lacūnōsus adj sunken.

lacus, -ūs m vat, tank; lake; reservoir, cistern.

laedō, -dere, -sī, -sum vt to hurt, strike, wound; (fig) to offend, annoy, break.

Laelius, -ī m Roman family name (esp the friend of Scipio).

laena, -ae f a lined cloak.

Lāērtēs, -ae m father of Ulysses.

Lāērtiadēs m Ulysses.

Lāērtius adj see n.

laesī perf of **laedō**.

laesiō, -ōnis f attack.

Laestrygonēs, -um mpl fabulous cannibals of Campania, founders of Formiae.

Laestrygonius adj see n.

laesus ppp of **laedō**.

laetābilis adj joyful.

laetē adv gladly.

laetificō, -āre vt to gladden.

laetificus adj glad, joyful.

laetitia, -ae f joy, delight, exuberance.

laetor, -ārī, -ātus vi to rejoice, be glad.

laetus adj glad, cheerful; delighting (in); pleasing, welcome; (growth) fertile, rich; (style) exuberant.

laevē adv awkwardly.

laevus adj left; stupid; ill-omened, unfortunate; (augury) lucky, favourable ♦ f left hand.

laganum, -ī nt a kind of oilcake.

lageōs, -ī f a Greek vine.

lagoena, -ae f flagon.

lagōis, -idis f a kind of grouse.

lagōna, -ae f flagon.

Lāiadēs, -ae m Oedipus.

Lāius, -ī m father of Oedipus.

lallō, -āre vi to sing a lullaby.

lāma, -ae f bog.

lamberō, -āre vt to tear to pieces.

lambō, -ere, -ī vt to lick, touch; (river) to wash.

lāmenta, -ōrum ntpl lamentation.

lāmentābilis adj mournful, sorrowful.

lāmentārius adj sorrowful.

lāmentātiō, -ōnis f weeping, lamentation.

lāmentor, -ārī, -ātus vi to weep, lament ♦ vt to weep for, bewail.

lamia, -ae f witch.

lāmina (lammina, lāmna), -ae f plate, leaf (of metal, wood); blade; coin.

lampas, -dis f torch; brightness, day.

Lamus, -ī m Laestrygonian king.

lāna, -ae f wool.

lānārius, -ī and **iī** m wool-worker.

lānātus adj woolly.

lancea, -ae f spear, lance.

lancinō, -āre, vt to tear up; to squander.

lāneus adj woollen.

languefaciō, -ere vt to make weary.

langueō, -ēre vi to be weary, be weak, droop; to be idle, dull.

languēscō, -ēscere, -uī vi to grow faint, droop.

languidē adv see adj.

languidulus adj languid.

languidus adj faint, languid, sluggish; listless, feeble.

languor, -ōris m faintness, fatigue, weakness; dullness, apathy.

laniātus, -ūs m mangling; (mind) anguish.

laniēna, -ae f butcher's shop.

lānificium, -ī and **iī** nt woolworking.

lānificus adj wool-working.

lāniger, -ī adj fleecy ♦ m/f ram, sheep.

laniō, -āre, -āvī, -ātum vt to tear to pieces, mangle.

lanista, -ae m trainer of gladiators, fencing master; (fig) agitator.

lānitium, -ī and **iī** nt woolgrowing.

lanius, -ī and **iī** m butcher.

lanterna, -ae f lamp.

lanternārius, -ī and **iī** m guide.

lānūgō, -inis f down, woolliness.

Lānuvīnus adj see n.

Lānuvium, -ī nt Latin town on the Appian Way.

lānx, lancis f dish, platter; (balance) scale.

Lāomedōn, -ontis m king of Troy (father of Priam).

Lāomedontēus adj and **ontiadēs, -ae** m son of Lāomedon; (pl) Trojans.

Lāomedontius adj Trojan.

lapathum, -ī nt, **-us, -ī** f sorrel.

lapicīda, -ae m stonecutter.

lapicīdīnae, -ārum fpl quarries.

lapidārius adj stone- (in cpds).

lapidātiō, -ōnis f throwing of stones.

lapidātor, -ōris m stone thrower.

lapideus adj of stones, stone- (in cpds).

lapidō, -āre vt to stone ♦ vi to rain stones.

lapidōsus adj stony; hard as stone.

lapillus, -ī m stone, pebble; precious stone, mosaic piece.

lapis, -dis m stone; milestone; boundary stone, tombstone; precious stone; marble; auctioneer's stand; (abuse) blockhead; **bis ad eundem**

The present infinitive verb endings are as follows: -āre = 1st; -ēre = 2nd; -ere = 3rd and -īre = 4th. See sections on irregular verbs and noun declensions.

(offendere) ≈ make the same mistake twice; **Juppiter ~** the Jupiter stone.
Lapithae, -ārum and **-um** mpl Lapiths (mythical people of Thessaly).
Lapithaeus, -ēius adj see n.
lappa, -ae f goosegrass.
lāpsiō, -ōnis f tendency.
lāpsō, -āre vi to slip, stumble.
lāpsus ppa of **lābor.**
lāpsus, -ūs m fall, slide, course, flight; error, failure.
laqueāria, -ium ntpl panelled ceiling.
laqueātus adj panelled, with a panelled ceiling.
laqueus, -ī m noose, snare, halter; (fig) trap.
Lār, Laris m tutelary deity, household god; hearth, home.
lārdum etc see **lāridum.**
largē adv plentifully, generously, very much.
largificus adj bountiful.
largifluus adj copious.
largiloquus adj talkative.
largior, -īrī, -ītus vt to give freely, lavish; to bestow, confer ♦ vi to give largesses.
largitās, -ātis f liberality, abundance.
largiter adv = **large.**
largītiō, -ōnis f giving freely, distributing; bribery.
largītor, -ōris m liberal giver, dispenser; spendthrift; briber.
largus adj copious, ample; liberal, bountiful.
lāridum, -ī nt bacon fat.
Lārissa (Lārīsa), -ae f town in Thessaly.
Lārissaeus, -ēnsis adj see n.
Lārius, -ī m lake Como.
larix, -cis f larch.
larva, -ae f ghost; mask.
larvātus adj bewitched.

lasanum, -ī nt pot.
lasārpicifer, -ī adj producing asafoetida.
lascīvia, -ae f playfulness; impudence, lewdness.
lascīviō, -īre vi to frolic, frisk; to run wild, be irresponsible.
lascīvus adj playful, frisky; impudent, lustful.
laserpīcium, -ī and **iī** nt silphium.
lassitūdō, -inis f fatigue, heaviness.
lassō, -āre vt to tire, fatigue.
lassulus adj rather weary.
lassus adj tired, exhausted.
lātē adv widely, extensively; **longē ~que** far and wide, everywhere.
latebra, -ae f hiding place, retreat; (fig) loophole, pretext.
latebricola, -ae adj low-living.
latebrōsē adv in hiding.
latebrōsus adj secret, full of coverts; porous.
latēns, -entis pres p of **lateō** ♦ adj hidden, secret.
latenter adv in secret.
lateō, -ēre, -uī vi to lie hid, lurk, skulk; to be in safety, live a retired life; to be unknown, escape notice.
later, -is m brick, tile; **~em lavāre** ≈ waste one's time.
laterāmen, -inis nt earthenware.
laterculus, -ī m small brick, tile; kind of cake.
latericius adj of bricks ♦ nt brickwork.
lāterna etc see **lanterna.**
latēscō, -ere vi to hide oneself.
latex, -icis m water; any other liquid.
Latiar, -iaris nt festival of Jupiter Latiaris.
Latiaris adj Latin.
latibulum, -ī nt hiding place, den, lair.
lāticlāvius adj with a broad purple

stripe ♦ *m* senator, patrician.

lātifundium, **-ī** *and* **iī** *nt* large estate.

Latīnē *adv* in Latin, into Latin; ~ loquī speak Latin, speak plainly, speak correctly; ~ **reddere** translate into Latin.

Latīnitās, **-ātis** *f* good Latin, Latinity; Latin rights.

Latīnus *adj* Latin ♦ *m legendary king of the Laurentians.*

lātiō, **-ōnis** *f* bringing; proposing.

latitō, **-āre** *vi* to hide away, lurk, keep out of the way.

lātitūdō, **-inis** *f* breadth; width; size; broad pronunciation.

Latium, **-ī** *nt* district of Italy including Rome; Latin rights.

Latius = **Latiaris, Latinus.**

Lātōis, **-idis** *f* Diana.

Lātōis, **-ius** *adj see* n.

lātom- *etc see* **lautum-.**

Lātōna, **-ae** *f* mother of Apollo and Diana.

Lātōnigenae, **-ārum** *pl* Apollo and Diana.

Lātōnius *adj* , *f* Diana.

lātor, **-ōris** *m* proposer.

Lātōus *adj* of Latona ♦ *m* Apollo.

lātrātor, **-ōris** *m* barker.

lātrātus, **-ūs** *m* barking.

lātrō, **-āre** *vi* to bark; to rant, roar ♦ *vt* to bark at; to clamour for.

latrō, **-ōnis** *m* mercenary soldier; bandit, brigand; (*chess*) man.

latrōcinium, **-ī** *and* **iī** *nt* highway robbery, piracy.

latrōcinor, **-ārī**, **-ātus** *vi* to serve as a mercenary; to be a brigand *or* pirate.

latrunculus, **-ī** *m* brigand, (*chess*) man.

lātumiae *etc see* **lautumiae.**

lātus *ppp of* **ferō.**

lātus *adj* broad, wide; extensive;

(*pronunciation*) broad; (*style*) diffuse.

latus, **-eris** *nt* side, flank; lungs; body; ~ **dare** expose oneself; ~ **tegere** walk beside; ~ **dolor** pleurisy; **ab ~ere** on the flank.

latusculum, **-ī** *nt* little side.

laudābilis *adj* praiseworthy.

laudābiliter *adv* laudably.

laudātiō, **-ōnis** *f* commendation, eulogy; panegyric, testimonial.

laudātor, **-ōris** *m*, **-rīx**, **-rīcis** *f* praiser, eulogizer; speaker of a funeral oration.

laudātus *adj* excellent.

laudō, **-āre**, **-āvī**, **-ātum** *vt* to praise, commend, approve; to pronounce a funeral oration over; to quote, name.

laurea, **-ae** *f* bay tree; crown of bay; triumph.

laureātus *adj* crowned with bay; (*despatches*) victorious.

Laurentēs, **-um** *mpl* Laurentians (*people of ancient Latium*).

Laurentius *adj see* n.

laureola, **-ae** *f* triumph.

laureus *adj* of bay.

lauricomus *adj* bay-covered.

lauriger, **-ī** *adj* crowned with bay.

laurus, **-ī** *f* bay tree; bay crown; victory, triumph.

laus, **laudis** *f* praise, approval; glory, fame; praiseworthy act, merit, worth.

lautē *adv* elegantly, splendidly; excellently.

lautia, **-ōrum** *ntpl* State banquet.

lautitia, **-ae** *f* luxury.

lautumiae, **-ārum** *fpl* stone quarry; prison.

lautus *ppp of* **lavō** ♦ *adj* neat, elegant, sumptuous; fine, grand, distinguished.

lavābrum, **-ī** *nt* bath.

*The present infinitive verb endings are as follows: **-āre** = 1st; **-ēre** = 2nd; **-ere** = 3rd and -**ire** = 4th. See sections on irregular verbs and noun declensions.*

lavātiō   200   lēniō

lavātiō, -ōnis f washing, bath; bathing gear.

Lāvīnium, -ī nt town of ancient Latium.

Lāvīnius adj see n.

lavō, -āre, lāvī, lautum (lavātum and **lōtum**) vt to wash, bathe; to wet, soak, wash away.

laxāmentum, -ī nt respite, relaxation.

laxē adv loosely, freely.

laxitās, -ātis f roominess.

laxō, -āre, -āvī, -ātum vt to extend, open out; to undo; to slacken; (fig) to release, relieve; to relax, abate ◆ vi (price) to fall off.

laxus adj wide, loose, roomy; (time) deferred; (fig) free, easy.

lea, -ae f lioness.

leaena, -ae f lioness.

Lēander, -rī m Hero's lover (who swam the Hellespont).

lebēs, -ētis m basin, pan, cauldron.

lectīca, -ae f litter, sedan chair.

lectīcārius, -ī and iī m litter-bearer.

lectīcula, -ae f small litter; bier.

lēctiō, -ōnis f selecting; reading, calling the roll.

lectisterniātor, -ōris m arranger of couches.

lectisternium, -ī and iī nt religious feast.

lēctitō, -āre vt to read frequently.

lēctiuncula, -ae f light reading.

lēctor, -ōris m reader.

lectulus, -ī m couch, bed.

lectus, -ī m couch, bed; bier.

lēctus ppp of **legō** ◆ adj picked; choice, excellent.

Lēda, -ae and ē, -ēs f mother of Castor, Pollux, Helen and Clytemnestra.

Lēdaeus adj see n.

lēgātiō, -ōnis f mission, embassy; members of a mission; (MIL) staff appointment, command of a

legion; **lībera ~** free commission (to visit provinces); **vōtīva ~** free commission for paying a vow in a province.

lēgātor, -ōris m testator.

lēgātum, -ī nt legacy, bequest.

lēgātus, -ī m delegate, ambassador; deputy, lieutenant; commander (of a legion).

lēgifer, -ī adj law-giving.

legiō, -ōnis f legion (up to 6000 men); (pl) troops, army.

legiōnārius adj legionary.

lēgirupa, -ae; -iō, -iōnis m lawbreaker.

lēgitimē adv lawfully, properly.

lēgitimus adj lawful, legal; right, proper.

legiuncula, -ae f small legion.

lēgō, -āre, -āvī, -ātum vt to send, charge, commission; to appoint as deputy or lieutenant; (will) to leave, bequeath.

legō, -ere, lēgī, lēctum vt to gather, pick; to choose, select; (sail) to furl; (places) to traverse, pass, coast along; (view) to scan; (writing) to read, recite; **senātum ~** call the roll of the senate.

lēguleïus, -ī and iī m pettifogging lawyer.

legūmen, -inis nt pulse, bean.

lembus, -ī m pinnace, cutter.

Lemnias f Lemnian woman.

Lemnicola, -ae m Vulcan.

lēmniscātus adj beribboned.

lēmniscus, -ī m ribbon (hanging from a victor's crown).

Lēmnius adj see n.

Lēmnos (-us), -ī f Aegean island, abode of Vulcan.

Lemurēs, -um mpl ghosts.

lēna, -ae f procuress; seductress.

Lēnaeus adj Bacchic ◆ m Bacchus.

lēnīmen, -inis nt solace, comfort.

lēnīmentum, -ī nt sop.

lēniō, -īre, -īvī and iī, -ītum vt to

soften, soothe, heal, calm.

lēnis adj soft, smooth, mild, gentle, calm.

lēnitās, -ātis f softness, smoothness, mildness, tenderness.

lēniter adv softly, gently; moderately, half-heartedly.

lēnitūdō, -inis f smoothness, mildness.

lēnō, -ōnis m pander, brothel keeper; go-between.

lēnōcinium, -ī and **iī** nt pandering; allurement; meretricious ornament.

lēnōcinor, -ārī, -ātus vi to pay court to; to promote.

lēnōnius adj pander's.

lēns, lentis f lentil.

lentē adv slowly; calmly, coolly.

lentēscō, -ere vi to become sticky, soften; to relax.

lentiscifer, -ī adj bearing mastic trees.

lentiscus, -ī f mastic tree.

lentitūdō, -inis f slowness, dullness, apathy.

lentō, -āre vt to bend.

lentulus adj rather slow.

lentus adj sticky, sluggish; pliant; slow, lasting, lingering; (person) calm, at ease, indifferent.

lēnunculus, -ī m skiff.

leō, -ōnis m lion.

Leōnidās, -ae m Spartan king who fell at Thermopylae.

leōnīnus adj lion's.

Leontīnī, -ōrum mpl town in Sicily.

Leontīnus adj see n.

lepas, -dis f limpet.

lepidē adv neatly, charmingly; (reply) very well, splendidly.

lepidus adj pleasant, charming, neat, witty.

lepōs (lepor), -ōris m

pleasantness, charm; wit.

lepus, -oris m hare.

lepusculus, -ī m young hare.

Lerna, -ae and **ē, -ēs** f marsh near Argos (where Hercules killed the Hydra).

Lernaeus adj Lernaean.

Lesbias, -iadis f Lesbian woman.

Lesbis, Lesbius adj see n.

Lesbos (-us), -ī f Aegean island (home of Alcaeus and Sappho).

Lesbous f Lesbian woman.

lētālis adj deadly.

Lēthaeus adj of Lethe; infernal; soporific.

lēthargicus, -ī m lethargic person.

lēthargus, -ī m drowsiness.

Lēthē, -ēs f river in the lower world, which caused forgetfulness.

lētifer, -ī adj fatal.

lētō, -āre vt to kill.

lētum, -ī nt death; destruction.

Leucadius adj see n.

Leucas, -dis and **dia, -diae** f island off W. Greece.

Leucothea, -ae; -ē, -ēs f Ino (a sea goddess).

Leuctra, -orum ntpl battlefield in Boeotia.

Leuctricus adj see n.

levāmen, -inis nt alleviation, comfort.

levāmentum, -ī nt mitigation, consolation.

levātiō, -ōnis f relief; diminishing.

levī perf of **linō**.

leviculus adj rather vain.

levidēnsis adj slight.

levipēs, -edis f light-footed.

levis adj (weight) light; (MIL) light-armed; (fig) easy, gentle; (importance) slight, trivial; (motion) nimble, fleet; (character) fickle, unreliable.

lēvis adj smooth; (youth) beardless,

The present infinitive verb endings are as follows: -āre = 1st; -ēre = 2nd; -ere = 3rd and -īre = 4th. See sections on irregular verbs and noun declensions.

delicate.

levisomnus adj light-sleeping.

levitās, -ātis f lightness; nimbleness; fickleness, frivolity.

lēvitās, -ātis f smoothness; fluency.

leviter adv lightly; slightly; easily.

levō, -āre vt to lighten, ease; (fig) to alleviate, lessen; to comfort, relieve; to impair; (danger) to avert; **sē ~** rise.

lēvō, -āre vt to smooth, polish.

lēvor, -ōris m smoothness.

lēx, lēgis f law, statute; bill; rule, principle; contract, condition; **lēgem ferre** propose a bill; **lēgem perferre** carry a motion; **lēge agere** proceed according to law; **sine lēge** out of control.

lībāmen, -inis nt offering, libation.

lībāmentum, -ī nt offering, libation.

lībātiō, -ōnis f libation.

lībella, -ae f small coin, as; level; **ad ~am** exactly; **ex ~a** sole heir.

libellus, -ī m small book; notebook, diary, letter; notice, programme; handbill; petition, complaint; lampoon.

libēns, -entis adj willing, glad.

libenter adv willingly, with pleasure.

liber, -rī m inner bark (of a tree); book; register.

Līber, -ī m Italian god of fertility (identified with Bacchus).

līber, -ī adj free, open, unrestricted, undistorted; (with abl) free from; (speech) frank; (POL) free, not slave, democratic.

Lībera, -ae f Proserpine; Ariadne.

Līberālia, -ālium ntpl festival of Liber in March.

līberālis adj of freedom, of free citizens, gentlemanly, honourable; generous, liberal; handsome.

līberālitās, -ātis f courtesy, kindness; generosity; bounty.

līberāliter adv courteously, nobly; generously.

līberātiō, -ōnis f delivery, freeing; (law) acquittal.

līberātor, -ōris m liberator, deliverer.

līberē adv freely, frankly, boldly.

līberī, -ōrum mpl children.

līberō, -āre, -āvī, -ātum vt to free, set free, release; to exempt; (law) to acquit; (slave) to give freedom to; **fidem ~** keep one's promise; **nōmina ~** cancel debts.

līberta, -ae f freedwoman.

lībertās, -ātis f freedom, liberty; status of a freeman; (POL) independence; freedom of speech, outspokenness.

lībertīnus adj of a freedman, freed ♦ m freedman ♦ f freedwoman.

lībertus, -ī m freedman.

libet (lubet), -ēre, -uit and **itum est** vi (impers) it pleases; **mihi ~** I like; **ut ~** as you please.

lībidinōsē adv wilfully.

lībidinōsus adj wilful, arbitrary, extravagant; sensual, lustful.

lībīdō (lubīdō), -inis f desire, passion; wilfulness, caprice; lust.

lībita, -ōrum ntpl pleasure, fancy.

Lībītīna, -ae f goddess of burials.

lībō, -āre, -āvī, -ātum vt to taste, sip, touch; to pour (a libation); offer; to extract, take out; to impair.

lībra, -ae f pound; balance, pair of scales; **ad ~am** of equal size.

lībrāmentum, -ī nt level surface, weight (to give balance or movement); (water) fall.

lībrāria, -ae f head spinner.

lībrāriolus, -ī m copyist.

lībrārium, -ī and **iī** nt bookcase.

lībrārius, -ī adj of books ♦ m copyist.

lībrātus adj level; powerful.

lībrīlis adj weighing a pound.

lībritor, -ōris m slinger.

lībrō, -āre, -āvī, -ātum vt to poise, hold balanced; to swing, hurl.

lībum, -ī nt cake.

Liburna, -ae f a fast galley, frigate.

Liburnī, -ōrum mpl people of Illyria.

Liburnus adj Liburnian.

Libya, -ae; -ē, -ēs f Africa.

Libycus adj African.

Libyes, -um mpl Libyans, people in N. Africa.

Libyssus, Libystinus, Libystis adj = Libycus.

licēns, -entis adj free, bold, unrestricted.

licenter adv freely, lawlessly.

licentia, -ae f freedom, license; lawlessness, licentiousness.

liceō, -ēre, -uī vi to be for sale, value at.

liceor, -ērī, -itus vt, vi to bid (at an auction), bid for.

licet, -ēre, -uit and **itum est** vi (impers) it is permitted, it is lawful; (reply) all right ♦ conj although; **mihi ~** I may.

Licinius, -ī m Roman family name (esp with surname Crassus).

Licinius adj see n.

licitātiō, -ōnis f bidding (at a sale).

licitor, -ārī, vi to make a bid.

licitus adj lawful.

licium, -ī and **iī** nt thread.

lictor, -ōris m lictor (an attendant with fasces preceding a magistrate).

licuī perf of **liceō**; perf of **liquēscō**.

liēn, -ēnis m spleen.

ligāmen, -inis nt band, bandage.

ligāmentum, -ī nt bandage.

Liger, -is m river Loire.

lignārius, -ī and **iī** m carpenter.

lignātiō, -ōnis f fetching wood.

lignātor, -ōris m woodcutter.

ligneolus adj wooden.

ligneus adj wooden.

lignor, -ārī vi to fetch wood.

lignum, -ī nt wood, firewood, timber; **in silvam ~a ferre** ≈ carry coals to Newcastle.

ligō, -āre, -āvī, -ātum vt to tie up, bandage; (fig) to unite.

ligō, -ōnis m mattock, hoe.

ligula, -ae f shoestrap.

Ligur, -ris m/f Ligurian.

Liguria, -riae f district of N.W. Italy.

ligūriō (ligurriō), -īre vt to lick; to eat daintily; (fig) to feast on, lust after.

ligūrītiō, -ōnis f daintiness.

Ligus, -ris m/f Ligurian.

Ligusticus, -stīnus adj see n.

ligustrum, -ī nt privet.

līlium, -ī and **iī** nt lily; (MIL) spiked pit.

līma, -ae f file; (fig) revision.

līmātius adv more elegantly.

līmātulus adj refined.

līmāx, -ācis f slug, snail.

limbus, -ī m fringe, hem.

līmen, -inis nt threshold, lintel; doorway, entrance; house, home; (fig) beginning.

līmes, -itis m path between fields, boundary; path, track, way; frontier, boundary line.

līmō, -āre, -āvī, -ātum vt to file; (fig) to polish, refine; to file down, investigate carefully; to take away from.

līmōsus adj muddy.

limpidus adj clear, limpid.

līmus adj sidelong, askance.

līmus, -ī m mud, slime, dirt.

līmus, -ī m ceremonial apron.

līnea, -ae f line, string; plumbline; boundary; **ad ~am, rectā ~ā** vertically; **extrēmā ~ā amāre** love at a distance.

līneāmentum, -ī nt line; feature;

The present infinitive verb endings are as follows: -āre = 1st; -ēre = 2nd; -ere = 3rd and -īre = 4th. See sections on irregular verbs and noun declensions.

outline.
līneus adj flaxen, linen.
lingō, -ere vt to lick.
lingua, -ae f tongue; speech,
language; tongue of land; **~ Latīna**
Latin.
lingula, -ae f tongue of land.
līniger, -ī adj linen-clad.
linō, -ere, lēvī, litum vt to daub,
smear; to overlay; (*writing*) to rub
out; (*fig*) to befoul.
linquō, -ere, līquī vt to leave, quit;
to give up, let alone; (*pass*) to
faint, swoon; **~itur ut** it remains
to.
linteātus adj canvas.
linteō, -ōnis m linen weaver.
linter, -ris f boat; trough.
linteum, -ī nt linen cloth, canvas;
sail.
linteus adj linen.
lintriculus, -ī m small boat.
līnum, -ī nt flax; linen; thread, line,
rope; net.
Lipara, -ae; -ē, -ēs f island N. of
Sicily (*now Lipari*).
Liparaeus, -ēnsis adj see in.
lippiō, -īre vi to have sore eyes.
lippitūdō, -inis f inflammation of
the eyes.
lippus adj blear-eyed, with sore
eyes; (*fig*) blind.
liquefaciō, -facere, -fēcī, -factum
(*pass* -fīō) vt to melt, dissolve; to
decompose; (*fig*) to enervate.
liquēns, -entis adj fluid, clear.
liquēscō, -ere, licuī vi to melt; to
clear; (*fig*) to grow soft, waste
away.
liquet, -ēre, licuit vi (*impers*) it is
clear, it is evident; **nōn ~** not
proven.
liquī perf of **linquō**
liquidō adv clearly.
liquidus adj fluid, liquid, flowing;
clear, transparent, pure; (*mind*)
calm, serene ♦ nt liquid water.

liquō, -āre vt to melt; to strain.
līquor, -ī vi to flow; (*fig*) to waste
away.
liquor, -ōris m fluidity; liquid, the
sea.
Līris, -is m river between Latium and
Campania.
līs, lītis f quarrel, dispute; lawsuit;
matter in dispute; **lītem aestimāre**
assess damages.
lītātiō, -ōnis f favourable sacrifice.
lītera etc see **littera**.
lītigātor, -ōris m litigant.
lītigiōsus adj quarrelsome,
contentious; disputed.
lītigium, -ī and **iī** nt quarrel.
lītigō, -āre vi to quarrel; to go to
law.
litō, -āre, -āvī, -ātum vi to offer an
acceptable sacrifice, obtain
favourable omens; (*with dat*) to
propitiate ♦ vt to offer
successfully.
lītorālis adj of the shore.
lītoreus adj of the shore.
littera, -ae f letter (of the
alphabet).
litterae, -ārum fpl writing; letter,
dispatch; document, ordinance;
literature; learning, scholarship;
~ās discere learn to read and
write; **homō trium ~ārum** thief (of
fur); **sine ~īs** uncultured.
litterārius adj of reading and
writing.
litterātē adv in clear letters;
literally.
litterātor, -ōris m grammarian.
litterātūra, -ae f writing, alphabet.
litterātus adj with letters on it,
branded; educated, learned.
litterula, -ae f small letter; short
note; (*pl*) studies.
litūra, -ae f correction, erasure,
blot.
litus ppp of **linō**.
lītus, -oris nt shore, beach, coast;

bank; **~ arāre** labour in vain.

lituus, -ī m augur's staff; trumpet; (fig) starter.

līvēns, -entis pres p of **līveō** ♦ adj bluish, black and blue.

līveō, -ēre vi to be black and blue; to envy.

līvēscō, -ere vi to turn black and blue.

Līviānus adj = **Līvius**.

līvidulus adj a little jealous.

līvidus adj bluish, black and blue; envious, malicious.

Līvius, -ī m Roman family name (esp the first Latin poet); the famous historian, Livy.

Līvius adj see n.

līvor, -ōris m bluish colour; envy, malice.

lixa, -ae m sutler, camp-follower.

locātiō, -ōnis f leasing; lease, contract.

locātōrius adj concerned with leases.

locitō, -āre vt to let frequently.

locō, -āre, -āvī, -ātum vt to place, put; to give in marriage; to let, lease, hire out; to contract for; (money) to invest.

loculus, -ī m little place; (pl) satchel, purse.

locuplēs, -ētis adj rich, opulent; reliable, responsible.

locuplētō, -āre vt to enrich.

locus, -ī m (pl -ī m and -a nt) place, site, locality, region; (MIL) post; (theatre) seat; (book) passage; (speech) topic, subject, argument; (fig) room, occasion, situation, state; rank, position, -ī individual spots; **~a** regions, ground; **-ī commūnēs** general arguments; **-ō** (with gen) instead of; **in -ō** opportunely; **eō -ī** in the position; **intereā -ī** meanwhile.

lōcusta, -ae f locust.

locūtiō, -ōnis f speech; pronunciation.

locūtus ppa of **loquor**.

lōdīx, -īcis f blanket.

logica, -ōrum ntpl logic.

logos (-us), -ī m word; idle talk; witticism.

lōlīg- etc see **lollīg-**.

lolium, -ī and **iī** nt darnel.

lollīgō, -inis f cuttlefish.

lōmentum, -ī nt face cream.

Londinium, -ī nt London.

longaevus adj aged.

longē adv far, far off; (time) long; (compar) by far, very much; **~ esse** be far away, of no avail; **~ latēque** everywhere.

longinquitās, -ātis f length; distance; duration.

longinquus adj distant, remote; foreign, strange; lasting, wearisome; (hope) long deferred.

longitūdō, -inis f length, duration; **in -inem** lengthwise.

longiusculus adj rather long.

longulē adv rather far.

longulus adj rather long.

longurius, -ī and **iī** m long pole.

longus adj long; vast; (time) long, protracted tedious; (hope) far-reaching; **~a nāvis** warship; **~um est** it would be tedious; **nē ~um faciam** ≈ to cut a long story short.

loquācitās, -ātis f talkativeness.

loquāciter adv see adj.

loquāculus adj somewhat talkative.

loquāx, -ācis adj talkative, chattering.

loquella, -ae f language, words.

loquor, -quī, cūtus vi to speak, talk, say; to talk about, mention; (fig) to indicate; **rēs ~quitur ipsa** the facts speak for themselves.

The present infinitive verb endings are as follows: -āre = 1st; -ēre = 2nd; -ere = 3rd and -īre = 4th. See sections on irregular verbs and noun declensions.

lōrārius, -ī *and* **iī** *m* flogger.

lōrātus *adj* strapped.

lōreus *adj of* leather strips.

lōrīca, -ae *f* breastplate; parapet.

lōrīcātus *adj* mailed.

lōripēs, -edis *adj* bandylegged.

lōrum, -ī *nt* strap; whip, lash; leather charm; (*pl*) reins.

lōtos (-us), -ī *f* lotus.

lōtus *ppp of* lavō.

lubēns *see* libēns.

lubentia, -ae *f* pleasure.

lubet, lubīdō *see* libet, libīdō.

lūbricō, -āre *vt* to make slippery.

lūbricus *adj* slippery, slimy; gliding, fleeting; (*fig*) dangerous, hazardous.

Lūca bōs *f* elephant.

Lūcānia, -iae *f district of S. Italy*.

Lūcānica *f* kind of sausage.

Lūcānus, -ī *m the epic poet Lucan.*

lūcar, -āris *nt* forest tax.

lucellum, -ī *nt* small gain.

lūceō, -cēre, -xī *vi* to shine, be light; (*impers*) to dawn, be daylight; (*fig*) to shine, be clear; **meridiē nōn ~cēre** ≈ (argue) that black is white.

Lūcerēs, -um *mpl a Roman patrician tribe.*

Lūceria, -iae *f town in Apulia.*

Lūcerīnus *adj see n.*

lucerna, -ae *f* lamp; (*fig*) ≈ midnight oil.

lūcēscō, -ere *vi* to begin to shine, get light, dawn.

lūcidē *adv* clearly.

lūcidus *adj* bright, clear; (*fig*) lucid.

lūcifer, -ī *adj* light-bringing ♦ *m* morning star, Venus; day.

lūcifugus *adj* shunning the light.

Lūcīlius, -ī *m* Roman family name (*esp the first Latin satirist*).

Lūcīna, -ae *f goddess of childbirth.*

lūcīscō *etc see* lūcēscō.

Lucmō (Lucumō), -ōnis *m* Etruscan prince *or* priest.

Lucrētia, -iae *f wife of Collatinus, ravished by Tarquin.*

Lucrētius, -ī *m* Roman family name (*esp the philosophic poet*).

lucrifuga, -ae *m* non-profiteer.

Lucrīnēnsis *adj see n.*

Lucrīnus, -ī *m* lake near Baiae (*famous for oysters*).

lucror, -ārī, -ātus *vt* to gain, win, acquire.

lucrōsus *adj* profitable.

lucrum, -ī *nt* profit, gain; greed; wealth; **~ī facere** gain, get the credit of; **~ō esse** be of advantage; **in ~īs pōnere** count as gain.

luctāmen, -inis *nt* struggle, exertion.

luctātiō, -ōnis *f* wrestling; fight, contest.

luctātor, -ōris *m* wrestler.

lūctificus *adj* baleful.

lūctisonus *adj* mournful.

luctor, -ārī, -ātus *vi* to wrestle; to struggle, fight.

lūctuōsus *adj* sorrowful, lamentable.

lūctus, -ūs *m* mourning, lamentation; mourning (dress).

lūcubrātiō, -ōnis *f* work by lamplight, nocturnal study.

lūcubrō, -āre, -āvī, -ātum *vi* to work by night ♦ *vt* to compose by night.

lūculentē *adv* splendidly, right.

lūculenter *adv* very well.

lūculentus *adj* bright; (*fig*) brilliant, excellent, rich, fine.

Lūcullus, -ī *m* Roman surname (*esp the conqueror of Mithridates*).

lūcus, -ī *m* grove; wood.

lūdia, -ae *f* woman gladiator.

lūdibrium, -ī *and* **iī** *nt* mockery, derision; laughing stock; sport, play; **~iō habēre** make fun of.

lūdibundus *adj* playful; safely,

easily.

lūdicer, -rī adj playful; theatrical.

lūdicum, -ī nt public show, play; sport.

lūdificātiō, -ōnis f ridicule; tricking.

lūdificātor, -ōris m mocker.

lūdificō, -āre; -or, -ārī, -ātus vt to make a fool of, ridicule; to delude, thwart.

lūdiō, -ōnis m actor.

lūdius, -ī and **iī** m actor; gladiator.

lūdō, -dere, -sī, -sum vi to play; to sport, frolic; to dally, make love ♦ vt to play at; to amuse oneself with; to mimic, imitate; to ridicule, mock; to delude.

lūdus, -ī m game, sport, play; (pl) public spectacle, games; school; (fig) child's play; fun, jest; (love) dalliance; **-um dare** humour; **-ōs facere** put on a public show; make fun of.

luella, -ae f atonement.

luēs, -is f plague, pest; misfortune.

Lugdūnēnsis adj see n.

Lugdūnum, -ī nt town in E. Gaul (now Lyons).

lūgeō, -gēre, -xī vt, vi to mourn; to be in mourning.

lūgubris adj mourning; disastrous; (sound) plaintive ♦ ntpl mourning dress.

lumbī, -ōrum mpl loins.

lumbricus, -ī m worm.

lūmen, -inis nt light; lamp, torch; day; eye; life; (fig) ornament, glory; clarity.

lūmināre, -is nt window.

lūminōsus adj brilliant.

lūna, -ae f moon; month; crescent.

lūnāris adj of the moon.

lūnātus adj crescent-shaped.

lūnō, -āre vt to bend into a crescent.

luō, -ere, -ī vt to pay; to atone for; to avert by expiation.

lupa, -ae f she-wolf; prostitute.

lupānar, -āris nt brothel.

lupātus adj toothed ♦ m and ntpl curb.

Lupercal, -ālis nt a grotto sacred to Pan.

Lupercālia, -ālium ntpl festival of Pan in February.

Lupercus, -ī m Pan; priest of Pan.

lupīnum, -ī nt lupin; sham money, counters.

lupīnus adj wolf's.

lupīnus, -ī m lupin; sham money, counters.

lupus, -ī m wolf; (fish) pike; toothed bit; grapnel; **~ in fābulā** ≈ talk of the devil.

lūridus adj pale yellow, ghastly pallid.

lūror, -ōris m yellowness.

lūscinia, -ae f nightingale.

lūscitiōsus adj purblind.

lūscus adj one-eyed.

lūsiō, -ōnis f play.

Lūsitānia, -iae f part of W. Spain (including what is now Portugal).

Lūsitānus adj see n.

lūsitō, -āre vi to play.

lūsor, -ōris m player; humorous writer.

lūstrālis adj lustral, propitiatory; quinquennial.

lūstrātiō, -ōnis f purification; roving.

lūstrō, -āre, -āvī, -ātum vt to purify; (motion) to go round, encircle, traverse; (MIL) to review; (eyes) to scan, survey; (mind) to consider; (light) to illuminate.

lūstror, -ōris m frequenter of brothels.

lūstrum, -ī nt den, lair; (pl) wild country; (fig) brothels, debauchery.

*The present infinitive verb endings are as follows: -**āre** = 1st; -**ēre** = 2nd; -**ere** = 3rd and -**īre** = 4th. See sections on irregular verbs and noun declensions.*

lūstrum, -ī nt purificatory sacrifice; (time) five years.

lūsus ppp of **lūdō**.

lūsus, -ūs m play, game, sport; dalliance.

lūteolus adj yellow.

Lutetia, -ae f town in N. Gaul (now Paris).

lūteus adj yellow, orange.

luteus adj of clay; muddy, dirty; (fig) vile.

lutitō, -āre vt to throw mud at.

lutulentus adj muddy, filthy; (fig) foul.

lūtum, -ī nt dyer's weed; yellow.

lutum, -ī nt mud, mire; clay.

lūx, lūcis f light; daylight; day; life; (fig) public view; glory, encouragement, enlightenment; **lūce** in the daytime; **prīmā lūce** at daybreak; **lūce carentēs** the dead.

lūxī perf of **lūceō**; perf of **lūgeō**.

luxor, -ārī vi to live riotously.

luxuria, -ae, -ēs, -ēī f rankness, profusion; extravagance, luxury.

luxuriō, -āre, -or, -ārī vi to grow to excess, be luxuriant; (fig) to be exuberant, run riot.

luxuriōsē adv voluptuously.

luxuriōsus adj luxuriant, excessive, extravagant; voluptuous.

luxus, -ūs m excess, debauchery, pomp.

Lyaeus, -ī m Bacchus; wine.

Lycaeus, -ī m mountain in Arcadia (sacred to Pan).

Lycāōn, -onis m father of Callisto, the Great Bear.

Lycāonius adj see n.

Lycēum (Lycīum), -ī nt Aristotle's school at Athens.

lychnūchus, -ī m lampstand.

lychnus, -ī m lamp.

Lycia, -ae f country in S.W. Asia Minor.

Lycius adj Lycian.

Lyctius adj Cretan.

Lycurgus, -ī m Thracian king killed by Bacchus; Spartan lawgiver; Athenian orator.

Lȳdia, -iae f country of Asia Minor.

Lȳdius adj Lydian; Etruscan.

Lȳdus, -ī m Lydian.

lympha, -ae f water.

lymphāticus adj crazy, frantic.

lymphātus adj distracted.

Lynceus, -eī m keen-sighted Argonaut.

lynx, lyncis m/f lynx.

lyra, -ae f lyre; lyric poetry.

lyricus adj of the lyre, lyrical.

Lysiās, -ae m Athenian orator.

M

Macedō, -onis m Macedonian.

Macedonia f Macedonia.

Macedonicus, -onius adj see n.

macellum, -ī nt market.

maceō, -ēre vi to be lean.

macer, -rī adj lean, meagre; poor.

māceria, -ae f wall.

mācerō, -āre vt to soften; (body) to enervate; (mind) to distress.

macēscō, -ere vi to grow thin.

machaera, -ae f sword.

machaerophorus, -ī m soldier armed with a sword.

Machāōn, -onis m legendary Greek surgeon.

Machāonius adj see n.

māchina, -ae f machine, engine; (fig) scheme, trick.

māchināmentum, -ī nt engine.

māchinātiō, -ōnis f mechanism, machine; (fig) contrivance.

māchinātor, -ōris m engineer; (fig) contriver.

māchinor, -ārī, -ātus vt to devise, contrive; (fig) to plot, scheme.

maciēs, -ēī f leanness, meagreness; poorness.

macilentus adj thin.

macrēscō, -ere vi to grow thin.
macritūdō, -inis f leanness.
macrocollum, -ī nt large size of paper.
mactābilis adj deadly.
mactātus, -ūs m sacrifice.
macte blessed; well done!
mactō, -āre, -āvī, -ātum vt to sacrifice; to punish, kill.
mactō, -āre vt to glorify.
macula, -ae f spot, stain; (net) mesh; (fig) blemish, fault.
maculō, -āre, -āvī, -ātum vt to stain, defile.
maculōsus adj dappled, mottled; stained, polluted.
madefaciō, -facere, -fēcī, -factum (pass -fīō, -fierī) vt to wet, soak.
madeō, -ēre vi to be wet, be drenched; to be boiled soft; (comedy) to be drunk; (fig) to be steeped in.
madēscō, -ere vi to get wet, become moist.
madidus adj wet, soaked; sodden; drunk.
madulsa, -ae m drunkard.
Maeander (-ros), -rī m a winding river of Asia Minor; winding, wandering.
Maecēnās, -ātis m friend of Augustus, patron of poets.
maena, -ae f sprat.
Maenala, -ōrum ntpl mountain range in Arcadia.
Maenalis, -ius adj of Maenalus; Arcadian.
Maenalus (-os), -ī m Maenala.
Maenas, -dis f Bacchante.
Maeniānum nt balcony.
Maenius, -ī m Roman family name; **~ia columna** whipping post in the Forum.
Maeonia, -ae f Lydia.
Maeonidēs, -dae m Homer.

Maeonius, -s adj Lydian; Homeric; Etruscan.
Maeōticus, -us adj Scythian, Maeotic.
Maeōtis, -dis f Sea of Azov.
maereō, -ēre vi to mourn, be sad.
maeror, -ōris m mourning, sorrow, sadness.
maestiter adv see adj.
maestitia, -ae f sadness, melancholy.
maestus adj sad, sorrowful; gloomy; mourning.
māgālia, -um ntpl huts.
mage etc see **magis.**
magicus adj magical.
magis (mage) adv more; eō ~ the more, all the more.
magister, -rī m master, chief, director; (school) teacher; (fig) instigator; **~ equitum** chief of cavalry, second in command to a dictator; **~ mōrum** censor; **~ sacrōrum** chief priest.
magisterium, -ī and **iī** nt presidency, tutorship.
magistra, -ae f mistress, instructress.
magistrātus, -ūs m magistracy, office; magistrate, official.
magnanimitās, -ātis f greatness.
magnanimus adj great, brave.
Magnēs, -ētis m Magnesian; magnet.
Magnēsia f district of Thessaly.
Magnēsius, -essus, -ētis adj see n.
magnidicus adj boastful.
magnificē adv grandly; pompously.
magnificentia, -ae f greatness, grandeur; pomposity.
magnificō, -āre vt to esteem highly.
magnificus (compar **-entior** superl **-entissimus**) adj great, grand,

The present infinitive verb endings are as follows: -āre = 1st; -ēre = 2nd; -ere = 3rd and -īre = 4th. See sections on irregular verbs and noun declensions.

splendid; pompous.

magniloquentia, -ae f elevated language; pomposity.

magniloquus adj boastful.

magnitūdō, -inis f greatness, size, large amount; dignity.

magnopere adv greatly, very much.

magnus (compar **māior** superl **māximus**) adj great, large, big, tall; (voice) loud; (age) advanced; (value) high, dear; (fig) grand, noble, important; **avunculus ~ great-uncle; ~a loquī** boast; **~ī aestimāre** think highly of; **~ī esse** be highly esteemed; **~ō stāre** cost dear; **~ō opere** very much.

magus, -ī m wise man; magician ♦ adj magic.

Māia, -ae f mother of Mercury.

māiestās, -ātis f greatness, dignity, majesty; treason; **~ātem laedere, minuere** offend against the sovereignty of; **lēx ~ātis** law against treason.

māior, -ōris compar of **māgnus; ~ nātū** older, elder.

māiōrēs, -ōrum mpl ancestors; **in ~us crēdere/ferre** exaggerate.

Māius, -ī m May ♦ adj of May.

māiusculus adj somewhat greater; a little older.

māla, -ae f cheek, jaw.

malacia, -ae f dead calm.

malacus adj soft.

male (compar **pēius,** superl **pessimē**) adv badly, wrongly, unfortunately; not; (with words having bad sense) very much; **~ est animō** I feel ill; **~ sānus** insane; **~ dīcere** abuse, curse; **~ facere** harm.

maledicē adv abusively.

maledictiō, -ōnis f abuse.

maledictum, -ī nt curse.

maledicus adj scurrilous.

malefactum, -ī nt wrong.

maleficē adv see adj.

maleficium, -ī and iī nt misdeed, wrong, mischief.

maleficus adj wicked ♦ m criminal.

malesuādus adj seductive.

malevolēns, -entis adj spiteful.

malevolentia, -ae f ill-will.

malevolus adj ill-disposed, malicious.

mālifer, -ī adj apple-growing.

malīgnē adv spitefully; grudgingly.

malīgnitās, -ātis f malice; stinginess.

malīgnus adj unkind, ill-natured, spiteful; stingy; (soil) unfruitful; (fig) small, scanty.

malitia, -ae f badness, malice; roguishness.

malitiōsē adv see adj.

malitiōsus adj wicked, crafty.

maliv- etc see **malev-.**

mālle infin of **mālō.**

malleolus, -ī m hammer; (MIL) fire-brand.

malleus, -ī m hammer, mallet, maul.

mālō, -le, -uī vt to prefer; would rather.

malobathrum, -ī nt an oriental perfume.

māluī perf of **mālō.**

mālum, -ī nt apple, fruit.

malum, -ī nt evil, wrong, harm, misfortune; (interj) mischief.

mālus, -ī f apple tree.

mālus, -ī m mast, pole.

malus (compar **pēior,** superl **pessimus**) adj bad, evil, harmful; unlucky; ugly; **ī in ~am rem** go to hell!

malva, -ae f mallow.

Māmers, -tis m Mars.

Māmertinī, -ōrum mpl mercenary troops who occupied Messana.

mamma, -ae f breast; teat.

mammilla, -ae f breast.
mānābilis adj penetrating.
manceps, -ipis m purchaser;
  contractor.
mancipium, -ī and **iī** nt formal
  purchase; property; slave.
mancipō, -āre vt to sell, deliver up.
mancup- etc see **mancip-**.
mancus adj crippled.
mandātum, -ī nt commission,
  command; (law) contract.
mandātus, -ūs m command.
mandō, -āre, -āvī, -ātum vt to
  entrust, commit; to commission,
  command.
mandō, -ere, -ī, mānsum vt to
  chew, eat, devour.
mandra, -ae f drove of cattle.
mandūcus, -ī m masked figure of a
  glutton.
māne nt (indecl) morning ♦ adv in
  the morning, early.
maneō, -ēre, mānsī, mānsum vi
  to remain; to stay, stop; to last,
  abide, continue ♦ vt to wait for,
  await; **in condiciōne ~** abide by an
  agreement.
Mānēs, -ium mpl ghosts, shades of
  the dead; the lower world; bodily
  remains.
mangō, -ōnis m dealer.
manicae, -ārum fpl sleeves,
  gloves; handcuffs.
manicātus adj with long sleeves.
manicula, -ae f little hand.
manifestō vt to disclose.
manifestō adv clearly, evidently.
manifestus adj clear, obvious;
  convicted, caught.
manipl- etc see **manipul-**.
manipulāris adj of a company ♦ m
  private (in the ranks); fellow
  soldier.
manipulātim adv by companies.
manipulus, -ī m bundle (esp of hay);

(MIL) company.
Manlius, -iānus adj see n.
Manlius, -ī m Roman family name
  (esp the saviour of the Capitol from the
  Gauls); a severe disciplinarian.
mannus, -ī m Gallic horse.
mānō, -āre, -āvī, -ātum vi to flow,
  drip, stream; (fig) to spread,
  emanate.
mānsī perf of **maneō**.
mānsiō, -ōnis f remaining, stay.
mānsitō, -āre vi to stay on.
**mānsuēfaciō, -facere, -fēcī,
  -factum** (pass -fiō, -fierī) vt to
  tame.
mānsuēscō, -scere, -vī, -tum vt to
  tame ♦ vi to grow tame, grow
  mild.
mānsuētē adv see adj.
mānsuētūdō, -inis f tameness;
  gentleness.
mānsuētus ppp of **mānsuēscō**
  ♦ adj tame; mild, gentle.
mānsus ppp of **mandō**; ppp of
  maneō.
mantēle, -is nt napkin, towel.
mantēlum, -ī nt cloak.
mantica, -ae f knapsack.
manticinor, -ārī, -ātus vi to be a
  prophet.
mantō, -āre vi to remain, wait.
Mantua, -ae f birthplace of Vergil in
  N. Italy.
manuālis adj for the hand.
manubiae, -ārum fpl money from
  sale of booty.
mānūbrium, -ī and **iī** nt handle,
  haft.
manuleātus adj with long sleeves.
manūmissiō, -ōnis f emancipation
  (of a slave).
manūmittō, -ittere, -īsī, -issum vt
  to emancipate, make free.
manupretium, -ī and **iī** nt pay,
  wages, reward.

*The present infinitive verb endings are as follows: -āre = 1st; -ēre = 2nd; -ere = 3rd and
-īre = 4th. See sections on irregular verbs and noun declensions.*

manus, -ūs f hand; corps, band, company; (*elephant*) trunk; (*art*) touch; (*work*) handiwork, handwriting; (*war*) force, valour, hand to hand fighting; (*fig*) power; **~ extrēma** finishing touch; **~ ferrea** grappling iron; **~um dare** give up, yield; **~ū** artificially; **~ū mittere** emancipate; **ad ~um** at hand; **in ~ū** obvious; subject; **in ~ūs venīre** come to hand; **in ~ibus** well known; at hand; **in ~ibus habēre** be engaged on; fondle; **per ~ūs** forcibly; **per ~ūs trādere** hand down.

mapālia, -um ntpl huts.

mappa, -ae f napkin, cloth.

Marathōn, -ōnis f *Attic village famous for Persian defeat.*

Marathōnius adj see n.

Marcellia, -iōrum ntpl *festival of the Marcelli.*

Marcellus, -ī m *Roman surname (esp the captor of Syracuse).*

marceō, -ēre vi to droop, be faint.

marcēscō, -ere vi to waste away, grow feeble.

Marciānus adj see n.

marcidus adj withered; enervated.

Marcius, -ī m *Roman family name (esp Ancus, fourth king).*

Marcius adj see n.

mare, -is nt sea; **~ nostrum** Mediterranean; **~ inferum** Tyrrhenian Sea; **~ superum** Adriatic.

Mareōticus adj Mareotic; Egyptian.

margarīta, -ae f pearl.

marginō, -āre vt to put a border or kerb on.

margō, -inis m/f edge, border, boundary; **~ cēnae** side dishes.

Mariānus adj see n.

Marica, -ae f *nymph of Minturnae.*

marīnus adj of the sea.

maritālis adj marriage- (*in cpds*).

maritimus adj of the sea, maritime, coastal ♦ ntpl coastal area.

marītō, -āre vt to marry.

marītus, -ī m husband ♦ adj nuptial.

Marius, -ī m *Roman family name (esp the victor over Jugurtha and the Teutons).*

Marius adj see n.

marmor, -is nt marble; statue, tablet; sea.

marmoreus adj of marble; like marble.

Marō, -ōnis m *surname of Vergil.*

marra, -ae f *kind of hoe.*

Mars, Martis m *god of war, father of Romulus*; war, conflict; planet Mars; **aequō Marte** on equal terms; **suō Marte** by one's own exertions.

Marsī, -ōrum mpl *people of central Italy, famous as fighters.*

Marsicus, -us adj Marsian.

marsuppium, -ī and **iī** nt purse.

Mārtiālis adj of Mars.

Mārticola, -ae m *worshipper of Mars.*

Mārtigena, -ae m *son of Mars.*

Mārtius adj of Mars; of March; warlike.

mās, maris m male, man ♦ adj male; manly.

māsculus adj male, masculine; manly.

Masinissa, -ae m *king of Numidia.*

massa, -ae f lump, mass.

Massicum, -ī nt Massic wine.

Massicus, -ī m *mountain in Campania, famous for vines.*

Massilia, -ae f *Greek colony in Gaul (now Marseilles).*

Massiliēnsis adj see n.

mastīgia, -ae nt scoundrel.

mastrūca, -ae f sheepskin.

mastrūcātus adj wearing sheepskin.

matara, -ae and **is, -is** f Celtic

javelin.
matelliō, -ōnis m pot.
māter, -ris f mother; **Māgna ~**
Cybele.
mātercula, -ae f poor mother.
māteria, -ae; -ēs, -ēī f matter,
substance; wood, timber; (fig)
subject matter, theme; occasion,
opportunity; (person) ability,
character.
māteriārius, -ī and **iī** m timber
merchant.
māteriātus adj timbered.
māteriēs etc see **māteria**.
māterior, -ārī vi to fetch wood.
māternus adj mother's.
mātertera, -ae f aunt (maternal).
mathēmaticus, -ī m
mathematician; astrologer.
mātricīda, -ae m matricide.
mātricīdium, -ī and **iī** nt a mother's
murder.
mātrimōnium, -ī and **iī** nt
marriage.
mātrimus adj whose mother is still
alive.
mātrōna, -ae f married woman,
matron, lady.
mātrōnālis adj a married woman's.
matula, -ae f pot.
mātūrē adv at the right time,
early, promptly.
mātūrēscō, -ēscere, -uī vi to ripen.
mātūritās, -ātis f ripeness; (fig)
maturity, perfection, height.
mātūrō, -āre, -āvī, -ātum vt to
bring to maturity; to hasten, be
too hasty with ♦ vi to make haste.
mātūrus adj ripe, mature; timely,
seasonable; early.
Mātūta, -ae f goddess of dawn.
mātūtinus adj morning, early.
Mauritānia, -ae f Mauretania (now
Morocco).
Maurus, -ī m Moor ♦ adj Moorish.

African.
Maurūsius adj see n.
Māvors, -tis m Mars.
Māvortius adj see n.
maxilla, -ae f jaw.
maximē adv most, very much,
especially; precisely; just;
certainly; yes; **cum ~** just as;
quam ~ as much as possible.
maximitās, -ātis f great size.
maximus superl of **magnus**.
māxum- etc see **māxim-**.
māzonomus, -ī m dish.
meāpte my own.
meātus, -ūs m movement, course.
mēcastor interj by Castor!
mēcum with me.
meddix tuticus m senior Oscan
magistrate.
Mēdēa, -ae f Colchian wife of Jason,
expert in magic.
Mēdēis adj magical.
medentēs, -entum mpl doctors.
medeor, -ērī vi (with dat) to heal,
remedy.
mediastīnus, -ī m drudge.
mēdica, -ae f lucern (kind of clover).
medicābilis adj curable.
medicāmen, -inis nt drug,
medicine; cosmetic; (fig) remedy.
medicāmentum, -ī nt drug,
medicine; potion, poison; (fig)
relief; embellishment.
medicātus, -ūs m charm.
medicīna, -ae f medicine; cure;
(fig) remedy, relief.
medicō, -āre, -āvī, -ātum vt to
cure; to steep, dye.
medicor, -ārī vt, vi to cure.
medicus adj healing ♦ m doctor.
medietās, -ātis f mean.
medimnum, -ī nt, **-us, -ī** m bushel.
mediocris adj middling, moderate,
average.
mediocritās, -ātis f mean,

*The present infinitive verb endings are as follows: -**āre** = 1st; -**ēre** = 2nd; -**ere** = 3rd and
-**īre** = 4th. See sections on irregular verbs and noun declensions.*

moderation; mediocrity.

mediocriter *adv* moderately, not particularly; calmly.

Mediolānēnsis *adj* see n.

Mediolānum, -ī *nt* town in N. Italy (*now* Milan).

meditāmentum, -ī *nt* preparation, drill.

meditātiō, -ōnis *f* thinking about; preparation, practice.

meditātus *adj* studied.

mediterrāneus *adj* inland.

meditor, -ārī, -ātus *vt, vi* to think over, contemplate, reflect; to practise, study.

medius *adj* middle, the middle of; intermediate; intervening; middling, moderate; neutral ♦ *nt* middle; public ♦ *m* mediator; **~um complectī** clasp round the waist; **~um sē gerere** be neutral; **-ō** midway; **~ō temporis** meanwhile; **in ~um** for the common good; **in ~um prōferre** publish; **dē ~ō tollere** do away with; **ē ~ō abīre** die, disappear; **in ~ō esse** be public; **in ~ō positus** open to all; **in ~ō relinquere** leave undecided.

medius fidius *interj* by Heaven!

medix *etc see* **meddix**.

medulla, -ae *f* marrow, pith.

medullitus *adv* from the heart.

medullula, -ae *f* marrow.

Mēdus, -ī *m* Mede, Persian.

Mēdus *adj* see n.

Medūsa, -ae *f* Gorgon, whose look turned everything to stone.

Medūsaeus *adj*: **~ equus** Pegasus.

Megalēnsia (Megalēsia), -um *ntpl* festival of Cybele in April.

Megara, -ae *f, -ōrum* *ntpl* town in Greece near the Isthmus.

Megarēus and icus *adj* Megarean.

megistānes, -um *mpl* grandees.

mehercle, mehercule,
mehercules *interj* by Hercules!

mēiō, -ere *vi* to make water.

mel, mellis *nt* honey.

melancholicus *adj* melancholy.

melē *pl* melos.

Meleager (-ros), -rī *m* prince of Calydon.

melicus *adj* musical; lyrical.

melilōtos, -ī *f* kind of clover.

melimēla, -ōrum *ntpl* honey apples.

Melīnum, -ī *nt* Melian white.

melior, -ōris *adj* better.

melisphyllum, -ī *nt* balm.

Melita, -ae *f* Malta.

Melitēnsis *adj* Maltese.

melius *nt* melior ♦ *adv* better.

meliusculē *adv* fairly well.

meliusculus *adj* rather better.

mellifer, -ī *adj* honey-making.

mellītus *adj* honeyed; sweet.

melos, -ī *nt* tune, song.

Melpomenē, -ēs *f* Muse of tragedy.

membrāna, -ae *f* skin, membrane, slough; parchment.

membrānula, -ae *f* piece of parchment.

membrātim *adv* limb by limb; piecemeal; in short sentences.

membrum, -ī *nt* limb, member; part, division; clause.

mēmet *emphatic form of* **mē**.

meminī, -isse *vi (with gen)* to remember, think of; to mention.

Memnōn, -onis *m* Ethiopian king, killed at Troy.

Memnonius *adj* see n.

memor, -is *adj* mindful, remembering; in memory (of).

memorābilis *adj* memorable, remarkable.

memorandus *adj* noteworthy.

memorātus, -ūs *m* mention.

memorātus *adj* famed.

memoria, -ae *f* memory, remembrance; time, lifetime; history; **haec ~** our day; **~ae prōdere** hand down to posterity;

post hominum ~am since the beginning of history.

memoriola, -ae f weak memory.

memoriter adv from memory; accurately.

memorō, -āre, -āvī, -ātum vt to mention, say, speak.

Memphis, -is and **idos** f town in middle Egypt.

Momphītēs and **ītis** and **īticus** adj of Memphis; Egyptian.

Menander (-ros), -rī m Greek writer of comedy.

Menandrēus adj see n.

menda, -ae f fault.

mendācium, -ī and **iī** nt lie.

mendāciunculum, -ī nt fib.

mendāx, -ācis adj lying; deceptive, unreal ♦ m liar.

mendīcitās, -ātis f beggary.

mendīcō, -āre, -or, -ārī, vi to beg, go begging.

mendīcus adj beggarly, poor ♦ m beggar.

mendōsē adv see adj.

mendōsus adj faulty; wrong, mistaken.

mendum, -ī nt fault, blunder.

Menelāeus adj see n.

Menelāus, -ī m brother of Agamemnon, husband of Helen.

Menoetiadēs, -ae m Patroclus.

mēns, mentis f mind, understanding; feelings; heart; idea, plan, purpose; courage; **venit in mentem** it occurs; **mente captus** insane; **eā mente ut** with the intention of.

mēnsa, -ae f table; meal, course; counter, bank; **secunda ~** dessert.

mēnsārius, -ī and **iī** m banker.

mēnsiō, -ōnis f (metre) quantity.

mēnsis, -is m month.

mēnsor, -ōris m measurer, surveyor.

mēnstruālis adj for a month.

mēnstruus adj monthly; for a month ♦ nt a month's provisions.

mēnsula, -ae f little table.

mēnsūra, -ae f measure, measurement; standard, standing; amount, size, capacity.

mēnsus ppa of **mētior**.

menta, -ae f mint.

Menteus adj see n.

mentiēns, -ientis f fallacy.

montiō, -ōnis f mention, hint.

mentior, -īrī, -ītus vi to lie, deceive ♦ vt to say falsely; to feign, imitate.

mentītus adj lying, false.

Mentor, -is m artist in metalwork; ornamental cup.

mentum, -ī nt chin.

meō, -āre vi to go, pass.

mephītis, -is f noxious vapour, malaria.

merācus adj pure.

mercābilis adj buyable.

mercātor, -ōris m merchant, dealer.

mercātūra, -ae f commerce; purchase; goods.

mercātus, -ūs m trade, traffic; market, fair.

mercēdula, -ae f poor wages, small rent.

mercēnārius adj hired, mercenary ♦ m servant.

mercēs, -ēdis f pay, wages, fee; bribe; rent; (fig) reward, retribution; cost

mercimōnium, -ī and **iī** nt wares, goods.

mercor, -ārī, -ātus vt to trade in, purchase.

Mercurius, -ī m messenger of the gods, god of trade, thieves, speech and the lyre; **stēlla ~ī** planet Mercury.

Mercuriālis adj see n.

The present infinitive verb endings are as follows: -āre = 1st; -ēre = 2nd; -ere = 3rd and -īre = 4th. See sections on irregular verbs and noun declensions.

merda, -ae f dung.

merenda, -ae f lunch.

mereō, -ēre, -uī; -eor, -ērī, -itus vt, vi to deserve; to earn, win, acquire; (MIL) to serve; **bene ~ dē** do a service to, serve well; **~ equō** serve in the cavalry.

meretrīcius adj a harlot's.

meretrīcula, -ae f pretty harlot.

meretrīx, -īcis f harlot.

mergae, -ārum fpl pitchfork.

merges, -itis f sheaf.

mergō, -gere, -sī, -sum vt to dip, immerse, sink; (fig) to bury, plunge, drown.

mergus, -ī m (bird) diver.

merīdiānus adj midday; southerly.

merīdiātiō, -ōnis f siesta.

merīdiēs, -ēī f midday, noon; south.

merīdiō, -āre, vi to take a siesta.

meritō, -āre vt to learn.

meritō adv deservedly.

meritōrius adj money-earning
   ♦ ntpl lodgings.

meritum, -ī nt service, kindness, merit; blame.

meritus ppp of **mereō** ♦ adj deserved, just.

merops, -is f bee-eater.

mersī perf of **mergō.**

mersō, -āre vt to immerse, plunge; to overwhelm.

mersus ppp of **mergō.**

merula, -ae f blackbird.

merum, -ī nt wine.

merus adj pure, undiluted; bare, mere.

merx, mercis f goods, wares.

Messalla, -ae m Roman surname
   (esp ~ **Corvīnus** Augustan orator, soldier and literary patron).

Messallīna, -īnae f wife of emperor Claudius; wife of Nero.

Messāna, -ae f Sicilian town (now Messina).

messis, -is f harvest.

messor, -ōris m reaper.

messōrius adj a reaper's.

messuī perf of **metō.**

messus ppp of **metō.**

mēta, -ae f pillar at each end of the Circus course; turning point, winning post; (fig) goal, end, limit.

metallum, -ī nt mine, quarry; metal.

mētātor, -ōris m surveyor.

Metaurus, -ī m river in Umbria, famous for the defeat of Hasdrubal.

Metellus, -ī m Roman surname
   (esp the commander against Jugurtha).

Mēthymna, -ae f town in Lesbos.

Mēthymnaeus adj see n.

mētior, -tīrī, -nsus vt to measure, measure out; to traverse; (fig) to estimate, judge.

metō, -tere, -ssuī, -ssum vt to reap, gather; to mow, cut down.

mētor, -ārī, -ātus vt to measure off, lay out.

metrēta, -ae f liquid measure
   (about 9 gallons).

metuculōsus adj frightful.

metuō, -uere, -uī, -ūtum vt to fear, be apprehensive.

metus, -ūs m fear, alarm, anxiety.

meus adj my, mine.

mī dat of **ego;** voc and mpl of **meus.**

mīca, -ae f crumb, grain.

micō, -āre, -uī vi to quiver, flicker, beat, flash, sparkle.

Midās, -ae m Phrygian king whose touch turned everything to gold.

migrātiō, -ōnis f removal, change.

migrō, -āre, -āvī, -ātum vi to remove, change, pass away ♦ vt to transport, transgress.

mīles, -itis m soldier, infantryman; army troops.

Mīlēsius adj see n.

Mīlētus, -ī f town in Asia Minor.

mīlia, -um ntpl thousands; ~ **passuum** miles.

mīliārium (milliārium), -ī *and* iī *nt* milestone.

mīlitāris *adj* military, a soldier's.

mīlitāriter *adv* in a soldierly fashion.

mīlitia, -ae *f* military service, war; the army; ~ae on service; **domī** ~**aeque** at home and abroad.

mīlitō, -āre *vi* to serve, be a soldier.

mīlium, -ī *and* iī *nt* millet.

mīlle, (*pl* -**ia**) *num* a thousand; ~ **passūs** a mile.

mīllēnsimus, -ēsimus -ē *adj* thousandth.

mīllia *etc see* mīlia.

mīlliārium *etc see* mīliārium.

mīlliēns, -ēs *adv* a thousand times.

Milō, -ōnis *m* tribune who killed Clodius and was defended by Cicero.

Milōniānus *adj see* n.

Miltiadēs, -is *m* Athenian general, victor at Marathon.

mīluīnus *adj* resembling a kite; rapacious.

mīluus (mīlvus), -ī *m* kite; gurnard.

mīma, -ae *f* actress.

Mimallonis, -dis *f* Bacchante.

mīmicē *adv see* adj.

mīmicus *adj* farcical.

Mimnermus, -ī *m* Greek elegiac poet.

mīmula, -ae *f* actress.

mīmus, -ī *m* actor; mime, farce.

mina, -ae *f* Greek silver coin.

mināciter *adv see* adj.

minae, -ārum *fpl* threats; (*wall*) pinnacles.

minanter *adv* threateningly.

minātiō, -ōnis *f* threat.

mināx, -ācis *adj* threatening; projecting.

Minerva, -ae *f* goddess of wisdom and arts, esp weaving; (*fig*) talent, genius; working in wool; **sūs ~am**

≈ "teach your grandmother!"

miniānus *adj* red-leaded.

miniātulus *adj* painted red.

minimē *adv* least, very little; (*reply*) no, not at all.

minimus *adj* least, smallest, very small; youngest.

miniō, -āre, -āvī, -ātum *vt* to colour red.

minister, -rī *m*, -**ra**, -**rae** *f* attendant, servant; helper, agent, tool.

ministerium, -ī *and* iī *nt* service, office, duty; retinue.

ministrātor, -ōris *m*, -**rīx, -rīcis** *f* assistant, handmaid.

ministrō, -āre *vt* to serve, supply; to manage.

minitābundus *adj* threatening.

minitor, -ārī, -ō, -āre *vt, vi* to threaten.

minium, -ī *and* iī *nt* vermilion, red lead.

Mīnōis, -idis *f* Ariadne.

Mīnōius, -us *adj see* n.

minor, -ārī, -ātus *vt, vi* to threaten; to project.

minor, -ōris *adj* smaller, less, inferior; younger; (*pl*) descendants.

Mīnōs, -is *m* king of Crete, judge in the lower world.

Mīnōtaurus, -ī *m* monster of the Cretan labyrinth, half bull, half man.

Minturnae, -ārum *fpl* town in S. Latium.

Minturnēnsis *adj see* n.

minum- *etc see* minim-.

minuō, -uere, -uī, -ūtum *vt* to make smaller, lessen; to chop up; to reduce, weaken ♦ *vi* (*tide*) to ebb.

minus *nt* minor ♦ *adv* less; not, not at all; **quō ~** (*prevent*) from.

minusculus *adj* smallish.

The present infinitive verb endings are as follows: -**āre** = 1st; -**ēre** = 2nd; -**ere** = 3rd *and* -**īre** = 4th. See sections on irregular verbs and noun declensions.

minūtal, -ālis nt mince.

minūtātim adv bit by bit.

minūtē adv in a petty manner.

minūtus ppp of **minuō ♦** adj small; paltry.

mīrābilis adj wonderful, extraordinary.

mīrābiliter adv see adj.

mīrābundus adj astonished.

mīrāculum, -ī nt marvel, wonder; amazement.

mīrandus adj wonderful.

mīrātiō, -ōnis f wonder.

mīrātor, -ōris m admirer.

mīrātrīx, -īcis adj admiring.

mīrē adv see adj.

mīrificē adv see adj.

mīrificus adj wonderful.

mirmillō see **murmillō.**

mīror, -ārī, -ātus vt to wonder at, be surprised at, admire ♦ vi to wonder, be surprised.

mīrus adj wonderful, strange; **~um quam, quantum** extraordinarily.

miscellānea, -ōrum ntpl (food) hotchpotch.

misceō, -scēre, -scuī, -xtum vt to mix, mingle, blend; to join, combine; to confuse, embroil.

misellus adj poor little.

Mīsēnēnsis adj see n.

Mīsēnum, -ī nt promontory and harbour near Naples.

miser, -ī adj wretched, poor, pitiful, sorry.

miserābilis adj pitiable, sad, plaintive.

miserābiliter adv see adj.

miserandus adj deplorable.

miserātiō, -ōnis f pity, compassion, pathos.

miserē adv see adj.

misereō, -ēre, -uī; -eor, -ērī, -itus vt, vi (with gen) to pity, sympathize with; **~et mē** I pity, I am sorry.

miserēscō, -ere vi to feel pity.

miseria, -ae f misery, trouble, distress.

misericordia, -ae f pity, sympathy, mercy.

misericors, -dis adj sympathetic, merciful.

miseriter adv sadly.

miseror, -ārī, -ātus vt to deplore; to pity.

mīsī perf of **mittō.**

missa, -ae f (ECCL) mass.

missilis adj missile.

missiō, -ōnis f sending; release; (MIL) discharge; (gladiators) quarter; (events) end; **sine ~ōne** to the death.

missitō, -āre vt to send repeatedly.

missus ppp of **mittō.**

missus, -ūs m sending; throwing; **~ sagittae** bowshot.

mitella, -ae f turban.

mītēscō, -ere vi to ripen; to grow mild.

Mithridātēs, -is m king of Pontus, defeated by Pompey.

Mithridātēus, -icus adj see n.

mītigātiō, -ōnis f soothing.

mītigō, -āre, -āvī, -ātum vt to ripen, soften; to calm, pacify.

mītis adj ripe, mellow; soft, mild; gentle.

mitra, -ae f turban.

mittō, -ere, mīsī, missum vt to send, dispatch; to throw, hurl; to let go, dismiss; to emit, utter; (news) to send word; (gift) to bestow; (event) to end; (speech) to omit, stop; **sanguinem ~** bleed; **ad cēnam ~** invite to dinner; **missum facere** forgo.

mītulus, -ī m mussel.

mixtim adv promiscuously.

mixtūra, -ae f mingling.

Mnēmosynē, -ēs f mother of the Muses.

mnēmosynon, -ī nt souvenir.

mōbilis adj movable; nimble, fleet; excitable, fickle.

mōbilitās, -ātis f agility, rapidity; fickleness.

mōbiliter adv rapidly.

mōbilitō, -āre vt to make rapid.

moderābilis adj moderate.

moderāmen, -inis nt control; government.

moderanter adv with control.

moderātē adv with restraint.

moderātim adv gradually.

moderātiō, -ōnis f control, government; moderation; rules.

moderātor, -ōris m controller, governor.

moderātrix, -īcis f mistress, controller.

moderātus adj restrained, orderly.

moderor, -ārī, -ātus vt, vi (with dat) to restrain, check; (with acc) to manage, govern, guide.

modestē adv with moderation; humbly.

modestia, -ae f temperate behaviour, discipline; humility.

modestus adj sober, restrained; well-behaved, disciplined; modest, unassuming.

modiālis adj holding a peck.

modicē adv moderately; slightly.

modicus adj moderate; middling, small, mean.

modificātus adj measured.

modius, -ī and iī m corn measure, peck.

modo adv only; at all, in any way; (with imp) just; (time) just now, a moment ago, in a moment ♦ conj if only; **nōn** ~ not only; **non** ~ ... **sed** not only ... but also ...; ~ **nōn** all but, almost; ~ ... ~ sometimes ... sometimes; ~ ... **tum** at first ... then.

modulātē adv melodiously.

modulātor, -ōris m musician.

modulātus adj played, measured.

modulor, -ārī, -ātus vt to modulate, play, sing.

modulus, -ī m measure.

modus, -ī m measure; size; metre; music; way, method; limit, end; **ēius -ī** such; ~ō, in, ~um like.

moecha, -ae f adulteress.

moechor, -ārī vi to commit adultery.

moechus, -ī m adulterer.

moenera etc see **mūnus**.

moenia, -um ntpl defences, walls; town, stronghold

moeniō etc see **mūniō**.

Moesī, -ōrum mpl people on lower Danube (now Bulgaria).

mola, -ae f millstone, mill; grains of spelt.

molāris, -is m millstone; (tooth) molar.

mōlēs, -is f mass, bulk, pile; dam, pier, massive structure; (fig) greatness, weight, effort, trouble.

molestē adv see adj

molestia, -ae f trouble, annoyance, worry; (style) affectation.

molestus adj irksome, annoying; (style) laboured

mōlīmen, -inis nt exertion, labour; importance.

mōlīmentum, -ī nt great effort.

mōlior, -īrī, -ītus vt to labour at, work, build; to wield, move, heave; to undertake, devise, occasion ♦ vi to exert oneself, struggle.

mōlītiō, -ōnis f laborious work.

mōlītor, -ōris m builder.

mollēscō, -ere vi to soften, become effeminate.

molliculus adj tender.

molliō, -īre, -īvī, -ītum vt to soften, make supple; to mitigate, make easier; to demoralize.

mollis adj soft, supple; tender;

The present infinitive verb endings are as follows: -āre = 1st; -ēre = 2nd; -ere = 3rd and -īre = 4th. See sections on irregular verbs and noun declensions.

gentle; (*character*) sensitive, weak,
unmanly; (*poetry*) amatory;
(*opinion*) changeable; (*slope*) easy.

molliter *adv* softly, gently; calmly;
voluptuously.

mollitia, -ae; -ēs, -ēī *f* softness,
suppleness, tenderness,
weakness, effeminacy.

mollitūdō, -inis *f* softness;
susceptibility.

molō, -ere *vt* to grind.

Molossī, -ōrum *mpl* Molossians,
people in Epirus.

Molossicus, -us *adj see* n.

Molossis, -idis *f country of the
Molossians.*

Molossus, -ī *m* Molossian hound.

mōly, -os *nt* a magic herb.

mōmen, -inis *nt* movement,
momentum.

mōmentum, -ī *nt* movement;
change; (*time*) short space,
moment; (*fig*) cause, influence,
importance; **nullius -ī**
unimportant.

momordī *perf of* **mordeō.**

Mona, -ae *f* Isle of Man; Anglesey.

monachus, -ī *m* monk.

monēdula, -ae *f* jackdaw.

moneō, -ēre, -uī, -itum *vt* to
remind, advise, warn; to instruct,
foretell.

monēris, -is *f* galley with one bank
of oars.

monērula *etc see* **monēdula.**

monēta, -ae *f* mint; money; stamp.

monīle, -is *nt* necklace, collar.

monim- *etc see* **monum-.**

monitiō, -ōnis *f* admonishing.

monitor, -ōris *m* admonisher;
prompter; teacher.

monitum, -ī *nt* warning; prophecy.

monitus, -ūs *m* admonition;
warning.

monogrammus *adj* shadowy.

monopodium, -ī *and* **iī** *nt* table
with one leg.

mōns, montis *m* mountain.

mōnstrātor, -ōris *m* shower,
inventor.

mōnstrātus *adj* distinguished.

mōnstrē *adv see adj.*

mōnstrō, -āre, -āvī, -ātum *vt* to
point out, show; to inform,
instruct; to appoint; to denounce.

mōnstrum, -ī *nt* portent, marvel;
monster.

mōnstruōsus *adj* unnatural.

montānus *adj* mountainous;
mountain- (*in cpds*), highland.

monticola, -ae *m* highlander.

montivagus *adj* mountain-roving.

montuōsus, montōsus *adj*
mountainous.

monumentum, -ī *nt* memorial,
monument; record.

Mopsopius *adj* Athenian.

mora, -ae *f* delay, pause;
hindrance; space of time,
sojourn; **moram facere** put off.

mora, -ae *f* division of the Spartan
army.

mōrālis *adj* moral.

morātor, -ōris *m* delayer.

mōrātus *adj* mannered, of a
nature; (*writing*) in character.

morbidus *adj* unwholesome.

morbus, -ī *m* illness, disease;
distress.

mordāciter *adv see adj.*

mordāx, -ācis *adj* biting, sharp,
pungent; (*fig*) snarling, carking.

mordeō, -dēre, momordī, -sum *vt*
to bite; to bite into, grip; (*cold*) to
nip; (*words*) to sting, hurt,
mortify.

mordicus *adv* with a bite; (*fig*)
doggedly.

mōres *pl of* **mōs.**

mōrētum, -ī *nt* salad.

moribundus *adj* dying, mortal;
deadly.

mōrigeror, -ārī, -ātus *vi* (*with dat*)
to gratify, humour.

mōrigerus adj obliging, obedient.

morior, -ī, -tuus vi to die; to decay, fade.

moritūrus fut p of **morior**.

mōrologus adj foolish.

moror, -ārī, -ātus vi to delay, stay, loiter ♦ vt to detain, retard; to entertain; (with neg) to heed, object; **nihil, nīl** ~ have no objection to; to not care for; to withdraw a charge against.

mōrōse adv see adj.

mōrōsitās, -ātis f peevishness.

mōrōsus adj peevish, difficult.

Morpheus, -eos m god of dreams.

mors, mortis f death; corpse; **mortem sibi cōnscīscere** commit suicide; **mortis poena** capital punishment.

morsiuncula, -ae f little kiss.

morsus ppp of **mordeō** ♦ ntpl little bits.

morsus, -ūs m bite; grip; (fig) sting, vexation.

mortālis adj mortal; transient; man-made ♦ m human being.

mortālitās, -ātis f mortality, death.

mortārium, -ī and **iī** nt mortar.

mortifer, -ī adj fatal.

mortuus ppa of **morior** ♦ adj dead ♦ m dead man.

mōrum, -ī nt blackberry, mulberry.

mōrus, -ī f black mulberry tree.

mōrus adj foolish ♦ m fool.

mōs, mōris m nature, manner; humour, mood; custom, practice, law; (pl) behaviour, character, morals; ~ **māiōrum** national tradition; **mōrem gerere** oblige, humour; **mōre, in mōrem** like.

Mosa, -ae m river Meuse.

Mōsēs, -is m Moses.

mōtiō, -ōnis f motion.

mōtō, -āre vt to keep moving.

mōtus ppp of **moveō**.

mōtus, -ūs m movement; dance, gesture; (mind) impulse, emotion; (POL) rising, rebellion; **terrae** ~ earthquake.

movēns, -entis pres p of **moveō** ♦ adj movable ♦ ntpl motives.

moveō, -ēre, mōvī, mōtum vt to move, set in motion; to disturb; to change; to dislodge, expel; to occasion, begin; (opinion) to shake; (mind) to affect, influence, provoke ♦ vi to move; **castra** ~ strike camp; **sē** ~ budge; to dance.

mox adv presently, soon, later on; next.

Mōysēs see **Mōsēs**.

mūcidus adj snivelling; mouldy.

Mūcius, -ī m Roman family name (esp Scaevola, who burned his right hand before Porsena).

mūcrō, -ōnis m point, edge; sword.

mūcus, -ī m mucus.

mūgilis, -is m mullet.

mūginor, -ārī vi to hesitate.

mūgiō, -īre vi to bellow, groan.

mūgītus, -ūs m lowing, roaring.

mūla, -ae f she-mule.

mulceō, -cēre, -sī, -sum vt to stroke, caress; to soothe, alleviate, delight.

Mulciber, -is and **ī** m Vulcan.

mulcō, -āre, -āvī, -ātum vt to beat, ill-treat, damage.

mulctra, -ae f, **-ārium, -ārī,** and **ārī, -um, -ī** nt milkpail.

mulgeō, -ēre, mulsī vt to milk.

muliebris adj woman's, feminine; effeminate.

muliebriter adv like a woman; effeminately.

mulier, -is f woman; wife.

mulierārius adj woman's.

The present infinitive verb endings are as follows: -āre = 1st; -ēre = 2nd; -ere = 3rd and -īre = 4th. See sections on irregular verbs and noun declensions.

muliercula, -ae f girl.
mulierōsitās, -ātis f fondness for women.
mulierōsus adj fond of women.
mūlīnus adj mulish.
mūliō, -ōnis m mule driver.
mūliōnius adj mule driver's.
mullus, -ī m red mullet.
mulsī perf of **mulceō**; perf of **mulgeō**.
mulsus ppp of **mulceō**.
mulsus adj honeyed, sweet ♦ nt honey-wine, mead.
multa, -ae f penalty, fine; loss.
multangulus adj many-angled;
multātīcius adj fine- (in cpds).
multātiō, -ōnis f fining.
multēsimus adj very small.
multicavus adj many-holed.
multīcia, -ōrum ntpl transparent garments.
multifāriam adv in many places.
multifidus adj divided into many parts.
multifōrmis adj of many forms.
multiforus adj many-holed.
multigeneris, -us adj of many kinds.
multiiugis, -us adj yoked together; complex.
multiloquium, -ī and iī nt talkativeness.
multiloquus adj talkative.
multimodīs adv variously.
multiplex, -icis adj with many folds, tortuous; many-sided, manifold, various; (comparison) far greater; (character) fickle, sly.
multiplicō, -āre, -āvī, -ātum vt to multiply, enlarge.
multipotēns, -entis adj very powerful.
multitūdō, -inis f great number, multitude, crowd.
multivolus adj longing for much.
multō adv much, far, by far; (time) long.

multō, -āre, -āvī, -ātum vt to punish, fine.
multum adv much, very, frequently.
multus (compar **plūs** superl **plūrimus**) adj much, many; (speech) lengthy, tedious; (time) late; **-ā nocte** late at night; **nē -a** = to cut a long story short.
mūlus, -ī m mule.
Mulvius adj Mulvian (a Tiber bridge above Rome).
mundānus, -ī m world citizen.
munditia, -ae; -ēs, -ēī f cleanness; neatness, elegance.
mundus adj clean, neat, elegant; **in -ō esse** be in readiness.
mundus, -ī m toilet gear; universe, world, heavens; mankind.
mūnerigerulus, -ī m bringer of presents.
mūnerō, -āre, -or, -ārī vt to present, reward.
mūnia, -ōrum ntpl official duties.
mūniceps, -ipis m/f citizen (of a municipium), fellow-citizen.
mūnicipālis adj provincial.
mūnicipium, -ī and iī nt provincial town, burgh.
mūnificē adv see adj.
mūnificentia, -ae f liberality.
mūnificō, -āre vt to treat generously.
mūnificus adj liberal.
mūnīmen, -inis nt defence.
mūnīmentum, -ī nt defencework, protection.
mūniō, -īre, -īī, -ītum vt to fortify, secure, strengthen; (road) to build; (fig) to protect.
mūnis adj ready to oblige.
mūnītiō, -ōnis f building; fortification; (river) bridging.
mūnītō, -āre vt (road) to open up.
mūnītor, -ōris m sapper, builder.
mūnus, -eris nt service, duty; gift; public show; entertainment; tax;

(*funeral*) tribute; (*book*) work.

mūnusculum, -ī *nt* small present.

mūraena, -ae *f* a fish.

mūrālis *adj* wall- (*in cpds*), mural, for fighting from or attacking walls.

mūrex, -icis *m* purple-fish; purple dye, purple; jagged rock.

muria, -ae *f* brine.

murmillō, -ōnis *m* kind of gladiator.

murmur, -is *nt* murmur, hum, rumbling, roaring.

murmurillum, -ī *nt* low murmur.

murmurō, -āre *vi* to murmur, rumble; to grumble.

murra, -ae *f* myrrh.

murreus *adj* perfumed; made of the stone called murra.

murrina, -ae *f* myrrh wine.

murrina, -ōrum *ntpl* murrine vases.

murt- *etc see* **myrt-**.

mūrus, -ī *m* wall, dam; defence

mūs, mūris *m/f* mouse; rat.

Mūsa, -ae *f* goddess inspiring an art, poem; (*pl*) studies.

mūsaeus *adj* poetic, musical.

musca, -ae *f* fly.

mūscipula, -ae *f*, **-um, -ī** *nt* mousetrap.

mūscōsus *adj* mossy.

mūsculus, -ī *m* mouse; muscle; (MIL) shed.

mūscus, -ī *m* moss.

mūsicē *adv* very pleasantly.

mūsicus *adj* of music, of poetry ♦ *m* musician ♦ *f* music, culture ♦ *ntpl* music.

mussitō, -āre *vi* to say nothing; to mutter ♦ *vt* to bear in silence.

mussō, -āre *vt, vi* to say nothing, brood over; to mutter, murmur.

mustāceum, -ī, -us, -ī *m* wedding cake.

mustēla, -ae *f* weasel.

mustum, -ī *nt* unfermented wine, must; vintage.

mūtābilis *adj* changeable, fickle.

mūtābilitās, -ātis *f* fickleness.

mūtātiō, -ōnis *f* change, alteration; exchange.

mutilō, -āre, -āvī, -ātum *vt* to cut off, maim; to diminish.

mutilus *adj* maimed.

Mutina, -ae *f* town in N. Italy (*now* Modena).

Mutinēnsis *adj see n*

mūtiō *etc see* **mutiō**.

mūtō, -āre, -āvī, -ātum *vt* to shift; to change, alter; to exchange, barter ♦ *vi* to change; **~āta verba** figurative language.

muttiō, -īre *vi* to mutter, mumble.

mūtuātiō, -ōnis *f* borrowing.

mūtuē *adv* mutually, in turns.

mūtuitō, -āre *vi* to try to borrow.

mūtuō *adv* = **mūtuē**.

mūtuor, -ārī, -ātus *vt* to borrow.

mūtus *adj* dumb, mute; silent, still.

mūtuum, -ī *nt* loan.

mūtuus *adj* borrowed, lent; mutual, reciprocal; **~um dare** lend; **~um sūmere** borrow; **~um facere** return like for like.

Mycēnae, -ārum *fpl* Agamemnon's capital in S. Greece.

Mycēnaeus, -ēnsis *adj*, **-is, -idis** *f* Iphigenia.

Mygdonius *adj* Phrygian.

myoparō, -ōnis *m* pirate galley.

myrica, -ae *f* tamarisk.

Myrmidones, -um *mpl* followers of Achilles.

Myrōn, -ōnis *m* famous Greek sculptor.

myropōla, -ae *m* perfumer.

myropōlium, -ī *and* **iī** *nt* perfumer's shop.

myrothēcium, -ī *and* **iī** *nt* perfume-box.

The present infinitive verb endings are as follows: **-āre** = 1st; **-ēre** = 2nd; **-ere** = 3rd and **-īre** = 4th. *See sections on irregular verbs and noun declensions.*

myrrh- *etc see* **murr-**.

myrtētum, -ī *nt* myrtlegrove.

myrteus *adj* myrtle- (*in cpds*).

Myrtoum mare *Sea N.W. of Crete*.

myrtum, -ī *nt* myrtle-berry.

myrtus, -ī *and* **ūs** *f* myrtle.

Mȳsia, -iae *f country of Asia Minor*.

Mȳsius, -us *adj see n*.

mysta, -ae *m* priest of mysteries.

mystagōgus, -ī *m* initiator.

mystērium, -ī *and* **iī** *nt* secret religion, mystery; secret.

mysticus *adj* mystic.

Mytilēnae, -ārum *fpl*: **-ē, -es** *f* capital of Lesbos.

Mytilēnaeus *adj see n*.

Mytilēnēnsis *adj see n*.

N

nablium, -ī *and* **iī** *nt* kind of harp.

nactus *ppa of* **nancīscor**.

nae *etc see* **nē**.

naenia *etc see* **nēnia**.

Naeviānus *adj see n*.

Naevius, -ī *m* early Latin poet.

naevus, -ī *m* mole (on the body).

Nāias, -adis *and* **s, -dis** *f* water nymph, Naiad.

Nāicus *adj see n*.

nam *conj* (*explaining*) for; (*illustrating*) for example; (*transitional*) now; (*interrog*) but; (*enclitic*) an emphatic particle.

namque *conj* for, for indeed, for example.

nancīscor, -ī, nactus *and* **nanctus** *vt* to obtain, get; to come upon, find.

nānus, -ī *m* dwarf.

Napaeae, -ārum *fpl* dell nymphs.

nāpus, -ī *m* turnip.

Narbō, -ōnis *m* town in S. Gaul.

Narbōnēnsis *adj see n*.

narcissus, -ī *m* narcissus.

nardus, -ī *f*, **-um, -ī** *nt* nard, nard oil.

nāris, -is *f* nostril; (*pl*) nose; (*fig*) sagacity, scorn.

nārrābilis *adj* to be told.

nārrātiō, -ōnis *f* narrative.

nārrātor, -ōris *m* storyteller, historian.

nārrātus, -ūs *m* narrative.

nārrō, -āre, -āvī, -ātum *vt* to tell, relate, say; **male ~** bring bad news.

narthēcium, -ī *and* **iī** *nt* medicine chest.

nāscor, -scī, -tus *vi* to be born; to originate, grow, be produced.

Nāsō, -ōnis *m surname of Ovid*.

nassa, -ae *f* wicker basket for catching fish; (*fig*) snare.

nasturtium, -ī *and* **iī** *nt* cress.

nāsus, -ī *m* nose.

nāsūtē *adv* sarcastically.

nāsūtus *adj* big-nosed; satirical.

nāta, -ae *f* daughter.

nātālicius *adj* of one's birthday, natal ♦ *f* birthday party.

nātālis *adj* of birth, natal ♦ *m* birthday ♦ *mpl* birth, origin.

natātiō, -ōnis *f* swimming.

natātor, -ōris *m* swimmer.

nātiō, -ōnis *f* tribe, race; breed, class.

natis, -is *f* (*usu pl*) buttocks.

nātīvus *adj* created; inborn, native, natural.

natō, -āre *vi* to swim, float; to flow, overflow; (*eyes*) to swim, fail; (*fig*) to waver.

nātrīx, -īcis *f* watersnake.

nātū *abl m* by birth, in age; **grandis ~, māgnō ~** quite old; **māior ~** older; **māximus ~** oldest.

nātūra, -ae *f* birth; nature, quality, character; natural order of things; the physical world; (*physics*) element; **rērum ~** Nature.

nātūrālis *adj* by birth; by nature, natural.

nātūrāliter adv by nature.

nātus ppa of **nāscor** ♦ m son ♦ adj born, made (for); old, of age; **prō, ē rē nātā** under the circumstances, as things are; **annōs vigintī ~** 20 years old.

nauarchus, -ī m captain.

naucī n gen: **nōn ~ esse, facere, habēre** to be worthless, consider worthless.

nauclēricus adj skipper's.

nauclērus, -ī m skipper.

naufragium, -ī and **iī** nt shipwreck, wreck; ~ **facere** be shipwrecked.

naufragus adj shipwrecked, wrecked; (sea) dangerous to shipping ♦ m shipwrecked man; (fig) ruined man.

naulum, -ī nt fare.

naumachia, -ae f mock sea fight.

nausea, -ae f seasickness.

nauseō, -āre vi to be sick, (fig) to disgust.

nauseola, -ae f squeamishness.

nauta, (nāvita), -ae m sailor, mariner.

nauticus adj nautical, sailors' ♦ mpl seamen.

nāvālis adj naval, of ships ♦ nt and ntpl dockyard; rigging.

nāvicula, -ae f boat.

nāviculāria, -ae f shipping business.

nāviculārius, -ī and **iī** m ship-owner.

nāvifragus adj dangerous.

nāvigābilis adj navigable.

nāvigātiō, -ōnis f voyage.

nāviger, -ī adj ship-carrying.

nāvigium, -ī and **iī** nt vessel, ship.

nāvigō, -āre, -āvī, -ātum vi to sail, put to sea ♦ vt to sail across, navigate.

nāvis, -is f ship; ~ **longa** warship; ~ **mercātōria** merchantman; ~

onerāria transport; ~ **praetōria** flagship; ~**em dēdūcere** launch; ~**em solvere** set sail; ~**em statuere** heave to; ~**em subdūcere** beach; ~**ibus atque quadrīgīs** with might and main.

nāvita etc see **nauta**.

nāvitās, -ātis f energy.

nāviter adv energetically; absolutely.

nāvō, -āre vt to perform energetically; **operam ~** be energetic; to come to the assistance (of).

nāvus adj energetic.

Naxos, -ī f Aegean island (famous for wines and the story of Ariadne).

nē interj truly, indeed.

nē adv not ♦ conj that not, lest; (fear) that; (purpose) so that ... not, to avoid, to prevent.

-ne enclitic (introducing a question).

Neāpolis, -is f Naples.

Neāpolītānus adj see n.

nebula, -ae f mist, vapour, cloud.

nebulō, -ōnis m idler, good-for-nothing.

nebulōsus adj misty, cloudy.

nec etc see **neque**.

necdum adv and not yet.

necessāriē, -ō adv of necessity, unavoidably.

necessārius adj necessary, inevitable; indispensable; (kin) related ♦ m/f relative ♦ ntpl necessities.

necesse adj (indecl) necessary, inevitable; needful.

necessitās, -ātis f necessity, compulsion; requirement, want; relationship, connection.

necessitūdō, -inis f necessity, need, want; connection; friendship (pl) relatives.

necessum etc see **necesse**.

necne adv or not.

---

*The present infinitive verb endings are as follows: -**āre** = 1st; -**ēre** = 2nd; -**ere** = 3rd and -**īre** = 4th. See sections on irregular verbs and noun declensions.*

necnōn *adv* also, besides.

necō, -āre, -āvī, -ātum *vt* to kill, murder.

necopīnāns, -antis *adj* unaware.

necopīnātō *adv* see adj.

necopīnātus *adj* unexpected.

necopīnus *adj* unexpected; unsuspecting.

nectar, -is *nt* nectar (*the drink of the gods*).

nectareus *adj* of nectar.

nectō, -ctere, -xī and xuī, -xum *vt* to tie, fasten, connect; to weave; (*fig*) to bind, enslave (*esp for debt*); to contrive, frame.

nēcubi *conj* so that nowhere.

nēcunde *conj* so that from nowhere.

nēdum *adv* much less, much more.

nefandus *adj* abominable, impious.

nefāriē *adv* see adj.

nefārius *adj* heinous, criminal.

nefās *nt* (*indecl*) wickedness, sin, wrong ♦ *interj* horror!, shame!

nefāstus *adj* wicked; unlucky; (*days*) closed to public business.

negātiō, -ōnis *f* denial.

negitō, -āre *vt* to deny, refuse.

neglēctiō, -ōnis *f* neglect.

neglēctus *ppp of* neglegō.

neglēctus, -ūs *m* neglecting.

neglegēns, -entis *pres p of* neglegō ♦ *adj* careless, indifferent.

neglegenter *adv* carelessly.

neglegentia, -ae *f* carelessness, neglect, coldness.

neglegō, -egere, -ēxī, -ēctum *vt* to neglect, not care for; to slight, disregard; to overlook.

negō, -āre, -āvī, -ātum *vt, vi* to say no; to say not, deny; refuse, decline.

negōtiālis *adj* business- (*in cpds*).

negōtiāns, -antis *m* businessman.

negōtiātiō, -ōnis *f* banking business.

negōtiātor, -ōris *m* businessman,

banker.

negōtiolum, -ī *nt* trivial matter.

negōtior, -ārī, -ātus *vi* to do business, trade.

negōtiōsus *adj* busy.

negōtium, -ī and iī *nt* business, work; trouble; matter, thing; **quid est ~i?** what is the matter?

Nēlēius *adj* see n.

Nēleus, -eī *m* father of Nestor.

Nēlēus *adj* see n.

Nemea, -ae *f* town in S. Greece, where Hercules killed the lion.

Nemea, -ōrum *ntpl* Nemean Games.

Nemeaeus *adj* Nemean.

nēmō, -inis *m/f* no one, nobody ♦ *adj* no; ~ **nōn** everybody; **nōn ~** many; ~ **ūnus** not a soul.

nemorālis *adj* sylvan.

nemorēnsis *adj* of the grove.

nemoricultrīx, -īcis *f* forest dweller.

nemorivagus *adj* forest-roving.

nemorōsus *adj* well-wooded; leafy.

nempe *adv* (*confirming*) surely, of course, certainly; (*in questions*) do you mean?

nemus, -oris *nt* wood, grove.

nēnia, -ae *f* dirge; incantation; song, nursery rhyme.

neō, nēre, nēvī, nētum *vt* to spin; to weave.

Neoptolemus, -ī *m* Pyrrhus (*son of Achilles*).

nepa, -ae *f* scorpion.

nepōs, -ōtis *m* grandson; descendant; spendthrift.

nepōtīnus, -ī *m* little grandson.

neptis, -is *f* granddaughter.

Neptūnius *adj* ~ **hērōs** Theseus.

Neptūnus, -ī *m* Neptune (*god of the sea*); sea.

nēquam *adj* (*indecl*) worthless, bad.

nēquāquam *adv* not at all, by no means.

neque, nec *adv* not ♦ *conj* and not, but not; neither, nor; ~ ... **et** not only not ... but also.

nequeō, -īre, -īvī, -ītum *vi* to be unable, cannot.

nēquīquam *adv* fruitlessly, for nothing; without good reason.

nēquior, nēquissimus *compar*, *superl of* **nēquam**

nēquiter *adv* worthlessly, wrongly.

nēquitia, -ae, -ēs *f* worthlessness, badness.

Nērēis, -ēidis *f* Nereid, sea nymph.

Nērēius *adj see n.*

Nēreus, -ei *m* a sea god; the sea.

Nērītius *adj* of Neritos; Ithacan.

Nēritos, -ī *m* island near Ithaca.

Nerō, -ōnis *m* Roman surname (*esp the emperor*).

Nerōniānus *adj see n.*

nervōsē *adv* vigorously.

nervōsus *adj* sinewy, vigorous.

nervulī, -ōrum *mpl* energy.

nervus, -ī *m* sinew; string; fetter, prison; (*shield*) leather; (*pl*) strength, vigour, energy.

nesciō, -īre, -īvī *and* **iī, -ītum** *vt* to not know, be ignorant of; to be unable; ~ **quis, quid** somebody, something; ~ **an** probably.

nescius *adj* ignorant, unaware; unable; unknown.

Nestor, -oris *m* Greek leader at Troy (*famous for his great age and wisdom*).

neu *etc see* **nēve**.

neuter, -rī *adj* neither; neuter.

neutiquam *adv* by no means, certainly not.

neutrō *adv* neither way.

nēve, neu *conj* and not; neither, nor.

nēvī *perf of* **neō**.

nex, necis *f* murder, death.

nexilis *adj* tied together.

nexum, -ī *nt* personal enslavement.

nexus *ppp of* **nectō**.

nexus, -ūs *m* entwining, grip; (*law*) bond, obligation, (*esp enslavement for debt*).

nī *adv* not ♦ *conj* if not, unless; that not; **quid nī?** why not?

nīcētērium, -ī *and* **iī** *nt* prize.

nictō, -āre *vi* to wink.

nīdāmentum, -ī *nt* nest.

nīdor, -ōris *m* steam, smell.

nīdulus, -ī *m* little nest.

nīdus, -ī *m* nest; (*pl*) nestlings; (*fig*) home.

niger, -rī *adj* black, dark; dismal, ill-omened; (*character*) bad.

nigrāns, -antis *adj* black, dusky.

nigrēscō, -ere *vi* to blacken, grow dark.

nigrō, -āre *vi* to be black.

nigror, -ōris *m* blackness.

nihil, nīl *nt* (*indecl*) nothing ♦ *adv* not; ~ **ad nōs** has nothing to do with us; ~ **est** it is no use; ~ **est quod** there is no reason why; ~ **nisi** nothing but, only; ~ **nōn** everything; **nōn** ~ something.

nihilum, -ī *nt* nothing; ~**ī esse** be worthless; ~**ō minus** none the less.

nīl, nīlum *see* **nihil, nihilum**.

Nīliacus *adj* of the Nile; Egyptian.

Nīlus, -ī *m* Nile; conduit.

nimbifer, -ī *adj* stormy.

nimbōsus *adj* stormy.

nimbus, -ī *m* cloud, rain, storm.

nimiō *adv* much, far.

nīmīrum *adv* certainly, of course.

nimis *adv* too much, very much; **nōn** ~ not very.

nimium *adv* too, too much; very, very much.

nimius *adj* too great, excessive; very great ♦ *nt* excess.

The present infinitive verb endings are as follows: -āre = 1st; -ēre = 2nd; -ere = 3rd and -īre = 4th. See sections on irregular verbs and noun declensions.

ningit, ninguit, -ere vi it snows.
ninguēs, -ium fpl snow.
Nioba, -ae; -ē, -ēs f daughter of
Tantalus (changed to a weeping
rock).
Niobēus adj see n.
Nīreus, -ei and **eos** m handsomest of
the Greeks at Troy.
Nīsaeus, -ēius adj see n.
Nīsēis, -edis f Scylla.
nisi conj if not, unless; except, but.
nisus ppa of **nītor**.
nisus, -ūs m pressure, effort;
striving, soaring.
Nīsus, -ī m father of Scylla.
nītēdula, -ae f dormouse.
nītēns, -entis pres p of **niteō** ♦ adj
bright; brilliant, beautiful.
niteō, -ēre vi to shine, gleam; to be
sleek, to be greasy; to thrive, look
beautiful.
nītēscō, -ere, nītuī vi to brighten,
shine, glow.
nitidiusculē adv rather more
finely.
nitidiusculus adj a little shinier.
nitidē adv magnificently.
nitidus adj bright, shining; sleek;
blooming; smart, spruce; (speech)
refined.
nitor, -ōris m brightness, sheen;
sleekness, beauty; neatness,
elegance.
nītor, -tī, -sus and **xus** vi to rest on,
lean on; to press, stand firmly; to
press forward, climb; to exert
oneself, strive, labour; to depend
on.
nitrum, -ī nt soda.
nivālis adj snowy.
niveus adj of snow, snowy, snow-
white.
nivōsus adj snowy.
nix, nivis f snow.
nixor, -ārī vi to rest on; to struggle.
nīxus ppp of **nītor**.
nīxus, -ūs m pressure; labour.

nō, nāre, nāvī vi to swim, float; to
sail, fly.
nōbilis adj known, noted, famous,
notorious; noble, high-born;
excellent.
nōbilitās, -ātis f fame; noble birth;
the nobility; excellence.
nōbilitō, -āre, -āvī, -ātum vt to
make famous or notorious.
nocēns, -entis pres p of **noceō** ♦ adj
harmful; criminal, guilty.
noceō, -ēre, -uī, -itum vi (with dat)
to harm, hurt.
nocīvus adj injurious.
noctifer, -ī m evening star.
noctilūca, -ae f moon.
noctivagus adj night-wandering.
noctū adv by night.
noctua, -ae f owl.
noctuābundus adj travelling by
night.
nocturnus adj night- (in cpds),
nocturnal.
nōdō, -āre, -āvī, -ātum vt to knot,
tie.
nōdōsus adj knotty.
nōdus, -ī m knot; knob; girdle; (fig)
bond, difficulty.
nōlō, -le, -uī vt, vi to not wish; to be
unwilling, refuse; **-ī, ~ite** do not.
Nomas, -dis m/f nomad;
Numidian.
nōmen, -inis nt name; title; (COMM)
demand, debt; (GRAM) noun; (fig)
reputation, fame; account,
pretext; ~ **dare profitērī** enlist; ~
dēferre accuse; **~ina facere** enter
the items of a debt.
nōmenclātor, -ōris m slave who told
his master the names of people.
nōminātim adv by name, one by
one.
nōminātiō, -ōnis f nomination.
nōminitō, -āre vt to usually name.
nōminō, -āre, -āvī, -ātum vt to
name, call; to mention; to make
famous; to nominate; to accuse,

denounce.

nomisma, -tis nt coin.

nōn adv not; no.

Nōnae, -ārum fpl Nones (7th day of March, May, July, October, 5th of other months).

nōnāgēsimus adj ninetieth.

nōnāgiēns, -ēs adv ninety times.

nōnāgintā num ninety.

nōnānus adj of the ninth legion.

nōndum adv not yet.

nōngentī, -ōrum num nine hundred.

nonna, -ae f nun.

nōnne adv do not?, is not? etc.; (indirect) whether not.

nōnnullus adj some.

nōnnunquam adv sometimes.

nōnus adj ninth ♦ f ninth hour.

nōnusdecimus adj nineteenth.

Nōricum, -ī nt country between the Danube and the Alps.

Nōricus adj see n.

nōrma, -ae f rule.

nōs pron we, us; I, me.

nōscitō, -āre vt to know, recognise; to observe, examine.

nōscō, -scere, -vī, -tum vt to get to know, learn; to examine; to recognise, allow; (perf) to know.

nōsmet pron (emphatic) see **nōs**.

noster, -rī adj our, ours; for us; my; (with names) my dear, good old ♦ m our friend ♦ mpl our side, our troops; ~rī, ~rum of us.

nostrās, -ātis adj of our country, native.

nota, -ae f mark, sign, note; (writing) note, letter; (pl) memoranda, shorthand, secret writing; (books) critical mark, punctuation; (wine, etc) brand, quality; (gesture) sign; (fig) sign, token; (censor's) black mark; (fig) stigma, disgrace.

notābilis adj remarkable; notorious.

notābiliter adv perceptibly.

notārius, -ī and iī m shorthand writer; secretary.

notātiō, -ōnis f marking; choice; observation; (censor) stigmatizing; (words) etymology.

nōtēscō, -ere, nōtuī vi to become known.

nothus adj bastard; counterfeit.

nōtiō, -ōnis f (law) cognisance, investigation; (PHIL OS) idea.

nōtitia, -ae, -ēs, -ēī f fame, acquaintance; (PHILOS) idea, preconception.

notō, -āre, -āvī, -ātum vt to mark, write; to denote; to observe; to brand, stigmatize.

nōtuī perf of **nōtēscō**.

nōtus ppp of **nōscō** ♦ adj known, familiar; notorious ♦ mpl acquaintances.

Notus (-os), -ī m south wind.

novācula, -ae f razor.

novālis, -is f, -e, -is nt fallow land; field; crops.

novātrix, -īcis f renewer.

novē adv unusually.

novellus adj young, fresh, new.

novem num nine.

November, -ris adj of November ♦ m November.

novendecim num nineteen.

novendiālis adj nine days'; on the ninth day.

novēnī, -ōrum adj in nines; nine.

Novēnsilēs, -ium mpl new gods.

noverca, -ae f stepmother.

novercālis adj stepmother's.

nōvī perf of **nōscō**.

novicius adj new.

noviēns, -ēs adv nine times.

novissimē adv lately; last of all.

novissimus adj latest, last, rear.

The present infinitive verb endings are as follows: -āre = 1st; -ēre = 2nd; -ere = 3rd and -īre = 4th. See sections on irregular verbs and noun declensions.

novitās, -ātis f newness, novelty; strangeness.

novō, -āre, -āvī, -ātum vt to renew, refresh; to change; (words) to coin; **rēs ~** effect a revolution.

novus adj new, young, fresh, recent; strange, unusual; inexperienced; **~ homō** upstart, first of his family to hold curule office; **-ae rēs** revolution; **-ae tabulae** cancellation of debts; **quid -ī** what news?

nox, noctis f night; darkness, obscurity; **nocte, noctū** by night; **dē nocte** during the night.

noxa, -ae f hurt, harm; offence, guilt; punishment.

noxia, -ae f harm, damage; guilt, fault.

noxius adj harmful; guilty.

nūbēcula, -ae f cloudy look.

nūbēs, -is f cloud; (fig) gloom; veil.

nūbifer, -ī adj cloud-capped; cloudy.

nūbigena, -ae m cloudborn, Centaur.

nūbilis adj marriageable.

nūbilus adj cloudy; gloomy, sad ♦ ntpl clouds.

nūbō, -bere, -psī, -ptum vi (women) to be married.

nucleus, -ī m nut, kernel.

nūdius day since, days ago; **~ tertius** the day before yesterday.

nūdō, -āre, -āvī, -ātum vt to bare, strip, expose; (MIL) to leave exposed; to plunder; (fig) to disclose, betray.

nūdus adj naked, bare; exposed, defenceless; wearing only a tunic; (fig) destitute, poor; mere; unembellished, plain; **vestīmenta dētrahere ~ō** ≈ draw blood from a stone.

nūgae, -ārum fpl nonsense, trifles; (person) waster.

nūgātor, -ōris m silly creature,

liar.

nūgātōrius adj futile.

nūgāx, -ācis adj frivolous.

nūgor, -ārī, -ātus vi to talk nonsense; to cheat.

nullus, -ius (dat -ī) adj no, none; not, not at all; non-existent, of no account ♦ m/f nobody.

num interrog particle surely not? (indirect) whether, if.

Numa, -ae m second king of Rome.

nūmen, -inis nt nod, will; divine will, power; divinity, god.

numerābilis adj easy to count.

numerātus adj in cash ♦ nt ready money.

numerō, -āre, -āvī, -ātum vt to count, number; (money) to pay out; (fig) to reckon, consider as.

numerō adv just now, quickly, too soon.

numerōsē adv rhythmically.

numerōsus adj populous; rhythmical.

numerus, -ī m number; many, numbers; (MIL) troop; (fig) a cipher; (pl) mathematics; rank, category, regard; rhythm, metre, verse; **in ~ō esse, habērī** be reckoned as; **nullō ~ō** of no account.

Numida adj see n.

Numidae, -ārum mpl Numidians (people of N. Africa).

Numidia, -iae f the country of the Numidians.

Numidicus adj see n.

Numitor, -ōris m king of Alba (grandfather of Romulus).

nummārius adj money- (in cpds); financial; mercenary.

nummātus adj moneyed.

nummulī, -ōrum mpl some money, cash.

nummus, -ī m coin, money, cash; (Roman coin) sestertius; (Greek coin) two-drachma piece.

numnam, numne see num.

numquam adv never; ~ nōn always; nōn ~ sometimes.

numquid (question) do you? does he? etc ; (indirect) whether.

nunc adv now; at present, nowadays; but as it is; ~ ... ~ at one time ... at another.

nuncupātiō -ōnis f pronouncing.

nuncupō, -āre, -āvī, -ātum vt to call, name; to pronounce formally.

nūndinae, -ārum fpl market day; market; trade.

nūndinātiō, -ōnis f trading.

nūndinor, -ārī vi to trade, traffic; to flock together ♦ vt to buy.

nūndinum, -ī nt market time; trīnum ~ 17 days.

nunq- etc see numq-.

nūntiātiō, -ōnis f announcing.

nūntiō, -āre, -āvī, -ātum vt to announce, report, tell.

nūntius adj informative, speaking ♦ m messenger; message, news; injunction; notice of divorce ♦ nt message.

nūper adv recently, lately.

nūpsī perf of nūbō.

nūpta, -ae f bride, wife.

nūptiae, -ārum fpl wedding, marriage.

nūptiālis adj wedding- (in cpds), nuptial.

nurus, -ūs f daughter-in-law; young woman.

nūsquam adv nowhere; in nothing, for nothing.

nūtō, -āre vi to nod; to sway, totter, falter.

nūtrīcius, -ī m tutor.

nūtrīcō, -āre, -or, -ārī vt to nourish, sustain.

nūtrīcula, -ae f nurse.

nūtrīmen, -inis nt nourishment.

nūtrīmentum, -ī nt nourishment, support.

nūtriō, -īre, -īvī, -ītum vt to suckle, nourish, rear, nurse.

nūtrīx, -īcis f nurse, foster mother.

nūtus, -ūs m nod; will, command; (physics) gravity.

nux, nucis f nut; nut tree, almond tree.

Nyctēis, -idis f Antiopa.

nympha, -ae; -ē, -ēs f bride; nymph; water.

Nysa, -ae f birthplace of Bacchus.

Nysaeus, -ēis, -ius adj see n.

O

ō interj (expressing joy, surprise, pain, etc) oh!; (with voc) O!

ob prep (with acc) in front of; for, on account of, for the sake of; quam ~ rem accordingly.

obaerātus adj in debt ♦ m debtor.

obambulō, -āre vi to walk past, prowl about.

obarmō, -āre vt to arm (against).

obarō, -āre vt to plough up.

obc- etc see occ-.

obdō, -ere, -idī, -itum vt to shut, to expose.

obdormiscō, -īscere, -īvī vi to fall asleep ♦ vt to sleep off.

obdūcō, -ūcere, -ūxī, -uctum vt to draw over, cover; to bring up; (drink) to swallow; (time) to pass.

obductō, -āre vt to bring as a rival.

obductus ppp of obdūcō.

obdūrēscō, -ēscere, -uī vi to harden; to become obdurate.

obdūrō, -āre vi to persist, stand firm.

obdūtiō, -ōnis f veiling.

obeō, -īre, -īvī, and iī, -itum vi to go to, meet; to die; (ASTRO) to set ♦ vt to visit, travel over; to

The present infinitive verb endings are as follows: -āre = 1st; -ēre = 2nd; -ere = 3rd and -īre = 4th. See sections on irregular verbs and noun declensions.

survey, go over; to envelop; (*duty*) to engage in, perform; (*time*) to meet; **diem ~** die; (*law*) to appear on the appointed day.

obequitō, -āre *vi* to ride up to.

oberrō, -āre *vi* to ramble about; to make a mistake.

obēsus *adj* fat, plump; coarse.

ōbex, -icis *m/f* bolt, bar, barrier.

obf- *etc see* **off-**.

obg- *etc see* **ogg-**.

obhaerēscō, -rēscere, -sī *vi* to stick fast.

obiaceō, -ēre *vi* to lie over against.

obiciō, -icere, -iēcī, -iectum *vt* to throw to, set before; (*defence*) to put up, throw against; (*fig*) to expose, give up; (*speech*) to taunt, reproach.

obiectātiō, -ōnis *f* reproach.

obiectō, -āre *vt* to throw against; to expose, sacrifice; to reproach; (*hint*) to let on.

obiectus *ppp of* **obiciō** ♦ *adj* opposite, in front of; exposed ♦ *ntpl* accusations.

obiectus, -ūs *m* putting in the way, interposing.

obīrātus *adj* angered.

obiter *adv* on the way; incidentally.

obitus *ppp of* **obeō**.

obitus, -ūs *m* death, ruin; (*ASTRO*) setting; visit.

obiūrgātiō, -ōnis *f* reprimand.

obiūrgātor, -ōris *m* reprover.

obiūrgātōrius *adj* reproachful.

obiūrgitō, -āre *vt* to keep on reproaching.

obiūrgō, -āre, -āvī, -ātum *vt* to scold, rebuke; to deter by reproof.

oblanguēscō, -ēscere, -uī *vi* to become feeble.

oblātrātrīx, -īcis *f* nagging woman.

oblātus *ppp of* **offerō**.

oblectāmentum, -ī *nt* amusement.

oblectātiō, -ōnis *f* delight.

oblectō, -āre, -āvī, -ātum *vt* to delight, amuse, entertain; to detain; (*time*) to spend pleasantly; **sē ~** enjoy oneself.

oblīdō, -dere, -sī, -sum *vt* to crush, strangle.

obligātiō, -ōnis *f* pledge.

obligō, -āre, -āvī, -ātum *vt* to tie up, bandage; to put under an obligation, embarrass; (*law*) to render liable, make guilty; to mortgage.

oblimō, -āre *vt* to cover with mud.

oblinō, -inere, -ēvī, -itum *vt* to smear over; to defile; (*fig*) to overload.

oblīquē *adv* sideways; indirectly.

oblīquō, -āre *vt* to turn aside, veer.

oblīquus *adj* slanting, downhill; from the side, sideways; (*look*) askance, envious; (*speech*) indirect.

oblīsus *ppp of* **oblīdō**.

oblitēscō, -ere *vi* to hide away.

oblitterō, -āre, -āvī, -ātum *vt* to erase, cancel; (*fig*) to consign to oblivion.

oblitus *ppp of* **oblinō**.

oblītus *ppa of* **oblīviscor**.

oblīviō, -ōnis *f* oblivion, forgetfulness.

oblīviōsus *adj* forgetful.

oblīviscor, -vīscī, -tus *vt, vi* to forget.

oblīvium, -ī *and* **iī** *nt* forgetfulness, oblivion.

oblocūtor, -ōris *m* contradicter.

oblongus *adj* oblong.

obloquor, -quī, -cūtus *vi* to contradict, interrupt; to abuse; (*music*) to accompany.

obluctor, -ārī *vi* to struggle against.

obmōlior, -īrī *vt* to throw up (*as a defence*).

obmurmurō, -āre *vi* to roar in answer.

obmūtēscō, -ēscere, -uī *vi* to
become silent; to cease.

obnātus *adj* growing on.

obnītor, -tī, -xus *vi* to push against,
struggle; to stand firm, resist.

obnīxē *adv* resolutely.

obnīxus *ppa of* **obnītor ♦** *adj*
steadfast.

obnoxiē *adv* slavishly.

obnoxiōsus *adj* submissive.

obnoxius *adj* liable, addicted;
culpable; submissive, slavish;
under obligation, indebted;
exposed (to danger).

obnūbō, -bere, -psī, -ptum *vt* to
veil, cover.

obnūntiātiō, -ōnis *f*
announcement of an adverse
omen.

obnūntiō, -āre *vt* to announce an
adverse omen.

oboediēns, -entis *pres p of* **oboediō
♦** *adj* obedient.

oboedienter *adv* readily.

oboedientia, -ae *f* obedience.

oboediō, -īre *vi* to listen; to obey,
be subject to.

oboleō, -ēre, -uī *vt* to smell of.

oborior, -īrī, -tus *vi* to arise, spring
up.

obp- *etc see* **opp-**.

obrēpō, -ere, -sī, -tum *vi, vt* to
creep up to, steal upon, surprise;
to cheat.

obrētiō, -īre *vt* to entangle.

obrigēscō, -ēscere, -uī *vi* to
stiffen.

obrogō, -āre, -āvī, -ātum *vt* to
invalidate (*by making a new law*).

obruō, -ere, -ī, -tum *vt* to cover
over, bury, sink; to overwhelm,
overpower **♦** *vi* to fall to ruin.

obrussa, -ae *f* test, touchstone.

obrutus *ppp of* **obruō**.

obsaepiō, -īre, -sī, -tum *vt* to

block, close.

obsaturō, -āre *vt* to sate, glut.

obscaen- *etc see* **obscen-**.

obscēnē *adv* indecently.

obscēnitās, -ātis *f* indecency.

obscēnus *adj* filthy; indecent;
ominous.

obscūrātiō, -ōnis *f* darkening,
disappearance.

obscūrē *adv* secretly.

obscūritās, -ātis *f* darkness; (*fig*)
uncertainty; (*rank*) lowliness.

obscūrō, -āre, -āvī, -ātum *vt* to
darken; to conceal, suppress;
(*speech*) to obscure; (*pass*) to
become obsolete.

obscūrus *adj* dark, shady, hidden;
(*fig*) obscure, indistinct; unknown,
ignoble; (*character*) reserved.

obsecrātiō, -ōnis *f* entreaty;
public prayer.

obsecrō, -āre *vt* to implore, appeal
to.

obsecundō, -āre *vi* to comply with,
back up.

obsēdī *perf of* **obsideō**.

obsēp- *etc see* **obsaep-**.

obsequēns, -entis *pres p of*
obsequor ♦ *adj* compliant; (*gods*)
gracious.

obsequenter *adv* compliantly.

obsequentia, -ae *f* complaisance.

obsequiōsus *adj* complaisant.

obsequium, -ī *nt*
compliance, indulgence;
obedience, allegiance.

obsequor, -quī, -cūtus *vi* to
comply with, yield to, indulge.

obserō, -āre *vt* to bar, close.

obserō, -erere, -ēvī, -itum *vt* to
sow, plant; to cover thickly.

observāns, -antis *pres p of* **observō
♦** *adj* attentive, respectful.

observantia, -ae *f* respect.

observātiō, -ōnis *f* watching;

The present infinitive verb endings are as follows: **-āre** = 1st; **-ēre** = 2nd; **-ere** = 3rd and
-īre = 4th. *See sections on irregular verbs and noun declensions.*

caution.

observitō, -āre vt to observe carefully.

observō, -āre, -āvī, -ātum vt to watch, watch for; to guard; (*laws*) to keep, comply with; (*person*) to pay respect to.

obses, -idis m/f hostage; guarantee.

obsessiō, -ōnis f blockade.

obsessor, -ōris m frequenter; besieger.

obsessus ppp of **obsideō**.

obsideō, -idēre, -ēdī, -essum vt to sit at, frequent; (MIL) to blockade, besiege; to block, fill, take up; to guard, watch for ♦ vi to sit.

obsidiō, -ōnis f siege, blockade; (*fig*) imminent danger.

obsidium, -ī and iī nt siege, blockade; hostageship.

obsidō, -ere vt to besiege, occupy.

obsignātor, -ōris m sealer; witness.

obsignō, -āre, -āvī, -ātum vt to seal up; to sign and seal; (*fig*) to stamp.

obsistō, -istere, -titī, -titum vi to put oneself in the way, resist.

obsitus ppp of **obserō**.

obsolefīō, -fierī vi to wear out, become degraded.

obsolēscō, -scere, -vī, -tum vi to wear out, become out of date.

obsolētius adv more shabbily.

obsolētus ppa of **obsolēscō** ♦ adj worn out, shabby; obsolete; (*fig*) ordinary, mean.

obsōnātor, -ōris m caterer.

obsōnātus, -ūs m marketing.

obsōnium, -ī and iī nt food eaten with bread, (*usu fish*).

obsōnō, -āre, -or, -ārī vi to cater, buy provisions; to provide a meal.

obsonō, -āre vi to interrupt.

obsorbeō, -ēre vt to swallow, bolt.

obstantia, -ium ntpl obstructions.

obstetrīx, -īcis f midwife.

obstinātiō, -ōnis f determination, stubbornness.

obstinātē adv firmly, obstinately.

obstinātus adj firm, resolute; stubborn.

obstinō, -āre vi to be determined, persist.

obstipēscō etc see **obstupēscō**.

obstīpus adj bent, bowed, drawn back.

obstitī perf of **obsistō**; perf of **obstō**.

obstō, -āre, -itī vi to stand in the way; to obstruct, prevent.

obstrepō, -ere, -uī, -itum vi to make a noise; to shout against, cry down, molest ♦ vt to drown (in noise); to fill with noise.

obstrictus ppp of **obstringō**.

obstringō, -ingere, -inxī, -ictum vt to bind up, tie round; (*fig*) to confine, hamper; to lay under an obligation.

obstructiō, -ōnis f barrier.

obstructus ppp of **obstruō**.

obstrūdō (obtrūdō), -dere, -sī, -sum vt to force on to; to gulp down.

obstruō, -ere, -xī, -ctum vt to build up against, block; to shut, hinder.

obstupefaciō, -facere, -fēcī, -factum (*pass* **-fīō, -fierī**) vt to astound, paralyse.

obstupēscō, -ēscere, -uī vi to be astounded, paralysed.

obstupidus adj stupefied.

obsum, -esse, -fuī vi to be against, harm.

obsuō, -uere, -uī, -ūtum vt to sew on, sew up.

obsurdēscō, -ēscere, -uī vi to grow deaf; to turn a deaf ear.

obsūtus ppp of **obsuō**.

obtegō, -egere, -ēxī, -ēctum vt to cover over; to conceal.

obtemperātiō, -ōnis f obedience.

obtemperō, -āre, -āvī, -ātum vi

(*with dat*) to comply with, obey.
obtendō, -dere, -dī, -tum *vt* to
spread over, stretch over against;
to conceal; to make a pretext of.
obtentus *ppp of* **obtendō**; *ppp of*
obtineō.
obtentus, -ūs *m* screen; pretext.
obterō, -erere, -rīvī, -rītum *vt* to
trample on, crush; to disparage.
obtestātiō, -ōnis *f* adjuring;
supplication.
obtestor, -ārī, -ātus *vt* to call to
witness; to entreat.
obtexō, -ere, -uī *vt* to overspread.
obticeō, -ēre *vi* to be silent.
obticēscō, -ēscere, -uī *vi* to be
struck dumb.
obtigī *perf of* **obtingō**.
obtigō *see* **obtegō**.
obtineō, -inēre, -inuī, -entum *vt* to
hold, possess; to maintain; to
gain, obtain ♦ *vi* to prevail,
continue.
obtingō, -ngere, -gī *vi* to fall to
one's lot; to happen.
obtorpēscō, -ēscere, -uī *vi* to
become numb, lose feeling.
obtorqueō, -quēre, -sī, -tum *vt* to
twist about, wrench.
obtrectātiō, -ōnis *f*
disparagement.
obtrectātor, -ōris *m* disparager.
obtrectō, -āre *vt, vi* to detract,
disparage
obtrītus *ppp of* **obterō**.
obtrūdō *etc see* **obstrūdō**.
obtruncō, -āre *vt* to cut down,
slaughter.
obtueor, -ērī, -or, -ī *vt* to gaze at,
see clearly.
obtulī *perf of* **offerō**.
obtundō, -undere, -udī, -ūsum
and **ūnsum** *vt* to beat, thump; to
blunt; (*speech*) to deafen, annoy.
obturbō, -āre *vt* to throw into

confusion; to bother, distract.
obturgēscō, -ere *vi* to swell up.
obtūrō, -āre *vt* to stop up, close.
obtūsus, obtūnsus *ppp of* **obtundō**
♦ *adj* blunt; (*fig*) dulled, blurred,
unfeeling.
obtūtus, -ūs *m* gaze.
obumbrō, -āre *vt* to shade, darken;
(*fig*) to cloak, screen.
obuncus *adj* hooked.
obūstus *adj* burnt, hardened in
fire.
obvallātus *adj* fortified.
obveniō, -enīre, -ēnī, -entum *vi* to
come up; to fall to; to occur.
obversor, -ārī *vi* to move about
before; (*visions*) to hover.
obversus *ppp of* **obvertō** ♦ *adj*
turned towards ♦ *mpl* enemy.
obvertō, -tere, -tī, -sum *vt* to
direct towards, turn against.
obviam *adv* to meet, against; ~ **īre**
to go to meet.
obvius *adj* in the way, to meet;
opposite, against; at hand,
accessible; exposed.
obvolvō, -vere, -vī, -ūtum *vt* to
wrap up, muffle up; (*fig*) to cloak.
occaecō, -āre, -āvī, -ātum *vt* to
blind, obscure, conceal; to
benumb.
occallēscō, -ēscere, -uī *vi* to grow
a thick skin; to become hardened.
occanō, -ere *vi* to sound the attack.
occāsiō, -ōnis *f* opportunity,
convenient time; (*MIL*) surprise.
occāsiuncula, -ae *f* opportunity.
occāsus, -ūs *m* setting; west;
downfall, ruin.
occātiō, -ōnis *f* harrowing.
occātor, -ōris *m* harrower.
occēdō, -ere *vi* to go up to.
occentō, -āre *vt, vi* to serenade; to
sing a lampoon.
occēpī *perf of* **occipiō**.

The present infinitive verb endings are as follows: **-āre** = 1st; **-ēre** = 2nd; **-ere** = 3rd and
-īre = 4th. *See sections on irregular verbs and noun declensions.*

occepsō *archaic fut of* occipiō.

occeptō, -āre *vt* to begin.

occidēns, -entis *pres p of* occidō
♦ *m* west.

occidiō, -ōnis *f* massacre; ~ōne
occidere annihilate.

occidō, -dere, -dī, -sum *vt* to fell;
to cut down, kill; to pester.

occidō, -idere, -idī, -āsum *vi* to
fall; to set; to die, perish, be
ruined.

occiduus *adj* setting; western;
failing.

occinō, -ere, -uī *vi* to sing
inauspiciously.

occipiō, -ipere, -ēpī, -eptum *vt, vi*
to begin.

occipitium, -ī *and* **iī** *nt* back of the
head.

occisiō, -ōnis *f* massacre.

occisor, -ōris *m* killer.

occisus *ppp of* occidō.

occlāmitō, -āre *vi* to bawl.

occlūdō, -dere, -sī, -sum *vt* to shut
up; to stop.

occō, -āre *vt* to harrow.

occubō, -āre *vi* to lie.

occulcō, -āre *vt* to trample down.

occulō, -ere, -uī, -tum *vt* to cover
over, hide.

occultātiō, -ōnis *f* concealment.

occultātor, -ōris *m* hider.

occultē *adv* secretly.

occultō, -āre, -āvī, -ātum *vt* to
conceal, secrete.

occultus *ppp of* occulō ♦ *adj*
hidden, secret; (*person*) reserved,
secretive ♦ *nt* secret, hiding.

occumbō, -mbere, -buī, -bitum *vt*
to fall, die.

occupātiō, -ōnis *f* taking
possession; business;
engagement.

occupātus *adj* occupied, busy.

occupō, -āre, -āvī, -ātum *vt* to take
possession of, seize; to occupy,
take up; to surprise, anticipate;

(*money*) to lend, invest.

occurrō, -rere, -rī, -sum *vi* to run
up to, meet; to attack; to fall in
with; to hurry to; (*fig*) to obviate,
counteract; (*words*) to object;
(*thought*) to occur, suggest itself.

occursātiō, -ōnis *f* fussy welcome.

occursō, -āre *vi* to run to meet,
meet; to oppose; (*thought*) to
occur.

occursus, -ūs *m* meeting.

Ōceanītis, -ītidis *f* daughter of
Ocean.

Ōceanus, -ī *m* Ocean, a stream
encircling the earth; the Atlantic.

ocellus, -ī *m* eye; darling, gem.

ōcior, -ōris *adj* quicker, swifter.

ōcius *adv* more quickly; sooner,
rather; quickly.

ocrea, -ae *f* greave.

ocreātus *adj* greaved.

Octāviānus *adj* of Octavius ♦ *m*
Octavian (*a surname of Augustus*).

Octāvius, -ī *m* a Roman family name
(*esp the emperor Augustus*; *his
father*).

octāvum *adv* for the eighth time.

octāvus *adj* eighth ♦ *f* eighth hour.

octāvusdecimus *adj* eighteenth.

octiēns, -ēs *adv* eight times.

octingentēsimus *adj* eight
hundredth.

octingentī, -ōrum *num* eight
hundred.

octipēs, -edis *adj* eight-footed.

octō *num* eight.

Octōber, -ris *adj* of October ♦ *m*
October.

octōgēnī, -ōrum *adj* eighty each.

octōgēsimus *adj* eightieth.

octōgiēns, -ēs *adv* eighty times.

octōgintā *num* eighty.

octōiugis *adj* eight together.

octōnī, -ōrum *adj* eight at a time,
eight each.

octōphoros *adj* (*litter*) carried by
eight bearers.

octuplicātus *adj* multiplied by eight.

octuplus *adj* eightfold.

octussis, -is *m* eight asses.

oculātus *adj* with eyes; visible; **~ā diē vēndere** sell for cash.

oculus, -ī *m* eye; sight; (*plant*) bud; (*fig*) darling, jewel; **~ōs adicere ad** glance at, covet; **ante ~ōs pōnere** imagine; **ex ~īs** out of sight; **esse in ~īs** be in view; be a favourite.

ōdī, -isse *vt* to hate, dislike.

odiōsē *adv see adj.*

odiōsus *adj* odious, unpleasant.

odium, -ī *and* **iī** *nt* hatred, dislike, displeasure; insolence; **~iō esse** be hateful, be disliked.

odor (-ōs), -ōris *m* smell, perfume, stench; (*fig*) inkling, suggestion.

odōrātiō, -ōnis *f* smelling.

odōrātus *adj* fragrant, perfumed.

odōrātus, -ūs *m* sense of smell; smelling.

odōrifer, -ī *adj* fragrant; perfume-producing.

odōrō, -āre *vt* to perfume.

odōror, -ārī, -ātus *vt* to smell, smell out; (*fig*) to search out; to aspire to; to get a smattering of.

odōrus *adj* fragrant; keen-scented.

odōs *etc see* **odor.**

Odrysius *adj* Thracian.

Odyssēa, -ae *f* Odyssey.

Oeagrius *adj* Thracian.

Oebalia, -iae *f* Tarentum.

Oebalidēs, -idae *m* Castor, Pollux.

Oebalis, -idis *f* Helen.

Oebalius *adj* Spartan.

Oebalus, -ī *m* king of Sparta.

Oedipūs, -odis *and* **ī** *m* king of Thebes; solver of riddles.

oenophorum, -ī *nt* wine basket.

Oenopia, -ae *f* Aegina.

Oenotria, -ae *f* S.E. Italy.

Oenotrius *adj* Italian.

oestrus, -ī *m* gadfly; (*fig*) frenzy.

Oeta, -ae, -ē, -ēs *f* mountain range in Thessaly, associated with Hercules.

Oetaeus *adj see n.*

ofella, -ae *f* morsel.

offa, -ae *f* pellet, lump; swelling.

offectus *ppp of* **officiō.**

offendō, -endere, -endī, -ēnsum *vt* to hit; to hit on, come upon; to offend, blunder; to take offence; to fail, come to grief.

offēnsa, -ae *f* displeasure, enmity; offence, injury.

offēnsiō, -ōnis *f* stumbling; stumbling block; misfortune, indisposition; offence, displeasure.

offēnsiuncula, -ae *f* slight displeasure; slight check.

offēnsō, -āre *vt, vi* to dash against.

offēnsus *ppp of* **offendō** ♦ *adj* offensive; displeased ♦ *nt* offence.

offēnsus, -ūs *m* shock; offence.

offerō, -re, obtulī, oblātum *vt* to present, show; to bring forward, offer; to expose; to cause, inflict; **sē ~** encounter.

offerumenta, -ae *f* present.

officīna, -ae *f* workshop factory.

officiō, -icere, -ēcī, -ectum *vi* to obstruct; to interfere with; to hurt, prejudice.

officiōsē *adv* courteously.

officiōsus *adj* obliging; dutiful.

officium, -ī *and* **iī** *nt* service, attention; ceremonial; duty, sense of duty; official duty, function.

offīgō, -ere *vt* to fasten, drive in.

offirmātus *adj* determined.

offirmō, -āre *vt, vi* to persevere in.

offlectō, -ere *vt* to turn about.

offrēnātus *adj* checked.

offūcia, -ae *f* (*cosmetic*) paint; (*fig*) trick.

The present infinitive verb endings are as follows: -āre = 1st; -ēre = 2nd; -ere = 3rd and -īre = 4th. See sections on irregular verbs and noun declensions.

offulgeō, -gēre, -sī vi to shine on.

offundō, -undere, -ūdī, -ūsum vt to pour out to; to pour over; to spread; to cover, fill.

offūsus ppp of **offundō**.

ogganniō, -īre vi to growl at.

oggerō, -ere vt to bring, give.

Ōgygius adj Theban.

oh interj (expressing surprise, joy, grief) oh!

ohē interj (expressing surfeit) stop!, enough!

oi interj (expressing complaint, weeping) oh!, oh dear!

oiei interj (lamenting) oh dear!

Oīleus, -eī m father of the less famous Ajax.

olea, -ae f olive; olive tree.

oleāginus adj of the olive tree.

oleārius adj oil- (in cpds) ♦ m oil seller.

oleaster, -rī m wild olive.

olēns, -entis pres p of **oleō** ♦ adj fragrant; stinking, musty.

oleō, -ēre, -uī vt, vi to smell, smell of; (fig) to betray.

oleum, -ī nt olive oil, oil; wrestling school; **~ et operam perdere** waste time and trouble.

olfaciō, -facere, -fēcī, -factum vt to smell, scent.

olfactō, -āre vt to smell at.

olidus adj smelling, rank.

ōlim adv once, once upon a time; at the time, at times; for a good while; one day (in the future).

olit- etc see **holit-**.

olīva, -ae f olive, olive tree; olive branch, olive staff.

olīvētum, -ī nt olive grove.

olīvifer, -ī adj olive-bearing.

olīvum, -ī nt oil; wrestling school; perfume.

olla, -ae f pot, jar.

olle, ollus etc see **ille**.

olor, -ōris m swan.

olōrīnus adj swan's.

olus etc see **holus**.

Olympia, -ae f site of the Greek games in Elis.

Olympia, -ōrum ntpl Olympic Games.

Olympiacus adj = **Olympicus**.

Olympias, -adis f Olympiad, period of four years.

Olympicus, -us adj Olympic.

Olympiōnīcēs, -ae m Olympic winner.

Olympus, -ī m mountain in N. Greece, abode of the gods; heaven.

omāsum, -ī nt tripe; paunch.

ōmen, -inis nt omen, sign; solemnity.

ōmentum, -ī nt bowels.

ōminor, -ārī, -ātus vt to forebode, prophesy.

ōmissus ppp of **ōmittō** ♦ adj remiss.

ōmittō, -ittere, -īsī, -issum vt to let go; to leave off, give up; to disregard, overlook; (speech) to pass over, omit.

omnifer, -ī adj all-sustaining.

omnigenus adj of all kinds.

omnimodīs adv wholly.

omninō adv entirely, altogether, at all; in general; (concession) to be sure, yes; (number) in all, just; **~ nōn** not at all.

omniparēns, -entis adj mother of all.

omnipotēns, -entis adj almighty.

omnis adj all, every, any; every kind of; the whole of ♦ nt the universe ♦ mpl everybody ♦ ntpl everything.

omnituēns, -entis adj all-seeing.

omnivagus adj roving everywhere.

omnivolus adj willing everything.

onager, -rī m wild ass.

onerārius adj (beast) of burden; (ship) transport.

onerō, -āre, -āvī, -ātum vt to load,

burden; (*fig*) to overload, oppress; to aggravate.

onerōsus *adj* heavy, burdensome, irksome.

onus, -eris *nt* load, burden, cargo; (*fig*) charge, difficulty.

onustus *adj* loaded, burdened; (*fig*) filled.

onyx, -chis *m/f* onyx; onyx box.

opācitās, -ātis *f* shade.

opācō, -āre *vt* to shade.

opācus *adj* shady; dark.

ope *abl of* ops.

opella, -ae *f* light work, small service.

opera, -ae *f* exertion, work; service; care, attention; leisure; time; (*person*) workman, hired rough; **~am dare** pay attention; do one's best; **~ae pretium** worth while; **~ā meā** thanks to me.

operārius *adj* working ♦ *m* workman.

operculum, -ī *nt* cover, lid.

operīmentum, -ī *nt* covering.

operiō, -īre, -uī, -tum *vt* to cover; to close; (*fig*) to overwhelm, conceal.

operor, -ārī, -ātus *vi* to work, take pains, be occupied.

operōsē *adv* painstakingly.

operōsus *adj* active, industrious, laborious, elaborate.

opertus *ppp of* operiō ♦ *adj* covered, hidden ♦ *nt* secret.

opēs *pl of* ops.

opicus *adj* barbarous, boorish.

opifer, -ī *adj* helping.

opifex, -icis *m/f* maker; craftsman, artisan.

ōpiliō, -ōnis *m* shepherd.

opīmitās, -ātis *f* abundance.

opīmus *adj* rich, fruitful, fat; copious, sumptuous; (*style*) overloaded; **spolia ~a** spoils of an

enemy commander killed by a Roman general.

opīnābilis *adj* conjectural.

opīnātiō, -ōnis *f* conjecture.

opīnātor, -ōris *m* conjecturer.

opīnātus, -ūs *m* supposition.

opīniō, -ōnis *f* opinion, conjecture, belief; reputation, esteem; rumour; **contrā, praeter ~ōnem** contrary to expectation.

opīniōsus *adj* dogmatic.

opīnor, -ārī, -ātus *vi* to think, suppose, imagine ♦ *adj* imagined.

opiparē *adv see adj.*

opiparus *adj* rich, sumptuous.

opitulor, -ārī, -ātus *vi* (*with dat*) to help.

oportet, -ēre, -uit *vt* (*impers*) ought, should.

oppedō, -ere *vi* to insult.

opperior, -īrī, -tus *vt, vi* to wait, wait for.

oppetō, -ere, -īvī, -ītum *vt* to encounter; to die.

oppidānus *adj* provincial ♦ *mpl* townsfolk.

oppidō *adv* quite, completely, exactly.

oppidulum, -ī *nt* small town.

oppidum, -ī *nt* town.

oppignerō, -āre *vt* to pledge.

oppilō, -āre *vt* to stop up.

oppleō, -ēre, -ēvī, -ētum *vt* to fill, choke up.

oppōnō, -ōnere, -osuī, -ositum *vt* to put against, set before; to expose; to present; (*argument*) to adduce, reply, oppose; (*property*) to pledge, mortgage.

opportūnitās, -ātis *f* suitableness, advantage; good opportunity.

opportūnē *adv* opportunely.

opportūnus *adj* suitable, opportune; useful; exposed.

oppositiō, -ōnis *f* opposing.

The present infinitive verb endings are as follows: **-āre** = 1st; **-ēre** = 2nd; **-ere** = 3rd and **-īre** = 4th. *See sections on irregular verbs and noun declensions.*

oppositus *ppp of* **oppōnō ♦** *adj* against, opposite.

oppositus, -ūs *m* opposing.

oppsuī *perf of* **oppōnō**.

oppressiō, -ōnis *f* violence; seizure; overthrow.

oppressus *ppp of* **opprimō**.

oppressus, -ūs *m* pressure.

opprimō, -imere, -essī, -essum *vt* to press down, crush; to press together, close; to suppress, overwhelm, overthrow; to surprise, seize.

opprobrium, -ī *and* **iī** *nt* reproach, disgrace, scandal.

opprobrō, -āre *vt* to taunt.

oppugnātiō, -ōnis *f* attack, assault.

oppugnātor, -ōris *m* assailant.

oppugnō, -āre, -āvī, -ātum *vt* to attack, assault.

ops, -opis *f* power, strength; help. **Ops** goddess of plenty.

ops- *etc see* **obs-**.

optābilis *adj* desirable.

optātiō, -ōnis *f* wish.

optātus *adj* longed for **♦** *nt* wish; **~ātō** according to one's wish.

optimās, -ātis *adj* aristocratic **♦** *mpl* the nobility.

optimē *adv* best, very well; just in time.

optimus *adj* best, very good; excellent; **~ō iūre** deservedly.

optiō, -ōnis *f* choice **♦** *m* assistant.

optīvus *adj* chosen.

optō, -āre, -āvī, -ātum *vt* to choose; to wish for.

optum- *etc see* **optim-**.

opulēns, -entis *adj* rich.

opulentia, -ae *f* wealth; power.

opulentō, -āre *vt* to enrich.

opulentē, -er *adv* sumptuously.

opulentus *adj* rich, sumptuous, powerful.

opum *fpl* resources, wealth.

opus, -eris *nt* work, workmanship;

(*art*) work, building, book; (*MIL*) siege work; (*colloq*) business; (*with* **esse**) need; **virō ~ est** a man is needed; **magnō ~ere** much, greatly.

opusculum, -ī *nt* little work.

ōra, -ae *f* edge, boundary; coast; country, region; (*NAUT*) hawser.

ōrāculum, -ī *nt* oracle, prophecy.

ōrātē *adv see adj*.

ōrātiō, -ōnis *f* speech, language; a speech, oration; eloquence; prose; emperor's message; **~ōnem habēre** deliver a speech.

ōrātiuncula, -ae *f* short speech.

ōrātor, -ōris *m* speaker, spokesman, orator.

ōrātōrius *adj* oratorical.

ōrātrīx, -īcis *f* suppliant.

ōrātus, -ūs *m* request.

orbātor, -ōris *m* bereaver.

orbiculātus *adj* round.

orbis, -is *m* circle, ring, disc, orbit; world; (*movement*) cycle, rotation; (*style*) rounding off; **~ lacteus** Milky Way; **~ signifer** Zodiac; **~ fortūnae** wheel of Fortune; **~ terrārum** the earth, world; **in ~em cōnsistere** form a circle; **in ~em īre** go the rounds.

orbita, -ae *f* rut, track, path.

orbitās, -ātis *f* childlessness, orphanhood, widowhood.

orbitōsus *adj* full of ruts.

orbō, -āre, -āvī, -ātum *vt* to bereave, orphan, make childless.

orbus *adj* bereaved, orphan, childless; destitute.

orca, -ae *f* vat.

orchas, -dis *f* kind of olive.

orchēstra, -ae *f* senatorial seats (in the theatre).

Orcus, -ī *m* Pluto; the lower world; death.

ōrdinārius *adj* regular.

ōrdinātim *adv* in order, properly.

ōrdinātiō, -ōnis *f* orderly

arrangement.

ōrdinātus *adj* appointed.

ōrdinō, -āre, -āvī, -ātum *vt* to arrange, regulate, set in order.

ōrdior, -dīrī, -sus *vt, vi* to begin, undertake.

ōrdō, -inis *m* line, row, series; order, regularity, arrangement; (MIL) rank, line, company, (*pl*) captains; (*building*) course, layer; (*seats*) row; (POL) class, order, station; **ex ~ine** in order, in one's turn; one after the other; **extrā ~inem** irregularly, unusually.

Orēas, -dis *f* mountain nymph.

Orestēs, -is and **ae** *m* son of Agamemnon, whom he avenged by killing his mother.

Orestēus *adj* see n.

orexis, -is *f* appetite.

organum, -ī *nt* instrument, organ.

orgia, -ōrum *ntpl* Bacchic revels; orgies.

orichalcum, -ī *nt* copper ore, brass.

ōriolla, -ae *f* lobe.

oriēns, -entis *pres p of* orior ♦ *m* morning; east.

orīgō, -inis *f* beginning, source; ancestry, descent; founder.

Orīōn, -onis and **ōnis** *m* mythical hunter and constellation.

orior, -īrī, -tus *vi* to rise; to spring, descend.

oriundus *adj* descended, sprung.

ōrnāmentum, -ī *nt* equipment, dress; ornament, decoration; distinction, pride of.

ōrnātē elegantly.

ōrnātus *ppp of* ōrnō ♦ *adj* equipped, furnished; embellished, excellent.

ōrnātus, -ūs *m* preparation; dress, equipment; embellishment.

ōrnō, -āre, -āvī, -ātum *vt* to fit out, equip, dress, prepare; to adorn,

embellish, honour.

ornus, -ī *f* manna ash.

ōrō, -āre, -āvī, -ātum *vt* to speak, plead; to beg, entreat; to pray.

Orontēs, -is and **ī** *m* river of Syria.

Orontēus *adj* Syrian.

Orpheus, -eī and **eos** (*acc* -ea) *m* legendary Thracian singer, who went down to Hades for Eurydice.

Orphēus, -icus *adj* see n.

ōrsus *ppa of* ōrdior ♦ *ntpl* beginning; utterance.

ōrsus, -ūs *m* beginning.

ortus *ppa of* orior ♦ *adj* born, descended.

ortus, -ūs *m* rising; east; origin, source.

Ortygia, -ae and **ē, -ēs** *f* Delos.

Ortygius *adj* see n.

oryx, -gis *m* gazelle.

oryza, -ae *f* rice.

os, ossis *nt* bone; (*fig*) very soul.

ōs, -ōris *nt* mouth; face; entrance, opening; effrontery; **ūnō ōre** unanimously; **in ōre esse** be talked about; **quō ōre redibō** how shall I have the face to go back?

oscen, -inis *m* bird of omen.

ōscillum, -ī *nt* little mask.

ōscitāns, -antis *pres p of* ōscito ♦ *adj* listless, drowsy.

ōscitanter *adv* half-heartedly.

ōscitō, -āre, -or, -ārī *vi* to yawn, be drowsy.

ōsculātiō, -ōnis *f* kissing.

ōsculor, -ārī, -ātus *vt* to kiss; to make a fuss of.

ōsculum, -ī *nt* sweet mouth; kiss.

Oscus *adj* Oscan.

Osiris, -is and **idis** *m* Egyptian god, husband of Isis.

Ossa, -ae *f* mountain in Thessaly.

osseus *adj* bony.

ossifraga, -ae *f* osprey.

ostendō, -dere, -dī, -tum *vt* to hold

The present infinitive verb endings are as follows: -āre = 1st; -ēre = 2nd; -ere = 3rd and -īre = 4th. See sections on irregular verbs and noun declensions.

out, show, display; to expose; to
disclose, reveal; (speech) to say,
make known.
ostentātiō, -ōnis f display;
showing off, ostentation;
pretence.
ostentātor, -ōris m displayer,
boaster.
ostentō, -āre vt to hold out,
proffer, exhibit; to show off,
boast of; to make known, indicate.
ostentum, -ī nt portent.
ostentus ppp of **ostendō**.
ostentus, -ūs m display,
appearance; proof.
Ostia, -ae f, **-ōrum** ntpl port at the
Tiber mouth.
ostiārium, -ī and **iī** nt door tax.
ostiātim adv from door to door.
Ostiēnsis adj see n.
ostium, -ī and **iī** nt door; entrance,
mouth.
ostrea, -ae f oyster.
ostreōsus adj rich in oysters.
ostreum, -ī nt oyster.
ostrifer, -ī adj oyster-producing.
ostrīnus adj purple.
ostrum, -ī nt purple; purple dress
or coverings.
ōsus, ōsūrus ppa and fut p of **ōdī**.
Othō, -ōnis m author of a law giving
theatre seats to Equites; Roman
emperor after Galba.
Othōniānus adj see n.
ōtiolum, -ī nt bit of leisure.
ōtior, -ārī vi to have a holiday, be
idle.
ōtiōsē adv leisurely; quietly;
fearlessly.
ōtiōsus adj at leisure, free; out of
public affairs; neutral,
indifferent; quiet, unexcited;
(things) free, idle ♦ m private
citizen, civilian.
ōtium, -ī nt leisure, time
(for), idleness, retirement; peace,
quiet.

ovātiō, -ōnis f minor triumph.
ovīle, -is nt sheep fold, goat fold.
ovillus adj of sheep.
ovis, -is f sheep.
ovō, -āre vi to rejoice; to celebrate
a minor triumph.
ōvum, -ī nt egg.

P

pābulātiō, -ōnis f foraging.
pābulātor, -ōris m forager.
pābulor, -ārī vi to forage.
pābulum, -ī nt food, fodder.
pācālis adj of peace.
pācātus adj peaceful, tranquil ♦ nt
friendly country.
Pachȳnum, -ī nt S.E. point of Sicily
(now Cape Passaro).
pācifer, -ī adj peace-bringing.
pācificātiō, -ōnis f peacemaking.
pācificātor, -ōris m peacemaker.
pācificātōrius adj peacemaking.
pācificō, -āre vi to make a peace
♦ vt to appease.
pācificus adj peacemaking.
pacīscor, -iscī, -tus vi to make a
bargain, agree ♦ vt to stipulate
for; to bargain.
pācō, -āre, -āvī, -ātum vt to pacify,
subdue.
pactiō, -ōnis f bargain, agreement,
contract; collusion; (words)
formula.
Pactōlus, -ī m river of Lydia
(famous for its gold).
pactor, -ōris m negotiator.
pactum, -ī nt agreement, contract.
pactus ppa of **pacīscor** ♦ adj
agreed, settled; betrothed.
Pācuvius, -ī m Latin tragic poet.
Padus, -ī m river Po.
paeān, -ānis m healer, epithet of
Apollo; hymn of praise, shout of
joy; (metre) paeon.
paedagōgus, -ī m slave who took
children to school.

paedor, -ōris m filth.

paelex, -icis f mistress, concubine.

paelicātus, -ūs m concubinage.

Paelignī, -ōrum mpl people of central Italy.

Paelignus adj see n.

paene adv almost, nearly.

paenīnsula, -ae f peninsula.

paenitendus adj regrettable.

paenitentia, -ae f repentance.

paenitet, -ēre, -uit vt, vi (impers) to repent, regret, be sorry; to be dissatisfied; **an ~et** is it not enough?

paenula, -ae f travelling cloak.

paenulātus adj wearing a cloak.

paeōn, -ōnis m metrical foot of one long and three short syllables.

paeōnius adj healing.

Paestānus adj see n.

Paestum, -ī nt town in S. Italy.

paetulus adj with a slight cast in the eye.

paetus adj with a cast in the eye.

pāgānus adj rural ♦ m villager, yokel.

pāgātim adv in every village.

pāgella, -ae f small page.

pāgina, -ae f (book) page, leaf.

pāginula, -ae f small page.

pāgus, -ī m village, country district; canton.

pāla, -ae f spade; (ring) bezel.

palaestra, -ae f wrestling school, gymnasium; exercise, wrestling; (RHET) exercise, training.

palaestricē adv in gymnastic fashion.

palaestricus adj of the wrestling school.

palaestrīta, -ae m head of a wrestling school.

palam adv openly, publicly, well-known ♦ prep (with abl) in the presence of.

Palātīnus adj Palatine; imperial.

Palātium, -ī nt Palatine Hill in Rome; palace.

palātum, -ī nt palate; taste, judgment.

palea, -ae f chaff.

paleāria, -ium ntpl dewlap.

Palēs, -is f goddess of shepherds.

Palīlis adj of Pales ♦ ntpl festival of Pales.

palimpsēstus, -ī m palimpsest.

Palinūrus, -ī m pilot of Aeneas; promontory in S. Italy.

paliūrus, -ī m Christ's thorn.

palla, -ae f woman's robe; tragic costume.

Palladium, -dī nt image of Pallas.

Palladius adj of Pallas.

Pallantēus adj see n.

Pallas, -dis and **dos** f Athene, Minerva; oil; olive tree.

Pallās, -antis m ancestor or son of Evander.

pallēns, -entis pres p ot **palleō** ♦ adj pale; greenish.

palleō, -ēre, -uī vi to be pale or yellow; to fade; to be anxious.

pallēscō, -escere, -uī vi to turn pale, turn yellow.

palliātus adj wearing a Greek cloak.

pallidulus adj palish.

pallidus adj pale, pallid, greenish; in love.

palliolum, -ī nt small cloak, cape, hood.

pallium, -ī and **iī** nt coverlet; Greek cloak.

pallor, -ōris m paleness, fading; fear.

palma, -ae f (hand) palm, hand; (oar) blade; (tree) palm, date; branch; (fig) prize, victory, glory.

palmāris adj excellent.

palmārius adj prizewinning.

palmātus adj palm-embroidered.

palmes, -itis m pruned shoot, branch.

palmētum, -ī nt palm grove.

palmifer, -ī adj palm-bearing.

palmōsus adj palm-clad.

palmula, -ae f oar blade.

pālor, -ārī, -ātus vi to wander about, straggle.

palpātiō, -ōnis f flatteries.

palpātor, -ōris m flatterer.

palpebra, -ae f eyelid.

palpitō, -āre vi to throb, writhe.

palpō, -āre; -or, -ārī vt to stroke; to coax, flatter.

palpus, -ī m coaxing.

palūdāmentum, -ī nt military cloak.

palūdātus adj in a general's cloak.

palūdōsus adj marshy.

palumbēs, -is m/f wood pigeon.

pālus, -ī m stake, pale.

palūs, -ūdis f marsh, pool, lake.

palūster, -ris adj marshy.

pampineus adj of vineshoots.

pampinus, -ī m vineshoot.

Pān, -ānos (acc -āna) m Greek god of shepherds, hills and woods, esp associated with Arcadia.

panacēa, -ae f a herb supposed to cure all diseases.

Panaetius, -ī m Stoic philosopher.

Panchāeus adj see n.

Panchāius adj see n.

Panchāia, -iae f part of Arabia.

panchrēstus adj good for everything.

pancratium, -ī and **iī** nt all-in boxing and wrestling match.

pandiculor, -āre vi to stretch oneself.

Pandīōn, -onis m king of Athens, father of Procne and Philomela.

Pandīonius adj see n.

pandō, -ere, -ī, pānsum and **passum** vt to spread out, stretch, extend; to open; (fig) to disclose,

explain.

pandus adj curved, bent.

pangō, -ere, panxī and **pepigī, pāctum** vt to drive in, fasten; to make, compose; to agree, settle.

pānicula, -ae f tuft.

pānicum, -ī nt Italian millet.

pānis, -is m bread, loaf.

Pāniscus, -ī m little Pan.

panniculus, -ī m rag.

Pannonia, -ae f country on the middle Danube.

Pannonius adj see n.

pannōsus adj ragged.

pannus, -ī m piece of cloth, rag, patch.

Panormus, -ī f town in Sicily (now Palermo).

pānsa adj splayfoot.

pānsus ppp of **pandō**.

panthēra, -ae f panther.

Panthoidēs, -ae m Euphorbus.

Panthūs, -ī m priest of Apollo at Troy.

panticēs, -um mpl bowels; sausages.

panxī perf of **pangō**.

papae interj (expressing wonder) ooh!

pāpas, -ae m tutor.

papāver, -is nt poppy.

papāvereus adj see n.

Paphius adj see n.

Paphos, -ī f town in Cyprus, sacred to Venus.

pāpiliō, -ōnis m butterfly.

papilla, -ae f teat, nipple; breast.

pappus, -ī m woolly seed.

papula, -ae f pimple.

papȳrifer, -ī adj papyrus-bearing.

papȳrum, -ī nt papyrus; paper.

papȳrus, -ī m/f papyrus; paper.

pār, paris adj equal, like; a match for; proper, right ♦ m peer, partner, companion ♦ nt pair; **pār parī respondēre** return like for like; **parēs cum paribus facillimē congregantur** ≈ birds of a feather

flock together ; **lūdere pār impār**
play at evens and odds.

parābilis *adj* easy to get.

parasīta, -ae *f* woman parasite.

parasītaster, -rī *m* sorry parasite.

parasīticus *adj* of a parasite.

parasītus, -ī *m* parasite, sponger.

parātē *adv* with preparation;
carefully; promptly.

parātiō, -ōnis *f* trying to get.

paratragoedō, -āre *vi* to talk
theatrically.

parātus *ppp of* **parō ✦** *adj* ready;
equipped; experienced.

parātus, -ūs *m* preparation,
equipment.

Parca, -ae *f* Fate.

parcē *adv* frugally; moderately.

parcō, -cere, pepercī, -sum *vt, vi*
(*with dat*) to spare, economize; to
refrain from, forgo; (*with inf*) to
forbear, stop.

parcus *adj* sparing, thrifty,
niggardly, scanty; chary.

pardus, -ī *m* panther.

pārēns, -entis *pres p of* **pāreō ✦** *adj*
obedient **✦** *mpl* subjects.

parēns, -entis *m/f* parent, father,
mother; ancestor; founder.

parentālis *adj* parental **✦** *ntpl*
festival in honour of dead ancestors
and relatives.

parentō, -āre *vi* to sacrifice in honour
of dead parents or relatives ; to
avenge (*with the death of another*).

pāreō, -ēre, -uī, -itum *vi* to be
visible, be evident; (*with dat*) to
obey, submit to, comply with; **~et**
it is proved.

pariēs, -etis *m* wall.

parietinae, -ārum *fpl* ruins.

Parīlia, -ium *ntpl* festival of Pales.

parīlis *adj* equal.

pariō, -ere, peperī, -tum *vt* to give
birth to; to produce, create,

cause; to procure.

Paris, -idis *m* son of Priam
(*abductor of Helen*).

pariter *adv* equally, alike; at the
same time, together.

paritō, -āre *vt* to get ready.

Parius *adj see* **Paros**.

parma, -ae *f* shield, buckler.

parmātus *adj* armed with a
buckler.

parmula, -ae *f* little shield.

Parnāsis, -idis *adj* Parnassian.

Parnāsius *adj* = **Parnāsis**.

Parnāsus, -ī *m* mount Parnassus in
central Greece, sacred to the Muses.

parō, -āre, -āvī, -ātum *vt* to
prepare, get ready, provide; to
intend, set about; to procure, get,
buy; to arrange.

parocha, -ae *f* provision of
necessaries (*to officials travelling*).

parochus, -ī *m* purveyor; host.

paropsic, -dis *f* dish.

Paros, -ī *f* Aegean island (*famous for
white marble*).

parra, -ae *f* owl.

Parrhasis, -idis, -ius *adj* Arcadian.

parricīda, -ae *m* parricide,
assassin; traitor.

parricīdium, -ī *and* **iī** parricide,
murder; high treason.

pars, -tis *f* part, share, fraction;
party, side; direction; respect,
degree; (*with pl verb*) some; (*pl*)
stage part, role; duty, function;
māgna ~ the majority; **māgnam
~tem** largely; **in eam ~tem** in that
direction, on that side, in that
sense; **nullā ~te** not at all; **omnī
~te** entirely; **ex ~te** partly; **ex
alterā ~te** on the other hand; **ex
māgnā ~te** to a large extent; **prō
~te** to the best of one's ability;
~tēs agere play a part; **duae ~tēs**
two-thirds; **trēs ~tēs** three-

The present infinitive verb endings are as follows: **-āre** *= 1st;* **-ēre** *= 2nd;* **-ere** *= 3rd and*
-īre *= 4th. See sections on irregular verbs and noun declensions.*

fourths; **multīs ~ibus** a great deal.
parsimōnia, -ae f thrift, frugality.
parthenicē, -ēs f a plant.
Parthenopē, -ēs f old name of
Naples.
Parthenopēius adj see n.
Parthī, -ōrum mpl Parthians
(Rome's great enemy in the East).
Parthicus, -us adj see n.
particeps, -ipis adj sharing,
partaking ♦ m partner.
participō, -āre vt to share, impart,
inform.
particula, -ae f particle.
partim adv partly, in part; mostly;
some ... others.
partiō, -īre, -īvī, -ītum vt, **-ior, -īrī** vt
to share, distribute, divide.
partītē adv methodically.
partītiō, -ōnis f distribution,
division.
parturiō, -īre vi to be in labour;
(fig) to be anxious ♦ vt to teem
with, be ready to produce; (mind)
to brood over.
partus ppp of **pariō** ♦ ntpl
possessions.
partus, -ūs m birth; young.
parum adv too little, not enough;
not very, scarcely.
parumper adv for a little while.
parvitās, -ātis f smallness.
parvulus, parvolus adj very small,
slight; quite young ♦ m child.
parvus (comp **minor**, superl
minimus) adj small, little, slight;
(time) short; (age) young; **~ī esse**
be of little value.
Pascha, -ae f Easter.
pāscō, -scere, -vī, -stum vt to feed,
put to graze; to keep, foster; (fig)
to feast, cherish ♦ vi to graze,
browse.
pāscuus adj for pasture ♦ nt
pasture.
Pāsiphaē, -ēs f wife of Minos
(mother of the Minotaur).

passer, -is m sparrow; (fish)
plaice; **~ marīnus** ostrich.
passerculus, -ī m little sparrow.
passim adv here and there, at
random; indiscriminately.
passum, -ī nt raisin wine.
passus ppp of **pandō** ♦ adj spread
out, dishevelled; dried.
passus ppa of **patior**.
passus, -ūs m step, pace; footstep;
mille ~ūs mile; **milia ~uum** miles.
pastillus, -ī m lozenge.
pāstor, -ōris m shepherd.
pāstōrālis adj shepherd's,
pastoral.
pāstōricius, pāstōrius adj
shepherd's.
pāstus ppp of **pāscō**.
pāstus, -ūs m pasture, food.
Patara, -ae f town in Lycia (with
oracle of Apollo).
Pataraeus and **eus** adj see n.
Patavīnus adj see n.
Patavium, -ī nt birthplace of Livy
(now Padua).
patefaciō, -facere, -fēcī, -factum
(pass **-fiō, -fierī**) vt to open, open
up; to disclose.
patefactiō, -ōnis f disclosing.
patefīō etc see **patefaciō**.
patella, -ae f small dish, plate.
patēns, -entis pres p of **pateō** ♦ adj
open, accessible, exposed; broad;
evident.
patenter adv clearly.
pateō, -ēre, -uī vi to be open,
accessible, exposed; to extend; to
be evident, known.
pater, -ris m father; (pl)
forefathers; senators.
patera, -ae f dish, saucer, bowl.
paterfamiliās, patrisfamiliās m
master of the house.
paternus adj father's, paternal;
native.
patēscō, -ere vi to open out; to
extend; to become evident.

patibilis adj endurable; sensitive.

patibulātus adj pilloried.

patibulum, -ī nt fork-shaped yoke, pillory.

patiēns, -entis pres p of **patior ♦** adj able to endure; patient; unyielding.

patienter adv patiently.

patientia, -ae f endurance, stamina; forbearance; submissiveness.

patina, -ae f dish, pan.

patior, -tī, -ssus vt to suffer, experience; to submit to; to allow, put up with; **facile ~** be well pleased with; **aegrē ~** be displeased with.

Patrae, -ārum fpl Greek seaport (now Patras).

patrātor, -ōris m doer.

patrātus adj : **pater ~** officiating priest.

Patrēnsis adj see n.

patria, -ae f native land, native town, home.

patricius adj patrician ♦ m aristocrat.

patrimōnium, -ī and iī nt inheritance, patrimony.

patrimus adj having a father living.

patrissō, -āre vi to take after one's father.

patrītus adj of one's father.

patrius adj father's; hereditary, native.

patrō, -āre, -āvī, -ātum vt to achieve, execute, complete.

patrōcinium, -ī and iī nt patronage, advocacy, defence.

patrōcinor, -ārī vi (with dat) to defend, support.

patrōna, -ae f patron goddess; protectress, safeguard.

patrōnus, -ī m patron, protector;

(law) advocate, counsel.

patruēlis adj cousin's ♦ m cousin.

patruus, -ī m (paternal) uncle ♦ adj uncle's.

patulus adj open; spreading, broad.

paucitās, -ātis f small number, scarcity.

pauculus adj very few.

paucus adj few, little ♦ mpl a few, the select few ♦ ntpl a few words.

paulātim adv little by little, gradually.

paulisper adv for a little while.

Paullus, -ī m = **Paulus**.

paulō adv a little, somewhat.

paululus adj very little ♦ nt a little bit.

paulum adv = **paulō**.

paulus adj little.

Paulus, -ī m Roman surname (esp victor of Pydna).

pauper, -is adj poor; meagre ♦ mpl the poor.

pauperculus adj poor.

pauperiēs, -ēī f poverty.

pauperō, -āre vt to impoverish; to rob.

paupertās, -ātis f poverty, moderate means.

pausa, -ae f stop, end.

pauxillātim adv bit by bit.

pauxillulus adj very little.

pauxillus adj little.

pavefactus adj frightened.

paveō, -ēre, pāvī vi to be terrified, quake ♦ vt to dread, be scared of.

pavēscō, -ere vt, vi to become alarmed (at).

pāvī perf of **pāscō**.

pavidē adv in a panic.

pavidus adj quaking, terrified.

pavīmentātus adj paved.

pavīmentum, -ī nt pavement, floor.

paviō, -īre vt to strike.

The present infinitive verb endings are as follows: -āre = 1st; -ēre = 2nd; -ere = 3rd and -īre = 4th. See sections on irregular verbs and noun declensions.

pavitō, -āre vi to be very frightened; to shiver.

pāvō, -ōnis m peacock.

pavor, -ōris m terror, panic.

pāx, pācis f peace; (*gods*) grace; (*mind*) serenity ♦ *interj* enough!; **pāce tuā** by your leave.

peccātum, -ī nt mistake, fault, sin.

peccō, -āre, -āvī, -ātum vi to make a mistake, go wrong, offend.

pecorōsus adj rich in cattle.

pecten, -inis m comb; (*fish*) scallop; (*loom*) reed; (*lyre*) plectrum.

pectō, -ctere, -xī, -xum vt to comb.

pectus, -oris nt breast; heart, feeling; mind, thought.

pecū nt flock of sheep; (*pl*) pastures.

pecuārius adj of cattle ♦ m cattle breeder ♦ *ntpl* herds.

pecūlātor, -ōris m embezzler.

pecūlātus, -ūs m embezzlement.

pecūliāris adj one's own; special.

pecūliātus adj provided with money.

pecūliōsus adj with private property.

pecūlium, -ī and **iī** nt small savings, private property.

pecūnia, -ae f property; money.

pecūniārius adj of money.

pecūniōsus adj moneyed, well-off.

pecus, -oris nt cattle, herd, flock; animal.

pecus, -udis f sheep, head of cattle, beast.

pedālis adj a (foot) long.

pedārius adj (*senator*) without full rights.

pedes, -itis m foot soldier, infantry ♦ adj on foot.

pedester, -ris adj on foot, pedestrian; infantry- (*in cpds*); on land; (*writing*) in prose, prosaic.

pedetemptim adv step by step, cautiously.

pedica, -ae f fetter, snare.

pedis, -is m louse.

pedisequa, -ae f handmaid.

pedisequus, -ī m attendant, lackey.

peditātus, -ūs m infantry.

pedum, -ī nt crook.

Pēgaseus and **is, -idis** adj Pegasean.

Pēgasus, -ī m mythical winged horse (*associated with the Muses*).

pēgma, -tis nt bookcase; stage elevator.

pēierō, -āre vi to perjure oneself.

pēior, -ōris compar of **malus**.

pēius adv worse.

pelagius adj of the sea.

pelagus, -ī (*pl -ē*) nt sea, open sea.

pelamys, -dis f young tunny fish.

Pelasgī, -ōrum mpl Greeks.

Pelasgias and **is** and **us** adj Grecian.

Pēleus, -eī and **eos** (*acc -ea*) m king of Thessaly (*father of Achilles*).

Peliās, -ae m uncle of Jason.

Pēlias and **iacus** and **ius** adj see **Pēlion**.

Pēlīdēs, -īdae m Achilles; Neoptolemus.

Pēlion, -ī nt mountain in Thessaly.

Pella, -ae; -ē, -ēs f town of Macedonia (*birthplace of Alexander*).

pellācia, -ae f attraction.

Pellaeus adj of Pella; Alexandrian; Egyptian.

pellāx, -ācis adj seductive.

pellēctiō, -ōnis f reading through.

pellectus ppp of **pelliciō**.

pellegō etc see **perlegō**.

pelliciō, -icere, -exī, -ectum vt to entice, inveigle.

pellicula, -ae f skin, fleece.

pelliō, -ōnis m furrier.

pellis, -is f skin, hide; leather, felt; tent.

pellītus adj wearing skins, with leather coats.

pellō, -ere, pepulī, pulsum vt to
push, knock, drive; to drive off,
rout, expel; (lyre) to play; (mind) to
touch, affect; (feeling) to banish.

pellūc- etc see **perlūc-**.

Pelopēis and **ēius** and **ēus** adj see n.

Pelopidae, -idārum mpl house of
Pelops.

Pelopīas adj see n.

Peloponnēsiacus, -ius adj see n.

Peloponnēsus, -ī f Peloponnese, S.
Greece.

Pelops, -is m son of Tantalus
(grandfather of Agamemnon).

pelōris, -idis f a large mussel.

pelta, -ae f light shield.

peltastae, -ārum mpl peltasts.

peltātus adj armed with the pelta.

Pēlūsiacus adj see n.

Pēlūsium, -ī nt Egyptian town at the
E. mouth of the Nile.

Pēlūsius adj see n.

pelvis, -is f basin.

penārius adj provision- (in cpds).

Penātēs, -ium mpl spirits of the
larder, household gods; home.

penatiger, -ī adj carrying his home
gods.

pendeō, -ēre, pependī vi to hang;
to overhang, hover; to hang down,
be flabby, (fig) to depend; to gaze,
listen attentively; (mind) to be in
suspense, be undecided.

pendō, -ere, pependī, pēnsum vt
to weigh; to pay; (fig) to ponder,
value ♦ vi to weigh.

pendulus adj hanging; in doubt.

Pēnēēls and **ēius** and **ēus** adj see n.

Pēnelopē, ēs and **a, -ae** f wife of
Ulysses (famed for her constancy).

Pēnelopēus adj see n.

penes prep (with acc) in the power
or possession of; in the house of,
with.

penetrābilis adj penetrable;

piercing.

penetrālis adj penetrating; inner,
inmost ♦ ntpl inner room, interior,
sanctuary; remote parts.

penetrō, -āre, -āvī, -ātum vt, vi to
put into, penetrate, enter.

Pēnēus, -ī m chief river of Thessaly.

pēnicillus, -ī m painter's brush,
pencil.

pēniculus, -ī m brush; sponge.

pēnis, -is m penis.

penitē adv inwardly.

penitus adv inside, deep within;
deeply, from the depths; utterly,
thoroughly.

penna, pinna, -ae f feather, wing;
flight.

pennātus adj winged.

penniger, -ī adj feathered.

pennipotēns, -entis adj winged.

pennula, -ae f little wing.

pēnsilis adj hanging, pendent.

pēnsiō, -ōnis f payment,
instalment.

pēnsitō, -āre vt to pay; to consider.

pēnsō, -āre, -āvī, -ātum vt to
weight out; to compensate, repay;
to consider; to judge.

pēnsum, -ī nt spinner's work; task,
duty; weight, value; **~ī esse** to be of
importance; **~ī habēre** care at all
about.

pēnsus ppp of **pendō**.

pentēris, -is f quinquereme.

Pentheus, -eī and **eos** m king of
Thebes (killed by Bacchantes).

pēnūria, -ae f want, need.

penus, -ūs and **ī** m/f, **-um, -ī; -us,
-oris** nt provisions, store of food.

pependī perf of **pendeō**; perf of
pendō.

poperci perf of **parcō**.

peperī perf of **pariō**.

pepigī perf of **pangō**.

peplum, -ī nt, **-us, -ī** m state robe of

The present infinitive verb endings are as follows: **-āre** = 1st; **-ēre** = 2nd; **-ere** = 3rd and
-īre = 4th. See sections on irregular verbs and noun declensions.

pepulī   250   **percipiō**

Athena.

pepulī *perf of* **pellō.**

per *prep (with acc : space)* through, all over; (*: time*) throughout, during; (*: means*) by, by means of, (*: cause*) by reason of, for the sake of; **~ īram** in anger; **~ manūs** from hand to hand; **~ mē** as far as I am concerned; **~ vim** forcibly; **~ ego tē deōs ōrō** in Heaven's name I beg you.

pēra, -ae *f* bag.

perabsurdus *adj* very absurd.

peraccommodātus *adj* very convenient.

perācer, -ris *adj* very sharp.

perācerbus *adj* very sour.

peracēscō, -ēscere, -uī *vi* to get vexed.

perāctiō, -ōnis *f* last act.

perāctus *ppp of* **peragō.**

peracūtē *adv* very acutely.

peracūtus *adj* very sharp, very clear.

peradulēscēns, -entis *adj* very young.

peraequē *adv* quite equally, uniformly.

peragitātus *adj* harried.

peragō, -agere, -ēgī, -actum *vt* to carry through, complete; to pass through, pierce; to disturb; (*law*) to prosecute to a conviction; (*words*) to go over, describe.

peragrātiō, -ōnis *f* travelling.

peragrō, -āre, -āvī, -ātum *vt* to travel through, traverse.

peramāns, -antis *adj* very fond.

peramanter *adv* devotedly.

perambulō, -āre *vt* to walk through, traverse.

peramoenus *adj* very pleasant.

peramplus *adj* very large.

perangustē *adv see adj.*

perangustus *adj* very narrow.

perantīquus *adj* very old.

perappositus *adj* very suitable.

perarduus *adj* very difficult.

perargūtus *adj* very witty.

perarō, -āre *vt* to furrow; to write (on wax).

perattentē *adv see adj.*

perattentus *adj* very attentive.

peraudiendus *adj* to be heard to the end.

perbacchor, -ārī *vt* to carouse through.

perbeātus *adj* very happy.

perbellē *adv* very nicely.

perbene *adv* very well.

perbenevolus *adj* very friendly.

perbenignē *adv* very kindly.

perbibō, -ere, -ī *vt* to drink up, imbibe.

perbītō, -ere *vi* to perish.

perblandus *adj* very charming.

perbonus *adj* very good.

perbrevis *adj* very short.

perbreviter *adv* very briefly.

perca, -ae *f* perch.

percalefactus *adj* quite hot.

percalēscō, -ēscere, -uī *vi* to become quite hot.

percallēscō, -ēscere, -uī *vi* to become quite hardened ♦ *vt* to become thoroughly versed in.

percārus *adj* very dear.

percautus *adj* very cautious.

percelebrō, -āre *vt* to talk much of.

perceler, -is *adj* very quick.

perceleriter *adv see adj.*

percellō, -ellere, -ulī, -ulsum *vt* to knock down, upset; to strike; (*fig*) to ruin, overthrow; to discourage, unnerve.

percēnseō, -ēre, -uī *vt* to count over; (*place*) to travel through; (*fig*) to review.

perceptiō, -ōnis *f* harvesting; understanding, idea.

perceptus *ppp of* **percipiō.**

percieō, -iēre, -iō, -īre *vt* to rouse, excite.

percipiō, -ipere, -ēpī, -eptum *vt* to

take, get hold of; to gather in; (senses) to feel; (mind) to learn, grasp, understand.

percitus ppp of **perciēo** ♦ adj roused, excited; excitable.

percoctus ppp of **percoquō**.

percolō, -āre vt to filter through.

percolō, -olere, -oluī, -ultum vt to embellish; to honour.

percōmis adj very friendly.

percommodē adv very conveniently.

percommodus adj very suitable.

percontātiō, -ōnis f asking questions.

percontātor, -ōris m inquisitive person.

percontor, -ārī, -ātus vt to question, inquire.

percontumāx, -ācis adj very obstinate.

percoquō, -quere, -xī, -ctum vt to cook thoroughly, heat, scorch, ripen.

percrēbēscō, percrēbrēscō, -ēscere, -uī vi to be spread abroad.

percrepō, -āre, -uī vi to resound.

perculī perf of **percellō**.

perculsus ppp of **percellō**.

percultus ppp of **percolō**.

percunct- etc see **percont-**.

percupidus adj very fond.

percupiō, -ere vi to wish very much.

percūriōsus adj very inquisitive.

percūrō, -āre vt to heal completely.

percurrō, -rrere, -currī and **rrī, -rsum** vt to run through, hurry over; (fig) to run over, look over ♦ vi to run along; to pass.

percursātiō, -ōnis f travelling through.

percursiō, -ōnis f running over.

percursō, -āre vi to rove about.

percursus ppp of **percurrō**.

percussiō, -ōnis f beating; (fingers) snapping; (music) time.

percussor, -ōris m assassin.

percussus ppp of **percutiō**.

percussus, -ūs m striking.

percutiō, -tere, -ssī, -ssum vt to strike, beat; to strike through, kill; (feeling) to shock, impress, move; (colloq) to trick.

perdēlirus adj quite crazy.

perdidī perf of **perdō**.

perdifficilis adj very difficult.

perdifficiliter adv with great difficulty.

perdignus adj most worthy.

perdīligēns, -entis adj very diligent.

perdīligenter adv see adj.

perdiscō, -scere, -dicī vt to learn by heart.

perdisertē adv very eloquently.

perditē adv desperately; recklessly.

perditor, -ōris m destroyer.

perditus ppp of **perdō** ♦ adj desperate, ruined; abandoned, profligate.

perdiū adv for a very long time.

perdiūturnus adj protracted.

perdīves, -itis adj very rich.

perdīx, -īcis m/f partridge.

perdō, -ere, -idī, -itum vt to destroy, ruin; to squander, waste; to lose; **dī tē —uint** curse you!

perdoceō, -ēre, -uī, -tum vt to teach thoroughly.

perdolēscō, -ēscere, -uī vi to take it to heart.

perdomō, -āre, -uī, -itum vt to subjugate, tame completely.

perdormiscō, -ere vi to sleep on.

perdūcō, -ūcere, -ūxī, -uctum vt to bring, guide to; to induce, seduce; to spread over; to prolong,

The present infinitive verb endings are as follows: -āre = 1st; -ēre = 2nd; -ere = 3rd and -īre = 4th. See sections on irregular verbs and noun declensions.

continue.

perductō, -āre vt to guide.

perductor, -ōris m guide; pander.

perductus ppp of **perdūcō**.

perduellīō, -ōnis f treason.

perduellis, -is m enemy.

perduint archaic subj of **perdō**.

perdūrō, -āre vi to endure, hold out.

peredō, -edere, -ēdī, -ēsum vt to consume, devour.

peregrē adv away from home, abroad; from abroad.

peregrīnābundus adj travelling.

peregrīnātiō, -ōnis f living abroad, travel.

peregrīnātor, -ōris m traveller.

peregrīnitās, -ātis f foreign manners.

peregrīnor, -ārī, -ātus vi to be abroad, travel; to be a stranger.

peregrīnus adj foreign, strange ♦ m foreigner, alien.

perēlegāns, -antis adj very polished.

perēleganter adv in a very polished manner.

perēloquēns, -entis adj very eloquent.

perēmī perf of **perimō**.

peremnia, -ium ntpl auspices taken on crossing a river.

peremptus ppp of **perimō**.

perendiē adv the day after tomorrow.

perendinus adj (the day) after tomorrow.

perennis adj perpetual, unfailing.

perennitās, -ātis f continuance.

perennō, -āre vi to last a long time.

pereō, -īre, -iī, -itum vi to be lost, pass away, perish, die; (fig) to be wasted, be in love, be undone.

perequitō, -āre vt, vi to ride up and down.

pererrō, -āre, -āvī, -ātum vt to roam over, cover.

perērudītus adj very learned.

perēsus ppp of **peredō**.

perexcelsus adj very high.

perexiguē adv very meagrely.

perexiguus adj very small, very short.

perfacētē adv very wittily.

perfacētus adj very witty.

perfacile adv very easily.

perfacilis adj very easy; very courteous.

perfamiliāris adj very intimate ♦ m very close friend.

perfectē adv fully.

perfectiō, -ōnis f completion, perfection.

perfector, -ōris m perfecter.

perfectus ppp of **perficiō** ♦ adj complete, perfect.

perferō, -ferre, -tulī, -lātum vt to carry through, bring, convey; to bear, endure, put up with; (work) to finish, bring to completion; (law) to get passed; (message) to bring news.

perficiō, -icere, -ēcī, -ectum vt to carry out, finish, complete; to perfect; to cause, make.

perficus adj perfecting.

perfidēlis adj very loyal.

perfidia, -ae f treachery, dishonesty.

perfidiōsē adv see adj.

perfidiōsus adj treacherous, dishonest.

perfidus adj treacherous, faithless.

perfīgō, -gere, -xī, -xum vt to pierce.

perflābilis adj that can be blown through.

perflāgitiōsus adj very wicked.

perflō, -āre vt to blow through, blow over.

perfluctuō, -āre vt to flood through.

perfluō, -ere, -xī vi to run out, leak.

perfodiō, -odere, -ōdī, -ossum vt

to dig through, excavate, pierce.

perforō, -āre, -āvī, -ātum vt to bore through, pierce.

perfortiter adv very bravely.

perfossor, -ōris m : ~ **parietum** burglar.

perfossus ppp of **perfodiō**.

perfrāctus ppp of **perfringō**.

perfrēgī perf of **perfringō**.

perfremō, -ere vi to snort along.

perfrequēns, -entis adj much frequented.

perfricō, -āre, -uī, -tum and **ātum** vt to rub all over; **ōs** ~ put on a bold face.

perfrīgefaciō, -ere vt to make shudder.

perfrīgēscō, -gēscere, -xī vi to catch a bad cold.

perfrīgidus adj very cold.

perfringō, -ingere, -ēgī, -āctum vt to break through, fracture, wreck; (fig) to violate; to affect powerfully.

perfrīxī perf of **perfrīgēscō**.

perfrūctus ppa of **perfruor**.

perfruor, -uī, -ūctus vi (with abl) to enjoy to the full; to fulfil.

perfuga, -ae m deserter.

perfugiō, -ugere, -ūgī vi to flee for refuge, desert to.

perfugium, -ī and **iī** nt refuge, shelter.

perfūnctiō, -ōnis f performing.

perfūnctus ppa of **perfungor**.

perfundō, -undere, -ūdī, -ūsum vt to pour over, drench, besprinkle; to dye; (fig) to flood, fill.

perfungor, -gī, perfūnctus vi (with abl) to perform, discharge; to undergo.

perfurō, -ere vi to rage furiously.

perfūsus ppp of **perfundō**.

Pergama, -ōrum ntpl Troy.

Pergamēnus adj see n.

Pergameus adj Trojan.

Pergamum, -ī nt town in Mysia (famous for its library).

pergaudeō, -ēre vi to be very glad.

pergō, -gere, -rēxī, -rēctum vi to proceed, go on, continue ♦ vt to go on with, continue.

pergraecor, -ārī vi to have a good time.

pergrandis adj very large; very old.

pergraphicus adj very artful.

pergrātus adj very pleasant.

pergravis adj very weighty.

pergraviter adv very seriously.

pergula, -ae f balcony; school; brothel.

perhibeō, -ēre, -uī, -itum vt to assert, call, cite.

perhīlum adv very little.

perhonōrificē adv very respectfully.

perhonōrificus adj very complimentary.

perhorrēscō, -ēscere, -uī vi to shiver, tremble violently ♦ vt to have a horror of.

perhorridus adj quite horrible.

perhūmāniter adv see adj.

perhūmānus adj very polite.

Periclēs, -is and **ī** m famous Athenian statesman and orator.

perīclitātiō, -ōnis f experiment.

perīclitor, -ārī, -ātus vt to test, try; to risk, endanger ♦ vi to attempt, venture; to run a risk, be in danger.

perīculōsē adv see adj.

perīculōsus adj dangerous, hazardous.

perīculum (perīclum), -ī nt danger, risk; trial, attempt; (law) lawsuit, writ.

perīdōneus adj very suitable.

periī perf of **pereō**.

perillūstris *adj* very notable;
highly honoured.

perimbēcillus *adj* very weak.

perimō, -imere, -ēmī, -emptum
vt to destroy, prevent, kill.

perincommodē *adv see adj.*

perincommodus *adj* very
inconvenient.

perinde *adv* just as, exactly as.

perindulgēns, -entis *adj* very
tender.

perīnfirmus *adj* very feeble.

peringeniōsus *adj* very clever.

perinīquus *adj* very unfair; very
discontented.

perinsignis *adj* very conspicuous.

perinvītus *adj* very unwilling.

periodus, -ī *f* sentence, period.

Peripatētici, -ōrum *mpl*
Peripatetics *(followers of Aristotle).*

peripetasmata, -um *ntpl* curtains.

perīrātus *adj* very angry.

periscelis, -dis *f* anklet.

peristrōma, -atis *nt* coverlet.

peristylum, -ī *nt* colonnade,
peristyle.

perītē *adv* expertly.

perītia, -ae *f* practical knowledge,
skill.

perītus *adj* experienced, skilled,
expert.

periūcundē *adv see adj.*

periūcundus *adj* very enjoyable.

periūrium, -ī and **iī** *nt* perjury.

periūrō *see* pēierō.

periūrus *adj* perjured, lying.

perlābor, -bī, -psus *vi* to glide
along *or* through, move on.

perlaetus *adj* very glad.

perlāpsus *ppa of* perlābor.

perlātē *adv* very extensively.

perlateō, -ēre *vi* to lie quite
hidden.

perlātus *ppp of* perferō.

perlegō, -egere, -ēgī, -ēctum *vt* to
survey; to read through.

perlevis *adj* very slight.

perleviter *adv see adj.*

perlibēns, -entis *adj* very willing.

perlibenter *adv see adj.*

perlīberālis *adj* very genteel.

perlīberāliter *adv* very liberally.

perlibet, -ēre *vi (impers)* (I) should
very much like.

perliciō *see* pelliciō.

perlītō, -āre, -āvī, -ātum *vi* to
sacrifice with auspicious results.

perlongē *adv* very far.

perlongus *adj* very long, very
tedious.

perlub- *etc see* perlib-.

perlūceō, -cēre, -xī *vi* to shine
through, be transparent; *(fig)* to
be quite intelligible.

perlūcidulus *adj* transparent.

perlūcidus *adj* transparent; very
bright.

perlūctuōsus *adj* very mournful.

perluō, -ere *vt* to wash thoroughly;
(pass) to bathe.

perlūstrō, -āre *vt* to traverse; *(fig)*
to survey.

permāgnus *adj* very big, very
great.

permānanter *adv* by flowing
through.

permānāscō, -ere *vi* to penetrate.

permaneō, -anēre, -ānsī, -ānsum
vi to last, persist, endure to the
end.

permānō, -āre, -āvī, -ātum *vi* to
flow *or* ooze through, penetrate.

permānsiō, -ōnis *f* continuing,
persisting.

permarīnus *adj* of seafaring.

permātūrēscō, -ēscere, -uī *vi* to
ripen fully.

permediocris *adj* very moderate.

permēnsus *ppa of* permētior.

permeō, -āre *vt, vi* to pass through,
penetrate.

permētior, -tīrī, -nsus *vt* to
measure out; to traverse.

permīrus *adj* very wonderful.

permisceō, -scēre, -scuī, -xtum *vt* to mingle, intermingle; to throw into confusion.

permissiō, -ōnis *f* unconditional surrender; permission.

permissus *ppp of* **permittō**.

permissus, -ūs *m* leave, permission.

permitiālis *adj* destructive.

permitiēs, -ēi *f* ruin.

permittō, -ittere, -īsī, -issum *vt* to let go, let pass; to hurl; to give up, entrust, concede; to allow, permit.

permixtē *adv see adj.*

permixtiō, -ōnis *f* mixture; disturbance.

permixtus *ppp of* **permisceō** ♦ *adj* promiscuous, disordered.

permodestus *adj* very moderate.

permolestē *adv* with much annoyance.

permolestus *adj* very troublesome.

permōtiō, -ōnis *f* excitement; emotion.

permōtus *ppp of* **permoveō**.

permoveō, -ovēre, -ōvī, -ōtum *vt* to stir violently; (*fig*) to influence, induce; to excite, move deeply.

permulceō, -cēre, -sī, -sum *vt* to stroke, caress; (*fig*) to charm, flatter; to soothe, appease.

permulsus *ppp of* **permulceō**.

permultus *adj* very much, very many.

permūniō, -īre, -īvī, -ītum *vt* to finish fortifying; to fortify strongly.

permūtātiō, -ōnis *f* change, exchange.

permūtō, -āre, -āvī, -ātum *vt* to change completely; to exchange; (*money*) to remit by bill of exchange.

perna, -ae *f* ham.

pernecessārius *adj* very necessary; very closely related.

pernecesse *adj* indispensable.

pernegō, -āre *vi* to deny flatly.

perniciābilis *adj* ruinous.

perniciēs, -ēi *f* destruction, ruin, death.

perniciōsē *adv see adj.*

perniciōsus *adj* ruinous.

pernicitās, -ātis *f* agility, swiftness.

perniciter *adv* nimbly.

pernimius *adj* much too much.

pernix, -icis *adj* nimble, agile, swift.

pernōbilis *adj* very famous.

pernoctō, -āre *vi* to stay all night.

pernōscō, -scere, -vī, -tum *vt* to examine thoroughly; to become fully acquainted with, know thoroughly.

pernōtēscō, -ēscere, -uī *vi* to become generally known.

pernōtus *ppp of* **pernōscō**.

pernox, -octis *adj* all night long.

pernumerō, -āre *vt* to count up.

pērō, -ōnis *m* rawhide boot.

perobscūrus *adj* very obscure.

perodiōsus *adj* very troublesome.

perofficiōsē *adv* very attentively.

peroleō, -ēre *vi* to give off a strong smell.

peropportūnē *adv* very opportunely.

peropportūnus *adj* very timely.

peroptātō *adv* very much to one's wish.

peropus est it is most essential.

perōrātiō, -ōnis *f* peroration.

perōrnātus *adj* very ornate.

perōrnō, -āre *vt* to give great distinction to.

perōrō, -āre, -āvī, -ātum *vt* to plead at length; (*speech*) to bring to a close; to conclude.

The present infinitive verb endings are as follows: **-āre** = 1st; **-ēre** = 2nd; **-ere** = 3rd and **-īre** = 4th. *See sections on irregular verbs and noun declensions.*

perōsus adj detesting.
perpācō, -āre vt to quieten completely.
perparcē adv very stingily.
perparvulus adj very tiny.
perparvus adj very small.
perpāstus adj well fed.
perpauculus adj very very few.
perpaucus adj very little, very few.
perpaulum, -ī nt a very little.
perpauper, -is adj very poor.
perpauxillum, -ī nt a very little.
perpellō, -ellere, -ulī, -ulsum vt to urge, force, influence.
perpendiculum, -ī nt plumbline; **ad ~** perpendicularly.
perpendō, -endere, -endī, -ēnsum vt to weigh carefully, judge.
perperam adv wrongly, falsely.
perpes, -etis adj continuous.
perpessiō, -ōnis f suffering, enduring.
perpessus ppa of **perpetior**.
perpetior, -tī, -ssus vt to endure patiently, allow.
perpetrō, -āre, -āvī, -ātum vt to perform, carry out.
perpetuitās, -ātis f continuity, uninterrupted duration.
perpetuō adv without interruption, forever, utterly.
perpetuō, -āre vt to perpetuate, preserve.
perpetuus adj continuous, entire; universal; in **~um** forever.
perplaceō, -ēre vi to please greatly.
perplexē adv obscurely.
perplexor, -ārī vi to cause confusion.
perplexus adj confused, intricate, obscure.
perplicātus adj interlaced.
perpluō, -ere vi to let the rain through, leak.
perpoliō, -īre, -īvī, -ītum vt to polish thoroughly.
perpolītus adj finished, refined.
perpopulor, -ārī, -ātus vt to ravage completely.
perpōtātiō, -ōnis f drinking bout.
perpōtō, -āre vi to drink continuously ♦ vt to drink off.
perprimō, -ere vt to lie on.
perpugnāx, -ācis adj very pugnacious.
perpulcher, -rī adj very beautiful.
perpulī perf of **perpellō**.
perpūrgō, -āre, -āvī, -ātum vt to make quite clean; to explain.
perpusillus adj very little.
perquam adv very, extremely.
perquīrō, -rere, -sīvī, -sītum vt to search for, inquire after; to examine carefully.
perquīsītius adv more accurately.
perrārō adv very seldom.
perrārus adj very uncommon.
perreconditus adj very abstruse.
perrēpō, -ere vt to crawl over.
perrēptō, -āre, -āvī, -ātum vt, vi to creep about or through.
perrēxī perf of **pergō**.
perrīdiculē adv see adj.
perrīdiculus adj very laughable.
perrogātiō, -ōnis f passing (of a law).
perrogō, -āre vt to ask one after another.
perrumpō, -umpere, -ūpī, -uptum vt, vi to break through, force a way through; (fig) to break down.
perruptus ppp of **perrumpō**.
Persae, -ārum mpl Persians.
persaepe adv very often.
persalsē adv see adj.
persalsus adj very witty.
persalūtātiō, -ōnis f greeting everyone in turn.
persalūtō, -āre vt to greet in turn.
persānctē adv most solemnly.
persapiēns, -entis adj very wise.
persapienter adv see adj.

perscienter adv very discreetly.

perscindō, -ndere, -dī, -ssum vt to tear apart.

perscītus adj very smart.

perscrībō, -bere, -psī, -ptum vt to write in full; to describe, report; (record) to enter; (money) to make over in writing.

perscrīptiō, -ōnis f entry; assignment.

perscrīptor, -ōris m writer.

perscrīptus ppp of **perscrībō**.

perscrūtor, -ārī, -ātus vt to search, examine thoroughly.

persecō, -āre, -uī, -tum vt to dissect; to do away with.

persector, -ārī vt to investigate.

persecūtiō, -ōnis f (law) prosecution.

persecūtus ppa of **persequor**.

persedeō, -dēre, -ēdī, -essum vi to remain sitting.

persegnis adj very slow.

Persēius adj see **Perseus**.

persentiō, -entīre, -ēnsī vt to see clearly; to feel deeply.

persentīscō, -ere vi to begin to see; to begin to feel.

Persephonē, -ēs f Proserpine.

persequor, -quī, -cūtus vt to follow all the way, to pursue, chase, hunt after; to overtake; (pattern) to be a follower of, copy; (enemy) to proceed against, take revenge on; (action) to perform, carry out; (words) to write down, describe.

Persēs, ae m last king of Macedonia.

Persēs, -ae m Persian.

Perseus, -eī and **eos** (acc -ea) m son of Danaë (killer of Medusa, rescuer of Andromeda).

Perseus adj see n.

perseverāns, -antis pres p of **persevērō ♦** adj persistent.

persevēranter adv see adj.

persevērantia, -ae f persistence.

persevērō, -āre, -āvī, -ātum vi to persist ♦ vt to persist in.

persevērus adj very strict.

Persicus adj Persian; of Perses.

Persicum nt peach.

persīdō, -idere, -ēdī, -essum vi to sink down into.

persignō, -āre vt to record.

persimilis adj very like.

persimplex, -icis adj very simple.

Persis, -idis f Persia.

persistō, -istere, -titī vi to persist.

persōlus adj one and only.

persolūtus ppp of **persolvō**.

persolvō, -vere, -vī, -ūtum vt to pay, pay up; to explain.

persōna, -ae f mask; character, part; person, personality.

persōnātus adj masked; in an assumed character.

personō, -āre, -uī, -itum vi to resound, ring (with); to play ♦ vt to make resound; to cry aloud.

perspectē adv intelligently.

perspectō, -āre vt to have a look through.

perspectus ppp of **perspiciō ♦** adj well-known.

perspeculor, -ārī vt to reconnoitre.

perspergō, -gere, -sī, -sum vt to besprinkle.

perspicāx, -ācis adj sharp, shrewd.

perspicientia, -ae f full understanding.

perspiciō, -icere, -exī, -ectum vt to see through; to examine, observe.

perspicuē adv clearly.

perspicuitās, -ātis f clarity.

perspicuus adj transparent; clear, evident.

persternō, -ernere, -rāvī, -rātum vt to pave all over.

perstimulō, -āre vt to rouse

violently.
perstitī *perf of* **persistō**; *perf of*
perstō.
perstō, -āre, -itī, -ātum *vi* to stand
fast; to last; to continue, persist.
perstrātus *ppp of* **persternō**.
perstrepō, -ere *vi* to make a lot of
noise.
perstrictus *ppp of* **perstringō**.
perstringō, -ingere, -inxī, -ictum
vt to graze, touch lightly; (*words*)
to touch on, belittle, censure;
(*senses*) to dull, deaden.
perstudiōsē *adv* very eagerly.
perstudiōsus *adj* very fond.
persuādeō, -dēre, -sī, -sum *vi*
(*with dat*) to convince, persuade;
~**sum habeō, mihi ~sum est** I am
convinced.
persuāsiō, -ōnis *f* convincing.
persuāsus, -ūs *m* persuasion.
persubtīlis *adj* very fine.
persultō, -āre *vt, vi* to prance
about, frisk over.
pertaedet, -dēre, -sum est *vt*
(*impers*) to be weary of, be sick of.
pertegō, -egere, -ēxī, -ēctum *vt* to
cover over.
pertemptō, -āre *vt* to test
carefully; to consider well; to
pervade, seize.
pertendō, -ere, -ī *vi* to push on,
persist ♦ *vt* to go on with.
pertenuis *adj* very small, very
slight.
perterebrō, -āre *vt* to bore
through.
pertergeō, -gēre, -sī, -sum *vt* to
wipe over; to touch lightly.
perterrefaciō, -ere *vt* to scare
thoroughly.
perterreō, -ēre, -uī, -itum *vt* to
frighten thoroughly.
perterricrepus *adj* with a
terrifying crash.
perterritus *adj* terrified.
pertexō, -ere, -uī, -tum *vt* to

accomplish.
pertica, -ae *f* pole, staff.
pertimefactus *adj* very
frightened.
pertimēscō, -ēscere, -uī *vt, vi* to be
very alarmed, be very afraid of.
pertinācia, -ae *f* perseverance,
stubbornness.
pertināciter *adv see adj*.
pertināx, -ācis *adj* very tenacious;
unyielding, stubborn.
pertineō, -ēre, -uī *vi* to extend,
reach; to tend, lead to, concern; to
apply, pertain, belong; **quod ~et**
ad as far as concerns.
pertingō, -ere *vi* to extend.
pertolerō, -āre *vt* to endure to the
end.
pertorqueō, -ēre *vt* to distort.
pertractātē *adv* in a hackneyed
fashion.
pertractātiō, -ōnis *f* handling.
pertractō, -āre *vt* to handle, feel all
over; (*fig*) to treat, study.
pertractus *ppp of* **pertrahō**.
pertrahō, -here, -xī, -ctum *vt* to
drag across, take forcibly; to
entice.
pertrect- *etc see* **pertract-**.
pertristis *adj* very sad, very
morose.
pertulī *perf of* **perferō**.
pertumultuōsē *adv* very
excitedly.
pertundō, -undere, -udī, -ūsum *vt*
to perforate.
perturbātē *adv* in confusion.
perturbātiō, -ōnis *f* confusion,
disturbance; emotion.
perturbātrīx, -īcis *f* disturber.
perturbātus *ppp of* **perturbō** ♦ *adj*
troubled; alarmed.
perturbō, -āre, -āvī, -ātum *vt* to
throw into disorder, upset, alarm.
perturpis *adj* scandalous.
pertūsus *ppp of* **pertundō** ♦ *adj* in
holes, leaky.

perungō, -ungere, -ūnxī, -ūnctum
vt to smear all over.

perurbānus *adj* very refined;
over-fine.

perūrō, -rere, -ssi, -stum *vt* to
burn up, scorch; to inflame, chafe;
to freeze, nip.

Perusia, -iae *f* Etruscan town (*now*
Perugia).

Perusīnus *adj see n.*

perūstus *ppp of* **perūrō.**

perūtilis *adj* very useful.

pervādō, -dere, -sī, -sum *vt, vi* to
pass through, spread through; to
penetrate, reach.

pervagātus *adj* widespread, well-
known; general.

pervagor, -ārī, -ātus *vi* to range,
rove about; to extend, spread ♦ *vt*
to pervade.

pervagus *adj* roving.

pervariē *adv* very diversely.

pervastō, -āre, -āvī, -ātum *vt* to
devastate.

pervāsus *ppp of* **pervādō.**

pervectus *ppp of* **pervehō.**

pervehō, -here, -xī, otum *vt* to
carry, convey, bring through;
(*pass*) to ride, drive, sail through;
to attain.

pervellō, -ere, -ī *vt* to pull, twitch,
pinch; to stimulate; to disparage.

perveniō, -enīre, -ēnī, -entum *vi*
to come to, arrive, reach; to attain
to.

pervēnor, -ārī *vi* to chase through.

perversē *adv* perversely.

perversitās, -ātis *f* perverseness.

perversus (pervorsus) *ppp of*
pervertō ♦ *adj* awry, squint;
wrong, perverse.

perverto, -tere, -tī, -sum *vt* to
overturn, upset; to overthrow,
undo; (*speech*) to confute.

pervesperī *adv* very late.

pervestīgātiō, -ōnis *f* thorough
search.

pervestīgō, -āre, -āvī, -ātum *vt* to
track down; to investigate.

pervetus, -eris *adj* very old.

pervetustus *adj* antiquated.

pervicācia, -ae *f* obstinacy;
firmness.

pervicāciter *adv see adj.*

pervicāx, -ācis *adj* obstinate,
wilful; dogged.

porvictus *ppp of* **pervincō.**

pervideō, -idēre, -īdī, -īsum *vt* to
look over, survey; to consider; to
discern.

pervigeō, -ēre, -uī *vi* to continue to
flourish.

pervigil, -is *adj* awake, watchful.

pervigilātiō, -ōnis *f* vigil.

pervigilium, -ī *and* **iī** *nt* vigil.

pervigilō, -āre, -āvī, -ātum *vt, vi* to
stay awake all night, keep vigil.

pervilis *adj* very cheap.

pervincō, -incere, -īcī, -īctum *vt, vi*
to conquer completely; to outdo,
surpass; to prevail upon, effect;
(*argument*) to carry a point,
maintain, prove.

pervīvō, -ere *vi* to survive.

pervius *adj* passable, accessible.

pervolgō *etc see* **pervulgō.**

pervolitō, -āre *vt, vi* to fly about.

pervolō, -āre, -āvī, -ātum *vt, vi* to
fly through or over, fly to.

pervolō, -elle, -oluī *vi* to wish very
much.

pervolūtō, -āre *vt* (*books*) to read
through.

pervolvō, -vere, -vī, -ūtum *vt* to
tumble about; (*book*) to read
through; (*pass*) to be very busy
(with).

pervor- *etc see* **perver-.**

pervulgātus *adj* very common.

pervulgō, -āre, -āvī, -ātum *vt* to

The present infinitive verb endings are as follows: **-āre** = 1st; **-ēre** = 2nd; **-ere** = 3rd *and*
-īre = 4th. *See sections on irregular verbs and noun declensions.*

make public, impart; to haunt.

pēs, pedis m foot; (length) foot; (verse) foot, metre; (sailrope) sheet; **pedem cōnferre** come to close quarters; **pedem referre** go back; **ante pedēs** self-evident; **pedibus** on foot, by land; **pedibus īre in sententiam** take sides; **pedibus aequīs** (NAUT) with the wind right aft; **servus ā pedibus** footman.

pessimē superl of **male**.

pessimus superl of **malus**.

pessulus, -ī m bolt.

pessum adv to the ground, to the bottom; ~ **dare** put an end to, ruin, destroy; ~ **īre** sink, perish.

pestifer, -ī adj pestilential; baleful, destructive.

pestilēns, -entis adj unhealthy; destructive.

pestilentia, -ae f plague, pest; unhealthiness.

pestilitās, -ātis f plague.

pestis, -is f plague, pest; ruin, destruction.

petasātus adj wearing the petasus.

petasunculus, -ī m small leg of pork.

petasus, -ī m broadbrimmed hat.

petessō, -ere vt to be eager for.

petītiō, -ōnis f thrust, attack; request, application; (office) candidature, standing for; (law) civil suit, right of claim.

petītor, -ōris m candidate; plaintiff.

petītūriō, -īre vt to long to be a candidate.

petītus ppp of **petō**.

petītus, -ūs m falling to.

petō, -ere, -īvī and **iī, -ītum** vt to aim at, attack; (place) to make for, go to; to seek, look for, demand, ask; to go and fetch; (law) to sue; (love) to court; (office) to stand for.

petorritum, -ī nt carriage.

petrō, -ōnis m yokel.

Petrōnius, -ī m arbiter of fashion under Nero.

petulāns, -antis adj pert, impudent, lascivious.

petulanter adv see adj.

petulantia, -ae f pertness, impudence.

petulcus adj butting.

pexus ppp of **pectō**.

Phaeāccius and **cus, -x** adj Phaeacian.

Phaeāces, -cum mpl fabulous islanders in the Odyssey.

Phaedra, -ae f stepmother of Hippolytus.

Phaedrus, -ī m pupil of Socrates; writer of Latin fables.

Phaethōn, -ontis m son of the Sun (killed while driving his father's chariot).

Phaethonteus adj see n.

Phaethontiades, -um fpl sisters of Phaethon.

phalangae, -ārum fpl wooden rollers.

phalangītae, -ārum mpl soldiers of a phalanx.

phalanx, -gis f phalanx; troops, battle order.

Phalaris, -dis m tyrant of Agrigentum.

phalerae, -ārum fpl medallions, badges; (horse) trappings.

phalerātus adj wearing medallions; ornamented.

Phalēreus, -icus adj see n.

Phalērum, -ī nt harbour of Athens.

pharetra, -ae f quiver.

pharetrātus adj wearing a quiver.

Pharius adj see n.

pharmaceutria, -ae f sorceress.

pharmacopōla, -ae m quack doctor.

Pharsālicus, -ius adj see n.

Pharsālus (-os), -ī f town in Thessaly (where Caesar defeated

Pompey).

Pharus (-os), -ī f *island off Alexandria with a famous lighthouse; lighthouse.*

phasēlus, -ī m/f *French beans; (boat) pinnace.*

Phāsiacus adj *Colchian.*

Phāsiānus, -āna m/f *pheasant.*

Phāsis, -dis and **dos** m *river of Colchis.*

Phasis adj *see n.*

phasma, -tis nt *ghost.*

Pherae, -ārum fpl *town in Thessaly (home of Admetus).*

Pheraeus adj *see n.*

phiala, -ae f *saucer.*

Phīdiacus adj *see n.*

Phīdiās, -ae m *famous Athenian sculptor.*

philēma, -tis nt *kiss.*

Philippī, -ōrum mpl *town in Macedonia (where Brutus and Cassius were defeated).*

Philippēus adj *see n.*

Philippicae fpl *Cicero's speeches against Antony.*

Philippicus adj *see n.*

Philippus, -ī m *king of Macedonia; gold coin.*

philitia, (phīditia), -ōrum ntpl *public meals at Sparta.*

Philō (-ōn), -ōnis m *Academic philosopher (teacher of Cicero).*

Philoctētēs, -ae m *Greek archer who gave Hercules poisoned arrows.*

philologia, -ae f *study of literature.*

philologus adj *scholarly, literary.*

Philomēla, -ae f *sister of Procne; nightingale.*

philosophē adv *see adj.*

philosophia, -ae f *philosophy.*

philosophor, -ārī, -ātus vi *to philosophize.*

philosophus, -ī m *philosopher*

♦ adj *philosophical.*

philtrum, -ī nt *love potion.*

philyra, -ae f *inner bark of the lime tree.*

phīmus, -ī m *dice box.*

Phlegethōn, -ontis m *a river of Hades.*

Phlegethontis adj *see n.*

Phliāsius adj *see n.*

Phliūs, -ūntis f *town in Peloponnese.*

phōca, -ae f *seal.*

Phōcaicus adj *see n.*

Phōceus adj *see n.*

Phōcis, -idis f *country of central Greece.*

Phōcius adj *see n.*

Phoebas, -adis f *prophetess.*

Phoebē, -ēs f *Diana, the moon.*

Phoebēius, -ēus adj *see n.*

Phoebigena, -ae m *son of Phoebus, Aesculapius.*

Phoebus, -ī m *Apollo; the sun.*

Phoenīcē, -cēs f *Phoenicia.*

Phoenīces, -cum mpl *Phoenicians.*

phoenīcopterus, -ī m *flamingo.*

Phoenissus adj *Phoenician* ♦ f *Dido.*

Phoenīx, -īcis m *friend of Achilles.*

phoenīx, -īcis m *phoenix.*

Phorcis, -idos f *Phorcynis.*

Phorcus, -ī m *son of Neptune (father of Medusa).*

Phorcynis, -ynidos f *Medusa.*

Phrāātēs, -ae m *king of Parthia.*

phrenēsis, -is f *delirium.*

phrenēticus adj *mad, delirious.*

Phrixeus adj *see n.*

Phrixus, -ī m *Helle's brother (who took the ram with the golden fleece to Colchis).*

Phryges, -um mpl *Phrygians; Trojans.*

Phrygia, -iae f *Phrygia (country of Asia Minor); Troy.*

Phrygius adj *Phrygian, Trojan.*

The present infinitive verb endings are as follows: -āre = 1st; -ēre = 2nd; -ere = 3rd and -īre = 4th. See sections on irregular verbs and noun declensions.

Phthīa, -ae f home of Achilles in Thessaly.
Phthīōta, -ōtēs, -ōtae m native of Phthia.
phthisis f consumption.
Phthīus adj see n.
phy interj bah!
phylaca, -ae f prison.
phylarchus, -ī m chieftain.
physica, -ae and **ē, -ēs** f physics.
physicē adv scientifically.
physicus adj of physics, natural ♦ m natural philosopher ♦ ntpl physics.
physiognōmōn, -onis m physiognomist.
physiologia, -ae f natural philosophy, science.
piābilis adj expiable.
piāculāris adj atoning ♦ ntpl sin offerings.
piāculum, -ī nt sin offering; victim; atonement, punishment; sin, guilt.
piāmen, -inis nt atonement.
pīca, -ae f magpie.
picāria, -ae f pitch hut.
picea, -ae f pine.
Picēns, -entis adj = **Picēnus.**
Picēnum, -ēnī nt Picenum.
Picēnus adj of Picenum in E. Italy.
piceus adj pitch black; of pitch.
pictor, -ōris m painter.
pictūra, -ae f painting; picture.
pictūrātus adj painted; embroidered.
pictus ppp of **pingō** ♦ adj coloured, tattooed; (style) ornate; (fear) unreal.
pīcus, -ī m woodpecker.
piē adv religiously, dutifully.
Pīeris, -dis f Muse.
Pīerius adj of the Muses, poetic.
pietās, -ātis f sense of duty (to gods, family, country), piety, filial affection, love, patriotism.
piger, -rī adj reluctant, slack, slow;

numbing, dull.
piget, -ēre, -uit (impers) to be annoyed, dislike; to regret, repent.
pigmentārius, -ī and **iī** m dealer in paints.
pigmentum, -ī nt paint, cosmetic; (style) colouring.
pignerātor, -ōris m mortgagee.
pignerō, -āre vt to pawn, mortgage.
pigneror, -ārī, -ātus vt to claim, accept.
pignus, -oris and **eris** nt pledge, pawn, security; wager, stake; (fig) assurance, token; (pl) children, dear ones.
pigritia, -ae, -ēs, -ēī f sluggishness, indolence.
pigrō, -āre, -or, -ārī vi to be slow, be slack.
pīla, -ae f mortar.
pīla, -ae f pillar; pier.
pila, -ae f ball, ball game.
pīlānus, -ī m soldier of the third line.
pīlātus adj armed with javelins.
pīlentum, -ī nt carriage.
pilleātus adj wearing the felt cap.
pilleolus, -ī m skullcap.
pilleum, -ī nt, **pilleus, -ī** m felt cap presented to freed slaves; (fig) liberty.
pilōsus adj hairy.
pīlum, -ī nt javelin.
pīlus, -ī m division of triarii; **prīmus ~** chief centurion.
pilus, -ī m hair; a whit.
Pimplēa, -ae and **is, -idis** f Muse.
Pimplēus adj of the Muses.
Pindaricus adj see n.
Pindarus, -ī m Pindar (Greek lyric poet).
Pindus, -ī m mountain range in Thessaly.
pīnētum, -ī nt pine wood.
pīneus adj pine- (in cpds).

pingŏ, -ere, pinxī, pictum vt to paint, embroider; to colour; (fig) to embellish, decorate.

pinguēscō, -ere vi to grow fat, become fertile.

pinguis adj fat, rich, fertile; (mind) gross, dull; (ease) comfortable, calm; (weather) thick ♦ nt grease.

pīnifer, -ī, piniger, -ī adj pine-clad.

pinna, -ae f feather; wing, arrow; battlement; (fish) fin.

pinnātus adj feathered, winged.

pinniger, -ī adj winged; finny.

pinnipēs, -edis adj wing-footed.

pinnirapus, -ī m plume-snatcher.

pinnula, -ae f little wing.

pīnotērēs, -ae m hermit crab.

pīnsō, -ere vt to beat, pound.

pīnus, -ūs and **ī** f stone pine, Scots fir; ship, torch, wreath.

pinxī perf of **pingō**.

plŏ, -āre vt to propitiate, worship; to atone for, avert; to avenge.

piper, -is nt pepper.

pīpilō, -āre vi to chirp.

Pīraea, -ōrum ntpl Piraeus (port of Athens).

Pīraeeus and **us, -ī** m main port of Athens.

Pīraeus see n.

pīrāta, -ae m pirate.

pīrāticus adj pirate ♦ f piracy.

Pīrēnē, -ēs f spring in Corinth.

Pīrēnis, -idis adj see n.

Pīrithous, -ī m king of the Lapiths.

pirum, -ī nt pear.

pirus, -ī f pear tree.

Pīsa, -ae f Greek town near the Olympic Games site.

Pīsae, -ārum fpl town in Etruria (now Pisa).

Pīsaeus see n.

Pīsānus adj see n.

piscārius adj fish- (in cpds), fishing- (in cpds).

piscātor, -ōris m fisherman.

piscātōrius adj fishing- (in cpds).

piscātus, -ūs m fishing; fish; catch, haul.

pisciculus, -ī m little fish.

piscīna, -ae f fishpond; swimming pool.

piscīnārius, -ī and **iī** m person keen on fish ponds.

piscis -is m fish; (ASTRO) Pisces.

piscor, -ārī, -ātus vi to fish.

piscōsus adj full of fish.

pisculentus adj full of fish.

Pīsistratidae, -idārum mpl sons of Pisistratus.

Pīsistratus, -ī m tyrant of Athens.

pistillum, -ī nt pestle.

pistor, -ōris m miller; baker.

pistrilla, -ae f little mortar.

pistrīnum, -ī nt mill, bakery; drudgery.

pistris, -is and **īx, -īcis** f sea monster, whale; swift ship.

pithēcium, -ī and **iī** nt little ape.

pītuīta, -ae f phlegm; catarrh, cold in the head.

pītuītōsus adj phlegmatic.

pius adj dutiful, conscientious; godly, holy; filial, affectionate; patriotic; good, upright ♦ mpl the blessed dead.

pix, picis f pitch.

plācābilis adj easily appeased.

plācābilitās, -ātis f readiness to condone.

plācāmen, -inis, plācāmentum, -ī nt peace-offering.

plācātē adv calmly.

plācātiō, -ōnis f propitiating.

plācātus ppp of **plācō** ♦ adj calm, quiet, reconciled.

placenta, -ae f cake.

Placentia, -iae f town in N. Italy (now Piacenza).

Placentīnus adj see n.

The present infinitive verb endings are as follows: -āre = 1st; -ēre = 2nd; -ere = 3rd and -īre = 4th. *See sections on irregular verbs and noun declensions.*

placeō, -ēre, -uī, -itum vi (with dat) to please, satisfy; **~et** it seems good, it is agreed, resolved; **mihi ~eō** I am pleased with myself.

placidē adv peacefully, gently.

placidus adj calm, quiet, gentle.

placitum,-ī nt principle, belief.

placitus ppa of **placeō** ♦ adj pleasing; agreed on.

plācō, -āre, -āvī, -ātum vt to calm, appease, reconcile.

plāga, -ae f blow, stroke, wound.

plaga, -ae f region, zone.

plaga, -ae f hunting net, snare, trap.

plagiārius, -ī and iī m plunderer, kidnapper.

plāgigerulus adj much flogged.

plāgōsus adj fond of punishing.

plagula, -ae f curtain.

planctus, -ūs m beating the breast, lamentation.

plānē adv plainly, clearly; completely, quite; certainly.

plangō, -gere, -xī, -ctum vt to beat noisily; to beat in grief; to lament loudly, bewail.

plangor, -ōris m beating; loud lamentation.

plānipēs, -edis m ballet dancer.

plānitās, -ātis f perspicuity.

plānitiēs, -ēī, (-a, -ae) f level ground, plain.

planta, -ae f shoot, slip; sole, foot.

plantāria, -ium ntpl slips, young trees.

plānus adj level, flat; plain, clear ♦ nt level ground; **dē ~ō** easily.

plānus, -ī m impostor.

platalea, -ae f spoonbill.

platea, -ae f street.

Platō, -ōnis m Plato (founder of the Academic school of philosophy).

Platōnicus adj see n.

plaudō, -dere, -sī, -sum vt to clap, beat, stamp ♦ vi to clap, applaud; to approve, be pleased with.

plausibilis adj praiseworthy.

plausor, -ōris m applauder.

plaustrum, -ī nt waggon, cart; (ASTRO) Great Bear; **~ percellere** ≃ upset the applecart.

plausus ppp of **plaudō**.

plausus, -ūs m flapping; clapping, applause.

Plautīnus adj see n.

Plautus, -ī m early Latin comic poet.

plēbēcula, -ae f rabble.

plēbēius adj plebeian; common, low.

plēbicola, -ae m friend of the people.

plēbiscītum, -ī nt decree of the people.

plēbs (plēbēs), -is f common people, plebeians; lower classes, masses.

plectō, -ere vt to punish.

plēctrum, -ī nt plectrum; lyre, lyric poetry.

Plēias, -dis f Pleiad; (pl) the Seven Sisters.

plēnē adv fully, entirely.

plēnus adj full, filled; (fig) sated; (age) mature; (amount) complete; (body) stout, plump; (female) pregnant; (matter) solid; (style) copious; (voice) loud; **ad ~um** abundantly.

plērumque adv generally, mostly.

plērusque adj a large part, most; (pl) the majority, the most; very many.

plexus adj plaited, interwoven.

Plīas see **Plēias**.

plicātrīx, -icis f clothes folder.

plicō, -āre, -āvī and uī, -ātum and itum vt to fold, coil.

Plīnius, -ī m Roman family name (esp Pliny the Elder, who died in the eruption of Vesuvius; Pliny the Younger, writer of letters).

plōrātus, -ūs m wailing.

plōrō, -āre, -āvī, -ātum vi to wail,

lament ♦ vt to weep for, bewail.

plōstellum, -ī nt cart.

ploxenum, -ī nt cart box.

pluit, -ere, -it vi (impers) it is raining.

plūma, -ae f soft feather, down.

plumbeus adj of lead; (fig) heavy, dull, worthless.

plumbum, -ī nt lead; bullet, pipe, ruler; ~ album tin.

plūmeus adj down, downy.

plūmipēs, -edis adj feather-footed.

plūmōsus adj feathered.

plūrimus superl of multus.

plūs, -ūris compar of multus ♦ adv more.

plūsculus adj a little more.

pluteus, -ī m shelter, penthouse; parapet; couch; bookcase.

Plūtō, -ōnis m king of the lower world.

Plūtōnius adj see n.

pluvia, -ae f rain.

pluviālis adj rainy.

pluvius adj rainy, rain- (in cpds).

pōcillum, -ī nt small cup.

pōculum, -ī nt cup; drink, potion.

podagra, -ae f gout.

podagrōsus adj gouty.

podium, -ī and **iī** nt balcony.

poēma, -tis nt poem.

poena, -ae f penalty, punishment; poenas dare to be punished.

Poenī, -ōrum mpl Carthaginians.

Poenus, Pūnicus adj Punic.

poēsis, -is f poetry, poem.

poēta, -ae m poet.

poēticē adv poetically.

poēticus adj poetic ♦ f poetry.

poētria, -ae f poetess.

pol interj by Pollux!, truly.

polenta, -ae f pearl barley.

poliō, -īre, -īvī, -ītum vt to polish; to improve, put in good order.

polītē adv elegantly.

polītia, -ae f Plato's Republic.

polīticus adj political.

polītus adj polished, refined, cultured.

pollen, -inis nt fine flour, meal.

pollēns, -entis pres p of polleō ♦ adj powerful, strong.

pollentia, -ae f power.

polleō, -ēre vi to be strong, be powerful.

pollex, -icis m thumb.

polliceor, -ērī, -itus vt to promise, offer.

pollicitātiō, -ōnis f promise.

pollicitor, -ārī, -ātus vt to promise.

pollicitum, -ī nt promise.

Polliō, -ōnis m Roman surname (esp C. Asinius, soldier, statesman and literary patron under Augustus).

pollis, -inis m/f see pollen.

pollūcibiliter adv sumptuously.

pollūctus adj offered up ♦ nt offering.

polluō, uere, -uī, -ūtum vt to defile, pollute, dishonour.

Pollūx, -ūcis m twin brother of Castor (famous as a boxer).

polus, -ī m pole, North pole; sky.

Polyhymnia, -ae f a Muse.

Polyphēmus, -ī m one-eyed Cyclops.

polypus, -ī m polypus.

pōmārium, -ī and **iī** nt orchard.

pōmārius, -ī and **iī** m fruiterer.

pōmerīdiānus adj afternoon.

pōmērium, -ī and **iī** nt free space round the city boundary.

pōmifer, -ī adj fruitful.

pōmoerium see pōmērium.

pōmōsus adj full of fruit.

pompa, -ae f procession; retinue, train; ostentation.

Pompeiānus adj see n.

Pompeiī, -ōrum mpl Campanian town buried by an eruption of Vesuvius.

Pompeius, -ī m Roman family

name (*esp* Pompey the Great).
Pompeius, -ānus *adj see* n.
Pompilius, -ī *m* Numa (*second king of Rome*).
Pompilius *adj see* n.
Pomptīnus *adj* Pomptine (*name of marshy district in S. Latium*).
pōmum, -ī *nt* fruit; fruit tree.
pōmus, -ī *f* fruit tree.
ponderō, -āre *vt* to weigh; to consider, reflect on.
ponderōsus *adj* heavy, weighty.
pondō *adv* in weight; pounds.
pondus, -eris *nt* weight; mass, burden; (*fig*) importance, authority; (*character*) firmness; (*pl*) balance.
pōne *adv* behind.
pōnō, -ere, posuī, positum *vt* to put, place, lay, set; to lay down, lay aside; (*fig*) to regard, reckon; (*art*) to make, build; (*camp*) to pitch; (*corpse*) to lay out, bury; (*example*) to take; (*food*) to serve; (*hair*) to arrange; (*hope*) to base, stake; (*hypothesis*) to suppose, assume; (*institution*) to lay down, ordain; (*money*) to invest; (*sea*) to calm; (*theme*) to propose; (*time*) to spend, devote; (*wager*) to put down ♦ *vi* (*wind*) to abate.
pōns, pontis *m* bridge; drawbridge; (*ship*) gangway, deck.
ponticulus, -ī *m* small bridge.
Ponticus *adj see* Pontus.
pontifex, -icis *m* high priest, pontiff.
pontificālis *adj* pontifical.
pontificātus, -ūs *m* high priesthood.
pontificius *adj* pontiff's.
pontō, -ōnis *m* ferryboat.
pontus, -ī *m* sea.
Pontus, -ī *m* Black Sea; *kingdom of Mithridates in Asia Minor.*

popa, -ae *m* minor priest.
popanum, -ī *nt* sacrificial cake.
popellus, -ī *m* mob.
popīna, -ae *f* eating house, restaurant.
popīnō, -ōnis *m* glutton.
popl- *etc see* **pūbl-**.
poples, -itis *m* knee.
poposcī *perf of* poscō.
poppysma, -tis *nt* clicking of the tongue.
populābilis *adj* destroyable.
populābundus *adj* ravaging.
populāris *adj* of, from, for the people; popular, democratic; native ♦ *m* fellow countryman ♦ *mpl* the people's party, the democrats.
populāritās, -ātis *f* courting popular favour.
populāriter *adv* vulgarly; democratically.
populātiō, -ōnis *f* plundering; plunder.
populātor, -ōris *m* ravager.
pōpuleus *adj* poplar- (*in cpds*).
pōpulifer, -ī *adj* rich in poplars.
populor, -ārī, -ātus; -ō, -āre *vt* to ravage, plunder; to destroy, ruin.
populus, -ī *m* people, nation; populace, the public; large crowds; district.
pōpulus, -ī *f* poplar tree.
porca, -ae *f* sow.
porcella, -ae *f*, **-us, -ī** *m* little pig.
porcīna, -ae *f* pork.
porcīnārius, -ī *and* **iī** *m* pork seller.
Porcius, -ī *m* family name of Cato.
Porcius *adj see* n.
porculus, -ī *m* porker.
porcus, -ī *m* pig, hog.
porgō *etc see* **porrigō**.
Porphyriōn, -ōnis *m* a Giant.
porrēctiō, -ōnis *f* extending.
porrēctus *ppp of* porrigō ♦ *adj* long, protracted; dead.
porrēxī *perf of* porrigō.

porriciō, -ere vt to make an offering of; **inter caesa et porrēcta** ≈ at the eleventh hour.

porrigō, -igere, -ēxī, -ēctum vt to stretch, spread out, extend; to offer, hold out.

porrigō, -inis f scurf, dandruff.

porrō adv forward, a long way off; (time) in future, long ago; (sequence) next, moreover, in turn.

porrum, -ī nt leek.

Porsenna, Porsonna, Porsinna, -ae f king of Clusium in Etruria.

porta, -ae f gate; entrance, outlet.

portātiō, -ōnis f carrying.

portendō, -dere, -dī, -tum vt to denote, predict.

portentificus adj marvellous.

portentōsus adj unnatural.

portentum, -ī nt omen, unnatural happening; monstrosity, monster; (story) marvel.

porthmeus, -eī and **eos** m ferryman.

porticula, -ae f small gallery.

porticus, -ūs m portico, colonnade; (MIL) gallery; (PHILOS) Stoicism.

portiō, -ōnis f share, instalment; **prō -ōne** proportionally.

portitor, -ōris m customs officer.

portitor, -ōris m ferryman.

portō, -āre, -āvī, -ātum vt to carry, convey, bring.

portōrium, -ī and **iī** nt customs duty, tax.

portula, -ae f small gate.

portuōsus adj well-off for harbours.

portus, -ūs m harbour, port; (fig) safety, haven.

pōsca, -ae f a vinegar drink.

poscō, -ere, poposcī vt to ask, require, demand; to call on.

Posidōnius, -ī m Stoic philosopher

(teacher of Cicero).

positiō, -ōnis f position, climate.

positor, -ōris m builder.

positūra, -ae f position; formation.

positus ppp of **pōnō ♦** adj situated.

posse infin of **possum**.

possēdī perf of **possideō**; perf of **possīdō**.

possessiō, -ōnis f seizing; occupation; possession, property.

possessiuncula, -ae f small estate.

possessor, -ōris m occupier, possessor.

possessus ppp of **possideō** and **possīdō**.

possideō, -idēre, -ēdī, -essum vt to hold, occupy; to have, possess.

possīdō, -idere, -ēdī, -essum vt to take possession of.

possum, -sse, -tuī vi to be able, can; to have power, avail.

post adv (place) behind; (time) after; (sequence) next ♦ prep (with acc) behind; after, since; **paulō ~** soon after; **~ urbem conditam** since the foundation of the city.

posteā adv afterwards, thereafter; next, then; **~ quam** conj aftor.

posterior, -ōris adj later, next; inferior, less important.

posteritās, -ātis f posterity, the future.

posterius adv later.

posterus adj next, following ♦ mpl posterity.

postferō, -re vt to put after, sacrifice.

postgenitī, -ōrum mpl later generations.

posthabeō, -ēre, -uī, -itum vt to put after, neglect.

posthāc adv hereafter, in future.

postibi adv then, after that.

postīculum, -ī nt small back building.

The present infinitive verb endings are as follows: **-āre** = 1st; **-ēre** = 2nd; **-ere** = 3rd and **-īre** = 4th. See sections on Irregular verbs and noun declensions.

posticus *adj* back- (*in cpds*), hind-
(*in cpds*) ♦ *nt* back door.
postideā *adv* after that.
postillā *adv* afterwards.
postis, -is *m* doorpost, door.
postlīminium, -ī and **iī** *nt* right of
recovery.
postmerīdiānus *adj* in the
afternoon.
postmodo, postmodum *adv*
shortly, presently.
postpōnō, -ōnere, -osuī, -ositum
vt to put after, disregard.
postputō, -āre *vt* to consider less
important.
postquam *conj* after, when.
postrēmō *adv* finally.
postrēmus *adj* last, rear; lowest,
worst.
postrīdiē *adv* next day, the day
after.
postscaenium, -ī and **iī** *nt* behind
the scenes.
postscrībō, -ere *vt* to write after.
postulātiō, -ōnis *f* demand, claim;
complaint.
postulātum, -ī *nt* demand, claim.
postulātus, -ūs *m* claim.
postulō, -āre, -āvī, -ātum *vt* to
demand, claim; (*law*) to summon,
prosecute; to apply for a writ (to
prosecute).
postumus *adj* last, last-born.
postus *etc see* **positus**.
posuī *perf of* **pōnō**.
pōtātiō, -ōnis *f* drinking.
pōtātor, -ōris *m* toper.
pote *etc see* **potis**.
potēns, -entis *adj* able, capable;
powerful, strong, potent; master
of, ruling over; successful in
carrying out.
potentātus, -ūs *m* political power.
potenter *adv* powerfully;
competently.
potentia, -ae *f* power, force,
efficacy; tyranny.

pōterium, -ī and **iī** *nt* goblet.
potesse *archaic infin of* **possum**.
potestās, -ātis *f* power, ability;
control, sovereignty, authority;
opportunity, permission; (*person*)
magistrate; (*things*) property;
~**ātem suī facere** allow access to
oneself.
potin can (you)?, is it possible?
pōtiō, -ōnis *f* drink, draught,
philtre.
pōtiō, -īre *vt* to put into the power
of.
potior, -īrī, -ītus *vi* (*with gen and
abl*) to take possession of, get hold
of, acquire; to be master of.
potior, -ōris *adj* better, preferable.
potis *adj* (*indecl*) able; possible.
potissimum *adv* especially.
potissimus *adj* chief, most
important.
pōtitō, -āre *vt* to drink much.
potius *adv* rather, more.
pōtō, -āre, -āvī, -ātum and **um** *vt*
to drink.
pōtor, -ōris *m* drinker.
pōtrīx, -īcis *f* woman tippler.
potuī *perf of* **possum**.
pōtulenta, -ōrum *ntpl* drinks.
pōtus *ppp of* **pōtō** ♦ *adj* drunk.
pōtus, -ūs *m* drink.
prae *adv* in front, before; in
comparison ♦ *prep* (*with abl*) in
front of; compared with; (*cause*)
because of, for; ~ **sē** openly; ~ **sē
ferre** display; ~ **manū** to hand.
praeacūtus *adj* pointed.
praealtus *adj* very high, very deep.
praebeō, -ēre, -uī, -itum *vt* to hold
out, proffer; to give, supply; to
show, represent; **sē** ~ behave,
prove.
praebibō, -ere, -ī *vt* to toast.
praebitor, -ōris *m* purveyor.
praecalidus *adj* very hot.
praecānus *adj* prematurely grey.
praecautus *ppp of* **praecaveō**.

praecaveō, -avēre, -āvī, -autum vt to guard against ♦ vi to beware, take precautions.

praecēdō, -dere, -ssī, -ssum vt to go before; to surpass ♦ vi to lead the way; to excel.

praecellō, -ere vi to excel, be distinguished ♦ vt to surpass.

praecelsus adj very high.

praecentiō, -ōnis f prelude.

praecentō, -āre vi to sing an incantation for.

praeceps, -ipitis adj head first, headlong; going down, precipitous; rapid, violent, hasty; inclined (to); dangerous ♦ nt edge of an abyss, precipice; danger ♦ adv headlong; into danger.

praeceptiō, -ōnis f previous notion; precept.

praeceptor, -ōris m teacher.

praeceptrix, -rīcis f teacher.

praeceptum, -ī nt maxim, precept; order.

praeceptus ppp of **praecipiō**.

praecerpō, -ere, -sī, -tum vt to gather prematurely; to forestall.

praecīdō, -dere, -dī, -sum vt to cut off, damage; (fig) to cut short, put an end to.

praecinctus ppp of **praecingō**.

praecingō, -ingere, -īnxī, -īnctum vt to gird in front; to surround.

praecinō, -inere, -inuī, -entum vt to play before; to chant a spell ♦ vt to predict.

praecipiō, -ipere, -ēpī, -eptum vt to take beforehand, get in advance; to anticipate; to teach, admonish, order.

praecipitanter adv at full speed.

praecipitem acc of **praeceps**.

praecipitō, -āre, -āvī, -ātum vt to throw down, throw away, hasten; (fig) to remove, carry away, ruin

♦ vi to rush headlong, fall; to be hasty.

praecipuē adv especially, chiefly.

praecipuus adj special; principal, outstanding.

praecīsē adv briefly, absolutely.

praecīsus ppp of **praecīdō** ♦ adj steep.

praeclārē adv very clearly; excellently.

praeclārus adj very bright; beautiful, splendid; distinguished, noble.

praeclūdō, -dere, -sī, -sum vt to close, shut against; to close to, impede.

praecō, -ōnis m crier, herald; auctioneer.

praecōgitō, -āre vt to premeditate.

praecognitus adj foreseen.

praecolō, -olere, -oluī, -ultum vt to cultivate early.

praecompositus adj studied.

praecōnium, -ī and **iī** nt office of a crier; advertisement; commendation.

praecōnius adj of a public crier.

praecōnsūmō, -ere, -ptum vt to use up beforehand.

praecontrectō, -āre vt to consider beforehand.

praecordia, -ōrum ntpl midriff; stomach; breast, heart; mind.

praecorrumpō, -umpere, -ūpī, -uptum vt to bribe beforehand.

praecox, -cis adj early, premature.

praecultus ppp of **praecolō**.

praecurrentia, -ium ntpl antecedents.

praecurrō, -rrere, -currī and **rrī, -rsum** vi to hurry on before, precede; to excel ♦ vt to anticipate; to surpass.

praecursiō, -ōnis f previous occurrence; (RHET) preparation.

The present infinitive verb endings are as follows: -āre = 1st; -ēre = 2nd; -ere = 3rd and -īre = 4th. See sections on irregular verbs and noun declensions.

praecursor, -ōris *m* advance guard; scout.

praecutiō, -ere *vt* to brandish before.

praeda, -ae *f* booty, plunder; (*animal*) prey; (*fig*) gain.

praedābundus *adj* plundering.

praedamnō, -āre *vt* to condemn beforehand.

praedātiō, -ōnis *f* plundering.

praedātor, -ōris *m* plunderer.

praedātōrius *adj* marauding.

praedēlassō, -āre *vt* to weaken beforehand.

praedēstinō, -āre *vt* to predetermine.

praediātor, -ōris *m* buyer of landed estates.

praediātōrius *adj* relating to the sale of estates.

praedicābilis *adj* laudatory.

praedicātiō, -ōnis *f* proclamation; commendation.

praedicātor, -ōris *m* eulogist.

praedicō, -āre, -āvī, -ātum *vt* to proclaim, make public; to declare; to praise, boast.

praedīcō, -īcere, -īxī, -ictum *vt* to mention beforehand, prearrange; to foretell; to warn, command.

praedictiō, -ōnis *f* foretelling.

praedictum, -ī *nt* prediction; command; prearrangement.

praedictus *ppp of* praedīcō.

praediolum, -ī *nt* small estate.

praediscō, -ere *vt* to learn beforehand.

praedispositus *adj* arranged beforehand.

praeditus *adj* endowed, provided.

praedium, -ī *and* **iī** *nt* estate.

praedīves, -itis *adj* very rich.

praedō, -ōnis *m* robber, pirate.

praedor, -ārī, -ātus *vt, vi* to plunder, rob; (*fig*) to profit.

praedūcō, -ūcere, -ūxī, -uctum *vt* to draw in front.

praedulcis *adj* very sweet.

praedūrus *adj* very hard, very tough.

praeēmineō, -ēre *vt* to surpass.

praeeō, -īre, -īvī *and* **iī, -itum** *vi* to lead the way, go first; (*formula*) to dictate, recite first ♦ *vt* to precede, outstrip.

praeesse *infin of* praesum.

praefātiō, -ōnis *f* formula; preface.

praefātus *ppa of* praefor.

praefectūra, -ae *f* superintendence; governorship; *Italian town governed by Roman edicts*, prefecture; district, province.

praefectus *ppp of* praeficiō ♦ *m* overseer, director, governor, commander; ~ **classis** admiral; ~ **legiōnis** colonel; ~ **urbis** *or* **urbī** city prefect (of Rome).

praeferō, -ferre, -tulī, -lātum *vt* to carry in front, hold out; to prefer; to show, display; to anticipate; (*pass*) to hurry past, outflank.

praeferōx, -ōcis *adj* very impetuous, very insolent.

praefervidus *adj* very hot.

praefestīnō, -āre *vi* to be too hasty; to hurry past.

praefica, -ae *f* hired mourner.

praeficiō, -icere, -ēcī, -ectum *vt* to put in charge, give command over.

praefidēns, -entis *adj* over-confident.

praefigō, -gere, -xī, -xum *vt* to fasten in front, set up before; to tip, point; to transfix.

praefiniō, -īre, -īvī *and* **iī, -ītum** *vt* to determine, prescribe.

praefiscinē, -ī *adv* without offence.

praeflōrō, -āre *vt* to tarnish.

praefluō, -ere *vt, vi* to flow past.

praefocō, -āre *vt* to choke.

praefodiō, -odere, -ōdī *vt* to dig in

front of; to bury beforehand.

praefor, -ārī, -ātus vt, vi to say in advance, preface; to pray beforehand; to predict.

praefrāctē adv resolutely.

praefrāctus ppp of **praefringō** ♦ adj abrupt; stern.

praefrīgidus adj very cold.

praefringō, -ingere, -ēgī, -āctum vt to break off, shiver.

praefuī perf of **praesum**.

praefulciō, -cīre, -sī, -tum vi to prop up; to use as a prop.

praefulgeō, -ulgēre, -ulsī vi to shine conspicuously; to outshine.

praegelidus adj very cold.

praegestiō, -īre vi to be very eager.

praegnāns, -antis adj pregnant; full.

praegracilis adj very slim.

praegrandis adj very large, very great.

praegravis adj very heavy; very wearisome.

praegravō, -āre vt to weigh down; to eclipse.

praegredior, -dī, -ssus vt, vi to go before; to go past; to surpass.

praegressiō, -ōnis f precession, precedence.

praegustātor, -ōris m taster

praegustō, -āre vt to taste beforehand.

praehibeō, -ēre vt to offer, give.

praeiaceō, -ēre vt to lie in front of.

praeiūdicium, -ī and **iī** nt precedent, example; prejudgment.

praeiūdicō, -āre, -āvī, -ātum vt to prejudge, decide beforehand

praeiuvō, -āre vt to give previous assistance to.

praelabor, -bī, -psus vt, vi to move past, move along.

praelambō, -ere vt to lick first.

praelātus ppp of **praeferō**.

praelegō, -ere vt to coast along.

praeligō, -āre vt to bind, tie up.

praelongus adj very long, very tall.

praeloquor, -quī, -cūtus vi to speak first.

praelūceō, -cēre, -xī vi to light, shine; to outshine.

praelūstris adj very magnificent.

praemandāta ntpl warrant of arrest.

praemandō, -āre, -āvī, -ātum vt to bespeak.

praemātūrē adv too soon.

praemātūrus adj too early, premature.

praemedicātus adj protected by charms.

praemeditātiō, -ōnis f thinking over the future.

praemeditātus adj premeditated.

praemeditor, -ārī, -ātus vt to think over, practise.

praemetuenter adv anxiously.

praemetuō, -ere vi to be anxious ♦ vt to fear the future.

praemissus ppp of **praemittō**.

praemittō, -ittere, -īsī, -issum vt to send in advance.

praemium, -ī and **iī** nt prize, reward.

praemolestia, -ae f apprehension.

praemōlior, -īrī vt to prepare thoroughly.

praemoneō, -ēre, -uī, -itum vt to forewarn, foreshadow.

praemonitus, -ūs m premonition.

praemōnstrātor, -ōris m guide.

praemōnstrō, -āre vt to guide; to predict.

praemordeō, -ēre vt to bite off; to pilfer.

praemorior, -ī, -tuus vi to die too

The present infinitive verb endings are as follows: **-āre** = 1st; **-ēre** = 2nd; **-ere** = 3rd and **-īre** = 4th. *See sections on irregular verbs and noun declensions.*

soon.

praemūniō, -īre, -īvī, -ītum vt to fortify, strengthen, secure.

praemūnītiō, -ōnis f (RHET) preparation.

praenārrō, -āre vt to tell beforehand.

praenatō, -āre vt to flow past.

Praeneste, -is nt/f Latin town (now Palestrina).

Praenestīnus adj see n.

praeniteō, -ēre, -uī vi to seem more attractive.

praenōmen, -inis nt first name.

praenōscō, -ere vt to foreknow.

praenōtiō, -ōnis f preconceived idea.

praenūbilus adj very gloomy.

praenūntia, -iae f harbinger.

praenūntiō, -āre vt to foretell.

praenūntius, -ī and iī m harbinger.

praeoccupō, -āre, -āvī, -ātum vt to take first, anticipate.

praeolit mihi I get a hint of.

praeoptō, -āre, -āvī, -ātum vt to choose rather, prefer.

praepandō, -ere vt to spread out; to expound.

praeparātiō, -ōnis f preparation.

praeparō, -āre, -āvī, -ātum vt to prepare, prepare for; **ex ~ātō** by arrangement.

praepediō, -īre, -īvī, -ītum vt to shackle, tether; to hamper.

praependeō, -ēre vi to hang down in front.

praepes, -etis adj swift, winged; of good omen ♦ f bird.

praepilātus adj tipped with a ball.

praepinguis adj very rich.

praepolleō, -ēre vi to be very powerful, be superior.

praeponderō, -āre vt to outweigh.

praepōnō, -ōnere, -osuī, -ositum vt to put first, place in front; to put in charge, appoint commander; to prefer.

praeportō, -āre vt to carry before.

praepositiō, -ōnis f preference; (GRAM) preposition.

praepositus ppp of **praepōnō** ♦ m overseer, commander.

praepossum, -sse, -tuī vi to gain the upper hand.

praeposterē adv the wrong way round.

praeposterus adj inverted, perverted; absurd.

praepotēns, -entis adj very powerful.

praeproperanter adv too hastily.

praeproperē adv too hastily.

praeproperus adj overhasty, rash.

praepūtium, -ī and iī nt foreskin.

praequam adv compared with.

praequestus adj complaining beforehand.

praeradiō, -āre vt to outshine.

praerapidus adj very swift.

praereptus ppp of **praeripiō**.

praerigēscō, -ēscere, -uī vi to become very stiff.

praeripiō, -ipere, -ipuī, -eptum vt to take before, forestall; to carry off prematurely; to frustrate.

praerōdō, -dere, -sum vt to bite the end of, nibble off.

praerogātīva, -ae f tribe or century with the first vote, the first vote; previous election; omen, sure token.

praerogātīvus adj voting first.

praerōsus ppp of **praerōdō**.

praerumpō, -umpere, -ūpī, -uptum vt to break off.

praeruptus ppp of **praerumpō** ♦ adj steep, abrupt; headstrong.

praes, -aedis m surety; property of a surety.

praesaep- etc see **praesēp-**.

praesāgiō, -īre vt to have a presentiment of, forebode.

praesāgītiō, -ōnis f foreboding.

praesāgium, -ī and iī nt

presentiment; prediction.
praesāgus adj foreboding,
prophetic.
praesciō, -īre, -īī vt to know
before.
praescīscō, -ere vt to find out
beforehand.
praescius adj foreknowing.
praescrībō, -bere, -psī, -ptum vt to
write first; to direct, command; to
dictate, describe; to put forward
as a pretext.
praescrīptiō, -ōnis f preface,
heading; order, rule; pretext.
praescrīptum, -ī nt order, rule.
praescrīptus ppp of **praescrībō**.
praesecō, -āre, -uī, -tum and
-ātum vt to cut off, pare.
praesēns, -entis adj present, in
person; (things) immediate, ready,
prompt; (mind) resolute; (gods)
propitious ♦ ntpl present state of
affairs; **in ~ēns** for the present;
~in rē ~entī on the spot.
praesēnsiō, -ōnis f foreboding;
preconception.
praesēnsus ppp of **praesentiō**.
praesentārius adj instant, ready.
praesentia, -ae f presence;
effectiveness.
praesentiō, -entīre, -ēnsī, -ēnsum
vt to presage, have a foreboding
of.
praesēpe, -is nt, **-ēs, -is** f stable,
fold, pen; hovel; hive.
praesēpiō, -īre, -sī, -tum vt to
barricade.
praesēpis f = **praesēpe**.
praesertim adv especially.
praeserviō, -īre vi to serve as a
slave.
praeses, -idis m guardian,
protector; chief, ruler.
praesideō, -idēre, -ēdī vi to guard,
defend; to preside over, direct.

praesidiārius adj garrison-.
praesidium, -ī and **iī** nt defence,
protection; support, assistance;
guard, garrison, convoy;
defended position, entrenchment.
praesignificō, -āre vt to
foreshadow.
praesignis adj conspicuous.
praesonō, -āre, -uī vi to sound
before.
praespargō, -ere vt to strew
before.
praestābilis adj outstanding;
preferable.
praestāns, -antis pres p of **praestō**
♦ adj outstanding, pre-eminent.
praestantia, -ae f pre-eminence.
praestes, -itis adj presiding,
guardian.
praestīgiae, -ārum fpl illusion,
sleight of hand.
praestīgiātor, -ōris m, **-rīx, -rīcis** f
conjurer, cheat.
praestinō, -āre vt to buy.
praestitī perf of **praestō**.
praestituō, -uere, -uī, -ūtum vt to
prearrange, prescribe.
praestitus ppp of **praestō**.
praestō adv at hand, ready.
praestō, -āre, -itī, -itum and **ātum**
vi to be outstanding, be superior;
(impers) it is better ♦ vt to excel;
to be responsible for, answer for;
(duty) to discharge, perform;
(quality) to show, prove; (things) to
give, offer, provide; **sē ~** behave,
prove.
praestōlor, -ārī, -ātus vt, vi to wait
for, expect.
praestrictus ppp of **praestringō**.
praestringō, -ingere, -īnxī, -ictum
vt to squeeze; to blunt, dull; (eyes)
to dazzle.
praestruō, -ere, -xī, -ctum vt to
block up; to build beforehand.

*The present infinitive verb endings are as follows: -āre = 1st; -ēre = 2nd; -ere = 3rd and
-īre = 4th. See sections on irregular verbs and noun declensions.*

praesul, -is m/f public dancer.

praesultātor, -ōris m public dancer.

praesultō, -āre vi to dance before.

praesum, -esse, -fuī vi (with dat) to be at the head of, be in command of; to take the lead; to protect.

praesūmō, -ere, -psī, -ptum vt to take first; to anticipate; to take for granted.

praesūtus adj sewn over at the point.

praetemptō, -āre vt to feel for, grope for; to test in advance.

praetendō, -dere, -dī, -tum vt to hold out, put before, spread in front of; to give as an excuse, allege.

praetentō etc see **praetemptō**.

praetentus ppp of **praetendō** ♦ adj lying over against.

praetepeō, -ēre, -uī vi to glow before.

praeter adv beyond; excepting ♦ prep (with acc) past, along; except, besides; beyond, more than, in addition to, contrary to.

praeteragō, -ere vt to drive past.

praeterbitō, -ere vt, vi to pass by.

praeterdūcō, -ere vt to lead past.

praptereā adv besides; moreover; henceforth.

praetereō, -īre, -iī, -itum vi to go past ♦ vt to pass, overtake; to escape, escape the notice of; to omit, leave out, forget, neglect; to reject, exclude; to surpass; to transgress.

praeterequitāns, -antis adj riding past.

praeterfluō, -ere vt, vi to flow past.

praetergredior, -dī, -ssus vt to pass, march past; to surpass.

praeterhāc adv further, more.

praeteritus ppp of **praetereō** ♦ adj past, gone by ♦ ntpl the past.

praeterlābor, -bī, -psus vt to flow

past, move past ♦ vi to slip away.

praeterlātus adj driving, flying past.

praetermeō, -āre vi to pass by.

praetermissiō, -ōnis f omission, passing over.

praetermittō, -ittere, -īsī, -issum vt to let pass; to omit, neglect; to make no mention of; to overlook.

praeterquam adv except, besides.

praetervectiō, -ōnis f passing by.

praetervehor, -hī, -ctus vt, vi to ride past, sail past; to march past; to pass by, pass over.

praetervolō, -āre vt, vi to fly past; to escape.

praetexō, -ere, -uī, -tum vt to border, fringe; to adorn; to pretend, disguise.

praetextātus adj wearing the toga praetexta, under age.

praetextus ppp of **praetexō** ♦ adj wearing the toga praetexta ♦ f toga with a purple border; Roman tragedy ♦ nt pretext.

praetextus, -ūs m splendour; pretence.

praetimeō, -ēre vi to be afraid in advance.

praetinctus adj dipped beforehand.

praetor, -ōris m chief magistrate, commander; praetor; propraetor, governor.

praetōriānus adj of the emperor's bodyguard.

praetōrium, -ī and **iī** nt general's tent, camp headquarters; governor's residence; council of war; palace, grand building; emperor's bodyguard.

praetōrius adj praetor's, praetorian; of a propraetor; of the emperor's bodyguard ♦ m ex-praetor; **~ia cohors** bodyguard of general or emperor; **porta ~ia** camp gate facing the enemy.

praetorqueō, -ēre *vt* to strangle first.

praetrepidāns, -antis *adj* very impatient.

praetruncō, -āre *vt* to cut off.

praetulī *perf of* **praeferō**.

praetūra, -ae *f* praetorship.

praeumbrāns, -antis *adj* obscuring.

praeut *adv* compared with.

praevaleō, -ēre, -uī *vi* to be very powerful, have most influence, prevail.

praevalidus *adj* very strong, very powerful; too strong.

praevāricātiō, -ōnis *f* collusion.

praevāricātor, -ōris *m* advocate guilty of collusion.

praevāricor, -ārī, -ātus *vi* (*with dat*) to favour by collusion

praevehor, -hī, -ctus *vi* to ride, fly in front, flow past.

praeveniō, -enīre, -ēnī, -entum *vt, vi* to come before; to anticipate, prevent.

praeverrō, -ere *vt* to sweep before.

praevertō, -ere, -ī, -or, -ī *vt* to put first, prefer; to turn to first, attend first to; to outstrip; to anticipate, frustrate, prepossess.

praevideō, -idēre, -īdī, -īsum *vt* to foresee.

praevitiō, -āre *vt* to taint beforehand.

praevius *adj* leading the way.

praevolō, -āre *vi* to fly in front.

pragmaticus *adj* of affairs ♦ *m* legal expert.

prandeō, -ēre, -ī *vi* to take lunch ♦ *vt* to eat.

prandium, -ī *and* **iī** *nt* lunch.

prānsor, -ōris *m* guest at lunch.

prānsus *adj* having lunched, fed.

prasinus *adj* green.

prātēnsis *adj* meadow.

prātulum, -ī *nt* small meadow.

prātum, -ī *nt* meadow; grass.

prāvē *adv* wrongly, badly.

prāvitās, -ātis *f* irregularity, perverseness, depravity.

prāvus *adj* crooked, deformed; perverse, bad, wicked.

Prāxitelēs, -is *m* famous Greek sculptor.

Prāxitelīus *adj* see n.

precāriō *adv* by request.

precārius *adj* obtained by entreaty.

precātiō, -ōnis *f* prayer.

precātor, -ōris *m* intercessor.

preces *pl of* **prex**.

preciae, -ārum *fpl* kind of vine.

precor, -ārī, -ātus *vi, vt* to pray, beg, entreat; to wish (well), curse.

prehendō, -endere, -endī, -ēnsum *vt* to take hold of, catch; to seize, detain; to surprise; (*eye*) to take in; (*mind*) to grasp.

prehēnsō *etc see* **prēnsō**.

prehēnsus *ppp of* **prehendō**.

prēlum, -ī *nt* wine press, oil press.

premō, -mere, -ssī, -ssum *vt* to press, squeeze; to press together, compress; (*eyes*) to close; (*reins*) to tighten; (*trees*) to prune; to press upon, lie, sit, stand on, cover, conceal, surpass; to press hard on, follow closely; (*coast*) to hug; to press down, lower, burden; (*fig*) to overcome, rule; (*words*) to disparage; to press in, sink, stamp, plant; to press back, repress, check, stop.

prendō *etc see* **prehendō**.

prēnsātiō, -ōnis *f* canvassing.

prēnsō (prehēnsō), -āre, -āvī, -ātum *vt* to clutch at, take hold of, buttonhole.

prēnsus *ppp of* **prehendō**.

The present infinitive verb endings are as follows: **-āre** = 1st; **-ēre** = 2nd; **-ere** = 3rd and **-īre** = 4th. *See sections on irregular verbs and noun declensions.*

presbyter, -ī m (ECCL) elder.

pressē adv concisely, accurately, simply.

pressī perf of **premō**.

pressiō, -ōnis f fulcrum.

pressō, -āre vt to press.

pressus ppp of **premō** ♦ adj (style) concise, compressed; (pace) slow; (voice) subdued.

pressus, -ūs m pressure.

prēstēr, -ēris m waterspout.

pretiōsē adv expensively.

pretiōsus adj valuable, expensive; extravagant.

pretium, -ī and **iī** nt price; value; worth; money, fee, reward; **māgnī ~ī, in ~iō** valuable; **operae ~** worth while.

prex, -ecis f request, entreaty; prayer; good wish; curse.

Priamēis, -ēidis f Cassandra.

Priamēius adj see **Priamus**.

Priamidēs, -idae m son of Priam.

Priamus, -ī m king of Troy.

Priāpus, -ī m god of fertility and of gardens.

prīdem adv long ago, long.

prīdiē adv the day before.

prīmaevus adj youthful.

prīmānī, -ōrum mpl soldiers of the 1st legion.

prīmārius adj principal, first-rate.

prīmigenus adj original.

prīmipīlāris, -is m chief centurion.

prīmipīlus, -ī m chief centurion.

prīmitiae, -ārum fpl first fruits.

prīmitus adv originally.

prīmō adv at first; firstly.

prīmōrdium, -ī and **iī** nt beginning; **~ia rērum** atoms.

prīmōris, -is adj first, foremost, tip of; principal ♦ mpl nobles; (MIL) front line.

prīmulum adv first.

prīmulus adj very first.

prīmum adv first, to begin with, in the first place; for the first time;

cum, ubi, ut ~ as soon as; **quam ~** as soon as possible; **~ dum** in the first place.

prīmus adj first, foremost, tip of; earliest; principal, most eminent; **~ veniō** I am the first to come; **prima lux** dawn, daylight; **~ō mēnse** at the beginning of the month; **~īs digitīs** with the fingertips; **~ās agere** play the leading part; **~ās dare** give first place to; **in ~īs** in the front line; especially.

prīnceps, -ipis adj first, in front, chief, most eminent ♦ m leader, chief; first citizen, emperor; (MIL) company, captain, captaincy ♦ pl (MIL) the second line.

prīncipālis adj original; chief; the emperor's.

prīncipātus, -ūs m first place; post of commander-in-chief; emperorship.

prīncipiālis adj from the beginning.

prīncipium, -ī and **iī** nt beginning, origin; first to vote ♦ pl first principles; (MIL) front line; camp headquarters.

prior, -ōris (nt **-us**) adj former, previous, first; better, preferable ♦ mpl forefathers.

prīscē adv strictly.

prīscus adj former, ancient, old-fashioned.

prīstinus adj former, original; of yesterday.

prius adv previously, before; in former times; **~ quam** before, sooner than.

prīvātim adv individually, privately; at home.

prīvātiō, -ōnis f removal.

prīvātus adj individual, private; not in public office ♦ m private citizen.

Prīvernās, -ātis adj see n.

Prīvernum, -ī nt old Latin town.

prīvīgna, -ae f stepdaughter.

prīvīgnus, -ī m stepson; pl stepchildren.

prīvilēgium, -ī and **iī** nt law in favour of or against an individual.

prīvō, -āre, -āvī, -ātum vt to deprive, rob; to free.

prīvus adj single, one each; own, private.

prō adv (with **ut** and **quam**) in proportion (as) ♦ prep (with abl) in front of, on the front of; for, on behalf of, instead of, in return for; as, as good as; according to, in proportion to, by virtue of; **~ eō ac** just as; **~ eō quod** just because; **~ eō quantum, ut** in proportion as.

prō interj (expressing wonder or sorrow) O!, alas!

proāgorus, -ī m chief magistrate (in Sicilian towns).

proavītus adj ancestral.

proavus, -ī m great-grandfather, ancestor.

probābilis adj laudable; credible, probable.

probābilitās, -ātis f credibility.

probābiliter adv credibly.

probātiō, -ōnis f approval, testing.

probātor, -ōris m approver.

probātus adj tried, excellent; acceptable.

probē adv well, properly; thoroughly, well done!

probitās, -ātis f goodness, honesty.

probō, -āre, -āvī, -ātum vt to approve, approve of; to appraise; to recommend; to prove, show.

probrōsus adj abusive; disgraceful.

probrum, -ī nt abuse, reproach; disgrace; infamy, unchastity.

probus adj good, excellent; honest, upright.

procācitās, -ātis f impudence.

procāciter adv insolently.

procāx, -ācis adj bold, forward, insolent.

prōcēdō, -ēdere, -essī, -essum vi to go forward, advance; to go out, come forth; (time) to go on, continue; (fig) to make progress, get on; (events) to turn out, succeed.

procella, -ae f hurricane, storm; (MIL) charge.

procellōsus adj stormy.

procer, -is m chief, noble, prince.

prōcēritās, -ātis f height; length.

prōcērus adj tall; long.

prōcessiō, -ōnis f advance.

prōcessus, -ūs m advance, progress.

prōcidō, -ere, -ī vi to fall forwards, fall down.

prōcinctus, -ūs m readiness (for action).

prōclāmātor, -ōris m bawler.

prōclāmō, -āre vi to cry out.

prōclīnātus adj tottering.

prōclīnō, -āre vt to bend.

prōclīve adv downwards; easily.

prōclīvis, -us adj downhill, steep; (mind) prone, willing; (act) easy; in **~ī** easy.

prōclīvitās, -ātis f descent; tendency.

prōclīvus etc see **prōclīvis**.

Procnē, -ēs f wife of Tereus (changed to a swallow); swallow.

prōcōnsul, -is m proconsul, governor.

prōcōnsulāris adj proconsular.

prōcōnsulātus, -ūs m proconsulship.

prōcrāstinātiō, -ōnis f procrastination.

prōcrāstinō, -āre vt to put off from

The present infinitive verb endings are as follows: -āre = 1st; -ēre = 2nd; -ere = 3rd and -īre = 4th. See sections on irregular verbs and noun declensions.

day to day.

prōcreātiō, -ōnis f begetting.

prōcreātor, -ōris m creator, parent.

prōcreātrīx, -īcis f mother.

prōcreō, -āre vt to beget, produce.

prōcrēscō, -ere vi to be produced, grow up.

Procrūstēs, -ae m Attic highwayman (who tortured victims on a bed).

prōcubō, -āre vi to lie on the ground.

prōcūdō, -dere, -dī, -sum vt to forge; to produce.

procul adv at a distance, far, from afar.

prōculcō, -āre vt to trample down.

prōcumbō, -mbere, -buī, -bitum vi to fall forwards, bend over; to sink down, be broken down.

prōcūrātiō, -ōnis f management; (religion) expiation.

prōcūrātor, -ōris m administrator, financial agent; (province) governor.

prōcūrātrīx, -īcis f governess.

prōcūrō, -āre, -āvī, -ātum vt to take care of, manage; to expiate ♦ vi to be a procurator.

prōcurrō, -rrere, -currī and **rrī, -rsum** vi to rush forward; to jut out.

prōcursātiō, -ōnis f charge.

prōcursātor, -ōris m skirmisher.

prōcursō, -āre vi to make a sally.

prōcursus, -ūs m charge.

prōcurvus adj curving forwards.

procus, -ī m nobleman.

procus, -ī m wooer, suitor.

Procyōn, -ōnis m Lesser Dog Star.

prōdeambulō, -āre vi to go out for a walk.

prōdeō, -īre, -iī, -itum vi to come out, come forward, appear; to go ahead, advance; to project.

prōdesse infin of **prōsum**.

prōdīcō, -īcere, -īxī, -ictum vt to appoint, adjourn.

prōdictātor, -ōris m vice-dictator.

prōdigē adv extravagantly.

prōdigentia, -ae f profusion.

prōdigiāliter adv unnaturally.

prōdigiōsus adj unnatural, marvellous.

prōdigium, -ī and **iī** nt portent; unnatural deed; monster.

prōdigō, -igere, -ēgī, -āctum vt to squander.

prōdigus adj wasteful; lavish, generous.

prōditiō, -ōnis f betrayal.

prōditor, -ōris m traitor.

prōditus ppp of **prōdō**.

prōdō, -ere, -idī, -itum vt to bring forth, produce; to make known, publish; to betray, give up; (tradition) to hand down.

prōdoceō, -ēre vt to preach.

prōdromus, -ī m forerunner.

prōdūcō, -ūcere, -ūxī, -uctum vt to bring forward, bring out; to conduct; to drag in front; to draw out, extend; (acting) to perform; (child) to beget, bring up; (fact) to bring to light; (innovation) to introduce; (rank) to promote; (slave) to put up for sale; (time) to prolong, protract, put off; (tree) to cultivate; (vowel) to lengthen.

prōductē adv long.

prōductiō, -ōnis f lengthening.

prōductō, -āre vt to spin out.

prōductus ppp of **prōdūcō** ♦ adj lengthened, long.

proēgmenon, -ī nt a preferred thing.

proeliātor, -ōris m fighter.

proelior, -ārī, -ātus vi to fight, join battle.

proelium, -ī and **iī** nt battle, conflict.

profānō, -āre vt to desecrate.

profānus adj unholy, common;

impious; ill-omened.

profātus ppa of profor.

profectiō, -ōnis f departure;
source.

profectō adv really, certainly.

profectus ppa of proficiscor.

prōfectus ppp of prōficiō.

prōfectus, -ūs m growth, progress,
profit.

prōferō, -ferre, -tulī, -lātum vt to
bring forward, forth or out; to
extend, enlarge; (time) to prolong,
defer; (instance) to mention,
quote; (knowledge) to publish,
reveal; **pedem ~** proceed; **signa ~**
advance.

professiō, -ōnis f declaration;
public register; profession.

professor, -ōris m teacher.

professōrius adj authoritative.

professus ppa of profiteor.

profēstus adj not holiday, working.

prōficiō, -icere, -ēcī, -ectum vi to
make progress, profit; to be of
use.

proficīscor, -icīscī, -ectus vi to set
out, start; to originate, proceed.

profiteor, -itērī, -essus vt to
declare, profess; to make an
official return of; to promise,
volunteer.

prōflīgātor, -ōris m spendthrift.

prōflīgātus adj dissolute.

prōflīgō, -āre, -āvī, -ātum vt to
dash to the ground; to destroy,
overthrow; to bring almost to an
end; to degrade.

prōflō, -āre vi to breathe out.

prōfluēns, -entis pres p of prōfluō
♦ adj flowing; fluent ♦ f running
water.

prōfluenter adv easily.

prōfluentia, -ae f fluency.

prōfluō, -ere, -xī vi to flow on, flow
out; (fig) to proceed.

prōfluvium, -ī and **iī** nt flowing.

profor, -ārī, -ātus vi to speak, give
utterance.

profugiō, -ugere, -ūgī vi to flee,
escape; to take refuge (with) ♦ vt
to flee from.

profugus adj fugitive; exiled;
nomadic.

prōfuī perf of prōsum.

profundō, -undere, -ūdī, -ūsum vt
to pour out, shed; to bring forth,
produce; to prostrate; to
squander; **sē ~** burst forth, rush
out.

profundus adj deep, vast, high;
infernal; (fig) profound,
immoderate ♦ nt depths, abyss.

profūsē adv in disorder,
extravagantly.

profūsus ppp of profundō ♦ adj
lavish; excessive.

prōgener, -ī m grandson-in-law.

prōgenerō, -āre vt to beget.

prōgeniēs, -ēī f descent;
offspring, descendants.

prōgenitor, -ōris m ancestor.

prōgignō, -ignere, -enuī, -enitum
vt to beget, produce.

prōgnātus adj born, descended
♦ m son, descendant.

Prognē see Procnē.

prōgnōstica, -ōrum ntpl weather
signs.

prōgredior, -dī, -ssus vi to go
forward, advance; to go out.

prōgressiō, -ōnis f advancing,
increase; (RHET) climax.

prōgressus pp of prōgredior.

prōgressus, -ūs m advance,
progress; (events) march.

prōh see prō interj.

prohibeō, -ēre, -uī, -itum vt to
hinder, prevent; to keep away,
protect; to forbid.

prohibitiō, -ōnis f forbidding.

---

*The present infinitive verb endings are as follows: -āre = 1st; -ēre = 2nd; -ere = 3rd and
-īre = 4th. See sections on irregular verbs and noun declensions.*

prōiciō, -icere, -iēcī, -iectum *vt* to throw down, fling forwards; to banish; *(building)* to make project; *(fig)* to discard, renounce; to forsake; *(words)* to blurt out; *(time)* to defer; **sē ~** rush forward, run into danger; to fall prostrate.

prōiectiō, -ōnis *f* forward stretch.

prōiectus *ppp of* **prōiciō** ♦ *adj* projecting, prominent; abject, useless; downcast; addicted (to).

prōiectus, -ūs *m* jutting out.

proinde, proin *adv* consequently, therefore; just (as).

prōlābor, -bī, -psus *vi* to slide, move forward; to fall down; *(fig)* to go on, come to; to slip out; to fail, fall, sink into ruin.

prōlāpsiō, -ōnis *f* falling.

prōlāpsus *ppa of* **prōlābor**.

prōlātiō, -ōnis *f* extension; postponement; adducing.

prōlātō, -āre *vt* to extend; to postpone.

prōlātus *ppp of* **prōferō**.

prōlectō, -āre *vt* to entice.

prōlēs, -is *f* offspring, child; descendants, race.

prōlētārius, -ī *and* **iī** *m* citizen of the lowest class.

prōliciō, -cere, -xī *vt* to entice.

prōlixē *adv* fully, copiously, willingly.

prōlixus *adj* long, wide, spreading; *(person)* obliging; *(CIRCS)* favourable.

prōlōgus, -ī *m* prologue.

prōloquor, -quī, -cūtus *vt* to speak out.

prōlubium, -ī *and* **iī** *nt* inclination.

prōlūdō, -dere, -sī, -sum *vi* to practise.

prōluō, -uere, -uī, -ūtum *vt* to wash out, wash away.

prōlūsiō, -ōnis *f* prelude.

prōluviēs, -ēī *f* flood; excrement.

prōmereō, -ēre, -uī; prōmereor,

-ērī, -itus *vt* to deserve, earn.

prōmeritum, -ī *nt* desert, merit, guilt.

Promētheus, -eī *and* **eos** *m* demigod who stole fire from the gods.

Promētheus *adj see n.*

prōminēns, -entis *pres p of* **prōmineō** ♦ *adj* projecting ♦ *nt* headland, spur.

prōmineō, -ēre, -uī *vi* to jut out, overhang; to extend.

prōmiscam, -ē, -uē *adv* indiscriminately.

prōmiscuus (prōmiscus) *adj* indiscriminate, in common; ordinary; open to all.

prōmīsī *perf of* **prōmittō**.

prōmissiō, -ōnis *f* promise.

prōmissor, -ōris *m* promiser.

prōmissum, -ī *nt* promise.

prōmissus *ppp of* **prōmittō** ♦ *adj* long.

prōmittō, -ittere, -īsī, -issum *vt* to let grow; to promise, give promise of.

prōmō, -ere, -psī, -ptum *vt* to bring out, produce; to disclose.

prōmont- *etc see* **prōmunt-**.

prōmōtus *ppp of* **prōmoveō** ♦ *ntpl* preferable things.

prōmoveō, -ovēre, -ōvī, -ōtum *vt* to move forward, advance; to enlarge; to postpone; to disclose.

prōmpsī *perf of* **prōmō**.

prōmptē *adv* readily; easily.

prōmptō, -āre *vt* to distribute.

prōmptū *abl m* : **in ~** at hand, in readiness; obvious, in evidence; easy.

prōmptus *ppp of* **prōmō** ♦ *adj* at hand, ready; prompt, resolute; easy.

prōmulgātiō, -ōnis *f* promulgating.

prōmulgō, -āre, -āvī, -ātum *vt* to make public, publish.

prōmulsis, -idis *f* hors d'oeuvre.

prōmunturium, -ī and **iī** nt headland, promontory, ridge.

prōmus, -ī m cellarer, butler.

prōmūtuus adj as a loan in advance.

prōnepōs, -ōtis m great-grandson.

pronoea, -ae f providence.

prōnōmen, -inis nt pronoun.

prōnuba, -ae f matron attending a bride.

prōnūntiātiō, -ōnis f declaration; (RHET) delivery; (logic) proposition.

prōnūntiātor, -ōris m narrator.

prōnūntiātum, -ātī nt proposition.

prōnūntiō, -āre, -āvī, -ātum vt to declare publicly, announce; to recite, deliver; to narrate; to nominate.

prōnurus, -ūs f granddaughter-in-law.

prōnus adj leaning forward; headlong, downwards; sloping, sinking; (fig) inclined, disposed, favourable; easy.

prooemium, -ī and **iī** nt prelude, preface.

propāgātiō, -ōnis f propagating; extension.

propāgātor, -ōris m enlarger.

propāgō, -āre, -āvī, -ātum vt to propagate; to extend; to prolong.

propāgō, -inis f (plant) layer, slip; (men) offspring, posterity.

prōpalam adv openly, known.

prōpatulum, -ī nt open space.

prōpatulus adj open.

prope adv (comp **propius**, superl **proximē**) near; nearly ♦ prep (with acc) near, not far from.

propediem adv very soon.

prōpellō, -ellere, -ulī, -ulsum vt to drive, push forward, impel; to drive away, keep off.

propemodum, -o adv almost.

prōpendeō, -endēre, -endī,

-ēnsum vi to hang down; to preponderate; to be disposed (to).

propēnsē adv willingly.

prōpēnsiō, -ōnis f inclination.

propēnsus adj inclining; inclined, well-disposed; important.

properanter adv hastily, quickly.

properantia, -ae f haste.

properātiō, -ōnis f haste.

properātō adv quickly.

properātus adj speedy.

properē adv quickly.

properipēs, -edis adj swiftfooted.

properō, -āre, -āvī, -ātum vi to hasten, do with haste ♦ vi to make haste, hurry.

Propertius, -ī m Latin elegiac poet.

properus adj quick, hurrying.

prōpexus adj combed forward.

propīnō, -āre vt to drink as a toast; to pass on (a cup).

propinquitās, -ātis f nearness; relationship, friendship.

propinquō, -āre vi to approach ♦ vt to hasten.

propinquus adj near, neighbouring; related ♦ m/f relation ♦ nt neighbourhood.

propior, -ōris adj nearer; more closely related, more like; (time) more recent.

propitiō, -āre vt to appease.

propitius adj favourable, gracious.

propius adv nearer, more closely.

prōpōla, -ae f retailer.

prōpolluō, -ere vt to defile further.

prōpōnō, -ōnere, -osuī, -ositum vt to set forth, display; to publish, declare; to propose, resolve; to imagine; to expose; (logic) to state the first premise; **ante oculōs ~** picture to oneself.

Propontiacus adj see n.

Propontis, -idis and **idos** f Sea of Marmora.

The present infinitive verb endings are as follows: **-āre** = 1st; **-ēre** = 2nd; **-ere** = 3rd and **-īre** = 4th. *See sections on irregular verbs and noun declensions.*

prōporrō adv furthermore; utterly.

prōportiō, -ōnis f symmetry, analogy.

prōpositiō, -ōnis f purpose; theme; (logic) first premise.

prōpositum, -ī nt plan, purpose; theme; (logic) first premise.

prōpositus ppp of **prōpōnō**.

prōpraetor, -ōris m propraetor, governor; vice-praetor.

propriē adv properly, strictly; particularly.

proprietās, -ātis f peculiarity, property.

proprītim adv properly.

proprius adj one's own, peculiar; personal, characteristic; permanent; (words) literal, regular.

propter adv near by ♦ prep (with acc) near, beside; on account of; by means of.

proptereā adv therefore.

prōpudium, -ī and **iī** nt shameful act; villain.

prōpugnāculum, -ī nt bulwark, tower; defence.

prōpugnātiō, -ōnis f defence.

prōpugnātor, -ōris m defender, champion.

prōpugnō, -āre vi to make a sortie; to fight in defence.

prōpulsātiō, -ōnis f repulse.

prōpulsō, -āre, -āvī, -ātum vt to repel, avert.

prōpulsus ppp of **prōpellō**.

Propylaea, -ōrum ntpl gateway to the Acropolis of Athens.

prō quaestōre m proquaestor.

prōquam conj according as.

prōra, -ae f prow, bows; ship.

prōrēpō, -ere, -sī, -tum vi to crawl out.

prōrēta -ae m man at the prow.

prōreus, -eī m man at the prow.

prōripiō, -ipere, -ipuī, -eptum vt to

drag out; to hurry away; sē ~ rush out, run away.

prōrogātiō, -ōnis f extension; deferring.

prōrogō, -āre, -āvī, -ātum vt to extend, prolong, continue; to defer.

prōrsum adv forwards; absolutely.

prōrsus adv forwards; absolutely; in short.

prōrumpō, -umpere, -ūpī, -uptum vt to fling out; (pass) to rush forth ♦ vi to break out, burst forth.

prōruō, -ere, -ī, -tum vt to throw down, demolish ♦ vi to rush forth.

prōruptus ppp of **prōrumpō**.

prōsāpia, -ae f lineage.

proscaenium, -ī and **iī** nt stage.

proscindō, -ndere, -dī, -ssum vt to plough up; (fig) to revile.

prōscrībō, -bere, -psī, -ptum vt to publish in writing; to advertise; to confiscate; to proscribe, outlaw.

prōscriptiō, -ōnis f advertisement; proscription.

prōscripturiō, -īre vi to want to have a proscription.

prōscriptus ppp of **prōscrībō** ♦ m outlaw.

prōsecō, -āre, -uī, -tum vt to cut off (for sacrifice).

prōsēminō, -āre vt to scatter; to propagate.

prōsentiō, -entīre, -ēnsī vt to see beforehand.

prōsequor, -quī, -cūtus vt to attend, escort; to pursue, attack; to honour (with); (words) to proceed with, continue.

Proserpina, -ae f Proserpine (daughter of Ceres and wife of Pluto).

proseucha, -ae f place of prayer.

prōsiliō, -īre, -uī vi to jump up, spring forward; to burst out, spurt.

prōsocer, -ī m wife's grandfather.

prōspectō, -āre vt to look out at,

view; to look forward to, await;
(place) to look towards.
prōspectus ppp of **prōspiciō**.
prōspectus, -ūs m sight, view,
prospect; gaze.
prōspeculor, -ārī vi to look out,
reconnoitre ♦ vt to watch for.
prosper, prosperus adj
favourable, successful.
prospere adv see adj.
prosperitās, -ātis f good fortune.
prosperō, -āre vt to make
successful, prosper.
prosperus etc see **prosper.**
prōspicientia, -ae f foresight.
prōspiciō, -icere, -exī, -ectum vi to
look out, watch; to see to, take
precautions ♦ vt to descry, watch
for; to foresee; to provide; (place)
to command a view of.
prōsternō, -ernere, -rāvī, -rātum
vt to throw in front, prostrate; to
overthrow, ruin; sē ~ fall
prostrate; to demean oneself.
prōstibulum, -ī nt prostitute.
prōstituō, -uere, -uī, -ūtum vt to
put up for sale, prostitute.
prōstō, -āre, -itī vi to project; to be
on sale; to prostitute oneself.
prōstrātus ppp of **prōsternō.**
prōsubigō, -ere vt to dig up.
prōsum, -desse, -fuī vi (with dat) to
be useful to, benefit.
Prōtagorās, -ae m Greek sophist
(native of Abdera).
prōtectus ppp of **prōtegō.**
prōtegō, -egere, -exī, -ectum vt to
cover over, put a projecting roof
on; (fig) to shield, protect.
prōtēlō, -āre vt to drive off.
prōtēlum, -ī nt team of oxen; (fig)
succession.
prōtendō, -dere, -dī, -tum vt to
stretch out, extend.
prōtentus ppp of **prōtendō.**

prōterō, -erere, -rīvī, -rītum vt to
trample down, crush; to
overthrow.
prōterreō, -ēre, -uī, -itum vt to
scare away.
prōtervē adv insolently; boldly.
prōtervitās, -ātis f forwardness,
insolence.
prōtervus adj forward, insolent,
violent.
Prōtesilāeus adj see n.
Prōtesilāus, -ī m first Greek killed at
Troy.
Prōteus, -eī and **eos** m seagod with
power to assume many forms.
prothȳmē adv gladly.
prōtinam adv immediately.
prōtinus adv forward, onward;
continuously; right away,
forthwith.
prōtollō, -ere vt to stretch out; to
put off.
prōtractus ppp of **prōtrahō.**
prōtrahō, -here, -xī, -ctum vt to
draw on (to); to drag out; to bring
to light, reveal.
prōtrītus ppp of **prōterō.**
prōtrūdō, -dere, -sī, -sum vt to
thrust forward, push out; to
postpone.
prōtuli perf of **prōferō.**
prōturbō, ārn, -āvī, -ātum vt to
drive off; to overthrow.
prout conj according as.
prōvectus ppp of **prōvehō ♦** adj
advanced.
prōvehō, -here, -xī, -ctum vt to
carry along, transport; to
promote, advance, bring to;
(speech) to prolong; (pass) to
drive, ride, sail on.
prōveniō, -enīre, -ēnī, -entum vi
to come out, appear; to arise,
grow; to go on, prosper, succeed.
prōventus, -ūs m increase; result,

success.

prōverbium, -ī *and* **iī** *nt* saying, proverb.

prōvidēns, -entis *pres p of* **prōvideō ♦** *adj* prudent.

prōvidenter *adv* with foresight.

prōvidentia, -ae *f* foresight, forethought.

prōvideō, -idēre, -īdī, -īsum *vi* to see ahead; to take care, make provision **♦** *vt* to foresee; to look after, provide for; to obviate.

prōvidus *adj* foreseeing, cautious, prudent; provident.

prōvincia, -ae *f* sphere of action, duty, province.

prōvinciālis *adj* provincial **♦** *mpl* provincials.

prōvīsiō, -ōnis *f* foresight; precaution.

prōvīsō *adv* with forethought.

prōvīsō, -ere *vi* to go and see.

prōvīsor, -ōris *m* foreseer; provider.

prōvīsus *ppp of* **prōvideō.**

prōvīsus, -ūs *m* looking forward; foreseeing; providing providence.

prōvīvō, -vere, -xī *vi* to live on.

prōvocātiō, -ōnis *f* challenge; appeal.

prōvocātor, -ōris *m* kind of gladiator.

prōvocō, -āre, -āvī, -ātum *vt* to challenge, call out; to provoke; to bring about **♦** *vi* to fly out, rush out.

prōvolō, -āre *vi* to fly out, rush out.

prōvolvō, -vere, -vī, -ūtum *vt* to roll forward, tumble over; (*pass*) to fall down, humble oneself, be ruined; **sē ~** wallow.

prōvomō, -ere *vi* to belch forth.

proximē *adv* next, nearest; (*time*) just before *or* after; (*with acc*) next to, very close to, very like.

proximitās, -ātis *f* nearness; near relationship; similarity.

proximus *adj* nearest, next; (*time*) previous, last, following, next; most akin, most like **♦** *m* next of kin **♦** *nt* next door.

proxum *etc see* **proxim-.**

prūdēns, -entis *adj* foreseeing, aware; wise, prudent, circumspect; skilled, versed (in).

prūdenter *adv* prudently; skilfully.

prūdentia, -ae *f* prudence, discretion; knowledge.

pruīna, -ae *f* hoar frost.

pruīnōsus *adj* frosty.

prūna, -ae *f* live coal.

prūnitius *adj* of plum tree wood.

prūnum, -ī *nt* plum.

prūnus, -ī *f* plum tree.

prūriō, -īre *vi* to itch.

prytanēum, -ī *nt* Greek town hall.

prytanis, -is *m* Greek chief magistrate.

psallō, -ere *vi* to play the lyre *or* lute.

psaltērium, -ī *and* **iī** *nt* kind of lute.

psaltria, -ae *f* girl musician.

psecas, -adis *f* slave who perfumed the lady's hair.

psēphisma, -tis *nt* decree of the people.

Pseudocatō, -ōnis *m* sham Cato.

pseudomenos, -ī *m* sophistical argument.

pseudothyrum, -ī *nt* back door.

psithius *adj* psithian (*kind of Greek vine*).

psittacus, -ī *m* parrot.

psychomantēum (-īum), -ī *nt* place of necromancy.

ptisanārium, -ī *nt* gruel.

-pte *enclitic* (*to pronouns*) self, own.

Ptolemaeēus, -us *adj see* n.

Ptolemaeus, -ī *m* Ptolemy (*name of Egyptian kings*).

pūbēns, -entis *adj* full-grown; (*plant*) juicy.

pūbertās, -ātis *f* manhood; signs

of puberty.

pūbēs (pūber), -eris adj grown up, adult; (plant) downy.

pūbēs, -is f hair at age of puberty; groin; youth, men, people.

pūbēscō, -ēscere, -uī vi to grow to manhood, become mature; to become clothed.

pūblicānus adj of public revenue ♦ m tax farmer.

pūblicātiō, -ōnis f confiscation.

pūblicē adv by or for the State, at the public expense; all together.

pūblicitus adv at the public expense; in public.

pūblicō, -āre, -āvī, -ātum vt to confiscate; to make public.

Pūblicola, -ae m P. Valerius (an early Roman consul).

pūblicum, -ī nt State revenue; State territory; public.

pūblicus adj of the State, public, common ♦ m public official; ~a causa criminal trial; rēs ~a the State; dē ~ō at the public expense; in ~ō in public.

Pūblius, -ī m Roman first name.

pudendus adj shameful.

pudēns, -entis adj bashful, modest.

pudenter adv modestly.

pudet, -ēre, -uit and itum est vt (impers) to shame, be ashamed.

pudibundus adj modest.

pudīcē adv see adj.

pudīcitia, -ae f modesty, chastity.

pudīcus adj modest, chaste.

pudor, -ōris m shame, modesty, sense of honour; disgrace.

puella, -ae f girl; sweetheart, young wife.

puellāris adj girlish, youthful.

puellula, -ae f little girl.

puellus, -ī m little boy.

puer, -ī m boy, child; son; slave.

puerīlis adj boyish, child's; childish, trivial.

puerīliter adv like a child; childishly.

pueritia, -ae f childhood, youth.

puerperium, -ī and iī nt childbirth.

puerperus adj to help childbirth ♦ f woman in labour.

puertia etc see **pueritia**.

puerulus, -ī m little boy, slave.

pugil, -is m boxer.

pugilātiō, -iōnis f, -us, -ūs m boxing.

pugillāris adj that can be held in the hand ♦ mpl, ntpl writing tablets.

pugillātōrius adj : follis ~ punchball.

pugiō, -ōnis m dirk, dagger.

pugiunculus, -ī m small dagger.

pugna, -ae f fight, battle.

pugnācitās, -ātis f fondness for a fight.

pugnāciter adv aggressively.

pugnāculum, -ī nt fortress.

pugnātor, -ōris m fighter.

pugnāx, -ācis adj fond of a fight, aggressive; obstinate.

pugneus adj with the fist.

pugnō, -āre, -āvī, -ātum vi to fight; to disagree; to struggle; sēcum ~ be inconsistent; ~ātum est the battle was fought.

pugnus, -ī m fist.

pulchellus adj pretty little.

pulcher, -rī adj beautiful, handsome; fine, glorious.

pulchrē adv excellently; well done!

pulchritūdō, -inis f beauty, excellence.

pūlēium, pūleglum, -ī and iī nt pennyroyal.

pūlex, -icis m flea.

pullārius, -ī and iī m keeper of the sacred chickens.

The present infinitive verb endings are as follows: -āre = 1st; -ēre = 2nd; -ere = 3rd and -īre = 4th. See sections on irregular verbs and noun declensions.

pullātus *adj* dressed in black.

pullulō, -āre *vi* to sprout.

pullus, -ī *m* young (of animals), chicken.

pullus *adj* dark-grey; mournful
♦ *nt* dark grey clothes.

pulmentārium, -ārī and āriī, -um, -ī *nt* relish; food.

pulmō, -ōnis *m* lung.

pulmōneus *adj* of the lungs.

pulpa, -ae *f* fleshy part.

pulpāmentum, -ī *nt* tit-bits.

pulpitum, -ī *nt* platform, stage.

puls, pultis *f* porridge.

pulsātiō, -ōnis *f* beating.

pulsō, -āre, -āvī, -ātum *vt* to batter, knock, strike.

pulsus *ppp of* pellō.

pulsus, -ūs *m* push, beat, blow; impulse.

pultiphagus, -ī *m* porridge eater.

pultō, -āre *vt* to beat, knock at.

pulvereus *adj* of dust, dusty, fine as dust; raising dust.

pulverulentus *adj* dusty; laborious.

pulvillus, -ī *m* small cushion.

pulvīnar, -āris *nt* sacred couch; seat of honour.

pulvīnus, -ī *m* cushion, pillow.

pulvis, -eris *m* dust, powder; arena; effort.

pulvisculus, -ī *m* fine dust.

pūmex, -icis *m* pumice stone; stone, rock.

pūmiceus *adj* of soft stone.

pūmicō, -āre *vt* to smooth with pumice stone.

pūmiliō, -ōnis *m/f* dwarf, pygmy.

pūnctim *adv* with the point.

pūnctum, -ī *nt* point, dot; vote; (*time*) moment; (*speech*) short section.

pūnctus *ppp of* pungō.

pungō, -ere, pupugī, pūnctum *vt* to prick, sting, pierce; (*fig*) to vex.

Pūnicānus *adj* in the Carthaginian style.

Pūnicē *adv* in Punic.

pūniceus *adj* reddish, purple.

Pūnicum, -ī *nt* pomegranate.

Pūnicus *adj* Punic, Carthaginian; purple-red.

pūniō (poeniō), -īre; -ior, -īrī *vt* to punish; to avenge.

pūnītor, -ōris *m* avenger.

pūpa, -ae *f* doll.

pūpilla, -ae *f* ward; (*eye*) pupil.

pūpillāris, -is *adj* of a ward, of an orphan.

pūpillus, -ī *m* orphan, ward.

puppis, -is *f* after part of a ship, stern; ship.

pupugī *perf of* pungō.

pūpula, -ae *f* (*eye*) pupil.

pūpulus, -ī *m* little boy.

pūrē *adv* cleanly, brightly; plainly, simply, purely, chastely.

pūrgāmen, -inis *nt* sweepings, dirt; means of expiation.

pūrgāmentum, -ī *nt* refuse, dirt.

pūrgātiō, -ōnis *f* purging; justification.

pūrgō, -āre, -āvī, -ātum *vt* to cleanse, purge, clear away; to exculpate, justify; to purify.

pūriter *adv* cleanly, purely.

purpura, -ae *f* purple-fish, purple; purple cloth; finery, royalty.

purpurātus *adj* wearing purple
♦ *m* courtier.

purpureus *adj* red, purple, black; wearing purple; bright, radiant.

purpurissum, -ī *nt* kind of rouge.

pūrus *adj* clear, unadulterated, free from obstruction or admixture; pure, clean; plain, unadorned; (*moral*) pure, chaste
♦ *nt* clear sky.

pūs, pūris *nt* pus; (*fig*) malice.

pusillus *adj* very little; petty, paltry.

pusiō, -ōnis *m* little boy.

pūstula, -ae *f* pimple, blister.

putāmen, -inis nt peeling, shell, husk.

putātiō, -ōnis f pruning.

putātor, -ōris m pruner.

puteal, -ālis nt low wall round a well or sacred place.

puteālis adj well- (in cpds).

pūteō, -ēre vi to stink.

Puteolānus adj see n.

Puteolī, -ōrum mpl town on the Campanian coast.

puter, putris, -ris adj rotten, decaying; crumbling; flabby.

putēscō, -ēscere, -uī vi to become rotten.

puteus, -ī m well; pit.

pūtidē adv see **pūtidus**.

pūtidiusculus adj somewhat nauseating.

pūtidus adj rotten, stinking; (speech) affected, nauseating.

putō, -āre, -āvī, -ātum vt to think, suppose; to think over; to reckon, count; (money) to settle; (tree) to prune.

pūtor, -ōris m stench.

putrefaciō, -facere, -fēcī, -factum vt to make rotten; to make crumble.

putrēscō, -ere vi to rot, moulder.

putridus adj rotten, decayed; withered.

putris etc see **puter**.

putus adj perfectly pure.

putus, -ī m boy.

pycta, -ēs, -ae m boxer.

Pydna, -ae f town in Macedonia.

Pydnaeus adj see n.

pȳga, -ae f buttocks.

Pygmaeus adj Pygmy.

Pyladēs, -ae and **is** m friend of Orestes.

Pyladēus adj see n.

Pylae, -ārum fpl Thermopylae.

Pylaicus adj see n.

Pylius adj see n.

Pylos, -ī f Pylus (Peloponnesian town, home of Nestor).

pyra, -ae f funeral pyre.

Pȳramaeus adj see **Pȳramus**.

pȳramis, -idis f pyramid.

Pȳramus, -ī m lover of Thisbe.

Pȳrēnē, -ēs f Pyrenees.

pyrethrum, -ī nt Spanish camomile.

Pyrgēnsis adj see **Pyrgī**.

Pyrgī, -ōrum mpl ancient town in Etruria.

pyrōpus, -ī m bronze.

Pyrrha, -ae and **ē, -ēs** f wife of Deucalion.

Pyrrhaeus adj see n.

Pyrrhō, -ōnis m Greek philosopher (founder of the Sceptics).

Pyrrhōnēus adj see n.

Pyrrhus, -ī m son of Achilles; king of Epirus, enemy of Rome.

Pythagorās, -ae m Greek philosopher who founded a school in S. Italy.

Pȳthagorēus, -icus adj Pythagorean.

Pȳthius, -icus adj Pythian, Delphic
 ♦ m Apollo ♦ f priestess of Apollo
 ♦ ntpl Pythian Games.

Pȳthō, -ūs f Delphi.

Pȳthōn, -ōnis m serpent killed by Apollo.

pȳtisma, -tis nt what is spit out.

pȳtissō, -āre vi to spit out wine.

pyxis, -dis f small box, toilet box.

Q

quā adv where, which way; whereby; as far as; partly ... partly.

quācumque adv wherever; anyhow.

quādam: ~ tenus adv only so far.

The present infinitive verb endings are as follows: **-āre** = 1st; **-ēre** = 2nd; **-ere** = 3rd and **-īre** = 4th. *See sections on irregular verbs and noun declensions.*

quadra, -ae f square; morsel; table.

quadrāgēnī, -ōrum adj forty each.

quadrāgēsimus adj fortieth ♦ f 2½ per cent tax.

quadrāgiēns, -ēs adv forty times.

quadrāgintā num forty.

quadrāns, -antis m quarter; (coin) quarter as.

quadrantārius adj of a quarter.

quadrātum, -ī nt square; (ASTRO) quadrature.

quadrātus ppp of **quadrō** ♦ adj square; **~ō agmine** in battle order.

quadriduum, -ī nt four days.

quadriennium, -ī and iī nt four years.

quadrifāriam adv in four parts.

quadrifidus adj split in four.

quadrigae, -ārum fpl team of four; chariot.

quadrigārius, -ī and iī m chariot racer.

quadrigātus adj stamped with a chariot.

quadrigulae, -ārum fpl little four horse team.

quadriiugī, -ōrum mpl team of four.

quadriiugis, -us adj of a team of four.

quadrilībris adj weighing four pounds.

quadrimulus adj four years old.

quadrimus adj four years old.

quadringēnārius adj of four hundred each.

quadringēnī, -ōrum adj four hundred each.

quadringentēsimus adj four-hundredth.

quadringentī, -ōrum num four hundred.

quadringentiēns, -ēs adv four hundred times.

quadripertītus adj fourfold.

quadrirēmis, -is f quadrireme.

quadrivium, -ī and iī nt crossroads.

quadrō, -āre vt to make square; to complete ♦ vi to square, fit, agree.

quadrum, -ī nt square.

quadrupedāns, -antis adj galloping.

quadrupēs, -edis adj four-footed, on all fours ♦ m/f quadruped.

quadruplātor, -ōris m informer, twister.

quadruplex, -icis adj four-fold.

quadruplum, -ī nt four times as much.

quaeritō, -āre vt to search diligently for; to earn (a living); to keep on asking.

quaerō, -rere, -sīvī and siī, -sītum vt to look for, search for; to seek, try to get; to acquire, earn; (plan) to think out, work out; (question) to ask, make inquiries; (law) to investigate; (with infin) to try, wish; **quid ~ris?** in short; **sī ~ris/~rimus** to tell the truth.

quaesītiō, -ōnis f inquisition.

quaesītor, -ōris m investigator, judge.

quaesītus ppp of **quaerō** ♦ adj special; far-fetched ♦ nt question ♦ ntpl gains.

quaesīvī perf of **quaerō**.

quaesō, -ere vt to ask, beg.

quaesticulus, -ī m slight profit.

quaestiō, -ōnis f seeking, questioning; investigation, research; criminal trial; court; **servum in ~ōnem ferre** take a slave for questioning by torture; **~ōnēs perpetuae** standing courts.

quaestiuncula, -ae f trifling question.

quaestor, -ōris m quaestor, treasury official.

quaestōrius adj of a quaestor ♦ m ex-quaestor ♦ nt quaestor's tent or residence.

quaestuōsus *adj* lucrative, productive; money-making; wealthy.

quaestūra, -ae *f* quaestorship; public money.

quaestus, -ūs *m* profit, advantage; money-making, occupation; ~uī habēre make money out of; ~um facere make a living.

quālibet *adv* anywhere, anyhow.

quālis *adj* (*interrog*) what kind of?; (*relat*) such as, even as.

quāliscumque *adj* of whatever kind; any, whatever.

quāliscunque *adj* = **quāliscumque.**

quālitās, -ātis *f* quality, nature.

quāliter *adv* just as.

quālubet *adv* anywhere; anyhow.

quālus, -ī *m* wicker basket.

quam *adv* (*interrog, excl*) how?, how much?; (*comparison*) as, than; (*with superl*) as … as possible; (*emphatic*) very; dīmidium ~ quod half of what; quīntō diē ~ four days after.

quamdiū *adv* how long?; as long as.

quamlibet, quamlubet *adv* as much as you like, however.

quamobrem *adv* (*interrog*) why?; (*relat*) why ♦ *conj* therefore.

quamquam *conj* although; and yet.

quamvīs *adv* however, ever so ♦ *conj* however much, although.

quānam *adv* what way.

quandō *adv* (*interrog*) when?; (*relat*) when; (*with* sī, nē, num) ever ♦ *conj* when; since.

quandōcumque, quandocunque *adv* whenever, as often as; some day.

quandōque *adv* whenever; some day ♦ *conj* seeing that.

quandō quidem *conj* seeing that,

since.

quanquam *etc see* **quamquam.**

quantillus *adj* how little, how much.

quantopere *adv* how much; (*after* tantopere) as.

quantulus *adj* how little, how small.

quantuluscumque *adj* however small, however trifling.

quantum *adv* how much; as much as; ~cumque as much as ever; ~libet however much, ~vīs as much as you like; although.

quantus *adj* how great; so great as, such as; ~ī how dear, how highly; ~ō (*with compar*) how much; the; in ~um as far as.

quantuscumque *adj* however great, whatever size.

quantuslibet *adj* as great as you like.

quantus quantus *adj* however great.

quantusvīs *adj* however great.

quāpropter *adv* why; and therefore.

quāquā *adv* whatever way.

quārē *adv* how, why; whereby; and therefore.

quartadecumānī, -ōrum *mpl* men of the fourteenth legion.

quartānus *adj* every four days ♦ *f* quartan fever ♦ *mpl* men of the fourth legion.

quartārius, -ī and **iī** *m* quarter pint.

quartus *adj* fourth; **quartum/ quartō** for the fourth time.

quartusdecimus *adj* fourteenth.

quasi *adv* as if; as it were; (*numbers*) about.

quasillus, -ī *m,* **-um, -ī** *nt* wool basket.

quassātiō, -ōnis *f* shaking.

The present infinitive verb endings are as follows: -āre = 1st; -ēre = 2nd; -ere = 3rd and -īre = 4th. *See sections on irregular verbs and noun declensions.*

quassō, -āre, -āvī, -ātum vt to
shake, toss; to shatter, damage.
quassus ppp of **quatiō** ♦ adj
broken.
quatefaciō, -facere, -fēcī vt to
shake, give a jolt to.
quātenus adv (interrog) how far?;
how long?; (relat) as far as; in so
far as, since.
quater adv four times; ~ deciēs
fourteen times.
quaternī, -ōrum adj four each, in
fours.
quatiō, -tere, -ssum vt to shake,
disturb, brandish; to strike,
shatter; (fig) to agitate, harass.
quattuor num four.
quattuordecim num fourteen.
quattuorvirātus, -ūs m
membership of quattuorviri.
quattuorvirī, -ōrum mpl board of
four officials.
-que conj and; both ... and; (after
neg) but.
quemadmodum adv (interrog)
how?; (relat) just as.
queō, -īre, -īvī and **iī, -itum** vi to be
able, can.
quercētum, -ī nt oak forest.
querceus adj of oak.
quercus, -ūs f oak; garland of oak
leaves; acorn.
querēla, querella, -ae f complaint;
plaintive sound.
queribundus adj complaining.
querimōnia, -ae f complaint;
elegy.
queritor, -ārī vi to complain much.
quernus adj oak- (in cpds).
queror, -rī, -stus vt, vi to complain,
lament; (birds) to sing.
querquetulānus adj of oakwoods.
querulus adj complaining,
plaintive, warbling.
questus ppa of **queror**.
questus, -ūs m complaint, lament.
quī, quae, quod pron (interrog)

what?, which?; (relat) who, which,
that; what; and this, he, etc.; (with
sī, nisi, nē, num) any.
quī adv (interrog) how?; (relat) with
which, whereby; (indef) somehow;
(excl) indeed.
quia conj because; ~nam why?
quicquam nt see **quisquam**.
quicque nt see **quisque**.
quicquid nt see **quisquis**.
quīcum with whom, with which.
quīcumque, quīcunque pron
whoever, whatever, all that;
every possible.
quid nt see **quis** ♦ adv why?
quīdam, quaedam, quoddam
pron a certain, a sort of, a ....
quiddam nt something.
quidem adv (emphatic) in fact;
(qualifying) at any rate; (conceding)
it is true; (alluding) for instance;
nē ... ~ not even.
quidlibet nt anything.
quidnam nt see **quisnam**.
quidnī adv why not?
quidpiam nt = quispiam.
quidquam nt = quisquam.
quidquid nt = quisquis.
quiēs, -ētis f rest, peace, quiet;
sleep, dream, death; neutrality;
lair.
quiēscō, -scere, -vī, -tum vi to
rest, keep quiet; to be at peace,
keep neutral; to sleep; (with acc
and infin) to stand by and see; (with
infin) to cease.
quiētē adv peacefully, quietly.
quiētus ppa of **quiēscō** ♦ adj at
rest; peaceful, neutral; calm,
quiet, asleep.
quīlibet, quaelibet, quodlibet
pron any, anyone at all.
quīn adv (interrog) why not?;
(correcting) indeed, rather ♦ conj
who not; but that, but, without;
(preventing) from; (doubting) that.
quīnam, quaenam, quodnam

pron which?, what?

Quīnct- *etc see* **Quīnt-**.

quīncūnx, -ūncis *m* five-twelfths; number five on a dice; **in ~ūncem dispositī** arranged in oblique lines.

quindeciēns, -ēs *adv* fifteen times.

quīndecim *num* fifteen; **~ prīmī** fifteen chief magistrates.

quīndecimvirālis *adj* of the council of fifteen

quīndecimvirī, -ōrum *mpl* council of fifteen.

quīngēnī, -ōrum *adj* five hundred each.

quīngentēsimus *adj* five-hundredth.

quīngentī, -ōrum *num* five hundred.

quīngentiēns, -ēs *adv* five hundred times.

quīnī, -ōrum *adj* five each; five; **~ dēnī** fifteen each; **~ vīcēnī** twenty-five each.

quīnquāgēnī, -ōrum *adj* fifty each.

quīnquāgēsimus *adj* fiftieth ♦ *f 2* per cent tax.

quīnquāgintā *num* fifty.

Quīnquātria, -iōrum *and* **ium** *ntpl* festival of Minerva.

Quīnquātrūs, -uum *fpl* festival of Minerva.

quīnque *num* five.

quīnquennālis *adj* quinquennial; lasting five years.

quīnquennis *adj* five years old; quinquennial.

quīnquennium, -ī *and* **iī** *nt* five years.

quīnquepartītus *adj* fivefold.

quīnqueprīmī, -ōrum *mpl* five leading men.

quīnquerēmis *adj* five-banked ♦ *f* quinquereme

quīnquevirātus, -ūs *m*

membership of the board of five.

quīnquevirī, -ōrum *mpl* board of five.

quīnquiēns, -ēs *adv* five times.

quīnquiplicō, -āre *vt* to multiply by five.

quīntadecimānī, -ōrum *mpl* men of the fifteenth legion.

quīntānus *adj* of the fifth ♦ *f* street in a camp between the 5th and 6th maniples ♦ *mpl* men of the fifth legion.

Quīntiliānus, -ī *m* Quintilian (famous teacher of rhetoric in Rome).

Quīntīlis *adj* of July.

quīntum, -ō *adv* for the fifth time.

Quīntus, -ī *m* Roman first name.

quīntus *adj* fifth.

quīntusdecimus *adj* fifteenth.

quippe *adv* (affirming) certainly, of course ♦ *conj* (explaining) for in fact, because, since; **~ quī** since I, he *etc*.

quippiam *etc see* **quispiam**.

quippinī *adv* certainly.

Quirīnālis *adj* of Romulus; Quirinal (hill).

Quirīnus, -ī *m* Romulus ♦ *adj* of Romulus.

Quirīs, -ītis *m* inhabitant of Cures; Roman citizen; citizen.

quirītātiō, -ōnis *f* shriek.

Quirītēs *pl* inhabitants of Cures; Roman citizens.

quirītō, -āre *vi* to cry out, wail.

quis, quid *pron* who?, what?; (indef) anyone, anything.

quis *poetic form of* **quibus**.

quisnam, quaenam, quidnam *pron* who?, what?

quispiam, quaepiam, quodpiam *and* **quidpiam** *pron* some, some one, something.

quisquam, quaequam, quicquam *and* **quidquam** *pron* any, anyone,

anything; **nec ~** and no one.
quisque, quaeque, quodque *pron*
each, every, every one; **quidque,**
quicque everything; **decimus ~**
every tenth; **optimus ~** all the
best; **prīmus ~** the first possible.
quisquiliae, -ārum *fpl* refuse,
rubbish.
quisquis, quaequae, quodquod,
quidquid *and* **quicquid** *pron*
whoever, whatever, all.
quīvīs, quaevīs, quodvīs, quidvīs
pron any you please, anyone,
anything.
quīvīscumque, quaevīscumque,
quodvīscumque *pron* any
whatsoever.
quō *adv* (*interrog*) where?;
whither?; for what purpose?,
what for?; (*relat*) where, to which
(place), to whom; (*with compar*)
(the more); (*with* **sī**) anywhere ♦ *conj*
(*with subj*) in order that; **nōn ~** not
that.
quoad *adv* how far?; how long?
♦ *conj* as far as, as long as; until.
quōcircā *conj* therefore.
quōcumque *adv* whithersoever.
quod *conj* as for, in that, that;
because; why; **~ sī** but if.
quōdam modo *adv* in a way.
quoi, quōius old forms of **cui, cūius.**
quōlibet *adv* anywhere, in any
direction.
quom *etc see* **cum** *conj.*
quōminus *conj* that not;
(*preventing*) from.
quōmodo *adv* (*interrog*) how?;
(*relat*) just as; **~cumque**
howsoever; **~nam** how?
quōnam *adv* where, where to?
quondam *adv* once, formerly;
sometimes; (*fut*) one day.
quōniam *conj* since, seeing that.
quōpiam *adv* anywhere.
quōquam *adv* anywhere.
quoque *adv* also, too.

quōquō *adv* to whatever place,
wherever.
quōquō modo *adv* howsoever.
quōquō versus, -um *adv* in every
direction.
quōrsus, quōrsum *adv* where to?,
in what direction?; what for?, to
what end?
quot *adj* how many; as many as,
every.
quotannīs *adv* every year.
quotcumque *adj* however many.
quotēnī, -ōrum *adj* how many.
quotīd- *etc see* **cottīd-**
quotiēns, -ēs *adv* how often?;
(*relat*) as often as.
quotiēnscumque *adv* however
often.
quotquot *adj* however many.
quotumus *adj* which number?,
what date?
quotus *adj* what number, how
many; **~ quisque** how few; **~a**
hōra what time.
quotuscumque *adj* whatever
number, however big.
quōusque *adv* how long, till when;
how far.
quōvīs *adv* anywhere.
quum *etc see* **cum** *conj.*

R

rabidē *adv* furiously.
rabidus *adj* raving, mad;
impetuous.
rabiēs, -em, -ē *f* madness, rage,
fury.
rabiō, -ere *vi* to rave.
rabiōsē *adv* wildly.
rabiōsulus *adj* somewhat rabid.
rabiōsus *adj* furious, mad.
rabula, -ae *m* wrangling lawyer.
racēmifer, -ī *adj* clustered.
racēmus, -ī *m* stalk of a cluster;
bunch of grapes; grape.
radiātus *adj* radiant.

rādīcitus *adv* by the roots; utterly.

rādīcula, -ae *f* small root.

radiō, -āre *vt* to irradiate ♦ *vi* to radiate, shine.

radius, -ī and iī *m* stick, rod; (*light*) beam, ray; (*loom*) shuttle; (*MATH*) rod for drawing figures, radius of a circle; (*plant*) long olive; (*wheel*) spoke.

rādīx, -īcis *f* root; radish; (*hill*) foot; (*fig*) foundation, origin.

radō, -dere, -sī, -sum *vi* to scrape, shave, scratch; to erase; to touch in passing, graze, pass along.

raeda, -ae *f* four-wheeled carriage.

raedārius, -ī *m* driver.

Raetī, -ōrum *mpl* Alpine people between Italy and Germany.

Raetia, -iae *f* country of the Raetī.

Raeticus and ius and us *adj* see n.

rāmālia, -ium *ntpl* twigs, brushwood.

rāmentum, -ī *nt* shavings, chips.

rāmeus *adj* of branches.

rāmex, -icis *m* rupture, blood vessels of the lungs.

Ramnēnsēs, Ramnēs, -ium *mpl* one of the original Roman tribes; a century of equites.

rāmōsus *adj* branching.

rāmulus, -ī *m* twig, sprig.

rāmus, -ī *m* branch, bough.

rāna, -ae *f* frog; frogfish.

rancēns, -entis *adj* putrid.

rancidulus *adj* rancid.

rancidus *adj* rank, rancid, disgusting.

rānunculus, -ī *m* tadpole.

rapācida, -ae *m* son of a thief.

rapācitās, -ātis *f* greed.

rapāx, -ācis *adj* greedy, grasping, ravenous.

raphanus, -ī *m* radish.

rapidē *adv* swiftly, hurriedly.

rapiditās, -ātis *f* rapidity.

rapidus *adj* tearing, devouring; swift, rapid; hasty, impetuous.

rapīna, -ae *f* pillage, robbery; booty, prey.

rapiō, -ere, -uī, -tum *vt* to tear, snatch, carry off; to seize, plunder; to hurry, seize quickly.

raptim *adv* hastily, violently.

raptiō, -ōnis *f* abduction.

raptō, -āre, -āvī, -ātum *vt* to seize and carry off, drag away, move quickly; to plunder, lay waste; (*passion*) to agitate.

raptor, -ōris *m* plunderer, robber, ravisher.

raptus *ppp of* **rapiō** ♦ *nt* plunder.

raptus, -ūs *m* carrying off, abduction; plundering.

rāpulum, -ī *nt* small turnip.

rāpum, -ī *nt* turnip.

rārēfaciō, -facere, -fēcī, -factum (*pass* **-fīō, -fierī**) *vt* to rarefy.

rārēscō, -ere *vi* to become rarefied, grow thin; to open out.

rāritās, -ātis *f* porousness, open texture; thinness, fewness.

rārō, -ē *adv* seldom.

rārus *adj* porous, open in texture; thin, scanty; scattered, straggling, here and there; (*MIL*) in open order; few, infrequent; uncommon, rare.

rāsī *perf of* **rādō**.

rāsilis *adj* smooth, polished.

rāstrum, -ī *nt* hoe, mattock.

rāsus *ppp of* **rādō**.

ratiō, -ōnis *f* 1. (*reckoning of*) account, calculation; list, register; affair, business. 2. (*relation*) respect, consideration; procedure, method, system, way, kind. 3. (*reason*) reasoning, thought; cause, motive; science, knowledge, philosophy; ~ **atque** **ūsus** theory and practice; ~ **est** it

The present infinitive verb endings are as follows: -āre = 1st; -ēre = 2nd; -ere = 3rd and -īre = 4th. See sections on irregular verbs and noun declensions.

is reasonable; Stōicōrum ~
Stoicism; ~ōnem dūcere, inīre
calculate; ~ōnem habēre take
account of, have to do with,
consider; ~ōnem reddere give an
account of; cum ~ōne reasonably;
meae ~ōnēs my interests; ā
~ōnibus accountant.
ratiōcinātiō, -ōnis f reasoning;
syllogism.
ratiōcinātīvus adj syllogistic.
ratiōcinātor, -ōris m accountant.
ratiōcinor, -ārī, -ātus vt, vi to
calculate; to consider; to argue,
infer.
ratiōnālis adj rational; syllogistic.
ratis, -is f raft; boat.
ratiuncula, -ae f small calculation;
slight reason; petty syllogism.
ratus ppa of **reor** ♦ adj fixed,
settled, sure; valid; prō ~ā (parte)
proportionally; ~um dūcere,
facere, habēre ratify.
raucisonus adj hoarse.
raucus adj hoarse; harsh, strident.
raudus, -eris nt copper coin.
raudusculum, -ī nt bit of money.
Ravenna, -ae f port in N.E. Italy.
Ravennās, -ātis adj see n.
rāvis, -im f hoarseness.
rāvus adj grey, tawny.
rea, -ae f defendant, culprit.
reāpse adv in defact, actually.
Reāte, -is nt ancient Sabine town.
Reātīnus adj see n.
rebellātiō, -ōnis f revolt.
rebellātrīx, -īcis f rebellious.
rebelliō, -ōnis f revolt.
rebellis adj rebellious ♦ mpl
rebels.
rebellium, -ī and **iī** nt revolt.
rebellō, -āre vi to revolt.
rebītō, -ere vi to return.
reboō, -āre vi to re-echo ♦ vt to
make resound.
recalcitrō, -āre vi to kick back.
recaleō, -ēre vi to be warm again.

recalēscō, -ere vi to grow warm
again.
recalfaciō, -facere, -fēcī vt to
warm again.
recalvus adj bald in front.
recandēscō, -ēscere, -uī vi to
whiten (in response to); to glow.
recantō, -āre, -āvī, -ātum vt to
recant; to charm away.
reccidī perf of **recidō**.
recēdō, -ēdere, -essī, -essum vi to
move back, withdraw, depart;
(place) to recede; (head) to be
severed.
recellō, -ere vi to spring back.
recēns, -entis adj fresh, young,
recent; (writer) modern; (with ab)
immediately after ♦ adv newly,
just.
recēnseō, -ēre, -uī, -um vt to
count; to review.
recēnsiō, -ōnis f revision.
recēnsus ppp of **recēnseō**.
recēpī perf of **recipiō**.
receptāculum, -ī nt receptacle,
reservoir; refuge, shelter.
receptō, -āre vt to take back; to
admit, harbour; to tug hard at.
receptor, -ōris m (male) receiver,
shelterer.
receptrīx, -īcis f (female) receiver,
shelterer.
receptum, -ī nt obligation.
receptus ppp of **recipiō**.
receptus, -ūs m withdrawal;
retreat; return; refuge; ~uī
canere sound the retreat.
recessī perf of **recēdō**.
recessim adv backwards.
recessus, -ūs m retreat,
departure; recess, secluded spot;
(tide) ebb.
recidīvus adj resurrected;
recurring.
recidō, -idere, -cidī, -āsum vi to
fall back; to recoil, relapse; (fig)
to fall, descend.

recīdō, -dere, -dī, -sum vt to cut back, cut off.

recingō, -gere, -ctum vt to ungird, loose.

recinō, -ere vt, vi to re-echo, repeat; to sound a warning.

reciper- etc see **recuper-**.

recipiō, -ipere, -ēpī, -eptum vt to take back, retake; to get back, regain, rescue; to accept, admit; (MIL) to occupy, (duty) to undertake; (promise) to pledge, guarantee; **sē ~** withdraw, retreat; **nōmen ~** receive notice of a prosecution.

reciprocō, -āre vt to move to and fro; (ship) to bring round to another tack; (proposition) to reverse ♦ vi (tide) to rise and fall.

reciprocus adj ebbing.

recīsus ppp of **recīdō**.

recitātiō, -ōnis f reading aloud, recital.

recitātor, -ōris m reader, reciter.

recitō, -āre, -āvī, -ātum vt to read out, recite.

reclāmātiō, -ōnis f outcry (of disapproval).

reclāmitō, -āre vi to cry out against.

reclāmō, -āre vi to cry out, protest; to reverberate.

reclīnis adj leaning back.

reclīnō, -āre, -āvī, -ātum vt to lean back.

reclūdō, -dere, -sī, -sum vt to open up; to disclose.

reclūsus ppp of **reclūdō**.

recoctus ppp of **recoquō**.

recōgitō, -āre vi to think over, reflect.

recognitiō, -ōnis f review.

recognōscō, -ōscere, -ōvī, -itum vt to recollect; to examine, review.

recolligō, -igere, -ēgī, -ēctum vt to gather up; (fig) to recover, reconcile.

recolō, -olere, -oluī, -ultum vt to recultivate; to resume; to reflect on, contemplate; to revisit.

recomminiscor, -ī vi to recollect.

recompositus adj rearranged.

reconciliātiō, -ōnis f restoration, reconciliation.

reconciliō, -āre, -āvī, -ātum vt to win back again, restore, reconcile.

reconcinnō, -āre vt to repair.

reconditus ppp of **recondō** ♦ adj hidden, secluded; abstruse, profound; (disposition) reserved.

recondō, -ere, -idī, -itum vt to store away, stow; to hide away, bury.

reconflō, -āre vt to rekindle.

recoquō, -quere, -xī, -ctum vt to cook again, boil again; to forge again, recast; (fig) to rejuvenate.

recordātiō, -ōnis f recollection.

recordor, -ārī, -ātus vt, vi to recall, remember; to ponder over.

recreō, -āre, -āvī, -ātum vt to remake, reproduce; to revive, refresh.

recrepō, -āre vt, vi to ring, re-echo.

recrēscō, -scere, -vī vi to grow again.

recrūdēscō, -ēscere, -uī vi (wound) to open again; (war) to break out again.

rēctā adv straight forward, right on.

rēctē adv straight; correctly, properly, well; quite; (inf) good, all right, no thank you.

rēctiō, -ōnis f government.

rēctor, -ōris m guide, driver, helmsman; governor, master.

rēctum, -ī nt right, virtue.

The present infinitive verb endings are as follows: -āre = 1st; -ēre = 2nd; -ere = 3rd and -īre = 4th. See sections on irregular verbs and noun declensions.

rēctus ppp of **regō** ♦ adj straight;
upright, steep; right, correct,
proper; (moral) good, virtuous.

recubō, -āre vi to lie, recline.

recultus ppp of **recolō**.

recumbō, -mbere, -buī vi to lie
down, recline; to fall, sink down.

recuperātiō, -ōnis f recovery.

recuperātor, -ōris m recapturer;
(pl) board of justices who tried civil
cases requiring a quick decision, esp
cases involving foreigners.

recuperātōrius adj of the
recuperatores.

recuperō, -āre, -āvī, -ātum vt to
get back, recover, recapture.

recūrō, -āre vt to restore.

recurrō, -ere, -ī vi to run back; to
return, recur; to revert.

recursō, -āre vi to keep coming
back, keep recurring.

recursus, -ūs m return, retreat.

recurvō, -āre vt to bend back,
curve.

recurvus adj bent, curved.

recūsātiō, -ōnis f refusal,
declining; (law) objection,
counterplea.

recūsō, -āre, -āvī, -ātum vt to
refuse, decline, be reluctant; (law)
to object, plead in defence.

recussus, -ūs adj reverberating.

redāctus ppp of **redigō**.

redambulō, -āre vi to come back.

redamō, -āre vt to love in return.

redārdēscō, -ere vi to blaze up
again.

redarguō, -ere, -ī vt to refute,
contradict.

redauspicō, -āre vi to take
auspices for going back.

redditus ppp of **reddō**.

reddō, -ere, -idī, -itum vt to give
back, return, restore; to give in,
response, repay; to give up,
deliver, pay; (copy) to represent,
reproduce; (speech) to report,

repeat, recite, reply; to translate;
(with adj) to make; iūdicium ~ fix
the date for a trial; iūs ~
administer justice.

redēgī perf of **redigō**.

redēmī perf of **redimō**.

redemptiō, -ōnis f ransoming;
bribing; (revenue) farming.

redemptō, -āre vt to ransom.

redemptor, -ōris m contractor.

redemptūra, -ae f contracting.

redemptus ppp of **redimō**.

redeō, -īre, -iī, -itum vi to go back,
come back, return; (speech) to
revert; (money) to come in; (CIRCS)
to be reduced to, come to.

redhālō, -āre vt to exhale.

redhibeō, -ēre vt to take back.

redigō, -igere, -ēgī, -āctum vt to
drive back, bring back; (money) to
collect, raise; (to a condition) to
reduce, bring; (number) to reduce;
ad irritum ~ make useless.

rediī perf of **redeō**.

redimīculum, -ī nt band.

redimiō, -īre, -iī, -ītum vt to bind,
crown, encircle.

redimō, -imere, -ēmī, -emptum vt
to buy back; to ransom, redeem;
to release, rescue; (good) to
procure; (evil) to avert; (fault) to
make amends for; (COMM) to
undertake by contract, hire.

redintegrō, -āre, -āvī, -ātum vt to
restore, renew, refresh.

redipīscor, -ī vt to get back.

reditiō, -ōnis f returning.

reditus, -ūs m return, returning;
(money) revenue.

redivīvus adj renovated.

redoleō, -ēre, -uī vi to give out a
smell ♦ vt to smell of, smack of.

redomitus adj broken in again.

redōnō, -āre vt to restore; to give
up.

redūcō, -ūcere, -ūxī, -uctum vt to
draw back; to lead back, bring

back; to escort home; to marry
again; (*troops*) to withdraw; (*fig*) to
restore; (*to a condition*) to make
into.
reductiō, -ōnis f restoration.
reductor, -ōris m man who brings
back.
reductus ppp of **redūcō** ♦ adj
secluded, aloof.
reduncus adj curved back.
redundantia, -ae f extravagance.
redundō, -āre, -āvī, -ātum vi to
overflow; to abound, be in excess;
(*fig*) to stream.
reduvia, -ae f hangnail.
redux, -cis adj (*gods*) who brings
back; (*men*) brought back,
returned.
refectus ppp of **reficiō**.
refellō, -ere, -ī vt to disprove,
rebut.
referciō, -cīre, -sī, -tum vt to stuff,
cram, choke full.
referiō, -īre vt to hit back; to
reflect.
referō, -ferre, -ttulī, -lātum vt to
bring back, carry back; to give
back, pay back, repay; to repeat,
renew; (*authority*) to refer to, trace
back to; (*blame, credit*) to ascribe;
(*likeness*) to reproduce, resemble;
(*memory*) to recall; (*news*) to
report, mention; (*opinion*) to
reckon amongst; (*record*) to enter;
(*senate*) to lay before, move;
(*speech*) to reply, say in answer;
grātiam ~ be grateful, requite;
pedem, gradum ~ return; retreat;
ratiōnēs ~ present an account; **sē
~** return.
refert, -ferre, -tulit vi (*impers*) it is
of importance, it matters, it
concerns; **meā ~** it matters to me.
refertus ppp of **referciō** ♦ adj
crammed, full.

referveō, -ēre vi to boil over.
refervēscō, -ere vi to bubble up.
reficiō, -icere, -ēcī, -ectum vt to
repair, restore; (*body, mind*) to
refresh, revive; (*money*) to get
back, get in return; (*POL*) to
re-elect.
refīgō, -gere, -xī, -xum vt to
unfasten, take down; (*fig*) to
annul.
refingō, -ere vt to remake.
refīxus ppp of **refīgo**.
reflāgitō, -āre vt to demand back.
reflātus, -ūs m contrary wind.
reflectō, -ctere, -xī, -xum vt to
bend back, turn back; (*fig*) to
bring back ♦ vi to give way.
reflexus ppp of **reflectō**.
reflō, -āre, -āvī, -ātum vi to blow
contrary ♦ vt to breathe out again.
refluō, -ere vi to flow back,
overflow.
refluus adj ebbing.
reformīdō, -āre vt to dread; to
shun in fear.
reformō, -āre vt to reshape.
refōtus ppp of **refoveō**.
refoveō, -ovēre, -ōvī, -ōtum vt to
refresh, revive.
refrāctāriolus adj rather stubborn.
refrāctus ppp of **refringō**.
refrāgor, -ārī, -ātus vi (*with dat*) to
oppose, thwart.
refrēgī perf of **refringō**.
refrēnō, -āre, -um vt to curb, restrain.
refricō, -āre, -uī, -ātum vt to
scratch open; to reopen, renew
♦ vi to break out again.
refrigerātiō, -ōnis f coolness.
refrigerō, -āre, -āvī, -ātum vt to
cool, cool off; (*fig*) to flag.
refrigēscō, -gēscere, -xī vi to grow
cold; (*fig*) to flag, grow stale.
refringō, -ingere, -ēgī, -āctum vt
to break open; to break off; (*fig*) to

The present infinitive verb endings are as follows: **-āre** = 1st; **-ēre** = 2nd; **-ere** = 3rd and
-īre = 4th. *See sections on irregular verbs and noun declensions.*

break, check.
refrīxī *perf of* **refrīgēscō.**
refugiō, -ugere, -ūgī *vi* to run
  back, flee, shrink ♦ *vt* to run away
  from, shun.
refugium, -ī *and* **iī** *nt* refuge.
refugus *adj* fugitive, receding.
refulgeō, -gēre, -sī *vi* to flash back,
  reflect light.
refundō, -undere, -ūdī, -ūsum *vt*
  to pour back, pour out; (*pass*) to
  overflow.
refūsus *ppp of* **refundō.**
refūtātiō, -ōnis *f* refutation.
refūtātus, -ūs *m* refutation.
refūtō, -āre, -āvī, -ātum *vt* to
  check, repress; to refute,
  disprove.
rēgālis *adj* king's, royal, regal.
rēgāliter *adv* magnificently;
  tyrannically.
regerō, -rere, -ssī, -stum *vt* to
  carry back, throw back.
rēgia, -ae *f* palace; court; (*camp*)
  royal tent; (*town*) capital.
rēgiē *adv* regally; imperiously.
rēgificus *adj* magnificent.
regignō, -ere *vt* to reproduce.
Rēgillānus *and* **ēnsis** *adj see*
  Rēgillus.
Rēgillus, -ī *m* Sabine town ; lake in
  Latium (*scene of a Roman victory
  over the Latins*).
regimen, -inis *nt* guiding,
  steering; rudder; rule, command,
  government; ruler.
rēgīna, -ae *f* queen, noblewoman.
Rēgīnus *adj see* **Rēgium.**
regiō, -ōnis *f* direction, line;
  boundary line; quarter, region;
  district, ward, territory; (*fig*)
  sphere, province; **ē ~ōne** in a
  straight line; (*with gen*) exactly
  opposite.
regiōnātim *adv* by districts.
Rēgium, -ī *and* **iī** *nt* town in
  extreme S. of Italy, (*now* Reggio).

rēgius *adj* king's, kingly, royal;
  princely, magnificent.
reglūtinō, -āre *vt* to unstick.
rēgnātor, -ōris *m* ruler.
rēgnātrīx, -īcis *adj* imperial.
rēgnō, -āre, -āvī, -ātum *vi* to be
  king, rule, reign; to be supreme,
  lord it; (*things*) to prevail,
  predominate ♦ *vt* to rule over.
rēgnum, -ī *nt* kingship, monarchy;
  sovereignty, supremacy;
  despotism; kingdom; domain.
regō, -ere, rēxī, rēctum *vt* to keep
  straight, guide, steer; to manage,
  direct; to control, rule, govern; **~
  fīnēs** (*law*) mark out the limits.
regredior, -dī, -ssus *vi* to go back,
  come back, return; (*MIL*) to retire.
regressus *ppa of* **regredior.**
regressus, -ūs *m* return; retreat.
rēgula, -ae *f* rule, ruler; stick,
  board; (*fig*) rule, pattern,
  standard.
rēgulus, -ī *m* petty king, chieftain;
  prince.
Rēgulus, -ī *m* Roman consul taken
  prisoner by the Carthaginians.
regustō, -āre *vt* to taste again.
rēiciō, -icere, -iēcī, -iectum *vt* to
  throw back, throw over the
  shoulder, throw off; to drive back,
  repel; to cast off, reject; to reject
  with contempt, scorn; (*jurymen*)
  to challenge, refuse; (*matter for
  discussion*) to refer; (*time*) to
  postpone; **sē ~** fling oneself.
rēiectāneus *adj* to be rejected.
rēiectiō, -ōnis *f* rejection; (*law*)
  challenging.
rēiectō, -āre *vt* to throw back.
rēiectus *ppp of* **rēiciō.**
relābor, -bī, -psus *vi* to glide back,
  sink back, fall back.
relanguēscō, -ēscere, -ī *vi* to faint;
  to weaken.
relātiō, -ōnis *f* (*law*) retorting; (*pl*)
  magistrate's report; (*RHET*)

repetition.

relātor, -ōris *m* proposer of a motion.

relātus *ppp of* **referō**.

relātus, -ūs *m* official report; recital.

relaxātiō, -ōnis *f* easing.

relaxō, -āre, -āvī, -ātum *vt* to loosen, open up; (*fig*) to release, ease, relax, cheer.

relēctus *ppp of* **relegō**.

relegātio, -ōnis *f* banishment.

relēgō, -āre, -āvī, -ātum *vt* to send away, send out of the way; to banish; (*fig*) to reject; to refer, ascribe.

relegō, -egere, -ēgī, -ēctum *vt* to gather up; (*place*) to traverse, sail over again; (*speech*) to go over again, reread.

relentēscō, -ere *vi* to slacken off.

relēvī *perf of* **relinō**.

relevō, -āre, -āvī, -ātum *vt* to lift up; to lighten; (*fig*) to relieve, ease, comfort.

relictiō, -ōnis *f* abandoning.

relictus *ppp of* **relinquō**.

relicuus *etc see* **reliquus**.

religātiō, -ōnis *f* tying up.

religiō, -ōnis *f* religious scruple, reverence, awe; religion; superstition; scruples, conscientiousness; holiness, sanctity (*in anything*); object of veneration, sacred place; religious ceremony, observance.

religiōsē *adv* devoutly; scrupulously, conscientiously.

religiōsus *adj* devout, religious; superstitious; involving religious difficulty; scrupulous, conscientious; (*objects*) holy, sacred.

religō, -āre, -āvī, -ātum *vt* to tie up, fasten behind; (*ship*) to make fast,

moor; (*fig*) to bind.

relinō, -inere, -ēvī *vt* to unseal.

relinquō, -inquere, -īquī, -ictum *vt* to leave, leave behind; to bequeath; to abandon, forsake; (*argument*) to allow; (*pass*) to remain.

rēliquiae, -ārum *fpl* leavings, remainder, relics.

reliquus *adj* remaining, left; (*time*) subsequent, future; (*debt*) outstanding ♦ *nt* remainder, rest; arrears ♦ *mpl* the rest; **~um est** it remains, the next point is; **~ī facere** leave behind, leave over, omit; **in ~um** for the future.

rell- *etc see* **rel-**.

relūceō, -cēre, -xī *vi* to blaze.

relūcēscō, -cēscere, -xī *vi* to become bright again.

reluctor, -ārī, -ātus *vi* to struggle against, resist.

remaneō, -anēre, -ānsī *vi* to remain behind; to remain, continue, endure.

remānō, -āre *vi* to flow back.

remānsiō, -ōnis *f* remaining behind.

remedium, -ī *and* **iī** *nt* cure, remedy, medicine.

remēnsus *ppa of* **remētior**.

remeō, -āre *vi* to come back, go back, return.

remētior, -tīrī, -nsus *vt* to measure again; to go back over.

rēmex, -igis *m* rower, oarsman.

Rēmī, -ōrum *mpl* people of Gaul (*in region of what is now* Rheims).

rēmigātiō, -ōnis *f* rowing.

rēmigium, -ī *and* **iī** *nt* rowing; oars; oarsmen.

rēmigō, -āre *vi* to row.

remigrō, -āre *vi* to move back, return (home).

reminīscor, -ī *vt, vi* (*usu with gen*) to

The present infinitive verb endings are as follows: -**āre** = 1st; -**ēre** = 2nd; -**ere** = 3rd and -**īre** = 4th. *See sections on Irregular verbs and noun declensions.*

remember, call to mind.
remisceō, -scēre, -xtum vt to mix up, mingle.
remissē adv mildly, gently.
remissiō, -ōnis f release; (tension) slackening, relaxing; (payment) remission; (mind) slackness, mildness, relaxation; (illness) abating.
remissus ppp of **remittō** ♦ adj slack; negligent; mild, indulgent, cheerful.
remittō, -ittere, -īsī, -issum vt to let go back, send back, release; to slacken, loosen, relax; to emit, produce; (mind) to relax, relieve; (notion) to discard, give up; (offence, penalty) to let off, remit; (right) to resign, sacrifice; (sound) to give back ♦ vi to abate.
remixtus ppp of **remisceō**.
remōlior, -īrī, -ītus vt to heave back.
remollēscō, -ere vi to become soft again, be softened.
remolliō, -īre vt to weaken.
remora, -ae f hindrance.
remorāmina, -um ntpl hindrances.
remordeō, -dēre, -sum vt (fig) to worry, torment.
remoror, -ārī, -ātus vi to linger, stay behind ♦ vt to hinder, delay, defer.
remorsus ppp of **remordeō**.
remōtē adv far.
remōtiō, -ōnis f removing.
remōtus ppp of **removeō** ♦ adj distant, remote; secluded; (fig) far removed, free from.
removeō, -ovēre, -ōvī, -ōtum vt to move back, withdraw, set aside; to subtract.
remūgiō, -īre vi to bellow in answer, re-echo.
remulceō, -cēre, -sī vt to stroke; (tail) to droop.
remulcum, -ī nt towrope.

remūnerātiō, -ōnis f recompense, reward.
remūneror, -ārī, -ātus vt to repay, reward.
remurmurō, -āre vi to murmur in answer.
rēmus, -ī m oar.
Remus, -ī m brother of Romulus.
rēnarrō, -āre vt to tell over again.
renāscor -scī, -tus vi to be born again; to grow, spring up again.
renātus ppa of **renāscor**.
renāvigō, -āre vi to sail back.
reneō, -ēre vt to unspin, undo.
rēnēs, -um mpl kidneys.
renīdeō, -ēre vt to shine back, be bright; to be cheerful, smile, laugh.
renīdēscō, -ere vi to reflect the gleam of.
renītor, -ī vi to struggle, resist.
renō, -āre vi to swim back.
rēnō, -ōnis m fur.
renōdō, -āre vt to tie back in a knot.
renovāmen, -inis nt new condition.
renovātiō, -ōnis f renewal; compound interest.
renovō, -āre, -āvī, -ātum vt to renew, restore; to repair, revive, refresh; (speech) to repeat; **faenus ~** take compound interest.
renumerō, -āre vt to pay back.
renūntiātiō, -ōnis f report, announcement.
renūntiō, -āre, -āvī, -ātum vt to report, bring back word; to announce, make an official statement; (election) to declare elected, return; (duty) to refuse, call off, renounce.
renūntius, -ī and **iī** m reporter.
renuō, -ere, -ī vt, vi to deny, decline, refuse.
renūtō, -āre vi to refuse firmly.
reor, rērī, ratus vi to think,

suppose.

repāgula, -ōrum ntpl (door) bolts, bars.

repandus adj curving back, turned up.

reparābilis adj retrievable.

reparcō, -ere vi to be sparing with, refrain.

reparō, -āre, -āvī, -ātum vt to retrieve, recover; to restore, repair; to purchase; (mind, body) to refresh; (troops) to recruit.

repastinātiō, -ōnis f digging up again.

repellō, -ellere, -pulī, -ulsum vt to push back, drive back, repulse; to remove, reject.

rependō, -endere, -endī, -ēnsum vt to return by weight; to pay, repay; to requite, compensate.

repēns, -entis adj sudden; new.

repēnsus ppp of **rependō.**

repente adv suddenly.

repentīnō adv suddenly.

repentīnus adj sudden, hasty; upstart.

repercō etc see **reparcō.**

repercussus ppp of **repercutiō.**

repercussus, -ūs m reflection, echo.

repercutiō, -tere, -ssī, -ssum vt to make rebound, reflect, echo.

reperiō, -īre, repperī, -tum vt to find, find out; to get, procure; to discover, ascertain; to devise, invent.

repertor, -ōris m discoverer, inventor, author.

repertus ppp of **reperiō** ♦ ntpl discoveries.

repetītiō, -ōnis f repetition; (RHET) anaphora.

repetītor, -ōris m reclaimer.

repetītus ppp of **repetō** ♦ adj: **altē/longē ~** far-fetched.

repetō, -ere, -īvī and iī, -ītum vt to go back to, revisit; to fetch back, take back; (MIL) to attack again; (action, speech) to resume, repeat; (memory) to recall, think over; (origin) to trace, derive; (right) to claim, demand back; **rēs ~** demand satisfaction; reclaim one's property; **pecūniae ~undae** extortion.

repetundae, -ārum fpl extortion (by a provincial governor).

repexus adj combed.

repleō, -ēre, -ēvī, -ētum vt to fill up, refill; to replenish, make good, complete; to satiate, fill to overflowing.

replētus adj full.

replicātiō, -ōnis f rolling up.

replicō, -āre vt to roll back, unroll, unfold.

rēpō, -ere, -sī, -tum vi to creep, crawl.

repōnō, -ōnere, -osuī, -ositum vt to put back, replace, restore; to bend back; to put (in the proper place); (performance) to repeat; (something received) to repay; (store) to lay up, put away; (task) to lay aside, put down; (hope) to place, rest; (with prō) substitute; **in numerō, in numerum ~** count, reckon among.

reportō, -āre, -āvī, -ātum vt to bring back, carry back; (prize) to win, carry off; (words) to report.

reposcō, -ere vt to demand back; to claim, require.

repositus ppp of **repōnō** ♦ adj remote.

repostor, -ōris m restorer.

repostus etc see **repositus.**

repōtia, -ōrum ntpl second drinking.

repperī perf of **reperiō.**

The present infinitive verb endings are as follows: -āre = 1st; -ēre = 2nd; -ere = 3rd and -īre = 4th. See sections on irregular verbs and noun declensions.

reppulī perf of **repellō**.

repraesentātiō, -ōnis f vivid presentation; (COMM) cash payment.

repraesentō, -āre, -āvī, -ātum vt to exhibit, reproduce; to do at once, hasten; (COMM) to pay cash.

reprehendō, -endere, -endī, -ēnsum vt to hold back, catch, restrain; to hold fast, retain; to blame, rebuke, censure; to refute.

reprehēnsiō, -ōnis f check; blame, reprimand, refutation.

reprehēnsō, -āre vt to keep holding back.

reprehēnsor, -ōris m censurer, critic, reviser.

reprehēnsus ppp of **reprehendō**.

reprendō etc see **reprehendō**.

repressor, -ōris m restrainer.

repressus ppp of **reprimō**.

reprimō, -imere, -essī, -essum vt to keep back, force back; to check, restrain, suppress.

reprōmissiō, -ōnis f counterpromise.

reprōmittō, -ittere, -īsī, -issum vt to promise in return, engage oneself.

rēptō, -āre vi to creep about, crawl along.

repudiātiō, -ōnis f rejection.

repudiō, -āre, -āvī, -ātum vt to reject, refuse, scorn; (wife) to divorce.

repudium, -ī and **iī** nt divorce, repudiation.

repuerāscō, -ere vi to become a child again; to behave like a child.

repugnanter adv reluctantly.

repugnantia, -ium ntpl contradictions.

repugnō, -āre, -āvī, -ātum vi to oppose, resist; to disagree, be inconsistent.

repulsa, -ae f refusal, denial, repulse; (election) rebuff.

repulsō, -āre vi to throb, reverberate.

repulsus ppp of **repellō**.

repulsus, -ūs m (light) reflection; (sound) echoing.

repungō, -ere vt to prod again.

repūrgō, -āre, -āvī, -ātum vt to clear again, cleanse again; to purge away.

reputātiō, -ōnis f pondering over.

reputō, -āre, -āvī, -ātum vt to count back; to think over, consider.

requiēs, -ētis f rest, relaxation, repose.

requiēscō, -scere, -vī, -tum vi to rest, find rest; to cease ♦ vt to stay.

requiētus adj rested, refreshed.

requīritō, -āre vt to keep asking after.

requīrō, -rere, -sīvī and **siī, -sītum** vt to search for, look for; to ask, inquire after; (with ex or ab) to question; to need, want, call for; to miss, look in vain for.

requīsītus ppp of **requīrō**.

rēs, reī f thing, object; circumstance, case, matter, affair; business, transaction; fact, truth, reality; possessions, wealth, money; advantage, interest; (law) case; (MIL) campaign, operations; (POL) politics, power, the State; (writing) subject matter, story, history; ~ mihi est tēcum I have to do with you; ~ dīvīna sacrifice; ~ mīlitāris war; ~ pūblica public affairs, politics, the State, republic; ~ rūstica agriculture; rem facere get rich; rem gerere wage war, fight; ad rem to the point, to the purpose; in rem usefully; ob rem to the purpose; ob eam rem therefore; ī in malam rem go to the devil!; contrā rem pūblicam unconstitutionally; **ē rē pūblicā** constitutionally; **rē vērā** in fact, actually; **eā rē** for that reason; **tuā rē, ex tuā rē** to your advantage; **ab rē** unhelpfully; **ē rē (nātā)** as things are; **prō rē** according to circumstances; **rēs adversae** failure, adversity; **rēs dubiae** danger; **rēs gestae** achievements, career; **rēs novae** revolution, **rēs prosperae, secundae** success, prosperity; **rērum māximus** greatest in the world; **rērum scriptor** historian.

resacrō etc see **resecrō.**

resaeviō, -īre vi to rage again.

resalūtō, -āre vt to greet in return.

resānēscō, -ēscere, -uī vi to heal up again.

resarciō, -cīre, -tum vt to patch up, repair.

rescindō, -ndere, -dī, -ssum vt to cut back, cut open, break down; to open up; (law, agreement) to repeal, annul.

rescīscō, -īscere, -īvī and **iī, -ītum** vt to find out, learn.

rescissus ppp of **rescindō.**

rescrībō, -bere, -psī, -ptum vt to write back, reply; to rewrite, revise; (emperors) to give a decision; (MIL) to transfer, re-enlist; (money) to place to one's credit, pay back.

rescrīptus ppp of **rescrībō ♦** nt imperial rescript.

resecō, -āre, -uī, -tum vt to cut back, cut short; to curtail; **ad vīvum ~** cut to the quick.

resecrō, -āre vt to pray again; to free from a curse.

resectus ppp of **resecō.**

resecūtus ppa of **resequor.**

resēdī perf of **resideō**; perf of **resīdō.**

resēminō, -āre vt to reproduce.

resequor, -quī, -cūtus vt to answer.

reserō, -āre, -āvī, -ātum vt to unbar, unlock; to disclose.

reservō, -āre, -āvī, -ātum vt to keep back, reserve; to preserve, save.

reses, -idis adj remaining; inactive; idle; calm.

resideō, -idēre, -ēdī vi to remain behind; to be idle, be listless; (fig) to remain, rest.

resīdō, -īdere, -ēdī vi to sit down, sink down, settle; to subside; (fig) to abate, calm down.

residuus adj remaining, left over; (money) outstanding.

resignō, -āre vt to unseal, open; (fig) to reveal; (COMM) to cancel, pay back.

resiliō, -īre, -uī vi to spring back; to recoil, rebound, shrink.

resīmus adj turned up.

resīna, -ae f resin.

resīnātus adj smeared with resin.

resipiō, -ere vt to savour of, smack of.

resipīscō, -īscere, iī and **uī** vi to come to one's senses.

resistō, -istere, -titī vi to stand still, stop, halt; to resist, oppose; to rise again.

resolūtus ppp of **resolvō.**

resolvō, -vere, -vī, -ūtum vt to unfasten, loosen, open, release; to melt, dissolve; to relax; (debt) to pay up; (difficulty) to banish, dispel; (tax) to abolish; (words) to explain.

resonābilis adj answering.

resonō, -āre vi to resound, re-echo **♦** vt to echo the sound of; to make resound.

resonus adj echoing.

resorbeō, -ēre vt to suck back,

*The present infinitive verb endings are as follows: -**āre** = 1st; -**ēre** = 2nd; -**ere** = 3rd and -**īre** = 4th. See sections on irregular verbs and noun declensions.*

swallow again.

respectō, -āre vi to look back; to gaze about, watch ♦ vt to look back at, look for; to have regard for.

respectus ppp of **respiciō**.

respectus, -ūs m looking back; refuge; respect, regard.

respergō, -gere, -sī, -sum vt to besprinkle, splash.

respersiō, -ōnis f sprinkling.

respersus ppp of **respergō**.

respiciō, -icere, -exī, -ectum vt to look back at, see behind; (help) to look to; (care) to have regard for, consider, respect ♦ vi to look back, look.

respirāmen, -inis nt windpipe.

respirātiō, -ōnis f breathing; exhalation; taking breath, pause.

respirātus, -ūs m inhaling.

respirō, -āre, -āvī, -ātum vt, vi to breathe, blow back; to breathe again, revive; (things) to abate.

resplendeō, -ēre vi to flash back, shine brightly.

respondeō, -ondēre, -ondī, -ōnsum vt to answer, reply; (lawyer, priest, oracle) to advise, give a response; (law court) to appear; (pledge) to promise in return; (things) to correspond, agree, match; **pār parī ~ return like for like, give tit for tat.**

respōnsiō, -ōnis f answering; refutation.

respōnsitō, -āre vi to give advice.

respōnsō, -āre vt, vi to answer back; to defy.

respōnsor, -ōris m answerer.

respōnsum, -ī nt answer, reply; response, opinion, oracle.

rēspūblica, reīpūblicae f public affairs, politics, the State, republic.

respuō, -ere, -ī vt to spit out, eject; to reject, refuse.

restagnō, -āre vi to overflow; to be flooded.

restaurō, -āre vt to repair, rebuild.

resticula, -ae f rope, cord.

restinctiō, -ōnis f quenching.

restinctus ppp of **restinguō**.

restinguō, -guere, -xī, -ctum vt to extinguish, quench; (fig) to destroy.

restiō, -ōnis m rope maker.

restipulātiō, -ōnis f counter-obligation.

restipulor, -ārī vt to stipulate in return.

restis, -is f rope.

restitī perf of **resistō**; perf of **restō**.

restitō, -āre vi to stay behind, hesitate.

restituō, -uere, -uī, -ūtum vt to replace, restore; to rebuild, renew; to give back, return; (to a condition) to reinstate; (decision) to quash, reverse; (character) to reform.

restitūtiō, -ōnis f restoration; reinstating.

restitūtor, -ōris m restorer.

restitūtus ppp of **restituō**.

restō, -āre, -itī vi to stand firm; to resist; to remain, be left; to be in store (for); **quod ~at for the future.**

restrictē adv sparingly; strictly.

restrictus ppp of **restringō** ♦ adj tight, short; niggardly; severe.

restringō, -ngere, -nxī, -ctum vt to draw back tightly, bind fast; (teeth) to bare; (fig) to check.

resultō, -āre vi to rebound; to re-echo.

resūmō, -ere, -psī, -ptum vt to take up again, get back, resume.

resupīnō, -āre vt to turn back, throw on one's back.

resupīnus adj lying back, face upwards.

resurgō, -gere, -rēxī, -rēctum vi to

rise again, revive.

resuscitō, -āre vt to revive.

retardātiō, -ōnis f hindering.

retardō, -āre, -āvī, -ātum vt to retard, detain, check.

rēte, -is nt net; (fig) snare.

retēctus ppp of **retegō.**

retegō, -egere, -ēxī, -ēctum vt to uncover, open; to reveal.

retemptō, -āre vt to try again.

retendō, -endere, -endī, -entum and **ūnsum** vt to slacken, relax.

retēnsus ppp of **retendō.**

retentiō, -ōnis f holding back.

retentō etc see **retemptō.**

retentō, -āre vt to keep back, hold fast.

retentus ppp of **retendō;** ppp of **retineō.**

retēxī perf of **retegō.**

retexō, -ere, -uī, -tum vt to unravel; (fig) to break up, cancel; to renew.

rētiārius, -ī and **iī** m net-fighter.

reticentia, -ae f saying nothing; pause.

reticeō, -ēre, -uī vi to be silent, say nothing ♦ vt to keep secret.

rēticulum, -ī nt small net, hairnet; network bag.

retināculum, -ī nt tether, hawser.

retinēns, -entis pres p of **retineō** ♦ adj tenacious, observant.

retinentia, -ae f memory.

retineō, -inēre, -inuī, -entum vt to hold back, detain, restrain; to keep, retain, preserve.

retinniō, -īre vi to ring.

retonō, -āre vi to thunder in answer.

retorqueō, -quēre, -sī, -tum vt to turn back, twist.

retorridus adj dried up, wizened.

retortus ppp of **retorqueō.**

retractātiō, -ōnis f hesitation.

retractō, -āre, -āvī, -ātum vt to rehandle, take up again; to reconsider, revise; to withdraw ♦ vi to draw back, hesitate.

retractus ppp of **retrahō** ♦ adj remote.

retrahō, -here, -xī, -ctum vt to draw back, drag back; to withdraw, remove.

retrectō etc see **retractō.**

retribuō, -uere, -uī, -ūtum vt to restore, repay.

retrō adv back, backwards, behind; (time) back, past.

retrōrsum adv backwards, behind, in reverse order.

retrūdō, -dere, -sum vt to push back; to withdraw.

rettulī perf of **referō.**

retundō, -undere, -udī and **tudī, -ūsum** and **ūnsum** vt to blunt; (fig) to check, weaken.

retūsus, retūsus ppp of **retundō** ♦ adj blunt, dull.

reus, -ī m the accused, defendant; guarantor, debtor, one responsible; culprit, criminal; **vōtī ~** one who has had a prayer granted.

revalēscō, -ēscere, -uī vi to recover.

revehō, -here, -xī, -ctum vt to carry back, bring back; (pass) to ride, drive, sail back.

revellō, -ellere, -ellī, -ulsum (olsum) vt to pull out, tear off; to remove.

revēlō, -āre vt to unveil, uncover.

reveniō, -enīre, -ēnī, -entum vi to come back, return.

rēvērā adv in fact, actually.

reverendus adj venerable, awe-inspiring.

reverēns, -entis pres p of **revereor** ♦ adj respectful, reverent.

---

*The present infinitive verb endings are as follows: -**āre** = 1st; -**ēre** = 2nd; -**ere** = 3rd and -**īre** = 4th. See sections on irregular verbs and noun declensions.*

reverenter adv respectfully.
reverentia, -ae f respect, reverence, awe.
revereor, -ērī, -itus vt to stand in awe of; to respect, revere.
reversiō (revorsiō), -ōnis f turning back; recurrence.
reversus ppa of revertor.
revertō, -ere, -ī; revertor, -tī, -sus vi to turn back, return; to revert.
revexī perf of revehō.
revictus ppp of revincō.
revinciō, -cīre, -xī, -ctum vt to tie back, bind fast.
revincō, -incere, -īcī, -ictum vt to conquer, repress; (words) to refute, convict.
revinctus ppp of revinciō.
revirēscō, -ēscere, -uī vi to grow green again; to be rejuvenated; to grow strong again, flourish again.
revīsō, -ere vt, vi to come back to, revisit.
revīvēscō, -vīscō, -vīscere, -xī vi to come to life again, revive.
revocābilis adj revocable.
revocāmen, -inis nt recall.
revocātiō, -ōnis f recalling; (word) withdrawing.
revocō, -āre, -āvī, -ātum vt to call back, recall; (action) to revoke; (former state) to recover, regain; (growth) to check; (guest) to invite in return; (judgment) to apply, refer; (law) to summon again; (performer) to encore; (troops) to withdraw.
revolō, -āre vi to fly back.
revolsus etc see revulsus.
revolūbilis adj that may be rolled back.
revolūtus ppp of revolvō.
revolvō, -vere, -vī, -ūtum vt to roll back, unroll, unwind; (speech) to relate, repeat; (thought) to think over; (writing) to read over; (pass) to revolve, return, come round.

revomō, -ere, -uī vt to disgorge.
revor- etc see rever-.
revulsus ppp of revellō.
rēx, rēgis m king; tyrant, despot; leader; patron, rich man.
rēxī perf of regō.
Rhadamanthus, -ī m judge in the lower world.
Rhaetī etc see Raetī.
Rhamnūs, -ūntis f town in Attica (famous for its statue of Nemesis).
Rhamnūsis, -ūsidis f Nemesis.
Rhamnūsius adj see n.
rhapsōdia, -ae f a book of Homer.
Rhea, -ae f Cybele.
Rhea Silvia, -ae, -ae f mother of Romulus and Remus.
Rhēgium etc see Rēgium.
Rhēnānus adj Rhenish.
rhēnō etc see rēnō.
Rhēnus, -ī m Rhine.
Rhēsus, -ī m Thracian king (killed at Troy).
rhētor, -oris m teacher of rhetoric; orator.
rhētorica, -ae and **ē, -ēs** f art of oratory, rhetoric.
rhētoricē adv rhetorically, in an oratorical manner.
rhētoricī, -ōrum mpl teachers of rhetoric.
rhētoricus adj rhetorical, on rhetoric.
rhīnocerōs, -ōtis m rhinoceros.
rhō nt (indecl) Greek letter rho.
Rhodanus, -ī m Rhone.
Rhodius adj see Rhodopē.
Rhodopē, -ēs f mountain range in Thrace.
Rhodopēius adj Thracian.
Rhodos (Rhodus), -ī f island of Rhodes.
Rhoetēum, -ī nt promontory on the Dardanelles (near Troy).
Rhoetēus adj Trojan.
rhombus, -ī m magician's circle; (fish) turbot.

rhomphaea, -ae f long barbarian javelin.

rhythmicus, -ī m teacher of prose rhythm.

rhythmos (-us), -i m rhythm, symmetry.

rīca, -ae f sacrificial veil.

rīcinium, -ī and **lī** nt small cloak with hood.

rictum, -ī nt, **-us, -ūs** m open mouth, gaping jaws.

rideo, -dēre, -sī, -sum vi to laugh, smile ♦ vt to laugh at; smile at; to ridicule

rīdibundus adj laughing.

rīdiculāria, -ium ntpl jokes.

rīdiculē adv jokingly; absurdly.

rīdiculus adj amusing, funny; ridiculous, silly ♦ m jester ♦ nt joke.

rigēns, -entis pres p of **rigeō** ♦ adj stiff, rigid, frozen.

rigeō, -ēre vi to be stiff.

rigēscō, -ēscere, -uī vi to stiffen, harden; to bristle.

rigidē adv rigorously.

rigidus adj stiff, rigid, hard; (fig) hardy, strict, inflexible.

rigō, -āre vt to water, moisten, bedew; to convey (water).

rigor, -ōris m stiffness, hardness; numbness, cold; strictness, severity.

riguī perf of **rigēscō**.

riguus adj irrigating; watered.

rīma, -ae f crack, chink.

rīmor, -ārī, -ātus vt to tear open; to search for, probe, examine; to find out.

rīmōsus adj cracked, leaky.

ringor, -ī vi to snarl.

rīpa, -ae f river bank; shore.

Rīphaeī, -ōrum mpl mountain range in N. Scythia.

Rīphaeus adj see **Rīphaeī**.

rīpula, -ae f riverbank.

riscus, -ī m trunk, chest.

risī perf of **rīdeō**.

risor, -ōris m scoffer.

risus, -ūs m laughter, laugh; laughing stock.

rīte adv with the proper formality or ritual; duly, properly, rightly; in the usual manner; fortunately.

rītus, -ūs m ritual, ceremony; custom, usage; **~u** after the manner of.

rīvālis, -is m rival in love.

rīvālitās, -ātis f rivalry in love.

rīvulus, -ī m brook.

rīvus, -ī m stream, brook; **ē ~ō flūmina māgna facere** = make a mountain of a molehill.

rixa, -ae f quarrel, brawl, fight.

rixor, -ārī, -ātus vi to quarrel, brawl, squabble.

rōbīginōsus adj rusty.

rōbīgō, -inis f rust; blight, mould, mildew.

rōboreus adj of oak.

rōborō, -āre vt to strengthen, invigorate.

rōbur, -oris nt oak; hard wood; prison, dungeon (at Rome); (fig) strength, hardness, vigour; best part, élite, flower.

rōbustus adj of oak; strong, hard; robust, mature.

rōdō, -dere, -sī, -sum vt to gnaw; (rust) to corrode; (words) to slander.

rogālis adj of a pyre.

rogātiō, -ōnis f proposal, motion, bill; request; (RHET) question.

rogātiuncula, -ae f unimportant bill; question.

rogātor, -ōris m proposer; polling clerk.

rogātus, -ūs m request.

rogitō, -āre vt to ask for, inquire

The present infinitive verb endings are as follows: -āre = 1st; -ēre = 2nd; -ere = 3rd and -īre = 4th. See sections on irregular verbs and noun declensions.

eagerly.

rogō, -āre, -āvī, -ātum vt to ask, ask for; (bill) to propose, move; (candidate) to put up for election; **lēgem ~, populum ~** introduce a bill; **magistrātum populum ~** nominate for election to an office; **milītēs sacrāmentō ~** administer the oath to the troops; **mālō emere quam rogāre** I'd rather buy it than borrow it.

rogus, -ī m funeral pyre.

Rōma, -ae f Rome.

Rōmānus adj Roman.

Rōmuleus, -us adj of Romulus; Roman.

Rōmulidae, -idārum mpl the Romans.

Rōmulus, -ī m founder and first king of Rome.

rōrāriī, -ōrum mpl skirmishers.

rōridus adj dewy.

rōrifer, -ī adj dew-bringing.

rōrō, -āre vi to distil dew; to drip, trickle ♦ vt to bedew, wet.

rōs, rōris m dew; moisture, water; (plant) rosemary; **~ marīnus** rosemary.

rosa, -ae f rose; rose bush.

rosāria, -ōrum ntpl rose garden.

rōscidus adj dewy; wet.

Rōscius, -ī m: **L. ~ Othō** tribune in 67 BC, whose law reserved theatre seats for the equites ; **Q. ~ Gallus** famous actor defended by Cicero ; **Sex. ~** of Ameria, defended by Cicero.

Rōscius, -iānus adj see n.

rosētum, -ī nt rosebed.

roseus adj rosy; of roses.

rōsi perf of **rōdō**.

rōstrātus adj beaked, curved; **columna ~a** column commemorating a naval victory.

rōstrum, -ī nt (bird) beak, bill; (animal) snout, muzzle; (ship) beak, end of prow; (pl) orators' platform in the Forum.

rōsus ppp of **rōdō**.

rota, -ae f wheel; potter's wheel, torture wheel; car, disc.

rotō, -āre, -āvī, -ātum vt to turn, whirl, roll; (pass) to revolve.

rotunde adv elegantly.

rotundō, -āre vt to round off.

rotundus adj round, circular, spherical; (style) well-turned, smooth.

rubefaciō, -facere, -fēcī, -factum vt to redden.

rubēns, -entis pres p of **rubeō** ♦ adj red; blushing.

rubeō, -ēre vi to be red; to blush.

ruber, -rī adj red; **mare ~rum** Red Sea; Persian Gulf; **ōceanus ~** Indian Ocean; **Saxa ~ra** stone quarries between Rome and Veii.

rubēscō, -ēscere, -uī vi to redden, blush.

rubēta, -ae f toad.

rubēta, -ōrum ntpl bramble bushes.

rubeus adj of bramble.

Rubicō, -ōnis m stream marking the frontier between Italy and Gaul.

rubicundulus adj reddish.

rubicundus adj red, ruddy.

rūbīg- etc see **rōbīg-**.

rubor, -ōris m redness; blush; bashfulness; shame.

rubrīca, -ae f red earth, red ochre.

rubuī perf of **rubēscō**.

rubus, -ī m bramble bush; bramble, blackberry.

ructō, -āre, -or, -ārī vt, vi to belch.

ructus, -us m belching.

rudēns, -entis pres p of **rudō** ♦ m rope; (pl) rigging.

Rudiae, -iārum fpl town in S. Italy (birthplace of Ennius).

rudiārius, -ī and **iī** m retired gladiator.

rudimentum, -ī nt first attempt, beginning.

Rudīnus adj see **Rudiae**.

rudis adj unwrought, unworked, raw; coarse, rough, badly-made; (age) new, young; (person) uncultured, unskilled, clumsy; ignorant (of), inexperienced (in).

rudis, -is f stick, rod; foil (for fighting practice); (fig) discharge.

rudō, -ere, -īvī, -ītum vi to roar, bellow, bray; to creak.

rūdus, -eris nt rubble, rubbish; piece of copper.

rūdus, -eris nt copper coin.

Rūfulī, -ōrum mpl military tribunes (chosen by the general).

rūfulus adj red-headed.

rūfus adj red, red-haired.

rūga, -ae f wrinkle, crease.

rūgō, -āre vi to become creased.

rūgōsus adj wrinkled, shrivelled, corrugated.

ruī perf of **ruō**.

ruīna, -ae f fall, downfall; collapse, falling in; debris, ruins; destruction, disaster, ruin (fig).

ruīnōsus adj collapsing; ruined.

rumex, -icis f sorrel.

rūmificō, -āre vt to report.

Rūmina, -ae f goddess of nursing mothers; **ficus -ālis** the fig tree of Romulus and Remus (under which the she-wolf suckled them).

rūminātiō, -ōnis f chewing the cud; (fig) ruminating.

rūminō, -āre vt, vi to chew the cud.

rūmor, -ōris m noise, cheering; rumour, hearsay; public opinion; reputation.

rumpia etc see **rhomphaea**.

rumpō, -ere, rūpī, ruptum vt to break, burst, tear; to break down, burst through; (activity) to interrupt; (agreement) to violate, annul; (delay) to put an end to; (voice) to give vent to; (way) to force through.

rūmusculī, -ōrum mpl gossip.

rūna, -ae f dart.

runcō, -āre vt to weed.

ruō, -ere, -ī, -tum vi to fall down, tumble; to rush, run, hurry; to come to ruin ♦ vt to dash down, hurl to the ground; to throw up, turn up.

rūpēs, -is f rock, cliff.

rūpī perf of **rumpō**.

ruptor, -ōris m violator.

ruptus ppp of **rumpō**.

rūricola, -ae adj rural, country- (in cpds).

rūrigena, -ae m countryman.

rūrsus, rūrsum (rūsum) adv back, backwards; on the contrary, in return; again.

rūs, rūris nt the country, countryside; estate, farm; **rūs** to the country; **rūrī** in the country; **rūre** from the country.

ruscum, -ī nt butcher's broom.

russus adj red.

rūsticānus adj country- (in cpds), rustic.

rūsticātiō, -ōnis f country life.

rūsticē adv in a countrified manner, awkwardly.

rūsticitās, -ātis f country manners, rusticity.

rūsticor, -ārī vi to live in the country.

rūsticulus, -ī m yokel.

rūsticus adj country- (in cpds), rural; simple, rough, clownish ♦ m countryman.

rūsum see **rūrsus**.

rūta, -ae f (herb) rue; (fig) unpleasantness.

ruta caesa ntpl minerals and timber on an estate.

rutilō, -āre vt to colour red ♦ vi to glow red.

rutilus adj red, auburn.

The present infinitive verb endings are as follows: -āre = 1st; -ēre = 2nd; -ere = 3rd and -īre = 4th. See sections on irregular verbs and noun declensions.

rutrum, -ī nt spade, shovel, trowel.

rūtula, -ae f little piece of rue.

Rutulī, -ōrum mpl ancient Latin people.

Rutulus adj Rutulian.

Rutupiae, -iārum fpl seaport in Kent (now Richborough).

Rutupīnus adj see n.

rutus ppp of **ruō**.

S

Saba, -ae f town in Arabia Felix.

Sabaeus adj see n.

Sabāzia, -iōrum ntpl festival of Bacchus.

Sabāzius, -ī m Bacchus.

sabbata, -ōrum ntpl Sabbath, Jewish holiday.

Sabellus, -ī m Sabine, Samnite.

Sabellus, -icus adj see n.

Sabīnī, -ōrum mpl Sabines (a people of central Italy).

Sabīnus adj Sabine ♦ f Sabine woman ♦ nt Sabine estate; Sabine wine; **herba ~a** savin (a kind of juniper).

Sabrīna, -ae f river Severn.

saburra, -ae f sand, ballast.

Sacae, -ārum mpl tribe of Scythians.

saccipērium, -ī and iī nt purse-pocket.

saccō, -āre vt to strain, filter.

sacculus, -ī m little bag, purse.

saccus, -ī m bag, purse, wallet.

sacellum, -ī nt chapel.

sacer, -rī adj sacred, holy; devoted for sacrifice, forfeited; accursed, criminal, infamous; **Mōns ~** hill to which the Roman plebs seceded ; **Via ~ra** street from the Forum to the Capitol.

sacerdōs, -ōtis m/f priest, priestess.

sacerdōtium, -ī and iī nt priesthood.

sacrāmentum, -ī nt deposit made by parties to a lawsuit; civil lawsuit, dispute; (MIL) oath of allegiance, engagement.

sacrārium, -ī and iī nt shrine, chapel.

sacrātus adj holy, hallowed; **~āta lēx** a law whose violation was punished by devotion to the infernal gods.

sacricola, -ae m/f sacrificing priest or priestess.

sacrifer, -ī adj carrying holy things.

sacrificālis adj sacrificial.

sacrificātiō, -ōnis f sacrificing.

sacrificium, -ī and iī nt sacrifice.

sacrificō, -āre vt, vi to sacrifice.

sacrificulus, -ī m sacrificing priest; **rēx ~** high priest.

sacrificus adj sacrificial.

sacrilēgium, -ī and iī nt sacrilege.

sacrilegus adj sacrilegious; profane, wicked ♦ m templerobber.

sacrō, -āre, -āvī, -ātum vt to consecrate; to doom, curse; to devote, dedicate; to make inviolable; (poetry) to immortalize.

sacrōsanctus adj inviolable, sacrosanct.

sacrūficō etc see **sacrificō**.

sacrum, -rī nt holy thing, sacred vessel; shrine; offering, victim; rite; (pl) sacrifice, worship, religion; **~ra facere** sacrifice; **inter ~rum saxumque** ≈ with one's back to the wall; **hērēditās sine ~rīs** a gift with no awkward obligations.

saeclum etc see **saeculum**.

saeculāris adj centenary; (ECCL) secular, pagan.

saeculum, -ī nt generation, lifetime, age; the age, the times; century; **in ~a** (ECCL) for ever.

saepe adv often, frequently.

saepe numerō adv very often.

saepēs, -is f hedge, fence.

saepīmentum, -ī *nt* enclosure.
saepiō, -īre, -sī, -tum *vt* to hedge round, fence in, enclose; (*fig*) to shelter, protect.
saeptus *ppp of* **saepiō** ♦ *nt* fence, wall; stake, pale; (*sheep*) fold; (*Rome*) voting area in the Campus Martius.
saeta, -ae *f* hair, bristle.
saetiger, -ī *adj* bristly.
saetōsus *adj* bristly, hairy.
saevē, **-iter** *adv* fiercely, cruelly.
saevidicus *adj* furious.
saeviō, -īre, -iī, -ītum *vi* to rage, rave.
saevitia, -ae *f* rage; ferocity, cruelty.
saevus *adj* raging, fierce; cruel.
sāga, -ae *f* fortune teller.
sagācitās, -ātis *f* (*dogs*) keen scent; (*mind*) shrewdness.
sagāciter *adv* keenly; shrewdly.
sagātus *adj* wearing a soldier's cloak.
sagāx, -ācis *adj* (*senses*) keen, keen-scented; (*mind*) quick, shrewd.
sagina, -ae *f* stuffing, fattening; food, rich food; fatted animal.
saginō, -are *vt* to cram, fatten; to feed, feast.
sāgiō, -īre *vi* to perceive keenly.
sagitta, -ae *f* arrow.
sagittārius, -ī and iī *m* archer.
sagittifer, -ī *adj* armed with arrows.
sagmen, -inis *nt* tuft of sacred herbs (*used as a mark of inviolability*).
sagulum, -ī *nt* short military cloak.
sagum, -ī *nt* military cloak; woollen mantle.
Saguntīnus *adj see* **Saguntum**.
Saguntum, -ī *nt*, **-us (os)**, -ī *f* town in E. Spain.
sāgus *adj* prophetic.

sāl, **salis** *m* salt; brine, sea; (*fig*) shrewdness, wit, humour, witticism; good taste.
salacō, -ōnis *m* swaggerer.
Salamīnius *adj see* **Salamis**.
Salamis, -īnis *f* Greek island near Athens; town in Cyprus.
salapūtium, -ī and iī *nt* manikin.
salārius *adj* salt- (*in cpds*) ♦ *nt* allowance, salary.
salāx, -ācis *adj* lustful, salacious.
salebra, -ae *f* roughness, rut.
Saliāris *adj of* the Salii; sumptuous.
salictum, -ī *nt* willow plantation.
salientēs, -ium *fpl* springs.
salignus *adj* of willow.
Saliī, -ōrum *mpl* priests of Mars.
salillum, -ī *nt* little saltcellar.
salīnae, -ārum *fpl* saltworks.
salīnum, -ī *nt* saltcellar.
saliō, -īre, -uī, -tum *vi* to leap, spring; to throb.
saliunca, -ae *f* Celtic nard.
salīva, -ae *f* saliva, spittle; taste.
salix, -icis *f* willow.
Sallustiānus *adj see* **Sallustius**.
Sallustius, -ī *m* Sallust (*Roman historian*); his wealthy grand nephew.
Salmōneus, -eos *m* son of Aeolus (*punished in Tartarus for imitating lightning*).
Salmōnis, -idis *f* Salmoneus' daughter Tyro.
salsāmentum, -ī *nt* brine, pickle; salted fish
salsē *adv* wittily.
salsus *adj* salted; salt, briny; (*fig*) witty.
saltātiō, -ōnis *f* dancing, dance.
saltātor, -ōris *m* dancer.
saltātōrius *adj* dancing- (*in cpds*).
saltātrīx, -icis *f* dancer.
saltātus, -ūs *m* dance.
saltem *adv* at least, at all events;

The present infinitive verb endings are as follows: -**āre** = 1st; -**ēre** = 2nd; -**ere** = 3rd and -**īre** = 4th. *See sections on irregular verbs and noun declensions.*

nōn ~ not even.

saltō, -āre vt, vi to dance.

saltuōsus adj wooded.

saltus, -ūs m leap, bound.

saltus, -ūs m woodland pasture, glade; pass, ravine.

salūber adj see **salūbris**.

salūbris adj health-giving, wholesome; healthy, sound.

salūbritās, -ātis f healthiness; health.

salūbriter adv wholesomely; beneficially.

saluī perf of **saliō**.

salum, -ī nt sea, high sea.

salūs, -ūtis f health; welfare; life; safety; good wish, greeting; ~ūtem dīcere greet; bid farewell.

salūtāris adj wholesome, healthy; beneficial; ~ littera letter A (for absolvō = acquittal).

salūtāriter adv beneficially.

salūtātiō, -ōnis f greeting; formal morning visit, levee.

salūtātor, -ōris m morning caller; male courtier.

salūtātrīx, -rīcis f morning caller; female courtier.

salūtifer, -ī adj health-giving.

salūtigerulus adj carrying greetings.

salūtō, -āre, -āvī, -ātum vt to greet, salute, wish well; to call on, pay respects to.

salvē adv well, in good health; all right.

salvē impv of **salveō**.

salveō, -ēre vi to be well, be in good health; ~ē, ~ētō, ~ēte hail!, good day!, goodbye!; ~ēre iubeō I bid good day.

salvus, salvos adj safe, alive, intact, well, without violating; all right; ~ sīs good day to you!; ~a rēs est all is well; ~ā lēge without breaking the law.

Samaous adj see **Samē**.

Samarobrīva, -ae f Belgian town (now Amiens).

sambūca, -ae f harp.

sambūcistria, -ae f harpist.

Samē, -ēs f old name of the Greek island Cephallenia.

Samius adj Samian ♦ ntpl Samian pottery.

Samnis, -ītis adj Samnite.

Samnium, -ī and **iī** nt district of central Italy.

Samos (-us), -ī f Aegean island off Asia Minor (famous for its pottery and as the birthplace of Pythagoras).

Samothrāces, -um mpl Samothracians.

Samothrācia, -iae and **a, -ae** f Samothrace (island in the N. Aegean).

Samothrācius adj see n.

sānābilis adj curable.

sānātiō, -ōnis f healing.

sanciō, -cīre, -xī, -ctum vt to make sacred or inviolable; to ordain, ratify; to enact a punishment against.

sanctimōnia, -ae f sanctity; chastity.

sanctiō, -ōnis f decree, penalty for violating a law.

sanctitās, -ātis f sacredness; integrity, chastity.

sanctitūdō, -inis f sacredness.

sanctō adv solemnly, religiously.

sanctor, -ōris m enacter.

sanctus ppp of **sanciō** ♦ adj sacred, inviolable; holy, venerable; pious, virtuous, chaste.

sandaligerula, -ae f sandalbearer.

sandalium, -ī and **iī** nt sandal, slipper.

sandapila, -ae f common bier.

sandyx, -ycis f scarlet.

sānē adv sensibly; (intensive) very, doubtless; (ironical) to be sure, of course; (concessive) of course, indeed; (in answer) certainly, surely; (*with impv*) then, if you please; **~ quam** very much; **haud ~** not so very, not quite.

sanguen *etc see* **sanguis**.

sanguinäns, -äntis *adj* bloodthirsty.

sanguinärius *adj* bloodthirsty.

sanguineus *adj* bloody, of blood; blood-red.

sanguinolentus *adj* bloody; blood-red; sanguinary.

sanguis, -inis *m* blood, bloodshed; descent, family; offspring; (*fig*) strength, life; **~inem dare** shed one's blood; **~inem mittere** let blood.

saniés, -em, -ē *f* diseased blood, matter; venom.

sānitās, -ātis *f* (*body*) health, sound condition; (*mind*) sound sense, sanity; (*style*) correctness, purity.

sanna, -ae *f* grimace, mocking.

sanniō, -ōnis *m* clown.

sānō, -āre, -āvī, -ātum *vt* to cure, heal; (*fig*) to remedy, relieve.

Sanquālis avis *f* osprey.

sānus *adj* (*body*) sound, healthy; (*mind*) sane, sensible; (*style*) correct; **male ~** mad, inspired; **sānun es?** are you in your senses?

sanxī *perf of* **sanciō**.

sāpa, -ae *f* new wine.

sapiēns, -entis *pres p of* **sapiō ♦** *adj* wise, discreet **♦** *m* wise man, philosopher; man of taste.

sapienter *adv* wisely, sensibly.

sapientia, -ae *f* wisdom, discernment; philosophy; knowledge.

sapiō, -ere, -īvī *and* **uī** *vi* to have a flavour or taste; to have sense, be wise **♦** *vt* to taste of, smell of, smack of; to understand.

sapor, -ōris *m* taste, flavour; (*food*) delicacy; (*fig*) taste, refinement.

Sapphicus *adj see* **Sapphō**.

Sapphō, -ūs *f* famous Greek lyric poetess, native of Lesbos.

sarcina, -ae *f* bundle, burden; (*MIL*) pack.

sarcinārius *adj* baggage- (*in cpds*).

sarcinātor, -ōris *m* patcher.

sarcinula, -ae *f* little pack.

sarciō, -īre, -sī, -tum *vt* to patch, mend, repair.

sarcophagus, -ī *m* sepulchre.

sarculum, -ī *nt* light hoe.

Sardēs (-is), -ium *fpl* Sardis (*capital of Lydia*).

Sardiānus *adj see* **Sardēs**.

Sardinia, -iniae *f* island of Sardinia.

sardonyx, -chis *f* sardonyx.

Sardus, -ōus, -iniēnsis *adj see* **Sardinia**.

sariō, -īre, -īvī *and* **uī** *vt* to hoe, weed.

sarīsa, -ae *f* Macedonian lance.

sarīsophorus, -ī *m* Macedonian lancer.

Sarmatae, -ārum *mpl* Sarmatians (*a people of S.E. Russia*).

Sarmaticus, -is *adj see* **Sarmatae**.

sarmentum, -ī *nt* twigs, brushwood.

Sarpēdōn, -onis *m* king of Lycia.

sarrācum, -ī *nt* cart.

Sarrānus *adj* Tyrian.

sarriō *etc see* **sariō**.

sarsī *perf of* **sarciō**.

sartāgō, -inis *f* frying pan.

sartor, -ōris *m* hoer, weeder.

sartus *ppp of* **sarciō**.

sat *etc see* **satis**.

satagō, -ere *vi* to have one's hands full, be in trouble; to bustle about, fuss.

satelles, -itis *m/f* attendant, follower; assistant, accomplice.

The present infinitive verb endings are as follows: -āre = 1st; -ēre = 2nd; -ere = 3rd and -īre = 4th. See sections on irregular verbs and noun declensions.

satiās, -ātis f sufficiency; satiety.

satietās, -ātis f sufficiency; satiety.

satin, satine see **satisne**.

satiō, -āre, -āvī, -ātum vt to satisfy, appease; to fill, saturate; to glut, cloy, disgust.

satiō, -ōnis f sowing, planting; (pl) fields.

satis, sat adj enough, sufficient ♦ adv enough, sufficiently; tolerably, fairly, quite; **~ accipiō** take sufficient bail; **~ agō, agitō** have one's hands full, be harassed; **~ dō** offer sufficient bail; **~ faciō** satisfy; give satisfaction, make amends; (creditor) pay.

satisdatiō, -ōnis f giving security.

satisdō see **satis**.

satisfaciō see **satis**.

satisfactiō, -ōnis f amends, apology.

satisne adv quite, really.

satius compar of **satis**; better, preferable.

sator, -ōris m sower, planter; father; promoter.

satrapēs, -is m satrap (Persian governor).

satur, -ī adj filled, sated; (fig) rich.

satura, -ae f mixed dish; medley; (poem) satire; **per ~am** confusingly.

saturēia, -ōrum ntpl (plant) savory.

saturitās, -ātis f repletion; fulness, plenty.

Saturnālia, -ium and **iōrum** ntpl festival of Saturn in December.

Saturnia, -iae f Juno.

Saturnīnus, -ī m revolutionary tribune in 103 and 100 B.C.

Saturnius adj see n.

Saturnus, -ī m Saturn (god of sowing, ruler of the Golden Age); the planet Saturn.

saturō, -āre, -āvī, -ātum vt to fill, glut, satisfy; to disgust.

satus ppp of **serō** ♦ m son ♦ f daughter ♦ ntpl crops.

satus, -ūs m sowing, planting; begetting.

satyriscus, -ī m little satyr.

satyrus, -ī m satyr.

sauciātiō, -ōnis f wounding.

sauciō, -āre vt to wound, hurt.

saucius adj wounded, hurt; ill, stricken.

Sauromatae etc see **Sarmatae**.

sāviātiō, -ōnis f kissing.

sāviolum, -ī nt sweet kiss.

sāvior, -ārī vt to kiss.

sāvium, -ī and **iī** nt kiss.

saxātilis adj rock- (in cpds).

saxētum, -ī nt rocky place.

saxeus adj of rock, rocky.

saxificus adj petrifying.

saxōsus adj rocky, stony.

saxulum, -ī nt small rock.

saxum, -ī nt rock, boulder; the Tarpeian Rock.

scaber, -rī adj rough, scurfy; mangy, itchy.

scabiēs, -em, -ē f roughness; scurf; mange, itch.

scabillum, -ī nt stool; a castanet played with the foot.

scabō, -ere, scābī vt to scratch.

Scaea porta, -ae, -ae f the west gate of Troy.

scaena, -ae f stage, stage setting; (fig) limelight, public life; outward appearance, pretext.

scaenālis adj theatrical.

scaenicus adj stage- (in cpds), theatrical ♦ m actor.

Scaevola, -ae m early Roman who burned his hand off before Porsenna; famous jurist of Cicero's day.

scaevus adj on the left; perverse ♦ f omen.

scālae, -ārum fpl steps, ladder, stairs.

scalmus -ī m tholepin.

scalpellum, -ī nt scalpel, lancet.
scalpō, -ere, -sī, -tum vt to carve, engrave; to scratch.
scalprum, -ī nt knife, penknife; chisel.
scalpurriō, -īre vi to scratch.
Scamander, -rī m river of Troy (also called Xanthus).
scammōnea, -ae f (plant) scammony.
scamnum, -ī nt bench, stool; throne.
scandō, -ere vt, vi to climb, mount.
scapha, -ae f boat, skiff.
scaphium, -ī and **iī** nt a boat-shaped cup.
scapulae, -ārum fpl shoulder blades; shoulders.
scāpus, -ī m shaft; (loom) yarnbeam.
scarus, -ī m (fish) scar.
scatebra, -ae f gushing water.
scateō, -ēre; o, -ēre vi to bubble up, gush out; (fig) to abound, swarm.
scatūriginēs, -um fpl springs.
scatūriō, -īre vi to gush out; (fig) to be full of.
scaurus adj large-ankled.
scelerātē adv wickedly.
scelerātus adj desecrated; wicked, infamous, accursed; pernicious.
scelerō, -āre vt to desecrate.
scelerōsus adj vicious, accursed.
scelestē adv wickedly.
scelestus adj wicked, villainous, accursed; unlucky.
scelus, -eris nt wickedness, crime, sin; (person) scoundrel; (event) calamity.
scēn- etc see **scaen-**.
scēptrifer, -ī adj sceptered.
scēptrum, -ī nt staff, sceptre; kingship, power.
scēptūchus, -ī m sceptre-bearer.

scheda etc see **scida**.
schēma, -ae f form, figure, style.
Schoenēis, -ēidis f Atalanta.
Schoenēius adj see **Schoenēis**.
Schoeneus, -eī m father of Atalanta.
schoenobatēs, -ae m rope dancer.
schola, -ae f learned discussion, dissertation; school; sect, followers.
scholasticus adj of a school ♦ m rhetorician.
scida, -ae f sheet of paper.
sciēns, -entis pres p of **sciō** ♦ adj knowing, purposely; versed in, acquainted with.
scienter adv expertly.
scientia, -ae f knowledge, skill.
scīlicet adv evidently, of course; (concessive) no doubt; (ironical) I suppose, of course.
scilla etc see **squilla**.
scindō, -ndere, -dī, -ssum vt to cut open, tear apart, split, break down; to divide, part.
scintilla, -ae f spark.
scintillō, -āre vi to sparkle.
scintillula, -ae f little spark.
sciō, -īre, -īvī, -ītum vt to know; to have skill in; (with infin) to know how to; **quod -iam** as far as I know; **-ītō** you may be sure.
Scīpiadēs, -ae m Scipio.
scīpiō, -ōnis m staff.
Scīpiō, -ōnis m famous Roman family name (esp the conqueror of Hannibal Africanus); Aemilianus (destroyer of Carthage and patron of literature).
scirpeus adj rush (in cpds) ♦ f wickerwork frame.
scirpiculus, -ī m rush basket.
scirpus, -ī m bulrush.
scīscitor, -ārī, -ātus; -ō, -āre vt to inquire; to question.
scīscō, -scere, -vī, -tum vt to

The present infinitive verb endings are as follows: **-āre** = 1st; **-ēre** = 2nd; **-ere** = 3rd and **-īre** = 4th. *See sections on irregular verbs and noun declensions.*

inquire, learn; (*POL*) to approve, decree, appoint.

scissus *ppp of* **scindō ♦** *adj* split; (*voice*) harsh.

scītāmenta, -ōrum *ntpl* dainties.

scītē *adv* cleverly, tastefully.

scītor, -ārī, -ātus *vt, vi* to inquire; to consult.

scītulus *adj* neat, smart.

scītum, -ī *nt* decree, statute.

scītus *ppp of* **sciō**; *ppp of* **scīscō ♦** *adj* clever, shrewd, skilled; (*words*) sensible, witty; (*appearance*) fine, smart.

scītus, -ūs *m* decree.

sciūrus, -ī *m* squirrel.

scīvī *perf of* **sciō**; *perf of* **scīscō**.

scobis, -is *f* sawdust, filings.

scomber, -rī *m* mackerel.

scōpae, -ārum *fpl* broom.

Scopās, -ae *m* famous Greek sculptor.

scopulōsus *adj* rocky.

scopulus, -ī *m* rock, crag, promontory; (*fig*) danger.

scorpiō, -ōnis, -us *and* **os, -ī** *m* scorpion; (*MIL*) a kind of catapult.

scortātor, -ōris *m* fornicator.

scorteus *adj* of leather.

scortor, -ārī *vi* to associate with harlots.

scortum, -ī *nt* harlot, prostitute.

screātor, -ōris *m* one who clears his throat noisily.

screātus, -ūs *m* clearing the throat.

scrība, -ae *m* clerk, writer.

scrībō, -bere, -psī, -ptum *vt* to write, draw; to write down, describe; (*document*) to draw up; (*law*) to designate; (*MIL*) to enlist.

scrīnium, -ī *and* **iī** *nt* book box, lettercase.

scrīptiō, -ōnis *f* writing; composition; text.

scrīptitō, -āre, -āvī, -ātum *vt* to write regularly, compose.

scrīptor, -ōris *m* writer, author; secretary; **rērum ~** historian.

scrīptula, -ōrum *ntpl* lines of a squared board.

scrīptum, -ī *nt* writing, book, work; (*law*) ordinance; **duodecim ~a** Twelve Lines (*a game played on a squared board*).

scrīptūra, -ae *f* writing; composition; document; (*POL*) tax on public pastures; (*will*) provision.

scrīptus *ppp of* **scrībō**.

scrīpulus, -ūs *m* clerkship.

scrīpulum, -ī *nt* small weight, scruple.

scrobis, -is *f* ditch, trench; grave.

scrōfa, -ae *f* breeding sow.

scrōfipāscus, -ī *m* pig breeder.

scrūpeus *adj* stony, rough.

scrūpōsus *adj* rocky, jagged.

scrūpulōsus *adj* stony, rough; (*fig*) precise.

scrūpulum *etc see* **scrīpulum**.

scrūpulus, -ī *m* small sharp stone; (*fig*) uneasiness, doubt, scruple.

scrūpus, -ī *m* sharp stone; (*fig*) uneasiness.

scrūta, -ōrum *ntpl* trash.

scrūtor, -ārī, -ātus *vt* to search, probe into, examine; to find out.

sculpō, -ere, -sī, -tum *vt* to carve, engrave.

sculpōneae, -ārum *fpl* clogs.

sculptilis *adj* carved.

sculptor, -ōris *m* sculptor.

sculptus *ppp of* **sculpō**.

scurra, -ae *m* jester; dandy.

scurrīlis *adj* jeering.

scurrīlitās, -ātis *f* scurrility.

scurror, -ārī *vi* to play the fool.

scūtāle, -is *nt* sling strap.

scūtātus *adj* carrying a shield.

scutella, -ae *f* bowl.

scutica, -ae *f* whip.

scutra, -ae *f* flat dish.

scutula, -ae *f* small dish.

scutula f wooden roller; secret letter.

scutulāta, -ae f a checked garment.

scūtulum, -ī nt small shield.

scūtum, -ī nt shield.

Scylla, -ae f dangerous rock or sea monster (in the Straits of Messina).

Scyllaeus adj see **Scylla**.

scymnus, -ī m cub.

scyphus, -ī m wine cup.

Scyrius, -ias adj see **Scyros**.

Scyros and **us, -ī** f Aegean island near Euboea.

scytala see **scutula**.

Scytha and **ēs, -ae** m Scythian.

Scythia, -iae f Scythia (country N.E. of the Black Sea).

Scythicus adj Scythian.

Scythis, -idis f Scythian woman.

sē pron himself, herself, itself, themselves; one another; **apud ~** at home; **in his senses, inter ~** mutually.

sēbum, -ī nt tallow, suet, grease.

sēcēdō, -ēdere, -essī, -essum vi to withdraw, retire; to revolt, secede.

sēcernō, -ernere, -rēvī, -rētum vt to separate, set apart; to dissociate; to distinguish.

sēcessiō, -ōnis f withdrawal; secession.

sēcessus, -ūs m retirement, solitude; retreat, recess.

sēclūdō, -dere, -sī, -sum vt to shut off, seclude; to separate, remove.

sēclūsus ppp of **sēclūdō** ♦ adj remote.

secō, -āre, -uī, -tum vt to cut; to injure; to divide; (MED) to operate on; (motion) to pass through; (dispute) to decide.

sēcrētiō, -ōnis f separation.

sēcrētō adv apart, in private, in secret.

sēcrētum, -ī nt privacy, secrecy; retreat, remote place; secret, mystery.

sēcrētus ppp of **sēcernō** ♦ adj separate; solitary, remote; secret, private.

secta, -ae f path; method, way of life; (POL) party; (PHILOS) school.

sectārius adj leading.

sectātor, -ōris m follower, adherent.

sectilis adj cut; for cutting.

sectiō, -ōnis f auctioning of confiscated goods.

sector, -ōris m cutter; buyer at a public sale.

sector, -ārī, -ātus vt to follow regularly, attend; to chase, hunt.

sectūra, -ae f digging.

sectus ppp of **secō**.

sēcubitus, -ūs m lying alone.

sēcubō, -āre, -uī vi to sleep by oneself; to live alone.

secuī perf of **secō**.

sēcul- etc see **saecul-**.

sēcum with himself etc.

secundānī, -ōrum mpl men of the second legion.

secundārius adj second-rate.

secundō adv secondly.

secundō, -āre vt to favour, make prosper.

secundum prep (place) behind, along; (time) after; (rank) next to; (agreement) according to, in favour of ♦ adv behind.

secundus adj following, next, second; inferior; favourable, propitious, fortunate ♦ fpl (play) subsidiary part; (fig) second fiddle ♦ ntpl success, good fortune; **~ō flūmine** downstream; **rēs ~ae** prosperity, success.

secūricula, -ae f little axe.

The present infinitive verb endings are as follows: **-āre** = 1st; **-ēre** = 2nd; **-ere** = 3rd and **-īre** = 4th. See sections on irregular verbs and noun declensions.

securifer, -ī *adj* armed with an axe.

securiger, -ī *adj* armed with an axe.

securis, -is *f* axe; (*fig*) death blow; (*POL*) authority, supreme power.

securitas, -atis *f* freedom from anxiety, composure; negligence; safety, feeling of security.

securus *adj* untroubled, unconcerned; carefree, cheerful; careless.

secus *nt* (*indecl*) sex.

secus *adv* otherwise, differently; badly; nōn ~ even so.

secutor, -ōris *m* pursuer.

sed *conj* but; but also, but in fact.

sedate *adv* calmly.

sedatio, -ōnis *f* calming.

sedatus *ppp of* sēdō ♦ *adj* calm, quiet, composed.

sedecim *num* sixteen.

sedecula, -ae *f* low stool.

sedentarius *adj* sitting.

sedeo, -ēre, sēdī, sessum *vi* to sit; (*army*) to be encamped, blockade; (*magistrates*) to be in session; (*clothes*) to suit, fit; (*places*) to be low-lying; (*heavy things*) to settle, subside; (*weapons*) to stick fast; (*inactivity*) to be idle; (*thought*) to be firmly resolved.

sedes, -is *f* seat, chair; abode, home; site, ground, foundation.

sedī *perf of* sedeō.

sedile, -is *nt* seat, chair.

seditio, -ōnis *f* insurrection, mutiny.

seditiose *adv* seditiously.

seditiosus *adj* mutinous, factious; quarrelsome; troubled.

sedo, -āre, -āvī, -ātum *vt* to calm, allay, lull.

seduco, -ucere, -uxī, -uctum *vt* to take away, withdraw; to divide.

seductio, -ōnis *f* taking sides.

seductus *ppp of* sēdūcō ♦ *adj* remote.

sedulitas, -ātis *f* earnestness,

assiduity; officiousness.

sedulo *adv* busily, diligently; purposely.

sedulus *adj* busy, diligent, assiduous; officious.

seges, -itis *f* cornfield; crop.

Segesta, -ae *f* town in N.W. Sicily.

Segestanus *adj see* Segesta.

segmentatus *adj* flounced.

segmentum, -ī *nt* brocade.

segne, -iter *adv* slowly, lazily.

segnipes, -edis *adj* slow of foot.

segnis *adj* slow, sluggish, lazy.

segnitia, -ae *and* ēs, -em, -ē *f* slowness, sluggishness, sloth.

segrego, -āre, -āvī, -ātum *vt* to separate, put apart; to dissociate.

seiugatus *adj* separated.

seiugis, -is *m* chariot and six.

seiunctim *adv* separately.

seiunctio, -ōnis *f* separation.

seiunctus *ppp of* sēiungō.

seiungo, -gere, sēiunxī, sēiunctum *vt* to separate, part.

selectio, -ōnis *f* choice.

selectus *ppp of* sēligō.

Seleucus, -ī *m* king of Syria.

selibra, -ae *f* half pound.

seligo, -igere, -ēgī, -ēctum *vt* to choose, select.

sella, -ae *f* seat, chair, stool, sedan chair; ~ curulis chair of office for higher magistrates.

sellisternia, -ōrum *ntpl* sacred banquets to goddesses.

sellula, -ae *f* stool; sedan chair.

sellularius, -ī *and* iī *m* mechanic.

semanimus *etc see* sēmianimis.

semel *adv* once; once for all; first; ever; ~ atque iterum again and again; ~ aut iterum once or twice.

Semele, -ēs *f* mother of Bacchus.

Semeleius *etc see* Semele.

semen, -inis *nt* seed; (*plant*) seedling, slip; (*men*) race, child; (*physics*) particle; (*fig*) origin, instigator.

sēmentifer, -ī adj fruitful.

sēmentis, -is f sowing, planting; young corn.

sēmentīvus adj of seed time.

sēmermis etc see **sēmiermis.**

sēmēstris adj half-yearly, for six months.

sēmēsus adj half-eaten.

sēmet pron self, selves.

sēmiadapertus adj half-open.

sēmianimis, -us adj half-dead.

sēmiapertus adj half-open.

sēmibōs, -ovis adj half-ox.

sēmicaper, -rī adj half-goat.

sēmicremātus, sēmicremus adj half-burned.

sēmicubitālis adj half a cubit long.

sēmideus adj half-divine ♦ m demigod.

sēmidoctus adj half-taught.

sēmiermis, -us adj half-armed.

sēmiēsus adj half-eaten.

sēmifactus adj half-finished.

sēmifer, -ī adj half-beast; half-savage.

sēmigermānus adj half-German.

sēmigravis adj half overcome.

sēmigrō, -āre vi to go away.

sēmihiāns, -antis adj half-opened.

sēmihomō, -inis m half-man, half-human.

sēmihōra, -ae f half an hour.

sēmilacer, -ī adj half-mangled.

sēmilautus adj half-washed.

sēmilīber, -ī adj half-free.

sēmilixa, -ae m not much better than a camp follower.

sēmimarīnus adj half in the sea.

sēmimās, -āris m hermaphrodite ♦ adj castrated.

sēmimortuus adj half-dead.

sēminārium, -ī and **iī** nt nursery, seed plot.

sēminātor, -ōris m originator.

sēminecis adj half-dead.

sēminium, -ī and **iī** nt procreation; breed.

sēminō, -āre vt to sow; to produce; to beget.

sēminūdus adj half-naked; almost unarmed.

sēmipāgānus adj half-rustic.

sēmiplēnus adj half-full, half-manned.

sēmiputātus adj half-pruned.

Semiramis, -is and **idis** f queen of Assyria.

Semiramius adj see n.

sēmirāsus adj half-shaven.

sēmireductus adj half turned back.

sēmirefectus adj half-repaired.

sēmirutus adj half-demolished, half in ruins.

sēmis, -issis m (coin) half an as; (interest) ½ per cent per month (i.e. 6 per cent per annum); (area) half an acre.

sēmisepultus adj half-buried.

sēmisomnus adj half-asleep.

sēmisupīnus adj half lying back.

sēmita, -ae f path, way.

sēmitālis adj of byways.

sēmitārius adj frequenting byways.

sēmiūst- etc see **sēmūst-.**

sēmivir, -ī adj half man; emasculated; unmanly.

sēmivīvus adj half dead.

sēmodius, -ī and **iī** m half a peck.

sēmōtus ppp of **sēmoveō** ♦ adj remote; distinct.

sēmoveō, -ovēre, -ōvī, -ōtum vt to put aside, separate.

semper adv always, ever, every time.

sempiternus adj everlasting, lifelong.

Semprōnius, -ī m Roman family name (esp the Gracchi).

*The present infinitive verb endings are as follows: -**āre** = 1st; -**ēre** = 2nd; -**ere** = 3rd and -**īre** = 4th. See sections on irregular verbs and noun declensions.*

Semprōnius, -iānus adj see n.

sēmūncia, -ae f half an ounce; a twenty-fourth.

sēmūnciārius adj (interest) at the rate of one twenty-fourth.

sēmūstulātus adj half-burned.

sēmūstus adj half-burned.

senāculum, -ī nt open air meeting place (of the Senate).

sēnāriolus, -ī m little trimeter.

sēnārius, -ī and iī m (iambic) trimeter.

senātor, -ōris m senator.

senātōrius adj senatorial, in the Senate.

senātus, -ūs m Senate; meeting of the Senate.

senātūscōnsultum, -ī nt decree of the Senate.

Seneca, -ae m Stoic philosopher, tutor of Nero.

senecta, -ae f old age.

senectus adj old, aged.

senectūs, -ūtis f old age; old men.

seneō, -ēre vi to be old.

senēscō, -ēscere, -uī vi to grow old; (fig) to weaken, wane, pine away.

senex, -is (compar -ior) adj old (over 45) ♦ m/f old man, old woman.

sēnī, -ōrum adj six each, in sixes; six; ~ dēnī sixteen each.

senīlis adj of an old person, senile.

sēniō, -ōnis m number six on a dice.

senior compar of **senex**.

senium, -ī and iī nt weakness of age, decline; affliction; peevishness.

Senonēs, -um mpl tribe of S. Gaul.

sēnsī perf of **sentiō**.

sēnsifer, -ī adj sensory.

sēnsilis adj having sensation.

sēnsim adv tentatively, gradually.

sēnsus ppp of **sentiō** ♦ ntpl thoughts.

sēnsus, -ūs m (body) feeling, sensation, sense; (intellect) understanding, judgment, thought; (emotion) sentiment, attitude, frame of mind; (language) meaning, purport, sentence; commūnis ~ universal human feelings, human sympathy, social instinct.

sententia, -ae f opinion, judgment; purpose, will; (law) verdict, sentence; (POL) vote, decision; (language) meaning, sentence, maxim, epigram; meā ~ā in my opinion; dē meā ~ā in accordance with my wishes; ex meā ~ā to my liking; ex animi meī ~ā to the best of my knowledge and belief; in ~am pedibus īre support a motion.

sententiola, -ae f phrase.

sententiōsē adv pointedly.

sententiōsus adj pithy.

senticētum, -ī nt thornbrake.

sentīna, -ae f bilge water; (fig) dregs, scum.

sentiō, -īre, sēnsī, sēnsum vt (senses) to feel, see, perceive; (CIRCS) to experience, undergo; (mind) to observe, understand; (opinion) to think, judge; (law) to vote, decide.

sentis, -is m thorn, brier.

sentīscō, -ere vt to begin to perceive.

sentus adj thorny; untidy.

senuī perf of **senēscō**.

seorsum, seorsus adv apart, differently.

sēparābilis adj separable.

sēparātim adv apart, separately.

sēparātiō, -ōnis f separation, severing.

sēparātius adv less closely.

sēparātus adj separate, different.

sēparō, -āre, -āvī, -ātum vt to part, separate, divide; to distinguish.

sepeliō, -elīre, -elīvī and elī, -ultum vt to bury; (fig) to overwhelm, overcome.

sēpia, -ae f cuttlefish.

Sēplasia, -ae f street in Capua where perfumes were sold.

sēpōnō, -ōnere, -osuī, -ositum vt to put aside, pick out; to reserve; to banish; to appropriate; to separate.

sepositus ppp of **sēpōnō** ♦ adj remote; distinct, choice.

sēpse pron oneself.

septem num seven.

September, -ris m September ♦ adj of September.

septemdecim etc see **septendecim.**

septemfluus adj with seven streams.

septemgeminus adj sevenfold.

septemplex, -icis adj sevenfold.

septemtriō etc see **septentriōnēs.**

septemvirālis adj of the septemviri ♦ mpl the septemviri.

septemvirātus, -ūs m office of septemvir.

septemvirī, -ōrum mpl board of seven officials.

septēnārius, -ī and iī m verse of seven feet.

septendecim num seventeen.

septēnī, -ōrum adj seven each, in sevens.

septentriō, -ōnis m, **-ōnēs, -ōnum** mpl Great Bear, Little Bear; north; north wind.

septentriōnālis adj northern ♦ ntpl northern regions.

septiēns, -ēs adv seven times.

septimānī, -ōrum mpl men of the seventh legion.

septimum adv for the seventh time; ~ **decimus** seventeenth.

septimus adj seventh.

septingentēsimus adj seven hundredth.

septingentī, -ōrum adj seven

hundred.

septuāgēsimus adj seventieth.

septuāgintā adj seventy.

septuennis adj seven years old.

septumus adj see **septimus.**

septūnx, -ūncis m seven ounces, seven-twelfths.

sepulcrālis adj funeral.

sepulcrētum, -ī nt cemetery.

sepulcrum, -ī nt grave, tomb.

sepultūra, -ae f burial, funeral.

sepultus ppp of **sepeliō.**

Sequāna, -ae f river Seine.

Sequānī, -ōrum mpl people of N. Gaul.

sequāx, -ācis adj pursuing, following.

sequēns, -entis pres p of **sequor** ♦ adj following, next.

sequester, -rī and ris m trustee; agent, mediator.

sequestrum, -rī nt deposit.

sēquius compar of **secus;** otherwise; **nihilō ~** nonetheless.

sequor, -quī, -cūtus vt, vi to follow; to accompany, go with; (time) to come after, come next, ensue; (enemy) to pursue; (objective) to make for, aim at; (pulling) to come away easily; (share, gift) to go to, come to; (words) to come naturally.

sera, -ae f door bolt, bar.

Serāpēum, -ēī nt temple of Serapis.

Serāpis, -is and idis m chief Egyptian god.

serēnitās, -atis f fair weather.

serēnō, -āre vt to clear up, brighten up.

serēnus adj fair, clear; (wind) fair-weather; (fig) cheerful, happy ♦ nt clear sky, fair weather.

Sērēs, -um mpl Chinese.

serēscō, -ere vi to dry off.

sēria, -ae f tall jar.

The present infinitive verb endings are as follows: **-āre** = 1st; **-ēre** = 2nd; **-ere** = 3rd and **-īre** = 4th. *See sections on irregular verbs and noun declensions.*

sērica, -ōrum ntpl silks.

Sēricus adj Chinese; silk.

seriēs, -em, -ē f row, sequence, succession.

sēriō adv in earnest, seriously.

sēriola, -ae f small jar.

Sēriphius adj see Sēriphus.

Sēriphus (-os), -ī f Aegean island.

sērius adj earnest, serious.

sērius compar of sērō.

sermō, -ōnis m conversation, talk; learned discussion, discourse; common talk, rumour; language, style; everyday language, prose; (pl) Satires (of Horace).

sermōcinor, -ārī vi to converse.

sermunculus, -ī m gossip, rumour.

serō, -ere, sēvī, -satum vt to sow, plant; (fig) to produce, sow the seeds of.

serō, -ere, -tum vt to sew, join, wreathe; (fig) to compose, devise, engage in.

sērō (compar -ius) adv late; too late.

serpēns, -entis m/f snake, serpent; (constellation) Draco.

serpentigena, -ae m offspring of a serpent.

serpentipēs, -edis adj serpent-footed.

serperastra, -ōrum ntpl splints.

serpō, -ere, -sī, -tum vi to creep, crawl; (fig) to spread slowly.

serpyllum, -ī nt wild thyme.

serra, -ae f saw.

serrācum etc see sarrācum.

serrātus adj serrated, notched.

serrula, -ae f small saw.

Sertōriānus adj see Sertōrius.

Sertōrius, -ī m commander under Marius, who held out against Sulla in Spain.

sertus ppp of serō ♦ ntpl garlands.

serum, -ī nt whey, serum.

sērum, -ī nt late hour.

sērus adj late; too late; **~ā nocte** late at night.

serva, -ae f maidservant, slave.

servābilis adj that cannot be saved.

servātor, -ōris m deliverer; watcher.

servātrīx, -īcis f deliverer.

servīlis adj of slaves, servile.

servīliter adv slavishly.

Servīlius, -ī m Roman family name of many consuls.

Servīlius, -ānus adj see n.

serviō, -īre, -īvī and **iī, -ītum** vi to be a slave; (with dat) to serve, be of use to, be good for; (property) to be mortgaged.

servitium, -ī and **iī** nt slavery, servitude; slaves.

servitūdō, -inis f slavery.

servitūs, -ūtis f slavery, service; slaves; (property) liability.

Servius, -ī m sixth king of Rome; famous jurist of Cicero's day.

servō, -āre, -āvī, -ātum vt to save, rescue; to keep, preserve, retain; to store, reserve; to watch, observe, guard; (place) to remain in.

servolus, -ī m young slave.

servos, -ī m see servus.

servula, -ae f servant girl.

servulus, -ī m young slave.

servus, -ī m slave, servant ♦ adj slavish, serving; (property) liable to a burden.

sescēnāris adj a year and a half old.

sescēnī, -ōrum adj six hundred each.

sescentēsimus adj six hundredth.

sescentī, -ōrum num six hundred; an indefinitely large number.

sescentiēns, -ēs adv six hundred times.

sēsē etc see sē.

seselis, -is f (plant) seseli.

sesqui adv one and a half times.

sesquialter, -ī adj one and a half.

sesquimodius, -ī and **iī** m a peck

and a half.

sesquioctāvus adj of nine to eight.

sesquiopus, -eris nt a day and a half's work.

sesquipedālis adj a foot and a half.

sesquipēs, -edis m a foot and a half.

sesquiplāga, -ae f a blow and a half.

sesquiplex, -icis adj one and a half times.

sesquitertius adj of four to three.

sessilis adj for sitting on.

sessiō, -ōnis f sitting; seat; session; loitering.

sessitō, -āre, -āvī vi to sit regularly.

sessiuncula, -ae f small meeting.

sessor, -ōris m spectator; resident.

sēstertium, -ī nt 1000 sesterces; **dēna ~ia** 10,000 sesterces; **centēna mīlia ~ium** 100,000 sesterces; **deciēns ~ium** 1,000,000 sesterces.

sēstertius, -ī and **iī** m sesterce, a silver coin.

Sestius, -ī m tribune defended by Cicero.

Sestius, -iānus adj of a Sestius.

Sestos (-us), -ī f town on Dardanelles (home of Hero).

Sestus adj see **Sestos**.

sēt- etc see **saet-**.

Sētia, -iae f town in S. Latium (famous for wine).

Sētiānus adj see **Sētia**.

sētius compar of **secus**.

seu etc see **sīve**.

sevērē adv sternly, severely.

sevēritās, -ātis f strictness, austerity.

sevērus adj strict, stern; severe, austere; grim, terrible.

sēvī perf of **serō**.

sēvocō, -āre vt to call aside; to withdraw, remove.

sēvum etc see **sēbum**.

sex num six.

sexāgēnārius adj sixty years old.

sexāgēnī, -ōrum adj sixty each.

sexāgēsimus adj sixtieth.

sexāgiēns, -ēs adv sixty times.

sexāgintā num sixty.

sexangulus adj hexagonal.

sexcēn- etc see **sescēn-**.

sexcenārius adj of six hundred.

sexennis adj six years old, after six years.

sexennium, -ī and **iī** nt six years.

sexiēns, -ēs adv six times.

sexprīmī, -ōrum mpl a provincial town, council.

sextadecimānī, -ōrum mpl men of the sixteenth legion.

sextāns, -antis m a sixth; (coin, weight) a sixth of an as.

sextārius, -ī and **iī** m pint.

Sextīlis, -is m August ♦ adj of August.

sextula, -ae f a sixth of an ounce.

sextum adv for the sixth time.

sextus adj sixth; **~ decimus** sixteenth.

sexus, -ūs m sex.

sī conj if; if only; to see if; **sī forte** in the hope that; **sī iam** assuming for the moment; **sī minus** if not; **sī quandō** whenever; **sī quidem** if indeed; since; **sī quis** if anyone, whoever; **mīrum sī** surprising that; **quod sī** and if, but if.

sībila, -ōrum ntpl whistle, hissing.

sībilō, -āre vi to hiss, whistle ♦ vt to hiss at.

sībilus, -ī m whistle, hissing.

sībilus adj hissing.

Sibulla, Sibylla, -ae f prophetess, Sibyl.

Sibyllīnus adj see **Sibylla**.

The present infinitive verb endings are as follows: **-āre** = 1st; **-ēre** = 2nd; **-ere** = 3rd and **-īre** = 4th. *See sections on irregular verbs and noun declensions.*

sīc adv so, thus, this way, as follows; as one is, as things are; on this condition; yes

sīca, -ae f dagger.

Sicānī, -ōrum mpl ancient people of Italy (later of Sicily).

Sicānia, -iae f Sicily.

Sicānus, -ius adj Sicanian, Sicilian.

sīcārius, -ī and **iī** m assassin, murderer.

siccē adv (speech) firmly.

siccitās, -ātis f dryness, drought; (body) firmness; (style) dullness.

siccō, -āre, -āvī, -ātum vt to dry; to drain, exhaust; (sore) to heal up.

siccoculus adj dry-eyed.

siccus adj dry; thirsty, sober; (body) firm, healthy; (argument) solid, sound; (style) flat, dull ♦ nt dry land.

Sicilia, -ae f Sicily.

sicilicula, -ae f little sickle.

Siciliēnsis, -s, -dis adj Sicilian.

sīcine is this how?

sīcubi adv if anywhere, wheresoever.

Siculus adj Sicilian.

sīcunde adv if from anywhere.

sīcut, sīcutī adv just as, as in fact; (comparison) like, as; (example) as for instance; (with subj) as if.

Sicyōn, -ōnis f town in N. Peloponnese.

Sicyōnius adj see **Sicyōn**.

sīdereus, -ī adj starry; (fig) radiant.

Sidicīnī, -ōrum mpl people of Campania.

Sidicīnus adj see n.

sīdō, -ere, -ī vi to sit down, settle; to sink, subside; to stick fast.

Sīdōn, -ōnis f famous Phoenician town.

Sīdōnis, -ōnidis adj Phoenician ♦ f Europa; Dido.

Sīdōnius adj Sidonian, Phoenician.

sīdus, -eris nt constellation; heavenly body, star; season;

climate, weather; destiny; (pl) sky; (fig) fame, glory.

siem archaic subj of **sum**.

Sigambrī etc see **Sugambrī**.

Sigēum, -ī nt promontory near Troy.

Sigēus, -ius adj Sigean.

sigilla, -ōrum ntpl little figures; seal.

sigillātus adj decorated with little figures.

signātor, -ōris m witness (to a document).

signifer, -ī adj with constellations; ~ orbis Zodiac ♦ m (MIL) standard-bearer.

significanter adv pointedly, tellingly.

significātiō, -ōnis f indication, signal, token; sign of approval; (RHET) emphasis; (word) meaning.

significō, -āre, -āvī, -ātum vt to indicate, show; to betoken, portend; (word) to mean.

signō, -āre, -āvī, -ātum vt to mark, stamp, print; (document) to seal; (money) to coin, mint; (fig) to impress, designate, note.

signum, -ī nt mark, sign, token; (MIL) standard; signal, password; (art) design, statue; (document) seal; (ASTRO) constellation; ~a cōnferre join battle; ~a cōnstituere halt; ~a convertere wheel about; ~a ferre move camp; attack; ~a inferre attack; ~a prōferre advance; ~a sequī march in order; ab ~īs discēdere leave the ranks; sub ~īs īre march in order.

Sīla, -ae f forest in extreme S. Italy

sīlānus, -ī m fountain, jet of water.

silēns, -entis pres p of **sileō** ♦ adj still, silent ♦ mpl the dead.

silentium, -ī and **iī** nt stillness, silence; (fig) standstill, inaction.

Sīlēnus, -ī m old and drunken companion of Bacchus.

sileō, -ēre, -uī vi to be still, be
silent; to cease ♦ vt to say nothing
about.

siler, -is nt willow.

silēscō, -ere vi to calm down, fall
silent.

silex, -icis m flint, hard stone; rock.

silicernium, -ī and **iī** nt funeral
feast.

silīgō, -inis f winter wheat; fine
flour.

siliqua, -ae f pod, husk; (pl) pulse.

sillybus, -ī m label bearing a book's
title.

Silurēs, -um mpl British tribe in S.
Wales.

silūrus, -ī m sheatfish.

silus adj snub-nosed.

silva, -ae f wood, forest;
plantation, shrubbery; (plant)
flowering stem; (LIT) material.

Silvānus, -ī m god of uncultivated
land.

silvēscō, -ere vi to run to wood.

silvestris adj wooded, forest- (in
cpds); wild; pastoral.

silvicola, -ae m/f sylvan.

silvicultrix, -īcis adj living in the
woods.

silvifragus adj tree-breaking.

silvōsus adj woody.

sīmia, -ae f ape.

simile, -is nt comparison, parallel.

similis adj like, similar; ~ atque
like what; **vērī ~** probable.

similiter adv similarly.

similitūdō, -inis f likeness,
resemblance; imitation; analogy;
monotony; (RHET) simile.

simiolus, -ī m monkey.

simītū adv at the same time,
together.

simius, -ī and **iī** m ape.

Simoīs, -entis m river of Troy.

Simōnidēs, -is m Greek lyric poet

of Ceos (famous for dirges).

Simōnidēus adj see n.

simplex, -icis adj single, simple;
natural, straightforward;
(character) frank, sincere.

simplicitās, -ātis f singleness;
frankness, innocence.

simpliciter adv simply, naturally;
frankly.

simplum, -ī nt simple sum.

simpulum, -ī nt small ladle;
excitāre fluctūs in ~ō ≈ raise a
storm in a teacup.

simpuvium, -ī and **iī** nt libation
bowl.

simul adv at the same time,
together, at once; likewise, also;
both ... and; **~ ac atque, ut** as soon
as ♦ conj as soon as.

simulācrum, -ī nt likeness, image,
portrait, statue; phantom, ghost;
(writing) symbol; (fig) semblance,
shadow.

simulāmen, -inis nt copy.

simulāns, -antis pres p of **simulō**
♦ adj imitative.

simulātē adv deceitfully.

simulātiō, -ōnis f pretence,
shamming, hypocrisy.

simulātor, -ōris m imitator;
pretender, hypocrite.

simulatque conj as soon as.

simulō, -āre, -āvī, -ātum vt to
imitate, represent; to
impersonate; to pretend,
counterfeit.

simultās, -ātis f feud, quarrel.

simulus adj snub-nosed.

sīmus adj snub-nosed.

sīn conj but if; **~ aliter, minus** but if
not.

sināpi, -is nt, **-is, -is** f mustard.

sincērē adv honestly.

sincēritās, -ātis f integrity.

sincērus adj clean, whole, genuine;

*The present infinitive verb endings are as follows: -āre = 1st; -ēre = 2nd; -ere = 3rd and
-īre = 4th. See sections on irregular verbs and noun declensions.*

(fig) pure, sound, honest.

sincipitāmentum, **-ī** *nt* half a head.

sinciput, **-itis** *nt* half a head; brain.

sine *prep (with abl)* without, -less *(in cpds)*.

singillātim *adv* singly, one by one.

singulāris *adj* one at a time, single, sole; unique, extraordinary.

singulāriter *adv* separately; extremely.

singulārius *adj* single.

singulī, **-ōrum** *adj* one each, single, one.

singultim *adv* in sobs.

singultō, **-āre** *vi* to sob, gasp, gurgle ♦ *vt* to gasp out.

singultus, **-ūs** *m* sob, gasp, death rattle.

singulus *etc see* **singulī**.

sinister, **-rī** *adj* left; *(fig)* perverse, unfavourable; *(Roman auspices)* lucky; *(Greek auspices)* unlucky.

sinistra, **-rae** *f* left hand, left-hand side.

sinistrē *adv* badly.

sinistrōrsus, **-um** *adv* to the left.

sinō, **-ere**, **sīvī**, **situm** *vt* to let, allow; to let be; **nē dī sīrint** God forbid!

Sinōpē, **-ēs** *f Greek colony on the Black Sea.*

Sinōpēnsis, **-eus** *adj see* **Sinōpē**.

Sinuessa, **-ae** *f town on the borders of Latium and Campania.*

Sinuessānus *adj see* **Sinuessa**.

sīnum *etc see* **sīnus**.

sinuō, **-āre**, **-āvī**, **-ātum** *vt* to wind, curve.

sinuōsus *adj* winding, curved.

sinus, **-ūs** *m* curve, fold; *(fishing)* net; *(GEOG)* bay, gulf, valley; *(hair)* curl; *(ship)* sail; *(toga)* fold, pocket, purse; *(person)* bosom; *(fig)* protection, love, heart, hiding place; **in ~ū gaudēre** be secretly glad.

sīnus, **-ī** *m* large cup.

sīparium, **-ī** *and* **iī** *nt* act curtain.

siphō, **-ōnis** *m* siphon; fire engine.

sīquandō *adv* if ever.

sīquī, **sīquis** *pron* if any, if anyone, whoever.

sīquidem *adv* if in fact ♦ *conj* since.

sīrempse *adj* the same.

Sīrēn, **-ēnis** *f* Siren.

sīris, **sīrit** *perf subj of* **sinō**.

Sīrius, **-ī** *m* Dog Star ♦ *adj of Sirius.*

sīrpe, **-is** *nt* silphium.

sīrus, **-ī** *m* corn pit.

sīs *(for* **sī vīs***) adv* please.

sistō, **-ere**, **stitī**, **statum** *vt* to place, set, plant; *(law)* to produce in court; *(monument)* to set up; *(movement)* to stop, arrest, check ♦ *vi* to stand, rest; *(law)* to appear in court; *(movement)* to stand still, stop, stand firm; **sē ~** appear, present oneself; **tūtum ~** see safe; **vadimōnium ~** duly appear in court; **~ī nōn potest** the situation is desperate.

sistrum, **-ī** *nt* Egyptian rattle, cymbal.

sisymbrium, **-ī** *and* **iī** *nt* fragrant herb, perhaps mint.

Sīsyphius *adj*, **-idēs**, **-idae** *m* Ulysses.

Sīsyphus, **-ī** *m criminal condemned in Hades to roll a rock repeatedly up a hill.*

sitella, **-ae** *f* lottery urn.

Sīthonis, **-idis** *adj* Thracian.

Sīthonius *adj* Thracian.

siticulōsus *adj* thirsty, dry.

sitiēns, **-entis** *pres p of* **sitiō** ♦ *adj* thirsty, dry; parching; *(fig)* eager.

sitienter *adv* eagerly.

sitiō, **-īre** *vi* to be thirsty; to be parched ♦ *vt* to thirst for, covet.

sitis, **-is** *f* thirst; drought.

sittybus *etc see* **sillybus**.

situla, **-ae** *f* bucket.

situs *ppp of* **sinō ♦** *adj* situated,
  lying; founded; (*fig*) dependent.
situs, -ūs *m* situation, site;
  structure; neglect, squalor,
  mould; (*mind*) dullness.
sīve *conj* or if; or; whether ... or.
sīvī *perf of* **sinō**.
smaragdus, -ī *m/f* emerald.
smīlax, -acis *f* bindweed.
Smintheus, -eī *m* Apollo.
Smyrna, -ae *f Ionian town in Asia
  Minor*.
Smyrnaeus *adj see* **Smyrna**.
sobol- *etc see* **subol-**.
sobriē *adv* temperately; sensibly.
sobrīna, -ae *f* cousin (*on the
  mother's side*).
sobrīnus, -ī *m* cousin (*on the
  mother's side*).
sobrius *adj* sober; temperate,
  moderate; (*mind*) sane, sensible.
soccus, -ī *m* slipper (*esp the sock
  worn by actors in comedy*); comedy.
socer, -ī *m* father-in-law.
sociābilis *adj* compatible.
sociālis *adj* of allies, confederate;
  conjugal.
sociāliter *adv* sociably.
soclennus, -ī *m* friend.
societās, -ātis *f* fellowship,
  association; alliance.
sociō, -āre, -āvī, -ātum *vt* to unite,
  associate, share.
sociofraudus, -ī *m* deceiver of
  friends.
socius *adj* associated, allied **♦** *m*
  friend, companion; partner, ally.
sōcordia, -ae *f* indolence, apathy;
  folly.
sōcordius *adv* more carelessly,
  lazily.
sōcors, -dis *adj* lazy, apathetic;
  stupid.
Sōcratēs, -is *m famous Athenian
  philosopher*.

Sōcraticus *adj* of Socrates,
  Socratic **♦** *mpl* the followers of
  Socrates.
socrus, -ūs *f* mother-in-law.
sodālicium, -ī and iī *nt* fellowship;
  secret society.
sodālicius *adj* of fellowship.
sodālis, -is *m/f* companion, friend;
  member of a society, accomplice.
sodālitās, -ātis *f* companionship,
  friendship; society, club, secret
  society.
sodālitius *etc see* **sodālicius**.
sodēs *adv* please.
sōl, sōlis *m* sun; sunlight, sun's
  heat; (*poetry*) day; (*myth*) Sun god;
  ~ **oriēns, -is ortus** east; ~
  occidēns, -is occāsus west.
sōlāciolum, -ī *nt* a grain of
  comfort.
sōlācium, -ī and iī *nt* comfort,
  consolation, relief.
sōlāmen, -inis *nt* solace, relief.
sōlāris *adj* of the sun.
sōlārium, -ī and iī *nt* sundial;
  clock; balcony, terrace.
sōlātium *etc see* **sōlācium**.
sōlātor, -ōris *m* consoler.
soldūrlī, -ōrum *mpl* retainers.
soldus *etc see* **solidus**.
solea, -ae *f* sandal, shoe; fetter;
  (*fish*) sole.
soleārius, -ī and iī *m* sandal
  maker.
soleātus *adj* wearing sandals.
soleō, -ēre, -itus *vi* to be
  accustomed, be in the habit,
  usually do; **ut** ~ as usual.
solidē *adv* for certain.
soliditās, -ātis *f* solidity.
solidō, -āre *vt* to make firm,
  strengthen.
solidus *adj* solid, firm, dense,
  whole, complete; (*fig*) sound,
  genuine, substantial **♦** *nt* solid

*The present infinitive verb endings are as follows: -āre = 1st; -ēre = 2nd; -ere = 3rd and
-īre = 4th. See sections on irregular verbs and noun declensions.*

matter, firm ground.

sōliferreum, -ī *nt* an all-iron javelin.

sōlistimus *adj* (AUG) most favourable.

sōlitārius *adj* solitary, lonely.

sōlitūdō, -inis *f* solitariness, loneliness; destitution; (*place*) desert.

solitus *ppa of* soleō ♦ *adj* usual, customary ♦ *nt* custom; **plūs ~ō** more than usual.

solium, -ī *and* **iī** *nt* seat, throne; tub; (*fig*) rule.

sōlivagus *adj* going by oneself; single.

sollemne, -is *nt* religious rite, festival; usage, practice.

sollemnis *adj* annual, regular; religious, solemn; usual, ordinary.

sollemniter *adv* solemnly.

sollers, -tis *adj* skilled, clever, expert; ingenious.

sollerter *adv* cleverly.

sollertia, -ae *f* skill, ingenuity.

sollicitātiō, -ōnis *f* inciting.

sollicitō, -āre, -āvī, -ātum *vt* to stir up, disturb; to trouble, distress, molest; to rouse, urge, incite, tempt, tamper with.

sollicitūdō, -inis *f* uneasiness, anxiety.

sollicitus *adj* agitated, disturbed; (*mind*) troubled, worried, alarmed; (*things*) anxious, careful; (*cause*) disquieting.

solliferreum *etc see* **sōliferreum**.

sollistimus *etc see* **sōlistimus**.

soloecismus, -ī *m* grammatical mistake.

Solōn, -ōnis *m* famous Athenian lawgiver.

sōlor, -ārī, -ātus *vt* to comfort, console; to relieve, ease.

sōlstitiālis *adj* of the summer solstice; midsummer.

sōlstitium, -ī *and* **iī** *nt* summer solstice; midsummer, summer heat.

solum, -ī *nt* ground, floor, bottom; soil, land, country; (*foot*) sole; (*fig*) basis; **~ō aequāre** raze to the ground.

sōlum *adv* only, merely.

sōlus (*gen* **-īus**, *dat* **-ī**) *see* vicis ♦ *adj* only, alone; lonely, forsaken; (*place*) lonely, deserted.

solūtē *adv* loosely, freely, carelessly, weakly, fluently.

solūtiō, -ōnis *f* loosening; payment.

solūtus *ppp of* solvō ♦ *adj* loose, free; (*from distraction*) at ease, at leisure, merry; (*from obligation*) exempt; (*from restraint*) free, independent, unprejudiced; (*moral*) lax, weak, insolent; (*language*) prose, unrhythmical; (*speaker*) fluent; **ōrātiō ~a, verba ~a** prose.

solvō, -vere, -vī, -ūtum *vt* to loosen, undo; to free, release, acquit, exempt; to dissolve, break up, separate; to relax, slacken, weaken; to cancel, remove, destroy; to solve, explain; to pay, fulfil; (*argument*) to refute; (*discipline*) to undermine; (*feelings*) to get rid of; (*hair*) to let down; (*letter*) to open; (*sail*) to unfurl; (*siege*) to raise; (*troops*) to dismiss ♦ *vi* to set sail; to pay; **nāvem ~** set sail; **poenās ~** be punished; **praesēns ~** pay cash; **rem ~** pay; **sacrāmentō ~** discharge; **~vendō esse** be solvent.

Solyma, -ōrum *ntpl* Jerusalem.

Solymus *adj* of the Jews.

somniculōsē *adv* sleepily.

somniculōsus *adj* sleepy.

somnifer, -ī *adj* soporific; fatal.

somniō, -āre *vt* to dream, dream about; to talk nonsense.

somnium, -ī and iī nt dream; nonsense, fancy.

somnus, -ī m sleep; sloth.

sonābilis adj noisy.

sonipēs, -edis m steed.

sonitus, -ūs m sound, noise.

sonivius adj noisy.

sonō, -āre, -uī, -itum vi to sound, make a noise ♦ vt to utter, speak, celebrate; to sound like.

sonor, -ōris m sound, noise.

sonōrus adj noisy, loud.

sōns, sontis adj guilty.

sonticus adj critical; important.

sonus, -ī m sound, noise; (fig) tone.

sophistēs, -ae m sophist.

Sophoclēs, -is m famous Greek tragic poet.

Sophoclēus adj of Sophocles, Sophoclean.

sophus adj wise.

sōpiō, -īre, -īvī, -ītum vt to put to sleep; (fig) to calm, lull.

sopor, -ōris m sleep; apathy.

sopōrifer, -ī adj soporific, drowsy.

sopōrō, -āre vt to lull to sleep; to make soporific.

sopōrus adj drowsy.

Sōracte, -is nt mountain in S. Etruria.

sorbeō, -ēre, -uī vt to suck, swallow; (fig) to endure.

sorbillō, -āre vt to sip.

sorbitiō, -ōnis f drink, broth.

sorbum, -ī nt service berry.

sorbus, -ī f service tree.

sordeō, -ēre vi to be dirty, be sordid; to seem shabby; to be of no account.

sordēs, -is f dirt, squalor, shabbiness; mourning; meanness; vulgarity; (people) rabble.

sordēscō, -ere vi to become dirty.

sordidātus adj shabbily dressed, in mourning.

sordidē adv meanly, vulgarly.

sordidulus adj soiled, shabby.

sordidus adj dirty, squalid, shabby; in mourning; poor, mean; base, vile.

sōrex, -icis m shrewmouse.

sōricinus adj of the shrewmouse.

sōrītēs, -ae m chain syllogism.

soror, -ōris f sister.

sorōricida, -ae m murderer of a sister.

sorōrius adj of a sister.

sors, sortis f lot; allotted duty; oracle, prophecy; fate, fortune; (money) capital, principal.

sōrsum etc see **seōrsum**.

sortilegus adj prophetic ♦ m soothsayer.

sortior, -īrī, -ītus vi to draw or cast lots ♦ vt to draw lots for, allot, obtain by lot; to distribute, share; to choose; to receive.

sortitiō, -ōnis f drawing lots, choosing by lot.

sortītus ppa of **sortior** ♦ adj assigned, allotted; -ō by lot.

sortītus, -ūs m drawing lots.

Sosius, -ī m Roman family name (esp two brothers Sosii, famous booksellers in Rome).

sōspes, -itis adj safe and sound, unhurt; favourable, lucky.

sōspita, -ae f saviour.

sōspitālis adj beneficial.

sōspitō, -āre vt to preserve, prosper.

sōtēr, -ēris m saviour.

spādīx, -icis adj chestnut-brown.

spadō, -ōnis m eunuch.

spargō, -gere, -sī, -sum vt to throw, scatter, sprinkle; to strew, spot, moisten; to disperse, spread abroad.

sparsus ppp of **spargō** ♦ adj freckled.

The present infinitive verb endings are as follows: -āre = 1st; -ēre = 2nd; -ere = 3rd and -īre = 4th. See sections on irregular verbs and noun declensions.

Sparta, -ae; -ē, -ēs f *famous Greek city.*

Spartacus, -ī m *gladiator who led a revolt against Rome.*

Spartānus, -icus adj Spartan.

Spartiātēs, -iātae m Spartan.

spartum, -ī nt Spanish broom.

sparulus, -ī m bream.

sparus, -ī m hunting spear.

spatha, -ae f broadsword.

spatior, -ārī, -ātus vi to walk; to spread.

spatiōsē adv greatly; after a time.

spatiōsus adj roomy, ample, large; (*time*) prolonged.

spatium, -ī and **iī** nt space, room, extent; (*between points*) distance; (*open space*) square, walk, promenade; (*race*) lap, track, course; (*time*) period, interval; (*opportunity*) time, leisure; (*metre*) quantity.

speciēs, -ēī f seeing, sight; appearance, form, outline; (*thing seen*) sight; (*mind*) idea; (*in sleep*) vision, apparition; (*fair show*) beauty, splendour; (*false show*) pretence, pretext; (*classification*) species; **in ~em** for the sake of appearances; like; **per ~em** under the pretence; **sub ~e** under the cloak.

specillum, -ī nt probe.

specimen, -inis nt sign, evidence, proof; pattern, ideal.

speciōsē adv handsomely.

speciōsus adj showy, beautiful; specious, plausible.

spectābilis adj visible; notable, remarkable.

spectāclum, spectāculum, -ī nt sight, spectacle; public show, play; theatre, seats.

spectāmen, -inis nt proof.

spectātiō, -ōnis f looking; testing.

spectātor, -ōris m onlooker, observer, spectator; critic.

spectātrīx, -īcis f observer.

spectātus ppp of **spectō ♦** adj tried, proved; worthy, excellent.

spectiō, -ōnis f the right to take auspices.

spectō, -āre, -āvī, -ātum vt to look at, observe, watch; (*place*) to face; (*aim*) to look to, bear in mind, contemplate, tend towards; (*judging*) to examine, test.

spectrum, -ī nt spectre.

specula, -ae f watchtower, lookout; height.

spēcula, -ae f slight hope.

speculābundus adj on the lookout.

speculāris adj transparent ♦ ntpl window.

speculātor, -ōris m explorer, investigator; (MIL) spy, scout.

speculātōrius adj for spying, scouting ♦ f spy boat.

speculātrīx, -īcis f watcher.

speculor, -ārī, -ātus vt to spy out, watch for, observe.

speculum, -ī nt mirror.

specus, -ūs m, nt cave; hollow, chasm.

spēlaeum, -ī nt cave, den.

spēlunca, -ae f cave, den.

spērābilis adj to be hoped for.

spērāta, -ātae f bride.

Sperchēis, -idis adj see **Sperchēus.**

Sperchēus (-os), -ī m river in Thessaly.

spernō, -ere, sprēvī, sprētum vt to remove, reject, scorn.

spērō, -āre, -āvī, -ātum vt to hope, hope for, expect; to trust; to look forward to.

spēs, speī f hope, expectation; **praeter spem** unexpectedly; **spē dēiectus** disappointed.

Speusippus, -ī m successor of Plato in the Academy.

sphaera, -ae f ball, globe, sphere.

Sphinx, -ingis f fabulous monster near Thebes.

spīca, -ae f (*grain*) ear; (*plant*) tuft; (ASTRO) brightest star in Virgo.

spīceus adj of ears of corn.

spīculum, -ī nt point, sting; dart, arrow.

spīna, -ae f thorn; prickle; fish bone; spine, back; (*pl*) difficulties, subtleties.

spīnētum, -ī nt thorn hedge.

spīneus adj of thorns.

spīnifer, -ī adj prickly.

spīnōsus adj thorny, prickly; (*style*) difficult.

spinter, -ēris nt elastic bracelet.

spīnus, -ī f blackthorn, sloe.

spīra, -ae f coil; twisted band.

spīrābilis adj breathable, life-giving.

spīrāculum, -ī nt vent.

spīrāmentum, -ī nt vent, pore; breathing space.

spīritus, -ūs m breath, breathing; breeze, air; inspiration; character, spirit, courage, arrogance.

spīrō, -āre, -āvī, -ātum vi to breathe, blow; to be alive; to be inspired ♦ vt to emit, exhale; (*fig*) to breathe, express.

spissātus adj condensed.

spissē adv closely; slowly.

spissēscō, -ere vi to thicken.

spissus adj thick, compact, crowded; slow; (*fig*) difficult.

splendeō, -ēre vi to be bright, shine; to be illustrious.

splendēscō, -ere vi to become bright.

splendidē adv brilliantly, magnificently, nobly.

splendidus adj bright, brilliant, glittering; (*sound*) clear; (*dress, house*) magnificent; (*person*) illustrious; (*appearance*) showy.

splendor, -ōris m brightness,

lustre; magnificence; clearness; nobility.

spoliātiō, -ōnis f plundering.

spoliātor, -ōris m robber.

spoliātrīx, -īcis f robber.

spoliō, -āre, -āvī, -ātum vt to strip; to rob, plunder.

spolium, -ī and **iī** nt (*beast*) skin; (*enemy*) spoils, booty.

sponda, -ae f bed frame; bed, couch.

spondālium, -ī and **iī** nt hymn accompanied by the flute.

spondeō, -ēre, spopondī, spōnsum vt to promise, pledge, vow; (*law*) to go bail for; (*marriage*) to betroth.

spondēus, -ī m spondee.

spongia, -ae f sponge; coat of mail.

spōnsa, -ae f fiancée, bride.

spōnsālia, -ium ntpl engagement.

spōnsiō, -ōnis f promise, guarantee; (*law*) agreement that the loser in a suit pays the winner a sum; bet.

spōnsor, -ōris m guarantor, surety.

spōnsus ppp of spondeō ♦ m fiancé, bridegroom ♦ nt agreement, covenant.

spōnsus, -ūs m contract, surety.

sponte f (*abl*) voluntarily, of one's own accord; unaided; by oneself; spontaneously.

spopondī perf of spondeō.

sportella, -ae f fruit basket.

sportula, -ae f small basket; gift to clients, dole.

sprētiō, -ōnis f contempt.

sprētor, -ōris m despiser.

sprētus ppp of spernō.

sprēvī perf of spernō.

spūma, -ae f foam, froth.

spūmēscō, -ere vi to become

frothy.

spūmeus *adj* foaming, frothy.

spūmifer, -ī *adj* foaming.

spūmiger, -ī *adj* foaming.

spūmō, -āre *vi* to foam, froth.

spūmōsus *adj* foaming.

spuō, -uere, -uī, -ūtum *vi* to spit
♦ *vt* to spit out.

spurcē *adv* obscenely.

spurcidicus *adj* obscene.

spurcificus *adj* obscene.

spurcitia, -ae and **ēs, -ēī** *f* filth,
smut.

spurcō, -āre *vt* to befoul.

spurcus *adj* filthy, nasty, foul.

spūtātilicus *adj* despicable.

spūtātor, -ōris *m* spitter.

spūtō, -āre *vt* to spit out.

spūtum, -ī *nt* spittle.

squāleō, -ēre, -uī *vi* to be rough,
stiff, clotted; to be parched; to be
neglected, squalid, filthy; to be in
mourning.

squālidē *adv* rudely.

squālidus *adj* rough, scaly;
neglected, squalid, filthy; (*speech*)
unpolished.

squālor, -ōris *m* roughness; filth,
squalor.

squāma, -ae *f* scale; scale armour.

squāmeus *adj* scaly.

squāmifer, -ī *adj* scaly.

squāmiger, -ī *adj* scaly ♦ *mpl*
fishes.

squāmōsus *adj* scaly.

squilla, -ae *f* prawn, shrimp.

st *interj* sh!

stabilīmentum, -ī *nt* support.

stabiliō, -īre *vt* to make stable; to
establish.

stabilis *adj* firm, steady; (*fig*)
steadfast, unfailing.

stabilitās, -ātis *f* firmness,
steadiness, reliability.

stabulō, -āre *vt* to house, stable
♦ *vi* to have a stall.

stabulum, -ī *nt* stall, stable,

steading; lodging, cottage;
brothel.

stacta, -ae *f* myrrh oil.

stadium, -ī and **iī** *nt* stade, furlong;
racetrack.

Stagīra, -ōrum *ntpl* town in
Macedonia (*birthplace of Aristotle*).

Stagīrītēs, -ītae *m* Aristotle.

stagnō, -āre *vi* to form pools; to be
inundated ♦ *vt* to flood.

stagnum, -ī *nt* standing water,
pool, swamp; waters.

stāmen, -inis *nt* warp; thread;
(*instrument*) string; (*priest*) fillet.

stāmineus *adj* full of threads.

stata *adj* : **Stata māter** Vesta.

statārius *adj* standing, stationary,
steady; calm ♦ *f* refined comedy
♦ *mpl* actors in this comedy.

statēra, -ae *f* scales.

statim *adv* steadily; at once,
immediately; ~ **ut** as soon as.

statiō, -ōnis *f* standing still;
station, post, residence; (*pl*)
sentries; (*NAUT*) anchorage.

Statius, -ī *m* Caecilius (*early writer
of comedy*); Papinius (*epic and lyric
poet of the Silver Age*).

statīvus *adj* stationary ♦ *ntpl*
standing camp.

stator, -ōris *m* attendant, orderly.

Stator, -ōris *m* the Stayer (*epithet
of Jupiter*).

statua, -ae *f* statue.

statūmen, -inis *nt* (*ship*) rib.

statuō, -uere, -uī, -ūtum *vt* to set
up, place; to bring to a stop; to
establish, constitute; to
determine, appoint; to decide,
settle; to decree, prescribe; (*with
infin*) to resolve, propose; (*with acc
and infin*) to judge, consider,
conclude; (*army*) to draw up;
(*monument*) to erect; (*price*) to fix;
(*sentence*) to pass; (*tent*) to pitch;
(*town*) to build; **condiciōnem ~
dictate** (to); **finem ~** put an end

(to); **iūs ~** lay down a principle;
modum ~ impose restrictions;
apud animum ~ make up one's
mind; **dē sē ~** commit suicide;
gravius ~ in deal severely with.
statūra, -ae f height, stature.
status ppp of **sistō ♦** adj appointed,
due.
status, -ūs m posture, attitude;
position; (social) standing, status,
circumstances; (POL) situation,
state, form of government;
(nature) condition; **reī pūblicae ~**
the political situation;
constitution; **dē ~ū movēre**
dislodge.
statūtus ppp of **statuō**.
stega, -ae f deck.
stēliō see **stēlliō**.
stēlla, -ae f star; **~ errāns** planet.
stēllāns, -antis adj starry.
stēllātus adj starred; set in the
sky.
stēllifer, -ī adj starry.
stēlliger, -ī adj starry.
stēlliō, -ōnis m newt.
stemma, -tis nt pedigree.
stercoreus adj filthy.
stercorō, -āre vt to manure.
stercus, -oris nt dung.
sterilis adj barren, sterile; bare,
empty, unprofitable, fruitless.
sterilitās, -ātis f barrenness.
sternāx, -ācis adj bucking.
sternō, -ere, strāvī, strātum vt to
spread, strew; to smooth,
level; to stretch out, extend; to
throw to the ground, prostrate; to
overthrow; (bed) to make; (horse)
to saddle; (road) to pave.
sternūmentum, -ī nt sneezing.
sternuō, -ere, -ī vt, vi to sneeze.
Steropē, -ēs f a Pleiad.
sterquilīnium, -ī and iī, (-um, -ī) nt
dung heap.

stertō, -ere, -uī vi to snore.
Stēsichorus, -ī m Greek lyric poet.
stetī perf of **stō**.
Sthenelēius and eis and ēidis adj
see n.
Sthenelus, -ī m father of Eurystheus;
father of Cycnus.
stigma, -tis nt brand.
stigmatiās, -ae m branded slave.
stilla, -ae f drop.
stillicidium, -ī and iī nt dripping
water, rainwater from the eaves.
stillō, -āre, -āvī, -ātum vi to drip,
trickle ♦ vt to let fall in drops,
distil.
stilus, -ī m stake; pen; (fig) writing,
composition, style; **~um vertere**
erase.
stimulātiō, -ōnis f incentive.
stimulātrix, -īcis f provocative
woman.
stimuleus adj smarting.
stimulō, -āre, -āvī, -ātum vt to
goad; to trouble, torment; to
rouse, spur on, excite.
stimulus, -ī m goad; (MIL) stake;
(pain) sting, pang; (incentive) spur,
stimulus.
stinguō, -ere vt to extinguish.
stīpātiō, -ōnis f crowd, retinue.
stīpātor, -ōris m attendant; (pl)
retinue, bodyguard.
stīpendiārius adj tributary, liable
to a money tax; (MIL) receiving pay
♦ mpl tributary peoples.
stīpendium, -ī and iī nt tax tribute;
soldier's pay; military service,
campaign; **~ merēre, merērī**
serve; **~ ēmerērī** complete one's
period of service.
stīpes, -itis m log, trunk; tree;
(insult) blockhead.
stīpō, -āre, -āvī, -ātum vt to press,
pack together; to cram, stuff full;
to crowd round, accompany in a

body.

stips, stipis f donation, contribution.

stipula, -ae f stalk, blade, stubble; reed.

stipulātiō, -ōnis f promise, bargain.

stipulātiuncula, -ae f slight stipulation.

stipulātus adj promised.

stipulor, -ārī vt, vi to demand a formal promise, bargain, stipulate.

stīria, -ae f icicle.

stirpēs etc see **stirps.**

stirpitus adv thoroughly.

stirps, -is f lower trunk and roots, stock; plant, shoot; family, lineage, progeny; origin; **ab ~e** utterly.

stīva, -ae f plough handle.

stlattārius adj seaborne.

stō, stāre, stetī, statum vi to stand; to remain in position, stand firm; to be conspicuous; (fig) to persist, continue; (battle) to go on; (hair) to stand on end; (NAUT) to ride at anchor; (play) to be successful; (price) to cost; (with ab, cum, prō) to be on the side of, support; (with in) to rest, depend on; (with per) to be the fault of; **stat sententia** one's mind is made up; **per Āfrānium stetit quōminus dīmicārētur** thanks to Afranius there was no battle.

Stōicē adv like a Stoic.

Stōicus adj Stoic ♦ m Stoic philosopher ♦ ntpl Stoicism.

stola, -ae f long robe (esp worn by matrons).

stolidē adv stupidly.

stolidus adj dull, stupid.

stomachor, -ārī, -ātus vi to be vexed, be annoyed.

stomachōsē adv see adj.

stomachōsus adj angry, irritable.

stomachus, -ī m gullet; stomach; taste, liking; dislike, irritation, chagrin.

stōrea (storia), -ae f rush mat, rope mat.

strabō, -ōnis m squinter.

strāgēs, -is f heap, confused mass; havoc, massacre.

strāgulus adj covering ♦ nt bedspread, rug.

strāmen, -inis nt straw, litter.

strāmentum, -ī nt straw, thatch; straw bed; covering, rug.

strāmineus adj straw-thatched.

strangulō, -āre, -āvī, -ātum vt to throttle, choke.

strangūria, -ae f difficult discharge of urine.

stratēgēma, -tis nt a piece of generalship, stratagem.

stratēgus, -ī m commander, president.

stratiōticus adj military.

strātum, -ī nt coverlet, blanket; bed, couch; horsecloth, saddle; pavement.

strātus ppp of **sternō** ♦ adj prostrate.

strāvī perf of **sternō.**

strēnuē adv energetically, quickly.

strēnuitās, -ātis f energy, briskness.

strēnuus adj brisk, energetic, busy; restless.

strepitō, -āre vi to make a noise, rattle, rustle.

strepitus, -ūs m din, clatter, crashing, rumbling; sound.

strepō, -ere, -uī vi to make a noise, clang, roar, rumble, rustle etc ♦ vt to bawl out.

striāta, -ae f scallop.

strictim adv superficially, cursorily.

strictūra, -ae f mass of metal.

strictus ppp of **stringō** ♦ adj close, tight.

strīdeō, -ēre, -ī; -ō, -ere, -ī *vi* to creak, hiss, shriek, whistle.

strīdor, -ōris *m* creaking, hissing, grating.

strīdulus *adj* creaking, hissing, whistling.

strigilis *f* scraper, strigil.

strigō, -āre *vi* to stop, jib.

strigōsus *adj* thin, scraggy; (*style*) insipid.

stringō, -ngere, -nxī, -ctum *vt* to draw together, draw tight; to touch, graze; to cut off, prune, trim; (*sword*) to draw; (*mind*) to affect, pain.

stringor, -ōris *m* twinge.

strix, -igis *f* screech owl.

stropha, -ae *f* trick.

Strophades, -um *fpl* islands off S. Greece.

strophiārius, -ī and **iī** *m* maker of breastbands.

strophium, -ī and **iī** *nt* breastband; headband.

structor, -ōris *m* mason, carpenter; (*at table*) server, carver.

structūra, -ae *f* construction, structure; works.

structus *ppp of* struō.

struēs, -is *f* heap, pile.

struix, -icis *f* heap, pile.

strūma, -ae *f* tumour.

strūmōsus *adj* scrofulous.

struō, -ere, -xī, -ctum *vt* to pile up; to build, erect; to arrange in order; to make, prepare; to cause, contrive, plot.

strūtheus *adj* sparrow- (*in cpds*).

strūthiocamēlus, -ī *m* ostrich.

Strȳmōn, -onis *m* river between Macedonia and Thrace (*now* Struma).

Strȳmonius *adj* Strymonian, Thracian.

studeō, -ēre, -uī *vi* (*usu with dat*) to be keen, be diligent, apply oneself to; to study; (*person*) to be a supporter of.

studiōsē *adv* eagerly, diligently.

studiōsus *adj* (*usu with gen*) keen on, fond of, partial to; studious
♦ *m* student.

studium, -ī and **iī** *nt* enthusiasm, application, inclination; fondness, affection; party spirit, partisanship; study, literary work.

stultē *adv* foolishly.

stultiloquentia, -ae *f* foolish talk.

stultiloquium, -ī and **iī** *nt* foolish talk.

stultitia, -ae *f* folly, silliness.

stultividus *adj* simple-sighted.

stultus *adj* foolish, silly ♦ *m* fool.

stupefaciō, -facere, -fēcī, -factum (*pass* -fīō, -fierī) *vt* to stun, astound.

stupeō, -ēre, -uī *vi* to be stunned, be astonished; to be brought to a standstill ♦ *vt* to marvel at.

stupēscō, -ere *vi* to become amazed.

stupeus *etc see* stuppeus.

stupiditās, -ātis *f* senselessness.

stupidus *adj* senseless, astounded; dull, stupid.

stupor, -ōris *m* numbness, bewilderment; dullness, stupidity.

stuppa, -ae *f* tow.

stuppeus *adj* of tow.

stuprō, -āre, -āvī, -ātum *vt* to defile; to ravish.

stuprum, -ī *nt* debauchery, unchastity.

sturnus, -ī *m* starling.

Stygius *adj* of the lower world, Stygian.

stylus *etc see* stilus.

Stymphalicus, (-ius, -is) *adj*

The present infinitive verb endings are as follows: -āre = 1st; -ēre = 2nd; -ere = 3rd and
-īre = 4th. *See sections on irregular verbs and noun declensions.*

Stymphalian.

Stymphalum, -ī nt, **Stymphalus, -ī** m district of Arcadia (famous for birds of prey killed by Hercules).

Styx, -ygis and **ygos** f river of Hades.

Styxius adj see n.

suādēla, -ae f persuasion.

suādeō, -dēre, -sī, -sum vi (with dat) to advise, urge, recommend.

suāsiō, -ōnis f speaking in favour (of a proposal); persuasive type of oratory.

suāsor, -ōris m adviser; advocate.

suāsus ppp of **suādeō**.

suāsus, -ūs m advice.

suāveolēns, -entis adj fragrant.

suāviātiō etc see **sāviātiō**.

suāvidicus adj charming.

suāviloquēns, -entis adj charming.

suāviloquentia, -ae f charm of speech.

suāvior etc see **sāvior**.

suāvis adj sweet, pleasant, delightful.

suāvitās, -ātis f sweetness, pleasantness, charm.

suāviter adv see **suāvis**.

suāvium etc see **sāvium**.

sub prep **1.** with abl (place) under, beneath; (hills, walls) at the foot of, close to; (time) during, at; (order) next to; (rule) under, in the reign of. **2.** with acc (place) under, along under; (hills, walls) up to, to; (time) up to, just before, just after; **~ ictum venīre** come within range; **~ manum** to hand.

subabsurdē adv see adj.

subabsurdus adj somewhat absurd.

subaccūsō, -āre vt to find some fault with.

subāctiō, -ōnis f working (the soil).

subāctus ppp of **subigō**.

subadroganter adv a little

conceitedly.

subagrestis adj rather boorish.

subalāris adj carried under the arms.

subamārus adj rather bitter.

subaquilus adj brownish.

subauscultō, -āre vt, vi to listen secretly, eavesdrop.

subbasilicānus, -ī m lounger.

subblandior, -īrī vi (with dat) to flirt with.

subc- etc see **succ-**.

subdidī perf of **subdō**.

subdifficilis adj rather difficult.

subdiffīdō, -ere vi to be a little doubtful.

subditīcius adj sham.

subditīvus adj sham.

subditus ppp of **subdō** ♦ adj spurious.

subdō, -ere, -idī, -itum vt to put under, plunge into; to subdue; to substitute, forge.

subdoceō, -ēre vt to teach as an assistant.

subdolē adv slily.

subdolus adj sly, crafty, underhand.

subdubitō, -āre vi to be a little undecided.

subdūcō, -ūcere, -ūxī, -uctum vt to pull up, raise; to withdraw, remove; to take away secretly, steal; (account) to balance; (ship) to haul up, beach; **sē ~** steal away, disappear.

subductiō, -ōnis f (ship) hauling up; (thought) reckoning.

subductus ppp of **subdūcō**.

subedō, -ēsse, -ēdī vt to wear away underneath.

subēgī perf of **subigō**.

subeō, -īre, -iī, -itum vi to go under, go in; to come up to, climb, advance; to come immediately after; to come to the assistance; to come as a substitute, succeed;

to come secretly, steal in; to come to mind, suggest itself ♦ *vt* to enter, plunge into; to climb; to approach, attack; to take the place of; to steal into; to submit to, undergo, suffer; (*mind*) to occur to.

sūber, -is *nt* cork tree; cork.

subesse *infin of* **subsum**.

subf- *etc see* **suff-**.

subg- *etc see* **sugg-**.

subhorridus *adj* somewhat uncouth.

subiaceō, -ēre, -uī *vi* to lie under, be close (to); to be connected (with).

subiciō, -icere, -iēcī, -iectum *vt* to put under, bring under; to bring up, throw up; to bring near; to submit, subject, expose; to subordinate, deal with under; to append, add on, answer; to adduce, suggest; to substitute, to forge; to suborn; **sē ~** grow up.

subiectē *adv* submissively.

subiectiō, -ōnis *f* laying under; forging.

subiectō, -āre *vt* to lay under, put to; to throw up.

subiector, -ōris *m* forger.

subiectus *ppp of* **subiciō** ♦ *adj* neighbouring, bordering; subject, exposed.

subigitātiō, -ōnis *f* lewdness.

subigitō, -āre *vt* to behave improperly to.

subigō, -igere, -ēgī, -āctum *vt* to bring up to; to impel, compel; to subdue, conquer; (*animal*) to tame, break in; (*blade*) to sharpen; (*boat*) to row, propel; (*cooking*) to knead; (*earth*) to turn up, dig; (*mind*) to train.

subiī *perf of* **subeō**.

subimpudēns, -entis *adj* rather

impertinent.

subinānis *adj* rather empty.

subinde *adv* immediately after; repeatedly.

subīnsulsus *adj* rather insipid.

subinvideō, -ēre *vi* to be a little envious of.

subinvīsus *adj* somewhat odious.

subinvītō, -āre *vt* to invite vaguely.

subīrāscor, -scī, -tus *vi* to be rather angry.

subīrātus *adj* rather angry.

subitārius *adj* sudden, emergency (*in cpds*).

subitō *adv* suddenly.

subitus *ppp of* **subeō** ♦ *adj* sudden, unexpected; (*man*) rash; (*troops*) hastily raised ♦ *nt* surprise, emergency.

subiūnctus *ppp of* **subiungō**.

subiungō, -ungere, -ūnxī, -ūnctum *vt* to harness; to add, affix; to subordinate, subdue.

sublābor, -bī, -psus *vi* to sink down; to glide away.

sublāpsus *ppa of* **sublābor**.

sublātē *adv* loftily.

sublātiō, -ōnis *f* elevation.

sublātus *ppp of* **tollō** ♦ *adj* elated.

sublectō, -āre *vt* to coax.

sublēctus *ppp of* **sublegō**.

sublegō, -egere, -ēgī, -ēctum *vt* to gather up; to substitute; (*child*) to kidnap; (*talk*) to overhear.

sublestus *adj* slight.

sublevātiō, -ōnis *f* alleviation.

sublevō, -āre, -āvī, -ātum *vt* to lift up, hold up; to support, encourage; to lighten, alleviate.

sublica, -ae *f* pile, palisade.

subliciius *adj* on piles.

subligāculum, -ī, subligar, -āris *nt* loincloth.

subligō, -āre *vt* to fasten on.

sublīmē adv aloft, in the air.
sublīmis adj high, raised high,
  lifted up; (*character*) eminent,
  aspiring; (*language*) lofty,
  elevated.
sublīmitās, -ātis f loftiness.
sublīmus etc see **sublīmis**.
sublingiō, -ōnis m scullion.
sublinō, -inere, -ēvī, -itum vt : ōs ~
  to fool, bamboozle.
sublitus ppp of **sublinō**.
sublūceō, -ēre vi to glimmer.
sublūō, -ere vt (*river*) to flow past
  the foot of.
sublūstris adj faintly luminous.
sublūtus ppp of **subluō**.
subm- etc see **summ-**.
subnātus adj growing up
  underneath.
subnectō, -ctere, -xuī, -xum vt to
  tie under, fasten to.
subnegō, -āre vt to half refuse.
subnexus ppp of **subnectō**.
subniger, -rī adj darkish.
subnīxus and **sus** adj supported,
  resting (on); relying (on).
subnuba, -ae f rival.
subnūbilus adj overcast.
subō, -āre vi to be in heat.
subobscēnus adj rather indecent.
subobscūrus adj somewhat
  obscure.
subodiōsus adj rather odious.
suboffendō, -ere vi to give some
  offence.
subolēs, -is f offspring, children.
subolēscō, -ere vi to grow up.
subolet, -ēre vi (*impers*) there is a
  faint scent; ~ mihi I detect, have
  an inkling.
suborior, -īrī vi to spring up in
  succession.
subōrnō, -āre, -āvī, -ātum vt to fit
  out, equip; to instigate secretly,
  suborn.
subortus, -ūs m rising up
  repeatedly.

subp- etc see **supp-**.
subrancidus adj slightly tainted.
subraucus adj rather hoarse.
subrēctus ppp of **subrigō**.
subrēmigō, -āre vi to paddle under
  (water).
subrēpō, -ere, -sī, -tum vi to creep
  along, steal up to.
subreptus ppp of **subripiō**.
subrīdeō, -dēre, -sī vi to smile.
subrīdiculē adv rather funnily.
subrigō, -igere, -ēxī, -ēctum vt to
  lift, raise.
subringor, -ī vi to make a wry face,
  be rather vexed.
subripiō, -ipere, -ipuī and **upuī,
  -eptum** vt to take away secretly,
  steal.
subrogō, -āre vt to propose as
  successor.
subrōstrānī, -ōrum mpl idlers.
subrubeō, -ēre vi to blush slightly.
subrūfus adj ginger-haired.
subruō, -ere, -ī, -tum vt to
  undermine, demolish.
subrūsticus adj rather countrified.
subrutus ppp of **subruō**.
subscrībō, -bere, -psī, -ptum vt to
  write underneath; (*document*) to
  sign, subscribe; (*censor*) to set
  down; (*law*) to add to an
  indictment, prosecute; (*fig*) to
  record; (*with dat*) to assent to,
  approve.
subscrīptiō, -ōnis f inscription
  underneath; signature; (*censor*)
  noting down; (*law*) subscription
  (to an indictment); register.
subscrīptor, -ōris m subscriber (to
  an indictment).
subscrīptus ppp of **subscrībō**.
subsecīvus etc see **subsicīvus**.
subsecō, -āre, -uī, -ctum vt to cut
  off, clip.
subsēdī perf of **subsīdō**.
subsellium, -ī and **iī** nt bench, seat;
  (*law*) the bench, the court.

subsentiō, -entīre, -ēnsī vt to have an inkling of.

subsequor, -quī, -cūtus vt, vi to follow closely; to support; to imitate.

subserviō, -īre vi to be a slave; (fig) to comply (with).

subsicīvus adj left over; (time) spare; (work) overtime.

subsidiārius adj in reserve ♦ mpl reserves.

subsidium, -ī and iī nt reserve ranks, reserve troops; relief, aid, assistance.

subsīdō, -īdere, -ēdī, -essum vi to sit down, crouch, squat; to sink down, settle, subside; (ambush) to lie in wait; (residence) to stay, settle ♦ vt to lie in wait for.

subsignānus adj special reserve (troops).

subsignō, -āre vt to register; to guarantee.

subsiliō, -īre, -uī vi to leap up.

subsistō, -istere, -titī vi to stand still, make a stand; to stop, halt; to remain, continue, hold out; (with dat) to resist ♦ vt to withstand.

subsortior, -īrī, -ītus vt to choose as a substitute by lot.

subsortītiō, -ōnis f choosing of substitutes by lot.

substantia, -ae f means, wealth.

substernō, -ernere, -rāvī, -rātum vt to scatter under, spread under; (fig) to put at one's service.

substitī perf of **subsistō**.

substituō, -uere, -uī, -ūtum vt to put next; to substitute; (idea) to present, imagine.

substitūtus ppp of **substituō**.

substō, -āre vi to hold out.

substrātus ppp of **substernō**.

substrictus ppp of **substringō** ♦ adj narrow, tight.

substringō, -ngere, -nxī, -ctum vt to bind up; to draw close; to check.

substructiō, -ōnis f foundation.

substruō, -ere, -xī, -ctum vt to lay, pave.

subsultō, -āre vi to jump up.

subsum, -esse vi to be underneath; to be close to, be at hand; (fig) to underlie, be latent in.

subsūtus adj fringed at the bottom.

subtēmen, -inis nt woof; thread.

subter adv below, underneath ♦ prep (with acc and abl) beneath; close up to.

subterdūcō, -cere, -xī vt to withdraw secretly.

subterfugiō, -ugere, -ūgī vt to escape from, evade.

subterlābor, -ī vt, vi to flow past under; to slip away.

subterrāneus adj underground.

subtexō, -ere, -uī, -tum vt to weave in; to veil, obscure.

subtīlis adj slender, fine; (senses) delicate, nice; (judgment) discriminating, precise; (style) plain, direct.

subtīlitās, -ātis f fineness; (judgment) acuteness, exactness, (style) plainness, directness.

subtīliter adv finely; accurately; simply.

subtimeō, -ēre vt to be a little afraid of.

subtractus ppp of **subtrahō**.

subtrahō, -here, -xī, -ctum vt to draw away from underneath; to take away secretly; to withdraw, remove.

subtristis adj rather sad.

subturpiculus adj a little bit mean.

subturpis adj rather mean.

subtus adv below, underneath.

The present infinitive verb endings are as follows: -āre = 1st; -ēre = 2nd; -ere = 3rd and -īre = 4th. See sections on irregular verbs and noun declensions.

subtūsus *adj* slightly bruised.
subūcula, -ae *f* shirt, vest.
sūbula, -ae *f* awl.
subulcus, -ī *m* swineherd.
Subūra, -ae *f* a disreputable quarter of Rome.
Subūrānus *adj see* **Subūra**.
suburbānitās, -ātis *f* nearness to Rome.
suburbānus *adj* near Rome ♦ *nt* villa near Rome ♦ *mpl* inhabitants of the towns near Rome.
suburbium, -ī and **iī** *nt* suburb.
suburgeō, -ēre *vt* to drive close (to).
subvectiō, -ōnis *f* transport.
subvectō, -āre *vt* to carry up regularly.
subvectus, -ūs *m* transport.
subvehō, -here, -xī, -ctum *vt* to carry up, transport upstream.
subveniō, -enīre, -ēnī, -entum *vi* (*with dat*) to come to the assistance of, relieve, reinforce.
subventō, -āre *vi* (*with dat*) to come quickly to help.
subvereor, -ērī *vi* to be a little afraid.
subversor, -ōris *m* subverter.
subversus *ppp of* **subvertō**.
subvertō, -tere, -tī, -sum *vt* to turn upside down, upset; to overthrow, subvert.
subvexī *perf of* **subvehō**.
subvexus *adj* sloping upwards.
subvolō, -āre *vi* to fly upwards.
subvolvō, -ere *vt* to roll uphill.
subvortō *etc see* **subvertō**.
succavus *adj* hollow underneath.
succēdō, -ēdere, -essī, -essum *vt, vi* (*with dat*) to go under, pass into, take on; (*with acc*) to go up, climb; (*with dat, acc, ad, sub*) to march on, advance to; (*with dat, in*) to come to take the place of, relieve; (*with dat, in, ad*) to follow

after, succeed, succeed to; (*result*) to turn out, be successful.
succendō, -endere, -endī, -ēnsum *vt* to set fire to, kindle; (*fig*) to fire, inflame.
succēnseō *etc see* **suscēnseō**.
succēnsus *ppp of* **succendō**.
succenturiātus *adj* in reserve.
succenturiō, -ōnis *m* under-centurion.
successī *perf of* **succēdō**.
successiō, -ōnis *f* succession.
successor, -ōris *m* successor.
successus *ppp of* **succēdō**.
successus, -ūs *m* advance uphill; result, success.
succīdia, -ae *f* leg or side of meat, flitch.
succīdō, -dere, -dī, -sum *vt* to cut off, mow down.
succīdō, -ere, -ī *vi* to sink, give way.
succiduus *adj* sinking, failing.
succinctus *ppp of* **succingō**.
succingō, -gere, -xī, -ctum *vt* to gird up, tuck up; to equip, arm.
succingulum, -ī *nt* girdle.
succinō, -ere, -ī *vi* to chime in.
succīsus *ppp of* **succīdō**.
succlāmātiō, -ōnis *f* shouting, barracking.
succlāmō, -āre, -āvī, -ātum *vt* to shout after, interrupt with shouting.
succontumēliōsē *adv* somewhat insolently.
succrēscō, -ere *vi* to grow up (from or to).
succrispus *adj* rather curly.
succumbō, -mbere, -buī, -bitum *vi* to fall, sink under; to submit, surrender.
succurrō, -rere, -rī, -sum *vi* to come quickly up; to run to the help of, succour; (*idea*) to occur.
succus *etc see* **sūcus**.
successus, -ūs *m* shaking.

succustōs, -ōdis m assistant keeper.

succutiō, -tere, -ssī, -ssum vt to toss up.

sūcidus adj juicy, fresh, plump.

sūcinum, -ī nt amber.

sūctus ppp of **sūgō**.

sucula, -ae f winch, windlass.

sucula, -ae f piglet; (pl) the Hyads.

sūcus, -ī m juice, sap; medicine, potion; taste, flavour; (fig) strength, vigour, life.

sūdārium, -ī and iī nt handkerchief.

sūdātōrius adj for sweating ♦ nt sweating bath.

sudis, -is f stake, pile, pike, spike.

sūdō, -āre, -āvī, -ātum vi to sweat, perspire; to be drenched with; to work hard ♦ vt to exude.

sūdor, -ōris m sweat, perspiration; moisture; hard work, exertion.

sudus adj cloudless, clear ♦ nt fine weather.

sueō, -ēre vi to be accustomed.

suēscō, -scere, -vī, -tum vi to be accustomed ♦ vt to accustom.

Suessa, -ae f town in Latium.

Suessiōnēs, um mpl people of Gaul (near Soissons).

suētus ppp of **suēscō** ♦ adj accustomed; usual.

Suēvī, -ōrum mpl people of N.E. Germany.

sūfes, -etis m chief magistrate of Carthage.

suffarcinātus adj stuffed full.

suffectus ppp of **sufficiō** ♦ adj (consul) appointed to fill a vacancy during the regular term of office.

sufferō, -re vt to support, undergo, endure.

suffes etc see **sūfes**.

sufficiō, -icere, -ēcī, -ectum vt to dye, tinge; to supply, provide; to appoint in place (of another), substitute ♦ vi to be adequate, suffice.

suffīgō, -gere, -xī, -xum vt to fasten underneath, nail on.

suffīmen, -inis, suffīmentum, -ī nt incense.

suffiō, -īre vt to fumigate, perfume.

suffīxus ppp of **suffīgō**.

sufflāmen, -inis nt brake.

sufflō, āre vt to blow up; to puff up.

suffocō, -āre vt to choke, stifle.

suffodiō, -odere, -ōdī, -ossum vt to stab; to dig under, undermine.

suffossus ppp of **suffodiō**.

suffrāgātiō, -ōnis f voting for, support.

suffrāgātor, -ōris m voter, supporter.

suffrāgātōrius adj supporting a candidate.

suffrāgium, -ī and iī nt vote, ballot; right of suffrage; (fig) judgment, approval; ~ ferre vote.

suffrāgor, -ārī, -ātus vi to vote for; to support, favour.

suffringō, -ere vt to break.

suffugiō, ugere, ūgī vi to run for shelter ♦ vt to elude.

suffugium, -ī and iī nt shelter, refuge.

suffulciō, -cīre, -sī, -tum vt to prop up, support.

suffundō, -undere, -ūdī, -ūsum vt to pour in; to suffuse, fill; to tinge, colour, blush; to overspread.

suffūror, -ārī vi to filch.

suffuscus adj darkish.

suffūsus ppp of **suffundō**.

Sugambrī, -ōrum mpl people of N.W. Germany.

suggerō, -rere, -ssī, -stum vt to bring up to, supply; to add on, put

The present infinitive verb endings are as follows: -āre = 1st; -ēre = 2nd; -ere = 3rd and -īre = 4th. See sections on irregular verbs and noun declensions.

next.

suggestum, -ī nt platform.

suggestus ppp of **suggerō**.

suggestus, -ūs m platform, stage.

suggrandis adj rather large.

suggredior, -dī, -ssus vi to come up close, approach ♦ vt to attack.

sūgillātiō, -ōnis f affronting.

sūgillātus adj bruised; insulted.

sūgō, -gere, -xī, -ctum vt to suck.

suī gen of **sē**.

suī perf of **suō**.

suillus adj of pigs.

sulcō, -āre vt to furrow, plough.

sulcus, -ī m furrow; trench; track.

sulfur etc see **sulpur**.

Sulla, -ae m famous Roman dictator.

Sullānus adj see n.

sullāturiō, -īre vi to hanker after being a Sulla.

Sulmō, -ōnis m town in E. Italy (birthplace of Ovid).

Sulmōnēnsis adj see n.

sultis adv please.

sum, esse, fuī vi to be, exist; ~ **ab** belong to; ~ **ad** be designed for; ~ **ex** consist of; **est, sunt** there is, are; **est mihi** I have; **mihi tēcum nīl est** I have nothing to do with you; **est quod** something; there is a reason for; **est ubi** sometimes; **est ut** it is possible that; **est** (with gen) to belong to, be the duty of, be characteristic of; (with infin) it is possible, it is permissible; **sunt quī** some; **fuit Ilium** Troy is no more.

sūmen, -inis nt udder, teat; sow.

summa, -ae f main part, chief point, main issue; gist, summary; sum, amount, the whole; supreme power; ~ **rērum** the general interest, the whole responsibility; ~ **summārum** the universe; **ad** ~**am** in short, in fact; in conclusion; **in** ~**ā** in all; after all.

Summānus, -ī m god of nocturnal thunderbolts.

summās, -ātis adj high-born, eminent.

summātim adv cursorily, summarily.

summātus, -ūs m sovereignty.

summē adv in the highest degree, extremely.

summergō, -gere, -sī, -sum vt to plunge under, sink.

summersus ppp of **summergō**.

sumministrō, -āre, -āvī, -ātum vt to provide, furnish.

summissē adv softly; humbly, modestly.

summissiō, -ōnis f lowering.

summissus ppp of **summittō** ♦ adj low; (voice) low, calm; (character) mean, grovelling, submissive, humble.

summittō, -ittere, -īsī, -issum vt (growth) to send up, raise, rear; to despatch, supply; to let down, lower, reduce, moderate; to supersede; to send secretly; **animum** ~ submit; **sē** ~ condescend.

summolestē adv with some annoyance.

summolestus adj a little annoying.

summoneō, -ēre, -uī vt to drop a hint to.

summōrōsus adj rather peevish.

summōtor, -ōris m clearer.

summōtus ppp of **summoveō**.

summoveō, -overe, -ōvī, -ōtum vt to move away, drive off; to clear away (to make room); to withdraw, remove, banish; (fig) to dispel.

summum, -ī nt top, surface.

summum adv at the most.

summus adj highest, the top of, the surface of; last, the end of; (fig) utmost, greatest, most important; (person) distinguished, excellent ♦ m head of the table.

summūtō, -āre vt to substitute.

sūmō, -ere, -psī, -ptum vt to take, take up; to assume, arrogate; (action) to undertake; (argument) to assume, take for granted; (dress) to put on; (punishment) to exact; (for a purpose) to use, spend.

sūmptiō, -ōnis f assumption.

sūmptuārius adj sumptuary.

sūmptuōsē adv see adj.

sūmptuōsus adj expensive, lavish, extravagant.

sūmptus ppp of **sūmō**.

sūmptus, -ūs m expense, cost.

Sūnium, -ī and **iī** nt S.E. promontory of Attica.

suō, suere, suī, sūtum vt to sew, stitch, join together.

suōmet, suōpte emphatic abl of **suus**.

suovetaurīlia, -ium ntpl sacrifice of a pig, sheep and bull.

supellex, -ectilis f furniture, goods, outfit.

super etc adj see **superus**.

super adv above, on the top; besides; moreover; left, remaining ♦ prep (with abl) upon, above; concerning; besides; (time) at; (with acc) over, above, on; beyond; besides, over and above.

superā etc see **suprā**.

superābilis adj surmountable, conquerable.

superaddō, -ere, -itum vt to add over and above.

superāns, -antis pres p of **superō**
♦ adj predominant.

superātor, -ōris m conqueror.

superbē adv arrogantly, despotically.

superbia, -ae f arrogance, insolence, tyranny; pride, lofty spirit.

superbiloquentia, -ae f arrogant

speech.

superbiō, -īre vi to be arrogant, take a pride in; to be superb.

superbus adj arrogant, insolent, overbearing; fastidious; superb, magnificent.

supercilium, -ī and **iī** nt eyebrow; (hill) brow, ridge; (fig) arrogance.

superēmineō, -ēre vt to overtop.

superesse infin of **supersum**.

superficiēs, -ēī f surface; (law) a building (esp on another's land).

superfīō, -ierī vi to be left over.

superfīxus adj fixed on top.

superfluō, -ere vi to overflow.

superfuī perf of **supersum**.

superfundō, -undere, -ūdī, -ūsum vt, vi to pour over, shower; (pass) to overflow, spread out.

superfūsus ppp of **superfundō**.

supergredior, -dī, -ssus vt to surpass.

superiaciō, -iacere, -iēcī, -iectum and **iactum** vt to throw over, overspread; to overtop; (fig) to exaggerate.

superiectus ppp of **superiaciō**.

superimmineō, -ēre vi to overhang.

superimpendēns, -entis adj overhanging.

superimpendēns, -entis adj
overhanging.

superimpōnō, -ōnere, -osuī, -ositum vt to place on top.

superimpositus ppp of **superimpōnō**.

superincidēns, -entis adj falling from above.

superincubāns, -antis adj lying upon.

superincumbō, -ere vi to fling oneself down upon.

superingerō, -ere vt to pour down.

superiniciō, -icere, -iēcī, -iectum vt to throw upon, put on top.

superiniectus ppp of **superinicō**.

The present infinitive verb endings are as follows: -āre = 1st; -ēre = 2nd; -ere = 3rd and -īre = 4th. See sections on irregular verbs and noun declensions.

superīnsternō, -ere vt to lay over.

superior, -ōris adj higher, upper; (time, order) preceding, previous, former; (age) older; (battle) victorious, stronger; (quality) superior, greater.

superlātiō, -ōnis f exaggeration.

superlātus adj exaggerated.

supernē adv at the top, from above.

supernus adj upper; celestial.

superō, -āre, -āvī, -ātum vi to rise above, overtop; to have the upper hand; to be in excess, be abundant; to be left over, survive ♦ vt to pass over, surmount, go beyond; to surpass, outdo; (MIL) to overcome, conquer; (NAUT) to sail past, double.

superobruō, -ere vt to overwhelm.

superpendēns, -entis adj overhanging.

superpōnō, -ōnere, -osuī, -ositum vt to place upon; to put in charge of.

superpositus ppp of **superpōnō**.

superscandō, -ere vt to climb over.

supersedeō, -edēre, -ēdī, -essum vi to forbear, desist from.

superstes, -itis adj standing over; surviving.

superstitiō, -ōnis f awful fear, superstition.

superstitiōsē adv superstitiously; scrupulously.

superstitiōsus adj superstitious; prophetic.

superstō, -āre vt, vi to stand over, stand on.

superstrātus adj spread over.

superstruō, -ere, -xī, -ctum vt to build on top.

supersum, -esse, -fuī vi to be left, remain; to survive; to be in abundance, be sufficient; to be in excess.

supertegō, -ere vt to cover over.

superurgēns, -entis adj pressing from above.

superus (compar **-ior**, superl **suprēmus, summus**) adj upper, above ♦ mpl the gods above; the living ♦ ntpl the heavenly bodies; higher places; **mare ~um** Adriatic Sea.

supervacāneus adj extra, superfluous.

supervacuus adj superfluous, pointless.

supervādō, -ere vt to climb over, surmount.

supervehor, -hī, -ctus vt to ride past, sail past.

superveniō, -enīre, -ēnī, -entum vt to overtake, come on top of ♦ vi to come on the scene, arrive unexpectedly.

superventus, -ūs m arrival.

supervolitō, -āre vt to fly over.

supervolō, -āre vt, vi to fly over.

supīnō, -āre, -āvī, -ātum vt to upturn, lay on its back.

supīnus adj lying back, face up; sloping, on a slope; backwards; (mind) indolent, careless.

suppāctus ppp of **suppingō**.

suppaenitet, -ēre vt impers to be a little sorry.

suppalpor, -ārī vi to coax gently.

suppār, -aris adj nearly equal.

supparasitor, -ārī vi to flatter gently.

supparus, -ī m, **supparum, -ī** nt woman's linen garment; topsail.

suppeditātiō, -ōnis f abundance.

suppeditō, -āre, -āvī, -ātum vi to be at hand, be in full supply, be sufficient; to be rich in ♦ vt to supply, furnish.

suppēdō, -ere vi to break wind quietly.

suppetiae, -ārum fpl assistance.

suppetiōr, -ārī, -ātus vi to come to

the assistance of.

suppetō, -ere, -īvī, *and* **iī, -ītum** *vi* to be available, be in store; to be equal to, suffice for.

suppīlō, -āre *vt* to steal.

suppingō, -ingere, -āctum *vt* to fasten underneath.

supplantō, -āre *vt* to trip up.

supplēmentum, -ī *nt* full complement; reinforcements.

suppleō, -ēre *vt* to fill up, make good, make up to the full complement.

supplex, -icis *adj* suppliant, in entreaty.

supplicātiō, -ōnis *f* day of prayer, public thanksgiving.

suppliciter *adv* in supplication.

supplicium, -ī *and* **iī** *nt* prayer, entreaty; sacrifice; punishment, execution, suffering; **~iō afficere** execute.

supplicō, -āre, -āvī, -ātum *vi* (*with dat*) to entreat, pray to, worship.

supplōdō, -dere, -sī *vt* to stamp.

supplōsiō, -ōnis *f* stamping.

suppōnō, -ōnere, -osuī, -ositum *vt* to put under, apply; to subject; to add on; to substitute, falsify.

supportō, -āre *vt* to bring up, transport.

suppositīcius *adj* spurious.

suppositiō, -ōnis *f* substitution.

suppositus *ppp of* **suppōnō**.

supposuī *perf of* **suppōnō**.

suppressiō, -ōnis *f* embezzlement.

suppressus *ppp of* **supprimō** ♦ *adj* (*voice*) low.

supprimō, -imere, -essī, -essum *vt* to sink; to restrain, detain, put a stop to; to keep secret, suppress.

suppromus, -ī *m* underbutler.

suppudet, -ēre *vt* (*impers*) to be a little ashamed.

suppūrō, -āre *vi* to fester.

suppus *adj* head downwards.

supputō, -āre *vt* to count up.

suprā *adv* above, up on top; (*time*) earlier, previously; (*amount*) more; **~ quam** beyond what ♦ *prep* (*with acc*) over, above; beyond; (*time*) before; (*amount*) more than, over.

suprāscandō, -ere *vt* to surmount.

suprēmum *adv* for the last time.

suprēmus *adj* highest; last, latest; greatest, supreme ♦ *ntpl* moment of death; funeral rites; testament.

sūra, -ae *f* calf (*of the leg*).

sūrculus, -ī *m* twig, shoot; graft, slip.

surdaster, -rī *adj* rather deaf.

surditās, -ātis *f* deafness.

surdus *adj* deaf; silent.

surēna, -ae *m* grand vizier (*of the Parthians*).

surgō, -ere, surrēxī, surrēctum *vi* to rise, get up, stand up; to arise, spring up, grow.

surpere *etc* = **surripere** *etc*.

surr- *etc see* **subr-**.

surrēxī *perf of* **surgō**.

surruptīcius *adj* stolen.

surrupuī *perf of* **subripiō**.

sūrsum, sūrsus *adv* upwards, up, high up; **~ deōrsum** up and down.

sūs, suis *m/f* pig, boar, hog, sow.

Sūsa, -ōrum *ntpl* ancient Persian capital.

suscēnseō, -ēre, -uī *vi* to be angry, be irritated.

susceptiō, -ōnis *f* undertaking.

susceptus *ppp of* **suscipiō**.

suscipiō, -ipere, -ēpī, -eptum *vt* to take up, undertake; to receive, catch; (*child*) to acknowledge; to beget; to take under one's protection.

suscitō, -āre, -āvī, -ātum *vt* to lift, raise; to stir, rouse, awaken; to

---

The present infinitive verb endings are as follows: **-āre** = 1st; **-ēre** = 2nd; **-ere** = 3rd and **-īre** = 4th. *See sections on irregular verbs and noun declensions.*

encourage, excite.

suspectō, -āre vt, vi to look up at, watch; to suspect, mistrust.

suspectus ppp of **suspiciō ♦** adj suspected, suspicious.

suspectus, -ūs m looking up; esteem.

suspendium, -ī and **iī** nt hanging.

suspendō, -endere, -endī, -ēnsum vt to hang, hang up; (death) to hang; (building) to support; (mind) to keep in suspense; (movement) to check, interrupt; (pass) to depend.

suspēnsus ppp of **suspendō ♦** adj raised, hanging, poised; with a light touch; (fig) in suspense, uncertain, anxious; dependent; **~ō gradū** on tiptoe.

suspicāx, -ācis adj suspicious.

suspiciō, -icere, -exī, -ectum vt to look up at, look up to; to admire, respect; to mistrust.

suspiciō, -ōnis f mistrust, suspicion.

suspiciōsē adv suspiciously.

suspiciōsus adj suspicious.

suspicor, -ārī, -ātus vt to suspect; to surmise, suppose.

suspīrātus, -ūs m sigh.

suspīritus, -ūs m deep breath, difficult breathing; sigh.

suspīrium, -ī and **iī** nt deep breath, sigh.

suspīrō, -āre, -āvī, -ātum vi to sigh **♦** vt to sigh for; to exclaim with a sigh.

susque dēque adv up and down.

sustentāculum, -ī nt prop.

sustentātiō, -ōnis f forbearance.

sustentō, -āre, -āvī, -ātum vt to hold up, support; (fig) to uphold, uplift; (food, means) to sustain, support; (enemy) to check, hold; (trouble) to suffer; (event) to hold back, postpone.

sustineō, -inēre, -inuī, -entum vt to hold up, support; to check,

control; (fig) to uphold, maintain; (food, means) to sustain, support; (trouble) to bear, suffer, withstand; (event) to put off.

sustollō, -ere vt to lift up, raise; to destroy.

sustulī perf of **tollō**.

susurrātor, -ōris m whisperer.

susurrō, -āre vt, vi to murmur, buzz, whisper.

susurrus, -ūs m murmuring, whispering.

susurrus adj whispering.

sūtēla, -ae f trick.

sūtilis adj sewn.

sūtor, -ōris m shoemaker; **~ nē suprā crepidam** ≈ let the cobbler stick to his last.

sūtōrius adj shoemaker's; ex-cobbler.

sūtrīnus adj shoemaker's.

sūtūra, -ae f seam.

sūtus ppp of **suō**.

suus adj his, her, its, their; one's own, proper, due, right **♦** mpl one's own troops, friends, followers etc **♦** nt one's own property.

Sybaris, -is f town in S. Italy (noted for its debauchery).

Sybarīta, -ītae m Sybarite.

Sӯchaeus, -ī m husband of Dido.

sӯcophanta, -ae m slanderer, cheat, sycophant.

sӯcophantia, -ae f deceit.

sӯcophantiōsē adv deceitfully.

sӯcophantor, -ārī, vi to cheat.

Syēnē, -ēs f town in S. Egypt (now Assuan).

syllaba, -ae f syllable.

syllabātim adv syllable by syllable.

symbola, -ae f contribution.

symbolus, -ī m token, symbol.

symphōnia, -ae f concord, harmony.

symphōniacus adj choir (in cpds).

Symplēgades, -um *fpl* clashing rocks in the Black Sea.

synedrus, -ī *m* senator (*in Macedonia*).

Synephēbī, -ōrum *mpl* Youths Together (*comedy by Caecilius*).

syngrapha, -ae *f* promissory note.

syngraphus, -ī *m* written contract; passport, pass.

Synnada, -ōrum *ntpl* town in Phrygia (*famous for marble*).

Synnadēnsis *adj* see n.

synodūs, -ontis *m* bream.

synthesis, -is *f* dinner service; suit of clothes; dressing gown.

Syphāx, -ācis *m* king of Numidia.

Syrācūsae, -ārum *fpl* Syracuse.

Syrācūsānus, Syrācūsānius, Syrācosius *adj* Syracusan.

Syria, -iae *f* country at the E. end of the Mediterranean.

Syrius, -us and **iacus, -iscus** *adj* Syrian.

syrma, -ae *f* robe with a train; (*fig*) tragedy.

Syrtis, -is *f* Gulf of Sidra in N. Africa; sandbank.

T

tabella, -ae *f* small board, sill; writing tablet, voting tablet, votive tablet; picture; (*pl*) writing, records, dispatches.

tabellārius *adj* about voting ♦ *m* courier.

tābeō, -ēre *vi* to waste away; to be wet.

taberna, -ae *f* cottage; shop; inn; (*circus*) stalls.

tabernāculum, -ī *nt* tent; ~ capere choose a site (for auspices).

tabernāriī, -ōrum *mpl* shopkeepers.

tābēs, -is *f* wasting away,

decaying, melting; putrefaction; plague, disease.

tābēscō, -ēscere, -uī *vi* to waste away, melt, decay; (*fig*) to pine, languish.

tābidulus *adj* consuming.

tābidus *adj* melting, decaying; pining; corrupting, infectious.

tābificus *adj* melting, wasting.

tabula, -ae *f* board, plank; writing tablet; votive tablet; map; picture, auction; (*pl*) account books, records, lists, will; ~ Sullae Sulla's proscriptions; **XII ~ae** Twelve Tables of Roman laws; **~ae novae** cancellation of debts.

tabulārium, -ī and **iī** *nt* archives.

tabulātiō, -ōnis *f* flooring, storey.

tabulātum, -ī *nt* flooring, storey; (*trees*) layer, row.

tābum, -ī *nt* decaying matter; disease, plague.

taceō, -ēre, -uī, -itum *vi* to be silent, say nothing; to be still, be hushed ♦ *vt* to say nothing about, not speak of.

tacitē *adv* silently; secretly.

taciturnitās, -ātis *f* silence, taciturnity.

taciturnus *adj* silent, quiet.

tacitus *ppp* of **taceō** ♦ *adj* silent, mute, quiet; secret, unmentioned; tacit, implied; per ~um quietly.

Tacitus, -ī *m* famous Roman historian.

tāctilis *adj* tangible.

tāctiō, -ōnis *f* touching; sense of touch.

tāctus *ppp* of **tangō.**

tāctus, -ūs *m* touch, handling, sense of touch; influence.

taeda, -ae *f* pitch pine, pinewood; torch; plank; (*fig*) wedding.

taedet, -ēre, -uit and **taesum est**

The present infinitive verb endings are as follows: -āre = 1st; -ēre = 2nd; -ere = 3rd and -īre = 4th. See sections on irregular verbs and noun declensions.

vt (*impers*) to be weary (of), loathe.

taedifer, -ī *adj* torch-bearing.

taedium, -ī *and* **iī** *nt* weariness, loathing.

Taenaridēs, -idae *m* Spartan (*esp Hyacinthus*).

Taenarius, -is *adj* of Taenarus; Spartan.

Taenarum (-on), -ī *nt*, **Taenarus (-os), -ī** *m/f* town and promontory in S. Greece (*now Matapan*); the lower world.

taenia, -ae *f* hairband, ribbon.

taesum est *perf of* **taedet**.

taeter, -rī *adj* foul, hideous, repulsive.

taetrē *adv* hideously.

taetricus *see* **tetricus**.

tagāx, -ācis *adj* light-fingered.

Tagus, -ī *m* river of Lusitania (*now Tagus*).

tālāris *adj* reaching to the ankles ♦ *ntpl* winged sandals; a garment reaching to the ankles.

tālārius *adj* of dice.

Talāsius, -ī *and* **iī** *m* god of weddings; wedding cry.

tālea, -ae *f* rod, stake.

talentum, -ī *nt* talent, *a Greek weight about 25.4kg* ; a large sum of money (*esp the Attic talent of 60 minae*).

tāliō, -ōnis *f* retaliation in kind.

tālis *adj* such; the following.

talpa, -ae *f* mole.

tālus, -ī *m* ankle; heel; (*pl*) knuckle bones, oblong dice.

tam *adv* so, so much, so very.

tamdiū *adv* so long, as long.

tamen *adv* however, nevertheless, all the same.

Tāmesis, -is *and* **a, -ae** *m* Thames.

tametsī *conj* although.

tamquam *adv* as, just as, just like ♦ *conj* as if.

Tanagra, -ae *f* town in Boeotia.

Tanais, -is *m* river in Sarmatia

(*now Don*).

Tanaquil, -ilis *f* wife of the elder Tarquin.

tandem *adv* at last, at length, finally; (*question*) just.

tangō, -ere, tetigī, tāctum *vt* to touch, handle; (*food*) to taste; (*with force*) to hit, strike; (*with liquid*) to sprinkle; (*mind*) to affect, move; (*place*) to reach; to border on; (*task*) to take in hand; (*by trick*) to take in, fool; (*in words*) to touch on, mention; **dē caelō tāctus** struck by lightning.

tanquam *see* **tamquam**.

Tantaleus *adj*, **-idēs, -idae** *m* Pelops, Atreus, Thyestes *or* Agamemnon.

Tantalis, -idis *f* Niobe *or* Hermione.

Tantalus, -ī *m* father of Pelops (*condemned to hunger and thirst in Tartarus, or to the threat of an overhanging rock*).

tantillus *adj* so little, so small.

tantisper *adv* so long, just for a moment.

tantopere *adv* so much.

tantulus *adj* so little, so small.

tantum *adv* so much, so, as; only, merely; ~ **modo** only; ~ **nōn** all but, almost; ~ **quod** only just.

tantummodo *adv* only.

tantundem *adv* just as much, just so much.

tantus *adj* so great; so little ♦ *nt* so much; so little; ~**ī esse** be worth so much, be so dear, be so important; ~**ō** so much, by so much, so far; (*with compar*) so much the; ~**ō opere** so much; **in ~um** to such an extent; **tria ~a** three times as much.

tantusdem *adj* just so great.

tapēta, -ae *m*, **-ia, -ium** *ntpl* carpet, tapestry, hangings.

Taprobanē, -ēs *f* Ceylon.

tardē adv slowly, tardily.

tardēscō, -ere vi to become slow, falter.

tardipēs, -edis adj limping.

tarditās, -ātis f slowness, tardiness; (mind) dullness.

tardiusculus adj rather slow.

tardō, -āre, -āvī, -ātum vt to retard, impede ♦ vi to delay, go slow.

tardus adj slow, tardy, late; (mind) dull, (speech) deliberate.

Tarentīnus adj Tarentine.

Tarentum, -ī nt town in S. Italy (now Taranto).

tarmes, -itis m woodworm.

Tarpēius adj Tarpeian; **mōns ~** the Tarpeian Rock on the Capitoline Hill from which criminals were thrown.

tarpezīta, -ae m banker.

Tarquiniēnsis adj of Tarquinii.

Tarquiniī, -iōrum mpl ancient town in Etruria.

Tarquinius adj of Tarquin.

Tarquinius, -ī m Tarquin (esp Priscus, the fifth king of Rome, and Superbus, the last king).

Tarracīna, -ae f, **-ae, -ārum** fpl town in Latium.

Tarracō, -ōnis f town in Spain (now Tarragona).

Tarracōnēnsis adj see n.

Tarsēnsis adj see n.

Tarsus, -ī f capital of Cilicia.

Tartareus adj infernal.

Tartarus (-os), -ī m, **-a, -ōrum** ntpl Tartarus, the lower world (esp the part reserved for criminals).

tat interj hallo there!

Tatius, -ī m Sabine king (who ruled jointly with Romulus).

Tatlus adj see n.

Taum, -ī nt Firth of Tay.

taureus adj bull's ♦ f whip of bull's hide.

Taurī, -ōrum mpl Thracians of the Crimea.

Tauricus adj see n.

taurifōrmis adj bull-shaped.

Taurīnī, -ōrum mpl people of N. Italy (now Turin).

taurīnus adj bull's.

Tauromenītānus adj see n.

Tauromenium, -ī and **iī** nt town in E. Sicily.

taurus, -ī m bull.

Taurus, -ī m mountain range in S.E. Asia Minor.

taxātiō, -ōnis f valuing.

taxeus adj of yews.

taxillus, -ī m small dice.

taxō, -āre vt to value, estimate.

taxus, -ī f yew.

Tāygeta, -ōrum ntpl, **Tāygetus, -ī** m mountain range in S. Greece.

Tāygetē, -ēs f a Pleiad.

tē acc and abl of **tū**.

-te suffix for **tū**.

Teānēnsis adj see n.

Teānum, -ī nt town in Apulia ; town in Campania.

techina, -ae f trick.

Tecmessa, -ae f wife of Ajax.

tēctor, -ōris m plasterer.

tēctōriolum, -ī nt a little plaster.

tēctōrium, -ī and **iī** nt plaster, stucco.

tēctōrius adj of a plasterer.

tēctum, -ī nt roof, ceiling, canopy; house, dwelling, shelter.

tēctus ppp of **tegō** ♦ adj hidden; secret, reserved, close.

tēcum with you.

Tegea, -ae f town in Arcadia.

Tegeaeus adj Arcadian ♦ m the god Pan ♦ f Atalanta.

Tegeātae, ātārum mpl Tegeans.

teges, -etis f mat.

tegillum, -ī nt hood, cowl.

tegimen, -inis nt covering.

The present infinitive verb endings are as follows: -āre = 1st; -ēre = 2nd; -ere = 3rd and -īre = 4th. See sections on irregular verbs and noun declensions.

tegimentum, **-ī** *nt* covering.

tegm- *etc see* **tegim-**.

tegō, **-ere**, **tēxī**, **tēctum** *vt* to cover; to hide, conceal; to protect, defend; to bury; **latus ~** walk by the side of.

tēgula, **-ae** *f* tile; (*pl*) tiled roof.

tegum- *etc see* **tegim**.

Tēius *adj* of Teos.

tēla, **-ae** *f* web; warp; yarnbeam, loom; (*fig*) plan.

Telamōn, **-ōnis** *m* father of Ajax.

Tēlegonus, **-ī** *m* son of Ulysses and Circe.

Tēlemachus, **-ī** *m* son of Ulysses and Penelope.

Tēlephus, **-ī** *m* king of Mysia (wounded by Achilles' spear).

tellūs, **-ūris** *f* the earth; earth, ground; land, country.

tēlum, **-ī** *nt* weapon, missile; javelin, sword; (*fig*) shaft, dart.

temerārius *adj* accidental; rash, thoughtless.

temere *adv* by chance, at random; rashly, thoughtlessly; **nōn ~** not for nothing; not easily; hardly ever.

temeritās, **-ātis** *f* chance; rashness, thoughtlessness.

temerō, **-āre**, **-āvī**, **-ātum** *vt* to desecrate, disgrace.

tēmētum, **-ī** *nt* wine, alcohol.

temnō, **-ere** *vt* to slight, despise.

tēmō, **-ōnis** *m* beam (of plough or carriage); cart; (*ASTRO*) the Plough.

Tempē *ntpl* famous valley in Thessaly.

temperāmentum, **-ī** *nt* moderation, compromise.

temperāns, **-antis** *pres p of* **temperō** ♦ *adj* moderate, temperate.

temperanter *adv* with moderation.

temperantia, **-ae** *f* moderation, self-control.

temperātē *adv* with moderation.

temperātiō, **-ōnis** *f* proper mixture, composition, constitution; organizing power.

temperātor, **-ōris** *m* organizer.

temperātus *ppp of* **temperō** ♦ *adj* moderate, sober.

temperī *adv* in time, at the right time.

temperiēs, **-ēī** *f* due proportion; temperature, mildness.

temperō, **-āre**, **-āvī**, **-ātum** *vt* to mix in due proportion, blend, temper; to regulate, moderate, tune; to govern, rule ♦ *vi* to be moderate, forbear, abstain; (*with dat*) to spare, be lenient to.

tempestās, **-ātis** *f* time, season, period; weather; storm; (*fig*) storm, shower.

tempestīvē *adv* at the right time, appropriately.

tempestīvitās, **-ātis** *f* seasonableness.

tempestīvus *adj* timely, seasonable, appropriate; ripe, mature; early.

templum, **-ī** *nt* space marked off for taking auspices; open space, region, quarter; sanctuary; temple.

temporārius *adj* for the time, temporary.

temptābundus *adj* making repeated attempts.

temptāmentum, **-ī** *nt* trial, attempt, proof.

temptāmina, **-um** *ntpl* attempts, essays.

temptātiō, **-ōnis** *f* trial, proof; attack.

temptātor, **-ōris** *m* assailant.

temptō, **-āre**, **-āvī**, **-ātum** *vt* to feel, test by touching; to make an attempt on, attack; to try, essay, attempt; to try to influence, tamper with, tempt, incite; **vēnās ~** feel the pulse.

tempus, -oris nt time; right time, opportunity; danger, emergency, circumstance; (head) temple; (verse) unit of metre; (verb) tense; **~ore** at the right time, in time; **ad ~us** at the right time; for the moment; **ante ~us** too soon; **ex ~ore** on the spur of the moment; to suit the circumstances; **in ~ore** in time; **in ~us** temporarily; **per ~us** just in time; **prō ~ore** to suit the occasion.

tēmulentus adj intoxicated.

tenācitās, -ātis f firm grip; stinginess.

tenāciter adv tightly, firmly.

tenāx, -ācis adj gripping, tenacious; sticky; (fig) firm, persistent; stubborn; stingy.

tendicula, -ae f little snare.

tendō, -ere, tetendī, tentum and **tēnsum** vt to stretch, spread; to strain; (arrow) to aim, shoot; (bow) to bend; (course) to direct; (lyre) to tune; (tent) to pitch; (time) to prolong; (trap) to lay ♦ vi to encamp; to go, proceed; to aim, tend; (with infin) to endeavour, exert oneself.

tenebrae, -ārum fpl darkness, night; unconsciousness, death, blindness, (place) dungeon, haunt, the lower world; (fig) ignorance, obscurity.

tenebricōsus adj gloomy.

tenebrōsus adj dark, gloomy.

Tenedius adj see one n.

Tenedos (-us), -ī f Aegean island near Troy.

tenellulus adj dainty little.

teneō, -ēre, -uī vt to hold, keep; to possess, occupy, be master of; to attain, acquire; (argument) to maintain, insist; (category) to comprise; (goal) to make for;

(interest) to fascinate; (law) to bind, be binding on; (mind) to grasp, understand, remember; (movement) to hold back, restrain ♦ vi to hold on, last, persist; (rumour) to prevail; **cursum ~** keep on one's course; **sē ~** remain; to refrain.

tener, -ī adj tender, delicate; young, weak; effeminate; (poet) erotic.

tenerāscō, -ere vi to grow weak.

tenerē adv softly.

teneritās, -ātis f weakness.

tenor, -ōris m steady course; **ūnō ~ōre** without a break, uniformly.

tēnsa, -ae f carriage bearing the images of the gods in procession.

tēnsus ppp of **tendō** ♦ adj strained.

tentā- etc see **temptā-**.

tentīgō, -inis f lust.

tentō etc see **temptō**.

tentōrium, -ī and **iī** nt tent.

tentus ppp of **tendō**.

tenuiculus adj paltry.

tenuis adj thin, fine; small, shallow; (air) rarefied; (water) clear; (condition) poor, mean, insignificant; (style) refined, direct, precise.

tenuitās, -ātis f thinness, fineness; poverty, insignificance; (style) precision.

tenuiter adv thinly; poorly; with precision; superficially.

tenuō, -āre, -āvī, -ātum vt to make thin, attenuate, rarefy; to lessen, reduce.

tenus prep (with gen or abl) as far as, up to, down to; **verbō ~** in name, nominally.

Teos, -ī f town on coast of Asia Minor (birthplace of Anacreon).

tepefaciō, -facere, -fēcī, -factum vt to warm.

*The present infinitive verb endings are as follows: **-āre** = 1st; **-ēre** = 2nd; **-ere** = 3rd and **-īre** = 4th. See sections on irregular verbs and noun declensions.*

tepeō, -ēre *vi* to be warm, be lukewarm; (*fig*) to be in love.

tepēscō, -ēscere, -uī *vi* to grow warm; to become lukewarm, cool off.

tepidus *adj* warm, lukewarm.

tepor, -ōris *m* warmth; coolness.

ter *adv* three times, thrice.

terdeciēns *and* **ēs** *adv* thirteen times.

terebinthus, -ī *f* turpentine tree.

terebra, -ae *f* gimlet.

terebrō, -āre *vt* to bore.

terēdō, -inis *f* grub.

Terentia, -iae *f* Cicero's wife.

Terentius, -ī *m* Roman family name (*esp the comic poet Terence*).

Terentius, -iānus *adj see n*.

teres, -etis *adj* rounded (*esp cylindrical*), smooth, shapely; (*fig*) polished, elegant.

Tēreus, -eī *and* **eos** *m* king of Thrace (*husband of Procne, father of Itys*).

tergeminus *adj* threefold, triple.

tergeō, -gēre, -sī, -sum *vt* to wipe off, scour, clean; to rub up, burnish.

tergīnum, -ī *nt* rawhide.

tergiversātiō, -ōnis *f* refusal, subterfuge.

tergiversor, -ārī, -ātus *vi* to hedge, boggle, be evasive.

tergō *etc see* **tergeō.**

tergum, -ī *nt* back; rear; (*land*) ridge; (*water*) surface; (*meat*) chine; (*skin*) hide, leather, anything made of leather; **~a vertere** take to flight; **ā ~ō** behind, in the rear.

tergus, -oris *see* **tergum.**

termes, -itis *m* branch.

Termīnālia, -ium *ntpl* Festival of the god of Boundaries.

terminātiō, -ōnis *f* decision; (*words*) clausula.

terminō, -āre, -āvī, -ātum *vt* to set

bounds to, limit; to define, determine; to end.

terminus, -ī *m* boundary line, limit, bound; god of boundaries.

ternī, -ōrum *adj* three each; three.

terō, -ere, -trīvī, -trītum *vt* to rub, crush, grind; to smooth, sharpen; to wear away, use up; (*road*) to frequent; (*time*) to waste; (*word*) to make commonplace.

Terpsichorē, -ēs *f* Muse of dancing.

terra, -ae *f* dry land, earth, ground, soil; land, country; **orbis ~ārum** the world; **ubi ~ārum** where in the world.

terrēnus *adj* of earth; terrestrial, land- (*in cpds*) ♦ *nt* land.

terreō, -ēre, -uī, -itum *vt* to frighten, terrify; to scare away; to deter.

terrestris *adj* earthly, on earth, land- (*in cpds*).

terribilis *adj* terrifying, dreadful.

terricula, -ōrum *ntpl* scare, bogy.

terrificō, -āre *vt* to terrify.

terrificus *adj* alarming, formidable.

terrigena, -ae *m* earth-born.

terriloquus *adj* alarming.

territō, -āre *vt* to frighten, intimidate.

territōrium, -ī *and* **iī** *nt* territory.

territus *adj* terrified.

terror, -ōris *m* fright, alarm, terror; a terror.

tersī *perf of* **tergeō.**

tersus *ppp of* **tergeō** ♦ *adj* clean; neat, terse.

tertiadecimānī, -ōrum *mpl* men of the thirteenth legion.

tertiānus *adj* recurring every second day ♦ *f* a fever ♦ *mpl* men of the third legion.

tertiō *adv* for the third time; thirdly.

tertium *adv* for the third time.

tertius *adj* third; **~ decimus**

(decumus) thirteenth.

terūncius, -ī *and* **iī** *m* quarter-as; a fourth; (*fig*) farthing.

tesqua (tesca), -ōrum *ntpl* waste ground, desert.

tessella, -ae *f* cube of mosaic stone.

tessera, -ae *f* cube, dice; (*MIL*) password; token (*for mutual recognition of friends*); ticket (*for doles*).

tesserārius, -ī *and* **iī** *m* officer of the watch.

testa, -ae *f* brick, tile; (*earthenware*) pot, jug, sherd; (*fish*) shell, shellfish.

testāmentārius *adj* testamentary ♦ *m* forger of wills.

testāmentum, -ī *nt* will, testament.

testātiō, -ōnis *f* calling to witness.

testātus *ppa of* **testor** ♦ *adj* public.

testiculus, -ī *m* testicle.

testificātiō, -ōnis *f* giving evidence, evidence.

testificor, -ārī, -ātus *vt* to give evidence, vouch for; to make evident, bring to light; to call to witness.

testimōnium, -ī *and* **iī** *nt* evidence, testimony; proof.

testis, -is *m/f* witness; eyewitness.

testis, -is *m* testicle.

testor, -ārī, -ātus *vt* to give evidence, testify; to prove, vouch for; to call to witness, appeal to ♦ *vi* to make a will.

testū (*abl* -ū) *nt* earthenware lid, pot.

testūdineus *adj* of tortoiseshell, tortoise- (*in cpds*).

testūdō, -inis *f* tortoise; tortoiseshell; lyre, lute; (*MIL*) shelter for besiegers, covering of shields; (*building*) vault.

testum, -ī *nt* earthenware lid, pot.

tēte *emphatic acc of* **tū**.

tetendī *perf of* **tendō**.

tēter *etc see* **taeter**.

Tēthys, -os *f* sea goddess; the sea.

tetigī *perf of* **tangō**.

tetrachmum, tetradrachmum, -ī *nt* four drachmas.

tetraō, -ōnis *m* blackcock, grouse or capercailzie.

tetrarchēs, -ae *m* tetrarch, ruler.

tetrarchia, -ae *f* tetrarchy.

tetricus *adj* gloomy, sour.

tetulī *archaic perf of* **ferō**.

Teucer, -rī *m* son of Telamon of Salamis; son-in-law of Dardanus.

Teucrī, -rōrum *mpl* Trojans.

Teucria, -riae *f* Troy.

Teutonī, -ōrum *and* **es, -um** *mpl* Teutons (*a German people*).

Teutonicus *adj* Teutonic, German.

tēxī *perf of* **tegō**.

texō, -ere, -uī, -tum *vt* to weave; to plait; to build, make; (*fig*) to compose, contrive.

textilis *adj* woven ♦ *nt* fabric.

textor, -ōris *m* weaver.

textrīnum, -ī *nt* weaving; shipyard.

textūra, -ae *f* web, fabric.

textus *ppp of* **texō** ♦ *nt* web, fabric.

textus, -ūs *m* texture.

texuī *perf of* **texo**.

Thāis, -idis *f* an Athenian courtesan.

thalamus, -ī *m* room, bedroom; marriage bed; marriage.

thalassicus *adj* sea-green.

thalassinus *adj* sea-green.

Thalēs, -is *and* **ētis** *m* early Greek philosopher (*one of the seven wise men*).

Thalīa, -ae *f* Muse of comedy.

thallus, -ī *m* green bough.

Thamyrās *m* blinded Thracian poet.

The present infinitive verb endings are as follows: -āre = 1st; -ēre = 2nd; -ere = 3rd and -īre = 4th. See sections on irregular verbs and noun declensions.

Thapsitānus adj see **Thapsus**.

Thapsus (-os), -ī f town in N. Africa (scene of Caesar's victory).

Thasius adj see **Thasus**.

Thasus (-os), -ī f Greek island in N. Aegean.

Thaumantias, -dis f Iris.

theātrālis adj of the theatre, in the theatre.

theātrum, -ī nt theatre; audience; (fig) theatre, stage.

Thēbae, -ārum fpl Thebes (capital of Boeotia); town in Upper Egypt.

Thēbais, -aidis f Theban woman; epic poem by Statius.

Thēbānus adj Theban.

thēca, -ae f case, envelope.

Themis, -idis f goddess of justice.

Themistoclēs, -ī and **is** m famous Athenian statesman.

Themistoclēus adj see **Themistoclēs**.

thēnsaurārius adj of treasure.

thēnsaurus see **thēsaurus**.

theologus, -ī m theologian.

Theophrastus, -ī m Greek philosopher (successor to Aristotle).

Theopompēus, -īnus adj see n.

Theopompus, -ī m Greek historian.

thermae, -ārum fpl warm baths.

Thermōdōn, -ontis m river of Pontus (where the Amazons lived).

Thermōdontēus, -ontiacus adj Amazonian.

thermopōlium nt restaurant serving warm drinks.

thermopōtō, -āre vt to refresh with warm drinks.

Thermopylae, -ārum fpl famous Greek pass defended by Leonidas.

thēsaurus, -ī m treasure, store; storehouse, treasury.

Thēseus, -eī and **eos** m Greek hero (king of Athens).

Thēsēus, -ēius adj, **-īdēs, -īdae** m Hippolytus; (pl) Athenians.

Thespiae, -ārum fpl Boeotian town near Helicon.

Thespiēnsis and **as, -adis** adj Thespian.

Thespis, -is m traditional founder of Greek tragedy.

Thessalia, -iae f Thessaly (district of N. Greece).

Thessalicus, -us and **is, -idis** adj Thessalian.

Thetis, -idis and **idos** f sea nymph (mother of Achilles); the sea.

thiasus, -ī m Bacchic dance.

Thoantēus adj see n.

Thoās, -antis m king of Crimea (killed by Orestes); king of Lemnos (father of Hypsipyle).

tholus, -ī m rotunda.

thōrāx, -ācis m breastplate.

Thrāca, -ae, (ē, -ēs), (-ia, -iae) f Thrace.

Thracius (Thrēicius) adj Thracian.

Thrasea, -ae m Stoic philosopher under Nero.

Thrasymachus, -ī m Greek sophist.

Thrāx, -ācis m Thracian; kind of gladiator.

Thrēssa, -ae, (Thrēissa, -ae) f Thracian woman.

Thrēx, -ēcis m kind of gladiator.

Thūcydidēs, -is m famous Greek historian.

Thūcydidius adj Thucydidean.

Thūlē, -ēs f island in the extreme N. (perhaps Shetland).

thunnus see **thynnus**.

thūr, -is nt = tūs, tūris.

Thūriī, -iōrum mpl town in S. Italy.

Thūrīnus adj see n.

thūs see **tūs**.

thȳa (thȳia), -ae f citrus tree.

Thybris, -is and **idis** m river Tiber.

Thyestēs, -ae m brother of Atreus (whose son's flesh he served up to him to eat).

Thyestēus adj, **-iadēs, -iadae** m Aegisthus.

Thyias (Thȳas), -adis f Bacchante.

Thȳlē see **Thūlē**.

thymbra, -ae f savory.

thymum, -ī nt garden thyme.

Thȳnia, -iae f Bithynia.

thynnus, -ī m tunnyfish.

Thȳnus, (-iacus), (-ias) adj
Bithynian.

Thyōneus, -eī m Bacchus.

thyrsus, -ī m Bacchic wand.

tiāra, -ae f, **-ās, -ae** m turban.

Tiberiānus adj see n.

Tiberīnus, -īnis adj, **-īnus, -īnī** m
Tiber.

Tiberis (Tibris), -is m river Tiber.

Tiberius, -ī m Roman praenomen
(esp the second emperor).

tibi dat of **tū**.

tībia, -ae f shinbone; pipe, flute.

tībicen, -inis m flute player; pillar.

tībicina, -ae f flute player.

tībicinium, -ī and **iī** nt flute
playing.

Tibullus, -ī m Latin elegiac poet.

Tibur, -is nt town on the river Anio
(now Tivoli).

Tiburs, -tis, (-tīnus), (-nus) adj
Tiburtine.

Ticīnus, -ī m tributary of the river Po.

Tigellīnus, -ī m favourite of Nero.

tigillum, -ī nt small log, small
beam.

tignārius adj working in wood;
faber ~ carpenter.

tignum, -ī nt timber, trunk, log.

Tigrānēs, -is m king of Armenia.

tigris, -is and **Idis** f tiger.

tīlia, -ae f lime tree.

Tīmaeus, -ī m Sicilian historian ;
Pythagorean philosopher ; a dialogue
of Plato.

timefactus adj frightened.

timeō, -ēre, -uī vt, vi to fear, be
afraid.

timidē adv timidly.

timiditās, -ātis f timidity,

cowardice.

timidus adj timid, cowardly.

timor, -ōris m fear, alarm; a
terror.

tinctilis adj dipped in.

tinctus ppp of **tingō**.

tinea, -ae f moth, bookworm.

tingō, -gere, -xī, -ctum vt to dip,
soak; to dye, colour; (fig) to
imbue.

tinnīmentum, -ī nt ringing noise.

tinniō, -īre vt, vi to ring, tinkle.

tinnītus, -ūs m ringing, jingle.

tinnulus adj ringing, jingling.

tintinnābulum, -ī nt bell.

tintinō, -āre vi to ring.

tīnus, -ī m a shrub, laurustinus.

tinxī perf of **tingō**.

Tīphys, -os m helmsman of the Argo.

tippula, -ae f water spider.

Tīresiās, -ae m blind soothsayer of
Thebes.

Tīridātēs, -ae m king of Armenia.

tīrō, -ōnis m recruit, beginner.

Tīrō, -ōnis m Cicero's freedman
secretary.

tīrōcinium, -ī and **iī** nt first
campaign; recruits; (fig) first
attempt, inexperience.

Tīrōniānus adj see **Tīrō**.

tīrunculus, -ī m young beginner.

Tīryns, this f ancient town in S.E.
Greece (home of Hercules).

Tīrynthius adj of Tiryns, of
Hercules ♦ m Hercules.

tis archaic gen of **tū**.

Tīsiphonē, -ēs f a Fury

Tīsiphonēus adj guilty.

Tītān, -ānis, (-ānus, -ānī) m Titan
(an ancient race of gods); the sun.

Tītānius, (-āniacus), (-ānis) adj see
n.

Tīthōnius adj see n.

Tīthōnus, -ī m consort of Aurora
(granted immortality without youth).

The present infinitive verb endings are as follows: **-āre** = 1st; **-ēre** = 2nd; **-ere** = 3rd and
-ire = 4th. See sections on irregular verbs and noun declensions.

tītillātiō, -ōnis *f* tickling.

tītillō, -āre *vt* to tickle.

titubanter *adv* falteringly.

titubātiō, -ōnis *f* staggering.

titubō, -āre *vi* to stagger, totter; to stammer; to waver, falter.

titulus, -ī *m* inscription, label, notice; title of honour; fame; pretext.

Tityos, -ī *m* giant punished in Tartarus.

Tmōlus, -ī *m* mountain in Lydia.

toculiō, -ōnis *m* usurer.

tōfus, -ī *m* tufa.

toga, -ae *f* toga (*dress of the Roman citizen*); (*fig*) peace; ~ **candida** dress of election candidates; ~ **picta** ceremonial dress of a victor in triumph; ~ **praetexta** purple-edged toga of magistrates and children; ~ **pūra, virīlis** plain toga of manhood.

togātus *adj* wearing the toga ♦ *m* Roman citizen; client ♦ *f* drama on a Roman theme.

togula, -ae *f* small toga.

tolerābilis *adj* bearable, tolerable; patient.

tolerābiliter *adv* patiently.

tolerāns, -antis *pres p of* **tolerō** ♦ *adj* patient.

toleranter *adv* patiently.

tolerantia, -ae *f* endurance.

tolerātiō, -ōnis *f* enduring.

tolerātus *adj* tolerable.

tolerō, -āre, -āvī, -ātum *vt* to bear, endure; to support, sustain.

tollēnō, -ōnis *m* crane, derrick, lift.

tollō, -ere, sustulī, sublātum *vt* to lift, raise; to take away, remove; to do away with, abolish, destroy; (*anchor*) to weigh; (*child*) to acknowledge, bring up; (*mind*) to elevate, excite, cheer; (*passenger*) to take on board; **signa** ~ decamp.

Tolōsa, -ae *f* Toulouse.

Tolōsānus *adj see* **Tolōsa**.

tolūtim *adv* at a trot.

tomāculum, -ī *nt* sausage.

tōmentum, -ī *nt* stuffing, padding.

Tomis, -is *f* town on the Black Sea (*to which Ovid was exiled*).

Tomītānus *adj see* **Tomis**.

Tonāns, -antis *m* Thunderer (*epithet of Jupiter*).

tondeō, -ēre, totondī, tōnsum *vt* to shear, clip, shave; to crop, reap, mow; to graze, browse on; (*fig*) to fleece, rob.

tonitrālis *adj* thunderous.

tonitrus, -ūs *m*, **-ua, -uōrum** *ntpl* thunder.

tonō, -āre, -uī *vi* to thunder ♦ *vt* to thunder out.

tōnsa, -ae *f* oar.

tōnsillae, -ārum *fpl* tonsils.

tōnsor, -ōris *m* barber.

tōnsōrius *adj* for shaving.

tōnstrīcula, -ae *f* barber girl.

tōnstrīna, -ae *f* barber's shop.

tōnstrīx, -īcis *f* woman barber.

tōnsūra, -ae *f* shearing, clipping.

tōnsus *ppp of* **tondeō**.

tōnsus, -ūs *m* coiffure.

tōphus *see* **tōfus**.

topiārius *adj* of ornamental gardening ♦ *m* topiarist ♦ *f* topiary.

topicē, -ēs *f* the art of finding topics.

toral, -ālis *nt* valance.

torcular, -āris and um, -ī *nt* press.

toreuma, -tis *nt* embossed work, relief.

tormentum, -ī *nt* windlass, torsion catapult, artillery; shot; rack, torture; (*fig*) torment, anguish.

tormina, -um *ntpl* colic.

torminōsus *adj* subject to colic.

tornō, -āre, -āvī, -ātum *vt* to turn (in a lathe), round off.

tornus, -ī *m* lathe.

torōsus *adj* muscular.

torpēdō, -inis f numbness, lethargy; (fish) electric ray.

torpeō, -ēre vi to be stiff, be numb; to be stupefied.

torpēscō, -ēscere, -uī vi to grow stiff, numb, listless.

torpidus adj benumbed.

torpor, -ōris m numbness, torpor, listlessness.

torquātus adj wearing a neckchain.

Torquātus, -ī m surname of Manlius.

torqueō, -quēre, -sī, -tum vt to turn, twist, bend, wind; (missile) to whirl, hurl, brandish; (body) to rack, torture; (mind) to torment.

torques and **is, -is** m/f neckchain, necklace, collar.

torrēns, -entis pres p of **torreō** ♦ adj scorching, hot; rushing, rapid ♦ m torment.

torreō, -ēre, -uī, tostum vt to parch, scorch, roast.

torrēscō, -ere vi to become parched.

torridus adj parched, dried up; frostbitten.

torris, -is m brand, firebrand.

torsī perf of **torqueō**.

tortē adv awry.

tortilis adj twisted, winding.

tortor, -arī vi to writhe.

tortor, -ōris m torturer, executioner.

tortuōsus adj winding; (fig) complicated.

tortus ppp of **torqueō** ♦ adj crooked; complicated.

tortus, -ūs m twisting, writhing.

torulus, -ī m tuft (of hair).

torus, -ī m knot, bulge; muscle, brawn; couch, bed; (earth) bank, mound; (language) ornament.

torvitās, -ātis f wildness, grimness.

torvus adj wild, grim, fierce.

tostus ppp of **torreō**.

tot adj (indecl) so many, as many.

totidem adj (indecl) just as many, the same number of.

totiēns, totiēs adv so often, as often.

totondī perf of **tondeō**.

tōtus (gen -īus, dat -ī) adj entire, the whole, all; entirely, completely taken up with; **ex ~ō** totally; **in ~ō** on the whole.

toxicum, -ī nt poison.

trabālis adj for beams; **clāvus ~** large nail.

trabea, -ae f ceremonial robe.

trabeātus adj wearing a ceremonial robe.

trabs, -abis f beam, timber; tree; ship; roof.

Trāchīn, -īnis f town in Thessaly (where Hercules cremated himself).

Trāchīnius adj see **Trāchīn**.

tractābilis adj manageable, tractable.

tractātiō, -ōnis f handling, treatment.

tractātus, -ūs m handling.

tractim adv slowly, little by little.

tractō, -āre, -āvī, -ātum vt to maul; to handle, deal with, manage; (activity) to conduct, perform; (person) to treat; (subject) to discuss, consider.

tractus ppp of **trahō** ♦ adj fluent.

tractus, -ūs m dragging, pulling, drawing; train, track; (place) extent, region, district; (movement) course; (time) lapse; (word) drawling.

trādidī perf of **trādō**.

trāditiō, -ōnis f surrender; handing down.

trāditor, -ōris m traitor.

trāditus ppp of **trādō**.

trādō, -ere, -idī, -itum vt to hand over, deliver, surrender; to commit, entrust; to betray; to bequeath, hand down; (narrative) to relate, record; (teaching) to propound; **sē ~** surrender, devote oneself.

trādūcō (trānsdūcō), -ūcere, -ūxī, -uctum vt to bring across, lead over, transport across; to transfer; to parade, make an exhibition of (in public); (time) to pass, spend.

trāductiō, -ōnis f transference; (time) passage; (word) metonymy.

trāductor, -ōris m transferrer.

trāductus ppp of **trādūcō**.

trādux, -ucis m vine layer.

tragicē adv dramatically.

tragicocōmoedia, -ae f tragicomedy.

tragicus adj of tragedy, tragic; in the tragic manner, lofty; terrible, tragic ♦ m writer of tragedy.

tragoedia, -ae f tragedy; (fig) bombast.

tragoedus, -ī m tragic actor.

trāgula, -ae f kind of javelin.

trahea, -ae f sledge.

trahō, -here, -xī, -ctum vt to draw, drag, pull, take with one; to pull out, lengthen; to draw together, contract; to carry off, plunder; (liquid) to drink, draw; (money) to squander; (wool) to spin; (fig) to attract; (appearance) to take on; (consequence) to derive, get; (praise, blame) to ascribe, refer; (thought) to ponder; (time) to spin out.

trāiciō, -icere, -iēcī, -iectum vt to throw across, shoot across; (troops) to get across, transport; (with weapon) to pierce, stab; (river, etc) to cross; (fig) to transfer ♦ vi to cross.

trāiectiō, -ōnis f crossing,

passage; (fig) transferring; (RHET) exaggeration; (words) transposition.

trāiectus ppp of **trāiciō**.

trāiectus, -ūs m crossing, passage.

trālāt- etc see **trānslāt-**.

Trallēs, -ium fpl town in Lydia.

Tralliānus adj see n.

trālūceō etc see **trānslūceō**.

trāma, -ae f woof, web.

trāmes, -itis m footpath, path.

trāmittō etc see **trānsmittō**.

trānatō etc see **trānsnatō**.

trānō, -āre, -āvī, -ātum vt, vi to swim across; (air) to fly through.

tranquillē adv quietly.

tranquillitās, -ātis f quietness, calm; (fig) peace, quiet.

tranquillō, -āre vt to calm.

tranquillus adj quiet, calm ♦ nt calm sea.

trāns prep (with acc) across, over, beyond.

trānsabeō, -īre, -iī vt to pierce.

trānsāctor, -ōris m manager.

trānsāctus ppp of **trānsigō**.

trānsadigō, -ere vt to drive through, pierce.

Trānsalpīnus adj Transalpine.

trānscendō (trānsscendō), -endere, -endī, -ēnsum vt, vi to pass over, surmount; to overstep, surpass, transgress.

trānscrībō (trānsscrībō), -bere, -psī, -ptum vt to copy out; (fig) to make over, transfer.

trānscurrō, -rere, -rī, -sum vt, vi to run across, run past, traverse.

trānscursus, -ūs m running through; (speech) cursory remark.

trānsd- etc see **trānsd-**.

trānsēgī perf of **trānsigō**.

trānsenna, -ae f net, snare; trellis, latticework.

trānseō, -īre, -iī, -itum vt, vi to pass over, cross over; to pass along or through; to pass by; to outstrip, surpass, overstep; (*change*) to turn into; (*speech*) to mention briefly, leave out, pass on; (*time*) to pass, pass away.

trānsferō, -ferre, -tulī, -lātum *vt* to bring across, transport, transfer; (*change*) to transform; (*language*) to translate; (ÞÞÞÞ) to use figuratively; (*time*) to postpone; (*writing*) to copy.

trānsfīgō, -gere, -xī, -xum *vt* to pierce; to thrust through.

trānsfīxus *ppp of* **trānsfīgō**.

trānsfodiō, -odere, -ōdī, -ossum *vt* to run through, stab.

trānsfōrmis *adj* changed in shape.

trānsfōrmō, -āre *vt* to change in shape.

trānsfossus *ppp of* **trānsfodiō**.

trānsfuga, -ae *m/f* deserter.

trānsfugiō, -ugere, -ūgī *vi* to desert, come over.

trānsfugium, -ī *and* **iī** *nt* desertion.

trānsfundō, -undere, -ūdī, -ūsum *vt* to decant, transfuse.

trānsfūsiō, -ōnis *f* transmigration.

trānsfūsus *ppp of* **trānsfundō**.

trānsgredior, -dī, -ssus *vi* to step across, cross over, cross; to pass on; to exceed.

trānsgressiō, -ōnis *f* passage; (*words*) transposition.

trānsgressus *ppa of* **trānsgredior**.

trānsgressus, -ūs *m* crossing.

trānsiciō *etc see* **trāiciō**.

trānsigō, -igere, -ēgī, -āctum *vt* to carry through, complete, finish; (*difference*) to settle; (*time*) to pass, spend; (*with* **cum**) to put an end to; (*with weapon*) to stab.

trānsiī *perf of* **trānseō**.

trānsiliō, trānssiliō, -īre, -uī *vi* to jump across ♦ *vt* to leap over; (*fig*) to skip, disregard; to exceed.

trānsitiō, -ōnis *f* passage;

desertion; (*disease*) infection.

trānsitō, -āre *vi* to pass through.

trānsitus *ppp of* **trānseō**.

trānsitus, -ūs *m* passing over, passage; desertion; passing by; transition.

trānslātīcius, trālātīcius *adj* traditional, customary, common.

trānslātiō, trālātiō, -ōnis *f* transporting, transferring; (*language*) metaphor.

trānslātīvus *adj* transferable.

trānslātor, -ōris *m* transferrer.

trānslātus *ppp of* **trānsferō**.

trānslegō, -ere *vt* to read through.

trānslūceō, -ēre *vi* to be reflected; to shine through.

trānsmarīnus *adj* overseas.

trānsmeō, -āre *vi* to cross.

trānsmigrō, -āre *vi* to emigrate.

trānsmissiō, -ōnis *f* crossing.

trānsmissus *ppp of* **trānsmittō**.

trānsmissus, -ūs *m* crossing.

trānsmittō, -ittere, -īsī, -issum *vt* to send across, put across; to let pass through; to transfer, entrust, devote; to give up, pass over; (*place*) to cross over, go through, pass ♦ *vi* to cross.

trānsmontānus *adj* beyond the mountains.

trānsmoveō, -ovēre, -ōvī, -ōtum *vt* to move, transfer.

trānsmūtō, -āre *vt* to shift.

trānsnatō, trānatō, -āre *vi* to swim across ♦ *vt* to swim.

trānsnō *etc see* **trānō**.

Trānspadānus *adj* north of the Po.

trānspectus, -ūs *m* view.

trānspiciō, -ere *vt* to look through.

trānspōnō, -ōnere, -osuī, -ositum *vt* to transfer.

trānsportō, -āre *vt* to carry across, transport, remove.

trānspositus *ppp of* **trānspōnō**.

The present infinitive verb endings are as follows: **-āre** = 1st; **-ēre** = 2nd; **-ere** = 3rd and **-īre** = 4th. *See sections on irregular verbs and noun declensions.*

Trānsrhēnānus *adj east of the Rhine.*

trānss- *etc see* **trāns-.**

Trānstiberīnus *adj across the Tiber.*

trānstineō, -ēre *vi* to get through.

trānstrum, -ī *nt* thwart.

trānstulī *perf of* **trānsferō.**

trānsultō, -āre *vi* to jump across.

trānsūtus *adj* pierced.

trānsvectiō, -ōnis *f* crossing.

trānsvectus *ppp of* **trānsvehō.**

trānsvehō, -here, -xī, -ctum *vt* to
carry across, transport.

trānsvehor, -hī, -ctus *vi* to cross,
pass over; (*parade*) to ride past;
(*time*) to elapse.

trānsverberō, -āre *vt* to pierce
through, wound.

trānsversus (trāversus) *adj* lying
across, crosswise, transverse;
digitum ~um a finger's breadth;
dē ~ō unexpectedly; **ex ~ō**
sideways.

trānsvolitō, -āre *vt* to fly through.

trānsvolō, -āre *vt, vi* to fly across,
fly through; to move rapidly
across; to fly past, disregard.

trānsvorsus *etc see* **trānsversus.**

trapētus, -ī *m* olive mill, oil mill.

trapezīta *etc see* **tarpezīta.**

Trapezūs, -ūntis *f* Black Sea town
(*now* Trebizond).

Trasumennus (Trasimēnus), -ī *m*
lake in Etruria (*where Hannibal
defeated the Romans*).

trāv- *see* **trānsv-.**

trāvectiō *etc see* **trānsvectiō.**

traxī *perf of* **trahō.**

trecēnī, -ōrum *adj* three hundred
each.

trecentēsimus *adj* three-
hundredth.

trecentī, -ōrum *num* three
hundred.

trecentiēns, -ēs *adv* three hundred
times.

trechedīpna, -ōrum *ntpl* dinner
shoes (of parasites).

tredecim *num* thirteen.

tremebundus *adj* trembling.

tremefaciō, -facere, -fēcī, -factum
vt to shake.

tremendus *adj* formidable,
terrible.

tremēscō (tremīscō), -ere *vi* to
begin to shake ♦ *vt* to be afraid of.

tremō, -ere, -uī *vi* to tremble,
quake, quiver ♦ *vt* to tremble at,
dread.

tremor, -ōris *m* shaking, quiver,
tremor; earthquake.

tremulus *adj* trembling, shivering.

trepidanter *adv* with agitation.

trepidātiō, -ōnis *f* agitation, alarm,
consternation.

trepidē *adv* hastily, in confusion.

trepidō, -āre, -āvī, -ātum *vi* to be
agitated, bustle about, hurry; to
be alarmed; to flicker, quiver ♦ *-vt*
to start at.

trepidus *adj* restless, anxious,
alarmed; alarming, perilous.

trēs, trium *num* three.

trēssis, -is *m* three asses.

trēsvirī, triumvirōrum *mpl* three
commissioners, triumvirs.

Trēverī, -ōrum *mpl* people of E.
Gaul (*about what is now* Trèves).

Trēvericus *adj see* n.

triangulum, -ī *nt* triangle.

triangulus *adj* triangular.

triāriī, -ōrum *mpl* the third line (*in
Roman battle order*), the reserves.

tribuārius *adj* of the tribes.

tribūlis, -is *m* fellow tribesman.

tribulum, -ī *nt* threshing sledge.

tribulus, -ī *m* star thistle.

tribūnal, -ālis *nt* platform;
judgment seat; camp platform,
cenotaph.

tribūnātus, -ūs *m* tribuneship,
rank of tribune.

tribūnicius *adj* of a tribune ♦ *m*
ex-tribune.

tribūnus, -ī *m* tribune; ~ **plēbis**

tribune of the people, a magistrate who defended the rights of the plebeians; ~ **mīlitum** or **mīlitāris** military tribune, an officer under the legatus; ~**ī aerāriī** paymasters.

tribuō, -uere, -uī, -ūtum vt to assign, allot; to give, bestow, pay; to concede, allow; to ascribe, attribute; (subject) to divide; (time) to devote.

tribus, -ūs m tribe.

tribūtāriụs adj : **-ae tabellae** letters of credit.

tribūtim adv by tribes.

tribūtiō, -ōnis f distribution.

tribūtum, -ī nt contribution, tribute, tax.

tribūtus ppp of **tribuō**.

tribūtus adj arranged by tribes.

trīcae, -ārum fpl nonsense; tricks, vexations.

trīcēnī, -ōrum adj thirty each, in thirties.

triceps, -ipitis adj three-headed.

trīcēsimus adj thirtieth.

trichila, -ae f arbour, summerhouse.

trīciēns, -ēs adv thirty times.

trīclīnium, -ī and **iī** nt dining couch, dining room.

tricō, -ōnis m mischief-maker.

tricor, -ārī vi to make mischief, play tricks.

tricorpor, -is adj three-bodied.

tricuspis, -idis adj three-pointed.

trīdēns, -entis adj three-pronged ♦ m trident.

trīdentifer, -ī adj trident-wielding.

trīdentiger, -ī adj trident-wielding.

trīduum, -ī nt three days.

triennia, -ium ntpl a triennial festival.

triennium, -ī and **iī** nt three years.

triēns, -entis m a third; (coin) a

third of an as; (measure) a third of a pint.

trientābulum, -ī nt land given by the State as a third of a debt.

trientius adj sold for a third.

triērarchus, -ī m captain of a trireme.

trīēris, -is f trireme.

trietēricus adj triennial ♦ ntpl festival of Bacchus.

trietēris, -idio f three years; a triennial festival.

trifāriam adv in three parts, in three places.

trifaux, -aucis adj three-throated.

trifidus adj three-forked.

trifōrmis adj triple.

trifūr, -ūris m archthief.

trifurcifer, -ī m hardened criminal.

trigeminus adj threefold, triple ♦ mpl triplets.

trigintā num thirty.

trigōn, -ōnis m a ball game.

trilībris adj three-pound.

trilinguis adj three-tongued.

trilīx, -īcis adj three-ply, three-stranded.

trimēstris adj of three months.

trimetrus, -ī m trimeter.

trīmus adj three years old.

Trīnacria, -iae f Sicily.

Trīnacrius, -is, -idis adj Sicilian.

trīnī, -ōrum adj three each, in threes; triple.

Trinobantēs, -um mpl British tribe in East Anglia.

trinōdis adj three-knotted.

triōbolus, -ī m half-a-drachma.

Triōnēs, -um mpl the Plough; the Little Bear.

tripartītō adv in or into three parts.

tripartītus, tripertītus adj divided into three parts.

tripectorus adj three-bodied.

tripedālis adj three-foot.

The present indicative verb endings are as follows: **-āre** *= 1st;* **-ēre** *= 2nd;* **-ere** *= 3rd and* **-īre** *= 4th. See sections on irregular verbs and noun declensions.*

tripert- *etc see* **tripart-**.

tripēs, -edis *adj* three-legged.

triplex, -icis *adj* triple, threefold
♦ *nt* three times as much ♦ *mpl*
three-leaved writing tablet.

triplus *adj* triple.

Triptolemus, -ī *m* inventor of
agriculture, judge in Hades.

tripudiō, -āre *vi* to dance.

tripudium, -ī *and* **iī** *nt* ceremonial
dance, dance; a favourable omen
(*when the sacred chickens ate*
greedily).

tripūs, -odis *f* tripod; the Delphic
oracle.

triquetrus *adj* triangular; Sicilian.

trirēmis *adj* with three banks of
oars ♦ *f* trireme.

trīs *etc see* **trēs**.

triscurria, -ōrum *ntpl* sheer
fooling.

tristē *adv* sadly; severely.

tristī = trīvistī.

tristiculus *adj* rather sad.

tristificus *adj* ominous.

tristimōnia, -ae *f* sadness.

tristis *adj* sad, glum, melancholy;
gloomy, sombre, dismal; (*taste*)
bitter; (*smell*) offensive; (*temper*)
severe, sullen, ill-humoured.

tristitia, -ae *f* sadness, sorrow,
melancholy; moroseness,
severity.

tristitiēs, -ēī *f* sorrow.

trisulcus *adj* three-forked.

tritavus, -ī *m* great-great-great-
grandfather.

trīticeus *adj* of wheat, wheaten.

trīticum, -ī *nt* wheat.

Trītōn, -ōnis *m* sea god (*son of*
Neptune); African lake (*where*
Minerva was born).

Trītōnius, -ōniacus, -ōnis *adj of*
Lake Triton, of Minerva ♦ *f*
Minerva.

trītūra, -ae *f* threshing.

trītus *ppp of* **terō** ♦ *adj* well-worn;

(*judgment*) expert; (*language*)
commonplace, trite.

trītus, -ūs *m* rubbing, friction.

triumphālis *adj* triumphal ♦ *ntpl*
insignia of a triumph.

triumphō, -āre, -āvī, -ātum *vi* to
celebrate a triumph; to triumph,
exult ♦ *vt* to triumph over, win by
conquest.

triumphus, -ī *m* triumphal
procession, victory parade;
triumph, victory.

triumvir, -ī *m* commissioner,
triumvir; mayor (*of a provincial*
town).

triumvirālis *adj* triumviral.

triumvirātus, -ūs *m* office of
triumvir, triumvirate.

triumvirī, -ōrum *mpl* three
commissioners, triumvirs.

trivenēfica, -ae *f* old witch.

trīvī *perf of* **terō**.

Trivia, -ae *f* Diana.

triviālis *adj* common, popular.

trivium, -ī *and* **iī** *nt* crossroads;
public street.

trivius *adj* of the crossroads.

Trōas, -adis *f* the district of Troy,
Troad; Trojan woman ♦ *adj*
Trojan.

trochaeus, -ī *m* trochee; tribrach.

trochlea, -ae *f* block and tackle.

trochus, -ī *m* hoop.

Trōglodytae, -ārum *mpl* cave
dwellers of Ethiopia.

Trōia, -ae *f* Troy.

Trōilus, -ī *m* son of Priam.

Trōiugena, -ae *m/f* Trojan; Roman.

Trōius *and* **ānus** *and* **cus** *adj*
Trojan.

tropaeum, -ī *nt* victory memorial,
trophy; victory; memorial, token.

Trōs, -ōis *m* king of Phrygia; Trojan.

trucīdātiō, -ōnis *f* butchery.

trucīdō, -āre, -āvī, -ātum *vt* to
slaughter, massacre.

truculentē *adv see* **truculentus**.

truculentia, -ae f ferocity, inclemency.

truculentus adj ferocious, grim, wild.

trudis, -is f pike.

trūdō, -dere, -sī, -sum vt to push, thrust, drive; (buds) to put forth.

trulla, -ae f ladle, scoop; washbasin.

truncō, -āre, -āvī, -ātum vt to lop off, maim, mutilate.

truncus, -ī m (tree) trunk, bole; (human) trunk, body; (abuse) blockhead ♦ adj maimed, broken, stripped (of); defective.

trūsī perf of **trūdō**.

trūsitō, -āre vt to keep pushing.

trūsus ppp of **trūdō**.

trutina, -ae f balance, scales.

trux, -ucis adj savage, grim, wild.

trygōnus, -ī m stingray.

tū pron you, thou.

tuātim adv in your usual fashion.

tuba, -ae f trumpet, war trumpet.

tūber, -is nt swelling, lump; (food) truffle.

tuber, -is f kind of apple tree.

tubicen, -inis m trumpeter.

tubilūstria, -ōrum ntpl festival of trumpets.

tuburcinor, -ārī vi to gobble up, guzzle.

tubus, -ī m pipe.

tuditō, -āre vt to strike repeatedly.

tueor, -ērī, -itus and **tūtus** vt to see, watch, look; to guard, protect, keep.

tugurium, -ī and **iī** nt hut, cottage.

tuitiō, -ōnis f defence.

tuitus ppa of **tueor**.

tulī perf of **ferō**.

Tulliānum, -ī nt State dungeon of Rome.

Tulliānus adj see **Tullius**.

Tulliola, -ae f little Tullia (Cicero's

daughter).

Tullius, -ī and **iī** m Roman family name (esp the sixth king); the orator Cicero.

Tullus, -ī m third king of Rome.

tum adv (time) then, at that time; (sequence) then, next ♦ conj moreuver, besides; ~ ... ~ at one time ... at another; ~ ... cum at the time when, whenever; cum ... ~ not only ... but; ~ dēmum only then; ~ ipsum even then; ~ māximē just then; ~ vērō then more than ever.

tumefaciō, -facere, -fēcī, -factum vt to make swell; (fig) to puff up.

tumeō, -ēre vi to swell, be swollen; (emotion) to be excited; (pride) to be puffed up; (language) to be turgid.

tumēscō, -ēscere, -uī vi to begin to swell, swell up.

tumidus adj swollen, swelling; (emotion) excited, enraged; (pride) puffed up; (language) bombastic.

tumor, -ōris m swelling, bulge; hillock; (fig) commotion, excitement.

tumulō, -āre vt to bury.

tumulōsus adj hilly.

tumultuārius adj hasty; (troops) emergency.

tumultuātiō, -ōnis f commotion.

tumultuō, -āre, -or, -ārī vi to make a commotion, be in an uproar.

tumultuōsē adv see **tumultuōsus**.

tumultuōsus adj uproarious, excited, turbulent.

tumultus, -ūs m commotion, uproar, disturbance; (MIL) rising, revolt, civil war; (weather) storm; (mind) disorder.

tumulus, -ī m mound, hill; burial mound, barrow.

tunc adv (time) then, at that time;

The present infinitive verb endings are as follows: -āre = 1st; -ēre = 2nd; -ere = 3rd and -īre = 4th. See sections on irregular verbs and noun declensions.

(*sequence*) then, next; **~ dēmum** only then; **~ quoque** then too; even so.

tundō, -ere, tutudī, tūnsum and **tūsum** *vt* to beat, thump, hammer; (*grain*) to pound; (*speech*) to din, importune.

Tūnēs, -ētis *m* Tunis.

tunica, -ae *f* tunic; (*fig*) skin, husk.

tunicātus *adj* wearing a tunic.

tunicula, -ae *f* little tunic.

tūnsus *ppp of* **tundō.**

tuor *etc see* **tueor.**

turba, -ae *f* disorder, riot, disturbance; brawl, quarrel; crowd, mob, troop, number.

turbāmenta, -ōrum *ntpl* propaganda.

turbātē *adv* in confusion.

turbātiō, -ōnis *f* confusion.

turbātor, -ōris *m* agitator.

turbātus *ppp of* **turbō ♦** *adj* troubled, disorderly.

turbellae, -ārum *fpl* stir, row.

turben *etc see* **turbō.**

turbidē *adv* in disorder.

turbidus *adj* confused, wild, boisterous; (*water*) troubled, muddy; (*fig*) disorderly, troubled, alarmed, dangerous.

turbineus *adj* conical.

turbō, -āre, -āvī, -ātum *vt* to disturb, throw into confusion; (*water*) to trouble, make muddy.

turbō, -inis *m* whirl, spiral, rotation; reel, whorl, spindle; (*toy*) top; (*wind*) tornado, whirlwind; (*fig*) storm.

turbulentē and **er** *adv* wildly.

turbulentus *adj* agitated, confused, boisterous, stormy; troublemaking, seditious.

turdus, -ī *m* thrush.

tūreus *adj* of incense.

turgeō, -gēre, -sī *vi* to swell, be swollen; (*speech*) to be bombastic.

turgēscō, -ere *vi* to swell up, begin

to swell; (*fig*) to become enraged.

turgidulus *adj* poor swollen.

turgidus *adj* swollen, distended; bombastic.

tūribulum, -ī *nt* censer.

tūricremus *adj* incense-burning.

tūrifer, -ī *adj* incense-producing.

tūrilegus *adj* incense-gathering.

turma, -ae *f* troop, squadron (*of cavalry*); crowd.

turmālis *adj* of a troop; equestrian.

turmātim *adv* troop by troop.

Turnus, -ī *m* Rutulian king (*chief opponent of Aeneas*).

turpiculus *adj* ugly little; slightly indecent.

turpificātus *adj* debased.

turpilucricupidus *adj* fond of filthy lucre.

turpis *adj* ugly, deformed, unsightly; base, disgraceful ♦ *nt* disgrace.

turpiter *adv* repulsively; shamefully.

turpitūdō, -inis *f* deformity; disgrace, infamy.

turpō, -āre *vt* to disfigure, soil.

turriger, -ī *adj* turreted.

turris, -is *f* tower, turret; siege tower; (*elephant*) howdah; (*fig*) mansion.

turrītus *adj* turreted; castellated; towering.

tursī *perf of* **turgeō.**

turtur, -is *m* turtledove.

tūs, tūris *nt* incense, frankincense.

Tusculānēnsis *adj* at Tusculum.

Tusculānum, -ānī *nt* villa at Tusculum (*esp Cicero's*).

Tusculānus *adj* Tusculan.

tūsculum, -ī *nt* a little incense.

Tusculum, -ī *nt* Latin town near Rome.

Tusculus *adj* Tuscan.

Tuscus *adj* Etruscan.

tussiō, -īre *vi* to cough, have a cough.

tussis, -is *f* cough.

tūsus *ppp of* tundō.

tūtāmen, -inis *nt* defence.

tūtāmentum, -ī *nt* protection.

tūte *emphatic form of* tū.

tūtē *adv* safely, in safety.

tūtēla, -ae *f* keeping, charge, protection; (*of minors*) guardianship, wardship; (*person*) watcher, guardian; ward, charge.

tūtemet *emphatic form of* tū.

tūtor, -ārī, -ātus; -ō, -āre *vt* to watch, guard, protect; to guard against.

tūtor, -ōris *m* protector; (*law*) guardian.

tutudī *perf of* tundō.

tūtus *ppp of* tueō ♦ *adj* safe, secure; cautious ♦ *nt* safety.

tuus *adj* your, yours, thy, thine; your own, your proper; of you.

Tȳdeus, -eī *and* **eos** *m* father of Diomede.

Tȳdīdēs, -īdae *m* Diomede.

tympanotrība, -ae *m* timbrel player.

tympanum (typanum), -ī *nt* drum, timbrel (*esp of the priests of Cybele*); (*mechanism*) wheel.

Tyndareus, -eī *m* king of Sparta (*husband of Leda*).

Tyndaridae, -idārum *mpl* Castor and Pollux.

Tyndaris, -idis *f* Helen; Clytemnestra.

Typhōeus, -eos *m* giant under Etna.

Typhōius, -is *adj see* n.

typus, -ī *m* figure.

tyrannicē *adv see* tyrannius.

tyrannicīda, -ae *m* tyrannicide.

tyrannicus *adj* tyrannical.

tyrannis, -idis *f* despotism, tyranny.

tyrannoctonus, -ī *m* tyrannicide.

tyrannus, -ī *m* ruler, king; despot, tyrant.

Tyrās, -ae *m* river Dniester.

Tyrius *adj* Tyrian, Phoenician, Carthaginian; purple.

tȳrotarichos, -ī *m* dish of salt fish and cheese.

Tyrrhēnia, -iae *f* Etruria.

Tyrrhēnus *adj* Etruscan, Tyrrhenian.

Tyrtaeus, -ī *m* Spartan war poet.

Tyrus (-os), -ī *f* Tyre (*famous Phoenician seaport*).

U

ūber, -is *nt* breast, teat; (*fig*) richness.

ūber, -is *adj* fertile, plentiful, rich (in); (*language*) full, copious.

ūberius (superl -rime) *compar adj* more fully, more copiously.

ūbertās, -ātis *f* richness, plenty, fertility.

ubertim *adv* copiously.

ubi *adv* (*interrog*) where?; (*relat*) where, in which, with whom; when.

ubicumque *adv* wherever; everywhere.

Ubiī, -ōrum *mpl* German tribe on the lower Rhine.

ubinam *adv* where (in fact)?

ubiquāque *adv* everywhere.

ubīque *adv* everywhere, anywhere.

ubiubī *adv* wherever.

ubīvīs *adv* anywhere.

ūdus *adj* wet, damp.

ulcerō, -āre *vt* to make sore, wound.

ulcerōsus *adj* full of sores; wounded.

ulcīscor, -ī, ultus *vt* to take vengeance on, punish; to take vengeance for, avenge.

ulcus, -eris *nt* sore, ulcer; ~

The present infinitive verb endings are as follows: -āre = 1st; -ēre = 2nd; -ere = 3rd and -īre = 4th. See sections on irregular verbs and noun declensions.

tangere touch on a delicate subject.

ūlīgō, -inis f moisture, marshiness.

Ulixēs, -is m Ulysses, Odysseus (*king of Ithaca, hero of Homer's Odyssey*).

ullus (*gen* -**īus**, *dat* -ī) *adj* any.

ulmeus *adj* of elm.

ulmus, -ī f elm; (*pl*) elm rods.

ulna, -ae f elbow; arm; (*measure*) ell.

ulterior, -ōris *compar adj* farther, beyond, more remote.

ulterius *compar of* **ultrā**.

ultimus *superl adj* farthest, most remote, the end of; (*time*) earliest, latest, last; (*degree*) extreme, greatest, lowest ♦ *ntpl* the end; ~**um** for the last time; **ad** ~**um** finally.

ultiō, -ōnis f vengeance, revenge.

ultor, -ōris m avenger, punisher.

ultrō *adv* beyond, farther, besides ♦ *prep* (*with acc*) beyond, on the far side of; (*time*) past; (*degree*) over and above.

ultrīx, -īcis *adj* avenging.

ultrō *adv* on the other side, away; besides; of one's own accord, unasked, voluntarily.

ultrō tribūta *ntpl* State expenditure for public works.

ultus *ppa of* **ulcīscor**.

ulula, -ae f screech owl.

ululātus, -ūs m wailing, shrieking, yells, whoops.

ululō, -āre, -āvī, -ātum *vi* to shriek, yell, howl ♦ *vt* to cry out to.

ulva, -ae f sedge.

umbella, -ae f parasol.

Umber, -rī *adj* Umbrian ♦ m Umbrian dog.

umbilīcus, -ī m navel; (*fig*) centre; (*book*) roller end; (*sea*) cockle or pebble.

umbō, -ōnis m boss (*of a shield*); shield; elbow.

umbra, -ae f shadow, shade; (*dead*) ghost; (*diner*) uninvited guest; (*fish*) grayling; (*painting*) shade; (*place*) shelter, school, study; (*unreality*) semblance, mere shadow.

umbrāculum, -ī nt arbour; school; parasol.

umbrāticola, -ae m lounger.

umbrāticus, -a, -um *adj* fond of idling; in retirement.

umbrātilis *adj* in retirement, private, academic.

Umbria, -riae f Umbria (*district of central Italy*).

umbrifer, -ī *adj* shady.

umbrō, -āre *vt* to shade.

umbrōsus *adj* shady.

ūmectō, -āre *vt* to wet, water.

ūmectus *adj* damp, wet.

ūmeō, -ēre *vi* to be damp, be wet.

umerus, -ī m upper arm, shoulder.

ūmēscō, -ere *vi* to become damp, get wet.

ūmidē *adv* with damp.

ūmidulus *adj* dampish.

ūmidus *adj* wet, damp, dank, moist.

ūmor, -ōris m liquid, fluid, moisture.

umquam, unquam *adv* ever, at any time.

ūnā *adv* together.

ūnanimāns, -antis *adj* in full agreement.

ūnanimitās, -ātis f concord.

ūnanimus *adj* of one accord, harmonious.

ūncia, -ae f a twelfth; (*weight*) ounce; (*length*) inch.

ūnciārius *adj* of a twelfth; (*interest*) 8½ per cent.

ūnciātim *adv* little by little.

ūncinātus *adj* barbed.

ūnciola, -ae f a mere twelfth.

ūnctiō, -ōnis f anointing.

ūnctitō, -āre *vt* to anoint regularly.

ūnctiusculus *adj* rather too unctuous.

ūnctor, -ōris *m* anointer.

ūnctūra, -ae *f* anointing (of the dead).

ūnctus *ppp of* ungō ♦ *adj* oiled; greasy, resinous; (*fig*) rich, sumptuous ♦ *nt* sumptuous dinner.

uncus, -ī *m* hook, grappling-iron.

uncus *adj* hooked, crooked, barbed.

unda, -ae *f* wave, water; (*fig*) stream, surge.

unde *adv* from where, whence; from whom, from which; ~ **petitur** the defendant; ~ **unde** from wherever; somehow or other.

ūndeciēns *and* **ēs** *adv* eleven times.

ūndecim *num* eleven.

ūndecimus *adj* eleventh.

undecumque *adv* from wherever.

ūndēnī, -ōrum *adj* eleven each, eleven.

ūndēnōnāgintā *num* eighty-nine.

ūndēoctōgintā *num* seventy-nine.

ūndēquadrāgintā *num* thirty-nine.

ūndēquīnquāgēsimus *adj* forty-ninth.

ūndēquīnquāgintā *num* forty-nine.

ūndēsexāgintā *num* fifty-nine.

ūndētrīcēsimus *adj* twenty-ninth.

ūndēvīcēsimānī, -ōrum *mpl* men of the nineteenth legion.

ūndēvīcēsimus *adj* nineteenth.

ūndēvīgintī *num* nineteen.

undique *adv* from every side, on all sides, everywhere; completely.

undisonus *adj* sea-roaring.

undō, -āre *vi* to surge; (*fig*) to roll, undulate.

undōsus *adj* billowy.

ūnetvīcēsimānī, -ōrum *mpl* men of the twenty-first legion.

ūnetvīcēsimus *adj* twenty-first.

ungō (unguō), -gere, ūnxī, ūnctum *vt* to anoint, smear, grease.

unguen, -inis *nt* fat, grease, ointment.

unguentārius, -ī *and* **iī** *m* perfumer.

unguentātus *adj* perfumed.

unguentum, -ī *nt* ointment, perfume.

unguiculus, -ī *m* fingernail.

unguis, -is *m* nail (*of finger or toe*); claw, talon, hoof; **ad ~em** with perfect finish; **trānsversum ~em** a hair's breadth; **dē tenerō ~ī** from earliest childhood.

ungula, -ae *f* hoof, talon, claw.

unguō *etc see* ungō.

ūnicē *adv* solely, extraordinarily.

ūnicolor, -ōris *adj* all one colour.

ūnicus *adj* one and only, sole; unparalleled, unique.

ūnifōrmis *adj* simple.

ūnigena, -ae *adj* only-begotten; of the same parentage.

ūnimanus *adj* with only one hand.

ūniō, -ōnis *m* a single large pearl.

ūniter *adv* together in one.

ūniversālis *adj* general.

ūniversē *adv* in general.

ūniversitās, -ātis *f* the whole; the universe.

ūniversus *adj* all taken together, entire, general ♦ *mpl* the community as a whole ♦ *nt* the universe; **in ~um** in general.

unquam *etc see* umquam.

ūnus *num* one ♦ *adj* sole, single, only; one and the same; the outstanding one; an individual; ~ **et alter** one or two; ~ **quisque**

---

every single one; **nēmō ~** not a single one; **ad ~um** to a man.

ūnxī *perf of* **ungō**.

ūpiliō, -ōnis *m* shepherd.

ūpupa, -ae *f* hoopoe; crowbar.

Ūrania, -ae *and* **ē, -ēs** *f* Muse of astronomy.

urbānē *adv* politely; wittily, elegantly.

urbānitās, -ātis *f* city life; refinement, politeness; wit.

urbānus *adj* town (*in cpds*), city (*in cpds*); refined, polite; witty, humorous; impertinent ♦ *m* townsman.

urbicapus, -ī *m* taker of cities.

urbs, urbis *f* city; Rome.

urceolus, -ī *m* jug.

urceus, -ī *m* pitcher, ewer.

ūrēdō, -inis *f* blight.

urgeō, -gēre, -sī *vt, vi* to force on, push forward; to press hard on, pursue closely; to crowd, hem in; to burden, oppress; (*argument*) to press, urge; (*work, etc*) to urge on, ply hard, follow up.

ūrīna, -ae *f* urine.

ūrīnātor, -ōris *m* diver.

urna, -ae *f* water jar, urn; voting urn, lottery urn, cinerary urn, money jar.

urnula, -ae *f* small urn.

ūrō, -ere, ūssī, ūstum *vt* to burn; to scorch, parch; (*cold*) to nip; (*MED*) to cauterize; (*rubbing*) to chafe, hurt; (*passion*) to fire, inflame; (*vexation*) to annoy, oppress.

ursa, -ae *f* she-bear, bear; (*ASTRO*) Great Bear, Lesser Bear.

ursī *perf of* **urgeō**.

ursīnus *adj* bear's.

ursus, -ī *m* bear.

urtīca, -ae *f* nettle.

ūrus, -ī *m* wild ox.

Usipetēs, -etum, (-iī, -iōrum) *mpl* German tribe on the Rhine.

ūsitātē *adv* in the usual manner.

ūsitātus *adj* usual, familiar.

uspiam *adv* anywhere, somewhere.

usquam *adv* anywhere; in any way, at all.

usque *adv* all the way (to, from), right on, right up to; (*time*) all the time, as long as, continuously; (*degree*) even, as much as; **~ quāque** everywhere; every moment, on every occasion.

ūssī *perf of* **ūrō**.

ūstor, -ōris *m* cremator.

ūstulō, -āre *vt* to burn.

ūstus *ppp of* **ūrō**.

ūsūcapiō, -apere, -ēpī, -aptum *vt* to acquire ownership of, take over.

ūsūcapiō, -ōnis *f* ownership by use or possession.

ūsūra, -ae *f* use, enjoyment; interest, usury.

ūsūrārius *adj* for use and enjoyment; paying interest.

ūsurpātiō, -ōnis *f* making use (of).

ūsurpō, -āre, -āvī, -ātum *vt* to make use of, employ, exercise; (*law*) to take possession of, enter upon; (*senses*) to perceive, make contact with; (*word*) to call by, speak of.

ūsus *ppa of* **ūtor**.

ūsus, -ūs *m* use, enjoyment, practice; experience, skill; usage, custom; intercourse, familiarity; usefulness, benefit, advantage; need, necessity; **~ est** there is need (of); **~uī esse, ex ~ū esse** be of use, be of service; **~ū venīre** happen; **~ frūctus** use and enjoyment, usufruct.

ut, utī *adv* how; (*relat*) as; (*explaining*) considering how, according as; (*place*) where; **~ in ōrātōre** for an orator ♦ *conj* **1.** with *indic*: (*manner*) as; (*concessive*) while, though; (*time*) when, as soon as. 2. *with subj* : (*expressing the idea of a verb*) that, to; (*purpose*) so that, to; (*causal*) seeing that; (*concessive*) granted that, although; (*result*) that, so that; (*fear*) that not; ~ ... ita while ... nevertheless; ~ nōn without; quī *seeing* that I, he, *etc* ; ~ quisque māximē the more.

utcumque (utcunque) *adv* however; whenever; one way or another.

ūtēnsilis *adj* of use ♦ *ntpl* necessaries.

ūter, -ris *m* bag, skin, bottle.

uter (*gen* -rīus, *dat* -rī), -ra, -rum *pron* which (of two), the one that; one or the other.

utercumque, utracumque, utrumcumque *pron* whichever (of two).

uterlibet, utralibet, utrumlibet *pron* whichever (of the two) you please, either one.

uterque, utraque, utrumque *pron* each (of two), either, both.

uterum, -ī *nt*, **uterus, -ī** *m* womb, child, belly.

utervīs, utravīs, utrumvīs *pron* whichever (of two) you please; either.

ūtī *infin of* **ūtor**.

utī *etc see* **ut**.

ūtibilis *adj* useful, serviceable.

Utica, -ae *f* town near Carthage (*where Cato committed suicide*).

Uticēnsis *adj see* **n**.

ūtilis *adj* useful, expedient, profitable; fit (for).

ūtilitās, -ātis *f* usefulness, expediency, advantage.

ūtiliter *adv* usefully, advantageously.

utinam *adv* I wish!, would that!, if only!

utique *adv* at least, by all means, especially.

ūtor, ūtī, ūsus *vi* (*with abl*) to use, employ; to possess, enjoy; to practise, experience; (*person*) to be on intimate terms with, find; **ūtendum rogāre** borrow.

utpote *adv* inasmuch as, as being.

ūtrārius, -ī *and* **iī** *m* water-carrier.

ūtriculārius, -ī *and* **iī** *m* bagpiper.

utrimque (utrinque) *adv* on both sides, on either side.

utrō *adv* in which direction.

utrobīque *see* **utrubīque**.

utrōque *adv* in both directions, both ways.

utrubī *adv* on which side.

utrubīque *adv* on both sides, on either side.

utrum *adv* whether.

utut *adv* however.

ūva, -ae *f* grape, bunch of grapes; vine; cluster.

ūvēscō, -ere *vi* to become wet.

ūvidulus *adj* moist.

ūvidus *adj* wet, damp, drunken.

uxor, -ōris *f* wife.

uxorcula, -ae *f* little wife.

uxōrius *adj* of a wife; fond of his wife.

V

vacāns, -antis *pres p of* **vacō** ♦ *adj* unoccupied; (*woman*) single.

vacātiō, -ōnis *f* freedom, exemption; exemption from military service; payment for exemption from service.

vacca, -ae *f* cow.

vaccinium, -ī *and* **iī** *nt* hyacinth.

vaccula, -ae *f* heifer.

vacēfīō, -ierī *vi* to become empty.

vacillō, -āre *vi* to stagger, totter; to

The present infinitive verb endings are as follows: -āre = 1st; -ēre = 2nd; -ere = 3rd and -īre = 4th. See sections on irregular verbs and noun declensions.

waver, be unreliable.

vacīvē adv at leisure.

vacīvitās, -ātis f want.

vacīvus adj empty, free.

vacō, -āre, -āvī, -ātum vi to be empty, vacant, unoccupied; to be free, aloof (from); to have time for, devote one's time to; ~at there is time.

vacuātus adj empty.

vacuēfaciō, -facere, -fēcī, -factum vt to empty, clear.

vacuitās, -ātis f freedom, exemption; vacancy.

vacuus adj empty, void, wanting; vacant; free (from), clear; disengaged, at leisure; (value) worthless; (woman) single ♦ nt void, space.

vadimōnium, -ī and **iī** nt bail, security; ~ sistere appear in court; ~ dēserere default.

vādō, -ere vi to go, go on, make one's way.

vador, -ārī, -ātus vt to bind over by bail.

vadōsus adj shallow.

vadum, -ī nt shoal, shallow, ford; water, sea; bottom.

vae interj woe!, alas!

vafer, -rī adj crafty, subtle.

vafrē adv artfully.

vagē adv far afield.

vāgīna, -ae f sheath, scabbard; (grain) husk.

vāgiō, -īre vi to cry.

vāgītus, -ūs m crying, bleating.

vagor, -ārī, -ātus vi to wander, rove, go far afield; (fig) to spread.

vāgor, -ōris m cry.

vagus adj wandering, unsettled; (fig) fickle, wavering, vague.

vah interj (expressing surprise, joy, anger) oh!, ah!

valdē adv greatly, intensely; very.

valē, valēte interj goodbye, farewell.

valēns, -entis pres p of **valeō** ♦ adj strong, powerful, vigorous; well, healthy.

valenter adv strongly.

valentulus adj strong.

valeō, -ēre, -uī, -itum vi to be strong; to be able, have the power (to); to be well, fit, healthy; (fig) to be powerful, effective, valid; (force) to prevail; (money) to be worth; (word) to mean; ~ apud have influence over, carry weight with; ~ēre iubeō say goodbye to; ~ē dīcō say goodbye; ~eās away with you!

valēscō, -ere vi to grow strong, thrive.

valētūdinārium, -ī and **iī** nt hospital.

valētūdō, -inis f state of health, health; illness.

valgus adj bow-legged.

validē adv powerfully, very.

validus adj strong, powerful, able; sound, healthy; effective.

vallāris adj (decoration) for scaling a rampart.

vallēs, vallis, -is f valley.

vallō, -āre, -āvī, -ātum vt to palisade, entrench, fortify.

vallum, -ī nt rampart, palisade, entrenchment.

vallus, -ī m stake; palisade, rampart; (comb) tooth.

valvae, -ārum fpl folding door.

vānēscō, -ere vi to disappear, pass away.

vānidicus, -ī m liar.

vāniloquentia, -ae f idle talk.

vāniloquus adj untruthful; boastful.

vānitās, -ātis f emptiness; falsehood, worthlessness, fickleness; vanity.

vānitūdō, -inis f falsehood.

vannus, -ī f winnowing fan.

vānus adj empty; idle, useless,

groundless; false, untruthful, unreliable; conceited.

vapidus *adj* spoilt, corrupt.

vapor, -ōris *m* steam, vapour; heat.

vapōrārium, -ī *and* **iī** *nt* steam pipe.

vapōrō, -āre *vt* to steam, fumigate, heat ♦ *vi* to burn.

vappa, -ae *f* wine that has gone flat; (*person*) good-for-nothing.

vāpulō, -āre *vi* to be flogged, beaten; to be defeated.

variantia, -ae *f* diversity.

variātiō, -ōnis *f* difference.

vāricō, -āre *vi* to straddle.

vāricōsus *adj* varicose.

vāricus *adj* with feet wide apart.

variē *adv* diversely, with varying success.

varietās, -ātis *f* difference, diversity.

variō, -āre, -āvī, -ātum *vt* to diversify, variegate; to make different, change, vary ♦ *vi* to change colour; to differ, vary.

varius *adj* coloured, spotted, variegated; diverse, changeable, various; (*ability*) versatile; (*character*) fickle.

Varius, -ī *m* epic poet (*friend of Vergil and Horace*).

varix, -icis *f* varicose vein.

Varrō, -ōnis *m* consul defeated at Cannae; antiquarian writer of Cicero's day.

Varrōniānus *adj see* **Varro**.

vārus *adj* knock-kneed; crooked; contrary.

vas, vadis *m* surety, bail.

vās, vasis (*pl* **vāsa, -ōrum**) *nt* vessel, dish; utensil, implement; (*MIL*) baggage.

vāsārium, -ī *and* **iī** *nt* furnishing allowance (of a governor).

vāsculārius, -ī *and* **iī** *m* metalworker.

vāsculum, -ī *nt* small dish.

vastātiō, -ōnis *f* ravaging.

vastātor, -ōris *m* ravager.

vastē *adv* (*size*) enormously; (*speech*) coarsely.

vastificus *adj* ravaging.

vastitās, -ātis *f* desolation, desert; devastation, destruction.

vastitiēs, -ēī *f* ruin.

vastō, -āre, -āvī, -ātum *vt* to make desolate, denude; to lay waste, ravage.

vastus *adj* empty, desolate, uncultivated; ravaged, devastated; (*appearance*) uncouth, rude; (*size*) enormous, vast.

vāsum *etc see* **vās**.

vātēs, -is *m/f* prophet, prophetess; poet, bard.

Vāticānus *adj* Vatican (*hill on right bank of Tiber*).

vāticinātiō, -ōnis *f* prophesying, prediction.

vāticinātor, -ōris *m* prophet.

vāticinor, -ārī, -ātus *vt, vi* to prophesy, to celebrate in verse; to rave, rant.

vāticinus *adj* prophetic.

-ve *conj* or; either ... or.

vēcordia, -ae *f* senselessness; insanity.

vēcors, -dis *adj* senseless, foolish, mad.

vectīgal, -ālis *nt* tax; honorarium (to a magistrate); income.

vectiō, -ōnis *f* transport.

vectis, -is *m* lever, crowbar; (*door*) bolt, bar.

Vectis, -is *f* Isle of Wight.

vectō, -āre *vt* to carry; (*pass*) to ride.

vector, -ōris *m* carrier; passenger, rider.

The present infinitive verb endings are as follows: -āre = 1st; -ēre = 2nd; -ere = 3rd and -īre = 4th. See sections on irregular verbs and noun declensions.

vectōrius *adj* transport (*in cpds*).

vectūra, -ae *f* transport; (*payment*) carriage, fare.

vectus *ppp of* **vehō**.

Vediovis, -is = **Vēiovis**.

vegetus *adj* lively, sprightly.

vēgrandis *adj* small.

vehemēns, -entis *adj* impetuous, violent; powerful, strong.

vehementer *adv* violently, eagerly; powerfully, very much.

vehementia, -ae *f* vehemence.

vehiculum, -ī *nt* carriage, cart; (*sea*) vessel.

vehō, -here, -xī, -ctum *vt* to carry, convey; (*pass*) to ride, sail, drive.

Vēiēns, -entis, (-entānus), (-us) *adj see* **Vēiī**.

Vēiī, -ōrum *mpl* ancient town in S. Etruria.

Vēiovis, -is *m* ancient Roman god (*anti-Jupiter*).

vel *conj* or, or perhaps; or rather; or else; either ... or ♦ *adv* even, if you like; perhaps; for instance; ~ **māximus** the very greatest.

Vēlābrum, -ī *nt* low ground between Capitol and Palatine hills.

vēlāmen, -inis *nt* covering, garment.

vēlāmentum, -ī *nt* curtain; (*pl*) draped olive branches carried by suppliants.

vēlārium, -ī and iī *nt* awning.

vēlātī, -ōrum *mpl* supernumerary troops.

vēles, -itis *m* light-armed soldier, skirmisher.

vēlifer, -ī *adj* carrying sail.

vēlificātiō, -ōnis *f* sailing.

vēlificō, -āre *vi* to sail ♦ *vt* to sail through.

vēlificor, -ārī *vi* to sail; (*with dat*) to make an effort to obtain.

Velīnus, -ī *m* a Sabine lake.

vēlitāris *adj* of the light-armed troops.

vēlitātiō, -ōnis *f* skirmishing.

vēlitēs *pl of* **vēles**.

vēlitor, -ārī *vi* to skirmish.

vēlivolus *adj* sail-winged.

velle *infin of* **volō**.

vellicō, -āre *vt* to pinch, pluck, twitch; (*speech*) to taunt, disparage.

vellō, -ere, vellī and vulsī, vulsum *vt* to pluck, pull, pick; to pluck out, tear up.

vellus, -eris *nt* fleece, pelt; wool; fleecy clouds.

vēlō, -āre, -āvī, -ātum *vt* to cover up, clothe, veil; (*fig*) to conceal.

vēlōcitās, -ātis *f* speed, rapidity.

vēlōciter *adv* rapidly.

vēlōx, -ōcis *adj* fast, quick, rapid.

vēlum, -ī *nt* sail; curtain, awning; **rēmis ~īsque** with might and main; **~a dare** set sail.

velut, velutī *adv* as, just as; for instance; just as if.

vēmēns *etc see* **vehemēns**.

vēna, -ae *f* vein, artery; vein of metal; water course; (*fig*) innermost nature of feelings, talent, strength; **~ās temptāre** feel the pulse; **~ās tenēre** have one's finger on the pulse (of).

vēnābulum, -ī *nt* hunting spear.

Venāfrānus, -ī *adj see* n.

Venāfrum, -ī *nt* Samnite town famous for olive oil.

vēnālicius *adj* for sale ♦ *m* slave dealer.

vēnālis *adj* for sale; bribable ♦ *m* slave offered for sale.

vēnāticus *adj* hunting (*in cpds*).

vēnātiō, -ōnis *f* hunting, a hunt; public show of fighting wild beasts; game.

vēnātor, -ōris *m* hunter.

vēnātōrius *adj* hunter's.

vēnātrīx, -īcis *f* huntress.

vēnātūra, -ae *f* hunting.

vēnātus, -ūs *m* hunting.

vēndibilis *adj* saleable; *(fig)* popular.

vēnditātiō, -ōnis *f* showing off, advertising.

vēnditātor, -ōris *m* braggart.

vēnditiō, -ōnis *f* sale.

vēnditō, -āre *vt* to try to sell; to praise up, advertise; **sē ~ ingratiate oneself (with).**

vēnditor, -ōris *m* seller.

vēndō *(pass* **vēneō)**, **-ere, -idī, -itum** *vt* to sell; to betray; to praise up.

venēficium, -ī *and* **iī** *nt* poisoning; sorcery.

venēficus *adj* poisonous; magic ♦ *m* sorcerer ♦ *f* sorceress.

venēnātus *adj* poisonous; magic.

venēnifer, -ī *adj* poisonous.

venēnō, -āre *vt* to poison.

venēnum, -ī *nt* drug, potion; dye; poison; magic charm; *(fig)* mischief; charm.

vēneō, -īre, -iī, -itum *vi* to be sold

venerābilis *adj* honoured, venerable.

venerābundus *adj* reverent.

venerātiō, -ōnis *f* respect, reverence.

venerātor, -ōris *m* reverencer.

Venereus, Venerius *adj* of Venus ♦ *m* highest throw at dice.

veneror, -ārī, -ātus *vt* to worship, revere, pray to; to honour, respect; to ask for, entreat.

Venetia, -iae *f* district of the Veneti.

Veneticus *adj* see n.

Venetus *adj* Venetian; *(colour)* blue.

vēnī *perf of* **veniō.**

venia, -ae *f* indulgence, favour, kindness; permission, leave; pardon, forgiveness; **bonā tuā ~ā** by your leave; **bonā ~ā audīre** give a fair hearing.

vēniī *perf of* **vēneō.**

veniō, -īre, vēnī, ventum *vi* to come; *(fig)* to fall into, incur, go as far as; **in amīcitiam ~** make friends (with); **in spem ~** entertain hopes.

vēnor, -ārī, -ātus *vt, vi* to hunt, chase.

venter, -ris *m* stomach, belly; womb, unborn child.

ventilātor, -ōris *m* juggler.

ventilō, -āre *vt* to fan, wave, agitate.

ventiō, -ōnis *f* coming.

ventitō, -āre *vi* to keep coming, come regularly.

ventōsus *adj* windy; like the wind; fickle; conceited.

ventriculus, -ī *m* belly; *(heart)* ventricle.

ventriōsus *adj* pot-bellied.

ventulus, -ī *m* breeze.

ventus, -ī *m* wind.

vēnūcula, -ae *f* kind of grape.

vēnum, vēnō for sale.

vēnumdō (vēnundō), -āre, -edī, -atum *vt* to sell, put up for sale.

venus, -eris *f* charm, beauty; love, mating.

Venus, -eris *f* goddess of love; planet Venus; highest throw at dice.

Venusia, -iae *f* town in Apulia *(birthplace of Horace).*

Venusīnus *adj* see **Venusia.**

venustās, -ātis *f* charm, beauty.

venustē *adv* charmingly.

venustulus *adj* charming little.

venustus *adj* charming, attractive, beautiful.

vēpallidus *adj* very pale.

veprēcula, -ae *f* little brier bush.

veprēs, -is *m* thornbush, bramblebush.

vēr, vēris *nt* spring; **~ sacrum** offerings of firstlings.

The present infinitive verb endings are as follows: **-āre** = 1st; **-ēre** = 2nd; **-ere** = 3rd and **-īre** = 4th. *See sections on irregular verbs and noun declensions.*

vērātrum, -ī *nt* hellebore.

vērāx, -ācis *adj* truthful.

verbēna, -ae *f* vervain; (*pl*) *sacred boughs carried by heralds or priests.*

verber, -is *nt* lash, scourge; (*missile*) strap; (*pl*) flogging, strokes.

verberābilis *adj* deserving a flogging.

verberātiō, -ōnis *f* punishment.

verbereus *adj* deserving a flogging.

verberō, -āre, -āvī, -ātum *vt* to flog, beat, lash.

verberō, -ōnis *m* scoundrel.

verbōsē *adv* verbosely.

verbōsus *adj* wordy.

verbum, -ī *nt* word; saying; expression; (*GRAM*) verb; (*pl*) language, talk; ~ ē (dē, prō) ~ō literally; **ad ~um** word for word; **~ī causā (grātiā)** for instance; **~ō** orally; briefly; **~a dare** cheat, fool; **~a facere** talk; **meīs ~is** in my name.

vērē *adv* really, truly, correctly.

verēcundē *adv* see *adj*.

verēcundia, -ae *f* modesty, shyness; reverence, dread; shame.

verēcundor, -ārī *vi* to be bashful, feel shy.

verēcundus *adj* modest, shy, bashful.

verendus *adj* venerable.

vereor, -ērī, -itus *vt, vi* to fear, be afraid; to revere, respect.

verētrum, -ī *nt* the private parts.

Vergiliae, -ārum *fpl* the Pleiads.

Vergilius, -ī *m* Vergil, Virgil (*famous epic poet*).

vergō, -ere *vt* to turn, incline ♦ *vi* to turn, incline, decline; (*place*) to face.

vēridicus *adj* truthful.

vērī similis *adj* probable.

vērī similitūdō, -inis *f* probability.

vēritās, -ātis *f* truth, truthfulness; reality, real life; (*character*) integrity; (*language*) etymology.

veritus *ppa of* vereor.

vermiculātus *adj* inlaid with wavy lines, mosaic.

vermiculus, -ī *m* grub.

vermina, -um *ntpl* stomach pains.

vermis, -is *m* worm.

verna, -ae *f* slave born in his master's home.

vernāculus *adj* of home-born slaves; native.

vernīlis *adj* slavish; (*remark*) smart.

vernīliter *adv* slavishly.

vernō, -āre *vi* to bloom, be springlike; to be young.

vernula, -ae *f* young home-born slave; native.

vērnus *adj* of spring.

vērō *adv* in fact, assuredly; (*confirming*) certainly, yes; (*climax*) indeed; (*adversative*) but in fact; **minimē ~** certainly not.

Vērōna, -ae *f* town in N. Italy (*birthplace of Catullus*).

Vērōnēnsis *adj* see **Vērōna**.

verpus, -ī *m* circumcised man.

verrēs, -is *m* boar.

Verrēs, -is *m* praetor prosecuted by Cicero.

verrīnus *adj* boar's, pork (*in cpds*).

verrō, -rere, -rī, -sum *vt* to sweep, scour; to sweep away, carry off.

verrūca, -ae *f* wart; (*fig*) slight blemish.

verrūcōsus *adj* warty.

verruncō, -āre *vi* to turn out successfully.

versābundus *adj* rotating.

versātilis *adj* revolving; versatile.

versicolor, -ōris *adj* of changing or various colours.

versiculus, -ī *m* short line; (*pl*) unpretentious verses.

versificātor, -ōris *m* versifier.

versipellis adj of changed appearance; crafty ♦ m werewolf.

versō, -āre, -āvī, -ātum vt to keep turning, wind, twist; (fig) to upset, disturb, ruin; (mind) to ponder, consider.

versor, -ārī, -ātus vi to live, be, be situated; to be engaged (in), be busy (with).

versum adv turned, in the direction.

versūra, -ae f borrowing to pay a debt; loan.

versus ppp of **vertō** ♦ adv turned, in the direction.

versus, -ūs m line, row; verse; (dance) step.

versūtē adv craftily.

versūtiae, -ārum fpl tricks.

versūtiloquus adj sly.

versūtus adj clever; crafty, deceitful.

vertex, -icis m whirlpool, eddy; whirlwind; crown of the head, head; top, summit; (sky) pole.

verticōsus adj eddying, swirling.

vertīgō, -inis f turning round; dizziness.

vertō, -tere, -tī, -sum vt to turn; to turn over, invert; to turn round; to turn into, change, exchange; (cause) to ascribe, impute; (language) to translate; (war) to overthrow, destroy; (pass) to be (in), be engaged (in) ♦ vi to turn; to change; to turn out, **in fugam ~** put to flight; **terga ~** flee; **solum ~** emigrate; **vitiō ~** blame; **annō ~tente** in the course of a year.

Vertumnus, -ī m god of seasons.

verū, -ūs nt spit; javelin.

vērum adv it truly, yes; but actually; but, yet; **~ tamen** nevertheless.

vērum, -ī nt truth, reality; right; **~**

similis probable.

vērus adj true, real, actual; truthful; right, reasonable.

verūtum, -ī nt javelin.

verūtus adj armed with the javelin.

vervēx, -ēcis m wether.

vēsānia, -ae f madness.

vēsāniēns, -entis adj raging.

vēsānus adj mad, insane; furious, raging.

vescor, -ī vi (with abl) to feed, eat; to enjoy.

vescus adj little, feeble; corroding.

vēsīca, -ae f bladder; purse; football.

vēsīcula, -ae f small bladder, blister.

vespa, -ae f wasp.

Vespasiānus, -ī m Roman emperor.

vesper, -is and **ī** m evening; supper; evening star; west; **~e, ~ī** in the evening.

vespera, -ae f evening.

vesperāscō, -ere vi to become evening, get late.

vespertīliō, -ōnis m bat.

vespertīnus adj evening (in cpds), in the evening; western.

vesperūgō, -inis f evening star.

Vesta, -ae f Roman goddess of the hearth.

Vestālis adj Vestal ♦ f virgin priestess of Vesta.

vester, -rī adj your, yours.

vestibulum, -ī nt forecourt, entrance.

vestīgium, -ī and **iī** nt footstep, footprint, track; (fig) trace, sign, vestige; (time) moment, instant; **ē ~iō** instantly.

vestīgō, -āre, -āvī, -ātum vt to track, trace, search for, discover.

vestīmentum, -ī nt clothes.

vestiō, -īre, -iī, -ītum vt to clothe, dress; to cover, adorn.

The present infinitive verb endings are as follows: -āre = 1st; -ēre = 2nd; -ere = 3rd and -īre = 4th. See sections on irregular verbs and noun declensions.

vestipica, -ae f wardrobe woman.

vestis, -is f clothes, dress; coverlet, tapestry, blanket; (*snake*) slough; **~em mūtāre** change one's clothes; go into mourning.

vestispica *etc see* **vestipica**.

vestītus, -ūs m clothes, dress; covering; **mūtāre ~um** go into mourning; **redīre ad suum ~um** come out of mourning.

Vesuvius, -ī m the volcano Vesuvius.

veterānus *adj* veteran.

veterāscō, -scere, -vī *vi* to grow old.

veterātor, -ōris m expert, old hand; sly fox.

veterātōriē *adv see* **veterātōrius**.

veterātōrius *adj* crafty.

veterīnus *adj* of burden ♦ f *and* *ntpl* beasts of burden.

veternōsus *adj* lethargic, drowsy.

veternus, -ī m lethargy, drowsiness.

vetitus *ppp of* **vetō** ♦ *nt* prohibition.

vetō, -āre, -uī, -itum *vt* to forbid, prohibit, oppose; (*tribune*) to protest.

vetulus *adj* little old, poor old.

vetus, -eris *adj* old, former ♦ *mpl* the ancients ♦ *fpl* the old shops (*in the Forum*) ♦ *ntpl* antiquity, tradition.

vetustās, -ātis f age, long standing; antiquity; great age, future age.

vetustus *adj* old, ancient; old-fashioned.

vexāmen, -inis *nt* shaking.

vexātiō, -ōnis f shaking; trouble, distress.

vexātor, -ōris m troubler, opponent.

vexī *perf of* **vehō**.

vexillārius, -ī *and* **iī** m standard-bearer, ensign; (*pl*) special reserve of veterans.

vexillum, -ī *nt* standard, flag; company, troop; **~ prōpōnere** hoist the signal for battle.

vexō, -āre, -āvī, -ātum *vt* to shake, toss, trouble, distress, injure, attack.

via, -ae f road, street, way; journey, march; passage; (*fig*) way, method, fashion; the right way; **~ā** properly; **inter ~ās** on the way.

viālis *adj* of the highways.

viārius *adj* for the upkeep of roads.

viāticātus *adj* provided with travelling money.

viāticus *adj* for a journey ♦ *nt* travelling allowance; (*MIL*) prizemoney, savings.

viātor, -ōris m traveller; (*law*) summoner.

vībix, -īcis f weal.

vibrō, -āre, -āvī, -ātum *vt* to wave, shake, brandish, hurl, launch ♦ *vi* to shake, quiver, vibrate; to shimmer, sparkle.

viburnum, -ī *nt* wayfaring-tree *or* guelder rose.

vīcānus *adj* village (*in cpds*) ♦ *mpl* villagers.

Vīca Pota, -ae, -ae f goddess of victory.

vicārius *adj* substituted ♦ *m* substitute, proxy; underslave.

vīcātim *adv* from street to street; in villages.

vice (*with gen*) on account of; like.

vicem in turn; (*with gen*) instead of; on account of; like; **tuam ~** on your account.

vīcēnārius *adj* of twenty.

vīcēnī, -ōrum *adj* twenty each, in twenties.

vīcēs *pl of* **vicis**.

vīcēsimānī, -ōrum *mpl* men of the twentieth legion.

vīcēsimārius adj derived from the 5 per cent tax.

vīcēsimus adj twentieth ♦ f a 5 per cent tax.

vīcī perf of **vincō**.

vicia, -ae f vetch.

viciēns and **ēs** adv twenty times.

vīcīnālis adj neighbouring.

vīcīnia, -ae f neighbourhood, nearness.

vīcīnitās, -ātis f neighbourhood, nearness.

vīcīnus adj neighbouring, nearby; similar, kindred ♦ m/f neighbour ♦ nt neighbourhood.

vicis gen (acc **-em**, abl **-e**) f interchange, alternation, succession; recompense, retaliation; fortune, changing conditions; duty, function, place; in **-em** in turn, mutually.

vicissim adv in turn, again.

vicissitūdō, -inis f interchange, alternation.

victima, -ae f victim, sacrifice.

victimārius, -ī and **iī** m assistant at sacrifices.

victitō, -āre vi to live, subsist.

victor, -ōris m conqueror, victor, winner ♦ adj victorious.

victōria, -ae f victory.

victōriātus, -ūs m silver coin stamped with Victory.

Victōriola, -ae f little statue of Victory.

victrīx, -īcis f conqueror ♦ adj victorious.

victus ppp of **vincō**.

victus, -ūs m sustenance, livelihood; way of life.

vīculus, -ī m hamlet.

vīcus, -ī m (city) quarter, street; (country) village, estate.

vidēlicet adv clearly, evidently; (ironical) of course; (explaining) namely.

videō, -ēre, vīdī, vīsum vt to see, look at; (mind) to observe, be aware, know; to consider, think over; to see to, look out for; to live to see; (pass) to seem, appear; to seem right, be thought proper; **mē ~ē** rely on me; **vīderit** let him see to it; **mihi ~eor esse** I think I am; **sī (tibi) vidētur** if you like.

viduāta adj widowed.

viduitās, -ātis f bereavement, want; widowhood.

vīdulus, -ī m trunk, box.

viduō, -āre vt to bereave.

viduus adj bereft, bereaved; unmarried; (with abl) without ♦ f widow; spinster.

Vienna, -ae f town in Gaul on the Rhone.

viētus adj shrivelled.

vigeō, -ēre, -uī vi to thrive, flourish.

vigēscō, -ere vi to begin to flourish, become lively.

vigēsimus etc see **vicēsimus**.

vigil, -is adj awake, watching, alert ♦ m watchman, sentinel; (pl) the watch, police.

vigilāns, -antis pres p of **vigilo** ♦ adj watchful.

vigilanter adv vigilantly.

vigilantia, -ae f wakefulness; vigilance.

vigilāx, -ācis adj watchful.

vigilia, -ae f lying awake, sleeplessness; keeping watch, guard; a watch; the watch, sentries; vigil; vigilance.

vigilō, -āre, -āvī, -ātum vi to remain awake; to keep watch; to be vigilant ♦ vt to spend awake, make while awake at night.

vīgintī num twenty.

vīgintīvirātus, -ūs m membership of

---

a board of twenty.

vīgintīvirī, -ōrum mpl a board or commission of twenty men.

vigor, -ōris m energy, vigour.

vīlica, -ae f wife of a steward.

vīlicō, -āre vi to be an overseer.

vīlicus, -ī m overseer, manager of an estate, steward.

vīlis adj cheap; worthless, poor, mean, common.

vīlitās, -ātis f cheapness, low price; worthlessness.

vīliter adv cheaply.

vīlla, -ae f country house, villa.

vīllic- etc see **vīlic-.**

vīllōsus adj hairy, shaggy.

vīllula, -ae f small villa.

vīllum, -ī nt a drop of wine.

vīllus, -ī m hair, fleece; (cloth) nap.

vīmen, -inis nt osier; basket.

vīmentum, -ī nt osier.

Vīminālis adj Viminal (hill of Rome).

vīmineus adj of osiers, wicker.

vīnāceus adj grape (in cpds).

Vīnālia, -ium ntpl Wine festival.

vīnārius adj of wine, wine (in cpds) ♦ m vintner ♦ nt wine flask.

vincibilis adj easily won.

vinciō, -cīre, -xī, -ctum vt to bind, fetter; to encircle; (fig) to confine, restrain, envelop, attach.

vinclum nt see **vinculum.**

vincō, -ere, vīcī, victum vt to conquer, defeat, subdue; to win, prevail, be successful; (fig) to surpass, excel; (argument) to convince, refute, prove conclusively; (life) to outlive.

vinctus ppp of **vinciō.**

vinculum, -ī nt bond, fetter, chain; (pl) prison.

vīndēmia, -ae f vintage grape harvest.

vīndēmiātor, -ōris m vintager.

vīndēmiola, -ae f small vintage.

Vīndēmitor, -ōris m the Vintager (a star in Virgo).

vindex, -icis m champion, protector; liberator; avenger ♦ adj avenging.

vindicātiō, -ōnis f punishment of offences.

vindiciae, -ārum fpl legal claim; **~ās ab lībertāte in servitūtem dare** condemn a free person to slavery.

vindicō, -āre, -āvī, -ātum vt to lay claim to; to claim, appropriate; to liberate, protect, champion; to avenge, punish; **in lībertātem ~** emancipate.

vindicta, -ae f rod used in manumitting a slave; defence, deliverance; revenge, punishment.

vīnea, -ae f vineyard; vine; (MIL) penthouse (for besiegers).

vīnētum, -ī nt vineyard.

vīnitor, -ōris m vine-dresser.

vinnulus adj delightful.

vīnolentia, -ae f wine drinking.

vīnolentus adj drunk.

vīnōsus adj fond of wine, drunken.

vīnum, -ī nt wine.

vinxī perf of **vinciō.**

viola, -ae f violet; stock.

violābilis adj vulnerable.

violāceus adj violet.

violārium, -ī nt violet bed.

violārius, -ī and **iī** m dyer of violet.

violātiō, -ōnis f desecration.

violātor, -ōris m violator, desecrator.

violēns, -entis adj raging, vehement.

violenter adv violently, furiously.

violentia, -ae f violence, impetuosity.

violentus adj violent, impetuous, boisterous.

violō, -āre, -āvī, -ātum vt to do violence to, outrage, violate; (agreement) to break.

vīpera, -ae f viper, adder, snake.

vīpereus adj snake's, serpent's.

vīperīnus adj snake's, serpent's.

vir, virī m man; grown man; brave man, hero; husband; (MIL) footsoldier.

virāgō, -inis f heroine, warrior maid.

virecta, -ōrum ntpl grassy sward.

vireō, -ēre, -uī vi to be green; (fig) to be fresh, flourish.

vīrēs pl of **vīs**.

virēscō, -ere vi to grow green.

virga, -ae f twig; graft; rod, staff, walking stick, wand; (colour) stripe.

virgātor, -ōris m flogger.

virgātus adj made of osiers; striped.

virgētum, -ī nt thicket of osiers.

virgeus adj of brushwood.

virgidēmia, -ae f crop of flogging.

virginālis adj maidenly, of maids.

virginārius adj of maids.

virgineus adj maidenly, virgin, of virgins.

virginitās, -ātis f maidenhood.

virgō, -inis f maid, virgin; young woman, girl; constellation Virgo; a Roman aqueduct.

virgula, -ae f wand.

virgulta, -ōrum ntpl thicket, shrubbery; cuttings, slips.

virguncula, -ae f little girl.

viridāns, -antis adj green.

viridārium, -ī and **iī** nt plantation, garden.

viridis adj green; fresh, young, youthful ♦ ntpl greenery.

viriditās, -ātis f verdure, greenness; freshness.

viridor, -ārī vi to become green.

virīlis adj male, masculine; man's; adult; manly, brave, bold; ~ **pars** one's individual part or duty; **prō ~ī parte, portiōne** to the best of one's ability.

virīlitās, -ātis f manhood.

virīliter adv manfully.

virītim adv individually, separately.

vīrōsus adj slimy; rank.

virtūs, -ūtis f manhood, full powers; strength, courage, ability, worth; (MIL) valour; prowess, heroism; (moral) virtue; (things) excellence, worth.

vīrus, -ī nt slime; poison; offensive smell; salt taste.

vīs (acc **vim**, abl **vī**, pl **vīrēs**) f power, force, strength; violence, assault; quantity, amount; (mind) energy, vigour; (word) meaning, import; (pl) strength; (MIL) troops; **per vim** forcibly; **dē vī damnārī** be convicted of assault; **prō vīribus** with all one's might.

vīs 2nd pers sg of **volō**.

viscātus adj limed.

viscerātiō, -ōnis f public distribution of meat.

viscō, -āre vt to make sticky.

viscum, -ī nt mistletoe; bird lime.

viscus, -eris (usu pl **-era, -erum**) nt internal organs; flesh, womb, child, (fig) heart, bowels.

vīsendus adj worth seeing.

vīsiō, -ōnis f apparition; idea.

vīsitō, -āre vt to see often; to visit.

vīsō, -ere, -ī, -un vt to look at, survey; to see to; to go and see, visit.

Visurgis, -is m river Weser.

vīsus ppp of **videō** ♦ nt vision.

vīsus, -ūs m sight, the faculty of seeing; a sight, vision.

vīta, -ae f life, livelihood; way of life; career, biography.

vītābilis adj undesirable.

vītābundus adj avoiding, taking evasive action.

vītālis adj of life, vital ♦ nt

subsistence ♦ *ntpl* vitals.

vītāliter *adv* with life.

vītātiō, -ōnis *f* avoidance.

Vitellius, -ī *m* Roman emperor in AD 69.

Vitellius, -iānus *adj see n.*

vitellus, -ī *m* little calf; *(egg)* yolk.

vīteus *adj* of the vine.

vīticula, -ae *f* little vine.

vītigenus *adj* produced from the vine.

vītilēna, -ae *f* procuress.

vitiō, -āre, -āvī, -ātum *vt* to spoil, corrupt, violate; to falsify.

vitiōsē *adv* badly, defectively.

vitiōsitās, -ātis *f* vice.

vitiōsus *adj* faulty, corrupt; wicked, depraved; ~ **cōnsul** *a consul whose election had a religious flaw in it.*

vītis, -is *f* vine; vine branch; centurion's staff, centurionship.

vītisator, -ōris *m* vine planter.

vitium, -ī *and* **iī** *nt* fault, flaw, defect; *(moral)* failing, offence, vice; *(religion)* flaw in the auspices.

vītō, -āre, -āvī, -ātum *vt* to avoid, evade, shun.

vītor, -ōris *m* basket maker, cooper.

vitreus *adj* of glass; glassy ♦ *ntpl* glassware.

vitricus, -ī *m* stepfather.

vitrum, -ī *nt* glass; woad.

vitta, -ae *f* headband, sacrificial fillet.

vittātus *adj* wearing a fillet.

vitula, -ae *f* (*of cow*) calf.

vitulīnus *adj* of veal ♦ *f* veal.

vītulor, -ārī *vi* to hold a celebration.

vitulus, -ī *m* calf; foal; ~ **marīnus** seal.

vituperābilis *adj* blameworthy.

vituperātiō, -ōnis *f* blame, censure; scandalous conduct.

vituperātor, -ōris *m* critic.

vituperō, -āre *vt* to find fault with, disparage; *(omen)* to spoil.

vīvārium, -ī *and* **iī** *nt* fishpond, game preserve.

vīvātus *adj* animated.

vīvāx, -ācis *adj* long-lived; lasting; *(sulphur)* inflammable.

vīvēscō, -ere *vi* to grow, become active.

vīvidus *adj* full of life; *(art)* true to life, vivid; *(mind)* lively.

vīvirādīx, -īcis *f* a rooted cutting, layer.

vīviscō *etc see* **vīvēscō.**

vīvō, -vere, -xī, -ctum *vi* to live, be alive; to enjoy life; *(fame)* to last, be remembered; *(with abl)* to live on; ~**ve** farewell!; ~**xērunt** they are dead.

vīvus *adj* alive, living; *(light)* burning; *(rock)* natural; *(water)* running; ~**ō vīdentique** before his very eyes; **mē ~ō** as long as I live, in my lifetime; **ad ~um resecāre** cut to the quick; **dē ~ō dētrahere** take out of capital.

vix *adv* with difficulty, hardly, scarcely.

vixdum *adv* hardly, as yet.

vīxī *perf of* **vīvō.**

vocābulum, -ī *nt* name, designation; *(GRAM)* noun.

vōcālis *adj* speaking, singing, tuneful ♦ *f* vowel.

vocāmen, -inis *nt* name.

vocātiō, -ōnis *f* invitation; *(law)* summons.

vocātus, -ūs *m* summons, call.

vōciferātiō, -ōnis *f* loud cry, outcry.

vōciferor, -ārī *vt* to cry out loud, shout.

vocitō, -āre, -āvī, -ātum *vt* to usually call; to shout.

vocīvus *etc see* **vacīvus.**

vocō, -āre, -āvī, -ātum *vt* to call, summon; to call, name; *(gods)* to

call upon; (*guest*) to invite; (MIL) to
challenge; (*fig*) to bring (*into some
condition or plight*); **~ dē** name
after; **~in dubium ~** call in
question; **in iūdicium ~** call to
account.

vōcula, -ae *f* weak voice; soft tone;
gossip.

volaema *ntpl* kind of large pear.

Volaterrae, -ārum *fpl* old Etruscan
town (*now* Volterra).

Volaterrānus *adj see* n.

volāticus *adj* winged; fleeting,
inconstant.

volātilis *adj* winged; swift;
fleeting.

volātus, -ūs *m* flight.

Volcānius *adj see* n.

Volcānus, -ī *m* Vulcan (*god of fire*);
fire.

volēns, -entis *pres p of* volō ♦ *adj*
willing, glad, favourable; **mihi
~entī est** it is acceptable to me.

volg- *etc see* vulg-.

volitō, -āre *vi* to fly about, flutter;
to hurry, move quickly; (*fig*) to
hover, soar; to get excited.

voln- *etc see* vuln-.

volō, -āre, -āvī, -ātum *vi* to fly; to
speed.

volō, velle, voluī *vt* to wish, want;
to be willing; to will, purpose,
determine; (*opinion*) to hold,
maintain; (*word, action*) to mean; **~
dicere** I mean; **bene ~** like; **male
~** dislike; **ōrātum tē ~** I beg you;
paucīs tē ~ a word with you!;
numquid vīs? (*before leaving*) is
there anything else?; **quid sibi
vult?** what does he mean?; what is
he driving at?; **velim faciās** please
do it; **vellem fēcissēs** I wish you
had done it.

volōnēs, -um *mpl* volunteers.

volpēs *etc see* vulpēs.

Volscī, -ōrum *mpl* people in S.
Latium.

Volscus *adj* Volscian.

volsella, -ae *f* tweezers.

volsus *ppp of* vellō.

volt, voltis *older forms of* vult,
vultis.

Voltumna, -ae *f* patron goddess of
Etruria.

voltus *etc see* vultus.

volūbilis *adj* spinning, revolving;
(*fortune*) fickle; (*speech*) fluent.

volūbilitās, -ātis *f* whirling motion;
roundness; fluency; inconstancy.

volūbiliter *adv* fluently.

volucer, -ris *adj* winged; flying,
swift; fleeting.

volucris, -is *f* bird; insect.

volūmen, -inis *nt* book, roll; coil,
eddy, fold.

voluntārius *adj* voluntary ♦ *mpl*
volunteers.

voluntās, -ātis *f* will, wish,
inclination; attitude, goodwill;
last will, testament; **suā ~āte** of
one's own accord; **ad ~atem** with
the consent (of).

volup *adv* agreeably, to one's
satisfaction.

voluptābilis *adj* agreeable.

voluptās, -ātis *f* pleasure,
enjoyment; (*pl*) entertainments,
sports.

voluptuārius *adj* pleasurable,
agreeable; voluptuous.

volūtābrum, -ī *nt* wallowing place.

volūtātiō, -ōnis *f* wallowing.

volūtō, -āre *vt* to roll about, turn
over; (*mind*) to occupy, engross;
(*thought*) to ponder, think over;
(*pass*) to wallow, flounder.

volūtus *ppp of* volvō.

volva, -ae *f* womb; (*dish*) sow's
womb.

volvō, -vere, -vī, -ūtum *vt* to roll,

The present infinitive verb endings are as follows: **-āre** = 1st; **-ēre** = 2nd; **-ere** = 3rd and
-īre = 4th. *See sections on irregular verbs and noun declensions.*

turn round; to roll along; (*air*) to breathe; (*book*) to open; (*circle*) to form; (*thought*) to ponder, reflect on; (*time*) to roll on; (*trouble*) to undergo; (*pass*) to roll, revolve ♦ *vi* to revolve, elapse.

vōmer, -eris *m* ploughshare.

vomica, -ae *f* sore, ulcer, abscess, boil.

vōmis *etc see* **vōmer.**

vomitiō, -ōnis *f* vomiting.

vomitus, -ūs *m* vomiting, vomit.

vomō, -ere, -uī, -itum *vt* to vomit, throw up; to emit, discharge.

vorāgō, -inis *f* abyss, chasm, depth.

vorāx, -ācis *adj* greedy, ravenous; consuming.

vorō, -āre, -āvī, -ātum *vt* to swallow, devour; (*sea*) to swallow up; (*reading*) to devour.

vors-, vort- *etc see* **vers-, vert-** *etc.*

vōs *pron* you.

Vosegus, -ī *m* Vosges mountains.

voster *etc see* **vester.**

vōtīvus *adj* votive, promised in a vow.

votō *etc see* **vetō.**

vōtum, -ī *nt* vow, prayer; votive offering; wish, longing; **~ī damnārī** have one's prayer granted.

vōtus *ppp of* **voveō.**

voveō, -ēre, vōvī, vōtum *vt* to vow, promise solemnly; to dedicate; to wish.

vōx, vōcis *f* voice; sound, cry, call; word, saying, expression; accent; **ūnā vōce** unanimously.

Vulcānus *see* **Volcānus.**

vulgāris *adj* common, general.

vulgāriter *adv* in the common fashion.

vulgātor, -ōris *m* betrayer.

vulgātus *adj* common; generally known, notorious.

vulgivagus *adj* roving; inconstant.

vulgō *adv* publicly, commonly, usually, everywhere.

vulgō, -āre, -āvī, -ātum *vt* to make common, spread; to publish, divulge, broadcast; to prostitute; to level down.

vulgus, -ī *nt* (*occ m*) the mass of the people, the public; crowd, herd; rabble, populace.

vulnerātiō, -ōnis *f* wounding, injury.

vulnerō, -āre, -āvī, -ātum *vt* to wound, hurt; to damage.

vulnificus *adj* wounding, dangerous.

vulnus, -eris *nt* wound, injury; (*things*) damage, hole; (*fig*) blow, misfortune, pain.

vulpēcula, -ae *f* little fox.

vulpēs, -is *f* fox; (*fig*) cunning.

vulsī *perf of* **vellō.**

vulsus *ppp of* **vellō.**

vulticulus, -ī *m* a mere look (from).

vultum *etc see* **vultus.**

vultuōsus *adj* affected.

vultur, -is *m* vulture.

vulturius, -ī *and* **iī** *m* vulture, bird of prey; (*dice*) an unlucky throw.

Vulturnus, -ī *m* river in Campania.

vultus, -ūs *m* look, expression (*esp* in the eyes); face; (*things*) appearance.

vulva *etc see* **volva.**

X

Xanthippē, -ēs *f* wife of Socrates.

Xanthus, -ī *m* river of Troy (*identified with Scamander*); river of Lycia.

xenium, -ī *and* **iī** *nt* present.

Xenocratēs, -is *m* disciple of Plato.

Xenophanēs, -is *m* early Greek philosopher.

Xenophōn, -ontis *m* famous Greek historian.

Xenophontēus *adj* see n.

xērampelinae, -ārum *fpl* dark-coloured clothes.

Xerxēs, -is *m* Persian king defeated at Salamis.

xiphiās, -ae *m* swordfish.

xystum, -ī *nt,* **xystus, -ī** *m* open colonnade, walk, avenue.

Z

Zacynthius *adj see n.*

Zacynthus (-os), -ī *f* island off W. Greece (*now* Zante).

Zama, -ae *f* town in Numidia (*where Scipio defeated Hannibal*).

Zamēnsis *adj see n.*

zāmia, -ae *f* harm.

Zanclaeus *and* **ēius** *adj see n.*

Zanclē, -ēs *f* old name of Messana.

zēlotypus *adj* jealous.

Zēnō *and* **ōn, -ōnis** *m* founder of Stoicism; *a philosopher of Elea; an Epicurean teacher of Cicero.*

Zephyrītis, -idis *f* Arsinoe (*queen of Egypt*).

Zephyrus, -ī *m* west wind, zephyr; wind.

Zēthus, -ī *m* brother of Amphion.

Zeuxis, -is *and* **idis** *m* famous Greek painter.

zmaragdus *etc see* ~~smaragdus~~.

Zmyrna *etc see* **Smyrna**.

zōdiacus, -ī *m* zodiac.

zōna, -ae *f* belt, girdle; (*GEOG*) zone; (*ASTRO*) Orion's Belt.

zōnārius *adj* of belts; **sector ~** cutpurse ♦ *m* belt maker.

zōnula, -ae *f* little belt.

zōthēca, -ae *f* private room.

zōthēcula, -ae *f* cubicle.

The present infinitive verb endings are as follows: **-āre** = 1st; **-ēre** = 2nd; **-ere** = 3rd and **-īre** = 4th. *See sections on irregular verbs and noun declensions.*

LATIN GRAMMAR AND VERSE

DECLENSIONS OF NOUNS

1st Declension

	mainly f			*m*
SING				
Nom.	terra	crambē	Aenēās	Anchīsēs
Voc.	terra	crambē	Aenēā	Anchīsā, -ē
Acc.	terram	crambēn	Aenēam, -ān	Anchīsam, -ēn
Gen.	terrae	crambes	Aenēae	Anchīsae
Dat.	terrae	crambæ	Aenēae	Anchīsae
Abl.	terra	crambā	Aenēā	Anchīsā
PLURAL				
Nom.	terrae	crambae		
Voc.	terrae	crambae		
Acc.	terrās	crambās		
Gen.	terrārum	crambārum		
Dat.	terrīs	crambīs		
Abl.	terrīs	crambīs		

2nd Declension

mainly m

SING					
Nom.	modus	Lūcius	Dēlos (f)	puer	liber
Voc.	mode	Lūcī	Dēle	puer	liber
Acc.	modum	Lūcium	Dēlon	puerum	librum
Gen.	modī	Lūcī	Dēlī	puerī	librī
Dat.	modō	Lūciō	Dēlō	puerō	librō
Abl.	modō	Lūciō	Dēlō	puerō	librō
PLURAL					
Nom.	modī			puerī	librī
Voc.	modī			puerī	librī
Acc.	modōs			puerōs	librōs
Gen.	modōrum			puerōrum	librōrum
Dat.	modīs			puerīs	librīs
Abl.	modīs			puerīs	librīs

		nt		nt

	SING		*PLURAL*	
Nom.	dōnum		*Nom.*	dōna
Voc.	dōnum		*Voc.*	dōna
Acc.	dōnum		*Acc.*	dōna
Gen.	dōnī		*Gen.*	dōnōrum
Dat.	dōnō		*Dat.*	dōnīs
Abl.	dōnō		*Abl.*	dōnīs

3rd Declension

Group I: *Vowel stems, with gen pl in* **-ium**

	m and f		nt	
SING				
Nom.	clādēs	nāvis	rēte	animal
Voc.	clādēs	nāvis	rēte	animal
Acc.	clādem	nāvem, -im	rēte	animal
Gen.	clādis	nāvis	rētis	animālis
Dat.	clādī	nāvī	rētī	animālī
Abl.	clāde	nāve, -ī	rētī	animālī
SING				
Nom.	clādēs	nāvēs	rētia	animālia
Voc.	clādēs	nāvēs	rētia	animālia
Acc.	clādēs, -īs	nāvēs, -īs	rētia	animālia
Gen.	clādium	nāvium	rētium	animālium
Dat.	clādibus	nāvibus	rētibus	animālibus
Abl.	clādibus	nāvibus	rētibus	animālibus

Group II: *Consonant stems, some with gen pl in* **-ium**, *some in* **-um**
and some in either. Monosyllabic nouns ending in two
consonants (e.g. **urbs** *below) regularly have* **-ium**.

	m and f			*nt*	
SING					
Nom.	urbs	amāns	laus	aetās	os
Voc.	urbs	amāns	laus	aetās	os
Acc.	urbem	amantem	laudem	aetātem	os
Gen.	urbis	amantis	laudis	aetātis	ossis
Dat.	urbī	amantī	laudī	aetātī	ossī
Abl.	urbe	amante	laude	aetāte	osse
PLURAL					
Nom.	urbēs	amantēs	laudēs	aetātēs	ossa
Voc.	urbēs	amantēs	laudēs	aetātēs	ossa
Acc.	urbēs	amantēs	laudēs	aetātēs	ossa
Gen.	urbium	amantium,	laudum,	aetātum,	ossium
		-um	-ium	-ium	
Dat.	urbibus	amantibus	laudibus	aetātibus	ossibus
Abl.	urbibus	amantibus	laudibus	aetātibus	ossibus

Group III: *Consonant stems, with gen pl in* **-um**

	m and f			*nt*	
SING					
Nom.	mōs	ratiō	pater	nōmen	opus
Voc.	mōs	ratiō	pater	nōmen	opus
Acc.	mōrem	ratiōnem	patrem	nōmen	opus
Gen.	mōris	ratiōnis	patris	nōminis	operis
Dat.	mōrī	ratiōnī	patrī	nōminī	operī
Abl.	mōre	ratiōne	patre	nōmine	opere
PLURAL					
Nom.	mōrēs	ratiōnēs	patrēs	nōmina	opera
Voc.	mōrēs	ratiōnēs	patrēs	nōmina	opera
Acc.	mōrēs	ratiōnēs	patrēs	nōmina	opera
Gen.	mōrum	ratiōnum	patrum	nōminum	operum
Dat.	mōribus	ratiōnibus	patribus	nōminibus	operibus
Abl.	mōribus	ratiōnibus	patribus	nōminibus	operibus

Group IV: *Greek nouns*

			m	f	nt
SING					
Nom.	āēr	hērōs	Periclēs	Naias	poēma
Voc.	āēr	hērōs	Periclē	Naias	poēma
Acc.	āera	hērōa	{ Periclem,	Naiada	poēma
			Periclea		
Gen.	āeris	hērōis	Periclis, ī	Naiadis, -os	poēmatis
Dat.	āerī	hērōī	Periclī	Naiadī	poēmatī
Abl.	āere	hērōe	Periclē	Naiade	poēmate
PLURAL					
Nom.	āeres	hērōes		Naiades	poēmata
Voc.	āeres	hērōes		Naiades	poēmata
Acc.	āeras	hērōas		Naiadas	poēmata
Gen.	āerum	hērōum		Naiadum	poēmatōrum
Dat.	āeribus	hērōibus		Naiadibus	poēmatīs
Abl.	āeribus	hērōibus		Naiadibus	poēmatīs

	4th Declension		**5th Declension**	
	mainly m	*nt*	*mainly f*	
SING				
Nom.	portus	genū	diēs	rēs
Voc.	portus	genū	diēs	rēs
Acc.	portum	genū	diem	rem
Gen.	portūs	genūs	diēī	reī
Dat.	portuī	genū	diēī	reī
Abl.	portū	genū	diē	rē
PLURAL				
Nom.	portūs	genua	diēs	rēs
Voc.	portūs	genua	diēs	rēs
Acc.	portūs	genua	diēs	rēs
Gen.	portuum	genuum	diērum	rērum
Dat.	portibus,	genibus,	diēbus	rēbus
	-ubus	-ubus		
Abl.	portibus,	genibus,	diēbus	rēbus
	-ubus	-ubus		

CONJUGATIONS OF VERBS

ACTIVE

PRESENT TENSE

	First parāre *prepare*	**Second** habēre *have*	**Third** sūmere *take*	**Fourth** audīre *hear*

Indicative

SING				
1st pers	parō	habeō	sūmō	audiō
2nd pers	parās	habēs	sūmis	audīs
3rd pers	parat	habet	sūmit	audit
PLURAL				
1st pers	parāmus	habēmus	sūmimus	audīmus
2nd pers	parātis	habētis	sūmitis	audītīs
3rd pers	parant	habent	sūmunt	audiunt

Subjunctive

SING				
1st pers	parem	habeam	sūmam	audiam
2nd pers	parēs	habeās	sūmās	audiās
3rd pers	paret	habeat	sūmat	audiat
PLURAL				
1st pers	parēmus	habeāmus	sūmāmus	audiāmus
2nd pers	parētis	habeātis	sūmātis	audiātis
3rd pers	parent	habeant	sūmant	audiant

IMPERFECT TENSE

Indicative

SING				
1st pers	parābam	habēbam	sūmēbam	audiēbam
2nd pers	parābās	habēbās	sūmēbās	audiēbās
3rd pers	parābat	habēbat	sūmēbat	audiēbat

1st pers	parābāmus	habēbāmus	sūmēbāmus	audiēbāmus
2nd pers	parābātis	habēbātis	sūmēbātis	audiēbātis
3rd pers	parābant	habēbant	sūmēbant	audiēbant

Subjunctive

SING

1st pers	parārem	habērem	sūmerem	audīrem
2nd pers	parārēs	habērēs	sūmerēs	audīrēs
3rd pers	parāret	habēret	sūmeret	audīret

PLURAL

1st pers	parārēmus	habērēmus	sūmerēmus	audīrēmus
2nd pers	parārētis	habērētis	sūmerētis	audīrētis
3rd pers	parārent	habērent	sūmerent	audīrent

FUTURE TENSE

Indicative

SING

1st pers	parābō	habēbō	sūmam	audiam
2nd pers	parābis	habēbis	sūmēs	audiēs
3rd pers	parābit	habēbit	sūmet	audiet

PLURAL

1st pers	parābimus	habēbimus	sūmēmus	audiēmus
2nd pers	parābitis	habēbitis	sūmētis	audiētis
3rd pers	parābunt	habēbunt	sūment	audient

Subjunctive

SING

parātūrus, -a, -um	sim	*or*	essem
habitūrus, -a, -um	sīs		essēs
sūmptūrus, -a, -um	sit		esset
audītūrus, -a, -um			

parātūrī, -ac, -a
habitūrī, -ae, -a
sūmptūrī, -ae, -a
audītūrī, -ae, -a

sīmus	*or*	essēmus
sītis		essētis
sint		essent

PERFECT TENSE
Indicative

SING

1st pers	parāvī	habuī	sūmpsī	audīvī
2nd pers	parāvistī	habuistī	sūmpsistī	audīvistī
3rd pers	parāvit	habuit	sūmpsit	audīvit

PLURAL

1st pers	parāvimus	habuimus	sūmpsimus	audīvimus
2nd pers	parāvistis	habuistis	sūmpsistis	audīvistis
3rd pers	parāvērunt, -e	habuērunt, -e	sūmpsērunt, -e	audīvērunt, -e

Subjunctive

SING

1st pers	parāverim	habuerim	sūmpserim	audīverim
2nd pers	parāveris	habueris	sūmpseris	audīveris
3rd pers	parāverit	habuerit	sūmpserit	audīverit

PLURAL

1st pers	parāverimus	habuerimus	sūmpserimus	audīverimus
2nd pers	parāveritis	habueritis	sūmpseritis	audīveritis
3rd pers	parāverint	habuerint	sūmpserint	audīverint

Indicative

SING

1st pers	parāveram	habueram	sūmpseram	audīveram
2nd pers	parāverās	habuerās	sūmpserās	audīverās
3rd pers	parāverat	habuerat	sūmpserat	audīverat

PLURAL

1st pers	parāverā-mus	habuerā-mus	sūmpserā-mus	audīverā-mus
2nd pers	parāverātis	habuerātis	sūmpserātis	audīverātis
3rd pers	parāverant	habuerant	sūmpserant	audīverant

Subjunctive

SING

1st pers	parāvissem	habuissem	sūmpsissem	audīvissem
2nd pers	parāvissēs	habuissēs	sūmpsissēs	áudīvissēs
3rd pers	parāvisset	habuisset	sūmpsisset	audīvisset

PLURAL

1st pers	parāvissē-mus	habuissē-mus	sūmpsissē-mus	audīvissē-mus
2nd pers	parāvissētis	habuissētis	sūmpsissētis	audīvissētis
3rd pers	parāvissent	habuissent	sūmpsissent	audīvissent

Indicative

SING

1st pers	parāverō	habuerō	sūmpserō	audīverō
2nd pers	parāveris	habueris	sūmpseris	audīveris
3rd pers	parāverit	habuerit	sūmpserit	audīverit

PLURAL

1st pers	parāveri-mus	habueri-mus	sūmpseri-mus	audīveri-mus
2nd pers	parāveritis	habueritis	sūmpseritis	audīveritis
3rd pers	parāverint	habuerint	sūmpserint	audīverint

Present

SING	parā	habē	sūme	audī
PLURAL	parāte	habēte	sūmite	audīte

Future

SING

2nd pers	parātō	habētō	sūmitō	audītō
3rd pers	parātō	habētō	sūmitō	audītō

PLURAL

2nd pers	parātōte	habētōte	sūmitōte	audītōte
3rd pers	parantō	habentō	sūmuntō	audiuntō

INFINITIVE
Present

parāre	habēre	sūmere	audīre

Perfect

parāvisse	habuisse	sūmpsisse	audīvisse

Future

parātūrus	habitūrus	sūmptūrus	audītūrus

-a, -um, esse *etc*

PASSIVE

PRESENT TENSE

Indicative

SING

1st pers	paror	habeor	sūmor	audior
2nd pers	parāris	habēris	sūmeris	audīris
3rd pers	parātur	habētur	sūmitur	audītur

PLURAL

1st pers	parāmur	habēmur	sūmimur	audīmur
2nd pers	parāminī	habēminī	sūmiminī	audīminī
3rd pers	parantur	habentur	sūmuntur	audiuntur

Subjunctive

SING

1st pers	parer	habear	sūmar	audiar
2nd pers	parēris	habeāris	sūmāris	audiāris
3rd pers	parētur	habeātur	sūmātur	audiātur

PLURAL

1st pers	parēmur	habeāmur	sūmāmur	audiāmur
2nd pers	parēminī	habeāminī	sūmāminī	audiāminī
3rd pers	parentur	habeantur	sūmantur	audiantur

IMPERFECT TENSE

Indicative

SING

1st pers	parābar	habēbar	sūmēbar	audiēbar
2nd pers	parābāris	habēbāris	sūmēbāris	audiēbāris
3rd pers	parābātur	habēbātur	sūmēbātur	audiēbātur

PLURAL

1st pers	parābāmur	habēbāmur	sūmēbāmur	audiēbāmur
2nd pers	parābāminī	habēbāminī	sūmēbāminī	audiēbāminī
3rd pers	parābāntur	habēbantur	sūmēbantur	audiēbantur

Subjunctive

1st pers	parārer	habērer	sūmerer	audīrer
2nd pers	parārēris	habērēris	sūmerēris	audīrēris
3rd pers	parārētur	habērētur	sūmerētur	audīrētur

PLURAL

1st pers	parārēmur	habērēmur	sūmerēmur	audīrēmur
2nd pers	parārēminī	habērēminī	sūmerēminī	audīrēminī
3rd pers	parārentur	habērentur	sūmerentur	audīrentur

FUTURE TENSE

Indicative

SING

1st pers	parābor	habēbor	sūmar	audiar
2nd pers	parāberis	habēberis	sūmēris	audiēris
3rd pers	parābitur	habēbitur	sūmētur	audiētur

PLURAL

1st pers	parābimur	habēbimur	sūmēmur	audiēmur
2nd pers	parābiminī	habēbiminī	sūmeminī	audiēminī
3rd pers	parābuntur	habēbuntur	sūmentur	audientur

PERFECT TENSE

Indicative

SING	parātus -a, -um sum/es/est *etc*	habitus	sūmptus	audītus
PLURAL	parātī -ae, -a sumus/estis/sunt *etc*	habitī	sūmptī	audītī

Subjunctive

SING	parātus -a, -um sim/sīs/sit *etc*	habitus	sūmptus	audītus
PLURAL	parātī -ae, -a sīmus/sītis/sint *etc*	habitī	sūmptī	audītī

Indicative

SING	parātus	habitus	sūmptus	audītus
	-a, -um	eram/erās/erat *etc*		
PLURAL	parātī	habītī	sūmptī	audītī
	-ae, -a	erāmus/erātis/erant *etc*		

Subjunctive

SING	parātus	habitus	sūmptus	audītus
	-a, -um	essem/essēs/esset *etc*		
PLURAL	parātī	habītī	sūmptī	audītī
	-ae, -a	essēmus/essētis/essent *etc*		

FUTURE PERFECT TENSE

Indicative

SING	parātus	habitus	sūmptus	audītus
	-a, -um	erō/eris/erit *etc*		
PLURAL	parātī	habītī	sumptī	audītī
	-ae, -a	erimus/eritis/erunt *etc*		

IMPERATIVE

Present

SING	parāre	habēre	sūmere	audīre
PLURAL	parāminī	habēminī	sūmiminī	audīminī

Future

2nd pers	parātor	habētor	sūmitor	audītor
3rd pers	parātor	habētor	sūmitor	audītor

PLURAL
3rd pers	parantor	habentor	sūmuntor	audiuntor

INFINITIVE

Present

parārī	habērī	sūmī	audīrī

Perfect

parātus	habitus	sūmptus	audītus
-a, -um esse *etc*			

Future

parātum	habitum	sūmptum	audītum
īrī	īrī	īrī	īrī

VERBAL NOUNS AND ADJECTIVES

Present Participle Active

parāns	habēns	sūmēns	audiēns

Perfect Participle Passive

parātus	habitus	sūmptus	audītus

Future Participle Active

parātūrus	habitūrus	sūmptūrus	audītūrus

Gerund

(acc, gen, dat and abl)

parandum, -ī, -ō	habendum, -ī, -ō	sūmendum, -ī, -ō	audiendum, -ī, -ō

Gerundive

parandus	habendus	sūmendus	audiendus

Supines

1st	parātum	habitum	sūmptum	audītum
2nd	parātū	habitū	sūmptū	audītū

Note. *Some verbs of the 3rd conjugation have the present indicative ending in* -io; *e.g.* **capio**, *I capture.*

PRESENT TENSE

	Indicative		Subjunctive	
Active	**Passive**	**Active**	**Passive**
capio	capior	capiam	capiar
capis	caperis	capias	capiāris
capit	capitur	capiat	capiātur
capimus	capimur	capiāmus	capiāmur
capitis	capiminī	capiātis	capiāminī
capiunt	capiuntur	capiant	capiantur

IMPERFECT TENSE

capiēbam *etc.* capiēbar *etc.* caperem *etc.* caperer *etc.*

FUTURE TENSE

INFINITIVE MOOD

capiam capiar **Present Active** capere
capiēs *etc.* capiēris *etc.* **Present Passive** capī

PRESENT IMPERATIVE

Active **Passive**

cape capite capere capiminī

PARTICIPLE GERUND GERUNDIVE

Present capiēns capiendum capiendus, -a, um

In all other tenses and moods **capere** is similar to **sumere**.

IRREGULAR VERBS

	Esse *be*	**Posse** *be able*	**Velle** *wish*	**Ire** *go*

Present Indicative

SING

1st Pers	sum	possum	volō	eō
2nd Pers	es	potes	vīs	īs
3rd Pers	est	potest	vult, volt	it

PLURAL

1st Pers	sumus	possumus	volumus	īmus
2nd Pers	estis	potestis	vultis, voltis	ītis
3rd Pers	sunt	possunt	volunt	eunt

Present Subjunctive

SING

1st Pers	sim	possim	velim	eam
2nd Pers	sīs	possīs	velīs	eās
3rd Pers	sit	possit	velit	eat

PLURAL

1st Pers	sīmus	possīmus	velīmus	eāmus
2nd Pers	sītis	possītis	velītis	eātis
3rd Pers	sint	possint	velint	eant

Imperfect Indicative

1st Pers	eram	poteram	volēbam	ībam

Imperfect Subjunctive

1st Pers	essem	possem	vellem	īrem

Future Indicative

1st Pers	erō	poterō	volam	ībō

Future Subjunctive

1st Pers	futūrus, -a, -um sim *or* essem	—	—	itūrus, -a, -um sim *or* essem

Perfect Indicative

1st Pers	fuī	potuī	voluī	īvī, iī

Perfect Subjunctive

1st Pers	fuerim	potuerim	volucrim	īverim, ierim

Pluperfect Indicative

1st Pers	fueram	potueram	volueram	īveram, ieram

Pluperfect Subjunctive

1st Pers	fuissem	potuissem	voluissem	īvissem, iissem

Future Perfect Indicative

1st Pers	fuerō	potuerō	voluerō	īverō, ierō

Present Imperative

SING	es	—	—	ī
PLURAL	este	—	—	īte

Future Imperative

SING	estō	—	—	ītō
PLURAL	estōte	—	—	ītōte

Infinitives

PRESENT	esse	posse	velle	īre
PERFECT	fuisse	potuisse	voluisse	īvisse, iisse
FUTURE	futūrus, -a, -um esse	—	—	itūrus, -a, -um esse

Participles

PRESENT	—	—	—	iēns, euntis
FUTURE	futūrus	—	—	itūrus

Gerund and Supine

GERUND	—	—	—	eundum
SUPINE	—	—	—	itum

404

LATIN VERSE

QUANTITY

Both vowels and syllables in Latin may be described as long or short. A long vowel or syllable is one on which the voice dwells for a longer time than on a short one, in much the same way as a minim is long compared with a crotchet in musical notation.

A syllable is long if the vowel in it is either long in itself or followed by two or more consonants. The letter **x** counts as a double consonant, the letter **h** not at all, and the following pairs of consonants occurring in the same word after a short vowel do not necessarily make the syllable long:

br, cr, dr, fr, gr, pr, tr; fl, gl, pl.

A syllable is short if its vowel is a short one and not followed by two or more consonants (except for the groups noted in the preceding paragraph).

Examples:

In **dūcō** both the vowels are long ("by nature") and therefore the two syllables are long.

In **deus** both the vowels are short, neither is followed by more than one consonant, and therefore the two syllables are short; but if a word beginning with a consonant follows, then the syllable **-us** will become long.

In **adsunt** both the vowels are short, but they are both followed by two consonants, and the two syllables are therefore "long by position".

This long or short characteristic of Latin vowels and syllables is called "quantity." To determine the quantities of vowels no general rules can be given, and some of them are now not known for certain. The vowel quantities of words will have to be learned when the words are learned, or else looked up when the need arises. In final syllables, however, there is a certain regularity to be found, and the following table shows the commonest of these:

ENDING

	Long	Short
-a	1st decl abl sing	1st decl nom and voc sing
	1st conj impv sing numerals and most adverbs	all nom and acc ntpl **ita, quia**
-e	5th decl abl sing 2nd conj impv sing most adverbs Greek nouns	all other noun and verb endings **bene, male** enclitics
-i	all endings, except	**quasi, nisi**: and sometimes **mihi, tibi, sibi, ibi, ubi**
-o	all endings, except	sometimes iambic words, esp **cito, duo, ego, homo, modo, puto, rogo, scio**
-u	all endings	
-as	all endings, except	Greek nouns
-es	all endings, except	3rd decl nom sing with short -e in stem **es** (be) and compounds **penes**
-is	1st and 2nd decl dat and abl pl 3rd decl acc pl 4th conj 2nd pers sing **vīs, sīs, velīs**	all others
-os	all endings, except	2nd decl nom sing **os** (bone) **compos, impos**
-us	3rd decl nom sing with	all others

long -u- in stem
4th decl gen sing and
nom and acc pl

METRES

Latin Verse is a pattern of long and short syllables, grouped together in "feet" or in lyric lines.

FEET

The commonest Feet employed in Latin metres are:

Anapaest	(short—short—long)	˘ ˘ –
Dactyl	(long—short—short)	– ˘ ˘
Iambus	(short—long)	˘ –
Proceleusmatic	(short—short—short—short)	˘ ˘ ˘ ˘
Spondee	(long—long)	– –
Tribrach	(short—short—short)	˘ ˘ ˘
Trochee	(long—short)	– ˘

CAESURA AND DIAERESIS

The longer lines usually have a regular break near the middle, occurring either in the middle of a foot (**Caesura**) or at the end of a foot (**Diaeresis**). This break need not imply a pause in the sense of the words, but merely the end of a word, provided that it does not go too closely with the word following, as in the case of a preposition before a noun. See examples on pages 409–414 where the caesura is marked †, and the diaeresis //.

ELISION

A vowel or a vowel followed by **m** at the end of a word ("open vowel") is regularly elided before a vowel at the beginning of the next word in the same line. In reciting, the elided syllable should not be dropped entirely, but slurred into the following vowel. An open vowel at the end of a line does not elide before a vowel at the beginning of the next line.

FINAL SYLLABLES

Where the metre requires the final syllable in a line to be long, this syllable may in fact be a short one. This position in the line is commonly called a **syllaba anceps**, and marked down as being either long or short. It is perhaps better to regard this syllable, when the vowel is short, as long by position, since metrical length is a matter of duration, and the end of a line calls naturally for a slight pause in reading, even if the sense runs on to the next line. In the metrical schemes which follow, a long final syllable should be understood in this sense: it may in itself be a short one.

Latin metres fall into three fairly distinct categories, associated with three different genres of verse: 1. *Dactylic*
2. *Iambic and Trochaic*
3. *Lyric*

DACTYLIC VERSE

The Dactylic metres are the **Hexameter** and the **Pentameter**. The Hexameter is the medium of epic, didactic and pastoral poetry, of satires and epistles, and other examples of occasional verse. In conjunction with the Pentameter it forms the **Elegiac Couplet**, the metre most commonly used for love poetry, occasional pieces, and the epigram.

Dactylic Hexameter

The first four feet may be either **dactyls** or **spondees**, the 5th is regularly a dactyl, the 6th always a spondee. In Virgil and later poets the last word is either disyllabic or trisyllabic. A **Caesura** normally occurs in either the 3rd or the 4th foot, and pastoral poetry often has the "**Bucolic Diaeresis**" at the end of the 4th foot. In Virgilian and later usage there is a tendency for words and feet to overlap in the first four feet and to coincide in the last two. Similarly in the first part of the line the metrical ictus and the normal accent of the spoken word tend to fall on different syllables, whereas they regularly coincide in the last two feet.

Example:

Clāss(em) āp|tēnt tăcĭ|tī† sŏcĭ|ōsqu(e) ād | lītŏră| tōrquēnt
(*Virgil, Aen. 4, 289*)

Occasional lines will be found in the poets, which deliberately violate the above rules for the sake of obtaining some special effect,

pĕr cō|nūbĭă| nōstrā,† pĕr| īncēp|tōs hў̆mĕ|nāeōs
(*Aen. 4, 316*)

The above echoes Greek hexameter, where the final word is Greek and has four syllables, and the caesura comes between the two short syllables of the dactyl in the 3rd foot:

cūm sŏcĭ|īs nā|tōquĕ† pĕ|nātĭbŭs| ēt māg|nīs dīs
(*Aen. 3, 12*)

Note the solemn, archaic touch, suggesting a line of Ennius, where the 5th foot is a spondee, and the last word is monosyllabic.

pārtŭrĭ|ēnt mōn|tēs,† nā|scētŭr| rīdĭcŭ|lūs mūs
(*Hor, A. P. 139*)

The monosyllabic ending, above, creates a comic effect.

Dactylic Pentameter

This line has two equal parts of 2½ feet each. The two feet in the first part may be either **dactyls** or **spondees**, those in the second part are always dactylic. The two half-feet are long (though the final syllable may be a short one), and there is always a diaeresis between the two parts of the line. In Ovid and later poets the last word in the line is regularly disyllabic.

Example:

Aēnē|ān ănĭ|mō // nōxquĕ dĭ|ēsquĕ rĕ|fērt
(*Ovid, Her. 7, 26*)

IAMBIC AND TROCHAIC VERSE

The Iambic and Trochaic metres occur mainly in dramatic verse, but some are found elsewhere, as in the lyrics of Catullus and Horace. The principal Iambic metres are the **Senarius**, the **Septenarius**, and the **Octonarius**; the principal Trochaic metres are the Septenarius and Octonarius.

Iambic Senarius

Basically this line consists of six iambic feet, but in practice such a line is very rare.

Example:

> Phăsēl|lŭs īl|lĕ quēm| vĭdē|tĭs, hōs|pĭtēs
>
> (*Cat.* 4, 1)

In drama the last foot is always iambic, and the 5th regularly a spondee. The **spondee** is also very common in the first four feet, the **dactyl** and the **tribrach** are frequent, occasionally the **anapaest** is found, and, more rarely, the **proceleusmatic**. There is usually a **caesura** in either the third or the fourth foot.

Example:

> In hāc| hăbĭtās|sĕ plătĕ|ā dīc|tūmst Chrȳ|sĭdēm
>
> (*Ter, And.* 796)

Iambic Septenarius

This line consists of seven and a half feet, basically iambic, but allowing the same variations as in the Senarius. The 4th foot is regularly an Iambus, and is usually followed by a diaeresis: this is an aid to identifying the line.

Example:

> N(am) īdcīr|c(o) āccēr|sōr nūp|tĭās| quŏd m(i) ād|părā|rī sēn|sīt
>
> (*Ter, And.* 690)

Iambic Octonarius

This line has eight iambic feet, with the same variations as in the other iambic lines. The 4th and 8th feet are regularly iambic, and a diaeresis follows the 4th foot.

Example:

Cūrā|bĭtŭr.| sēd pătĕr| ădēst.| căvĕt(e) ēs|sĕ trīs|tēm sēn|tĭāt
(Ter, And. 403)

Trochaic Septenarius

Apart from drama, this line is common in popular verses, and comes into its own in later Latin poetry. It consists of seven and a half **trochees**, but in practice only the seventh foot is regularly trochaic, while the others may be **spondee, dactyl, tribrach**, or (more rarely) **anapaest**. There is usually a **diaeresis** after the 4th foot.

Example:

Crās ă|mēt quī| nūnqu(am) ă|māvĭt,| quīqu(e) ă| māvĭt| crās ă|mēt
(Pervigilium Veneris)

Trochaic Octonarius

This is a line of eight trochees, allowing the same variations as above. There is a diaeresis after the 4th foot.

Example:

Prōin tū| sōllĭcĭ|tūdĭn|(em) īstām| fālsām| quae t(e) ēx|crŭcĭăt|
mīttās

(Ter, Heaut. 177)

LYRIC VERSE

In most lyric metres the line is not to be subdivided into feet, but is itself the unit of scansion, and has a fixed number of syllables. The commonest, which are those used by Catullus and Horace, are the **Hendecasyllabic**, the **Asclepiads**, the **Glyconic** and the **Pherecratic**, which occur either singly or in combinations to form either couplets or stanzas of four lines. Beside these groupings there are the **Alcaic** and **Sapphic** stanzas. Elisions occur much more rarely than in the other metres.

Hendecasyllabic

This is Catullus's favourite line. It consists of eleven syllables in the following pattern:

$$- \ - \ - \ \smile\smile \ - \ \smile \ - \ \smile \ - \ -$$

Either the first or the second syllable may occasionally be short, and there is usually a caesura after the 5th syllable.

Example:

> Vīvāmŭs, mĕă Lēsbĭ(a), ătqu(e) ămēmŭs

> (*Cat.* 5, 1).

Asclepiads

There are two Asclepiad lines, of which the **Lesser** is by far the commoner. It has twelve syllables, in the following pattern with a caesura after the 6th syllable:

$$- \ - \ - \ \smile\smile \ - \ \| \ - \ \smile\smile \ - \ \smile \ -$$

> Māecēnās, ătăvīs† ēdĭtĕ rēgĭbŭs

> (*Hor., Od. I,* 1, 1)

The **Greater Asclepiad** is formed by adding a **choriambus** $- \ \smile \ \smile \ -$ after the 6th syllable with a **diaeresis** both before and after it.

412

Nūllām, Varĕ, sắcrā vītĕ priŭs sēvĕrĭs ārbŏrēm

(Hor, Od. I, 18, 1)

Glyconic

The **Glyconic** occurs by itself in Catullus, but more usually it is found in combination with the **Lesser Asclepiad** or the **Pherecratic**. It consists of eight syllables (_ _ _ _ _ _ _ _), so that it is like a Lesser Asclepiad minus the **choriambus**. It has no regular caesura.

Example:

Dōnĕc grātŭs ĕrām tĭbī

(Hor. Od. III, 9, 1)

Pherecratic

The **Pherecratic** is a Glyconic minus the second last (short) syllable. It is found only in combination with other lines.

Example:

Sŭspēndīssĕ pŏtēntī

(Hor, Od. I, 5, 11)

Alcaic Stanza

The **Alcaic stanza** has four lines, of which the first two have the same pattern _ _ _ _ _ _ _ _ _ _ _ . In these there is a regular **caesura** after the 5th syllable. The third line is _ _ _ _ _ _ _ _ _ _ and the 4th _ _ _ _ _ _ _ _ _ _ Neither of the last two lines has a regular break in it.

Example:

Nūnc ēst bĭbēndŭm,† nūnc pĕdĕ lībĕrō

pūlsāndă tēllūs,† nūnc Sălĭārĭbŭs

ōrnārĕ pūlvīnār dĕōrŭm

tēmpŭs ĕrāt dăpĭbŭs, sŏdālēs

(Hor, Od. I. 37, 1-4)

Sapphic Stanza

The **Sapphic stanza** also has four lines, of which the first three are the same: $- \smile - - - \smile \smile - \smile - -$. As in the Alcaic there is a **caesura** after the 5th syllable. The last line is a short **Adonic** $- \smile \smile - -$

Example:

> Intĕgēr vītāe† scĕlĕrīsquĕ pūrŭs
>
> nōn ĕgĕt Māurīs† iăcŭlīs nĕqu(e) ārcū
>
> nēc vĕnēnātīs† grăvĭdā săgīttīs,
>
> Fūscĕ, phărĕtrā.

(Hor, Od. I. 22, 1-4)

SCANSION

The following procedure may assist beginners to scan a normal hexameter or pentameter correctly:—

1. Mark off elisions.
2. Mark the first syllable long, and (Hexameter) the last five a dactyl and spondee, or (Pentameter) the last seven syllables, two dactyls and a long syllable.
3. Mark all diphthongs long.
4. Mark all syllables that are long by position, omitting any doubtful cases.
5. Mark any other syllables known to be long.
6. Mark any syllables known to be short.
7. Fill in the few (if any) remaining syllables, and identify the principal caesura.
8. Read the line aloud.

ENGLISH – LATIN

A

a, an *art not translated;* (*a certain*) quīdam; **twice a day** bis in diē; **four acres a man** quaterna in singulōs iūgera.

aback *adv:* **taken ~** dēprehēnsus.

abaft *adv* in puppi ♦ *prep* post, pōne.

abandon *vt* relinquere; (*wilfully*) dērelinquere, dēserere; (*to danger*) ōbicere; (*to pleasure*) dēdere; (*plan*) abicere; **~ hope** spem abicere.

abandoned *adj* perditus.

abase *vt* dēprimere; **~ oneself** sē prōsternere.

abash *vt* perturbāre; rubōrem incutere (*dat*).

abate *vt* minuere, imminuere; (*a portion*) remittere ♦ *vi* (*fever*) dēcēdere; (*passion*) dēfervēscere; (*price*) laxāri; (*storm*) cadere.

abatement *n* remissiō f, dēminūtiō f.

abbess *n* abbātissa f.

abbey *n* abbātia f.

abbot *n* abbās m.

abbreviate *vt* imminuere.

abbreviation *n* (*writing*) nota f.

abdicate *vt* sē abdicāre (*abl*).

abdication *n* abdicātiō f.

abduct *vt* abripere.

abduction *n* raptus m.

aberration *n* error m.

abet *vt* adiuvāre, adesse (*dat*), favēre (*dat*).

abettor *n* adiūtor m, minister m, fautor m, socius m.

abeyance *n:* **in ~** intermissus; **be in ~** iacēre.

abhor *vt* ōdisse, invīsum habēre.

abhorrence *n* odium nt.

abhorrent *adj:* **~ to** aliēnus ab.

abide *vi* (*dwell*) habitāre; (*tarry*) commorārī; (*last*) dūrāre; **~ by** *vt fus* stāre (*abl*), perstāre in (*abl*).

abiding *adj* perpetuus, diūturnus.

ability *n* (*to do*) facultās f, potestās f; (*physical*) vīrēs fpl; (*mental*) ingenium nt; **to the best of my ~** prō meā parte, prō virīlī parte.

abject *adj* abiectus, contemptus; (*downcast*) dēmissus.

abjectly *adv* humiliter, dēmissē.

abjure *vt* ēiūrāre.

ablative *n* ablātīvus m.

ablaze *adj* flagrāns, ārdēns.

able *adj* perītus, doctus; **be ~** posse, valēre.

able-bodied *adj* rōbustus.

ablution *n* lavātiō f.

ably *adv* perītē, doctē.

abnegation *n* abstinentia f.

abnormal *adj* inūsitātus; (*excess*) immodicus.

abnormally *adv* inūsitātē, praeter mōrem.

aboard *adv* in nāvī; **go ~** nāvem cōnscendere; **put ~** impōnere.

abode *n* domicilium nt, sēdes f.

abolish *vt* tollere, ē mediō tollere, abolēre; (*law*) abrogāre.

abolition *n* dissolūtiō f; (*law*) abrogātiō f.

abominable *adj* dētestābilis, nefārius.

abominably *adv* nefāriē, foedē.

abominate *vt* dētestārī.

abomination *n* odium nt; (*thing*) nefas nt.

aboriginal *adj* prīscus.

aborigines *n* aborīginēs mpl.

abortion *n* abortus m.

abortive adj abortīvus; (fig)
inritus; **be ~ ad** inritum redigī.

abound vi abundāre, superesse; **~
in** abundāre (abl), adfluere (abl).

abounding adj abundāns, adfluēns;
cōpiōsus ab.

about adv (place) usu expressed by
cpd verbs; (number) circiter, ferē,
fermē ♦ prep (place) circā, circum
(acc); (number) circā, ad (acc);
(time) sub (acc); (concerning) dē
(abl); **~ to die** moritūrus; **I am ~ to
go** in eō est ut eam.

above adv suprā; **from ~** dēsuper;
over and ~ īnsuper ♦ prep suprā
(acc); (motion) super (acc); (rest)
super (abl); **be ~** (conduct)
indignārī.

abreast adv (ships) aequātīs prōrīs;
walk ~ of latus tegere (dat).

abridge vt contrahere, compendī
facere.

abridgement n epitomē f.

abroad adv peregrē; (out of doors)
forīs; **be ~** peregrīnārī; **from ~**
peregrē.

abrogate vt dissolvere; (law)
abrogāre.

abrupt adj subitus, repentīnus;
(speech) concīsus.

abscess n vomica f.

abscond vi aufugere.

absence n absentia f; **in my ~** mē
absente; **leave of ~** commeātus m.

absent adj absēns; **be ~** abesse; **~
oneself** vi discēre, nōn adesse.

absent-minded adj immemor,
parum attentus.

absolute adj absolūtus, perfectus;
(not limited) īnfīnītus; (not relative)
simplex; **~ power** rēgnum nt,
dominātus m; **~ ruler** rēx.

absolutely adv absolūtē, omnīnō.

absolution n venia f.

absolve vt absolvere, exsolvere;
(from punishment) condōnāre.

absorb vt bibere, absorbēre; (fig)

distringere; **I am ~ed in** tōtus sum
in (abl).

absorbent adj bibulus.

abstain vi abstinēre, sē abstinēre;
(from violence) temperāre.

abstemious adj sobrius.

abstinence n abstinentia f,
continentia f.

abstinent adj abstinēns, sobrius.

abstract adj mente perceptus,
cōgitātiōne comprehēnsus ♦ n
epitomē f ♦ vt abstrahere,
dēmere.

abstraction n (idea) nōtiō f;
(inattention) animus parum
attentus.

abstruse adj reconditus, obscūrus,
abstrūsus.

absurd adj ineptus, absurdus.

absurdity n ineptiae fpl, īnsulsitās
f.

absurdly adv ineptē, absurdē.

abundance n cōpia f, abundantia f;
there is ~ of abundē est (gen).

abundant adj cōpiōsus, abundāns,
largus; **be ~** abundāre.

abundantly adv abundē,
abundanter, adfātim.

abuse vt abūtī (abl); (words)
maledīcere (dat) ♦ n probra ntpl,
maledicta ntpl, convīcium nt,
contumēlia f.

abusive adj maledicus,
contumēliōsus.

abut vi adiacēre; **~ting on** cōnfīnis
(dat), fīnitimus (dat).

abysmal adj profundus.

abyss n profundum nt, vorāgō f;
(water) gurges m; (fig) barathrum
nt.

academic adj scholasticus; (style)
umbrātilis; (sect) Acadēmicus.

academy n schola f; (Plato's)
Acadēmīa f.

accede vi adsentīrī; **~ to** accipere.

accelerate vt, vi adcelerāre,
festīnāre; (process) mātūrāre.

accent n vōx f; (intonation) sonus m; (mark) apex m ♦ vt (syllable) acuere; (word) sonum admovēre (dat).

accentuate vt exprimere.

accept vt accipere.

acceptable adj acceptus, grātus, probābilis; be ~ placēre.

acceptation n significātiō f.

access n aditus m; (addition) accessiō f; (illness) impetus m.

accessary n socius m, particeps m.

accessible adj (person) adfābilis, facilis; be ~ (place) patēre; (person) facilem sē praebēre.

accession n (addition) accessiō f; (king's) initium rēgnī.

accident n cāsus m, calamitās f.

accidental adj fortuītus.

accidentally adv cāsū, fortuītō.

acclaim vt adclāmāre.

acclamation n clāmor m, studium nt.

acclimatize vt aliēnō caelō adsuēfacere.

accommodate vt accommodāre, aptāre; (lodging) hospitium parāre (dat); ~ oneself to mōrigerārī (dat).

accommodating adj facilis.

accommodation n hospitium nt.

accompany vt comitārī; (courtesy) prōsequī; (to Forum) dēdūcere; (music) concinere (dat).

accomplice n socius m, particeps m, cōnscius m.

accomplish vt efficere, perficere, patrāre.

accomplished adj doctus, perītus.

accomplishment n effectus m, perfectiō f, fīnis m; ~s pl artēs fpl.

accord vi inter sē congruere, cōnsentīre ♦ vt dare, praebēre, praestāre ♦ n cōnsēnsus m, concordia f; (music) concentus m; of one's own ~ suā sponte, ultrō; with one ~ unā vōce.

accordance n: in ~ with ex, ē (abl),

secundum (acc).

according adv: ~ to ex, ē (abl), secundum (acc); (proportion) prō (abl); ~ as prout.

accordingly adv itaque, igitur, ergō.

accost vt appellāre, adloquī, compellāre.

account n ratiō f; (story) nārrātiō f, expositiō f; on ~ of ob (acc); propter (acc), causā (gen); be of no ~ (person) nihilī aestimārī, nēquam esse; on that ~ idcircō ideō; on your ~ tuā grātiā, tuō nōmine; give an ~ ratiōnem reddere; present an ~ ratiōnem referre; take ~ of ratiōnem habēre (gen); put down to my ~ mihī expēnsum ferre; the ~s balance ratiō cōnstat/convenit.

account vi: ~ for ratiōnes reddere, adferre (cūr); that ~s for it haec causa est; (PROV) hinc illae lacrimae.

accountant n ā ratiōnibus, ratiōcinātor m.

accountable adj reus; I am ~ for mihi ratiō reddenda est (gen).

account book n tabulae fpl; cōdex acceptī et expēnsī.

accoutred adj īnstructus, ōrnātus.

accoutrements n ōrnāmenta ntpl, arma ntpl.

accredited adj pūblicā auctōritāte missus.

accretion n accessiō f

accrue vi (addition) cēdere; (advantage) redundāre.

accumulate vt cumulāre, congerere, coacervāre ♦ vi crēscere, cumulārī.

accumulation n cumulus m, acervus m.

accuracy n cūra f; (writing) subtīlitās f.

accurate adj (work) exāctus, subtīlis; (worker) dīligēns.

accurately adv subtīliter, ad
amussim, dīligenter.

accursed adj sacer; (fig)
exsecrātus, scelestus.

accusation n (act) accūsātiō f;
(charge) crīmen nt; (unfair)
īnsimulātiō f; (false) calumnia f;
bring an ~ against (crime in a
magistrate) nōmen dēferre (gen).

accusative n (case) accūsātīvus m.

accuse vt accūsāre, crīminārī,
reum facere; (falsely) īnsimulāre;
the ~d reus; (said by prosecutor)
iste.

accuser n accūsātor m; (civil suit)
petītor m; (informer) dēlātor m.

accustom vt adsuēfacere; ~
oneself adsuēscere, consuēscere.

accustomed adj adsuētus; **be ~**
solēre; **become ~** adsuēscere,
consuēscere.

ace n ūniō f; **I was within an ~ of
going** minimum āfuit quin īrem.

acerbity n acerbitās f.

ache n dolor m ♦ vi dolēre.

achieve vt cōnficere, patrāre; (win)
cōnsequī, adsequī.

achievement n factum nt, rēs
gesta.

acid adj acidus.

acknowledge vt (fact) agnōscere;
(fault) fatērī, cōnfitērī; (child)
tollere; (service) grātiās agere prō
(abl); **I have to ~ your letter of 1st
March** accēpī litterās tuās Kal.
Mart. datās.

acknowledgement n cōnfessiō f;
grātia f.

acme n fastīgium nt, flōs m.

aconite n aconītum nt.

acorn n glāns f.

acoustics n rēs audītōria f.

acquaint vt certiōrem facere,
docēre; ~ **oneself with** cognōscere; **~ed with** gnārus (gen),
perītus (gen).

acquaintance n (with fact) cognitiō

f, scientia f; (with person)
familiāritās f, ūsus m; (person)
nōtus m, familiāris m.

acquiesce vi (assent) adquiēscere;
(submit) aequō animō patī.

acquiescence n: **with your ~** tē nōn
adversante, pāce tuā.

acquire vt adquīrere, adipīscī,
cōnsequī; nancīscī.

acquirements n artēs fpl.

acquisition n (act) comparātiō f,
quaestus m; (thing) quaesītum nt.

acquisitive adj quaestuōsus.

acquit vt absolvere; ~ **oneself** sē
praestāre, officiō fungī.

acquittal n absolūtiō f.

acre n iūgerum nt.

acrid adj asper, ācer.

acrimonious adj acerbus,
truculentus.

acrimony n acerbitās f.

acrobat n fūnambulus m.

acropolis n arx f.

across adv trānsversus ♦ prep
trāns (acc).

act n factum nt, facinus nt; (play)
āctus m; (POL) āctum nt, senātūs
cōnsultum nt, dēcrētum nt; **I was
in the ~ of saying** in eō erat ut
dīcerem; **caught in the ~**
dēprehēnsus ♦ vi facere, agere;
(conduct) sē gerere; (stage)
histriōnem esse, partēs agere;
(pretence) simulāre ♦ vt: ~ **a part**
partēs agere, persōnam
sustinēre; **the ~ part of** agere; ~
as esse, munere fungī (gen); ~
upon (instructions) exsequī.

action n (doing) āctiō f; (deed)
factum nt, facinus nt; (legal) āctiō
f, līs f; (MIL) proelium nt; (of play)
āctiō f; (of speaker) gestus m; **bring
an ~ against** lītem intendere,
āctiōnem īnstituere (dat); **be in ~**
agere, rem gerere; (MIL) pugnāre,
in aciē dīmicāre; **man of ~** vir
strēnuus.

active *adj* impiger, strēnuus, sēdulus, nāvus.

actively *adv* impigrē, strēnuē, nāviter.

activity *n* (*motion*) mōtus *m*; (*energy*) industria *f*, sēdulitās *f*.

actor *n* histriō *m*; (*in comedy*) cōmoedus *m*; (*in tragedy*) tragoedus *m*.

actress *n* mīma *f*.

actual *adj* vērus, ipse.

actually *adv* rē vērā.

actuate *vt* movēre, incitāre.

acumen *n* acūmen *nt*, ingenī aciēs, argūtiae *fpl*.

acute *adj* acūtus, ācer; (*pain*) ācer; (*speech*) argūtus, subtīlis.

acutely *adv* acūtē, ācriter, argūtē.

acuteness *n* (*mind*) acūmen *nt*, aciēs *f*, subtīlitās *f*.

adage *n* prōverbium *nt*.

adamant *n* adamās *m* ♦ *adj* obstinātus.

adamantine *adj* adamantinus.

adapt *vt* accommodāre.

adaptable *adj* flexibilis, facile accommodandus.

adaptation *n* accommodātiō *f*.

add *vt* addere, adicere, adiungere; **be ~ed** accēdere.

adder *n* vīpera *f*.

addicted *adj* dēditus.

addition *n* adiūnctiō *f*, accessiō *f*; additāmentum *nt*, incrēmentum *nt*; **in ~** īnsuper, praetereā; **in ~ to** praeter (*acc*).

additional *adj* novus, adiūnctus.

addled *adj* (*egg*) irritus; (*brain*) inānis.

address *vt* compellāre, alloquī; (*crowd*) cōntiōnem habēre apud (*acc*); (*letter*) īnscrībere; **~ oneself** (*to action*) accingī ♦ *n* alloquium *nt*; (*public*) cōntiō *f*, ōrātiō *f*; (*letter*) īnscrīptiō *f*.

adduce *vt* (*argument*) adferre; (*witness*) prōdūcere.

adept *adj* perītus.

adequate *adj* idōneus, dignus, pār; **be ~** sufficere.

adequately *adv* satis, ut pār est.

adhere *vi* haerēre, adhaerēre; **~ to** inhaerēre (*dat*), inhaerēscere in (*abl*); (*agreement*) manēre, stāre in (*abl*).

adherent *n* adsectātor *m*; (*of party*) fautor *m*; (*of person*) cliēns *m*.

adhesive *adj* tenax.

adieu *interj* valē, valēte; **bid ~ to** valēre iubēre.

adjacent *adj* fīnitimus, vīcīnus; **be ~ to** adiacēre (*dat*).

adjoin *vi* adiacēre (*dat*).

adjoining *adj* fīnitimus, adiūnctus, proximus.

adjourn *vt* (*short time*) differre; (*longer time*) prōferre; (*case*) ampliāre ♦ *vi* rem differre, prōferre.

adjournment *n* dīlātiō *f*, prōlātiō *f*.

adjudge *vt* addīcere, adiūdicāre.

adjudicate *vi* dēcernere.

adjudicator *n* arbiter *m*.

adjunct *n* appendix *f*, accessiō *f*.

adjure *vt* obtestārī, obsecrāre.

adjust *vt* (*adapt*) accommodāre; (*put in order*) compōnere.

adjutant *n* (*MIL*) optiō *m*; (*civil*) adiūtor *m*.

administer *vt* administrāre, gerere; (*justice*) reddere; (*oath to*) iūreiūrandō adigere; (*medicine*) dare, adhibēre.

administration *n* administrātiō *f*.

administrator *n* administrātor *m*, prōcūrātor *m*.

admirable *adj* admīrābilis, ēgregius.

admirably *adv* ēgregiē.

admiral *n* praefectus classis; **~'s ship** nāvis praetōria.

admiralty *n* praefectī classium.

admiration *n* admīrātiō *f*, laus *f*.

admire *vt* admīrārī; mīrārī.

admirer n laudātor m; amātor m.

admissible adj aequus.

admission n (entrance) aditus m; (of guilt etc) cōnfessiō f.

admit vt (let in) admittere, recipere, accipere; (to membership) adscīscere; (argument) concēdere; (fault) fatērī; **~ of** patī, recipere.

admittedly adv sānē.

admonish vt admonēre, commonēre, hortārī.

admonition n admonitiō f.

ado n negōtium nt; **make much ~ about nothing** flūctūs in simpulō excitāre; **without more ~** prōtinus, sine morā.

adolescence n prīma adulēscentia f.

adolescent adj adulēscēns ♦ n adulēscentulus m.

adopt vt (person) adoptāre; (custom) adscīscere; **~ a plan** cōnsilium capere.

adoption n (person) adoptiō f; (custom) adsūmptiō f; **by ~** adoptīvus.

adoptive adj adoptīvus.

adorable adj amābilis, venustus.

adorably adv venustē.

adoration n (of gods) cultus m; (of kings) venerātiō f; (love) amor m.

adore vt (worship) venerārī; (love) adamāre.

adorn vt ōrnāre, exōrnāre, decorāre.

adornment n ōrnāmentum nt, decus nt; ōrnātus m.

adrift adj flūctuāns; **be ~** flūctuāre.

adroit adj sollers, callidus.

adroitly adv callidē, scītē.

adroitness n sollertia f, calliditās f.

adulation n adūlātiō f, adsentātiō f.

adulatory adj blandus.

adult adj adultus.

adulterate vt corrumpere, adulterāre.

adulterer n adulter m.

adulteress n adultera f.

adulterous adj incestus.

adultery n adulterium nt; **commit ~** adulterāre.

adults npl pūberēs mpl.

adumbrate vt adumbrāre.

advance vt prōmovēre; (a cause) fovēre; (money) crēdere; (opinion) dīcere; (to honours) prōvehere; (time) mātūrāre ♦ vi prōcēdere, prōgredī, adventāre; (MIL) signa prōferre, pedem īnferre; (progress) prōficere; (walk) incēdere; **~ to the attack** signa īnferre ♦ n prōgressus m, prōcessus m; (attack) impetus m; (money) mūtuae pecūniae; **in ~** mātūrius; **fix in ~** praefīnīre; **get in ~** praecipere.

advanced adj prōvectus; **well ~** (task) adfectus.

advancement n (POL) honōs m.

advantage n (benefit) commodum nt, bonum nt, ūsus m; (of place or time) opportūnitās f; (profit) frūctus m; (superiority) praestantia f; **it is an ~** bonō est; **be of ~ to** prōdesse (dat), ūsuī esse (dat); **to your ~** in rem tuam; **it is to your ~** tibi expedit, tuā interest; **take ~ of** (circs) ūtī; (person) dēcipere, fallere; **have an ~ over** praestāre (dat); **be seen to ~** māximē placēre.

advantageous adj ūtilis, opportūnus.

advantageously adv ūtiliter, opportūnē.

advent n adventus m.

adventitious adj fortuītus.

adventure n (exploit) facinus memorābile nt; (hazard) perīculum nt.

adventurer n vir audāx m; (social) parasītus m.

adventurous adj audāx.

adversary n adversārius m, hostis m.

adverse adj adversus, contrārius, inimīcus.

adversely adv contrāriē, inimīcē, male.

adversity n rēs adversae fpl, calamitās f.

advert vi: ~ **to** attingere.

advertise vt prōscrībere; vēnditāre.

advertisement n prōscrīptiō f, libellus m.

advice n cōnsilium nt; (POL) auctōritās f; (legal) respōnsum nt; **ask ~ of** cōnsulere; **on the ~ of Sulla** auctōre Sullā.

advisable adj ūtilis, operae pretium.

advise vt monēre, suādēre (dat), cēnsēre (dat); ~ **against** dissuādēre.

advisedly adv cōnsultō.

adviser n auctor m, suāsor m.

advocacy n patrōcinium nt.

advocate n patrōnus m, causidicus m; (supporter) auctor m; **be an ~** causam dīcere ♦ vt suādēre, cēnsēre.

adze n ascia f.

aedile n aedīlis m.

aedile's adj aedīlicius.

aedileship n aedīlitās f.

aegis n aegis f; (fig) praesidium nt.

Aeneid n Aenēis f.

aerial adj āerius.

aesthetic adj pulchritūdinis amāns, artificiōsus.

afar adv procul; **from ~** procul.

affability n cōmitās f, facilitās f, bonitās f.

affable adj cōmis, facilis, commodus.

affably adv cōmiter.

affair n negōtium nt, rēs f.

affect vt afficere, movēre, commovēre; (concern) attingere;

(pretence) simulāre.

affectation n simulātiō f; (RHET) adfectātiō f; (in diction) īnsolentia f, quaesīta ntpl.

affected adj (style) molestus, pūtidus.

affectedly adv pūtidē.

affecting adj miserābilis.

affection n amor m, cāritās f, studium nt; (family) pietās f.

affectionate adj amāns, pius.

affectionately adv amanter, piē.

affiance vt spondēre.

affidavit n testimōnium nt.

affinity n affīnitās f, cognātiō f.

affirm vt adfirmāre, adsevērāre.

affirmation n adfirmātiō f.

affirmative adj: **I reply in the ~** āiō.

affix vt adfīgere, adiungere.

afflict vt adflīctāre, angere, vexāre; afflīgere.

affliction n miseria f, dolor m, rēs adversae fpl.

affluence n cōpia f, opēs fpl.

affluent adj dīves, opulentus, locuplēs.

afford vt praebēre, dare; **I cannot ~** rēs mihi nōn suppetit ad.

affray n rixa f, pugna f.

affright vt terrēre ♦ n terror m, pavor m.

affront vt offendere, contumēliam dīcere (dat) ♦ n iniūria f, contumēlia f.

afield adv forīs; **far ~** peregrē.

afloat adj natāns; **be ~** natāre.

afoot adv pedibus; **be ~** gerī.

aforesaid adj suprā dictus.

afraid adj timidus; **be ~ of** timēre, metuere; verērī.

afresh adv dēnuō, dē integrō.

Africa n Africa f.

aft adv in puppī, puppim versus.

after adj posterior ♦ adv post (acc), posteā; **the day ~** postrīdiē ♦ conj postquam; **the day ~** postrīdiē quam ♦ prep post (acc); (in rank) secundum (acc); (in imitation) ad (acc), dē (abl); ~ **all** tamen, dēnique; ~ **reading the book** librō lēctō; **one thing** ~ **another** aliud ex aliō; **immediately** ~ statim ab.

aftermath n ēventus m.

afternoon n: **in the** ~ post merīdiem ♦ adj postmerīdiānus.

afterthought n posterior cōgitātiō f.

afterwards adv post, posteā, deinde.

again adv rūrsus, iterum; ~ **and** ~ etiam atque etiam, identidem; **once** ~ dēnuō; (new point in a speech) quid?

against prep contrā (acc), adversus (acc), in (acc); ~ **the stream** adversō flūmine; ~ **one's will** invitus.

agape adj hiāns.

age n (life) aetās f; (epoch) aetās f, saeculum nt; **old** ~ senectūs f; **he is of** ~ suī iūris est; **he is eight years of** ~ octō annōs nātus est, nōnum annum agit; **of the same** ~ aequālis.

aged adj senex, aetāte prōvectus; (things) antīquus.

agency n opera f; **through the** ~ **of** per (acc).

agent n āctor m, prōcūrātor m; (in crime) minister m.

aggrandize vt augēre, amplificāre.

aggrandizement n amplificātiō f.

aggravate vt (wound) exulcerāre; (distress) augēre; **become** ~ **d** ingravēscere.

aggravating adj molestus.

aggregate n summa f.

aggression n incursiō f, iniūria f.

aggressive adj ferōx.

aggressiveness n ferōcitās f.

aggressor n oppugnātor m.

aggrieved adj īrātus; **be** ~ indignārī.

aghast adj attonitus, stupefactus;

stand ~ obstupēscere.

agile adj pernix, vēlōx.

agility n pernīcitās f.

agitate vt agitāre; (mind) commovēre, perturbāre.

agitation n commōtiō f, perturbātiō f, trepidātiō f; (POL) tumultus m.

agitator n turbātor m, concitātor m.

aglow adj fervidus ♦ adv: **be** ~ fervēre.

ago adv abhinc (acc); **three days** ~ abhinc trēs diēs; **long** ~ antīquitus, iamprīdem, iamdūdum; **a short time** ~ dūdum.

agog adj sollicitus, ērēctus.

agonize vt cruciāre, torquēre.

agonizing adj horribilis.

agony n cruciātus m, dolor m.

agrarian adj agrārius; ~ **party** agrāriī mpl.

agree vi (together) cōnsentīre, congruere; (with) adsentīrī (dat), sentīre cum; (bargain) pacīscī; (facts) cōnstāre, convenīre; (food) facilem esse ad concoquendum; ~ **upon** cōnstituere, compōnere; **it is agreed** constat (inter omnes).

agreeable adj grātus, commodus, acceptus.

agreeableness n dulcēdō f, iūcunditās f.

agreeably adv iūcundē.

agreement n (together) cōnsēnsus m, concordia f; (with) adsēnsus m; (pact) pactiō f, conventum nt, foedus nt; **according to** ~ compactō, ex compositō; **be in** ~ cōnsentīre, congruere.

agricultural adj rūsticus, agrestis.

agriculture n rēs rūstica f, agrī cultūra f.

aground adv: **be** ~ sīdere; **run** ~ in lītus ēicī, offendere.

ague n horror m, febris f.

ahead adv ante; **go** ~ anteīre,

praeīre; **go~** adj impiger; **ships
in line ~** agmen nāvium.

aid vt adiuvāre, succurrere (dat),
subvenīre (dat) ♦ n auxilium nt,
subsidium nt.

aide-de-camp n optiō m.

ail vt dolēre ♦ vi aegrōtāre,
labōrāre, languēre.

ailing adj aeger, īnfirmus.

ailment n morbus m, valētūdō f.

aim vt intendere; **~ at** petere; (fig)
adfectāre, spectāre, sequī; (with
verb) id agere ut ♦ n fīnis m,
prōpositum nt.

aimless adj inānis, vānus.

aimlessly adv sine ratiōne.

aimlessness n vānitās f.

air n āēr m; (breeze) aura f, (look)
vultus m, speciēs f; (tune) modus
m; **in the open ~** sub dīvō; **~s**
fastus m; **give oneself ~s** sē
iactāre.

airily adv hilarē.

airy adj (of air) āerius m; (light) tenuis;
(place) apertus; (manner) hilaris.

aisle n āla f.

ajar adj sēmiapertus.

akin adj cōnsanguineus, cognātus.

alacrity n alacritās f.

alarm n terror m, formīdō f,
trepidātiō f; (sound) clāmor m;
sound an ~ ad arma conclāmāre;
give the ~ incrēpāre; **be in a state
of ~** trepidāre ♦ vt terrēre,
perterrēre, perturbāre.

alarming adj formīdolōsus.

alas interj heu.

albeit conj etsī, etiamsī.

alcove n zōthēca f.

alder n alnus f.

alderman n decuriō m.

ale n cervīsia f.

alehouse n caupōna f, taberna f.

alert adj prōmptus, alacer,
vegetus.

alertness n alacritās f.

alien adj externus; **~ to** abhorrēns

ab ♦ n peregrīnus m.

alienate vt aliēnāre, abaliēnāre,
āvertere, āvocāre.

alienation n aliēnātiō f.

alight vi (from horse) dēscendere,
dēsilīre; (bird) īnsīdere.

alight adj: **be ~** ārdēre; **set ~**
accendere.

alike adj pār, similis ♦ adv aequē,
pariter.

alive adj vīvus; **be ~** vīvere.

all adj omnis; (together) ūniversus,
cūnctus; (whole) tōtus; **~ but**
paene; **~ for** studiōsus (gen); **~ in**
cōnfectus; **~ of** tōtus; **~ over with**
āctum dē (abl); **~ the best men**
optimus quisque; **~ the more** eō
plūs, tantō plūs; **at ~** ullō modō,
quid; **it is ~ up with** actum est de
(abl); **not at ~** haudquāquam ♦ n
fortūnae fpl.

allay vt sēdāre, mītigāre, lēnīre.

allegation n adfirmātiō f; (charge)
īnsimulātiō f.

allege vt adfirmāre, praetendere;
(in excuse) excūsāre.

allegiance n fidēs f; **owe ~ to** in
fidē esse (gen); **swear ~ to** in
verba iūrāre (gen).

allegory n allēgoria f, immūtāta
ōrātiō f.

alleviate vt mītigāre, adlevāre,
sublevāre.

alleviation n levātiō f, levāmentum
nt.

alley n (garden) xystus m; (town)
angiportus m.

alliance n societās f, foedus nt.

allied adj foederātus, socius;
(friends) coniūnctus.

alligator n crocodīlus m.

allocate vt adsignāre, impertīre.

allot vt adsignāre, distribuere; **be
~ted** obtingere.

allotment n (land) adsignātiō f.

allow vt sinere, permittere (dat),
concēdere (dat), patī; (admit)

fatērī, concēdere; (approve)
comprobāre; it is ~ed licet (dat
+ infin); ~ for vt fus ratiōnem
habēre (gen).
allowance n venia f, indulgentia f;
(pay) stīpendium nt; (food) cibāria
ntpl; (for travel) viāticum nt; **make
~ for** indulgēre (dat), ignōscere
(dat), excusāre.
alloy n admixtum nt.
all right adj rēctē; **it is ~** bene est.
allude vi: **~ to** dēsignāre, attingere,
significāre.
allure vt adlicere, pellicere.
allurement n blanditia f,
blandīmentum nt, illecebra f.
alluring adj blandus.
alluringly adv blandē.
allusion n mentiō f, indicium nt.
alluvial adj: **~ land** adluviō f.
ally n socius m ♦ vt sociāre,
coniungere.
almanac n fāstī mpl.
almighty adj omnipotēns.
almond n (nut) amygdalum nt;
(tree) amygdala f.
almost adv paene, ferē, fermē,
propemodum.
alms n stipem (no nom) f.
aloe n aloē f.
aloft adj sublīmis ♦ adv sublīmē.
alone adj sōlus, sōlitārius, ūnus
♦ adv sōlum.
along prep secundum (acc), praeter
(acc) ♦ adv porrō; **all ~** iamdūdum,
ab initiō; **~ with** unā cum (abl).
alongside adv: **bring ~** adpellere;
come ~ ad crepīdinem accēdere.
aloof adv procul; **stand ~** sē
removēre ♦ adj sēmōtus.
aloofness n sōlitūdō f, sēcessus m.
aloud adv clārē, māgnā vōce.
alphabet n elementa ntpl.
Alps n Alpēs fpl.
already adv iam.
also adv etiam, et, quoque; īdem.
altar n āra f.

alter vt mūtāre, commūtāre;
(order) invertere.
alteration n mūtātiō f, commūtātiō f.
altercation n altercātiō f, iūrgium
nt.
alternate adj alternus ♦ vt variāre.
alternately adv invicem.
alternation n vicem (no nom) f,
vicissitūdō f.
alternative adj alter, alius ♦ n
optiō f.
although conj quamquam (indic),
etsī/etiamsī (+ cond clause);
quamvīs (+ subj).
altitude n altitūdō f.
altogether adv omnīnō; (emphasis)
plānē, prōrsus.
altruism n beneficentia f.
alum n alūmen nt.
always adv semper.
amalgamate vt miscēre,
coniungere.
amalgamation n coniūnctiō f,
temperātiō f.
amanuensis n librārius m.
amass vt cumulāre, coacervāre.
amateur n idiōta m.
amatory adj amātōrius.
amaze vt obstupefacere; attonāre;
be ~d obstupēscere.
amazement n stupor m; **in ~**
attonitus, stupefactus.
ambassador n lēgātus m.
amber n sūcinum nt.
ambidextrous adj utrīusque
manūs compos.
ambiguity n ambiguitās f; (RHET)
amphibolia f.
ambiguous adj ambiguus, anceps,
dubius.
ambiguously adv ambiguē.
ambition n glōria f, laudis
studium.
ambitious adj glōriae cupidus,
laudis avidus.
amble vi ambulāre.

ambrosia n ambrosia f.

ambrosial adj ambrosius.

ambuscade n īnsidiae fpl.

ambush n īnsidiae fpl ♦ vt
īnsidiārī (dat).

ameliorate vt corrigere, meliōrem
reddere.

amelioration n prōfectus m.

amenable adj facilis, docilis.

amend vt corrigere, ēmendāre.

amendment n ēmendātiō f.

amends n (apology) satisfactiō f;
make ~ for expiāre; **make ~ to**
satisfacere (dat).

amenity n (scenery) amoenitās f;
(comfort) commodum nt.

amethyst n amethystus f.

amiability n benignitās f, suāvitās
f.

amiable adj benignus, suāvis.

amiably adv benignē, suāviter.

amicable adj amīcus, cōmiter.

amicably adv amīcē, cōmiter.

amid, amidst prep inter (acc).

amiss adv perperam, secus,
incommodē; **take ~** aegrē ferre.

amity n amīcitia f.

ammunition n tēla ntpl.

amnesty n venia f.

among, amongst prep inter (acc),
apud (acc).

amorous adj amātōrius, amāns.

amorously adv cum amōre.

amount vi: **~ to** efficere; (fig) esse
♦ n summa f.

amours n amōrēs mpl.

amphibious adj anceps.

amphitheatre n amphitheātrum
nt.

ample adj amplus, satis.

amplification n amplificātiō f.

amplify vt amplificāre.

amplitude n amplitūdō f, cōpia f.

amputate vt secāre, amputāre.

amuck adv: **run ~** bacchārī.

amulet n amulētum nt.

amuse vt dēlectāre, oblectāre.

amusement n oblectāmentum
nt, dēlectātiō f; **for ~** animī causā.

amusing adj rīdiculus, facētus.

an indef art see **a**.

anaemic adj exsanguis.

analogous adj similis.

analogy n prōportiō f, comparātiō
f.

analyse vt excutere, perscrūtārī.

analysis n explicātiō f.

anapaest n anapaestus m.

anarchical adj sēditiōsus.

anarchy n reī pūblicae
perturbātiō, lēgēs nullae fpl,
licentia f.

anathema n exsecrātiō f; (object)
pestis f.

ancestor n proavus m; **~s** pl
māiōrēs mpl.

ancestral adj patrius.

ancestry n genus nt, orīgō f.

anchor n ancora f; **lie at ~** in
ancorīs stāre; **weigh ~** ancoram
tollere ♦ vi ancoram iacere.

anchorage n statiō f.

ancient adj antīquus, prīscus,
vetustus; **~ history, ~ world**
antīquitās f; **from/in ~ times**
antīquitus; **the ~s** veterēs.

and conj et, atque, ac, -que; **~
...not** nec, neque; **~ so** itaque.

anecdote n fābella f.

anent prep dē (abl).

anew adv dēnuō, ab integrō.

angel n angelus m.

angelic adj angelicus; (fig) dīvīnus,
eximius.

anger n īra f ♦ vt inrītāre.

angle n angulus m ♦ vi hāmō
piscārī.

angler n piscātor m.

Anglesey n Mona f.

angrily adv īrātē.

angry adj īrātus; **be ~** īrāscī (dat).

anguish n cruciātus m, dolor m;
(mind) angor m.

angular adj angulātus.

animal n animal nt; (domestic) pecus f; (wild) fera f.

animate vt animāre.

animated adj excitātus, vegetus.

animation n ārdor m, alacritās f.

animosity n invidia f, inimīcitia f.

ankle n tālus m.

annalist n annālium scrīptor.

annals n annālēs mpl.

annex vt addere.

annexation n adiectiō f.

annihilate vt dēlēre, exstinguere, perimere.

annihilation n exstinctiō f, interneciō f.

anniversary n diēs anniversārius; (public) sollemne nt.

annotate vt adnotāre.

annotation n adnotātiō f.

announce vt nūntiāre; (officially) dēnūntiāre, prōnūntiāre; (election result) renūntiāre.

announcement n (official) dēnūntiātiō f; (news) nūntius m.

announcer n nūntius m.

annoy vt inrītāre, vexāre; **be ~ed with** aegrē ferre.

annoyance n molestia f, vexātiō f; (felt) dolor m.

annoying adj molestus.

annual adj annuus, anniversārius.

annually adv quotannīs.

annuity n annua ntpl.

annul vt abrogāre, dissolvere, tollere.

annulment n abrogātiō f.

anoint vt ungere, illinere.

anomalous adj novus.

anomaly n novitās f.

anon adv mox.

anonymous adj incertī auctōris.

anonymously adv sine nōmine.

another adj alius; (second) alter; **of ~** aliēnus; **one after ~** alius ex aliō; **one ~** inter sē, alius alium; **in ~ place** alibī; **to ~ place** aliō; **in ~ way** aliter; **at ~ time** aliās.

answer vt respondēre (dat); (by letter) rescrībere (dat); (agree) respondēre, congruere; **~ a charge** crīmen dēfendere; **~ for** vt fus (surety) praestāre; (account) ratiōnem referre; (substitute) īnstar esse (gen) ♦ n respōnsum nt; (to a charge) dēfēnsiō f; **~ to the name of** vocārī; **give an ~** respondēre.

answerable adj reus; **I am ~ for ...** ratiō mihī reddenda est ... (gen).

ant n formīca f.

antagonism n simultās f, inimīcitia f.

antagonist n adversārius m, hostis m.

antarctic adj antarcticus.

antecedent adj antecēdēns, prior.

antediluvian adj prīscus, horridus, Deucaliōneus.

antelope n dorcas f.

anterior adj prior.

anteroom n vestibulum nt.

anthology n excerpta ntpl; **make an ~** excerpere.

anthropology n rēs hūmānae fpl.

anticipate vt (expect) exspectāre; (forestall) antevenīre, occupāre; (in thought) animō praecipere.

anticipation n exspectātiō f, spēs f; praesūmptiō f.

antics n gestus m, ineptiae fpl.

anticyclone n serēnitās f.

antidote n remedium nt, medicāmen nt.

antipathy n fastīdium nt, odium nt; (things) repugnantia f.

antiphonal adj alternus.

antiphony n alterna ntpl.

antipodes n contrāria pars terrae.

antiquarian adj historicus.

antiquary n antīquārius m.

antiquated adj prīscus, obsolētus.

antique adj antīquus, prīscus.

antiquity n antīquitās f, vetustas f, veterēs mpl.

antithesis *n* contentiō *f*, contrārium *nt*.

antlers *n* cornua *ntpl*.

anvil *n* incūs *f*.

anxiety *n* sollicitūdō *f*, metus *m*, cūra *f*; anxietās *f*.

anxious *adj* sollicitus, anxius; avidus; cupidus.

any *adj* ullus; (*interrog*) ecquī; (*after* **sī, nisi, num, nē**) quī; (*indef*) quīvīs, quīlibet; **hardly ~** nullus ferē; **~ further** longius; **~ longer** (*of time*) diutius.

anybody *pron* aliquis; (*indef*) quīvīs, quīlibet; (*after* **sī, nisi, num, nē**) quis; (*interrog*) ecquis, numquis; (*after neg*) quisquam; **hardly ~** nēmō ferē.

anyhow *adv* ullō modō, quōquō modō.

anyone *pron see* **anybody.**

anything *pron* aliquid; quidvīs, quidlibet; (*interrog*) ecquid, numquid; (*after neg*) quicquam; (*after* **sī, nisi, num, nē**) quid; **hardly ~** nihil ferē.

anywhere *adv* usquam, ubīvīs.

apace *adv* citō, celeriter.

apart *adv* seōrsus, sēparātim ♦ *adj* dīversus; **be six feet ~** sex pedēs distāre; **set ~** sēpōnere; **stand ~** distāre; **joking ~** remōtō iocō; **~ from** praeter (*acc*).

apartment *n* cubiculum *nt*, conclāve *nt*.

apathetic *adj* lentus, languidus, ignāvus.

apathy *n* lentitūdō *f*, languor *m*, ignāvia *f*.

ape *n* sīmia *f* ♦ *vt* imitārī.

aperture *n* hiātus *m*, forāmen *nt*, rīma *f*.

apex *n* fastīgium *nt*.

aphorism *n* sententia *f*.

apiary *n* alveārium *nt*.

apiece *adv* in singulōs; **two ~** bīnī.

aplomb *n* cōnfīdentia *f*.

apocryphal *adj* commentīcius.

apologetic *adj* cōnfitēns, veniam petēns.

apologize *vi* veniam petere, sē excūsāre.

apology *n* excūsātiō *f*.

apoplectic *adj* apoplēcticus.

apoplexy *n* apoplēxis *f*.

apostle *n* apostolus *m*.

apothecary *n* medicāmentārius *m*.

appal *vt* perterrēre, cōnsternere.

appalling *adj* dīrus.

apparatus *n* īnstrūmenta *ntpl*, ōrnāmenta *ntpl*.

apparel *n* vestis *f*, vestīmenta *ntpl*.

apparent *adj* manifestus, apertus, ēvidēns.

apparently *adv* speciē, ut vidētur.

apparition *n* vīsum *nt*, speciēs *f*.

appeal *vi* (*to magistrate*) appellāre; (*to people*) prōvocāre ad; (*to gods*) invocāre, testārī; (*to senses*) placēre (*dat*) ♦ *n* appellātiō *f*, prōvocātiō *f*, testātiō *f*.

appear *vi* (*in sight*) appārēre; (*in court*) sistī; (*in public*) prōdīre; (*at a place*) adesse, advenīre; (*seem*) vidērī.

appearance *n* (*coming*) adventus *m*; (*look*) aspectus *m*, faciēs *f*; (*semblance*) speciēs *f*; (*thing*) vīsum *nt*; **for the sake of ~s** in speciem; (*formula*) dicis causā; **make one's ~** prōcēdere, prōdīre.

appeasable *adj* plācābilis.

appease *vt* plācāre, lēnīre, mītigāre, sēdāre.

appeasement *n* plācātiō *f*; (*of enemy*) pācificātiō *f*.

appellant *n* appellātor *m*.

appellation *n* nōmen *nt*.

append *vt* adiungere, subicere.

appendage *n* appendix *f*, adiūnctum *nt*.

appertain *vi* pertinēre.

appetite *n* adpetītus *m*; (*for food*) famēs *f*.

applaud vt plaudere; (fig) laudāre.
applause n plausus m; (fig) adsēnsiō f, adprobātiō f.
apple n pōmum nt; mālum nt; ~-tree mālus f; ~ of my eye ocellus meus; **upset the ~ cart** plaustrum percellere.
appliance n māchina f, īnstrūmentum nt.
applicable adj aptus, commodus; **be ~** pertinēre.
applicant n petītor m.
application n (work) industria f; (mental) intentiō f; (asking) petītiō f; (MED) fōmentum nt.
apply vt adhibēre, admovēre; (use) ūtī (abl); ~ **oneself to** sē adplicāre, incumbere in (acc) ♦ vi pertinēre; (to a person) adīre (acc); (for office) petere.
appoint vt (magistrate) creāre, facere, cōnstituere; (commander) praeficere; (guardian, heir) īnstituere; (time) dīcere, statuere; (for a purpose) dēstināre; (to office) creāre.
appointment n cōnstitūtum nt; (duty) mandātum nt; (office) magistrātus m; **have an ~ with** cōnstitūtum habēre cum; **keep an ~** ad cōnstitūtum venīre.
apportion vt dispertīre, dīvidere; (land) adsignāre.
apposite adj aptus, appositus.
appraisal n aestimātiō f.
appraise vt aestimāre.
appreciable adj haud exiguus.
appreciate vt aestimāre.
appreciation n aestimātiō f.
apprehend vt (person) comprehendere; (idea) intellegere, mente comprehendere; (fear) metuere, timēre.
apprehension n comprehēnsiō f; metus m, formīdō f.
apprehensive adj anxius, sollicitus; **be ~ of** metuere.

apprentice n discipulus m, tīrō m.
apprenticeship n tīrōcinium nt.
apprise vt docēre, certiōrem facere.
approach vt appropinquāre ad (acc), accēdere ad; (person) adīre ♦ vi (time) adpropinquāre; (season) appetere ♦ n (act) accessus m, aditus m; (time) adpropinquātiō f; (way) aditus m; **make ~es to** adīre ad, ambīre, petere.
approachable adj (place) patēns; (person) facilis.
approbation n adprobātiō f, adsēnsiō f.
appropriate adj aptus, idōneus, proprius ♦ vt adscīscere, adsūmere.
appropriately adv aptē, commodē.
approval n adprobātiō f, adsēnsus m, favor m.
approve vt, vi adprobāre, comprobāre, adsentīrī (dat); (law) scīscere.
approved adj probātus, spectātus.
approximate adj propinquus ♦ vi: ~ **to** accēdere ad.
approximately adv prope, propemodum; (number) ad (acc).
appurtenances n īnstrūmenta ntpl, apparātus m.
apricot n armēniacum nt; ~-tree n armēniaca f.
April n mēnsis Aprīlis m; **of ~** Aprīlis.
apron n operīmentum nt.
apropos of prep quod attinet ad.
apse n apsis f.
apt adj aptus, idōneus; (pupil) docilis, prōmptus; ~ **to** prōnus, prōclīvis ad; **be ~ to** solēre.
aptitude n ingenium f, facultās f.
aptly adv aptē.
aquarium n piscīna f.
aquatic adj aquātilis.

aqueduct n aquae ductus m.
aquiline adj (nose) aduncus.
arable land n arvum nt.
arbiter n arbiter m.
arbitrarily adv ad libīdinem,
licenter.
arbitrary adj libīdinōsus (act);
(ruler) superbus.
arbitrate vi diiūdicāre, disceptāre.
arbitration n arbitrium nt,
diiūdicātiō f.
arbitrator n arbiter m, disceptātor
m.
arbour n umbrāculum nt.
arbutus n arbutus f.
arc n arcus m.
arcade n porticus f.
arch n fornix m, arcus m ♦ vt
arcuāre ♦ adj lascīvus, vafer.
archaeologist n antīquitātis
investīgātor m.
archaeology n antīquitātis
investīgātiō f.
archaic adj prīscus.
archaism n verbum obsolētum nt.
archbishop n archiepiscopus m.
arched adj fornicātus.
archer n sagittārius m.
archery n sagittāriōrum ars f.
architect n architectus m.
architecture n architectūra f.
architrave n epistylium nt.
archives n tabulae (pūblicae) fpl.
arctic adj arcticus, septentriōnālis
♦ n septentriōnēs mpl.
ardent adj ārdēns, fervidus,
vehemēns.
ardently adv ārdenter, ācriter,
vehementer.
ardour n ārdor m, fervor m.
arduous adj difficilis, arduus.
area n regiō f; (MATH) superficiēs f.
arena n harēna f.
argonaut n argonauta m.
argosy n onerāria f.
argue vi (discuss) disserere,
disceptāre; (dispute) ambigere;

disputāre; (reason) argūmentārī
♦ vt (prove) arguere.
argument n (discussion)
contrōversia f, disputātiō f;
(reason) ratiō f; (proof, theme)
argūmentum nt.
argumentation n argūmentātiō f.
argumentative adj lītigiōsus.
aria n canticum nt.
arid adj āridus, siccus.
aright adv rēctē, vērē.
arise vi orīrī, coorīrī, exsistere; ~
from nāscī ex, proficīscī ab.
aristocracy n optimātēs mpl,
nōbilēs mpl; (govt) optimātium
dominātus m.
aristocrat n optimās m.
aristocratic adj patricius,
generōsus.
arithmetic n numerī mpl,
arithmētica f.
ark n arca f.
arm n bracchium nt; (upper)
lacertus m; (sea) sinus m;
(weapon) tēlum nt ♦ vt armāre
♦ vi arma capere.
armament n bellī apparātus m,
cōpiae fpl.
armed adj (men) armātus; **light-
troops** levis armātūra f, vēlitēs
mpl.
armistice n indūtiae fpl.
armlet n armilla f.
armour n arma ntpl, (kind of)
armātūra f.
armourer n (armōrum) faber m.
armoury n armāmentārium nt.
armpit n āla f.
arms npl (MIL) arma ntpl; **by force of
~** vī et armīs; **under ~** in armīs.
army n exercitus m; (in battle)
aciēs f; (on march) agmen nt.
aroma n odor m.
aromatic adj frāgrāns.
around adv circum (acc), circā
(acc) ♦ prep circum (acc).
arouse vt suscitāre, ērigere,

excitāre.

arraign vt accūsāre.

arrange vt (in order) compōnere, ōrdināre, dīgerere, dispōnere; (agree) pacīscī; ~ **a truce** indūtiās compōnere.

arrangement n ōrdō m, collocātiō f, dispositiō f; pactum nt, cōnstitūtum nt.

arrant adj summus.

array n vestis f, habitus m; (MIL) aciēs f ♦ vt vestīre, exōrnāre; (MIL) īnstruere.

arrears n residuae pecūniae fpl, reliqua ntpl.

arrest vt comprehendere, adripere; (attention) in sē convertere; (movement) morārī, tardāre ♦ n comprehēnsiō f.

arrival n adventus m.

arrive vi advenīre (ad + acc), pervenīre (ad + acc).

arrogance n superbia f, adrogantia f, fastus m.

arrogant adj superbus, adrogāns.

arrogantly adv superbē, adroganter.

arrogate vt adrogāre.

arrow n sagitta f.

arsenal n armāmentārium nt.

arson n incēnsiōnis crīmen nt.

art n ars f, artificium nt; **fine ~s** ingenuae artēs.

artery n artēria f.

artful adj callidus, vafer, astūtus.

artfully adv callidē, astūtē.

artfulness n astūtia f, dolus m.

artichoke n cinara f.

article n rēs f, merx f; (clause) caput nt; (term) condiciō f.

articulate adj explānātus, distīnctus ♦ vt explānāre, exprimere.

articulately adv explānātē, clārē.

articulation n prōnūntiātiō f.

artifice n ars f, artificium nt, dolus m.

artificer n artifex m, opifex m, faber m.

artificial adj (work) artificiōsus; (appearance) fūcātus.

artificially adv arte, manū.

artillery n tormenta ntpl.

artisan n faber m, opifex m.

artist n artifex m; pictor m.

artistic adj artificiōsus, ēlegāns.

artistically adv artificiōsē, ēleganter.

artless adj (work) inconditus; (person) simplex.

artlessly adv inconditē; simpliciter, sine dolō.

artlessness n simplicitās f.

as adv (before adj, adv) tam; (after aequus, īdem, similis) ac, atque; (correlative) quam, quālis, quantus ♦ conj (compar) ut (+ indic), sīcut, velut, quemadmodum; (cause) cum (+ indic), quoniam, quippe quī; (time) dum, ut ♦ relat pron quī, quae, quod (+ subj); ~ **being** utpote; ~ **follows** ita; ~ **for** quod attinet ad; ~ **if** quasī, tamquam sī, velut; (= while) usu expressed by pres part; ~ **it were** ut ita dīcam; ~ **yet** adhūc; ~ **soon** ~ simul ac/atque (+ perf indic); ~ . . . ~ **as possible** quam (+ superl).

as n (coin) as m.

ascend vt, vi ascendere.

ascendancy n praestantia f, auctōritās f.

ascendant adj surgēns, potēns; **be in the** ~ praestāre.

ascent n ascēnsus m; (slope) clīvus m.

ascertain vt comperīre, cognōscere.

ascetic adj nimis abstinēns, austērus.

asceticism n dūritia f.

ascribe vt adscrībere, attribuere, adsignāre.

ash n (tree) fraxinus f ♦ adj

fraxineus.

ashamed adj: **I am** ~ pudet mē; ~ **of** pudet (+ acc of person, + gen of thing).

ashen adj pallidus.

ashes n cinis m.

ashore adv (motion) in lītus; (rest) in lītore; **go** ~ ēgredī.

Ασia n Λsia f.

aside adv sēparatim, sē- (in cpd).

ask vt (question) rogāre, quaerere; (request) petere, poscere; (beg, entreat) ōrāre; ~ **for** vt fus petere; rogāre; scīscitārī; percontārī.

askance adv oblīquē; **look** ~ **at** līmīs oculīs aspicere, invidēre (dat).

askew adv prāvē.

aslant adv oblīquē.

asleep adj sōpītus; **be** ~ dormīre; **fall** ~ obdormīre, somnum inīre.

asp n aspis f.

asparagus n asparagus m.

aspect n (place) aspectus m; (person) vultus m; (CIRCS) status m; **have a southern** ~ ad merīdiem spectāre; **there is another** ~ **to the matter** aliter sē rēs habet.

aspen n pōpulus f.

asperity n acerbitās f.

asperse vt maledīcere (dat), calumniārī.

aspersion n calumnia f; **cast** ~**s on** calumniārī, īnfāmiā aspergere.

asphalt n bitūmen n.

asphyxia n strangulātiō f.

asphyxiate vt strangulāre.

aspirant n petītor m.

aspirate n (GRAM) aspīrātiō f.

aspiration n spēs f; (POL) ambitiō f.

aspire vi: ~ **to** adfectāre, petere, spērāre.

ass n asinus m, asellus m; (fig) stultus m.

assail vt oppugnāre, adorīrī, aggredī.

assailable adj expugnābilis.

assailant n oppugnātor m.

assassin n sīcārius m, percussor m.

assassinate vt interficere, occīdere, iugulāre.

assassination n caedēs f, parricīdium nt.

assault vt oppugnāre, adorīrī, aggredī; (speech) invehī in (acc) ♦ n impetus m, oppugnātiō f; (personal) vīs f.

assay vt (metal) spectāre; temptāre, cōnārī.

assemble vt convocāre, congregāre, cōgere ♦ vi convenīre, congregārī.

assembly n coetus m, conventus m; (plebs) concilium nt; (Roman people) comitia ntpl; (troops) cōntiō f; (things) congeriēs f.

assent vi adsentīrī, adnuere ♦ n adsēnsus m.

assert vt adfirmāre, adsevērāre, dīcere.

assertion n adfirmātiō f, adsevērātiō f, dictum nt, sententia f.

assess vt cēnsēre, aestimāre; ~ **damages** lītem aestimāre.

assessment n cēnsus m, aestimātiō f.

assessor n cēnsor m; (assistant) cōnsessor m.

assets n bona ntpl.

assiduity n dīligentia f, sēdulitās f, industria f.

assiduous adj dīligēns, sedulus, industrius.

assign vt tribuere, attribuere; (land) adsignāre; (in writing) perscrībere; (task) dēlēgāre; (reason) adferre.

assignation n cōnstitūtum nt.

assignment n adsignātiō f, perscrīptiō f; (task) mūnus nt, pēnsum nt.

assimilate vt aequāre; (food)

concoquere; (*knowledge*) concipere.

assist vt adiuvāre, succurrere (*dat*), adesse (*dat*).

assistance n auxilium nt, opem (*no nom*) f; **come to the ~ of** subvenīre (*dat*); **be of ~ to** auxiliō esse (*dat*).

assistant n adiūtor m, minister m.

assize n conventus m; **hold ~s** conventūs agere.

associate vt cōnsociāre, coniungere ♦ vi rem inter sē cōnsociāre; **~ with** familiāriter ūtī (*abl*) ♦ n socius m, sodālis m.

association n societās f; (*club*) sodālitās f.

assort vt dīgerere, dispōnere ♦ vi congruere.

assortment n (*of goods*) variae mercēs fpl.

assuage vt lēnīre, mītigare, sēdāre.

assume vt (*for oneself*) adsūmere, adrogāre; (*hypothesis*) pōnere; (*office*) inīre.

assumption n (*hypothesis*) sūmptiō f, positum nt.

assurance n (*given*) fidēs f, pignus nt; (*felt*) fīdūcia f; (*boldness*) cōnfīdentia f.

assure vt cōnfirmāre, prōmittere (*dat*).

assured adj (*person*) fīdēns; (*fact*) explōrātus, certus.

assuredly adv certō, certē, profectō, sānē.

astern adv ā puppī; (*movement*) retrō; **~ of** post.

asthma n anhēlitus m.

astonish vt obstupefacere; attonāre.

astonished adj attonitus, stupefactus; **be ~ed at** admīrārī.

astonishing adj mīrificus, mīrus.

astonishment n stupor m, admīrātiō f.

astound vt obstupefacere.

astray adj vagus; **go ~** errāre, aberrāre, deerrāre.

astride adj vāricus.

astrologer n Chaldaeus m, mathēmaticus m.

astrology n Chaldaeōrum dīvīnātiō f.

astronomer n astrologus m.

astronomy n astrologia f.

astute adj callidus, vafer.

astuteness n calliditās f.

asunder adv sēparātim, dis- (*in cpd*).

asylum n asȳlum nt.

at prep in (*abl*), ad (*acc*); (*time*) usu expressed by abl; (*towns, small islands*) loc; **~ the house of** apud (*acc*); **~ all events** saltem; *see also* dawn, hand, house *etc.*

atheism n deōs esse negāre.

atheist n atheos m; **be an ~** deōs esse negāre.

Athenian adj Atheniensis.

Athens n Athenae fpl; **at/from ~** Athenis; **to ~** Athenas.

athirst adj sitiens; (*fig*) avidus.

athlete n athlēta m.

athletic adj rōbustus, lacertōsus.

athletics n athlētica ntpl.

athwart prep trāns (*acc*).

atlas n orbis terrārum dēscriptiō f.

atmosphere n āēr m.

atom n atomus f, corpus indīviduum nt.

atone vi: **~ for** expiāre.

atonement n expiātiō f, piāculum nt.

atrocious adj immānis, nefārius, scelestus.

atrociously adv nefāriē, scelestē.

atrociousness n immānitās f.

atrocity n nefas nt, scelus nt, flāgitium nt.

atrophy vi marcēscere.

attach vt adiungere, adfīgere, illigāre; (*word*) subicere; **~ed to** amāns (*gen*).

attachment n vinculum nt; amor m, studium nt.

attack vt oppugnāre, adorīrī, aggredī; impetum facere in (acc); (speech) īnsequī, invehī in (acc); (disease) ingruere in (acc) ♦ n impetus m, oppugnātiō f, incursus m.

attacker n oppugnātor m.

attain vt adsequī, adipīscī, cōnsequī; **~ to** pervenīre ad.

attainable adj impetrābilis, in prōmptū.

attainder n: **bill of ~** prīvilēgium nt.

attainment n adeptiō f.

attainments npl doctrīna f, ērudītiō f.

attaint vt maiestātis condemnāre.

attempt vt cōnārī, temptāre; (with effort) mōlīrī ♦ n cōnātus m, inceptum nt; (risk) perīculum nt; **first ~s** rudīmenta ntpl.

attend vt (meeting) adesse (dat), interesse (dat); (person) prōsequī, comitārī; (master) appārēre (dat); (invalid) cūrāre ♦ vi animum advertere, animum attendere; **~ to** (task) adcūrāre; **~ upon** prōsequī, adsectārī; **~ the lectures of** audīre; **not ~** aliud agere; **~ first to** praevenīre (dat); **well ~ed** frequēns; **thinly ~ed** īnfrequēns.

attendance n (courtesy) adsectātiō f; (MED) cūrātiō f; (service) apparitiō f; **constant ~** adsiduitās f; **full ~** frequentia f; **poor ~** īnfrequentia f, **dance ~ on** haerēre (dat).

attendant n famulus m, minister m; (on candidate) sectātor m; (on nobleman) adsectātor m; (on magistrate) appāritor m.

attention n animadversiō f, animī attentiō f; (to work) cūra f; (respect) observantia f; **attract ~** digitō mōnstrārī; **call ~ to** indicāre; **pay ~ to** animadvertere, observāre;

ratiōnem habēre (gen); **~!** hōc age!

attentive adj intentus; (to work) dīligēns.

attentively adv intentē, dīligenter.

attenuate vt attenuāre.

attest vt cōnfirmāre, testārī.

attestation n testificātiō f.

attestor n testis m.

attic n cēnāculum n.

attire vt vestīre ♦ n vestis f, habitus m.

attitude n (body) gestus m, status m, habitus m; (mind) ratiō f.

attorney n āctor m; advocātus m.

attract vt trahere, attrahere, adlicere.

attraction n vīs attrahendī; illecebra f, invītāmentum n.

attractive adj suāvis, venustus, lepidus.

attractively adv suāviter, venustē, lepidē.

attractiveness n venustās f, lepōs m.

attribute vt tribuere, attribuere, adsignāre ♦ n proprium nt.

attrition n attrītus m.

attune vt modulārī.

auburn adj flāvus.

auction n auctiō f; (public) hasta f; **hold an ~** auctiōnem facere; **sell by ~** sub hastā vēndere.

auctioneer n praecō m.

audacious adj audāx; protervus.

audaciously adv audācter, protervē.

audacity n audācia f, temeritās f.

audible adj: **be ~** exaudīrī posse.

audibly adv clārā vōce.

audience n audītōrēs mpl; (interview) aditus m; **give an ~ to** admittere.

audit vt īnspicere ♦ n ratiōnum īnspectiō f.

auditorium n cavea f.

auditory adj audītōrius.

auger n terebra f.

augment vt augēre, adaugēre ♦ vi crēscere, augērī.

augmentation n incrēmentum nt.

augur n augur m; ~'s staff lituus m ♦ vi augurārī; (fig) portendere.

augural adj augurālis.

augurship n augurātus m.

augury n augurium nt, auspicium nt; ōmen nt; **take ~ies** augurārī; **after taking ~ies** augurātō.

august adj augustus.

August n mēnsis Augustus, Sextīlis; **of ~** Sextīlis.

aunt n (paternal) amita f; (maternal) mātertera f.

auspices n auspicium nt; **take ~** auspicārī; **after taking ~** auspicātō; **without taking ~** inauspicātō.

auspicious adj faustus, fēlīx.

auspiciously adv fēlīciter, prosperē.

austere adj austērus, sevērus, dūrus.

austerely adv sevērē.

austerity n sevēritās f, dūritia f.

authentic adj vērus, certus.

authenticate vt recognōscere.

authenticity n auctōritās f, fidēs f.

author n auctor m, inventor m; scrīptor m.

authoress n auctor f.

authoritative adj fīdus; imperiōsus.

authority n auctōritās f, potestās f, iūs nt; (MIL) imperium nt; (LIT) auctor m, scrīptor m; **enforce ~** iūs suum exsequī; **have great ~** multum pollēre; **on Caesar's ~** auctōre Caesare; **an ~ on** perītus (gen).

authorize vt potestātem facere (dat), mandāre; (law) sancīre.

autobiography n dē vītā suā scrīptus liber m.

autocracy n imperium singulāre

nt, tyrannis f.

autocrat n tyrannus m, dominus m.

autocratic adj imperiōsus.

autograph n manus f, chīrographum m.

automatic adj necessārius.

automatically adv necessāriō.

autonomous adj līber.

autonomy n lībertās f.

Autumn n auctumnus m.

autumnal adj auctumnālis.

auxiliaries npl auxilia ntpl, auxiliāriī mpl.

auxiliary adj auxiliāris ♦ n adiūtor m; ~ **forces** auxilia ntpl; novae copiae fpl.

avail vi valēre ♦ vt prōdesse (dat); ~ **oneself of** ūtī (abl) ♦ n ūsus m; **of no ~** frustrā.

available adj ad manum, in prōmptū.

avalanche n montis ruīna f.

avarice n avāritia f, cupiditās f.

avaricious adj avārus, cupidus.

avariciously adv avārē.

avenge vt ulcīscī (+ abl), vindicāre.

avenger n ultor m, vindex m.

avenue n xystus m; (fig) aditus m, iānua f.

aver vt adfirmāre, adsevērāre.

average n medium nt; **on the ~** ferē.

averse adj āversus (ab); **be ~ to** abhorrēre ab.

aversion n odium nt, fastīdium nt.

avert vt arcēre, dēpellere; (by prayer) dēprecārī.

aviary n aviārium nt.

avid adj avidus.

avidity n aviditās f.

avidly adv avidē.

avoid vt vītāre, fugere, dēclīnāre; (battle) dētrectāre.

avoidance n fuga f, dēclīnātiō f.

avow vt fatērī, cōnfitērī.

avowal n cōnfessiō f.

avowed adj apertus.

avowedly adv apertē, palam.
await vt exspectāre; (future) manēre.
awake vt suscitāre, exsuscitāre ♦ vi expergīscī ♦ adj vigil.
awaken vt exsuscitāre.
award vt tribuere; (law) adiūdicāre ♦ n (decision) arbitrium nt, iūdicium nt; (thing) praemium nt.
aware adj gnārus ♦ adj conscius (gen); **be ~** scīre; **become ~ of** percipere.
away adv ā-, ab- (in cpd); **be ~** abesse ab (abl); **far ~** procul, longē; **make ~ with** dē mediō tollere.
awe n formīdō f, reverentia f, rēligiō f; **stand in ~ of** vererī; (gods) venerārī.
awe-struck adj stupidus.
awful adj terrībilis, formīdolōsus, dīrus.
awfully adv formīdolōsē.
awhile adv aliquamdiū, aliquantisper, parumper.
awkward adj incallidus, inconcinnus; (to handle) inhabilis; (fig) molestus.
awkwardly adv incallidē, imperītē.
awkwardness n imperītia f, īnscītia f.
awl n sūbula f.
awning n vēlum nt.
awry adj prāvus, dissidēns.
axe n secūris f.
axiom n prōnūntiātum nt, sententia f.
axiomatic adj ēvidēns, manifestus.
axis n axis m.
axle n axis m.
aye adv semper; **for ~** in aeternum.
azure adj caeruleus.

B

baa vi bālāre ♦ n bālātus m.
babble vi garrīre, blaterāre.
babbler n garrulus m.
babbling adj garrulus.
babe n īnfāns m/f.
babel n dissonae vōcēs fpl.
baboon n sīmia f.
baby n īnfāns m/f.
Bacchanalian adj Bacchicus.
Bacchante n Baccha f.
bachelor n caelebs m; (degree) baccalaureus m.
back n tergum nt; (animal) dorsum nt; (head) occipitium nt; **at one's ~** ā tergō; **behind one's ~** (fig) clam (acc); **put one's up** stomachum movēre (dat); **turn one's ~ on** sē āvertere ab ♦ adj āversus, postīcus ♦ adv retrō, retrōrsum, re- (in cpds) ♦ vt obsecundāre (dat), adesse (dat); **~ water** inhibēre rēmīs, inhibēre nāvem ♦ vi: **~ out of** dētrectāre, dēfugere.
backbite vt obtrectāre (dat), maledīcere (dat).
backbone n spīna f.
backdoor n postīcum nt.
backer n fautor m.
background n recessus m, umbra f.
backing n fidēs f, favor m.
backslide vi dēscīscere.
backward adj āversus; (slow) tardus; (late) sērus.
backwardness n tardītās f, pigritia f.
backwards adv retrō, retrōrsum.
bacon n lārdum nt.
bad adj malus, prāvus, improbus, turpis; **go ~** corrumpī; **be ~ for** obesse (dat), nocēre (dat).
badge n īnsigne nt, īnfula f.
badger n mēles f ♦ vt sollicitāre.

badly adv male, prāvē, improbē, turpiter.

badness n prāvitās f, nēquitia f, improbitās f.

baffle vt ēlūdere, fallere, frustrārī.

bag n saccus m, folliculus m; **hand~** mantica f.

bagatelle n nūgae fpl, floccus m.

baggage n impedīmenta ntpl, vāsa ntpl, sarcinae fpl; **~ train** impedīmenta ntpl; **without ~** expedītus.

bail n vadimōnium nt; (person) vas m; **become ~ for** spondēre prō (abl); **accept ~ for** vadārī; **keep one's ~** vadimōnium obīre ♦ vt spondēre prō (abl).

bailiff n (POL) apparitor m; (private) vīlicus m.

bait n esca f, illecebra f ♦ vt lacessere.

bake vt coquere, torrēre.

bakehouse n pistrīna f.

baker n pistor m.

bakery n pistrīna f.

balance n (scales) lībra f, trutina f; (equilibrium) lībrāmentum nt; (money) reliqua ntpl ♦ vt lībrāre; (fig) compēnsāre; **the account ~s** ratiō cōnstat.

balance sheet n ratiō acceptī et expēnsī.

balcony n podium nt, Maeniānum nt.

bald adj calvus; (style) āridus, iēiūnus.

baldness n calvitium nt; (style) iēiūnitās f.

bale n fascis m; **~ out** vt exhaurīre.

baleful adj fūnestus, perniciōsus, tristis.

balk n tignum nt ♦ vt frustrārī, dēcipere.

ball n globus m; (play) pila f; (wool) glomus nt; (dance) saltātiō f.

ballad n carmen nt.

ballast n saburra f.

ballet n saltātiō f.

ballot n suffrāgium nt.

ballot box urna f.

balm n unguentum nt; (fig) sōlātium nt.

balmy adj lēnis, suāvis.

balsam n balsamum nt.

balustrade n cancellī mpl.

bamboozle vt cōnfundere.

ban vt interdīcere (dat), vetāre ♦ n interdictum nt.

banal adj trītus.

banana n ariēna f; (tree) pāla f.

band n vinculum nt, redimīculum nt; (head) īnfula f; (men) caterva f, manus f, grex f ♦ vi: **~ together** cōnsociārī.

bandage n fascia f, īnfula f ♦ vt obligāre, adligāre.

bandbox n: **out of a ~** (fig) dē capsulā.

bandeau n redimīculum nt.

bandit n latrō m.

bandy vt iactāre; **~ words** altercārī ♦ adj vārus.

bane n venēnum nt, pestis f, perniciēs f.

baneful adj perniciōsus, pestifer.

bang vt pulsāre ♦ n fragor m.

bangle n armilla f.

banish vt pellere, expellere, ēicere; (law) aquā et ignī interdīcere (dat); (temporarily) relēgāre; (feeling) abstergēre.

banishment n (act) aquae et ignis interdictiō f; relēgātiō f; (state) exsilium nt, fuga f.

bank n (earth) agger m; (river) rīpa f; (money) argentāria f.

banker n argentārius m; (public) mēnsārius m.

bankrupt adj: **be ~** solvendō nōn esse; **declare oneself ~** bonam cōpiam ēiūrāre; **go ~** dēcoquere ♦ n dēcoctor m.

banner n vexillum nt.

banquet n cēna f, epulae fpl;
convīvium nt; (religious) daps f
♦ vi epulārī.

banter n cavillātiō f ♦ vi cavillārī.

baptism n baptisma nt.

baptize vt baptizāre.

bar n (door) sera f; (gate) claustrum
nt; (metal) later m; (wood) asser
m; (lever) vectis m; (obstacle)
impedīmentum nt; (law-court)
cancellī mpl; (barristers) advocātī
mpl; (profession) forum nt; **of the ~**
forēnsis; **practise at the ~** causās
agere.

bar vt (door) obserāre; (way)
obstāre (dat), interclūdere,
prohibēre; (exception) excipere,
exclūdere.

barb n aculeus m, dēns m, hāmus
m.

barbarian n barbarus m ♦ adj
barbarus.

barbarism n barbaria f.

barbarity n saevitia f, ferōcia f,
immānitās f, inhūmānitās f.

barbarous adj barbarus, saevus,
immānis, inhūmānus.

barbarously adv barbarē,
inhūmānē.

barbed adj hāmātus.

barber n tōnsor m; **~'s shop**
tōnstrīna f.

bard n vātēs m/f; (Gallic) bardus m.

bare adj nūdus; (mere) merus; **lay ~**
nūdāre, aperīre, dētegere ♦ vt
nūdāre.

barefaced adj impudēns.

barefoot adj nūdīs pedibus.

bare-headed adj capite aperto.

barely adv vix.

bargain n pactum nt, foedus nt;
make a ~ pacīscī; **make a bad ~**
male emere; **into the ~** grātiīs
♦ vi pacīscī.

barge n linter f.

bark n cortex m; (dog) lātrātus m;
(ship) nāvis f, ratis f ♦ vi lātrāre.

barking n lātratus m.

barley n hordeum nt; **of ~**
hordeāceus.

barn n horreum nt.

barrack vt obstrepere (dat).

barracks n castra ntpl.

barrel n cūpa f; (ligneum vās nt.

barren adj sterilis.

barrenness n sterilitās f.

barricade n claustrum nt,
mūnīmentum nt ♦ vt obsaepīre,
obstruere; **~ off** intersaepīre.

barrier n impedīmentum nt;
(racecourse) carcer m.

barrister n advocātus m, patrōnus
m, causidicus m.

barrow n ferculum nt; (mound)
tumulus m.

barter vt mūtāre ♦ vi mercēs
mūtāre ♦ n mūtātiō f,
commercium nt.

base adj turpis, vīlis; (birth)
humilis, ignōbilis; (coin)
adulterīnus.

base n fundāmentum nt; (statue)
basis f; (hill) rādīcēs fpl; (MIL)
castra ntpl.

baseless adj falsus, inānis.

basely adv turpiter.

basement n basis f; (storey) īmum
tabulātum nt.

baseness n turpitūdō f.

bashful adj pudīcus, verēcundus.

bashfulness n pudor m,
verēcundia f.

basic adj prīmus.

basin n alveolus m, pelvis f; **wash-**
aquālis m.

basis n fundāmentum nt.

bask vi aprīcārī.

basket n corbis f, fiscus m; (for
bread) canistrum nt; (for wool)
quasillum nt.

basking n aprīcātiō f.

bas-relief n toreuma nt.

bass adj (voice) gravis.

bastard adj nothus.

bastion n prōpugnāculum nt.

bat n vespertīliō m; (games) clāva f.

batch n numerus m.

Bath n Aquae Sulis fpl.

bath n balneum nt; (utensil) lābrum nt, lavātiō f; **Turkish ~** Lacōnicum nt; **cold ~** frīgidārium nt; **hot ~** calidārium nt; **~ superintendent** balneātor m ♦ vt lavāre.

bathe vt lavāre ♦ vi lavārī, perluī.

bathroom n balneāria ntpl.

baths n (public ~) balneae fpl.

batman n cālō m.

baton n virga f, scīpiō m.

battalion n cohors f.

batter vt quassāre, pulsāre, verberāre.

battering ram n ariēs m.

battery n (assault) vīs f.

battle n pugna f, proelium nt, certāmen nt; **a ~ was fought** pugnātum est; **pitched ~** iūstum proelium nt; **line of ~** aciēs f; **drawn ~** anceps proelium ♦ vi pugnāre, contendere; **~ order** aciēs f.

battle-axe n bipennis f.

battlefield, battle-line n aciēs f.

battlement n pinna f.

bawl vt vōciferārī, clāmitāre.

bay n (sea) sinus m; (tree) laurus f, laurea f; **of ~** laureus; **at ~** interclūsus ♦ adj (colour) spādīx ♦ vi (dog) lātrāre.

be vi esse, (CIRCS) versārī; (condition) sē habēre; **~ at** adesse (dat); **~ amongst** interesse (dat); **~ in** inesse (dat); **consul-to~** cōnsul dēsignātus; **how are you?** quid agis?; **so~it** estō; see also **absent, here** etc.

beach n lītus nt, acta f ♦ vt (ship) subdūcere.

beacon n ignis m.

bead n pilula f.

beadle n apparitor m.

beak n rōstrum nt.

beaked adj rōstrātus.

beaker n cantharus m, scyphus m.

beam n (wood) trabs f, tignum nt; (balance) iugum nt; (light) radius m; (ship) latus nt; **on the ~** ā latere ♦ vi fulgēre; (person) adrīdēre.

beaming adj hilaris.

bean n faba f.

bear n ursus m, ursa f; **Great B~** septentriōnēs mpl, Arctos f; **Little B~** septentriō minor m, Cynosūra f; **~'s** ursīnus ♦ vt (carry) ferre, portāre; (endure) ferre, tolerāre, patī; (produce) ferre, fundere; (child) parere; **~ down upon** appropinquāre; **~ off** ferre; **~ out** vt arguere; **~ up** vi: **~ up under** obsistere (dat), sustinēre; **~ upon** innītī (dat); (refer) pertinēre ad; **~ with** vt fus indulgēre (dat); **~ oneself** sē gerere; **I cannot ~ to** addūcī nōn possum ut.

bearable adj tolerābilis.

beard n barba f ♦ vt ultrō lacessere.

bearded adj barbātus.

beardless adj imberbis.

bearer n bāiulus m; (letter) tabellārius m; (litter) lectīcārius m; (news) nūntius m.

bearing n (person) gestus m, vultus m; (direction) regiō f; **have no ~ on** nihil pertinēre ad; **I have lost my ~s** ubi sim nesciō.

beast n bestia f; (large) bēlua f; (wild) fera f; (domestic) pecus f.

beastliness n foeditās f, stuprum nt.

beastly adj foedus.

beast of burden n iūmentum nt.

beat n ictus m; (heart) palpitātiō f; (music) percussiō f; (oars, pulse) pulsus m.

beat vt ferīre, percutere, pulsāre; (the body in grief) plangere; (punish) caedere; (whip) verberāre; (conquer) vincere, superāre ♦ vi palpitāre, micāre; ~ **back** repellere; ~ **in** perfringere; ~ **out** excutere; (*metal*) extundere; ~ **a retreat** receptuī canere; ~ **about the bush** circuitiōne ūtī; **be ~en** vāpulāre; **dead ~** cōnfectus.

beating n verbera ntpl; (*defeat*) clādes f; (*time*) percussiō f; **get a ~** vāpulāre.

beatitude n beātitūdō f, fēlīcitās f.

beau n nitidus homō m; (*lover*) amāns m.

beauteous adj pulcher, fōrmōsus.

beautiful adj pulcher, formōsus; (*looks*) decōrus; (*scenery*) amoenus.

beautifully adv pulchrē.

beautify vt exōrnāre, decorāre.

beauty n fōrma f, pulchritūdō f, amoenitās f.

beaver n castor m, fiber m; (*helmet*) buccula f.

becalmed adj ventō dēstitūtus.

because conj quod, quia, quoniam (+ indic); quippe quī; ~ **of** propter (acc).

beck n nūtus m.

beckon vt innuere, vocāre.

become vi fierī; **what will ~ of me?** quid me fīet? ◆ vt decēre, convenīre in (acc).

becoming adj decēns, decōrus.

becomingly adv decōrē, convenienter.

bed n cubīle nt, lectus m, lectulus m; **go to ~** cubitum īre; **make a ~** lectum sternere; **be ~ridden** lectō tenērī; **camp ~** grabātus m; **flower~** pulvīnus m; **marriage ~** lectus geniālis m; **river~** alveus m.

bedaub vt illinere, oblinere.

bedclothes n strāgula ntpl.

bedding n strāgula ntpl.

bedeck vt ōrnāre, exōrnāre.

bedew vt inrōrāre.

bedim vt obscūrāre.

bedpost n fulcrum nt.

bedraggled adj sordidus, madidus.

bedroom n cubiculum nt.

bedstead n sponda f.

bee n apis f; **queen ~** rēx m.

beech n fāgus f ◆ adj fāginus.

beef n būbula f.

beehive n alvus f.

beekeeper n apiārius m

beer n cervīsia f, fermentum nt.

beet n bēta f.

beetle n (*insect*) scarabaeus m; (*implement*) fistūca f.

beetling adj imminēns, mināx.

befall vi, vt accidere, ēvenīre (dat); (*good*) contingere (dat).

befit vt decēre, convenīre in (acc).

before adv ante, anteā, antehāc ◆ prep ante (acc); (*place*) prō (abl); (*presence*) apud (acc), cōram (abl) ◆ conj antequam, priusquam.

beforehand adv ante, anteā; prae (in cpd).

befoul vt inquināre, foedāre.

befriend vt favēre (dat), adiuvāre; (*in trouble*) adesse (dat).

beg vt ōrāre, obsecrāre, precārī, poscere ab, petere ab; ~ **for** petere ◆ vi mendīcāre.

beget vt gignere, prōcreāre, generāre.

begetter n generātor m, creātor m.

beggar n mendīcus m.

beggarly adj mendīcus, indigēns.

beggary n mendīcitās f, indigentia f.

begin vi, vt incipere, coepisse; (*speech*) exōrdīrī; (*plan*) īnstituere, incohāre; (*time*) inīre; ~ **with** incipere ab.

beginning n initium nt, prīncipium nt, exōrdium nt, inceptiō f; (*learning*) rudīmenta ntpl, elementa ntpl; (*origin*) orīgō f, fōns m; **at the ~ of spring** ineunte vēre.

begone interj apage, tē āmovē.

begotten adj genitus, nātus.

begrudge vt invidēre (dat).

beguile vt dēcipere, fallere.

behalf n: on ~ of prō (abl); on my ~ meō nōmine.

behave vi sē gerere, sē praebēre (with adj); **well ~d** bene mōrātus.

behaviour n mōrēs mpl.

behead vt dētruncāre, secūrī percutere.

behest n iūssum nt.

behind adv pōne, post, ā tergō ♦ prep post (acc), pōne (acc).

behindhand adv sērō; be ~ parum prōficere.

behold vt aspicere, cōnspicere, intuērī ♦ interj ecce, ēn.

beholden adj obnoxius, obstrictus, obligātus.

behoof n ūsus m.

behove vt oportēre.

being n (life) animātiō f; (nature) nātūra f; (person) homō m/f.

bejewelled adj gemmeus, gemmātus.

belabour vt verberāre, caedere.

belated adj sērus.

belch vi ructāre, ēructāre.

beldam n anus f.

beleaguer vt obsidēre, circumsedēre.

belie vt abhorrēre ab, repugnāre.

belief n fidēs f, opīniō f; (opinion) sententia f; **to the best of my ~** ex animī meī sententiā; **past ~** incrēdibilis.

believe vt, vi (thing) crēdere; (person) crēdere (dat); (suppose) crēdere, putāre, arbitrārī, opīnārī; **~ in gods** deōs esse crēdere; **make ~** simulāre.

believer n deōrum cultor m; Christiānus m.

belike adv fortasse.

belittle vt obtrectāre.

bell n tintinnābulum nt; (public) campāna f.

belle n fōrmōsa f, pulchra f.

belles-lettres n litterae fpl.

bellicose adj ferōx.

belligerent adj bellī particeps.

bellow vi rūdere, mūgīre ♦ n mūgītus m.

bellows n follis m.

belly n abdōmen nt, venter m; (sail) sinus m ♦ vi tumēre.

belong vi esse (gen), proprium esse (gen), inesse (dat); (concern) attinēre, pertinēre.

belongings n bona ntpl.

beloved adj cārus, dīlectus, grātus.

below adv īnfrā, subter ♦ adj īnferus ♦ prep īnfrā (acc), sub (abl, acc).

belt n zōna f, (sword) balteus m.

bemoan vt dēplōrāre, lāmentārī.

bemused adj stupefactus, stupidus.

bench n subsellium nt; (rowing) trānstrum nt; (law) iūdicēs mpl; **seat on the ~** iūdicātus m.

bend vt flectere, curvāre, inclīnāre; (bow) intendere; (course) tendere, flectere; (mind) intendere ♦ vi sē īnflectere; (person) sē dēmittere; ~ **back** reflectere; ~ **down** vi dēflectere; sē dēmittere ♦ n flexus m, ānfrāctus m.

beneath adv subter ♦ prep sub (acc or abl).

benediction n bonae precēs fpl.

benedictory adj faustus.

benefaction n beneficium nt, dōnum nt.

benefactor n patrōnus m; **be a ~** bene merērī (dē).

beneficence n beneficentia f, līberālitās f.

beneficent adj beneficus.

beneficial adj ūtilis, salūbris.

benefit n beneficium nt; (derived) frūctus m; **have the ~ of** fruī (abl) ♦ vt prōdesse (dat), ūsuī esse (dat).

benevolence n benevolentia f, benignitās f.

benevolent adj benevolus, benignus.

benevolently adv benevolē, benignē.

benighted adj nocte oppressus; (fig) ignārus, indoctus.

benign adj benignus, cōmis.

bent n (mind) inclīnātiō f, ingenium nt ♦ adj curvus, flexus; (mind) attentus; **be ~ on** studēre (dat).

benumb vt stupefacere.

benumbed adj stupefactus, torpidus; **be ~** torpēre.

bequeath vt lēgāre.

bequest n lēgātum nt.

bereave vt orbāre, prīvāre.

bereavement n damnum nt.

bereft adj orbus, orbātus, prīvātus.

berry n bāca f.

berth n statiō f; **give a wide ~ to** dēvītāre.

beryl n bēryllus m.

beseech vt implōrāre, ōrāre, obsecrāre.

beset vt obsidēre, circumsedēre.

beside prep ad (acc), apud (acc); (close) iuxtā (acc); **~ the point** nihil ad rem; **be ~ oneself** nōn esse apud sē.

besides adv praetereā, accēdit quod; (in addition) īnsuper ♦ prep praeter (acc).

besiege vt obsidēre, circumsedēre.

besieger n obsessor m.

besmear vt illinere.

besmirch vt maculāre.

besom n scōpae fpl.

besotted adj stupidus.

bespatter vt aspergere.

bespeak vt (order) imperāre; (denote) significāre.

besprinkle vt aspergere.

best adj optimus; **the ~ part** māior pars ♦ n flōs m, rōbur nt; **do one's ~** prō virīlī parte agere; **do one's ~ to** operam dare ut; **have the ~ of**

it vincere; **make the ~ of (a situation)** aequō animō accipere; **to the ~ of one's ability** prō virīlī parte; **to the ~ of my knowledge** quod sciam ♦ adv optimē.

bestial adj foedus.

bestir vt movēre; **~ oneself** expergīscī.

bestow vt dōnāre, tribuere, dare, cōnferre.

bestride vt (horse) sedēre in (abl).

bet n pignus nt ♦ vt opponere ♦ vi pignore contendere.

betake vt cōnferre, recipere; **~ o.s.** sē cōnferre.

bethink vt: **~ oneself** sē colligere; **~ oneself of** respicere.

betide vi accidere, ēvenīre.

betoken vt significāre; (foretell) portendere.

betray vt prōdere, trādere; (feelings) arguere; **without ~ing one's trust** salvā fidē.

betrayal n prōditiō f.

betrayer n prōditor m; (informer) index m.

betroth vt spondēre, dēspondēre.

betrothal n spōnsālia ntpl.

better adj melior; **it is ~ to** praestat (infin); **get the ~ of** vincere, superāre; **I am ~** (in health) melius est mihi, **I had ~ go** praestat īre; **get ~** convalēscere; **think ~ of** sententiam mūtāre dē ♦ adv melius ♦ vt corrigere; **~ oneself** prōficere.

betterment n prōfectus m.

between prep inter (acc).

beverage n pōtiō f.

bevy n manus f, grex f.

bewail vt dēflēre, lāmentārī, dēplōrāre.

beware vt cavēre.

bewilder vt cōnfundere, perturbāre.

bewildered adj attonitus.

bewilderment n perturbātiō f,

admīrātiō f.

bewitch vt fascināre; (fig) dēlēnīre.

beyond adv ultrā, suprā ♦ prep ultrā (acc), extrā (acc); (motion) trāns (acc); (amount) ultrā, suprā (acc); **go/pass** ~ excēdere, ēgredī.

bezel n pāla f.

bias n inclīnātiō f; (party) favor m ♦ vt inclīnāre.

biassed adj prōpēnsior.

bibber n pōtor m, pōtātor m.

Bible n litterae sacrae fpl.

bibulous adj bibulus.

bicephalous adj biceps.

bicker vi altercārī, iūrgāre.

bid vt iubēre; (guest) vocāre, invītāre ♦ vi (at auction) licērī; ~ **for** licērī; ~ **good day** salvēre iubēre; **he ~s fair to make progress** spēs est eum prōfectūrum esse.

biddable adj docilis.

bidding n iussum nt; (auction) licitātiō f.

bide vt manēre, opperīrī.

biennial adj biennālis.

bier n ferculum nt.

bifurcate vi sē scindere.

bifurcation n (road) trivium nt.

big adj māgnus, grandis, amplus; (with child) gravida; **very ~** permāgnus; **talk ~** glōriārī.

bight n sinus m.

bigness n māgnitūdō f, amplitūdō f.

bigot n nimis obstinātus fautor m.

bigoted adj contumāx.

bigotry n contumācia f, nimia obstinātiō f.

bile n bīlis f, fel nt.

bilgewater n sentīna f.

bilk vt fraudāre.

bill n (bird) rōstrum nt; (implement) falx f; (law) rogātiō f, lēx f; (money) syngrapha f; (notice) libellus m, titulus m; **introduce a ~**

populum rogāre, lēgem ferre; **carry a ~** lēgem perferre.

billet n hospitium nt ♦ vt in hospitia dīvidere.

billhook n falx f.

billow n fluctus m.

billowy adj undōsus.

billy goat n caper m.

bin n lacus m.

bind vt adligāre, dēligāre, vincīre; (by oath) adigere; (by obligation) obligāre, obstringere; (wound) obligāre; ~ **fast** dēvincīre; ~ **together** conligāre; ~ **over** vt vadārī.

binding n compāgēs f ♦ adj (law) ratus; **it is ~ on** oportet.

bindweed n convolvulus m.

biographer n vītae nārrātor m.

biography n vīta f.

bipartite adj bipartītus.

biped n bipēs m.

birch n bētula f; (flogging) virgae ulmeae fpl.

bird n avis f; **~s of a feather** parēs cum paribus facillimē congregantur; **kill two ~s with one stone** ūnō saltū duōs aprōs capere, dē eādem fidēliā duōs parietēs dealbāre; **~'s-eye view of** dēspectus in (acc).

birdcatcher n auceps m.

birdlime n viscum m.

birth n (act) partus m; (origin) genus nt; **low ~** ignōbilitās f; **high ~** nōbilitās f; **by ~** nātū, ortū.

birthday n nātālis m.

birthday party n nātālicia ntpl.

birthplace n locus nātālis m; (fig) incūnābula ntpl.

birthright n patrimōnium nt.

bisect vt dīvidere.

bishop n episcopus m.

bison n ūrus m.

bit n pars f; (food) frustum nt; (broken off) fragmentum nt; (horse) frēnum nt; **~ by ~** minūtātim; **a ~**

adv aliquantulum; **a ~ sad** tristior.
bitch *n* canis *f.*
bite *vt* mordēre; (*frost*) ūrere ♦ *n*
morsus *m;* **with a ~** mordicus.
biting *adj* mordāx.
bitter *adj* (*taste*) acerbus, amārus;
(*words*) asper.
bitterly *adv* acerbē, asperē.
bittern *n* būtio *m,* ardea *f.*
bitterness *n* acerbitās *f.*
bitumen *n* bitūmen *nt.*
bivouac *n* excubiae *fpl* ♦ *vi*
excubāre.
bizarre *adj* īnsolēns.
blab *vt, vi* garrīre, effūtīre.
black *adj* (*dull*) āter; (*glossy*) niger;
(*dirt*) sordidus; (*eye*) līvidus;
(*looks*) trux; **~ and blue** līvidus;
♦ *n* ātrum *nt,* nigrum *nt;* **dressed
in ~** ātrātus; (*in mourning*)
sordidātus.
blackberry *n* mōrum *nt.*
blackbird *n* merula *f.*
blacken *vt* nigrāre, nigrum
reddere; (*character*) īnfāmāre,
obtrectāre (*dat*).
blackguard *n* scelestus, scelerātus
m.
blacking *n* ātrāmentum *nt.*
blacklist *n* prōscrīptiō *f.*
black magic *n* magicae artēs *fpl.*
blackmail *n* minae *fpl* ♦ *vt* minīs
cōgere.
black mark *n* nota *f.*
blacksmith *n* faber *m.*
bladder *n* vēsīca *f.*
blade *n* (*grass*) herba *f,* (*oar*) palma
f; (*sword*) lāmina *f.*
blame *vt* reprehendere, culpāre; **I
am to ~** reus sum ♦ *n* reprehēnsiō
f, culpa *f.*
blameless *adj* innocēns.
blamelessly *adv* innocenter.
blamelessness *n* innocentia *f,*
integritās *f.*
blameworthy *adj* accūsābilis,
nocēns.

blanch *vi* exalbēscere, pallēscere.
bland *adj* mītis, lēnis.
blandishment *n* blanditiae *fpl.*
blank *adj* vacuus, pūrus; (*look*)
stolidus.
blanket *n* lōdīx *f;* **wet ~** nimium
sevērus.
blare *vi* canere, strīdere ♦ *n*
clangor *m,* strīdor *m.*
blarney *n* lēnōcinium *nt.*
blaspheme *vi* maledīcere.
blasphemous *adj* maledicus,
impius.
blasphemy *n* maledicta *ntpl,*
impietās *f.*
blast *n* flātus *m,* īnflātus *m* ♦ *vt*
disicere, discutere; (*crops*)
rōbīgine adficere.
blatant *adj* raucus.
blaze *n* flamma *f,* ignis *m,* fulgor *m*
♦ *vi* flāgrāre, ārdēre, fulgēre; **~
up** exārdēscere ♦ *vt:* **~ abroad**
pervulgāre.
blazon *vt* prōmulgāre.
bleach *vt* candidum reddere.
bleak *adj* dēsertus, tristis,
inamoenus.
bleary-eyed *adj* lippus.
bleat *vi* bālāre ♦ *n* bālātus *m.*
bleed *vi* sanguinem fundere ♦ *vt*
sanguinem mittere (*dat*); **my heart
~s** animus mihī dolet.
bleeding *adj* crūdus, sanguineus
♦ *n* sanguinis missiō *f.*
blemish *n* macula *f,* vitium *nt* ♦ *vt*
maculāre, foedāre.
blend *vt* miscēre, immiscēre,
admiscēre ♦ *n* coniūnctiō *f.*
bless *vt* beāre; laudāre; (*ECCL*)
benedīcere; **~ with** augēre (*abl*); **~
my soul!** ita mē dī ament!
blessed *adj* beātus, fortūnātus;
(*emperors*) dīvus.
blessing *n* (*thing*) commodum *nt,*
bonum *nt;* (*ECCL*) benedictiō *f.*
blight *n* rōbīgō *f,* ūrēdō *f* ♦ *vt*
rōbīgine adficere; (*fig*) nocēre

(*dat*).

blind *adj* caecus; (*in one eye*) luscus; (*fig*) ignārus, stultus; (*alley*) nōn pervius; (*forces*) necessārius; **turn a ~ eye to** cōnīvēre in (*abl*) ♦ *vt* excaecāre, caecāre; (*fig*) occaecāre; (*with light*) praestringere.

blindfold *adj* capite obvolūtō.

blindly *adv* temerē.

blindness *n* caecitās *f*; (*fig*) temeritās *f*, īnspientia *f*.

blink *vi* nictāre.

bliss *n* fēlicitās *f*, laetitia *f*.

blissful *adj* fēlix, beātus, laetus.

blissfully *adv* fēliciter, beātē.

blister *n* pustula *f*.

blithe *adj* hilaris, laetus.

blithely *adv* hilare, laetē.

blizzard *n* hiems *f*.

bloated *adj* tumidus, turgidus.

blob *n* gutta *f*, particula *f*.

block *n* (*wood*) stīpes *m*, caudex *m*; (*stone*) massa *f*; (*houses*) īnsula *f*; **~ letter** quadrāta littera; **stumbling ~** offēnsiō *f*.

block *vt* claudere, obstruere, interclūdere; **~ the way** obstāre.

blockade *n* obsidiō *f*; **raise a ~** obsidiōnem solvere ♦ *vt* obsidēre, interclūdere.

blockhead *n* caudex *m*, bārō *m*, truncus *m*.

blockhouse *n* castellum *nt*.

blond *adj* flāvus.

blood *n* sanguis *m*; (*shed*) cruor *m*; (*murder*) caedēs *f*; (*kin*) genus *nt*; **let ~** sanguinem mittere; **staunch ~** sanguinem supprimere; **bad ~** simultās *f*; **in cold ~** cōnsultō; **own flesh and ~** cōnsanguineus.

bloodless *adj* exsanguis; (*victory*) incruentus.

bloodshed *n* caedēs *f*.

bloodshot *adj* sanguineus.

bloodstained *adj* cruentus.

bloodsucker *n* hirūdō *f*.

bloodthirsty *adj* sanguinārius.

blood vessel *n* vēna *f*.

bloody *adj* cruentus.

bloom *n* flōs *m*; **in ~** flōrēns ♦ *vi* flōrēre, flōrēscere, vigēre.

blossom *n* flōs *m* ♦ *vi* efflōrēscere, flōrēre.

blot *n* macula *f*; (*erasure*) litūra *f* ♦ *vt* maculāre; **~ out** dēlēre, oblitterāre.

blotch *n* macula *f*.

blotched *adj* maculōsus.

blow *vt*, *vi* (*wind*) flāre; (*breath*) adflāre, anhēlāre; (*instrument*) canere; (*flower*) efflōrēscere; (*nose*) ēmungere; **~ out** *vi* exstinguere; **~ over** *vi* (*storm*) cadere; (*fig*) abīre; **~ up** *vt* īnflāre; (*destroy*) discutere, disturbāre ♦ *n* ictus *m*; (*on the cheek*) alapa *f*; (*fig*) plāga *f*; (*misfortune*) calamitās *f*; **aim a ~ at** petere; **come to ~s** ad manūs venīre.

blowy *adj* ventōsus.

bludgeon *n* fustis *m*.

blue *adj* caeruleus; **black and ~** līvidus; **true ~** fīdissimus; **~ blood** nōbilitās *f*.

bluff *n* rūpēs *f*, prōmunturium *nt* ♦ *adj* inurbānus ♦ *vt* fallere, dēcipere, verba dare (*dat*), impōnere (*dat*).

blunder *vi* errāre, offendere ♦ *n* error *m*, errātum *nt*; (*in writing*) mendum *nt*.

blunt *adj* hebes; (*manners*) horridus, rūsticus, inurbānus; **be ~** hebēre ♦ *vt* hebetāre, obtundere, retundere.

bluntly *adv* līberius, plānē et apertē.

blur *n* macula *f* ♦ *vt* obscūrāre.

blurt *vt*: **~ out** ēmittere.

blush *vi* rubēre, ērubēscere ♦ *n* rubor *m*.

bluster *vi* dēclāmitāre, lātrāre.

boa *n* boa *f*.

Boadicea n Boudicca f.
boar n verrēs m; (wild) aper m.
board n tabula f; (table) mēnsa f; (food) vīctus m; (committee) concilium nt; (judicial) quaestiō f; (of ten men) decemvirī mpl; (gaming) abacus m, alveus m; on ~ in nāvī; **go on** ~ in nāvem cōnscendere; **go by the** ~ intercidere, perīre; **above** ~ sine fraude ♦ vt (building) contabulāre; (ship) cōnscendere; (person) vīctum praebēre (dat) ♦ vi: ~ **with** dēvertere ad.
boarder n hospes m.
boast vi glōriārī, sē iactāre; ~ **of** glōriārī dē (abl) ♦ n glōria f, glōriātiō f, iactātiō f.
boastful adj glōriōsus.
boastfully adv glōriōsē.
boasting n glōriātiō f ♦ adj glōriōsus.
boat n linter f, scapha f, cymba f; (ship) nāvis f; **be in the same** ~ (fig) in eādem nāvī esse.
boatman n nauta m.
boatswain n hortātor m.
bobbin n fūsus m.
bode vt portendere, praesāgīre.
bodiless adj sine corpore.
bodily adj corporeus.
bodkin n acus f.
body n corpus nt; (dead) cadāver nt; (small) corpusculum nt; (person) homō m/f; (of people) globus m, numerus m; (of troops) manus f, caterva f; (of cavalry) turma f; (of officials) collēgium nt; (heavenly) astrum nt; **in a** ~ ūniversī, frequentēs.
bodyguard n custōs m, stīpātōrēs mpl; (emperor's) praetōriānī mpl.
bog n palūs f.
bogey n mōnstrum nt.
boggle vi tergiversārī, haesitāre.
boggy adj palūster.
bogus adj falsus, fictus.

Bohemian adj līberior, solūtior, libīdinōsus.
boil vt coquere; (liquid) fervefacere; ~ **down** dēcoquere ♦ vi fervēre, effervēscere; (sea) exaestuāre; (passion) exārdēscere, aestuāre; ~ **over** effervēscere ♦ n (MED) fūrunculus m.
boiler n cortīna f.
boiling adj (hot) fervēns.
boisterous adj (person) turbulentus, vehemēns; (sea) turbidus, agitātus; (weather) procellōsus, violentus.
boisterously adv turbidē, turbulentē.
boisterousness n tumultus m, violentia f.
bold adj audāx, fortis, intrepidus; (impudent) impudēns, protervus; (language) līber; (headland) prōminēns; **make** ~ audēre.
boldly adv audācter, fortiter, intrepidē; impudenter.
boldness n audācia f, cōnfīdentia f; impudentia f, petulantia f; (speech) lībertās f.
bolster n pulvīnus m ♦ vt: ~ **up** sustinēre, cōnfirmāre.
bolt n (door) claustrum nt, pessulus m, sera f; (missile) tēlum nt, sagitta f; (lightning) fulmen nt; **make a** ~ **for it** sē prōripere, aufugere; **a** ~ **from the blue** rēs subita, rēs inopīnāta ♦ vi (door) obserāre, obdere.
bombard vt tormentīs verberāre; (fig) lacessere.
bombast n ampullae fpl.
bombastic adj tumidus, īnflātus; **bo** ~ ampullārī.
bond n vinculum nt, catēna f, compes f; (of union) cōpula f, iugum nt, nōdus m; (document) syngrapha f; (agreement) foedus nt ♦ adj servus, addictus.

bondage n servitūs f, famulātus m.
bone n os nt; (fish) spīna f ♦ vt exossāre.
boneless adj exos.
bonfire n ignis festus m.
bonhomie n festīvitās f.
bon mot n dictum nt, sententia f.
bonny adj pulcher, bellus.
bony adj osseus.
boo vt explōdere.
book n liber m; (small) libellus m; (scroll) volūmen nt; (modern form) cōdex, m; ~s (COMM) rationēs fpl, tabulae fpl; **bring to ~** in iūdicium vocāre.
bookbinder n glūtinātor m.
bookcase n librārium nt, pēgma nt.
bookish adj litterārum studiōsus.
book-keeper n āctuārius m.
bookseller n librārius m, bibliopōla m.
bookshop n bibliothēca f, librāria taberna f.
bookworm n tinea f.
boom n (spar) longurius m; (harbour) ōbex m/f ♦ vi resonāre.
boon n bonum nt, beneficium nt, dōnum nt ♦ adj festīvus; ~ **companion** sodālis m, compōtor m.
boor n agrestis m, rūsticus m.
boorish adj agrestis, rūsticus, inurbānus.
boorishly adv rūsticē.
boost vt efferre; (wares) vēnditāre.
boot n calceus m; (MIL) caliga f; (rustic) pērō m; (tragic) cothurnus m ♦ vi prōdesse; **to ~** īnsuper, praetereā.
booted adj calceātus, caligātus.
booth n taberna f.
bootless adj inūtilis, vānus.
bootlessly adv frūstrā.
booty n praeda f, spolia ntpl.
border n ōra f, margō f; (country) fīnis m; (dress) limbus m ♦ vt praetexere, margināre; fīnīre

♦ vi: ~ **on** adiacēre (dat), imminēre (dat), attingere; (fig) fīnitimum esse (dat).
bordering adj fīnitimus.
bore vt perforāre, perterebrāre; (person) obtundere, fatīgāre; ~ **out** exterebrāre ♦ n terebra f; (hole) forāmen nt; (person) homō importūnus m, ineptus m.
boredom n lassitūdō f.
borer n terebra f.
born adj nātus; **be ~** nāscī.
borough n mūnicipium nt.
borrow vt mūtuārī.
borrowed adj mūtuus; (fig) aliēnus.
borrowing n mūtuātiō f; (to pay a debt) versūra f.
bosky adj nemorōsus.
bosom n sinus m; (fig) gremium nt; ~ **friend** familiāris m/f, sodālis m; **be a ~ friend of** ab latere esse (gen).
boss n bulla f; (shield) umbō m.
botanist n herbārius m.
botany n herbāria f.
botch vt male sarcīre, male gerere.
both pron ambō, uterque (gen utriusque, each of two ♦) ♦ adv: ~ ... and et ... et, cum ... tum.
bother n negōtium nt ♦ vt vexāre, molestus esse (dat) ♦ vi operam dare.
bothersome adj molestus.
bottle n lagoena f, amphora f ♦ vt (wine) diffundere.
bottom n fundus m; (ground) solum nt; (ship) carīna f; **the ~ of** īmus; **be at the ~ of** (cause) auctōrem esse; **go to the ~** pessum īre, perīre; **send to the ~** pessum dare; **from the ~** funditus, ab īnfimō.
bottomless adj profundus, fundō carēns.
bottommost adj īnfimus.

bough n rāmus m.

boulder n saxum nt.

boulevard n platea f.

bounce vi salīre, resultāre.

bound n fīnis m, modus m,
terminus m; (leap) saltus m; **set ~s
to** modum facere ♦ vt fīnīre,
dēfīnīre, termināre ♦ vi salīre,
saltāre ♦ adj adligātus, obligātus,
obstrictus; **be ~ to** (duty) dēbēre;
it is ~ to happen necesse est
ēveniat; **be ~ for** tendere in (acc);
be storm~ tempestāte tenērī.

boundaries npl fīnes mpl.

boundary n fīnis m; (of fields)
terminus m; (fortified) līmes m; **~
stone** terminus m.

boundless adj immēnsus,
īnfīnītus.

boundlessness n īnfīnītās f,
immēnsum nt.

bounteous adj see **bountiful**.

bounteously adv largē, līberāliter,
cōpiōsē.

bountiful adj largus, līberālis,
benignus.

bounty n largitās f, līberālitās f;
(store) cōpia f.

bouquet n corollārium nt; (of wine)
flōs m.

bourn n fīnis m.

bout n certāmen nt; (drinking)
cōmissātiō f.

bovine adj būbulus; (fig) stolidus.

bow n arcus m; (ship) prōra f;
(courtesy) salūtātiō f; **have two
strings to one's ~** duplicī spē ūtī;
rain~ arcus m ♦ vi flectere,
inclīnāre ♦ vt caput dēmittere.

bowels n alvus f, (fig) viscera ntpl.

bower n umbrāculum nt, trichila f.

bowl n (cooking) catīnus m;
(drinking) calix m; (mixing wine)
crātēra f; (ball) pila f ♦ vt volvere;
~ over prōruere.

bow-legged adj valgus.

bowler n (game) dator m.

bowstring n nervus m.

box n arca f, capsa f; (for clothes)
cista f; (for medicine) pyxis f; (for
perfume) alabaster m; (tree) buxus
f; (wood) buxum nt; (blow on ears)
alapa f ♦ vt inclūdere; **~ the ears
of** alapam dūcere (dat), colaphōs
īnfringere (dat) ♦ vi (fight) pugnīs
certāre.

boxer n pugil m.

boxing n pugilātiō f.

boxing glove n caestus m.

boy n puer m; **become a ~ again**
repuerāscere.

boycott vt repudiāre.

boyhood n pueritia f; **from ~ ā**
puerō.

boyish adj puerīlis.

boyishly adv puerīliter.

brace n (building) fībula f; (strap)
fascia f; (pair) pār nt ♦ vt
adligāre; (strengthen) firmāre.

bracelet n armilla f.

bracing adj (air) salūbris.

bracken n filix f.

bracket n uncus m.

brackish adj amārus.

bradawl n terebra f.

brag vi glōriārī, sē iactāre.

braggart n glōriōsus m.

braid vt nectere.

brain n cerebrum nt; ingenium nt.

brainless adj sōcors, stultus.

brainy adj ingeniōsus.

brake n (wood) dūmētum nt; (on
wheel) sufflāmen nt.

bramble n rubus m.

bran n furfur m.

branch n rāmus m; (kind) genus nt
♦ vi: **~ out** rāmōs porrigere.

branching adj rāmōsus.

brand n (fire) torris m, fax f; (mark)
nota f; (sword) ēnsis m; (variety)
genus nt ♦ vt (mark) inūrere;
(stigma) notāre; **~ new** recēns.

brandish vt vibrāre.

brass n orichalcum nt.

bravado n ferōcitās f; **out of ~** per speciem ferōcitātis.

brave adj fortis, ācer ♦ vt adīre, patī.

bravely adv fortiter, ācriter.

bravery n fortitūdō f, virtūs f.

bravo interj bene, euge, macte.

brawl n rixa f, iūrgium nt ♦ vi rixārī.

brawn n lacertī mpl.

brawny adj lacertōsus, rōbustus.

bray vi rūdere.

brazen adj aēneus; (fig) impudēns.

brazier n foculus m.

breach n (in wall) ruīna f; (of friendship) dissēnsiō f ♦ vt perfringere; **~ of trust** mala fidēs; **commit a ~ of promise** prōmissīs nōn stāre.

breach of the peace n iūrgium nt, tumultus m.

bread n pānis m.

breadth n lātitūdō f; **in ~** in lātitūdinem (acc).

break vt frangere, perfringere; **~ down** vt īnfringere, dīruere; **~ in** vt (animal) domāre; **~ into pieces** dīrumpere; **~ off** vt abrumpere, dēfringere; (action) dīrimere; **~ open** effringere, solvere; **~ through** vt fus interrumpere; **~ up** vt dissolvere, interrumpere; **~ one's word** fidem fallere, violāre; **without ~ing the law** salvīs lēgibus ♦ vi rumpī, frangī; (day) illūcēscere; (strength) dēficere; **~ off** vi dēsinere; **~ into** intrāre; **~ out** vi ērumpere; (sore) recrūdēscere; (trouble) exārdēscere; **~ up** vi dīlābī, dissolvī; (meeting) dīmittī; **~ through** vi inrumpere; **~ with** dissidēre ab ♦ n intermissiō f, intervallum nt.

breakable adj fragilis.

breakage n frāctum nt.

breakdown n (activity) mora f;

(health) dēbilitās f.

breaker n fluctus m.

breakfast n ientāculum nt, prandium nt ♦ vi ientāre, prandēre.

breakwater n mōlēs f.

bream n sparulus m.

breast n pectus nt; (woman's) mamma f; **make a clean ~ of** cōnfitērī.

breastplate n lōrīca f.

breastwork n lōrīca f, pluteus m.

breath n spīritus m, anima f; (bad) hālitus m; (quick) anhēlitus m; (of wind) aura f, adflātus m; **below one's ~** mussitāns; **catch one's ~** obstipēscere; **hold one's ~** animam comprimere, continēre; **take a ~** spīritum dūcere; **take one's ~ away** exanimāre; **waste one's ~** operam perdere; **out of ~** exanimātus.

breathable adj spīrābilis.

breathe vt, vi spīrāre, respīrāre; (quickly) anhēlāre; **~ again** respīrāre; **~ in** vt, vi spīritum dūcere; **~ out** vt, vi exspīrāre, exhālāre; **~ upon** īnspīrāre (dat), adflāre (dat); **~ one's last** animam agere, efflāre.

breathing n hālitus m, respīrātiō f.

breathing space n respīrātiō f.

breathless adj exanimātus.

breeches n brācae fpl.

breed n genus nt ♦ vt generāre, prōcreāre; (raise) ēducāre, alere; (fig) adferre, efficere; **well-bred** generōsus.

breeder n (animal) mātrīx f; (man) generātor m; (fig) nūtrīx f.

breeding n (act) fētūra f; (manners) mōrēs mpl; **good ~** hūmānitās f.

breeze n aura f, flātus m.

breezy adj ventōsus; (manner) hilaris.

brevity n brevitās f.

brew vt coquere ♦ vi (fig) parārī,

imminēre.

bribe vt corrumpere ♦ vi largīrī
♦ n pecūnia f, mercēs f.

briber n corruptor m, largītor m.

bribery n ambitus m, largītiō f.

brick n later m ♦ adj latericius.

brickwork n latericium nt.

bridal adj nūptiālis; (bed) geniālis
♦ n nūptiae fpl.

bride n nūpta f.

bridegroom m marītus m.

bridge n pōns m ♦ vt pontem
impōnere (dat).

bridle n frēnum nt ♦ vt frēnāre,
īnfrēnāre.

brief adj brevis; **to be ~** nē longum
sit, nē multa.

briefly adv breviter, paucīs verbīs.

briefness n brevitās f.

brier n veprēs m, sentis m.

brig n liburna f.

brigade n legiō f; (cavalry) turma f.

brigadier n lēgātus m.

brigand n latrō m, praedō m.

brigandage n latrōcinium nt.

bright adj clārus, lūculentus; (sky)
serēnus; (intellect) ingeniōsus;
(manner) hilaris, laetus; **be ~**
lūcēre, splendēre.

brighten vt illūstrāre; laetificāre
♦ vi lūcēscere; (person) hilarem
fierī.

brightly adv clārē.

brightness n fulgor m, candor m;
(sky) serēnitās f.

brilliance n splendor m, fulgor m;
(style) nitor m, lumen nt, īnsignia
ntpl.

brilliant adj clārus, illūstris,
splendidus; (fig) īnsignis,
praeclārus, lūculentus.

brilliantly adv splendidē,
praeclārē, lūculentē.

brim n labrum nt, margō m; **fill to
the ~** explēre.

brimstone n sulfur nt.

brindled adj varius.

brine n salsāmentum nt.

bring vt ferre; (person) dūcere;
(charge) intendere; (to a place)
adferre, addūcere, advehere,
dēferre; (to a destination)
perdūcere; (to a worse state)
redigere; **~ about** vt efficere; **~
before** dēferre ad, referre ad; **~
back** vt (thing) referre; (person)
redūcere; **~ down** vt dēdūcere,
dēferre; **~ forth** (from store)
dēprōmere; (child) parere; (crops)
ferre, ēdere; **~ forward** vt (for
discussion) iactāre, iacere; (reason)
adferre; **~ home** (bride) dēdūcere;
(in triumph) dēportāre; **~ home to**
pervincere; **~ in** vt invehere,
indūcere, intrōdūcere; (import)
importāre; (revenue) reddere; **~
off** vt (success) reportāre; **~ on**
īnferre, importāre; (stage)
indūcere; **~ out** vt efferre; (book)
ēdere; (play) dare; (talent) ēlicere;
~ over perdūcere, trādūcere; **~ to
bear** adferre; **~ to light** nūdāre,
dētegere; **~ to pass** perficere,
peragere; **~ to shore** ad lītus
appellere; **~ together** contrahere,
cōgere; (enemies) conciliāre; **~ up**
vt (child) ēducāre, tollere; (troops)
admovēre; (topic) prōferre; **~
upon oneself** sibī cōnscīscere,
sibī contrahere.

brink n ōra f, margō f.

briny adj salsus.

brisk adj alacer, vegetus, ācer.

briskly adv ācriter.

briskness n alacritās f.

bristle n sēta f ♦ vi horrēre,
horrēscere.

bristly adj horridus, hirsūtus.

Britain n Brittania f.

Britons n Brittani mpl.

brittle adj fragilis.

broach vt (topic) in medium
prōferre.

broad adj lātus; (accent) lātus;

(*joke*) inurbānus; (*daylight*) multus.
broadcast vt dissēmināre.
broaden vt dīlātāre.
broadly adv lātē.
broadsword n gladius m.
brocade n Attalica ntpl.
brochure n libellus m.
brogue n pērō m.
broil n rixa f, iūrgium nt ♦ vt
torrēre.
broiling adj torridus.
broken adj frāctus; (*fig*) cōnfectus;
(*speech*) īnfrāctus.
broken-hearted adj dolōre
cōnfectus.
broker n īnstitor m.
bronze n aes nt ♦ adj aēneus,
aerātus.
brooch n fībula f.
brood n fētus m; (*fig*) gēns f ♦ vi
incubāre (*dat*); (*fig*) incubāre (*dat*),
fovēre; ~ over meditārī.
brook n rīvus m ♦ vt ferre, patī.
brooklet n rīvulus m.
broom n (*plant*) genista f; (*brush*)
scōpae fpl.
broth n iūs nt.
brother n frāter m; (*full*) germānus
m; ~ and sister frātrēs marītus mpl.
brotherhood n frāternitās f.
brother-in-law n lēvir m, uxōris
frāter m, sorōris marītus m.
brotherly adj frāternus.
brow n frōns f; (*eye*) supercilium
nt; (*hill*) dorsum nt.
browbeat vt obiūrgāre, exagitāre.
brown adj fulvus, spādīx; (*skin*)
adūstus.
browse vi pāscī, dēpāscī.
bruise vt atterere, frangere,
contundere ♦ n vulnus nt.
bruit vt pervulgāre.
brunt n vīs f; **bear the ~ of**
exhaurīre.
brush n pēniculus m; (*artist's*)
pēnicillus m; (*quarrel*) rixa f ♦ vt
verrere, dētergēre; (*teeth*)

dēfricāre; ~ **aside** vt aspernārī,
neglegere; ~ **up** vt (*fig*) excolere.
brushwood n virgulta ntpl; (*for
cutting*) sarmenta ntpl.
brusque adj parum cōmis.
brutal adj atrōx, saevus,
inhūmānus.
brutality n atrōcitās f, saevitia f.
brutally adv atrōciter, inhūmānē.
brute n bēlua f, bestia f.
brutish adj stolidus.
bubble n bulla f ♦ vi bullāre; ~
over effervēscere; ~ **up** scatēre.
buccaneer n praedō m, pīrāta m.
buck n cervus m ♦ vi exsultāre.
bucket n situla f, fidēlia f.
buckle n fībula f ♦ vt fībulā
nectere; ~ **to** accingī.
buckler n parma f.
buckram n carbasus m.
bucolic adj agrestis.
bucolics n būcolica ntpl.
bud n gemma f, flōsculus m ♦ vi
gemmāre.
budge vi movērī, cēdere.
budget n pūblicae pecūniae ratiō f
♦ vi: ~ **for** prōvidēre (*dat*).
buff adj lūteus.
buffalo n ūrus m.
buffet n (*blow*) alapa f; (*fig*) plāga f;
(*sideboard*) abacus m ♦ vt iactāre,
tundere.
buffoon n scurra m, balatrō m.
buffoonery n scurrīlitās f.
bug n cīmex m.
bugbear n terricula ntpl, terror m.
bugle n būcina f.
bugler n būcinātor m.
build vt aedificāre, struere; (*bridge*)
facere; (*road*) mūnīre; ~ **on** vt
(*add*) adstruere; (*hopes*) pōnere; ~
on sand in aquā fundāmenta
pōnere; ~ **up** vt exstruere; (*to
block*) inaedificāre; (*knowledge*)
īnstruere; ~ **castles in the air**
spem inānem pāscere ♦ n statūra
f.

builder n aedificātor m, structor m.
building n (act) aedificātiō f;
  (structure) aedificium nt.
bulb n bulbus m.
bulge vi tumēre, tumēscere,
  prōminēre ♦ vi tuberculum nt; (of
  land) locus prōminēns m.
bulk n māgnitūdō f, amplitūdō f;
  (mass) mōlēs f; (most) plērīque,
  māior pars.
bulky adj amplus, grandis.
bull n taurus m; ~'s taurīnus; **take
  the ~ by the horns** rem fortiter
  adgredī.
bulldog n Molossus m.
bullet n glāns f.
bulletin n libellus m.
bullion n aurum īnfectum nt,
  argentum īnfectum nt.
bullock n iuvencus m.
bully n obiūrgātor m, patruus m.
  ♦ vt obiūrgāre, exagitāre.
bulrush n scirpus m.
bulwark n prōpugnāculum nt; (fig)
  arx f.
bump n (swelling) tuber nt,
  tuberculum nt; (knock) ictus m
  ♦ vi: **~ against** offendere.
bumper n plēnum pōculum nt
  ♦ adj plēnus, māximus.
bumpkin n rūsticus m.
bumptious adj adrogāns.
bunch n fasciculus m; (of berries)
  racēmus m.
bundle n fascis m; (of hay)
  manipulus m ♦ vt obligāre.
bung n obtūrāmentum nt ♦ vt
  obtūrāre.
bungle vt male gerere.
bunk n lectus m, lectulus m.
buoy n cortex m ♦ vt sublevāre.
buoyancy n levitās f.
buoyant adj levis; (fig) hilaris.
bur n lappa f.
burden n onus nt; beast of ~
  iūmentum nt ♦ vt onerāre; **be a ~**
  oneri esse.

burdensome adj gravis, molestus.
bureau n scrīnium nt.
burgeon vi gemmāre.
burgess n mūniceps m.
burgh n mūnicipium nt.
burgher n mūniceps m.
burglar n fūr m.
burglary n fūrtum nt.
burial n fūnes nt, humātiō f,
  sepultūra f.
burin n caelum nt.
burlesque n imitātiō f ♦ vt per
  iocum imitārī.
burly adj crassus.
burn vt incendere, ūrere; (to ashes)
  cremāre ♦ vi ārdēre, flāgrāre; ~
  up ambūrere, combūrere,
  exūrere; **be ~ed down** dēflagrāre;
  ~ out exstinguī; ~ **the midnight
  oil** lūcubrāre ♦ n (MED) ambūstum
  nt.
burning adj igneus.
burnish vt polīre.
burrow n cunīculus m ♦ vi
  dēfodere.
burst vt rumpere, dīrumpere ♦ vi
  rumpī, dīrumpī; ~ in inrumpere;
  ~ **into tears** in lacrimās effundī; ~
  open refringere; ~ out
  ērumpere, prōrumpere; ~ out
  laughing cachinnum tollere; ~
  through perrumpere per (acc); ~
  upon offerrī (dat), invādere ♦ n
  ēruptiō f; (noise) fragor m; ~ of
  applause clāmōrēs mpl; **with a ~
  of speed** citātō gradū, citātō equō.
bury vt sepelīre, humāre;
  (ceremony) efferre; (hiding)
  condere; (things) dēfodere; (fig)
  obruere; ~ **the hatchet** amīcitiam
  reconciliāre.
bush n frutex m; dūmus m; **beat
  about the ~** circuitiōne ūtī.
bushel n medimnus m.
bushy adj fruticōsus; (thick)
  dēnsus; (hair) hirsūtus.
busily adv strēnuē, impigrē.

business n negōtium nt;
(*occupation*) ars f, quaestus m;
(*public life*) forum nt; (*matter*) rēs f;
it is your ~ tuum est; **make it one's**
~ **to** id agere ut; **you have no** ~ **to**
nōn tē decet (*infin*); **mind one's**
own ~ suum negōtium agere; ~
days diēs fāstī mpl.
businessman n negōtiātor m.
buskin n cothurnus m.
bust n imāgō f.
bustle vi trepidāre, festīnāre; ~
about discurrere.
busy adj negōtiōsus, occupātus;
(*active*) operōsus, impiger,
strēnuus; ~ **in** occupātus (*abl*); ~
on intentus (*dat*); **keep** ~ vt
exercēre; ~ **oneself with**
pertractāre, studēre (*dat*).
busybody n **be a** ~ aliēnīs negōtīs
sē immiscēre.
but conj sed, at; (*2nd place*) autem,
tamen ♦ adv modo ♦ prep praeter
(*acc*); **nothing** ~ nihil nisī; ~ **that,**
what quīn; **not** ~ **what** nihilōminus.
butcher n lanius m ♦ vt trucīdāre.
butcher's shop n laniēna f
butchery n strāgēs f, occīdiō f.
butler n prōmus m.
butt n (*cask*) cadus m; (*of ridicule*)
lūdibrium nt ♦ vi arietāre; ~ **in**
interpellāre.
butter n būtyrum nt.
butterfly n pāpiliō m.
buttock n clūnis m/f.
button n bulla f.
buttonhole vt (*fig*) dētinēre,
prēnsāre.
buttress n antērides fpl ♦ vt
fulcīre.
buxom adj nitidus.
buy vt emere; ~ **provisions**
obsōnāre; ~ **back** vt redimere; ~
off vt redimere; ~ **up** vt coemere.
buyer n emptor m; (*at auctions*)
manceps m.

buzz n strīdor m, susurrus m ♦ vi
strīdere, susurrāre.
buzzard n būteō m.
by prep (*near*) ad (*acc*), apud (*acc*);
prope (*acc*); (*along*) secundum
(*acc*); (*past*) praeter (*acc*); (*agent*) ā,
ab (*abl*); (*instrument*) abl; (*time*)
ante (*acc*); (*oath*) per (*acc*) ♦ adv
prope, iuxtā; ~ **and** ~ mox; **be** ~
adesse, astāre; ~ **force of arms** vī
et armās; ~ **land and sea** terrī
marique.
bygone adj praeteritus.
bystander n arbiter m; pl
circumstantēs mpl.
byway n dēverticulum nt, trāmes
m, sēmita f.
byword n prōverbium nt.

C

cabal n factiō f.
cabbage n brassica f, caulis m.
cabin n casa f; (*ship*) cubiculum nt.
cabinet n armārium nt.
cable n fūnis m; (*anchor*) ancorāle
nt.
cache n thēsaurus m.
cachet n nota f.
cackle vi strepere n ♦ strepitus m,
clangor m.
cacophonous adj dissonus.
cacophony n vōcēs dissonae fpl.
cadaverous adj cadāverōsus.
cadence n clausula numerōsa f,
numerus m.
cadet n (*son*) nātū minor; (*MIL*)
contubernālis m.
cage n cavea f ♦ vt inclūdere.
caitiff n ignāvus m.
cajole vt blandīrī, dēlēnīre.
cake n placenta f.
calamitous adj exitiōsus,
calamitōsus.
calamity n calamitās f, malum nt;
(*MIL*) clādēs f.
calculate vt ratiōnem dūcere,

inīre.
calculation n ratiō f.
calculator n ratiōcinātor m.
calendar n fāstī mpl.
calends n Kalendae fpl.
calf n (animal) vitulus m, vitula f;
(leg) sūra f.
calibre n (fig) ingenium nt,
auctōritās f.
call vt vocāre; (name) appellāre,
nōmināre; (aloud) clāmāre; (to a
place) advocāre, convocāre; ~
aside sēvocāre; ~ **down** (curse)
dētestārī; ~ **for** vt fus postulāre,
requīrere; ~ **forth** ēvocāre,
excīre, ēlicere; ~ **in** vt advocāre;
~ **together** convocāre; ~ **on** vt fus
(for help) implōrāre; (visit)
salūtāre; ~ **off** vt āvocāre,
revocāre; ~ **out** vi exclāmāre; ~
up vt (dead) excitāre, ēlicere;
(MIL) ēvocāre ♦ n vōx f, clāmor m;
(summons) invītātiō f; (visit)
salūtātiō f.
caller n salūtātor m.
calling n ars f, quaestus m.
callous adj dūrus; **become** ~
obdūrēscere.
callow adj rudis.
calm adj tranquillus, placidus;
(mind) aequus ♦ vi: ~ **down** (fig)
dēfervēscere ♦ vt sēdāre,
tranquillāre ♦ n tranquillitās f;
dead ~ (at sea) malacia f.
calmly adv tranquillē, placidē;
aequō animō.
calumniate vt obtrectāre,
crīminārī; (falsely) calumniārī.
calumniator n obtrectātor m.
calumny n opprobria ntpl,
obtrectātiō f.
calve vi parere.
cambric n linteum nt.
camel n camēlus m.
camouflage n dissimulātiō f ♦ vt
dissimulāre.
camp n castra ntpl; **summer** ~

aestīva ntpl; **winter** ~ hīberna ntpl;
in ~ sub pellibus; **pitch** ~ castra
pōnere; **strike** ~ castra movēre
♦ adj castrēnsis ♦ vi tendere.
campaign n stīpendium nt, bellum
nt; (rapid) expedītiō f ♦ vi bellum
gerere, stīpendium merēre.
campaigner n mīles m; **old** ~
veterānus m; (fig) veterātor m.
campbed n grabātus m.
camp followers n lixae mpl.
oan n hirnea f.
can vi posse (+ infin); (know how)
scīre.
canaille n vulgus nt, plebs f.
canal n fossa nāvigābilis f, eurīpus
m.
cancel vt indūcere, abrogāre.
cancellation n (writing) litūra f;
(law) abrogātiō f.
cancer n cancer m; (fig) carcinōma
nt, ulcus nt.
cancerous adj (fig) ulcerōsus.
candelabrum n candēlābrum nt.
candid adj ingenuus, apertus,
līber, simplex.
candidate n petītor m; **be a** ~ **for**
petere.
candidature n petītiō f.
candidly adv ingenuē.
candle n candēla f.
candlestick n candēlabrum nt.
candour n ingenuitās f, simplicitās
f, lībertās f.
cane n (reed) harundō f; (for
walking, punishing) virga f ♦ vt
verberāre.
canine adj canīnus.
canister n capsula f.
canker n (plants) rōbigō f; (fig)
aerūgō f, carcinōma nt ♦ vt
corrumpere.
Cannae n Cannae fpl.
cannibal n anthrōpophagus m.
cannon n tormentum nt.
cannot nōn posse, nequīre; **I** ~ **help
but** . . . facere nōn possum quīn . . .

(*subj*), nōn possum nōn ... (*infin*).

canny *adj* prūdens, prōvidus, cautus, circumspectus.

canoe *n* linter *f*.

canon *n* nōrma *f*, rēgula *f*; (*ECCL*) canonicus *m*.

canopy *n* aulaeum *nt*.

cant *n* fūcus *m*, fūcāta verba *ntpl* ♦ *vt* oblīquāre.

cantankerous *adj* importūnus.

cantankerousness *n* importūnitās *f*.

canter *n* lēnis cursus *m* ♦ *vi* lēniter currere.

canticle *n* canticum *nt*.

canto *n* carmen *nt*.

canton *n* pāgus *m*.

canvas *n* carbasus *m*, linteum *nt* ♦ *adj* carbaseus; **under ~** sub pellibus.

canvass *vi* ambīre ♦ *vt* prēnsāre, circumīre.

canvassing *n* ambitus *m*, ambitiō *f*.

cap *n* pilleus *m*; (*priest's*) galērus *m*, apex *m*.

capability *n* facultās *f*, potestās *f*.

capable *adj* capāx, doctus, perītus.

capably *adv* bene, doctē.

capacious *adj* capāx, amplus.

capacity *n* capācitās *f*, amplitūdō *f*; (*mind*) ingenium *nt*.

caparison *n* ephippium *nt*.

cape *n* (*GEOG*) prōmunturium *nt*; (*dress*) chlamys *f*.

caper *vi* saltāre; (*animal*) lascīvīre ♦ *n* saltus *m*.

capering *n* lascivia *f*.

capital *adj* (*chief*) praecipuus, prīnceps; (*excellent*) ēgregius; (*law*) capitālis; **convict of a ~ offence** capitis damnāre ♦ *n* (*town*) caput *nt*; (*money*) sors *f*; (*class*) negōtiātorēs *mpl*; **make ~ out of** ūtī (*abl*).

capitalist *n* faenerātor *m*.

capital punishment *n* capitis supplicum *nt*.

capitation tax *n* capitum exāctiō *f*.

Capitol *n* Capitolium *nt*.

capitulate *vi* sē dēdere; **troops who have ~d** dēditīciī *mpl*.

capitulation *n* dēditiō *f*.

capon *n* capō *m*.

caprice *n* libīdō *f*, incōnstantia *f*.

capricious *adj* incōnstāns, levis.

capriciously *adv* incōnstanter, leviter.

capriciousness *n* incōnstantia *f*, libīdō *f*.

capsize *vt* ēvertere ♦ *vi* ēvertī.

captain *n* dux *m*, praefectus *m*, prīnceps *m*; (*MIL*) centuriō *m*; (*naval*) nāvarchus *m*; (*of merchant ship*) magister *m* ♦ *vt* praeesse (*dat*), dūcere.

captaincy *n* centuriātus *m*.

caption *n* caput *nt*.

captious *adj* mōrōsus; (*question*) captiōsus.

captiously *adv* mōrōsē.

captiousness *n* mōrōsitās *f*.

captivate *vt* capere, dēlēnīre, adlicere.

captive *n* captīvus *m*.

captivity *n* captīvitās *f*, vincula *ntpl*.

captor *n* (*by storm*) expugnātor *m*; victor *m*.

capture *n* (*by storm*) expugnātiō *f* ♦ *vt* capere.

car *n* currus *m*.

caravan *n* commeātus *m*.

carbuncle *n* (*MED*) fūrunculus *m*; (*stone*) acaustus *m*.

carcass *n* cadāver *nt*.

card *n* charta *f*; (*ticket*) tessera *f*; (*wool*) pecten *m* ♦ *vt* pectere.

cardamom *n* amōmum *nt*.

cardinal *adj* praecipuus; **~ point** cardō *m* ♦ *n* (*ECCL*) cardinālis.

care *n* cūra *f*; (*anxiety*) sollicitūdō *f*; (*attention*) dīligentia *f*; (*charge*) custōdia *f*; **take ~** cavēre; **take ~ of** cūrāre ♦ *vi* cūrāre; **~ for** *vt fus* (*look after*) cūrāre; (*like*) amāre; **I don't ~** nīl moror; **I couldn't care less about ...** flocci nōn faciō ..., pendō; **I don't ~ about** mittō, nihil moror; **for all I ~** per mē.

career *n* curriculum *nt*; (*POL*) cursus honōrum; (*completed*) rēs gestae *fpl* ♦ *vi* ruere, volāre.

carefree *adj* sēcūrus.

careful *adj* (*cautious*) cautus; (*attentive*) dīligēns, attentus; (*work*) accūrātus.

carefully *adv* cautē, dīligenter, attentē; accūrātē.

careless *adj* incautus, neglegēns.

carelessly *adv* incautē, neglegenter.

carelessness *n* incūria *f*, neglegentia *f*.

caress *vt* fovēre, blandīrī ♦ *n* blandīmentum *nt*, amplexus *m*.

cargo *n* onus *nt*.

caricature *n* (*picture*) gryllus *m*; (*fig*) imāgō dētorta *f* ♦ *vt* dētorquēre.

carmine *n* coccum *nt* ♦ *adj* coccineus.

carnage *n* strāgēs *f*, caedēs *f*.

carnal *adj* corporeus; (*pleasure*) libīdinōsus.

carnival *n* fēriae *fpl*.

carol *n* carmen *nt* ♦ *vi* cantāre.

carouse *vi* perpōtāre, cōmissārī ♦ *n* cōmissātiō *f*.

carp *vi* obtrectāre; **~ at** carpere, rōdere.

carpenter *n* faber *m*, lignārius *m*.

carpet *n* tapēte *m*.

carriage *n* (*conveying*) vectūra *f*; (*vehicle*) vehiculum *nt*; (*for journeys*) raeda *f*, petorritum *nt*; (*for town*) carpentum *nt*, pīlentum *nt*; (*deportment*) gestus *m*, incessus *m*; **~ and pair** bīgae *fpl*; **~ and four** quadrīgae *fpl*.

carrier *n* vector *m*; (*porter*) bāiulus *m*; **letter ~** tabellārius *m*.

carrion *n* cadāver *nt*.

carrot *n* carōta *f*.

carry *vt* portāre, vehere, ferre, gerere; (*law*) perferre; (*by assault*) expugnāre; **~ away** auferre, āvehere; (*by force*) rapere; (*with emotion*) efferre; **~ all before one** ēvincere; **~ along** (*building*) dūcere; **~ back** reportāre; revehere, referre; **~ down** dēportāre, dēvehere; **~ in** invehere, intrōferre; **~ off** auferre, asportāre, āvehere; (*by force*) abripere, ēripere; (*prize*) ferre, reportāre; (*success*) bene gerere; **~ on** vi gerere; (*profession*) exercēre; **~ out** *vi* efferre, ēgerere, ēvehere; (*task*) exsequī; **~ out an undertaking** rem suscipere; **~ over** trānsportāre, trānsferre; **~ the day** vincere; **~ one's point** pervincere; **~ through** perferre; **~ to** adferre, advehere; **~ up** subvehere ♦ *vi* (*sound*) audīrī; **~ on** vi pergere; (*flirt*) lascīvīre.

cart *n* plaustrum *nt*; carrus *nt*; **put the ~ before the horse** praeposterum dīcere ♦ *vt* plaustrō vehere.

Carthage *n* Carthāgō, Carthāginis *f*.

Carthaginian *adj* Carthāginiēnsis; Pūnicus; **the ~s** Poenī *mpl*.

carthorse *n* iūmentum *nt*.

carve *vt* sculpere; (*on surface*) caelāre; (*meat*) secāre; **~ out** exsculpere.

carver *n* caelātor *m*.

carving *n* caelātūra *f*.

cascade *n* cataracta *f*.

case *n* (*instance*) exemplum *nt*, rēs *f*; (*legal*) āctiō *f*, līs *f*, causa *f*; (*plight*) tempus *nt*; (*GRAM*) cāsus *m*; (*receptacle*) thēca *f*, involucrum *nt*; **in ~** sī; (*to prevent*) nē; **in any ~** utut est rēs; **in that ~** ergō; **such is**

the ~ sic sē rēs habet; **civil ~**
causa prīvāta; **criminal ~** causa
pūblica; **win a ~** causam, lītem
obtinēre; **lose a ~** causam, lītem
āmittere.

casement n fenestra f.

cash n nummī mpl; (ready)
numerātum nt, praesēns pecūnia
f; **pay ~** ex arcā absolvere,
repraesentāre.

cash box n arca f.

cashier n dispēnsātor m ♦ vt (MIL)
exauctōrāre.

cash payment n repraesentātiō f.

cask n cūpa f.

casket n arcula f, pyxis f.

casque n galea f, cassis f.

cast vt iacere; (account) inīre;
(eyes) conicere; (lots) conicere;
(covering) exuere; (metal) fundere;
~ ashore ēicere; **~ away** prōicere;
~ down dēicere; (humble) abicere;
~ in one's teeth exprobrāre; **~
lots** sortīrī; **~ off** vi abicere,
exuere; **~ out** prōicere, ēicere,
pellere ♦ n iactus m; (moulding)
typus m, fōrma f; **with a ~ in the
eye** paetus m.

castanet n crotalum nt.

castaway n ēiectus m.

caste n ōrdō m.

castigate vt animadvertere,
castīgāre.

castigation n animadversiō f,
castīgātiō f.

castle n arx f, castellum nt.

castrate vt castrāre.

casual adj fortuītus; (person)
neglegēns.

casually adv temerē.

casualty n īnfortūnium nt, pl:
casualties occīsī mpl.

casuist n sophistēs m.

cat n fēlēs f.

cataclysm n dīluvium nt, ruīna f.

catalogue n index m.

catapult n catapulta f, ballista f.

cataract n cataracta f.

catarrh n gravēdō f; **liable to ~**
gravēdinōsus.

catastrophe n calamitās f, ruīna f.

catastrophic adj calamitōsus,
exitiōsus.

catch vt capere, dēprehendere,
excipere; (disease) contrahere,
nancīscī; (fire) concipere,
comprehendere; (meaning)
intellegere; **~ at** captāre; **~ out** vi
dēprehendere; **~ up with** adsequī;
~ birds aucupārī; **~ fish** piscārī
♦ n bolus m.

categorical adj (statement) plānus.

categorically adv sine exceptiōne.

category n numerus m, genus nt.

cater vi obsōnāre.

cateran n praedātor m.

caterer n obsōnātor m.

caterpillar n ērūca f.

caterwaul vi ululāre.

catgut n chorda f.

catharsis n pūrgātiō f.

cathedral n aedēs f.

catholic adj generālis.

catkin n iūlus m.

cattle n (collectively) pecus nt;
(singly) pecus f; (for plough)
armenta ntpl.

cattle breeder n pecuārius m.

cattle market n forum boārium nt.

cattle thief n abāctor m.

cauldron n cortīna f.

cause n causa f, (person) auctor m;
(law) causa f, (party) partēs fpl;
give ~ for māteriam dare (gen);
make common ~ with facere cum,
stāre ab; **plead a ~** causam
dīcere; **in the ~ of** prō (abl);
without ~ iniūriā ♦ vt efficere ut
(+ subj), facere, facessere (with
ut); cūrāre (with gerundive);
(feelings) movēre, inicere, ciēre.

causeless adj vānus, sine causā.

causeway n agger m.

caustic adj (fig) mordāx.

cauterize vt adūrere.
caution n (wariness) cautiō f,
prūdentia f; (warning) monitum nt
♦ vt monēre, admonēre.
cautious adj cautus, prōvidus,
prūdens.
cautiously adv cautē, prūdenter.
cavalcade n pompa f.
cavalier n eques m ♦ adj adrogāns.
cavalierly adv adroganter.
cavalry n equitēs mpl, equitātus m
♦ adj equester; **troop of ~** turma f.
cavalryman n eques m.
cave n spēlunca f, caverna f;
antrum nt; **~ in** vi concidere,
conlābī.
cavern n spēlunca f, caverna f.
cavil vi cavillārī; **~ at** carpere,
cavillārī ♦ n captiō f, cavillātiō f.
cavity n caverna f, cavum nt.
cavort vi saltāre.
caw vi cornīcārī.
cease vi dēsinere, dēsistere.
ceaseless adj adsiduus, perpetuus.
ceaselessly adv adsiduē, perpetuō.
cedar n cedrus f ♦ adj cedrinus.
cede vt cēdere, concēdere.
ceiling n tēctum nt; (panelled)
lacūnar nt, laqueārium nt.
celebrate vt (rite) celebrāre,
agitāre; (in crowds) frequentāre;
(person, theme) laudāre, celebrāre,
dīcere.
celebrated adj praeclārus,
illūstris, nōtus; **the ~** ille.
celebration n celebrātiō f; (rite)
sollemne nt.
celebrity n celebritās f, fāma f;
(person) vir illūstris.
celerity n celeritās f, vēlōcitās f.
celery n apium nt.
celestial adj caelestis; dīvīnus.
celibacy n caelibātus m.
celibate n caelebs m.
cell n cella f.
cellar n cella f.
cement n ferrūmen nt ♦ vt

coagmentāre.
cemetery n sepulchrētum nt.
cenotaph n tumulus honōrārius,
tumulus inānis m.
censer n tūribulum nt, acerra f.
censor n cēnsor m ♦ vt cēnsēre.
censorious adj cēnsōrius,
obtrectātor.
censorship n cēnsūra f.
censure n reprehēnsiō f,
animadversiō f; (censor's) nota f
♦ vt reprehendere,
animadvertere, incrēpāre;
notāre.
census n cēnsus m.
cent n: **one per ~** centēsima f; **12**
per ~ per annum centēsima f (ie
monthly).
centaur n centaurus m.
centaury n (plant) centaurēum nt.
centenarian n centum annōs nātus
m, nāta f.
centenary n centēsimus annus m.
centesimal adj centēsimus.
central adj medius.
centralize vt in ūnum locum
cōnferre; (power) ad ūnum
dēferre.
centre n centrum nt, media pars f;
the ~ of medius.
centuple adj centuplex.
centurion n centuriō m.
century n (MIL) centuria f; (time)
saeculum nt.
ceramic adj fictilis.
cereal n frūmentum nt.
ceremonial adj sollemnis ♦ n rītus
m.
ceremonious adj (rite) sollemnis;
(person) officiōsus.
ceremoniously adv sollemniter;
officiōsē.
ceremony n caerimōnia f, rītus m;
(politeness) officium nt; (pomp)
apparātus m; **master of**
ceremonies dēsignātor m.
cerise n coccum nt ♦ adj

coccineus.

certain adj (*sure*) certus; (*future*) explōrātus; **a ~** quīdam, quaedam, quoddam; **be ~** (*know*) prō certō scīre/habēre.

certainly adv certē, certō, sine dubiō; (*yes*) ita, māximē, (*concessive*) quidem.

certainty n (*thing*) certum nt; (*belief*) fidēs f; **for a ~** prō certō, explōrātē; **regard as a ~** prō explōrātō habēre.

certificate n testimōnium nt.

certify vt (*writing*) recognōscere; (*fact*) adfirmāre, testificārī.

cessation n fīnis m; (*from labour*) quiēs f; (*temporary*) intermissiō f; (*of hostilities*) indutiae fpl.

chafe vt ūrere; (*fig*) inrītāre ♦ vi stomachārī.

chaff n palea f ♦ vt lūdere.

chaffinch n fringilla f.

chagrin n dolor m, stomachus m ♦ vt stomachum facere (*dat*), sollicitāre.

chain n catēna f; (*for neck*) torquis m; (*sequence*) seriēs f; **~s** pl vincula ntpl ♦ vt vincīre.

chair n sella f; (*of office*) sella curūlis f; (*sedan*) sella gestātōria f, lectīca f; (*teacher's*) cathedra f.

chairman n (*at meeting*) magister m; (*of debate*) disceptātor m.

chalet n casa f.

chalice n calix m.

chalk n crēta f.

chalky adj crētōsus.

challenge n prōvocātiō f ♦ vt prōvocāre, lacessere; (*statement*) in dubium vocāre; (*fig*) invītāre, dēposcere.

challenger n prōvocātor m.

chamber n conclāve nt; (*bed*) cubiculum nt; (*bridal*) thalamus m; (*parliament*) cūria f.

chamberlain n cubiculārius m.

chambermaid n serva f, ancilla f.

chameleon n chamaeleōn f.

chamois n rūpicapra f.

champ vt mandere.

champion n prōpugnātor m, patrōnus m; (*winner*) victor m ♦ vt favēre (*dat*), adesse (*dat*).

chance n fors f, fortūna f, cāsus m; (*opportunity*) occāsiō f; potestās f, facultās f; (*prospect*) spēs f; **game of ~** ālea f; **by ~** cāsū, fortuītō; **have an eye to the main ~** forō ūtī; **on the ~ of** sī forte ♦ adj fortuītus ♦ vi accidere, ēvenīre; **it chanced that ... accidit ut ... (+*subj*); **~ upon** vt fus incidere in, invenīre ♦ vi periclitārī.

chancel n absis f.

chancellor n cancellārius m.

chancy adj dubius, perīculōsus.

chandelier n candēlābrum nt.

chandler n candēlārum prōpōla m.

change n mūtātiō f, commūtātiō f, permūtātiō f; (*POL*) rēs novae fpl; (*alternation*) vicēs fpl, vicissitūdō f; (*money*) nummī minōrēs mpl ♦ vt mūtāre, commūtāre, permūtāre ♦ vi mūtārī; **~ hands** abaliēnarī; **~ places** ōrdinem permūtāre, inter sē loca permūtāre.

changeable adj incōnstāns, mūtābilis.

changeableness n incōnstantia f, mūtābilitās f.

changeful adj varius.

changeless adj cōnstāns, immūtābilis.

changeling adj subditus m.

channel n canālis m; (*sea*) fretum nt; (*irrigation*) rīvus m; (*groove*) sulcus m.

chant vt cantāre, canere ♦ n cantus m.

chaos n chaos nt; (*fig*) perturbātiō f.

chaotic adj perturbātus.

chap n rīma f; (*man*) homō m.

chapel n sacellum nt, aedicula f.

chaplain n diāconus m.
chaplet n corōna f, sertum nt.
chaps n (animal) mālae fpl.
chapter n caput nt.
char vt ambūrere.
character n (inborn) indolēs f, ingenium nt, nātūra f; (moral) mōrēs mpl; (reputation) existimātiō f; (kind) genus nt; (mark) signum nt, littera f; (THEAT) persōna f, partēs fpl; **sustain a ~** persōnam gerere, I know his ~ sciō quālis sit.
characteristic adj proprius ♦ n proprium nt.
characteristically adv suō mōre.
characterize vt dēscrībere; proprium esse (gen).
charcoal n carbō m.
charge n (law) accūsātiō f, crīmen nt; (MIL) impetus m, dēcursus m; (cost) impēnsa f; (task) mandātum nt, onus nt; (trust) cūra f, tūtēla f; **bring a ~ against** lītem intendere (dat); **entertain a ~ against** nōmen recipere (gen); **give in ~** in custōdiam trādere; **put in ~ of** praeficere (acc, dat); **be in ~ of** praeesse (dat) ♦ vt (law) accūsāre; (falsely) īnsimulāre; (MIL) incurrere in (acc), signa īnferre in (acc), impetum facere in (acc); (duty) mandāre; (cost) ferre, īnferre; (empty space) complēre; (trust) committere; (speech) hortārī; **~ to the account of** expēnsum ferre (dat).
chargeable adj obnoxius.
charger n (dish) lānx f; (horse) equus m.
charily adv cautē, parcē.
chariot n currus m; (racing) quadrīgae fpl; (war) essedum nt.
charioteer n aurīga m; (war) essedārius m.
charitable adj benevolus, benignus.

charitably adv benevolē, benignē.
charity n amor m, benignitās f; līberālitās f.
charlatan n planus m.
charm n (spell) carmen nt; (amulet) bulla f, (fig) blanditiae fpl, dulcēdō f, illecebra f; (beauty) venus f, lepōs m ♦ vt (magic) fascināre; (delight) dēlectāre, dēlēnīre.
charming adj venustus, lepidus; (speech) blandus; (scenery) amoenus.
charmingly adv venustē, blandē.
chart n tabula f.
charter n diplōma nt ♦ vt condūcere.
chary adj (cautious) cautus; (sparing) parcus.
chase vt fugāre; (hunt) vēnārī; (pursue) persequī, īnsequī; (engrave) caelāre; **~ away** pellere, abigere ♦ n vēnātus m, vēnātiō f; (pursuit) īnsectātiō f.
chaser n (in metal) caelātor m.
chasm n hiātus m.
chaste adj castus, pudīcus; (style) pūrus.
chasten vt castīgāre, corrigere.
chastener n castīgātor m, corrēctor m.
chastise vt castīgāre, animadvertere.
chastisement n castīgātiō f, poena f.
chastity n castitās f, pudīcitia f.
chat vi colloquī, sermōcinārī ♦ n sermō m, colloquium nt.
chatelaine n domina f.
chattels n bona ntpl, rēs mancipī.
chatter vi garrīre; (teeth) crepitāre ♦ n garrulitās f, loquācitās f.
chatterbox n lingulāca m/f.
chatterer n garrulus m, loquāx m.
chattering adj garrulus, loquāx ♦ n garrulitās f, loquācitās f; (teeth) crepitus m.
cheap adj vīlis; **hold ~** parvī

cheapen vt pretium minuere (gen).

cheaply adv vīliter, parvō pretiō.

cheapness n vīlitās f.

cheat vt dēcipere, fraudāre, dēfraudāre, frustrārī ♦ n fraudātor m.

check vt cohibēre, coercēre; (movement) impedīre, inhibēre; (rebuke) reprehendere; (test) probāre ♦ n impedīmentum nt, mora f; (MIL) offēnsiō f; (rebuke) reprehēnsiō f; (test) probātiō f; (ticket) tessera f.

checkmate n incitae calcēs fpl ♦ vt ad incitās redigere.

cheek n gena f; (impudence) ōs nt; ~s pl mālae fpl; **how have you the ~ to say?** quō ōre dīcis?

cheekbone n maxilla f.

cheeky adj impudēns.

cheep vi pīpilāre.

cheer vt hilarāre, exhilarāre; hortārī; (in sorrow) cōnsōlārī ♦ vi clāmāre, adclāmāre; **~ up!** bonō animō es! ♦ n (shout) clāmor m, plausus m; (food) hospitium nt; (mind) animus m.

cheerful adj alacer, hilaris, laetus.

cheerfully adv hilare, laetē.

cheerfulness n hilaritās f.

cheerily adv hilare.

cheerless adj tristis, maestus.

cheerlessly adv triste.

cheery adj hilaris.

cheese n cāseus m.

chef n coquus m.

cheque n perscrīptiō f, syngrapha f.

chequer vt variāre.

chequered adj varius; (mosaic) tessellātus.

cherish vt fovēre, colere.

cherry n (fruit) cerasum nt; (tree) cerasus f.

chess n latrunculī mpl.

chessboard n abacus m.

chest n (box) arca f, arcula f; (body) pectus nt; **~ of drawers** armārium nt.

chestnut n castanea f ♦ adj (colour) spādīx.

chevalier n eques m.

chevaux-de-frise n ēricius m.

chew vt mandere.

chic adj expolītus, concinnus.

chicanery n (law) calumnia f; (fig) dolus m.

chick n pullus m.

chicken n pullus m; **don't count your ~s before they're hatched** adhūc tua messis in herbā est.

chicken-hearted adj timidus, ignāvus.

chick-pea n cicer nt.

chide vt reprehendere, increpāre, obiūrgāre.

chief n prīnceps m, dux m ♦ adj praecipuus, prīmus; **~ point** caput nt.

chief command n summa imperī.

chiefly adv in prīmīs, praesertim, potissimum.

chieftain n prīnceps m, rēgulus m.

chilblain n perniō m.

child n īnfāns m/f; puer m, puerulus m, puella f; fīlius m, fīlia f; **~'s play** lūdus m.

childbed n puerperium nt.

childbirth n partus m.

childhood n pueritia f; **from ~** ā puerō.

childish adj puerīlis.

childishly adv puerīliter.

childless adj orbus.

childlessness n orbitās f.

childlike adj puerīlis.

children n (pl) līberī mpl.

chill n frīgus nt ♦ adj frīgidus ♦ vt refrīgerāre.

chilly adj frīgidus, frīgidior.

chime n sonāre, canere; **~ in** interpellāre; (fig) cōnsonāre ♦ n sonus m.

chimera n chimaera f; (fig)
  somnium nt.
chimerical adj commentīcius.
chimney n camīnus m.
chin n mentum nt.
china n fictilia ntpl.
chink n rīma f; (sound) tinnītus m
  ♦ vi crepāre, tinnīre.
chip n assula f, fragmentum nt ♦ vt
  dolāre.
chirp vi pīpilare.
chirpy adj hilaris.
chisel n scalprum nt, scalpellum nt
  ♦ vt sculpere.
chit n (child) pūsiō m, puerulus m.
chitchat n sermunculī mpl.
chitterlings n hillae fpl.
chivalrous adj generōsus.
chivalry n virtūs f; (men) iuventūs
  f; (class) equitēs mpl.
chive n caepe nt.
chock n cuneus m.
chock-full adj refertus.
choice n dēlēctus m, ēlēctiō f; (of
  alternatives) optiō f ♦ adj lēctus,
  eximius, exquīsītus.
choiceness n ēlegantia f,
  praestantia f.
choir n chorus m.
choke vt suffocāre; (emotion)
  reprimere; (passage) obstruere.
choler n bīlis f; (anger) īra f,
  stomachus m.
choleric adj īrācundus.
choose vt legere, ēligere, dēligere;
  (alternative) optāre; (for office)
  dēsignāre; (with infin) velle, mālle.
chop vt concīdere; ~ off
  praecīdere ♦ n (meat) offa f.
chopper n secūris f.
choppy adj (sea) asper.
choral adj symphōniacus.
chord n (string) nervus m, chorda f.
chortle vi cachinnāre.
chorus n (singers) chorus m; (song)
  concentus m, symphōnia f; in ~
  unā vōce.

christen vt baptizāre.
Christian adj Christiānus.
Christianity n Christiānismus m.
chronic adj inveterātus; become ~
  inveterāscere.
chronicle n annālēs mpl, ācta
  pūblica ntpl ♦ vt in annālēs
  referre.
chronicler n annālium scrīptor m.
chronological adj: in ~ order
  servātō temporum ōrdine; make a
  ~ error temporibus errāre.
chronology n temporum ratiō f,
  temporum ōrdō m.
chronometer n hōrologium nt.
chubby adj pinguis.
chuck vt conicere; ~ out
  extrūdere.
chuckle vi rīdēre ♦ n rīsus m.
chum n sodālis m.
church n ecclēsia f.
churl n rūsticus m.
churlish adj difficilis, importūnus;
  avārus.
churlishly adv rūsticē, avārē.
churlishness n mōrōsitās f,
  avāritia f.
chute n (motion) lāpsus m; (place)
  dēclīve nt.
cicada n cicāda f.
cincture n cingulum nt.
cinder n cinis m.
cipher n numerus m, nihil nt; (code)
  notae fpl; in ~ per notās.
circle n orbis m, circulus m, gȳrus
  m; form a ~ in orbem cōnsistere
  ♦ vi sē circumagere, circumīre.
circlet n īnfula f.
circuit n ambitus m, circuitus m;
  (assizes) conventus m.
circuitous adj longus; a ~ route
  circuitus m; (speech) ambāgēs fpl.
circular adj rotundus.
circulate vt (news) pervulgāre ♦ vi
  circumagī; (news) circumferrī,
  percrēbrēscere.
circulation n ambitus m; be in ~ in

manibus esse; **go out of ~**
obsolēscere.
circumcise vt circumcīdere.
circumference n ambitus m.
circumlocution n ambāgēs fpl,
circuitiō f.
circumnavigate vt circumvehī.
circumscribe vt circumscrībere;
(restrict) coercēre, fīnīre.
circumspect adj cautus, prūdēns.
circumspection n cautiō f,
prūdentia f, circumspectiō f.
circumspectly adv cautē,
prūdenter.
circumstance n rēs f; **~s** rērum
status m; (wealth) rēs f; **as ~s arise**
ē rē nātā; **under the ~s** cum haec
ita sint, essent; **under no ~s**
nēquāquam.
circumstantial adj adventīcius;
(detailed) accūrātus; **~ evidence**
coniectūra f.
circumstantially adv accūrātē,
subtīliter.
circumvallation n circummūnītiō
f.
circumvent vt circumvenīre,
fallere.
circus n circus m.
cistern n lacus m, cisterna f.
citadel n arx f.
citation n (law) vocātiō f; (mention)
commemorātiō f.
cite vt in iūs vocāre; (quote)
commemorāre, prōferre.
citizen n cīvis m/f; (of provincial
town) mūniceps m; **fellow ~** cīvis
m/f; **Roman ~s** Quirītēs mpl ♦ adj
cīvīlis, cīvicus.
citizenship n cīvitās f; **deprived of
~** capite dēminūtus; **loss of ~**
capitis dēminūtiō f.
citron n (fruit) citrum nt; (tree)
citrus f.
city n urbs f, oppidum nt.
civic adj cīvīlis, cīvicus.
civil adj (of citizens) cīvīlis; (war)

cīvīlis, intestīnus, domesticus;·
(manners) urbānus, cōmis,
officiōsus; (lawsuit) prīvātus.
civilian n togātus m.
civility n urbānitās f, cōmitās f;
(act) officium nt.
civilization n exculta hominum
vīta f, cultus atque hūmānitās.
civilize vt excolere, expolīre, ad
hūmānum cultum dēdūcere.
civil war n bellum cīvīle, bellum
domesticum, bellum intestīnum.
clad adj vestītus.
claim vt (for oneself) adrogāre,
adserere; (something due) poscere,
postulāre, vindicāre; (at law)
petere; (statement) adfirmāre ♦ n
postulātiō f, postulātum nt; (at law)
petītiō f, vindiciae fpl.
claimant n petītor m.
clam n chāma f.
clamber vi scandere.
clammy adj ūmidus, lentus.
clamorous adj vōciferāns.
clamour n strepitus m, clāmōrēs
mpl ♦ vi: **~ against** obstrepere
(dat).
clamp n cōnfībula f.
clan n gēns f.
clandestine adj fūrtivus.
clandestinely adv clam, fūrtim.
clang n clangor m, crepitus m ♦ vi
increpāre.
clangour n clangor m.
clank n crepitus m ♦ vi crepitāre.
clansman n gentīlis m.
clap vi plaudere, applaudere; **~
eyes on** cōnspicere; **~ in prison** in
vincula conicere ♦ n plausus m;
(thunder) fragor m.
clapper n plausor m.
claptrap n iactātiō f.
claque n plausōrēs mpl, operae fpl.
clarify vt pūrgāre; (knowledge)
illūstrāre ♦ vi liquēre.
clarinet n tībia f.
clarion n lituus m, cornū nt.

clarity n perspicuitās f.

clash n concursus m; (sound) strepitus m, crepitus m; (fig) discrepantia f ♦ vi concurrere; (sound) increpāre; (fig) discrepāre ♦ vt cōnflīgere.

clasp n fībula f; (embrace) amplexus m ♦ vt implicāre; amplectī, complectī; ~ together interiungere.

class n (POL) ōrdō m, classis f; (kind) genus nt; (school) classis f ♦ vi dēscrībere; ~ **as** in numerō (gen pl) referre, repōnere, habēre.

classic n scrīptor classicus m.

classical adj classicus; ~ **literature** litterae Graecae et Rōmānae.

classics npl scrīptōrēs Graecī et Rōmānī.

classify vt dēscrībere, in ōrdinem redigere.

class-mate n condiscipulus m.

clatter n crepitus m ♦ vi increpāre.

clause n (GRAM) incīsum nt, membrum nt; (law) caput nt; (will) ēlogium nt; **in short ~s** incīsim.

claw n unguis m, ungula f ♦ vt (unguibus) lacerāre.

clay n argilla f, **made of ~** fictilis.

clayey adj argillāceus.

claymore n gladius m.

clean adj mundus; (fig) pūrus, castus; ~ **slate** novae tabulae fpl; **make a ~ sweep of** omnia tollere; **show a ~ pair of heels** sē in pedēs conicere; **my hands are ~** innocēns sum ♦ adv prōrsus, tōtus ♦ vt pūrgāre.

cleanliness n munditia f.

cleanly adj mundus, nitidus ♦ adv mundē, pūrē.

cleanse vt pūrgāre, abluere, dētergēre.

clear adj clārus; (liquid) limpidus; (space) apertus, pūrus; (sound) clārus; (weather) serēnus; (fact)

manifestus, perspicuus; (language) illūstris, dīlūcidus; (conscience) rēctus, innocēns; **it is ~** liquet; **~ of** līber (abl), expers (gen); **be ~ about** rēctē intellegere; **keep ~ of** ēvītāre; **the coast is ~** arbitrī absunt ♦ vt (of obstacles) expedīre, pūrgāre; (of a charge) absolvere; (self) pūrgāre; (profit) lucrārī; **~ away** āmovēre, tollere; **~ off** vt (debt) solvere, exsolvere ♦ vi facessere; **~ out** ēluere, dētergēre; **~ up** vt (difficulty) illūstrāre, ēnōdāre, explicāre ♦ vi (weather) disserēnāscere.

clearance n pūrgātiō f; (space) intervallum nt.

clearing n (in forest) lūcus m.

clearly adv clārē; manifestē, apertē, perspicuē; (with clause) vidēlicet.

clearness n clāritās f; (weather) serēnitās f; (mind) acūmen nt; (style) perspicuitās f.

clear-sighted adj sagāx, perspicāx.

cleavage n discidium nt.

cleave vt (out) findere, discindere ♦ vi (cling): **~ to** haerēre (dat), adhaerēre (dat).

cleaver n dolabra f.

cleft n rīma f, hiātus m ♦ adj fissus, discissus.

clemency n clēmentia f, indulgentia f; **with ~** clēmenter.

clement adj clēmēns, misericors.

clench vt (nail) retundere; (hand) comprimere.

clerk n scrība m; (of court) lēctor m.

clever adj callidus, ingeniōsus, doctus, astūtus.

cleverly adv doctē, callidē, ingeniōsē.

cleverness n calliditās f, sollertia f.

clew n glomus nt.

cliché n verbum trītum nt.

client n cliēns m/f; (lawyer's)

cōnsultor *m*; **body of ~s** clientēla
f.

clientele *n* clientēla *f*.

cliff *n* rūpēs *f*, scopulus *m*.

climate *n* caelum *nt*.

climax *n* (*RHET*) gradātiō *f*; (*fig*)
culmen *nt*.

climb *vt, vi* scandere, ascendere; **~
down** dēscendere ♦ *n* ascēnsus
m.

climber *n* scandēns *m*.

clime *n* caelum *nt*, plāga *f*.

clinch *vt* cōnfirmāre.

cling *vi* adhaerēre; **~ together**
cohaerēre.

clink *vi* tinnīre ♦ *n* tinnītus *m*.

clip *vt* tondēre; praecīdere.

clippers *n* forfex *f*.

clique *n* factiō *f*.

cloak *n* (*rain*) lacerna *f*, (*travel*)
paenula *f*, (*MIL*) sagum *nt*;
palūdāmentum *nt*; (*Greek*) pallium
nt; (*fig*) involūcrum *nt*; (*pretext*)
speciēs *f* ♦ *vt* tegere, dissimulāre.

clock *n* hōrologium *nt*; (*sun*)
sōlārium *nt*; (*water*) clepsydra *f*;
ten o'~ quārta hōra.

clockwise *adv* dextrōvorsum,
dextrōrsum.

clod *n* glaeba *f*.

clog *n* (*shoe*) sculpōnea *f*; (*fig*)
impedīmentum *nt* ♦ *vt* impedīre.

cloister *n* porticus *f*.

cloistered *adj* (*fig*) umbrātilis.

close *adj* (*shut*) clausus; (*tight*)
artus; (*narrow*) angustus; (*near*)
propinquus; (*compact*) refertus,
dēnsus; (*stingy*) parcus; (*secret*)
obscūrus; (*weather*) crassus; **~
together** dēnsus, refertus; **~ at
quarters** comminus; **be ~ at hand**
īnstāre; **keep ~ to** adhaerēre; **~ to**
prope (*acc*), iuxtā (*acc*) ♦ *adv*
prope, iuxtā ♦ *n* angiportus *m*.

close *vt* claudere, operīre; (*finish*)
perficere, fīnīre, conclūdere,
termināre; (*ranks*) dēnsāre ♦ *vi*

claudī; conclūdī, termināri; (*time*)
exīre; (*wound*) coīre; (*speech*)
perōrāre; **~ with** (*fight*) manum
cōnserere, signa cōnferre; (*deal*)
pacīscī; (*offer*) accipere ♦ *n* fīnis
m, terminus *m*; (*action*) exitus *m*;
(*sentence*) conclūsiō *f*; **at the ~ of
summer** aestāte exeunte.

closely *adv* prope; (*attending*)
attentē; (*associating*) coniūnctē;
follow ~ īnstāre (*dat*).

closeness *n* propinquitās *f*;
(*weather*) gravitās *f*, crassitūdō *f*;
(*with money*) parsimōnia *f*; (*friends*)
coniūnctiō *f*; (*manner*) cautiō *f*.

closet *n* cubiculum *nt*, cella *f* ♦ *vt*
inclūdere.

clot *n* (*blood*) concrētus sanguis *m*
♦ *vi* concrēscere.

cloth *n* textīle *nt*; (*piece*) pannus *m*;
(*linen*) linteum *nt*; (*covering*)
strāgulum *nt*.

clothe *vt* vestīre.

clothes *n* vestis *f*, vestītus *m*,
vestīmenta *ntpl*.

clothier *n* vestiārius *m*.

clothing *n* vestis *f*, vestītus *m*,
vestīmenta *ntpl*.

clotted *adj* concrētus.

cloud *n* nūbēs *f*; (*storm*) nimbus *m*;
(*dust*) globus *m*; (*disfavour*) invidia
f ♦ *vt* nūbibus obdūcere; (*fig*)
obscūrāre.

clouded *adj* obnūbilus.

cloudiness *n* nūbilum *nt*.

cloudless *adj* pūrus, serēnus.

cloudy *adj* obnūbilus.

clout *n* pannus *m*.

clover *n* trifolium *nt*.

cloven *adj* (*hoof*) bifidus.

clown *n* (*boor*) rūsticus *m*; (*comic*)
scurra *m*.

clownish *adj* rūsticus, inurbānus.

clownishness *n* rūsticitās *f*.

cloy *vt* satiāre.

cloying *adj* pūtidus.

club *n* (*stick*) fustis *m*, clāva *f*;

(society) sodālitās f; ~ **together** vi in commūne cōnsulere, pecūniās cōnferre.

club-footed adj scaurus.

cluck vi singultīre ♦ n singultus m.

clue n indicium nt, vestīgium nt.

clump n massa f; (earth) glaeba f; (trees) arbustum nt; (willows) salictum nt.

clumsily adv ineptē, inēleganter; inconditē, īnfābrē.

clumsiness n īnscītia f.

clumsy adj (person) inconcinnus, ineptus; (thing) inhabilis; (work) inconditus.

cluster n cumulus m; (grapes) racēmus m; (people) corōna f ♦ vi congregārī.

clutch vt prehendere, adripere; ~ **at** captāre, comprehēnsiō f; **from one's ~es** ē manibus; **in one's ~es** in potestāte.

clutter n turba f ♦ vt impedīre, obstruere.

coach n currus m, raeda f, pīlentum nt; (trainer) magister m ♦ vt ēdocēre, praecipere (dat).

coachman n aurīga m, raedārius m.

coagulate vt cōgere ♦ vi concrēscere.

coagulation n concrētiō f.

coal n carbō m; **carry ~s to Newcastle** in silvam ligna ferre.

coalesce vi coīre, coālēscere.

coalition n coitiō f, cōnspīrātiō f.

coarse adj (quality) crassus; (manners) rūsticus, inurbānus; (speech) īnfacētus.

coarsely adv inurbānē, inēleganter.

coarseness n crassitūdō f; rūsticitās f.

coast n lītus nt, ōra maritima f ♦ vi: ~ **along** legere, praetervehī.

coastal adj lītorālis, maritimus.

coastline n lītus nt.

coat n pallium nt; (animals) pellis f ♦ vt indūcere, inlinere.

coating n corium nt.

coax vt blandīrī, dēlēnīre.

coaxing adj blandus ♦ n blanditiae fpl.

cob n (horse) mannus m; (swan) cygnus m.

cobble n lapis m ♦ vt sarcīre.

cobbler n sūtor m.

cobweb n arāneum nt.

cock n gallus m, gallus gallīnāceus m; (other birds) mās m; (tap) epitonium nt; (hay) acervus m.

cockatrice n basiliscus m.

cockchafer n scarabaeus m.

cockcrow n gallī cantus m ♦ vt ērigere.

cockerel n pullus m.

cockroach n blatta f.

cocksure adj cōnfīdēns.

cod n callariās m.

coddle vt indulgēre (dat), permulcēre.

code n fōrmula f; (secret) notae fpl.

codicil n cōdicillī mpl.

codify vt in ōrdinem redigere.

coequal adj aequālis.

coerce vt cōgere.

coercion n vīs f.

coffer n arca f, cista f; (public) fiscus m.

coffin n arca f.

cog n dēns m.

cogency n vīs f, pondus nt.

cogent adj gravis, validus.

cogitate vt cōgitāre, meditārī.

cogitation n cōgitātiō f; meditātiō f.

cognate adj cognātus.

cognition n cognitiō f.

cognizance n cognitiō f; **take ~ of** cognōscere.

cognizant adj gnārus.

cohabit vi cōnsuēscere.

cohabitation n cōnsuētūdō f.

coheir n cohērēs m/f.

cohere vi cohaerēre; (*statement*) congruere.

coherence n coniūnctiō f; (*fig*) convenientia f.

coherent adj congruēns.

cohesion n coagmentātiō f.

cohesive adj tenāx.

cohort n cohors f.

coil n spīra f ♦ vt glomerāre.

coin n nummus m ♦ vt cūdere; (*fig*) fingere.

coinage n monēta f; (*fig*) fictum nt.

coincide vi concurrere; (*opinion*) cōnsentīre.

coincidence n concursus m; cōnsēnsus m; **by a ~** cāsū.

coincidental adj fortuītus.

coiner n (*of money*) signātor m.

col n iugum nt.

colander n cōlum nt.

cold adj frīgidus; (*icy*) gelidus; **very ~** perfrīgidus; **be, feel ~** algēre, frīgēre; **get ~** algēscere, frīgēscere ♦ n frīgus nt; (*felt*) algor m; (*malady*) gravēdō f; **catch ~** algēscere, frīgus colligere; **catch a ~** gravēdinem contrahere; **have a ~** gravēdine labōrāre.

coldish adj frīgidulus, frīgidior.

coldly adv (*manner*) sine studiō.

coldness n frīgus nt, algor m.

cold water n frīgida f.

colic n tormina ntpl.

collar n collāre nt.

collarbone n iugulum nt.

collate vt cōnferre, comparāre.

collateral adj adiūnctus; (*evidence*) cōnsentāneus.

collation n collātiō f; (*meal*) prandium nt, merenda f.

colleague n collēga m.

collect vt colligere, cōgere, congerere; (*persons*) congregāre, convocāre; (*taxes*) exigere; (*something due*) recipere; **~ oneself** animum colligere; **cool and ~ed** aequō animō ♦ vi

convenīre, congregārī.

collection n (*persons*) coetus m, conventus m; (*things*) congeriēs f; (*money*) exāctiō f.

collective adj commūnis.

collectively adv commūniter.

collector n (*of taxes*) exāctor m.

college n collēgium nt.

collide vi concurrere, cōnflīctārī.

collier n carbōnārius m.

collision n concursus m.

collocation n collocātiō f.

collop n offa f.

colloquial adj cottīdiānus.

colloquy n sermō m, colloquium nt.

collude vi praevāricārī.

collusion n praevāricātiō f.

collusive adj praevāricātor.

colonel n lēgātus m.

colonial adj colōnicus ♦ n colōnus m.

colonist n colōnus m.

colonization n dēductiō f.

colonize vt colōniam dēdūcere, cōnstituere in (*acc*).

colonnade n porticus f.

colony n colōnia f.

colossal adj ingēns, vastus.

colossus n colossus m.

colour n color m; (*paint*) pigmentum nt; (*artificial*) fūcus m; (*complexion*) color m; (*pretext*) speciēs f; **take on a ~** colōrem dūcere; **under ~ of** per speciem (*gen*); **local ~** māteria dē regiōne sūmpta ♦ vt colōrāre; (*dye*) īnficere, fūcāre; (*fig*) praetendere (*dat*) ♦ vi rubēre, ērubēscere.

colourable adj speciōsus.

coloured adj (*naturally*) colōrātus; (*artificially*) fūcātus.

colourful adj fūcōsus, varius.

colouring n pigmentum nt; (*dye*) fūcus m.

colourless adj perlūcidus; (*person*) pallidus; (*fig*) īnsulsus.

colours n (*MIL*) signum nt, vexillum

nt; (POL) partēs fpl; **sail under false ~** aliēnō nōmine ūtī; **with flying ~** māximā cum glōriā.
colour sergeant n signifer m.
colt n equuleus m, equulus m.
coltsfoot n farfarus m.
column n columna f; (MIL) agmen nt.
coma n sopor m.
comb n pecten m; (bird) crista f; (loom) pecten m; (honey) favus m ♦ vt pectere.
combat n pugna f, proelium nt, certāmen nt ♦ vi pugnāre, dīmicāre, certāre ♦ vt pugnāre cum (abl), obsistere (dat).
combatant n pugnātor m ♦ adj pugnāns; **non~** imbellis.
combative adj ferōx, pugnāx.
combination n coniūnctiō f, cōnfūsiō f; (persons) cōnspīrātiō f; (illegal) coniūrātiō f.
combine vt coniungere, iungere ♦ vi coīre, coniungī ♦ n societās f.
combustible adj ignī obnoxius.
combustion n dēflagrātiō f, incendium nt.
come vi venīre, advenīre; (after a journey) dēvenīre; (interj) age!; **how ~s it that...?;** quī fit ut ...?; **~ across** vi invenīre, offendere; **~ after** sequī, excipere, succēdere (dat); **~ again** revenīre, redīre; **~ away** vi abscēdere; (when pulled) sequī; **~ back** vi revenīre, redīre, regredī; **~ between** intervenīre, intercēdere; **~ down** vi dēvenīre, dēscendere; (from the past) trādī, prōdī; **~ forward** vi prōcēdere, prōdīre; **~ from** vi (origin) dēfluere; **~ in** vi inīre, introīre; ingredī; (revenue) redīre; **~ near** accēdere ad (acc), appropinquāre (dat); **~ nearer and nearer** adventāre; **~ of** vi (family) ortum esse ab, ex (abl); **~ off** vi ēvādere, discēdere; **~ on** vi prōcēdere;

(progress) prōficere; (interj) age, agite; **~ on the scene** intervenīre, supervenīre, adesse; **~ out** vi exīre, ēgredī; (hair, teeth) cadere; (flower) flōrēscere; (book) ēdī; **~ over** vi trānsīre; (feeling) subīre, occupāre; **~ to** vi advenīre ad, in (acc); (person) adīre; (amount) efficere; **~ to the help of** subvenīre (dat); succurrere (dat); **~ to nought** ad nihilum recidere; **~ to pass** ēvenīre, fierī; **~ together** convenīre, coīre; **~ up** vi subīre, succēdere; (growth) prōvenīre; **~ upon** vt fus invenīre; **he is coming to** animus eī redit.
comedian n (actor) cōmoedus m; (writer) cōmicus m.
comedienne n mīma f.
comedy n cōmoedia f.
comeliness n decor m, decōrum nt.
comely adj decōrus, pulcher.
comestibles n vīctus m.
comet n comētēs m.
comfort vt sōlārī, cōnsōlārī, adlevāre ♦ n sōlācium nt, cōnsōlātiō f.
comfortable adj commodus; **make oneself ~** corpus cūrāre.
comfortably adv commodē.
comforter n cōnsōlātor m.
comfortless adj incommodus; **be ~** sōlātiō carēre.
comforts npl commoda ntpl.
comic adj cōmicus; facētus ♦ n scurra m.
comical adj facētus, rīdiculus.
coming adj futūrus ♦ n adventus m.
comity n cōmitās f.
command vt iubēre (+ acc and infin), imperāre (dat and ut +subj), dūcere; (feelings) regere; (resources) fruī (abl); (view) prōspectāre ♦ n (MIL) imperium nt; (sphere) prōvincia f; (order) imperium nt, iussum nt,

mandātum *nt*; **be in ~ (of)**
praeesse (*dat*); **put in ~ of**
praeficere (*dat*); **~ of language**
fācundia *f*.

commandant *n* praefectus *m*.

commandeer *vt* pūblicāre.

commander *n* dux *m*, praefectus
m.

commander in chief *n* imperātor
m.

commandment *n* mandātum *nt*.

commemorate *vt* celebrāre,
memoriae trādere.

commemoration *n* celebrātiō *f*.

commence *vt* incipere, exōrdīrī,
initium facere (*gen*).

commencement *n* initium *nt*,
exōrdium *nt*, prīncipium *nt*.

commend *vt* laudāre; (*recommend*)
commendāre; (*entrust*) mandāre; ~
oneself sē probāre.

commendable *adj* laudābilis,
probābilis.

commendation *n* laus *f*, commendātiō *f*.

commendatory *adj* commendātīcius.

commensurable *adj* pār.

commensurate *adj* congruēns,
conveniēns.

comment *vi* dīcere, scrībere; **~ on**
interpretārī; (*with notes*) adnotāre
♦ *n* dictum *nt*, sententia *f*.

commentary *n* commentāriī *mpl*.

commentator *n* interpres *m*.

commerce *n* mercātūra *f*,
commercium *nt*; **engage in ~**
mercātūrās facere, negōtiārī.

commercial dealings *n*
commercium *nt*.

commercial traveller *n* īnstitor *m*.

commination *n* minae *fpl*.

comminatory *adj* mināx.

commingle *vt* intermīscēre.

commiserate *vt* miserērī (*gen*).

commiseration *n* misericordia *f*,
(*RHET*) commiserātiō *f*.

commissariat *n* rēs frūmentāria *f*,
commeātus *m*; (*staff*) frūmentāriī
mpl.

commissary *n* lēgātus *m*; reī
frūmentāriae praefectus *m*.

commission *n* (*charge*) mandātum
nt; (*persons*) triumvirī *mpl*,
decemvirī *mpl*, etc; (*abroad*)
lēgātiō *f*; **get a ~** (*MIL*) tribūnum
fierī; (*standing ~*) (*law*) quaestiō
perpetua ♦ *vt* mandāre,
adlēgāre.

commissioner *n* lēgātus *m*; **three
~s** triumvirī *mpl*; **ten ~s**
decemvirī *mpl*.

commit *vt* (*charge*) committere,
mandāre; (*crime*) admittere; (*to
prison*) conicere; (*to an undertaking*)
obligāre, obstringere; **~ to
memory** memoriae trādere; **~ to
writing** litterīs mandāre; **~ an
error** errāre; **~ a theft** fūrtum
facere; *see also* **suicide**.

commitment *n* mūnus *nt*, officium
nt.

committee *n* dēlēctī *mpl*.

commodious *adj* capāx.

commodity *n* merx *f*, rēs *f*.

commodore *n* praefectus classis
m.

common *adj* (*for all*) commūnis;
(*ordinary*) vulgāris, cottīdiānus;
(*repeated*) frequēns, crēber;
(*inferior*) nēquam ♦ *n* compāscuus
ager *m*, prātum *nt*; **~ man** homō
plēbēius *m*; **~ soldier** gregārius
mīles *m*.

commonalty *n* plēbs *f*.

commoner *n* homō plēbēius *m*.

common law *n* mōs māiōrum *m*.

commonly *adv* ferē, vulgō.

common people *n* plēbs *f*, vulgus
nt.

commonplace *n* trītum
prōverbium *nt*; (*RHET*) locus
commūnis *m* ♦ *adj* vulgāris,
trītus.

commons n plēbs f; (food) diāria
ntpl.

common sense n prūdentia f.

commonwealth n cīvitās f, rēs
pūblica f.

commotion n perturbātiō f,
tumultus m; **cause a ~** tumultuārī.

communal adj commūnis.

commune n pāgus m ♦ vi colloquī,
sermōnēs cōnferre.

communicate vt commūnicāre;
(information) nūntiāre, patefacere
♦ vi: **~ with** commūnicāre (dat),
commercium habēre (gen), agere
cum (abl).

communication n (dealings)
commercium nt; (information)
litterae fpl, nūntius m; (passage)
commeātus m; **cut off the ~s of**
interclūdere.

communicative adj loquāx.

communion n societās f.

communiqué n litterae fpl,
praedicātiō f.

communism n bonōrum aequātiō
f.

community n cīvitās f, commūne
nt; (participation) commūniō f.

commutation n mūtātiō f.

commute vt mūtāre, commūtāre.

compact n foedus nt, conventum
nt ♦ adj dēnsus vt vt densāre.

companion n socius m, comes m/f;
(intimate) sodālis m; (at school)
condiscipulus m; (in army)
commīlitō m, contubernālis m.

companionable adj facilis,
commodus.

companionship n sodālitās f,
cōnsuētūdō f; (MIL) contubernium
nt.

company n societās f, cōnsuētūdō
f; (gathering) coetus m, conventus
m; (guests) cēnantēs mpl;
(commercial) societās f;
(magistrates) collēgium nt; (MIL)
manipulus m; (THEAT) grex m,

caterva f; **~ of ten** decuria f.

comparable adj comparābilis,
similis.

comparative adj māgnus, sī cum
aliīs cōnfertur.

comparatively adv ut in tālī
tempore, ut in eā regiōne, ut est
captus hominum; **~ few** perpaucī,
nullus ferē.

compare vt comparāre, cōnferre;
~d with ad (acc).

comparison n comparātiō f,
collātiō f; (RHET) similitūdō f; **in ~
with** prō (abl).

compartment n cella f, pars f.

compass n ambitus m, spatium nt,
modus m; **pair of ~es** circinus m
♦ vt circumdare, cingere; (attain)
cōnsequī.

compassion n misericordia f.

compassionate adj misericors,
clēmēns.

compassionately adv clēmenter.

compatibility n convenientia f.

compatible adj congruēns,
conveniēns; **be ~** congruere.

compatibly adv congruenter,
convenienter.

compatriot n cīvis m, populāris m.

compeer n pār m; aequālis m.

compel vt cōgere.

compendious adj brevis.

compendiously adv summātim.

compendium n epitomē f.

compensate vt compēnsāre,
satisfacere (dat).

compensation n compēnsātiō f;
pretium nt, poena f.

compete vi certāre, contendere.

competence n facultās f; (law) iūs
nt; (money) quod sufficit.

competent adj perītus, satis
doctus, capāx; (witness) locuplēs;
it is ~ licet.

competition n certāmen nt,
contentiō f.

competitor n competītor m,

aemulus m.

compilation n collectānea ntpl,
liber m.

compile vt compōnere.

compiler n scrīptor m.

complacency n amor suī m.

complacent adj suī contentus.

complain vi querī, conquerī; ~ of
(person) nōmen dēferre (gen).

complainant n accūsātor m,
petītor m.

complaint n questus m,
querimōnia f; (law) crīmen nt;
(MED) morbus m, valētūdō f.

complaisance n cōmitās f,
obsequium nt, indulgentia f.

complaisant adj cōmis, officiōsus,
facilis.

complement n complēmentum nt;
numerus suus m; **make up the ~ of**
complēre.

complete vt (amount, time)
complēre, explēre; (work)
cōnficere, perficere, absolvere,
peragere ♦ adj perfectus,
absolūtus, integer; (victory)
iūstus; (amount) explētus.

completely adv funditus, omnīnō,
absolūtē, plānē; penitus.

completeness n integritās f;
(perfection) perfectiō f.

completion n (process) absolūtiō f,
cōnfectiō f; (end) fīnis m; **bring to
~** absolvere.

complex adj implicātus, multiplex.

complexion n color m.

complexity n implicātiō f.

compliance n accommodātiō f,
obsequium n, obtemperātiō f.

compliant adj obsequēns, facilis.

complicate vt implicāre, impedīre.

complicated adj implicātus,
involūtus, impedītus.

complication n implicātiō f.

complicity n cōnscientia f.

compliment n blandīmentum nt,
honōs m ♦ vt blandīrī, laudāre; ~

on grātulārī (dat) dē (abl).

complimentary adj honōrificus,
blandus.

compliments npl (as greeting) salūs
f.

comply vi obsequī (dat), obtemperāre (dat); mōrem gerere (dat),
mōrigerārī (dat).

component n elementum nt, pars
f.

comport vt gerere.

compose vt (art) compōnere,
condere, pangere; (whole)
efficere, cōnflāre; (quarrel)
compōnere, dīrimere;
(disturbance) sēdāre; **be ~d of**
cōnsistere ex (abl), cōnstāre ex
(abl).

composed adj tranquillus,
placidus.

composer n auctor m, scrīptor m.

composite adj multiplex.

composition n (process)
compositiō f, scrīptūra f; (product)
opus nt, poēma nt, carmen nt;
(quality) structūra f.

composure n sēcūritās f, aequus
animus m; (face) tranquillitās f.

compound vt miscēre; (words)
duplicāre, iungere ♦ vi (agree)
pacīscī ♦ adj compositus ♦ n
(word) iūnctum verbum nt; (area)
saeptum m.

compound interest n anatocismus
m.

comprehend vt intellegere,
comprehendere; (include)
continēre, complectī.

comprehensible adj perspicuus.

comprehension n intellegentia f,
comprehēnsiō f.

comprehensive adj capāx; **be ~**
lātē patēre, multa complectī.

compress vt comprimere,
coartāre ♦ n fōmentum nt.

compression n compressus m.

comprise vt continēre, complectī,

comprehendere.

compromise n (by one side)
accommodātiō f; (by both sides)
comprōmissum nt ♦ vi com-
prōmittere ♦ vt implicāre, in suspiciōnem vocāre; **be ~d** in suspiciōnem venīre.

comptroller n moderātor m.

compulsion n necessitās f, vīs f;
under ~ coāctus.

compulsory adj necesse, lēge
imperātus; **use ~ measures** vim
adhibēre.

compunction n paenitentia f.

computation n ratiō f.

compute vt computāre, ratiōnem
dūcere.

comrade n socius m, contubernālis
m.

comradeship n contubernium nt.

concatenation n seriēs f.

concave adj concavus.

conceal vt cēlāre, abdere,
abscondere; (fact) dissimulāre.

concealment n occultātiō f; (place)
latebrae fpl; (of facts) dissimulātiō
f, in ~ abditus, occultus; **be in ~**
latēre, latitāre; **go into ~**
dēlitēscere.

concede vt concēdere.

conceit n (idea) nōtiō f; (wit)
facētiae fpl; (pride) superbia f,
adrogantia f, vānitās f.

conceited adj glōriōsus, adrogāns.

conceitedness n adrogantia f,
vānitās f.

conceive vt concipere,
comprehendere, intellegere.

concentrate vt (in one place)
cōgere, congregāre; (attention)
intendere, dēfigere.

concentrated adj dēnsus.

concentration n animī intentiō f.

concept n nōtiō f.

conception n conceptus m; (mind)
intellegentia f, īnfōrmātiō f; (idea)
nōtiō f, cōgitātiō f, cōnsilium nt.

concern vt (refer) attinēre ad (acc),
interesse (gen); (worry) sollicitāre;
it ~s me meā rēfert, meā interest;
as far as I am ~ed per mē ♦ n rēs f,
negōtium nt; (importance) mōmentum nt; (worry) sollicitūdō f, cūra f;
(regret) dolor m.

concerned adj sollicitus, anxius;
be ~ dolēre; **be ~ about** molestē
ferre.

concerning prep dē (abl).

concernment n sollicitūdō f.

concert n (music) concentus m;
(agreement) cōnsēnsus m; **in ~** ex
compositō, ūnō animō ♦ vt
compōnere; (plan) inīre.

concession n concessiō f; **by the ~
of** concessū (gen); **make a ~**
concēdere, tribuere.

conciliate vt conciliāre.

conciliation n conciliātiō f.

conciliator n arbiter m.

conciliatory adj pācificus.

concise adj brevis; (style) dēnsus.

concisely adv breviter.

conciseness n brevitās f.

conclave n sēcrētus cōnsessus m.

conclude vt (end) termināre,
fīnīre, cōnficere; (settle) facere,
compōnere, pangere; (infer)
īnferre, colligere.

conclusion n (end) fīnis m; (of
action) exitus m; (of speech)
perōrātiō f; (inference) coniectūra
f; (decision) placitum nt, sententia
f; **in ~** dēnique; **try ~s with**
contendere cum.

conclusive adj certus, manifestus,
gravis.

conclusively adv sine dubiō.

concoct vt coquere; (fig) cōnflāre.

concoction n (fig) māchinātiō f.

concomitant adj adiūnctus.

concord n concordia f; (music)
harmonia f.

concordant adj concors.

concordat n pactum nt, foedus nt.

concourse n frequentia f,
celebrātiō f; (moving) concursus
m.

concrete adj concrētus; **in the ~** rē.

concretion n concrētiō f.

concubine n concubīna f.

concupiscence n libīdō f.

concur vi (time) concurrere;
(opinion) cōnsentīre, adsentīre.

concurrence n (time) concursus m;
(opinion) cōnsēnsus m.

concurrent adj (time) aequālis;
(opinion) cōnsentāneus; **be ~**
concurrere, cōnsentīre.

concurrently adv simul, ūnā.

concussion n ictus m.

condemn vt damnāre,
condemnāre; (disapprove)
improbāre; **~ to death** capitis
damnāre; **~ for treason** dē
māiestāte damnāre.

condemnation n damnātiō f;
condemnātiō f.

condemnatory adj damnātōrius.

condense vt dēnsāre; (words)
premere.

condescend vi dēscendere, sē
submittere.

condescending adj cōmis.

condescension n cōmitās f.

condiment n condīmentum nt.

condition n (of body) habitus m;
(external) status m, condiciō f, rēs
f; (in society) locus m, fortūna f; (of
agreement) condiciō f, lēx f; **~s of
sale** mancipī lēx f; **on ~ that** eā
condicione ut (subj); **in ~** (animals)
nitidus ♦ vt fōrmāre, regere.

conditional adj: **the assistance is ~
on** eā condiciōne succurritur ut
(subj).

conditionally adv sub condiciōne.

conditioned adj (character)
mōrātus.

condole vi: **~ with** cōnsōlārī.

condolence n cōnsōlātiō f.

condonation n venia f.

condone vt condōnāre, ignōscere
(dat).

conduce vi condūcere (ad),
prōficere (ad).

conducive adj ūtilis, accommodātus.

conduct vt dūcere; (escort)
dēdūcere; (to a place) addūcere,
perdūcere; (business) gerere,
administrāre; (self) gerere ♦ n
mōrēs mpl; (past) vīta f, facta ntpl;
(business) administrātiō f; **safe ~**
praesidium nt.

conductor m dux m, ductor m.

conduit n canālis m, aquae ductus
m.

cone n cōnus m.

coney n cunīculus m.

confabulate vi colloquī.

confection n cuppēdō f.

confectioner n cuppēdinārius m.

confectionery n dulcia ntpl.

confederacy n foederātae
cīvitātēs fpl, societās f.

confederate adj foederātus ♦ n
socius m ♦ vi coniūrāre, foedus
facere.

confederation n societās f.

confer vt cōnferre, tribuere ♦ vi
colloquī, sermōnem cōnferre; **~
about** agere dē (abl).

conference n colloquium nt,
congressus m.

conferment n dōnātiō f.

confess vt fatērī, cōnfitērī.

confessedly adv manifestō.

confession n cōnfessiō f.

confidant n cōnscius m.

confide vi fīdere (dat), cōnfīdere
(dat) ♦ vt crēdere, committere.

confidence n fidēs f, fīdūcia f; **have
~ in** fīdere (dat), cōnfīdere (dat);
inspire ~ in fidem facere (dat); **tell
in ~** tūtīs auribus dēpōnere.

confident adj fīdēns; **~ in** frētus
(abl); **be ~ that** certō scīre, prō
certō habēre.

confidential adj arcānus, intimus.
confidentially adv inter nōs.
confidently adv fīdenter.
confiding adj crēdulus.
configuration n figūra f, fōrma f.
confine vt (prison) inclūdere, in vincula conicere; (limit) termināre, circumscrībere; (restrain) coercēre, cohibēre; (to bed) dētinēre; **be ~d** (women) parturīre.
confinement n custōdia f, vincula ntpl, inclūsiō f; (women) puerperium nt.
confines n fīnēs mpl.
confirm vt (strength) corrōborāre, firmāre; (decision) sancīre, ratum facere; (fact) adfirmāre, comprobāre.
confirmation n cōnfirmātiō f, adfirmātiō f.
confirmed adj ratus.
confiscate vt pūblicāre.
confiscation n pūblicātiō f.
conflagration n incendium f, dēflāgrātiō f.
conflict n (physical) concursus m; (hostile) certāmen nt, proelium nt; (verbal) contentiō f, contrōversia f; (contradiction) repugnantia f, discrepantia f ♦ vi inter sē repugnāre.
conflicting adj contrārius.
confluence n cōnfluēns m.
confluent adj cōnfluēns.
conform vt accommodāre ♦ vi sē cōnfōrmāre (ad), obsequī (dat), mōrem gerere (dat).
conformable adj accommodātus, conveniēns.
conformably adv convenienter.
conformation n structūra f, cōnfōrmātiō f.
conformity n convenientia f, cōnsēnsus m.
confound vt (mix) cōnfundere, permiscēre; (amaze) obstupefacere; (thwart) frustrārī; (suppress) opprimere, obruere; **~ you!** dī tē perduint.
confounded adj miser, sacer, nefandus.
confoundedly adv mīrum quantum nefārīē.
confraternity n frāternitās f.
confront vt sē oppōnere (dat), obviam īre (dat), sē cōram offerre.
confuse vt permiscēre, perturbāre.
confused adj perturbātus.
confusedly adv perturbātē, prōmiscuē.
confusion n perturbātiō f; (shame) rubor m.
confutation n refūtātiō f.
confute vt refūtāre, redarguere, convincere.
congé n commeātus m.
congeal vt congelāre, dūrāre ♦ vi concrēscere.
congealed adj concrētus.
congenial adj concors, congruēns, iūcundus.
congeniality n concordia f, mōrum similitūdō f.
congenital adj nātīvus.
conger n conger m.
congested adj refertus, dēnsus; (with people) frequentissimus.
congestion n congeriēs f; frequentia f.
conglomerate vt glomerāre.
conglomeration n congeriēs f, cumulus m.
congratulate vt grātulārī (dat).
congratulation n grātulātiō f.
congratulatory adj grātulābundus.
congregate vt congregāre, cōgere ♦ vi convenīre, congregārī.
congregation n conventus m, coetus m.
congress n conventus m, cōnsessus m, concilium nt; senātus m.

congruence n convenientia f.

congruent adj conveniēns, congruēns.

congruently adv convenienter, congruenter.

congruous adj see congruent.

conical adj turbinātus.

coniferous adj cōnifer.

conjectural adj opīnābilis.

conjecturally adv coniectūrā.

conjecture n coniectūra f ♦ vt conicere, augurārī.

conjoin vt coniungere.

conjoint adj coniūnctus.

conjointly adv coniūnctē, ūnā.

conjugal adj coniugālis.

conjugate vt dēclīnāre.

conjugation n (GRAM) dēclīnātiō f.

conjunct adj coniūnctus.

conjunction n coniūnctiō f, concursus m.

conjure vt (entreat) obtestārī, obsecrāre; (spirits) ēlicere, ciēre ♦ vi praestigiīs ūtī.

conjurer n praestigiātor m.

conjuring n praestigiae fpl.

connate adj innātus, nātūrā īnsitus.

connect vt iungere, coniungere, cōpulāre, connectere.

connected adj coniūnctus; (unbroken) continēns; (by marriage) adfīnis; **be ~ed with** contingere; **be closely ~ed with** inhaerēre (dat), cohaerēre cum (abl).

connectedly adv coniūnctē, continenter.

connection n coniūnctiō f, contextus m, seriēs f; (kin) necessitūdō f; (by marriage) adfīnitās f; **~ between ... and ...** ratiō (gen) ... cum ... (abl); **I have no ~ with you** nīl mihi tēcum est.

connivance n venia f, dissimulātiō f.

connive vi conīvēre in (abl), dissimulāre.

connoisseur n intellegēns m.

connotation n vīs f, significātiō f.

connote vt significāre.

connubial adj coniugālis.

conquer vt vincere, superāre.

conquerable adj superābilis, expugnābilis.

conqueror n victor m.

conquest n victōria f; (town) expugnātiō f; (prize) praemium nt, praeda f; **the ~ of Greece** Graecia capta.

conscience n cōnscientia f; **guilty ~** mala cōnscientia; **have a clear ~** nullīus culpae sibi cōnscium esse; **have no ~** nullam religiōnem habēre.

conscientious adj probus, religiōsus.

conscientiously adv bonā fidē, religiōsē.

conscientiousness n fidēs f, religiō f.

conscious adj sibī cōnscius; (aware) gnārus; (physically) mentis compos; **be ~** sentīre.

consciously adv sciēns.

consciousness n animus m; (of action) cōnscientia f; **he lost ~** animus eum relīquit.

conscript n tīrō m ♦ vt cōnscrībere.

conscription n dēlēctus m; (of wealth) pūblicātiō f.

consecrate vt dēdicāre, cōnsecrāre; (self) dēvovēre.

consecrated adj sacer.

consecration n dēdicātiō f, cōnsecrātiō f; (self) dēvōtiō f.

consecutive adj dēinceps, continuus.

consecutively adv dēinceps, ōrdine.

consensus n cōnsēnsus m.

consent vi adsentīre (dat), adnuere (infin); (together) cōnsentīre ♦ n (one side) adsēnsus m; (all)

cōnsēnsus *m*; **by common ~**
omnium cōnsēnsū.

consequence *n* ēventus *m*, exitus
m; (*logic*) conclūsiō *f*; (*importance*)
mōmentum *nt*, auctōritās *f*; **it is of
~ interest**; **what will be the ~ of ?**
quō ēvādet?

consequent *adj* cōnsequēns.

consequential *adj* cōnsentāneus;
(*person*) adrogāns.

consequently *adv* itaque, igitur,
proptereā.

conservation *n* cōnservātiō *f*.

conservative *adj* reī pūblicae
cōnservandae studiōsus;
(*estimate*) mediōcris; **~ party**
optimātēs *mpl*.

conservator *n* custōs *m*,
cōnservātor *m*.

conserve *vt* cōnservāre, servāre.

consider *vt* cōnsīderāre,
contemplārī; (*reflect*) sēcum
volūtāre, meditārī, dēlīberāre,
cōgitāre; (*deem*) habēre, dūcere;
(*respect*) respicere, observāre.

considerable *adj* aliquantus,
nōnnūllus; (*person*) illūstris.

considerably *adv* aliquantum,
(*with compar*) aliquantō, multō.

considerate *adj* hūmānus,
benignus.

considerately *adv* hūmānē,
benignē.

consideration *n* cōnsīderātiō *f*,
contemplātiō *f*, dēlīberātiō *f*;
(*respect*) respectus *m*, ratiō *f*;
(*importance*) mōmentum *nt*;
(*reason*) ratiō *f*; (*pay*) pretium *nt*;
for a ~ mercēde, datā mercēde; **in
~ of** propter (*acc*), prō (*abl*); **on no
~** nēquāquam; **with ~** cōnsultō;
without ~ temerē; **take into ~** ad
cōnsilium dēferre; **show ~ for**
respectum habēre (*gen*).

considered *adj* (*reasons*)
exquīsītus.

considering *prep* prō (*abl*), propter

(*acc*) ♦ *conj* ut, quōniam.

consign *vt* mandāre, committere.

consist *vi* cōnstāre; **~ in** cōnstāre
ex (*abl*), continērī (*abl*), positum
esse in (*abl*); **~ with** congruere
(*dat*), convenīre (*dat*).

consistence *n* firmitās *f*.

consistency *n* cōnstantia *f*.

consistent *adj* cōnstāns; (*with*)
cōnsentāneus, congruēns; (*of
movement*) aequābilis; **be ~**
cohaerēre.

consistently *adv* cōnstanter.

consolable *adj* cōnsōlābilis.

consolation *n* cōnsōlātiō *f*; (*thing*)
sōlācium *nt*.

consolatory *adj* cōnsōlātōrius.

console *vt* cōnsōlārī.

consoler *n* cōnsōlātor *m*.

consolidate *vt* (*liquid*) cōgere;
(*strength*) corrōborāre; (*gains*)
obtinēre ♦ *vi* concrēscere.

consolidation *n* concrētiō *f*;
cōnfirmātiō *f*.

consonance *n* concentus *m*.

consonant *adj* cōnsonus, haud
absōnus ♦ *n* cōnsonāns *f*.

consort *n* cōnsors *m/f*, socius *m*;
(*married*) coniunx *m/f* ♦ *vi*: **~ with**
familiāriter ūtī (*abl*), coniūnc-
tissimē vīvere cum (*abl*).

conspectus *n* summārium *nt*.

conspicuous *adj* ēminēns,
īnsignis, manifestus; **be ~**
ēminēre.

conspicuously *adv* manifestō,
palam, ante oculōs.

conspiracy *n* coniūrātiō *f*.

conspirator *n* coniūrātus *m*.

conspire *vi* coniūrāre; (*for good*)
cōnspīrāre.

constable *n* lictor *m*.

constancy *n* cōnstantia *f*, firmitās
f; **with ~** cōnstanter.

constant *adj* cōnstāns; (*faithful*)
fīdus, fidēlis; (*continuous*)
adsiduus.

constantly adv adsiduē, saepe, crēbrō.

constellation n sīdus nt.

consternation n trepidātiō f, pavor m; **throw into ~** perterrēre, cōnsternere.

constituency n suffrāgātōrēs mpl.

constituent adj: **~ part** elementum nt ♦ n **(voter)** suffrāgātor m.

constitute vt creāre, cōnstituere; esse.

constitution n nātūra f, status m; **(body)** habitus m; **(POL)** cīvitātis fōrma f, reī pūblicae status m, lēgēs fpl.

constitutional adj lēgitimus, iūstus.

constitutionally adv ē rē pūblicā.

constrain vt cōgere.

constraint n vīs f; **under ~** coāctus; **without ~** suā sponte.

constrict vt comprimere, cōnstringere.

constriction n contractiō f.

construct vt aedificāre, exstruere.

construction n aedificātiō f; **(method)** structūra f; **(meaning)** interpretātiō f; **put a wrong ~ on** in malam partem interpretārī.

construe vt interpretārī.

consul n cōnsul m; **~ elect** cōnsul dēsignātus; **ex~** cōnsulāris m.

consular adj cōnsulāris.

consulship n cōnsulātus m; **stand for the ~** cōnsulātum petere; **hold the ~** cōnsulātum gerere; **in my ~** mē cōnsule.

consult vt cōnsulere; **~ the interests of** cōnsulere (dat) ♦ vi dēlīberāre, cōnsiliārī.

consultation n **(asking)** cōnsultātiō f; **(discussion)** dēlīberātiō f.

consume vt cōnsūmere, absūmere; **(food)** edere.

consumer n cōnsūmptor m.

consummate adj summus, perfectus ♦ vt perficere,

absolvere.

consummation n absolūtiō f; fīnis m, ēventus m.

consumption n cōnsūmptiō f; **(disease)** tābēs f, phthisis f.

consumptive adj pulmōnārius.

contact n tāctus m, contāgiō f; **come in ~ with** contingere.

contagion n contāgiō f.

contagious adj tābificus; **be ~** contāgiīs vulgārī.

contain vt capere, continēre; **(self)** cohibēre.

container n vās nt.

contaminate vt contāmināre, īnficere.

contamination n contāgiō f, lābēs f.

contemplate vt contemplārī, intuērī; **(action)** in animō habēre; **(prospect)** spectāre.

contemplation n contemplātiō f; **(thought)** cōgitātiō f.

contemplative adj cōgitāns, meditāns; **in a ~ mood** cōgitātiōnī dēditus.

contemporaneous adj aequālis.

contemporaneously adv simul.

contemporary adj aequālis.

contempt n contemptiō f; **be an object of ~** contemptuī esse; **treat with ~** contemptum habēre, conculcāre.

contemptible adj contemnendus, abiectus, vīlis.

contemptuous adj fastīdiōsus.

contemptuously adv contemptim, fastīdiōsē.

contend vi certāre, contendere; **(in battle)** dīmicāre, pugnāre; **(in words)** affirmāre, adsevērāre.

contending adj contrārius.

content adj contentus ♦ n aequus animus m ♦ vt placēre (dat); satisfacere (dat); **be ~ed** satis habēre.

contentedly adv aequō animō.

contention n certāmen nt; contrōversia f; (*opinion*) sententia f.

contentious adj pugnāx, lītigiōsus.

contentiously adv pugnāciter.

contentiousness n contrōversiae studium nt.

contentment n aequus animus m.

contents n quod inest, quae insunt; (*of speech*) argūmentum nt.

conterminous adj affīnis.

contest n certāmen nt, contentiō f ♦ vt (*law*) lēge agere dē (*abl*); (*office*) petere; (*dispute*) repugnāre (*dat*), resistere (*dat*).

contestable adj contrōversus.

contestant n petītor m, aemulus m.

context n contextus m.

contiguity n vīcīnia f, propinquitās f.

contiguous adj vīcīnus, adiacēns; **be ~ to** adiacēre (*dat*), contingere.

continence n continentia f, abstinentia f.

continent adj continēns, abstinēns ♦ n continēns f.

continently adv continenter, abstinenter.

contingency n cāsus m, rēs f.

contingent adj fortuītus ♦ n (*MIL*) numerus m.

continual adj adsiduus, perpetuus.

continually adv adsiduē, semper.

continuance n perpetuitās f, adsiduitās f.

continuation n continuātiō f; (*of a command*) prōrogātiō f; (*of a story*) reliqua pars f.

continue vt continuāre; (*time*) prōdūcere; (*command*) prōrogāre ♦ vi (*action*) pergere; (*time*) manēre; (*endurance*) perstāre, dūrāre; **~ to** *imperf indic*.

continuity n continuātiō f; (*of speech*) perpetuitās f.

continuous adj continuus,

continēns, perpetuus.

continuously adv perpetuō, continenter.

contort vt contorquēre, dētorquēre.

contortion n distortiō f.

contour n fōrma f.

contraband adj interdictus, vetitus.

contract n pactum nt, mandātum nt, conventum nt; (*POL*) foedus nt; **trial for a breach of ~** mandātī iūdicium nt ♦ vt (*narrow*) contrahere, addūcere; (*short*) dēminuere; (*illness*) contrahere; (*agreement*) pacīscī; (*for work*) locāre; (*to do work*) condūcere ♦ vi pacīscī.

contraction n contractiō f; (*word*) compendium nt.

contractor n redemptor m, conductor m.

contradict vt (*person*) contrādīcere (*dat*), refrāgārī (*dat*); (*statement*) īnfitiās īre (*dat*); (*self*) repugnāre (*dat*).

contradiction n repugnantia f, īnfitiae fpl.

contradictory adj repugnāns, contrārius; **be ~** inter sē repugnāre.

contradistinction n oppositiō f.

contraption n māchina f.

contrariety n repugnantia f.

contrariwise adv ē contrāriō.

contrary adj contrārius, adversus; (*person*) difficilis, mōrōsus; **~ to** contrā (*acc*), praeter (*acc*); **~ to expectations** praeter opiniōnem ♦ n contrārium nt; **on the ~** ē contrāriō, contrā; (*retort*) immo.

contrast n discrepantia f ♦ vt comparāre, oppōnere ♦ vi discrepāre.

contravene vt (*law*) violāre; (*statement*) contrādīcere (*dat*).

contravention n violātiō f.

contribute vt cōnferre, adferre, contribuere. ♦ vi: ~ **towards** cōnferre ad (acc), adiuvāre; ~ **to the cost** impēnsās cōnferre.

contribution n conlātiō f; (money) stipem (no nom) f.

contributor n quī cōnfert.

contributory adj adiūnctus.

contrite adj paenitēns.

contrition n paenitentia f.

contrivance n māchinātiō f; excōgitātiō f; (thing) māchina f; (idea) cōnsilium nt; (deceit) dolus m.

contrive vt māchinārī, excōgitāre, struere; (to do) efficere ut.

contriver n māchinātor m, artifex m, auctor m.

control n (restraint) frēnum nt; (power) moderātiō f, potestās f, imperium nt; **have ~ of** praeesse (dat); **out of ~** impotēns ♦ vt moderārī (dat), imperāre (dat).

controller n moderātor m.

controversial adj concertātōrius.

controversy n contrōversia f, disceptātiō f.

controvert vt redarguere, impugnāre, in dubium vocāre.

contumacious adj contumāx, pervicāx.

contumaciously adv contumāciter, pervicāciter.

contumacy n contumācia f, pervicācia f.

contusion n sūgillātiō f.

conundrum n aenigma nt.

convalesce vi convalēscere.

convalescence n melior valētūdō f.

convalescent adj convalēscēns.

convene vt convocāre.

convenience n opportūnitās f, commoditās f; (thing) commodum nt; **at your ~** commodō tuō.

convenient adj idōneus, commodus, opportūnus; **be ~**

convenīre; very ~ percommodus.

conveniently adv opportūnē, commodē.

convention n (meeting) conventus m; (agreement) conventum nt; (custom) mōs m, iūsta ntpl.

conventional adj iūstus, solitus.

conventionality n mōs m, cōnsuētūdō f.

converge vi in medium vergere, in eundem locum tendere.

conversant adj perītus, doctus, exercitātus; **be ~ with** versārī in (abl).

conversation n sermō m, colloquium nt.

converse n sermō m, colloquium nt; (opposite) contrārium nt ♦ vi colloquī, sermōnem cōnferre ♦ adj contrārius.

conversely adv ē contrāriō, contrā.

conversion n mūtātiō f; (moral) mōrum ēmendātiō f.

convert vt mūtāre, convertere; (to an opinion) dēdūcere ♦ n discipulus m.

convertible adj commūtābilis.

convex adj convexus.

convexity n convexum nt.

convey vt vehere, portāre, convehere; (property) abaliēnāre; (knowledge) commūnicāre; (meaning) significāre; ~ **across** trānsmittere, trādūcere, trānsvehere; ~ **away** auferre, āvehere; ~ **down** dēvehere, dēportāre; ~ **into** importāre, invehere; ~ **to** advehere, adferre; ~ **up** subvehere.

conveyance n vehiculum nt; (property) abaliēnātiō f.

convict vt (prove guilty) convincere; (sentence) damnāre ♦ n reus m.

conviction n (law) damnātiō f; (argument) persuāsiō f; (belief) fidēs f; **carry ~** fidem facere; **have a ~** persuāsum habēre.

convince vt persuādēre (dat); **I am firmly ~d** mihi persuāsum habeō.

convincing adj (argument) gravis; (evidence) manifestus.

convincingly adv manifestō.

convivial adj convīvālis, festīvus.

conviviality n festīvitās f.

convocation n conventus m.

convoke vt convocāre.

convolution n spīra f.

convoy n praesidium nt ♦ vt prōsequī.

convulse vt agitāre; **be ~d with laughter** sē in cachinnōs effundere.

convulsion n (MED) convulsiō f; (POL) tumultus m.

convulsive adj spasticus.

coo vi gemere.

cook vt coquere ♦ n coquus m.

cookery n ars coquīnāria f.

cool adj frīgidus; (conduct) impudens; (mind) impavidus, lentus ♦ n frīgus nt ♦ vt refrīgerāre; (passion) restinguere, sēdāre ♦ vi refrīgēscere, refrīgerārī, dēfervēscere.

coolly adv aequō animō; impudenter.

coolness n frīgus nt; (mind) aequus animus m; impudentia f.

coop n hara f; (barrel) cūpa f ♦ vt inclūdere.

co-operate vi operam cōnferre; **~ with** adiuvāre, socius esse (gen).

co-operation n cōnsociātiō f; auxilium nt, opera f.

co-operative adj (person) officiōsus.

co-operator n socius m.

co-opt vt cooptāre.

coot n fulica f.

copartner n socius m.

copartnership n societās f.

cope vi: **~ with** contendere cum (abl); **able to ~ with** pār (dat); **unable to ~ with** impār (dat).

copier n librārius m.

coping n fastīgium nt.

copious adj cōpiōsus, largus, plēnus, abundāns.

copiously adv cōpiōsē, abundanter.

copiousness n cōpia f, ūbertās f.

copper n aes nt ♦ adj aēneus.

coppersmith n faber aerārius m.

coppice, copse n dūmētum nt, virgultum nt.

copy n exemplar nt ♦ vt imitārī; (writing) exscrībere, trānscrībere.

copyist n librārius m.

coracle n linter f.

coral n cūrālium nt.

cord n fūniculus m.

cordage n fūnēs mpl.

cordial adj cōmis, festīvus, amīcus; (greetings) multus.

cordiality n cōmitās f, studium nt.

cordially adv cōmiter, libenter, ex animō.

cordon n corōna f.

core n (fig) nucleus m.

cork n sūber nt; (bark) cortex m.

corn n frūmentum nt ♦ adj frūmentārius; (on the foot) clāvus m; **price of ~** annōna f.

corndealer n frūmentārius m.

cornfield n seges f.

cornel n (tree) cornus f.

corner n angulus m.

cornet n cornū nt.

cornice n corōna f.

coronet n diadēma nt.

corporal adj corporeus.

corporal punishment n verbera ntpl.

corporation n collēgium nt; (civic) magistrātūs mpl.

corporeal adj corporeus.

corps n manus f.

corpse n cadāver nt.

corpulence n obēsum corpus nt.

corpulent adj obēsus, pinguis.

corpuscle n corpusculum nt.

corral n praesēpe nt.

correct vt corrigere, ēmendāre; (person) castīgāre ♦ adj vērus; (language) integer; (style) ēmendātus.

correction n ēmendātiō f; (moral) corrēctiō f; (punishment) castīgātiō f.

correctly adv bene, vērē.

correctness n (fact) vēritās f; (language) integritās f; (moral) probitās f.

corrector n ēmendātor m, corrēctor m.

correspond vi (agree) respondēre (dat), congruere (dat); (by letter) inter sē scrībere.

correspondence n similitūdō f; epistulae fpl.

correspondent n epistulārum scrīptor m.

corresponding adj pār.

correspondingly adv pariter.

corridor n porticus f.

corrigible adj ēmendābilis.

corroborate vt cōnfirmāre.

corroboration n cōnfirmātiō f.

corrode vt ērōdere, edere.

corrosive adj edāx.

corrugate vt rūgāre.

corrugated adj rūgōsus.

corrupt vt corrumpere, dēprāvāre; (text) vitiāre ♦ adj corruptus, vitiātus; (person) prāvus, vēnālis; (text) vitiātus.

corrupter n corruptor m.

corruptible adj (matter) dissolūbilis; (person) vēnālis.

corruption n (of matter) corruptiō f; (moral) corruptēla f, dēprāvātiō f; (bribery) ambitus m.

corsair n pīrāta m.

cortège n pompa f.

coruscate vi fulgēre.

coruscation n fulgor m.

Corybant n Corybās m.

Corybantic adj Corybantius.

cosmetic n medicāmen nt.

cosmic adj mundānus.

cosmopolitan adj mundānus.

cosmos n mundus m.

cost vt ēmī, stāre (dat); it ~ me dear māgnō mihi stetit, male ēmī; it ~ me a talent talentō mihi stetit, talentō ēmī; it ~ me my freedom lībertātem perdidī ♦ n pretium m, impēnsa f; ~ of living annōna f; to your ~ incommodō tuō, dētrīmentō tuō; at the ~ of one's reputation violātā fāmā, nōn salvā existimātiōne; I sell at ~ price quantī ēmī vēndō.

costliness n sūmptus m; cāritās f.

costly adj cārus; (furnishings) lautus, sūmptuōsus.

costume n habitus m.

cosy adj commodus.

cot n lectulus m.

cote n columbārium nt.

cottage n casa f, tugurium nt.

cottager n rūsticus m.

cotton n (tree) gossypinus f; (cloth) xylinum nt.

couch n lectus m ♦ vi recumbere ♦ vt (lance) intendere; (words) exprimere, reddere.

cough n tussis f ♦ vi tussīre.

council n concilium nt; (small) cōnsilium nt.

councillor n (town) decuriō m.

counsel n (debate) cōnsultātiō f; (advice) cōnsilium nt; (law) advocātus m, patrōnus m; take ~ cōnsiliārī, dēlīberāre; take ~ of cōnsulere ♦ vt suādēre (dat), monēre.

counsellor n cōnsiliārius m.

count vt numerāre, computāre; ~ as dūcere, habēre; ~ amongst pōnere in (abl); ~ up vt ēnumerāre; ~ upon cōnfīdere (dat); be ~ed among vi aestimārī, habērī ♦ n ratiō f; (in indictment) caput nt;

(title) comes m.

countenance n faciēs f, vultus m, ōs nt; *(fig)* favor m; **put out of ~** conturbāre ♦ vt favēre *(dat)*, indulgēre *(dat)*.

counter n *(for counting)* calculus m; *(for play)* tessera f; *(shop)* mēnsa f ♦ adj contrārius ♦ adv contrā, obviam ♦ vt obsistere *(dat)*, respondēre *(dat)*.

counteract vt obsistere *(dat)*, adversārī *(dat)*; *(malady)* medērī *(dat)*.

counterattack vt in vicem oppugnāre, adgredī.

counterattraction n altera illecebra f.

counterbalance vt compēnsāre, exaequāre.

counterclockwise adv sinistrōrsus.

counterfeit adj falsus, fūcātus, adsimulātus, fictus ♦ vt fingere, simulāre, imitārī.

countermand vt renūntiāre.

counterpane n lōdīx f, strāgulum nt.

counterpart n pār m/f/nt.

counterpoise n aequum pondus nt ♦ vt compēnsāre, exaequāre.

countersign n *(MIL)* tessera f.

counting table n abacus m.

countless adj innumerābilis.

countrified adj agrestis, rūsticus.

country n *(region)* regiō f, terra f; *(territory)* fīnēs mpl; *(native)* patria f; *(not town)* rūs nt; *(open)* agrī mpl; **of our ~** nostrās; **live in the ~** rūsticārī; **living in the ~** rūsticātiō f.

country house n vīlla f.

countryman n agricola m; **fellow ~** populāris m, cīvis m.

countryside n agrī mpl, rus nt.

couple n pār nt; **a ~ of** duo ♦ vt cōpulāre, coniungere.

couplet n distichon nt.

courage n fortitūdō f, animus m; *(MIL)* virtūs f; **have the ~ to** audēre; **lose ~** animōs dēmittere; **take ~** bonō animō esse.

courageous adj fortis, ācer; audāx.

courageously adv fortiter, ācriter.

courier n tabellārius m.

course n *(movement)* cursus m; *(route)* iter nt; *(sequence)* seriēs f; *(career)* dēcursus; *(for races)* stadium nt, circus m; *(of dinner)* ferculum nt; *(of stones)* ōrdō m; *(of water)* lāpsus m; **of ~** certē, sānē, scīlicet; **as a matter of ~** continuō; **in due ~** mox; **in the ~ of** inter *(acc)*, in *(abl)*; **keep on one's ~** cursum tenēre; **be driven off one's ~** dēicī; **second ~** secunda mēnsa.

court n *(space)* ārea f; *(of house)* ātrium nt; *(of king)* aula f; *(suite)* cohors f, comitēs mpl; *(law)* iūdicium nt, iūdicēs mpl; **pay ~ to** ambīre, īnservīre *(dat)*; **hold a ~** forum agere; **bring into ~** in iūs vocāre ♦ vt colere, ambīre; *(danger)* sē offerre *(dat)*; *(woman)* petere.

courteous adj cōmis, urbānus, hūmānus.

courteously adv cōmiter, urbānē.

courtesan n meretrīx f.

courtesy n *(quality)* cōmitās f, hūmānitās f; *(act)* officium nt.

courtier n aulicus m; **~s** pl aula f.

courtly adj officiōsus.

cousin n cōnsobrīnus m, cōnsobrīna f.

cove n sinus m.

covenant n foedus nt, pactum nt ♦ vi pacīscī.

cover vt tegere, operīre; *(hide)* vēlāre; *(march)* claudere; **~ over** obdūcere; **~ up** vi obtegere ♦ n integumentum nt, operculum nt; *(shelter)* latebrae fpl, suffugium nt; *(pretence)* speciēs f; **under ~ of** sub (*abl*), sub speciē (*gen*); **take ~** dēlitēscere.

covering n integumentum nt, involucrum nt, operculum nt; (*of couch*) strāgulum nt.

coverlet n lōdīx f.

covert adj occultus; (*language*) oblīquus ♦ n latebra f, perfugium nt; (*thicket*) dūmētum nt.

covertly adv occultē, sēcrētō.

covet vt concupīscere, expetere.

covetous adj avidus, cupidus.

covetously adv avidē, cupidē.

covetousness n aviditās f, cupiditās f.

covey n grex f.

cow n vacca f ♦ vt terrēre.

coward n ignāvus m.

cowardice n ignāvia f.

cowardly adj ignāvus.

cower vi subsīdere.

cowherd m bubulcus m.

cowl n cucullus m.

coxswain n rēctor m.

coy adj pudēns, verēcundus.

coyly adv pudenter, modestē.

coyness n pudor m, verēcundia f.

cozen vt fallere, dēcipere.

crab n cancer m.

crabbed adj mōrōsus, difficilis.

crack n (*chink*) rīma f; (*sound*) crepitus m ♦ vt findere, frangere; (*whip*) crepitāre (*abl*) ♦ vi (*open*) fatīscere; (*sound*) crepāre, crepitāre.

crackle vi crepitāre.

crackling n crepitus m.

cradle n cūnae fpl; (*fig*) incūnābula ntpl.

craft n ars f; (*deceit*) dolus m; (*boat*) nāvigium nt.

craftily adv callidē, sollerter; dolōsē.

craftsman n artifex m, faber m.

craftsmanship n ars f, artificium nt.

crafty adj callidus, sollers; dolōsus.

crag n rūpēs f, scopulus m.

cram vt farcīre, refercīre; (*with food*) sagīnāre.

cramp n convulsiō f; (*tool*) cōnfībula f ♦ vt coercēre, coartāre.

crane n (*bird*) grus f; (*machine*) māchina f, trochlea f.

crank n uncus m; (*person*) ineptus m.

crannied adj rīmōsus.

cranny n rīma f.

crash n (*fall*) ruīna f; (*noise*) fragor m ♦ vi ruere; strepere.

crass adj crassus; **~ stupidity** mera stultitia.

crate n crātēs fpl.

crater n crātēr m.

cravat n fōcāle nt.

crave vt (*desire*) concupīscere, adpetere, exoptāre; (*request*) ōrāre, obsecrāre.

craven adj ignāvus.

craving n cupīdō f, dēsīderium nt, adpetītiō f.

crawl vi (*animal*) serpere; (*person*) rēpere.

crayfish n commarus m.

craze n libīdō f ♦ vt mentem aliēnāre.

craziness n dēmentia f.

crazy adj dēmēns, fatuus.

creak vi crepāre.

creaking n crepitus m.

cream n spūma lactis f; (*fig*) flōs m.

crease n rūga f ♦ vt rūgāre.

create vt creāre, facere, gignere.

creation n (*process*) fabricātiō f; (*result*) opus nt; (*human*) hominēs mpl.

creative adj (*nature*) creātrīx; (*mind*) inventor, inventrīx.

creator n creātor m, auctor m, opifex m.

creature n animal nt; (*person*) homō m/f.

credence n fidēs f.

credentials n litterae
commendātīciae fpl; (fig)
auctōritās f.
credibility n fidēs f; (source)
auctōritās f.
credible adj crēdibilis; (witness)
locuplēs.
credit n (belief) fidēs f; (repute)
existimātiō f; (character)
auctōritās f, grātia f; (comm) fidēs
f; **be a ~ to** decus esse (gen); **it is to
your ~** tibī laudī est; **give ~ for**
laudem tribuere (gen); **have ~** fidē
stāre ♦ vt crēdere (dat); (with
money) acceptum referre (dat).
creditable adj honestus, laudābilis.
creditably adv honestē, cum laude.
creditor n crēditor m.
credulity n crēdulitās f.
credulous adj crēdulus.
creed n dogma nt.
creek n sinus m.
creel n vīdulus m.
creep vi (animal) serpere; (person)
rēpere; (flesh) horrēre.
cremate vt cremāre.
crescent n lūna f.
crescent-shaped adj lūnātus.
cress n nasturtium nt.
crest n crista f.
crested adj cristātus.
crestfallen adj dēmissus.
crevasse n hiātus m.
crevice n rīma f.
crew n nautae mpl, rēmigēs mpl,
grex f, turba f.
crib n (cot) lectulus m, (manger)
praesēpe nt.
cricket n gryllus m.
crier n praecō m.
crime n scelus nt, facinus nt,
flāgitium nt.
criminal adj scelestus, facinorōsus,
flāgitiōsus ♦ n reus m.
criminality n scelus nt.
criminally adv scelestē, flāgitiōsē.
crimson n coccum nt ♦ adj

coccineus.
cringe vi adūlārī, adsentārī.
crinkle n rūga f.
cripple vt dēbilitāre, mūtilāre; (fig)
frangere ♦ adj claudus.
crisis n discrīmen nt.
crisp adj fragilis; (manner) alacer;
(hair) crispus.
crisscross adj in quīncuncem
dispositus.
criterion n index m, indicium nt;
take as a ~ referre ad (acc).
critic n iūdex m; (literary) criticus,
grammaticus m; (adverse)
castīgātor m.
critical adj (mind) accūrātus,
ēlegāns; (blame) cēnsōrius,
sevērus; (danger) perīculōsus,
dubius; **~ moment** discrīmen nt.
critically adv accūrātē, ēleganter;
sevērē; cum perīculō.
criticism n iūdicium nt; (adverse)
reprehēnsiō f.
criticize vt iūdicāre; reprehendere,
castīgāre.
croak vi (raven) crōcīre; (frog)
coaxāre.
croaking n cantus m ♦ adj raucus.
crock n olla f.
crockery n fictilia ntpl.
crocodile n crocodīlus m; **weep ~
tears** lacrimās cōnfingere.
crocus n crocus m.
croft n agellus m.
crone n anus f.
crony n sodālis m.
crook n pedum nt ♦ vt incurvāre.
crooked adj incurvus, aduncus;
(deformed) prāvus; (winding)
flexuōsus; (morally) perversus.
crookedly adv perversē, prāvē.
crookedness n prāvitās f.
croon vt, vi cantāre.
crop n (grain) seges f, messis f;
(tree) fructus m; (bird) ingluviēs f
♦ vt (reap) metere; (graze)
carpere, tondēre; **~ up** vi

intervenīre.

cross n (*mark*) decussis m; (*torture*)
crux f ♦ *adj* trānsversus,
oblīquus; (*person*) acerbus, īrātus
♦ *vt* trānsīre; (*water*) trāicere;
(*mountain*) trānscendere;
superāre; (*enemy*) obstāre (dat),
frustrārī; **~ out** *vt* (*writing*)
expungere ♦ *vi* trānsīre; **~ over**
(*on foot*) trānsgredī; (*by sea*)
trānsmittere.

crossbar n iugum nt.

crossbow n scorpiō m.

cross-examination n interrogātiō
f.

cross-examine *vt* interrogāre,
percontārī.

cross-grained *adj* (*fig*) mōrōsus.

crossing n trānsitus m; (*on water*)
trāiectus m.

cross purpose n: **be at ~s** dīversa
spectāre.

cross-question *vt* interrogāre.

crossroads n quadrivium nt.

crosswise *adv* ex trānsversō;
divide ~ decussāre.

crotchety *adj* mōrōsus, difficilis.

crouch *vi* subsīdere, sē submittere.

crow n cornīx f; **as the ~ flies** rēctā
regiōne ♦ *vi* cantāre; (*fig*)
exsultāre, gestīre.

crowbar n vectis m.

crowd n turba f, concursus m,
frequentia f; (*small*) grex m;
multitūdō f; **in ~s** gregātim ♦ *vi*
frequentāre, celebrāre ♦ *vt* (*place*)
complēre; (*person*) stīpāre.

crowded *adj* frequēns.

crown n corōna f; (*royal*) diadēma
nt; (*of head*) vertex m; (*fig*) apex m,
flōs m; **the ~ of** summus ♦ *vt*
corōnāre; (*fig*) cumulāre,
fastīgium impōnere (dat).

crucial *adj* gravissimus, māximī
mōmentī; **~ moment** discrīmen nt.

crucifixion n crucis supplicium nt.

crucify *vt* crucī suffīgere.

crude *adj* crūdus; (*style*) dūrus,
inconcinnus.

crudely *adv* dūrē, asperē.

crudity n asperitās f.

cruel *adj* crūdēlis, saevus, atrōx.

cruelly *adv* crūdēliter, atrōciter.

cruelty n crūdēlitās f, saevitia f,
atrōcitās f.

cruise n nāvigātiō f ♦ *vi* nāvigāre.

cruiser n speculātōria nāvis f.

crumb n mīca f.

crumble *vi* corruere, putrem fierī
♦ *vt* putrefacere, friāre.

crumbling *adj* putris.

crumple *vt* rūgāre.

crunch *vt* dentibus frangere.

crupper n postilēna f.

crush *vt* frangere, contundere,
obterere; (*fig*) adflīgere,
opprimere, obruere ♦ n turba f,
frequentia f.

crust n crusta f; (*bread*) frustum nt.

crusty *adj* (*fig*) stomachōsus.

crutch n baculum nt.

cry *vt, vi* clāmāre, clāmitāre;
(*weep*) flēre; (*infant*) vāgīre; **~
down** dētrectāre; **~ out**
exclāmāre, vōciferārī; **~ out
against** adclāmāre, reclāmāre; **~
up** laudāre, vēnditāre ♦ n clāmor
m, vōx f; (*child's*) vāgītus m; (*of
grief*) plōrātus m.

cryptic *adj* arcānus.

crystal n crystallum nt ♦ *adj*
crystallinus.

cub n catulus m.

cube n cubus m.

cubit n cubitum nt.

cuckoo n coccyx m.

cucumber n cucumis m.

cud n: **chew the ~** rūmināri.

cudgel n fustis m ♦ *vt* verberāre.

cue n signum nt, indicium nt.

cuff n (*blow*) alapa f.

cuirass n lōrīca f.

culinary *adj* coquīnārius.

cull *vt* legere, carpere, dēlībāre.

culminate vi ad summum fastīgium venīre.

culmination n fastīgium nt.

culpability n culpa f, noxa f.

culpable adj nocēns.

culprit n reus m.

cultivate vt (land) colere, subigere; (mind) excolere; (interest) fovēre, studēre (dat).

cultivation n cultus m, cultūra f.

cultivator n cultor m, agricola m.

cultural adj hūmānior.

culture n hūmānitās f, bonae artēs fpl.

cultured adj doctus, litterātus.

culvert n cloāca f.

cumber vt impedīre, obesse (dat); (load) onerāre.

cumbersome adj molestus, gravis.

cumulative adj alius ex aliō; **be ~** cumulārī.

cuneiform adj cuneātus.

cunning adj callidus, astūtus ♦ n ars f, astūtia f, calliditās f.

cunningly adv callidē, astūtē.

cup n pōculum nt; **drink the ~ of** (fig) exanclāre, exhaurīre; **in one's ~s** ēbrius, pōtus.

cupboard n armārium nt.

Cupid n Cupīdō m, Amor m.

cupidity n avāritia f.

cupola n tholus m.

cupping glass n cucurbita f.

cur n canis m.

curable adj sānābilis.

curative adj salūbris.

curator n custōs m.

curb vt frēnāre, īnfrēnāre; (fig) coercēre, cohibēre ♦ n frēnum nt.

curdle vt cōgere ♦ vi concrēscere.

curds n concrētum lac nt.

cure vt sānāre, medērī (dat) ♦ n remedium nt; (process) sānātiō f.

curio n dēliciae fpl.

curiosity n studium nt; (thing) mīrāculum nt.

curious adj (inquisitive) cūriōsus,

cupidus; (artistic) ēlabōrātus; (strange) mīrus, novus.

curiously adv cūriōsē; summā arte; mīrum in modum.

curl n (natural) cirrus m; (artificial) cincinnus m ♦ vt (hair) crīspāre ♦ vi (smoke) volvī.

curling irons n calamistrī mpl.

curly adj crispus.

currency n (coin) monēta f; (use) ūsus m; **gain ~** (rumour) percrēbrēscere.

current adj vulgātus, ūsitātus; (time) hīc ♦ n flūmen nt; **with the ~** secundō flūmine; **against the ~** adversō flūmine.

currently adv vulgō.

curriculum n īnstitūtiō f.

curry vt (favour) aucupārī.

curse n exsecrātiō f, maledictum nt; (formula) exsecrābile carmen nt; (fig) pestis f; ~s (interj) malum! ♦ vt exsecrārī, maledīcere (dat).

cursed adj exsecrātus, sacer; scelestus.

cursorily adv breviter, strictim.

cursory adj brevis.

curt adj brevis.

curtail vt minuere, contrahere.

curtailment n dēminūtiō f, contractiō f.

curtain n aulaeum nt ♦ vt vēlāre.

curule adj curūlis.

curve n flexus m, arcus m ♦ vt flectere, incurvāre, arcuāre.

cushion n pulvīnus m.

custodian n custōs m.

custody n custōdia f, tūtēla f; (prison) carcer m; **hold in ~** custōdīre.

custom n mōs m, cōnsuētūdō f; (national) īnstitūtum nt; ~s pl portōria ntpl.

customarily adv plērumque, dē mōre, vulgō.

customary adj solitus, ūsitātus; (rite) sollemnis; **it is ~** mōs est.

customer n emptor m.
customs officer n portitor m.
cut vt secāre, caedere, scindere;
  (corn) metere; (branch) amputāre;
  (acquaintance) āversārī; (hair)
  dētondēre; ~ **away** abscindere,
  resecāre; ~ **down** rescindere,
  caedere, succīdere; ~ **into**
  incīdere; ~ **off** vt abscīdere,
  praecīdere; (exclude) exclūdere;
  (intercept) interclūdere,
  intercipere; (head) abscindere; ~
  out vt excīdere, exsecāre; (omit)
  ōmittere; ~ **out for** aptus ad, nātus
  ad (acc); ~ **round** circumcīdere; ~
  short praecīdere; (speech)
  incīdere, interrumpere; ~
  through intercīdere; ~ **up** vt
  concīdere ♦ n vulnus nt.
cutlass n gladius m.
cutlery n cultrī mpl.
cutter n sector m; (boat) lembus m.
cutthroat n sīcārius m.
cutting n (plant) propāgō f ♦ adj
  acūtus; (fig) acerbus, mordāx.
cuttlefish n sēpia f.
cyclamen n baccar nt.
cycle n orbis m.
cyclone n turbō f.
cylinder n cylindrus m.
cymbal n cymbalum nt.
cynic n (PHILOS) cynicus m.
cynical adj mordāx, acerbus.
cynically adv mordāciter, acerbē.
cynicism n acerbitās f.
cynosure n cynosūra f.
cypress n cypressus f.

D

dabble vi: ~ **in** gustāre, leviter
  attingere.
dactyl n dactylus m.
dactylic adj dactylicus.
dagger n sīca f, pugiō f.
daily adj diūrnus, cottīdiānus ♦ adv
  cottīdiē, in diēs.

daintily adv molliter, concinnē;
  fastīdiōsē.
daintiness n munditia f,
  concinnitās f; (squeamish)
  fastīdium nt.
dainty adj mundus, concinnus,
  mollis; fastīdiōsus ♦ npl: **dainties**
  cuppēdia ntpl.
dais n suggestus m.
daisy n bellis f.
dale n vallis f.
dalliance n lascīvia f.
dally vi lūdere; morārī.
dam n mōlēs f, agger m; (animal)
  māter f ♦ vt obstruere,
  exaggerāre.
damage n damnum nt,
  dētrīmentum nt, malum nt;
  (inflicted) iniūria f; (law) damnum
  nt; **assess ~s** lītem aestimāre ♦ vt
  laedere, nocēre (dat); (by evidence)
  laedere; (reputation) violāre.
damageable adj fragilis.
dame n mātrōna f, domina f.
damn vt damnāre, exsecrārī.
damnable adj dētestābilis,
  improbus.
damnably adv improbē.
damnation n malum nt.
damp adj ūmidus ♦ n ūmor m ♦ vt
  madefacere; (enthusiasm)
  restinguere, dēmittere.
damsel n puella f, virgō f.
damson n Damascēnum nt.
dance vi saltāre ♦ n saltātiō f;
  (religious) tripudium nt.
dancer n saltātor m, saltātrīx f.
dandruff n porrīgō f.
dandy n dēlicātus m.
danger n perīculum nt, discrīmen
  nt.
dangerous adj perīculōsus,
  dubius; (in attack) īnfestus.
dangerously adv perīculōsē.
dangle vt suspendere ♦ vi
  pendēre.
dank adj ūmidus.

dapper adj concinnus, nitidus.
dapple vt variāre, distinguere.
dappled adj maculōsus, distinctus.
dare vt audēre; (challenge) prōvocāre; **I ~ say** haud sciō an.
daring n audācia f ♦ adj audāx.
daringly adv audācter.
dark adj obscūrus, opācus; (colour) fuscus, āter; (fig) obscūrus; **it is getting ~** advesperāscit; **keep ~** silēre ♦ n tenebrae fpl; (mist) cālīgō f; **keep in the ~** cēlāre.
darken vt obscūrāre, occaecāre.
darkish adj subobscūrus.
darkling adj obscūrus.
darkness n tenebrae fpl; (mist) cālīgō f.
darksome adj obscūrus.
darling adj cārus, dīlēctus ♦ n dēliciae fpl, voluptās f.
darn vt resarcīre.
darnel n lolium nt.
dart n tēlum nt; iaculum nt ♦ vi ēmicāre, sē conicere ♦ vt iaculārī, iacere.
dash vt adflīgere; (hope) frangere; **~ against** illīdere, incutere; **~ down** dēturbāre; **~ out** ēlīdere; **~ to pieces** discutere; **~ to the ground** prōsternere ♦ vi currere, sē incitāre, ruere ♦ n impetus m; (quality) ferōcia f.
daybook n adversāria ntpl.
dashing adj ferōx, animōsus.
dastardly adj ignāvus.
date n (fruit) palmula f; (time) tempus nt, diēs m/f; **out of ~** obsolētus; **become out of ~** exolēscere; **to ~** adhūc; **be up to ~** praesentī mōre ūtī ♦ vt (letter) diem adscrībere; (past event) repetere ♦ vi initium capere.
dative n datīvus m.
daub vt inlinere.
daughter n fīlia f; (little) fīliola f.
daughter-in-law n nurus f.
daunt vt terrēre, perterrēre.
dauntless adj impavidus,

intrepidus.
dauntlessly adv impavidē, intrepidē.
dawdle vi cessāre, cunctārī.
dawdler n cunctātor m.
dawn n aurōra f, dīlūculum nt; (fig) orīgō f; prima lux f; **at ~** prīmā lūce ♦ vi dīlūcēscere, **day ~s** diēs illūcēscit; **it ~s upon me** mente concipiō.
day n diēs m/f; (period) aetās f; **~ about** alternīs diēbus; **~ by ~** in diēs; cotīdiē; **by ~** adj diūrnus ♦ adv interdiū; **during the ~** interdiū; **every ~** cotīdiē; **from ~ to ~** in diēs, dies in diem; **late in the ~** multō diē; **next ~** postrīdiē; **one ~/some ~** ōlim; **the ~ after** adv postrīdiē ♦ conj postrīdiē quam; **the ~ after tomorrow** perendiē; **the ~ before** adv prīdiē ♦ conj prīdiē quam; **the ~ before yesterday** nūdius tertius; **the present ~** haec aetās; **time of ~** hōra; **twice a ~** bis (in) diē; **~s of old** praeteritum tempus; **~s to come** posterītās; **better ~s** rēs prosperae; **evil ~s** rēs adversae; **three ~s** trīduum nt; **two ~s** bīduum nt; **win the ~** vincere.
daybook n adversāria ntpl.
daybreak n aurōra f, prima lūx f.
daylight n diēs m; (become) ~ illūcēscere.
daystar n lūcifer m.
daytime n diēs m; **in the ~** interdiū.
daze vt obstupefacere ♦ n stupor m.
dazzle vt praestringere.
dazzling adj splendidus, nitēns.
deacon n diāconus m.
deaconess n diāconissa f.
dead adj mortuus; (in battle) occīsus; (ur) frīgidus; (place) iners, sōlitārius; (senses) hebes; **~ of night** nox intempesta f; **be ~ to**

nōn sentīre; **in ~ earnest** sēriō ac
vērō; **rise from the ~** revīvīscere
♦ *adv* prōrsus, omnīnō.
dead beat *adj* cōnfectus.
dead body *n* cadāver *m.*
dead calm *n* malacia *f.*
dead certainty *n* rēs certissima.
deaden *vt* (*senses*) hebetāre,
obtundere; (*pain*) restinguere.
deadlock *n* incitae *fpl*; **reach a ~** ad
incitās redigī.
dead loss *n* mera iactūra.
deadly *adj* fūnestus, exitiōsus,
exitiābilis; (*enmity*) implācābilis;
(*pain*) acerbissimus.
dead weight *n* mōlēs *f.*
deaf *adj* surdus; **become ~**
obsurdēscere; **be ~ to** nōn audīre,
obdūrēscere contrā.
deafen *vt* (*with noise*) obtundere.
deafness *n* surditās *f.*
deal *n* (*amount*) cōpia *f*; **a good ~**
aliquantum *nt*, bona pars *f*; (*wood*)
abiēs *f* ♦ *adj* abiēgnus ♦ *vt* (*blow*)
dare, īnflīgere; (*share*) dīvidere,
partīrī ♦ *vi* agere, negōtiārī; **~
with** *vt fus* (*person*) agere cum
(*abl*); (*matter*) tractāre.
dealer *n* (*wholesale*) negōtiātor *m,*
mercātor *m*; (*retail*) caupō *m.*
dealings *n* commercium *nt,*
negōtium *nt*, rēs *f.*
dean *n* decānus *m.*
dear *adj* (*love*) cārus, grātus; (*cost*)
cārus, pretiōsus; **my ~ Quintus** mī
Quīnte; (*beginning of letter from
Marcus*) Marcus Quintō salūtem; **~
me!** (*surprise*) ehem!; (*sorrow*) hei!; **buy ~** male emere; **sell ~**
bene vēndere.
dearly *adv* (*love*) valdē, ārdenter;
(*value*) magnī.
dearness *n* cāritās *f.*
dearth *n* inopia *f*, pēnūria *f.*
death *n* mors *f*; (*natural*) obitus *m*;
(*violent*) nex *f*, interitus *m*;
condemn to ~ capitis damnāre;

put to ~ interficere; **give the ~
blow to** interimere.
deathbed *n*: **on one's ~** moriēns,
moribundus.
deathless *adj* immortālis.
deathly *adj* pallidus.
debar *vt* prohibēre, exclūdere.
debase *vt* dēprāvāre, corrumpere;
(*coin*) adulterāre; (*self*)
prōsternere, dēmittere.
debasement *n* dēdecus *nt*; (*coin*)
adulterium *nt.*
debatable *adj* ambiguus, dubius.
debate *vt* disputāre, disceptāre
♦ *n* contrōversia *f*, disceptātiō *f,*
altercātiō *f.*
debater *n* disputātor *m.*
debauch *vt* corrumpere, pellicere
♦ *n* cōmissātiō *f.*
debauched *adj* perditus, prāvus.
debauchee *n* cōmissātor *m.*
debaucher *n* corruptor *m.*
debauchery *n* luxuria *f*, stuprum
nt.
debilitate *vt* dēbilitāre.
debility *n* īnfirmitās *f.*
debit *n* expēnsum *nt* ♦ *vt* in
expēnsum referre.
debonair *adj* urbānus, cōmis.
debouch *vi* exīre.
debris *n* rūdus *nt.*
debt *n* aes aliēnum *nt*; (*booked*)
nōmen *nt*; (*fig*) dēbitum *nt*; **be in ~**
in aere aliēnō esse; **pay off ~** aes
aliēnum persolvere; **run up ~** aes
aliēnum contrahere; **collect ~s**
nōmina exigere; **abolition of ~s**
novae tabulae *fpl.*
debtor *n* dēbitor *m.*
decade *n* decem annī *mpl.*
decadence *n* occāsus *m.*
decadent *adj* dēgener, dēterior.
decamp *vi* (*MIL*) castra movēre;
(*fig*) discēdere, aufugere.
decant *vt* dēfundere, diffundere.
decanter *n* lagoena *f.*
decapitate *vt* dētruncāre.

decay vi dīlābī, perīre, putrēscere; (fig) tābēscere, senēscere ♦ n ruīna f, lāpsus m; (fig) occāsus m, dēfectiō f.

deceased adj mortuus.

deceit n fraus f, fallācia f, dolus m.

deceitful adj fallāx, fraudulentus, dolōsus.

deceitfully adv fallāciter, dolōsē.

deceive vt dēcipere, fallere, circumvenīre, fraudāre.

deceiver n fraudātor m.

December n mēnsis December m; of ~ December.

decemvir n decemvir m; of the ~s decemvirālis.

decemvirate n decemvirātus m.

decency n honestum nt, decōrum nt, pudor m.

decent adj honestus, pudēns.

decently adv honestē, pudenter.

deception n fraus f, fallācia f.

deceptive adj fallāx, fraudulentus.

decide vt, vi (dispute) diiūdicāre, dēcernere, dīrimere; ~ to do statuere, cōnstituere (infin); I have ~d mihī certum est; ~ the issue dēcernere.

decided adj certus, firmus.

decidedly adv certē, plānē.

deciduous adj cadūcus.

decimate vt decimum quemque occīdere.

decipher vt expedīre, ēnōdāre.

decision n (of judge) iūdicium nt; (of council) dēcrētum nt; (of senate) auctōritās f; (of referee) arbitrium nt; (personal) sententia f; (quality) cōnstantia f.

decisive adj certus; ~ moment discrīmen nt.

decisively adv sine dubiō.

deck vt ōrnāre, exōrnāre ♦ n (ship) pōns m; with a ~ cōnstrātus.

decked adj ōrnātus; (ship) cōnstrātus.

declaim vt, vi dēclāmāre, prōnūntiāre.

declamation n dēclāmātiō f.

declamatory adj dēclāmātōrius.

declaration n affirmātiō f, adsevērātiō f; (formal) professiō f; (of war) dēnūntiātiō f.

declare vt affirmāre, adsevērāre; (secret) aperīre, expōnere; (proclamation) dēnūntiāre, ēdīcere; (property in census) dēdicāre; (war) indīcere.

declension n dēclīnātiō f.

declination n dēclīnātiō f.

decline n (slope) dēclīve nt, dēiectus m; (of age) senium nt; (of power) dēfectiō f; (of nation) occāsus m ♦ vi inclīnāre, occidere; (fig) ruere, dēlābī, dēgenerāre ♦ vt dētrectāre, recūsāre; (GRAM) dēclīnāre.

decode vt expedīre, ēnōdāre.

decompose vt dissolvere ♦ vi putrēscere.

decomposed adj putridus.

decomposition n dissolūtiō f.

decorate vt ōrnāre, decorāre.

decoration n ōrnāmentum nt; (medal) īnsigne nt.

decorous adj pudēns, modestus, decōrus.

decorously adv pudenter, modestē.

decorum n pudor m, honestum nt.

decoy n illecebra f ♦ vt adlicere, inescāre.

decrease n dēminūtiō f, dēcessiō f ♦ vt dēminuere, extenuāre ♦ vi dēcrēscere.

decree n (of magistrate) dēcrētum nt, ēdictum nt; (of senate) cōnsultum nt, auctōritās f; (of people) scītum nt ♦ vt ēdīcere, dēcernere; (people) iubēre; the senate ~s placet senātuī.

decrepit adj īnfirmus, dēbilis, dēcrepitus.

decrepitude n īnfirmitās f, dēbilitās f.

decry vt obtrectāre, reprehendere.

decurion n decuriō m.

dedicate vt dēdicāre, cōnsecrāre; (life) dēvovēre.

dedication n dēdicātiō f; dēvōtiō f.

dedicatory adj commendātīcius.

deduce vt colligere, conclūdere.

deduct vt dēmere, dētrahere.

deduction n (inference) conclūsiō f, cōnsequēns nt; (subtraction) dēductiō f, dēminūtiō f.

deed n factum m, facinus nt; gestum nt; (legal) tabulae fpl; ~s pl rēs gestae fpl.

deem vt dūcere, cēnsēre, habēre.

deep adj altus, profundus; (discussion) abstrūsus; (sleep) artus; (sound) gravis; (width) lātus; **three ~** (MIL) ternī in lātitūdinem ♦ n altum nt.

deepen vt dēfodere, altiōrem reddere; (fig) augēre ♦ vi altiōrem fierī; (fig) crēscere.

deepest adj īmus.

deeply adv altē, graviter; (inside) penitus; **very ~** valdē, vehementer.

deep-seated adj (fig) inveterātus.

deer n cervus m, cerva f; (fallow) dāma f.

deface vt dēfōrmāre, foedāre.

defaced adj dēfōrmis.

defacement n dēfōrmitās f.

defalcation n peculātus m.

defamation n calumnia f, opprobrium nt.

defamatory adj contumēliōsus, probrōsus.

defame vt īnfāmāre, obtrectāre, calumniārī.

default vi deesse; (money) nōn solvere ♦ n dēfectiō f, culpa f; **let judgment go by ~** vadimōnium dēserere, nōn respondēre.

defaulter n reus m.

defeat vt vincere, superāre; (completely) dēvincere; (plan) frustrārī, disicere ♦ n clādēs f; (at election) repulsa f, offēnsiō f; (of plan) frustrātiō f.

defeatism n patientia f.

defeatist n imbellis m.

defect n vitium nt.

defection n dēfectiō f, sēditiō f.

defective adj mancus, vitiōsus.

defence n praesidium nt, tūtēla f; patrōcinium nt; (speech) dēfēnsiō f; **speak in ~** dēfendere.

defenceless adj inermis, indēfēnsus; **leave ~** nūdāre.

defences npl mūnīmenta ntpl, mūnītiōnēs fpl.

defend vt dēfendere, tuērī, custōdīre.

defendant n reus m.

defender n dēfēnsor m, prōpugnātor m; (law) patrōnus m.

defensible adj iūstus.

defensive adj dēfēnsiōnis causā; **be on the ~** sē dēfendere.

defensively adv dēfendendō.

defer vt differre, prōlātāre ♦ vi mōrem gerere (dat); **I ~ to you in this** hōc tibī tribuō.

deference n obsequium nt, observantia f; **show ~ to** observāre, īnservīre (dat).

deferential adj observāns, officiōsus.

deferment n dīlātiō f, prōlātiō f.

defiance n ferōcia f, minae fpl.

defiant adj ferōx, mināx.

defiantly adv ferōciter, mināciter.

deficiency n vitium nt; (lack) pēnūria f, inopia f.

deficient adj vitiōsus, inops; **be ~** deesse, dēficere.

deficit n lacūna f.

defile n faucēs fpl, angustiae fpl ♦ vt inquināre, contāmināre.

defilement n sordēs f, foedītās f.

define vt (limits) fīnīre, dēfīnīre,

terminăre; (*meaning*) explicăre.
definite *adj* certus, dēfīnītus.
definitely *adv* dēfīnītē; prōrsus.
definition *n* dēfīnītiō *f*, explicātiō *f*.
definitive *adj* dēfīnītīvus.
deflate *vt* laxāre.
deflect *vt* dēdūcere, dēclīnāre ♦ *vi* dēflectere, dēgredī.
deflection *n* dēclīnātiō *f*, flexus *m*.
deform *vt* dēfōrmāre.
deformed *adj* dēfōrmis, distortus.
deformity *n* dēfōrmitās *f*, prāvitās *f*.
defraud *vt* fraudāre, dēfraudāre.
defrauder *n* fraudātor *m*.
defray *vt* solvere, suppeditāre.
deft *adj* habilis.
deftly *adv* habiliter.
defunct *adj* mortuus.
defy *vt* contemnere, spernere, adversārī (*dat*); (*challenge*) prōvocāre, lacessere.
degeneracy *n* dēprāvātiō *f*.
degenerate *adj* dēgener ♦ *vi* dēgenerāre, dēscīscere.
degradation *n* īnfāmia *f*, ignōminia *f*, nota *f*.
degrade *vt* notāre, abicere; (*from office*) movēre.
degrading *adj* turpis, indignus.
degree *n* gradus; (*social*) locus *m*; **in some ~** aliquā ex parte; **by ~s** gradātim, sēnsim.
deification *n* apotheōsis *f*.
deified *adj* (*emperor*) dīvus.
deify *vt* cōnsecrāre, inter deōs referre.
deign *vi* dignārī.
deity *n* deus *m*.
dejected *adj* afflīctus, dēmissus.
dejectedly *adv* animō dēmissō.
dejection *n* maestitia *f*.
delay *vt* dēmorārī, dētinēre, retardāre ♦ *vi* cunctārī, cessāre ♦ *n* mora *f*, cunctātiō *f*.
delayer *n* morātor *m*, cunctātor *m*.
delectable *adj* iūcundus, amoenus.

delegate *vt* lēgāre, mandāre, committere ♦ *n* lēgātus *m*.
delegation *n* lēgātiō *f*, lēgātī *mpl*.
delete *vt* dēlēre.
deleterious *adj* perniciōsus, noxius.
deletion *n* (*writing*) litūra *f*.
deliberate *vi* dēlīberāre, cōnsulere ♦ *adj* (*act*) cōnsīderātus; (*intention*) certus; (*manner*) cōnsīderātus; (*speech*) lentus.
deliberately *adv* dē industriā.
deliberation *n* dēlīberātiō *f*.
deliberative *adj* dēlīberātīvus.
delicacy *n* (*judgment*) subtīlitās *f*, ēlegantia *f*; (*manners*) mollitia *f*, luxus *m*; (*health*) valētūdō *f*; (*food*) cuppēdia *ntpl*.
delicate *adj* mollis; (*health*) īnfīrmus; (*shape*) gracilis; (*feelings*) hūmānus.
delicately *adv* molliter; hūmānē.
delicious *adj* suāvis, lautus.
delight *n* voluptās *f*, gaudium *nt*, dēlectātiō *f* ♦ *vt* dēlectāre, oblectāre, iuvāre ♦ *vi* gaudēre, dēlectārī.
delightful *adj* iūcundus, dulcis, festīvus; (*scenery*) amoenus.
delightfully *adv* iūcundē, suāviter.
delimitation *n* dēfīnītiō *f*.
delineate *vt* dēscrībere, dēpingere.
delineation *n* dēscrīptiō *f*.
delinquency *n* culpa *f*, dēlictum *nt*, noxa *f*.
delinquent *n* nocēns *m/f*, reus *m*.
delirious *adj* dēlīrus, āmēns, furiōsus; **be ~** furere, dēlīrāre.
delirium *n* furor *m*, āmentia *f*.
deliver *vt* (*from*) līberāre, exsolvere, ēripere; (*blow*) intendere; (*message*) referre; (*speech*) habēre; **~ to** dēferre, trādere, dare; **~ up** dēdere, trādere; **be ~ed of** parere.
deliverance *n* līberātiō *f*.

deliverer n līberātor m.
delivery n (of things due) trāditiō f;
(of speech) āctiō f, prōnūntiātiō f;
(of child) partus m.
dell n convallis f.
Delphi n Delphī mpl.
delude vt dēcipere, frustrārī,
dēlūdere.
deluge n ēluviō f ♦ vt inundāre.
delusion n error m, fraus f.
delusive adj fallāx, inānis.
delve vt fodere.
demagogue n plēbicola m.
demand vt poscere, postulāre,
imperāre; (urgently) flāgitāre,
poscere; (this due) exigere;
(answer) quaerere; ~ **back**
repetere ♦ n postulātiō f,
postulātum nt.
demarcation n līmes m.
demean vt (self) dēmittere.
demeanour n gestus m, mōs m,
habitus m.
demented adj dēmēns, furiōsus.
demerit n culpa f, vitium nt.
demesne n fundus m.
demigod n hērōs m.
demise n obitus m ♦ vt lēgāre.
democracy n cīvitās populāris f.
democrat n homō populāris m/f.
democratic adj populāris.
demolish vt dēmōlīrī, dīruere,
dēstruere; (argument) discutere.
demolition n ruīna f, ēversiō f.
demon n daemōn m.
demonstrate vt (show) mōnstrāre,
ostendere, indicāre; (prove)
dēmōnstrāre.
demonstration n exemplum nt;
(proof) dēmōnstrātiō f.
demonstrative adj (manner)
vehemēns, (RHET) dēmōnstrātīvus.
demoralization n corruptiō f,
dēprāvātiō f.
demoralize vt corrumpere,
dēprāvāre, labefactāre.
demote vt locō movēre.

demur vi gravārī, recūsāre ♦ n
mora f, dubitātiō f.
demure adj modestus, verēcundus.
demurely adv modestē,
verēcundē.
demureness n modestia f,
verēcundia f, pudor m.
demurrer n (law) exceptiō f.
den n latibulum nt, latebra f; (of
vice) lustrum nt.
denarius n dēnārius m.
denial n īnfitiātiō f, negātiō f.
denigrate vt obtrectāre,
calumniārī.
denizen n incola m/f.
denominate vt nōmināre,
appellāre.
denomination n nōmen nt;
(religious) secta f.
denote vt notāre, significāre.
denouement n exitus m.
denounce vt dēferre, incūsāre.
denouncer n dēlātor m.
dense adj dēnsus; (crowd)
frequēns; (person) stolidus.
density n crassitūdō f; (crowd)
frequentia f.
dent n nota f.
dentate adj dentātus.
denture n dentēs mpl.
denudation n spoliātiō f.
denude vt spoliāre, nūdāre.
denunciation n (report) indicium
nt, dēlātiō f; (threat) minae fpl.
deny vt īnfitiārī, īnfitiās īre,
negāre, abnuere; (on oath)
abiūrāre; ~ **oneself** genium
dēfraudāre.
depart vi discēdere (abl), abīre,
exīre, ēgredī.
department n (district) regiō f, pars
f; (duty) prōvincia f, mūnus nt.
departure n discessus m, abitus m,
dīgressus m, exitus m; (change)
mūtātiō f; (death) obitus m.
depend vi pendēre; (be dependent)
pendēre ex (abl), nītī (abl); (rely)

fīdere, cōnfīdere; **~ing on** frētus (*abl*).

dependable *adj* fīdus.

dependant *n* cliēns *m/f*.

dependence *n* clientēla *f*; (*reliance*) fīdūcia *f*.

dependency *n* prōvincia *f*.

dependent *adj* subiectus, obnoxius.

depict *vt* dēscrībere, dēpingere; (*to the life*) expingere.

deplete *vt* dēminuere.

depletion *n* dēminūtiō *f*.

deplorable *adj* turpis, nefandus, pessimus.

deplorably *adv* turpiter, pessimē, miserē.

deplore *vt* dēplōrāre, dēflēre, conquerī.

deploy *vt* explicāre; instruere, dispōnere.

depopulate *vt* vāstāre, nūdāre.

depopulation *n* vāstitās *f*, sōlitūdō *f*.

deport *vt* (*banish*) dēportāre; (*self*) gerere.

deportation *n* exsilium *nt*.

deportment *n* gestus *m*, habitus *m*.

depose *vt* dēmovēre, dēpellere; (*evidence*) testārī.

deposit *n* fīdūcia *f*, dēpositum *nt*
♦ *vt* dēpōnere, mandāre.

depositary *n* sequester *m*.

deposition *n* (*law*) testimōnium *nt*, indicium *nt*.

depository *n* apothēca *f*.

depot *n* (*for arms*) armāmentārium *nt*; (*for trade*) emporium *nt*.

deprave *vt* dēprāvāre, corrumpere.

depraved *adj* prāvus.

depravity *n* dēprāvātiō *f*, turpitūdō *f*.

deprecate *vt* abōminārī, dēprecārī.

deprecation *n* dēprecātiō *f*.

depreciate *vt* obtrectāre, dētrec-

tāre.

depreciation *n* obtrectātiō *f*; (*price*) vīlitās *f*.

depredation *n* praedātiō *f*, dīreptiō *f*.

depress *vt* dēprimere; (*mind*) afflīgere, frangere; **be ~ed** iacēre, animum dēspondēre.

depressing *adj* maestus, tristis.

depression *n* (*place*) cavum *nt*; (*mind*) tristitia *f*, sollicitūdō *f*.

deprivation *n* prīvātiō *f*, spoliātiō *f*.

deprive *vt* prīvāre, spoliāre.

depth *n* altitūdō *f*; (*place*) profundum *nt*, gurges *m*.

deputation *n* lēgātiō *f*, lēgātī *mpl*.

depute *vt* lēgāre, mandāre.

deputy *n* lēgātus *m*; (*substitute*) vicārius *m*.

derange *vt* conturbāre.

deranged *adj* īnsānus, mente captus.

derangement *n* perturbātiō *f*; (*mind*) īnsānia *f*, dēmentia *f*.

derelict *adj* dēsertus.

dereliction *n* (*of duty*) neglegentia *f*.

deride *vt* dērīdēre, inlūdere.

derision *n* rīsus *m*, irrīsiō *f*.

derisive *adj* mordāx.

derivation *n* orīgō *f*.

derive *vt* dūcere, trahere; (*advantage*) capere, parāre; (*pleasure*) dēcerpere, percipere; **be ~d** dēfluere.

derogate *vi* dērogāre, dētrahere; **~ from** imminuere, obtrectāre.

derogation *n* imminūtiō *f*, obtrectātiō *f*.

derogatory *adj* indignus; **~ remarks** obtrectātiō *f*.

derrick *n* trochlea *f*.

descant *vt* disserere ♦ *n* cantus *m*.

descend *vi* dēscendere; (*water*) dēlābī; (*from heaven*) dēlābī; (*by inheritance*) pervenīre, prōdī; (*morally*) dēlābī, sē dēmittere; **be**

~ed from orīrī ex (abl).

descendant n prōgeniēs f; ~s pl minōrēs mpl, posterī mpl.

descent n dēscensus m; (slope) clīvus m, dēiectus m; (birth) genus nt; (hostile) dēcursus m, incursiō f; **make a ~ upon** inrumpere in (acc), incursāre in (acc).

describe vt dēscrībere; (tell) nārrāre; (portray) dēpingere, exprimere.

description n dēscrīptiō f; (tale) nārrātiō f; (kind) genus nt.

descry vt cernere, cōnspicere, prōspectāre.

desecrate vt prōfānāre, exaugurāre.

desecration n exaugurātiō f, violātiō f.

desert vt dēserere, dērelinquere, dēstituere ♦ vi dēscīscere, dēficere ♦ adj dēsertus, sōlitārius ♦ n (place) sōlitūdō f, loca dēserta ntpl; (merit) meritum nt.

deserted adj dēsertus.

deserter n dēsertor m; (MIL) trānsfuga m.

desertion n dēfectiō f, trāns-fugium nt.

deserve vt merērī; dignus esse quī (+ subj); ~ **well of** bene merērī dē (abl).

deserved adj meritus.

deservedly adv meritō.

deserving adj dignus.

desiccate vt siccāre.

design n (drawing) adumbrātiō f; (plan) cōnsilium nt, prōpositum nt; **by ~** cōnsultō ♦ vt adumbrāre; in animō habēre.

designate vt dēsignāre, mōnstrāre; (as heir) scrībere; (as official) dēsignāre ♦ adj dēsignātus.

designation n nōmen nt, titulus m.

designedly adv dē industriā, cōnsultō.

designer n auctor m, inventor m.

designing adj vafer, dolōsus.

desirable adj optābilis, expetendus, grātus.

desire n cupiditās f; studium nt; (uncontrolled) libīdō f; (natural) adpetītiō f ♦ vt cupere; (much) exoptāre, expetere; (command) iubēre.

desirous adj cupidus, avidus, studiōsus.

desist vi dēsistere.

desk n scrīnium nt.

desolate adj dēsertus, sōlitārius; (place) vastus ♦ vt vastāre.

desolation n sōlitūdō f, vastitās f; (process) vastātiō f.

despair vi dēspērāre dē (abl), animum dēspondēre ♦ n dēspērātiō f.

despairingly adv dēspēranter.

dispatch see **dispatch**.

desperado n homō dēspērātus m.

desperate adj (hopeless) dēspērātus; (wicked) perditus; (dangerous) perīculōsus.

desperately adv dēspēranter.

desperation n dēspērātiō f.

despicable adj dēspectus, abiectus, turpis.

despicably adv turpiter.

despise vt contemnere, dēspicere, spernere.

despiser n contemptor m.

despite n malevolentia f, odium nt.

despoil vt spoliāre, nūdāre.

despoiler n spoliātor m, praedātor m.

despond vi animum dēspondēre, dēspērāre.

despondency n dēspērātiō f.

despondent adj abiectus, adflīctus, dēmissus; **be ~** animum dēspondēre.

despondently adv animō dēmissō.

despot n dominus m, rēx m.

despotic adj imperiōsus, superbus.

despotically adv superbē.

despotism n dominātiō f, superbia f, rēgnum nt.

dessert n secunda mēnsa f.

destination n fīnis m.

destine vt dēstināre, dēsignāre; **-d to be** futūrus.

destiny n fātum nt; **of ~** fātālis.

destitute adj inops, pauper, prīvātus; **~ of** expers (gen).

destitution n inopia f, egestās f.

destroy vt dēlēre, ēvertere, dīrimere, perdere.

destroyer n ēversor m.

destructible adj fragilis.

destruction n exitium nt, ēversiō f, excidium nt.

destructive adj exitiābilis, perniciōsus.

destructively adv perniciōsē.

desuetude n dēsuētūdō f.

desultorily adv carptim.

desultory adj varius, incōnstāns.

detach vt abiungere, sēiungere, āmovēre, sēparāre.

detachment n (MIL) manus f, cohors f; (mind) integer animus m, līber animus.

detail n: **~s** pl singula ntpl; **in ~** singillātim ♦ vt exsequī.

detain vt dēmorārī, dētinēre, distinēre, morārī.

detect vt dēprehendere, patefacere.

detection n dēprehēnsiō f.

detective n inquīsītor m.

detention n retentiō f; (prison) vincula ntpl.

deter vt dēterrēre, absterrēre, impedīre.

deteriorate vi dēgenerāre.

deterioration n dēprāvātiō f, lāpsus m.

determinate adj certus, fīnītus.

determination n obstinātiō f, cōnstantia f; (intention) prōpositum nt, sententia f.

determine vt (fix) fīnīre; (decide) statuere, cōnstituere.

determined adj obstinātus; (thing) certus; **I am ~ to** mihī certum est (infin).

determinedly adv cōnstanter.

deterrent n: **act as a ~ to** dēterrēre.

detest vt ōdisse, dētestārī.

detestable adj dētestābilis, odiōsus.

detestation n odium nt, invidia f.

dethrone vt rēgnō dēpellere.

detour n circuitus m; **make a ~** iter flectere; (MIL) agmen circumdūcere.

detract vi: **~ from** dērogāre, dētrahere.

detraction n obtrectātiō f.

detractor n obtrectātor m, invidus m.

detriment n damnum nt, dētrīmentum m.

detrimental adj damnōsus; **be ~ to** dētrīmentō esse (dat).

devastate vt vāstāre, populārī.

devastation n vāstātiō f, populātiō f; (state) vāstitās f.

develop vt ēvolvere, explicāre; (person) ēducāre, alere ♦ vi crēscere; **~ into** ēvādere in (acc).

development n explicātiō f; (of men) ēducātiō f; (of resources) cultus m; (of events) exitus m.

deviate vi dēcēdere dē viā, aberrāre, dēclīnāre; (speech) dēgredī.

deviation n dēclīnātiō f; (from truth) error m; (in speech) dīgressus m.

device n (plan) cōnsilium nt; (machine) māchina f; (emblem) īnsigne nt.

devil n diabolus m; **go to the ~** abī in malam crucem!; **talk of the ~** lupus in fābulā!

devilish adj scelestus, impius.

devil-may-care adj praeceps, lascīvus.

devilment n malitia f.

devilry n magicae artēs fpl.

devious adj dēvius, errābundus.

devise vt excōgitāre, commentārī, fingere.

devoid adj vacuus, expers; **be ~ of** carēre (abl).

devolve vi obtingere, obvenīre ♦ vt dēferre, committere.

devote vt dēdicāre; (attention) dēdere, trādere; (life) dēvovēre.

devoted adj dēditus, studiōsus; (victim) dēvōtus, sacer; **be ~ to** studēre (dat), incumbere (dat).

devotee n cultor m.

devotion n amor m, studium nt; rēligiō f.

devour vt dēvorāre, cōnsūmere; (fig) haurīre.

devout adj pius, rēligiōsus.

devoutly adv piē, rēligiōsē.

dew n rōs m.

dewy adj rōscidus.

dexterity n ars f, sollertia f.

dexterous adj sollers, habilis.

dexterously adv sollerter, habiliter.

diabolical adj scelestus, nefārius.

diadem n diadēma nt.

diagnose vt discernere, diiūdicāre.

diagnosis n iūdicium nt.

diagonal adj oblīquus.

diagram n fōrma f.

dial n sōlārium nt.

dialect n dialectus f, sermō m.

dialectic n ars disserendī f, dialecticē f ♦ adj dialecticus.

dialectician n dialecticus m.

dialogue n dialogus m, colloquium nt.

diameter n diametros f.

diamond n adamās m.

diaphanous adj perlūcidus.

diaphragm n praecordia ntpl.

diary n ephēmeris f.

diatribe n convīcium nt.

dice n tālus m, tessera f; **game of ~** ālea f.

dictate vt dictāre ♦ n praeceptum nt; **~s of nature** nātūrae iūdicia ntpl.

dictation n dictāta ntpl; (fig) arbitrium nt.

dictator n dictātor m; **~'s** dictātōrius.

dictatorial adj imperiōsus, superbus.

dictatorship n dictātūra f.

diction n (enunciation) ēlocūtiō f; (words) ōrātiō f.

dictionary n verbōrum thēsaurus m.

die n signum nt; **the ~ is cast** iacta ālea est ♦ vi morī, perīre, obīre; (in battle) cadere, occumbere; **~ off** dēmorī; **~ out** ēmorī; **be dying to** exoptāre.

diet n (food) diaeta f; (meeting) conventus m.

differ vi differre, discrepāre, dissentīre.

difference n discrepantia f, dissimilitūdō f; (of opinion) dissēnsiō f; **there is a ~** interest.

different adj dīversus, varius, dissimilis; **~ from** alius ... ac; **in ~ directions** dīversī; **they say ~ things** alius aliud dīcit.

differentiate vt discernere.

differently adv dīversē, variē, alius aliter; **~ from** aliter ... ac.

difficult adj difficilis, arduus; **very ~** perdifficilis, perarduus.

difficulty n difficultās f, labor m, negōtium nt; **with ~** difficulter, aegrē, vix; **be in ~** labōrāre.

diffidence n diffīdentia f; (shyness) pudor m; **with ~** modestē.

diffident adj diffīdēns; (shy) modestus, verēcundus.

diffidently adv modestē.

diffuse vt diffundere, dispergere; be ~d diffluere ♦ adj fūsus, diffūsus, cōpiōsus.

diffusely adv diffūsē, cōpiōsē.

diffuseness n cōpia f.

dig vt fodere, dūcere; (nudge) fodicāre; ~ up vt effodere, ēruere.

digest vt coquere, concoquere ♦ n summārium nt.

digestion n concoctiō f; with a bad ~ crūdus.

digger n fossor m.

dignified adj gravis, augustus.

dignify vt honōrāre, honestāre.

dignity n gravitās f, māiestās f, amplitūdō f.

digress vi dēvertere, dīgredī, dēclīnāre.

digression n dēclīnātiō f, dīgressus m.

dike n (ditch) fossa f; (mound) agger m.

dilapidated adj ruīnōsus.

dilapidation n ruīna f.

dilate vt dīlātāre; (speech) plūra dīcere.

dilatorily adv tardē, cunctanter.

dilatoriness n mora f, cunctātiō f.

dilatory adj tardus, lentus, segnis.

dilemma n nōdus m, angustiae fpl; be in a ~ haerēre; be on the horns of a ~ auribus tenēre lupum.

diligence n dīligentia f, industria f, cūra f.

diligent adj dīligēns, industrius, sēdulus.

diligently adv dīligenter, sēdulō.

dill n anēthum nt.

dilly-dally vi cessāre.

dilute vt dīluere, temperāre.

dim adj obscūrus; (fig) hebes ♦ vt obscūrāre, hebetāre.

dimension n modus m; ~s pl amplitūdō f, māgnitūdō f.

diminish vt minuere, imminuere, extenuāre, īnfringere ♦ vi

dēcrēscere.

diminution n imminūtiō f, dēminūtiō f.

diminutive adj parvulus, exiguus ♦ n (word) dēminūtum nt.

diminutiveness n exiguitās f.

dimly adv obscūrē.

dimness n tenebrae fpl, cālīgō f.

dimple n gelasīnus m.

din n fragor m, strepitus m; make a ~ strepere ♦ vt obtundere.

dine vi cēnāre.

diner n convīva m.

dinghy n scapha f.

dingy adj sordidus; (colour) fuscus.

dining room n cēnātiō f.

dinner n cēna f.

dinner party convīvium nt.

dint n ictus m; by ~ of per (acc).

dip vt imbuere, mergere ♦ vi mergī; ~ into (study) perstringere.

diploma n diplōma nt.

diplomacy n (embassy) lēgātiō f; (tact) iūdicium nt, sagācitās f.

diplomat n lēgātus m.

diplomatic adj sagāx, circumspectus.

diptych n tabellae fpl.

dire adj dīrus, horridus.

direct vt regere, dīrigere; (attention) attendere, advertere; (course) tendere; (business) administrāre, moderārī; (letter) īnscrībere; (order) imperāre (dat), iubēre; (to a place) viam mōnstrāre (dat); (weapon) intendere ♦ adj rēctus, dīrēctus; (person) simplex; (language) apertus ♦ adv rēctā.

direction n (of going) cursus m, iter nt; (of looking) pars f, regiō f; (control) administrātiō f, regimen nt; (order) praeceptum nt, iussum nt; in the ~ of Rome Rōmam versus; in all ~s passim, undique; in both ~s utrōque.

directly adv (place) rēctā; (time)

prōtinus, continuō, statim;
(*language*) apertē ♦ *conj* simulac.
directness *n* (*fig*) simplicitās *f.*
director *n* dux *m*, gubernātor *m*,
moderātor *m.*
dirge *n* nēnia *f.*
dirk *n* pūgiō *m.*
dirt *n* sordēs *f*; (*mud*) lūtum *nt.*
dirty *adj* sordidus, foedus; (*speech*)
inquinātus ♦ *vt* foedāre,
inquināre.
disability *n* vitium *nt.*
disable *vt* dēbilitāre, imminuere.
disabled *adj* mutilus, dēbilis.
disabuse *vt* errōrem dēmere (*dat*).
disaccustom *vt* dēsuēfacere.
disadvantage *n* incommodum *nt*,
dētrīmentum *nt*; **it is a ~**
dētrīmentō est.
disadvantageous *adj* incommodus, inīquus.
disadvantageously *adv* incommodē.
disaffected *adj* aliēnātus, sēditiōsus.
disaffection *n* aliēnātiō *f*, sēditiō *f.*
disagree *vi* discrepāre, dissentīre,
dissidēre.
disagreeable *adj* molestus,
incommodus, iniūcundus.
disagreeably *adv* molestē,
incommodē.
disagreement *n* discordia *f*,
dissēnsiō *f*, discrepantia *f.*
disallow *vt* improbāre, abnuere,
vetāre.
disappear *vi* dēperīre, perīre,
abīre, diffugere, ēvānēscere.
disappearance *n* dēcessiō *f*, fuga *f.*
disappoint *vt* dēcipere, spē
dēicere, frustrārī; **be ~ed in a**
hope ā spē dēcidere, dē spē dēicī.
disappointment *n* frustrātiō *f*,
malum *nt.*
disapprobation *n* reprehēnsiō *f*,
improbātiō *f.*
disapproval *n* improbātiō *f.*

disapprove *vt*, *vi* improbāre,
reprehendere.
disarm *vt* exarmāre, dearmāre;
(*fig*) mītigāre.
disarrange *vt* turbāre, cōnfundere.
disarranged *adj* incompositus.
disarrangement *n* turbātiō *f.*
disarray *n* perturbātiō *f* ♦ *vt*
perturbāre.
disaster *n* calamitās *f*, cāsus *m*;
(*MIL*) clādēs *f.*
disastrous *adj* īnfēlīx, exitiōsus,
calamitōsus.
disavow *vt* diffitērī, īnfitiārī.
disavowal *n* īnfitiātiō *f.*
disband *vt* dīmittere.
disbelief *n* diffidentia *f*, suspiciō *f.*
disbelieve *vt* diffīdere (*dat*).
disburden *vt* exonerāre.
disburse *vt* ērogāre, expendere.
disbursement *n* impēnsa *f.*
disc *n* orbis *m.*
discard *vt* mittere, pōnere,
prōicere.
discern *vt* cōnspicere, dīspicere,
cernere; (*fig*) intellegere.
discernment *n* iūdicium *nt*,
intellegentia *f*, sagācitās *f.*
discharge *vt* (*load*) exonerāre;
(*debt*) exsolvere; (*duty*) fungī (*abl*),
exsequī; (*officer*) exauctōrāre;
(*troops*) missōs facere, dīmittere;
(*weapon*) iacere, iaculārī;
(*prisoner*) absolvere; (*from body*)
ēdere, reddere ♦ *vi* (*river*) effundī,
īnfluere ♦ *n* (*bodily*) dēfluxiō *f*;
(*MIL*) missiō *f*, dīmissiō *f*; (*of a duty*)
perfūnctiō *f.*
disciple *n* discipulus *m.*
discipline *n* (*MIL*) modestia *f*;
(*punishment*) castīgātiō *f*; (*study*)
disciplīna *f* ♦ *vt* coercēre,
castīgāre.
disciplined *adj* modestus.
disclaim *vt* renūntiāre, repudiāre,
rēicere.
disclaimer *n* repudiātiō *f.*

disclose vt aperīre, patefacere, indicāre.

disclosure n indicium nt.

discoloration n dēcolōrātiō f.

discolour vt dēcolōrāre.

discoloured adj dēcolor.

discomfit vt vincere, conturbāre, dēprehendere.

discomfiture n clādēs f; (POL) repulsa f.

discomfort n molestia f, incommodum nt.

disconcert vt conturbāre, percellere.

disconcerting adj molestus.

disconnect vt abiungere, sēiungere.

disconnected adj dissolūtus, abruptus.

disconnectedly adv dissolūtē.

disconsolate adj maestus, dēmissus.

disconsolately adv animō dēmissō.

discontent n offēnsiō f, fastīdium nt, taedium nt.

discontented adj invidus, fastīdiōsus, parum contentus.

discontentedly adv invītus, inīquō animō.

discontinuance n intermissiō f.

discontinue vt intermittere ♦ vi dēsistere, dēsinere.

discord n discordia f; (music) dissonum nt.

discordance n discrepantia f, dissēnsiō f.

discordant adj discors, discrepāns; (music) dissonus, absonus.

discount vt dētrahere; (fig) praetermittere ♦ n dēcessiō f; **be at a ~** incēre.

discountenance vt improbāre.

discourage vt dēhortārī, dēterrēre; **be ~d** animum dēmittere, animō dēficere.

discouragement n animī abiectiō f; (cause) incommodum nt.

discourse n sermō m; (lecture) ōrātiō f ♦ vi conloquī, disserere, disputāre.

discourteous adj inurbānus, asper, inhūmānus.

discourteously adv inhūmānē, rūsticē.

discourtesy n inhūmānitās f, acerbitās f.

discover vt (find) invenīre, reperīre; (detect) dēprehendere; (reveal) aperīre, patefacere; (learn) cognōscere.

discoverer n inventor m.

discovery n inventum nt.

discredit vt notāre, fidem imminuere (gen) ♦ n invidia f, lābēs f; **be in ~** iacēre.

discreditable adj inhonestus, turpis.

discreditably adv inhonestē, turpiter.

discreet adj prūdēns, sagāx, cautus.

discreetly adv prūdenter, sagāciter, cautē.

discrepancy n discrepantia f, dissēnsiō f.

discretion n prūdentia f; (tact) iūdicium nt; (power) arbitrium nt, arbitrātus m; **at your ~** arbitrātū tuō; **surrender at ~** in dēditiōnem venīre, sine ullā pactiōne sē tradere; **years of ~** adulta aetās f.

discretionary adj līber.

discriminate vt, vi discernere, internōscere, distinguere.

discriminating adj perspicāx, sagāx.

discrimination n discrīmen nt, iūdicium nt.

discursive adj vagus, loquāx; **be ~** excurrere.

discuss vt agere, disputāre, disceptāre dē (abl); **~ terms of**

peace dē pāce agere.
discussion n disceptātiō f,
disputātiō f.
disdain vt contemnere, aspernārī,
fastīdīre ♦ n contemptiō f,
fastīdium nt.
disdainful adj fastīdiōsus,
superbus.
disdainfully adv fastīdiōsē,
superbē.
disease n morbus m; pestilentia f.
diseased adj aeger, aegrōtus.
disembark vi ē nave ēgredī ♦ vt
mīlitēs ē nāve expōnere.
disembarkation n ēgressus m.
disembodied adj sine corpore.
disembowel vt exenterāre.
disencumber vt exonerāre.
disengage vt expedīre, līberāre;
(mind) abstrahere, abdūcere.
disengaged adj vacuus, ōtiōsus.
disentangle vt expedīre,
explicāre, exsolvere.
disfavour n invidia f.
disfigure vt dēfōrmāre, foedāre.
disfigured adj dēfōrmis.
disfigurement n dēfōrmātiō f.
disfranchise vt cīvitātem adimere
(dat).
disfranchised adj capite
dēminūtus.
disfranchisement n capitis
dēminūtiō f.
disgorge vt ēvomere.
disgrace n dēdecus nt, ignōminia f,
īnfāmia f ♦ vt dēdecorāre,
dēdecorī esse (dat).
disgraceful adj ignōminiōsus,
flāgitiōsus, turpis; ~ thing
flāgitium nt.
disgracefully adv turpiter,
flāgitiōsē.
disgruntled adj mōrōsus, invidus.
disguise n integumentum nt; (fig)
speciēs f, simulātiō f; in ~ mūtātā
veste ♦ vt obtegere, involvere;
(fact) dissimulāre; ~ oneself

vestem mūtāre.
disgust vt displicēre (dat),
fastīdium movēre (dat); be ~ed
stomachārī; I am ~ed mē taedet,
mē piget ♦ n fastīdium nt,
taedium nt.
disgusting adj taeter, foedus,
dēfōrmis.
disgustingly adv foedē.
dish n lanx f; (course) ferculum nt.
dishearten vt percellere; be ~ed
animō dēficere, animum
dēmittere.
dishevelled adj solūtus, passus.
dishonest adj perfidus, inīquus,
improbus.
dishonestly adv improbē, dolō
malō.
dishonesty n mala fidēs f, perfidia
f, fraus f.
dishonour n dēdecus nt, ignōminia
f, turpitūdō f ♦ vt dēdecorāre.
dishonourable adj ignōminiōsus,
indecōrus, turpis.
dishonourably adv turpiter,
inhonestē.
disillusion vt errōrem adimere
(dat).
disinclination n odium nt.
disinclined adj invītus, āversus.
disinfect vt pūrgāre.
disingenuous adj dolōsus, fallāx.
disingenuously adv dolōsē.
disinherit vt abdicāre, exhērēdāre.
disinherited adj exhērēs.
disintegrate vt dissolvere ♦ vi
dīlābī, dissolvī.
disinter vt effodere, ēruere.
disinterested adj grātuītus,
favōris expers.
disinterestedly adv sine favōre.
disinterestedness n innocentia f,
integritās f.
disjoin vt sēiungere.
disjointed adj parum cohaerēns.
disk n orbis m.
dislike n odium nt, offēnsiō f,

invidia f ♦ vt ōdisse; **I ~** mihī
displicet, mē piget (gen).
dislocate vt extorquēre.
dislocated adj luxus.
dislodge vt dēmovēre, dēicere,
dēpellere, dētrūdere.
disloyal adj īnfīdus, īnfidēlis; (to
gods, kin, country) impius.
disloyally adv īnfīdēliter.
disloyalty n perfidia f, īnfidēlitās f;
impietās f.
dismal adj fūnestus, maestus.
dismally adv miserē.
dismantle vt nūdāre; (building)
dīruere.
dismay n pavor m, formīdō f ♦ vt
terrēre, perturbāre.
dismember vt discerpere.
dismiss vt dīmittere; (troops)
missōs facere; (from service)
exauctōrāre; (fear) mittere,
pōnere.
dismissal n missiō f, dīmissiō f.
dismount vi dēgredī, (ex equō)
dēscendere.
disobedience n contumācia f.
disobedient adj contumāx.
disobediently adv contrā iussa.
disobey vt nōn pārēre (dat),
aspernārī.
disoblige vt displicēre (dat),
offendere.
disobliging adj inofficiōsus,
difficilis.
disobligingly adv contrā officium.
disorder n turba f, cōnfūsiō f; (MED)
morbus m; (POL) mōtus m,
tumultus m ♦ vt turbāre, miscēre,
sollicitāre.
disorderly adj immodestus,
inōrdinātus, incompositus; (POL)
turbulentus, sēditiōsus; **in a ~
manner** nullō ōrdine, temerē.
disorganize vt dissolvere,
perturbāre.
disown vt (statement) īnfitiārī;
(thing) abnuere, repudiāre; (heir)

abdicāre.
disparage vt obtrectāre,
dētrectāre.
disparagement n obtrectātiō f,
probrum m.
disparager n obtrectātor m,
dētrectātor m.
disparate adj dispār.
disparity n discrepantia f,
dissimilitūdō f.
dispassionate adj studiī expers.
dispassionately adv sine īrā et
studiō.
dispatch vt mittere, dīmittere;
(finish) absolvere, perficere; (kill)
interficere ♦ n (letter) litterae fpl;
(speed) celeritās f.
dispel vt dispellere, discutere.
dispensation n (distribution)
partītiō f; (exemption) venia f; (of
heaven) sors f; **by divine ~**
dīvīnitus.
dispense vt dispertīrī, dīvidere ♦
vi: **~ with** ōmittere,
praetermittere, repudiāre.
dispersal n dīmissiō f, diffugium
nt.
disperse vt dispergere, dissipāre,
dīsicere ♦ vi diffugere, dīlābī.
dispirited adj dēmissō animō; **be ~**
animō dēficere, animum
dēmittere.
displace vt locō movēre.
display n ostentātiō f, iactātiō f; **for
~** per speciem ♦ vt exhibēre,
ostendere, praestāre, ac ferre.
displease vt displicēre (dat),
offendere; **be ~d** aegrē ferre,
stomachārī, indignārī.
displeasing adj ingrātus, odiōsus.
displeasure n invidia f, offēnsiō f,
odium nt.
disport vt: **~ oneself** lūdere.
disposal n (sale) vēnditiō f; (power)
arbitrium nt.
dispose vt (troops) dispōnere;
(mind) inclīnāre, addūcere ♦ vi: **~**

of abaliēnāre, vēndere; (*get rid*)
tollere; (*argument*) refellere.

disposed *adj* adfectus, inclīnātus,
prōnus; **well ~** benevolus, bonō
animō.

disposition *n* animus *m*, adfectiō *f*,
ingenium *nt*, nātūra *f*; (*of troops*)
dispositiō *f*.

dispossess *vt* dētrūdere, spoliāre.

disproportion *n* inconcinnitās *f*.

disproportionate *adj* impār,
inconcinnus.

disproportionately *adv*
inaequāliter.

disprove *vt* refūtāre, redarguere,
refellere.

disputable *adj* dubius, ambiguus.

disputation *n* disputātiō *f*.

dispute *n* altercātiō *f*, contrōversia
f; (*violent*) iūrgium *nt*; **beyond ~**
certissimus ♦ *vt* altercārī,
certāre, rixārī ♦ *vt* negāre, in
dubium vocāre.

disqualification *n* impedīmentum
nt.

disqualify *vt* impedīre.

disquiet *n* sollicitūdō *f* ♦ *vt*
sollicitāre.

disquisition *n* disputātiō *f*.

disregard *n* neglegentia *f*,
contemptiō *f* ♦ *vt* neglegere,
contemnere, ōmittere.

disrepair *n* vitium *nt*; **in ~** male
sartus.

disreputable *adj* inhonestus,
īnfāmis.

disrepute *n* īnfāmia *f*.

disrespect *n* neglegentia *f*,
contumācia *f*.

disrespectful *adj* contumāx,
īnsolēns.

disrespectfully *adv* īnsolenter.

disrobe *vt* nūdāre, vestem exuere
(*dat*) ♦ *vi* vestem exuere.

disrupt *vt* dīrumpere, dīvellere.

disruption *n* discidium *nt*.

dissatisfaction *n* molestia *f*,

aegritūdō *f*, dolor *m*.

dissatisfied *adj* parum contentus; **I
am ~ with . . .** mē taedet (*gen*) . . . .

dissect *vt* incīdere; (*fig*)
investīgāre.

dissemble *vt*, *vi* dissimulāre;
mentīrī.

dissembler *n* simulātor *m*.

disseminate *vt* dīvulgāre,
dissēmināre.

dissension *n* discordia *f*, dissēnsiō
f; (*violent*) iūrgium *nt*.

dissent *vi* dissentīre, dissidēre ♦ *n*
dissēnsiō *f*.

dissertation *n* disputātiō *f*.

disservice *n* iniūria *f*,
incommodum *nt*.

dissimilar *adj* dispār, dissimilis.

dissimilarity *n* discrepantia *f*,
dissimilitūdō *f*.

dissident *adj* discors.

dissimulation *n* dissimulātiō *f*.

dissipate *vt* dissipāre, diffundere,
disperdere.

dissipated *adj* dissolūtus, lascīvus,
luxuriōsus.

dissipation *n* dissipātiō *f*; (*vice*)
luxuria *f*, licentia *f*.

dissociate *vt* dissociāre,
sēiungere.

dissociation *n* sēparātiō *f*,
discidium *nt*.

dissoluble *adj* dissolūbilis.

dissolute *adj* dissolūtus, perditus,
libīdinōsus.

dissolutely *adv* libīdinōsē,
luxuriōsē.

dissoluteness *n* luxuria *f*.

dissolution *n* dissolūtiō *f*,
discidium *nt*.

dissolve *vt* dissolvere; (*ice*)
liquefacere; (*meeting*) dīmittere;
(*contract*) dīrimere ♦ *vi*
liquēscere; (*fig*) solvī.

dissonance *n* dissonum *nt*.

dissonant *adj* dissonus.

dissuade *vt* dissuādēre (*dat*),

dēhortārī.

dissuasion n dissuāsiō f.

distaff n colus f.

distance n intervallum nt, spatium nt; (long way) longinquitās f; at a ~ (far) longē; (within sight) procul; (fight) ēminus; at a ~ of ... spatiō (gen) ...; within striking ~ intrā iactum tēlī.

distant adj longinquus; (measure) distāns; (person) parum familiāris; be ~ abesse (abl).

distaste n fastīdium nt.

distasteful adj molestus, iniūcundus.

distemper n morbus m.

distend vt distendere.

distil vt, vi stillāre.

distinct adj (different) dīversus; (separate) distinctus; (clear) clārus, argūtus; (marked) distinctus; (sure) certus; (well-drawn) expressus.

distinction n discrīmen nt; (dissimilarity) discrepantia f; (public status) amplitūdō f; (honour) honōs m, decus nt; (mark) īnsigne nt; there is a ~ interest; without ~ prōmiscuē.

distinctive adj proprius, īnsignītus.

distinctively adv propriē, īnsignītē.

distinctly adv clārē, distinctē, certē, expressē.

distinguish vt distinguere, internōscere, dīiūdicāre, discernere; (honour) decorāre, ōrnāre; ~ oneself ēminēre.

distinguished adj īnsignis, praeclārus, ēgregius, amplissimus.

distort vt dētorquēre; (fig) dēprāvāre.

distorted adj distortus.

distortion n distortiō f; dēprāvātiō f.

distract vt distrahere, distinēre; āvocāre; (mind) aliēnāre.

distracted adj āmēns, īnsānus.

distraction n (state) indīligentia f; (cause) invītāmentum nt; (madness) furor m, dēmentia f; to ~ efflīctim.

distraught adj āmēns, dēmēns.

distress n labor m, dolor m, aegrimōnia f, aerumna f; be in ~ labōrāre ♦ vt adflīgere, sollicitāre.

distressed adj adflīctus, sollicitus; be ~ at rem aegrē ferre.

distressing adj tristis, miser, acerbus.

distribute vt distribuere, dīvidere, dispertīre.

distribution n partītiō f, distribūtiō f.

district n regiō f, pars f.

distrust n diffīdentia f ♦ vt diffīdere (dat), nōn crēdere (dat).

distrustful adj diffīdēns.

distrustfully adv diffīdenter.

disturb vt perturbāre, conturbāre; commovēre; (mind) sollicitāre.

disturbance n turba f, perturbātiō f; (POL) mōtus m, tumultus m.

disturber n turbātor m.

disunion n discordia f, discidium nt.

disunite vt dissociāre, sēiungere.

disuse n dēsuētūdō f; fall into ~ obsolēscere.

disused adj dēsuētus, obsolētus.

disyllabic adj disyllabus.

ditch n fossa f, scrobis m.

dithyrambic adj dithyrambicus.

dittany n dictamnum nt.

ditty n carmen nt, cantilēna f.

diurnal adj diūrnus.

divan n lectus m, lectulus m.

dive vi dēmergī.

diver n ūrīnātor m.

diverge vi dēvertere, dīgredī; (road) sē scindere; (opinions) discrepāre.

divergence n dīgressiō f; discrepantia f.

divers adj complūrēs.

diverse adj varius, dīversus.

diversify vt variāre.

diversion n (of water) dērīvātiō f; (of thought) āvocātiō f; (to amuse) oblectāmentum nt; **create a ~** (MIL) hostēs dīstringere; **for a ~** animī causā.

diversity n varietās f, discrepantia f.

divert vt dēflectere, āvertere; (attention) āvocāre, abstrahere; (water) dērīvāre; (to amuse) oblectāre, placēre (dat).

diverting adj iūcundus; (remark) facētus.

divest vt exuere, nūdāre; **~ oneself of** (fig) pōnere, mittere.

divide vt dīvidere; (troops) dīdūcere; **~ among** partīrī, distribuere; **~ from** sēparāre ab, sēiungere ab; **~ out** dispertīrī, dīvidere ♦ vi discēdere, sē scindere; (senate) in sententiam īre, **be ~d** (opinions) discrepāre.

divination n dīvīnātiō f; (from birds) augurium nt; (from entrails) haruspicium nt.

divine adj dīvīnus ♦ vt dīvīnāre, augurārī, hariolārī; **by ~ intervention** dīvīnitus.

divinely adv dīvīnē.

diviner n dīvīnus m, augur m, haruspex m.

divinity n (status) dīvīnitās f; (god) deus m, dea f.

divisible adj dīviduus.

division n (process) dīvīsiō f, partītiō f; (variance) discordia f, dissēnsiō f; (section) pars f; (grade) classis f; (of army) legiō f; (of time) discrīmen nt; (in senate) discessiō f.

divorce n dīvortium nt, repudium

nt ♦ vt (wife) nūntium mittere (dat); (things) dīvellere, sēparāre.

divulge vt aperīre, patefacere, ēvulgāre, ēdere.

dizziness n vertīgō f.

dizzy adj vertīginōsus; (fig) attonitus.

do vt facere, agere; (duty) fungī (abl); (wrong) admittere; **~ away with** vt fus tollere; (kill) interimere; **~ one's best to** id agere ut (subj); **~ without** repudiāre; **~ not ...** nōlī/nōlīte (+ infin); **how ~ you ~?** quid agis?; **I have nothing to ~ with you** mihī tēcum nihil est commercī; **it has nothing to ~ with me** nihil est ad mē; **that will ~** iam satis est; **be done** fierī; **have done with** dēfungī (abl).

docile adj docilis.

docility n docilitās f.

dock n (ships) nāvāle nt; (law) cancellī mpl ♦ vt praecīdere.

dockyard n nāvālia ntpl.

doctor n medicus m; (UNIV) doctor m ♦ vt cūrāre.

doctrine n dogma nt, dēcrētum nt; (system) ratiō f.

document n litterae fpl, tabula f.

dodge vt dēclīnāre, ēvādere ♦ n dolus m.

doe n cerva f.

doer n āctor m, auctor m.

doff vt exuere.

dog n canis m/f; **~ star** Canīcula f; **~'s** canīnus ♦ vt īnsequī, īnstāre (dat).

dogged adj pertināx.

doggedly adv pertināciter.

dogma n dogma nt, praeceptum nt.

dogmatic adj adrogāns.

dogmatically adv adroganter.

doing n factum nt.

dole n sportula f ♦ vt: **~ out** dispertīrī, dīvidere.

doleful adj lūgubris, flēbilis,

maestus.

dolefully adv flēbiliter.

dolefulness n maestitia f, miseria f.

doll n pūpa f.

dolorous adj lūgubris, maestus.

dolour n maestitia f, dolor m.

dolphin n delphīnus m.

dolt n stīpes m, caudex m.

domain n ager m; (king's) rēgnum nt.

dome n tholus m, testūdō f.

domestic adj domesticus, familiāris; (animal) mānsuētus ♦ n famulus m, servus m, famula f, ancilla f; **~s** pl familia f.

domesticate vt mānsuēfacere.

domesticated adj mānsuētus.

domesticity n larēs suī mpl.

domicile n domicilium nt, domus f.

dominant adj superior, praepotēns.

dominate vt dominārī in (acc), imperāre (dat); (view) dēspectāre.

domination n dominātiō f, dominātus m.

domineer vi dominārī, rēgnāre.

dominion n imperium nt, rēgnum nt.

don vt induere ♦ n scholasticus m.

donate vt dōnāre.

donation n dōnum nt.

donkey n asellus m.

donor n dōnātor m.

doom n fātum nt ♦ vt damnāre.

door n (front) iānua f; (back) postīcum nt; (double) forēs fpl; **folding ~s** valvae fpl; **out of ~s** forīs; (to) forās; **next ~ to** iuxtā (acc).

doorkeeper n iānitor m.

doorpost n postis m.

doorway n ōstium nt.

dormant adj sōpītus; **lie ~** iacēre.

dormitory n cubiculum nt.

dormouse n glīs m.

dose n pōculum nt.

dot n pūnctum nt.

dotage n senium nt.

dotard n senex dēlīrus m.

dote vi dēsipere; **~ upon** dēamāre.

doting adj dēsipiēns, peramāns.

dotingly adv perditē.

double adj duplex; (amount) duplus; (meaning) ambiguus ♦ n duplum nt ♦ vt duplicāre; (promontory) superāre; (fold) complicāre ♦ vi duplicārī; (MIL) currere.

double-dealer n fraudātor m.

double-dealing adj fallāx, dolōsus ♦ n fraus f, dolus m.

doublet n tunica f.

doubly adv bis, dupliciter.

doubt n dubium nt; (hesitancy) dubitātiō f; (distrust) suspiciō f; **give one the benefit of the ~** innocentem habēre; **no ~** sānē; **I do not ~ that** ... nōn dubitō quīn ... (+ subj); **there is no ~ that** nōn dubium est quīn (subj) ♦ vt dubitāre; (distrust) diffīdere (dat), suspicārī.

doubtful adj dubius, incertus; (result) anceps; (word) ambiguus.

doubtfully adv dubiē; (hesitation) dubitanter.

doubtless adv scīlicet, nīmīrum.

doughty adj fortis, strēnuus.

dove n columba f.

dovecote n columbārium nt.

dowdy adj inconcinnus.

dower n dōs f ♦ vt dōtāre.

dowerless adj indōtātus.

down n plūmae fpl, lānūgō f; (thistle) pappus m.

down adv deōrsum; **be ~** iacēre; **~ with!** perea(n)t; **up and ~** sūrsum deōrsum ♦ prep dē (abl); **~ from** dē (abl).

downcast adj dēmissus, maestus.

downfall n ruīna f; (fig) occāsus m.

downhearted adj dēmissus, frāctus animī.

downhill adj dēclīvis; (fig)
prōclīvis ♦ adv in praeceps.
downpour n imber m.
downright adj dīrectus; (intensive)
merus.
downstream adv secundō flūmine.
downtrodden adj subiectus,
oppressus.
downward adj dēclīvis, prōclīvis.
downwards adv deōrsum.
downy adj plūmeus.
dowry n dōs f.
doyen n pater m.
doze vi dormītāre.
dozen n duodecim.
drab adj sordidior.
drachma n drachma f.
draft n (writing) exemplum nt; (MIL)
dīlectus m; (money) syngrapha f;
(literary) silva f ♦ vt scrībere; (MIL)
mittere.
drag vt trahere ♦ vi (time) trahī; ~
on vi (war) prōdūcere ♦ n
harpagō m; (fig) impedīmentum
nt.
dragnet n ēverriculum nt.
dragon n dracō m.
dragoon n eques m.
drain n cloāca f ♦ vt (water)
dērīvāre; (land) siccāre; (drink)
exhaurīre; (resources) exhaurīre.
drainage n dērīvātiō f.
drake n anas m.
drama n fābula f; **the ~** scaena f.
dramatic adj scaenicus.
dramatist n fābulārum scrīptor m.
dramatize vt ad scaenam
compōnere.
drape vt vēlāre.
drapery n vestīmenta ntpl.
drastic adj vehemēns, efficāx.
draught n (air) aura f; (drink)
haustus m; (net) bolus m.
draughts n latrunculī mpl.
draw vt dūcere, trahere; (bow)
addūcere; (inference) colligere;
(picture) scrībere, pingere; (sword)

stringere, dēstringere; (tooth)
eximere; (water) haurīre; **~ aside**
sēdūcere; **~ away** āvocāre; **~
back** vt retrahere ♦ vi recēdere; **~
near** adpropinquāre; **~ off**
dētrahere; (water) dērīvāre; **~ out**
vi ēdūcere; (lengthen) prōdūcere;
~ over obdūcere; **~ taut**
addūcere; **~ together** contrahere;
~ up vt (MIL) īnstruere; (document)
scrībere.
drawback n scrūpulus m; **this was
the only ~** hōc ūnum dēfuit.
drawing n dēscrīptiō f; (art)
graphicē f.
drawing room n sellāria f.
drawings npl līneāmenta ntpl.
drawl vi lentē dīcere.
drawling adj lentus in dīcendō.
dray n plaustrum nt.
dread n formīdō f, pavor m, horror
m ♦ adj dīrus ♦ vt expavēscere,
extimēscere, formīdāre.
dreadful adj terribilis, horribilis,
formīdolōsus, dīrus.
dreadfully adv vehementer,
atrōciter.
dream n somnium nt ♦ vt, vi
somniāre.
dreamy adj somniculōsus.
dreariness n (place) vastitās f;
(mind) trīstitia f.
dreary adj (place) vastus; (person)
trīstis.
dregs n faex f; (of oil) amurca f;
drain to the ~ exhaurīre.
drench vt perfundere.
dress n vestis f, vestītus m,
vestīmenta ntpl; (style) habitus m
♦ vt vestīre; (wound) cūrāre; (tree)
amputāre ♦ vi induī; **~ up** vi
vestum induere.
dressing n (MED) fōmentum nt.
drift n (motion) mōtus m; (snow)
agger m; (language) vīs f; **I see the
~ of your speech** videō quōrsum
ōrātiō tua tendat ♦ vi fluitāre; (fig)

lābī, ferrī.

drill n terebra f; (MIL) exercitātiō f
♦ vt (hole) terebrāre; (MIL)
exercēre; (pupil) īnstruere.

drink vt, vi bibere, pōtāre; ~ **a**
health propīnāre, Graecō mōre
bibere; ~ **deep of** exhaurīre; ~ **in**
haurīre; ~ **up** ēpōtāre ♦ n pōtiō f.

drinkable adj pōtulentus.

drinker n pōtor m.

drinking bout n pōtātiō f.

drip vi stillāre, dēstillāre.

drive vt agere; (force) cōgere; ~
away abigere; (fig) pellere,
prōpulsāre; ~ **back** repellere; ~
home dēfīgere; ~ **in/into** īnfīgere
in (acc); (flock) cōgere in (acc); ~ **off**
dēpellere; ~ **out** exigere,
expellere, exturbāre; ~ **through**
trānsfīgere ♦ vi vehī; ~ **away**
āvehī; ~ **back** revehī; ~ **in** invehī;
~ **on** vt impellere; ~ **round**
circumvehī; ~ **past** praetervehī;
what are you driving at? quōrsum
tua spectat ōrātiō? ♦ n gestātiō f.

drivel vi dēlīrāre.

drivelling adj dēlīrus, ineptus ♦ n
ineptiae fpl.

driver n aurīga m; rēctor m.

drizzle vi rōrāre.

droll adj facētus, ioculāris.

drollery n facētiae fpl.

dromedary n dromas m.

drone n (bee) fūcus m; (sound)
bombus m ♦ vi fremere.

droop vi dēmittī; (flower)
languēscere; (mind) animum
dēmittere.

drooping adj languidus.

drop n gutta f ♦ vi cadere; (liquid)
stillāre ♦ vt mittere; (anchor)
iacere; (hint) ēmittere; (liquid)
īnstillāre; (work) dēsistere ab (abl)
♦ vi: ~ **behind** cessāre; ~ **in**
vīsere, supervenīre; ~ **out**
excidere.

dross n scōria f; (fig) faex f.

drought n siccitās f.

drouth n sitis f.

drove n grex f.

drover n bubulcus m.

drown vt mergere, obruere; (noise)
obscūrāre ♦ vi aquā perīre.

drowse vi dormītāre.

drowsily adv somniculōsē.

drowsiness n sopor m.

drowsy adj sēmisomnus,
somniculōsus.

drub vt pulsāre, verberāre.

drudge n mediastīnus m ♦ vi
labōrāre.

drudgery n labor m.

drug n medicāmentum nt ♦ vt
medicāre.

Druids n Druidae, Druidēs mpl.

drum n tympanum nt; (container)
urna f.

drummer n tympanista m.

drunk adj pōtus, ēbrius,
tēmulentus.

drunkard n ēbriōsus m.

drunken adj ēbriōsus, tēmulentus.

drunkenness n ēbrietās f.

dry adj siccus, āridus; (thirst)
sitiēns, (speech) āridus, frīgidus;
(joke) facētus; **be** ~ ārēre ♦ vt
siccāre ♦ vi ārēscere; ~ **up**
exārēscere.

dryad n dryas f.

dry rot n rōbīgō f.

dual adj duplex.

duality n duplex nātūra f.

dubiety n dubium nt.

dubious adj dubius, incertus;
(meaning) ambiguus.

dubiously adv dubiē; ambiguē.

duck n anas f ♦ vt dēmergere ♦ vi
dēmergī, sē dēmittere.

duckling n anaticula f.

duct n ductus m.

dudgeon n dolor m, stomachus m.

due adj dēbitus, meritus, iūstus; **be**
~ dēbērī; **it is** ~ **to me that ... not**
per mē stat quōminus (+ subj); **be**

~ to orīrī ex, fierī *(abl)* ♦ *n* iūs *nt*, dēbitum *nt; (tax)* vectīgal *nt; (harbour)* portōrium *nt;* **give every man his ~** suum cuīque tribuere ♦ *adv* rēctā; **~ to** ob *(+ acc);* propter *(+ acc).*

duel *n* certāmen *nt.*

dug *n* über *nt.*

duke *n* dux *m.*

dulcet *adj* dulcis.

dull *adj* hebes; *(weather)* subnūbilus; *(language)* frīgidus; *(mind)* tardus; **be ~** hēbēre; **become ~** hebēscere ♦ *vt* hebetāre, obtundere, retundere.

dullard *n* stolidus *m.*

dulness *n (mind)* tardītās *f,* stultitia *f.*

duly *adv* rītē, ut pār est.

dumb *adj* mūtus; **be struck ~** obmūtēscere.

dun *n* flāgitātor *m* ♦ *vt* flāgitāre ♦ *adj* fuscus.

dunce *n* bārō *m.*

dune *n* tumulus *m.*

dung *n* fimus *m.*

dungeon *n* carcer *m,* rōbur *nt.*

dupe *vt* dēlūdere, fallere ♦ *n* crēdulus *m.*

duplicate *n* exemplar *nt* ♦ *vt* duplicāre.

duplicity *n* fraus *f,* perfidia *f.*

durability *n* firmitās *f,* firmitūdō *f.*

durable *adj* firmus, perpetuus.

durably *adv* firmē.

duration *n* spatium *nt; (long)* diūturnitās *f.*

duresse *n* vīs *f.*

during *prep* inter *(acc),* per *(acc).*

dusk *n* crepusculum *nt,* vesper *m;* **at ~** prīmā nocte, prīmīs tenebrīs.

dusky *adj* fuscus.

dust *n* pulvis *m;* **throw ~ in the eyes of** tenebrās offundere *(dat)* ♦ *vt* dētergēre.

dusty *adj* pulverulentus.

dutiful *adj* pius, officiōsus.

dutifully *adv* piē, officiōsē.

dutifulness *n* pietās *f.*

duty *n (moral)* officium *nt; (task)* mūnus *nt; (tax)* vectīgal *nt;* **be on ~** *(MIL)* statiōnem agere, excubāre; **do one's ~** officiō fungī; **do ~ for** *(pers)* in locum sufficī *(gen); (thing)* adhibērī prō *(abl);* **it is my ~** dēbeō, mē oportet, meum est; **it is the ~ of a commander** ducis est; **sense of ~** pietās *f.*

duty call *n* salūtātiō *f.*

duty-free *adj* immūnis.

dwarf *n* nānus *m.*

dwell *vi* habitāre; **~ in** incolere; **~ upon** *(theme)* commorārī in *(abl).*

dweller *n* incola *m.*

dwelling *n* domus *f,* domicilium *nt; (place)* sēdēs *f.*

dwindle *vi* dēcrēscere, extenuārī.

dye *n* fūcus *m,* color *m* ♦ *vt* īnficere, fūcāre.

dyer *n* īnfector *m.*

dying *adj* moribundus, moriēns.

dynasty *n* domus *(rēgia) f.*

dyspepsia *n* crūditās *f.*

E

each *adj, pron* quisque; *(of two)* uterque; **~ other** inter sē; **one ~** singulī; **~ year** quotannīs.

eager *adj* avidus, cupidus, alācer; **~ for** avidus *(+ gen).*

eagerly *adv* avidē, cupidē, ācriter.

eagerness *n* cupīdō *f,* ārdor *m,* studium *nt;* alacritās *f.*

eagle *n* aquila *f.*

ear *n* auris *f; (of corn)* spīca *f;* **give ~** aurem praebēre, auscultāre; **go in at one ~ and out at the other** surdīs auribus nārrārī; **prick up one's ~s** aurēs ērigere; **with long ~s** aurītus.

earl *n* comes *m.*

earlier *adv* ante; anteā.

early *adj (in season)* mātūrus; *(in*

day) mātūtīnus; (*at beginning*)
prīmus; (*in history*) antīquus ♦ *adv*
(*in day*) māne; (*before time*) mātūrē,
temperī; ~ **in life** ab ineunte
aetāte.

earn *vt* merērī, cōnsequī; ~ **a living**
vīctum quaerere, quaestum
facere.

earnest *adj* (*serious*) sērius; (*eager*)
ācer, sēdulus ♦ *n* pignus *nt*;
(*money*) arrabō *m*; **in** ~ sēdulō,
ēnīxē.

earnestly *adv* sēriō, graviter,
sēdulō.

earnestness *n* gravitās *f*, studium
nt.

earnings *n* quaestus *m*.

earring *n* elenchus *m*.

earth *n* (*planet*) tellūs *f*; (*inhabited*)
orbis terrārum *m*; (*land*) terra *f*;
(*soil*) solum *nt*, humus *f*; (*fox's*)
latibulum *nt*; **where on** ~? ubī
gentium?; **of the** ~ terrestris.

earthen *adj* (*ware*) fictilis; (*mound*)
terrēnus.

earthenware *n* fictilia *ntpl* ♦ *adj*
fictilis.

earthly *adj* terrestris.

earthquake *n* terrae mōtus *m*.

earthwork *n* agger *m*.

earthy *adj* terrēnus.

ease *n* facilitās *f*; (*leisure*) ōtium *nt*;
at ~ ōtiōsus; (*in mind*) sēcūrus; **ill**
at ~ sollicitus ♦ *vt* laxāre,
relevāre; (*pain*) mītigāre.

easily *adv* facile; (*gladly*) libenter;
(*at leisure*) ōtiōsē; **not** ~ nōn
temerē.

easiness *n* facilitās *f*.

east *n* Oriēns *m*, sōlis ortus *m*; ~
wind eurus *m*.

Eactor *n* Pascha *f*.

easterly, eastern *adj* orientālis.

eastward *adv* ad orientem.

easy *adj* facilis; (*manner*) adfābilis,
facilis; (*mind*) sēcūrus; (*speech*)
expedītus; (*discipline*) remissus; ~

circumstances dīvitiae *fpl*,
abundantia *f*.

eat *vt* edere; cōnsūmere; vescī
(*abl*); ~ **away** rōdere; ~ **up**
exedere.

eatable *adj* esculentus.

eating *n* cibus *m*.

eaves *n* suggrunda *f*.

eavesdropper *n* sermōnis auceps
m.

ebb *n* dēcessus *m*, recessus *m*; **at**
~ **tide** minuente aestū; **be at a low**
~ (*fig*) iacēre ♦ *vi* recēdere.

ebony *n* ebenus *f*.

ebullient *adj* fervēns.

ebullition *n* fervor *m*.

eccentric *adj* īnsolēns.

eccentricity *n* īnsolentia *f*.

echo *n* imāgō *f* ♦ *vt*, *vi* resonāre.

eclipse *n* dēfectus *m*, dēfectiō *f*
♦ *vt* obscūrāre; **be** ~**d** dēficere,
labōrāre.

eclogue *n* ecloga *f*.

economic *adj* quaestuōsus, sine
iactūrā.

economical *adj* (*person*) frūgī,
parcus.

economically *adv* nūllā iactūrā
factā.

economics *n* reī familiāris
dispēnsātiō *f*.

economize *vi* parcere.

economy *n* frūgālitās *f*.

ecstasy *n* alacritās *f*, furor *m*.

ecstatic *adj* gaudiō ēlātus.

eddy *n* vertex *m* ♦ *vi* volūtārī.

edge *n* ōra *f*, margō *f*; (*of dish*)
labrum *nt*; (*of blade*) aciēs *f*; **take**
the ~ **off** obtundere; **on** ~ (*fig*)
suspēnsō animō ♦ *vt* (*garment*)
praetexere; (*blade*) acuere ♦ *vi*: ~
in sē īnsinuāre.

edging *n* limbus *m*.

edible *adj* esculentus.

edict *n* ēdictum *nt*, dēcrētum *nt*.

edification *n* ērudītiō *f*.

edifice *n* aedificium *nt*.

edify vt ērudīre.

edit vt recognōscere, recēnsēre.

edition n ēditiō f.

educate vt ērudīre, īnfōrmāre; ~ **in** īnstituere ad (acc).

education n doctrīna f; (process) īnstitūtiō f.

eel n anguilla f.

eerie adj mōnstruōsus.

efface vt dēlēre, tollere.

effect n (result) ēventus m; (impression) vīs f, effectus m; (show) iactātiō f; ~s pl bona ntpl; **for** ~ iactātiōnis causā; **in** ~ rē vērā; **to this** ~ in hanc sententiam; **without** ~ irritus ♦ vt efficere, facere, patrāre.

effective adj valēns, validus; (RHET) gravis, ōrnātus.

effectively adv validē, graviter, ōrnātē.

effectiveness n vīs f.

effectual adj efficāx, idōneus.

effectually adv efficāciter.

effectuate vt efficere, cōnsequī.

effeminacy n mollitiēs f.

effeminate adj mollis, effēminātus.

effeminately adv molliter, effēminātē.

effervesce vi effervēscere.

effete adj effētus.

efficacious adj efficāx.

efficaciously adv efficāciter.

efficacy n vīs f.

efficiency n virtūs f, perītia f.

efficient adj capāx, perītus; (logic) efficiēns.

efficiently adv perītē, bene.

effigy n simulācrum nt, effigiēs f.

effloresce vi flōrēscere.

efflorescence n (fig) flōs m.

effluvium n hālitus m.

effort n opera f, cōnātus m; (of mind) intentiō f; **make an** ~ ēnītī.

effrontery n audācia f, impudentia f.

effusive adj officiōsus.

egg n ōvum nt; **lay an** ~ ōvum parere ♦ vt impellere, īnstīgāre.

egoism n amor suī m.

egoist n suī amāns m.

egotism n iactātiō f.

egotist n glōriōsus m.

egregious adj singulāris.

egress n exitus m.

eight num octō; ~ **each** octōnī; ~ **times** octiēns.

eighteen num duodēvīgintī.

eighteenth adj duodēvīcēsimus.

eighth adj octāvus.

eight hundred num octingentī.

eight hundredth adj octingentēsimus.

eightieth adj octōgēsimus.

eighty num octōgintā; ~ **each** octōgēnī; ~ **times** octōgiēns.

either pron alteruter, uterlibet, utervīs ♦ conj aut, vel; ~ ... **or** aut ... aut; vel ... vel.

ejaculation n clāmor m.

eject vt ēicere, expellere.

ejection n expulsiō f.

eke vt: **eke out** parcendō prōdūcere.

elaborate vt ēlabōrāre ♦ adj ēlabōrātus, exquīsītus.

elaborately adv summō labōre, exquīsītē.

elan n ferōcia f.

elapse vi abīre, intercēdere; **allow to** ~ intermittere; **a year has ~d since** annus est cum (indic).

elated adj ēlātus; **be** ~ efferrī.

elation n laetitia f.

elbow n cubitum nt.

elder adj nātū māior, senior ♦ n (tree) sambūcus f.

elderly adj aetāte prōvectus.

elders npl patrēs mpl.

eldest adj nātū māximus.

elecampane n inula f.

elect vt ēligere, dēligere; (magistrate) creāre; (colleague) coöptāre ♦ *adj* dēsignātus; (*special*) lēctus.

election *n* (POL) comitia *ntpl*.

electioneering *n* ambitiō *f*.

elector *n* suffrāgātor *m*.

elegance *n* ēlegantia *f*, lepōs *m*, munditia *f*, concinnitās *f*.

elegant *adj* ēlegāns, concinnus, nitidus.

elegantly *adv* ēleganter, concinnē.

elegiac *adj*: ~ **verse** elegī *mpl*, versūs alternī *mpl*.

elegy *n* elegīa *f*.

element *n* elementum *nt*; ~**s** *pl* initia *ntpl*, prīncipia *ntpl*; **out of one's** ~ peregrīnus.

elementary *adj* prīmus.

elephant *n* elephantus *m*, elephās *m*.

elevate *vt* efferre, ērigere.

elevated *adj* ēditus, altus.

elevation *n* altitūdō *f*; (*style*) ēlātiō *f*.

eleven *num* ūndecim; ~ **each** ūndēnī; ~ **times** ūndeciēns.

eleventh *adj* ūndecimus.

elf *n* deus *m*.

elicit *vt* ēlicere; (*with effort*) ēruere.

elide *vt* ēlīdere.

eligible *adj* idōneus, aptus.

eliminate *vt* tollere, āmovēre.

elilus *n* flius *m*, robur *nt*.

elk *n* alcēs *f*.

ell *n* ulna *f*.

ellipse *n* (RHET) dētractiō *f*; (*oval*) ōvum *nt*.

elm *n* ulmus *f* ♦ *adj* ulmeus.

elocution *n* prōnūntiātiō *f*.

elongate *vt* prōdūcere.

elope *vi* aufugere.

eloquence *n* ēloquentia *f*; (*natural*) fācundia *f*, dīcendī vīs *f*.

eloquent *adj* ēloquēns; (*natural*) fācundus; (*fluent*) disertus.

eloquently *adv* fācundē, disertē.

else *adv* aliōquī, aliter ♦ *adj* alius; **or** ~ aliōquī; **who** ~ quis alius.

elsewhere *adv* alibī; ~ **to** aliō.

elucidate *vt* ēnōdāre, illūstrāre.

elucidation *n* ēnōdātiō *f*, explicātiō *f*.

elude *vt* ēvītāre, frustrārī, fallere.

elusive *adj* fallāx.

emaciated *adj* macer.

emaciation *n* maciēs *f*.

emanate *vi* mānāre; (*fig*) ēmānāre, orīrī.

emanation *n* exhālātiō *f*.

emancipate *vt* ēmancipāre, manū mittere, līberāre.

emancipation *n* lībertās *f*.

emasculate *vt* ēnervāre, dēlumbāre.

embalm *vt* condīre.

embankment *n* agger *m*, mōlēs *f*.

embargo *n* interdictum *nt*.

embark *vi* cōnscendere, nāvem cōnscendere; ~ **upon** (*fig*) ingredī ♦ *vt* impōnere.

embarkation *n* cōnscēnsiō *f*.

embarrass *vt* (*by confusing*) perturbāre; (*by obstructing*) impedīre; (*by revealing*) dēprehendere; **be ~ed** haerēre.

embarrassing *adj* incommodus, intempestīvus.

embarrassment *n* (*in speech*) haesitātiō *f*; (*in mind*) sollicitūdō *f*; (*in business*) angustiae *fpl*, difficultās *f*; (*cause*) molestia *f*, impedīmentum *nt*.

embassy *n* lēgātiō *f*.

embedded *adj* dēfīxus.

embellish *vt* adōrnāre, exōrnāre, decorāre.

embellishment *n* decus *nt*, exōrnātiō *f*, ōrnāmentum *nt*.

embers *n* cinis *m*, favilla *f*.

embezzle *vt* pecūlārī, dēpecūlārī.

embezzlement *n* pecūlātus *m*.

embezzler *n* pecūlātor *m*.

embitter *vt* exacerbāre.

emblazon *vt* īnsignīre.

emblem *n* īnsigne *nt*.

embodiment n exemplar nt.
embody vt repraesentāre; (MIL) cōnscrībere.
embolden vt cōnfirmāre; ~ **the hearts of** animōs cōnfirmāre.
emboss vt imprimere, caelāre.
embrace vt amplectī, complectī; (items) continēre, comprehendere; (party) sequī; (opportunity) adripere ♦ n amplexus m, complexus m.
embroider vt acū pingere.
embroidery n vestis picta f.
embroil vt miscēre, implicāre.
emend vt ēmendāre, corrigere.
emendation n ēmendātiō f, corrēctiō f.
emerald n smaragdus m.
emerge vi ēmergere, exsistere; ēgredī.
emergency n tempus nt, discrīmen nt ♦ adj subitārius.
emigrate vi migrāre, ēmigrāre.
emigration n migrātiō f.
eminence n (ground) tumulus m, locus ēditus m; (rank) praestantia f, amplitūdō f.
eminent adj ēgregius, ōminēns, īnsignis, amplus.
eminently adv ēgregiē, prae cēterīs, in prīmīs.
emissary n lēgātus m.
emit vt ēmittere.
emolument n lucrum nt, ēmolumentum nt.
emotion n animī mōtus m, commōtiō f, adfectus m.
emotional adj (person) mōbilis; (speech) flexanimus.
emperor n prīnceps m, imperātor m.
emphasis n pondus nt; (words) impressiō f.
emphasize vt exprimere.
emphatic adj gravis.
emphatically adv adsevēranter, vehementer.

empire n imperium nt.
employ vt ūtī (abl); (for purpose) adhibēre; (person) exercēre.
employed adj occupātus.
employees npl operae fpl.
employer n redemptor m.
employment n (act) ūsus m; (work) quaestus m.
empower vt permittere (dat), potestātem facere (dat).
emptiness n inānitās f.
empty adj inānis, vacuus; (fig) vānus, inritus ♦ vt exhaurīre, exinānīre ♦ vi (river) īnfluere.
emulate vt aemulārī.
emulation n aemulātiō f.
emulous adj aemulus.
emulously adv certātim.
enable vt potestātem facere (dat); efficere ut (subj).
enact vt dēcernere, ēdīcere, scīscere; (part) agere.
enactment n dēcrētum nt, lēx f.
enamoured adj amāns; **be ~ of** dēamāre.
encamp vi castra pōnere, tendere.
encampment n castra ntpl.
encase vt inclūdere.
enchant vt fascināre; (fig) dēlectāre.
enchantment n fascinātiō f; blandīmentum nt.
enchantress n sāga f.
encircle vt cingere, circumdare, amplectī.
enclose vt inclūdere, saepīre.
enclosure n saeptum nt, māceria f.
encompass vt cingere, circumdare, amplectī.
encounter vt obviam īre (dat), occurrere (dat); (in battle) concurrere cum (abl), congredī cum ♦ n occursus m, concursus m.
encourage vt cōnfirmāre, (co) hortārī, sublevāre, favēre (dat).
encouragement n hortātiō f, favor

m, auxilium nt.
encroach vi invādere; ~ **upon**
occupāre; (fig) imminuere.
encrust vt incrustāre.
encumber vt impedīre, onerāre.
encumbrance n impedīmentum nt,
onus nt.
end n fīnis m; (aim) prōpositum nt;
(of action) ēventus m, exitus m; (of
speech) perōrātiō f; ~ **to** ~
continuī; **at a loose** ~ vacuus,
ōtiōsus; **for two days on** ~ biduum
continenter; **in the** ~ dēnique; **the**
~ **of** extrēmus; (time) exāctus; **put**
an ~ **to** fīnem facere (dat), fīnem
impōnere (dat); **to the** ~ **that** eō
cōnsiliō ut (subj); **to what** ~? quō?,
quōrsum? ♦ vt fīnīre, cōnficere;
(mutual dealings) dīrimere ♦ vi
dēsinere; (event) ēvādere;
(sentence) cadere; (speech)
perōrāre; (time) exīre; ~ **up as**
ēvādere; ~ **with** dēsinere in (acc).
endanger vt perīclitārī, in
discrīmen addūcere.
endear vt dēvincīre.
endearing adj blandus.
endearment n blanditiae fpl.
endeavour vt cōnārī, ēnītī ♦ n
cōnātus m.
ending n fīnis m, exitus m.
endless adj īnfīnītus; (time)
aeternus, perpetuus.
endlessly adv sine fīne, īnfīnītē.
endorse vt ratum facere.
endow vt dōnāre, īnstruere.
endowed adj praeditus (+ abl).
endowment n dōnum nt.
endurance n patientia f.
endure vi dūrāre, permanēre ♦ vt
ferre, tolerāre, patī.
enemy n (public) hostis, hostēs
mpl; (private) inimīcus m; **greatest**
~ inimīcissimus m; ~ **territory**
hosticum nt.
energetic adj impiger, nāvus,

strēnuus; (style) nervōsus.
energetically adv impigrē, nāviter,
strēnuē.
energy n impigritās f, vigor m,
incitātiō f; (mind) contentiō f;
(style) nervī mpl.
enervate vt ēnervāre, ēmollīre.
enervation n languor m.
enfeeble vt īnfirmāre, dēbilitāre.
enfold vt involvere, complectī.
enforce vt (law) exsequī;
(argument) cōnfirmāre.
enfranchise vt cīvitāte dōnāre;
(slave) manū mittere.
engage vt (affection) dēvincīre;
(attention) distinēre, occupāre;
(enemy) manum cōnserere cum
(abl); (hire) condūcere; (promise)
spondēre, recipere; ~ **the enemy**
proelium cum hostibus
committere; **be ~d in** versārī in
(abl) ♦ vi: ~ **in** ingredī, suscipere.
engagement n (comm) occupātiō f,
(MIL) pugna f, certāmen nt;
(agreement) spōnsiō f; **keep an** ~
fidem praestāre; **break an** ~ fidem
fallere; **I have an** ~ **at your house**
prōmisī ad tē.
engaging adj blandus.
engender vt ingenerāre,
ingignere.
engine n māchina f.
engineer n māchinātor m ♦ vt
mōlīrī.
engraft vt īnserere.
engrave vt īnsculpere, incīdere,
caelāre.
engraver n sculptor m, caelātor m.
engraving n sculptūra f, caelātūra
f.
engross vt dīstringere, occupāre;
~**ed in** tōtus in (abl).
engulf vt dēvorāre, obruere.
enhance vt amplificāre, augēre,
exaggerāre.
enigma n aenigma nt, ambāgēs fpl.
enigmatic adj ambiguus, obscūrus.

enigmatically *adv* per ambāgēs, ambiguē.

enjoin *vt* imperāre (*dat*), iniungere (*dat*).

enjoy *vt* fruī (*abl*); (*advantage*) ūtī (*abl*); (*pleasure*) percipere, dēcerpere; **~ oneself** dēlectārī, geniō indulgēre.

enjoyable *adj* iūcundus.

enjoyment *n* frūctus *m*; dēlectātiō *f*, voluptās *f*.

enlarge *vt* augēre, amplificāre, dīlātāre; (*territory*) prōpāgāre; **~ upon** amplificāre.

enlargement *n* amplificātiō *f*, prōlātiō *f*.

enlighten *vt* inlūstrāre; docēre, ērudīre.

enlightenment *n* ērudītiō *f*, hūmānitās *f*.

enlist *vt* scrībere, cōnscrībere; (*sympathy*) conciliāre ♦ *vi* nōmen dare.

enliven *vt* excitāre.

enmesh *vt* impedīre, implicāre.

enmity *n* inimīcitia *f*, simultās *f*.

ennoble *vt* honestāre, excolere.

ennui *n* taedium *nt*.

enormity *n* immānitās *f*; (*deed*) scelus *nt*, nefās *nt*.

enormous *adj* immānis, ingēns.

enormously *adv* immēnsum.

enough *adj* satis (*indecl gen*) ♦ *adv* satis; **more than ~** satis superque; **I have had ~ of ...** mē taedet (*gen*) . . . .

enquire *vi* quaerere, percontārī; **~ into** cognōscere, inquīrere in (*acc*).

enquiry *n* percontātiō *f*; (*legal*) quaestiō *f*.

enrage *vt* inrītāre, incendere.

enrapture *vt* dēlectāre.

enrich *vt* dītāre, locuplētāre; **~ with** augēre (*abl*).

enrol *vt* adscrībere, cōnscrībere ♦ *vi* nōmen dare.

enshrine *vt* dēdicāre; (*fig*) sacrāre.

enshroud *vt* involvere.

ensign *n* signum *nt*, īnsigne *nt*; (*officer*) signifer *m*.

enslave *vt* in servitūtem redigere.

enslavement *n* servitūs *f*.

ensnare *vt* dēcipere, inlaqueāre, inrētīre.

ensue *vi* īnsequī.

ensure *vt* praestāre; **~ that** efficere ut (*subj*).

entail *vt* adferre.

entangle *vt* impedīre, implicāre, inrētīre.

entanglement *n* implicātiō *f*.

enter *vi* inīre, ingredī, intrāre; (*riding*) invehī; **~ into** introīre in (*acc*); **~ upon** inīre, ingredī ♦ *vt* (*place*) intrāre; (*account*) ferre, indūcere; (*mind*) subīre.

enterprise *n* inceptum *nt*; (*character*) prōmptus animus *m*.

enterprising *adj* prōmptus, strēnuus.

entertain *vt* (*guest*) invītāre, excipere; (*state of mind*) habēre, concipere; (*to amuse*) oblectāre.

entertainer *n* acroāma *nt*.

entertainment *n* hospitium *nt*; oblectāmentum *nt*; acroāma *nt*.

enthral *vt* capere.

enthusiasm *n* studium *nt*, fervor *m*; **~ for** studium *nt* (+*gen*).

enthusiastic *adj* studiōsus, fervidus.

enthusiastically *adv* summō studiō.

entice *vt* inlicere, ēlicere, invītāre.

enticement *n* illecebra *f*, lēnōcinium *nt*.

entire *adj* integer, tōtus, ūniversus.

entirely *adv* omnīnō, funditus, penitus.

entitle *vt* (*book*) īnscrībere; **be ~d to** merērī, dignum esse quī (*subj*), iūs habēre (*gen*).

entity *n* rēs *f*.

entomb vt humāre, sepelīre.
entrails n intestīna ntpl, exta ntpl.
entrance n aditus m, introitus m;
(act) ingressiō f; (of house)
vestibulum nt; (of harbour) ōstium
nt.
entrance vt fascināre, cōnsōpīre,
capere.
entreat vt implōrāre, obsecrāre;
(successfully) exōrāre.
entreaty n precēs fpl.
entrenchment n mūnītiō f.
entrust vt committere, crēdere,
mandāre; (for keeping) dēpōnere.
entry n introitus m, aditus m; **make
an ~** (book) in tabulās referre.
entwine vt implicāre, involvere.
enumerate vt numerāre,
dīnumerāre.
enunciate vt ēdīcere; (word)
exprimere.
envelop vt implicāre, involvere.
envelope n involucrum nt.
enviable adj beātus.
envious adj invidus, invidiōsus.
enviously adv invidiōsē.
environment n vīcīnia f; **our ~** ea
in quibus versāmur.
envoy n lēgātus m.
envy n invidia f ♦ vt invidēre (dat).
enwrap vt involvere.
ephemeral adj brevis.
ephor n ephorus m.
epic adj epicus ♦ n epos nt.
epicure n dēlicātus m.
epigram n sententia f; (poem)
epigramma nt.
epilepsy n morbus comitiālis m.
epilogue n epilogus m.
episode n ēventum nt.
epistle n epistula f, litterae fpl.
epitaph n epigramma nt, titulus m.
epithet n adsūmptum nt.
epitome n epitomē f.
epoch n saeculum nt.
equable adj aequālis; (temper)
aequus.

equal adj aequus, pār; **be ~ to**
aequāre; (task) sufficere (dat) ♦ n
pār m/f ♦ vt aequāre, adaequāre.
equality n aequālitās f.
equalize vt adaequāre, exaequāre.
equally adv aequē, pariter.
equanimity n aequus animus m.
equate vt aequāre.
equator n aequinoctiālis circulus
m.
equestrian adj equester.
equidistant adj: **be ~** aequō spatiō
abesse, idem distāre.
equilibrium n lībrāmentum nt.
equine adj equīnus.
equinoctial adj aequinoctiālis.
equinox n aequinoctium nt.
equip vt armāre, īnstruere, ōrnāre.
equipment n arma ntpl,
īnstrūmenta ntpl, adparātus m.
equipoise n lībrāmentum nt.
equitable adj aequus, iūstus.
equitably adv iūstē, aequē.
equity n aequum nt, aequitās f.
equivalent adj pār, īdem īnstar
(gen).
equivocal adj anceps, ambiguus.
equivocally adv ambiguē.
equivocate vi tergiversārī.
era n saeculum nt.
eradicate vt ēvellere, exstirpāre.
erase vt dēlēre, indūcere.
erasure n litūra f.
ere conj priusquam.
erect vt ērigere; (building)
exstruere; (statute) pōnere ♦ adj
ērēctus.
erection n (process) exstructiō f;
(product) aedificium nt.
erode vt rōdere.
erotic adj amātōrius.
err vi errāre, peccāre.
errand n mandātum nt.
errant adj vagus.
erratic adj incōnstāns.
erroneous adj falsus.
erroneously adv falsō, perperam.

error *n* error *m*; (*moral*) peccātum *nt*; (*writing*) mendum *nt*.
erudite *adj* doctus.
erudition *n* doctrīna *f*, ērudītiō *f*.
erupt *vi* ērumpere.
eruption *n* ēruptiō *f*.
escapade *n* ausum *nt*.
escape *vi* effugere, ēvādere ♦ *vt* fugere, ēvītāre; (*memory*) excidere ex (*abl*); **~ the notice of** fallere, praeterīre ♦ *n* effugium *nt*, fuga *f*; **way of ~** effugium *nt*.
eschew *vt* vītāre.
escort *n* praesidium *nt*; (*private*) dēductor *m* ♦ *vt* comitārī, prōsequī; (*out of respect*) dēdūcere.
especial *adj* praecipuus.
especially *adv* praecipuē, praesertim, māximē, in prīmīs.
espionage *n* inquīsītiō *f*.
espouse *vt* (*wife*) dūcere; (*cause*) fovēre.
espy *vt* cōnspicere, cōnspicārī.
essay *n* cōnātus *m*; (*test*) perīculum *nt*; (*literary*) libellus *m* ♦ *vt* cōnārī, incipere.
essence *n* vīs *f*, nātūra *f*.
essential *adj* necesse, necessārius.
essentially *adv* necessāriō.
establish *vt* īnstituere, condere; (*firmly*) stabilīre.
established *adj* firmus, certus; **be ~** cōnstāre; **become ~** (*custom*) inveterāscere.
establishment *n* (*act*) cōnstitūtiō *f*; (*domestic*) familia *f*.
estate *n* fundus *m*, rūs *nt*; (*in money*) rēs *f*; (*rank*) ōrdō *m*.
esteem *vt* aestimāre, respicere ♦ *n* grātia *f*, opīniō *f*.
estimable *adj* optimus.
estimate *vt* aestimāre, ratiōnem inīre (*gen*) ♦ *n* aestimātiō *f*, iūdicium *nt*.
estimation *n* opīniō *f*, sententia *f*.
estrange *vt* aliēnāre, abaliēnāre.
estrangement *n* aliēnātiō *f*,

discidium *nt*.
estuary *n* aestuārium *nt*.
eternal *adj* aeternus, perennis.
eternally *adv* semper, aeternum.
eternity *n* aeternitās *f*.
etesian winds *n* etēsiae *fpl*.
ether *n* (*sky*) aethēr *m*.
ethereal *adj* aetherius, caelestis.
ethic, ethical *adj* mōrālis.
ethics *n* mōrēs *mpl*, officia *ntpl*.
Etruscan *n* Etruscus *m* ♦ *adj like* bonus.
etymology *n* verbōrum notātiō *f*.
eulogist *n* laudātor *m*.
eulogize *vt* laudāre, conlaudāre.
eulogy *n* laudātiō *f*.
eunuch *n* eunūchus *m*.
euphony *n* sonus *m*.
evacuate *vt* (*place*) exinānīre; (*people*) dēdūcere.
evacuation *n* discessiō *f*.
evade *vt* dēclīnāre, dēvītāre, ēlūdere.
evaporate *vt* exhālāre ♦ *vi* exhālārī.
evaporation *n* exhālātiō *f*.
evasion *n* tergiversātiō *f*.
evasive *adj* ambiguus.
eve *n* vesper *m*; (*before festival*) pervigilium *nt*; **on the ~ of** prīdiē (*gen*).
even *adj* aequus, aequālis; (*number*) pār ♦ *adv* et, etiam; (*tentative*) vel; **~ if** etsī, etiamsī; tametsī; **~ more** etiam magis; **~ so** nihilōminus; **~ yet** etiamnum; **not ~ ...** nē quidem ♦ *vt* aequāre.
evening *n* vesper *m* ♦ *adj* vespertīnus; **~ is drawing on** invesperāscit; **in the ~** vesperī.
evening star *n* Vesper *m*, Hesperus *m*.
evenly *adv* aequāliter, aequābiliter.
evenness *n* aequālitās *f*, aequābilitās *f*.
event *n* ēventum *nt*; (*outcome*)

ēventus m.
eventide n vespertīnum tempus nt.
eventuality n cāsus m.
eventually adv mox, aliquandō, tandem.
ever adv unquam; (after sī, nisi, num, nē) quandō; (always) semper; (after interrog) -nam, tandem; ~ **so** nimium, nimium quantum; ~ **best** ~ omnium optimus; **for** ~ in aeternum.
everlasting adj aeternus, perpetuus, immortālis.
evermore adv semper, in aeternum.
every adj quisque, omnis; ~ **four years** quīntō quōque annō; ~ **now and then** interdum; in ~ direction passim; undique; ~ **other day** alternīs diēbus; ~ **day** cottīdiē
♦ adj cottīdiānus.
everybody pron quisque, omnēs mpl; ~ **agrees** inter omnēs constat; ~ **knows** nēmō est quīn sciat.
everyday adj cottīdiānus.
everyone pron see **everybody**.
everything omnia ntpl; **your health is** ~ **to me** meā māximē interest tē valēre.
everywhere adv ubīque, passim.
evict vt dēicere, dētrūdere.
eviction n dēiectiō f.
evidence n testimōnium nt, indicium nt; (person) testis m/f; (proof) argūmentum nt; **on the** ~ **of fidē** (gen); **collect** ~ **against** inquīrere in (acc); **turn King's** ~ indicium profitērī.
evident adj manifestus, ēvidēns, clārus; **it is** ~ appāret.
evidently adv manifestō, clārē.
evil adj malus, improbus, scelerātus.
evildoer n scelerātus m, maleficus m.
evil eye n fascinum nt, malum nt,

improbitās f.
evil-minded adj malevolus.
evince vt praestāre.
evoke vt ēvocāre, ēlicere.
evolution n seriēs f, prōgressus m; (MIL) dēcursus m, dēcursiō f.
evolve vt explicāre, ēvolvere ♦ vi crēscere.
ewe n ovis f.
ewer n hydria f.
exacerbate vt exacerbāre, exasperāre.
exact vt exigere ♦ adj accūrātus; (person) dīligēns; (number) exāctus.
exaction n exāctiō f.
exactly adv accūrātē; (reply) ita prōrsus; ~ **as** perinde que.
exactness n cūra f, dīligentia f.
exaggerate vt augēre, in māius extollere.
exalt vt efferre, extollere; laudāre.
exaltation n ēlātiō f.
examination n inquīsītiō f, scrūtātiō f; (of witness) interrogātiō f; (test) probātiō f.
examine vt investīgāre, scrūtārī; īnspicere; (witness) interrogāre; (case) quaerere dē (abl); (candidate) probāre.
examiner n scrūtātor m.
example n exemplum nt, documentum nt; **for** ~ exemplī grātiā; **make an** ~ **of** animadvertere in (acc); **I am an** ~ exemplō sum.
exasperate vt exacerbāre, irrītāre.
exasperation n irrītātiō f.
excavate vt fodere.
excavation n fossiō f.
excavator n fossor m.
exceed vt excēdere, superāre.
exceedingly adv nimis, valdē, nimium quantum.
excel vt praestāre (dat), exsuperāre ♦ vi excellere.

excellence n praestantia f, virtūs f.
excellent adj ēgregius, praestāns, optimus.
excellently adv ēgregiē, praeclārē.
except vt excipere ♦ prep praeter (acc) ♦ adv nisī ♦ conj praeterquam, nisī quod.
exception n exceptiō f; **make an ~ of** excipere; **take ~ to** gravārī quod; **with the ~ of** praeter (acc).
exceptional adj ēgregius, eximius.
exceptionally adv ēgregiē, eximiē.
excerpt vt excerpere ♦ n excerptum nt.
excess n immoderātiō f, intemperantia f ♦ adj supervacāneus; **be in ~** superesse.
excessive adj immoderātus, immodestus, nimius.
excessively adv immodicē, nimis.
exchange vt mūtāre, permūtāre ♦ n permūtātiō f; (of currencies) collybus m.
exchequer n aerārium nt; (emperor's) fiscus m.
excise n vectīgālia ntpl ♦ vt excīdere.
excision n excīsiō f.
excitable adj mōbilis.
excite vt excitāre, concitāre; (to action) incitāre, incendere; (to hope) ērigere, exacuere; (emotion) movēre, commovēre.
excitement n commōtiō f.
exclaim vt exclāmāre; **~ against** adclāmāre (dat).
exclamation n clāmor m, exclāmātiō f.
exclude vt exclūdere.
exclusion n exclūsiō f.
exclusive adj proprius.
exclusively adv sōlum.
excogitate vt excōgitāre.
excrescence n tūber m.
excruciating adj acerbissimus.
exculpate vt pūrgāre, absolvere.
excursion n iter nt; (MIL) excursiō f.

excuse n excūsātiō f; (false) speciēs f ♦ vt excūsāre, ignōscere (dat); (something due) remittere; **plead in ~** excūsāre; **put forward as an ~** praetendere.
execrable adj dētestābilis, sacer, nefārius.
execrate vt dētestārī, exsecrārī.
execration n dētestātiō f, exsecrātiō f.
execute vt efficere, patrāre, exsequī; suppliciō afficere; (behead) secūrī percutere.
execution n effectus m; (penalty) supplicium m, mors f.
executioner n carnifex m.
exemplar n exemplum nt.
exempt vt immūnis, līber ♦ vt līberāre.
exemption n (from tax) immūnitās f; (from service) vacātiō f.
exercise n exercitātiō f, ūsus m; (school) dictāta ntpl ♦ vt exercēre, ūtī (abl); (mind) acuere.
exert vt extendere, intendere, ūtī (abl); **~ oneself** mōlīrī, ēnītī, sē intendere.
exertion n mōlīmentum nt; (mind) intentiō f.
exhalation n exhālātiō f, vapor m.
exhale vt exhālāre, exspīrāre.
exhaust vt exhaurīre; (tire) dēfatīgāre, cōnficere.
exhaustion n dēfatīgātiō f.
exhaustive adj plēnus.
exhibit vt exhibēre, ostendere, expōnere; (on stage) ēdere.
exhibition n expositiō f, ostentātiō f.
exhilarate vt exhilarāre.
exhort vt hortārī, cohortārī.
exhortation n hortātiō f, hortāmen nt.
exhume vt ēruere.
exigency n necessitās f.
exile n exsilium nt, fuga f;

(*temporary*) relēgātiō f; (*person*)
exsul m; **live in ~** exsulāre ♦ vt in
exsilium pellere, dēportāre;
(*temporarily*) relēgāre.
exist vi esse.
existence n vīta f.
exit n exitus m, ēgressus m.
exodus n discessus m.
exonerate vt absolvere.
exorbitant adj nimius,
immoderātus.
exotic adj peregrīnus.
expand vt extendere, dīlātāre.
expanse n spatium nt, lātitūdō f.
expatiate vi: **~ upon** amplificāre.
expatriate vt extermināre ♦ n
extorris m.
expect vt exspectāre, spērāre.
expectancy, expectation n spēs f,
exspectātiō f; opīniō f.
expediency n ūtile nt, ūtilitās f.
expedient adj ūtilis, commodus; **it
is ~** expedit ♦ n modus m, ratiō f.
expediently adv commodē.
expedite vt mātūrāre.
expedition n (MIL) expedītiō f.
expeditious adj prōmptus, celer.
expeditiously adv celeriter.
expel vt pellere, expellere, ēicere.
expend vt impendere, expendere.
expenditure n impēnsae fpl,
sūmptus m.
expense n impēnsae fpl, impendia
ntpl; **at my ~** meō sūmptū; **at the
public ~** dē pūblicō.
expensive adj cārus, pretiōsus;
(*furnishings*) lautus.
expensively adv sūmptuōsē,
māgnō pretiō.
experience n ūsus m, experientia f
♦ vt experīrī, patī.
experienced adj perītus, expertus
(+ gen).
experiment n experīmentum nt
♦ vi: **~ with** experīrī.
expert adj perītus, sciēns.
expertly adv perītē, scienter.

expertness n perītia f.
expiate vt expiāre, luere.
expiation n (*act*) expiātiō f; (*penalty*)
piāculum nt.
expiatory adj piāculāris.
expiration n (*breath*) exspīrātiō f;
(*time*) exitus m.
expire vi exspīrāre; (*die*) animam
agere, animam efflāre; (*time*)
exīre.
expiry n exitus m, fīnis m.
explain vt explicāre, expōnere,
explānāre, interpretārī; (*lucidly*)
ēnōdāre; (*in detail*) ēdisserere.
explanation n explicātiō f,
ēnōdātiō f, interpretātiō f.
explicit adj expressus, apertus.
explicitly adv apertē.
explode vt discutere ♦ vi dīrumpī.
exploit n factum nt, ausum nt; **~s**
pl rēs gestae fpl ♦ vt ūtī (*abl*), fruī
(*abl*).
explore vt, vi explōrāre, scrūtārī.
explorer n explōrātor m.
explosion n fragor m.
exponent n interpres m, auctor m.
export vt exportāre ♦ n exportātiō
f.
exportation n exportātiō f.
expose vt dētegere, dēnūdāre,
patefacere; (*child*) expōnere; (*to
danger*) obicere; (MIL) nūdāre; (*for
sale*) prōpōnere; **~ o.s.** sē obicere.
exposed adj apertus, obnoxius.
exposition n explicātiō f,
interpretātiō f.
expostulate vi expostulāre,
conquerī.
expostulation n expostulātiō f.
exposure n (*of child*) expositiō f; (*of
guilt*) dēprehēnsiō f; (*to hardship*)
patientia f.
expound vt expōnere,
interpretārī.
expounder n interpres m.
express vt (*in words*) exprimere,
dēclārāre, ēloquī; (*in art*) effingere

♦ adj expressus; (speed)
celerrimus.
expression n significātiō f; (word)
vōx f, verbum nt; (face) vultus m.
expressive adj significāns; ~ of
index (gen); **be very ~** māximam
vim habēre.
expressively adv significanter.
expressiveness n vīs f.
expressly adv plānē.
expulsion n expulsiō f, ēiectiō f.
expurgate vt pūrgāre.
exquisite adj ēlegāns, exquīsītus,
eximius; (judgment) subtīlis.
exquisitely adv ēleganter,
exquīsītē.
ex-service adj ēmeritus.
extant adj superstes; **be ~** exstāre.
extempore adv ex tempore, subitō
♦ adj extemporālis.
extemporize vi subita dīcere.
extend vt extendere, dīlātāre;
(hand) porrigere; (line) dūcere;
(office) prōrogāre; (territory)
propāgāre ♦ vi patēre, porrigī; ~
into incurrere in (acc).
extension n prōductiō f, prōlātiō f;
(of office) prōrogātiō f; (of territory)
propāgātiō f; (extra) incrēmentum
nt.
extensive adj effūsus, amplus,
lātus.
extensively adv lātē.
extent n spatium nt, amplitūdō f;
to a large ~ māgnā ex parte; **to
some ~** aliquā ex parte; **to this ~**
hāctenus; **to such an ~** adeō.
extenuate vt levāre, mītigāre.
exterior adj externus, exterior ♦ n
speciēs f.
exterminate vt occīdiōne
occīdere, interimere.
extermination n occīdiō f,
interneciō f.
external adj externus.
externally adv extrīnsecus.
extinct adj mortuus; (custom)

obsolētus.
extinction n exstinctiō f, interitus
m.
extinguish vt exstinguere,
restinguere.
extinguisher n exstinctor m.
extirpate vt exstīrpāre, excīdere.
extol vt laudāre, laudibus efferre.
extort vt extorquēre, exprimere.
extortion n (offence) rēs
repetundae fpl.
extortionate adj inīquus, rapāx.
extra adv īnsuper, praetereā ♦ adj
additus.
extract vt excerpere, extrahere
♦ n: **make ~s** excerpere.
extraction n ēvulsiō f; (descent)
genus nt.
extraneous adj adventīcius,
aliēnus.
extraordinarily adv mīrificē,
eximiē.
extraordinary adj extraōrdinārius;
(strange) mīrus, novus;
(outstanding) eximius, īnsignis.
extravagance n intemperantia f;
(language) immoderātiō f, luxuria
f; (spending) sūmptus m.
extravagant adj immoderātus,
immodestus; (spending)
sūmptuōsus, prōdigus.
extreme adj extrēmus, ultimus.
extremely adv valdē, vehementer.
extremity n extrēmum nt, fīnis m;
(distress) angustiae fpl; **the ~ of**
extrēmus.
extricate vt expedīre, absolvere; ~
oneself ēmergere.
exuberance n ūbertās f, luxuria f.
exuberant adj ūber, laetus,
luxuriōsus.
exuberantly adv ūbertim.
exude vt exsūdāre ♦ vi mānāre.
exult vi exsultārī, laetārī, gestīre.
exultant adj laetus.
exultantly adv laetē.
exultation n laetitia f.

eye n oculus m; (*needle*) forāmen nt; **cast ~s on** oculōs conicere in (*acc*); **have an ~ to** spectāre; **in your ~s** iūdice tē; **keep one's ~s on** oculōs dēfigere in (*abl*); **lose an ~** alterō oculō capī; **see ~ to ~** cōnsentīre; **set ~s on** cōnspicere; **shut one's ~s to** cōnīvēre in (*abl*); **take one's ~s off** oculōs dēicere ab (*abl*); **up to the ~s in** tōtus in (*abl*); **with a cast in the ~** paetus; **with sore ~s** lippus; **sore ~s** lippitūdō f; **with one's own ~s** cōram; **with one's ~s open** sciēns ♦ vt intuērī, aspicere.

eyeball n pūpula f.

eyebrow n supercilium nt.

eyelash n palpebrae pilus m.

eyelid n palpebra f.

eyeshot n oculōrum coniectus m.

eyesight n aciēs f, oculī mpl.

eyesore n turpe nt; **it is an ~ to me** oculī meī dolent.

eye tooth n dēns canīnus m.

eyewash n sycophantia f.

eyewitness n arbiter m; **be an ~ of** interesse (*dat*).

F

fable n fābula f, apologus m.

fabled adj fābulōsus.

fabric n (*built*) structūra f; (*woven*) textile nt.

fabricate vt fabricārī, (*fig*) comminīscī, fingere.

fabricated adj commentīcius.

fabrication n (*process*) fabricātiō f; (*thing*) commentum nt.

fabricator n auctor m.

fabulous adj commentīcius, fictus.

fabulously adv incrēdibiliter

facade n frōns f.

face n faciēs f, ōs nt; (*aspect*) aspectus m; (*impudence*) ōs nt; **~ to ~** cōram; **how shall I have the ~ to go back?** quō ōre redībō?; **on the**

~ of it ad speciem, prīmō aspectū; **put a bold ~ on** fortem sē praebēre; **save ~** factum pūrgāre; **set one's ~ against** adversārī (*dat*) ♦ vt spectāre ad (*acc*); **obviam īre** (*dat*), sē oppōnere (*dat*) ♦ vi (*place*) spectāre, vergere; **~ about** (*MIL*) signa convertere.

facetious adj facētus, salsus.

facetiously adv facētē, salsē.

facetiousness n facētiae fpl, salēs mpl.

facile adj facilis.

facilitate vt expedīre.

facilities npl opportūnitās f.

facility n facilitās f.

facing adj adversus ♦ prep exadversus (*acc*).

facsimile n exemplār nt.

fact n rēs f, vērum nt; **as a matter of ~** enimvērō; **the ~ that** quod; **in rē vērā** conj etenim; (*climax*) dēnique.

faction n factiō f.

factious adj factiōsus, sēditiōsus.

factiously adv sēditiōsē.

factor n prōcūrātor m.

factory n officīna f.

faculty n facultās f, vīs f.

fad n libīdō f.

fade vi dēflōrēscere, marcēscere.

faded adj marcidus.

faggot n sarmentum nt.

fail vi dēficere, dēesse; (*fig*) cadere, dēcidere; (*in business*) forō cēdere; **~ to** nōn posse; **~ to come** nōn venīre ♦ vt dēficere, dēstituere.

failing n culpa f, vitium nt.

failure n (*of supply*) dēfectiō f; (*in action*) offēnsiō f; (*at election*) repulsa f.

fain adv libenter.

faint adj (*body*) languidus, dēfessus; (*impression*) hebes, levis; (*courage*) timidus; (*colour*) pallidus; **be ~** languēre; hebēre

♦ *vi* intermorī, animō linquī; **I feel**
~ animō male est.
faint-hearted *adj* animo dēmissus;
timidus.
faintly *adv* languidē; leviter.
faintness *n* dēfectiō *f*, languor *m*;
levitās *f*.
fair *adj* (*appearance*) pulcher,
fōrmōsus; (*hair*) flāvus; (*skin*)
candidus; (*weather*) serēnus;
(*wind*) secundus; (*copy*) pūrus;
(*dealings*) aequus; (*speech*)
speciōsus, blandus; (*ability*)
mediocris; (*reputation*) bonus ♦ *n*
nūndinae *fpl*; **~ and square** sine
fūcō ac fallāciīs.
fairly *adv* iūre, iūstē; mediocriter.
fairness *n* aequitās *f*.
fair play *n* aequum et bonum *nt*.
fairy *n* nympha *f*.
faith *n* fidēs *f*; **in good ~** bonā fidē.
faithful *adj* fidēlis, fīdus.
faithfully *adv* fidēliter.
faithfulness *n* fidēlitās *f*.
faithless *adj* īnfidēlis, īnfīdus,
perfidus.
faithlessly *adv* īnfidēliter.
faithlessness *n* īnfidēlitās *f*.
fake *vt* simulāre.
falchion *n* falx *f*.
falcon *n* falcō *m*.
fall *vi* cadere; (*gently*) lābī; (*morally*)
prōlābī; (*dead*) concidere,
occidere; (*fortress*) expugnārī,
capī; **~ at** accidere; **~ away**
dēficere, dēscīscere; **~ back**
recidere; (*MIL*) pedem referre; **~
between** intercidere; **~ behind**
cessāre; **~ by the way**
intercidere; **~ down** dēcidere,
dēlābī; (*building*) ruere, corruere;
~ due cadere; **~ flat** sē
prōsternere; (*speech*) frīgēre; **~
forward** prōlābī; **~ foul of**
incurrere in (*acc*); **~ headlong** sē
praecipitāre; **~ in, into** incidere; **~
in with** occurrere (*dat*); **~ off**

dēcidere; (*fig*) dēscīscere; **~ on**
incumbere in (*acc*), incidere in
(*acc*); **~ out** excidere; (*event*)
ēvenīre; (*hair*) dēfluere; **~ short of**
deesse *ad*; **~ to** (*by lot*) obtingere,
obvenīre (*dat*); **~ to the ground**
(*case*) iacēre; **~ upon** invādere,
ingruere in (*acc*); (*one's neck*) in
collum invādere ♦ *n* cāsus *m*;
(*building*) ruīna *f*; (*moral*) lāpsus *m*;
(*season*) autumnus *m*; **the ~ of
Capua** Capua capta.
fallacious *adj* captiōsus, fallāx.
fallaciously *adv* fallāciter.
fallacy *n* captiō *f*.
fallible *adj*: **be ~** errāre solēre.
fallow *adj* (*land*) novālis ♦ *n* novāle
nt; **lie ~** cessāre.
false *adj* falsus, fictus.
falsehood *n* falsum *nt*, mendācium
nt; **tell a ~** mentīrī.
falsely *adv* falsō.
falsify *vt* vitiāre, interlinere.
falter *vi* (*speech*) haesitāre; (*gait*)
titubāre.
faltering *adj* (*speech*) īnfrāctus;
(*gait*) titubāns ♦ *n* haesitātiō *f*.
fame *n* fāma *f*, glōria *f*; nōmen *nt*.
famed *adj* illūstris, praeclārus.
familiar *adj* (*friend*) intimus; (*fact*)
nōtus; (*manner*) cōmis; **~ spirit**
genius *m*; **be ~ with** nōvisse; **be
on ~ terms with** familiāriter ūtī
(*abl*).
familiarity *n* ūsus *m*, cōnsuētūdō *f*.
familiarize *vt* adsuēfacere.
familiarly *adv* familiāriter.
family *n* domus *f*, gēns *f* ♦ *adj*
domesticus, familiāris; **~
property** rēs familiāris *f*.
famine *n* famēs *f*.
famished *adj* famēlicus.
famous *adj* illūstris, praeclārus,
nōbilis; **make ~** nōbilitāre; **the ~**
ille.
fan *n* flābellum *nt*; (*winnowing*)
vannus *f* ♦ *vt* ventilāre; **~ the**

flames of (*fig*) īnflammāre.
fanatic *n* (*religious*) fānāticus *m*.
fanciful *adj* (*person*) incōnstāns; (*idea*) commentīcius.
fancy *n* (*faculty*) mēns *f*; (*idea*) opīnātiō *f*; (*caprice*) libīdō *f*; **take a ~ to** amāre incipere; **~oneself** se amāre ♦ *vt* animō fingere, imāginārī, sibi prōpōnere; **~you thinking...! tē crēdere...! ♦ *adj* dēlicātus.
fancy-free *adj* sēcūrus, vacuus.
fang *n* dēns *m*.
fantastic *adj* commentīcius, mōnstruōsus.
fantasy *n* imāginātiō *f*; (*contemptuous*) somnium *nt*.
far *adj* longinquus ♦ *adv* longē, procul; (*with compar*) multō; **be ~ from** longē abesse ab; **be not ~ from doing** haud multum abest quin (+*subj*); **by ~** longē; **how ~?** quātenus?, quoūsque?; **so ~** hāctenus, eātenus; (*limited*) quādam tenus; **thus ~** hāctenus; **~ and wide** lātē; **~ be it from me to say** equidem dīcere nōlim; **~ from thinking...I** adeō nōn crēdō...ut; **as ~ as** *prep* tenus (*abl*) ♦ *adv* ūsque ♦ *conj* quātenus; (*know*) quod.
farce *n* mīmus *m*.
farcical *adj* rīdiculus.
fare *vi* sē habēre, agere ♦ *n* vectūra *f*; (*boat*) naulum *nt*; (*food*) cibus *m*.
farewell *interj* valē, valēte; **say ~ to** valēre iubēre.
far-fetched *adj* quaesītus, accessītus, altē repetītus.
farm *n* fundus *m*, praedium *nt* ♦ *vt* (*soil*) colere; (*taxes*) redimere; **~out** locāre.
farmer *n* agricola *m*; (*of taxes*) pūblicānus *m*.
farming *n* agrīcultūra *f*.
farrow *vt* parere ♦ *n* fētus *m*.

far-sighted *adj* prōvidus, prūdēns.
farther *adv* longius, ultrā ♦ *adj* ulterior.
farthest *adj* ultimus, extrēmus ♦ *adv* longissimē.
fasces *n* fascēs *mpl*.
fascinate *vt* dēlēnīre, capere.
fascination *n* dulcēdō *f*, dēlēnīmenta *ntpl*, lēnōcinia *ntpl*.
fashion *n* mōs *m*, ūsus *m*; (*manner*) modus *m*, ratiō *f*; (*shape*) fōrma *f* ♦ *vt* fingere, fōrmāre; **after the ~ of** rītū (*gen*); **come into ~** in mōrem venīre; **go out of ~** obsolēscere.
fashionable *adj* ēlegāns; **it is ~** mōris est.
fashionably *adv* ēleganter.
fast *adj* (*firm*) firmus; (*quick*) celer; **make ~** dēligāre ♦ *adv* firmē, celeriter; **be ~ asleep** artē dormīre ♦ *vi* iēiūnus esse, cibō abstinēre ♦ *n* iēiūnium *nt*.
fasten *vt* fīgere, ligāre; **~ down** dēfīgere; **~ on** inligāre; **~ to** adligāre; **~ together** conligāre, cōnfīgere.
fastening *n* iūnctūra *f*.
fastidious *adj* dēlicātus, ēlegāns.
fastidiously *adv* fastīdiōsē.
fastidiousness *n* fastīdium *nt*.
fasting *n* iēiūnium *nt*, inedia *f* ♦ *adj* iēiūnus.
fastness *n* arx *f*, castellum *nt*.
fat *adj* pinguis, opīmus, obēsus; **grow ~** pinguēscere ♦ *n* adeps *m/f*.
fatal *adj* (*deadly*) fūnestus, exitiābilis; (*fated*) fātālis.
fatality *n* fātum *nt*, cāsus *m*.
fatally *adv*: **be ~ wounded** vulnere perīre.
fate *n* fātum *nt*, fortūna *f*, sors *f*.
fated *adj* fātālis.
fateful *adj* fātālis; fūnestus.
Fates *npl* (*goddesses*) Parcae *fpl*.
father *n* pater *m*; (*fig*) auctor *m*

♦ vt gignere; ~ **upon** addīcere, tribuere.

father-in-law n socer m.

fatherland n patria f.

fatherless adj orbus.

fatherly adj paternus.

fathom n sex pedēs mpl ♦ vt (fig) exputāre.

fathomless adj profundus.

fatigue n fatīgātiō f, dēfatīgātiō f ♦ vt fatīgāre, dēfatīgāre.

fatness n pinguitūdō f.

fatten vt sagīnāre.

fatty adj pinguis.

fatuity n īnsulsitās f, ineptiae fpl.

fatuous adj fatuus, īnsulsus, ineptus.

fault n culpa f, vitium nt; (written) mendum nt; **count as a** ~ vitiō vertere; **find** ~ **with** incūsāre; **it is not your** ~ **that...** nōn per tē stat quōminus (subj).

faultily adv vitiōsē, mendōsē.

faultiness n vitium nt.

faultless adj ēmendātus, integer.

faultlessly adv ēmendātē.

faulty adj vitiōsus, mendōsus.

faun n faunus m.

fauna n animālia ntpl.

favour n grātia f, favor m; (done) beneficium nt; **win** ~ **with** grātiam inīre apud; **by your** ~ bonā veniā tuā ♦ vt favēre (dat), indulgēre (dat).

favourable adj faustus, prosperus, secundus.

favourably adv faustē, fēlīciter, benignē.

favourite adj dīlectus, grātissimus ♦ n dēliciae fpl.

favouritism n indulgentia f, studium nt.

fawn n hinnuleus m ♦ adj (colour) gilvus ♦ vi: ~ **upon** adūlārī.

fawning adj blandus ♦ n adūlātiō f.

fear n timor m, metus m, formīdō f ♦ vt timēre, metuere, formīdāre,

verērī; **fearing that** veritus ne (+ imperf subj).

fearful adj timidus; horrendus, terribilis, formīdolōsus.

fearfully adv timidē; formīdolōsē.

fearless adj impavidus, intrepidus.

fearlessly adv impavidē, intrepidē.

fearlessness n fīdentia f, audācia f.

fearsome adj formīdolōsus.

feasible adj: **it is** ~ fierī potest.

feast n epulae fpl; (private) convīvium nt; (public) epulum nt; (religious) daps f; (festival) festus diēs m ♦ vi epulārī, convīvārī; (fig) pāscī ♦ vt: ~ **one's eyes on** oculōs pāscere (abl).

feat n factum nt, facinus nt.

feather n penna f; (downy) plūma f; **birds of a** ~ **flock together** parēs cum paribus facillimē congregantur.

feathered adj pennātus.

feathery adj plūmeus.

feature n līneāmentum nt; (fig) proprium nt.

February n mēnsis Februārius m; **of** ~ Februārius.

federal adj sociālis, foederātus.

federate vi societātem facere.

federated adj foederātus.

federation n societās f, foederātae cīvitātēs fpl.

fee n honōs m, mercēs f.

feeble adj imbēcillus, īnfirmus, dēbilis.

feebleness n imbēcillitās f, īnfirmitās f.

feebly adv īnfirmē.

feed vt alere, pāscere ♦ vi pāscī; ~ **on** vescī (abl) ♦ n pābulum nt.

feel vt sentīre; (with hand) tractāre, tangere; (emotion) capere, adficī (abl); (opinion) cēnsēre, sentīre; ~ **one's way** pedetemptim prōgredī ♦ vi sentīre; **I** ~ **glad** gaudeō; ~ **sure** prō certō habēre.

feeling n sēnsus m, tāctus m;

(*mind*) animus *m*, adfectus *m*;
(*pity*) misericordia *f*; **good ~**
voluntās *f*; **bad ~** invidia *f*.
feign *vt* simulāre, fingere.
feignedly *adv* simulātē, fictē.
feint *n* simulātiō *f*.
felicitate *vt* grātulārī (*dat*).
felicitation *n* grātulātiō *f*.
felicitous *adj* fēlīx, aptus.
felicity *n* fēlīcitās *f*.
feline *adj* fēlīnus.
fell *vt* (*tree*) succīdere; (*enemy*)
sternere, caedere ♦ *adj* dīrus,
crūdēlis, atrōx ♦ *n* mōns *m*; (*skin*)
pellis *f*.
fellow *n* socius *m*, aequālis *m*;
(*contemptuous*) homō *m*.
fellow citizen *n* cīvis *m/f*.
fellow countryman *n* cīvis *m/f*,
populāris *m/f*.
fellow feeling *n* misericordia *f*.
fellowship *n* societās *f*, sodālitās *f*.
fellow slave *n* cōnservus *m*.
fellow soldier *n* commīlitō *m*.
fellow student *n* condiscipulus *m*.
felon *n* nocēns *m*.
felonious *adj* scelestus, scelerātus.
felony *n* scelus *m*, noxa *f*.
felt *n* coāctum *nt*.
female *adj* muliebris ♦ *n* fēmina *f*.
feminine *adj* muliebris.
fen *n* palūs *f*.
fence *n* saepēs *f*; **sit on the ~**
quiēscere, medium sē gerere ♦ *vt*
saepīre; **~ off** intersaepīre ♦ *vi*
bātuere, rudibus lūdere.
fencing *n* rudium lūdus *m*; **~
master** lānista *m*.
fend *vt* arcēre ♦ *vi* prōvidēre.
fennel *n* ferula *f*.
fenny *adj* palūster.
ferment *n* fermentum *nt*; (*fig*)
aestus *m* ♦ *vt* fermentāre; (*fig*)
excitāre, accendere ♦ *vi* fervēre.
fermentation *n* fervor *m*.
fern *n* filix *f*.
ferocious *adj* ferōx, saevus,

truculentus.
ferociously *adv* truculentē.
ferocity *n* ferōcitās *f*, saevitia *f*.
ferret *n* viverra *m* ♦ *vt*: **~ out**
rīmārī, ēruere.
ferry *n* trāiectus *m*; (*boat*) cymba *f*,
pontō *m* ♦ *vt* trānsvehere.
ferryman *n* portitor *m*.
fertile *adj* fertilis, fēcundus.
fertility *n* fertilitās *f*, fēcunditās *f*.
fertilize *vt* fēcundāre, laetificāre.
fervent *adj* fervidus, ārdēns.
fervently *adv* ārdenter.
fervid *adj* fervidus.
fervour *n* ārdor *m*, fervor *m*.
festal *adj* festus.
fester *vi* exulcerārī.
festival *n* diēs festus *m*, sollemne
nt.
festive *adj* (*time*) festus; (*person*)
fēstīvus.
festivity *n* hilaritās *f*; (*event*)
sollemne *nt*.
festoon *n* sertum *m* ♦ *vt* corōnāre.
fetch *vt* arcessere, addūcere;
(*price*) vēnīre (*gen*); **~ out**
dēprōmere; **~ water** aquārī.
fetching *adj* lepidus, blandus.
fetid *adj* foetidus, pūtidus.
fetter *n* compēs *f*, vinculum *nt* ♦ *vt*
compedēs inicere (*dat*), vincīre;
(*fig*) impedīre.
fettle *n* habitus *m*, animus *m*.
feud *n* simultās *f*, inimīcitia *f*.
fever *n* febris *f*.
feverish *adj* febrīculōsus; (*fig*)
sollicitus.
few *adj* paucī; **very ~** perpaucī;
how ~? quotus quisque?
fewness *n* paucitās *f*.
fiancé *n* spōnsus *m*.
fiasco *n* calamitās *f*; **be a ~** frīgēre.
fiat *n* ēdictum *nt*.
fibre *n* fibra *f*.
fickle *adj* inconstāns, levis, mōbilis.
fickleness *n* inconstantia *f*, levitās
f, mōbilitās *f*.

fiction n fābula f, commentum nt.

fictitious adj fictus, falsus, commentīcius; (character) persōnātus.

fictitiously adv fictē.

fidelity n fidēlitās f, fidēs f.

fidget vi sollicitārī.

field n ager m; (ploughed) arvum nt; (of grain) seges f; (MIL) campus m, aciēs f; (scope) campus m, locus m; **in the ~** (MIL) mīlitiae; **hold the ~** vincere, praevalēre; **~ of vision** cōnspectus m.

fiend n diabolus m.

fiendish adj nefārius, improbus.

fierce adj saevus, ācer, atrōx; (look) torvus.

fiercely adv ācriter, atrōciter, saevē.

fierceness n saevitia f, atrōcitās f.

fieriness n ārdor m, fervor m.

fiery adj igneus, flammeus, (fig) ārdēns, fervidus.

fife n tībia f.

fifteen num quīndecim; **~ each** quīndēnī; **~ times** quīndeciēns.

fifteenth adj quīntus decimus.

fifth adj quīntus ♦ n quīnta pars f.

fiftieth adj quīnquāgēsimus.

fifty num quīnquāgintā.

fig n fīcus f; (tree) fīcus f; **of ~** ficulnus; **not care a ~ for** floccī nōn facere.

fight n pugna f, proelium nt ♦ vi pugnāre, dīmicāre; **~ it out** dēcernere, dēcertāre; **~ to the end** dēpugnāre ♦ vt (battle) committere; (enemy) pugnāre cum (abl).

fighter n pugnātor m.

fighting n dīmicātiō f.

figment n commentum nt.

figurative adj trānslātus; **in ~ language** trānslātīs per similitūdinem verbīs; **use ~ly** trānsferre.

figure n figūra f, fōrma f; (in art)

signum nt; (of speech) figūra f, trānslātiō f; (pl, on pottery) sigilla ntpl ♦ vt figūrāre, fōrmāre; (art) fingere, effingere; **~ to oneself** sibi prōpōnere.

figured adj sigillātus.

figurehead n (of ship) īnsigne nt.

filament n fibra f.

filch vt fūrārī, surripere.

file n (tool) līma f; (line) ōrdō m, agmen nt; (of papers) fasciculus m; **~s** pl tabulae fpl; **in single ~** simplicī ōrdine; **the rank and ~** gregāriī mīlitēs ♦ vt līmāre.

filial adj pius.

filigree n diatrēta ntpl.

fill vt implēre, explēre, complēre; (office) fungī (abl); **~ up** supplēre.

fillet n īnfula f, vitta f ♦ vt (fish) exossāre.

fillip n stimulus m.

filly n equula f.

film n membrāna f.

filter n cōlum nt ♦ vt dēliquāre ♦ vi percōlārī.

filth n sordēs f, caenum nt.

filthily adv foedē, inquinātē.

filthiness n foedītās f, impūritās f.

filthy adj foedus, impūrus; (speech) inquinātus.

fin n pinna f.

final adj ultimus, postrēmus, extrēmus.

finally adv dēnique, tandem, postrēmō.

finance n rēs nummāria f; (state) vectīgālia ntpl.

financial adj aerārius.

financier n faenerātor m.

finch n fringilla f.

find vt invenīre, reperīre; (supplies) parāre; (verdict) iūdicāre; (pleasure) capere; **~ fault with** incūsāre; **~ guilty** damnāre; **~ out** comperīre, cognōscere.

finder n inventor m.

finding n iūdicium nt, sententia f.

fine n (*law*) multa f, damnum nt; in ~ dēnique ♦ vt multāre ♦ adj (*thin*) tenuis, subtīlis; (*refined*) ēlegāns, mundus, decōrus; (*beautiful*) pulcher, venustus; (*showy*) speciōsus; (*of weather*) serēnus.

finely adv pulchrē, ēleganter, subtīliter.

fineness n tenuitās f; ēlegantia f; pulchritūdō f; speciēs f; serēnitās f.

finery n ōrnātus m, munditiae fpl.

finesse n astūtia f, ars f, argūtiae fpl.

finger n digitus m; a ~'s breadth trānsversus digitus; not lift a ~ (*in offort*) nē manum quidem vertere ♦ vt pertractāre.

fingertips n extrēmī digitī.

finish n fīnis m; (*art*) perfectiō f ♦ vt fīnīre, perficere; cōnficere; (*with art*) perficere, expolīre ♦ vi dēsinere; ~ off trānsigere, peragere, absolvere.

finishing post n mēta f.

finishing touch n manus extrēma.

finite adj circumscrīptus.

fir n abiēs f, of ~ abiēgnus.

fire n ignis m; (*conflagration*) incendium nt; (*in hearth*) focus m; (*fig*) ārdor m, calor m, impetus m; be on ~ ārdēre, flagrāre; catch ~ flammam concipere, ignem comprehendere; set on ~ accendere, incendere ♦ vt incendere; (*fig*) īnflammāre; (*missile*) iaculārī.

firebrand n fax f.

fire brigade n vigilēs mpl.

fireplace n focus m.

fireside n focus m.

firewood n lignum nt.

firm n societās f ♦ adj firmus, stabilis; (*mind*) cōnstāns; **stand ~** perstāre.

firmament n caelum nt.

firmly adv firmē, cōnstanter.

firmness n firmitās f, firmitūdō f; cōnstantia f.

first adj prīmus, prīnceps; (*of two*) prior ♦ adv prīmum; **at ~** prīmō, prīncipiō; **at ~ hand** ipse, ab ipsō; **come in ~** vincere; **give ~ aid to** ad tempus medērī (*dat*); **I was the ~ to see** prīmus vīdī.

first-class adj classicus.

first fruits npl prīmitiae fpl.

firstly adv prīmum.

first-rate adj eximius, lūculentus.

firth n aestuārium nt, fretum nt.

fiscal adj vectīgālis, aerārius.

fish n piscis m ♦ vi piscārī; (*fig*) expiscārī.

fisher, fisherman n piscātor m.

fishing n piscātus m ♦ adj piscātōrius.

fishing-rod n harundō f.

fish market n forum piscārium nt.

fishmonger n piscārius m.

fish pond n piscīna f.

fissile adj fissilis.

fissure n rīma f.

fist n pugnus m.

fit n (*MED*) convulsiō f; (*of anger, illness*) impetus m; **by ~s and starts** temerē, carptim ♦ vt aptāre, accommodāre; (*dress*) sedēre (*dat*); **~ out** armāre, īnstruere ♦ adj aptus, idōneus, dignus; **I see ~ to** mihi vidētur; **~ for** aptus ad (+ *acc*).

fitful adj dubius, incōnstāns.

fitfully adv incōnstanter.

fitly adv dignē, aptē.

fitness n convenientia f.

fitting n adparātus m, īnstrūmentum nt ♦ adj idōneus, dignus; **it is ~** convenit, decet.

fittingly adv dignē, convenienter.

five num quīnque; **~ each** quīnī; **~ times** quīnquiēns; **~ years** quīnquennium nt, lūstrum nt; **~ sixths** quīnque partēs.

five hundred num quīngentī; ~

each quīngēnī; **~ times**
quīngentiēns.

five hundredth adj quīngentēsimus.

fix vt fīgere; (time) dīcere,
cōnstituere; (decision) statuere
♦ n angustiae fpl; **put in a ~**
dēprehendere.

fixed adj fīxus; (attention) intentus;
(decision) certus; (star) inerrāns;
be firmly ~ in īnsidēre (dat).

fixedly adv intentē.

fixity n stabilitās f; (of purpose)
cōnstantia f.

fixtures npl adfīxa ntpl.

flabbergast vt obstupefacere.

flabbiness n mollitia f.

flabby adj flaccidus, mollis.

flag n vexillum nt; **~ officer**
praefectus classis m ♦ vi flaccēre,
flaccēscere, languēscere.

flagellate vt verberāre.

flagon n lagoena f.

flagrant adj manifestus;
flāgitiōsus.

flagrantly adv flāgitiōsē.

flagship n nāvis imperātōria f.

flail n fūstis m.

flair n iūdicium nt.

flake n squāma f; **~s** pl (snow) nix f.

flame n flamma f ♦ vi flagrāre,
exārdēscere.

flaming adj flammeus.

flamingo n phoenīcopterus m.

flank n latus nt; cornū m; **on the ~**
ab latere, ad latus ♦ vt latus
tegere (gen).

flap n flābellum nt; (dress) lacinia f
♦ vt plaudere (abl).

flare n flamma f, fulgor m ♦ vi
exārdēscere, flagrāre.

flash n fulgor m; (lightning) fulgur
nt; (time) mōmentum nt ♦ vi
fulgēre; (motion) micāre.

flashy adj speciōsus.

flask n ampulla f.

flat adj plānus; (ground) aequus; (on

back) supīnus; (on face) prōnus;
(music) gravis; (style) āridus,
frīgidus; **fall ~** (fig) frīgēre ♦ n
(land) plāniēs f; (sea) vadum nt;
(house) tabulātum nt.

flatly adv prōrsus.

flatness n plāniēs f.

flatten vt aequāre, complānāre.

flatter vt adūlārī (dat); adsentārī
(dat), blandīrī (dat).

flatterer n adsentātor m.

flattering adj blandus.

flatteringly adv blandē.

flattery n adūlātiō f, adsentātiō f,
blanditiae fpl.

flatulence n īnflātiō f.

flatulent adj īnflātus.

flaunt vt iactāre ♦ vi iactāre,
glōriārī.

flaunting n iactātiō f ♦ adj
glōriōsus.

flauntingly adv glōriōsē.

flautist n tībīcen m.

flavour n gustātus m, sapor m ♦ vt
imbuere, condīre.

flavouring n condītiō f.

flavourless adj īnsulsus.

flaw n vitium nt.

flawless adj ēmendātus.

flax n līnum nt.

flaxen adj flāvus.

flay vt dēglūbere.

flea n pūlex m.

fleck n macula f ♦ vt variāre.

fledged adj pennātus.

flee vi fugere, effugere; (for refuge)
cōnfugere.

fleece n vellus nt ♦ vt tondēre; (fig)
spoliāre.

fleecy adj lāneus.

fleet n classis f ♦ adj vēlōx, celer.

fleeting adj fugāx.

fleetness n vēlōcitās f, celeritās f.

flesh n cārō f; (fig) corpus nt; **in the
~** vīvus; **one's own ~ and blood**
cōnsanguineus; **put on ~**
pinguēscere.

fleshiness n corpus nt.

fleshliness n lībīdō f.

fleshly adj lībīdinōsus.

fleshy adj pinguis.

flexibility n lentitia f.

flexible adj flexibilis, lentus.

flicker vi coruscāre.

flickering adj tremulus.

flight n (flying) volātus m; (fleeing)
fuga f; (steps) scāla f; **put to ~**
fugāre, in fugam conicere; **take to
~** sē in fugam dare, terga vertere.

flightiness n mōbilitās f.

flighty adj mōbilis, incōnstāns.

flimsy adj tenuis, pertenuis.

flinch vi recēdere.

fling vt iacere, conicere; (missile)
intorquēre; **~ away** abicere,
prōicere; **~ open** patefacere; **~ in
one's teeth** obicere (dat); **~ to the
ground** prōsternere ♦ vi sē
incitāre ♦ n iactus m.

flint n silex m.

flinty adj siliceus.

flippancy n lascīvia f.

flippant adj lascīvus, protervus.

flippantly adv petulanter.

flirt vi lūdere, lascīvīre ♦ n
lascīvus m, lascīva f.

flit vi volitāre.

flitch n succīdia f.

float vi innāre, fluitāre; (in air)
volitāre; **~ down** dēfluere.

flock n grex m; (wool) floccus m
♦ vi concurrere, congregārī,
cōnfluere; **~ in** adfluere.

flog vt verberāre, virgīs caedere.

flogging n verbera ntpl.

flood n (deluge) ēluviō f; (river)
torrēns m; (tide) accessus m; (fig)
flūmen nt ♦ vt inundāre.

floodgate n cataracta f.

fluor n sōlum nt; (paved)
pavīmentum nt; (storey)
tabulātum nt; (threshing) ārea f
♦ vt contabulāre; **be ~ed** (in
argument) iacēre.

flora n herbae fpl.

floral adj flōreus.

florid adj flōridus.

flotilla n classicula f.

flounce vi sē concīre ♦ n īnstita f.

flounder vi volutāre; (in speech)
haesitāre.

flour n farīna f.

flourish n flōrēre, vigēre ♦ vt
vibrāre, iactāre ♦ n (RHET)
calamistrī mpl; (music) clangor m.

flout vt spernere, inlūdere (dat).

flow vi fluere, mānāre; (tide)
accēdere; **~ back** recēdere;
~ between interfluere; **~ down**
dēfluere; **~ into** īnfluere in (acc);
~ out prōfluere, ēmānāre; **~ past**
praeterfluere; **~ through**
permānāre; **~ together** cōnfluere;
~ towards adfluere ♦ n flūmen nt,
cursus m; (tide) accessus m;
(words) flūmen nt.

flower n flōs m, flōsculus m ♦ vi
flōrēre, flōrēscere.

floweret n flōsculus m.

flowery adj flōridus.

flowing adj prōfluēns; **~ with**
abundāns (abl).

flowingly adv prōfluenter.

flown adj īnflātus.

fluctuate vi aestuāre, fluctuāre.

fluctuating adj incōnstāns,
incertus.

fluctuation n aestus m, dubitātiō f.

fluency n fācundia f, verbōrum
cōpia f.

fluent adj disertus, prōfluēns.

fluently adv disertē, prōfluenter.

fluid adj liquidus ♦ n liquor m.

fluidity n liquor m.

fluke n (anchor) dēns m; (luck)
fortuītum nt.

flurry n trepidātiō f ♦ vt
sollicitāre, turbāre.

flush n rubor m; **in the first ~ of
victory** victōriā ēlātus ♦ vi
ērubēscere ♦ adj (full) abundāns;

(level) aequus.

fluster n trepidātiō f ♦ vt turbāre, sollicitāre.

flute n tībia f; **play the ~** tībiā canere.

fluted adj striātus.

flutter n tremor m; (fig) trepidātiō f ♦ vi (heart) palpitāre; (mind) trepidāre; (bird) volitāre.

fluvial adj fluviātilis.

flux n fluxus m; **be in a state of ~** fluere.

fly n musca f ♦ vi volāre; (flee) fugere; **~ apart** dissilīre; **~ at** involāre in (acc); **~ away** āvolāre; **~ from** fugere; **~ in the face of** obviam īre (dat); **~ out** ēvolāre; **~ to** advolāre ad (acc); **~ up** ēvolāre, subvolāre; **let ~ at** immittere in (acc).

flying adj volucer, volātilis; (time) fugāx.

foal n equuleus m, equulus m ♦ vt parere.

foam n spūma f ♦ vi spūmāre; (with rage) saevīre.

foaming adj spūmeus.

focus vt (mind) intendere.

fodder n pābulum nt.

foe n hostis m; (private) inimīcus m.

fog n cālīgō f, nebula f.

foggy adj cālīginōsus, nebulōsus.

foible n vitium nt.

foil n (metal) lāmina f; (sword) rudis f ♦ vt ēlūdere, ad inritum redigere.

foist vt inculcāre, interpōnere.

fold n sinus m; (sheep) ovīle nt ♦ vt plicāre, complicāre; (hands) comprimere; (sheep) inclūdere; **~ back** replicāre; **~ over** plicāre; **~ together** complicāre; **~ up in** involvere in (abl).

folding doors npl valvae fpl.

foliage n frondēs fpl.

folk n hominēs mpl ♦ adj patrius.

follow vt sequī; (calling) facere; (candidate) adsectārī; (enemy) īnsequī; (example) imitārī; (instructions) pārēre (dat); (predecessor) succēdere (dat); (road) pergere; (speaker) intellegere; **~ closely** īnsequī; **~ hard on the heels of** īnsequī, īnstāre (dat), īnstāre (dat); **~ out** exsequī; **~ to the grave** exsequī; **~ up** subsequī, īnsistere (dat) ♦ vi (time) īnsequī; (inference) sequī; **as ~s** ita, in hunc modum.

follower n comes m; (of candidate) adsectātor m; (of model) imitātor m; (of teacher) audītor m.

following adj īnsequēns, proximus, posterus; **on the ~ day** postrīdiē, posterō diē, proximō diē ♦ n adsectātōrēs mpl.

folly n stultitia f, dēmentia f, īnsipientia f.

foment vt fovēre; (fig) augēre.

fond adj amāns, studiōsus; ineptus; **be ~ of** amāre.

fondle vt fovēre, mulcēre.

fondly adv amanter, ineptē.

food n cibus m; (fig) pābulum nt.

fool n stultus m, ineptus m; (jester) scurra m; **make a ~ of** ludibriō habēre; **play the ~** dēsipere ♦ vt dēcipere, lūdere; **~ away** disperdere ♦ vi dēsipere.

foolery n ineptiae fpl, nūgae fpl.

foolhardy adj temerārius.

foolish adj stultus, ineptus, īnsipiēns.

foolishly adv stultē, ineptē.

foolishness n stultitia f, īnsipientia f.

foot n pēs m; (MIL) peditātus m; **a ~ long** pedālis; **on ~** pedes; **set ~ on** īnsistere (dat); **set on ~** īnstituere; **the ~ of** īmus ♦ vt (bill) solvere.

football n follis m.

footing n locus m, status m; **keep one's ~** īnsistere; **on an equal ~** ex aequō.

footman n pedisequus m.
footpad n grassātor m.
footpath n sēmita f, trāmes m.
footprint n vestīgium nt.
foot soldier n pedes m.
footstep n vestīgium nt; **follow in the ~s of** vestīgiīs ingredī (gen).
foppish adj dēlicātus.
for prep (advantage) dat; (duration) acc; (after noun) gen; (price) abl; (behalf) prō (abl); (cause) propter (acc), causā (gen); (after neg) prae (abl); (feelings) ergā (acc); (lieu) prō (abl); (purpose) ad, in (acc); (time fixed) in (acc) ♦ conj namque; nam (1st word), enim (2nd word); (with pron) quippe quī; ~ **a long time** diū; ~ **some time** aliquamdiū.
forage n pābulum nt ♦ vi pābulārī, frūmentārī.
forager n pābulātor m, frūmentātor m.
foraging n pābulātiō f, frūmentātiō f.
forasmuch as conj quōniam.
foray n incursiō f.
forbear vi parcere (dat), supersedēre (infin).
forbearance n venia f, indulgentia f.
forbears n māiōrēs mpl.
forbid vt vetāre (+ acc and infin), interdīcere (dat and quominus and subj); **Heaven ~!** dī meliōra!
forbidding adj tristis.
force n vīs f; (band of men) manus m; **by ~ of arms** vī et armīs ♦ vt cōgere, impellere; (way) rumpere, mōlīrī; (growth) festīnāre; ~ **an engagement** hostēs proeliārī cogere; ~ **down** dētrūdere; ~ **out** extrūdere, expellere, exturbāre; ~ **upon** inculcāre; ~ **a way in** intrōrumpere, inrumpere.
forced adj (march) magnus; (style) quaesītus; ~ **march** magnum iter.
forceful adj validus.

forceps n forceps m/f.
forces npl (MIL) cōpiae fpl.
forcible adj validus; (fig) gravis.
forcibly adv vī, violenter; (fig) graviter.
ford n vadum nt ♦ vt vadō trānsīre.
fore adj prior; **to the ~** praestō ♦ adv: ~ **and aft** in longitūdinem.
forearm n bracchium nt ♦ vt: **be ~ed** praecavēre.
forebode vt ōminārī, portendere; praesentīre.
foreboding n praesēnsiō f; ōmen nt.
forecast n praedictiō f ♦ vt praedīcere, prōvidēre.
forecourt n vestibulum nt.
forefathers n māiōrēs mpl.
forefinger n index m.
foreground n ēminentia ntpl.
forehead n frōns f.
foreign adj peregrīnus, externus; (goods) adventīcius; ~ **to** aliēnus ab; ~ **ways** peregrīnitās f.
foreigner n peregrīnus m, advena m.
foreknow vt praenōscere.
foreknowledge n prōvidentia f.
foreland n prōmunturium nt.
foremost adj prīmus, prīnceps.
forenoon n antemerīdiānum tempus nt.
forensic adj forēnsis.
forerunner n praenūntius m.
foresee vt praevidēre.
foreshadow vt praemonēre.
foresight n prōvidentia f.
forest n silva f.
forestall vt occupāre, antevenīre.
forester n silvicola m.
foretaste vt praegustāre.
foretell vt praedīcere, vāticinārī.
forethought n prōvidentia f.
forewarn vt praemonēre.
foreword n praefātiō f.
forfeit n multa f, damnum nt ♦ vt āmittere, perdere, multārī (abl);

(*bail*) dēserere.

forfeiture *n* damnum *nt*.

forgather *vi* congregārī, convenīre.

forge *n* fornāx *f* ♦ *vt* fabricārī, excūdere; (*document*) subicere; (*will*) suppōnere; (*signature*) imitārī; (*money*) adulterīnōs nummōs percutere.

forged *adj* falsus, adulterīnus, commentīcius.

forger *n* (*of will*) subiector *m*.

forgery *n* falsum *nt*, commentum *nt*.

forget *vt* oblīvīscī (*gen*); (*thing learnt*) dēdiscere; **be forgotten** memoriā cadere, ex animō effluere.

forgetful *adj* immemor; (*by habit*) oblīviōsus.

forgetfulness *n* oblīviō *f*.

forgive *vt* ignōscere (*dat*), veniam dare (*dat*).

forgiveness *n* venia *f*.

forgo *vt* dīmittere, renūntiāre; (*rights*) dēcēdere dē iūre.

fork *n* furca *f*; (*small*) furcula *f*; (*road*) trivium *nt*.

forlorn *adj* inops, dēstitūtus, exspes.

form *n* fōrma *f*, figūra *f*; (*of procedure*) fōrmula *f*; (*condition*) vigor *m*; (*etiquette*) mōs *m*; (*seat*) scamnum *nt*; (*school*) schola *f*; (*hare's*) latibulum *nt* ♦ *vt* fōrmāre, fingere, efficere; (*MIL*) īnstruere; (*plan*) inīre, capere.

formal *adj* iūstus; (*rite*) sollemnis.

formality *n* iūsta *ntpl*, rītus *m*; **as a ~** dicis causā; **with due ~** rītē.

formally *adv* rītē.

formation *n* fōrma *f*, figūra *f*; (*process*) cōnfōrmātiō *f*; **in ~** (*MIL*) īnstructus.

former *adj* prior, prīstinus, vetus; **the ~** ille.

formerly *adv* anteā, ōlim,

quondam.

formidable *adj* formīdolōsus.

formidably *adv* formīdolōsē.

formula *n* fōrmula *f*; (*dictated*) praefātiō *f*.

formulate *vt* compōnere.

forsake *vt* dērelinquere, dēstituere, dēserere.

forswear *vt* pēierāre, abiūrāre.

fort *n* castellum *nt*.

forth *adv* forās; (*time*) posthāc.

forthwith *adv* extemplō, statim, prōtinus.

fortieth *adj* quadrāgēsimus.

fortification *n* (*process*) mūnītiō *f*; (*place*) mūnīmentum *nt*, arx *f*.

fortify *vt* mūnīre, ēmūnīre, commūnīre; (*fig*) cōnfīrmāre.

fortitude *n* fortitūdō *f*.

fortnight *n* quīndecim diēs *mpl*.

fortnightly *adv* quīntō decimō quōque diē.

fortress *n* arx *f*, castellum *nt*.

fortuitous *adj* fortuītus.

fortuitously *adv* fortuītō, cāsū.

fortunate *adj* fēlīx, fortūnātus.

fortunately *adv* fēlīciter, bene.

fortune *n* fortūna *f*, fors *f*; (*wealth*) rēs *f*, dīvitiae *fpl*; **good ~** fēlīcitās *f*, secundae rēs *fpl*; **bad ~** adversae rēs *fpl*; **make one's ~** rem facere, rem quaerere; **tell ~s** hariolārī.

fortune-hunter *n* captātor *m*.

fortune-teller *n* hariolus *m*, sāga *f*.

forty *num* quadrāgintā; **each ~** quadrāgēnī; **~ times** quadrāgiēns.

forum *n* forum *nt*.

forward *adj* (*person*) protervus, audāx; (*fruit*) praecox ♦ *adv* porrō, ante; **bring ~** prōferre; **come ~** prōdīre ♦ *vt* (*letter*) perferre; (*cause*) adiuvāre, favēre (*dat*).

forwardness *n* audācia *f*, alacritās *f*.

forwards *adv* porrō, prōrsus; **backwards and ~** rursum

prōrsum, hūc illūc.
fosse n fossa f.
foster vt alere, nūtrīre; (fig)
fovēre.
foster child n alumnus m, alumna f.
foster father n altor m, ēducātor
m.
foster mother n altrīx f, nūtrīx f.
foul adj foedus; (speech)
inquinātus; **fall ~ of** inruere in
(acc).
foully adv foedē, inquinātē.
foul-mouthed adj maledicus.
foulness n foedītās f.
found vt condere, fundāre,
īnstituere; (metal) fundere.
foundation n fundāmenta ntpl.
founder n fundātor m, conditor m
♦ vi submergī, naufragium
facere.
foundling n expositīcia f.
fount n fōns m.
fountain n fōns m.
fountainhead n fōns m, orīgō f.
four num quattuor (indecl); ~ **each**
quaternī; ~ **times** quater; ~ **days**
quadriduum nt; ~ **years**
quadriennium nt.
fourfold adj quadruplex ♦ adv
quadrifāriam.
four hundred num quadringentī; ~
each quadringēnī; ~ **times**
quadringentiēns.
four hundredth adj quadringentēsimus.
fourteen num quattuordecim; ~
each quaternī dēnī; ~ **times**
quater deciēns.
fourteenth adj quartus decimus.
fourth adj quartus ♦ n quadrāns
m; **three ~s** dōdrāns m, trēs
partēs fpl.
fowl n avis f; gallīna f.
fowler n auceps m.
fox n vulpēs f; ~'**s** vulpīnus.
foxy adj astūtus, vafer.
fracas n rīxa f.

fraction n pars f.
fractious adj difficilis.
fracture n frāctum os nt ♦ vt
frangere.
fragile adj fragilis.
fragility n fragilitās f.
fragment n fragmentum nt.
fragrance n odor m.
fragrant adj suāvis.
fragrantly adv suāviter.
frail adj fragilis, īnfirmus, dēbilis.
frailty n dēbilitās f; (moral) error m.
frame vt fabricārī, fingere,
effingere; (document) compōnere
♦ n fōrma f; (of mind) adfectiō f,
habitus m; **in a ~ of mind**
animātus.
framer n fabricātor m, opifex m;
(of law) lātor m.
framework n compāgēs f.
franchise n suffrāgium nt, cīvitās f.
frank adj ingenuus, apertus;
(speech) līber.
frankincense n tūs nt.
frankly adv ingenuē, apertē; līberē.
frankness n ingenuitās f; (speech)
lībertās f.
frantic adj furēns, furiōsus,
dēlīrus.
frantically adv furenter.
fraternal adj frāternus.
fraternally adv frāternē.
fraternity n frāternitās f; (society)
sodālitās f; (guild) collēgium nt.
fraternize vi amīcitiam iungere.
fratricide n frātricīda m; (act)
frātris parricīdium nt.
fraud n fraus f, dolus m, falsum nt;
(criminal) dolus malus m.
fraudulence n fraus f.
fraudulent adj fraudulentus,
dolōsus.
fraudulently adv dolōsē, dolō malō.
fraught adj plēnus.
fray n pugna f, rīxa f ♦ vt terere.
freak n mōnstrum nt; (caprice)
libīdō f.

freckle n lentīgō f.

freckly adj lentīginōsus.

free adj līber; (*disengaged*) vacuus; (*generous*) līberālis; (*from cost*) grātuītus; (*from duty*) immūnis; (*from encumbrance*) expedītus; **be ~ from** vacāre (abl); **I am still ~ to** integrum est mihī (infin); **set ~** absolvere, līberāre; (*slave*) manū mittere ♦ adv grātīs, grātuītō ♦ vt līberāre, expedīre, exsolvere.

freebooter n praedō m.

freeborn adj ingenuus.

freedman n lībertus m.

freedom n lībertās f; (*from duty*) immūnitās f.

freehold n praedium līberum nt ♦ adj immūnis.

freely adv līberē; (*lavishly*) cōpiōsē, largē; (*frankly*) apertē; (*voluntarily*) ultrō, suā sponte.

freeman n cīvis m.

free will n voluntās f; **of one's own ~** suā sponte.

freeze vt gelāre, glaciāre ♦ vi concrēscere.

freezing adj gelidus; **it is ~** gelat.

freight n vectūra f; (*cargo*) onus nt ♦ vt onerāre.

freighter n nāvis onerāria f.

frenzied adj furēns, furiōsus, fānāticus.

frenzy n furor m, īnsānia f.

frequency n adsiduitās f.

frequent adj frequēns, crēber ♦ vt frequentāre, commeāre in (acc).

frequently adv saepe, saepenumerō, frequenter.

fresh adj (*new*) recēns, novus; (*vigorous*) integer; (*water*) dulcis; (*wind*) ācer.

freshen vt renovāre ♦ vi (*wind*) incrēbrēscere.

freshly adv recenter.

freshman n tīrō m.

freshness n novitās f, viriditās f.

fret vi maerēre, angī ♦ vt

fretful adj mōrōsus, querulus.

fretfulness n mōrōsitās f.

fretted adj laqueātus.

friable adj puter.

friction n trītus m.

friend n amīcus m, familiāris m/f, hospes m, sodālis m; **make ~s with** sē cōnferre ad amīcitiam (gen).

friendless adj sine amīcīs.

friendliness n cōmitās f, officium nt.

friendly adj cōmis, facilis, benīgnus; **on ~ terms** familiāriter.

friendship n amīcitia f, familiāritās f.

frigate n liburna f.

fright n horror m, pavor m, terror m; **take ~** extimēscere, expavēscere.

frighten vt terrēre, exterrēre, perterrēre; **~ away** absterrēre; **~ off** dēterrēre; **~ the life out of** exanimāre.

frightful adj horribilis, immānis; (*look*) taeter.

frightfully adv foedē.

frigid adj frīgidus.

frigidity n frīgus nt.

frill n fimbriae fpl; (RHET) calamistrī mpl.

fringe n fimbriae fpl.

frisk vi lascīvīre, exsultāre.

frisky adj lascīvus.

fritter vt: **~ away** dissipāre; (*time*) extrahere.

frivolity n levitās f.

frivolous adj levis, inānis.

frivolously adv ināniter.

fro adv: **to and ~** hūc illūc.

frock n stola f.

frog n rāna f.

frolic n lūdus m ♦ vi lūdere, lascīvīre.

frolicsome adj lascīvus, hilaris.

from prep ab (abl); ā (before consonants); (out) ē, ex (abl); (cause) propter (acc); (prevention) quōminus, quīn; ~ **all directions** undique.

front n frōns f; **in ~** ā fronte, adversus; **in ~ of** prō (+ abl).

frontier n līmes m, cōnfīnia ntpl; ~s fīnēs mpl.

front line n prima aciēs.

frost n gelū nt.

frostbitten adj: **he ~** vī frīgoris ambūrī.

frosty adj gelidus, glaciālis.

froth n spūma f ♦ vi spūmās agere.

frothy adj spūmeus.

froward adj contumāx.

frown n frontis contractiō f ♦ vi frontem contrahere.

frozen adj glaciālis.

fructify vt fēcundāre.

frugal adj parcus, frūgī.

frugality n frūgālitās f, parsimōnia f.

frugally adv parcē, frūgāliter.

fruit n frūctus m; (tree) māla ntpl; (berry) bāca f; (fig) frūctus m; ~s pl (of earth) frūgēs fpl.

fruiterer n pōmārius m.

fruitful adj fēcundus, frūctuōsus.

fruitfully adv ferāciter.

fruitfulness n fēcunditās f, ūbertās f.

fruition n frūctus m.

fruitless adj inūtilis, vānus.

fruitlessly adv nēquīquam, frustrā.

fruit tree n pōmum nt.

frustrate vt frustrārī, ad inritum redigere.

frustration n frustrātiō f.

fry vt frīgere.

frying pan n sartāgō f; **out of the ~ into the fire** incidit in Scyllam quī vult vītāre Charybdim.

fuel n fōmes m.

fugitive adj fugitīvus ♦ n fugitīvus m, trānsfuga m; (from abroad)

extorris m.

fulfil vt (duty) explēre, implēre; (promise) praestāre; (order) exsequī, perficere.

fulfilment n absolūtiō f.

full adj plēnus (+ abl), refertus, explētus; (entire) integer; (amount) solidus; (brother) germānus; (measure) iūstus; (meeting) frequēns; (style) cōpiōsus; **at ~ length** porrēctus; **at ~ speed** citātō gradū, citātō equō.

fuller n fullō m.

full-grown adj adultus.

full moon n lūna plēna.

fullness n (style) cōpia f; (time) mātūritās f.

fully adv plēnē, penitus, funditus.

fulminate vi intonāre.

fulsome adj fastīdiōsus, pūtidus.

fumble vi haesitāre.

fume n fūmus m, hālitus m ♦ vi stomachārī.

fumigate vt suffīre.

fun n iocus m, lūdus m; **for ~** animī causā; **make ~ of** inlūdere, dēlūdere, lūdibriō habēre.

function n officium nt, mūnus nt.

fund n cōpia f.

fundamental adj prīmus ♦ n prīncipium nt, elementum nt.

funds npl nora f, pecūliae ipl.

funeral n fūnus nt, exsequiae fpl ♦ adj fūnebris.

funeral pile n rogus m.

funeral pyre n rogus m.

funeral rites npl exsequiae fpl, īnferiae fpl.

funereal adj fūnebris, lūgubris.

funnel n īnfundibulum nt.

funny adj ioculāris, rīdiculus.

fur n pellis m.

furbelow n īnstita f.

furbish vt expolīre; ~ **up** interpolāre.

Furies npl Furiae fpl.

furious adj saevus, vehemēns,

perīrātus.
furiously adv furenter, saevē, vehementer.
furl vt (sail) legere.
furlong n stadium nt.
furlough n commeātus m.
furnace n fornāx f.
furnish vt praebēre, suppeditāre; (equip) īnstruere, ōrnāre.
furniture n supellex f.
furrow n sulcus m ♦ vt sulcāre.
furry adj villōsus.
further adj ulterior ♦ adv ultrā, porrō; amplius ♦ vt adiuvāre, cōnsulere (dat).
furtherance n prōgressus m; (means) īnstrūmentum nt.
furthermore adv praetereā, porrō.
furthest adj ultimus ♦ adv longissimē.
furtive adj fūrtīvus, clandestīnus.
furtively adv clam, fūrtim.
fury n furor m, saevitia f; īra f.
fuse vt fundere; (together) coniungere.
fusion n coniūnctiō f.
fuss n importūnitās f, querimōnia f ♦ vi conquerī, sollicitārī.
fussy adj importūnus, incommodus.
fusty adj mūcidus.
futile adj inānis, inūtilis, futtilis.
futility n vānitās f, futtilitās f.
future adj futūrus, posterus ♦ n posterum nt, reliquum nt; in ~ posthāc; **for the** ~ in posterum.
futurity n posterum tempus nt, posteritās f.

G

gabble vi garrīre.
gable n fastīgium nt.
gadfly n tabānus m.
gag vt ōs praeligāre (dat), ōs obvolvere (dat).
gage n pignus nt.

gaiety n laetitia f, hilaritās f, festīvitās f.
gaily adv hilare, festīve.
gain n lucrum nt, quaestus m ♦ vt comparāre; adipīscī; (profit) lucrārī; (thing) parāre, cōnsequī, capere; (case) vincere; (place) pervenīre ad; (possession of) potīrī (gen); (victory) reportāre; ~ **over** conciliāre; ~ **ground** incrēbrēscere; ~ **possession of** potior (+ abl); ~ **the upper hand** rem obtinēre.
gainful adj quaestuōsus.
gainsay vt contrādīcere (dat).
gait n incessus m, ingressiō f.
gaiters n ocreae fpl.
gala n diēs festus m.
galaxy n circulus lacteus m.
gale n ventus m.
gall n fel nt, bīlis f ♦ vt ūrere.
gallant adj fortis, audāx; (courteous) officiōsus.
gallantly adv fortiter; officiōsē.
gallantry n virtūs f; urbānitās f.
gall bladder n fel nt.
gallery n porticus f.
galley n nāvis āctuāria f; (cook's) culīna f.
galling adj amārus, mordāx.
gallon n congius m.
gallop n cursus m; **at the** ~ citātō equō, admissō equō ♦ vi admissō equō currere.
gallows n īnfēlīx arbor m, furca f.
gallows bird n furcifer m.
galore adv adfatim.
gamble n ālea f ♦ vi āleā lūdere.
gambler n āleātor m.
gambling n ālea f.
gambol n lūsus m ♦ vi lūdere, lascīvīre, exsultāre.
game n lūdus m; (with dice) ālea f; (hunt) praeda f; **play the** ~ rēctē facere; **public** ~ s lūdī mpl; **Olympic** ~s Olympia npl; **the** ~'**s up** āctum est ♦ adj animōsus.

gamester n āleātor m.

gammon n perna f.

gander n ānser m.

gang n grex m, caterva f.

gangster n grassātor m.

gangway n forus m.

gaol n carcer m.

gaoler n custōs m.

gap n hiātus m, lacūna f.

gape vi hiāre, inhiāre; (opening) dēhiscere.

garb n habitus m, amictus m ♦ vt amicīre.

garbage n quisquiliae fpl.

garden n hortus m; (public) hortī mpl.

gardener n hortulānus m; (ornamental) topiārius m.

gardening n hortī cultūra f; (ornamental) topiāria f.

gargle vi gargarissāre.

garish adj speciōsus, fūcātus.

garland n sertum nt, corōna f ♦ vt corōnāre.

garlic n ālium nt.

garment n vestis f, vestīmentum nt.

garnish vt ōrnāre, decorāre.

garret n cēnāculum nt.

garrison n praesidium nt, dēfēnsōrēs mpl ♦ vt praesidiō mūnīre, praesidium collocāre in (abl).

garrotte vt laqueō gulam frangere (dat).

garrulity n garrulitās f.

garrulous adj garrulus, loquāx.

gas n vapor m.

gash n vulnus nt ♦ vt caedere, lacerāre.

gasp n anhēlitus m, singultus m ♦ vi anhēlāre.

gastronomy n gula f.

gate n porta f.

gather vt colligere, cōgere; (fruit) legere; (inference) colligere, conicere ♦ vi congregārī.

gathering n conventus m, coetus m.

gauche adj inconcinnus, illepidus.

gaudily adv splendidē, speciōsē.

gaudy adj speciōsus, fūcātus, lautus.

gauge n modulus m ♦ vt mētīrī.

Gaul n Gallia f; (person) Gallus m.

gaunt adj macer.

gauntlet n manica f.

gauze n Cōa ntpl.

gay adj hilaris, festīvus, laetus.

gaze vi intuērī; ~ at intuērī, adspectāre, contemplārī.

gazelle n oryx m.

gazette n ācta diūrna ntpl, ācta pūblica ntpl.

gear n īnstrūmenta ntpl; (ship's) armāmenta ntpl.

gelding n cantērius m.

gelid adj gelidus.

gem n gemma f.

gender n genus nt.

genealogical adj dē stirpe.

genealogical table n stemma nt.

genealogist n geneālogus m.

genealogy n geneālogia f.

general adj generālis, ūniversus; (usual) vulgāris, commūnis; in ~ omninō ♦ n dux m, imperātor m; ~'s tent praetōrium nt.

generalissimo n imperātor m.

generality n vulgus nt, plērīque mpl.

generalize vi ūnīversē loquī.

generally adv ferē, plērumque; (discuss) īnfīnītē.

generalship n ductus m.

generate vt gignere, generāre.

generation n aetās f, saeculum nt.

generic adj generālis.

generically adv genere.

generosity n līberālitās f, largitās f.

generous adj līberālis, largus, benīgnus.

generously adv līberāliter, largē,

benīgnē.

genesis n orīgō f, prīncipium nt.

genial adj cōmis, hilaris.

geniality n cōmitās f, hilaritās f.

genially adv cōmiter, hilare.

genitive n genitīvus m.

genius n (deity) genius m; (talent) ingenium nt, indolēs f; of ~ ingeniōsus.

genre n genus nt.

genteel adj urbānus, polītus.

gentility n urbānitās f, ēlegantia f.

gentle adj (birth) ingenuus; (manner) hūmānus, indulgēns, mītis; (slope) lēnis, mollis; (thing) placidus, lēnis.

gentleman n vir m, ingenuus m, vir honestus m.

gentlemanly adj ingenuus, līberālis, honestus.

gentleness n hūmānitās f, indulgentia f, lēnitās f.

gentlewoman n ingenua f, mulier honesta f.

gently adv lēniter, molliter, placidē.

gentry n ingenuī mpl, optimātēs mpl; (contempt) hominēs mpl.

genuine adj vērus, germānus, sincērus.

genuinely adv germānē, sincērē.

genuineness n fidēs f.

geographical adj geōgraphicus; ~ position situs m.

geography n geōgraphia f.

geometrical adj geōmetricus.

geometry n geōmetria f.

Georgics n Geōrgica ntpl.

germ n germen nt, sēmen nt.

germane adj affīnis.

germinate vi gemmāre.

gesticulate vi sē iactāre, gestū ūtī.

gesticulation n gestus m.

gesture n gestus m, mōtus m.

get vt adipīscī, nancīscī, parāre; (malady) contrahere; (request) impetrāre; (return) capere;

(reward) ferre; ~ sth done cūrāre (with gerundive); ~ sb to do persuādēre (dat), addūcere; ~ by heart ēdiscere; ~ in repōnere; ~ the better of superāre; go and ~ arcessere ♦ vi fierī; ~ about (rumour) palam fierī, percrēbrēscere; ~ away effugere; ~ at (intent) spectāre; ~ behind cessāre; ~ off absolvī; ~ on prōficere; ~ out effugere, ēvādere; ~ out of hand lascīvīre; ~ out of the way dē viā dēcēdere; ~ ready parāre; ~ rid of abicere, tollere; ~ to pervenīre ad; ~ to know cognōscere; ~ off abicere; ~ together congregārī; ~ up exsurgere.

get-up n ōrnātus m.

ghastliness n pallor m.

ghastly adj pallidus; (sight) taeter.

ghost n larva f, īdōlon nt; ~s pl mānēs mpl; **give up the ~** animam agere, efflāre.

giant n Gigas m.

gibberish n barbaricus sermō m.

gibbet n furca f.

gibe vi inrīdēre.

giddiness n vertīgō f.

giddy adj vertīginōsus; (fig) levis.

gift n dōnum nt; (small) mūnusculum nt; ~s pl (mind) ingenium nt.

gifted adj ingeniōsus.

gig n cisium nt.

gigantic adj ingēns, immānis.

gild vt inaurāre.

gill n (measure) quartārius m; (fish) branchia f.

gilt adj aurātus.

gimlet n terebra f.

gin n pedica f, laqueus m.

ginger n zingiberī nt.

gingerly adv pedetemptim.

giraffe n camēlopardālis f.

gird vt circumdāre; ~ on accingere; ~ oneself cingī; ~ up succingere.

girder n tignum nt.
girdle n cingulus m ♦ vt cingere.
girl n puella f, virgō f.
girlhood n aetās puellāris f.
girlish adj puellāris.
girth n ambitus m, amplitūdō f.
gist n firmāmentum nt.
give vt dare, dōnāre, tribuere;
  (thing due) reddere; ~ away
  largīrī; (bride) in matrimōnium
  collocāre; (secret) prōdere; ~ back
  reddere, restituere; **birth (to)**
  parēre; ~ in (name) profitērī; ~ off
  ēmittere; ~ out (orders) ēdere;
  (sound) ēmittere; ~ thanks grātiās
  agere; ~ up dēdere, trādere; (hope
  of) dēspērāre; (rights) dēcēdere
  dē, renūntiāre; ~ way cēdere;
  (MIL) inclīnāre ♦ vi labāre; ~ in sē
  victum fatērī; (MIL) manūs dare; ~
  out (fail) dēficere; (pretend) ferre;
  ~ up dēsistere; ~ way cēdere.
giver n dator m.
glacial adj glaciālis.
glad adj laetus, alacer, hilaris; **be**
  ~ gaudēre.
gladden vt exhilarāre, oblectāre.
glade n saltus m.
gladiator n gladiātor m.
gladiatorial adj gladiātōrius;
  present a ~ **show** gladiātōrēs
  dare.
gladly adv laetē, libenter.
gladness n laetitia f, alacritās f,
  gaudium nt.
glamorous adj venustus.
glamour n venustās f.
glance n aspectus m ♦ vi oculōs
  conicere; ~ **at** aspicere; (fig)
  attingere, perstringere; ~ off
  stringere.
glare n fulgor m ♦ vi fulgēre; ~ at
  torvīs oculīs intuērī.
glaring adj (look) torvus; (fault)
  manifestus; **be** ~ ante pedēs
  positum esse.
glass n vitrum nt; (mirror)

speculum nt.
glassy adj vitreus.
glaze vt vitrō obdūcere.
gleam n fulgor m, lūx f ♦ vi
  fulgēre, lūcēre.
gleaming adj splendidus, nitidus.
glean vi spīcās legere.
gleaning n spīcilegium nt.
glebe n fundus m.
glee n hilaritās f, gaudium nt.
gleeful adj hilaris, festīvus, laetus.
gleefully adv hilare, laetē.
glen n vallis f.
glib adj prōfluēns, fācundus.
glibly adv prōfluenter.
glide n lāpsus m ♦ vi lābī; ~ away
  ēlābī.
glimmer vi sublūcēre ♦ n: a ~ of
  hope spēcula f.
glimpse n aspectus m ♦ vt
  cōnspicārī.
glint vi renīdēre.
glisten vi fulgēre, nitēre.
glitter vi micāre.
gloaming n crepusculum nt.
gloat vi: ~ **over** inhiāre, animō
  haurīre, oculōs pāscere (abl).
globe n globus m, sphaera f;
  (inhabited) orbis terrārum m.
globular adj globōsus.
globule n globulus m, pilula f.
gloom n tenebrae fpl; trīstitia f.
gloomy adj tenebricōsus; trīstis,
  dēmissus.
glorify vt illūstrāre, extollere,
  laudāre.
glorious adj illūstris, praeclārus,
  splendidus.
gloriously adv praeclārē,
  splendidē.
glory n laus f, glōria f, decus nt ♦ vi
  glōriārī, sē iactāre.
gloss n nitor m ♦ vt: ~ **over** (fig)
  dissimulāre.
glossy adj nitidus.
glove n manica f.
glow n (light) lūmen nt; (heat) ārdor

m; (*passion*) calor *m* ♦ *vi* lūcēre,
ārdēre, calēre, candēre.
glowing *adj* candēns, ārdēns,
calidus.
glue *n* glūten *nt* ♦ *vt* glūtināre.
glum *adj* tristis, maestus.
glut *vt* explēre, saturāre ♦ *n*
satietās *f*, abundantia *f*.
glutton *n* gāneō *m*, helluō *m*.
gluttonous *adj* edāx, vorāx,
avidus.
gluttony *n* gula *f*, edācitās *f*.
gnarled *adj* nōdōsus.
gnash *vt*, *vi* frendere; **~ one's teeth**
dentibus frendere.
gnat *n* culex *m*.
gnaw *vt* rōdere; **~ away** ērōdere.
gnawing *adj* mordāx.
go *vi* īre, vādere; (*depart*) abīre,
discēdere; (*event*) ēvādere;
(*mechanism*) movērī; **~ about**
incipere, adgredī; **~ after** īnsequī;
~ away abīre, discēdere; **~ back**
redīre, regredī; **~ before** anteīre,
praeīre; by praeterīre; (*rule*)
sequī, ūtī (*abl*); **~ down**
dēscendere; (*storm*) cadere; (*star*)
occidere, **~ for** pctere; **~ forward**
prōgredī; **~ in** intrāre, ingredī; **~**
in for (*profession*) facere,
exercēre; **~ off** abīre; **~ on**
pergere; (*event*) agī; **~ out** exīre,
ēgredī; (*fire*) extinguī; **~ over**
trānsīre; (*to enemy*) dēscīscere;
(*preparation*) meditārī; (*reading*)
legere; (*work done*) retractāre; **~**
round circumīre, ambīre; **~**
through percurrere; penetrāre;
(*suffer*) perferre; **~ to** adīre,
petere; **~ to the help of** subvenīre
(+ *dat*); **~ to meet** obviam īre;
~ up ascendere; **~ with** comitārī;
~ without carēre (*abl*),
sē abstinēre (*abl*) ♦ *n* vīs *f*,
ācrimōnia *f*.
goad *n* stimulus *m* ♦ *vt* irrītāre;
pungere; (*fig*) stimulāre.

go-ahead *adj* impiger.
goal *n* fīnis *m*, mēta *f*.
goat *n* caper *m*, capra *f*.
gobble *vt* dēvorāre.
go-between *n* internūntius *m*,
internūntia *f*; (*bribery*) sequester
m.
goblet *n* pōculum *nt*, scyphus *m*.
god *n* deus *m*.
goddess *n* dea *f*.
godhead *n* dīvīnitās *f*, nūmen *nt*.
godless *adj* impius.
godlike *adj* dīvīnus.
godliness *n* pietās *f*, religiō *f*.
godly *adj* pius.
godsend *n* quasi caelō dēmissus.
going *n* itiō *f*; (*way*) iter *nt*;
(*departure*) profectiō *f*, discessus
m.
goitre *n* strūma *f*.
gold *n* aurum *nt* ♦ *adj* aureus.
golden *adj* aureus; (*hair*) flāvus.
gold leaf *n* bractea *f*.
goldmine *n* aurāria *f*.
goldsmith *n* aurārius *m*, aurifex
m.
good *adj* bonus, probus; (*fit*)
idōneus, aptus; (*considerable*)
magnus; **~ day!** salvē, salvēte!; **~**
looks fōrma *f*, pulchritūdō *f*; **~**
nature facilitās *f*, cōmitās *f* ♦ *n*
bonum *nt*, commodum *nt*; **do ~** to
prōdesse (*dat*); **make ~** supplēre,
praestāre; **seem ~** vidērī; ♦ *interj*
bene.
goodbye *interj* valē, valēte; **say ~**
to valēre iubēre.
good-for-nothing *adj* nēquam.
good-humoured *adj* cōmis.
good-looking *adj* pulcher.
goodly *adj* pulcher; (*size*) amplus.
good nature *n* facilitās *f*, cōmitās
f.
good-natured *adj* facilis,
benīgnus, benevolus.
goodness *n* bonitās *f*; (*character*)
virtūs *f*, probitās *f*, pietās *f*.

goods npl bona ntpl, rēs f; (for sale)
merx f.
good-tempered adj mītis, lēnis.
goodwill n benevolentia f, favor m,
grātia f.
goose n ānser m/f.
goose flesh n horror m.
gore n cruor m ♦ vt cornibus
cōnfodere.
gorge n faucēs fpl, gula f; (GEOG)
angustiae fpl ♦ vt: ~ oneself sē
ingurgitāre.
gorgeous adj lautus, splendidus.
gorgeously adv lautē, splendidē.
gorgeousness n lautitia f.
gormandize vi helluārī.
gory adj cruentus.
gospel n ēvangelium nt.
gossip n (talk) sermunculus m,
rūmusculus m, fāma f; (person)
lingulāca f ♦ vi garrīre.
gouge vt ēruere.
gourd n cucurbita f.
gourmand n helluō m, gāneō m.
gout n podagra f, articulāris
morbus m.
gouty adj arthrīticus.
govern vt (subjects) regere; (state)
administrāre, gubernāre;
(emotion) moderārī (dat), cohibēre.
governess n ēducātrīx f.
government n gubernātiō f,
administrātiō f; (men)
magistrātūs mpl.
governor n gubernātor m,
moderātor m; (province) prōcōnsul
m, prōcūrātor m.
gown n (men) toga f; (women) stola
f.
grab vt adripere, corripere.
grace n grātia f, lepōs m, decor m;
(favour) grātia f, venia f; (of gods)
pāx f; **be in the good ~s of** in
grātiā esse apud (acc); **with a bad
~** invītus ♦ vt decorāre, ōrnāre.
graceful adj decōrus, venustus,
lepidus.

gracefully adv venustē, lepidē.
graceless adj illepidus, impudēns.
gracious adj benīgnus, prōpitius,
misericors.
graciously adv benīgnē,
līberāliter.
graciousness n benīgnitās f,
līberālitās f.
gradation n gradus m.
grade n gradus m.
gradient n clīvus m.
gradual adj lēnis.
gradually adv gradātim, sēnsim,
paulātim.
graft n surculus m; (POL) ambitus
m ♦ vt īnserere.
grafting n īnsitiō f.
grain n frūmentum nt; (seed)
grānum nt; **against the ~** invītā
Minervā.
grammar n grammatica f.
grammarian n grammaticus m.
granary n horreum nt.
grand adj (person) amplus, illūstris,
ēgregius; (way of life) lautus,
māgnificus; (language) grandis,
sublīmis.
granddaughter n neptis f; **great ~**
prōneptis f.
grandeur n māiestās f,
māgnificentia f; (style) granditās f.
grandfather n avus m; **great-~**
proavus m; **great-great-~** abavus
m; **of a ~** avītus.
grandiloquence n māgniloquentia
f.
grandiloquent adj grandiloquus,
tumidus.
grandiose adj māgnificus.
grandmother n avia f; **great ~**
proavia f.
grandson n nepōs m; **great ~**
prōnepōs m.
grant vt dare, concēdere, tribuere;
(admit) fatērī ♦ n concessiō f.
grape n ūva f.
graphic adj expressus; **give a ~**

account of ante oculōs pōnere, oculīs subicere.

grapnel n manus ferrea f, harpagō f.

grapple vi luctārī.

grappling iron n manus ferrea f.

grasp vt prēnsāre, comprehendere; (with mind) complectī, adsequī, percipere, intellegere; ~ **at** captāre, adpetere ♦ n manus f, comprehēnsiō f; (mind) captus m.

grasping adj avārus, rapāx.

grass n herba f.

grasshopper n gryllus m.

grassy adj herbōsus; herbidus.

grate n focus m ♦ vt atterere; ~ **upon** offendere.

grateful adj grātus; **feel** ~ grātiam habēre.

gratefully adv grātē.

gratification n voluptās f.

gratify vt mōrem gerere (dat), mōrigerārī (dat), grātificārī (dat).

gratifying adj iūcundus.

gratis adv grātuītō, grātīs.

gratitude n grātia f; **show** ~ grātiam referre.

gratuitous adj grātuītus.

gratuitously adv grātuītō.

gratuity n stips f; (MIL) dōnātīvum nt.

grave n sepulchrum nt ♦ adj gravis, austērus ♦ vt scalpere.

gravel n glārea f.

gravely adv graviter, sevērē.

gravitate vi vergere.

gravity n (person) sevēritās f, tristitia f; (CIRCS) gravitās f, mōmentum nt; (physics) nūtus m; **by force of** ~ nūtū suō.

gray adj rāvus; (hair) cānus.

graze vi pāscī ♦ vt (cattle) pāscere; (by touch) stringere.

grazing n pāstus m.

grease n arvīna f ♦ vt ungere.

greasy adj pinguis, ūnctus.

great adj māgnus, grandis, ingēns, amplus; (fame) īnsignis, praeclārus; **as** ~ **as** … tantus … quantus; ~ **deal** plūrimum; ~ **many** plūrimī; **how** ~ quantus; **very** ~ permāgnus.

greatcoat n lacerna f.

greatest adj māximus.

greatly adv multum, māgnopere.

greave n ocrea f.

greed n avāritia f.

greedily adv avārē, cupidē.

greedy adj avārus, cupidus; avidus.

Greek adj Graecus.

green adj viridis; (unripe) crūdus; **be** ~ virēre.

greenness n viriditās f.

greens n olus nt.

greet vt salūtāre.

greeting n salūs f, salūtātiō f.

grey adj rāvus; (hair) cānus.

greyhound n vertagus m.

grief n dolor m, maeror m, lūctus m; **come to** ~ perīre.

grievance n querimōnia f; iniūria f.

grieve vi dolēre, maerēre, lūgēre.

grievous adj tristis, lūctuōsus; molestus, gravis, acerbus.

grievously adv graviter, valdē.

grim adj trux, truculentus; atrōx.

grimace n ōris dēprāvātiō f; **make a** ~ ōs dūcere.

grime n sordēs f, lutum nt.

grimy adj sordidus, lutulentus.

grin n rīsus m ♦ vi adrīdēre.

grind vt contundere; (corn) molere; (blade) acuere; ~ **down** (fig) opprimere.

grindstone n cōs f.

grip vt comprehendere, arripere ♦ n comprehēnsiō f; **come to ~s with** in complexum venīre (gen).

gripe n tormina ntpl.

grisly adj horridus, dīrus.

grist n (fig) ēmolumentum nt.

grit n harēna f.

groan n gemitus m ♦ vi gemere, ingemere.

groin n inguen nt.

groom n agāsō m.

groove n canālis m, stria f.

grope vi praetentāre.

gross adj crassus, pinguis; (morally) turpis, foedus.

grossly adv foedē, turpiter; (very) valdē.

grossness n crassitūdō f; turpitūdō f.

grotto n spēlunca f, antrum nt.

ground n (bottom) solum nt; (earth) terra f, humus f; (cause) ratiō f, causa f; (sediment) faex f; on the ~ humī; on the ~ that quod (+ subj); to the ~ humum; gain ~ prōficere; (rumour) incrēbrēscere; lose ~ cēdere; (MIL) inclīnāre ♦ vt īnstituere ♦ vi (ship) sīdere.

grounding n īnstitūtiō f.

groundless adj vānus, inānis.

groundlessly adv frustrā, temerē.

grounds n faex f; (property) praedium nt; (reason) causa f; I have good ~ for doing nōn sine causā faciō, iūstīs dē causīs faciō.

groundwork n fundāmentum nt.

group n globus m, circulus m ♦ vt dispōnere.

grouse n (bird) tetraō m; (complaint) querēla f ♦ vi querī.

grove n nemus nt, lūcus m.

grovel vi serpere, sē prōsternere, sē advolvere.

grovelling adj humilis, abiectus.

grow vi crēscere, glīscere; (spread) percrēbrēscere; (become) fierī; ~ old (con)senēscere; ~ up adolēscere, pūbēscere; let ~ (hair) prōmittere ♦ vt (crops) colere; (beard) dēmittere.

growl n fremitus m ♦ vi fremere.

grown-up n adj adultus, grandis.

growth n incrēmentum nt, auctus m.

grub n vermiculus m.

grudge n invidia f ♦ vt invidēre (dat); (thing) gravārī.

grudgingly adv invītus, gravātē.

gruesome adj taeter.

gruff adj acerbus, asper.

grumble vi querī, mussāre ♦ n querēla f.

grumpy adj mōrōsus, querulus.

grunt n grunnītus m ♦ vi grunnīre.

guarantee n (money) spōnsiō f; (promise) fīdēs f; (person) praes m ♦ vt spondēre, praestāre.

guarantor n spōnsor m.

guard n custōdia f, praesidium nt; (person) custōs m; on ~ in statiōne; be on one's ~ cavēre; keep ~ statiōnem agere; off one's ~ imprūdēns, inopīnāns; be taken off one's ~ dē gradū dēicī ♦ vt custōdīre, dēfendere; (keep) cōnservāre; ~ against cavēre.

guarded adj cautus.

guardedly adv cautē.

guardhouse n custōdia f.

guardian n custōs m; (of minors) tūtor m.

guardianship n custōdia f, tūtēla f.

guardian spirit n genius m.

gudgeon n gōbius m.

guerdon n praemium nt, mercēs f.

guess n coniectūra f ♦ vt dīvīnāre, conicere.

guest n hospes m, hospita f; (at dinner) convīva m; uninvited ~ umbra f; ~'s hospitālis.

guffaw n cachinnus m ♦ vi cachinnāre.

guidance n moderātiō f; under the ~ of God dūcente deō.

guide n dux m, ductor m; (in policy) auctor m ♦ vt dūcere; (steer) regere; (control) moderārī.

guild n collēgium nt.

guile n dolus m, fraus f.

guileful adj dolōsus, fraudulentus.

guilefully adv dolōsē.

guileless adj simplex, innocēns.

guilelessly adv sine fraude.

guilt n culpa f, scelus nt.

guiltless adj innocēns, īnsōns.

guiltlessly adv integrē.

guilty adj nocēns, sōns; **find ~** damnāre.

guise n speciēs f.

guitar n fidēs fpl; **play the ~** fidibus canere.

gulf n sinus m; (chasm) hiātus m.

gull n mergus m ♦ vt dēcipere.

gullet n gula f, guttur nt.

gullible adj crēdulus.

gulp vt dēvorāre, haurīre.

gum n gummī nt; (mouth) gingīva f.

gumption n prūdentia f.

gurgle vi singultāre.

gush vi sē profundere, ēmicāre ♦ n scatūrīginēs fpl.

gust n flāmen nt, impetus m.

gusto n studium nt.

gusty adj ventōsus.

gut n intestīnum nt ♦ vt exenterāre; (fig) extergēre.

gutter n canālis m.

guzzle vi sē ingurgitāre.

gymnasium n gymnasium nt, palaestra f; **head of a ~** gymnasiarchus m.

gymnastic adj gymnicus; **~s** pl palaestra f.

gyrate vi volvī.

H

habit n mōs m, cōnsuētūdō f; (dress) habitus m, vestītus m; **be in the ~ of** solēre.

habitable adj habitābilis.

habitation n domus f, domicilium nt; (place) sēdēs f.

habitual adj ūsitātus.

habitually adv ex mōre, persaepe.

habituate vt adsuēfacere, īnsuēscere.

hack vt caedere, concīdere ♦ n

(horse) caballus m.

hackneyed adj trītus.

Hades n Īnferī mpl.

haft n manubrium nt.

hag n anus f.

haggard adj ferus.

haggle vi altercārī.

hail n grandō f ♦ vi: **it ~s** grandinat ♦ vt salūtāre, adclāmāre ♦ interj avē, avēte; salvē, salvēte; **I ~ from Rome** Rōma mihi patria est.

hair n capillus m; crīnis m; (single) pīlus m; (animals) sēta f, villus nt; **deviate a ~'s breadth** trānsversum digitum discēdere ab; **split ~s** cavillārī.

hairdresser n tōnsor m.

hairless adj (head) calvus; (body) glaber.

hairpin n crīnāle nt.

hairsplitting adj captiōsus ♦ n cavillātiō f.

hairy adj pīlōsus.

halberd n bipennis f.

halcyon n alcēdō f; **~ days** alcēdōnia ntpl.

hale adj validus, rōbustus ♦ vt trahere, rapere.

half n dīmidium nt, dīmidia pars f ♦ adj dīmidius, dīmidiātus; **~ as much again** sesquī; **well begun is ~ done** dīmidium factī quī coepit habet.

half-asleep adj sēmisomnus.

half-baked adj (fig) rudis.

half-dead adj sēmianimis, sēmivīvus.

half-full adj sēmiplēnus.

half-hearted adj incūriōsus, sōcors.

half-heartedly adv sine studiō.

half-hour n sēmihōra f.

half-moon n lūna dīmidiāta f.

half-open adj sēmiapertus.

half pound n sēlībra f.

half-way adj medius; **~ up the hill** in mediō colle.

half-yearly *adj* sēmestris.
hall *n* ātrium *nt*; (*public*) exedra *f*.
hallo *interj* heus.
hallow *vt* sacrāre.
hallucination *n* error *m*, somnium *nt*.
halo *n* corōna *f*.
halt *vi* īnsistere, cōnsistere ♦ *vt* sistere ♦ *n*: **come to a ~** cōnsistere, agmen cōnstituere ♦ *adj* claudus.
halter *n* capistrum *nt*; (*fig*) laqueus *m*.
halve *vt* bipartīre.
ham *n* perna *f*.
hamlet *n* vīcus *m*.
hammer *n* malleus *m* ♦ *vt* tundere; **~ out** excūdere.
hamper *n* corbis *f* ♦ *vt* impedīre; (*with debt*) obstrigillāre.
hamstring *vt* poplitem succīdere (*dat*).
hand *n* manus *f*; **left ~** laeva *f*, sinistra *f*; **right ~** dextra *f*; **an old ~** veterātor *m*; **at ~** praestō, ad manum; **be at ~** adesse; **at first ~** ipse; **at second ~** ab aliō; **on the one ~** ... **on the other** et ... et, quidem ... at; **near at ~** in expedītō, inibī; **the matter in ~** quod nunc īnstat, quae in manibus sunt; **get out of ~** lascīvīre; **have a ~ in** interesse (*dat*); **have one's ~s full** satis agere; **lay ~s on** manum adferre, inicere (*dat*); **live from ~ to mouth** ad hōram vīvere; **pass from ~ to ~** per manūs trādere; **take in ~** suscipere; **~s** *pl* (*workmen*) operae *fpl* ♦ *vt* trādere, porrigere; **~ down** trādere, prōdere; **~ over** dēferre, reddere.
handbill *n* libellus *m*.
handbook *n* ars *f*.
handcuffs *n* manicae *fpl*.
handful *n* manipulus *m*.
handicap *n* impedīmentum *nt*.
handicraft *n* artificium *nt*, ars

operōsa *f*.
handily *adv* habiliter.
handiness *n* habilitās *f*; commoditās *f*.
handiwork *n* opus *nt*, manus *f*.
handkerchief *n* sūdārium *nt*.
handle *n* (*cup*) ānsa *f*; (*knife*) manubrium *nt*; (*fig*) ānsa *f*, occāsiō *f* ♦ *vt* tractāre.
handling *n* tractātiō *f*.
handmaid *n* famula *f*.
handsome *adj* fōrmōsus, pulcher; (*gift*) līberālis.
handsomely *adv* pulchrē; līberāliter.
handsomeness *n* pulchritūdō *f*, fōrma *f*.
hand-to-hand *adv*: **fight ~** manum cōnserere, comminus pugnāre.
handwriting *n* manus *f*.
handy *adj* (*to use*) habilis; (*near*) praestō.
hang *vt* suspendere; (*head*) dēmittere; (*wall*) vestīre ♦ *vi* pendēre; **~ back** gravārī, dubitāre; **~ down** dēpendēre; **~ on** to haerēre (*dat*); **~ over** imminēre (*dat*), impendēre (*dat*); **go and be ~ed!** abī in malam crucem!
hanger-on *n* cliēns *m/f*, assecla *m/f*.
hanging *n* (*death*) suspendium *nt*; **~s** *pl* aulaea *ntpl* ♦ *adj* pendulus.
hangman *n* carnifex *m*.
hanker *vi*: **~ after** appetere, exoptāre.
hap *n* fors *f*.
haphazard *adj* fortuītus.
hapless *adj* miser, īnfēlīx.
haply *adv* fortasse.
happen *vi* accidere, ēvenīre, contingere; (*become*) fierī; **as usually ~s** ut fit; **~ upon** incidere in (*acc*); **it ~s that** accidit ut (+*subj*).
happily *adv* fēlīciter, beātē, bene.
happiness *n* fēlīcitās *f*.
happy *adj* fēlīx, beātus; laetus; (*in*

some respect) fortūnātus.

harangue n cōntiō f ♦ vt cōntiōnārī apud (+ acc), hortārī.

harass vt vexāre, lacessere, exagitāre, sollicitāre.

harassing adj molestus.

harbinger n praenūntius m.

harbour n portus m ♦ vt recipere.

harbour dues n portōria ntpl.

hard adj dūrus; (CIRCS) asper, inīquus; (task) difficilis, arduus; **~ of hearing** surdaster; **grow ~** dūrēscere ♦ adv sēdulō, valdē; **~ by** prope, iuxtā; **I am ~ put to it to do** aegerrimē faciō.

hard cash n praesēns pecūnia f.

harden vt dūrāre ♦ vi dūrēscere; (fig) obdūrēscere; **become ~ed** obdūrēscere.

hard-fought adj atrōx.

hard-hearted adj crūdēlis, dūrus, inhūmānus.

hardihood n audācia f.

hardily adv sevērē.

hardiness n rōbur nt; dūritia f.

hardly adv vix, aegrē; (severely) dūriter, acerbē; **~ any** nullus ferē.

hardness n dūritia f; (fig) asperitās f, inīquitās f; (difficulty) difficultās f; **~ of hearing** surditās f.

hard-pressed n **be ~** labōrāre.

hardship n labor m, malum nt, iniūria f.

hard-working adj industrius, nāvus, sēdulus.

hardy adj dūrus, rōbustus, sevērus.

hare n lepus m.

hark interj auscultā, auscultāte ♦ vi: **~ back to** repetere.

harm n iniūria f, damnum nt, malum nt, dētrīmentum nt; **come to ~** dētrīmentum capere, accipere ♦ vt laedere, nocēre (dat).

harmful adj damnōsus, noxius.

harmfully adv male.

harmless adj innocēns.

harmlessly adv innocenter; (escape) salvus, incolumis, inviolātus.

harmonious adj cōnsonus, canōrus; (fig) concors; (things) congruēns.

harmoniously adv modulātē; concorditer; convenienter.

harmonize vi concinere, cōnsentīre, congruere.

harmony n concentus m; (fig) concordia f, cōnsēnsus m.

harness n arma ntpl ♦ vt īnfrēnāre, iungere.

harp n fidēs fpl; **play the ~** fidibus canere ♦ vi: **~ on** (fig) cantāre, dictitāre; **be always ~ing on the same thing** cantilēnam eandem canere.

harpist n fidicen m, fidicina f.

harpoon n iaculum nt.

harpy n Harpyia f.

harrow n rāstrum nt ♦ vt occāre.

harrower n occātor m.

harrowing adj horrendus.

harry vt vexāre, dīripere.

harsh adj dūrus, acerbus, asper; (person) inclēmens, sevērus.

harshly adv acerbē, asperē; sevērē.

harshness n acerbitās f, asperitās f; crūdēlitās f.

hart n cervus m.

harvest n messis f ♦ vt metere, dēmetere.

harvester n messor m.

hash n farrāgō f ♦ vt comminuere.

haste n festīnātiō f, properātiō f; **in ~** festīnanter; **in hot ~** incitātus; **make ~** festīnāre.

hasten vt mātūrāre, adcelerāre ♦ vi festīnāre, properāre, mātūrāre.

hastily adv properē, raptim; temerē, incōnsultē; īrācundē.

hastiness n temeritās f; (temper) īrācundia f.

hasty adj properus, celer; (action) incōnsultus, temerārius; (temper) īrācundus, ācer; **over ~** praeproperus.

hat n petasus m.

hatch vt exclūdere, parere.

hatchet n dolābra f.

hate n odium nt, invidia f ♦ vt ōdisse.

hated adj: **to be ~ (by sb)** odiō esse (+ dat).

hateful adj odiōsus, invīsus.

hatefully adv odiōsē.

hatred n odium nt.

haughtily adv adroganter, superbē, insolenter.

haughtiness n fastus m, adrogantia f, superbia f.

haughty adj adrogāns, superbus, īnsolēns.

haul vt trahere ♦ n bolus m.

haulage n vectūra f.

haulm n culmus m.

haunch n femur nt.

haunt vt frequentāre ♦ n locus m; (animals) lustrum nt.

have vt habēre, tenēre; (get done) cūrāre (gerundive); **I ~ a house** est mihī domus; **I ~ to go** mihī abeundum est; **~ it out with** rem dēcernere cum; **~ on** gerere, gestāre, induī; **I had better go** melius est īre, praestat īre; **I had rather** mālim, māllem.

haven n portus m; (fig) perfugium nt.

havoc n exitium nt, vastātiō f, ruīna f.

hawk n accipiter m ♦ vt (wares) circumferre.

hawker n īnstitor m.

hay n faenum nt; **make ~ while the sun shines** forō ūtī.

hazard n perīculum nt, discrīmen nt, ālea f ♦ vt perīclitārī, in āleam dare.

hazardous adj perīculōsus.

haze n nebula f.

hazel n corylus f.

hazy adj nebulōsus; (fig) incertus.

he pron hic, ille, is.

head n caput nt; (person) dux m, prīnceps m; (composition) caput nt; (mind) animus m, ingenium nt; **~ over heels** cernuus; **off one's ~** dēmēns; **be at the ~ of** dūcere, praeesse (dat); **come to a ~** caput facere; (fig) in discrīmen addūcī; **give one's ~ to** indulgēre (dat), habēnās immittere (dat); **keep one's ~** praesentī animō ūtī; **lose one's ~** suī compotem nōn esse; **shake one's ~** abnuere ♦ vt dūcere, praeesse (dat); **~ off** intercipere ♦ vi (in a direction) tendere.

headache n capitis dolor m.

headfirst adj praeceps.

heading n caput nt.

headland n prōmunturium nt.

headlong adj praeceps ♦ adv in praeceps; **rush ~** sē praecipitāre.

headquarters n (MIL) praetōrium nt.

headship n prīncipātus m.

headsman n carnifex m.

headstrong adj impotēns, pervicāx.

headway n prōfectus m.

heady adj incōnsultus; (wine) vehemēns.

heal vt sānāre, medērī (dat) ♦ vi sānēscere; **~ over** obdūcī.

healer n medicus m.

healing adj salūbris.

health n valētūdō f, salūs f; **state of ~** valētūdō f; **ill ~** valētūdō f; **be in good ~** valēre; **drink the ~ of** propīnāre (dat).

healthful adj salūbris.

healthiness n sānitās f.

healthy adj sānus, integer; (conditions) salūber.

heap n acervus m, cumulus m; **in**

~s acervātim ♦ vt acervāre; ~ **together** congerere; ~ **up** accumulāre, coacervāre, congerere.

hear vt audīre; (case) cognōscere; ~ **clearly** exaudīre; ~ **in secret** inaudīre.

hearer n audītor m.

hearing n (sense) audītus m; (act) audītiō f; (of case) cognitiō f; **get a** ~ sibī audientiam facere; **hard of** ~ surdaster; **without a** ~ indictā causā.

hearken vi auscultāre.

hearsay n fāma f, rūmor m.

heart n cor nt; (emotion) animus m, pectus nt; (courage) animus m; (interior) viscera ntpl; **by** ~ memoriā, memoriter; **learn by** ~ ēdiscere; **the ~ of the matter** rēs ipsa; **lose** ~ animum dēspondēre; **take to** ~ graviter ferre.

heartache n dolor m, angor m.

heartbroken adj animī frāctus, aeger; **be** ~ animō labōrāre.

heartburning n invidia f.

heartfelt adj sincērus.

hearth n focus m; **~ and home** ārae et focī.

heartily adv vehementer, valdē.

heartiness n studium nt, vigor m.

heartless adj dūrus, inhūmānus, crūdēlis.

heartlessly adv inhūmānē.

heartlessness n inhūmānitās f, crūdēlitās f.

hearty adj studiōsus, vehemēns; (health) rōbustus; (feeling) sincērus.

heat n ārdor m, calor m; (emotion) ārdor m, aestus m; (race) missus m ♦ vt calefacere, fervefacere; (fig) accendere; **become ~ed** incalēscere.

heatedly adv ferventer, ārdenter.

heath n inculta loca ntpl.

heathcock n attagēn m.

heathen n pāgānus m.

heather n ericē f.

heave vt tollere; (missile) conicere; (sigh) dūcere ♦ vi tumēre, fluctuāre.

heaven n caelum nt, dī mpl; ~ **forbid!** dī meliōra; **from** ~ dīvīnitus; **in ~'s name** prō deum fidem!; **be in seventh** ~ digitō caelum attingere.

heavenly adj caelestis, dīvīnus.

heavily adv graviter.

heaviness n gravitās f, pondus nt; (of spirit) maestitia f.

heavy adj gravis; (air) crassus; (spirit) maestus; (shower) māgnus, dēnsus.

heckle vt interpellāre.

heckler n interpellātor m.

hectic adj violēns, ācer, fervidus.

hector vt obstrepere (dat).

hedge n saepēs f ♦ vt saepīre; ~ **off** intersaepīre ♦ vi tergiversārī.

hedgehog n echīnus m, ēricius m.

heed vt cūrāre, respicere ♦ n cūra f, opera f; **pay** ~ animum attendere; **take** ~ cavēre.

heedful adj attentus, cautus, dīligēns.

heedfully adv attentē, cautē.

heedfulness n cūra f, dīligentia f.

heedless adj incautus, immemor, neglegēns.

heedlessly adv incautē, neglegenter, temerē.

heedlessness n neglegentia f.

heel n calx f; **take to one's ~s** sē in pedēs conicere ♦ vi sē inclīnāre.

hegemony n principātus m.

heifer n būcula f.

height n altitūdō f; (person) prōcēritās f; (hill) collis m, iugum nt; (fig) fastīgium nt; **the ~ of** summus.

heighten vt augēre, exaggerāre.

heinous adj atrōx, nefārius.

heinously adv atrōciter, nefāriē.

heinousness n atrōcitās f.
heir n hērēs m; **sole ~** hērēs ex asse.
heiress n hērēs f.
heirship n hērēditās f.
hell n Tartarus m, Înfernī mpl.
hellish adj Înfernus, scelestus.
helm n gubernāculum nt, clāvus m.
helmet n galea f.
helmsman n gubernātor m.
helots n Hīlōtae mpl.
help n auxilium nt, subsidium nt; **I am a ~** auxiliō sum ♦ vt iuvāre (+ acc), auxiliārī, subvenīre (dat), succurrere (dat) ♦ vi prōdesse; **I cannot ~** facere nōn possum quīn (subj); **it can't be ~ed** fierī nōn potest aliter; **so ~ me God** ita me dī ament.
helper n adiūtor m, adiūtrix f.
helpful adj ūtilis; **be ~ to** auxiliō esse (dat).
helpless adj inops.
helplessness n inopia f.
hem n ōra f, limbus m ♦ vt: **~ in** interclūdere, circumsedēre.
hemlock n cicūta f.
hemp n cannabis f.
hen n gallīna f.
hence adv hinc; (consequence) igitur, ideō.
henceforth, henceforward adv dehinc, posthāc, ex hōc tempore.
her adj suus, ēius.
herald n praecō m; (POL) fētiālis m ♦ vt praenūntiāre.
herb n herba f, olus nt.
herbage n herbae fpl.
herd n pecus nt; grex f, armentum nt ♦ vi congregārī.
herdsman n pāstor m.
here adv hīc; **be ~** adesse; **~ and there** passim; **... there** alibī ... alibī; **from ~** hinc; **~ is ...** ecce (acc) ....
hereabouts adv hīc ferē.
hereafter adv posthāc, posteā.

hereat adv hīc.
hereby adv ex hōc, hinc.
hereditary adj hērēditārius, patrius.
heredity n genus nt.
herein adv hīc.
hereinafter adv înfrā.
hereof adv ēius reī.
hereupon adv hīc, quō factō.
herewith adv cum hōc, ūnā.
heritable adj hērēditārius.
heritage n hērēditās f.
hermaphrodite n androgynus m.
hermit n homō sōlitārius m.
hero n vir fortissimus m; (demigod) hērōs m.
heroic adj fortissimus, magnanimus; (epic) hērōicus; (verse) hērōus.
heroically adv fortissimē, audācissimē.
heroism n virtūs f, fortitūdō f.
heron n ardea f.
hers pron suus, ēius.
herself pron ipsa f; (reflexive) sē.
hesitancy n dubitātiō f.
hesitant adj incertus, dubius.
hesitate vi dubitāre, haesitāre.
hesitating adj dubius.
hesitatingly adv cunctanter.
hesitation n dubitātiō f; **with ~** dubitanter.
heterogeneous adj dīversus, aliēnigenus.
hew vt dolāre, caedere; **~ down** excīdere, interscindere.
hexameter n hexameter m.
heyday n flōs m.
hiatus n hiātus m.
hiccup n singultus m ♦ vi singultīre.
hide vt cēlāre, abdere, abscondere, occultāre; **~ away** abstrūdere; **~ from** cēlāre (acc) ♦ vi sē abdere, latēre; **~ away** dēlitēscere ♦ n pellis f, corium nt.
hideous adj foedus, dēfōrmis,

turpis.

hideously adv foedē.

hideousness n foeditās f, dēfōrmitās f.

hiding n (place) latebra f.

hierarchy n ōrdinēs mpl.

high adj altus, excelsus; (ground) ēditus; (pitch) acūtus; (rank) amplus; (price) cārus; (tide) māximus; (wind) māgnus; **~ living** luxuria f, **~ treason** māiestās f; **~ and mighty** superbus; **on ~** sublīmis ♦ adv altē.

highborn adj nōbilis, generōsus.

high-class adj (goods) lautus.

high-flown adj īnflātus, tumidus.

high-handed adj superbus, īnsolēns.

high-handedly adv superbē, licenter.

high-handedness n licentia f, superbia f.

highland adj montānus.

highlander n montānus m.

highlands npl montāna ntpl.

highly adv (value) māgnī; (intensity) valdē.

highly-strung adj trepidus.

high-minded adj generōsus.

high-spirited adj ferōx, animōsus.

highway n via f.

highwayman n grassātor m, latrō m.

hilarious adj festīvus, hilaris.

hilariously adv festīvē, hilare.

hilarity n festīvitās f, hilaritās f.

hill n collis m, mōns m; (slope) clīvus m.

hillock n tumulus m.

hilly adj montuōsus, clīvōsus.

hilt n manubrium nt, capulus m.

himself pron ipse; (reflexive) sē.

hind n cerva f.

hinder vt impedīre, obstāre (dat), morārī.

hindmost adj postrēmus; (in column) novissimus.

hindrance n impedīmentum nt, mora f.

hinge n cardō f.

hint n indicium nt, suspiciō f; **throw out a ~** inicere ♦ vt subicere, significāre.

hip n coxendīx f.

hippodrome n spatium nt.

hire vt condūcere; **~ out** locāre ♦ n conductiō f, locātiō f; (wages) mercēs f.

hired adj mercennārius, conductus.

hireling n mercennārius m.

hirsute adj hirsūtus.

his adj suus, ēius.

hiss vi sībilāre ♦ vt: **~ off stage** explōdere, exsībilāre ♦ n sībilus m.

historian n historicus m, rērum scrīptor m.

historical adj historicus.

history n historia f; the **~ of Rome** rēs Rōmānae fpl; **since the beginning of ~** post hominum memoriam; **ancient ~** antīquitās f.

histrionic adj scaenicus.

hit n ictus m, plāga f; **a ~!** (in duel) habet! ♦ vt ferīre, icere, percutere; **~ against** offendere; **~ upon** invenīre.

hitch n mora f ♦ vt implicāre; **~ up** succingere.

hither adv hūc; **~ and thither** hūc illūc ♦ adj citerior.

hitherto adv adhūc, hāctenus, hūcusque.

hive n alveārium nt.

hoar adj cānus ♦ n pruīna f.

hoard n thēsaurus m, acervus m ♦ vt condere, recondere.

hoarfrost n pruīna f.

hoarse adj raucus, fuscus.

hoarsely adv raucā vōce.

hoary adj cānus.

hoax n fraus f, fallācia f, lūdus m ♦ vt dēcipere, fallere.

hobble vi claudicāre.

hobby n studium nt.

hob-nob vi familiāriter ūtī (abl).

hocus-pocus n trīcae fpl.

hoe n sarculum nt ♦ vt sarrīre.

hog n sūs m, porcus m; ~'s porcīnus.

hogshead n dōlium nt.

hoist vt tollere; (sail) vēla dare.

hold n (grasp) comprehēnsiō f; (power) potestās f; (ship) alveus m; **gain a ~ over** obstringere, sibi dēvincīre; **get ~ of** potīrī (abl); **keep ~ of** retinēre; **lose ~ of** ōmittere; **take ~ of** prehendere, comprehendere ♦ vt tenēre, habēre; (possession) obtinēre, possidēre; (office) gerere, fungī (abl); (capacity) capere; (meeting) habēre; **~ a meeting** concilium habēre; **~ one's own with** parem esse (dat); **~ over** differre, prōlātāre; **~ water** (fig) stāre ♦ vi manēre, dūrāre; (opinion) dūcere, existimāre, affirmāre; **~ back** vt retinēre, inhibēre ♦ vi gravārī, dubitāre; **~ cheap** parvī facere; **~ fast** vt retinēre, amplectī ♦ vi haerēre; **~ good** valēre; **~ out** vt porrigere, extendere; (hope) ostendere ♦ vi dūrāre, perstāre; **~ together** vt cohaerēre; **~ up** tollere; (falling) sustinēre; (movement) obstāre (dat), morārī, **~ with** adsentīre.

holdfast n fībula f.

holding n (land) agellus m.

hole n forāmen nt, cavum nt; **make a ~ in** pertundere, perforāre.

holiday n ōtium nt; festus diēs m; **on ~** fēriātus; **~s** pl fēriae fpl.

holily adv sanctē.

holiness n sanctitās f.

hollow adj cavus, concavus; (fig) inānis, vānus ♦ n cavum nt, caverna f ♦ vt excavāre.

hollowness n (fig) vānitās f.

holly n aquifolium nt.

holy adj sanctus.

homage n observantia f, venerātiō f; **pay ~ to** venerārī, colere.

home n domus f; (town, country) patria f; **at ~** domī; **from ~** domō ♦ adj domesticus ♦ adv domum.

homeless adj profugus.

homely adj simplex, rūsticus; (speech) plēbēius.

homestead n fundus m.

homewards adv domum.

homicide n (act) homicīdium nt, caedēs f; (person) homicīda m.

homily n sermō m.

homogeneous adj aequābilis.

homologous adj cōnsimilis.

hone n cōs f ♦ vt acuere.

honest adj probus, frūgī, integer.

honestly adv probē, integrē.

honesty n probitās f, fidēs f.

honey n mel nt.

honeycomb n favus m.

honeyed adj mellītus, mulsus.

honorarium n stips f.

honorary adj honōrārius.

honour n honōs m; (repute) honestās f; existimātiō f; (chastity) pudor m; (trust) fidēs f; (rank) dignitās f; (award) decus nt, īnsigne nt; (respect) observantia f ♦ vt honōrāre, decorāre; (respect) observāre, colere; **do ~ to** honestāre.

honourable adj honestus, probus; (rank) illūstris, praeclārus.

honourably adv honestē.

hood n cucullus m.

hoodwink vt verba dare (dat).

hoof n ungula f.

hook n uncus m, hāmus m ♦ vt hāmō capere.

hooked adj aduncus, hāmātus.

hoop n circulus m; (toy) trochus m.

hoot vi obstrepere; **~ off** (stage) explōdere.

hop n saltus m; **catch on the ~** in

ipsō articulō opprimere ♦ *vi* salīre.

hope *n* spēs *f*; **in the ~ that** sī forte; **give up ~** spem dēpōnere, dēspērāre; **past ~** dēspērātus; **entertain ~s** spem habēre ♦ *vt* spērāre.

hopeful *adj* bonae speī; **be ~** aliquam spem habēre.

hopefully *adv* nōn sine spē.

hopeless *adj* dēspērātus.

hopelessly *adv* dēspēranter.

hopelessness *n* dēspērātiō *f*.

horde *n* multitūdō *f*.

horizon *n* fīniēns *m*.

horizontal *adj* aequus, lībrātus.

horizontally *adv* ad lībram.

horn *n* cornū *nt*; (*shepherd's*) būcina *f*.

horned *adj* corniger.

hornet *n* crabrō *m*; **stir up a ~'s nest** crabrōnēs inrītāre.

horny *adj* corneus.

horoscope *n* sīdus nātālicium *nt*.

horrible *adj* horrendus, horribilis, dīrus, foedus.

horribly *adv* foedē.

horrid *adj* horribilis.

horrify *vt* terrēre, perterrēre.

horror *n* horror *m*, terror *m*; odium *nt*.

horse *n* equus *m*; (*cavalry*) equitēs *mpl*; **flog a dead ~** asellum currere docēre; **spur a willing ~** currentem incitāre; **~'s** equīnus.

horseback *n*: **ride on ~** in equō vehī; **fight on ~** ex equō pugnāre.

horseman *n* eques *m*.

horseradish *n* armoracia *f*.

horse soldier *n* eques *m*.

horticulture *n* hortōrum cultus *m*.

hospitable *adj* hospitālis.

hospitably *adv* hospitāliter.

hospital *n* valētūdinārium *nt*.

hospitality *n* hospitālitās *f*, hospitium *nt*.

host *n* hospes *m*; (*inn*) caupō *m*; (*number*) multitūdō *f*; (MIL) exercitus *m*.

hostage *n* obses *m/f*.

hostelry *n* taberna *f*, dēversōrium *nt*.

hostile *adj* hostīlis, īnfēnsus, inimīcus; īnfestus; **in a ~ manner** īnfēnsē, hostīliter, inimīcē.

hostility *n* inimīcitia *f*; **hostilities** *pl* bellum *nt*.

hot *adj* calidus, fervidus, aestuōsus; (*boiling*) fervēns; (*fig*) ārdēns; **be ~** calēre, fervēre, ārdēre; **get ~** calēscere.

hotch-potch *n* farrāgō *f*.

hotel *n* dēversōrium *nt*.

hot-headed *adj* ārdēns, temerārius, praeceps.

hotly *adv* ārdenter, ācriter.

hot-tempered *adj* īrācundus.

hot water *n* calida *f*.

hound *n* canis *m* ♦ *vt* īnstāre (*dat*).

hour *n* hōra *f*.

hourly *adv* in hōrās.

house *n* domus *f*, aedēs *fpl*; (*country*) vīlla *f*; (*family*) domus *f*, gēns *f*, **at the ~ of** apud (*acc*); **full ~** frequēns senātus, frequēns theātrum ♦ *vt* hospitiō accipere, recipere; (*things*) condere.

household *n* familia *f*, domus *f* ♦ *adj* familiāris, domesticus.

householder *n* paterfamiliās *m*, dominus *m*.

housekeeping *n* reī familiāris cūra *f*.

housemaid *n* ancilla *f*.

housetop *n* fastīgium *nt*.

housewife *n* māterfamiliās *f*, domina *f*.

housing *n* hospitium *nt*; (*horse*) ōrnāmenta *ntpl*.

hovel *n* gurgustium *nt*.

hover *vi* pendēre; (*fig*) impendēre.

how *adv* (*interrog*) quemadmodum; quōmodō, quō pactō; (*excl*) quam;

~ **great/big/large** quantus; ~ **long**
(*time*) quamdiū; ~ **many** quot; ~
much quantum; ~ **often** quotiēns.
howbeit *adv* tamen.
however *adv* tamen; autem,
nihilōminus; utcumque, quōquō
modō; ~ **much** quamvīs,
quantumvīs; ~ **great**
quantuscumque.
howl *n* ululātus *m* ♦ *vi* ululāre;
(*wind*) fremere.
howsoever *adv* utcumque.
hub *n* axis *m*.
hubbub *n* tumultus *m*.
huckster *n* īnstitor *m*, propōla *m*.
huddle *n* turba *f* ♦ *vi* congregārī.
hue *n* color *m*; ~ **and cry** clāmor *m*.
huff *n* offēnsiō *f* ♦ *vt* offendere.
hug *n* complexus *m* ♦ *vt*
complectī.
huge *adj* ingēns, immānis,
immēnsus, vastus.
hugely *adv* vehementer.
hugeness *n* immānitās *f*.
hulk *n* alveus *m*.
hull *n* alveus *m*.
hum *n* murmur *nt*, fremitus *m* ♦ *vi*
murmurāre, fremere.
human *adj* hūmānus.
human being *n* homo *m*/*f*.
humane *adj* hūmānus, misericors.
humanely *adv* hūmānē, hūmāniter.
humanism *n* litterae *fpl*.
humanist *n* homō litterātus *m*.
humanity *n* hūmānitās *f*;
misericordia *f*.
humanize *vt* excolere.
humanly *adv* hūmānitus.
human nature *n* hūmānitās *f*.
humble *adj* humilis, modestus ♦ *vt*
dēprimere; (*oneself*) summittere.
humbleness *n* humilitās *f*.
humbly *adv* summissē, modestē.
humbug *n* trīcae *fpl*.
humdrum *adj* vulgāris; (*style*)
pedester.
humid *adj* ūmidus, madidus; **be** ~

madēre.
humidity *n* ūmor *m*.
humiliate *vt* dēprimere,
dēdecorāre.
humiliation *n* dēdecus *nt*.
humility *n* modestia *f*, animus
summissus *m*.
humorist *n* homō facētus *m*.
humorous *adj* facētus, ioculāris,
rīdiculus.
humorously *adv* facētē.
humour *n* facētiae *fpl*; (*disposition*)
ingenium *nt*; (*mood*) libīdō *f*; **be in
a bad** ~ sibī displicēre ♦ *vt*
indulgēre (*dat*), mōrem gerere
(*dat*), mōrigerārī (*dat*).
hump *n* gibbus *m*.
hunchback *n* gibber *m*.
hundred *num* centum; ~ **each**
centēnī; ~ **times** centiēns.
hundredth *adj* centēsimus.
hundredweight *n*
centumpondium *nt*.
hunger *n* famēs *f* ♦ *vi* ēsurīre.
hungrily *adv* avidē.
hungry *adj* ēsuriēns, iēiūnus,
avidus; **be** ~ ēsurīre.
hunt *n* vēnātiō *f*, vēnātus *m* ♦ *vt*
vēnārī, indāgāre, exagitāre.
hunter *n* vēnātor *m*.
hunting *n* vēnātiō *f*; (*fig*) aucupium
nt.
hunting spear *n* vēnābulum *nt*.
huntress *n* vēnātrīx *f*.
huntsman *n* vēnātor *m*.
hurdle *n* crātēs *f*; (*obstacle*) obex
m/*f*.
hurl *vt* conicere, ingerere, iaculārī,
iācere.
hurly-burly *n* turba *f*, tumultus *m*.
hurrah *interj* euax, iō.
hurricane *n* procella *f*.
hurried *adj* praeproperus,
praeceps, trepidus.
hurriedly *adv* properātō, cursim,
festīnanter.
hurry *vt* adcelerāre, mātūrāre ♦ *vi*

festīnāre, properāre; ~ **along** vt
rapere; ~ **away** vi discēdere,
properāre; ~ **about** vi discurrere;
~ **on** vi mātūrāre; ~ **up** vi
properāre ♦ n festīnātiō f; **in a ~**
festīnanter, raptim.
hurt n iniūria f, damnum nt; vulnus
nt ♦ vt laedere, nocēre (dat); **it ~s**
dolet.
hurtful adj nocēns, damnōsus.
hurtfully adv nocenter, damnōsē.
hurtle vi volāre; sē praecipitāre.
husband n vir m, marītus m ♦ vt
parcere (dat).
husbandry n agrī cultūra f;
(economy) parsimōnia f.
hush n silentium nt ♦ vt silentium
facere (dat), lēnīre ♦ vi tacēre,
silēre; ~ **up** comprimere, cēlāre
♦ interj st!
hushed adj tacitus.
husk n folliculus m, siliqua f ♦ vt
dēglūbāre.
husky adj fuscus, raucus.
hustle vt trūdere, īnstāre (dat).
hut n casa f, tugurium nt.
hutch n cavea f.
hyacinth n hyacinthus m.
hybrid n hibrida m/f.
hydra n hydra f.
hyena n hyaena f.
hygiene n salūbritās f.
hygienic adj salūbris.
hymeneal adj nūptiālis.
hymn n carmen nt ♦ vt canere.
hyperbole n superlātiō f.
hypercritical adj Aristarchus m.
hypocaust n hypocaustum nt.
hypocrisy n simulātiō f,
dissimulātiō f.
hypocrite n simulātor m,
dissimulātor m.
hypocritical adj simulātus, fictus.
hypothesis n positum nt, sūmptiō
f, coniectūra f.
hypothetical adj sūmptus.

I

I pron ego.
iambic adj iambēus.
iambus n iambus m.
ice n glaciēs f.
icicle n stīria f.
icon n simulacrum nt.
icy adj glaciālis, gelidus.
idea n nōtiō f, nōtitia f, imāgō f;
(Platonic) fōrma f; (expressed)
sententia f; **conceive the ~ of**
īnfōrmāre; **with the ~ that** eō
cōnsiliō ut (+ subj).
ideal adj animō comprehēnsus;
(perfect) perfectus, optimus ♦ n
specimen nt, speciēs f, exemplar
nt.
identical adj Īdem, cōnsimilis.
identify vt agnōscere.
identity n: **establish the ~ of**
cognōscere quis sit.
Ides n Īdūs fpl.
idiocy n animī imbēcillitās f.
idiom n proprium nt, sermō m.
idiomatic adj proprius.
idiomatically adv sermōne suō,
sermōne propriō.
idiosyncrasy n proprium nt, libīdō
f.
idiot n excors m.
idiotic adj fatuus, stultus.
idiotically adv stultē, ineptē.
idle adj ignāvus, dēses, iners;
(unoccupied) ōtiōsus, vacuus;
(useless) inānis, vānus; **be ~**
cessāre, dēsidēre; **lie ~** (money)
iacēre ♦ vi cessāre.
idleness n ignāvia f, dēsidia f,
inertia f; ōtium nt.
idler n cessātor m.
idly adv ignāvē; ōtiōsē; frustrā,
nēquīquam.
idol n simulacrum nt; (person)
dēliciae fpl.
idolater n falsōrum deōrum

cultor m.
idolatry n falsōrum deōrum cultus m.
idolize vt venerārī.
idyll n carmen Theocrītēum nt.
if conj sī; (interrog) num, utrum; ~ **anyone** sī quis; ~ **ever** sī quandō; ~ **not** nisī; ~ **only** dum, dummodo; ~ ... **or** sīve ... sīve; **as** ~ quasi, velut; **but** ~ sīn, quodsī; **even** ~ etiamsī.
igneous adj īgneus.
ignite vt accendere, incendere ♦ vi ignem concipere.
ignoble adj (birth) ignōbilis; (repute) illīberālis, turpis.
ignominious adj ignōminiōsus, īnfāmis, turpis.
ignominiously adv turpiter.
ignominy n ignōminia f, īnfāmia f, dēdecus nt.
ignoramus n idiōta m, indoctus m.
ignorance n īnscītia f, ignōrātiō f.
ignorant adj īgnārus, indoctus; (of something) īnscītus, rudis; (unaware) īnscius; **be** ~ **of** nescīre, ignōrāre.
ignorantly adv īnscienter, īnscītē, indoctē.
ignore vt praetermittere.
ilex n īlex f.
Iliad n Īlias f.
ill adj aeger, aegrōtus, invalidus; (evil) malus; **be** ~ aegrōtāre; **fall** ~ in morbum incidere; ~ **at ease** sollicitus ♦ adv male, improbē ♦ n malum nt, incommodum nt, aerumna f, damnum nt.
ill-advised adj incōnsultus.
ill-bred adj agrestis, inurbānus.
ill-disposed adj malevolus, invidus.
illegal adj illicitus, vetitus.
illegally adv contrā lēgēs.
ill-fated adj īnfēlīx.
ill-favoured adj turpis.
ill-gotten adj male partus.

ill-health n valētūdō f.
illicit adj vetitus.
illimitable adj īnfīnītus.
illiteracy n litterārum īnscītia f.
illiterate adj illitterātus, inērudītus.
ill-natured adj malevolus, malignus.
illness n morbus m, valētūdō f.
illogical adj absurdus.
ill-omened adj dīrus, īnfaustus.
ill-starred adj īnfēlīx.
ill-tempered adj īrācundus, amārus, stomachōsus.
ill-timed adj immātūrus, intempestīvus.
ill-treat vt malefacere (dat)
illuminate vt illūmināre, illūstrāre.
illumination n lūmina ntpl.
illusion n error m, somnium nt.
illusive, illusory adj fallāx.
illustrate vt illūstrāre; (with instances) exemplō cōnfirmāre.
illustration n exemplum nt.
illustrious adj illūstris, īnsignis, praeclārus.
illustriously adv praeclārē.
ill will n invidia f.
image n imāgō f, effigiēs f; (idol) simulacrum nt; (verbal) figūra f, similitūdō f.
imagery n figūrae fpl.
imaginary adj commentīcius, fictus.
imagination n cōgitātiō f, opīnātiō f.
imaginative adj ingeniōsus.
imagine vt animō fingere, animum indūcere, ante oculōs pōnere; (think) opīnārī, arbitrārī.
imbecile adj animō imbēcillus, fatuus, mente captus.
imbecility n animī imbēcillitās f.
imbibe vt adbibere; (fig) imbuī (abl).
imbrue vt īnficere.

imbue vt imbuere, īnficere, tingere.

imitable adj imitābilis.

imitate vt imitārī.

imitation n imitātiō f; (copy) imāgō f.

imitator n imitātor m, imitātrix f, aemulātor m.

immaculate adj integer, ēmendātus.

immaculately adv integrē, sine vitiō.

immaterial adj indifferēns.

immature adj immātūrus.

immeasurable adj immēnsus, īnfīnītus.

immediate adj īnstāns, praesēns; (neighbour) proximus.

immediately adv statim, extemplō, cōnfestim.

immemorial adj antīquissimus; **from time ~** post hominum memoriam.

immense adj immēnsus, immānis, ingēns, vastus.

immensely adv vehementer.

immensity n immēnsum nt, māgnitūdō f.

immerse vt immergere, mergere.

immigrant n advena m.

immigrate vi migrāre.

imminent adj īnstāns, praesēns; **be ~** imminēre, impendēre.

immobile adj fīxus, immōbilis.

immoderate adj immoderātus, immodestus.

immoderately adv immoderātē, immodestē.

immodest adj impudīcus, inverēcundus.

immolate vt immolāre.

immoral adj prāvus, corruptus, turpis.

immorality n corruptī mōrēs mpl, turpitūdō f.

immorally adv prāvē, turpiter.

immortal adj immortālis,

aeternus.

immortality n immortālitās f.

immortalize vt in astra tollere.

immortally adv aeternum.

immovable adj fīxus, immōbilis.

immune adj immūnis, vacuus.

immunity n immūnitās f, vacātiō f.

immure vt inclūdere.

immutability n immūtābilitās f.

immutable adj immūtābilis.

imp n puer improbus m.

impact n ictus m, incussus m.

impair vt imminuere, corrumpere.

impale vt induere, īnfīgere.

impalpable adj tenuissimus.

impart vt impertīre, commūnicāre; (courage) addere.

impartial adj aequus, medius.

impartiality n aequābilitās f.

impartially adv sine favōre.

impassable adj invius; (mountains) inexsuperābilis; (fig) inexplicābilis.

impasse n mora f, incitae fpl.

impassioned adj ārdēns, fervidus.

impassive adj rigidus, sēnsū carēns.

impatience n aviditās f; (of anything) impatientia f.

impatient adj trepidus, avidus; impatiēns.

impatiently adv aegrē.

impeach vt diem dīcere (dat), accūsāre.

impeachment n accūsātiō f, crīmen nt.

impeccable adj ēmendātus.

impecunious adj pauper.

impede vt impedīre, obstāre (dat).

impediment n impedīmentum nt.

impel vt impellere, incitāre.

impend vi impendēre, imminēre, īnstāre.

impenetrable adj impenetrābilis; (country) invius, impervius.

impenitent adj: **I am ~** nīl mē paenitet.

imperative adj necessārius.

imperceptible adj tenuissimus, obscurus.

imperceptibly adv sēnsim.

imperfect adj imperfectus, vitiōsus.

imperfection n vitium nt.

imperfectly adv vitiōsē.

imperial adj imperātōrius, rēgius.

imperil vt in discrīmen addūcere, labefactāre.

imperious adj imperiōsus, superbus.

imperiously adv superbē.

imperishable adj immortālis, aeternus.

impersonate vt partēs agere (gen).

impertinence n importūnitās f, protervitās f.

impertinent adj importūnus, protervus, ineptus.

impertinently adv importūnē, ineptē, protervē.

imperturbable adj immōtus, gravis.

impervious adj impervius, impenetrābilis.

impetuosity n ārdor m, violentia f, vīs f.

impetuous adj violēns, fervidus, effrēnātus.

impetuously adv effrēnātē.

impetus n impetus m.

impiety n impietās f.

impinge vi incidere.

impious adj impius, profānus; **it is ~** nefās est.

impiously adv impiē.

impish adj improbus.

implacable adj implācābilis, inexōrābilis, dūrus.

implacably adv dūrē.

implant vt īnserere, ingignere.

implement n īnstrūmentum nt ♦ vt implēre, exsequī.

implicate vt implicāre, impedīre.

implication n indicium nt.

implicit adj tacitus; absolūtus.

implicitly adv absconditē; (trust) omnīnō, summā fidē.

implore vt implōrāre, obsecrāre.

imply vt significāre, continēre; **be implied** inesse.

impolite adj inurbānus, illepidus.

impolitely adv inurbānē.

impolitic adj inconsultus, imprūdēns.

imponderable adj levissimus.

import vt importāre, invehere, (mean) velle ♦ n significātiō f.

importance n gravitās f, mōmentum nt; (rank) dignitās f, amplitūdō f, auctōritās f; **it is of great ~ to me** meā māgnī rēfert.

important adj gravis, magnī mōmentī; **it is ~** interest (+ gen) rēfert; **more ~, most ~** antīquior, antīquissimus.

importation n invectiō f.

imports npl importātīcia ntpl.

importunate adj molestus.

importune vt flāgitāre, īnstāre (dat).

impose vt impōnere; (by order) indīcere, iniungere; **~ upon** illūdere, fraudāre, abūtī (abl).

imposing adj māgnificus, lautus.

imposition n fraus f; (tax) tribūtum nt.

impossible adj: **it is ~** fierī nōn potest.

impost n tribūtum nt, vectīgal nt.

impostor n planus m, fraudātor m.

imposture n fraus f, fallācia f.

impotence n īnfirmitās f.

impotent adj īnfirmus, dēbilis; (with rage) impotēns.

impotently adv frustrā; (rage) impotenter.

impound vt inclūdere; (confiscate) pūblicāre.

impoverish vt in inopiam redigere.

impracticable adj: **be ~** fierī nōn posse.

imprecate vt exsecrārī.

imprecation n exsecrātiō f.

impregnable adj inexpugnābilis.

impregnate vt imbuere, īnficere.

impress vt imprimere; (on mind) īnfīgere; (person) permovēre; (MIL) invītum scrībere.

impression n (copy) exemplar nt; (mark) signum nt; (feeling) impulsiō f; (belief) opīniātiō f; **make an ~ of** exprimere; **make an ~ on** commovēre; **have the ~** opīnārī.

impressionable adj crēdulus.

impressive adj gravis.

impressively adv graviter.

impressiveness n gravitās f.

imprint n impressiō f, signum nt ♦ vt imprimere; (on mind) īnfīgere, inūrere.

imprison vt inclūdere, in vincula conicere.

imprisonment n custōdia f, vincula ntpl.

improbable adj incrēdibilis, haud vērīsimilis.

impromptu adv ex tempore.

improper adj indecōrus, ineptus.

improperly adv prāvē, perperam.

impropriety n culpa f, offēnsa f.

improve vt ēmendāre, corrigere; (mind) excolere ♦ vi prōficere, meliōrem fierī.

improvement n ēmendātiō f, prōfectus m.

improvident adj imprōvidus; (with money) prōdigus.

improvidently adv imprōvidē; prōdigē.

improvise vt ex tempore compōnere, excōgitāre.

imprudence n imprūdentia f.

imprudent adj imprūdēns.

imprudently adv imprūdenter.

impudence n impudentia f, audācia f.

impudent adj impudēns, audāx.

impudently adv impudenter,

protervē.

impugn vt impugnāre, in dubium vocāre.

impulse n impetus m, impulsus m.

impulsive adj praeceps, violentus.

impulsively adv impetū quōdam animī.

impulsiveness n impetus m, violentia f.

impunity n impūnitās f; **with ~** impūne.

impure adj impūrus, incestus, inquinātus.

impurely adv impūrē, incestē, inquinātē.

impurity n impūritās f, sordēs fpl.

imputation n crīmen nt.

impute vt attribuere, adsignāre; **~ as a fault** vitiō vertere.

in prep (in abl); (with motion) in (acc); (authors) apud (acc); (time) abl; **~ doing this** dum hoc faciō; **~ my youth** adulēscēns; **~ that** quod ♦ adv (rest) intrā; (motion) intrō.

inaccessible adj inaccessus.

inaccuracy n neglegentia f, incūria f; (error) mendum nt.

inaccurate adj parum dīligēns, neglegēns.

inaccurately adv neglegenter.

inaction n inertia f.

inactive adj iners, quiētus; **be ~** cessāre.

inactivity n inertia f, ōtium nt.

inadequate adj impār, parum idōneus.

inadequately adv parum.

inadvertency n imprūdentia f.

inadvertent adj imprūdēns.

inadvertently adv imprūdenter.

inane adj inānis, vānus; ineptus, stultus.

inanely adv ineptē.

inanimate adj inanimus.

inanity n ineptiae fpl, stultitia f.

inapplicable adj: **be ~** nōn valēre.

inappropriate adj aliēnus, parum

aptus.

inarticulate adj īnfāns.

inartistic adj sine arte, dūrus, inēlegāns.

inasmuch as conj quōniam, cum (subj).

inattention n incūria f, neglegentia f.

inattentive adj neglegēns.

inattentively adv neglegenter.

inaudible adj: be ~ audīrī nōn posse.

inaugurate vt inaugurāre, cōnsecrāre.

inauguration n cōnsecrātiō f.

inauspicious adj īnfaustus, īnfēlix.

inauspiciously adv malīs ōminibus.

inborn adj innātus.

incalculable adj inaestimābilis.

incantation n carmen nt.

incapable adj inhabilis, indocilis; be ~ nōn posse.

incapacitate vt dēbilitāre.

incapacity n inertia f, īnscītia f.

incarcerate vt inclūdere, in vincula conicere.

incarnate adj hūmānā speciē indūtus.

incautious adj incautus, temerārius.

incautiously adv incautē.

incendiary adj incendiārius.

incense n tūs nt ♦ vt irritāre, stomachum movēre (dat); be ~d stomachārī.

incentive n incitāmentum nt, stimulus m.

inception n initium nt, exōrdium nt.

incessant adj adsiduus.

incessantly adv adsiduē.

incest n incestus m.

inch n digitus m, ūncia f.

incident n ēventum nt, cāsus m, rēs f.

incidental adj fortuītus.

incidentally adv cāsū.

incipient adj prīmus.

incisive adj ācer.

incite vt īnstīgāre, impellere, hortārī, incitāre.

incitement n invītāmentum nt, stimulus m.

inciter n īnstimulātor m.

incivility n importūnitās f, inhūmānitās f.

inclemency n (weather) intemperiēs f.

inclement adj asper, tristis.

inclination n inclīnātiō f, animus m, libīdō f; (slope) clīvus m.

incline vt inclīnāre; (person) indūcere ♦ vi inclīnāre, incumbere; ~ **towards** sē adclīnāre ♦ n adclīvitās f, clīvus m.

inclined adj inclīnātus, prōpēnsus; **I am ~ to think** haud sciō an.

include vt inclūdere, continēre, complectī.

incognito adv clam.

incoherent adj interruptus; be ~ nōn cohaerēre.

income n fructus m, mercēs f.

incommensurate adj dispār.

incommode vt molestiam adferre (dat).

incomparable adj singulāris, eximius.

incompatibility n discrepantia f, repugnantia f.

incompatible adj īnsociābilis, repugnāns; be ~ **with** dissidēre ab, repugnāre (dat).

incompetence n inertia f, īnscītia f.

incompetent adj iners, īnscītus.

incomplete adj imperfectus.

incomprehensible adj incrēdibilis.

inconceivable adj incrēdibilis.

inconclusive adj inānis.

incongruous adj absonus, aliēnus.

inconsiderable adj exiguus.

inconsiderate adj imprōvidus, incōnsultus.

inconsistency n discrepantia f, incōnstantia f.

inconsistent adj incōnstāns; be ~ discrepāre; be ~ with abhorrēre ab, repugnāre (dat).

inconsistently adv incōnstanter.

inconsolable adj nōn cōnsōlābilis.

inconspicuous adj obscūrus; be ~ latēre.

inconstancy n incōnstantia f, levitās f.

inconstant adj incōnstāns, levis, mōbilis.

inconstantly adv incōnstanter.

incontestable adj certus.

incontinence n incontinentia f.

incontinent adj intemperāns.

inconvenience n incommodum nt ♦ vt incommodāre.

inconvenient adj incommodus.

inconveniently adv incommodē.

incorporate vt īnserere, adiungere.

incorrect adj falsus; be ~ nōn cōnstāre.

incorrectly adv falsō, perperam.

incorrigible adj improbus, perditus.

incorruptibility n integritās f.

incorruptible adj incorruptus.

increase n incrēmentum nt, additāmentum nt, auctus m ♦ vt augēre, amplificāre ♦ vi crēscere, incrēscere.

increasingly adv magis magisque.

incredible adj incrēdibilis.

incredibly adv incrēdibiliter.

incredulous adj incrēdulus.

increment n incrēmentum nt.

incriminate vt crīminārī.

inculcate vt inculcāre, īnfīgere.

incumbent adj: it is ~ on oportet.

incur vt subīre; (guilt) admittere.

incurable adj īnsānābilis.

incursion n incursiō f.

indebted adj obnoxius; be ~ dēbēre.

indecency n obscēnitās f.

indecent adj obscēnus, impudīcus.

indecently adv obscēnē.

indecision n dubitātiō f.

indecisive adj anceps, dubius; the battle is ~ ancipitī Marte pugnātur.

indecisively adv incertō ēventū.

indecorous adj indecōrus.

indeed adv profectō, sānē; (concessive) quidem; (interrog) itane vērō?; (reply) certē, vērō; (with pron) dēmum; (with adj, adv, conj) adeō.

indefatigable adj impiger.

indefensible adj: be ~ dēfendī nōn posse; (belief) tenērī nōn posse; (offence) excūsārī nōn posse.

indefinite adj incertus, ambiguus, īnfīnītus.

indefinitely adv ambiguē; (time) in incertum.

indelicate adj pūtidus, indecōrus.

independence n lībertās f.

independent adj līber, suī iūris.

indescribable adj incnārrābilis.

indestructible adj perennis.

indeterminate adj incertus.

index n index m.

indicate vt indicāre, significāre.

indication n indicium nt, signum nt.

indict vt diem dīcere (dat), accūsāre, nōmen dēferre (gen).

indictment n accūsātiō f.

indifference n neglegentia f, languor m.

indifferent adj (manner) neglegēns, frīgidus, sēcūrus; (quality) mediocris.

indifferently adv neglegenter; mediocriter; (without distinction) promiscuē, sine discrīmine.

indigence n indigentia f, egestās f.

indigenous adj indigena.

indigent adj indigēns, egēnus.
indigestible adj crūdus.
indigestion n crūditās f.
indignant adj indignābundus,
irātus; **be ~** indignārī.
indignantly adv irātē.
indignation n indignātiō f, dolor m.
indignity n contumēlia f,
indignitās f.
indigo n Indicum nt.
indirect adj oblīquus.
indirectly adv oblīquē, per
ambāgēs.
indirectness n ambāgēs fpl.
indiscipline n lascīvia f, licentia f.
indiscreet adj incōnsultus,
imprūdēns.
indiscreetly adv incōnsultē,
imprūdenter.
indiscretion n imprūdentia f; (act)
culpa f.
indiscriminate adj prōmiscuus.
indiscriminately adv prōmiscuē,
sine discrīmine.
indispensable adj necesse,
necessārius.
indisposed adj infirmus, aegrōtus,
(will) āversus, aliēnātus; **be ~**
aegrōtāre; abhorrēre, aliēnārī.
indisposition n īnfirmitās f,
valētūdō f.
indisputable adj certus,
manifestus.
indisputably adv certē, sine dubiō.
indissoluble adj indissolūbilis.
indistinct adj obscūrus, obtūsus;
(speaker) balbus.
indistinctly adv obscūrē;
pronounce ~ opprimere; **speak ~**
balbūtīre.
individual adj proprius ♦ n homō
m/f, prīvātus m; **-s** pl singulī mpl.
individuality n proprium nt.
individually adv singulātim,
prīvātim.
indivisible adj indīviduus.
indolence n dēsidia f, ignāvia f,

inertia f.
indolent adj dēses, ignāvus, iners.
indolently adv ignāvē.
indomitable adj indomitus.
indoor adj umbrātilis.
indoors adv intus; (motion) intrā.
indubitable adj certus.
indubitably adv sine dubiō.
induce vt indūcere, addūcere,
persuādēre (dat).
inducement n illecebra f,
praemium m.
induction n (logic) inductiō f.
indulge vt indulgēre (dat).
indulgence n indulgentia f, venia f;
(favour) grātia f.
indulgent adj indulgēns, lēnis.
indulgently adv indulgenter.
industrious adj industrius,
impiger, dīligēns.
industriously adv industriē.
industry n industria f, dīligentia f,
labor m.
inebriated adj ēbrius.
inebriation n ēbrietās f.
ineffable adj eximius.
ineffective adj inūtilis, invalidus.
ineffectively adv ināniter.
ineffectual adj inritus.
inefficient adj inscitus, parum
strēnuus.
inelegant adj inēlegāns,
inconcinnus.
inelegantly adv inēleganter.
inept adj ineptus.
ineptly adv ineptē.
inequality n dissimilitūdō f,
inīquitās f.
inert adj iners, sōcors, immōbilis.
inertia n inertia f.
inertly adv tardē, lentē.
inestimable adj inaestimābilis.
inevitable adj necessārius.
inevitably adv necessāriō.
inexact adj parum subtīlis.
inexhaustible adj perennis.
inexorable adj inexōrābilis.

inexpediency n inūtilitās f,
incommodum nt.
inexpedient adj inūtilis; **it is ~** nōn
expedit.
inexpensive adj vīlis.
inexperience n imperītia f, īnscītia
f.
inexperienced adj imperītus,
rudis, īnscītus.
inexpert adj imperītus.
inexpiable adj inexpiābilis.
inexplicable adj inexplicābilis,
inēnōdābilis.
inexpressible adj inēnārrābilis.
inextricable adj inexplicābilis.
infallible adj certus, errōris
expers.
infamous adj īnfāmis, flāgitiōsus.
infamously adv flāgitiōsē.
infamy n īnfāmia f, flāgitium nt,
dēdecus nt.
infancy n īnfantia f; (fig)
incūnābula ntpl.
infant n īnfāns m/f.
infantile adj puerīlis.
infantry n peditēs mpl, peditātus m.
infantryman n pedes m.
infatuate vt īnfatuāre.
infatuated adj dēmēns.
infatuation n dēmentia f.
infect vt īnficere.
infection n contāgiō f.
infer vt īnferre, colligere.
inference n conclūsiō f.
inferior adj (position) īnferior;
(quality) dēterior.
infernal adj īnfernus.
infest vt frequentāre.
infidel adj impius.
infidelity n perfidia f, īnfidēlitās f.
infiltrate vi sē īnsinuāre.
infinite adj īnfīnītus, immēnsus.
infinitely adv longē, immēnsum.
infinitesimal adj minimus.
infinity n īnfīnitās f.
infirm adj īnfirmus, invalidus.
infirmary n valētūdinārium nt.

infirmity n morbus m.
inflame vt accendere, incendere,
īnflammāre. **be ~d** exārdēscere.
inflammation n (MED) īnflātiō f.
inflate vt īnflāre.
inflated adj (fig) īnflātus, tumidus.
inflexible adj rigidus.
inflexion n (GRAM) flexūra f; (voice)
flexiō f.
inflict vt īnflīgere, incutere;
(burden) impōnere; (penalty)
sūmere; **be ~ed with** labōrāre ex.
infliction n poena f; malum nt.
influence n (physical) impulsiō f,
mōmentum nt; (moral) auctōritās
f; (partial) grātia f; **have ~** valēre;
have great ~ with plūrimum posse
apud; **under the ~ of** īnstinctus
(abl) ♦ vt impellere, movēre,
addūcere.
influential adj gravis, potēns;
grātiōsus.
influenza n gravēdō f.
inform vt docēre, certiōrem
facere; **~ against** nōmen dēferre
(gen).
informant n index m, auctor m.
information n indicium nt, nūntius
m.
informer n index m, dēlātor m;
turn ~ indicium profitērī.
infrequent adj rārus.
infrequently adv rārō.
infringe vt violāre, imminuere.
infringement n violātiō f.
infuriate vt efferāre.
infuriated adj furibundus.
infuse vt īnfundere; (fig) inicere.
ingenious adj ingeniōsus, callidus;
(thing) artificiōsus.
ingeniously adv callidē, summā
arte.
ingenuity n ars f, artificium nt,
acūmen nt.
ingenuous adj ingenuus, simplex.
ingenuously adv ingenuē,
simpliciter.

ingenuousness n ingenuitās f.

ingle n focus m.

inglorious adj inglōrius, ignōbilis, inhonestus.

ingloriously adv sine glōriā, inhonestē.

ingot n later m.

ingrained adj īnsitus.

ingratiate vt: ~ oneself with grātiam inīre ab, sē īnsinuāre in familiāritātem (gen); ~ oneself into sē īnsinuāre in (acc).

ingratitude n ingrātus animus m.

ingredient n pars f.

inhabit vt incolere, habitāre in (abl).

inhabitable adj habitābilis.

inhabitant n incola m/f.

inhale vt haurīre.

inharmonious adj dissonus.

inherent adj īnsitus; **be ~ in** inhaerēre (dat), inesse (dat).

inherently adv nātūrā.

inherit vt excipere.

inheritance n hērēditās f, patrimōnium nt; **divide an ~** herctum ciēre; **come into an ~** hērēditātem adīre.

inheritor n hērēs m/f.

inhibit vt prohibēre, inhibēre.

inhospitable adj inhospitālis.

inhuman adj inhūmānus, immānis, crūdēlis.

inhumanity n inhūmānitās f, crūdēlitās f.

inhumanly adv inhūmānē, crūdēliter.

inimical adj inimīcus.

inimitable adj singulāris, eximius.

iniquitous adj inīquus, improbus, nefārius.

iniquity n scelus nt, flāgitium nt

initial adj prīmus.

initiate vt initiāre; (with knowledge) imbuere.

initiative n initium nt; **take the ~** initium capere, facere; occupāre

(inf).

inject vt inicere.

injudicious adj incōnsultus, imprūdēns.

injunction n iussum nt, praeceptum nt.

injure vt laedere, nocēre (dat).

injurious adj damnōsus, nocēns.

injury n iniūria f, damnum nt; (bodily) vulnus nt.

injustice n iniūria f, inīquitās f.

ink n ātrāmentum nt.

inkling n audītiō f, suspiciō f.

inland adj mediterrāneus; **further ~** interior.

inlay vt īnserere.

inlet n sinus m, aestuārium nt.

inly adv penitus.

inmate n inquilīnus m.

inmost adj intimus.

inn n dēversōrium nt; (caupōna f, taberna f.

innate adj innātus, īnsitus.

inner adj interior.

innermost adj intimus.

innkeeper n caupō m.

innocence n innocentia f.

innocent adj innocēns, īnsōns; (character) integer, castus.

innocently adv innocenter, integrē, castē.

innocuous adj innoxius.

innovate vt novāre.

innovation n novum nt, nova rēs f.

innovator n novārum rērum auctor m.

innuendo n verbum inversum nt.

innumerable adj innumerābilis.

inoffensive adj innocēns.

inoffensively adv innocenter.

inopportune adj intempestīvus.

inopportunely adv intempestīvē.

inordinate adj immodicus, immoderātus.

inordinately adv immoderātē.

inquest n quaestiō f; **hold an ~ on** quaerere dē.

inquire vi exquīrere, rogāre; ~
into inquīrere in (acc),
investigāre.
inquiry n quaestiō f, investīgātiō f;
(asking) interrogātiō f; make ~
exquīrere; **make inquiries about**
inquīrere in (acc); **hold an ~ on**
quaerere dē, quaestiōnem
īnstituere dē.
inquisition n inquīsītiō f.
inquisitive adj cūriōsus.
inquisitiveness n cūriōsitās f.
inquisitor n inquīsītor m.
inroad n incursiō f, impressiō f;
make an ~ incursāre.
insane adj īnsānus, mente captus;
be ~ īnsānīre.
insanity n īnsānia f, dēmentia f.
insatiable adj īnsatiābilis,
inexplēbilis, īnsaturābilis.
insatiably adv īnsaturābiliter.
inscribe vt īnscrībere.
inscription n epigramma nt;
(written) īnscrīptiō f.
inscrutable adj obscūrus.
insect n bēstiola f.
insecure adj īnstabilis, intūtus.
insecurity n perīcula ntpl.
insensate adj ineptus, stultus.
insensible adj torpidus; (fig) dūrus.
insensitive adj dūrus.
inseparable adj coniūnctus; **be the
~ companion of** ab latere esse
(gen).
inseparably adv coniūnctē.
insert vt īnserere, immittere,
interpōnere.
insertion n interpositiō f.
inshore adv prope lītus.
inside adv intus; (motion) intrō
♦ adj interior ♦ n pars f interior
♦ prep intrā (acc); **get right ~** sē
īnsinuāre in (acc); **turn ~ out**
excutere; **on the ~** interior.
insidious adj īnsidiōsus, subdolus.
insidiously adv īnsidiōsē.
insight n intellegentia f, cognitiō f.

insignia n īnsignia ntpl.
insignificance n levitās f.
insignificant adj levis, exiguus,
nullīus mōmentī; (position)
humilis.
insincere adj simulātus, fūcōsus.
insincerely adv simulātē.
insincerity n simulātiō f, fraus f.
insinuate vt īnsinuāre; (hint)
significāre ♦ vi sē īnsinuāre.
insinuating adj blandus.
insinuation n ambigua verba ntpl.
insipid adj īnsulsus, frīgidus.
insipidity n īnsulsitās f.
insist vi īnstāre; **~ on** postulāre.
insistence n pertinācia f.
insistent adj pertināx.
insolence n īnsolentia f,
contumācia f, superbia f.
insolent adj īnsolēns, contumāx,
superbus.
insolently adv īnsolenter.
insoluble adj inexplicābilis.
insolvency n reī familiāris
naufragium nt.
insolvent adj: **be ~** solvendō nōn
esse.
inspect vt īnspicere; (MIL)
recēnsēre.
inspection n cognitiō f; (MIL)
recēnsiō f.
inspector n cūrātor m.
inspiration n adflātus m, īnstinctus
m.
inspire vt īnstinguere, incendere.
instability n mōbilitās f.
install vt inaugurāre.
instalment n pēnsiō f.
instance n exemplum nt; **for ~**
exemplī causā, grātiā; at my ~
admonitū; **at my ~** mē auctōre
♦ vt memorāre.
instant adj īnstāns, praesēns ♦ n
temporis pūnctum nt, mōmentum
nt.
instantaneous adj praesēns.
instantaneously adv continuō,

īlicō.

instantly adv īlicō, extemplō.

instead of prep prō (abl), locō (gen); (with verb) nōn ... sed.

instigate vt īnstīgāre, impellere.

instigation n impulsus m, stimulus m; auctōritās f; **at my ~** mē auctōre

instigator n īnstimulātor m, auctor m.

instil vt imbuere, adspīrāre, inicere.

instinct n nātūra f, ingenium nt, sēnsus m.

instinctive adj nātūrālis.

instinctively adv nātūrā, ingeniō suō

institute vt īnstituere, inaugurāre.

institution n īnstitūtum nt; societās f.

instruct vt docēre, īnstituere, īnstruere; ērudīre; (order) praecipere (dat).

instruction n doctrīna f, disciplīna f; praeceptum nt; **give ~s** dēnūntiāre, praecipere.

instructor n doctor m, praeceptor m.

instructress n magistra f.

instrument n īnstrūmentum nt; (music) fidēs fpl; (legal) tabulae fpl.

instrumental adj ūtilis.

instrumentalist n fidicen m, fidicina f.

instrumentality n opera f.

insubordinate adj turbulentus, sēditiōsus.

insubordination n intemperantia f, licentia f.

insufferable adj intolerandus, intolerābilis.

insufficiency n inopia f.

insufficient adj minor; **be ~** nōn sufficere.

insufficiently adv parum.

insulate vt sēgregāre.

insult n iniūria f, contumēlia f,

probrum nt ♦ vt maledīcere (dat), contumēliam impōnere (dat).

insulting adj contumēliōsus.

insultingly adv contumēliōsē.

insuperable adj inexsuperābilis.

insupportable adj intolerandus, intolerābilis.

insurance n cautiō f.

insure vi cavēre.

insurgent n rebellis m.

insurmountable adj inexsuperābilis.

insurrection n mōtus m, sēditiō f.

intact adj integer, intāctus, incolumis.

integrity n integritās f, innocentia f, fidēs f.

intellect n ingenium nt, mēns f, animus m.

intellectual adj ingeniōsus.

intelligence n intellegentia f, acūmen nt; (MIL) nūntius m.

intelligent adj ingeniōsus, sapiēns, argūtus.

intelligently adv ingeniōsē, sapienter, satis acūtē.

intelligible adj perspicuus, apertus.

intemperance n intemperantia f, licentia f.

intemperate adj intemperāns, intemperātus.

intemperately adv intemperanter.

intend vt (with inf) in animō habēre, velle; (with object) dēstināre.

intense adj ācer, nimius.

intensely adv valdē, nimium.

intensify vt augēre, amplificāre; **be intensified** ingravēscere.

intensity n vīs f.

intensive adj ācer, multus, adsiduus.

intensively adv summō studiō.

intent adj ērēctus, intentus; **be ~ on** animum intendere in (acc) ♦ n cōnsilium nt; **with ~** cōnsultō.

intention n cōnsilium nt,

prōpositum nt; **it is my ~** mihī in
animō est; **with the ~ of** eā mente,
eō cōnsiliō ut (subj).
intentionally adv cōnsultō, dē
industriā.
inter vt humāre.
intercalary adj intercalāris.
intercalate vt intercalāre.
intercede vi intercēdere,
dēprecārī.
intercept vt excipere, intercipere;
(cut off) interclūdere.
intercession n dēprecātiō f;
(tribune's) intercessiō f.
intercessor n dēprecātor m.
interchange vt permūtāre ♦ n
permūtātiō f, vicissitūdō f.
intercourse n commercium nt,
ūsus m, cōnsuētūdō f.
interdict n interdictum nt ♦ vt
interdīcere (dat), vetāre.
interest n (advantage) commodum
nt; (study) studium nt; (money)
faenus nt, ūsūra f; **compound ~**
anatocismus m; **rate of ~** faenus
nt; **~ at 12 per cent (per annum)**
centēsimae fpl; **it is of ~** interest;
it is in my ~s meā interest; **consult
the ~s of** cōnsulere (dat); **take an ~
in** animum intendere (dat) ♦ vt
dēlectāre, capere; (audience)
tenēre; **~ oneself in** studēre (dat).
interested adj attentus; (for gain)
ambitiōsus.
interesting adj iūcundus, novus.
interfere vi intervenīre: (with) sē
interpōnere (dat), sē admiscēre
ad; (hinder) officere (dat).
interference n interventus m,
intercessiō f.
interim n: **in the ~** interim, intereā.
interior adj interior ♦ n pars
interior f; (country) interiōra ntpl.
interject vt exclāmāre.
interjection n interiectiō f.
interlace vt intexere.
interlard vt variāre.

interlock vt implicāre.
interloper n interpellātor m.
interlude n embolium nt.
intermarriage n cōnūbium nt.
intermediary adj medius ♦ n
internūntius m.
intermediate adj medius.
interment n humātiō f.
interminable adj sempiternus,
longus.
intermingle vt intermiscēre ♦ vi
sē immiscēre.
intermission n intercapēdō f,
intermissiō f.
intermittent adj interruptus.
intermittently adv interdum.
intern vt inclūdere.
internal adj internus; (POL)
domesticus.
internally adv intus, domī.
international adj: **~ law** iūs
gentium.
internecine adj internecīvus.
interplay n vicēs fpl.
interpolate vt interpolāre.
interpose vt interpōnere ♦ vi
intercēdere.
interposition n intercessiō f.
interpret vt interpretārī.
interpretation n interpretātiō f.
interpreter n interpres m/f.
interrogate vt interrogāre,
percontārī.
interrogation n interrogātiō f,
percontātiō f.
interrupt vt (action) intercipere;
(speaker) interpellāre; (talk)
dirimere; (continuity) intermittere.
interrupter n interpellātor m.
interruption n interpellātiō f;
intermissiō f.
intersect vt dīvidere, secāre.
intersperse vt distinguere.
interstice n rīma f.
intertwine vt intexere, implicāre.
interval n intervallum nt, spatium
nt; **after an ~** spatiō interpositō;

after an ~ of a year annō
interiectō; at ~s interdum; at
frequent ~s identidem; leave an ~
intermittere.
intervene vt intercēdere,
intervenīre.
intervention n intercessiō f,
interventus m; **by the ~ of**
intercursū (gen).
interview n colloquium nt, aditus
m ♦ vt convenīre.
interweave vt implicāre, intexere.
intestate adj intestātus ♦ adv
intestātō.
intestine adj intestīnus; (POL)
domesticus ♦ npl intestīna ntpl;
(victim's) exta ntpl.
intimacy n familiāritās f.
intimate adj familiāris; **be an ~
friend of** ab latere esse (gen); **a
very ~ friend** perfamiliāris m/f
♦ vt dēnūntiāre.
intimately adv familiāriter.
intimation n dēnūntiātiō f; (hint)
indicium nt.
intimidate vt minārī (dat),
terrōrem inicere (dat).
intimidation n metus m, minae fpl.
into prep in (acc), intrā (acc).
intolerable adj intolerandus,
intolerābilis.
intolerably adv intoleranter.
intolerance n impatientia f.
intolerant adj impatiēns,
intolerāns.
intonation n sonus m, flexiō f.
intone vt cantāre.
intoxicate vt ēbrium reddere.
intoxicated adj ēbrius.
intoxication n ēbrietās f.
intractable adj indocilis, difficilis.
intransigent adj obstinātus.
intrepid adj intrepidus, impavidus.
intrepidity n audācia f, fortitūdō f.
intricacy n implicātiō f.
intricate adj implicātus, involūtus.
intricately adv implicitē.

intrigue n factiō f, artēs fpl, fallācia
f ♦ vi māchinārī, fallāciīs ūtī.
intriguing adj factiōsus; blandus.
intrinsic adj vērus, innātus.
intrinsically adv per sē.
introduce vt indūcere, īnferre,
importāre; (acquaintance)
commendāre; (custom) īnstituere.
introduction n exōrdium nt,
prooemium nt; (of person)
commendātiō f; **letter of ~** litterae
commendātīciae fpl.
intrude vi sē interpōnere,
intervenīre.
intruder n interpellātor m, advena
m; (fig) aliēnus m.
intrusion n interpellātiō f.
intuition n sēnsus m, cognitiō f.
inundate vt inundāre.
inundation n ēluviō f.
inure vt dūrāre, adsuēfacere.
invade vt invādere.
invalid adj aeger, dēbilis; (null)
inritus.
invalidate vt īnfirmāre.
invaluable adj inaestimābilis.
invariable adj cōnstāns,
immūtābilis.
invariably adv semper.
invasion n incursiō f.
invective n convīcium nt.
inveigh vi: **~ against** invehī in (acc),
īnsectārī.
inveigle vt illicere, pellicere.
invent vt fingere, comminīscī,
invenīre.
invention n inventum nt; (faculty)
inventiō f.
inventor n inventor m, auctor m.
inverse adj inversus.
inversely adv inversō ōrdine.
invert vt invertere.
invest vt (in office) inaugurāre; (MIL)
obsidēre, circumsedēre; (money)
locāre.
investigate vt investīgāre,
indāgāre; (case) cognōscere.

investigation n investīgātiō f,
indāgātiō f; (*case*) cognitiō f.
investment n (*MIL*) obsessiō f;
(*money*) locāta pecūnia f.
inveterate adj inveterātus, vetus;
become ~ inveterāscere.
invidious adj invidiōsus.
invidiously adv invidiōsē.
invigorate vt recreāre, reficere.
invincible adj invictus.
inviolable adj inviolātus; (*person*)
sacrōsanctus.
inviolably adv inviolātē.
inviolate adj integer.
invisible adj caecus; **be ~** vidērī
nōn posse.
invitation n invītātiō f; **at the ~ of**
invītātū (*gen*).
invite vt invītāre, vocāre.
inviting adj suāvis, blandus.
invitingly adv blandē, suāviter.
invocation n testātiō f.
invoke vt invocāre, testārī.
involuntarily adv īnscienter,
invītus.
involuntary adj coāctus.
involve vt implicāre, involvere; **be
~d in** inligārī (*abl*).
invulnerable adj inviolābilis; **be ~**
vulnerārī nōn posse.
inward adj interior.
inwardly adv intus.
inwards adv intrōrsus.
inweave vt intexere.
inwrought adj intextus.
irascibility n īrācundia f.
irascible adj īrācundus.
irate adj īrātus.
ire n īra f.
iris n hyacinthus m.
irk vt incommodāre; **I am ~ed** mē
piget.
irksome adj molestus.
irksomeness n molestia f.
iron n ferrum nt; **of ~** ferreus ♦ adj
ferreus.
ironical adj inversus.

ironically adv inversīs verbīs.
iron mine n ferrāria f.
ironmonger n negōtiātor ferrārius
m.
ironmongery n ferrāmenta ntpl.
iron ore n ferrum īnfectum nt.
iron-tipped adj ferrātus.
irony n illūsiō f, verbōrum inversiō
f, dissimulātiō f.
irradiate vt illūstrāre.
irrational adj absurdus, ratiōnis
expers; (*animal*) brūtus.
irrationally adv absurdē, sine
ratiōne.
irreconcilable adj repugnāns,
īnsociābilis.
irrefutable adj certus, invictus.
irregular adj incompositus;
(*ground*) inaequālis; (*meeting*)
extraōrdinārius; (*troops*)
tumultuārius.
irregularity n inaequālitās f;
(*conduct*) prāvitās f, licentia f;
(*election*) vitium nt.
irregularly adv nullō ōrdine;
(*elected*) vitiō.
irrelevant adj aliēnus.
irreligion n impietās f.
irreligious adj impius.
irremediable adj īnsānābilis.
irreparable adj inrevocābilis.
irreproachable adj integer,
innocēns.
irresistible adj invictus.
irresolute adj dubius, anceps.
irresolutely adv dubitanter.
irresolution n dubitātiō f.
irresponsibility n licentia f.
irresponsible adj lascīvus, levis.
irretrievable adj inrevocābilis.
irreverence n impietās f.
irreverent adj impius.
irreverently adv impiē.
irrevocable adj inrevocābilis.
irrigate vt inrigāre.
irrigation n inrigātiō f.
irritability n īrācundia f.

irritable adj īrācundus.

irritate vt inrītāre, stomachum movēre (dat).

irritation n īrācundia f, stomachus m.

island n īnsula f.

islander n īnsulānus m.

isle n īnsula f.

isolate vt sēgregāre, sēparāre.

isolation n sōlitūdō f.

issue n (result) ēventus m, exitus m; (children) prōlēs f; (question) rēs f, (book) ēditiō f, **decide the ~** dēcernere, dēcertāre; **the point at ~** quā dē rē agitur ♦ vt distribuere; (book) ēdere; (announcement) prōmulgāre; (coin) ērogāre ♦ vi ēgredī, ēmānāre; (result) ēvādere, ēvenīre.

isthmus n isthmus m.

it pron hōc, id.

itch n (disease) scabiēs f; (fig) cacoēthes nt ♦ vi prūrīre.

item n nōmen nt, rēs f.

iterate vt iterāre.

itinerant adj vāgus, circumforāneus.

itinerary n iter nt.

its adj suus, ēius.

itself pron ipse, ipsa, ipsum.

ivory n ebur nt ♦ adj eburneus.

ivy n hedera f.

J

jabber vi blaterāre.

jackdaw n graculus m.

jaded adj dēfessus, fatīgātus.

jagged adj serrātus.

jail n carcer m.

jailer n custōs m, carcerārius m.

jam vt comprimere; (way) obstruere.

jamb n postis m.

jangle vi crepitāre; rixārī.

janitor n iānitor m.

January n mēnsis Iānuārius m; of ~ Iānuārius.

jar n urna f; (for wine) amphora f; (for water) hydria f; (sound) offēnsa f; (quarrel) rixa f ♦ vi offendere.

jasper n iaspis f.

jaundice n morbus arquātus.

jaundiced adj ictericus.

jaunt n: **take a ~** excurrere.

jauntily adv hilare, festīvē.

jauntiness n hilaritās f.

jaunty adj hilaris, festīvus.

javelin n iaculum nt, pīlum nt, **throw the ~** iaculārī.

jaw n māla f, **~s** pl faucēs fpl.

jay n grāculus m.

jealous adj invidus; **be ~ of** invidēre (dat).

jealousy n invidia f.

jeer n irrīsiō f ♦ vi irrīdēre; **~ at** illūdere.

jejune adj iēiūnus, exīlis.

jeopardize vt in perīculum addūcere.

jeopardy n perīculum nt.

jerk n subitus mōtus m.

jest n iocus m.

jester n scurra m.

jet n (mineral) gagātēs m; (of water) saltus m ♦ vi salīre.

jetsam n ēiectāmenta ntpl.

jettison vt ēicere.

jetty n mōlēs f.

Jew n Iūdaeus.

jewel n gemma f

Jewish adj Iūdaicus.

jig n tripudium nt.

jilt vt repudiāre.

jingle n nēnia f ♦ vi crepitāre, tinnīre.

job n opus nt.

jocose adj see jocular.

jocular adj facētus, ioculāris.

jocularity n facētiae fpl.

jocularly adv facētē, per iocum.

jocund adj hilaris, festīvus.

jog vt fodicāre; (fig) stimulāre ♦ vi

ambulāre.

join vt iungere, coniungere, cōpulāre ♦ vi coniungī, sē coniungere; ~ **in** interesse (dat), sē immiscēre (dat); ~ **battle with** proelium committere (+ abl).

joiner n faber m.

joint adj commūnis ♦ n commissūra f; (of body) articulus m, nōdus m; ~ **by** ~ articulātim.

jointed adj geniculātus.

joint-heir n cohērēs m/f.

jointly adv ūnā, coniūnctē.

joist n tignum n.

joke n iocus m ♦ vi iocārī, lūdere.

joking n iocus m; ~ **apart** remōtō iocō.

jokingly adv per iocum.

jollity n hilaritās f, festīvitās f.

jolly adj hilaris, festīvus.

jolt vt iactāre.

jolting n iactātiō f.

jostle vt agitāre, offendere.

jot n minimum nt; **not a** ~ nihil; **not care a** ~ nōn floccī facere.

journal n ācta diūrna ntpl.

journey n iter nt.

journeyman n opifex m.

Jove n Iuppiter m.

jovial adj hilaris.

joviality n hilaritās f.

jovially adv hilare.

jowl n māla f; **cheek by** ~ iuxtā.

joy n gaudium n, laetitia f, alacritās f.

joyful adj laetus, hilaris.

joyfully adv laetē, hilare.

joyfulness n gaudium nt, laetitia f.

joyless adj tristis, maestus.

joyous adj see joyful.

joyously adv see joyfully.

jubilant adj laetus, gaudiō exsultāns.

judge n iūdex m, arbiter m ♦ vt iūdicāre; (think) exīstimāre, cēnsēre; ~ **between** diiūdicāre.

judgeship n iūdicātus m.

judgment n iūdicium nt, arbitrium nt; (opinion) sententia f; (punishment) poena f; (wisdom) iūdicium nt; **in my** ~ meō animō, meō arbitrātū; **pass** ~ **on** statuere dē; **sit in** ~ iūdicium exercēre.

judgment seat n tribūnal nt.

judicature n iūrisdictiō f; (men) iūdicēs mpl.

judicial adj iūdiciālis; (law) iūdiciārius.

judiciary n iūdicēs mpl.

judicious adj prūdēns, cōnsīderātus.

judiciously adv prūdenter.

jug n hydria f, urceus m.

juggler n praestīgiātor m.

juggling n praestīgiae fpl.

juice n liquor m, sūcus m.

juicy adj sūcī plēnus.

July n mēnsis Quīnctilis, Iūlius m; **of** ~ Quīnctilis, Iūlius.

jumble n congeriēs f ♦ vt cōnfundere.

jump n saltus m ♦ vi salīre; ~ **across** trānsilīre; ~ **at** (opportunity) captāre, adripere, amplectī; ~ **down** dēsilīre; ~ **on to** īnsilīre in (acc).

junction n coniūnctiō f.

juncture n tempus nt.

June n mēnsis Iūnius; **of** ~ Iūnius.

junior adj iūnior, nātū minor.

juniper n iūniperus f.

Juno n Iūnō, Iūnōnis f.

Jupiter n Iuppiter, Iovis m.

juridical adj iūdiciārius.

jurisconsult n iūriscōnsultus m.

jurisdiction n iūrisdictiō f, diciō f; **exercise** ~ iūs dīcere.

jurisprudence n iūrisprūdentia f.

jurist n iūriscōnsultus m.

juror n iūdex m.

jury n iūdicēs mpl.

just adj iūstus, aequus ♦ adv (exactly) prōrsus; (only) modo; (time) commodum, modo; (with

adv) dēmum, dēnique; (*with pron*)
adeō dēmum, ipse; ~ **as**
(*comparison*) aequē ac, perinde ac,
quemadmodum; sīcut; ~ **before**
(*time*) cum māximē, sub (*acc*); ~
now modo, nunc; ~ **so** ita
prōrsus, sānē; **only** ~ vix.

justice *n* iūstitia *f*, aequitās *f*, iūs
nt; (*person*) praetor *m*; **administer**
~ iūs reddere.

justiciary *n* praetor *m*.

justifiable *adj* iūstus.

justifiably *adv* iūre.

justification *n* pūrgātiō *f*,
excūsātiō *f*.

justify *vt* excūsāre, pūrgāre.

justly *adv* iūstē, aequē; iūre,
meritō.

jut *vi* prōminēre, excurrere.

jutting *adj* prōiectus.

juvenile *adj* iuvenīlis, puerīlis.

K

keel *n* carīna *f*.

keen *adj* ācer; (*mind*) acūtus,
argūtus; (*sense*) sagāx; (*pain*)
acerbus; **I am ~ on** studeō.

keenly *adv* ācriter, sagāciter,
acūtē, acerbē.

keenness *n* (*scent*) sagācitās *f*;
(*sight*) aciēs *f*; (*pain*) acerbitās *f*;
(*eagerness*) studium *nt*, ārdor *m*.

keep *vt* servāre, tenēre, habēre;
(*celebrate*) agere, celebrāre;
(*guard*) custōdīre; (*obey*)
observāre; (*preserve*) cōnservāre;
(*rear*) alere, pāscere; (*store*)
condere; ~ **apart** distinēre; ~
away arcēre; ~ **back** dētinēre,
reservāre; ~ **down** comprimere;
(*exuberance*) dēpāscere; ~ **in**
cohibēre, claudere; ~ **in** with
grātiam sequī (*gen*); ~ **off** arcēre,
dēfendere; ~ **one's word** fidem
praestāre; ~ **one's hands off**
manūs abstinēre; ~ **house** domī sē

retinēre; ~ **secret** cēlāre; ~
together continēre; ~ **up**
sustinēre, cōnservāre; ~ **up with**
subsequī; ~ **waiting** dēmorārī ♦ *vi*
dūrāre, manēre ♦ *n* arx *f*.

keeper *n* custōs *m*.

keeping *n* custōdia *f*; **in ~ with** prō
(*abl*); **be in ~ with** convenīre (*dat*).

keg *n* cadus *m*.

ken *n* cōnspectus *m*.

kennel *n* stabulum *nt*.

kerb *n* crepīdō *f*.

kernel *n* grānum *nt*, nucleus *m*.

kettle *n* lebēs *f*.

key *n* clāvis *f*; (*fig*) claustra *ntpl*,
iānua *f*; ~ **position** cardō *m*.

kick *vi* calcitrāre ♦ *vt* calce ferīre.

kid *n* haedus *m*.

kidnap *vt* surripere.

kidnapper *n* plagiārius *m*.

kidney *n* rēn *m*.

kidney bean *n* phasēlus *m*.

kid's *adj* haedīnus.

kill *vt* interficere, interimere; (*in
battle*) occīdere; (*murder*) necāre,
iugulāre; (*time*) perdere.

killer *n* interfector *m*.

kiln *n* fornāx *f*.

kin *n* cognātī *mpl*, propinquī *mpl*;
next of ~ proximī *mpl*.

kind *adj* bonus, benīgnus,
benevolus ♦ *n* genus *nt*; **of such a
~** tālis; **what ~ of** quālis ♦ *adj*
cōmis.

kindle *vt* incendere, succendere,
īnflammāre.

kindliness *n* cōmitās *f*, hūmānitās
f.

kindling *n* (*fuel*) fōmes *m*.

kindly *adv* benīgnē.

kindness *n* benīgnitās *f*,
benevolentia *f*; (*act*) beneficium *nt*,
officium *nt*, grātia *f*.

kindred *n* necessitūdō *f*, cognātiō *f*;
propinquī *mpl*, cognātī *mpl* ♦ *adj*
cognātus, adfīnis.

king *n* rēx *m*.

kingdom n rēgnum nt.
kingfisher n alcēdō f.
kingly adj rēgius, rēgālis.
kingship n rēgnum nt.
kink n vitium nt.
kinsfolk n cognātī mpl, necessāriī mpl.
kinsman n cognātus m, propinquus m, necessārius m.
kinswoman n cognāta f, propinqua f, necessāria f.
kismet n fātum nt.
kiss n ōsculum nt ♦ vt ōsculārī.
kit n (MIL) sarcina f.
kitchen n culīna f.
kitchen garden n hortus m.
kite n mīluus m.
kite's adj mīluīnus.
knack n calliditās f, artificium nt; **have the ~ of** callēre.
knapsack n sarcina f.
knave n veterātor m.
knavish adj improbus.
knavishly adv improbē.
knead vt depsere, subigere.
knee n genū nt.
kneel vi genibus nītī.
knife n culter m; (surgeon's) scalprum nt.
knight n eques m ♦ vt in ōrdinem equestrem recipere.
knighthood n ōrdō equester m.
knightly adj equester.
knit vt texere; (brow) contrahere.
knob n bulla f.
knock vt ferīre, percutere; ~ **against** offendere; ~ **at** pulsāre; ~ **down** dēicere, adflīgere; (at auction) addīcere; ~ **off** dēcutere; (work) dēsistere ab; ~ **out** ēlīdere, excutere; (unconscious) exanimāre; (fig) dēvincere; ~ **up** suscitāre ♦ n pulsus m, ictus m.
knock-kneed adj vārus.
knoll n tumulus m.
knot n nōdus m ♦ vt nectere.
knotty adj nōdōsus; ~ **point** nōdus

m.
know vt scīre; (person) nōvisse; ~ **all about** explōrātum habēre; ~ **again** agnōscere; ~ **how to** scīre; **not** ~ ignōrāre, nescīre; **let me** ~ fac sciam, fac mē certiōrem; **get to** ~ cognōscere ♦ n **in the** ~ cōnscius.
knowing adj prūdēns, callidus.
knowingly adv cōnsultō, sciēns.
knowledge n scientia f, doctrīna f; (practical) experientia f; (of something) cognitiō f.
knowledgeable adj gnārus, doctus.
known adj nōtus; **make** ~ dēclārāre.
knuckle n articulus m.
knuckle bone n tālus m.
kotow vi adulārī.
kudos n glōria f, laus f.

L

label n titulus m ♦ vt titulō īnscrībere.
laboratory n officīna f.
laborious adj labōriōsus, operōsus.
laboriously adv operōsē.
laboriousness n labor m.
labour n labor m, opera f; (work done) opus nt; (work allotted) pēnsum nt; (workmen) operae fpl; **be in** ~ parturīre ♦ vi labōrāre, ēnītī; ~ **at** ēlabōrāre; ~ **under a delusion** errōre fallī.
laboured adj adfectātus.
labourer n operārius m; ~**s** pl operae fpl.
labyrinth n labyrinthus m.
lace n texta rēticulāta ntpl; (shoe) ligula f ♦ vt nectere.
lacerate vt lacerāre.
laceration n lacerātiō f.
lack n inopia f, dēfectiō f ♦ vt egēre (abl), carēre (abl).
lackey n pedisequus m.

laconic adj brevis.

laconically adv ūnō verbō, paucīs verbīs.

lacuna n lacūna f.

lad n puer m.

ladder n scāla f.

lade vt onerāre.

laden adj onustus, oncrātus.

lading n onus nt.

ladle n trulla f.

lady n domina f, mātrōna f, mulier f.

ladylike adj līberālis, honestus.

lag vi cessāre.

lagoon n stagnum nt.

lair n latibulum nt.

lake n lacus m.

lamb n agnus m; (flesh) agnīna f; ewe ~ agna f.

lame adj claudus; (argument) inānis; **be ~** claudicāre.

lameness n claudicātiō f.

lament n lāmentātiō f, lāmentum nt ♦ vt lūgēre, lāmentārī; (regret) dēplōrāre.

lamentable adj lāmentābilis, miserābilis.

lamentably adv miserābiliter.

lamentation n lāmentātiō f.

lamp n lucerna f, lychnus m.

lampoon n satura f ♦ vt carmine dēstringere.

lance n hasta f, lancea f.

lancer n hastātus m.

lancet n scalpellum nt.

land n terra f; (country) terra f, regiō f; (territory) fīnēs mpl; (native) patria f; (property) praedium nt, ager m; (soil) solum nt ♦ vt expōnere ♦ vi ē nāve ēgredī ♦ adj terrēnus, terrestris.

landfall n adpulsus m.

landing place n ēgressus m.

landlady n caupōna f.

landlord n dominus m; (inn) caupō m.

landmark n lapis m; **be a ~**

eminēre.

landscape n agrōrum prōspectus m.

landslide n terrae lābēs f, lāpsus m.

landwards adv terram versus.

lane n (country) sēmita f; (town) angiportus m.

language n lingua f; (style) ōrātiō f, sermō m; (diction) verba ntpl; **bad ~** maledicta ntpl.

languid adj languidus, remissus.

languidly adv languidē.

languish vi languēre, languēscere; (with disease) tābēscere.

languor n languor m.

lank, lanky adj exīlis, gracilis.

lantern n lanterna f, lucerna f.

lap n gremium nt, sinus m ♦ vt lambere; (cover) involvere.

lapse n (time) lāpsus m; (mistake) errātum nt; **after the ~ of a year** interiectō annō ♦ vi lābī; (agreement) inritum fierī; (property) revertī.

larceny n fūrtum nt.

larch n larix f ♦ adj larignus.

lard n adeps m/f.

larder n cella penāria f.

large adj māgnus, grandis, amplus; **at ~** solūtus; **very ~** permāgnus; **as ~ as ...** tantus ... quantus.

largely adv plērumque.

largesse n largitiō f; (MIL) dōnātīvum nt; (civil) congiārium nt; **give ~** largīrī.

lark n alauda f.

lascivious adj libīdinōsus.

lasciviously adv libīdinōsē.

lasciviousness n libīdō f.

lash n flagellum nt, lōrum nt; (eye) cilium nt ♦ vt verberāre; (tie) adligāre; (with words) castīgāre.

lashing n verbera ntpl.

lass n puella f.

lassitude n languor m.

last adj ultimus, postrēmus,

suprēmus; *(in line)* novissimus; *(preceding)* proximus; **at ~** tandem, dēmum, dēnique; **for the ~ time** postrēmum ♦ *n* fōrma *f*; **let the cobbler stick to his ~** nē sūtor suprā crepidam ♦ *vi* dūrāre, permanēre.

lasting *adj* diūtinus, diūturnus.

lastly *adv* postrēmō, dēnique.

latch *n* pessulus *m*.

latchet *n* corrigia *f*.

late *adj* sērus; *(date)* recēns; *(dead)* dēmortuus; *(emperor)* dīvus; **~ at night** multā nocte; **till ~ in the day** ad multum diem ♦ *adv* sērō; **too ~** sērō; **too ~ to** sērius quam quī *(subj)*; **of ~** nūper.

lately *adv* nūper.

latent *adj* occultus, latitāns.

later *adj* posterior ♦ *adv* posteā, posthāc, mox.

latest *adj* novissimus.

lath *n* tigillum *nt*.

lathe *n* tornus *m*.

lather *n* spūma *f*.

Latin *adj* Latīnus; **speak ~** Latīnē loquī; **understand ~** Latīnē scīre; **translate into ~** Latīnē reddere; **in ~** latīnē.

Latinity *n* Latīnitās *f*.

latitude *n* (GEOG) caelum *nt*; *(scope)* lībertās *f*.

latter *adj* posterior; **the ~** hīc.

latterly *adv* nūper.

lattice *n* trānsenna *f*.

laud *n* laus *f* ♦ *vt* laudāre.

laudable *adj* laudābilis, laude dignus.

laudatory *adj* honōrificus.

laugh *n* rīsus *m*; *(loud)* cachinnus *m* ♦ *vi* rīdēre, cachinnāre; **~ at** *(joke)* rīdēre; *(person)* dērīdēre; **~ up one's sleeve** in sinū gaudēre.

laughable *adj* rīdiculus.

laughing stock *n* lūdibrium *nt*.

laughter *n* rīsus *m*.

launch *vt* *(missile)* contorquēre;

(ship) dēdūcere; **~ an attack** impetum dare ♦ *vi*: **~ out into** ingredī in *(acc)* ♦ *n* celōx *f*, lembus *m*.

laureate *adj* laureātus.

laurel *n* laurus *m* ♦ *adj* laureus.

lave *vt* lavāre.

lavish *adj* prōdigus, largus ♦ *vt* largīrī, profundere.

lavishly *adv* prōdigē, effūsē.

lavishness *n* largitās *f*.

law *n* lēx *f*; *(system)* iūs *nt*; *(divine)* fās *nt*; **civil ~** iūs cīvīle; **constitutional ~** iūs pūblicum; **international ~** iūs gentium; **go to ~** lēge agere, lītigāre; **break the ~** lēgēs violāre; **pass a ~** *(magistrate)* lēgem perferre; *(people)* lēgem iubēre.

law-abiding *adj* bene mōrātus.

law court *n* iūdicium *nt*; *(building)* basilica *f*.

lawful *adj* lēgitimus; *(morally)* fās.

lawfully *adv* lēgitimē, lēge.

lawgiver *n* lēgum scrīptor *m*.

lawless *adj* exlēx.

lawlessly *adv* licenter.

lawlessness *n* licentia *f*.

lawn *n* prātulum *nt*.

law-suit *n* līs *f*, āctiō *f*.

lawyer *n* iūriscōnsultus *m*, causidicus *m*.

lax *adj* dissolūtus, remissus.

laxity *n* dissolūtiō *f*.

lay *vt* pōnere, locāre; *(ambush)* collocāre, tendere; *(disorder)* sēdāre; *(egg)* parere; *(foundation)* iacere; *(hands)* inicere; *(plan)* capere, inīre; *(trap)* tendere; *(wager)* facere; **~ aside** pōnere; *(in store)* repōnere; **~ by** repōnere; **~ down** dēpōnere; *(rule)* statuere; **~ hold of** prehendere, adripere; **~ in** condere; **~ a motion before** referre ad; **~ on** impōnere; **~ open** patefacere; *(to attack)* nūdāre; **~ out** *(money)* impendere;

ērogāre; (camp) mētārī; ~ siege to
obsidēre; ~ to heart in pectus
dēmittere; ~ up recondere; ~
upon iniungere, impōnere; ~
violent hands on vim adferre,
adhibēre (dat); whatever they
could ~ hands on quod cuīque in
manum vēnisset; ~ waste vastāre
♦ n carmen nt, melos nt.

lay adj (eccl) lāicus.

layer n corium nt; (stones) ōrdō m;
(plant) propāgō f.

layout n dēsignātiō f.

laze vi ōtiārī.

lazily adv ignāvē, ōtiōsē.

laziness n ignāvia f, dēsidia f,
pigritia f.

lazy adj ignāvus, dēsidiōsus, piger.

lea n prātum nt.

lead vt dūcere; (life) agere; (wall)
perdūcere; (water) dērīvāre; ~
across trādūcere; ~ around
circumdūcere; ~ astray in
errōrem indūcere; ~ away
abdūcere; ~ back redūcere; ~
down dēdūcere; ~ in
intrōdūcere; ~ on addūcere; ~
out ēdūcere; ~ over trādūcere; ~
the way dūcere, praeīre; ~ up to
tendere ad, spectāre ad; the road
~s... via fert....

lead n plumbum nt ♦ adj
plumbeus.

leaden adj (colour) līvidus.

leader n dux m, ductor m.

leadership n ductus m.

leading adj prīmus, prīnceps,
praecipuus.

leaf, pl **leaves** n folium nt, frōns f;
(paper) scheda f; put forth leaves
frondēscere.

leaflet n libellus m.

leafy adj frondōsus.

league n foedus nt, societās f;
(distance) tria mīlia passuum ♦ vi
coniūrāre, foedus facere.

leagued adj foederātus.

leak n rīma f ♦ vi mānāre, rimās
agere.

leaky adj rīmōsus.

lean adj macer, exīlis, gracilis ♦ vi
nītī; ~ back sē reclīnāre; ~ on
innītī in (abl), incumbere (dat); ~
over inclīnāre.

loaning n prōpēnsiō f ♦ adj
inclīnātus.

leanness n gracilitās f, maciēs f.

leap n saltus m ♦ vi salīre; (for joy)
exsultāre; ~ down dēsilīre; ~ on
to īnsilīre in (acc).

leap year n annus bissextilis m.

learn vt discere; (news) accipere,
audīre; (by heart) ēdiscere;
(discover) cognōscere.

learned adj doctus, ērudītus,
litterātus.

learnedly adv doctē.

learner n tīrō m, discipulus m.

learning n doctrīna f, ērudītiō f,
litterae fpl.

lease n (taken) conductiō f; (given)
locātiō f ♦ vt condūcere; locāre.

leash n cōpula f.

least adj minimus ♦ adv minimē; at
~ saltem; to say the ~ ut
levissimē dīcam; not in the ~
haudquāquam.

leather n corium nt, alūta f.

leathery adj lentus.

leave n (of absence) commeātus m;
(permission) potestās f, venia f; ask
~ veniam petere; give ~
potestātem facere; obtain ~
impetrāre; by your ~ pāce tuā,
bonā tuā veniā ♦ vt relinquere,
dēserere; (legacy) lēgāre; ~ alone
nōn tangere, manum abstinēre ab;
~ behind relinquere; ~ in the
lurch dōdituere, dērelinquere; ~
off dēsinere, dēsistere ab;
(temporarily) intermittere; (garment)
pōnere; ~ out
praetermittere, ōmittere ♦ vi
discēdere ab (+ abl), abīre.

leaven n fermentum nt.

leavings n rēliquiae fpl.

lecherous adj salāx.

lecture n acroāsis f, audītiō f ♦ vi docēre, scholam habēre.

lecturer n doctor m.

lecture room n audītōrium nt.

ledge n līmen nt.

ledger n cōdex acceptī et expēnsī.

lee n pars ā ventō tūta.

leech n hirūdō f.

leek n porrum nt.

leer vi līmīs oculīs intuērī.

lees n faex f; (of oil) amurca f.

left adj sinister, laevus ♦ n sinistra f, laeva f; **on the ~** ā laevā, ad laevam, ā sinistrā.

leg n crūs nt; (of table) pēs m.

legacy n lēgātum nt; **~ hunter** captātor m.

legal adj lēgitimus.

legalize vt sancīre.

legally adv secundum lēgēs, lēge.

legate n lēgātus m.

legation n lēgātiō f.

legend n fābula f; (inscription) titulus m.

legendary adj fābulōsus.

legerdemain n praestigiae fpl.

legging n ocrea f.

legible adj clārus.

legion n legiō f; **men of the 10th ~** decumānī mpl.

legionary n legiōnārius m.

legislate vi lēgēs scrībere, lēgēs facere.

legislation n lēgēs fpl, lēgēs scrībendae.

legislator n lēgum scrīptor m.

legitimate adj lēgitimus.

legitimately adv lēgitimē.

leisure n ōtium nt; **at ~** ōtiōsus, vacuus; **have ~ for** vacāre (dat).

leisured adj ōtiōsus.

leisurely adj lentus.

lend vt commodāre, mūtuum dare; (at interest) faenerārī; (ear) aurēs

praebēre, admovēre; **~ a ready ear** aurēs patefacere; **~ assistance** opem ferre.

length n longitūdō f; (time) diūturnitās f; **at ~** tandem, dēmum, dēnique; (speech) cōpiōsē.

lengthen vt extendere; (time) prōtrahere; (sound) prōdūcere.

lengthwise adv in longitūdinem.

lengthy adj longus, prōlixus.

leniency n clēmentia f.

lenient adj clēmēns, mītis.

leniently adv clēmenter.

lentil n lēns f.

leonine adj leōnīnus.

leopard n pardus m.

less adj minor ♦ adv minus; **~ than** (num) intrā (acc); **much ~, still ~** nēdum.

lessee n conductor m.

lessen vt minuere, imminuere, dēminuere ♦ vi dēcrēscere.

lesson n documentum nt; **be a ~ to** documento esse (dat); **~s** pl dictāta ntpl; **give ~s** scholās habēre; **give ~s in** docēre.

lessor n locātor m.

lest conj nē (+ subj).

let vt (allow) sinere; (lease) locāre; (imper) fac; **~ alone** ōmittere; (mention) nē dīcam; **~ blood** sanguinem mittere; **~ down** dēmittere; (word) ēmittere; **~ fly** ēmittere; **~ go** mittere, āmittere; (ship) solvere; **~ in** admittere; **~ loose** solvere; **~ off** absolvere, ignōscere (dat); **~ oneself go** geniō indulgēre; **~ out** ēmittere; **~ slip** āmittere, ōmittere.

lethal adj mortifer.

lethargic adj veternōsus.

lethargy n veternus m.

letter n epistula f, litterae fpl; (of alphabet) littera f; **the ~ of the law** scrīptum nt; **to the ~** ad

praescrīptum; **by ~** per litterās;
~s (*learning*) litterae *fpl*; **man of ~s**
scrīptor *m*.

lettered *adj* litterātus.

lettuce *n* lactūca *f*.

levee *n* salūtātiō *f*.

level *adj* aequus, plānus ♦ *n*
plānitiēs *f*; (*instrument*) lībra *f*; **do
one's ~ best** prō virīlī parte
agere; **put on a ~ with** exaequāre
cum ♦ *vt* aequāre, adaequāre,
inaequāre; (*to the ground*) solō
aequāre, sternere; (*weapon*)
intendere.

level-headed *adj* prūdēns.

levelled *adj* (*weapon*) īnfestus.

lever *n* vectis *m*

levity *n* levitās *f*; (*fun*) iocī *mpl*,
facētiae *fpl*.

levy *vt* (*troops*) scrībere; (*tax*)
exigere ♦ *n* dīlectus *m*.

lewd *adj* impudīcus.

lewdness *n* impudīcitia *f*.

liable *adj* obnoxius; **render ~**
obligāre.

liaison *n* cōnsuētūdō *f*.

liar *n* mendāx *m*.

libel *n* probrum *nt*, calumnia *f* ♦ *vt*
calumniārī.

libellous *adj* probrōsus, fāmōsus.

liberal *adj* līberālis; (*in giving*)
largus, liargus, liberigenus, = **education**
bonae artēs *fpl*.

liberality *n* līberālitās *f*, largitās *f*.

liberally *adv* līberāliter, largē,
benīgnē.

liberate *vt* līberāre; (*slave*) manū
mittere.

liberation *n* līberātiō *f*.

liberator *n* līberātor *m*.

libertine *n* libīdinōsus *m*.

liberty *n* lībertās *f*; (*excess*) licentia
f; **I am at ~ to** mihi licet (*inf*); **I am
still at ~ to** integrum est mihi (*inf*);
take a ~ with licentius ūtī (*abl*),
familiārius sē gerere in (*acc*).

libidinous *adj* libīdinōsus.

librarian *n* librārius *m*.

library *n* bibliothēca *f*.

licence *n* (*permission*) potestās *f*;
(*excess*) licentia *f*.

license *vt* potestātem dare (*dat*).

licentious *adj* dissolūtus.

licentiousness *n* libīdō *f*, licentia *f*.

lick *vt* lambere; mulcēre.

lictor *n* lictor *m*.

lid *n* operculum *nt*.

lie *n* mendācium *nt*; **give the ~ to**
redarguere; **tell a ~** mentīrī ♦ *vi*
mentīrī; (*lie down*) iacēre; (*place*)
situm esse; (*consist*) continērī; **as
far as in me ~s** quantum in mē est;
~ at anchor stāre; **~ between**
interiacēre; **~ down** cubāre,
discumbere; **~ heavy on** premere;
~ hid latēre; **~ in wait** īnsidiārī; **~
low** dissimulāre; **~ on** incumbere
(*dat*); **~ open** patēre; hiāre.

lien *n* nexus *m*.

lieu *n*: **in ~ of** locō (*gen*).

lieutenant *n* decuriō *m*; legātus *m*.

life *n* vīta *f*; (*in danger*) salūs *f*, caput
nt; (*biography*) vīta *f*; (*breath*)
anima *f*, (*RHET*) sanguis *m*; (*time*)
aetās *f*; **come to ~ again**
revīvīscere; **draw to the ~**
exprimere; **for ~** aetātem; **matter
of ~ and death** capitāle *nt*; **prime
of ~** flōs aetātis; **way of ~** mōrēs
mpl.

lifeblood *n* sanguis *m*.

life-giving *adj* almus, vītalis.

lifeguard *n* custōs *m*; (*emperor's*)
praetōriānus *m*.

lifeless *adj* exanimis; (*style*)
exsanguis.

lifelike *adj* expressus.

lifelong *adj* perpetuus.

lifetime *n* aetās *f*.

lift *vt* tollere, sublevāre; **~ up**
efferre, attollere.

light *n* lūx *f*, lūmen *nt*; (*painting*)
lūmen *nt*; **bring to ~** in lūcem
prōferre; **see in a favourable ~** in

meliōrem partem interpretārī;
 throw ~ on lūmen adhibēre (*dat*)
 ♦ *vt* accendere, incendere;
 (*illuminate*) illūstrāre, illūmināre;
 be lit up collūcēre ♦ *vi*: **~ upon**
 invenīre, offendere ♦ *adj* illūstris;
 (*movement*) agilis; (*weight*) levis;
 grow ~ illūcēscere, dīlūcēscere;
 make ~ of parvī pendere.
light-armed *adj* expedītus.
lighten *vi* fulgurāre ♦ *vt* levāre.
lighter *n* linter f.
light-fingered *adj* tagāx.
light-footed *adj* celer, pernīx.
light-headed *adj* levis, volāticus.
light-hearted *adj* hilaris, laetus.
lightly *adv* leviter; pernīciter.
lightness *n* levitās f.
lightning *n* fulgur nt; (*striking*)
 fulmen nt; **be hit by ~** dē caelō
 percutī; **of ~** fulgurālis.
like *adj* similis, pār; **~ this** ad hunc
 modum ♦ *adv* similiter, sīcut, rītū
 (*gen*) ♦ *vt* amāre; **I ~ mihī** placet,
 mē iuvat; **I ~ to** libet (*inf*); **I don't ~**
 nīl moror, mihī displicet; **look ~**
 similem esse, referre.
likelihood *n* vērī similitūdō f.
likely *adj* vērī similis ♦ *adv* sānē.
liken *vt* comparāre, aequiperāre.
likeness *n* imāgō f, īnstar nt,
 similitūdō f.
likewise *adv* item; (*also*) etiam.
liking *n* libīdō f, grātia f; **to one's ~**
 ex sententiā.
lily *n* līlium nt.
limb *n* membrum nt, artus m.
lime *n* calx f; (*tree*) tilia f.
limelight *n* celebritās f; **enjoy the**
 ~ mōnstrārī digitō.
limestone *n* calx f.
limit *n* fīnis m, terminus m, modus
 m; **mark the ~s of** dētermināre
 ♦ *vt* fīnīre, dēfīnīre, termināre;
 (*restrict*) circumscrībere.
limitation *n* modus m.
limp *adj* mollis, flaccidus ♦ *vi*

claudicāre.
limpid *adj* limpidus.
linden *n* tilia f.
line *n* līnea f; (*battle*) aciēs f; (*limit*)
 modus m; (*outline*) līneāmentum
 nt; (*writing*) versus m; **in a straight**
 ~ ē regiōne; **~ of march** agmen nt;
 read between the ~s dissimulātā
 dispicere; **ship of the ~** nāvis
 longa; **write a ~** pauca scrībere
 ♦ *vt* (*street*) saepīre.
lineage *n* genus nt, stirps f.
lineal *adj* (*descent*) gentīlis.
lineaments *n* līneāmenta ntpl, ōris
 ductūs mpl.
linen *n* linteum nt ♦ *adj* linteus.
liner *n* nāvis f.
linger *vi* cunctārī, cessāre,
 dēmorārī.
lingering *adj* tardus ♦ *n* cunctātiō
 f.
linguist *n*: **be a ~** complūrēs
 linguās callēre.
link *n* ānulus m; (*fig*) nexus m,
 vinculum nt ♦ *vt* coniungere.
lintel *n* līmen superum nt.
lion *n* leō m; **~'s** leōnīnus; **~'s**
 share māior pars.
lioness *n* leaena f.
lip *n* labrum nt; **be on everyone's**
 ~s in ōre omnium hominum esse,
 per omnium ōra ferrī.
lip service *n*: **pay ~ to** verbō tenus
 obsequī (*dat*).
liquefy *vt* liquefacere.
liquid *adj* liquidus ♦ *n* liquor m.
liquidate *vt* persolvere.
liquor *n* liquor m; vīnum nt.
lisp *vi* balbūtīre.
lisping *adj* blaesus.
lissom *adj* agilis.
list *n* index m, tabula f; (*ship*)
 inclīnātiō f ♦ *vt* scrībere ♦ *vi*
 (*lean*) sē inclīnāre; (*listen*)
 auscultāre; (*wish*) cupere.
listen *vi* auscultāre; **~ to**
 auscultāre, audīre.

listener n audītor m, auscultātor m.
listless adj languidus.
listlessness n languor m.
literally adv ad verbum.
literary adj (man) litterātus; ~
pursuits litterae fpl, studia ntpl.
literature n litterae fpl.
lithe adj mollis, agilis.
litigant n lītigātor m.
litigate vi lītigāre.
litigation n līs f.
litigious adj lītigiōsus.
litter n (carriage) lectīca f; (brood)
fētus m; (straw) strāmentum nt;
(mess) strāgēs f ♦ vt sternere;
(young) parere.
little adj parvus, exiguus; (time)
brevis; **very ~** perexiguus,
minimus; **~ boy** puerulus m ♦ n
paulum nt, aliquantulum nt; **for a**
~ paulisper, parumper; **~ or**
nothing vix quicquam ♦ adv
paulum, nonnihil; (with comp)
paulō; **~ by ~** paulātim, sēnsim,
gradātim; **think ~ of** parvī
aestimāre; **too ~** parum (+ gen).
littleness n exiguitās f.
littoral n lītus nt.
live vi vīvere, vītam agere; (dwell)
habitāre; **~ down** (reproach)
ēluere; **~ on** (food) vescī (abl)
♦ adj vīvus.
livelihood n vīctus m.
liveliness n alacritās f, hilaritās f.
livelong adj tōtus.
lively adj alacer, hilaris.
liven vt exhilārāre.
liver n iecur nt.
livery n vestis famulāris f.
livid adj līvidus; **be ~** līvēre.
living adj vīvus ♦ n vīctus m;
(earning) quaestus m.
lizard n lacerta f.
lo interj ecce.
load n onus nt ♦ vt onerāre.
loaf n pānis m ♦ vi grassārī.
loafer n grassātor m.

loam n lutum nt.
loan n mūtuum nt, mūtua pecūnia f.
loathe vt fastīdīre, ōdisse.
loathing n fastīdium nt.
loathsome adj odiōsus, taeter.
lobby n vestibulum nt.
lobe n fibra f.
lobster n astacus m.
local adj indigena, locī.
locality n locus m.
locate vt reperīre; **be ~d** situm
esse.
location n situs m.
loch n lacus m.
lock n (door) sera f; (hair) coma f
♦ vt obserāre.
locomotion n mōtus m.
locust n locusta f.
lodge n casa f ♦ vi dēversārī ♦ vt
īnfīgere; (complaint) dēferre.
lodger n inquilīnus m.
lodging n hospitium nt,
dēversōrium nt.
loftiness n altitūdō f, sublīmitās f.
lofty adj excelsus, sublīmis.
log n stīpes m; (fuel) lignum nt.
loggerhead n: **be at ~s** rixārī.
logic n dialecticē f.
logical adj dialecticus, ratiōne
frētus.
logically adv ex ratiōne.
logician n dialecticus m.
loin n lumbus m.
loiter vi grassārī, cessāre.
loiterer n grassātor m, cessātor m.
loll vi recumbere.
lone adj sōlus, sōlitārius.
loneliness n sōlitūdō f.
lonely, lonesome adj sōlitārius.
long adj longus; (hair) prōmissus;
(syllable) prōductus; (time) longus,
diūturnus; **in the ~ run** aliquandō;
for a ~ time diū; **to make a ~ story**
short nē longum sit, nē longum
faciam ♦ adv diū; **~ ago**
iamprīdem, iamdūdum; **as ~ as**

conj dum; **before ~** mox; **for ~** diū;
how ~ quamdiū, quōusque; **I have
~ been wishing** iam prīdem cupiō;
not ~ after haud multō post; **any
~er** (*time*) diūtius; (*distance*)
longius; **no ~er** nōn iam ♦ *vi:* **~ for**
dēsīderāre, exoptāre, expetere; **~
to** gestīre.
longevity *n* vīvācitās *f.*
longing *n* dēsīderium *nt*, cupīdō *f*
♦ *adj* avidus.
longingly *adv* avidē.
longitudinally *adv* in
longitūdinem.
long-lived *adj* vīvāx.
long-suffering *adj* patiēns.
long-winded *adj* verbōsus, longus.
longwise *adv* in longitūdinem.
look *n* aspectus *m*; (*expression*)
vultus *m* ♦ *vi* aspicere; (*seem*)
vidērī, speciem praebēre; **~
about** circumspicere; **~ after**
prōvidēre (*dat*), cūrāre; **~ at**
spectāre ad (+ *acc*), aspicere,
intuērī; (*with mind*) contemplārī; **~
back** respicere; **~ down on**
dēspectāre; (*fig*) dēspicere; **~ for**
quaerere, petere; **~ forward to**
exspectāre; **~ here** heus tu,
ehodum; **~ into** īnspicere,
intrōspicere; **~ out** prōspicere;
(*beware*) cavēre; **~ round**
circumspicere; **~ through**
perspicere; **~ to** ratiōnem habēre
(*gen*); (*leader*) spem pōnere in (*abl*);
~ towards spectāre ad; **~ up**
suspicere; **~ up to** suspicere; **~
upon** habēre.
looker-on *n* arbiter *m.*
lookout *n* (*place*) specula *f*; (*man*)
vigil *m*, excubiae *fpl.*
looks *npl* speciēs *f*; **good ~** fōrma *f*,
pulchritūdō *f.*
loom *n* tēla *f* ♦ *vi* in cōnspectum sē
dare.
loop *n* orbis *m*, sinus *m.*
loophole *n* fenestra *f.*

loose *adj* laxus, solūtus, remissus;
(*morally*) dissolūtus; **let ~ on**
immittere in (*acc*) ♦ *vt* (*undo*)
solvere; (*slacken*) laxāre.
loosely *adv* solūtē, remissē.
loosen *vt* (re)solvere; (*structure*)
labefacere.
looseness *n* dissolūtiō *f*, dissolūtī
mōrēs *mpl.*
loot *n* praeda *f*, rapīna *f.*
lop *vt* amputāre.
lopsided *adj* inaequālis.
loquacious *adj* loquāx.
loquacity *n* loquācitās *f.*
lord *n* dominus *m* ♦ *vi:* **~ it**
dominārī.
lordliness *n* superbia *f.*
lordly *adj* superbus; (*rank*) nōbilis.
lordship *n* dominātiō *f*, imperium
nt.
lore *n* litterae *fpl*, doctrīna *f.*
lose *vt* āmittere, perdere; **~ an eye**
alterō oculō capī; **~ heart** animum
dēspondēre; **~ one's way**
deerrāre ♦ *vi* (*in contest*) vincī.
loss *n* damnum *nt*, dētrīmentum *nt*;
be at a ~ haerēre, haesitāre;
suffer ~ damnum accipere,
facere; **~es** (*in battle*) caesī *mpl.*
lost *adj* āmissus, absēns; **be ~**
perīre, interīre; **give up for ~**
dēplōrāre.
lot *n* sors *f*; **be assigned by ~** sorte
obvenīre; **draw a ~** sortem
dūcere; **draw ~s for** sortīrī; **a ~ of**
multus, plūrimus.
loth *adj* invītus.
lottery *n* sortēs *fpl*; (*fig*) ālea *f.*
lotus *n* lōtos *f.*
loud *adj* clārus, māgnus.
loudly *adv* māgnā vōce.
loudness *n* māgna vōx *f.*
lounge *vi* ōtiārī.
louse *n* pedis *m/f.*
lout *n* agrestis *m.*
lovable *adj* amābilis.
love *n* amor *m*; **be hopelessly in ~**

dēperīre; **fall in ~ with** adamāre
♦ vt amāre, dīligere; **I ~ to mē**
iuvat (inf).

love affair n amor m.

loveless adj amōre carēns.

loveliness n grātia f, venustās f.

lovely adj pulcher, amābilis,
venustus.

love poem n carmen amātōrium
nt.

lover n amāns m, amātor m.

lovesick adj amōre aeger.

loving adj amāns.

lovingly adv amanter.

low adj humilis; (birth) ignōbilis;
(price) vīlis; (sound) gravis;
(spirits) dēmissus; (voice)
dēmissus; **at ~ water** aestus
dēcessū; **be ~** iacēre; **lay ~**
interficere ♦ vi mūgīre.

lower adj īnferior; **the ~ world**
īnferī mpl; **of the ~ world** īnfernus
♦ adv īnferius ♦ vt dēmittere,
dēprimere ♦ vi (cloud) obscūrārī,
minārī.

lowering adj mināx.

lowest adj īnfimus, īmus.

lowing n mūgītus m

lowland adj campestris.

lowlands n campī mpl.

lowliness n humilitās f.

lowly adj humilis, obscūrus.

low-lying adj dēmisssus; **be ~**
sedēre.

lowness n humilitās f; (spirit)
tristitia f.

loyal adj fidēlis, fīdus; (citizen)
bonus.

loyally adv fidēliter.

loyalty n fidēs f, fidēlitās f.

lubricate vt ungere.

lucid adj clārus, perspicuus

lucidity n perspicuitās f.

lucidly adv clārē, perspicuē.

luck n fortūna f, fors f; **good ~**
fēlicitās f; **bad ~** īnfortūnium nt.

luckily adv fēliciter, faustē,

prosperē.

luckless adj īnfēlīx.

lucky adj fēlīx, fortūnātus; (omen)
faustus.

lucrative adj quaestuōsus.

lucre n lucrum nt, quaestus m.

lucubration n lūcubrātiō f.

ludicrous adj rīdiculus.

ludicrously adv rīdiculē.

lug vt trahere.

luggage n impedīmenta ntpl,
sarcina f.

lugubrious adj lūgubris, maestus.

lukewarm adj tepidus; (fig) segnis,
neglegēns; **be ~** tepēre.

lukewarmly adv segniter,
neglegenter.

lukewarmness n tepor m; (fig)
neglegentia f, incūria f.

lull vt sōpīre; (storm) sēdāre ♦ n
intermissiō f.

lumber n scrūta ntpl.

luminary n lūmen nt, astrum nt.

luminous adj lūcidus, illūstris.

lump n massa f; (on body) tuber nt.

lumpish adj hebes, crassus,
stolidus.

lunacy n īnsānia f.

lunar adj lūnāris.

lunatic n īnsānus m.

lunch n prandium nt ♦ vi
prandēre.

lung n pulmō m; pl (RHET) latera
ntpl.

lunge n ictus m ♦ vi prōsilīre.

lurch n: **leave in the ~**
dērelinquere, dēstituere ♦ vi
titubāre.

lure n esca f ♦ vt allicere, illicere,
ēlicere.

lurid adj lūridus.

lurk vi latēre, latitāre, dēlitēscere.

luscious adj praedulcis.

lush adj luxuriōsus.

lust n libīdō f ♦ vi libīdine flagrāre,
concupīscere.

lustful adj libīdinōsus.

lustily adv validē, strēnuē.
lustiness n vigor m, nervī mpl.
lustration n lūstrum nt.
lustre n fulgor m, splendor m.
lustrous adj illūstris.
lusty adj validus, lacertōsus.
lute n cithara f, fidēs fpl.
lute player n citharista m,
  citharistria f, fidicen m, fidicina f.
luxuriance n luxuria f.
luxuriant adj luxuriōsus.
luxuriate vi luxuriārī.
luxuries pl lautitiae fpl.
luxurious adj luxuriōsus,
  sūmptuōsus, lautus.
luxuriously adv sūmptuōsē, lautē.
luxury n luxuria f, luxus m.
lynx n lynx m/f; **~-eyed** lynceus.
lyre n lyra f, fidēs fpl; **play the ~**
  fidibus canere.
lyric adj lyricus ♦ n carmen nt.
lyrist n fidicen m, fidicina f.

M

mace n scīpiō m.
machination n dolus m.
machine n māchina f.
mackerel n scomber m.
mad adj īnsānus, furiōsus, vēcors,
  dēmēns; **be ~** īnsānīre, furere.
madam n domina f.
madden vt furiāre, mentem
  aliēnāre (dat).
madly adv īnsānē, furiōsē,
  dēmenter.
madness n īnsānia f, furor m,
  dēmentia f; (animals) rabiēs f.
maelstrom n vertex m.
magazine n horreum nt, apothēca
  f.
maggot n vermiculus m.
magic adj magicus ♦ n magicae
  artēs fpl.
magician n magus m, veneficus m.
magistracy n magistrātus m.
magistrate n magistrātus m.

magnanimity n māgnanimitās f,
  līberālitās f.
magnanimous adj generōsus,
  līberālis, māgnanimus.
magnet n magnēs m.
magnificence n māgnificentia f,
  adparātus m.
magnificent adj māgnificus,
  amplus, splendidus.
magnificently adv māgnificē,
  amplē, splendidē.
magnify vt amplificāre,
  exaggerāre.
magnitude n māgnitūdō f.
magpie n pīca f.
maid n virgō f; (servant) ancilla f.
maiden n virgō f.
maidenhood n virginitās f.
maidenly adj virginālis.
mail n (armour) lōrīca f; (letters)
  epistulae fpl.
maim vt mutilāre.
maimed adj mancus.
main adj prīnceps, prīmus; **~ point**
  caput nt ♦ n (sea) altum nt,
  pelagus nt; **with might and ~**
  manibus pedibusque, omnibus
  nervīs.
mainland n continēns f.
mainly adv praecipuē, plērumque.
maintain vt (keep) tenēre, servāre;
  (keep up) sustinēre; (keep alive)
  alere, sustentāre; (argue)
  adfirmāre, dēfendere.
maintenance n (food) alimentum
  nt.
majestic adj augustus, māgnificus.
majestically adv augustē.
majesty n māiestās f.
major adj māior.
majority n māior pars f, plērīque;
  have attained one's ~ suī iūris
  esse.
make vt facere, fingere;
  (appointment) creāre; (bed)
  sternere; (cope) superāre;
  (compulsion) cōgere; (consequence)

efficere; (*craft*) fabricārī; (*harbour*)
capere; (*living*) quaerere; (*sum*)
efficere; (*with adj*) reddere; (*with
verb*) cōgere; ~ **away with** tollere,
interimere; ~ **good** supplēre,
resarcīre; ~ **light of** parvī facere;
~ **one's way** iter facere; ~ **much
of** māgnī aestimāre, multum
tribuere (*dat*); ~ **for** petere; ~ **out**
arguere; ~ **over** dēlēgāre,
trānsferre; ~ **ready** parāre; ~ **a
speech** ōrātiōnem habēre; ~ **a
truce** indutiās compōnere; ~ **war
on** bellum īnferre; ~ **up** (*loss*)
supplēre; (*total*) efficere; (*story*)
fingere; **be made fierī.**
make-believe *n* simulātiō *f*.
maker *n* fabricātor *m*, auctor *m*.
make-up *n* medicāmina *ntpl*.
maladministration *n* (*charge*)
repetundae *fpl*.
malady *n* morbus *m*.
malcontent *adj* novārum rērum
cupidus.
male *adj* mās, masculus.
malefactor *n* nocēns *m*, reus *m*.
malevolence *n* malevolentia *f*.
malevolent *adj* malevolus,
malignus.
malevolently *adv* malignē.
malformation *n* dēprāvātiō *f*.
malice *n* invidia *f*, malevolentia *f*;
bear ~ towards invidēre (*dat*).
malicious *adj* invidiōsus,
malevolus, malignus.
maliciously *adv* malignē.
malign *adj* malignus, invidiōsus
♦ *vt* obtrectāre.
malignant *adj* malevolus.
maligner *n* obtrectātor *m*.
malignity *n* malevolentia *f*.
malleable *adj* ductilis.
mallet *n* malleus *m*.
mallow *n* malva *f*.
malpractices *n* dēlicta *ntpl*.
maltreat *vt* laedere, vexāre.
malversation *n* pecūlātus *m*.

man *n* (*human being*) homō *m/f*;
(*male*) vir *m*; (*MIL*) mīles *m*; (*chess*)
latrunculus *m*; **to a ~** omnēs ad
ūnum; ~ **who** is qui; **old ~** senex
m; **young ~** adulēscēns *m*; ~ **of
war** nāvis longa *f* ♦ *vt* (*ship*)
complēre; (*walls*) praesidiō
firmāre.
manacle *n* manicae *fpl* ♦ *vt*
manicās inicere (*dat*).
manage *vt* efficere, gerere,
gubernāre, administrāre; (*horse*)
moderārī; (*with verb*) posse.
manageable *adj* tractābilis,
habilis.
management *n* administrātiō *f*,
cūra *f*; (*finance*) dispēnsātiō *f*.
manager *n* administrātor *m*,
moderātor *m*; dispēnsātor *m*.
mandate *n* mandātum *nt*.
mane *n* iuba *f*.
manful *adj* virīlis, fortis.
manfully *adv* virīliter, fortiter.
manger *n* praesēpe *nt*.
mangle *vt* dīlaniāre, lacerāre.
mangy *adj* scaber.
manhood *n* pūbertās *f*, toga virīlis
f.
mania *n* īnsānia *f*.
maniac *n* furiōsus *m*.
manifest *adj* manifestus, apertus,
clārus ♦ *vt* dēclārāre, aperīre.
manifestation *n* speciēs *f*.
manifestly *adv* manifestō, apertē.
manifesto *n* ēdictum *nt*.
manifold *adj* multiplex, varius.
manikin *n* homunciō *m*,
homunculus *m*.
manipulate *vt* tractāre.
manipulation *n* tractātiō *f*.
mankind *n* hominēs *mpl*, genus
hūmānum *nt*.
manliness *n* virtūs *f*.
manly *adj* fortis, virīlis.
manner *n* modus *m*, ratiō *f*;
(*custom*) mōs *m*, ūsus *m*; ~**s** *pl*
mōrēs *mpl*; **after the ~ of** rītū,

mōre (*gen*); **good ~s** hūmānitās *f*,
modestia *f*.

mannered *adj* mōrātus.

mannerism *n* mōs *m*.

mannerly *adj* bene mōrātus,
urbānus.

manoeuvre *n* (MIL) dēcursus *m*,
dēcursiō *f*; (*fig*) dolus *m* ♦ *vi*
dēcurrere; (*fig*) māchinārī.

manor *n* praedium *nt*.

mansion *n* domus *f*.

manslaughter *n* homicīdium *nt*.

mantle *n* pallium *nt*; (*women's*)
palla *f*.

manual *adj*: **~ labour** opera *f* ♦ *n*
libellus *m*, ars *f*.

manufacture *n* fabrica *f* ♦ *vt*
fabricārī.

manumission *n* manūmissiō *f*.

manumit *vt* manū mittere,
ēmancipāre.

manure *n* fimus *m*, stercus *nt* ♦ *vt*
stercorāre.

manuscript *n* liber *m*, cōdex *m*.

many *adj* multī; **as ~ as** tot … quot;
how ~? quot?; **so ~** tot; **in ~
places** multifāriam; **a good ~**
complūrēs; **too ~** nimis multī; **the
~** vulgus *nt*; **very ~** permultī,
plūrimī.

map *n* tabula *f* ♦ *vt*: **~ out**
dēscrībere, dēsignāre.

maple *n* acer *m* ♦ *adj* acernus.

mar *vt* corrumpere, dēfōrmāre.

marauder *n* praedātor *m*,
dēpopulātor *m*.

marble *n* marmor *nt* ♦ *adj*
marmoreus.

March *n* mēnsis Martius *m*; **of ~**
Martius.

march *n* iter *nt*; **line of ~** agmen *nt*;
by forced ~es māgnīs itineribus;
on the ~ ex itinere, in itinere;
quick ~ plēnō gradū; **a regular
day's ~** iter iūstum *nt* ♦ *vi*
contendere, iter facere, incēdere,
īre; **~ out** exīre; **~ on** signa

prōferre, prōgredī ♦ *vt* dūcere; **~
out** ēdūcere; **~ in** intrōdūcere.

mare *n* equa *f*.

margin *n* margō *f*; (*fig*) discrīmen
nt.

marigold *n* caltha *f*.

marine *adj* marīnus ♦ *n* mīles
classicus *m*.

mariner *n* nauta *m*.

marital *adj* marītus.

maritime *adj* maritimus.

marjoram *n* amāracus *m*.

mark *n* nota *f*; (*of distinction*)
īnsigne *nt*; (*target*) scopos *m*;
(*trace*) vestīgium *nt*; **beside the ~**
nihil ad rem; **it is the ~ of a wise
man to** sapientis est (*inf*); **be wide
of the ~** errāre ♦ *vt* notāre,
dēsignāre; (*observe*)
animadvertere, animum
attendere; **~ out** (*site*) mētārī,
dēsignāre; (*for purpose*) dēnotāre.

marked *adj* īnsignis, manifestus.

markedly *adv* manifestō.

marker *n* index *m*.

market *n* macellum *nt*; **~ day**
nūndinae *fpl*; **~ town** emporium
nt; **cattle ~** forum boārium *nt*; **fish
~** forum piscārium *nt*.

marketable *adj* vēndibilis.

marketplace *n* forum *nt*.

market prices *npl* annōna *f*.

market town *n* emporium *nt*.

marking *n* macula *f*.

maroon *vt* dērelinquere.

marriage *n* mātrimōnium *nt*,
coniugium *nt*; (*ceremony*) nūptiae
fpl; **give in ~** collocāre; **~ bed**
lectus geniālis *m*.

marriageable *adj* nūbilis.

marrow *n* medulla *f*.

marry *vt* (*a wife*) dūcere, in
mātrimōnium dūcere; (*a husband*)
nūbere (*dat*).

marsh *n* palūs *f*.

marshal *n* imperātor *m* ♦ *vt*
īnstruere.

marshy adj palūster.
mart n forum nt.
marten n mēlēs f.
martial adj bellicōsus, ferōx.
martyr n dēvōtus m; (ECCL) martyr m/f.
marvel n mīrāculum nt, portentum nt ♦ vi mīrārī; **~ at** admīrārī.
marvellous adj mīrus, mīrificus, mīrābilis.
marvellously adv mīrē, mīrum quantum.
masculine adj mās, virīlis.
mash n farrāgō f ♦ vt commiscēre, contundere.
mask n persōna f ♦ vt persōnam induere (dat); (fig) dissimulāre.
mason n structor m.
masonry n lapidēs mpl, caementum nt.
masquerade n simulātiō f ♦ vi vestem mūtāre; **~ as** speciem sibi induere (gen), persōnam ferre (gen).
mass n mōlēs f; (of small things) congeriēs f, (of people) multitūdō f; (ECCL) missa f; **the ~es** vulgus nt, plebs f ♦ vt congerere, coacervāre.
massacre n strāgēs f, caedēs f, internetiō f ♦ vt trucīdāre.
massive adj ingēns, solidus.
massiveness n mōlēs f, solidītās f.
mast n mālus m.
master n dominus m; (school) magister m; **be ~ of** dominārī in (abl); (skill) perītus esse (gen); **become ~ of** potīrī (abl); **be one's own ~** suī iūris esse; **not ~ of** impotēns (gen); **a past ~** veterātor m ♦ vt dēvincere; (skill) ēdiscere; (passion) continēre.
masterful adj imperiōsus.
masterly adj doctus, perītus.
masterpiece n praeclārum opus nt.
mastery n dominātiō f, imperium nt, arbitrium nt.

masticate vt mandere.
mastiff n Molossus m.
mat n storea f.
match n (person) pār m/f; (marriage) nūptiae fpl; (contest) certāmen nt; **a ~ for** pār (dat); **no ~ for** impār (dat) ♦ vt exaequāre, adaequāre ♦ vi congruere.
matchless adj singulāris, ūnicus.
mate n socius m; (married) coniunx m/f ♦ vi coniungī.
material adj corporeus; (significant) haud levis ♦ n māteriēs f; (literary) silva f.
materialize vi ēvenīre.
materially adv māgnopere.
maternal adj māternus.
mathematical adj mathēmaticus.
mathematician n mathēmaticus m, geōmetrēs m.
mathematics n ars mathēmatica f, numerī mpl.
matin adj mātūtīnus.
matricide n (act) mātrīcīdium nt; (person) mātrīcīda m.
matrimony n mātrimōnium nt.
matrix n fōrma f.
matron n mātrōna f.
matter n māteria f, corpus nt; (affair) rēs f; (MED) pūs nt; **what is the ~ with you?** quid tibī est? ♦ vi: **it ~s** interest, rēfert.
matting n storea f.
mattock n dolābra f.
mattress n culcita f.
mature adj mātūrus; (age) adultus ♦ vi mātūrēscere.
maturity n mātūritās f; (age) adulta aetās f.
maul n fistūca f ♦ vt contundere, dīlaniāre.
maw n ingluviēs f.
mawkish adj pūtidus.
mawkishly adv pūtidē.
maxim n dictum nt, praeceptum nt, sententia f.
maximum adj quam māximus,

quam plūrimus.
May n mēnsis Māius m; **of ~**
Māius.
may vi posse; **I ~** licet mihī.
mayor n praefectus m.
maze n labyrinthus m.
mead n (drink) mulsum nt; (land)
prātum nt.
meagre adj exīlis, ieiūnus.
meagrely adv exīliter, ieiūnē.
meagreness n exīlitās f.
meal n (flour) farīna f; (repast)
cibus m.
mealy-mouthed adj blandiloquus.
mean adj humilis, abiectus; (birth)
ignōbilis; (average) medius,
mediocris ♦ n modus m,
mediocritās f ♦ vt dīcere,
significāre; (word) valēre; (intent)
velle, in animō habēre.
meander vi sinuōsō cursū fluere.
meaning n significātiō f, vīs f,
sententia f; **what is the ~ of?** quid
sibī vult?, quōrsum spectat?
meanly adv abiectē, humiliter.
meanness n humilitās f, (conduct)
illīberālitās f, avāritia f.
means n īnstrūmentum nt; (of
doing) facultās f; (wealth) opēs fpl;
by ~ of per (acc); **by all ~** māximē;
by no ~ nūllō modō, haudquāquam; **of small ~** pauper.
meantime, meanwhile adv
intereā, interim.
measles n boa f.
measure n modus m, mēnsūra f,
(rhythm) numerī mpl; (plan)
cōnsilium nt; (law) rogātiō f, lēx f;
beyond ~ nimium; **in some ~**
aliquā ex parte; **take ~s**
cōnsulere; **take the ~ of** quālis sit
cognōscere; **without ~**
immoderātē ♦ vt mētīrī; **~ out**
dīmētīrī; (land) mētārī.
measured adj moderātus.
measureless adj īnfīnītus,
immēnsus.

measurement n mēnsūra f.
meat n carō f.
mechanic n opifex m, faber m.
mechanical adj mēchanicus.
mechanical device n māchinātiō f.
mechanics n māchinālis scientia f.
mechanism n māchinātiō f.
medal n īnsigne nt.
meddle vi sē interpōnere.
meddlesome adj cūriōsus.
Medes n Mīdi mpl.
mediate vi intercēdere; **~
between** compōnere, conciliāre.
mediator n intercessor m,
dēprecātor m.
medical adj medicus.
medicate vt medicāre.
medicinal adj medicus, salūbris.
medicine n (art) medicīna f; (drug)
medicāmentum nt.
medicine chest n narthēcium nt.
mediocre adj mediocris.
mediocrity n mediocritās f.
meditate vi meditārī, cōgitāre,
sēcum volūtāre.
meditation n cōgitātiō f, meditātiō
f.
medium n internūntius m; (means)
modus m ♦ adj mediocris.
medley n farrāgō f.
meek adj mītis, placidus.
meekly adv summissō animō.
meet adj idōneus, aptus ♦ n
conventus m ♦ vi convenīre ♦ vt
obviam īre (dat), occurrere (dat);
(fig) obīre; **~ with** invenīre,
excipere.
meeting n cōnsilium nt, conventus
m.
melancholic adj melancholicus.
melancholy n ātra bīlis f; tristitia
f, maestitia f ♦ adj tristis,
maestus.
mêlée n turba f, concursus m.
mellow adj mītis; (wine) lēnis;
become ~ mītēscere; **make ~**
mītigāre.

mellowness n mātūritās f.

melodious adj canōrus, numerōsus.

melodiously adv numerōsē.

melody n melos nt, modī mpl.

melt vt liquefacere, dissolvere; (fig) movēre ♦ vi liquēscere, dissolvī; (fig) commovērī; ~ away dēliquēscere.

member n membrum nt; (person) socius m.

membrane n membrāna f.

memento n monumentum nt.

memoir n commentārius m.

memorable adj memorābilis, commemorābilis.

memorandum n hypomnēma nt.

memorial n monumentum nt.

memorize vt ēdiscere.

memory n memoria f; from ~ memoriter.

menace n minae fpl ♦ vt minārī, minitārī; (things) imminēre (dat).

menacing adj mināx.

menacingly adv mināciter.

menage n familia f.

mend vt sarcīre, reficere ♦ vi meliōrem fierī; (health) convalēscere.

mendacious adj mendāx.

mendacity n mendācium nt.

mendicant n mendīcus m.

mendicity n mendīcitās f.

menial adj servīlis, famulāris ♦ n servus m, famulus m.

menstrual adj mēnstruus.

mensuration n mētiendī ratiō f.

mental adj cōgitātiōnis, mentis.

mentality n animī adfectus m, mēns f.

mentally adv cōgitātiōne, mente.

mention n mentiō f ♦ vt memorāre, mentiōnem facere (gen); (casually) inicere; (briefly) attingere; omit to ~ praetermittere.

mentor n auctor m, praeceptor m.

mercantile adj mercātōrius.

mercenary adj mercennārius, vēnālis ♦ n mercennārius mīles m.

merchandise n mercēs fpl.

merchant n mercātor m.

merchantman n nāvis onerāria f.

merchant ship n nāvis onerāria f.

merciful adj misericors, clēmens.

mercifully adv clēmenter.

merciless adj immisericors, inclēmens, inhūmānus.

mercilessly adv inhūmānē.

mercurial adj hilaris.

mercy n misericordia f, clēmentia f, venia f; at the ~ of obnoxius (dat), in manū (gen).

mere n lacus m ♦ adj merus, ipse.

merely adv sōlum, tantum, dumtaxat.

meretricious adj meretricius; ~ attractions lēnōcinia ntpl.

merge vt cōnfundere ♦ vi cōnfundī.

meridian n merīdiēs m ♦ adj merīdiānus.

merit n meritum nt, virtūs f ♦ vt merērī.

meritorious adj laudābilis.

meritoriously adv optimē.

mermaid n nympha f.

merrily adv hilare, fēstīvē.

merriment n hilaritās f, fēstīvitās f.

merry adj hilaris, fēstīvus; **make ~** lūdere.

merrymaking n lūdus m, fēstīvitās f.

mesh n macula f.

mess n (dirt) sordēs f, squālor m; (trouble) turba f; (food) cibus m; (MIL) contubernālēs mpl.

message n nūntius m.

messenger n nūntius m.

messmate n contubernālis m.

metal n metallum nt ♦ adj ferreus, aereus.

metamorphose vt mūtāre,
  trānsfōrmāre.
metamorphosis n mūtātiō f.
metaphor n trānslātiō f.
metaphorical adj trānslātus.
metaphorically adv per
  trānslātiōnem.
metaphysics n dialectica ntpl.
mete vt mētīrī.
meteor n fax caelestis f.
meteorology n prognōstica ntpl.
methinks vi: ~ **I am** mihi videor
  esse.
method n ratiō f, modus m.
methodical adj dispositus; (person)
  dīligēns.
methodically adv dispositē.
meticulous adj accūrātus.
meticulously adv accūrātē.
meticulousness n cūra f.
metonymy n immūtātiō f.
metre n numerī mpl, modī mpl.
metropolis n urbs f.
mettle n ferōcitās f, virtūs f.
mettlesome adj ferōx, animōsus.
mew n (bird) larus m; ~**s** pl stabula
  ntpl ♦ vi vāgīre.
miasma n hālitus m.
mid adj medius ♦ prep inter (acc).
midday n merīdiēs m ♦ adj
  merīdiānus.
middle adj medius ♦ n medium nt;
  in the ~ medius, in mediō; **~ of**
  medius.
middling adj mediocris.
midge n culex m.
midget n pūmiliō m/f.
midland adj mediterrāneus.
midnight n media nox f.
midriff n praecordia ntpl.
midst n medium nt; **in the ~**
  medius; **in the ~ of** inter (acc);
  through the ~ of per medium.
midsummer n sōlstitium nt ♦ adj
  sōlstitiālis.
midway adv medius.
midwife n obstetrix f.

midwinter n brūma f ♦ adj
  brūmālis.
mien n aspectus m, vultus m.
might n vīs f, potentia f; **with ~ and**
  main omnibus nervīs, manibus
  pedibusque.
mightily adv valdē, magnopere.
mighty adj ingēns, validus.
migrate vi abīre, migrāre.
migration n peregrīnātiō f.
migratory adj advena.
mild adj mītis, lēnis, clēmens.
mildew n rōbīgō f.
mildly adv lēniter, clēmenter.
mildness n clēmentia f,
  mānsuētūdō f; (weather) caelī
  indulgentia f.
mile n mīlle passūs mpl; ~**s** pl
  mīlia passuum.
milestone n lapis m, mīliārium nt.
militant adj ferōx.
military adj mīlitāris ♦ n mīlitēs
  mpl.
military service n mīlitia f.
militate vi: ~ **against** repugnāre
  (dat), facere contrā (acc).
militia n mīlitēs mpl.
milk n lac nt ♦ vt mulgēre.
milk pail n mulctra f.
milky adj lacteus.
mill n pistrīnum nt.
milled adj (coin) serrātus.
millennium n mīlle annī mpl.
miller n pistor m.
millet n mīlium nt.
million num deciēs centēna mīlia
  ntpl.
millionaire n rēx m.
millstone n mola f, molāris m.
mime n mīmus m.
mimic n imitātor m, imitātrīx f
  ♦ vt imitārī.
mimicry n imitātiō f.
minatory adj mināx.
mince vt concīdere; **not ~ words**
  plānē apertēque dīcere ♦ n
  minūtal nt.

mind n mēns f, animus m, ingenium nt; (*opinion*) sententia f; (*memory*) memoria f; **be in one's right ~** mentis suae esse; **be of the same ~** eadem sentīre; **be out of one's ~** īnsānīre; **bear in ~** meminisse (*gen*), memorem esse (*gen*); **call to ~** memoriā repetere, recordārī; **have a ~ to** libet; **have in ~** in animō habēre; **put one's ~ to** animum applicāre ad (+ *acc*); **make up one's ~** animum indūcere, animō obstināre, statuere; **put in ~ of** admonēre (*gen*); **speak one's ~** sententiam suam aperīre; **to one's ~** ex sententiā ♦ vt cūrāre, attendere; **~ one's own business** suom negōtium agere ♦ vi gravārī; **I don't ~** nīl moror; **never ~** mitte.

minded adj animātus.

mindful adj memor.

mine n metallum nt; (*MIL*) cunīculum m; (*fig*) thēsaurus m ♦ vi fodere; (*MIL*) cunīculum agere ♦ pron meus.

miner n fossor m.

mineral n metallum nt.

mingle vt miscēre, commiscēre ♦ vi sē immiscēre.

miniature n minima pictūra f.

minimize vt dētrectāre.

minimum n minimum nt ♦ adj quam minimus.

minion n cliēns m/f; dēlicātus m.

minister n administer m ♦ vi ministrāre, servīre.

ministry n mūnus nt, officium nt.

minor adj minor ♦ n pupillus m, pupilla f.

minority n minor pars f; **in one's ~** nōndum suī iūris.

Minotaur n Mīnōtaurus m.

minstrel n fidicen m.

minstrelsy n cantus m.

mint n (*plant*) menta f; (*money*) Monēta f ♦ vt cūdere.

minute n temporis mōmentum nt.

minute adj minūtus, exiguus, subtīlis.

minutely adv subtīliter.

minuteness n exiguitās f, subtīlitās f.

minutiae n singula ntpl.

minx n lascīva f.

miracle n mīrāculum nt, mōnstrum nt.

miraculous adj mīrus, mīrābilis.

miraculously adv dīvīnitus.

mirage n falsa speciēs f.

mire n lutum nt.

mirror n speculum nt ♦ vt reddere.

mirth n hilaritās f, laetitia f.

mirthful adj hilaris, laetus.

mirthfully adv hilare, laetē.

miry adj lutulentus.

misadventure n īnfortūnium nt, cāsus m.

misapply vt abūtī (*abl*); (*words*) invertere.

misapprehend vt male intellegere.

misapprehension n error m.

misappropriate vt intervertere.

misbegotten adj nothus.

misbehave vi male sē gerere.

miscalculate vi errāre, fallī.

miscalculation n error m.

miscall vt maledīcere (*dat*).

miscarriage n abortus m; (*fig*) error m.

miscarry vi abortīrī; (*fig*) cadere, inritum esse.

miscellaneous adj prōmiscuus, varius.

miscellany n farrāgō f.

mischance n īnfortūnium nt.

mischief n malum nt, facinus nt, maleficium nt; (*children*) lascīvia f.

mischievous adj improbus, maleficus; lascīvus.

misconceive vt male intellegere.

misconception n error m.

misconduct n dēlictum nt, culpa f.

misconstruction n prāva

interpretātiō f.
misconstrue vt male interpretārī.
miscreant n scelerātus m.
misdeed n maleficium nt, dēlictum nt.
misdemeanour n peccātum nt, culpa f.
miser n avārus m.
miserable adj miser, infēlīx; **make oneself ~** sē cruciāre.
miserably adv miserē.
miserliness n avāritia f.
miserly adj avārus.
misery n miseria f, aerumna f.
misfortune n malum nt, īnfortūnium nt, incommodum nt, rēs adversae fpl.
misgiving n suspīciō f, cūra f; **have ~s** parum cōnfīdere.
misgovern vt male regere.
misgovernment n prāva administrātiō f.
misguide vt fallere, dēcipere.
misguided adj dēmēns.
mishap n īnfortūnium nt.
misinform vt falsa docēre.
misinterpret vt male interpretārī.
misinterpretation n prāva interpretātiō f.
misjudge vt male iūdicāre.
mislay vt āmittere.
mislead vt dēcipere, indūcere, auferre.
mismanage vt male gerere.
misnomer n falsum nōmen nt.
misogyny n mulierum odium nt.
misplace vt in aliēnō locō collocāre.
misplaced adj (fig) vānus.
misprint n mendum nt.
mispronounce vt prāvē appellāre.
misquote vt perperam prōferre.
misrepresent vt dētorquēre, invertere; (person) calumniārī.
misrepresentation n calumnia f.
misrule n prāva administrātiō f.
miss vt (aim) aberrāre (abl); (loss)

requīrere, dēsīderāre; (notice) praetermittere ♦ n error m; (girl) virgō f.
misshapen adj distortus, dēfōrmis.
missile n tēlum nt.
missing adj absēns; **be ~** dēesse, dēsīderārī.
mission n lēgātiō f.
missive n litterae fpl.
misspend vt perdere, dissipāre.
misstatement n falsum nt, mendācium nt.
mist n nebula f, cālīgō f.
mistake n error m; (writing) mendum nt; **full of ~s** mendōsus ♦ vt: **~ for** habēre prō (abl); **be ~n** errāre, fallī.
mistletoe n viscum nt.
mistranslate vt prāvē reddere.
mistress n domina f, (school) magistra f, (lover) amīca f.
mistrust n diffīdentia f, suspīciō f ♦ vt diffīdere (dat).
mistrustful adj diffīdēns.
mistrustfully adv diffīdenter.
misty adj nebulōsus.
misunderstand vt male intellegere ♦ vi errāre.
misunderstanding n error m; (quarrel) discidium nt.
misuse n malus ūsus m ♦ vt abūtī (abl).
mite n parvulus m; (insect) vermiculus m.
mitigate vt mītigāre, lēnīre.
mitigation n mītigātiō f.
mix vt miscēre; **~ in** admiscēre; **~ together** commiscēre; **get ~ed up with** admiscērī cum, sē interpōnere (dat).
mixed adj prōmiscuus.
mixture n (act) temperātiō f; (state) dīversitās f.
mnemonic n artificium memoriae nt.
moan n gemitus m ♦ vi gemere.

moat n fossa f.

mob n vulgus nt, turba f ♦ vt circumfundī in (acc).

mobile adj mōbilis, agilis.

mobility n mōbilitas f, agilitās f.

mobilize vt (MIL) ēvocāre.

mock vt irrīdēre, lūdibriō habēre, lūdificārī; (ape) imitārī; **~ at** inlūdere ♦ n lūdibrium nt ♦ adj simulātus, fictus.

mocker n dērīsor m.

mockery n lūdibrium nt, irrīsus m.

mode n modus m, ratiō f.

model n exemplar nt, exemplum nt ♦ vt fingere.

modeller n fictor m.

moderate adj (size) modicus; (conduct) moderātus ♦ vt temperāre; (emotion) temperāre (dat) ♦ vi mītigārī.

moderately adv modicē, moderātē, mediocriter.

moderation n moderātiō f, modus m; (mean) mediocritās f.

moderator n praefectus m.

modern adj recēns.

modernity n haec aetās f.

modest adj pudīcus, verēcundus.

modestly adv verēcundē, pudenter.

modesty n pudor m, verēcundia f.

modicum n paullulum m, aliquantulum nt.

modification n mūtātiō f.

modify vt immūtāre; (law) derogāre aliquid dē.

modulate vt (voice) īnflectere.

modulation n flexiō f, inclīnātiō f.

moiety n dīmidia pars f.

moist adj ūmidus.

moisten vt ūmectāre, rigāre.

moisture n ūmor m.

molar n genuīnus m.

mole n (animal) talpa f; (on skin) naevus m; (pier) mōlēs f.

molecule n corpusculum nt.

molehill n: **make a mountain out of**

a ~ ē rīvō flūmina māgna facere, arcem facere ē cloācā.

molest vt sollicitāre, vexāre.

molestation n vexātiō f.

mollify vt mollīre, lēnīre.

molten adj liquefactus.

moment n temporis mōmentum nt, temporis pūnctum nt; **for a ~** parumper; **in a ~** iam, without a **~'s delay** nullā interpositā morā; **be of great ~** māgnō mōmentō esse; **it is of ~ interest.**

momentary adj brevis.

momentous adj gravis, māgnī mōmentī.

momentum n impetus m.

monarch n rēx m, tyrannus m.

monarchical adj rēgius.

monarchy n rēgnum nt.

monastery n monastērium nt.

monetary adj pecūniārius.

money n pecūnia f; (cash) nummī mpl; **for ~** mercēde; **ready ~** nummī, praesēns pecūnia; **make ~ rem** facere, quaestum facere.

moneybag n fiscus m.

moneyed adj nummātus, pecūniōsus.

moneylender n faenerator m.

moneymaking n quaestus m.

mongoose n ichneumōn m.

mongrel n hibrida m.

monitor n admonitor m.

monk n monachus m.

monkey n sīmia f.

monograph n libellus m.

monologue n ōrātiō f.

monopolize vt absorbēre, sibī vindicāre.

monopoly n arbitrium nt.

monosyllabic adj monosyllabus.

monosyllable n monosyllabum nt.

monotonous adj aequābilis.

monotony n taedium nt.

monster n mōnstrum nt, portentum nt, bēlua f.

monstrosity n mōnstrum nt.

monstrous adj immānis, mōnstruōsus; improbus.
month n mēnsis m.
monthly adj mēnstruus.
monument n monumentum nt.
monumental adj ingēns.
mood n affectiō f, adfectus m, animus m; (GRAM) modus m; **I am in the ~ for** libet (inf).
moody adj mōrōsus, tristis.
moon n lūna f; **new ~** interlūnium nt.
moonlight n: **by ~** ad lūnam.
moonshine n somnia ntpl.
moonstruck adj lūnāticus.
moor vt religāre ♦ n tesqua ntpl.
moorings n ancorae fpl.
moot n conventus m; **it is a ~ point** discrepat ♦ vt iactāre.
mop n pēniculus m ♦ vt dētergēre.
mope vi maerēre.
moral adj honestus, probus; (opposed to physical) animī; (PHILOS) mōrālis ♦ n documentum nt.
morale n animus m; **~ is low** iacet animus.
morality n bonī mōrēs mpl, virtūs f.
moralize vi dē officiīs disserere.
morally adv honestē.
morals npl mōrēs mpl.
morass n palūs f.
moratorium n mora f.
morbid adj aeger.
mordant adj mordāx.
more adj plūs, plūris (in sg + gen, in pl + adj) ♦ adv plūs, magis, amplius; (extra) ultrā; **~ than** amplius quam; **~ than three feet** amplius trēs pedēs; **~ and ~** magis magisque; **never ~** immō; **~ or less** ferē; **no ~** (time) nōn diūtius, nunquam posteā.
moreover adv tamen, autem, praetereā.
moribund adj moribundus.
morning n māne nt; **early in the ~** bene māne; **this ~** hodiē māne;

good ~ salvē ♦ adj mātūtīnus.
morning call n salūtātiō f.
morning watch n (NAUT) tertia vigilia f.
moron n sōcors m.
morose adj acerbus, tristis.
moroseness n acerbitās f, tristitia f.
morrow n posterus diēs m; **on the ~** posterō diē, postrīdiē.
morsel n offa f.
mortal adj mortālis, hūmānus; (wound) mortifer ♦ n mortālis m/f, homō m/f; **poor ~** homunculus m.
mortality n mortālitās f; (death) mors f; **the ~ was high** plūrimī periērunt.
mortally adv: **be ~ wounded** mortiferum vulnus accipere.
mortar n mortārium nt.
mortgage n pignus nt, fīdūcia f ♦ vt obligāre.
mortification n dolor m, angor m.
mortified adj: **be ~ at** aegrē ferre.
mortify vt mordēre, vexāre; (lust) coercēre ♦ vi putrēscere.
mortise vt immittere.
mosaic n emblēma nt, lapillī mpl ♦ adj tessellātus.
mosquito n culex m.
mosquito net n cōnōpēum nt.
moss n muscus m.
mossy adj muscōsus.
most adj plūrimus, plērusque; **for the ~ part** māximam partem ♦ adv māximē, plūrimum.
mostly adv plērumque, ferē.
mote n corpusculum nt.
moth n tinea f.
mother n māter f; **of a ~** māternus.
mother-in-law n socrus f.
motherless adj mātre orbus.
motherly adj māternus.
mother tongue n patrius sermō m.
mother wit n Minerva f.
motif n argūmentum nt.
motion n mōtus m; (for law) rogātiō

f; (*in debate*) sententia f; **propose a ~** ferre; **set in ~** movēre ♦ *vt* innuere.

motionless *adj* immōbilis.

motive *n* causa f, ratiō f; **I know your ~ in asking** sciō cūr rogēs.

motley *adj* versicolor, varius.

mottled *adj* maculōsus.

motto *n* sententia f.

mould *n* fōrma f; (*soil*) humus f; (*fungus*) mūcor m ♦ *vt* fingere, fōrmāre.

moulder *vi* putrēscere ♦ *n* fictor m.

mouldering *adj* puter.

mouldiness *n* situs m.

mouldy *adj* mūcidus.

moult *vi* pennas exuere.

mound *n* agger m, tumulus m.

mount *n* mōns m; (*horse*) equus m ♦ *vt* scandere, cōnscendere, ascendere ♦ *vi* ascendere; **~ up** ēscendere.

mountain *n* mōns m.

mountaineer *n* montānus m.

mountainous *adj* montuōsus.

mourn *vi* maerēre, lūgēre ♦ *vt* dēflēre, lūgēre.

mourner *n* plōrātor m; (*hired*) praefica f.

mournful *adj* (*cause*) lūctuōsus, acerbus; (*sound*) lūgubris, maestus.

mournfully *adv* maestē.

mourning *n* maeror nt, lūctus m; (*dress*) sordēs fpl; **in ~** fūnestus; **be in ~** lūgēre; **put on ~** vestem mūtāre, sordēs suscipere; **wearing ~** ātrātus.

mouse *n* mūs m.

mousetrap *n* mūscipulum nt.

mouth *n* ōs nt; (*river*) ōstium nt.

mouthful *n* bucca f.

mouthpiece *n* interpres m.

movable *adj* mōbilis ♦ *npl*: **~s** rēs fpl, supellex f.

move *vt* movēre; (*emotion*)

commovēre; **~ backwards and forwards** reciprocāre; **~ out of the way** dēmovēre; **~ up** admovēre ♦ *vi* movērī; (*residence*) dēmigrāre; (*proposal*) ferre, cēnsēre; **~ into** immigrāre in (*acc*); **~ on** prōgredī.

movement *n* mōtus m; (*process*) cursus m; (*society*) societās f.

mover *n* auctor m.

moving *adj* flēbilis, flexanimus.

mow *vt* secāre, dēmetere.

mower *n* faenisex m.

much *adj* multus ♦ *adv* multum; (*with compar*) multō; **as ~ as** tantum quantum; **so ~** tantum; (*with verbs*) adeō; **~ less** nēdum; **too ~** nimis ♦ *n* multum nt.

muck *n* stercus nt.

mud *n* lutum nt.

muddle *n* turba f ♦ *vt* turbāre.

muffle *vt* involvere; **~ up** obvolvere.

muffled *adj* surdus.

mug *n* pōculum nt.

mulberry *n* mōrum nt; (*tree*) mōrus f.

mule *n* mūlus m.

muleteer *n* mūliō m.

mulish *adj* obstinātus.

mullet *n* mullus m.

multifarious *adj* multiplex, varius.

multiform *adj* multifōrmis.

multiply *vt* multiplicāre ♦ *vi* crēscere.

multitude *n* multitūdō f.

multitudinous *adj* crēberrimus.

mumble *vt* (*words*) opprimere ♦ *vi* murmurāre.

munch *vt* mandūcāre.

mundane *adj* terrestris.

municipal *adj* mūnicipālis.

municipality *n* mūnicipium nt.

munificence *n* largitās f.

munificent *adj* largus, mūnificus.

munificently *adv* mūnificē.

munitions *n* bellī adparātus m.

mural adj mūrālis.

murder n parricīdium nt, caedēs f; **charge with ~** inter sīcāriōs accūsāre; **trial for ~** quaestiō inter sīcāriōs ♦ vt interficere, iūgulāre, necāre.

murderer n sīcārius m, homicīda m, parricīda m, percussor m.

murderess n interfectrīx f.

murderous adj cruentus.

murky adj tenebrōsus.

murmur n murmur nt; (angry) fremitus m ♦ vi murmurāre; fremere.

murmuring n admurmurātiō f.

muscle n torus m.

muscular adj lacertōsus.

muse vi meditārī ♦ n Mūsa f.

mushroom n fungus m, bōlētus m.

music n (art) mūsica f; (sound) cantus m, modī mpl.

musical adj (person) mūsicus; (sound) canōrus.

musician n mūsicus m; (strings) fidicen m; (wind) tībīcen m.

muslin n sindōn f.

must n (wine) mustum nt ♦ vi dēbēre; **I ~ go** mē oportet īre, mihi eundum est.

mustard n sināpi nt.

muster vt convocāre, cōgere; (review) recēnsēre ♦ vi convenīre, coīre ♦ n conventus m; (review) recēnsiō f.

muster roll n album nt.

mustiness n situs m.

musty adj mūcidus.

mutability n incōnstantia f.

mutable adj incōnstāns, mūtābilis.

mute adj mūtus.

mutilate vt mūtilāre, truncāre.

mutilated adj mutilus, truncus.

mutilation n lacerātiō f.

mutineer n sēditiōsus m.

mutinous adj sēditiōsus.

mutiny n sēditiō f ♦ vi sēditiōnem facere.

mutter vi mussitāre.

mutton n carō ovilla f.

mutual adj mūtuus.

mutually adv mūtuō, inter sē.

muzzle n ōs nt, rōstrum nt; (guard) fiscella f ♦ vt fiscellā capistrāre.

my adj meus.

myriad n decem mīlia; (any large no.) sēscentī.

myrmidon n satelles m.

myrrh n murra f.

myrtle n myrtus f ♦ adj myrteus.

myrtle grove n myrtētum nt.

myself pron ipse, egomet; (reflexive) mē.

mysterious adj arcānus, occultus.

mysteriously adv occultē.

mystery n arcānum nt; (rites) mystēria ntpl; (fig) latebra f.

mystic adj mysticus.

mystical adj mysticus.

mystification n fraus f, ambāgēs fpl.

mystify vt fraudāre, cōnfundere.

myth n fābula f.

mythical adj fābulōsus.

mythology n fābulae fpl.

N

nabob n rēx m.

nadir n fundus m.

nag n caballus m ♦ vt obiūrgitāre.

naiad n nāias f.

nail n clāvus m; (finger) unguis m; **hit the ~ on the head** rem acū tangere ♦ vt clāvīs adfīgere.

naive adj simplex.

naively adv simpliciter.

naiveté n simplicitās f.

naked adj nūdus.

nakedly adv apertē.

name n nōmen nt; (repute) existimātiō f; (term) vocābulum nt; **by ~** nōmine, nōminātim; **have a bad ~** male audīre; **have a good ~** bene audīre; **in the ~ of** verbīs (gen) (*oath*) per ♦ vt appellāre, vocāre, nōmināre; (*appoint*) dīcere.

nameless adj nōminis expers, sine nōmine.

namely adv nempe, dīcō.

namesake n gentilis m/f.

nanny goat n capra f.

nap n brevis somnus m; (*cloth*) villus nt.

napkin n linteum nt.

narcissus n narcissus m.

narcotic adj somnifer.

nard n nardus f.

narrate vt nārrāre, ēnārrāre.

narration n nārrātiō f.

narrative n fābula f.

narrator n nārrātor m.

narrow adj angustus ♦ vt coartāre ♦ vi coartārī.

narrowly adv aegrē, vix.

narrowness n angustiae fpl.

narrows n angustiae fpl.

nasal adj nārium.

nascent adj nāscēns.

nastily adv foedē.

nastiness n foediātas f.

nasty adj foedus, taeter, impūrus.

natal adj nātālis.

nation n populus m; (*foreign*) gēns f.

national adj pūblicus, cīvīlis; (*affairs*) domesticus.

nationality n cīvitās f.

native adj indigena; (*speech*) patrius ♦ n incola m, indigena m/f.

native land n patria f.

nativity n ortus m.

natural adj nātūrālis; (*innate*) nātīvus, genuīnus, īnsitus.

naturalization n cīvitās f.

naturalize vt cīvitāte dōnāre.

naturalized adj (*person*) cīvitāte dōnātus; (*thing*) īnsitus.

naturally adv nātūrāliter, secundum nātūram; (*of course*) scīlicet, certē.

nature n nātūra f; rērum nātūra f;

(*character*) indolēs f, ingenium nt; (*species*) genus nt; **course of** ~ nātūra f; **I know the** ~ **of** sciō quālis sit.

naught n nihil nt; **set at** ~ parvī facere.

naughty adj improbus.

nausea n nausea f; (*fig*) fastīdium nt.

nauseate vt fastīdium movēre (*dat*); **be** ~**d with** fastīdīre.

nauseous adj taeter.

nautical adj nauticus, maritimus.

naval adj nāvālis.

navel n umbilīcus m.

navigable adj nāvigābilis.

navigate vt, vi nāvigāre.

navigation n rēs nautica f; (*sailing*) nāvigātiō f.

navigator n nauta m, gubernātor m.

navy n classis f, cōpiae nāvālēs fpl.

nay adv nōn; ~ **more** immo.

near adv prope ♦ adj propinquus ♦ prep prope (*acc*), ad (*acc*); **lie** ~ adiacēre (*dat*) ♦ vt adpropinquāre (*dat*).

nearby adj iuxtā.

nearer adj propior.

nearest adj proximus.

nearly adv paene, prope, fermē.

neat adj nitidus, mundus, concinnus; (*wine*) pūrus.

neatly adv mundē, concinnē.

neatness n munditia f.

nebulous adj nebulōsus; (*fig*) incertus.

necessaries n rēs ad vīvendum necessāriae fpl.

necessarily adv necessāriō, necesse.

necessary adj necessārius, necesse; **it is** ~ oportet (+ *acc and infin* or *gerundive* of vt).

necessitate vt cōgere (*inf*), efficere ut (*subj*).

necessitous adj egēnus, pauper.

necessity n necessitās f; (thing) rēs
  necessāria f; (want) paupertās f,
  egestās f.
neck n collum nt.
neckcloth n fōcāle nt.
necklace n monīle nt, torquis m.
nectar n nectar nt.
need n (necessity) necessitās f;
  (want) egestās f, inopia f,
  indigentia f; **there is ~ of** opus est
  (abl); **there is no ~ to** nihil est
  quod, cūr (subj) ♦ vt egēre (abl),
  carēre, indigēre (abl); **I ~** opus est
  mihī (abl).
needful adj necessārius.
needle n acus f.
needless adj vānus, inūtilis.
needlessly adv frustrā, sine causā.
needs adv necesse ♦ npl
  necessitātēs fpl.
needy adj egēns, inops, pauper.
nefarious adj nefārius, scelestus.
negation n negātiō f, īnfitiātiō f.
negative adj negāns ♦ n negātiō f;
  answer in the ~ vt negāre ♦ vt
  vetāre, contrādīcere (dat).
neglect n neglegentia f, incūria f;
  (of duty) dērelictiō f ♦ vt
  neglegere, ōmittere.
neglectful adj neglegēns,
  immemor.
negligence n neglegentia f, incūria
  f.
negligent adj neglegēns,
  indīligēns.
negligently adv neglegenter,
  indīligenter.
negligible adj levissimus, minimī
  mōmentī.
negotiate vi agere dē ♦ vt (deal)
  peragere; (difficulty) superāre.
negotiation n āctiō f, pactum nt.
negotiator n lēgātus m, conciliātor
  m.
negro n Aethiops m.
neigh vi hinnīre.
neighbour n vīcīnus m,

fīnitimus m.
neighbourhood n vīcīnia f,
  vīcīnitās f.
neighbouring adj vīcīnus,
  finitimus, propinquus.
neighbourly adj hūmānus, amīcus.
neighing n hinnītus m.
neither adv neque, nec; nēve, neu
  ♦ pron neuter ♦ adj neuter,
  neutra, neutrum (like alter); **~ ...
  nor** nec/neque ... nec/neque.
neophyte n tīrō m.
nephew n frātris fīlius m, sorōris
  fīlius m.
Nereid n Nērēis f.
nerve n nervus m; (fig) audācia f;
  ~s pl pavor m, trepidātiō f; **have
  the ~ to** audēre ♦ vt cōnfirmāre.
nervous adj diffīdēns, sollicitus,
  trepidus.
nervously adv trepidē.
nervousness n sollicitūdō f,
  diffīdentia f.
nest n nīdus m ♦ vi nīdificāre.
nestle vi recubāre.
nestling n pullus m.
net n rēte nt ♦ vt inrētīre.
nether adj īnferior.
nethermost adj īnfimus, īmus.
netting n rēticulum nt.
nettle n urtīca f ♦ vt inrītāre,
  ūrere.
neuter adj neuter.
neutral adj medius; **be ~** neutrī
  partī sē adiungere, medium sē
  gerere.
neutralize vt compēnsāre.
never adv nunquam.
nevertheless adv nihilōminus, at
  tamen.
new adj novus, integer, recēns.
newcomer n advena m/f.
newfangled adj novus, inaudītus.
newly adv nūper, modo.
newness n novitās f.
news n nūntius m; **what ~?** quid
  novī?; **~ was brought that**

nūntiātum est (+ *acc and infin*).

newspaper *n* ācta diūrna/pūblica *ntpl*.

newt *n* lacerta *f*.

next *adj* proximus; (*time*) īnsequēns ♦ *adv* deinde, deinceps; ~ **day** postrīdiē; ~ **to** iuxtā; **come** ~ **to** excipere.

nibble *vi* rōdere.

nice *adj* bellus, dulcis; (*exact*) accūrātus; (*particular*) fastīdiōsus.

nicely *adv* bellē, probē.

nicety *n* subtīlitās *f*.

niche *n* aedicula *f*.

nick *n:* **in the ~ of time** in ipsō articulō temporis.

nickname *n* cognōmen *nt*.

niece *n* frātris fīlia *f*, sorōris fīlia *f*.

niggardliness *n* illīberālitās *f*, avāritia *f*.

niggardly *adj* illīberālis, parcus, avārus.

nigh *adv* prope.

night *n* nox *f*; **by** ~ noctū; **all** ~ pernox; **spend the** ~ pernoctāre; **be awake all** ~ pervigilāre ♦ *adj* nocturnus.

night bird *n* noctua *f*.

nightfall *n* prīmae tenebrae *fpl*; **at** ~ sub noctem.

nightingale *n* luscinia *f*.

nightly *adj* nocturnus ♦ *adv* noctū.

nightmare *n* incubus *m*.

night work *n* lūcubrātiō *f*.

nimble *adj* agilis, pernīx.

nimbleness *n* agilitās *f*, pernīcitās *f*; (*mind*) argūtiae *fpl*.

nimbly *adv* pernīciter.

nine *num* novem; ~ **each** novēnī; ~ **times** noviēns; ~ **days'** novendiālis.

nine hundred *num* nōngentī.

nine hundredth *adj* nōngentēsimus.

nineteen *num* ūndēvigintī; ~ **each** ūndēvīcēnī; ~ **times** deciēns et noviēns.

nineteenth *adj* ūndēvīcēsimus.

ninetieth *adj* nōnāgēsimus.

ninety *num* nōnāgintā; ~ **each** nōnāgēnī; ~ **times** nōnāgiēns.

ninth *adj* nōnus.

nip *vt* vellicāre; (*frost*) ūrere.

nippers *n* forceps *m*.

nipple *n* papilla *f*.

no *adv* nōn; (*correcting*) immo; **say** ~ negāre ♦ *adj* nullus.

nobility *n* nōbilitās *f*; (*persons*) optimātēs *mpl*, nōbilēs *mpl*.

noble *adj* nōbilis; (*birth*) generōsus; (*appearance*) decōrus.

nobleman *n* prīnceps *m*, optimās *m*.

nobly *adv* nōbiliter, praeclārē.

nobody *n* nēmō *m*.

nocturnal *adj* nocturnus.

nod *n* nūtus *m* ♦ *vi* nūtāre; (*sign*) adnuere; (*sleep*) dormītāre.

noddle *n* caput *nt*.

node *n* nōdus *m*.

noise *n* strepitus *m*, sonitus *m*; (*loud*) fragor *m*; **make a** ~ increpāre, strepere ♦ *vt:* ~ **abroad** ēvulgāre; **be** ~**d abroad** percrēbrēscere.

noiseless *adj* tacitus.

noiselessly *adv* tacitē.

noisily *adv* cum strepitū.

noisome *adj* taeter, gravis.

noisy *adj* clāmōsus.

nomadic *adj* vagus.

nomenclature *n* vocābula *ntpl*.

nominally *adv* nōmine, verbō.

nominate *vt* nōmināre, dīcere; (*in writing*) scrībere.

nomination *n* nōminātiō *f*.

nominative *adj* nōminātīvus.

nominee *n* nōminātus *m*.

nonappearance *n* absentia *f*.

nonce *n:* **for the** ~ semel.

nonchalance *n* aequus animus *m*.

nonchalantly *adv* aequō animō.

noncombatant *adj* imbellis.

noncommittal *adj* circumspectus.

nondescript *adj* īnsolitus.
none *adj* nūllus ♦ *pron* nēmō *m*.
nonentity *n* nihil *nt*, nūllus *m*.
nones *n* Nōnae *fpl*.
nonexistent *adj* quī nōn est.
nonplus *vt* ad incitās redigere.
nonresistance *n* patientia *f*.
nonsense *n* nūgae *fpl*, ineptiae *fpl*.
nonsensical *adj* ineptus, absurdus.
nook *n* angulus *m*.
noon *n* merīdiēs *m* ♦ *adj* merīdiānus.
no one *pron* nēmō *m* (*for gen/abl use* nūllus).
noose *n* laqueus *m*.
nor *adv* neque, nec; nēve, neu.
norm *n* nōrma *f*.
normal *adj* solitus.
normally *adv* plērumque.
north *n* septentriōnēs *mpl* ♦ *adj* septentriōnālis.
northeast *adv* inter septentriōnēs et orientem.
northerly *adj* septentriōnālis.
northern *adj* septentriōnālis.
North Pole *n* arctos *f*.
northwards *adv* ad septentriōnēs versus.
northwest *adv* inter septentriōnēs et occidentem ♦ *adj*: **~ wind** Cōrus *m*.
north wind *n* aquilō *m*.
nose *n* nāsus *m*, nārēs *fpl*; **blow the ~** ēmungere; **lead by the ~** labiīs ductāre ♦ *vi* scrūtārī.
nostril *n* nāris *f*.
not *adv* nōn, haud; **~ at all** haudquāquam; **~ as if** nōn quod, nōn quō; **~ but what** nōn quīn; **~ even** nē … quidem; **~ so very** nōn ita; **~ that** nōn quō; **and ~** neque; **does ~, did ~** (*interrog*) nonne; **if … ~** nisi; **that ~** (*purpose*) nē; (*fear*) nē nōn; **~ long after** haud multō post; **~ only … but also** nōn modo/ sōlum … sed etiam; **~ yet** nōndum.

notability *n* vir praeclārus *m*.
notable *adj* īnsignis, īnsignītus, memorābilis.
notably *adv* īnsignītē.
notary *n* scrība *m*.
notation *n* notae *fpl*.
notch *n* incīsūra *f* ♦ *vt* incīdere.
note *n* (*mark*) nota *f*; (*comment*) adnotātiō *f*; (*letter*) litterulae *fpl*; (*sound*) vōx *f*; **make a ~ of** in commentāriōs referre ♦ *vt* notāre; (*observe*) animadvertere.
notebook *n* pugillārēs *mpl*.
noted *adj* īnsignis, praeclārus, nōtus.
noteworthy *adj* memorābilis.
nothing *n* nihil, nīl *nt*; **~ but** merus, nīl nisi; **come to ~** in irritum cadere; **for ~** frūstrā; (*gift*) grātīs, grātuītō; **good for ~** nēquam; **think ~ of** nihilī facere.
notice *n* (*official*) prōscrīptiō *f*; (*private*) libellus *m*; **attract ~** cōnspicī; **escape ~** latēre; **escape the ~ of** fallere; **give ~ of** dēnūntiāre; **take ~ of** animadvertere ♦ *vt* animadvertere, cōnspicere.
noticeable *adj* cōnspicuus, īnsignis.
noticeably *adv* īnsignītē.
notification *n* dēnūntiātiō *f*.
notify *vt* (*event*) dēnūntiāre, indicāre; (*person*) renūntiāre (*dat*), certiōrem facere.
notion *n* nōtiō *f*, īnfōrmātiō *f*, suspiciō *f*.
notoriety *n* īnfāmia *f*.
notorious *adj* fāmōsus, īnfāmis; (*thing*) manifestus.
notoriously *adv* manifestō.
notwithstanding *adv* nihilōminus, tamen ♦ *prep*: **~ the danger** in tantō discrīmine.
nought *n* nihil, nīl *nt*.
noun *n* nōmen *nt*.
nourish *vt* alere, nūtrīre.

nourisher n altor m, altrīx f.

nourishment n cibus m, alimenta ntpl.

novel adj novus, inaudītus ♦ n fābella f.

novelty n rēs nova f; novitās f, īnsolentia f.

November n mēnsis November m; of ~ November.

novice n tīrō m.

now adv nunc; (past) iam; ~ **and then** interdum; just ~ nunc; (lately) dūdum, modo; ~...~ modo ...modo ♦ conj at, autem.

nowadays adv nunc, hodiē.

nowhere adv nusquam.

nowise adv nullō modō, haudquāquam.

noxious adj nocēns, noxius.

nuance n color m.

nucleus n sēmen nt.

nude adj nūdus.

nudge vt fodicāre.

nudity n nūdātum corpus nt.

nugget n massa f.

nuisance n malum nt, incommodum nt.

null adj inritus.

nullify vt inritum facere; (law) abrogāre.

numb adj torpēns, torpidus; be ~ torpēre; become ~ torpēscere.

number n numerus m; a ~ of complūrēs, aliquot; a great ~ multitūdō f, frequentia f; a small ~ īnfrequentia f; in large ~s frequentēs ♦ vt numerāre, ēnumerāre.

numberless adj innumerābilis.

numbness n torpor m.

numerous adj frequēns, crēber, plūrimī.

nun n monacha f.

nuptial adj nūptiālis.

nuptials n nūptiae fpl.

nurse n nūtrīx f ♦ vt (child) nūtrīre; (sick) cūrāre; (fig) fovēre.

nursery n (children) cubiculum nt; (plants) sēminārium nt.

nursling n alumnus m, alumna f.

nurture n ēducātiō f.

nut n nux f.

nutrition n alimenta ntpl.

nutritious adj salūbris.

nutshell n putāmen nt.

nut tree n nux f.

nymph n nympha f.

O

O interj ō!

oaf n agrestis m.

oak n quercus f; (evergreen) īlex f; (timber) rōbur nt ♦ adj quernus, īlignus, rōboreus; ~ **forest** quercētum nt.

oakum n stuppa f.

oar n rēmus m.

oarsman n rēmex m.

oaten adj avēnāceus.

oath n iūsiūrandum nt; (MIL) sacrāmentum nt; (imprecation) exsecrātiō f; false ~ periūrium nt; take an ~ iūrāre; take an ~ of allegiance to in verba iūrāre (gen).

oats n avēna f.

obduracy n obstinātus animus m.

obdurate adj obstinātus, pervicāx.

obdurately adv obstinātē.

obedience n oboedientia f, obsequium n.

obedient adj oboediēns, obsequēns; be ~ to pārēre (dat), obtemperāre (dat), obsequī (dat).

obediently adv oboedienter.

obeisance n obsequium nt; make ~ to adōrāre.

obelisk n obeliscus m.

obese adj obēsus, pinguis.

obesity n obēsitās f, pinguitūdō f.

obey vt pārēre (dat), obtemperāre (dat), oboedīre (dat); ~ **orders** dictō pārēre.

obituary n mortēs fpl.
object n rēs f; (aim) fīnis m,
prōpositum nt; **be an ~ of hate**
odiō esse; **with what ~** quō
cōnsiliō ♦ vi recūsāre, gravārī;
but, it is ~ed at enim; **~ to**
improbāre.
objection n recūsātiō f, mora f; **I
have no ~** nīl moror.
objectionable adj invīsus,
iniūcundus.
objective vt obiūrgāre ♦ n
prōpositum nt, fīnis m.
objurgate vt obiūrgāre, culpāre.
oblation n dōnum nt.
obligation n (legal) dēbitum nt;
(moral) officium nt; **lay under an ~**
obligāre, obstringere.
obligatory adj dēbitus,
necessārius.
oblige vt (force) cōgere; (contract)
obligāre, obstringere;
(compliance) mōrem gerere (dat);
mōrigerārī (dat); **I am ~d to**
(action) dēbeō (inf); (person) amāre,
grātiam habēre (dat).
obliging adj cōmis, officiōsus.
obligingly adv cōmiter, officiōsē.
oblique adj oblīquus.
obliquely adv oblīquē.
obliquity n (moral) prāvitās f.
obliterate vt dēlēre, oblitterāre.
obliteration n litūra f.
oblivion n oblīviō f.
oblivious adj oblīviōsus,
immemor.
oblong adj oblongus.
obloquy n vituperātiō f,
opprobrium nt.
obnoxious adj invīsus.
obscene adj obscaenus, impūrus.
obscenity n obscaenitās f,
impūritās f.
obscure adj obscūrus, caecus ♦ vt
obscūrāre, officere (dat).
obscurely adv obscūrē; (speech)
per ambāgēs.

obscurity n obscūritās f; (speech)
ambāgēs fpl.
obsequies n exsequiae fpl.
obsequious adj officiōsus,
ambitiōsus.
obsequiously adv officiōsē.
obsequiousness n adsentātiō f.
observance n observantia f; (rite)
rītus m.
observant adj attentus, dīligēns.
observation n observātiō f,
animadversiō f; (remark) dictum
nt.
observe vt animadvertere,
contemplārī; (see) cernere,
cōnspicere; (remark) dīcere;
(adhere to) cōnservāre, observāre.
observer n spectātor m,
contemplātor m.
obsess vt occupāre; **I am ~ed by**
tōtus sum in (abl).
obsession n studium nt.
obsolescent adj: **be ~** obsolēscere.
obsolete adj obsolētus; **become ~**
exolēscere.
obstacle n impedīmentum nt, mora
f.
obstinacy n pertinācia f,
obstinātus animus m.
obstinate adj pertināx, obstinātus.
obstinately adv obstinātō animō.
obstreperous adj clāmōsus, ferus.
obstruct vt impedīre, obstruere,
obstāre (dat); (POL) intercēdere
(dat); (fig) officere (dat).
obstruction n impedīmentum nt;
(POL) intercessiō f
obstructionist n intercessor m.
obtain vt adipīscī, nancīscī,
cōnsequī; comparāre; (by request)
impetrāre ♦ vi tenēre, obtinēre.
obtrude vi sē inculcāre ♦ vt
ingerere.
obtrusive adj importūnus,
molestus.
obtuse adj hebes, stolidus.
obtusely adv stolidē.

obtuseness n stupor m.

obverse adj obversus.

obviate vt tollere, praevertere.

obvious adj ēvidēns, manifestus, apertus; **it is ~** appāret.

obviously adv ēvidenter, apertē, manifestō.

occasion n occāsiō f, locus m; (reason) causa f ♦ vt movēre, facessere, auctōrem esse (gen).

occasional adj fortuītus.

occasionally adv interdum, nōnnunquam.

occidental adj occidentālis.

occult adj arcānus.

occupancy n possessiō f

occupant n habitātor m, possessor m.

occupation n quaestus m, occupātiō f.

occupier n possessor m.

occupy vt possidēre, (MIL) occupāre; (space) complēre; (attention) distinēre, occupāre.

occur vi ēvenīre, accidere; (to mind) occurrere, in mentem venīre.

occurrence n ēventum nt; rēs f.

ocean n mare nt, ōceanus m.

October n mēnsis October m; **of ~** October.

ocular adj oculōrum; **give ~ proof of** ante oculōs pōnere, videntī dēmōnstrāre.

odd adj (number) impār; (moment) subsecīvus; (appearance) novus, īnsolitus.

oddity n novitās f; (person) homō rīdiculus m.

oddly adv mīrum in modum.

odds n praestantīa f; **be at ~ with** dissidēre cum; **the ~ are against us** imparēs sumus; **the ~ are in our favour** superiōrēs sumus.

ode n carmen nt.

odious adj invīsus, odiōsus.

odium n invidia f.

odorous adj odōrātus.

odour n odor m.

of prep gen; (origin) ex, dē; (cause) abl; **all ~us** nōs omnēs; **the city ~ Rome** urbs Rōma.

off adv procul; (prefix) ab-; **~ and on** interdum; **~ with you** aufer tē; **come ~** ēvādere; **well ~** beātus; **well ~ for** abundāns (abl).

offal n quisquiliae fpl.

offence n offēnsiō f; (legal) dēlictum nt; **commit an ~** dēlinquere.

offend vt laedere, offendere; **be ~ed** aegrē ferre ♦ vi dēlinquere; **~ against** peccāre in (acc), violāre.

offender n reus m.

offensive adj odiōsus; (smell) gravis; (language) contumēliōsus; **take the ~** bellum īnferre.

offensively adv odiōsē; graviter.

offer vt offerre, dare, praebēre; (hand) porrigere; (violence) adferre; (honour) dēferre; (with verb) prōfitērī, pollicērī ♦ n condiciō f; **~ for sale** venditāre.

offering n dōnum nt; (to the dead) īnferiae fpl.

off-hand adj neglegēns, incūriōsus.

office n (POL) magistrātus m, mūnus nt, honōs m; (kindness) officium nt; (place) mēnsa f.

officer n praefectus m, lēgātus m.

official adj pūblicus ♦ n adiūtor m, minister m.

officially adv pūblicē.

officiate vi operārī, officiō fungī.

officious adj molestus.

officiously adv molestē.

officiousness n occursātiō f.

offing n: **in the ~** procul.

offset vt compēnsāre.

offspring n prōgeniēs f, līberī mpl; (animal) fētus m.

often adv saepe, saepenumerō; **as ~ as** quotiēs; **totiēs ... quotiēs;** **how ~?** quotiēns?; **so ~** totiēns;

very ~ persaepe.

ogle *vi*: **at** līmīs oculīs intuērī.

ogre *n* mōnstrum *nt*.

oh *interj* (*joy, surprise*) ōh!; (*sorrow*) prō!

oil *n* oleum *nt* ♦ *vt* ungere.

oily *adj* oleōsus.

ointment *n* unguentum *nt*.

old *adj* (*person*) senex; (*thing*) vetus; (*ancient*) antīquus, prīscus; **~ age** senectūs *f*; **be ten years ~** decem annōs habēre; **ten years ~** decem annōs nātus; **two years ~** bīmus; **good ~** antīquus; **good ~ days** antīquitās *f*; **grow ~** senēscere; **of ~** quondam.

olden *adj* prīscus, prīstinus.

older *adj* nātū māior, senior.

oldest *adj* nātū māximus.

old-fashioned *adj* antīquus, obsolētus.

old man *n* senex *m*.

oldness *n* vetustās *f*.

old woman *n* anus *f*.

oligarchy *n* paucōrum dominātiō *f*, optimātium factiō *f*.

olive *n* olea *f*; **~ orchard** olīvētum *nt*.

Olympiad *n* Olympias *f*.

Olympic *adj* Olympicus; **win an ~ victory** Olympia vincere.

Olympic Games *n* Olympia *ntpl*.

omen *n* ōmen *nt*, auspicium *nt*; **announce a bad ~** obnūntiāre; **obtain favourable ~s** litāre.

ominous *adj* īnfaustus, mināx.

omission *n* praetermissiō *f*, neglegentia *f*.

omit *vt* ōmittere, praetermittere.

omnipotence *n* īnfīnīta potestās *f*.

omnipotent *adj* omnipotēns.

on *prep* (*place*) in (*abl*), in- (*prefix*); (*time*) *abl*; (*coast of*) ad (*acc*); (*subject*) dē (*abl*); (*side*) ab (*abl*) ♦ *adv* porrō, usque; **and so ~** ac deinceps; **~ hearing the news** nūntiō acceptō; **~ equal terms** (*in*

battle) aequō Marte; **~ the following day** posterō/proximō diē; postrīdiē; **~ this side of** citrā (+ *acc*).

once *adv* semel; (*past*) ōlim, quondam; **at ~** extemplō, statim; (*together*) simul; **for ~** aliquandō; **~ and for all** semel; **~ more** dēnuō, iterum; **~ upon a time** ōlim, quondam.

one *num* ūnus ♦ *pron* quīdam; (*of two*) alter, altera, alterum; **~ and the same** ūnus; **~ another** inter sē, alius alium; **~ or the other** alteruter; **~ day** ōlim; **~ each** singulī; **~ would have thought** crēderēs; **be ~ of** in numerō esse (*gen*); **be at ~** idem sentīre; **it is all ~** nihil interest; **the ~** alter, hic; **this is the ~** hōc illud est.

one-eyed *adj* luscus.

oneness *n* ūnitās *f*.

onerous *adj* gravis.

oneself *pron* ipse; (*reflexive*) sē.

one-sided *adj* inaequālis, inīquus.

onion *n* caepe *nt*.

onlooker *n* spectātor *m*.

only *adj* ūnus, sōlus; (*son*) ūnicus ♦ *adv* sōlum, tantum, modo; (*with clause*) nōn nisi, nīl nisi, nihil aliud quam; (*time*) dēmum; **if ~** sī modo; (*wish*) utinam.

onrush *n* incursus *m*.

onset *n* impetus *m*.

onslaught *n* incursus *m*; **make an ~ on** (*words*) invehī in (*acc*).

onto *prep* in (+ *acc*).

onus *n* officium *nt*.

onward, onwards *adv* porrō.

onyx *n* onyx *m*.

ooze *vi* mānāre, stillāre.

opaque *adj* haud perlūcidus.

open *adj* apertus; (*wide*) patēns, hiāns; (*ground*) pūrus, apertus; (*question*) integer; **lie ~** patēre; **stand ~** hiāre; **throw ~** adaperīre, patefacere; **it is ~ to me to** mihī

integrum est (*inf*); **while the
question is still ~ rē integrā ♦** *vt*
aperīre, patefacere; (*book*)
ēvolvere; (*letter*) resolvere;
(*speech*) exōrdīrī; (*with ceremony*)
inaugurāre; (*will*) resignāre ♦ *vi*
aperīrī, hīscere; (*sore*)
recrūdēscere; **~ out** extendere,
pandere; **~ up** (*country*) aperīre.

open air *n*: **in the ~** sub dīvō.

open-handed *adj* largus,
mūnificus.

open-handedness *n* largitās *f.*

open-hearted *adj* ingenuus.

opening *n* forāmen *nt*, hiātus *m*;
(*ceremony*) cōnsecrātiō *f*;
(*opportunity*) occāsiō *f*, ānsa *f* ♦ *adj*
prīmus.

openly *adv* palam, apertē.

open-mouthed *adj*: **stand ~ at**
inhiāre.

operate *vi* rem gerere ♦ *vt*
movēre.

operation *n* opus *nt*, āctiō *f*; (*MED*)
sectiō *f.*

operative *adj* efficax.

ophthalmia *n* lippitūdō *f.*

opiate *adj* somnifer.

opine *vi* opīnārī, existimāre.

opinion *n* sententia *f*; (*of person*)
existimātiō *f*; **public ~**: **in my ~** meō iūdiciō, meō animō.

opponent *n* adversārius *m*, hostis
m.

opportune *adj* opportūnus,
tempestīvus.

opportunely *adv* opportūnē.

opportunity *n* occāsiō *f*; (*to act*)
facultās *f*, potestās *f.*

oppose *vt* (*barrier*) obicere;
(*contrast*) oppōnere ♦ *vi* adversārī
(*dat*), resistere (*dat*), obstāre (*dat*);
be ~d to adversārī (*dat*); (*opinion*)
dīversum esse ab.

opposite *adj* (*facing*) adversus;
(*contrary*) contrārius, dīversus
♦ *prep* contrā (*acc*), adversus (*acc*);

directly ~ ē regiōne (*gen*) ♦ *adv* ex
adversō.

opposition *n* repugnantia *f*; (*party*)
factiō adversa *f.*

oppress *vt* opprimere, adflīgere;
(*burden*) premere, onerāre.

oppression *n* iniūria *f*, servitūs *f.*

oppressive *adj* gravis, inīquus;
become more ~ ingravēscere.

oppressor *n* tyrannus *m.*

opprobrious *adj* turpis.

opprobriously *adv* turpiter.

opprobrium *n* dēdecus *nt*,
ignōminia *f.*

optical *adj* oculōrum.

optical illusion *n* oculōrum
lūdibrium *nt.*

optimism *n* spēs *f.*

option *n* optiō *f*, arbitrium *nt*; **I
have no ~** nōn est arbitriī meī.

optional *adj*: **it is ~ for you** optiō tua
est.

opulence *n* opēs *fpl*, cōpia *f.*

opulent *adj* dīves, cōpiōsus.

or *conj* aut, vel, -ve; (*after utrum*)
an; **~ else** aliōquīn; **~ not** (*direct*)
annōn; (*indirect*) necne.

oracle *n* ōrāculum *nt.*

oracular *adj* fātidicus; (*fig*)
obscūrus.

oral *adj*: **give an ~ message** vōce
nūntiāre.

orally *adv* vōce, verbīs.

oration *n* ōrātiō *f.*

orator *n* ōrātor *m.*

oratorical *adj* ōrātōrius.

oratory *n* ēloquentia *f*, rhētoricē *f*;
(*for prayer*) sacellum *nt*; **of ~**
dīcendī, ōrātōrius.

orb *n* orbis *m.*

orbit *n* orbis *m*, ambitus *m.*

orchard *n* pōmārium *nt.*

ordain *vt* ēdīcere, sancīre.

ordeal *n* labor *m.*

order *n* (*arrangement*) ōrdō *m*;
(*class*) ōrdō *m*; (*battle*) aciēs *f*;
(*command*) iussum *nt*, imperium

nt; (*money*) perscrīptiō *f*; **in ~**
dispositus; (*succession*) deinceps;
in ~ that/to ut (+ *subj*); **in ~ that
not** nē (+ *subj*); **put in ~** dispōnere,
ōrdināre; **by ~ of** iussū (*gen*); **out
of ~** incompositus; **without ~s
from** iniussū (*gen*) ♦ *vt* (*arrange*)
dispōnere, ōrdināre; (*command*)
iubēre (+ *acc and infin*), imperāre
(*dat and* ut/nē +*subj*).

orderly *adj* ōrdinātus; (*conduct*)
modestus ♦ *n* accēnsus *m*.

ordinance *n* ēdictum *nt*, institūtum
nt.

ordinarily *adv* plērumque, ferē.

ordinary *adj* ūsitātus, solitus,
cottīdiānus.

ordnance *n* tormenta *ntpl*.

ordure *n* stercus *m*.

ore *n* aes *nt*; **iron ~** ferrum
īnfectum *nt*.

Oread *n* (MYTH) Oreas *f*.

organ *n* (*bodily*) membrum *nt*;
(*musical*) organum *nt*, hydraulus
m.

organic *adj* nātūrālis.

organically *adv* nātūrā.

organization *n* ōrdinātiō *f*,
structūra *f*.

organize *vt* ōrdināre, īnstituere,
adparāre.

orgies *n* orgia *ntpl*.

orgy *n* cōmissātiō *f*.

orient *n* oriēns *m*.

oriental *adj* Asiāticus.

orifice *n* ōstium *nt*.

origin *n* orīgō *f*, prīncipium *nt*;
(*source*) fōns *m*; (*birth*) genus *nt*.

original *adj* prīmus, prīstinus, (LIT)
proprius ♦ *n* exemplar *nt*.

originally *adv* prīncipiō,
antīquitus.

originate *vt* īnstituere, auctōrem
esse (*gen*) ♦ *vi* exorīrī; **~ in**
innāscī in (*abl*), initium dūcere ab.

originator *n* auctor *m*.

orisons *n* precēs *fpl*.

ornament *n* ōrnāmentum *nt*; (*fig*)
decus *nt* ♦ *vt* ōrnāre, decorāre; **I
am ~** ōrnāmentō sum.

ornamental *adj* decōrus; **be ~**
decorī esse.

ornamentally *adv* ōrnātē.

ornate *adj* ōrnātus.

ornately *adv* ōrnātē.

orphan *n* orbus *m*, orba *f*.

orphaned *adj* orbātus.

orthodox *adj* antīquus.

orthography *n* orthographia *f*.

oscillate *vi* reciprocāre.

osculate *vt* ōsculārī.

osier *n* vīmen *nt* ♦ *adj* vīmineus.

osprey *n* haliaeetos *m*.

ostensible *adj* speciōsus.

ostensibly *adv* per speciem.

ostentation *n* iactātiō *f*, ostentātiō
f.

ostentatious *adj* glōriōsus,
ambitiōsus.

ostentatiously *adv* glōriōsē.

ostler *n* agāsō *m*.

ostrich *n* strūthiocamēlus *m*.

other *adj* alius; (*of two*) alter; **one
or the ~** alteruter; **every ~ year**
tertiō quōque annō; **on the ~ side**
of ultrā (+ *acc*); **of ~s** aliēnus.

otherwise *adv* aliter; (*if not*)
aliōquī.

otter *n* lutra *f*.

ought *vi* dēbēre (+ *infin or gerundive
of vt*); **I ~** mē oportet; **I ~ to have
said** dēbuī dīcere.

ounce *n* ūncia *f*; **two ~s** sextāns *m*;
three ~s quadrāns *m*; **four ~s**
triēns *m*; **five ~s** quīncūnx *m*; **six
~s** sēmis *m*; **seven ~s** septūnx *m*;
eight ~s bēs *m*; **nine ~s** dōdrāns
m; **ten ~s** dextāns *m*; **eleven ~s**
deūnx *m*.

our *adj* noster.

ourselves *pron* ipsī; (*reflexive*) nōs.

oust *vt* extrūdere, ēicere.

out *adv* (*rest*) forīs; (*motion*) forās;
~ of dē, ē/ex (*abl*); (*cause*) propter

(*acc*); (*beyond*) extrā, ultrā (*acc*); **be ~** (*book*) in manibus esse; (*calculation*) errāre; (*fire*) exstinctum esse; (*secret*) palam esse.

outbreak *n* initium *nt*, ēruptiō *f*.

outburst *n* ēruptiō *f*.

outcast *n* profugus *m*.

outcome *n* ēventus *m*, exitus *m*.

outcry *n* clāmor *m*, adclāmātiō *f*; **raise an ~ against** obstrepere (*dat*).

outdistance *vt* praevertere.

outdo *vt* superāre.

outdoor *adj* sub dīvō.

outer *adj* exterior.

outermost *adj* extrēmus.

outfit *n* īnstrūmenta *ntpl*; vestīmenta *ntpl*.

outflank *vt* circumīre.

outgrow *vt* excēdere ex.

outing *n* excursiō *f*.

outlandish *adj* barbarus.

outlaw *n* prōscrīptus *m* ♦ *vt* prōscrībere, aquā et ignī interdīcere (*dat*).

outlawry *n* aquae et ignis interdictiō *f*.

outlay *n* impēnsa *f*, sūmptus *m*.

outlet *n* ēmissārium *nt*, exitus *m*.

outline *n* ductus *m*, adumbrātiō *f* ♦ *vt* adumbrāre.

outlive *vt* superesse (*dat*).

outlook *n* prōspectus *m*.

outlying *adj* longinquus, exterior.

outnumber *vt* numerō superiōrēs esse, multitūdine superāre.

out-of-doors *adv* forīs.

outpost *n* statiō *f*.

outpouring *n* effūsiō *f*.

output *n* fructus *m*.

outrage *n* flāgitium *nt*, iniūria *f* ♦ *vt* laedere, violāre.

outrageous *adj* flāgitiōsus, indignus.

outrageously *adv* flāgitiōsē.

outrider *n* praecursor *m*.

outright *adv* penitus, prōrsus; semel.

outrun *vt* praevertere.

outset *n* initium *nt*.

outshine *vt* praelūcēre (*dat*).

outside *adj* externus ♦ *adv* extrā, forīs; (*motion to*) forās; **~ in** inversus; **from ~** extrīnsecus ♦ *n* exterior pars *f*; (*show*) speciēs *f*; **at the ~** summum, ad summum; **on the ~** extrīnsecus ♦ *prep* extrā (*acc*).

outsider *n* aliēnus *m*; (*POL*) novus homō *m*.

outskirts *n* suburbānus ager *m*; **on the ~** suburbānus.

outspoken *adj* līber.

outspokenness *n* lībertās *f*.

outspread *adj* patulus.

outstanding *adj* ēgregius, īnsignis, singulāris; (*debt*) residuus.

outstep *vt* excēdere.

outstretched *adj* passus, porrēctus, extentus.

outstrip *vt* praevertere.

outvote *vt* suffrāgiīs superāre.

outward *adj* externus; **~ form** speciēs *f* ♦ *adv* domō, forās.

outweigh *vt* praeponderāre.

outwit *vt* dēcipere, circumvenīre.

outwork *n* prōpugnāculum *nt*, bracchium *nt*.

outworn *adj* exolētus.

oval *adj* ōvātus ♦ *n* ōvum *nt*.

ovation *n* (*triumph*) ovātiō *f*; **receive an ~** cum laudibus excipī.

oven *n* furnus *m*, fornāx *f*.

over *prep* (*above*) super (*abl*), suprā (*acc*); (*across*) super (*acc*); (*extent*) per (*acc*); (*time*) inter (*acc*); **~ and above** super (*acc*), praeter (*acc*); **all ~** per; **~ against** adversus (*acc*) ♦ *adv* suprā; (*excess*) nimis; (*done*) cōnfectus; **~ again** dēnuō; **~ and above** īnsuper; **~ and ~** identidem; **be left ~** superesse, restāre; **it is all ~ with** āctum est dē.

overall adj tōtus ♦ adv ubīque, passim.

overawe vt formīdinem incicere (dat).

overbalance vi titubāre.

overbearing adj superbus.

overboard adv ē nāvī, in mare; **throw ~** excutere, iactāre.

overbold adj importūnus.

overburden vt praegravāre.

overcast adj nūbilus.

overcoat n paenula f, lacerna f.

overcome vt superāre, vincere.

overconfidence n cōnfīdentia f.

overconfident adj cōnfīdēns.

overdo vt modum excēdere in (abl).

overdone adj (style) pūtidus.

overdraw vt (style) exaggerāre.

overdue adj (money) residuus.

overestimate vt māiōris aestimāre.

overflow n ēluviō f ♦ vi abundāre, redundāre ♦ vt inundāre.

overgrown adj obsitus; **be ~** luxuriāre.

overhang vt, vi impendēre, imminēre (dat).

overhaul vt reficere.

overhead adv īnsuper.

overhear vt excipere, auscultāre.

overjoyed adj nimiō gaudiō ēlātus.

overladen adj praegravātus.

overland adv terrā.

overlap vt implicāre.

overlay vt indūcere.

overload vt (fig) obruere.

overlook vt (place) dēspectāre, imminēre (dat); (knowledge) ignōrāre; (notice) neglegere, praetermittere; (fault) ignōscere (dat).

overlord n dominus m.

overmaster vt dēvincere.

overmuch adv nimis, plūs aequō.

overnight adj nocturnus ♦ adv

noctū.

overpower vt superāre, domāre, obruere, opprimere.

overpraise vt in māius extollere.

overrate vt māiōris aestimāre.

overreach vt circumvenīre.

overriding adj praecipuus.

overrule vt rescindere.

overrun vt pervagārī; (fig) obsidēre.

oversea adj trānsmarīnus.

oversee vt praeesse (dat).

overseer n cūrātor m, custōs m.

overset vt ēvertere.

overshadow vt officere (dat).

overshoot vt excēdere.

oversight n neglegentia f.

overspread vt offendere (dat), obdūcere.

overstep vt excēdere.

overt adj apertus.

overtake vt cōnsequī; (surprise) opprimere, dēprehendere.

overtax vt (fig) abūtī (abl).

overthrow vt ēvertere; (destroy) prōflīgāre, dēbellārc ♦ n ēversiō f, ruīna f.

overtly adv palam.

overtop vt superāre.

overture n exōrdium nt; **make ~s to** temptāre, agere cum, lēgātōs mittere ad.

overturn vt ēvertere.

overweening adj superbus, adrogāns, īnsolēns.

overwhelm vt obruere, dēmergere, opprimere.

overwhelming adj īnsignis, vehementissimus.

overwhelmingly adv mīrum quantum.

overwork vi plūs aequō labōrāre ♦ vt cōnficere ♦ n immodicus labor m.

overwrought adj (emotion) ēlātus; (style) ēlabōrātus.

owe vt dēbēre.

owing adj: be ~ dēbērī; ~ to (person) per; (cause) ob/propter (acc).

owl n būbō m; ulula f.

own adj proprius; **my** ~ meus; **have of one's** ~ domī habēre; **hold one's** ~ parem esse ♦ vt possidēre, habēre; (admit) fatērī, cōnfitērī.

owner n dominus m, possessor m.

ownership n possessiō f, mancipium nt.

ox n bōs m.

ox herd n bubulcus m.

oyster n ostrea f.

P

pace n passus m; (speed) gradus m; **keep** ~ gradum cōnferre ♦ vi incēdere; ~ **up and down** spatiārī, inambulāre.

pacific adj pācificus; (quiet) placidus.

pacification n pācificātiō f.

pacifist n imbellis m.

pacify vt (anger) plācāre; (rising) sēdāre.

pack n (MIL) sarcina f; (animals) grex m; (people) turba f ♦ vt (kit) colligere; (crowd) stīpāre; ~ **together** coartāre; ~ **up** colligere, compōnere ♦ vi vāsa colligere; **send** ~**ing** missum facere ♦ adj (animal) clītellārius.

package n fasciculus m, sarcina f.

packet n fasciculus m; (ship) nāvis āctuāria f.

packhorse n iūmentum nt.

packsaddle n clītellae fpl.

pact n foedus nt, pactum nt.

pad n pulvillus m.

padding n tōmentum nt.

paddle n rēmus m ♦ vi rēmigāre.

paddock n saeptum nt.

paean n paeān m.

pagan adj pāgānus.

page n (book) pāgina f; (boy) puer m.

pageant n pompa f, spectāculum nt.

pageantry n adparātus m.

pail n situla f.

pain n dolor m; **be in** ~ dolēre ♦ vt dolōre adficere.

painful adj acerbus; (work) labōriōsus.

painfully adv acerbē, labōriōsē.

painless adj dolōris expers.

painlessly adv sine dolōre.

painlessness n indolentia f.

pains npl opera f; **take** ~ operam dare; **take** ~ **with** (art) ēlabōrāre.

painstaking adj dīligēns, operōsus.

painstakingly adv dīligenter, summā cūrā.

paint n pigmentum nt; (cosmetic) fūcus m ♦ vt pingere; (red) fūcāre; (in words) dēpingere; (portrait) dēpingere.

paintbrush n pēnicillus m.

painter n pictor m.

painting n pictūra f.

pair n pār nt ♦ vt coniungere, compōnere.

palace n rēgia f.

palatable adj suāvis, iūcundus.

palate n palātum nt.

palatial adj rēgius.

palaver n colloquium nt, sermunculī mpl.

pale n pālus m, vallus m; **beyond the** ~ extrāneus ♦ adj pallidus; **look** ~ pallēre; **grow** ~ pallēscere; ~ **brown** subfuscus; ~ **green** subviridis ♦ vi pallēscere.

paleness n pallor m.

palimpsest n palimpsēstus m.

paling n saepēs f.

palisade n (MIL) vallum nt.

palish adj pallidulus.

pall n (funeral) pallium nt ♦ vi taedēre.

pallet n grabātus m.

palliasse n strāmentum nt.

palliate vt extenuāre, excūsāre.

palliation n excūsātiō f.

palliative n lēnīmentum nt.

pallid adj pallidus.

pallor n pallor m.

palm n (hand) palma f; (tree) palma f ♦ vt: ~ **off** impōnere.

palmy adj flōrēns.

palpable adj tractābilis; (fig) manifestus.

palpably adv manifestō, propalam.

palpitate vi palpitāre, micāre.

palpitation n palpitātiō f.

palsied adj membrīs captus.

palsy n paralysis f.

paltry adj vīlis, frīvolus.

pamper vt indulgēre (dat).

pampered adj dēlicātus.

pamphlet n libellus m.

pan n patina f, patella f; (frying) sartāgō f; (of balance) lanx f.

pancake n laganum nt.

pander n lēnō m ♦ vi: ~ **to** lēnōcinārī (dat).

panegyric n laudātiō f.

panegyrist n laudātor m.

panel n (wall) abacus m; (ceiling) lacūnār nt; (judges) decuria f.

panelled adj laqueātus.

pang n dolor m.

panic n pavor m ♦ vi trepidāre.

panic-stricken adj pavidus.

panniers n clītellae fpl.

panoply n arma ntpl.

panorama n prōspectus m.

panpipe n fistula f.

pant vi anhēlāre.

panther n panthēra f.

panting n anhēlitus m.

pantomime n mīmus m.

pantry n cella penāria f.

pap n mamma f.

paper n charta f.

papyrus n papyrus f.

par n: on a ~ **with** pār (dat).

parable n parabolē f.

parade n pompa f; (show) adparātus m ♦ vt trādūcere, iactāre ♦ vi pompam dūcere, incēdere.

paradox n verba sēcum repugnantia; ~**es** pl paradoxa ntpl.

paragon n exemplar nt, specimen nt.

paragraph n caput nt.

parallel adj parallēlus f; (fig) cōnsimilis.

paralyse vt dēbilitāre; (with fear) percellere; **be ~d** torpēre.

paralysis n dēbilitās f; (fig) torpēdō f.

paramount adj prīnceps, summus.

paramour n adulter m.

parapet n lōrīca f.

paraphernalia n adparātus m.

paraphrase vt vertere.

parasite n parasītus m.

parasol n umbella f.

parboiled adj subcrūdus.

parcel n fasciculus m ♦ vt: ~ **out** distribuere, dispertīre.

parch vt torrēre.

parched adj torridus, āridus; **be ~** ārēre.

parchment n membrāna f.

pardon n venia f ♦ vt ignōscere (dat); (offence) condōnāre.

pardonable adj ignōscendus.

pare vt dēglūbere; (nails) resecāre.

parent n parēns m/f, genitor m, genetrīx f.

parentage n stirps f, genus m.

parental adj patrius.

parenthesis n interclūsiō f.

parings n praesegmina ntpl.

parish n (ECCL) paroecia f.

parity n aequālitās f.

park n hortī mpl.

parlance n sermō m.

parley n colloquium nt ♦ vi colloquī, agere.

parliament n senātus m; **house of**

~ cūria f.

parliamentary adj senātōrius.

parlour n exedrium nt.

parlous adj difficilis, perīculōsus.

parochial adj mūnicipālis.

parody n carmen ioculāre nt ♦ vt calumniārī.

parole n fidēs f.

paronomasia n agnōminātiō f.

paroxysm n accessus m.

parricide n (doer) parricīda m; (deed) parricīdium nt.

parrot n psittacus m.

parry vt ēlūdere, prōpulsāre.

parsimonious adj parcus.

parsimoniously adv parcē.

parsimony n parsimōnia f, frūgālitās f.

part n pars f; (play) partēs fpl, persōna f; (duty) officium nt; ~s loca ntpl; (ability) ingenium nt; for my ~ equidem; for the most ~ māximam partem; on the ~ of ab; act the ~ of persōnam sustinēre, partēs agere; have no ~ in expers esse (gen); in ~ partim; it is the ~ of a wise man sapientis est; play one's ~ officiō satisfacere; take ~ in interesse (dat), particeps esse (gen); take in good ~ in bonam partem accipere; take someone's ~ adesse alicui, dēfendere aliquem; from all ~s undique; in foreign ~s peregrē; in two ~s bifāriam; (MIL) bipartītō; in three ~s trifāriam; (MIL) tripartītō; of ~s ingeniōsus ♦ vt dīvidere, sēparāre, dirimere; ~ company dīversōs discēdere ♦ vi dīgredī, discēdere; (things) dissilīre; ~ with renūntiāre.

partake vi interesse, particeps esse; ~ of gustāre.

partial adj (biased) inīquus, studiōsus; (incomplete) mancus; be ~ to favēre (dat), studēre (dat); win a ~ victory aliquā ex parte vincere.

partiality n favor m, studium nt.

partially adv partim, aliquā ex parte.

participant n particeps m/f.

participate vi interesse, particeps esse.

participation n societās f.

particle n particula f.

parti-coloured adj versicolor, varius.

particular adj (own) proprius; (special) praecipuus; (exact) dīligēns, accūrātus; (fastidious) fastīdiōsus; a ~ person quīdam ♦ n rēs f; with full ~s subtīliter; give all the ~s omnia exsequī; in ~ praesertim.

particularity n subtīlitās f.

particularize vt singula exsequī.

particularly adv praecipuē, praesertim, in prīmīs, māximē.

parting n dīgressus m, discessus m ♦ adj ultimus.

partisan n fautor m, studiōsus m.

partisanship n studium nt.

partition n (act) partītiō f; (wall) pariēs m; (compartment) loculāmentum nt ♦ vt dīvidere.

partly adv partim, ex parte.

partner n socius m; (in office) collēga m.

partnership n societās f; form a ~ societātem inīre.

partridge n perdīx m/f.

parturition n partus m.

party n (POL) factiō f, partēs fpl; (entertainment) convīvium nt; (MIL) manus f; (individual) homō m/f; (associate) socius m, cōnscius m.

party spirit n studium nt.

parvenu n novus homō m.

pass n (hill) saltus m; (narrow) angustiae fpl, faucēs fpl; (crisis) discrīmen nt; (document) diplōma nt; (fighting) petītiō f; things have come to such a ~ in eum locum

ventum est, adeō rēs rediit ♦ *vi*
īre, praeterīre; (*time*) trānsīre;
(*property*) pervenīre; ~ **away**
abīre; (*die*) morī, perīre; (*fig*)
dēfluere; ~ **by** praeterīre; ~ **for**
haberī prō (*abl*); ~ **off** abīre; ~ **on**
pergere; ~ **over** praeterīre; **come to**
~ fierī, ēvenīre; **let** ~
intermittere, praetermittere ♦ *vt*
praeterīre; (*riding*) praetervehī;
(*by hand*) trādere; (*law*) iubēre;
(*limit*) excēdere; (*sentence*)
interpōnere, dīcere; (*test*)
satisfacere (*dat*); (*time*) dēgere,
agere; ~ **accounts** ratiōnēs ratās
habēre; ~ **the day** diem
cōnsūmere; ~ **a law** lēgem ferre;
~ **a decree** dēcernere; ~ **off** ferre;
~ **over** praeterīre, mittere; (*fault*)
ignōscere (*dat*); ~ **round** trādere;
~ **through** trānsīre.

passable *adj* (*place*) pervius;
(*standard*) mediocris.

passably *adv* mediocriter.

passage *n* iter nt, cursus m; (*land*)
trānsitus m; (*sea*) trānsmissiō f;
(*book*) locus m; **of** ~ (*bird*) advena.

passenger *n* vector m.

passer-by *n* praeteriēns m.

passing *n* obitus m ♦ *adj*
admodum.

passion *n* animī mōtus m,
permōtiō f, ārdor m; (*anger*) īra f;
(*lust*) libīdō f.

passionate *adj* ārdēns, impotēns,
ācer; īrācundus.

passionately *adv* vehementer,
ārdenter; īrācundē; **be ~ in love**
amōre ārdēre.

passive *adj* iners.

passiveness *n* inertia f, patientia f.

passport *n* diplōma nt.

password *n* tessera f.

past *adj* praeteritus; (*recent*)
proximus ♦ *n* praeterita *ntpl*
♦ *prep* praeter (*acc*); (*beyond*) ultrā
(*acc*).

paste *n* glūten nt ♦ *vt* glūtināre.

pastime *n* lūdus m,
oblectāmentum nt.

pastoral *adj* pāstōrālis; (*poem*)
būcolicus.

pastry *n* crustum nt.

pasture *n* pāstus m, pāscuum nt
♦ *vt* pāscere.

pat *vt* dēmulcēre ♦ *adj* opportūnus.

patch *n* pannus m ♦ *vt* resarcīre.

patchwork *n* centō m.

pate *n* caput nt.

patent *adj* apertus, manifestus ♦ *n*
prīvilēgium nt.

patently *adv* manifestō.

paternal *adj* paternus.

path *n* sēmita f, trāmes m.

pathetic *adj* miserābilis.

pathetically *adv* miserābiliter.

pathfinder *n* explorātor m.

pathless *adj* āvius.

pathos *n* misericordia f; (*RHET*)
dolor m.

pathway *n* sēmita f.

patience *n* patientia f.

patient *adj* patiēns ♦ *n* aeger m.

patiently *adv* patienter, aequō
animō.

patois *n* sermō m.

patrician *adj* patricius ♦ *n*
patricius m.

patrimony *n* patrimōnium nt.

patriot *n* amāns patriae m.

patriotic *adj* pius, amāns patriae.

patriotically *adv* prō patriā.

patriotism *n* amor patriae m.

patrol *n* excubiae *fpl* ♦ *vi*
circumīre.

patron *n* patrōnus m, fautor m.

patronage *n* patrōcinium nt.

patroness *n* patrōna f, fautrīx f.

patronize *vt* favēre (*dat*), fovēre.

patronymic *n* nōmen nt.

patter *vi* crepitāre ♦ *n* crepitus m.

pattern *n* exemplar m, exemplum
nt, nōrma f; (*ideal*) specimen nt;
(*design*) figūra f.

paucity n paucitās f.

paunch n abdōmen nt, venter m.

pauper n pauper m.

pause n mora f, intervallum nt ♦ vi īnsistere, intermittere.

pave vt sternere; **~ the way** (fig) viam mūnīre.

pavement n pavīmentum nt.

pavilion n tentōrium nt.

paw n pēs m ♦ vt pede pulsāre.

pawn n (chess) latrunculus m; (COMM) pignus nt, fīdūcia f ♦ vt oppignerāre.

pawnbroker n pignerātor m.

pay n mercēs f; (MIL) stīpendium nt; (workman) manuprētium nt ♦ vt solvere, pendere; (debt) exsolvere; (in full) persolvere; (honour) persolvere; (MIL) stīpendium numerāre (dat); (penalty) dāre, luere; **~ down** numerāre; **~ for** condūcere; **~ off** dissolvere, exsolvere; **~ out** expendere; (publicly) ērogāre; **~ up** dēpendere; **~ a compliment to** laudāre; **~ respects to** salūtāre ♦ vi respondēre; **it ~s** expedit.

payable adj solvendus.

paymaster n (MIL) tribūnus aerārius m.

payment n solūtiō f; (money) pēnsiō f.

pea n pisum n; **like as two ~s** tam similis quam lac lacti est.

peace n pāx f; **~ and quiet** ōtium nt; **breach of the ~** vīs f; **establish ~** pācem conciliāre; **hold one's ~** reticēre; **sue for ~** pācem petere.

peaceable adj imbellis, placidus.

peaceably adv placidē.

peaceful adj tranquillus, placidus, pācātus.

peacefully adv tranquillē.

peacemaker n pācificus m.

peace-offering n piāculum nt.

peach n Persicum nt.

peacock n pāvō m.

peak n apex m, vertex m.

peal n (bell) sonitus m; (thunder) fragor m ♦ vi sonāre.

pear n pirum nt; (tree) pirus f.

pearl n margarīta f.

pearly adj gemmeus; (colour) candidus.

peasant n agricola m, colōnus m.

peasantry n agricolae mpl.

pebble n calculus m.

pebbly adj lapidōsus.

peccadillo n culpa f.

peck n (measure) modius m ♦ vt vellicāre.

peculate vi pecūlārī.

peculation n pecūlātus m.

peculiar adj (to one) proprius; (strange) singulāris.

peculiarity n proprietās f, nota f.

peculiarly adv praecipuē, praesertim.

pecuniary adj pecūniārius.

pedagogue n magister m.

pedant n scholasticus m.

pedantic adj nimis dīligenter.

pedantically adv dīligentior.

pedantry n nimia dīligentia f.

poddle vt circumferre.

pedestal n basis f.

pedestrian adj pedester ♦ n pedes m.

pedigree n stirps f, stemma nt ♦ adj generōsus.

pediment n fastīgium nt.

podlar n īnstitor m, circumforāneus m.

peel n cortex m ♦ vt glūbere.

peep vi dīspicere ♦ n aspectus m; **at ~ of day** prīmā lūce.

peer vi: **~ at** intuērī ♦ n pār m; (rank) patricius m.

peerless adj ūnicus, ēgregius.

peevish adj stomachōsus, mōrōsus.

peevishly adv stomachōsē, mōrōsē.

peevishness n stomachus m,

mōrōsitās f.

peg n clāvus m; **put a round ~ in a square hole** bovī clītellās impōnere ♦ vt clāvīs dēfīgere.

pelf n lucrum nt.

pellet n globulus m.

pell-mell adv prōmiscuē, turbātē.

pellucid adj perlūcidus.

pelt n pellis f ♦ vt petere ♦ vi violenter cadere.

pen n calamus m, stilus m; (cattle) saeptum nt ♦ vt scrībere.

penal adj poenālis.

penalize vt poenā adficere, mulctāre.

penalty n poena f, damnum nt; (fine) multa f; **pay the ~** poenās dare.

penance n supplicium nt.

pencil n graphis f.

pending adj sub iūdice ♦ prep inter (acc).

penetrable adj pervius.

penetrate vt penetrāre.

penetrating adj ācer, acūtus; (mind) perspicāx.

penetration n (mind) acūmen nt.

peninsula n paenīnsula f.

penitence n paenitentia f.

penitent adj: **I am ~** mē paenitet.

penknife n scalpellum nt.

penmanship n scrīptiō f, manus f.

pennant n vexillum nt.

penny n dēnārius m.

pension n annua ntpl.

pensioner n ēmeritus m.

pensive adj attentus.

pensiveness n cōgitātiō f.

pent adj inclūsus.

penthouse n (MIL) vīnea f.

penurious adj parcus, avārus, tenāx.

penuriousness n parsimōnia f, tenācitās f.

penury n egestās f, inopia f.

people n hominēs mpl; (nation) populus m, gēns f; **common ~**

plēbs f ♦ vt frequentāre.

peopled adj frequēns.

pepper n piper nt.

peradventure adv fortasse.

perambulate vi spatiārī, inambulāre.

perceive vt sentīre, percipere, intellegere.

perceptible adj: **be ~** sentīrī posse, audīrī posse.

perception n sēnsus m.

perch n (bird's) pertica f; (fish) perca f ♦ vi īnsidēre.

perchance adv fortasse, forsitan (subj).

percolate vi permānāre.

percussion n ictus m.

perdition n exitium nt.

peregrinate vi peregrīnārī.

peregrination n peregrīnātiō f.

peremptorily adv praecīsē, prō imperiō.

peremptory adj imperiōsus.

perennial adj perennis.

perfect adj perfectus, absolūtus; (entire) integer; (faultless) ēmendātus ♦ vt perficere, absolvere.

perfection n perfectiō f, absolūtiō f.

perfectly adv perfectē, ēmendātē; (quite) plānē.

perfidious adj perfidus, perfidiōsus.

perfidiously adv perfidiōsē.

perfidy n perfidia f.

perforate vt perforāre, terebrāre.

perforation n forāmen nt.

perforce adv per vim, necessāriō.

perform vt perficere, peragere; (duty) exsequī, fungī (abl); (play) agere.

performance n (process) exsecūtiō f, fūnctiō f; (deed) factum nt; (stage) fābula f.

performer n āctor m; (music) tībīcen m, fidicen m; (stage) histriōm.

perfume n odor m, unguentum nt
♦ vt odōrāre.

perfumer n unguentārius m.

perfumery n unguenta ntpl.

perfunctorily adv neglegenter.

perfunctory adj neglegēns.

perhaps adv fortasse, forsitan
(subj), nescio an (subj); (tentative)
vel, (interrog) an.

peril n perīculum m, discrīmen nt.

perilous adj perīculōsus.

perilously adv perīculōsē.

perimeter n ambitus m.

period n tempus nt, spatium nt;
(history) aetās f; (end) terminus m;
(sentence) complexiō f, ambitus m.

periodic adj (style) circumscrīptus.

periodical adj status.

periodically adv certīs
temporibus, identidem.

peripatetic adj vagus; (sect)
peripatēticus.

periphery n ambitus m.

periphrasis n circuitus m.

perish vi perīre, interīre.

perishable adj cadūcus, fragilis,
mortālis.

peristyle n peristȳlium nt.

perjure vi: ~ o.s. pēierāre.

perjured adj periūrus.

perjurer n periūrus m.

perjury n periūrium nt; **commit ~**
pēierāre.

permanence n cōnstantia f,
stabilitās f.

permanent adj stabilis, diūturnus,
perpetuus.

permanently adv perpetuō.

permeable adj penetrābilis.

permeate vt penetrāre ♦ vi
permānāre.

permissible adj licitus, concessus;
it is ~ licet.

permission n potestās f; **ask ~**
veniam petere; **give ~** veniam
dare, potestātem facere; **by ~ of**

permissū (gen); **with your kind ~**
bonā tuā veniā; **without your ~** tē
invītō.

permit vt sinere, permittere (dat); **I
am ~ted** licet mihī.

pernicious adj perniciōsus,
exitiōsus.

perorate vi perōrāre.

peroration n perōrātiō f, epilogus
m.

perpendicular adj dīrēctus.

perpendicularly adv ad
perpendiculum, ad līneam.

perpetrate vt facere, admittere.

perpetual adj perpetuus, perennis,
sempiternus.

perpetually adv perpetuō.

perpetuate vt continuāre,
perpetuāre.

perpetuity n perpetuitās f.

perplex vt sollicitāre, cōnfundere.

perplexed adj ambiguus,
perplexus.

perplexity n haesitātiō f.

perquisite n pecūlium nt.

persecute vt īnsectārī, exagitāre;
persequi.

persecution n īnsectātiō f.

persecutor n īnsectātor m.

perseverance n pesevērantia f,
cōnstantia f.

persevere vi persevērāre,
perstāre; **~ in** tenēre.

Persian n Persa m.

persist vt īnstāre, perstāre,
persevērāre.

persistence, persistency n
pertinācia f, persevērantia f.

persistent adj pertināx.

persistently adv pertināciter,
persevēranter.

person n homō m/f; (counted) caput
nt; (character) persōna f; (body)
corpus nt; **in ~** ipse praesēns.

personage n vir m.

personal adj prīvātus, suus.

personality n nātūra f; (person) vir

ēgregius m.
personally adv ipse, cōram.
personal property n pecūlium nt.
personate vt persōnam gerere (gen).
personification n prosōpopoeia f.
personify vt hūmānam nātūram tribuere (dat).
personnel n membra ntpl, sociī mpl.
perspective n scaenographia f.
perspicacious adj perspicāx, acūtus.
perspicacity n perspicācitās f, acūmen nt.
perspicuity n perspicuitās f.
perspicuous adj perspicuus.
perspiration n sūdor m.
perspire vi sūdāre.
persuade vt persuādēre (dat); (by entreaty) exōrāre.
persuasion n persuāsiō f.
persuasive adj blandus.
persuasively adv blandē.
pert adj procāx, protervus.
pertain vi pertinēre, attinēre.
pertinacious adj pertināx.
pertinaciously adv pertināciter.
pertinacity n pertinācia f.
pertinent adj appositus; be ~ ad rem pertinēre.
pertinently adv appositē.
pertly adv procāciter, protervē.
perturb vt perturbāre.
perturbation n animī perturbātiō f, trepidātiō f.
peruke n capillāmentum nt.
perusal n perlēctiō f.
peruse vt perlegere; (book) ēvolvere.
pervade vt permānāre per, complēre; (emotion) perfundere.
pervasive adj crēber.
perverse adj perversus, prāvus.
perversely adv perversē.
perversion n dēprāvātiō f.
perversity n perversitās f.

pervert vt dēprāvāre; (words) dētorquēre; (person) corrumpere.
perverter n corruptor m.
pessimism n dēspērātiō f.
pest n pestis f.
pester vt sollicitāre.
pestilence n pestilentia f, pestis f.
pestilential adj pestilēns, nocēns.
pestle n pistillum nt.
pet n dēliciae fpl ♦ vt in dēliciīs habēre, dēlēnīre.
petard n: be hoist with his own ~ suō sibī gladiō iugulārī.
petition n precēs fpl; (POL) libellus m ♦ vt ōrāre.
petrify vt (fig) dēfigere; be petrified stupēre, obstupēscere.
pettifogger n lēguleius m.
pettiness n levitās f.
pettish adj stomachōsus.
petty adj levis, minūtus.
petulance n protervitās f.
petulant adj protervus, petulāns.
petulantly adv petulanter.
pew n subsellium nt.
phalanx n phalanx f.
phantasy n commentīcia ntpl.
phantom n simulacrum nt, īdōlon nt.
phases npl vicēs fpl.
pheasant n phāsiānus m.
phenomenal adj eximius, singulāris.
phenomenon n rēs f, novum nt, spectāculum nt.
philander vi lascīvīre.
philanthropic adj hūmānus, beneficus.
philanthropically adv hūmānē.
philanthropy n hūmānitās f, beneficia ntpl.
Philippic n Philippica f.
philologist n grammaticus m.
philology n grammatica ntpl.
philosopher n philosophus m, sapiēns m.
philosophical adj philosophus;

(*temperament*) aequābilis.

philosophize *vi* philosophārī.

philosophy *n* philosophia *f*, sapientia *f*.

philtre *n* philtrum *nt*.

phlegm *n* pītuīta *f*; (*temper*) lentitūdō *f*.

phlegmatic *adj* lentus.

phoenix *n* phoenīx *m*.

phrase *n* locūtiō *f*; (*GRAM*) incīsum *nt*.

phraseology *n* verba *ntpl*, ōrātiō *f*.

physic *n* medicāmentum *nt*; **~s** *pl* physica *ntpl*.

physical *adj* physicus; (*of body*) corporis.

physician *n* medicus *m*.

physicist *n* physicus *m*.

physique *n* corpus *nt*, vīrēs *fpl*.

piazza *n* forum *nt*.

pick *n* (*tool*) dolabra *f*; (*best part*) lēctī *mpl*, flōs *m* ♦ *vt* (*choose*) legere, dēligere; (*pluck*) carpere; **~ out** ēligere, excerpere; **~ up** colligere.

pickaxe *n* dolabra *f*.

picked *adj* ēlēctus, dēlēctus.

picket *n* (*MIL*) statiō *f*.

pickle *n* muria *f* ♦ *vt* condīre.

picture *n* pictūra *f*, tabula *f* ♦ *vt* dēpingere; (*to oneself*) ante oculōs pōnere.

picturesque *adj* (*scenery*) amoenus.

pie *n* crustum *nt*.

piebald *adj* bicolor, varius.

piece *n* pars *f*; (*broken off*) fragmentum *nt*; (*food*) frustum *nt*; (*coin*) nummus *m*; (*play*) fābula *f*; **break in ~s** comminuere; **fall to ~s** dīlābī; **take to ~s** dissolvere; **tear in ~s** dīlaniāre.

piecemeal *adv* membrātim, minūtātim.

pied *adj* maculōsus.

pier *n* mōlēs *f*.

pierce *vt* perfodere, trānsfīgere; (*bore*) perforāre; (*fig*) pungere.

piercing *adj* acūtus.

piety *n* pietās *f*, religiō *f*.

pig *n* porcus *m*, sūs *m/f*; **buy a ~ in a poke** spem pretiō emere; **~'s** suillus.

pigeon *n* columba *f*; **wood ~** palumbēs *f*.

pig-headed *adj* pervicāx.

pigment *n* pigmentum *nt*.

pigsty *n* hara *f*.

pike *n* dolō *m*, hasta *f*.

pikeman *n* hastātus *m*.

pile *n* acervus *m*, cumulus *m*; (*funeral*) rogus *m*; (*building*) mōlēs *f*; (*post*) sublica *f* ♦ *vt* cumulāre, congerere; **~ up** exstruere, adcumulāre, coacervāre.

pile-driver *n* fistūca *f*.

pilfer *vt* fūrārī, surripere.

pilferer *n* fūr *m*, fūrunculus *m*.

pilgrim *n* peregrīnātor *m*.

pilgrimage *n* peregrīnātiō *f*.

pill *n* pilula *f*.

pillage *n* rapīna *f*, dēpopulātiō *f*, expīlātiō *f* ♦ *vt* dīripere, dēpopulārī, expīlāre.

pillager *n* expīlātor *m*, praedātor *m*.

pillar *n* columen *nt*, columna *f*.

pillory *n* furca *f*.

pillow *n* pulvīnus *m*, culcita *f*.

pilot *n* gubernātor *m*, ductor *m* ♦ *vt* regere, gubernāre.

pimp *n* lēnō *m*.

pimple *n* pustula *f*.

pin *n* acus *f* ♦ *vt* adfīgere.

pincers *n* forceps *m/f*.

pinch *vt* pervellere, vellicāre; (*shoe*) ūrere; (*for room*) coartāre.

pine *n* pīnus *f* ♦ *vi* tābēscere; **~ away** intābēscere; **~ for** dēsīderāre.

pinion *n* penna *f*.

pink *adj* rubicundus.

pinnace *n* lembus *m*.

pinnacle *n* fastīgium *nt*.

pint *n* sextārius *m*.

pioneer n antecursor m.

pious adj pius, religiōsus.

piously adv piē, religiōsē.

pip n grānum nt.

pipe n (music) fistula f, tībia f; (water) canālis m ♦ vi fistulā canere.

piper n tībīcen m.

pipkin n olla f.

piquancy n sāl m, vīs f.

piquant adj salsus, argūtus.

pique n offēnsiō f, dolor m ♦ vt offendere.

piracy n latrōcinium nt.

pirate n pīrāta m praedō m.

piratical adj pīrāticus.

piscatorial adj piscātōrius.

piston n embolus m.

pit n fovea f, fossa f; (THEAT) cavea f.

pitch n pix f; (sound) sonus m ♦ vt (camp) pōnere; (tent) tendere; (missile) conicere.

pitch-black adj piceus.

pitched battle n proelium iustum nt.

pitcher n hydria f.

pitchfork n furca f.

pitch pine n picea f.

piteous adj miscrābilis, flēbilis.

piteously adv miserābiliter.

pitfall n fovea f.

pith n medulla f.

pithy adj (style) dēnsus; ~ saying sententia f.

pitiable adj miserandus.

pitiful adj miser, miserābilis; misericors.

pitifully adv miserē, miserābiliter.

pitiless adj immisericors, immītis.

pitilessly adv crūdēliter.

pittance n (food) dēmēnsum nt; (money) stips f.

pity n misericordia f; **take ~ on** miserērī (+acc of person, gen of things); **it is a ~ that** male accidit quod ♦ vt miserērī (gen); **I ~ me** miseret (gen).

pivot n cardō m.

placability n plācābilitās f.

placable adj plācābilis.

placard n libellus m.

placate vt plācāre.

place n locus m; **in another ~** alibī; **in the first ~** prīmum; **in ~ of** locō (gen), pro (+abl); **to this ~** hūc; **out of ~** intempestīvus; **give ~ to** cēdere (dat); **take ~** fierī, accidere; **take the ~ of** in locum (gen) succēdere ♦ vt pōnere, locāre, collocāre; **~ beside** adpōnere; **~ over** (in charge) praepōnere; **~ round** circumdare; **~ upon** impōnere.

placid adj placidus, tranquillus, quiētus.

placidity n tranquillitās f, sēdātus animus m.

placidly adv placidē, quiētē.

plagiarism n fūrtum nt.

plagiarize vt fūrārī.

plague n pestilentia f, pestis f.

plain adj (lucid) clārus, perspicuus; (unadorned) subtīlis, simplex; (frank) sincērus; (ugly) invenustus ♦ n campus m, plānitiēs f; **of the ~** campester.

plainly adv perspicuē; simpliciter, sincērē.

plainness n perspicuitās f; simplicitās f.

plaint n querella f.

plaintiff n petītor m.

plaintive adj flēbilis, queribundus.

plaintively adv flēbiliter.

plait vt implicāre, nectere.

plan n cōnsilium nt; (of a work) fōrma f, dēsignātiō f; (of living) ratiō f; (intent) prōpositum nt; (drawing) dēscrīptiō f ♦ vt (a work) dēsignāre, dēscrībere; (intent) cōgitāre, meditārī; cōnsilium capere or inīre; (with verb) in animō habēre (inf).

plane n (surface) plānitiēs f; (tree)

platanus f; (tool) runcīna f ♦ adj
aequus, plānus ♦ vt runcināre.

planet n stēlla errāns f.

plank n tabula f.

plant n herba f, planta f ♦ vt (tree)
serere; (field) cōnserere; (colony)
dēdūcere; (feet) pōnere; ~ firmly
īnfīgere.

plantation n arbustum nt.

planter n sator m, colōnus m.

plaque n tabula f.

plaster n albārium nt, tectōrium
nt; (MED) emplastrum nt; ~ of Paris
gypsum nt ♦ vt dealbāre.

plasterer n albārius m.

plastic adj ductilis, fūsilis.

plate n (dish) catillus m; (silver)
argentum nt; (layer) lāmina f ♦ vt
indūcere.

platform n suggestus m; rōstrum
nt, tribūnal nt.

platitude n trīta sententia f.

platter n patella f, lanx f.

plaudit n plausus m.

plausibility n vērīsimilitūdō f.

plausible adj speciōsus, vērī
similis.

play n lūdus m; (THEAT) fābula f;
(voice) inclīnātiō f; (scope) campus
m; (hands) gestus m; ~ on words
agnōminātiō f; fair ~ aequum et
bonum ♦ vi lūdere; (fountain)
scatēre ♦ vt (music) canere;
(instrument) canere; (game)
lūdere (abl); (part) agere; ~ the
part of agere; ~ a trick on
lūdificārī, impōnere (dat).

playbill n ēdictum nt.

player n lūsor m; (at dice) āleātor
m; (on flute) tībīcen m; (on lyre)
fidicen m; (on stage) histriō m.

playful adj lascīvus; (words)
facētus.

playfully adv per lūdum, per
iocum.

playfulness n lascīvia f; facētiae
fpl.

playground n ārea f.

playmate n collūsor m.

playwright n fābulārum scrīptor
m.

plea n causa f; (in defence) dēfēnsiō
f, excūsātiō f.

plead vi causam agere, causam
ōrāre, causam dīcere; (in excuse)
dēprecārī, excūsāre; ~ with
obsecrāre.

pleader n āctor m, causidicus m.

pleasant adj iūcundus, dulcis,
grātus; (place) amoenus.

pleasantly adv iūcundē, suāviter.

pleasantry n facētiae fpl, iocus m.

please vt placēre, dēlectāre;
try to ~ īnservīre (dat); just as you
~ quod commodum est; if you ~
sīs; ~d with contentus (abl); be ~d
with oneself sibī placēre ♦ adv
amābō.

pleasing adj grātus, iūcundus,
amoenus; be ~ to cordī esse (dat).

pleasurable adj iūcundus.

pleasure n voluptās f; (decision)
arbitrium nt; it is my ~ libet;
derive ~ voluptātem capere ♦ vt
grātificārī (dat).

pleasure grounds n hortī mpl.

pleasure-loving adj dēlicātus.

plebeian adj plēbēius ♦ n: the ~s
plēbs f.

plebiscite n suffrāgium nt.

plectrum n plēctrum nt.

pledge n pignus nt ♦ vt obligāre; ~
oneself prōmittere, spondēre; ~
one's word fidem obligāre, fidem
interpōnere.

Pleiads n Plēiadēs fpl.

plenary adj īnfīnītus.

plenipotentiary n lēgātus m.

plenitude n cōpia f, mātūritās f.

plentiful adj cōpiōsus, largus.

plentifully adv cōpiōsē, largē.

plenty n cōpia f, abundantia f;
(enough) satis.

pleonasm n redundantia f.

pleurisy n lateris dolor m.

pliable adj flexibilis, mollis, lentus.

pliant adj flexibilis, mollis, lentus.

pliers n forceps m/f.

plight n habitus m, discrimen nt ♦ vt spondēre.

plod vi labōrāre, operam īnsūmere.

plot n coniūrātiō f, īnsidiae fpl; (land) agellus m; (play) argūmentum nt ♦ vi coniūrāre, mōlīrī.

plotter n coniūrātus m.

plough n arātrum nt ♦ vt arāre; (sea) sulcāre; ~ **up** exarāre.

ploughing n arātiō f.

ploughman n arātor m.

ploughshare n vōmer m.

pluck n fortitūdō f ♦ vt carpere, legere; ~ **out** ēvellere; ~ **up courage** animum recipere, animō adesse.

plucky adj fortis.

plug n obtūrāmentum nt ♦ vt obtūrāre.

plum n prūnum nt; (tree) prūnus f.

plumage n plūmae fpl.

plumb n perpendiculum nt ♦ adj dīrēctus ♦ adv ad perpendiculum ♦ vt (building) ad perpendiculum exigere; (depth) scrūtārī.

plumber n artifex plumbārius m.

plumb line n līnea f, perpendiculum nt.

plume n crista f ♦ vt: ~ **oneself on** iactāre, prae sē ferre.

plummet n perpendiculum nt.

plump adj pinguis.

plumpness n nitor m.

plunder n (act) rapīna f; (booty) praeda f ♦ vi praedārī ♦ vt dīripere, expīlāre.

plunderer n praedātor m, spoliātor m.

plundering n rapīna f ♦ adj praedābundus.

plunge vt mergere, dēmergere;

(weapon) dēmittere ♦ vi mergī, sē dēmergere.

plural adj plūrālis.

plurality n multitūdō f, plūrēs pl.

ply vt exercēre.

poach vt surripere.

pocket n sinus m.

pocket money n pecūlium nt.

pod n siliqua f.

poem n poēma nt, carmen nt.

poesy n poēsis f.

poet n poēta m.

poetess n poētria f.

poetic adj poēticus.

poetical adj = **poetic**.

poetically adv poēticē.

poetry n (art) poētica f; (poems) poēmata ntpl, carmina ntpl.

poignancy n acerbitās f.

poignant adj acerbus, acūtus.

poignantly adv acerbē, acūtē.

point n (dot) pūnctum nt; (place) locus m; (item) caput nt; (sharp end) aciēs f; (of sword) mucrō m; (of epigram) acūleī mpl; ~ **of honour** officium nt; **beside the ~** ab rē; **to the ~** ad rem; **from this ~** hinc; **to that ~** eō; **up to this ~** hāctenus, adhūc; **without ~** īnsulsus; **in ~ of fact** nempe; **make a ~ of doing** cōnsultō facere; **on the ~ of death** moritūrus; **on the ~ of happening** inibī; **I was on the ~ of saying** in eō erat ut dīcerem; **matters have reached such a ~** eō rēs recidit; **come to the ~** ad rem redīre; **the ~ at issue** est illud quaeritur; **the main ~** cardō m, caput nt; **turning ~** articulus temporis m ♦ vt acuere, exacuere; (aim) intendere; (punctuate) distinguere; ~ **out** indicāre, dēmōnstrāre; ostendere.

point-blank adj simplex ♦ adv praecīsē.

pointed adj acūtus; (criticism) acūleātus; (wit) salsus.

pointedly adv apertē, dīlūcidē.

pointer n index m.

pointless adj īnsulsus, frīgidus.

pointlessly adv īnsulsē.

point of view n iūdicium nt, sententia f.

poise n lībrāmen nt; (fig) urbānitās f ♦ vt lībrāre.

poison n venēnum nt ♦ vt venēnō necāre; (fig) īnficere.

poisoned adj venēnātus.

poisoner n venēficus m.

poisoning n venēficium nt.

poisonous adj noxius.

puke vt trūdere, fodicāre.

polar adj septentriōnālis.

pole n asser m, contus m; (ASTRO) polus m.

poleaxe n bipennis f.

polemic n contrōversia f.

police n lictōrēs mpl; (night) vigilēs mpl.

policy n ratiō f, cōnsilium nt; **honesty is the best ~** ea māximē condūcunt quae sunt rēctissima.

polish n (appearance) nitor m; (character) urbānitās f; (LIT) līma f ♦ vt polīre; (fig) expolīre.

polished adj polītus, mundus; (person) excultus, urbānus; (style) līmātus.

polite adj urbānus, hūmānus, cōmis.

politely adv urbānē, cōmiter.

politeness n urbānitās f, hūmānitās f, cōmitās f.

politic adj prūdēns, circumspectus.

political adj cīvīlis, pūblicus; **~ life** rēs pūblica f.

politician n magistrātus m.

politics n rēs pūblica f; **take up ~** ad rem pūblicam accēdere.

polity n reī pūblicae fōrma f.

poll n caput nt; (voting) comitia ntpl ♦ vi suffrāgia inīre.

poll tax n tribūtum nt in singula

capita impositum.

pollute vt inquināre, contāmināre.

pollution n corruptēla f.

poltroon n ignāvus m.

pomegranate n mālum Pūnicum nt.

pomp n adparātus m.

pomposity n māgnificentia f, glōria f.

pompous adj māgnificus, glōriōsus.

pompously adv māgnificē, glōriōsē.

pompousness n māgnificentia f.

pond n stagnum nt, lacūna f.

ponder vi sēcum reputāre ♦ vt animō volūtāre, in mente agitāre.

ponderous adj gravis, ponderōsus.

ponderously adv graviter.

poniard n pugiō m.

pontiff n pontifex m.

pontifical adj pontificālis, pontificius.

pontoon n pontō m.

pony n mannus m.

pooh-pooh vt dērīdēre.

pool n lacūna f, stagnum nt ♦ vt cōnferre.

poop n puppis f.

poor adj pauper, inops; (meagre) exīlis; (inferior) improbus; (pitiable) miser; **~ little** misellus.

poorly adj aeger, aegrōtus ♦ adv parum, tenuiter.

pop n crepitus m ♦ vi ēmicāre.

pope n pāpa m.

poplar n pōpulus f.

poppy n papāver nt.

populace n vulgus nt, plēbs f.

popular adj grātus, grātiōsus; (party) populāris.

popularity n populī favor m, studium nt.

popularly adv vulgō.

populate vt frequentāre.

population n populus m, cīvēs mpl.

populous adj frequēns.

porcelain n fictilia ntpl.
porch n vestibulum nt.
porcupine n hystrīx f.
pore n forāmen nt ♦ vi: ~ **over**
scrūtārī, incumbere in (acc).
pork n porcīna f.
porous adj rārus.
porridge n puls f.
port n portus m ♦ adj (side) laevus,
sinister.
portage n vectūra f.
portal n porta f.
portcullis n cataracta f.
portend vt portendere.
portent n mōnstrum nt, portentum
nt.
portentous adj mōnstruōsus.
porter n iānitor m; (carrier) bāiulus
m.
portico n porticus f.
portion n pars f; (marriage) dōs f;
(lot) sors f.
portliness n amplitūdō f.
portly adj amplus, opīmus.
portrait n imāgō f, effigiēs f.
portray vt dēpingere, exprimere,
effingere.
pose n status m, habitus m ♦ vt
pōnere ♦ vi habitūm sūmere.
poser n nōdus m.
posit vt pōnere.
position n (GEOG) situs m; (body)
status m, gestus m; (rank) dignitās
f; (office) honōs m; (lot) locus m;
be in a ~ to habēre (inf); **take up a
~** (MIL) locum capere.
positive adj certus; **be ~ about**
adfirmāre.
positively adv certō, adfirmātē, rē
vērā.
posse n manus f.
possess vt possidēre, habēre;
(take) occupāre, potīrī (abl).
possession n possessiō f, ~**s** pl
bona ntpl, fortūnae fpl; **take ~ of**
potīrī (abl), occupāre, manum
inicere (dat); (inheritance) obīre;

(emotion) invādere, incēdere (dat);
gain ~ of potior (+ abl).
possessor n possessor m, dominus
m.
possibility n facultās f; **there is a ~**
fierī potest.
possible adj: **it is ~** fierī potest; **as
big as ~** quam māximus.
possibly adv fortasse.
post n pālus m; (MIL) statiō f;
(office) mūnus nt; (courier)
tabellārius m; **leave one's ~** locō
cēdere, signa relinquere ♦ vt
(troops) locāre, collocāre; (at
intervals) dispōnere; (letter) dare,
tabellāriō dare; (entry) in cōdicem
referre; **be ~ed** (MIL) in statiōne
esse.
postage n vectūra f.
poster n libellus m.
posterior adj posterior.
posterity n posterī mpl; (time)
posterītās f.
posthaste adv summā celeritāte.
posthumous adj postumus.
posthumously adv (born) patre
mortuō; (published) auctōre
mortuō.
postpone vt differre, prōferre.
postponement n dīlātiō f.
postscript n: **add a ~** adscrībere,
subicere.
postulate vt sūmere ♦ n sūmptiō f.
posture n gestus m, status m.
pot n olla f, matella f.
pot-bellied adj ventriōsus.
potency n vīs f.
potent adj efficāx, valēns.
potentate n dynastēs m, tyrannus
m.
potential adj futūrus.
potentiality n facultās f.
potentially adv ut fierī posse
vidētur; ~ **an emperor** capāx
imperiī.
potently adv efficienter.

potion n pōtiō f.
pot-pourri n farrāgō f.
potsherd n testa f.
pottage n iūs nt.
potter n figulus m; **~'s** figulāris.
pottery n fictilia ntpl.
pouch n pēra f, sacculus m.
poultice n fōmentum nt, emplastrum nt.
poultry n gallīnae fpl.
pounce vi involāre, īnsilīre.
pound n lībra f; **five ~s** (weight) of gold aurī quīnque pondo ♦ vt conterere; pulsāre.
pour vt fundere; **~ forth** effundere; **~ in** īnfundere; **~ on** superfundere; **~ out** effundere ♦ vi fundī, fluere; **~ down** ruere, sē praecipitāre.
pouring adj (rain) effūsus.
poverty n paupertās f, egestās f, inopia f; (style) iēiūnitās f.
powder n pulvis m.
powdery adj pulvereus.
power n potestās f; (strength) vīrēs fpl; (excessive) potentia f; (supreme) imperium nt; (divine) nūmen nt; (legal) auctōritās f; (of father) manus f; **as far as is in my ~** quantum in mē est; **have great ~** multum valēre, posse; **have of attorney** cognitōrem esse; **it is still in my ~ to** integrum est mihi (inf).
powerful adj validus, potēns.
powerfully adv valdē.
powerless adj impotēns, imbēcillus; **be ~** nihil valēre.
powerlessness n imbēcillitas f.
practicable adj in apertō; **be ~** fierī posse.
practical adj (person) habilis.
practical joke n lūdus m.
practical knowledge n ūsus m.
practically adv ferē, paene.
practice n ūsus m, exercitātiō f; (RHET) meditātiō f; (habit)

consuētūdō f, mōs m; **corrupt ~s** malae artēs.
practise vt (occupation) exercēre, facere; (custom) factitāre; (RHET) meditārī ♦ vi (MED) medicīnam exercēre; (law) causās agere.
practised adj exercitātus, perītus.
practitioner n (MED) medicus m.
praetor n praetor nt; **~'s** praetōrius.
praetorian adj praetōrius.
praetorian guards npl praetōriānī mpl.
praetorship n praetūra f.
praise n laus f ♦ vt laudāre.
praiser n laudātor m.
praiseworthy adj laudābilis, laude dignus.
prance vi exsultāre.
prank n lūdus m.
prate vi garrīre.
prating adj garrulus.
pray vi deōs precārī, deōs venerārī ♦ vt precārī, ōrāre; **~ for** petere, precārī; **~ to** adōrāre.
prayer(s) n precēs fpl.
prayerful adj supplex.
preach vt, vi docēre, praedicāre.
preacher n ōrātor m.
preamble n exōrdium nt.
prearranged adj cōnstitūtus.
precarious adj dubius, perīculōsus.
precariousness n discrīmen nt.
precaution n cautiō f, prōvidentia f; **take ~s** cavēre, praecavēre.
precede vt praecīre (dat), anteīre (dat), antecēdere.
precedence n prīmārius locus m; **give ~ to** cēdere (dat); **take ~** (thing) antīquius esse; (person) prīmās agere.
precedent n exemplum nt; (law) praeiūdicium nt; **breach of ~** īnsolentia f; **in defiance of ~** īnsolenter.
preceding adj prior, superior.
precept n praeceptum nt.

preceptor n doctor m, magister m.

precinct n terminus m, templum nt.

precious adj cārus; pretiōsus; (style) pūtidus.

precious stone n gemma f.

precipice n locus praeceps m, rūpēs f.

precipitancy n festīnātiō f.

precipitate vt praecipitāre ♦ adj praeceps; praeproperus.

precipitation n festīnātiō f.

precipitous adj dēruptus, praeceps, praeruptus.

precise adj certus, subtīlis; (person) accūrātus.

precisely adv dēmum.

precision n cūra f.

preclude vt exclūdere, prohibēre.

precocious adj praecox.

precocity n festīnāta mātūritās f.

preconceive vt praecipere; **~d idea** praeiūdicāta opīniō f.

preconception n praeceptiō f.

preconcerted adj ex compositō factus.

precursor n praenūntius m.

predatory adj praedātōrius.

predecessor n dēcessor m; **my ~** cui succēdō.

predestination n fātum nt, necessitās f.

predestine vt dēvovēre.

predetermine vt praefīnīre.

predicament n angustiae fpl, discrīmen nt.

predicate n attribūtum nt.

predict vt praedīcere, augurārī.

prediction n praedictiō f.

predilection n amor m, studium m.

predispose vt inclīnāre, praeparāre.

predisposition n inclīnātiō f.

predominance n potentia f, praestantia f.

predominant adj praepotēns, praecipuus.

predominantly adv plērumque.

predominate vi pollēre, dominārī.

pre-eminence n praestantia f.

pre-eminent adj ēgregius, praecipuus, excellēns.

pre-eminently adv ēgregiē, praecipuē, excellenter.

preface n prooemium nt, praefātiō f ♦ vi praefārī.

prefect n praefectus m.

prefecture n praefectūra f.

prefer vt (charge) dēferre; (to office) anteferre; (choice) antepōnere (acc and dat), posthabēre (dat and acc); (with verb) mālle.

preferable adj potior.

preferably adv potius.

preference n favor m; **give ~ to** antepōnere, praeoptāre; **in ~ to** potius quam.

preferment n honōs m, dignitās f.

prefix vt praetendere ♦ n praepositiō f.

pregnancy n graviditās f.

pregnant adj gravida.

prejudge vt praeiūdicāre.

prejudice n praeiūdicāta opīniō f; (harmful) invidia f, incommodum nt; **without ~** cum bonā veniā ♦ vt obesse (dat); **be ~d against** invidēre (dat), male opīnārī dē (abl).

prejudicial adj damnōsus; **be ~ to** obesse (dat), nocēre (dat), officere (dat), dētrīmentō esse (dat).

preliminaries npl praecurrentia ntpl.

preliminary adj prīmus ♦ n prōlūsiō f.

prelude n prooemium nt.

premature adj immātūrus; (birth) abortīvus.

prematurely adv ante tempus.

premeditate vt praecōgitāre, praemeditārī.

premeditated adj praemeditātus.

premier adj prīnceps, praecipuus.

premise n (major) prōpositiō f;

(*minor*) adsūmptiō f; **~s** *pl* aedēs fpl, domus f.

premium n praemium nt; **be at a ~** male emī.

premonition n monitus m.

preoccupation n sollicitūdō f.

preoccupied adj sollicitus, districtus.

preordain vt praefinīre.

preparation n (*process*) adparātiō f, comparātiō f; (*product*) adparātus m; (*of speech*) meditātiō f; **make ~ for** īnstruere, exōrnāre, comparāre.

prepare vt parāre, adparāre, comparāre; (*speech*) meditārī; (*with verb*) parāre; **~d for** parātus ad (+ acc).

preponderance n praestantia f.

preponderate vi praepollēre, vincere.

preposition n praepositiō f.

prepossess vt commendāre (*dat and acc*), praeoccupāre.

prepossessing adj suāvis, iūcundus.

prepossession n favor m.

preposterous adj absurdus.

prerogative n iūs nt.

presage n ōmen n ♦ vt ōminārī, portendere.

prescience n prōvidentia f.

prescient adj prōvidus.

prescribe vt imperāre; (MED) praescrībere; (*limit*) fīnīre.

prescription n (MED) compositiō f; (*right*) ūsus m.

presence n praesentia f; (*appearance*) aspectus m; **~ of mind** praesēns animus m; **in the ~ of** cōram (*abl*); apud (*abl*); **in my ~** mē praesente.

present adj praesēns, īnstāns; **be ~** adesse; **be ~ at** interesse (*dat*) ♦ n praesēns tempus nt; (*gift*) dōnum nt; **at ~** in praesentī, nunc; **for the ~** in praesēns ♦ vt dōnāre,

offerre; (*on stage*) indūcere; (*in court*) sistere; **~ itself** occurrere.

presentable adj spectābilis.

presentation n dōnātiō f.

presentiment n augurium nt.

presently adv mox.

preservation n cōnservātiō f.

preserve vt cōnservāre, tuērī; (*food*) condīre.

preside vi praesidēre (*dat*).

presidency n praefectūra f.

president n praefectus m.

press n prēlum nt ♦ vt premere; (*crowd*) stīpāre; (*urge*) īnstāre (*dat*); **~ for** flāgitāre; **~ hard** (*pursuit*) īnsequī, īnstāre (*dat*), īnsistere (*dat*); **~ out** exprimere; **~ together** comprimere.

pressing adj īnstāns, gravis.

pressure n pressiō f, nīsus m.

prestige n auctōritās f, opīniō f.

presumably adv sānē.

presume vt sūmere, conicere ♦ vi audēre, cōnfīdere; **I ~** opīnor, crēdō.

presuming adj adrogāns.

presumption n coniectūra f; (*arrogance*) adrogantia f, licentia f.

presumptuous adj adrogāns, audāx.

presumptuously adv adroganter, audācter.

presuppose vt praesūmere.

pretence n simulātiō f, speciēs f; **under ~ of** per speciem (*gen*); **under false ~** dolō malō.

pretend vt simulāre, fingere; **~ that ... not** dissimulāre.

pretender n captātor m.

pretension n postulātum nt; **make ~s to** adfectāre, sibī adrogāre.

pretentious adj adrogāns, glōriōsus.

pretext n speciēs f; **under ~ of** per speciem (*gen*); **on the ~ that** quod (+ *subj*).

prettily adv pulchrē, bellē.

prettiness n pulchritūdō f, lepōs m.

pretty adj formōsus, pulcher, bellus ♦ adv admodum, satis.

prevail vi vincere; (custom) tenēre, obtinēre; ~ **upon** persuādēre (dat); (by entreaty) exōrāre.

prevailing adj vulgātus.

prevalent adj vulgātus; **be** ~ obtinēre; **become** ~ incrēbrēscere.

prevaricate vi tergiversārī.

prevarication n tergiversātiō f.

prevaricator n veterātor m.

prevent vt impedīre (+ quōminus/ quin and subj), prohibēre (+ acc and infin).

prevention n impedītiō f.

previous adj prior, superior.

previously adv anteā, antehāc.

prevision n prōvidentia f.

prey n praeda f ♦ vi: ~ **upon** īnsectārī, (fig) vexāre, carpere.

price n pretium nt; (of corn) annōna f; **at a high** ~ māgnī; **at a low** ~ parvī ♦ vt pretium cōnstituere (gen).

priceless adj inaestimābilis.

prick vt pungere; (goad) stimulāre; ~ **up the ears** aurēs adrigere.

prickle n aculeus m.

prickly adj aculeātus, horridus.

pride n superbia f, fastus m; (boasting) glōria f; (object) decus nt; (best part) flōs m ♦ vt: ~ **oneself on** iactāre, prae sē ferre.

priest n sacerdōs m; (especial) flāmen m; **high** ~ pontifex m, antistes m.

priestess n sacerdōs f; **high** ~ antistita f.

priesthood n sacerdōtium nt, flāminium nt.

prig n homō fāstīdiōsus m.

priggish adj fāstīdiōsus.

prim adj modestior.

primarily adv prīncipiō, praecipuē.

primary adj prīmus, praecipuus.

prime adj prīmus, ēgregius; ~ **mover** auctor m ♦ n flōs m; **in one's** ~ flōrēns ♦ vt īnstruere, ērudīre.

primeval adj prīscus.

primitive adj prīstinus, incultus.

primordial adj prīscus.

prince n rēgulus m; rēgis fīlius m; prīnceps m.

princely adj rēgālis.

princess n rēgis fīlia f.

principal adj praecipuus, prīnceps, māximus ♦ n (person) prīnceps m/f; (money) sors f.

principally adv in prīmīs, māximē, māximam partem.

principle n prīncipium nt; (rule) fōrmula f, ratiō f; (character) fidēs f; ~s pl īnstitūta ntpl, disciplīna f; **first** ~s elementa ntpl, initia ntpl.

print n nota f, signum nt; (foot) vestīgium nt ♦ vt imprimere.

prior adj prior, potior.

priority n: **give** ~ **to** praevertere (dat).

prise vt sublevāre; ~ **open** vectī refringere.

prison n carcer m, vincula ntpl; **put in** ~ in vincula conicere.

prisoner n (for debt) nexus m; (of war) captīvus m; ~ **at the bar** reus m, rea f; **take** ~ capere.

pristine adj prīscus, prīstinus, vetus.

privacy n sēcrētum nt.

private adj (individual) prīvātus; (home) domesticus; (secluded) sēcrētus ♦ n (MIL) gregārius mīles m.

privately adv clam, sēcrētō.

private property n res familiāris f.

privation n inopia f, egestās f.

privet n ligustrum nt.

privilege n iūs nt, immūnitās f.

privileged adj immūnis.

privy adj sēcrētus; ~ **to** cōnscius (gen).

prize n praemium nt; (captured) praeda f; **~ money** manubiae fpl ♦ vt māgnī aestimāre.

pro-Athenian adj rērum Athēniēnsium studiōsus.

probability n vērī similitūdō f.

probable adj vērī similis; **more ~** vērō propior.

probably adv fortasse.

probation n probātiō f.

probationer n tīrō m.

probe vt īnspicere, scrūtārī.

probity n honestās f, integritās f.

problem n quaestiō f; **the ~ is** illud quaeritur.

problematical adj dubius, anceps.

procedure n ratiō f, modus m; (law) fōrmula f.

proceed vi pergere, prōcēdere, prōgredī; (narrative) īnsequī; **~ against** persequī, lītem intendere (dat); **~ from** orīrī, proficīscī ex.

proceedings n ācta ntpl.

proceeds n frūctus m, reditus m.

process n ratiō f; (law) āctiō f; **in the ~ of time** post aliquod tempus.

procession n pompa f, (fig) agmen nt.

proclaim vt ēdīcere, prōnūntiāre, praedicāre, dēclārāre; **~ war upon** bellum indīcere ⊢ dat.

proclamation n ēdictum nt.

proclivity n prōpēnsiō f.

proconsul n prōconsul m.

proconsular adj prōcōnsulāris.

proconsulship n prōcōnsulātus m.

procrastinate vt differre, prōferre ♦ vi cunctārī.

procrastination n prōcrāstinātiō f, mora f.

procreate vt generāre, prōcreāre.

procreation n prōcreātiō f.

procreator n generātor m.

procumbent adj prōnus.

procurator n prōcūrātor m.

procure vt parāre, adipīscī, adquīrere; (by request) impetrāre.

procurer n lēnō m.

prod vt stimulāre.

prodigal adj prōdigus ♦ n nepōs m.

prodigality n effūsiō f.

prodigally adv effūsē.

prodigious adj ingēns, immānis.

prodigy n prōdigium nt, portentum nt; (fig) mīrāculum nt.

produce vt ēdere; (young) parere; (crops) ferre; (play) dare, docēre; (line) prōdūcere; (in court) sistere; (into view) prōferre; (from store) prōmere, dēprōmere ♦ n frūctus m; (of earth) frūgēs fpl; (in money) reditus m.

product n opus nt; **~ of** frūctus (gen).

production n opus nt.

productive adj fēcundus, ferāx, frūctuōsus.

productivity n fēcunditās f, ūbertās f.

profanation n violātiō f.

profane adj profānus, impius ♦ vt violāre, polluere.

profanely adv impiē.

profanity n impietās f.

profess vt profitērī, prae sē ferre; **~ to be** profitērī sē.

profession n professiō f; (occupation) ars f, haeresis f.

professor n doctor m.

proffer vt offerre, pollicērī.

proficiency n prōgressus m, perītia f; **attain ~** prōficere.

proficient adj perītus.

profile n ōris līneāmenta ntpl; (portrait) oblīqua imāgō f.

profit n lucrum nt, ēmolumentum nt, frūctus m; **make a ~ out of** quaestuī habēre ♦ vt prōdesse (dat) ♦ vi: **~ by** fruī (abl), ūtī (abl); (opportunity) arripere.

profitable adj frūctuōsus, ūtilis.

profitably adv ūtiliter.

profligacy n flāgitium nt, perditī mōrēs mpl.

profligate adj perditus, dissolūtus
♦ n nepōs m.
profound adj altus; (discussion) abstrūsus.
profoundly adv penitus.
profundity n altitūdō f.
profuse adj prōdigus, effūsus.
profusely adv effūsē.
profusion n abundantia f, adfluentia f; in ~ abundē.
progenitor n auctor m.
progeny n prōgeniēs f, prōlēs f.
prognostic n signum nt.
prognosticate vt ōminārī, augurārī, praedīcere.
prognostication n ōmen nt, praedictiō f.
programme n libellus m.
progress n prōgressus m; **make ~** prōficere ♦ vi prōgredī.
progression n prōgressus m.
progressively adv gradātim.
prohibit vt vetāre, interdīcere (dat).
prohibition n interdictum nt.
project n prōpositum nt ♦ vi ēminēre, exstāre; (land) excurrere ♦ vt prōicere.
projectile n tēlum nt.
projecting adj ēminēns.
projection n ēminentia f.
proletarian adj plēbēius.
proletariat n plēbs f.
prolific adj fēcundus.
prolix adj verbōsus, longus.
prolixity n redundantia f.
prologue n prologus m.
prolong vt dūcere, prōdūcere; (office) prōrogāre.
prolongation n (time) propāgātiō f; (office) prōrogātiō f.
promenade n ambulātiō f ♦ vi inambulāre, spatiārī.
prominence n ēminentia f.
prominent adj ēminēns, īnsignis; **be ~** ēminēre.
promiscuous adj prōmiscuus.

promiscuously adv prōmiscuē.
promise n prōmissum nt; **break a ~** fidem fallere; **keep a ~** fidem praestāre; **make a ~** fidem dare; **a youth of great ~** summae speī adulēscēns ♦ vt prōmittere, pollicērī; (in marriage) dēspondēre; ~ **in return** reprōmittere ♦ vi: ~ **well** bonam spem ostendere.
promising adj bonae speī.
promissory note n syngrapha f.
promontory n prōmunturium nt.
promote vt favēre (dat); (growth) alere; (in rank) prōdūcere.
promoter n auctor m, fautor m.
promotion n dignitās f.
prompt adj alacer, prōmptus ♦ vt incitāre, commovēre; (speaker) subicere.
prompter n monitor m.
promptitude n alacritās f, celeritās f.
promptly adv extemplō, citō.
promulgate vt prōmulgāre, palam facere.
promulgation n prōmulgātiō f.
prone adj prōnus; (mind) inclīnātus.
prong n dēns m.
pronounce vt ēloquī, appellāre; (oath) interpōnere; (sentence) dīcere, prōnūntiāre.
pronounced adj manifestus, īnsignis.
pronouncement n ōrātiō f, adfirmātiō f.
pronunciation n appellātiō f.
proof n documentum nt, argūmentum nt; (test) probātiō f ♦ adj immōtus, impenetrābilis.
prop n adminiculum nt, firmāmentum nt ♦ vt fulcīre.
propaganda n documenta ntpl.
propagate vt prōpāgāre.
propagation n prōpāgātiō f.
propel vt incitāre, prōpellere.

propensity n inclīnātiō f.

proper adj idōneus, decēns, decōrus; rēctus; **it is ~** decet.

properly adv decōrē; rēctē.

property n rēs f, rēs mancipī, bona ntpl; (estate) praedium nt; (attribute) proprium nt; (slave's) pecūlium nt.

prophecy n vāticinium nt, praedictiō f.

prophesy vt vāticinārī, praedīcere.

prophet n vātēs m, fātidicus m.

prophetess n vātēs f.

prophetic adj dīvīnus, fātidicus.

prophetically adv dīvīnitus.

propinquity n (place) vīcīnitās f; (kin) propinquitās f.

propitiate vt plācāre.

propitiation n plācātiō f, litātiō f.

propitious adj fēlīx, faustus; (god) praesēns.

proportion n mēnsūra f; **in ~** portiōne, prō ratā parte; **in ~ to** prō (abl).

proportionately adv prō portiōne, prō ratā parte.

proposal n condiciō f.

propose vt prōpōnere; (motion) ferre, rogāre; (penalty) inrogāre; (candidate) rogāre magistrātum.

proposer n auctor m, lātor m.

proposition n (offer) condiciō f; (plan) cōnsilium nt, prōpositum nt; (logic) prōnūntiātum nt.

propound vt expōnere, in medium prōferre.

propraetor n prōpraetor m.

proprietor n dominus m.

propriety n decōrum nt; (conduct) modestia f; **with ~** decenter.

propulsion n impulsus m.

prorogation n prōrogātiō f.

prorogue vt prōrogāre.

prosaic adj pedester.

proscribe vt prōscrībere.

proscription n prōscrīptiō f.

prose n ōrātiō f, ōrātiō solūta f.

prosecute vt (task) exsequī, gerere; (at law) accūsāre, lītem intendere (dat).

prosecution n exsecūtiō f; (at law) accūsātiō f; (party) accūsātor m.

prosecutor n accūsātor m.

prosody n numerī mpl.

prospect n prōspectus m; (fig) spēs f ♦ vi explōrāre.

prospective adj futūrus, spērātus.

prosper vi flōrēre, bonā fortūnā ūtī ♦ vt fortūnāre.

prosperity n fortūna f, rēs secundae fpl, fēlīcitās f.

prosperous adj fēlīx, fortūnātus, secundus.

prosperously adv prosperē.

prostrate adj prōstrātus, afflīctus; **lie ~** iacēre ♦ vt prōsternere, dēicere; **~ oneself** prōcumbere, sē prōicere.

prostration n frāctus animus m.

prosy adj longus.

protagonist n prīmārum partium āctor m.

protect vt tuērī, dēfendere, custōdīre, prōtegere.

protection n tūtēla f, praesidium nt; (law) patrōcinium nt; (POL) fidēs f; **put oneself under the ~ of** in fidem venīre (gen); **take under one's ~** in fidem recipere.

protector n patrōnus m, dēfēnsor m, custōs m.

protectress n patrōna f.

protégé n clīēns m.

protest n obtestātiō f; (POL) intercessiō f ♦ vi obtestārī, reclāmāre; (POL) intercēdere.

protestation n adsevērātiō f.

prototype n archetypum nt.

protract vt dūcere, prōdūcere.

protrude vi prōminēre.

protruding adj exsertus.

protuberance n ēminentia f, tūber nt.

protuberant *adj* ēminēns,
turgidus.
proud *adj* superbus, adrogāns,
īnsolēns; **be ~** superbīre; **be ~ of**
iactāre.
proudly *adv* superbē.
prove *vt* dēmōnstrāre, arguere,
probāre; (*test*) experīrī ♦ *vi*
(*person*) sē praebēre; (*event*)
ēvādere; **~ oneself** sē praebēre, sē
praestāre; **not ~n** nōn liquet.
proved *adj* expertus.
provenance *n* orīgō f.
provender *n* pābulum nt.
proverb *n* prōverbium nt.
proverbial *adj* trītus; **become ~** in
prōverbium venīre.
provide *vt* parāre, praebēre; **~ for**
prōvidēre (*dat*); **the law ~s** lēx
iubet; **~ against** praecavēre.
provided that *conj* dum, dummodo
(+ *subj*).
providence *n* prōvidentia f; Deus
m.
provident *adj* prōvidus, cautus.
providential *adj* dīvīnus;
secundus.
providentially *adv* dīvīnitus.
providently *adv* cautē.
providing *conj* dum, dummodo.
province *n* prōvincia f.
provincial *adj* prōvinciālis;
(*contemptuous*) oppidānus,
mūnicipālis.
provision *n* parātus m; **make ~ for**
prōvidēre (*dat*); **make ~** cavēre.
provisionally *adv* ad tempus.
provisions *n* cibus m, commeātus
m, rēs frūmentāria f.
proviso *n* condiciō f; **with this ~**
hāc lēge.
provocation *n* inrītāmentum nt,
offēnsiō f.
provocative *adj* (*language*)
molestus, invidiōsus.
provoke *vt* inrītāre, lacessere; (*to
action*) excitāre.

provoking *adj* odiōsus, molestus.
provost *n* praefectus m.
prow *n* prōra f.
prowess *n* virtūs f.
prowl *vi* grassārī, vagārī.
proximate *adj* proximus.
proximity *n* propinquitās f, vīcīnia
f.
proxy *n* vicārius m.
prude *n* fastīdiōsa f.
prudence *n* prūdentia f.
prudent *adj* prūdēns, cautus,
sagāx.
prudently *adv* prūdenter, cautē.
prudery *n* fastīdiōsa quaedam
pudīcitia f.
prudish *adj* fastīdiōsus.
prune *vt* amputāre.
pruner *n* putātor m.
pruning hook *n* falx f.
pry *vi* inquīrere; **~ into** scrūtārī.
pseudonym *n* falsum nōmen nt.
psychology *n* animī ratiō f.
Ptolemy *n* Ptolemaeus m.
puberty *n* pūbertās f.
public *adj* pūblicus; (*speech*)
forēnsis; **~ life** rēs pūblica f,
forum nt; **in ~** forīs; **appear in ~** in
medium prōdīre; **make ~** in mediō
pōnere, forās perferre; **make a ~
case of** in medium vocāre; **act for
the ~ good** in medium cōnsulere;
be a ~ figure in lūce versārī, digitō
mōnstrārī ♦ *n* vulgus nt, hominēs
mpl.
publican *n* (*taxes*) pūblicānus m;
(*inn*) caupō m.
publication *n* ēditiō f, prōmulgātiō
f; (*book*) liber m.
publicity *n* lūx f, celebritās f.
publicly *adv* palam; (*by the state*)
pūblicē.
public opinion *n* fāma f.
publish *vt* vulgāre, dīvulgāre;
(*book*) ēdere.
pucker *vt* corrūgāre.
puerile *adj* puerīlis.

puerility n ineptiae fpl.

puff n aura ♦ vt īnflāre ♦ vi anhēlāre.

puffed up adj īnflātus, tumidus.

pugilism n pugilātus m.

pugilist n pugil m.

pugnacious adj pugnāx.

pugnacity n ferōcitās f.

puissance n potentia f, vīrēs fpl.

puissant adj potēns.

pull n tractus m; (of gravity) contentiō f ♦ vt trahere, tractāre; ~ **apart** distrahere; ~ **at** vellicāre; ~ **away** āvellere; ~ **back** retrahere; ~ **down** dēripere, dētrahere; (building) dēmōlīrī; ~ **off** āvellere; ~ **out** ēvellere, extrahere; ~ **through** vi pervincere; (illness) convalēscere; ~ **up** (plant) ēruere; (movement) coercēre; ~ **to pieces** dīlaniāre.

pullet n pullus gallīnāceus m.

pulley n trochlea f.

pulmonary adj pulmōneus.

pulp n carō f.

pulpit n suggestus m.

pulsate vi palpitāre, micāre.

pulse n (plant) legūmen nt; (of blood) vēnae fpl; **feel the ~** vēnās temptāre.

pulverize vt contundere.

pumice stone n pūmex m.

pummel vt verberāre.

pump n antlia f ♦ vt haurīre; ~ **out** exhaurīre.

pumpkin n cucurbita f.

pun n agnōminātiō f.

punch n ictus m ♦ vt pertundere, percutere.

punctilious adj riligiōsus.

punctiliousness n rīligiō f.

punctual adj accūrātus, dīligēns.

punctuality n dīligentia f.

punctually adv ad hōram, ad tempus.

punctuate vt distinguere.

punctuation n interpūnctiō f.

puncture n pūnctiō f ♦ vt pungere.

pundit n scholasticus m.

pungency n ācrimōnia f; (in debate) aculeī mpl.

pungent adj ācer, mordāx.

punish vt pūnīre, animadvertere in (acc); poenam sūmere dē (+ abl); **be ~ed** poenās dare

punishable adj poenā dignus.

punisher n vindex m, ultor m.

punishment n poena f, supplicium nt; (censors') animadversiō f; **capital ~** capitis supplicium nt; **corporal ~** verbera ntpl; **inflict ~ on** poenā adficere, poenam capere dē (abl), supplicium sūmere dē (abl); **submit to ~** poenam subīre; **undergo ~** poenās dare, pendere, solvere.

punitive adj ulcīscendī causā.

punt n pontō m.

puny adj pusillus.

pup n catulus m ♦ vi parere.

pupil n discipulus m, discipula f; (eye) aciēs f, pūpula f.

pupillage n tūtēla f.

puppet n pūpa f.

puppy n catulus m.

purblind adj luscus.

purchase n emptiō f; (formal) mancipium nt ♦ vt emere.

purchaser n emptor m; (at auction) manceps m.

pure adj pūrus, integer; (morally) castus; (mere) merus.

purely adv pūrē, integrē; (solely) sōlum, nīl nisi; (quite) omnīnō, plānē.

purgation n pūrgātiō f.

purge vt pūrgāre, expūrgāre.

purification n lūstrātiō f, pūrgātiō f.

purify vt pūrgāre, expūrgāre.

purist n fastīdiōsus m.

purity n integritās f, castitās f.

purloin vt surripere, fūrārī.

purple n purpura f ♦ adj

purpureus.

purport *n* sententia *f*; (*of words*) vīs *f*; **what is the ~ of?** quō spectat?, quid vult? ♦ *vt* velle spectāre ad.

purpose *n* prōpositum *nt*, cōnsilium *nt*, mēns *f*; **for that ~** eō; **for the ~ of** ad (*acc*), ut (*subj*), eā mente ut, eō cōnsiliō ut (*subj*); **on ~** cōnsultō, dē industriā; **to the ~** ad rem; **to what ~?** quō?, quōrsum?; **to no ~** frūstrā, nēquīquam; **without achieving one's ~** rē īnfectā ♦ *vt* in animō habēre, velle.

purposeful *adj* intentus.

purposeless *adj* inānis.

purposely *adv* cōnsultō, dē industriā.

purr *n* murmur *nt* ♦ *vi* murmurāre.

purse *n* marsupium *nt*, crumēna *f*; **privy ~** fiscus *m* ♦ *vt* adstringere.

pursuance *n* exsecūtiō *f*; **in ~ of** secundum (*acc*).

pursue *vt* īnsequī, īnsectārī, persequī; (*closely*) īnstāre (*dat*), īnsistere (*dat*); (*aim*) petere; (*course*) īnsistere.

pursuer *n* īnsequēns *m*; (*law*) accūsātor *m*.

pursuit *n* īnsectātiō *f*; (*hunt*) vēnātiō *f*; (*ambition*) studium *nt*.

purvey *vt* parāre; (*food*) obsōnāre.

purveyance *n* prōcūrātiō *f*.

purveyor *n* obsōnātor *m*.

purview *n* prōvincia *f*.

pus *n* pūs *nt*.

push *n* pulsus *m*, impetus *m* ♦ *vt* impellere, trūdere, urgēre; **~ away** āmovēre; **~ back** repellere; **~ down** dēprimere, dētrūdere; **~ forward** prōpellere; **~ in** intrūdere; **~ on** incitāre; **~ through** perrumpere.

pushing *adj* cōnfīdēns.

pusillanimity *n* ignāvia *f*, timor *m*.

pusillanimous *adj* ignāvus, timidus.

pustule *n* pustula *f*.

put *vt* (*in a state*) dare; (*in a position*) pōnere; (*in words*) reddere; (*argument*) pōnere; (*spur*) subdere; (*to some use*) adhibēre; **~ an end to** fīnem facere (*dat*); **~ a question to** interrogāre; **~ against** adpōnere; **~ among** intericere; **~ aside** sēpōnere; **~ away** pōnere, dēmovēre; (*store*) repōnere; **~ back** repōnere, repellere; **~ beside** adpōnere; **~ between** interpōnere; **~ by** condere; **~ down** dēpōnere; (*revolt*) opprimere; **~ forth** extendere; (*growth*) mittere; **~ forward** ostentāre; (*plea*) adferre; **~ in** immittere, īnserere; (*ship*) adpellere; **~ off** differre; (*clothes*) induere; (*play*) dare; **~ out** ēicere; (*eye*) effodere; (*fire*) exstinguere; (*money*) pōnere; (*tongue*) exserere; **~ out of the way** dēmovēre; **~ out to sea** in altum ēvehī, solvere; **~ over** superimpōnere; **~ to** adpōnere; (*flight*) dare in (*acc*), fugāre, prōflīgāre; **in fugam conicere**; (*sea*) solvere; **~ together** cōnferre; **~ under** subicere; **~ up** (*for sale*) prōpōnere; (*lodge*) dēvertere, dēversārī apud; **~ up with** ferre, patī; **~ upon** impōnere.

putrefaction *n* pūtor *m*.

putrefy *vi* putrēscere.

putrid *adj* putridus.

puzzle *n* nōdus *m* ♦ *vt* impedīre, sollicitāre; **be ~d** haerēre.

puzzling *adj* ambiguus, perplexus.

pygmy *n* pygmaeus *m*.

pyramid *n* pȳramis *f*.

pyramidal *adj* pȳramidātus.

pyre *n* rogus *m*.

Pyrenees *npl* Pyrenaeī (montēs) *mpl*.

python *n* pȳthōn *m*.

Q

quack n (*doctor*) circulātor m ♦ vi tetrinnīre.

quadrangle n ārea f.

quadruped n quadrupēs m/f.

quadruple adj quadruplex.

quaestor n quaestor m; **~'s** quaestōrius.

quaestorship n quaestūra f.

quaff vt ēpōtāre, haurīre.

quagmire n palūs f.

quail n (*bird*) coturnīx f ♦ vi pāvēscere, trepidāre.

quaint adj novus, īnsolitus.

quaintness n īnsolentia f.

quake vi horrēre, horrēscere ♦ n (*earth*) mōtus m.

quaking n horror m, tremor m ♦ adj tremulus.

qualification n condiciō f; (*limitation*) exceptiō f.

qualified adj (*for*) aptus, idōneus, dignus; (*in*) perītus, doctus.

qualify vi prōficere ♦ vt temperāre, mītigāre.

qualities npl ingenium nt.

quality n nātūra f, vīs f; indolēs f, (*rank*) locus m, genus nt; **I know the ~ of** sciō quālis sit.

qualm n religiō f, scrūpulus m.

quandary n angustiae fpl; **be in a ~** haerēre.

quantity n cōpia f, numerus m; (*metre*) vōcum mēnsiō f; **a large ~** multum nt, plūrimum nt; **a small ~** aliquantulum nt.

quarrel n dissēnsiō f, controversia f; (*violent*) rixa f, iūrgium nt ♦ vi rīxārī, altercārī.

quarrelsome adj pugnāx, lītigiōsus.

quarry n lapicīdinae fpl, metallum nt; (*prey*) praeda f ♦ vt excīdere.

quart n duō sextāriī mpl.

quartan n (*fever*) quartāna f.

quarter n quarta pars f, quadrāns m; (*sector*) regiō f; (*direction*) pars f, regiō f; (*respite*) missiō f; **~s** castra ntpl; (*billet*) hospitium nt; **come to close ~s** manum cōnserere; (*armies*) signa cōnferre; **winter ~s** hīberna ntpl ♦ vt quadrifidam dīvidere; (*troops*) in hospitia dīvidere.

quarterdeck n puppis f.

quarterly adj trimestris ♦ adv quartō quōque mēnse.

quartermaster n (*navy*) gubernātor m; (*army*) castrōrum praefectus m.

quarterstaff n rudis f.

quash vt comprimere; (*decision*) rescindere.

quatrain n tetrastichon nt.

quaver n tremor m ♦ vi tremere.

quavering adj tremebundus.

quay n crepīdō f.

queasy adj fastīdiōsus.

queen n rēgīna f; (*bee*) rēx m.

queer adj īnsolēns, rīdiculus.

quell vt opprimere, domāre, dēbellāre.

quench vt exstinguere, restinguere; (*thirst*) sēdāre, explēre.

querulous adj querulus, queribundus.

query n interrogātiō f ♦ vt in dubium vocāre ♦ vi rogāre.

quest n investīgātiō f; **go in ~ of** investīgāre, anquīrere.

question n interrogātiō f; (*at issue*) quaestiō f, rēs f; (*in doubt*) dubium nt; **ask a ~** rogāre, quaerere, scīscitārī, percontārī; **call in ~** in dubium vocāre, addubitāre; **out of the ~** indīgnus; **be out of the ~** improbārī, fierī nōn posse; **the ~ is** illud quaeritur; **there is no ~ that** nōn dubium est quīn (*subj*); **without ~** sine dubiō ♦ vt interrogāre; (*closely*) percontārī;

(*doubt*) in dubium vocāre ♦ *vi* dubitāre.

questionable *adj* incertus, dubius.

questioner *n* percontātor *m*.

questioning *n* interrogātiō *f*.

queue *n* agmen *nt*.

quibble *n* captiō *f* ♦ *vi* cavillārī.

quibbler *n* cavillātor *m*.

quibbling *adj* captiōsus.

quick *adj* (*speed*) celer, vēlōx, citus; (*to act*) alacer, impiger; (*to perceive*) sagāx; (*with hands*) facilis; (*living*) vīvus; **be ~** properāre, festīnāre; **cut to the ~** ad vīvum resecāre; (*fig*) mordēre.

quicken *vt* adcelerāre; (*with life*) animāre.

quickening *adj* vītālis.

quickly *adv* celeriter, citō; (*haste*) properē; (*mind*) acūtē; **as ~ as possible** quam celerrimē.

quickness *n* celeritās *f*, vēlōcitās *f*; (*to act*) alacritās *f*; (*to perceive*) sagācitās *f*, sollertia *f*.

quicksand *n* syrtis *f*.

quick-tempered *adj* īrācundus.

quick-witted *adj* acūtus, sagāx, perspicāx.

quiescence *n* inertia *f*, ōtium *nt*.

quiescent *adj* iners, ōtiōsus.

quiet *adj* tranquillus, quiētus, placidus; (*silent*) tacitus; **be ~** quiēscere; silēre ♦ *n* quiēs *f*, tranquillitās *f*, silentium *nt*; (*peace*) pāx *f* ♦ *vt* pācāre, compōnere.

quietly *adv* tranquillē, quiētē; tacitē, per silentium; aequō animō.

quietness *n* tranquillitās *f*; silentium *nt*.

quill *n* penna *f*.

quince *n* cydōnium *nt*.

quinquennial *adj* quīnquennālis.

quinquereme *n* quīnquerēmis *f*.

quintessence *n* flōs *m*, vīs *f*.

quip *n* sāl *m*, facētiae *fpl*.

quirk *n* captiuncula *f*; **~s** *pl* trīcae *fpl*.

quit *vt* relinquere ♦ *adj* līber, solūtus.

quite *adv* admodum, plānē, prōrsus; **not ~** minus, parum; (*time*) nōndum.

quits *n* parēs *mpl*.

quiver *n* pharetra *f* ♦ *vi* tremere, contremere.

quivering *adj* tremebundus, tremulus.

quoit *n* discus *m*.

quota *n* pars *f*, rata pars *f*.

quotation *n* (*act*) commemorātiō *f*; (*passage*) locus *m*.

quote *vt* prōferre, commemorāre.

quoth *vt* inquit.

R

rabbit *n* cunīculus *m*.

rabble *n* turba *f*; (*class*) vulgus *nt*, plēbēcula *f*.

rabid *adj* rabidus.

rabidly *adv* rabidē.

race *n* (*descent*) genus *nt*, stirps *f*; (*people*) gēns *f*, nātiō *f*; (*contest*) certāmen *nt*; (*fig*) cursus *m*, curriculum *nt*; (*water*) flūmen *nt*; **run a ~** cursū certāre; **run the ~** (*fig*) spatium dēcurrere ♦ *vi* certāre, contendere.

racecourse *n* (*foot*) stadium *nt*; (*horse*) spatium *m*.

racer *n* cursor *m*.

racial *adj* gentīlis.

rack *n* (*torture*) tormentum *nt*; (*shelf*) pluteus *m*; **be on the ~** (*fig*) cruciārī ♦ *vt* torquēre, cruciāre; **~ off** (*wine*) diffundere.

racket *n* (*noise*) strepitus *m*.

racy *adj* (*style*) salsus.

radiance *n* splendor *m*, fulgor *m*.

radiant *adj* splendidus, nitidus.

radiantly *adv* splendidē.

radiate *vi* fulgēre; (*direction*)

dīversōs tendere ♦ vt ēmittere.
radical adj īnsitus, innātus; (thorough) tōtus ♦ n novārum rērum cupidus m.
radically adv omnīnō, penitus, funditus.
radish n rādīx f.
radius n radius m.
raffish adj dissolūtus.
raffle n ālea f ♦ vt āleā vēndere.
raft n ratis f.
rafter n trabs f, tignum nt.
rag n pannus m.
rage n īra f, furor m; **be all the ~ in** ōre omnium esse; **spend one's ~** exsaevīre ♦ vi furere, saevīre; (furiously) dēbacchārī.
ragged adj pannōsus.
raid n excursiō f, incursiō f, impressiō f; **make a ~** excurrere ♦ vt incursiōnem facere in (acc).
rail n longurius m ♦ vt saepīre ♦ vi: **~ at** maledīcere (dat), convīcia facere (dat).
railing n saepēs f, cancellī mpl.
raillery n cavillātiō f.
raiment n vestis f.
rain n pluvia f, imber m ♦ vi pluere; **it is raining** pluit.
rainbow n arcus m.
rainstorm n imber m.
rainy adj pluvius.
raise vt tollere, ēlevāre; (army) cōgere, cōnscrībere; (children) ēducāre; (cry) tollere; (from dead) excitāre; (laugh) movēre; (money) cōnflāre; (price) augēre; (siege) exsolvere; (structure) exstruere; (to higher rank) ēvehere; **~ up** ērigere, sublevāre.
raisin n astaphis f.
rajah n dynastēs m.
rake n rastrum nt; (person) nepōs m ♦ vt rādere; **~ in** conrādere; **~ up** (fig) ēruere.
rakish adj dissolūtus.
rally n conventus m ♦ vt (troops)

ōrdinem revocāre; (with words) hortārī; (banter) cavillārī ♦ vi sē colligere.
ram n ariēs m; (battering) ariēs m ♦ vt: **~ down** fistūcāre; **~ home** (fact) inculcāre.
ramble n errātiō f ♦ vi vagārī, errāre.
rambling adj vagus; (plant) errāticus; (speech) fluēns.
ramification n rāmus m.
rammer n fistūca f.
rampage vi saevīre.
rampant adj ferōx.
rampart n agger m, vallum nt.
ranch n lātifundium nt.
rancid adj pūtidus.
rancour n odium nt, acerbitās f, invidia f.
random adj fortuītus; **at ~** temerē.
range n ōrdō m, seriēs f; (mountain) iugum nt; (of weapon) iactus m; **within ~** intrā tēlī iactum; **come within ~** sub ictum venīre ♦ vt ōrdināre ♦ vi ēvagārī, pervagārī; (in speech) excurrere.
rank n (line) ōrdō m; (class) ōrdō m; (position) locus m, dignitās f; ~ **and file** gregāriī mīlitēs mpl; **keep the ~s** ōrdinēs observāre; **the ~s** (MIL) aciēs, aciēī f; **leave the ~s** ōrdine ēgredī, ab signīs discēdere; **reduce to the ~s** in ōrdinem redigere ♦ vt numerāre ♦ vi in numerō habērī.
rank adj luxuriōsus; (smell) gravis, foetidus.
rankle vi exulcerāre.
rankness n luxuriēs f.
ransack vt dīripere, spoliāre.
ransom n redemptiō f, pretium nt ♦ vt redimere.
rant vi latrāre.
ranter n rabula m, latrātor m.
rap n ictus m ♦ vt ferīre.
rapacious adj rapāx, avidus.
rapaciously adv avidē.

rapacity n rapācitās f, avidītās f.
rape n raptus m.
rapid adj rapidus, vēlōx, citus, incitātus.
rapidity n celeritās f, vēlōcitās f, incitātiō f.
rapidly adv rapidē, vēlōciter, citō.
rapine n rapīna f.
rapt adj intentus.
rapture n laetitia f, alacritās f.
rare adj rārus; (occurrence) īnfrequēns; (quality) singulāris.
rarefy vt extenuāre.
rarely adv rārō.
rarity n rāritās f; (thing) rēs īnsolita f.
rascal n furcifer m, scelestus m.
rascally adj improbus.
rash adj temerārius, audāx, incōnsultus; praeceps.
rashly adv temerē, incōnsultē.
rashness n temeritās f, audācia f.
rat n mūs m/f.
rate n (cost) pretium nt; (standard) nōrma f; (tax) vectīgal nt; (speed) celeritās f; **at any ~** (concessive) utique, saltem; (adversative) quamquam, tamen ♦ vt (value) aestimāre; (scold) increpāre, obiūrgāre.
rather adv potius, satius; (somewhat) aliquantum; (with comp) aliquantō; (with verbs) mālō; (correcting) immo; **~ sad** tristior; **I would ~** mālō; **I ~ think** haud sciō an; **~ than** magis quam, potius quam.
ratification n (formal) sānctiō f.
ratify vt ratum facere, sancīre; (law) iubēre.
rating n taxātiō f, aestimātiō f; (navy) nauta m; (scolding) obiūrgātiō f.
ratiocinate vi ratiōcinārī.
ratiocination n ratiōcinātiō f.
ration n dēmēnsum nt.
rational adj animō praeditus; **be ~**

sapere.
rationality n ratiō f.
rationally adv ratiōne.
rations npl cibāria ntpl, diāria ntpl.
rattle n crepitus m; (toy) crotalum nt ♦ vi crepitāre, increpāre.
raucous adj raucus.
ravage vt dēpopulārī, vāstāre, dīripere.
rave vi furere, īnsānīre; (fig) bacchārī, saevīre.
raven n cornīx f.
ravenous adj rapāx, vorāx.
ravenously adv avidē.
ravine n faucēs fpl, hiātus m.
raving adj furiōsus, īnsānus ♦ n furor m.
ravish vt rapere; (joy) efferre.
raw adj crūdus; (person) rudis, agrestis.
ray n radius m; **the first ~ of hope appeared** prīma spēs adfulsit.
raze vt excīdere, solō aequāre.
razor n novācula f.
reach vi (space) spatium nt; (mind) captus m; (weapon) ictus m; **out of ~** extrā (acc); **within ~** ad manum ♦ vt advenīre ad (+ acc); attingere; (space) pertinēre ad; (journey) pervenīre ad.
react vi adficī; **~ to** ferre.
reaction n: **what was his ~ to?** quō animō tulit?
read vt legere; (a book) ēvolvere; (aloud) recitāre; **~ over** perlegere.
reader n lēctor m.
readily adv facile, libenter, ultrō.
readiness n facilitās f; **in ~** ad manum, in prōmptū, in expedītō.
reading n lēctiō f.
readjust vt dēnuō accommodāre.
ready adj parātus, prōmptus; (manner) facilis; (money) praesēns; **get, make ~** parāre, expedīre, adōrnāre.
reaffirm vt iterum adfirmāre.
real adj vērus, germānus.

real estate n fundus m, solum nt.

realism n vēritās f.

realistic adj vērī similis.

reality n rēs f, rēs ipsa f, vērum nt; **in ~** rēvērā.

realize vt intellegere, animadvertere; (aim) efficere, peragere; (money) redigere.

really adv vērē, rēvērā, profectō; **~?** itane vērō?

realm n rēgnum nt.

reap vt metere; **~ the reward of** fructum percipere ex.

reaper n messor m.

reappear vi revenīre.

rear vt alere, ēducāre, (structure) exstruere ♦ vi sē ērigere ♦ n tergum nt; (MIL) novissima aciēs f, novissimum agmen nt; **in the ~** ā tergō; **bring up the ~** agmen claudere, agmen cōgere ♦ adj postrēmus, novissimus.

rearguard n novissimum agmen nt, novissimī mpl.

rearrange vt ōrdinem mūtāre (gen).

reason n (faculty) mēns f, animus m, ratiō f; (sanity) sānitās f; (argument) ratiō f; (cause) causa f; (moderation) modus m; **by ~ of** propter (acc); **for this ~** idcircō, ideō, proptereā; **in ~** aequus, modicus; **with good ~** iūre; **without ~** temerē, sine causā; **without good ~** frustrā, iniūriā; **give a ~ for** ratiōnem adferre (gen); **I know the ~ for** sciō cūr, quamobrem (subj); **there is no ~ for** nōn est cūr, nihil est quod (subj); **lose one's ~** insānīre ♦ vi ratiōcinārī, disserere.

reasonable adj aequus, iūstus; (person) modestus; (amount) modicus.

reasonably adv ratiōne, iūstē; modicē.

reasoning n ratiō f, ratiōcinātiō f.

reassemble vt colligere, cōgere.

reassert vt iterāre.

reassume vt recipere.

reassure vt firmāre, cōnfirmāre.

rebate vt dēdūcere.

rebel n rebellis m ♦ adj sēditiōsus ♦ vi rebelliōnem facere, rebellāre, dēscīscere.

rebellion n sēditiō f, mōtus m.

rebellious adj sēditiōsus.

rebound vi resilīre.

rebuff n repulsa f ♦ vt repellere, āversārī.

rebuild vt renovāre, restaurāre.

rebuke n reprehēnsiō f, obiūrgātiō f ♦ vt reprehendere, obiūrgāre, increpāre.

rebut vt refūtāre, redarguere.

recalcitrant adj invītus.

recall n revocātiō f, reditus m ♦ vt revocāre; (from exile) redūcere; (to mind) reminīscī (gen), recordārī (gen).

recant vt retractāre.

recantation n receptus m.

recapitulate vt repetere, summātim dīcere.

recapitulation n ēnumerātiō f.

recapture vt recipere.

recast vt reficere, retractāre.

recede vi recēdere.

receipt n (act) acceptiō f; (money) acceptum nt; (written) apocha f.

receive vt accipere, capere; (in turn) excipere.

receiver n receptor m.

recent adj recēns.

recently adv nūper, recēns.

receptacle n receptāculum nt.

reception n aditus m, hospitium nt.

receptive adj docilis.

recess n recessus m, angulus m; (holiday) fēriae fpl.

recharge vt replēre.

recipe n compositiō f.

recipient n quī accipit.

reciprocal adj mūtuus.

reciprocally adv mūtuō, inter sē.
reciprocate vt referre, reddere.
reciprocity n mūtuum nt.
recital n nārrātiō f, ēnumerātiō f; (LIT) recitātiō f.
recitation n recitātiō f.
recite vt recitāre; (details) ēnumerāre.
reciter n recitātor m.
reck vt ratiōnem habēre (gen).
reckless adj temerārius, incautus, praeceps.
recklessly adv incautē, temerē.
recklessness n temeritās f, neglegentia f.
reckon vt (count) computāre, numerāre; (think) cēnsēre, dūcere; (estimate) aestimāre; ~ on cōnfīdere (dat); ~ up dīnumerāre; (cost) aestimāre; ~ with contendere cum.
reckoning n ratiō f.
reclaim vt repetere; (from error) revocāre.
recline vi recumbere; (at table) accumbere; (plur) discumbere.
recluse n homō sōlitārius m.
recognition n cognitiō f.
recognizance n vadimōnium nt.
recognize vt agnōscere; (approve) accipere; (admit) fatērī.
recoil vi resilīre; ~ from refugere; ~ upon recidere in (acc).
recollect vt reminīscī (gen).
recollection n memoria f, recordātiō f.
recommence vt renovāre, redintegrāre.
recommend vt commendāre; (advise) suādēre (dat).
recommendation n commendātiō f; (advice) cōnsilium nt; letter of ~ litterae commendātīciae.
recompense vt remūnerārī, grātiam referre (dat) ♦ n praemium nt, remūnerātiō f.
reconcile vt compōnere,

reconciliāre; **be ~d** in grātiam redīre.
reconciliation n reconciliātiō f, grātia f.
recondite adj reconditus, abstrūsus.
recondition vt reficere.
reconnaissance n explōrātiō f.
reconnoitre vt, vi explōrāre; **without reconnoitring** inexplōrātō.
reconquer vt recipere.
reconsider vt reputāre, retractāre.
reconstruct vt restituere, renovāre.
reconstruction n renovātiō f.
record n monumentum nt; (LIT) commentārius m; ~**s** pl tabulae fpl, fāstī mpl, ācta ntpl; **break the ~** priōrēs omnēs superāre ♦ vt in commentārium referre; (history) perscrībere, nārrāre.
recount vt nārrāre, commemorāre.
recourse n: **have ~ to** (for safety) cōnfugere ad; (as expedient) dēcurrere ad.
recover vt recipere, recuperāre; (loss) reparāre; ~ **oneself** sē colligere; ~ **one's senses** ad sānitātem revertī ♦ vi convalēscere.
recovery n recuperātiō f; (from illness) salūs f.
recreate vt recreāre.
recreation n requiēs f, remissiō f, lūdus m.
recriminate vi in vicem accūsāre.
recrimination n mūtua accūsātiō f.
recruit n tīrō m ♦ vt (MIL) cōnscrībere; (strength) reficere.
recruiting officer n conquīsītor m.
rectify vt corrigere, ēmendāre.
rectitude n probitās f.
recumbent adj supīnus.
recuperate vi convalēscere.
recur vi recurrere, redīre.

recurrence n reditus m, reversiō f.

recurrent adj adsiduus.

red adj ruber.

redden vi ērubēscere ♦ vt rutilāre.

reddish adj subrūfus.

redeem vt redimere, līberāre.

redeemer n līberātor m.

redemption n redemptiō f.

red-haired adj rūfus.

red-handed adj: **catch ~ in manifestō scelere dēprehendere.**

red-hot adj fervēns.

red lead n minium nt.

redness n rubor m.

redolent adj: **be ~ of** redolēre.

redouble vt ingemināre.

redoubt n prōpugnāculum nt.

redoubtable adj īnfestus, formīdolōsus.

redound vi redundāre; **it ~s to my credit** mihī honōrī est.

redress n remedium nt; **demand ~ rēs repetere** ♦ vt restituere.

reduce vt minuere, attenuāre; (to a condition) redigere, dēdūcere; (MIL) expugnāre; **~ to the ranks** in ōrdinem cōgere.

reduction n imminūtiō f, (MIL) expugnātiō f.

redundancy n redundantia f.

redundant adj redundāns; **be ~** redundāre.

reduplication n gemīnātiō f.

re-echo vt reddere, referre ♦ vi resonāre.

reed n harundō f.

reedy adj harundineus.

reef n saxa ntpl ♦ vt (sail) subnectere.

reek n fūmus m ♦ vi fūmāre.

reel vi vacillāre, titubāre.

re-enlist vt rescrībere.

re-establish vt restituere.

refashion vt reficere.

refer vt (person) dēlēgāre; (matter) rēicere, remittere ♦ vi: **~ to** spectāre ad; (in speech) attingere,

perstringere.

referee n arbiter m.

reference n ratiō f; (in book) locus m.

refine vt excolere, expolīre; (metal) excoquere.

refined adj hūmānus, urbānus, polītus.

refinement n hūmānitās f, cultus m, ēlegantia f.

refit vt reficere.

reflect vt reddere, repercutere ♦ vi meditārī; **~ upon** cōnsīderāre, sēcum reputāre; (blame) reprehendere.

reflection n (of light) repercussus m; (image) imāgō f; (thought) meditātiō f, cōgitātiō f; (blame) reprehēnsiō f; **cast ~s on** maculīs aspergere, vitiō vertere; **with due ~** cōnsīderātē; **without ~** incōnsultē.

reflux n recessus m.

reform n ēmendātiō f ♦ vt (lines) restituere; (error) corrigere, ēmendāre; (morals) meliōrem facere ♦ vi sē corrigere.

reformation n correctiō f.

reformer n corrector m, ēmendātor m.

refract vt īnfringere.

refractory adj contumāx.

refrain vi temperāre, abstinēre (dat), supersedēre (inf).

refresh vt recreāre, renovāre, reficere; (mind) integrāre.

refreshed adj requiētus.

refreshing adj dulcis, iūcundus.

refreshment n cibus m.

refuge n perfugium nt; (secret) latebra f; **take ~ with** perfugere ad (acc); **take ~ in** confugere.

refugee n profugus m.

refulgence n splendor m.

refulgent adj splendidus.

refund vt reddere.

refusal n recūsātiō f, dētrectātiō f.

refuse n pūrgāmenta ntpl; (fig)
faex f ♦ vt (request) dēnegāre;
(offer) dētrectāre, recūsāre; (with
verb) nōlle.
refutation n refūtātiō f,
reprehēnsiō f.
refute vt refellere, redarguere,
revincere.
regain vt recipere.
regal adj rēgius, rēgālis.
regale vt excipere, dēlectāre; ~
oneself epulārī.
regalia n īnsignia ntpl.
regally adv rēgāliter.
regard n respectus m, ratiō f;
(esteem) grātia f; **with ~ to** ad
(acc), quod attinet ad ♦ vt (look)
intuērī, spectāre; (deem) habēre,
dūcere; **send ~s to** salūtem dīcere
(dat).
regarding prep dē (abl).
regardless adj neglegēns,
immemor.
regency n interrēgnum nt.
regent n interrēx m.
regicide n (person) rēgis
interfector m; (act) rēgis caedēs f.
regime n administrātiō t.
regimen n vīctus m.
regiment n legiō f.
region n regiō f, tractus m.
register n tabulae fpl, album nt ♦ vt
in tabulās referre, perscrībere;
(emotion) ostendere, sūmere.
registrar n tabulārius m.
registry n tabulārium nt.
regret n dolor m; (for past)
dēsīderium nt; (for fault)
paenitentia f ♦ vt dolēre; **I ~**
paenitet, mē piget (gen).
regretful adj maestus.
regretfully adv dolenter.
regrettable adj īnfēlīx,
īnfortūnātus.
regular adj (consistent) cōnstāns;
(orderly) ōrdinātus; (habitual)
solitus, adsiduus; (proper) iūstus,

rēctus.
regularity n moderātiō f, ōrdō m;
(consistency) cōnstantia f.
regularly adv ōrdine; cōnstanter;
iūstē, rēctē.
regulate vt ōrdināre, dīrigere;
(control) moderārī.
regulation n lēx f, dēcrētum nt.
rehabilitate vt restituere.
rehearsal n meditātiō f.
rehearse vt meditārī.
reign n rēgnum nt; (emperor's)
prīncipātus m; **in the ~ of Numa**
rēgnante Numā ♦ vi rēgnāre; (fig)
dominārī.
reimburse vt rependere.
rein n habēna f; **give full ~ to**
habēnās immittere ♦ vt īnfrēnāre.
reindeer n rēnō m.
reinforce vt firmāre, cōnfirmāre.
reinforcement n subsidium nt; **~s**
pl novae cōpiae fpl.
reinstate vt restituere, redūcere.
reinstatement n restitūtiō f,
reductiō f; (to legal privileges)
postlīminium nt.
reinvigorate vt recreāre.
reiterate vt dictitāre, iterāre.
reiteration n iterātiō f.
reject vt rēicere; (with scorn)
respuere, aspernārī, repudiāre.
rejection n rēiectiō f, repulsa f.
rejoice vi gaudēre, laetārī ♦ vt
dēlectāre.
rejoicing n gaudium nt.
rejoin vt redīre ad ♦ vi respondēre.
rejoinder n respōnsum nt.
rejuvenate vt: **be ~d** repuerāscere.
rekindle vt suscitāre.
relapse vi recidere.
relate vt (tell) nārrāre,
commemorāre, expōnere;
(compare) cōnferre ♦ vi pertinēre.
related adj propinquus; (by birth)
cognātus; (by marriage) adfīnis;
(fig) fīnitimus.
relation n (tale) nārrātiō f;

(*connection*) ratiō f; (*kin*) necessārius m, cognātus m, adfīnis m.

relationship n necessitūdō f; (*by birth*) cognātiō f; (*by marriage*) adfīnitās f; (*connection*) vīcīnitās f.

relative adj cum cēterīs comparātus ♦ n propinquus m, cognātus m, adfīnis m, necessārius m.

relatively adv ex comparātiōne.

relax vt laxāre, remittere ♦ vi languēscere.

relaxation n remissiō f, requiēs f, lūdus m.

relay n: ~s of horses dispositī equī mpl.

release vt solvere, exsolvere, līberāre, expedīre; (*law*) absolvere ♦ n missiō f, līberātiō f.

relegate vt relēgāre.

relent vi concēdere, plācārī, flectī.

relentless adj immisericors, inexōrābilis; (*things*) improbus.

relevant adj ad rem.

reliability n fīdūcia f.

reliable adj fīdus.

reliance n fīdūcia f, fidēs f.

reliant adj frētus.

relic n reliquiae fpl.

relief n levātiō f, levāmen nt, adlevāmentum nt; (*aid*) subsidium nt; (*turn of duty*) vicēs fpl; (*art*) ēminentia f; (*sculpture*) toreuma nt; **bas ~** anaglypta ntpl; **in ~** ēminēns, expressus; **throw into ~** exprimere, distinguere.

relieve vt levāre, sublevāre; (*aid*) subvenīre (*dat*); (*duty*) succēdere (*dat*), excipere; (*art*) distinguere.

religion n religiō f, deōrum cultus m.

religious adj religiōsus, pius; ~ **feeling** religiō f.

religiously adv religiōsē.

relinquish vt relinquere; (*office*) sē abdicāre (*abl*).

relish n sapor m; (*sauce*) condīmentum nt; (*zest*) studium nt ♦ vt dēlectārī (*abl*).

reluctance n: **with ~** invītus.

reluctant adj invītus.

reluctantly adv invītē, gravātē.

rely vi fīdere (*dat*), cōnfīdere (*dat*).

relying adj frētus (*abl*).

remain vi manēre, morārī; (*left over*) restāre, superesse.

remainder n reliquum nt.

remaining adj reliquus; **the ~** cēterī pl.

remains n rēliquiae fpl.

remand vt (*law*) ampliāre.

remark n dictum nt ♦ vt dīcere; (*note*) observāre.

remarkable adj īnsignis, ēgregius, memorābilis.

remarkably adv īnsignītē, ēgregiē.

remediable adj sānābilis.

remedy n remedium nt ♦ vt medērī (*dat*), sānāre.

remember vt meminisse (*gen*); (*recall*) recordārī (*gen*), reminīscī (*gen*).

remembrance n memoria f, recordātiō f.

remind vt admonēre, commonefacere.

reminder n admonitiō f, admonitum nt.

reminiscence n recordātiō f.

remiss adj dissolūtus, neglegēns.

remission n venia f.

remissness n neglegentia f.

remit vt remittere; (*fault*) ignōscere (*dat*); (*debt*) dōnāre; (*punishment*) condōnāre; (*question*) referre.

remittance n pecūnia f.

remnant n fragmentum nt; ~**s** pl rēliquiae fpl.

remonstrance n obtestātiō f, obiūrgātiō f.

remonstrate vi reclāmāre; ~ **with** obiūrgāre; ~ **about** expostulāre.

remorse n paenitentia f,
cōnscientia f.
remorseless adj immisericors.
remote adj remōtus, reconditus.
remotely adv procul.
remoteness n longinquitās f.
removal n āmōtiō f; (going)
migrātiō f.
remove vt āmovēre, dēmere,
eximere, removēre; (out of the
way) dēmovēre ♦ vi migrāre,
dēmigrāre.
remunerate vt remūnērārī.
remuneration n mercēs f,
praemium nt.
rend vt scindere, dīvellere.
render vt reddere; (music)
interpretārī; (translation) vertere;
(thanks) referre.
rendering n interpretātiō f.
rendez-vous n cōnstitūtum nt.
renegade n dēsertor m.
renew vt renovāre, integrāre,
īnstaurāre, redintegrāre.
renewal n renovātiō f; (ceremony)
īnstaurātiō f.
renounce vt renūntiāre, mittere,
repudiāre.
renovate vt renovāre, reficere.
renown n fāma f, glōria f.
renowned adj praeclārus, īnsignis,
nōtus.
rent n (tear) fissum nt; (pay) mercēs
f ♦ vt (hire) condūcere; (lease)
locāre.
renunciation n cessiō f, repudiātiō
f.
repair vt reficere, sarcīre ♦ vi sē
recipere ♦ n: **keep in good ~** tuērī;
in bad ~ ruīnōsus.
reparable adj ēmendābilis.
reparation n satisfactiō f.
repartee n facētiae fpl, salēs mpl.
repast n cēna f, cibus m.
repay vt remūnērārī, grātiam
referre (dat); (money) repōnere.
repayment n solūtiō f.

repeal vt abrogāre ♦ n abrogātiō f.
repeat vt iterāre; (lesson) reddere;
(ceremony) īnstaurāre;
(performance) referre.
repeatedly adv identidem, etiam
atque etiam.
repel vt repellere, dēfendere.
repellent adj iniūcundus.
repent vi: **I ~** mē paenitet (+ gen of
thing).
repentance n paenitentia f.
repentant adj paenitēns.
repercussion n ēventus m.
repertory n thēsaurus m.
repetition n iterātiō f.
repine vi conquerī.
replace vt repōnere, restituere; **~
by** substituere.
replacement n supplēmentum nt.
replenish vt replēre, supplēre.
replete adj plēnus.
repletion n satietās f.
replica n apographon nt.
reply vi respondēre ♦ n respōnsum
nt.
report n (talk) fāma f, rūmor m;
(reputo) opīniō f; (account)
renūntiātiō f, litterae fpl; (noise)
fragor m; **make a ~** renūntiāre
♦ vt referre, dēferre, renūntiāre.
repose n quiēs f, requiēs f ♦ vt
repōnere, pōnere ♦ vi quiēscere.
repository n horreum nt.
reprehend vt reprehendere,
culpāre.
reprehensible adj accūsābilis,
improbus.
reprehension n reprehēnsiō f,
culpa f.
represent vt dēscrībere, effingere,
exprimere, imitārī; (character)
partēs agere (gen), persōnam
gerere (gen); (case) prōpōnere;
(substitute for) vicārium esse (gen).
representation n imāgō f, imitātiō
f; **make ~s to** admonēre.
representative n lēgātus m.

repress vt reprimere, cohibēre.

repression n coercitiō f.

reprieve n mora f, venia f ♦ vt veniam dare (dat).

reprimand vt reprehendere, increpāre ♦ n reprehēnsiō f.

reprisals n ultiō f.

reproach vt exprobāre, obicere (dat) ♦ n exprobrātiō f, probrum nt, (cause) opprobrium nt.

reproachful adj contumēliōsus.

reprobate adj perditus.

reproduce vt prōpāgāre; (likeness) referre.

reproduction n prōcreātiō f; (likeness) imāgō f.

reproductive adj genitālis.

reproof n reprehēnsiō f, obiūrgātiō f.

reprove vt reprehendere, increpāre, obiūrgāre.

reptile n serpēns f.

republic n lībera rēspublica f, cīvitās populāris f.

republican adj populāris.

repudiate vt repudiāre.

repudiation n repudiātiō f.

repugnance n fastīdium nt, odium nt.

repugnant adj invīsus, adversus.

repulse n dēpulsiō f; (at election) repulsa f ♦ vt repellere, āversārī, prōpulsāre.

repulsion n repugnantia f.

repulsive adj odiōsus, foedus.

reputable adj honestus.

reputation n fāma f, existimātiō f; (for something) opīniō f (gen); **have** ~ nōmen habēre.

repute n fāma f, existimātiō f; **bad** ~ īnfāmia f.

reputed adj: **I am ~ to be** dīcor esse.

request n rogātiō f, postulātum nt; **obtain a** ~ impetrāre ♦ vt rogāre, petere; (urgently) dēposcere.

require vt (demand) imperāre,

postulāre; (need) egēre (abl); (call for) requīrere.

requirement n postulātum nt, necessārium nt.

requisite adj necessārius.

requisition n postulātiō f ♦ vt imperāre.

requital n grātia f, vicēs fpl.

requite vt grātiam referre (dat), remūnerārī.

rescind vt rescindere, abrogāre.

rescript n rescrīptum nt.

rescue vt ēripere, expedīre, servāre ♦ n salūs f; **come to the** ~ **of** subvenīre (dat).

research n investīgātiō f.

resemblance n similitūdō f, imāgō f, īnstar nt.

resemble vt similem esse (dat), referre.

resent vt aegrē ferre, indignārī.

resentful adj īrācundus.

resentment n dolor m, indignātiō f.

reservation n (proviso) exceptiō f.

reserve vt servāre; (store) recondere; (in a deal) excipere ♦ nt (MIL) subsidium nt; (disposition) pudor m, reticentia f; (caution) cautiō f; **in** ~ in succenturiātus; **without** ~ palam.

reserved adj (place) adsignātus; (disposition) taciturnus, tēctus.

reservedly adv circumspectē.

reserves npl subsidia ntpl.

reservoir n lacus m.

reside vi habitāre; ~ **in** incolere.

residence n domicilium nt, domus f.

resident n incola m/f.

residual adj reliquus.

residue, residuum n reliqua pars f.

resign vt cēdere; (office) abdicāre mē, tē etc dē (+abl); ~ **oneself** acquiēscere ♦ vi sē abdicāre.

resignation n abdicātiō f; (state of mind) patientia f, aequus animus *m*.

resigned *adj* patiēns; **be ~ to** aequō animō ferre.

resilience *n* mollitia *f*.

resilient *adj* mollis.

resist *vt* resistere (*dat*), adversārī (*dat*), repugnāre (*dat*).

resistance *n* repugnantia *f*; **offer ~** obsistere (*dat*).

resistless *adj* invictus.

resolute *adj* fortis, cōnstāns.

resolutely *adv* fortiter, cōnstanter.

resolution *n* (*conduct*) fortitūdō *f*, cōnstantia *f*; (*decision*) dēcrētum *nt*, sententia *f*; (*into parts*) sēcrētiō *f*.

resolve *n* fortitūdō *f*, cōnstantia *f* ♦ *vt* dēcernere, cōnstituere; (*into parts*) dissolvere; **the senate ~s** placet senātuī.

resonance *n* sonus *m*.

resonant *adj* canōrus.

resort *n* locus celeber *m*; **last ~** ultimum auxilium *nt* ♦ *vi* frequentāre, ventitāre; (*have recourse*) dēcurrere, dēscendere, cōnfugere.

resound *vi* resonāre, personāre.

resource *n* subsidium *nt*; (*means*) modus *m*; **~s** *pl* opēs *fpl*, cōpiae *fpl*.

resourceful *adj* versūtus, callidus.

resourcefulness *n* calliditās *f*, versūtus animus *m*.

respect *n* (*esteem*) honōs *m*, observantia *f*; (*reference*) ratiō *f*; **out of ~** honōris causā; **pay one's ~s to** salūtāre; **for ~ for** observāre; **in every ~** ex omnī parte, in omnī genere; **in ~ of** ad (*acc*), ab (*abl*) ♦ *vt* honōrāre, observāre, verērī.

respectability *n* honestās *f*.

respectable *adj* honestus, līberālis, frūgī.

respectably *adv* honestē.

respectful *adj* observāns.

respectfully *adv* reverenter.

respectfulness *n* observantia *f*.

respective *adj* suus (*with quisque*).

respectively *adv* alius ... alius.

respiration *n* respīrātiō *f*, spīritus *m*.

respire *vi* respīrāre.

respite *n* requiēs *f*, intercapēdō *f*, intermissiō *f*.

resplendence *n* splendor *m*.

resplendent *adj* splendidus, illūstris.

resplendently *adv* splendidē.

respond *vi* respondēre.

response *n* respōnsum *nt*.

responsibility *n* auctōritās *f*, cūra *f*.

responsible *adj* reus; (*witness*) locuplēs; **be ~ for** praestāre.

responsive *adj* (*pupil*) docilis; (*character*) facilis.

rest *n* quiēs *f*, ōtium *nt*; (*after toil*) requiēs *f*; (*remainder*) reliqua pars *f*; **be at ~** requiēscere; **set at ~** tranquillāre; **the ~ of** reliquī ♦ *vi* requiēscere, acquiēscere; **~ on** nītī (*abl*), innītī in (*abl*) ♦ *vt* (*hope*) pōnere in (*abl*).

rest *n* cēterī *mpl*.

resting place *n* cubīle *nt*, sēdēs *f*.

restitution *n* satisfactiō *f*; **make ~** restituere; **demand ~** rēs repetere.

restive *adj* contumāx.

restless *adj* inquiētus, sollicitus; **be ~** fluctuārī.

restlessness *n* sollicitūdō *f*.

restoration *n* renovātiō *f*; (*of king*) reductiō *f*.

restore *vt* reddere, restituere; (*to health*) recreāre; (*to power*) redūcere; (*damage*) reficere, redintegrāre.

restorer *n* restitūtor *m*.

restrain *vt* coercēre, comprimere, cohibēre.

restraint *n* moderātiō *f*, temperantia *f*, frēnī *mpl*; **with ~**

abstinenter.

restrict vt continēre, circumscrībere.

restricted adj artus; **~ to** proprius (gen).

restriction n modus m, fīnis m; (limitation) exceptiō f.

result n ēventus m, ēventum nt, exitus m; **the ~ is that** quō fit ut ♦ vi ēvenīre, ēvādere.

resultant adj cōnsequēns.

resume vt repetere.

resuscitate vt excitāre, suscitāre.

retail vt dīvēndere, vēndere.

retailer n caupō m.

retain vt retinēre, tenēre, cōnservāre.

retainer n satelles m.

retake vt recipere.

retaliate vi ulcīscī.

retaliation n ultiō f.

retard vt retardāre, remorārī.

retention n cōnservātiō f.

retentive adj tenāx.

reticence n taciturnitās f.

reticent adj taciturnus.

reticulated adj rēticulātus.

retinue n satellitēs mpl, comitātus m.

retire vi recēdere, abscēdere; (from office) abīre; (from province) dēcēdere; (MIL) pedem referre, sē recipere.

retired adj ēmeritus; (place) remōtus.

retirement n (act) recessus m, dēcessus m; (state) sōlitūdō f, ōtium nt; **life of ~** vīta prīvāta.

retiring adj modestus, verēcundus.

retort vt respondēre, referre ♦ n respōnsum nt.

retouch vt retractāre.

retrace vt repetere, iterāre.

retract vt revocāre, renūntiāre.

retreat n (MIL) receptus m; (place) recessus m, sēcessus m; **sound the ~** receptuī canere ♦ vi sē

recipere, pedem referre; regredī.

retrench vt minuere, recīdere.

retrenchment n parsimōnia f.

retribution n poena f.

retributive adj ultor, ultrīx.

retrieve vt reparāre, recipere.

retrograde adj (fig) dēterior.

retrogression n regressus m.

retrospect n: **in ~** respicientī.

retrospective adj: **be ~** retrōrsum sē referre.

retrospectively adv retrō.

return n reditus m; (pay) remūnerātiō f; (profit) fructus m, pretium nt; (statement) professiō f; **make a ~ of** profitērī; **in ~ for** prō (+ abl), **in ~** in vicem, vicissim ♦ vt reddere, restituere, referre ♦ vi redīre, revenīre, revertī; (from province) dēcēdere.

reunion n convīvium nt.

reunite vt reconciliāre.

reveal vt aperīre, patefacere.

revel n cōmissātiō f, bacchātiō f; **~s** pl orgia ntpl ♦ vi cōmissārī, bacchārī; **~ in** luxuriārī.

revelation n patefactiō f.

reveller n cōmissātor m.

revelry n cōmissātiō f.

revenge n ultiō f; **take ~ on** vindicāre in (acc) ♦ vt ulcīscī.

revengeful adj ulcīscendī cupidus.

revenue n fructus m, reditus m, vectīgālia ntpl.

reverberate vi resonāre.

reverberation n repercussus m.

revere vt venerārī, colere.

reverence n venerātiō f; (feeling) religiō f; reverentia f.

reverent adj religiōsus, pius.

reverently adv religiōsē.

reverie n meditātiō f, somnium nt.

reversal n abrogātiō f.

reverse adj contrārius ♦ n contrārium nt; (MIL) clādēs f ♦ vt invertere; (decision) rescindere.

reversion n reditus m.

revert vi redīre, revertī.

review n recognitiō f, recēnsiō f ♦ vt (MIL) recēnsēre.

revile vt maledīcere (dat).

revise vt recognōscere, corrigere; (LIT) līmāre.

revision n ēmendātiō f; (LIT) līma f.

revisit vt revīsere.

revival n renovātiō f.

revive vt recreāre, excitāre ♦ vi revīvīscere, renāscī.

revocation n revocātiō f.

revoke vt renūntiāre, īnfectum reddere.

revolt n sēditiō f, dēfectiō f ♦ vi dēficere, rebellāre.

revolting adj taeter, obscēnus.

revolution n (movement) conversiō f; (change) rēs novae fpl; (revolt) mōtus m; **effect a ~** rēs novāre.

revolutionary adj sēditiōsus, novārum rērum cupidus.

revolve vi volvī, versārī, convertī ♦ vt (in mind) volūtāre.

revulsion n mūtātiō f.

reward n praemium nt, mercēs f ♦ vt remūnerārī, compēnsāre.

rhapsody n carmen nt; (epic) rhapsōdia f.

rhetoric n rhētorica f; **of ~** rhētoricus; **exercise in ~** dēclāmātiō f; **practise ~** dēclāmāre; **teacher of ~** rhētor m.

rhetorical adj rhētoricus, dēclāmātōrius.

rhetorically adv rhētoricē.

rhetorician n rhētor m, dēclāmātor m.

rhinoceros n rhīnocerōs m.

rhyme n homoeoteleuton nt; **without ~ or reason** temerē.

rhythm n numerus m, modus m.

rhythmical adj numerōsus.

rib n costa f.

ribald adj obscēnus.

ribaldry n obscēnitās f.

ribbon n īnfula f.

rice n oryza f.

rich adj dīves, locuplēs; opulentus; (fertile) ūber, opīmus; (food) pinguis.

riches n dīvitiae fpl, opēs fpl.

richly adv opulentē, largē, lautē.

richness n ūbertās f, cōpia f.

rid vt līberāre; **get ~ of** dēpōnere, dēmovēre, exuere.

riddle n aenigma nt; (sieve) cribrum nt ♦ vt (with wounds) cōnfodere.

ride vi equitāre, vehī; **~ a horse in** equō vehī; **~ at anchor** stāre; **~ away** abequitāre, āvehī; **~ back** revehī; **~ between** interequitāre; **~ down** dēvehī; **~ into** invehī; **~ off** āvehī; **~ out** ēvehī; **~ past** praetervehī; **~ round** circumvehī (dat), circumequitāre; **~ up and down** perequitāre; **~ up to** adequitāre ad, advehī ad.

rider n eques m.

ridge n iugum nt.

ridicule n lūdibrium nt, irrīsus m ♦ vt irrīdēre, illūdere, lūdibriō habēre.

ridiculous adj rīdiculus, dērīdiculus.

ridiculously adv rīdiculē.

riding n equitātiō f.

rife adj frequēns.

riff-raff n faex populī f.

rifle vt expīlāre, spoliāre.

rift n rīma f.

rig vt (ship) armāre, ōrnāre ♦ n habitus m.

rigging n rudentēs mpl.

right adj rēctus; (just) aequus, iūstus; (true) rēctus, vērus; (proper) lēgitimus, fās; (hand) dexter; **it is ~** decet (+ acc and infin); **it is not ~** dēdecet (+ acc and infin); **you are ~** vēra dīcis; **if I am ~** nisi fallor; **in the ~ place** in locō; **at the ~ time** ad tempus; **at ~ angles** ad parēs angulōs; **on the ~**

ā dextrā ♦ adv rēctē, bene, probē; (justifiably) iūre; ~ up to usque ad (+ acc); ~ on rēctā ♦ n (legal) iūs nt; (moral) fās nt ♦ vt (replace) restituere; (correct) corrigere; (avenge) ulcīscī.

righteous adj iūstus, sanctus, pius.

righteously adv iūstē, sanctē, piē.

righteousness n sanctitās f, pietās f.

rightful adj iūstus, lēgitimus.

rightfully adv iūstē, lēgitimē.

right hand n dextra f.

right-hand adj dexter; ~ man comes m.

rightly adv rēctē, bene; iūre.

right-minded adj sānus.

rigid adj rigidus.

rigidity n rigor m; (strictness) sevēritās f.

rigidly adv rigidē, sevērē.

rigmarole n ambāgēs fpl.

rigorous adj dūrus; (strict) sevērus.

rigorously adv dūriter, sevērē.

rigour n dūritia f; sevēritās f.

rile vt inrītāre, stomachum movēre (dat).

rill n rīvulus m.

rim n labrum nt.

rime n pruīna f.

rind n cortex m.

ring n ānulus m; (circle) orbis m; (of people) corōna f; (motion) gȳrus m ♦ vt circumdare; (bell) movēre ♦ vi tinnīre, sonāre.

ringing n tinnītus m ♦ adj canōrus.

ringleader n caput m, dux m.

ringlet n cincinnus m.

rinse vt colluere.

riot n tumultus m, rixa f; run ~ exsultāre, luxuriārī, tumultuārī, turbās efficere; (revel) bacchārī.

rioter n commissātor m.

riotous adj tumultuōsus, sēditiōsus; (debauched) dissolūtus; ~ living commissātiō f, luxuria f.

riotously adv tumultuōsē;

luxuriōsē.

rip vt scindere.

ripe adj mātūrus; of ~ judgment animī mātūrus.

ripen vt mātūrāre ♦ vi mātūrēscere.

ripeness n mātūritās f.

ripple n unda f ♦ vi trepidāre.

rise vi orīrī, surgere; (hill) ascendere; (wind) cōnsurgere; (passion) tumēscere; (voice) tollī; (in size) crēscere; (in rank) ascendere; (in revolt) coorīrī, arma capere; ~ and fall (tide) reciprocāre; ~ above superāre; ~ again resurgere; ~ in (river) orīrī ex (abl), ~ out ēmergere; ~ up exsurgere ♦ n ascēnsus m; (slope) clīvus m; (increase) incrēmentum nt; (start) ortus m; give ~ to parere.

rising n (sun) ortus m; (revolt) mōtus m ♦ adj (ground) ēditus.

risk n perīculum nt; run a ~ perīculum subīre, ingredī ♦ vt perīclitārī, in āleam dare.

risky adj perīculōsus.

rite n rītus m.

ritual n caerimōnia f.

rival adj aemulus ♦ n aemulus m, rīvālis m ♦ vt aemulārī.

rivalry n aemulātiō f.

river n flūmen nt, fluvius m ♦ adj fluviātilis.

riverbed n alveus m.

riverside n rīpa f.

rivet n clāvus m ♦ vt (attention) dēfīgere.

rivulet n rīvulus m, rīvus m.

road n via f, iter nt; on the ~ in itinere, ex itinere; off the ~ dēvius; make a ~ viam mūnīre.

roadstead n statiō f.

roam vi errāre, vagārī; ~ at large ēvagārī.

roar n fremitus m ♦ vi fremere.

roast vt torrēre ♦ adj āssus ♦ n

āssum nt.

rob vt spoliāre, exspoliāre, expīlāre; (of hope) dēicere dē.

robber n latrō m, fūr m; (highway) grassātor m.

robbery n latrōcinium nt.

robe n vestis f; (woman's) stola f; (of state) trabea f ♦ vt vestīre.

robust adj rōbustus, fortis.

robustness n rōbur nt, firmitās f.

rock n saxum nt; (steep) rūpēs f, scopulus m ♦ vt agitāre ♦ vi agitārī, vacillāre.

rocky adj saxōsus, scopulōsus.

rod n virga f; (fishing) harundō f.

roe n (deer) capreolus m, caprea f; (fish) ōva ntpl.

rogue n veterātor m.

roguery n fraus f, scelus nt.

roguish adj improbus, malus.

role n partēs fpl.

roll n (book) volūmen nt; (movement) gyrus m; (register) album nt; **call the ~ of** legere; **answer the ~ call** ad nōmen respondēre ♦ vt volvere ♦ vi volvī, volūtārī; **~ down** vt dēvolvere ♦ vi dēfluere; **~ over** vt prōvolvere ♦ vi prōlābī; **~ up** vt convolvere.

roller n (AGR) cylindrus m; (for moving) phalangae fpl; (in book) umbilīcus m.

rollicking adj hilaris.

rolling adj volūbilis.

Roman adj Rōmānus ♦ n: **the ~s** Rōmānī mpl.

romance n fābula f; amor m.

romantic adj fābulōsus; amātōrius.

Rome n Rōma f; **at ~** Rōmae; **from ~** Rōmā; **to ~** Rōmam.

romp vi lūdere.

roof n tēctum nt; (of mouth) palātum nt ♦ vt tegere, integere.

rook n corvus m.

room n conclāve nt; camera f; (small) cella f; (bed) cubiculum nt; (dining) cēnāculum nt; (dressing) apodytērium nt; (space) locus m; **make ~ for** locum dare (dat), cēdere (dat).

roominess n laxitās f.

roomy adj capāx.

roost vi stabulārī.

rooster n gallus gallīnāceus m.

rooted adj (fig) dēfixus; **deeply ~** (custom) inveterātus; **be ~ in** īnsidēre (dat); **become deeply ~** inveterāscere.

rope n fūnis m; (thin) restis f; (ship's) rudēns m; **know the ~s** perītum esse.

rose n rosa f.

rosemary n rōs marīnus m.

rostrum n rōstra ntpl, suggestus m.

rosy adj roseus, purpureus.

rot n tābēs f ♦ vi putrēscere, pūtēscere ♦ vt putrefacere.

rotate vi volvī, sē convertere.

rotation n conversiō f; (succession) ōrdō m, vicissitūdō f; **in ~** ōrdine; **move in ~** in ōrdinem īre.

rote n: **by ~** memoriter.

rotten adj putridus.

rotund adj rotundus.

rotundity n rotunditās f.

rouge n fūcus m ♦ vt fūcāre.

rough adj asper; (in manner) incultus, rudis; (manners) agrestis, inurbānus; (stone) impolītus; (treatment) dūrus, sevērus; (weather) atrōx, procellōsus ♦ vi: **~ it** dūram vītam vīvere.

rough-and-ready adj fortuītus.

rough draft n (lit) silva f.

roughen vt asperāre, exasperāre.

rough-hew vt dolāre.

roughly adv asperē, dūriter; (with numbers) circiter.

roughness n asperitās f.

round adj rotundus; (spherical)

globōsus; (*cylindrical*) teres ♦ *n* (*circle*) orbis *m*; (*motion*) gȳrus *m*; (*series*) ambitus *m*; **go the ~s** (MIL) vigiliās circumīre ♦ *vt* (*cape*) superāre; **~ off** rotundāre; **~ up** (*sentence*) concludere; **~ up** compellere ♦ *adv* circum, circā; **go ~** ambīre ♦ *prep* circum (*acc*), circā (*acc*).

roundabout *adj:* **~ story** ambāges *fpl*; **~ route** circuitus *m*, ānfrāctus *m*.

roundly *adv* (*speak*) apertē, līberē.

rouse *vt* excīre, excitāre; (*courage*) adrigere.

rousing *adj* vehemēns.

rout *n* fuga *f*; (*crowd*) turba *f* ♦ *vt* fugāre, fundere; **in fugam** conicere; prōfligāre.

route *n* cursus *m*, iter *nt*.

routine *n* ūsus *m*, ōrdō *m*.

rove *vi* errāre, vagārī.

rover *n* vagus *m*; (*sea*) pīrāta *m*.

row *n* (*line*) ōrdō *m*; (*noise*) turba *f*, rixa *f* ♦ *vi* (*boat*) rēmigāre ♦ *vt* rēmīs incitāre.

rowdy *adj* turbulentus.

rower *n* rēmex *m*.

rowing *n* rēmigium *nt*.

royal *adj* rēgius, rēgālis.

royally *adv* rēgiē, rēgāliter.

royalty *n* (*power*) rēgnum *nt*; (*persons*) rēgēs *mpl*, domus rēgia *f*.

rub *vt* fricāre, terere; **~ away** conterere; **~ hard** dēfricāre; **~ off** dētergēre; **~ out** dēlēre; **~ up** expolīre.

rubbing *n* trītus *m*.

rubbish *n* quisquiliae *fpl*; (*talk*) nūgae *fpl*.

rubble *n* rūdus *nt*.

rubicund *adj* rubicundus.

rudder *n* gubernāculum *nt*, clāvus *m*.

ruddy *adj* rubicundus, rutilus.

rude *adj* (*uncivilized*) barbarus, dūrus, inurbānus; (*insolent*) asper,

importūnus.

rudely *adv* horridē, rusticē; petulanter.

rudeness *n* barbariēs *f*; petulantia *f*, importūnitās *f*.

rudiment *n* elementum *nt*, initium *nt*.

rudimentary *adj* prīmus, incohātus.

rue *n* (*herb*) rūta *f* ♦ *vt:* **I ~ mē** paenitet (*gen*).

rueful *adj* maestus.

ruffian *n* grassātor *m*.

ruffle *vt* agitāre; (*temper*) sollicitāre, commovēre.

rug *n* strāgulum *nt*.

rugged *adj* horridus, asper.

ruggedness *n* asperitās *f*.

ruin *n* ruīna *f*; (*fig*) exitium *nt*, perniciēs *f*; **go to ~** pessum īre, dīlābī ♦ *vt* perdere, dēperdere, pessum dare; (*moral*) corrumpere, dēprāvāre; **be ~ed** perīre.

ruined *adj* ruīnōsus.

ruinous *adj* exitiōsus, damnōsus.

rule *n* (*instrument*) rēgula *f*, amussis *f*; (*principle*) norma *f*, lēx *f*, praeceptum *nt*; (*government*) dominātiō *f*, imperium *nt*; **ten-foot ~** decempeda *f*; **as a ~** ferē; **lay down ~s** praecipere; **make it a ~** tū īnstituere (*inf*); **of thumb** ūsus *m* ♦ *vt* regere, moderārī ♦ *vi* rēgnāre, dominārī; (*judge*) ēdīcere; (*custom*) obtinēre; **~ over** imperāre (*dat*).

ruler *n* (*instrument*) rēgula *f*; (*person*) dominus *m*, rēctor *m*.

ruling *n* ēdictum *nt*.

rumble *vi* mūgīre.

rumbling *n* mūgītus *m*.

ruminate *vi* rūminārī.

rummage *vi:* **~ through** rīmārī.

rumour *n* fāma *f*, rūmor *m*.

rump *n* clūnis *f*.

run *vi* currere; (*fluid*) fluere, mānāre, (*road*) ferre; (*time*) lābī

◆ *n* cursus *m*; ~ **about** discurrere, cursāre; ~ **across** incidere in (*acc*); ~ **after** sectārī; ~ **aground** offendere; ~ **away** aufugere, terga vertere; (*from*) fugere, dēfugere; ~ **down** dēcurrere, dēfluere ◆ *vt* (*in words*) obtrectāre; ~ **high** (*fig*) glīscere; ~ **into** incurrere in (*acc*), īnfluere in (*acc*); ~ **off with** abripere, abdūcere; ~ **on** pergere; ~ **out** (*land*) excurrere; (*time*) exīre; (*supplies*) dēficere; ~ **over** *vt* (*with car*) obterere; (*details*) percurrere; ~ **riot** luxuriārī; ~ **through** (*course*) dēcurrere; (*money*) disperdere; ~ **short** dēficere; ~ **up to** adcurrere ad; ~ **up against** incurrere in (*acc*); ~ **wild** lascīvīre ◆ *vt* gerere, administrāre.

runaway *adj* fugitīvus.

rung *n* gradus *m*.

runner *n* cursor *m*.

running *n* cursus *m* ◆ *adj* (*water*) vīvus.

rupture *n* (*fig*) dissidium *nt* ◆ *vt* dīrumpere.

rural *adj* rūsticus, agrestis.

ruse *n* fraus *f*, dolus *m*.

rush *n* (*plant*) cārex *f*, iuncus *m*; (*movement*) impetus *m* ◆ *vi* currere, sē incitāre, ruere; ~ **forward** sē prōripere; prōruere; ~ **in** inruere, incurrere; ~ **out** ēvolāre, sē effundere ◆ *adj* iunceus.

russet *adj* flāvus.

rust *n* (*iron*) ferrūgō *f*; (*copper*) aerūgō *f* ◆ *vi* rōbīginem trahere.

rustic *adj* rūsticus, agrestis.

rusticate *vi* rūsticārī ◆ *vt* relēgāre.

rusticity *n* mōrēs rūsticī *mpl*.

rustle *vi* increpāre, crepitāre ◆ *n* crepitus *m*.

rusty *adj* rōbīginōsus.

rut *n* orbita *f*.

ruthless *adj* inexōrābilis, crūdēlis.

ruthlessly *adv* crūdēliter.

rye *n* secāle *nt*.

S

sabbath *n* sabbata *ntpl*.

sable *adj* āter, niger.

sabre *n* acīnacēs *m*.

sacerdotal *adj* sacerdōtālis.

sack *n* saccus *m*; (*MIL*) dīreptiō *f* ◆ *vt* dīripere, expīlāre; spoliāre.

sackcloth *n* cilicium *nt*.

sacred *adj* sacer, sanctus.

sacredly *adv* sanctē.

sacredness *n* sanctitās *f*.

sacrifice *n* sacrificium *nt*, sacrum *nt*; (*act*) immolātiō *f*; (*victim*) hostia *f*; (*fig*) iactūra *f* ◆ *vt* immolāre, sacrificāre, mactāre; (*fig*) dēvovēre, addīcere ◆ *vi* sacra facere; (*give up*) prōicere.

sacrificer *n* immolātor *m*.

sacrilege *n* sacrilegium *nt*.

sacrilegious *adj* sacrilegus.

sacristan *n* aedituus *m*.

sacrosanct *adj* sacrōsanctus.

sad *adj* maestus, tristis; (*thing*) trīstis.

sadden *vt* dolōre adficere.

saddle *n* strātum *nt* ◆ *vt* sternere; (*fig*) impōnere.

saddlebags *n* clītellae *fpl*.

sadly *adv* maestē.

sadness *n* trīstitia *f*, maestitia *f*.

safe *adj* tūtus; (*out of danger*) incolumis, salvus; (*to trust*) fīdus. ~ **and sound** salvus ◆ *n* armārium *nt*.

safe-conduct *n* fidēs pūblica *f*.

safeguard *n* cautiō *f*, prōpugnāculum *nt* ◆ *vt* dēfendere.

safely *adv* tūtō, impūne.

safety *n* salūs *f*, incolumitās *f*; **seek ~ in flight** salutem fugā petere.

saffron *n* crocus *m* ◆ *adj* croceus.

sag *vi* dēmittī.

sagacious adj prūdēns, sagāx, acūtus.

sagaciously adv prūdenter, sagāciter.

sagacity n prūdentia f, sagācitās f.

sage n sapiēns m; (herb) salvia f
♦ adj sapiēns.

sagely adv sapienter.

sail n vēlum nt; **set ~** vēla dare, nāvem solvere; **shorten ~** vēla contrahere ♦ vi nāvigāre; **~ past** legere, praetervehī.

sailing n nāvigātiō f.

sailor n nauta m.

sail yard n antenna f.

saint n vir sanctus m.

sainted adj beātus.

saintly adj sanctus.

sake n: **for the ~ of** grātiā (gen), causā (gen), propter (acc); (behalf) prō (abl).

salacious adj salāx.

salad n morētum nt.

salamander n salamandra f.

salary n mercēs f.

sale n vēnditiō f; (formal) mancipium nt; (auction) hasta f; **for ~** vēnālis; **be for ~** prōstāre; **offer for ~** vēnum dare.

saleable adj vēndibilis.

sallent adj ēminēns, **~ points** capita ntpl.

saline adj salsus.

saliva n salīva f.

sallow adj pallidus.

sally n ēruptiō f, (wit) facētiae fpl
♦ vi ērumpere, excurrere.

salmon n salmō m.

salon n ātrium nt.

salt n sal m ♦ adj salsus.

saltcellar n salīnum nt.

saltpetre n nitrum nt.

salt-pits n salīnae fpl.

salty adj salsus.

salubrious adj salūbris.

salubriously adv salūbriter.

salubriousness n salūbritās f.

salutary adj salūāris, ūtilis.

salutation n salūs f.

salute vt salūtāre.

salvage vt servāre, ē:ripere.

salvation n salūs f.

salve n unguentum nt.

salver n scutella f.

same adj īdem; **~ as** īdem ac; **all the ~** nihilōminus; **one and the ~** ūnus et īdem; **from the ~ place** indidem; **in the ~ place** ibīdem; **to the ~ place** eōdem; **at the ~ time** simul, eōdem tempore; (adversative) tamen; **it is all the ~ to me** meā nōn interest.

Samnites n Samnītēs, Samnītium mpl.

sample n exemplum nt, specimen nt ♦ vt gustāre.

sanctify vt cōnsecrāre.

sanctimony n falsa rēligiō f.

sanction n comprobātiō f, auctōritās f ♦ vt ratum facere.

sanctity n sanctitās f.

sanctuary n fānum nt, dēlubrum nt; (for men) asȳlum nt.

sand n harēna f.

sandal n (outdoors) crepida f; (indoors) solea f.

sandalled adj crepidātus, soleātus.

sandpit n harēnāria f.

sandstone n tōfus m.

sandy adj harēnōsus; (colour) flāvus.

sane adj sānus.

sangfroid n aequus animus m.

sanguinary adj cruentus.

sanguine adj laetus.

sanitary adj salūbris.

sanity n mēns sāna f.

sap n sūcus m ♦ vt subruere.

sapience n sapientia f.

sapient adj sapiēns.

sapling n surculus m.

sapper n cunīculārius m.

sapphire n sapphīrus f.

sarcasm n aculeī mpl, dicācitās f.

sarcastic adj dicāx, acūleātus.
sardonic adj amārus.
sash n cingulum m.
satchel n loculus m.
sate vt explēre, satiāre.
satellite n satelles m.
satiate vt explēre, satiāre, saturāre.
satiety n satietās f.
satire n satura f; (pl, of Horace) sermōnēs mpl.
satirical adj acerbus.
satirist n saturārum scrīptor m.
satirize vt perstringere, notāre.
satisfaction n (act) explētiō f; (feeling) voluptās f; (penalty) poena f; demand ~ rēs repetere.
satisfactorily adv ex sententiā.
satisfactory adj idōneus, grātus.
satisfied adj: be ~ satis habēre, contentum esse.
satisfy vt satisfacere (dat); (desire) explēre.
satrap n satrapēs m.
saturate vt imbuere.
satyr n satyrus m.
sauce n condīmentum nt; (fish) garum m.
saucer n patella f.
saucily adv petulanter.
saucy adj petulāns.
saunter vi ambulāre.
sausage n tomāculum nt, hīllae fpl.
savage adj ferus, efferātus; (cruel) atrōx, inhūmānus; saevus.
savagely adv ferōciter, inhūmānē.
savagery n ferōcitās f, inhūmānitās f.
savant n vir doctus m.
save vt servāre; ~ up reservāre ♦ prep praeter (acc).
saving adj parcus; ~ clause exceptiō f ♦ n compendium nt; ~s pl pecūlium nt.
saviour n līberātor m.
savory n thymbra f.
savour n sapor m; (of cooking)

nīdor m ♦ vi sapere; ~ of olēre, redolēre.
savoury adj condītus.
saw n (tool) serra f; (saying) prōverbium nt ♦ vt serrā secāre.
sawdust n scobis f.
say vt dīcere; ~ that ... not negāre; ~ no negāre; he ~s (quoting) inquit; he ~s yes āit; they ~ ferunt (+ acc and infin).
saying n dictum nt.
scab n (disease) scabiēs f; (over wound) crusta f.
scabbard n vāgīna f.
scabby adj scaber.
scaffold, scaffolding n fala f.
scald vt ūrere.
scale n (balance) lanx f; (fish, etc) squāma f; (gradation) gradūs mpl; (music) diagramma nt ♦ vt scālīs ascendere.
scallop n pecten m.
scalp n capitis cutis f.
scalpel n scalpellum m.
scamp n verberō m.
scamper vi currere.
scan vt contemplārī; (verse) mētīrī.
scandal n īnfāmia f, opprobrium nt; (talk) calumnia f.
scandalize vt offendere.
scandalous adj flāgitiōsus, turpis.
scansion n syllabārum ēnārrātiō f.
scant adj exiguus, parvus.
scantily adv exiguē, tenuiter.
scantiness n exiguitās f.
scanty adj exiguus, tenuis, exīlis; (number) paucus.
scapegoat n piāculum nt.
scar n cicātrīx f.
scarce adj rārus; make oneself ~ sē āmovēre, dē mediō recēdere ♦ adv vix, aegrē.
scarcely adv vix, aegrē; ~ anyone nēmō ferē.
scarcity n inopia f, angustiae fpl.
scare n formīdō f ♦ vt terrēre; ~ away absterrēre.

scarecrow n formīdō f.

scarf n fōcāle nt.

scarlet n coccum nt ♦ adj coccinus.

scarp n rūpēs f.

scathe n damnum nt.

scatter vt spargere; dispergere, dissipāre; (violently) disicere ♦ vi diffugere.

scatterbrained adj dēsipiēns.

scattered adj rārus.

scene n spectāculum nt; (place) theātrum nt.

scenery n locī faciēs f, speciēs f; (beautiful) amoenitās f.

scent n odor m; (sense) odōrātus m; keen ~ sagācitās f ♦ vt odōrārī; (perfume) odōribus perfundere.

scented adj odōrātus.

sceptic n Pyrrhōnēus m.

sceptical adj incrēdulus.

sceptre n scēptrum nt.

schedule n tabulae fpl, ratiō f.

scheme n cōnsilium nt, ratiō f ♦ vt māchinārī, mōlīrī.

schemer n māchinātor m.

schism n discidium nt, sēcessiō f.

scholar n vir doctus, litterātus m; (pupil) discipulus m.

scholarly adj doctus, litterātus.

scholarship n litterae fpl, doctrīna f.

scholastic adj umbrātilis.

school n (elementary) lūdus m; (advanced) schola f; (high) gymnasium nt; (sect) secta f, domus f ♦ vt īnstituere.

schoolboy n discipulus m.

schoolmaster n magister m.

schoolmistress n magistra f.

science n doctrīna f, disciplīna f, ars f.

scimitar n acīnacēs m.

scintillate vi scintillāre.

scion n prōgeniēs f.

Scipio n Scīpiō, Scīpiōnis m.

scissors n forfex f.

scoff vi irrīdēre; ~ at dērīdēre.

scoffer n irrīsor m.

scold vt increpāre, obiūrgāre.

scolding n obiūrgātiō f.

scoop n trulla f ♦ vt: ~ out excavāre.

scope n (aim) fīnis m; (room) locus m, campus m; ample ~ laxus locus.

scorch vt exūrere, torrēre.

scorched adj torridus.

score n (mark) nota f; (total) summa f; (reckoning) ratiō f; (number) vīgintī ♦ vt notāre ♦ vi vincere.

scorn n contemptiō f ♦ vt contemnere, spernere.

scorner n contemptor m.

scornful adj fastīdiōsus.

scornfully adv contemptim.

scorpion n scorpiō m, nepa f.

scot-free adj immūnis, impūnītus.

scoundrel n furcifer m.

scour vt (clean) tergēre; (range) percurrere.

scourge n flagellum nt; (fig) pestis f ♦ vt verberāre, virgīs caedere.

scout n explōrātor m, speculātor m ♦ vi explōrāre, speculārī ♦ vt spernere, repudiāre.

scowl n frontis contractiō f ♦ vi frontem contrahere.

scraggy adj strigōsus.

scramble vi: ~ for certātim captāre; ~ up scandere.

scrap n frūstum nt.

scrape vt rādere, scabere; ~ off abrādere.

scraper n strigilis f.

scratch vt rādere; (head) perfricāre; ~ out exsculpere, ērādere.

scream n clāmor m, ululātus m ♦ vi clāmāre, ululāre.

screech n ululātus m ♦ vi ululāre.

screen n obex m/f; (from sun) umbra f; (fig) vēlāmentum nt ♦ vt

tegere.
screw n clāvus m; (of winepress) cochlea f.
scribble vt properē scrībere.
scribe n scrība m.
script n scrīptum nt; (handwriting) manus f.
scroll n volūmen nt.
scrub vt dētergēre, dēfricāre.
scruple n religiō f, scrūpulus m.
scrupulous adj religiōsus; (careful) dīligēns.
scrupulously adv religiōsē, dīligenter.
scrupulousness n religiō f; dīligentia f.
scrutinize vt scrūtārī, intrōspicere in (acc), excutere.
scrutiny n scrūtātiō f.
scud vi volāre.
scuffle n rixa f.
scull n calvāria f; (oar) rēmus m.
scullery n culīna f.
sculptor n fictor m, sculptor m.
sculpture n ars fingendī f; (product) statuae fpl ♦ vt sculpere.
scum n spūma f.
scurf n porrīgō f.
scurrility n maledicta ntpl.
scurrilous adj maledicus.
scurvy adj (fig) turpis, improbus.
scythe n falx f.

sea n mare nt; aequor nt; **open~** altum nt; **put to ~** solvere; **be at ~** nāvigāre; (fig) in errōre versārī ♦ adj marīnus; (coast) maritimus.
seaboard n lītus nt.
seafaring adj maritimus, nauticus.
seafight n nāvāle proelium nt.
seagull n larus m.
seal n (animal) phōca f; (stamp) signum nt ♦ vt signāre; **~ up** obsignāre.
seam n sūtūra f.
seaman n nauta m.
seamanship n scientia et ūsus nauticārum rērum.

seaport n portus m.
sear vt adūrere, torrēre.
search n investigātiō f ♦ vi investīgāre, explōrāre ♦ vt excutere, scrūtārī; **in ~ of** causā (+ gen); **~ for** quaerere, exquīrere, investīgāre; **~ into** inquīrere, anquīrere; **~ out** explōrāre, indāgāre.
searcher n inquīsītor m.
searching adj acūtus, dīligēns.
seashore n lītus nt.
seasick adj: **be ~** nauseāre.
seasickness n nausea f.
seaside n mare nt.
season n annī tempus nt, tempestās f; (right time) tempus nt, opportūnitās f; **in ~** tempestīvē ♦ vt condīre.
seasonable adj tempestīvus.
seasonably adv tempestīvē.
seasoned adj (food) condītus; (wood) dūrātus.
seasoning n condīmentum nt.
seat n sēdēs f; (chair) sedīle nt; (home) domus f, domicilium nt; **keep one's ~** (riding) in equō haerēre ♦ vt collocāre; **~ oneself** īnsidēre.
seated adj: **be ~** sedēre.
seaweed n alga f.
seaworthy adj ad nāvigandum ūtilis.
secede vi sēcēdere.
secession n sēcessiō f.
seclude vt sēclūdere, abstrūdere.
secluded adj sēcrētus, remōtus.
seclusion n sōlitūdō f, sēcrētum nt.
second adj secundus, alter; **a ~ time** iterum ♦ n temporis pūnctum nt; (person) fautor m; **~sight** hariolātiō f ♦ vt favēre (dat), adesse (dat).
secondary adj inferior, dēterior.
seconder n fautor m.
second-hand adj aliēnus, trītus.
secondly adv deinde.

secrecy n sēcrētum nt, silentium nt.

secret adj secretus; occultus, arcānus; (stealth) fūrtīvus ♦ n arcānum nt; **keep ~** dissimulāre, cēlāre; **in ~** clam; **be ~** latēre.

secretary n scrība m, ab epistolīs, ā manū.

secrete vt cēlāre, abdere.

secretive adj tēctus.

secretly adv clam, occultē, sēcrētō.

sect n secta f, schola f, domus f.

section n pars f.

sector n regiō f.

secular adj profānus.

secure adj tūtus ♦ vt (MIL) firmāre, ēmūnīre; (fasten) religāre; (obtain) parāre, nancīscī.

securely adv tūtō.

security n salūs f, impūnitās f; (money) cautiō f, pignus nt, spōnsiō f; **sense of ~** sēcūritās f; **give good ~** satis dare; **on good ~** (loan) nōminibus rēctīs cautus; **stand ~ for** praedem esse prō (abl).

sedan n lectīca f.

sedate adj placidus, temperātus, gravis.

sedately adv placidē.

sedateness n gravitās f.

sedge n ulva f.

sediment n faex f.

sedition n sēditiō f, mōtus m.

seditious adj sēditiōsus.

seditiously adv sēditiōsē.

seduce vt illicere, pellicere.

seducer n corruptor m.

seduction n corruptēla f.

seductive adj blandus.

seductively adv blandē.

sedulity n dīligentia f.

sedulous adj dīligēns, sēdulus.

sedulously adv dīligenter, sēdulō.

see vt vidēre, cernere; (suddenly) cōnspicārī; (performance) spectāre; (with mind) intellegere; **go and ~** vīsere, invīsere; **~ to**

vidēre, cōnsulere (dat); curare (+ acc and gerundive); **~ through** dīspicere; **~ that you are** vidē ut sīs, fac sīs; **~ that you are not** vidē nē sīs, cavē sīs.

seed n sēmen nt; (in a plant) grānum nt; (in fruit) acinum nt; (fig) stirps f, prōgeniēs f.

seedling n surculus m.

seed-time n sēmentis f.

seeing that conj quoniam, siquidem.

seek vt petere, quaerere.

seeker n indāgātor m.

seem vi vidērī.

seeming adj speciōsus ♦ n speciēs f.

seemingly adv ut vidētur.

seemly adj decēns, decōrus; **it is ~** decet.

seep vi mānāre, percōlārī.

seer n vātēs m/f.

seethe vi fervēre.

segregate vt sēcernere, sēgregāre.

segregation n sēparātiō f.

seize vt rapere, corripere, adripere, prehendere; (MIL) occupāre; (illness) adficere; (emotion) invādere, occupāre.

seizure n ēreptiō f, occupātiō f.

seldom adv rārō.

select vt ēligere, excerpere, dēligere ♦ adj lēctus, ēlēctus.

selection n ēlēctiō f, dēlēctus m; (LIT) ecloga f.

self n ipse m; (reflexive) sē; **a second ~** alter īdem.

self-centred adj glōriōsus.

self-confidence n cōnfīdentia f, fīdūcia f.

self-confident adj cōnfīdēns.

self-conscious adj pudibundus.

self-control n temperantia f.

self-denial n abstinentia f.

self-evident adj manifestus; **it is ~** ante pedēs positum est.

self-governing adj līber.
self-government n lībertās f.
self-important adj adrogāns.
self-interest n ambitiō f.
selfish adj inhūmānus, avārus; **be ~ suā causā facere.**
selfishly adv inhūmānē, avārē.
selfishness n inhūmānitās f, incontinentia f, avāritia f.
self-made adj (man) novus.
self-possessed adj aequō animō.
self-possession n aequus animus m.
self-reliant adj cōnfīdēns.
self-respect n pudor m.
self-restraint n modestia f.
self-sacrifice n dēvōtiō f.
selfsame adj ūnus et īdem.
sell vt vēndere; (in lots) dīvēndere; **be sold** vēnīre.
seller n vēnditor m.
selvage n limbus m.
semblance n speciēs f, imāgō f.
semicircle n hēmicyclium nt.
senate n senātus m; **hold a meeting of the ~** senātum habēre; **decree of the ~** senātus cōnsultum nt.
senate house n cūria f.
senator n senātor m; (provincial) decuriō m; **~s** pl patrēs mpl.
senatorial adj senātōrius.
send vt mittere; **~ across** trānsmittere; **~ ahead** praemittere; **~ away** dīmittere; **~ back** remittere; **~ for** accessere; (doctor) adhibēre; **~ forth** ēmittere; **~ forward** praemittere; **~ in** immittere, intrōmittere; **~ out** ēmittere; (in different directions) dīmittere; **~ out of the way** ablēgāre; **~ up** submittere.
senile adj senīlis.
senility n senium nt.
senior adj nātū māior; (thing) prior.
sensation n sēnsus m; (event) rēs

nova f; **lose ~** obtorpēscere; **create a ~** hominēs obstupefacere.
sensational adj novus, prōdigiōsus.
sense n (faculty) sēnsus m; (wisdom) prūdentia f; (meaning) vis f, sententia f; **common ~** prūdentia f; **be in one's ~s** apud sē esse, mentis suae esse; **out of one's ~s** dēmēns; **recover one's ~s** resipīscere; **what is the ~ of** quid sibī vult? ♦ vt sentīre.
senseless adj absurdus, ineptus, īnsipiēns.
senselessly adv īnsipienter.
senselessness n īnsipientia f.
sensibility n sēnsus m.
sensible adj prūdēns, sapiēns.
sensibly adv prūdenter, sapienter.
sensitive adj mollis, irrītābilis, patibilis.
sensitiveness n mollitia f.
sensual adj libīdinōsus.
sensuality n libīdō f, voluptās f.
sensually adv libīdinōsē.
sentence n (judge) iūdicium nt, sententia f; (GRAM) sententia f; **pass ~** iūdicāre; **execute ~** lēge agere ♦ vt damnāre; **~ to death** capitis damnāre.
sententious adj sententiōsus.
sententiously adv sententiōsē.
sentient adj patibilis.
sentiment n (feeling) sēnsus m; (opinion) sententia f; (emotion) mollitia f.
sentimental adj mollis, flēbilis.
sentimentality n mollitia f.
sentimentally adv molliter.
sentries npl statiōnēs fpl, excubiae fpl.
sentry n custōs m, vigil m; **be on ~ duty** in statiōne esse.
separable adj dīviduus, sēparābilis.
separate vt sēparāre, dīvidere,

disiungere; (*forcibly*) dīrimere, dīvellere ♦ *vi* dīgredī ♦ *adj* sēparātus, sēcrētus.

separately *adv* sēparātim, seōrsum.

separation *n* sēparātiō f; (*violent*) discidium *nt*.

September *n* mēnsis September *m*; of ~ September.

sepulchral *adj* fūnebris.

sepulchre *n* sepulcrum *nt*.

sepulture *n* sepultūra f.

sequel *n* exitus *m*, quae sequuntur.

sequence *n* seriēs f, ōrdō *m*.

sequestered *adj* sēcrētus.

serenade *vt* occentāre.

serene *adj* tranquillus, sēcūrus.

serenely *adv* tranquillē.

serenity *n* sēcūritās f.

serf *n* servus *m*.

serfdom *n* servitūs f.

sergeant *n* signifer *m*.

series *n* seriēs f, ōrdō *m*.

serious *adj* gravis, sērius, sevērus.

seriously *adv* graviter, sēriō, sevērē.

seriousness *n* gravitās f.

sermon *n* ōrātiō f.

serpent *n* serpēns f.

serpentine *adj* tortuōsus.

serrated *adj* serrātus.

serried *adj* cōnfertus.

servant *n* (*domestic*) famulus *m*, famula f; (*public*) minister *m*, ministra f; **family** ~ familia f.

servant maid *n* ancilla f.

serve *vt* servīre (*dat*); (*food*) ministrāre, adpōnere; (*interest*) condūcere (*dat*) ♦ *vi* (*MIL*) stīpendia merēre, mīlitāre; (*suffice*) sufficere; ~ **as** esse prō (*abl*); ~ **in the cavalry** equō merēre; ~ **in the infantry** pedibus merēre; **having ~d one's time** ēmeritus f; ~ **a sentence** poenam subīre; ~ **well** bene merērī dē (*abl*).

service *n* (*status*) servitium *nt*,

famulātus *m*; (*work*) ministerium *nt*; (*help*) opera f; (*by an equal*) meritum *nt*, beneficium *nt*; (*MIL*) mīlitia f, stīpendia *ntpl*; **be of** ~ **to** prōdesse (*dat*), bene merērī dē; **I am at your** ~ adsum tibī; **complete one's** ~ stīpendia ēmerērī.

serviceable *adj* ūtilis.

servile *adj* servīlis; (*fig*) abiectus, humilis.

servility *n* adūlātiō f.

servitude *n* servitūs f.

session *n* conventus *m*; **be in** ~ sedēre.

sesterce *n* sēstertius *m*; **10 ~s** decem sēstertiī; **10,000 ~s** dēna sēstertia *ntpl*; **1,000,000 ~s** deciēs sēstertium.

set *vt* pōnere, locāre, statuere, sistere; (*bone*) condere; (*course*) dīrigere; (*example*) dare; (*limit*) impōnere; (*mind*) intendere; (*music*) modulārī; (*sail*) dare; (*sentries*) dispōnere; (*table*) īnstruere; (*trap*) parāre ♦ *vi* (*ASTRO*) occidere; ~ **about** incipere; ~ **against** oppōnere; ~ **apart** sēpōnere; ~ **aside** sēpōnere; ~ **down** (*writing*) perscrībere; ~ **eyes on** cōnspicere; ~ **foot on** ingredī; ~ **forth** expōnere, ēdere; ~ **free** līberāre; ~ **in motion** movēre; ~ **in order** compōnere, dispōnere; ~ **off** (*decoration*) distinguere; (*art*) illūmināre; ~ **on** (*to attack*) immittere; ~ **on foot** īnstituere; ~ **on fire** incendere; ~ **one's heart on** exoptāre; ~ **out** vi proficīscī; ~ **over** praeficere, impōnere; ~ **up** statuere; (*fig*) cōnstituere.

set *adj* (*arrangement*) status, (*purpose*) certus; (*rule*) praescrīptus; (*speech*) compositus; of ~ **purpose** cōnsultō ♦ *n* (*persons*) numerus *m*; (*things*) congeriēs f; (*current*)

cursus m.
setback n repulsa f.
settee n lectulus m.
setting n (ASTRO) occāsus m; (event) locus m.
settle n sella f ♦ vt statuere; (annuity) praestāre; (business) trānsigere; (colony) dēdūcere; (debt) exsolvere; (decision) cōnstituere; (dispute) dēcīdere, compōnere ♦ vi (abode) cōnsīdere; (agreement) cōnstituere, convenīre; (sediment) dēsīdere; ~ in īnsidēre (dat).
settled adj certus, explōrātus.
settlement n (of a colony) dēductiō f; (colony) colōnia f; (of dispute) dēcīsiō f, compositiō f; (to wife) dōs f.
settler n colōnus m.
set to n pugna f.
seven num septem; ~ each septēnī; ~ times septiēns.
seven hundred num septingentī.
seven hundredth adj septingentēsimus.
seventeen num septendecim.
seventeenth adj septimus decimus.
seventh adj septimus; **for the ~ time** septimum.
seventieth adj septuāgēsimus.
seventy num septuāgintā; ~ each septuāgēnī; ~ times septuāgiēns.
sever vt incīdere, sēparāre, dīvidere.
several adj complūrēs, aliquot.
severally adv singulī.
severe adj gravis, sevērus, dūrus; (style) austērus; (weather) asper; (pain) ācer, gravis.
severely adv graviter, sevērē.
severity n gravitās f, asperitās f; sevērītās f.
sew vt suere; ~ up cōnsuere; ~ up in īnsuere in (acc).
sewer n cloāca f.

sex n sexus m.
shabbily adv sordidē.
shabbiness n sordēs fpl.
shabby adj sordidus.
shackle n compēs f, vinculum nt ♦ vt impedīre, vincīre.
shade n umbra f; (colour) color m; ~s pl mānēs mpl; **put in the ~** officere (dat) ♦ vt opācāre, umbram adferre (dat).
shadow n umbra f.
shadowy adj obscūrus; (fig) inānis.
shady adj umbrōsus, opācus.
shaft n (missile) tēlum nt, sagitta f; (of spear) hastīle nt; (of cart) tēmō m; (of light) radius m; (excavation) puteus m.
shaggy adj hirsūtus.
shake vt quatere, agitāre; (structure) labefacere, labefactāre; (belief) īnfirmāre; (resolution) labefactāre, commovēre; ~ hands with dextram dare (dat) ♦ vi quatī, agitārī, tremere, horrēscere; ~ off dēcutere, excutere; ~ out excutere.
shaking n tremor m.
shaky adj īnstābilis, tremebundus.
shall aux vb = fut indic.
shallot n caepa Ascalōnia f.
shallow adj brevis, vadōsus; (fig) levis.
shallowness n vada ntpl; (fig) levitās f.
shallows n brevia ntpl, vada ntpl.
sham adj fictus, falsus, fūcōsus ♦ n simulātiō f, speciēs f ♦ vt simulāre.
shambles n laniēna f.
shame n (feeling) pudor m; (cause) dēdecus nt, ignōminia f; **it ~s** pudet (+ acc of person, gen of thing); **it is a ~** flāgitium est ♦ vt rubōrem incutere (dat) ♦ interj prō pudor!
shamefaced adj verēcundus.
shameful adj ignōminiōsus, turpis.
shamefully adv turpiter.

shameless adj impudēns.

shamelessly adv impudenter.

shamelessness n impudentia f.

shank n crūs nt.

shape n fōrma f, figūra f ♦ vt fōrmāre, fingere; (fig) īnfōrmāre ♦ vi: ~ **well** prōficere.

shapeless adj īnfōrmis, dēfōrmis.

shapelessness n dēfōrmitās f.

shapeliness n fōrma f.

shapely adj fōrmōsus.

shard n testa f.

share n pars f; (plough) vōmer m; **go ~s with** inter sē partīrī ♦ vt (give) partīrī, impertīre; (have) commūnicāre, participem esse (gen).

sharer n particeps m/f, socius m.

shark n volpēs marīna f.

sharp adj acūtus; (fig) ācer, acūtus; (bitter) amārus.

sharpen vt acuere; (fig) exacuere.

sharply adv ācriter, acūtē.

sharpness n aciēs f; (mind) acūmen nt, argūtiae fpl; (temper) acerbitās f.

shatter vt quassāre, perfringere, adflīgere; (fig) frangere.

shave vt rādere; ~ **off** abrādere.

shavings n rāmenta ntpl.

she pron haec, ea, illa.

sheaf n manipulus m.

shear vt tondēre, dētondēre.

shears n forficēs fpl.

sheath n vāgīna f.

sheathe vt recondere.

shed vt fundere; (blood) effundere; (one's own) profundere; (tears) effundere; (covering) exuere; ~ **light on** (fig) lūmen adhibēre (dat).

sheen n nitor m.

sheep n ovis f; (flock) pecus m.

sheepfold n ovīle nt.

sheepish adj pudibundus.

sheepishly adv pudenter.

sheer adj (absolute) merus; (steep)

praeruptus.

sheet n (cloth) linteum nt; (metal) lāmina f; (paper) carta f, scheda f; (sail) pēs m; (water) aequor nt.

shelf n pluteus m, pēgma nt.

shell n concha f; (egg) putāmen nt; (tortoise) testa f.

shellfish n conchȳlium nt.

shelter n suffugium nt, tegmen nt; (refuge) perfugium nt, asȳlum nt; (lodging) hospitium nt; (fig) umbra f ♦ vt tegere, dēfendere; (refugee) excipere ♦ vi latēre; ~ **behind** (fig) dēlitēscere in (abl).

sheltered adj (life) umbrātilis.

shelve vt differre ♦ vi sē dēmittere.

shelving adj dēclīvis.

shepherd n pastor m.

shield n scūtum nt; clipeus m; (small) parma f; (fig) praesidium nt ♦ vt prōtegere, dēfendere.

shift n (change) mūtātiō f; (expedient) ars f, dolus m; **make ~ to efficere ut; in ~s** per vicēs ♦ vt mūtāre; (move) movēre ♦ vi mutārī; discēdere.

shiftless adj iners, inops.

shifty adj vafer, versūtus.

shilling n solidus m.

shimmer vi micāre ♦ n tremulum lūmen nt.

shin n tībia f.

shine vi lūcēre, fulgēre; (reflecting) nitēre; (fig) ēminēre; ~ **forth** ēlūcēre, ēnitēre; effulgēre; ~ **upon** adfulgēre (dat) ♦ n nitor m.

shingle n lapillī mpl, glārea f.

shining adj lūcidus, splendidus; (fig) illūstris.

shiny adj nitidus.

ship n nāvis f; **admiral's ~** nāvis praetōria; **decked ~** nāvis tēcta, nāvis cōnstrāta ♦ vt (cargo) impōnere; (to a place) nāvī invehere.

shipowner n nāviculārius m.

shipping n nāvēs fpl.
shipwreck n naufragium nt; **suffer ~** naufragium facere.
shipwrecked adj naufragus.
shirk vt dēfugere, dētrectāre.
shirt n subūcula f.
shiver n horror m ♦ vi horrēre, tremere ♦ vt perfringere, comminuere.
shivering n horror m.
shoal n (fish) exāmen nt; (water) vadum nt; **~s** pl brevia ntpl.
shock n impulsus m; (battle) concursus m, cōnflictus m; (hair) caesariēs f; (mind) offēnsiō f ♦ vt percutere, offendere.
shocking adj atrōx, dētestābilis, flāgitiōsus.
shoddy adj vīlis.
shoe n calceus m.
shoemaker n sūtor m.
shoot n surculus m; (vine) pampinus m ♦ vi frondēscere; (movement) volāre; **~ up** ēmicāre ♦ vt summā, ēmicāre, iaculārī; (missile) conīcere, iaculārī; (person) iaculārī, trānsfīgere.
shop n taberna f.
shore n lītus nt, ōra f ♦ vt fulcīre.
short adj brevis; (broken) curtus; (amount) exiguus; **for a ~ time** parumper, paulisper; **~ of** (number) intrā (acc); **be ~ of** indigēre (abl); **cut ~** interpellāre; **in ~** ad summam, dēnique; **very ~** perbrevis; **fall ~ of** nōn pervenīre ad, abesse ab; **run ~** dēficere; **to cut a long story ~** nē multīs morer, nē multa.
shortage n inopia f.
shortcoming n dēlictum nt, culpa f.
short cut n via compendiāria f.
shorten vt curtāre, imminuere, contrahere; (sail) legere.
shorthand n notae fpl.
shorthand writer n āctuārius m.
short-lived adj brevis.

shortly adv (time) brevī; (speak) breviter; **~ after** paulō post, nec multō post.
shortness n brevitās f, exiguitās f; (difficulty) angustiae fpl.
short-sighted adj (fig) imprōvidus, imprūdēns.
short-sightedness n imprūdentia f.
short-tempered adj īrācundus.
shot n ictus m; (range) iactus m.
should vi (duty) dēbēre.
shoulder n umerus m; (animal) armus m ♦ vt (burden) suscipere.
shout n clāmor m, adclāmātiō f ♦ vt, vi clāmāre, vōciferārī; **~ down** obstrepere (dat); **~ out** exclāmāre.
shove vt trūdere, impellere.
shovel n rutrum nt.
show n speciēs f; (entertainment) lūdī mpl, spectāculum nt; (stage) lūdicrum nt; **for ~** in speciem; **put on a ~** spectācula dare ♦ vt mōnstrāre, indicāre, ostendere, ostentāre; (point out) dēmōnstrāre; (qualities) praestāre; **~ off** vi sē iactāre ♦ vt ostentāre.
shower n imber m ♦ vt fundere, conicere.
showery adj pluvius.
showiness n ostentātiō f.
showing off n iactātiō f.
showy adj speciōsus.
shred n fragmentum nt; **in ~s** minūtātim; **tear to ~s** dīlaniāre ♦ vt concīdere.
shrew n virāgō f.
shrewd adj acūtus, ācer, sagāx.
shrewdly adv acūtē, sagāciter.
shrewdness n acūmen nt, sagācitās f.
shriek n ululātus m ♦ vi ululāre.
shrill adj acūtus, argūtus.
shrine n fānum nt, dēlubrum nt.
shrink vt contrahere ♦ vi contrahī;

~ **from** abhorrēre ab, refugere ab, dētrectāre.

shrivel vt corrūgāre ♦ vi exārēscere.

shroud n integumentum nt; ~**s** pl rudentēs mpl ♦ vt involvere.

shrub n frutex m.

shrubbery n fruticētum nt.

shudder n horror m ♦ vi exhorrēscere; ~ **at** horrēre.

shuffle vt miscēre ♦ vi claudicāre; (fig) tergiversārī.

shun vt vītāre, ēvītāre, dēfugere.

shut vt claudere; (with cover) operīre; (hand) comprimere; ~ **in** inclūdere; ~ **off** interclūdere; ~ **out** exclūdere; ~ **up** inclūdere.

shutter n foricula f, lūmināre nt.

shuttle n radius m.

shy adj timidus, pudibundus, verēcundus.

shyly adv timidē, verēcundē.

shyness n verēcundia f.

sibyl n sibylla f.

sick adj aeger, aegrōtus; **be** ~ aegrōtāre; **feel** ~ nauseāre; **I am** ~ **of** mē taedet (gen).

sicken vt fastīdium movēre (dat) ♦ vi nauseāre, aegrōtāre.

sickle n falx f.

sickly adj invalidus.

sickness n nausea f; (illness) morbus m, aegritūdō f.

side n latus nt; (direction) pars f; (faction) partēs fpl; (kin) genus nt; **on all** ~**s** undique; **on both** ~**s** utrimque; **on one** ~ ūnā ex parte; **on our** ~ ā nōbīs; **be on the** ~ **of** stāre ab, sentīre cum; **on the far** ~ **of** ultrā (acc); **on this** ~ hīnc; **on this** ~ **of** cis (acc), citrā (acc) ♦ vi: ~ **with** stāre ab, facere cum.

sideboard n abacus m.

sidelong adj oblīquus.

sideways adv oblīquē, in oblīquum.

sidle vi oblīquō corpore incēdere.

siege n obsidiō f, oppugnātiō f; **lay** ~ **to** obsidēre.

siege works n opera ntpl.

siesta n merīdiātiō f; **take a** ~ merīdiāre.

sieve n crībrum nt.

sigh n suspīrium nt; (loud) gemitus m ♦ vi suspīrāre, gemere.

sight n (sense) vīsus m; (process) aspectus m; (range) cōnspectus m; (thing seen) spectāculum nt, speciēs f; **at** ~ ex tempore; **at first** ~ prīmō aspectū; **in** ~ in cōnspectū; **come into** ~ in cōnspectum sē dare; **in the** ~ **of** in oculīs (gen); **catch** ~ **of** cōnspicere; **lose** ~ **of** ē cōnspectū āmittere; (fig) oblīviscī (gen) ♦ vt cōnspicārī.

sightless adj caecus.

sightly adj decōrus.

sign n signum nt, indicium nt; (distinction) īnsigne nt; (mark) nota f; (trace) vestīgium nt; (proof) documentum nt; (portent) ōmen nt; (Zodiac) signum nt; **give a** ~ innuere ♦ vi signum dare, innuere ♦ vt subscrībere (dat); (as witness) obsignāre.

signal n signum nt; **give the** ~ **for retreat** receptuī canere ♦ vi signum dare ♦ adj īnsignis, ēgregius.

signalize vt nōbilitāre.

signally adv ēgregiē.

signature n nōmen nt, manus f, chīrographum nt.

signet n signum nt.

signet ring n anulus m.

significance n interpretātiō f, significātiō f, vīs f; (importance) pondus nt.

significant adj gravis, clārus.

signification n significātiō f.

signify vt significāre, velle; (omen) portendere; **it does not** ~ nōn interest.

silence n silentium nt; **in ~** per silentium ♦ vt comprimere; (argument) refūtāre.

silent adj tacitus; (habit) taciturnus; **be ~** silēre, tacēre; **be ~ about** silēre, tacēre; **become ~** conticēscere.

silently adv tacitē.

silhouette n adumbrātiō f.

silk n bombȳx m; (clothes) sērica ntpl ♦ adj bombȳcius, sēricus.

silken adj bombȳcinus.

sill n līmen nt.

silliness n stultitia f, ineptiae fpl.

silly adj fatuus, ineptus; stultus; **be ~** dēsipere.

silt n līmus m.

silver n argentum nt ♦ adj argenteus.

silver mine n argentāria f.

silver plate n argentum nt.

silver-plated adj argentātus.

silvery adj argenteus.

similar adj similis.

similarity n similitūdō f.

similarly adv similiter.

simile n similitūdō f.

simmer vi lēniter fervēre.

simper vi molliter subrīdēre.

simple adj simplex; (mind) fatuus; (task) facilis.

simpleton n homō ineptus m.

simplicity n simplicitās f; (mind) stultitia f.

simplify vt faciliōrem reddere.

simply adv simpliciter; (merely) sōlum, tantum.

simulate vt simulāre.

simulation n simulātiō f.

simultaneously adv simul, ūnā, eōdem tempore.

sin n peccātum nt, nefās nt, dēlictum nt ♦ vi peccāre.

since adv abhinc; **long ~** iamdūdum ♦ conj (time) ex quō tempore, postquam; (reason) cum (+ subj), quoniam; **~ he** quippe quī

♦ prep ab (abl), ex (abl), post (acc); **ever ~** usque ab.

sincere adj sincērus, simplex, apertus.

sincerely adv sincērē, ex animō.

sincerity n fidēs f, simplicitās f.

sinew n nervus m.

sinewy adj nervōsus.

sinful adj improbus, impius, incestus.

sinfully adv improbē, impiē.

sing vt canere, cantāre; **~ of** canere.

singe vt adūrere.

singer n cantor m.

singing n cantus m ♦ adj canōrus.

single adj ūnus, sōlus, ūnicus; (unmarried) caelebs ♦ vt: **~ out** ēligere, excerpere.

single-handed adj ūnus.

singly adv singillātim, singulī.

singular adj singulāris; (strange) novus.

singularly adv singulāriter, praecipuē.

sinister adj īnfaustus, malevolus.

sink vi dēsīdere; (in water) dēmergī; **~ in** inlābī, īnsīdere ♦ vt dēprimere, mergere; (well) fodere; (fig) dēmergere.

sinless adj integer, innocēns, castus.

sinner n peccātor m.

sinuous adj sinuōsus.

sip vt gustāre, lībāre.

siphon n siphō m.

sir n (to master) ere; (to equal) optimē; (title) eques m.

sire n pater m.

siren n sīrēn f.

sirocco n Auster m.

sister n soror f; **~'s** sorōrius.

sisterhood n germānitās f; (society) sorōrum societās f.

sister-in-law n glōs f.

sisterly adj sorōrius.

sit vi sedēre; **~ beside** adsidēre

(*dat*); **~ down** cōnsīderāre; **~ on**
īnsīdere (*dat*); (*eggs*) incubāre; **~
at table** accumbere; **~ up** (*at night*)
vigilāre.
site *n* situs *m*, locus *m*; (*for building*)
ārea *f.*
sitting *n* sessiō *f.*
situated *adj* situs.
situation *n* situs *m*; (CIRCS) status
m, condiciō *f.*
six *num* sex; **~ each** sēnī; **~ or
seven** sex septem; **~ times**
sexiēns.
six hundred *num* sēscentī; **~ each**
sēscēnī; **~ times** sēscentiēns.
six hundredth *adj* sēscentēsimus.
sixteen *num* sēdecim; **~ each** sēnī
dēnī; **~ times** sēdeciēns.
sixteenth *adj* sextus decimus.
sixth *adj* sextus; **for the ~ time**
sextum.
sixtieth *adj* sexagēsimus.
sixty *num* sexāgintā; **~ each**
sexāgēnī; **~ times** sexāgiēns.
size *n* māgnitūdō *f*, amplitūdō *f*;
(*measure*) mēnsūra *f*, fōrma *f.*
skate *vi* per glaciem lābī; **~ on thin
ice** (*fig*) incēdere per ignēs
suppositōs cinerī dolōsō.
skein *n* glomus *nt.*
skeleton *n* ossa *ntpl.*
sketch *n* adumbrātiō *f*, dēscrīptiō *f*
♦ *vt* adumbrāre, īnfōrmāre.
skewer *n* verū *nt.*
skiff *n* scapha *f*, lēnunculus *m.*
skilful *adj* perītus, doctus, scītus,
(*with hands*) habilis.
skilfully *adv* perītē, doctē;
habiliter.
skill *n* ars *f*, perītia *f*, sollertia *f.*
skilled *adj* perītus, doctus; **~ in**
perītus (+ *gen*).
skim *vt* dēspūmāre; **~ over** (*fig*)
legere, perstringere.
skin *n* cutis *f*; (*animal*) pellis *f* ♦ *vt*
pellem dētrahere (*dat*).
skinflint *n* avārus *m.*

skinny *adj* macer.
skip *vi* exsultāre ♦ *vt* praeterīre.
skipper *n* magister *m.*
skirmish *n* leve proelium *nt* ♦ *vi*
vēlitārī.
skirmisher *n* vēles *m*, excursor *m.*
skirt *n* īnstita *f*; (*border*) limbus *m*
♦ *vt* contingere (*dat*); (*motion*)
legere.
skittish *adj* lascīvus.
skulk *vi* latēre, dēlitēscere.
skull *n* caput *nt.*
sky *n* caelum *nt*; **of the ~** caelestis.
skylark *n* alauda *f.*
slab *n* tabula *f.*
slack *adj* remissus, laxus; (*work*)
piger, neglegēns.
slacken *vt* remittere, dētendere
♦ *vi* laxārī.
slackness *n* remissiō *f*; pigritia *f.*
slag *n* scōria *f.*
slake *vt* restinguere, sēdāre.
slam *vt* adflīgere.
slander *n* maledicta *ntpl*,
obtrectātiō *f*; (*law*) calumnia *f* ♦ *vt*
maledīcere (*dat*), īnfāmāre,
obtrectāre (*dat*).
slanderer *n* obtrectātor *m.*
slanderous *adj* maledicus.
slang *n* vulgāria verba *ntpl.*
slant *vi* in trānsversum īre.
slanting *adj* oblīquus, trānsversus.
slantingly *adv* oblīquē, ex
trānsversō.
slap *n* alapa *f* ♦ *vt* palmā ferīre.
slapdash *adj* praeceps,
temerārius.
slash *vt* caedere ♦ *n* ictus *m.*
slate *n* (*roof*) tēgula *f*; (*writing*)
tabula *f* ♦ *vt* increpāre.
slatternly *adj* sordidus, incōmptus.
slaughter *n* caedēs *f*, strāgēs *f* ♦ *vt*
trucīdāre.
slaughterhouse *n* laniēna *f.*
slave *n* servus *m*; (*domestic*)
famulus *m*; (*home-born*) verna *m*;
be a ~ to īnservīre (*dat*);

household ~s familia f.
slave girl n ancilla f.
slavery n servitūs f.
slavish adj servīlis.
slavishly adv servīliter.
slay vt interficere, occīdere.
slayer n interfector m.
sleek adj nitidus, pinguis.
sleep n somnus m; **go to ~** obdormīscere ♦ vi dormīre; **~ off** vt ēdormīre.
sleeper n dormītor m.
sleepiness n sopor m.
sleepless adj īnsomnis, vigil.
sleeplessness n īnsomnia f.
sleepy adj somniculōsus; **be ~** dormītāre.
sleeve n manica f.
sleight of hand n praestīgiae fpl.
slender adj gracilis, exīlis.
slenderness n gracilitās f.
slice n frūstum n ♦ vt secāre.
slide n lāpsus m ♦ vi lābī.
slight adj levis, exiguus, parvus ♦ n neglegentia f ♦ vt neglegere, offendere.
slightingly adv contemptim.
slightly adv leviter, paululum.
slightness n levitās f.
slim adj gracilis.
slime n līmus m.
slimness n gracilitās f.
slimy adj līmōsus, mūcōsus.
sling n funda f ♦ vt mittere, iaculārī.
slinger n funditor m.
slink vi sē subdūcere.
slip n lāpsus m; (mistake) offēnsiuncula f; (plant) surculus m ♦ vi lābī; **~ away** ēlābī, dīlābī; **~ out** ēlābī; (word) excidere; **give the ~ to** ēlūdere; **let ~** āmittere, ēmittere; (opportunity) ōmittere; **there's many a ~ twixt the cup and the lip** inter ōs et offam multa intervenunt.
slipper n solea f.

slippery adj lūbricus.
slipshod adj neglegēns.
slit n rīma f ♦ vt findere, incīdere.
sloe n spīnus m.
slope n dēclīve nt, clīvus m; (steep) dēiectus m ♦ vi sē dēmittere, vergere.
sloping adj dēclīvis, dēvexus; (up) adclīvis.
slot n rīma f.
sloth n inertia f, segnitia f, dēsidia f, ignāvia f.
slothful adj ignāvus, iners, segnis.
slothfully adv ignāvē, segniter.
slouch vi languidē incēdere.
slough n (skin) exuviae fpl; (bog) palūs f.
slovenliness n ignāvia f, sordēs fpl.
slovenly adj ignāvus, sordidus.
slow adj tardus, lentus; (mind) hebes.
slowly adv tardē, lentē.
slowness n tarditās f.
sludge n līmus m.
slug n līmāx f.
sluggard n homō ignāvus m.
sluggish adj piger, segnis; (mind) hebes.
sluggishly adv pigrē, segniter.
sluggishness n pigritia f, inertia f.
sluice n cataracta f.
slumber n somnus m, sopor m ♦ vi dormīre.
slump n vīlis annōna f.
slur n nota f; **cast ~ on** dētrectāre ♦ vt: **~ words** balbūtīre.
sly adj astūtus, vafer, callidus; **on the ~** ex opīnātō.
slyly adv astūtē, callidē.
slyness n astūtia f.
smack n (blow) ictus m; (with hand) alapa f; (boat) lēnunculus m; (taste) sapor m ♦ vt ferīre ♦ vi: **~ of** olēre, redolēre.
small adj parvus, exiguus; **how ~** quantulus, quantillus; **so ~** tantulus; **very ~** perexiguus,

minimus; **a ~ meeting of** īnfrequēns.

smaller adj minor.

smallest adj minimus.

smallness n exiguitās f, brevitās f.

small talk n sermunculus m.

smart adj (action) ācer, alacer; (dress) concinnus, nitidus; (pace) vēlōx; (wit) facētus, salsus ♦ n dolor m ♦ vi dolēre; (fig) ūrī, mordērī.

smartly adv ācriter; nitidē; vēlōciter; facētē.

smartness n alacritās f; (dress) nitor m; (wit) facētiae fpl, sollertia f.

smash vt ruīna f ♦ vt frangere, comminuere.

smattering n: **get a ~ of** odōrārī, prīmīs labrīs attingere; **with a ~ of** imbūtus (abl).

smear vt oblinere, ungere.

smell n (sense) odōrātus m; (odour) odor m; (of cooking) nīdor m ♦ vt olfacere, odōrārī ♦ vi olēre.

smelly adj olidus.

smelt vt fundere.

smile n rīsus m ♦ vi subrīdēre; **~ at** adrīdēre (dat); **~ upon** rīdēre ad; (fig) secundum esse (dat).

smiling adj laetus.

smirk vi subrīdēre.

smith n faber m.

smithy n fabrica f.

smock n tunica f.

smoke n fūmus m ♦ vi fūmāre.

smoky adj fūmōsus.

smooth adj lēvis; (skin) glaber; (talk) blandus; (sea) placidus; (temper) aequus; (voice) lēvis, teres ♦ vt sternere, līmāre.

smoothly adv lēviter, lēniter.

smoothness n lēvitās f, lēnitās f.

smother vt opprimere, suffocāre.

smoulder vi fūmāre.

smudge n macula f.

smug adj suī contentus.

smuggle vt fūrtim importāre.

smugness n amor suī m.

smut n fūlīgō f.

snack n cēnula f; **take a ~** gustāre.

snag n impedīmentum nt, scrūpulus m.

snail n cochlea f.

snake n anguis m, serpēns f.

snaky adj vīpereus.

snap vt rumpere, praerumpere; **the fingers** digitīs concrepāre ♦ vi rumpī, dissilīre; **~ at** mordēre; **~ up** corripere.

snare n laqueus m, plaga f, pedica f ♦ vt inrētīre.

snarl n gannītus m ♦ vi gannīre.

snatch vt rapere, ēripere, adripere, corripere; **~ at** captāre.

sneak n perfidus m ♦ vi conrēpere; **~ in** sē īnsinuāre; **~ out** ēlābī.

sneaking adj humilis, fūrtīvus.

sneer n irrīsiō f ♦ vi irrīdēre, dērīdēre.

sneeze n sternūtāmentum nt ♦ vi sternuere.

sniff vt odōrārī.

snip vt praecīdere, secāre.

snob n homō ambitiōsus m.

snood n mitra f.

snooze vi dormītāre.

snore vi stertere.

snoring n rhoncus m.

snort n fremitus m ♦ vi fremere.

snout n rōstrum nt.

snow n nix f ♦ vi ningere; **~ed under** nive obrutus; **it is ~ing** ningit.

snowy adj nivālis; (colour) niveus.

snub vt neglegere, praeterīre.

snub-nosed adj sīmus.

snuff n (candle) fungus m.

snug adj commodus.

snugly adv commodē.

so adv (referring back) sīc; (referring forward) ita; (with adj and adv) tam; (with verb) adeō; (consequence) ergō, itaque, igitur; **and ~** itaque; **~ great** tantus; **so-so** sīc; **~ as to** ut; **~ be it** estō; **~ big** tantus; **~ far** usque adeō, adhūc; **~ far as** quod; **~ far from** adeō nōn; **~ little** tantillus; **~ long as** dum; **~ many** tot; **~ much** adj tantus ♦ adv tantum; (with compar) tantō; **~ often** totiēns; **~ that** (+ subj); **~ that ... not** (purpose) nē; (result) ut nōn; **and ~ on** deinceps; **not ~ very** haud ita; **say ~** id dīcere.

soak vt imbuere, madefacere.

soaking adj madidus.

soap n sāpō m.

soar vi in sublīme ferrī, subvolāre; **~ above** superāre.

sob n singultus m ♦ vi singultāre.

sober adj sobrius; (conduct) modestus; (mind) sānus.

soberly adv sobriē, modestē.

sobriety n modestia f, continentia f.

so-called adj quī dīcitur.

sociability n facilitās f.

sociable adj facilis, cōmis.

sociably adv faciliter, cōmiter.

social adj sociālis, commūnis.

socialism n populāris ratiō f.

socialist n homō populāris m/f.

society n societās f; (class) optimātēs mpl; (being with) convīctus m; **cultivate the ~ of** adsectārī; **secret ~** sodālitās f.

sod n caespes m, glaeba f.

soda n nitrum nt.

sodden adj madidus.

soever adv -cumque.

sofa n lectus m.

soft adj mollis; (fruit) mītis; (voice) submissus; (character) dēlicātus; (words) blandus.

soften vt mollīre; (body) ēnervāre; (emotion) lēnīre, mītigāre ♦ vi mollēscere, mītēscere.

soft-hearted adj misericors.

softly adv molliter, lēniter; blandē.

softness n mollitia f, mollitiēs f.

soil n sōlum nt, humus f ♦ vt inquināre, foedāre.

sojourn n commorātiō f, mānsiō f ♦ vi commorārī.

sojourner n hospes m, hospita f.

solace n sōlātium nt, levātiō f ♦ vt sōlārī, cōnsōlārī.

solar adj sōlis.

solder n ferrūmen nt ♦ vt ferrūmināre.

soldier n mīles m; **be a ~** mīlitāre; **common ~** manipulāris m, gregārius mīles m; **fellow ~** commīlitō m; **foot ~** pedes m; **old ~** veterānus m ♦ vi mīlitāre.

soldierly adj mīlitāris.

soldiery n mīles m.

sole adj sōlus, ūnus, ūnicus ♦ n (foot) planta f; (fish) solea f.

solecism n soloecismus m.

solely adv sōlum, tantum, modō.

solemn adj gravis; (religion) sanctus.

solemnity n gravitās f; sanctitās f.

solemnize vt agere.

solemnly adv graviter; rītē.

solicit vt flāgitāre, obsecrāre.

solicitation n flāgitātiō f.

solicitor n advocātus m.

solicitous adj anxius, trepidus.

solicitously adv anxiē, trepidē.

solicitude n cūra f, anxietās f.

solid adj solidus; (metal) pūrus; (food) firmus; (argument) firmus; (character) cōnstāns, spectātus; **become ~** concrēscere; **make ~** cōgere.

solidarity n societās f.

solidify vt cōgere ♦ vi concrēscere.

solidity n soliditās f.

solidly adv firmē, cōnstanter.

soliloquize vi sēcum loquī.

soliloquy n ūnīus ōrātiō f.

solitary adj sōlus, sōlitārius; (instance) ūnicus; (place) dēsertus.

solitude n sōlitūdō f.
solo n canticum nt.
solstice n (summer) sōlstitium nt; (winter) brūma f.
solstitial adj sōlstitiālis, brūmālis.
suluble adj dissolūbilis.
solution n (of puzzle) ēnōdātiō f
solve vt ēnōdāre, explicāre.
solvency n solvendī facultās f.
solvent adj: **be ~** solvendō esse.
sombre adj obscūrus; (fig) tristis.
some adj aliquī; (pl) nonnūllī, aliquot; **~ people** sunt quī (+ subj); **~ ... other** alius ... alius; **for ~ time** aliquamdiū; **with ~ reason** nōn sine causā ♦ pron aliquis; (pl) nonnūllī, sunt quī (subj), erant quī (subj).
somebody pron aliquis; **~ or other** nesciōquis.
somehow adv quōdammodō, nesciō quōmodō.
someone pron aliquis; (negative) quisquam; **~ or other** nesciōquis; **~ else** alius.
something pron aliquid; **~ or other** nesciōquid; **~ else** aliud.
sometime adv aliquandō; (past) quondam.
sometimes adv interdum, nōnnumquam; **~ ... ~** modo ... modo.
somewhat adv aliquantum, nōnnihil, paulum; (with compar) paulō, aliquantō.
somewhere adv alicubi; (to) aliquō; **~ else** alibī; (to) aliō; **from ~** alicunde; **from ~ else** aliunde.
somnolence n somnus m.
sumnolent adj sēmisomnus.
son n fīlius m; **small ~** fīliolus m.
song n carmen nt, cantus m.
son-in-law n gener m.
sonorous adj sonōrus, canōrus.
soon adv mox, brevī, citō; **as ~ as** prīmum, cum prīmum (+ fut perf), simul āc/atque (+ perf indic);

as ~ as possible quam prīmum; **too ~** praemātūrē, ante tempus.
sooner adv prius, mātūrius; (preference) libentius, potius; **~ or later** sērius ōcius; **no ~ said than done** dictum factum.
soonest adv mātūrissimē.
soot n fūlīgō f.
soothe vt dēlēnīre, permulcēre.
soothing adj lēnis, blandus.
soothingly adv blandē.
soothsayer n hariolus m, vātēs m/f, haruspex m.
sooty adj fūmōsus.
sop n offa f; (fig) dēlēnīmentum nt.
sophism n captiō f.
sophist n sophistēs m.
sophistical adj acūleātus, captiōsus.
sophisticated adj lepidus, urbānus.
sophistry n captiō f.
soporific adj sopōrifer, somnifer.
soprano adj acūtus.
sorcerer n venēficus m.
sorceress n venēfica f, saga f.
sorcery n venēficium nt; (means) venēna ntpl, carmina ntpl.
sordid adj sordidus; (conduct) illīberālis.
sordidly adv sordidē.
sordidness n sordēs fpl; illīberālitās f.
sore adj molestus, gravis, acerbus; **feel ~** dolēre ♦ n ulcus nt.
sorely adv graviter, vehementer.
sorrel n lapathus f, lapathum nt.
sorrow n dolor m, aegritūdō f; (outward) maeror m; (for death) lūctus m ♦ vi dolēre, maerēre, lūgēre.
sorrowful adj maestus, tristis.
sorrowfully adv maestē.
sorry adj paenitēns; (poor) miser; **I am ~ for** (remorse) mē paenitet, mē piget (gen); (pity) mē miseret (gen).

sort n genus nt; a ~ of quīdam; all ~s of omnēs; the ~ of tālis; this ~ of huiusmodī; the common ~ plēbs f; **I am not the ~ of man to** nōn is sum quī (+ *subj*); **I am out of ~s** mihī displiceō ♦ *vt* dīgerere, compōnere; (*votes*) dīribēre.

sortie n excursiō f, excursus m, ēruptiō f; **make a ~** ērumpere, excurrere.

sot n ēbriōsus m.

sottish *adj* ēbriōsus, tēmulentus.

sottishness n vīnolentia f.

soul n anima f, animus m; (*essence*) vīs f; (*person*) caput nt; **not a ~** nēmō ūnus; **the ~ of** (*fig*) medulla f.

soulless *adj* caecus, dūrus.

sound n sonitus m, sonus m; (*articulate*) vōx f; (*confused*) strepitus m; (*loud*) fragor m; (*strait*) fretum nt ♦ *vt* (*signal*) canere; (*instrument*) īnflāre; (*depth*) scrūtārī, temptāre; (*person*) animum temptāre (*gen*) ♦ *vi* canere, sonāre; (*seem*) vidērī; **~ a retreat** receptuī canere ♦ *adj* sānus, salūbris; (*health*) firmus; (*sleep*) artus; (*judgment*) exquīsītus; (*argument*) vērus; **safe and ~** salvus, incolumis.

soundly *adv* (*beat*) vehementer; (*sleep*) artē; (*study*) penitus, dīligenter.

soundness n sānitās f, integritās f.

soup n iūs nt.

sour *adj* acerbus, amārus, acidus; **turn ~** acēscere; (*fig*) coacēscere ♦ *vt* (*fig*) exacerbāre.

source n fōns m; (*river*) caput nt; (*fig*) fōns m, orīgō f; **have its ~ in** orīrī ex; (*fig*) proficīscī ex.

sourness n acerbitās f; (*temper*) mōrōsitās f.

souse *vt* immergere.

south n merīdiēs f ♦ *adj* austrālis ♦ *adv* ad merīdiem.

south-east *adv* inter sōlis ortum et merīdiem.

southerly *adj* ad merīdiem versus.

southern *adj* austrālis.

south-west *adv* inter occāsum sōlis et merīdiem.

south wind n auster m.

souvenir n monumentum nt.

sovereign n rēx m, rēgīna f ♦ *adj* prīnceps, summus.

sovereignty n rēgnum nt, imperium nt, prīncipātus m; (*of the people*) māiestās f.

sow n scrōfa f, sūs f.

sow *vt* serere; (*field*) cōnserere ♦ *vi* sementem facere.

sower n sator m.

sowing n sēmentis f.

spa n aquae fpl.

space n (*extension*) spatium nt; (*not matter*) ināne nt; (*room*) locus m; (*distance*) intervallum nt; (*time*) spatium nt; **open ~** ārea f; **leave a ~ of** intermittere ♦ *vt*: ~ **out** dispōnere.

spacious *adj* amplus, capāx.

spaciousness n amplitūdō f.

spade n pāla f, rūtrum nt.

span n (*measure*) palmus m; (*extent*) spatium nt ♦ *vt* iungere.

spangle n bractea f.

spangled *adj* distinctus.

spar n tignum nt.

spare *vt* parcere (*dat*); (*to give*) suppeditāre; **~ time for** vacāre (*dat*) ♦ *adj* exīlis; (*extra*) subsecīvus.

sparing *adj* parcus.

sparingly *adv* parcē.

spark n scintilla f; (*fig*) igniculus m.

sparkle *vi* scintillāre, nitēre, micāre.

sparrow n passer m.

sparse *adj* rārus.

spasm n convulsiō f.

spasmodically *adv* interdum.

spatter vt aspergere.

spawn n ōva ntpl.

speak vt, vi loquī; (make speech) dīcere, contiōnārī, ōrātiōnem habēre; ~ **out** ēloquī; ~ **to** adloquī; (converse) colloquī cum; ~ **well of** bene dīcere (dat); **it ~s for itself** rēs ipsa loquitur.

speaker n ōrātor m.

speaking n: **art of** ~ dīcendī ars f; **practise public** ~ dēclāmāre ♦ adj: **likeness** ~ vīvida imāgō.

spear n hasta f.

spearman n hastātus m.

special adj praecipuus, proprius.

speciality n proprium nt.

specially adv praecipuē, praesertim.

species n genus nt.

specific adj certus.

specification n dēsignātiō f.

specify vt dēnotāre, dēsignāre.

specimen n exemplar nt, exemplum nt.

specious adj speciōsus.

speciously adv speciōsē.

speciousness n speciēs f.

speck n macula f.

speckled adj maculīs distinctus.

spectacle n spectāculum nt.

spectacular adj spectābilis.

spectator n spectātor m.

spectral adj larvālis.

spectre n larva f.

speculate vi cōgitāre, coniectūrās facere; (COMM) forō ūtī.

speculation n cōgitātiō f, coniectūra f; (COMM) ālea f.

speculator n contemplātor m; (COMM) āleātor m.

speech n ōrātiō f; (language) sermō m, lingua f; (to people or troops) contiō f; **make a** ~ ōrātiōnem/contiōnem habēre.

speechless adj ēlinguis, mūtus.

speed n celeritās f, cursus m, vēlōcitās f; **with all** ~ summā

celeritāte; **at full** ~ magnō cursū, incitātus; (riding) citātō equō ♦ vt accelerāre, mātūrāre ♦ vi properāre, festīnāre.

speedily adv celeriter, citō.

speedy adj celer, vēlōx, citus.

spell n carmen nt.

spellbound adj: **be** ~ obstipēscere.

spelt n far nt.

spend vt impendere, īnsūmere; (public money) ērogāre; (time) agere, cōnsūmere, terere; (strength) effundere; ~ **itself** (storm) dēsaevīre; ~ **on** īnsūmere (acc & dat).

spendthrift n nepōs m, prōdigus m.

sphere n globus m; (of action) prōvincia f.

spherical adj globōsus.

sphinx n sphinx f.

spice n condīmentum nt; ~**s** pl odōrēs mpl ♦ vt condīre.

spicy adj odōrātus; (wit) salsus.

spider n arānea f; ~'**s web** arāneum nt.

spike n dēns m, clāvus m.

spikenard n nardus m.

spill vt fundere, profundere ♦ vi redundāre.

spin vt (thread) nēre, dēdūcere; (top) versāre; ~ **out** (story) prōdūcere ♦ vi circumagī, versārī.

spindle n fūsus m.

spine n spīna f.

spineless adj ēnervātus.

spinster n virgō f.

spiral adj intortus ♦ n spīra f.

spire n cōnus m.

spirit n (life) anima f; (intelligence) mēns f; (soul) animus m; (vivacity) spīritus m, vigor m, vīs f; (character) ingenium nt; (intention) voluntās f; (of an age) mōrēs mpl; (ghost) anima f; ~**s** pl mānēs mpl; **full of** ~ alacer, animōsus.

spirited adj animōsus, ācer.

spiritless 670 **spring**

spiritless adj iners, frāctus, timidus.

spiritual adj animī.

spit n verū nt ♦ vi spuere, spūtāre; ~ on cōnspūtāre; ~ out exspuere.

spite n invidia f, malevolentia f, līvor m; in ~ of me mē invītō; in ~ of the difficulties in his angustiīs ♦ vt incommodāre, offendere.

spiteful adj malevolus, malignus, invidus.

spitefully adv malevolē, malignē.

spitefulness n malevolentia f.

spittle n spūtum nt.

splash n fragor m ♦ vt aspergere.

spleen n splēn m; (fig) stomachus m.

splendid adj splendidus, lūculentus; īnsignis; (person) amplus.

splendidly adv splendidē, optimē.

splendour n splendor m, fulgor m; (fig) lautitia f, apparātus m.

splenetic adj stomachōsus.

splice vt iungere.

splint n ferula f.

splinter n fragmentum nt, assula f ♦ vt findere.

split vt findere ♦ vi dissilīre ♦ adj fissus ♦ n fissum nt; (fig) dissidium nt.

splutter vi balbūtīre.

spoil n praeda f ♦ vt (rob) spoliāre; (mar) corrumpere ♦ vi corrumpī.

spoiler n spoliātor m; corruptor m.

spoils npl spolia ntpl, exuviae fpl.

spoke n radius m; put a ~ in one's wheel inicere scrūpulum (dat).

spokesman n interpres m, ōrātor m.

spoliation n spoliātiō f, dīreptiō f.

spondee n spondēus m.

sponge n spongia f.

sponsor n spōnsor m; (fig) auctor m.

spontaneity n impulsus m, voluntās f.

spontaneous adj voluntārius.

spontaneously adv suā sponte, ultrō.

spoon n cochlear nt.

sporadic adj rārus.

sporadically adv passim.

sport n lūdus m; (in Rome) campus m; (fun) iocus m; (ridicule) lūdibrium nt; make ~ of illūdere (dat) ♦ vi lūdere.

sportive adj lascīvus.

sportiveness n lascīvia f.

sportsman n vēnātor m.

sportsmanlike adj honestus, generōsus.

spot n macula f; (place) locus m; (dice) pūnctum nt; on the ~ īlicō ♦ vt maculāre; (see) animadvertere.

spotless adj integer, pūrus; (character) castus.

spotted adj maculōsus.

spouse n coniunx m/f.

spout n (of jug) ōs nt; (pipe) canālis m ♦ vi ēmicāre.

sprain vt intorquēre.

sprawl vi sē fundere.

sprawling adj fūsus.

spray n aspergō f ♦ vt aspergere.

spread vt pandere, extendere; (news) dīvulgāre; (infection) vulgare ♦ vi patēre; (rumour) mānāre, incrēbrēscere; (feeling) glīscere.

spreadeagle vt dispandere.

spreading adj (tree) patulus.

spree n cōmissātiō f.

sprig n virga f.

sprightliness n alacritās f.

sprightly adj alacer, hilaris.

spring n (season) vēr nt; (water) fōns m; (leap) saltus m ♦ vi (grow) crēscere, ēnāscī; (leap) salīre; ~ from orīrī ex, proficīscī ex; ~ on to īnsilīre in (acc); ~ up exorīrī, exsilīre ♦ vt: ~ a leak rīmās agere; ~ a surprise on admīrātiōnem movēre (*dat*) ♦ *adj* vērnus.

springe *n* laqueus *m.*

sprinkle *vt* aspergere; ~ **on**
inspergere (*dat*).

sprint *vi* currere.

sprout *n* surculus *m* ♦ *vi* fruticārī.

spruce *adj* nitidus, concinnus.

sprung *adj* ortus, oriundus.

spume *n* spūma *f.*

spur *n* calcar *nt*; ~ **of a hill**
prōminēns collis; **on the ~ of the
moment** ex tempore ♦ *vt*
incitāre; ~ **the willing horse**
currentem incitāre; ~ **on**
concitāre.

spurious *adj* falsus, fūcōsus, fictus.

spurn *vt* spernere, aspernārī,
respuere.

spurt *vi* ēmicāre; (*run*) sē incitāre
♦ *n* impetus *m.*

spy *n* speculātor *m*, explōrātor *m*
♦ *vi* speculārī ♦ *vt* cōnspicere; ~
out explōrāre.

squabble *n* iūrgium *nt* ♦ *vi* rixārī.

squad *n* (MIL) decuria.

squadron *n* (*cavalry*) āla *f*, turma *f*;
(*ships*) classis *f.*

squalid *adj* sordidus, dēfōrmis.

squall *n* procella *f.*

squally *adj* procellōsus.

squalor *n* sordēs *fpl*, squālor *m.*

squander *vt* dissipāre, disperdere,
effundere.

squanderer *n* prōdigus *m.*

square *n* quadrātum *nt*; (*town*)
ārea *f* ♦ *vt* quadrāre; (*account*)
subdūcere ♦ *vi* cōnstāre,
congruere ♦ *adj* quadrātus.

squash *vt* conterere, contundere.

squat *vi* subsīdere ♦ *adj* brevis
atque obēsus.

squatter *n* (*on land*) agripeta *m.*

squawk *vi* crōcīre.

squeak *n* strīdor *m* ♦ *vi* strīdēre.

squeal *n* vāgītus *m* ♦ *vi* vāgīre.

squeamish *adj* fastīdiōsus; **feel ~**
nauseāre, fastīdīre.

squeamishness *n* fastīdium *nt*,
nausea *f.*

squeeze *vt* premere, comprimere;
~ **out** exprimere.

squint *adj* perversus ♦ *n*: **person
with a** ~ strabō *m* ♦ *vi* strabō
esse.

squinter *n* strabō *m.*

squinting *adj* paetus.

squire *n* armiger *m*; (*landed*)
dominus *m.*

squirm *vi* volūtārī.

squirrel *n* sciūrus *m.*

squirt *vt* ēicere, effundere ♦ *vi*
ēmicāre.

stab *n* ictus *m*, vulnus *nt* ♦ *vt*
fodere, ferīre, percutere.

stability *n* stabilitās *t*, firmitās *f*,
cōnstantia *f.*

stabilize *vt* stabilīre, firmāre.

stable *adj* firmus, stabilis ♦ *n*
stabulum *m*, equīle *nt*; **shut the ~
door after the horse is stolen**
clipeum post vulnera sūmere.

stack *n* acervus *m* ♦ *vt* congerere,
cumulāre.

stadium *n* spatium *nt.*

staff *n* scīpiō *m*, virga *f*; (*augur's*)
lituus *m*; (*officers*) contubernālēs
mpl.

stag *n* cervus *m.*

stage *n* pulpitum *nt*, proscēnium
nt; (*theatre*) scēna *f*, theātrum *nt*;
(*scene of action*) campus *m*; (*of
journey*) iter *nt*; (*of progress*)
gradus *m* ♦ *adj* scēnicus ♦ *vt*
(*play*) dare, docēre.

stage fright *n* horror *m.*

stagger *vi* titubāre ♦ *vt*
obstupefacere.

stagnant *adj* iners.

stagnate *vi* (*fig*) cessāre,
refrīgēscere.

stagnation *n* cessātiō *f*, torpor *m.*

stagy *adj* scēnicus.

staid *adj* sevērus, gravis.

stain *n* macula *f*, lābēs *f*; (*fig*)

dēdecus *nt*, ignōminia *f* ♦ *vt*
maculāre, foedāre, contāmināre;
~ **with** īnficere (*abl*).
stainless *adj* pūrus, integer.
stair *n* scālae *fpl*, gradus *mpl*.
staircase *n* scālae *fpl*.
stake *n* pālus *m*, stīpes *m*; (*pledge*)
pignus *nt*; **be at** ~ agī, in
discrīmine esse ♦ *vt* (*wager*)
dēpōnere.
stale *adj* obsolētus, effētus; (*wine*)
vapidus.
stalemate *n*: **reach a** ~ ad incitās
redigī.
stalk *n* (*corn*) calamus *m*; (*plant*)
stīpes *m* ♦ *vi* incēdere ♦ *vt*
vēnārī, īnsidiārī (*dat*).
stall *n* (*animal*) stabulum *nt*; (*seat*)
subsellium *nt*; (*shop*) taberna *f*
♦ *vt* stabulāre.
stallion *n* equus *m*.
stalwart *adj* ingēns, rōbustus,
fortis.
stamina *n* patientia *f*.
stammer *n* haesitātiō *f* ♦ *vi*
balbūtīre.
stammering *adj* balbus.
stamp *n* fōrma *f*; (*mark*) nota *f*,
signum *nt*; (*of feet*) supplōsiō *f* ♦ *vt*
imprimere; (*coin*) ferīre, signāre;
(*fig*) inūrere; ~ **one's feet** pedem
supplōdere; ~ **out** exstinguere.
stampede *n* discursus *m*; (*fig*)
pavor *m* ♦ *vi* discurrere; (*fig*)
expavēscere.
stance *n* status *m*.
stanchion *n* columna *f*.
stand *n* (*position*) statiō *f*; (*platform*)
suggestus *m*; **make a** ~ resistere,
restāre ♦ *vi* stāre; (*remain*)
manēre; (*matters*) sē habēre ♦ *vt*
statuere; (*tolerate*) ferre, tolerāre;
~ **against** resistere (*dat*); ~ **aloof**
abstāre; ~ **by** adsistere (*dat*);
(*friend*) adesse (*dat*); (*promise*)
praestāre; ~ **convicted**
manifestum tenērī; ~ **down**

concēdere; ~ **fast** cōnsistere; ~
one's ground in locō perstāre; ~
for (*office*) petere; (*meaning*)
significāre; (*policy*) postulāre; ~ **in**
awe of in metū habēre; ~ **in need**
of indigēre (*abl*); ~ **on** īnsistere in
(*abl*); ~ **on end** horrēre; ~ **on one's**
dignity gravitātem suam tuērī; ~
out ēminēre, exstāre; (*against*)
resistere (*dat*); (*to sea*) in altum
prōvehī; ~ **out of the way of**
dēcēdere (*dat*); ~ **over** (*case*)
ampliāre; ~ **still** cōnsistere,
īnsistere; ~ **to reason** sequī; ~
trial reum fierī; ~ **up** surgere,
cōnsurgere; ~ **up for** dēfendere,
adesse (*dat*); ~ **up to** respōnsāre
(*dat*).
standard *n* (MIL) signum *nt*;
(*measure*) nōrma *f*; ~ **author**
scrīptor classicus *m*; **up to** ~
iūstus; **judge by the** ~ **of** referre
ad.
standard-bearer *n* signifer *m*.
standing *adj* perpetuus *m* ~ status
m; (*social*) locus *m*, ōrdō *m*; **of long**
~ inveterātus; **be of long** ~
inveterāscere.
stand-offish *adj* tēctus.
standstill *n*: **be at a** ~ haerēre,
frīgēre; **bring to a** ~ ad incitās
redigere; **come to a** ~ īnsistere.
stanza *n* tetrastichon *m*.
staple *n* uncus *m* ♦ *adj* praecipuus.
star *n* stēlla *f*, astrum *nt*; sīdus *nt*;
shooting ~**s** acontiae *fpl*.
starboard *adj* dexter.
starch *n* amylum *nt*.
stare *n* obtūtus *m* ♦ *vi* intentīs
oculīs intuērī, stupēre; ~ **at**
contemplārī.
stark *adj* rigidus; simplex ♦ *adv*
plānē, omnīnō.
starling *n* sturnus *m*.
starry *adj* stēllātus.
start *n* initium *nt*; (*movement*)
saltus *m*; (*journey*) profectiō *f*; **by**

fits and ~s carptim; **have a day's ~ on** diē antecēdere ♦ vt incipere, īnstituere; (game) excitāre; (process) movēre ♦ vi (with fright) resilīre; (journey) proficīscī; **~ up** exsilīre.

starting place n carcerēs mpl.

startle vt excitāre, terrēre.

starvation n famēs f.

starve vi fame cōnficī; (cold) frīgēre ♦ vt fame ēnecāre.

starveling n famēlicus m.

state n (condition) status m, condiciō f; (pomp) apparātus m; (POL) cīvitās f, rēs pūblica f; **the ~ of affairs is** ita sē rēs habet; **I know the ~ of affairs** quō in locō rēs sit sciō; **of the ~** pūblicus ♦ adj pūblicus ♦ vt affirmāre, expōnere, profitērī; **~ one's case** causam dīcere.

stateliness n māiestās f, gravitās f.

stately adj gravis, grandis, nōbilis.

statement n affirmātiō f, dictum nt; (witness) testimōnium nt.

state of health n valētūdō f.

state of mind n adfectiō f.

statesman n vir reī pūblicae gerendae perītus m, cōnsilī pūblicī auctor m.

statesmanlike adj prūdēns.

statesmanship n cīvīlis prūdentia f.

static adj stabilis.

station n locus m; (MIL) statiō f; (social) locus m, ōrdō m ♦ vt collocāre, pōnere; (in different places) dispōnere.

stationary adj immōtus, statārius, stabilis.

statistics n cēnsus m.

statuary n fictor m.

statue n statua f, signum nt, imāgō f.

statuette n sigillum nt.

stature n fōrma f, statūra f.

status n locus m.

status quo n: **restore the ~** ad integrum restituere.

statutable adj lēgitimus.

statute n lēx f.

staunch vt (blood) sistere ♦ adj fīdus, cōnstāns.

stave vt perrumpere, perfringere; **~ off** arcēre.

stay n firmāmentum nt; (fig) columen nt; (sojourn) mānsiō f, commorātiō f ♦ vt (prop) fulcīre; (stop) dētinēre, dēmorārī ♦ vi manēre, commorārī.

stead n locus m; **stand one in good ~** prōdesse (dat).

steadfast adj firmus, stabilis, cōnstāns; **~ at home** tenēre sē domī.

steadfastly adv cōnstanter.

steadfastness n firmitās f, cōnstantia f.

steadily adv firmē, cōnstanter.

steadiness n stabilitās f; (fig) cōnstantia f.

steady adj stabilis, firmus; (fig) gravis, cōnstāns.

steak n offa f.

steal vt surripere, fūrārī ♦ vi: **~ away** sē subdūcere; **~ over** subrēpere (dat); **~ into** sē īnsinuāre in (acc); **~ a march on** occupāre.

stealing n fūrtum nt.

stealth n fūrtum nt; **by ~** fūrtim, clam.

stealthily adv fūrtim, clam.

stealthy adj fūrtīvus, clandestīnus.

steam n aquae vapor m, fūmus m ♦ vi fūmāre.

steed n equus m.

steel n ferrum nt, chalybs m ♦ vt dūrāre; **~ oneself** obdūrēscere.

steely adj ferreus.

steelyard n statēra f.

steep adj arduus, praeceps, praeruptus; (slope) dēclīvis ♦ vt imbuere.

steeple n turris f.

steepness n arduum nt.

steer vi gubernāre, regere, dīrigere ♦ n iuvencus m.

steering n gubernātiō f.

steersman n gubernātor m; rector m.

stellar adj stēllārum.

stem n stīpes m, truncus m; (ship) prōra f ♦ vt adversārī (dat); **~ the tide of** (fig) obsistere (dat).

stench n foetor m.

stenographer n exceptor m, āctuārius m.

stenography n notae fpl.

stentorian adj (voice) ingēns.

step n gradus m; (track) vestīgium nt; (of stair) gradus m; **~ by ~** gradātim; **flight of ~s** gradus mpl; **take a ~** gradum facere; **take ~s to** ratiōnem inīre ut, vidēre ut; **march in ~** in numerum īre; **out of ~** extrā numerum ♦ vi gradī, incēdere; **~ aside** dēcēdere; **~ back** regredī; **~ forward** prōdīre; **~ on** insistere (dat).

stepdaughter n prīvīgna f.

stepfather n vītricus m.

stepmother n noverca f.

stepson n prīvīgnus m.

stereotyped adj trītus.

sterile adj sterilis.

sterility n sterilitās f.

sterling adj integer, probus, gravis.

stern adj dūrus, sevērus; (look) torvus ♦ n puppis f.

sternly adv sevērē, dūriter.

sternness n sevēritās f.

stew vt coquere.

steward n prōcūrātor m; (of estate) vīlicus m.

stewardship n prōcūrātiō f.

stick n (for beating) fūstis m; (for walking) baculum nt ♦ vi haerēre; **~ at nothing** ad omnia

dēscendere; **~ fast in** inhaerēre (dat), inhaerēscere in (abl); **~ out** ēminēre; **~ to** adhaerēre (dat); **~ up** ēminēre; **~ up for** dēfendere ♦ vt (with glue) conglūtināre; (with point) fīgere; **~ into** īnfīgere; **~ top on** praefigere.

stickler n dīligēns (gen).

sticky adj lentus, tenāx.

stiff adj rigidus; (difficult) difficilis; **be ~** rigēre.

stiffen vt rigidum facere ♦ vi rigēre.

stiffly adv rigidē.

stiff-necked adj obstinātus.

stiffness n rigor m.

stifle vt suffocāre; (fig) opprimere, restinguere.

stigma n nota f.

stigmatize vt notāre.

stile n saepēs f.

still adj immōtus, tranquillus, quiētus; tacitus ♦ vt lēnīre, sēdāre ♦ adv etiam, adhūc, etiamnum; (past) etiam tum; (with compar) etiam; (adversative) tamen, nihilōminus.

stillness n quiēs f; silentium nt.

stilly adj tacitus.

stilted adj (language) īnflātus.

stilts n grallae fpl.

stimulant n stimulus m.

stimulate vt stimulāre, acuere, exacuere, excitāre.

stimulus n stimulus m.

sting n aculeus m; (wound) ictus m; (fig) aculeus m, morsus m ♦ vt pungere, mordēre.

stingily adv sordidē.

stinginess n avāritia f, sordēs fpl, tenācitās f.

stinging adj (words) aculeātus, mordāx.

stingy adj sordidus, tenāx.

stink n foetor m ♦ vi foetere; **~ of** olēre.

stinking adj foetidus.

stint n modus m; **without ~** abundē
♦ vt circumscrībere.
stipend n mercēs f.
stipulate vt pacīscī, stipulārī.
stipulation n condiciō f, pactum nt.
stir n tumultus m ♦ vt movēre,
agitāre; (fig) commovēre; **~ up**
excitāre, incitāre ♦ vi movērī.
stirring adj impiger, tumultuōsus;
(speech) ārdēns.
stitch vt suere ♦ n sūtūra f; (in side)
dolor m.
stock n stirps f, genus nt, gēns f;
(equipment) īnstrūmenta ntpl;
(supply) cōpia f; (investment)
pecūniae fpl; **live~** rēs pecuāria f
♦ vt īnstruere ♦ adj commūnis,
trītus.
stockade n vallum nt.
stock dove n palumbēs m/f.
stock in trade n īnstrūmenta ntpl.
stocks n (ship) nāvālia ntpl;
(torture) compedēs fpl.
stock-still adj plānē immōtus.
stocky adj brevis atque obēsus.
stodgy adj crūdus, īnsulsus.
stoic n Stōicus m ♦ adj Stōicus.
stoical adj dūrus, patiēns.
stoically adv patienter.
stoicism n Stōicōrum ratiō f,
Stōicōrum disciplīna f.
stoke n agitāre.
stole n stola f.
stolid adj stolidus.
stolidity n īnsulsitās f.
stolidly adv stolidē.
stomach n stomachus m; venter
m ♦ vt patī, tolerāre.
stone n lapis m, saxum nt;
(precious) gemma f, lapillus m; (of
fruit) acinum nt; **leave nō ~
unturned** omnia experīrī; **kill two
birds with one ~** ūnō saltū duōs
aprōs capere; **hewn ~** saxum
quadrātum; **unhewn ~**
caementum nt ♦ vt lapidibus
percutere ♦ adj lapideus; **~ blind**

plānē caecus; **~ deaf** plānē
surdus.
stonecutter n lapicīda m.
stony adj (soil) lapidōsus; (path)
scrūpōsus; (feeling) dūrus,
ferreus.
stool n sēdēcula f.
stoop vi sē dēmittere; **~ to**
dēscendere in (acc).
stop n mora f; (punctuation)
pūnctum nt; **come to a ~**
īnsistere; **put a ~ to** comprimere,
dirimere ♦ vt sistere, inhibēre,
fīnīre; (restrain) cohibēre; (hole)
obtūrāre; **~ up** occlūdere,
interclūdere ♦ vi dēsinere,
dēsistere; (motion) īnsistere.
stopgap n tībīcen m.
stoppage n interclūsiō f,
impedīmentum n.
stopper n obtūrāmentum nt.
store n cōpia f; (place) horreum nt;
(for wine) apothēca f; **be in ~ for**
manēre; **set great ~ by** māgnī
aestimāre ♦ vt condere, repōnere;
~ away recondere; **~ up**
repōnere, congerere.
storehouse n (fig) thēsaurus m.
storekeeper n cellārius m.
storeship n nāvis frūmentāria f.
storey n tabulātum nt.
stork n cicōnia f.
storm n tempestās f, procella f;
take by ~ expugnāre ♦ vt (MIL)
expugnāre ♦ vi saevīre; **~ at**
īnsectārī, invehī in (acc).
stormbound adj tempestāte
dētentus.
stormer n expugnātor m.
storming n expugnātiō f.
stormy adj turbidus, procellōsus;
(fig) turbulentus.
story n fābula f, nārrātiō f; (short)
fābella f; (untrue) mendācium nt.
storyteller n nārrātor m; (liar)
mendāx m.
stout adj pinguis; (brave) fortis;

(strong) validus, rōbustus;
(material) firmus.
stouthearted adj mágnanimus.
stoutly adv fortiter.
stove n camīnus m, fornāx f.
stow vt repōnere, condere; ~ away
vi in nāvī dēlitēscere.
straddle vi vāricāre.
straggle vi deerrāre, pālārī.
straggler n pālāns m.
straggling adj dispersus, rārus.
straight adj rēctus, dīrēctus; (fig)
apertus, vērāx; **in a ~ line** rēctā, ē
regiōne; **set ~** dīrigere ♦ adv
dīrēctō, rēctā.
straighten vt corrigere,
extendere.
straightforward adj simplex,
dīrēctus; (easy) facilis.
straightforwardness n
simplicitās f.
straightness n (fig) integritās f.
straightway adv statim, extemplō.
strain n contentiō f; (effort) labor
m; (music) modī mpl; (breed) genus
nt ♦ vt intendere, contendere;
(injure) nimiā contentiōne
dēbilitāre; (liquid) dēliquāre,
percōlāre ♦ vi ēnītī, vīrēs
contendere.
strained adj (language) accessītus.
strainer n cōlum nt.
strait adj angustus ♦ n fretum nt;
~s pl angustiae fpl.
straiten vt coartāre, contrahere;
~ed circumstances angustiae fpl.
strait-laced adj tristis, sevērus.
strand n lītus nt; (of rope) fīlum nt
♦ vt (ship) ēicere.
strange adj novus, īnsolitus,
(foreign) peregrīnus; (another's)
aliēnus; (ignorant) rudis, expers.
strangely adv mīrē, mīrum in
modum.
strangeness n novitās f, īnsolentia
f.
stranger n (from abroad) advena f;

peregrīnus m; (visiting) hospes m,
hospita f; (not of the family)
externus m; (unknown) ignōtus m.
strangle vt strangulāre, laqueō
gulam frangere.
strap n lōrum nt, habēna f.
strapping adj grandis.
stratagem n cōnsilium nt, fallācia
f.
strategic adj (action) prūdēns;
(position) idōneus.
strategist n artis bellicae perītus
m.
strategy n ars imperātōria f;
cōnsilia ntpl.
straw n (stalk) culmus m;
(collective) strāmentum nt; **not
care a ~ for** floccī nōn facere ♦ adj
strāmenticius.
strawberry n frāgum nt.
strawberry tree n arbutus m.
stray vt aberrāre, deerrāre; vagārī
♦ adj errābundus.
streak n līnea f, macula f; (light)
radius m; (character) vēna f ♦ vt
maculāre.
stream n flūmen nt, fluvius m;
down ~ secundō flūmine; **up ~**
adversō flūmine ♦ vi fluere, sē
effundere; **~ into** īnfluere in (acc).
streamlet n rīvus m, rīvulus m.
street n via f, platea f.
strength n vīrēs fpl; (of material)
firmitās f; (fig) rōbur nt, nervī mpl;
(MIL) numerus m; **know the
enemy's ~** quot sint hostēs scīre;
on the ~ of frētus (abl).
strengthen vt firmāre,
corrōborāre; (position) mūnīre.
strenuous adj impiger, strēnuus,
sēdulus.
strenuously adv impigrē, strēnuē.
strenuousness n industria f.
stress n (words) ictus m; (meaning)
vīs f; (importance) mōmentum nt;
(difficulty) labor m; **lay great ~ on**
in māgnō discrīmine pōnere ♦ vt

exprimere.

stretch n spatium nt, tractus m; **at a ~** sine ullā intermissiōne ♦ vt tendere, intendere; (length) prōdūcere, extendere; (facts) in malus crēdere; **~ a point** indulgēre; **~ before** obtendere; **~ forth** porrigere; **~oneself** (on ground) sternī; **~ out** porrigere, extendere ♦ vi extendī, patēscere.

strew vt (things) sternere; (place) cōnsternere.

stricken adj saucius.

strict adj (defined) ipse, certus; (severe) sevērus, rigidus; (accurate) dīligēns.

strictly adv sevērē; dīligenter; **~ speaking** scīlicet, immo.

strictness n sevēritās f; dīligentia f.

stricture n vītuperātiō f.

stride n passus m; **make great ~s** (fig) multum prōficere ♦ vi incēdere, ingentēs gradūs ferre.

strident adj asper.

strife n discordia f, pugna f.

strike vt ferīre, percutere; (instrument) pellere, pulsāre; (sail) subdūcere; (tent) dētendere; (mind) venīre in (with, acc), (camp) movēre; (fear into) incutere in (acc); **~ against** offendere; **~ out** dēlēre; **~ up** (music) incipere; **~ a bargain** pacīscī; **be struck** vāpulāre ♦ vi (work) cessāre.

striking adj īnsignis, īnsignītus, ēgregius.

strikingly adv īnsignītē.

string n (cord) resticula f; (succession) seriēs f; (instrument) nervus m; (bow) nervus m; **have two ~s to one's bow** duplicī spē ūtī ♦ vt (bow) intendere; (together) coniungere.

stringency n sevēritās f.

stringent adj sevērus.

strip vt nūdāre, spoliāre;

dēnūdāre; **~ off** exuere; (leaves) stringere, dēstringere ♦ n lacinia f.

stripe n virga f; (on tunic) clāvus m; **~s** pl verbera ntpl.

striped adj virgātus.

stripling n adulescentulus m.

strive vi nītī, ōnītī, contendere; (contend) certāre.

stroke n ictus m; (lightning) fulmen nt; (oar) pulsus m; (pen) līnea f; **~ of luck** fortūna secunda f ♦ vt mulcēre, dēmulcēre.

stroll vi deambulāre, spatiārī.

strong adj fortis, validus; (health) rōbustus, firmus; (material) firmus; (smell) gravis; (resources) pollēns, potēns; (feeling) ācer, magnus; (language) vehemēns, probrōsus; **be ~** valēre; **be twenty ~** vīgintī esse numerō.

strongbox n arca f.

stronghold n arx f.

strongly adv validē, vehementer, fortiter, ācriter, graviter.

strong-minded adj pertināx, cōnstans.

strophe n stropha f.

structure n aedificium nt; (form) structūra f; (arrangement) compositiō f.

struggle n (effort) cōnātus m; (fight) pugna f, certāmen nt ♦ vi nītī; certāre, contendere; (fight) luctārī; **~ upwards** ēnītī.

strut vi māgnificē incēdere.

stubble n stipula f.

stubborn adj pertināx, pervicāx.

stubbornly adv pertināciter, pervicāciter.

stubbornness n pertinācia f, pervicācia f.

stucco n gypsum nt.

stud n clāvus m; (horses) equī mpl.

studded adj distinctus.

student n discipulus m; **be a ~ of** studēre (dat).

studied adj meditātus, accūrātus; (language) exquīsītus.

studio n officīna f.

studious adj litterīs dēditus, litterārum studiōsus; (careful) attentus.

studiously adv dē industriā.

study vt studēre (dat); (prepare) meditārī; ~ **under** audīre ♦ n studium nt; (room) bibliothēca f.

stuff n māteria f; (cloth) textile nt ♦ vt farcīre, refercīre; (with food) sagīnāre.

stuffing n sagina f; (of cushion) tōmentum nt.

stultify vt ad inritum redigere.

stumble vi offendere; ~ **upon** incidere in (acc), offendere.

stumbling block n offēnsiō f.

stump n stīpes m.

stun vt stupefacere; (fig) obstupefacere, cōnfundere.

stunned adj attonitus.

stunt vt corporis auctum inhibēre.

stunted adj curtus.

stupefaction n stupor m.

stupefied adj: **be** ~ stupēre, obstupefacere.

stupefy vt obstupefacere.

stupendous adj mīrus, mīrificus.

stupid adj stultus, hebes, ineptus.

stupidity n stultitia f.

stupidly adv stultē, ineptē.

stupor n stupor m.

sturdily adv fortiter.

sturdiness n rōbur nt, firmitās f.

sturdy adj fortis, rōbustus.

sturgeon n acipēnser m.

stutter vi balbūtīre.

stuttering adj balbus.

sty n hara f.

style n (kind) genus nt, ratiō f; (of dress) habitus m; (of prose) ēlocūtiō f, ōrātiō f; (pen) stilus m ♦ vt appellāre.

stylish adj ēlegāns, lautus, expolītus.

stylishly adv ēleganter.

suasion n suāsiō f.

suave adj blandus, urbānus.

suavity n urbānitās f.

subaltern n succenturiō m.

subdivide vt dīvidere.

subdivision n pars f, mōmentum nt.

subdue vt subigere, dēvincere, redigere, domāre; (fig) cohibēre.

subdued adj dēmissus, summissus.

subject n (person) cīvis m/f; (matter) rēs f; (theme) locus m, argūmentum nt ♦ adj subiectus; ~ **to** obnoxius (dat) ♦ vt subicere; obnoxium reddere.

subjection n servitūs f.

subjective adj proprius.

subject matter n māteria f.

subjoin vt subicere, subiungere.

subjugate vt subigere, dēbellāre, domāre.

sublime adj sublīmis, ēlātus, excelsus.

sublimely adv excelsē.

sublimity n altitūdō f, ēlātiō f.

submarine adj submersus.

submerge vt dēmergere; (flood) inundāre ♦ vi sē dēmergere.

submersed adj submersus.

submission n obsequium nt, servitium nt; (fig) patientia f.

submissive adj submissus, docilis, obtemperāns.

submissively adv submissē, oboedienter, patienter.

submit vi sē dēdere; ~ **to** pārēre (dat), obtemperāre (dat), patī, subīre ♦ vt (proposal) referre.

subordinate adj subiectus, secundus ♦ vt subiungere, subicere.

suborn vt subicere, subōrnāre.

subpoena vt testimōnium dēnūntiāre (dat).

subscribe vt (name) subscrībere;

(*money*) cōnferre.
subscription n collātiō f.
subsequent adj sequēns, posterior.
subsequently adv posteā, mox.
subserve vt subvenīre (dat), commodāre.
subservience n obsequium nt.
subservient adj obsequēns; (*thing*) ūtilis, commodus.
subside vi dēsīdere, resīdere; (*fever*) dēcēdere; (*wind*) cadere; (*passion*) dēfervēscere.
subsidence n lābēs f.
subsidiary adj subiectus, secundus.
subsidize vt pecūniās suppeditāre (dat).
subsidy n pecūniae fpl, vectīgal nt.
subsist vi cōnstāre, sustentārī.
subsistence n vīctus m.
substance n (*matter*) rēs f, corpus nt; (*essence*) nātūra f; (*gist*) summa f; (*reality*) rēs f; (*wealth*) opēs fpl.
substantial adj solidus; (*real*) vērus; (*important*) gravis; (*rich*) opulentus, dīves.
substantially adv rē; māgnā ex parte.
substantiate vt cōnfirmāre.
substitute vt subicere, repōnere, substituere ♦ n vicārius m.
substratum n fundāmentum nt.
subterfuge n latebra f, perfugium nt.
subterranean adj subterrāneus.
subtle adj (*fine*) subtīlis; (*shrewd*) acūtus, astūtus.
subtlety n subtīlitās f; acūmen nt, astūtia f.
subtly adv subtīliter; acūtē, astūtē.
subtract vt dētrahere, dēmere; (*money*) dēdūcere.
subtraction n dētractiō f, dēductiō f.
suburb n suburbium nt.
suburban adj suburbānus.

subvention n pecūniae fpl.
subversion n ēversiō f, ruīna f.
subversive adj sēditiōsus.
subvert vt ēvertere, subruere.
subverter n ēversor m.
succeed vi (*person*) rem bene gerere; (*activity*) prosperē ēvenīre, ~ **in obtaining** impetrāre ♦ vt īnsequī, excipere, succēdere (dat).
success n bonus ēventus m, rēs bene gesta f.
successful adj fēlīx; (*thing*) secundus; **be** ~ rem bene gerere; (*play*) stāre.
successfully adv fēlīciter, prosperē, bene.
succession n (*coming next*) successiō f; (*line*) seriēs f, ōrdō m; **alternate** ~ vicissitūdō f; **in** ~ deinceps, ex ōrdine.
successive adj continuus, perpetuus.
successively adv deinceps, ex ōrdine; (*alternately*) vicissim.
successor n successor m.
succinct adj brevis, pressus.
succinctly adv breviter, pressē.
succour n auxilium nt, subsidium nt ♦ vt subvenīre (dat), succurrere (dat), opem ferre (dat).
succulence n sūcus m.
succulent adj sūcidus.
succumb vi succumbere, dēficere.
such adj tālis, ēiusmodī, hūiusmodī; (*size*) tantus; **at** ~ **a time** id temporis; ~ **great** tantus.
suchlike adj hūiusmodī, ēiusdem generis.
suck vt sūgere; ~ **in** sorbēre; ~ **up** exsorbēre, ēbibere.
sucker n surculus m.
sucking adj (*child*) lactēns.
suckle vt nūtrīcārī, mammam dare (dat).
suckling n lactēns m/f.
sudden adj subitus, repentīnus.

suddenly *adv* subitō, repente.

sue *vt* in iūs vocāre, lītem intendere (*dat*); **~ for** rogāre, petere, ōrāre.

suffer *vt* patī, ferre, tolerāre; (*injury*) accipere; (*loss*) facere; (*permit*) patī, sinere ♦ *vi* dolōre adficī; **~ defeat** clādem accipere; **~ from** labōrāre ex, adficī (*abl*); **~ for** poenās dare (*gen*).

sufferable *adj* tolerābilis.

sufferance *n* patientia *f*, tolerantia *f*.

suffering *n* dolor *m*.

suffice *vi* sufficere, suppetere.

sufficiency *n* satis.

sufficient *adj* idōneus, satis (*gen*).

sufficiently *adv* satis.

suffocate *vt* suffocāre.

suffrage *n* suffrāgium *nt*.

suffuse *vt* suffundere.

sugar *n* saccharon *nt*.

suggest *vt* admonēre, inicere, subicere; **~ itself** occurrere.

suggestion *n* admonitiō *f*; **at the ~ of** admonitū (*gen*); **at my ~** mē auctōre.

suicidal *adj* fūnestus.

suicide *n* mors voluntāria *f*; **commit ~** mortem sibī cōnscīscere.

suit *n* (*law*) līs *f*, āctiō *f*; (*clothes*) vestītus *m* ♦ *vt* convenīre (*dat*), congruere (*dat*); (*dress*) sedēre (*dat*), decēre; **it ~s** decet; **to ~ me** dē meā sententiā.

suitability *n* convenientia *f*.

suitable *adj* aptus (+ *acc*), idōneus (+ *acc*).

suitably *adv* aptē, decenter.

suite *n* comitēs *mpl*, comitātus *m*.

suitor *n* procus *m*, amāns *m*.

sulk *vi* aegrē ferre, mōrōsum esse.

sulky *adj* mōrōsus, tristis.

sullen *adj* tristis, mōrōsus.

sullenness *n* mōrōsitās *f*.

sully *vt* īnfuscāre, contāmināre.

sulphur *n* sulfur *nt*.

sultriness *n* aestus *m*.

sultry *adj* aestuōsus.

sum *n* summa *f*; **~ of money** pecūnia *f* ♦ *vt* subdūcere, computāre; **~ up** summātim dēscrībere; **to ~ up** ūnō verbō, quid plūra?

summarily *adv* strictim, summātim; sine morā.

summarize *vt* summātim dēscrībere.

summary *n* summārium *nt*, epitomē *f* ♦ *adj* subitus, praesēns.

summer *n* aestās *f* ♦ *adj* aestīvus; **of ~** aestīvus.

summit *n* vertex *m*, culmen *nt*; (*fig*) fastīgium *nt*; **the ~ of** summus.

summon *vt* arcessere; (*meeting*) convocāre; (*witness*) citāre; **~ up courage** animum sūmere.

summons *n* (*law*) vocātiō *f* ♦ *vt* in iūs vocāre, diem dīcere (*dat*).

sumptuary *adj* sūmptuārius.

sumptuous *adj* sūmptuōsus, adparātus, māgnificus, lautus.

sumptuously *adv* sūmptuōsē, māgnificē.

sun *n* sōl *m* ♦ *vt*: **~ oneself** aprīcārī.

sunbeam *n* radius *m*.

sunburnt *adj* adūstus.

sunder *vt* sēparāre, dīvidere.

sundial *n* sōlārium *nt*.

sundry *adj* dīversī, complūrēs.

sunlight *n* sōl *m*.

sunlit *adj* aprīcus.

sunny *adj* aprīcus, serēnus.

sunrise *n* sōlis ortus *m*.

sunset *n* sōlis occāsus *m*.

sunshade *n* umbella *f*.

sunshine *n* sōl *m*.

sup *vi* cēnāre.

superabundance *n* abundantia *f*.

superabundant *adj* nimius.

superabundantly *adv* satis

superque.
superannuated adj ēmeritus.
superb adj māgnificus.
superbly adv māgnificē.
supercilious adj adrogāns, superbus.
superciliously adv adroganter, superbē.
superciliousness n adrogantia f, fastus m.
supererogation n: of ~ ultrō factus.
superficial adj levis; **acquire a ~ knowledge of** prīmīs labrīs gustāre.
superficiality n levitās f.
superficially adv leviter, strictim.
superfluity n abundantia f.
superfluous adj supervacāneus, nimius; **be ~** redundāre.
superhuman adj dīvīnus, hūmānō māior.
superimpose vt superimpōnere.
superintend vt prōcūrāre, praeesse (dat).
superintendence n cūra f.
superintendent n cūrātor m, praefectus m.
superior adj melior, amplior; **be ~** praestāre, superāre ♦ n prīnceps m, praefectus m.
superiority n praestantia f; **have the ~** superāre; (in numbers) plūrēs esse.
superlative adj ēgregius, optimus.
supernatural adj dīvīnus.
supernaturally adv dīvīnitus.
supernumerary adj adscrīptīcius; **~ soldiers** accēnsī mpl.
superscription n titulus m.
supersede vt succēdere (dat), in locum succēdere (gen); **~ gold with silver** prō aurō argentum suppōnere.
superstition n religiō f, superstitiō f.
superstitious adj religiōsus,

superstitiōsus.
supervene vi īnsequī, succēdere.
supervise vt prōcūrāre.
supervision n cūra f.
supervisor n cūrātor m.
supine adj supīnus; (fig) neglegēns, segnis.
supinely adv segniter.
supper n cēna f; **after ~** cēnātus.
supperless adj iēiūnus.
supplant vt praevertere.
supple adj flexibilis, mollis.
supplement n appendix f ♦ vt amplificāre.
supplementary adj additus.
suppleness n mollitia f.
suppliant n supplex m/f.
supplicate vt supplicāre, obsecrāre.
supplication n precēs fpl.
supplies npl commeātus m.
supply n cōpia f ♦ vt suppeditāre, praebēre; (loss) supplēre.
support n firmāmentum nt; (help) subsidium nt, adiūmentum nt; (food) alimenta ntpl; (of party) favor m; (of needy) patrōcinium nt; **I ~ subsidio** sum (dat); **lend ~ to rumours** alimenta rumōribus addere ♦ vt fulcīre; (living) sustinēre, sustentāre; (with help) adiuvāre, opem ferre (dat); (at law) adesse (dat).
supportable adj tolerābilis.
supporter n fautor m; (at trial) advocātus m; (of proposal) auctor m.
supporting cast n adiūtōrēs mpl.
suppose vi (assume) pōnere; (think) existimāre, opīnārī, crēdere; **~ it is true** fac vērum esse.
supposedly adv ut fāma est.
supposing conj sī; (for the sake of argument) sī iam.
supposition n opīniō f; **on this ~** hōc positō.
supposititious adj subditus,

suppress 682 **sustain**

subditīvus.
suppress vt opprimere, comprimere; (knowledge) cēlāre, reticēre; (feelings) coercēre, reprimere.
suppression n (of fact) reticentia f.
supremacy n imperium nt, dominātus m, prīncipātus m.
supreme adj summus; **be ~** dominārī; **~ command** imperium nt.
supremely adv ūnicē, plānē.
sure adj certus; (fact) explōrātus; (friend) fīdus; **be ~ of** compertum habēre; **feel ~** persuāsum habēre, haud scīre an; pro certō habēre; **make ~ of** (fact) comperīre; (action) efficere ut; **to be ~** quidem; **~ enough** rē vērā.
surely adv certō, certē, nonne; (tentative) scīlicet, sānē; **~ you do not think?** num putās?; **~ not** num.
surety n (person) vās m, praes m, spōnsor m; (deposit) fīdūcia f; **be ~ for** spondēre prō.
surf n fluctus m.
surface n superficiēs f; **~ of the water** summa aqua.
surfeit n satietās f ♦ vt satiāre, explēre.
surge n aestus m, fluctus m ♦ vi tumēscere.
surgeon n chīrurgus m.
surgery n chīrurgia f.
surlily adv mōrōsē.
surliness n mōrōsitās f.
surly adj mōrōsus, difficilis.
surmise n coniectūra f ♦ vi suspicārī, conicere, augurārī.
surmount vt superāre.
surmountable adj superābilis.
surname n cognōmen nt.
surpass vt excellere, exsuperāre, antecēdere.
surpassing adj excellēns.
surplus n reliquum nt; (money)

pecūniae residuae fpl.
surprise n admīrātiō f; (cause) rēs inopīnāta f; **take by ~** dēprehendere ♦ adj subitus ♦ vt dēprehendere; (MIL) opprimere; **be ~d** dēmīrārī; **be ~d at** admīrārī.
surprising adj mīrus, mīrābilis.
surprisingly adv mīrē, mīrābiliter.
surrender vt dēdere, trādere, concēdere ♦ vi sē dēdere; **~ unconditionally to** sē suāque omnia potestātī permittere (gen) ♦ n dēditiō f; (legal) cessiō f.
unconditional ~ permissiō f.
surreptitious adj fūrtīvus.
surreptitiously adv fūrtim, clam; **get in ~** inrēpere in (acc).
surround vt circumdare, cingere, circumvenīre, circumfundere.
surrounding adj circumiectus; **~s** n vīcīnia f.
survey vt contemplārī, cōnsīderāre; (land) mētārī ♦ n contemplātiō f; (land) mēnsūra f.
surveyor n fīnītor m, agrimēnsor m, mētātor m.
survival n salūs f.
survive vt superāre ♦ vt superesse (dat).
survivor n superstes m/f.
susceptibility n mollitia f.
susceptible adj mollis.
suspect vt suspicārī; **be ~ed in** suspiciōnem venīre.
suspend vt suspendere; (activity) differre; (person) locō movēre; **be ~ed** pendēre.
suspense n dubitātiō f; **be in ~** animī pendēre, haerēre.
suspicion n suspiciō f; **direct ~ to** suspiciōnem adiungere ad.
suspicious adj (suspecting) suspiciōsus; (suspected) dubius, anceps.
sustain vt (weight) sustinēre; (life) alere, sustentāre; (hardship) ferre,

sustinēre; (*the part of*) agere.

sustenance n alimentum nt, victus m.

sutler n lixa m.

suzerain n dominus m.

swaddling clothes n incūnābula ntpl.

swagger vi sē iactāre.

swaggerer n homō glōriōsus m.

swallow n hirundō f ♦ vt dēvorāre; ~ **up** absorbēre.

swamp n palūs f ♦ vt opprimere.

swampy adj ūlīginōsus.

swan n cycnus m; ~'**s** cycnēus.

swank vi sē iactāre.

sward n caespes m.

swarm n exāmen nt; (*fig*) nūbēs f ♦ vi: ~ **round** circumfundī.

swarthy adj fuscus, aquilus.

swathe vt conligāre.

sway n diciō f, imperium nt; **bring under one's** ~ suae diciōnis facere ♦ vt regere ♦ vi vacillāre.

swear vi iūrāre; ~ **allegiance to** iūrāre in verba (*gen*).

sweat n sūdor m ♦ vi sūdāre.

sweep vt verrere; ~ **away** rapere; ~ **out** ēverrere.

sweet adj dulcis, suāvis.

sweeten vt dulcem reddere.

sweetheart n dēliciae fpl.

sweetly adv dulciter, suāviter.

sweetness n dulcitūdō f, suāvitās f.

sweet-tempered adj suāvis, cōmis.

swell n tumor m ♦ vi tumēre, tumēscere; (*fig*) glīscere ♦ vt inflāre.

swelling adj tumidus ♦ n tumor m.

swelter vi aestū labōrāre.

swerve vi dēclīnāre, dēvertere ♦ n dēclīnātiō f.

swift adj celer, vēlōx, incitātus.

swiftly adv celeriter, vēlōciter.

swiftness n celeritās f, vēlōcitās f.

swill vt (*rinse*) colluere; (*drink*) ēpōtāre.

swim vi nāre, innāre; (*place*) natāre; ~ **across** trānāre; ~ **ashore** ēnāre; ~ **to** adnāre.

swimming n natātiō f.

swindle vt circumvenīre, verba dare (*dat*) ♦ n fraus f.

swine n sūs m/f.

swineherd n subulcus m.

swing n (*motion*) oscillātiō f ♦ vi oscillāre ♦ vt lībrāre.

swinish adj obscēnus.

swirl n vertex m ♦ vi volūtārī.

switch n virga f ♦ vt flectere, torquēre.

swivel n cardō f.

swollen adj tumidus, turgidus, īnflātus.

swoon n dēfectiō f ♦ vi intermorī.

swoop n impetus m ♦ vi lābī; ~ **down on** involāre in (*acc*).

sword n gladius m; **put to the** ~ occīdere; **with fire and** ~ ferrō ignīque.

swordsman n gladiātor m.

sworn adj iūrātus.

sybarite n dēlicātus m.

sycophancy n adsentātiō f, adūlātiō f.

sycophant n adsentātor m, adūlātor m.

syllable n syllaba f.

syllogism n ratiōcinātiō f.

sylvan adj silvestris.

symbol n signum nt, īnsigne nt.

symmetrical adj concinnus, aequus.

symmetry n concinnitās f, aequitās f.

sympathetic adj concors, misericors.

sympathetically adv misericorditer.

sympathize vi cōnsentīre; ~ **with** miserērī (*gen*).

sympathy n concordia f, cōnsēnsus m; misericordia f.

symphony n concentus m.
symptom n signum nt, indicium nt.
syndicate n societās f.
synonym n verbum idem dēclārāns nt.
synonymous adj idem dēclārāns.
synopsis n summārium nt.
syringe n clystēr m.
system n ratiō f, fōrmula f; (PHILOS) disciplīna f.
systematic adj ōrdinātus, cōnstāns.
systematically adv ratiōne, ōrdine.
systematize vt in ōrdinem redigere.

T

tabernacle n tabernāculum nt.
table n mēnsa f; (inscribed) tabula f; (list) index m; **at ~** inter cēnam; **turn the ~s on** pār parī referre.
tablet n tabula f, tabella f.
taboo n rēligiō f.
tabulate vt in ōrdinem redigere.
tacit adj tacitus.
tacitly adv tacitē.
taciturn adj taciturnus.
taciturnity n taciturnitās f.
tack n clāvulus m; (of sail) pēs m ♦ vt: **~ on** adsuere ♦ vi (ship) reciprocārī, nāvem flectere.
tackle n armāmenta ntpl ♦ vt adgredī.
tact n iūdicium nt, commūnis sēnsus m, hūmānitās f.
tactful adj prūdēns, hūmānus.
tactfully adv prūdenter, hūmāniter.
tactician n reī mīlitāris perītus m.
tactics n rēs mīlitāris f, bellī ratiō f.
tactless adj ineptus.
tactlessly adv ineptē.
tadpole n rānunculus m.
tag n appendicula f.
tail n cauda f; **turn ~** terga vertere.

tailor n vestītor m.
taint n lābēs f, vitium nt ♦ vt inquināre, contāmināre, īnficere.
take vt capere, sūmere; (auspices) habēre; (disease) contrahere; (experience) ferre; (fire) concipere; (meaning) accipere, interpretārī; (in the act) dēprehendere; (person) dūcere; **~ after** similem esse (dat, gen); **~ across** trānsportāre; **~ arms** arma sūmere; **~ away** dēmere, auferre, adimere, abdūcere; **~ back** recipere; **~ by storm** expugnāre; **~ care that** cūrāre ut/ne (+ subj); **~ down** dētrahere; (in writing) exscrībere; **~ for** habēre prō; **~ hold of** prehendere; **~ in** (as guest) recipere; (information) percipere, comprehendere; (with deceit) dēcipere; **~ in hand** incipere, suscipere; **~ off** dēmere; (clothes) exuere; **~ on** suscipere; **~ out** eximere, extrahere; (from store) prōmere; **~ over** excipere; **~ place** fierī, accidere; **~ prisoner** capere; **~ refuge in** cōnfugere ad (+ infin); **~ the field** in aciem dēscendere; **~ to** sē dēdere (dat), amāre; **~ to oneself** suscipere; **~ up** sūmere, tollere; (task) incipere, adgredī ad; (in turn) excipere; (room) occupāre; **~ upon oneself** recipere, sibī sūmere.
taking adj grātus ♦ n (MIL) expugnātiō f.
tale n fābula f, fābella f.
talent n (money) talentum nt; (ability) ingenium nt, indolēs f.
talented adj ingeniōsus.
talk n sermō m; (with another) colloquium nt; **common ~** fāma f; **be the ~ of the town** in ōre omnium esse ♦ vi loquī; (to one) colloquī cum; **~ down to** ad intellectum audientis dēscendere; **~ over** cōnferre, disserere dē.

talkative adj loquāx.
talkativeness n loquācitās f.
tall adj prōcērus, grandis.
tallness n prōcēritās f.
tallow n sēbum nt.
tally n tessera f ♦ vi congruere.
talon n unguis m.
tamarisk n myrīca f.
tambourine n tympanum nt.
tame vt domāre, mānsuēfacere
♦ adj mānsuētus; (character)
ignāvus; (language) īnsulsus,
frīgidus.
tamely adv ignāvē, lentē.
tameness n mānsuētūdō f; (fig)
lentitūdō f.
tamer n domitor m.
tamper vi: ~ with (person)
sollicitāre; (writing) interpolāre.
tan vt imbuere.
tang n sapor m.
tangible adj tāctilis.
tangle n nōdus m ♦ vt implicāre.
tank n lacus m.
tanned adj (by sun) adūstus.
tanner n coriārius m.
tantalize vt lūdere.
tantamount adj pār, īdem.
tantrum n īra f.
tap n epitonium nt; (touch) plāga f
♦ vt (cask) relinere; (hit) ferīre.
tape n taenia f.
taper n cēreus m ♦ vi fastīgārī.
tapestry n aulaea ntpl.
tar n pix f.
tardily adv tardē, lentē.
tardiness n tarditās f, segnitia f.
tardy adj tardus, lentus.
tare n lolium nt.
targe n parma f.
target n scopus m.
tariff n portōrium nt.
tarn n lacus m.
tarnish vt īnfuscāre, inquināre ♦ vi
īnfuscārī.
tarry vi morārī, commorārī,
cunctārī.

tart adj acidus, asper ♦ n scrīblīta
f.
tartly adv acerbē.
tartness n asperitās f.
task n pēnsum nt, opus nt,
negōtium nt; **take to ~** obiūrgāre.
taskmaster n dominus m.
tassel n fimbriae fpl.
taste n (sense) gustātus m; (flavour)
sapor m; (artistic) iūdicium nt,
ēlegantia f; (for rhetoric) aurēs fpl;
of ~ doctus; **in good ~** ēlegāns
♦ vt gustāre, dēgustāre ♦ vi
sapere; **~ of** resipere.
tasteful adj ēlegāns.
tastefully adv eleganter.
tastefulness n ēlegantia f.
tasteless adj īnsulsus, inēlegāns.
tastelessly adv īnsulsē,
inēleganter.
tastelessness n īnsulsitās f.
taster n praegustātor m.
tasty adj dulcis.
tattered adj pannōsus.
tatters n pannī mpl.
tattoo vt compungere.
taunt n convīcium nt, probrum nt
♦ vt exprobrāre, obicere (dat of
pers, acc of charge).
taunting adj contumēliōsus.
tauntingly adv contumēliōsē.
taut adj intentus; **draw ~**
addūcere.
tavern n taberna f, hospitium nt.
tawdry adj vīlis.
tawny adj fulvus.
tax n vectīgal n, tribūtum nt; **a 5
per cent ~** vīcēsima f; **free from ~**
immūnis ♦ vt vectīgal impōnere
(dat); (strength) contendere; **~ with**
(charge) obicere (acc and dat),
īnsimulāre.
taxable adj vectīgālis.
taxation n vectīgālia ntpl.
tax collector n exāctor m.
tax farmer n pūblicānus m.
taxpayer n assiduus m.

teach vt docēre, ērudīre, īnstituere; (*thoroughly*) ēdocēre; (*pass*) discere; ~ **your grandmother** sūs Minervam.

teachable adj docilis.

teacher n magister m, magistra f, doctor m; (PHILOS) praeceptor m; (*of literature*) grammaticus m; (*of rhetoric*) rhētor m.

teaching n doctrīna f, disciplīna f.

team n (*animals*) iugum nt.

tear n lacrima f; **shed ~s** lacrimās effundere ♦ vt scindere; ~ **down** revellere; ~ **in pieces** dīlaniāre, discerpere, lacerāre; ~ **off** abscindere, dēripere; ~ **open** rescindere; ~ **out** ēvellere; ~ **up** convellere.

tearful adj flēbilis.

tease vt lūdere, inrītāre.

teat n mamma f.

technical adj (*term*) proprius.

technique n ars f.

tedious adj longus, lentus, odiōsus.

tediously adv moleste.

tedium n taedium nt, molestia f.

teem vi abundāre.

teeming adj fēcundus, refertus.

teens n: **in one's ~** adulescentulus m.

teethe vi dentīre.

tell vt (*story*) nārrāre; (*person*) dīcere (dat); (*number*) ēnumerāre; (*inform*) certiōrem facere; (*difference*) intellegere; (*order*) iubēre (+ acc and infin), imperāre (+ ut/ne and subj); ~ **the truth** vēra dīcere; ~ **lies** mentīrī ♦ vi valēre; ~ **the difference between** discernere; **I cannot ~** nesciō.

telling adj validus.

temerity n temeritās f.

temper n animus m, ingenium nt; (*bad*) īra f, īrācundia f; (*of metal*) temperātiō f ♦ vt temperāre; (*fig*) moderārī (dat).

temperament n animī habitus m, animus m.

temperamental adj incōnstāns.

temperance n temperantia f, continentia f.

temperate adj temperātus, moderātus, sobrius.

temperately adv moderātē.

temperature n calor m, frīgus nt; **mild ~** temperiēs f.

tempest n tempestās f, procella f.

tempestuous adj procellōsus.

temple n templum nt, aedēs f; (*head*) tempus nt.

temporal adj hūmānus, profānus.

temporarily adv ad tempus.

temporary adj brevis.

temporize vi temporis causā facere, tergiversārī.

tempt vt sollicitāre, pellicere, invītāre.

temptation n illecebra f.

tempter n impulsor m.

ten num decem; ~ **each** dēnī; ~ **times** deciēns.

tenable adj inexpugnābilis, stabilis, certus.

tenacious adj tenāx, firmus.

tenaciously adv tenāciter.

tenacity n tenācitās f.

tenant n inquilīnus m, habitātor m; (*on land*) colōnus m.

tenantry n colōnī mpl.

tend vi spectāre, pertinēre ♦ vt cūrāre, colere.

tendency n inclīnātiō f, voluntās f.

tender adj tener, mollis ♦ vt dēferre, offerre.

tenderhearted adj misericors.

tenderly adv indulgenter.

tenderness n indulgentia f, mollitia f.

tendon n nervus m.

tendril n clāviculus m.

tenement n habitātiō f; **block of ~s** īnsula f.

tenet n dogma nt, dēcrētum nt.

tennis court n sphaeristērium nt.

tenor n (*course*) tenor m; (*purport*)

sententia f.

tense adj intentus ♦ n tempus nt.

tension n intentiō f.

tent n tabernāculum nt; (general's) praetōrium nt.

tentacle n bracchium nt.

tentatively adv experiendō.

tenterhooks n: on ~ animī suspēnsus.

tenth adj decimus; for the ~ time decimum; men of the ~ legion decumānī mpl.

tenuous adj rārus.

tenure n possessiō f.

tepid adj tepidus; be ~ tepēre.

tergiversation n tergiversātiō f.

term n (limit) terminus m; (period) spatium nt; (word) verbum nt ♦ vt appellāre, nuncupāre.

terminate vt termināre, fīnīre ♦ vi dēsinere; (words) cadere.

termination n fīnis m, terminus m.

terminology n vocābula ntpl.

terms npl condiciō f, lēx f; propose ~ condiciōnem ferre; be on good ~ in grātiā esse; we come to ~ inter nōs convenit.

terrain n ager m.

terrestrial adj terrestris.

terrible adj terribilis, horribilis, horrendus.

terribly adv horrendum in modum.

terrific adj formīdolōsus; vehemēns.

terrify vt terrēre, perterrēre, exterrēre.

terrifying adj formīdolōsus.

territory n ager m, fīnēs mpl.

terror n terror m, formīdō f, pavor m; object of ~ terror m; be a ~ to terrōrī esse (dat).

terrorize vt metum inicere (dat).

terse adj pressus, brevis.

tersely adv pressē.

terseness n brevitās f.

tessellated adj tessellātus.

test n experīmentum nt, probātiō f;

(standard) obrussa f; put to the ~ experīrī, perīclitārī; stand the ~ spectārī ♦ vt experīrī, probāre, spectāre.

testament n testāmentum nt.

testamentary adj testāmentārius.

testator n testātor m.

testify vt testificārī.

testifying n testificātiō f.

testily adv stomachōsē.

testimonial n laudātiō f.

testimony n testimōnium nt.

testy adj difficilis, stomachōsus.

tether n retināculum nt, vinculum nt ♦ vt religāre.

tetrarch n tetrarchēs m.

tetrarchy n tetrarchia f.

text n verba ntpl.

textbook n ars f.

textile adj textilis.

textual adj verbōrum.

texture n textus m.

than conj quam abl; other ~ alius ac.

thank vt grātiās agere (dat); ~ you bene facis; no, ~ you benignē.

thankful adj grātus.

thankfully adv grātē.

thankfulness n grātia f.

thankless adj ingrātus.

thanklessly adv ingrātē.

thanks n grātiae fpl, grātēs fpl; return ~ grātiās agere, grātēs persolvere; ~ to you opera tuā, beneficiō tuō; it is ~ to sb that . . . not per aliquem stat quominus (+ subj).

thanksgiving n grātulātiō f; (public) supplicātiō f.

that pron (demonstrative) ille; (relat) quī ♦ conj (statement) acc and infin; (command, purpose, result) ut; (fearing) nē; (emotion) quod, oh ~ utinam.

thatch n culmus m, strāmenta ntpl ♦ vt tegere, integere.

thaw vt dissolvere ♦ vi liquēscere,

tabēscere.

the *art not expressed*; (*emphatic*) ille; (*with compar*) quō . . . eō.

theatre *n* theātrum *nt.*

theatrical *adj* scēnicus.

theft *n* fūrtum *nt.*

their *adj* eōrum; (*ref to subject*) suus.

theme *n* māteria *f*, argūmentum *nt.*

themselves *pron* ipsī; (*reflexive*) sē.

then *adv* (*time*) tum, tunc; (*succession*) deinde, tum, posteā; (*consequence*) igitur, ergō; **now and ~** interdum; **only ~** tum dēmum.

thence *adv* inde.

thenceforth *adv* inde, posteā, ex eō tempore.

theologian *n* theologus *m.*

theology *n* theologia *f.*

theorem *n* prōpositum *nt.*

theoretical *adj* contemplātīvus.

theory *n* ratiō *f*; **~ and practice** ratiō atque ūsus.

there *adv* ibī, illīc; (*thither*) eō, illūc; **from ~** inde, illinc; **here and ~** passim; **~ is** est; (*interj*) ecce.

thereabout(s) *adv* circā, circiter, prope.

thereafter *adv* deinde, posteā.

thereby *adv* eā rē, hōc factō.

therefore *adv* itaque, igitur, ergō, idcircō.

therein *adv* inibī, in eō.

thereof *adv* ēius, ēius reī.

thereon *adv* īnsuper, in eō.

thereupon *adv* deinde, statim, inde, quō facto.

therewith *adv* cum eō.

thesis *n* prōpositum *nt.*

thews *n* nervī *mpl.*

they *pron* iī, hī, illī.

thick *adj* dēnsus; (*air*) crassus.

thicken *vt* dēnsāre ♦ *vi* concrēscere.

thickening *n* concrētiō *f.*

thicket *n* dūmētum *nt.*

thickheaded *adj* stupidus, hebes.

thickly *adv* dēnsē; **~ populated** frequēns.

thickness *n* crassitūdō *f.*

thickset *adj* brevis atque obēsus.

thick-skinned *adj*: **be ~** callēre; **become ~** occallēscere.

thief *n* fūr *m.*

thieve *vt* fūrārī, surripere.

thievery *n* fūrtum *nt.*

thievish *adj* fūrāx.

thigh *n* femur *nt.*

thin *adj* exīlis, gracilis, tenuis; (*attendance*) īnfrequēns ♦ *vt* attenuāre, extenuāre; **~ out** rārefacere; **~ down** dīluere.

thine *adj* tuus.

thing *n* rēs *f*; **as ~s are** nunc, cum haec ita sint.

think *vi* cōgitāre; (*opinion*) putāre, existimāre, arbitrārī, rērī, crēdere; **as I ~** meā sententiā; **~ about** cōgitāre dē; **~ highly of** magnī aestimāre; **~ nothing of** nihilī facere; **~ out** excōgitāre; **~ over** reputāre, in mente agitāre.

thinker *n* philosophus *m.*

thinking *adj* sapiēns ♦ *n* cōgitātiō *f*; **~ that** ratus, arbitrātus.

thinly *adv* exīliter, tenuiter; rārē.

thinness *n* exīlitās *f*, gracilitās *f*; (*person*) maciēs *f*; (*number*) exiguitās *f*, īnfrequentia *f*; (*air*) tenuitās *f.*

thin-skinned *adj* inrītābilis.

third *adj* tertius; **for the ~ time** tertium ♦ *n* tertia pars *f*, triēns *m*; **two ~s** duae partēs, bēs *m.*

thirdly *adv* tertiō.

thirst *n* sitis *f* ♦ *vi* sitīre; **~ for** sitīre.

thirstily *adv* sitienter.

thirsty *adj* sitiēns.

thirteen *num* tredecim; **~ each** ternī dēnī; **~ times** terdeciēns.

thirteenth *adj* tertius decimus.

thirtieth *adj* trīcēsimus.

thirty *num* trīgintā; **~ each** trīcēnī;

~ **times** trīciēns.

this pron hīc.

thistle n carduus m.

thither adv eō, illūc.

thole n scalmus nt.

thong n lōrum nt, habēna f.

thorn n spīna f, sentis m.

thorny adj spīnōsus.

thorough adj absolūtus, germānus; (work) accūrātus.

thoroughbred adj generōsus.

thoroughfare n via f.

thoroughly adv penitus, omnīnō, funditus.

thoroughness n cūra f, diligentia f.

thou pron tū.

though conj etsī, etiamsī, quamvīs (+ subj), quamquam all (+ indic).

thought n (faculty) cōgitātiō f, mēns f, animus m; (an idea) cōgitātum nt, nōtiō f; (design) cōnsilium nt, prōpositum nt; (expressed) sententia f; (heed) cautiō f, prōvidentia f; (RHET) inventiō f; **second ~s** posteriōrēs cōgitātiōnēs.

thoughtful adj cōgitābundus; prōvidus.

thoughtfully adv prōvidē.

thoughtless adj incōnsīderātus, incōnsultus, imprōvidus, immemor.

thoughtlessly adv temerē, incōnsultē.

thoughtlessness n incōnsīderantia f, imprūdentia f.

thousand num mīlle; **~s** pl mīlia (+ gen) ntpl; **~ each** mīllēnī; **~ times** mīlliēns; **three ~** tria mīlia.

thousandth adj mīllēsimus.

thrall n servus m.

thraldom n servitūs f.

thrash vt verberāre.

thrashing n verbera ntpl.

thread n fīlum nt; **hang by a ~** (fig) fīlō pendēre ♦ vt: **~ one's way sē** īnsinuāre.

threadbare adj trītus, obsolētus.

threat n minae fpl, minātiō f.

threaten vt minārī (dat of pers), dēnūntiāre ♦ vi imminēre, impendēre.

threatening adj mināx, imminēns.

threateningly adv mināciter.

three num trēs; **~ each** ternī; **~ times** ter; **~ days** trīduum nt; **~ years** triennium nt; **~ quarters** trēs partēs fpl, dōdrāns m.

three-cornered adj triangulus, triquetrus.

threefold adj triplex.

three hundred num trecentī; **~ each** trecēnī; **~ times** trecentiēns.

three hundredth adj trecentēsimus.

three-legged adj tripēs.

three-quarters n dōdrāns m, trēs partēs fpl.

thresh vt terere, exterere.

threshing floor n ārea f.

threshold n līmen nt.

thrice adv ter.

thrift n frūgālitās f, parsimōnia f.

thriftily adv frūgāliter.

thrifty adj parcus, frūgī.

thrill n horror m ♦ vt percellere, percutere ♦ vi trepidāre.

thrilling adj mīrābilis.

thrive vi vigēre, valēre, crēscere.

thriving adj valēns, vegetus; (crops) laetus.

throat n faucēs fpl, guttur nt; **out the ~ of** iugulāre.

throaty adj gravis, raucus.

throb vi palpitāre, micāre ♦ n pulsus m.

throe n dolor m; **be in the ~s of** labōrāre ex.

throne n solium nt; (power) rēgnum nt.

throng n multitūdō f, frequentia f ♦ vt celebrāre; **~ round** stīpāre, circumfundī (dat).

throttle vt strangulāre.

through prep per (acc); (cause)
propter (acc), abl ♦ adv: **and ~**
penitus; **carry ~** exsequī,
peragere; **go ~** trānsīre; **run ~**
percurrere; **be ~ with**
perfūnctum esse (abl).

throughout adv penitus, omnīnō
♦ prep per (acc).

throw n iactus m, coniectus m ♦ vt
iacere, conicere; **~ about** iactāre;
~ across trāicere; **~ away**
abicere; (something precious)
prōicere; **~ back** rēicere; **~ down**
dēturbāre, dēicere; **~ into**
inicere; **~ into confusion**
perturbāre; **~ off** excutere,
exsolvere; **~ open** patefacere; **~
out** ēicere, prōicere; **~ over**
inicere; (fig) dēstituere; **~
overboard** iactūram facere (gen);
~ to (danger) obicere; **~ up** ēicere;
(building) exstruere; **~ a bridge
over** pontem inicere (dat), pontem
faciendum cūrāre in (abl); **~ light
on** (fig) lūmen adhibēre (dat); **~ a
rider** equitem excutere.

throwing n coniectiō f, iactus m.

thrum n līcium m.

thrush n turdus m.

thrust vt trūdere, pellere,
impingere; **~ at** petere; **~ away**
dētrūdere; **~ forward** prōtrūdere;
~ home dēfīgere; **~ into** īnfīgere,
impingere; **~ out** extrūdere.

thud n gravis sonitus m.

thug n percussor m, sīcārius m.

thumb n pollex m; **have under
one's ~** in potestāte suā habēre.

thump n plāga f ♦ vt tundere,
pulsāre.

thunder n tonitrus m ♦ vi tonāre,
intonāre; **it ~s** tonāt.

thunderbolt n fulmen nt.

thunderer n tonāns m.

thunderstruck adj attonitus.

thus adv (referring back) sīc;
(referring forward) ita; **~ far**
hāctenus.

thwack vt verberāre.

thwart vt obstāre (dat), officere
(dat), remorārī, frustrārī ♦ n
(boat's) trānstrum nt.

thy adj tuus.

thyme n thymum nt; (wild)
serpyllum nt.

tiara n diadēma nt.

ticket n tessera f.

tickle vt titillāre.

tickling n titillātiō f.

ticklish adj lūbricus.

tidal adj: **~ waters** aestuārium nt.

tide n aestus m; (time) tempus nt;
ebb ~ aestūs recessus m; **flood ~**
aestūs accessus m; **turn of the ~**
commūtātiō aestūs; **the ~ will turn**
(fig) circumagētur hīc orbis.

tidily adv concinnē, mundē.

tidiness n concinnitās f, munditia f.

tidings n nūntius m.

tidy adj concinnus, mundus.

tie n (bond) vinculum nt, cōpula f;
(kin) necessitūdō f ♦ vt ligāre;
(knot) nectere; **~ fast** dēvincīre,
cōnstringere; **~ on** illigāre; **~ to**
adligāre; **~ together** colligāre; **~
up** adligāre; (wound) obligāre.

tier n ōrdō m.

tiff n dissēnsiō f.

tiger n tigris m, more usu f.

tight adj strictus, astrictus,
intentus; (close) artus; **draw ~**
intendere, addūcere.

tighten vt adstringere,
contendere.

tightly adv artē, angustē.

tightrope n extentus fūnis; **~
walker** n fūnambulus m.

tigress n tigris f.

tile n tegula f, imbrex f, later nt.

till conj dum, dōnec ♦ prep usque
ad (in), in (acc); **not ~** dēmum ♦ n
arca f ♦ vt colere.

tillage n cultus m.

tiller n (AGR) cultor m; (ship) clāvus
m.

m, gubernāculum *nt*.

tilt *vt* inclīnāre.

tilth *n* cultus *m*, arvum *nt*.

timber *n* (*for building*) māteria *f*; (*firewood*) lignum *nt*.

timbrel *n* tympanum *nt*.

time *n* tempus *nt*; (*lifetime*) aetās *f*; (*interval*) intervallum *nt*, spatium *nt*; (*of day*) hōra *f*; (*leisure*) ōtium *nt*; (*rhythm*) numerus *m*; **another ~** aliās; **at ~s** aliquandō, interdum; **at all ~s** semper; **at any ~** umquam; **at one ~ ... at another ~** aliās ... aliās; **at that ~** tunc, id temporis; **at the right ~** ad tempus, mātūrē, tempestīvō; **at the same ~** simul; tamen; **at the wrong ~** intempestīvē; **beating ~** percussiō *f*; **convenient ~** opportūnitās *f*; **for a ~** aliquantisper, parumper; **for a long ~** diū; **for some ~** aliquamdiū; **for the ~ being** ad tempus; **from ~ to ~** interdum, identidem; **have a good ~** geniō indulgēre; **have ~ for** vacāre (*dat*); **in ~** ad tempus, tempore; **in a short ~** brevī; **in good ~** tempestīvus; **in the ~ of** apud (*acc*); **keep ~** (*marching*) gradum cōnferre; (*music*) modulārī; **many ~s** saepe, saepenumerō; **pass, spend ~** tempus sūmere, dēgere; **several ~s** aliquotiēns; **some ~** aliquandō; **waste ~** tempus terere; **what is the ~?** quota hōra est?; **~-expired** ēmeritus.

time-honoured *adj* antīquus.

timeliness *n* opportūnitās *f*.

timely *adj* opportūnus, tempestīvus, mātūrus.

timid *adj* timidus.

timidity *n* timiditās *f*.

timidly *adv* timidē.

timorous *adj* timidus.

timorously *adv* timidē.

tin *n* stannum *nt*, plumbum album

nt ♦ *adj* stanneus.

tincture *n* color *m*, sapor *m* ♦ *vt* īnficere.

tinder *n* fōmes *m*.

tinge *vt* imbuere, īnficere, tingere.

tingle *vi* horrēre.

tingling *n* horror *m*.

tinkle *vi* tinnīre ♦ *n* tinnītus *m*.

tinsel *n* bractea *f*; (*fig*) speciēs *f*, fūcus *m*.

tint *n* color *m* ♦ *vt* colōrāre.

tiny *adj* minūtus, pusillus, perexiguus.

tip *n* apex *m*, cacūmen *nt*, extrēmum *nt*; **the ~ of** prīmus, extrēmus ♦ *vt* praefīgere; **~ over** invertere.

tipple *vi* pōtāre.

tippler *n* pōtor *m*, ēbrius *m*.

tipsy *adj* tēmulentus.

tiptoes *n*: **on ~** suspēnsō gradū.

tirade *n* obiūrgātiō *f*, dēclāmātiō *f*.

tire *vt* fatīgāre; **~ out** dēfatīgāre ♦ *vi* dēfetīscī, fatīgārī; **I ~ of** mē taedet (*gen*); **it ~s** mē taedet (+ *acc of person, gen of thing*).

tired *adj* (dē)fessus, lassus; **~ out** dēfessus, **I am ~ of** mē taedet.

tiresome *adj* molestus, difficilis.

tiring *adj* labōriōsus, operōsus.

tiro *n* tīrō *m*, rudis *m*.

tissue *n* textus *m*.

tit *n*: **give ~ for tat** pār parī respondēre.

Titan *n* Tītān *m*.

titanic *adj* immānis.

titbit *n* cuppēdium *nt*.

tithe *n* decuma *f*.

tithe gatherer *n* decumānus *m*.

titillate *vt* titillāre.

titillation *n* titillātiō *f*.

title *n* (*book*) īnscrīptiō *f*, index *m*; (*inscription*) titulus *m*; (*person*) nōmen *nt*, appellātiō *f*; (*claim*) iūs *nt*, vindiciae *fpl*; **assert one's ~ to** vindicāre; **give a ~ to** īnscrībere.

titled *adj* nōbilis.

title deed n auctōritās f.

titter n rīsus m ♦ vi rīdēre.

tittle-tattle n sermunculus m.

titular adj nōmine.

to prep ad (acc), in (acc); (attitude) ergā (acc); (giving) dat; (towns, small islands, domus, rūs) acc ♦ conj (purpose) ut ♦ adv: **come ~ animum recipere; ~ and fro** hūc illūc.

toad n būfō m.

toady n adsentātor m, parasītus m ♦ vt adsentārī (dat).

toadyism n adsentātiō f.

toast n: **drink a ~** propīnāre ♦ vt torrēre; (drink) propīnāre (dat).

today adv hodiē; **~'s** hodiernus.

toe n digitus m; **big ~** pollex m.

toga n toga f.

together adv ūnā, simul; **bring ~** cōgere, congerere; **come ~** convenīre, congregārī; **put ~** cōnferre, compōnere.

toil n labor m; (snare) rēte nt ♦ vi labōrāre; **~ at** ēlabōrāre in (abl).

toilet n (lady's) cultus m.

toilsome adj labōriōsus, operōsus.

toil-worn adj labōre cōnfectus.

token n īnsigne nt, signum nt, indicium nt.

tolerable adj tolerābilis, patibilis; (quality) mediocris; (size) modicus.

tolerably adv satis, mediocriter.

tolerance n patientia f, tolerantia f.

tolerant adj indulgēns, tolerāns.

tolerantly adv indulgenter.

tolerate vt tolerāre, ferre, indulgēre (dat).

toleration n patientia f; (freedom) lībertās f.

toll n vectīgal nt; (harbour) portōrium nt.

toll collector n exāctor m; portitor m.

tomb n sepulcrum nt.

tombstone n lapis m.

tome n liber m.

tomorrow adv crās; **~'s** crāstinus; **the day after ~** perendiē; **put off till ~** in crāstinum differre.

tone n sonus m, vōx f; (painting) color m.

tongs n forceps m/f.

tongue n lingua f; (shoe) ligula f; **on the tip of one's ~** in prīmōribus labrīs.

tongue-tied adj ēlinguis, īnfāns.

tonnage n amphorae fpl.

tonsils n tōnsillae fpl.

tonsure n rāsūra f.

too adv (also) etiam, īnsuper, quoque; (excess) nimis ♦ compar adj: **~ far** extrā modum; **~ much** nimium; **~ long** nimium diū; **~ great to** māior quam quī (subj); **~ late** sērius; **~ little** parum (+ gen).

tool n īnstrūmentum nt; (AGR) ferrāmentum nt; (person) minister m.

tooth n dēns m; **~ and nail** tōtō corpore atque omnibus unguibus; **cast in one's teeth** exprobrāre, obicere; **cut teeth** dentīre; **in the teeth of** obviam (dat), adversus (acc); **with the teeth** mordicus.

toothache n dentium dolor m.

toothed adj dentātus.

toothless adj ēdentulus.

toothpick n dentiscalpium nt.

toothsome adj suāvis, dulcis.

top n vertex m, fastīgium nt; (tree) cacūmen nt; (toy) turbō m; **from ~ to toe** ab īmīs unguibus usque ad verticem summum; **the ~ of** summus ♦ vt exsuperāre; **~ up** supplēre ♦ adj superior, summus.

tope vi pōtāre.

toper n pōtor m.

topiary adj topiārius. ♦ n topiārium opus nt.

topic n rēs f; (RHET) locus m; **~ of conversation** sermō m.

topical adj hodiernus.

topmost adj summus.

topography n dēscrīptiō f.

topple vi titubāre; ~ **over** prōlābī.

topsail n dolō m.

topsyturvy adv praeposterē; **turn** ~ sūrsum deōrsum versāre, permiscēre

tor n mōns m.

torch n fax f, lampas f.

torment n cruciātus m; (mind) angor m ♦ vt cruciāre; (mind) discruciāre, excruciāre, angere.

tormentor n tortor m.

tornado n turbō m.

torpid adj torpēns; **be** ~ torpēre; **grow** ~ obtorpēscere.

torpor n torpor m, inertia f.

torrent n torrēns m.

torrid adj torridus.

torsion n tortus m.

torso n truncus m.

tortoise n testūdō f.

tortoiseshell n testūdō f.

tortuous adj flexuōsus.

torture n cruciātus m, supplicium nt; **instrument of** ~ tormentum nt ♦ vt torquēre, cruciāre, excruciāre.

torturer n tortor m, carnifex m.

toss n iactus m ♦ vt iactāre, excutere; ~ **about** agitāre; **be** ~ed (at sea) fluitāre.

total adj tōtus, ūniversus ♦ n summa f.

totality n ūniversitās f.

totally adv omnīnō, plānē.

totter vi lābāre, titubāre; **make** ~ labefactāre.

tottering n titubātiō f.

touch n tāctus m; **a** ~ **of** aliquantulum (gen); **finishing** ~ manus extrēma f ♦ vt tangere, attingere; (feelings) movēre, tangere ♦ vi inter sē contingere; ~ **at** nāvem appellere ad; ~ **on** (topic) attingere, perstringere; ~ **up** expolīre.

touch-and-go adj anceps ♦ n

discrīmen nt.

touching adj (place) contiguus; (emotion) flexanimus ♦ prep quod attinet ad (acc).

touchstone n (fig) obrussa f.

touchy adj inrītābilis, stomachōsus.

tough adj dūrus.

toughen vt dūrāre.

toughness n dūritia f.

tour n iter nt; (abroad) peregrīnātiō f.

tourist n viātor m, peregrīnātor m.

tournament n certāmen nt.

tow n stuppa f; **of** ~ stuppeus ♦ vt adnexum trahere, remulcō trahere.

toward(s) prep ad (acc), versus (after noun, acc); (feelings) in (acc), ergā (acc); (time) sub (acc).

towel n mantēle nt.

tower n turris f ♦ vi ēminēre.

towered adj turrītus

town n urbs f, oppidum nt; **country** ~ mūnicipium nt ♦ adj urbānus.

town councillor n decuriō m.

townsman n oppidānus m.

townspeople npl oppidānī mpl.

towrope n remulcum nt.

toy n crepundia ntpl ♦ vi lūdere.

trace n vestīgium nt, indicium nt ♦ vt investīgāre; (draw) dēscrībere; ~ **out** dēsignāre.

track n (mark) vestīgium nt; (path) callis m, sēmita f; (of wheel) orbita f; (of ship) cursus m ♦ vt investīgāre, indāgāre.

trackless adj invius.

tract n (country) tractus m, regiō f; (book) libellus m.

tractable adj tractābilis, facilis, docilis.

trade n mercātūra f, mercātus m, (a business) ars f, quaestus m; **freedom of** ~ commercium nt ♦ vi mercātūrās facere, negōtiārī; ~ **in** vēndere, vēnditāre.

trader n mercātor m, negōtiātor m.
tradesman n opifex m.
tradition n fāma f, mōs māiōrum
m, memoria f.
traditional adj ā māiōribus
trāditus, patrius.
traditionally adv mōre māiōrum.
traduce vt calumniārī, obtrectāre
(dat).
traducer n calumniātor m,
obtrectātor m.
traffic n commercium nt; (on road)
vehicula ntpl ♦ vi mercātūrās
facere; ~ **in** vēndere, vēnditāre.
tragedian n (author) tragoedus m;
(actor) āctor tragicus m.
tragedy n tragoedia f; (fig)
calamitās f, malum nt.
tragic adj tragicus m; (fig) tristis.
tragically adv tragicē; male.
tragicomedy n tragicocōmoedia f.
trail n vestīgia ntpl ♦ vt trahere
♦ vi trahī.
train n (line) agmen nt, ōrdō m; (of
dress) īnstita f; (army) impedīmenta ntpl; (followers) comitēs
mpl, satellitēs mpl, cohors f ♦ vt
īnstituere, īnstruere, docēre,
adsuēfacere; exercēre; (weapon)
dīrigere.
trainer n (sport) lanista m, aliptēs
m.
training n disciplīna f, īnstitūtiō f;
(practice) exercitātiō f.
trait n līneāmentum nt.
traitor n prōditor m.
traitorous adj perfidus,
perfidiōsus.
traitorously adv perfidiōsē.
trammel vt impedīre.
tramp n (man) plānus m; (of feet)
pulsus m ♦ vi gradī.
trample vi: ~ **on** obterere,
prōterere, prōculcāre.
trance n stupor m; (prophetic) furor
m.
tranquil adj tranquillus, placidus,

quiētus, sēdātus.
tranquility n tranquillitās f, quiēs f,
pāx f.
tranquillize vt pācāre, sēdāre.
tranquilly adv tranquillē, placidē,
tranquillō animō.
transact vt agere, gerere,
trānsigere.
transaction n rēs f, negōtium nt.
transactor n āctor m.
transalpine adj trānsalpīnus.
transcend vt superāre, excēdere.
transcendence n praestantia f.
transcendent adj eximius,
ēgregius, excellēns.
transcendental adj dīvīnus.
transcendentally adv eximiē,
ēgregiē, ūnicē.
transcribe vt dēscrībere,
trānscrībere.
transcriber n lībrārius m.
transcript n exemplar nt,
exemplum nt.
transfer n trānslātiō f; (of property)
aliēnātiō f ♦ vt trānsferre;
(troops) trādūcere; (property)
abaliēnāre; (duty) dēlēgāre.
transference n trānslātiō f.
transfigure vt trānsfōrmāre.
transfix vt trānsfīgere, trāicere,
trānsfodere; (mind)
obstupefacere; **be ~ed** stupēre,
stupēscere.
transform vt commūtāre, vertere.
transformation n commūtātiō f.
transgress vt violāre, perfringere
♦ vi dēlinquere.
transgression n dēlictum nt.
transgressor n violātor m.
transience n brevitās f.
transient adj fluxus, cadūcus,
brevis.
transit n trānsitus m.
transition n mūtātiō f; (speech)
trānsitus m.
transitory adj brevis, fluxus.
translate vt vertere, reddere; ~

into Latin Latīnē reddere.
translation n: **a Latin ~ of Homer**
Latīnē redditus Homērus.
translator n interpres m.
translucent adj perlūcidus.
transmarine adj trānsmarīnus.
transmission n mīssiō f.
transmit vt mittere; (legacy)
trādere, prōdere.
transmutable adj mūtābilis.
transmutation n mūtātiō f.
transmute vt mūtāre, commūtāre.
transom n trabs f.
transparency n perlūcida nātūra f.
transparent adj perlūcidus; (fig)
perspicuus.
transparently adv perspicuē.
transpire vi (get known) ēmānāre,
dīvulgārī; (happen) ēvenīre.
transplant vt trānsferre.
transport n vectūra f; (ship) nāvis
onerāria f; (emotion) ēlātiō f,
summa laetitia f ♦ vt
trānsportāre, trānsvehere,
trānsmittere; **be ~ed** (fig) efferrī,
gestīre.
transportation n vectūra f.
transpose vt invertere; (words)
trāicere.
transposition n (words) trāiectiō f.
transverse adj trānsversus,
oblīquus.
transversely adv in trānsversum,
oblīquē.
trap n laqueus m; (fig) īnsidiae fpl
♦ vt dēcipere, excipere; (fig)
inlaqueāre.
trappings n ōrnāmenta ntpl,
īnsignia ntpl; (horse's) phalerae fpl.
trash n nūgae fpl.
trashy adj vīlis.
Trasimene n Trasimēnus m.
travail n labor m, sūdor m;
(woman's) puerperium nt ♦ vi
labōrāre, sūdāre; parturīre.
travel n itinera ntpl; (foreign)
peregrīnātiō f ♦ vi iter facere;

(abroad) peregrīnārī; **~ through**
peragrāre; **~ to** contendere ad, in
(acc), proficīscī in (acc).
traveller n viātor m; (abroad)
peregrīnātor m.
traverse vt peragrāre, lūstrāre; **~ a
great distance** multa mīlia
passuum iter facere.
travesty n perversa imitātiō f ♦ vt
perversē imitārī.
tray n ferculum nt.
treacherous adj perfidus,
perfidiōsus; (ground) lūbricus.
treacherously adv perfidiōsē.
treachery n perfidia f.
tread vi incēdere, ingredī; **~ on**
īnsistere (dat) ♦ n gradus m,
incessus m.
treadle n (loom) īnsilia ntpl.
treadmill n pistrīnum nt.
treason n māiestās f, perduelliō f;
be charged with ~ māiestātis
accūsārī; **be guilty of high ~
against** māiestātem minuere,
laedere (gen).
treasonable adj perfidus,
perfidiōsus.
treasure n gāza f, thēsaurus m;
(person) dēliciae fpl ♦ vt māximī
aestimāre, dīligere, fovēre; **~ up**
condere, congerere.
treasure house n thēsaurus m.
treasurer n aerāriī praefectus m;
(royal) dioecētēs m.
treasury n aerārium nt; (emperor's)
fiscus m.
treat n convīvium nt; dēlectātiō f
♦ vt (in any way) ūtī (abl), habēre,
tractāre, accipere; (patient)
cūrāre; (topic) tractāre; (with
hospitality) invītāre; **~ with** agere
cum; **~ as a friend** amīcī locō
habēre.
treatise n liber m.
treatment n tractātiō f; (MED)
cūrātiō f.
treaty n foedus nt; **make a ~**

foedus ferīre.

treble adj triplus; (voice) acūtus ♦ n acūtus sonus m ♦ vt triplicāre.

tree n arbor f.

trek vi migrāre ♦ n migrātiō f.

trellis n cancellī mpl.

tremble vi tremere, horrēre.

trembling n tremor m, horror m ♦ adj tremulus.

tremendous adj immānis, ingēns, vastus.

tremendously adv immāne quantum.

tremor n tremor m.

tremulous adj tremulus.

trench n fossa f.

trenchant adj ācer.

trenchantly adv ācriter.

trend n inclīnātiō f ♦ vi vergere.

trepidation n trepidātiō f.

trespass n dēlictum nt ♦ vi dēlinquere; ~ on (property) invādere in (acc); (patience, time, etc) abūtī (abl).

trespasser n quī iniussū dominī ingreditur.

tress n crīnis m.

trial n (essay) experientia f; (test) probātiō f; (law) iūdicium nt, quaestiō f; (trouble) labor m, aerumna f; **make a ~ of** experīrī, perīculum facere (gen); **be brought to ~** in iūdicium venīre; **put on ~** in iūdicium vocāre; **hold a ~ on** quaestiōnem habēre dē (abl).

triangle n triangulum nt.

triangular adj triangulus, triquetrus.

tribe n tribus m; gēns f; (barbarian) nātiō f.

tribulation n aerumna f.

tribunal n iūdicium nt.

tribune n tribūnus m; (platform) rōstra ntpl.

tribuneship, tribunate n trib-

ūnātus m.

tribunician adj tribūnicius.

tributary adj vectīgālis ♦ n: **be a ~ of** (river) īnfluere in (acc).

tribute n tribūtum nt, vectīgal nt; (verbal) laudātiō f; **pay a ~ to** laudāre.

trice n: **in a ~** mōmentō temporis.

trick n dolus m, fallācia f, fraus f, īnsidiae fpl, ars f; (conjurer's) praestīgiae fpl; (habit) mōs m ♦ vt fallere, dēcipere, ēlūdere; (with words) verba dare (dat); **~ out** ōrnāre, distinguere.

trickery n dolus m, fraus f, fallāciae fpl.

trickle n guttae fpl ♦ vi mānāre, dēstillāre.

trickster n fraudātor m, veterātor m.

tricky adj lūbricus, difficilis.

trident n tridēns m, fuscina f.

tried adj probātus, spectātus.

triennial adj trietēricus.

triennially adv quartō quōque annō.

trifle n nūgae fpl, paululum nt ♦ vi lūdere, nūgārī; **~ with** lūdere.

trifling adj levis, exiguus.

triflingly adv leviter.

trig adj lepidus, concinnus.

trigger n manulea f.

trim adj nitidus, concinnus ♦ vt putāre, tondēre; (lamp) oleum īnstillāre (dat) ♦ vi temporibus servīre.

trimly adv concinnē.

trimness n nitor, munditia f.

trinket n crepundia ntpl.

trip n iter nt ♦ vt supplantāre ♦ vi lābī, titubāre; **~ along** currere; **~ over** incurrere in (acc).

tripartite adj tripartītus.

tripe n omāsum nt.

triple adj triplex, triplus ♦ vt triplicāre.

triply adv trifāriam.

tripod n tripus m.

trireme n trirēmis f.

trite adj trītus.

triumph n triumphus m; (victory) victōria f ♦ vi triumphāre; vincere; ~ **over** dēvincere.

triumphal adj triumphālis.

triumphant adj victor; laetus.

triumvir n triumvir m.

triumvirate n triumvirātus m.

trivial adj levis, tenuis.

triviality n nūgae fpl.

trochaic adj trochaicus.

trochee n trochaeus m.

Trojan n Trōiānus m.

troop n grex f, caterva f; (cavalry) turma f ♦ vi cōnfluere, congregārī.

trooper n eques m.

troops npl cōpiae fpl.

trope n figūra f, trānslātiō f.

trophy n tropaeum nt; **set up a ~** tropaeum pōnere.

tropic n sōlstitiālis orbis m; **~s** pl loca fervida ntpl.

tropical adj tropicus.

trot vi tolūtim īre.

troth n fidēs f.

trouble n incommodum nt, malum nt, molestia f, labor m; (effort) opera f, negōtium nt; (disturbance) turba f, tumultus m; **take the ~ to** operam dare ut; **be worth the ~** operae pretium esse ♦ vt (disturb) turbāre; (make uneasy) sollicitāre, exagitāre; (annoy) incommodāre, molestiam exhibēre (dat); **~ oneself about** cūrāre, respicere; **be ~d with** labōrāre ex.

troubler n turbātor m.

troublesome adj molestus, incommodus, difficilis.

troublesomeness n molestia f.

troublous adj turbidus, turbulentus.

trough n alveus m.

trounce vt castīgāre.

troupe n grex f, caterva f.

trousered adj brācātus.

trousers n brācae fpl.

trow vi opīnārī.

truant adj tardus ♦ n cessātor m; **play ~** cessāre, nōn compārēre.

truce n indutiae fpl.

truck n carrus m; **have no ~ with** nihil commercī habēre cum.

truckle vi adsentārī.

truculence n ferōcia f, asperitās f.

truculent adj truculentus, ferōx.

truculently adv ferōciter.

trudge vi rēpere, pedibus incēdere.

true adj vērus; (genuine) germānus, vērus; (loyal) fīdus, fidēlis; (exact) rēctus, iūstus.

truism n verbum trītum nt.

truly adv rēvērā, profectō, vērē.

trumpery n nūgae fpl ♦ adj vīlis.

trumpet n tuba f, būcina f.

trumpeter n būcinātor m, tubicen m.

trump up vt ēmentīrī, cōnfingere.

truncate vt praecīdere.

truncheon n fustis m, scīpiō m

trundle vt volvere.

trunk n truncus m; (elephant's) manus f; (box) cista f.

truss n fascia f ♦ vt colligāre.

trust n fidēs f, fīdūcia f; **breach of ~** mala fidēs f; **held in ~** fīdūciārius; **put ~ in** fidem habēre (dat) ♦ vt cōnfīdere (dat), crēdere (dat); (entrust) committere, concrēdere.

trustee n tūtor m.

trusteeship n tūtēla f.

trustful adj crēdulus, fīdēns.

trustfully adv fīdenter.

trustily adv fidēliter.

trustiness n fidēs f, fidēlitās f.

trusting adj fīdēns.

trustingly adv fīdenter.

trustworthily adv fidēliter.

trustworthiness n fidēs f, integritās f.

trustworthy *adj* fīdus, certus;
(*witness*) locuplēs; (*authority*)
certus, bonus.

trusty *adj* fīdus, fidēlis.

truth *n* vēritās *f*, vērum *nt*; **in ~ rē**
vērā.

truthful *adj* vērāx.

truthfully *adv* vērē.

truthfulness *n* fidēs *f*.

try *vt* (*attempt*) cōnārī; (*test*)
experīrī, temptāre; (*harass*)
exercēre; (*judge*) iūdicāre,
cognōscere; **~ for** petere,
quaerere.

trying *adj* molestus.

tub *n* alveus *m*, cūpa *f*.

tubby *adj* obēsus.

tube *n* fistula *f*.

tufa *n* tōfus *m*.

tuft *n* crista *f*.

tug *vt* trahere, tractāre.

tuition *n* īnstitūtiō *f*.

tumble *vi* concidere, corruere,
prōlābī ♦ *n* cāsus *m*.

tumbledown *adj* ruīnōsus.

tumbler *n* pōculum *nt*.

tumid *adj* tumidus, īnflātus.

tumour *n* tūber *nt*.

tumult *n* tumultus *m*, turba *f*; (*fig*)
perturbātiō *f*.

tumultuous *adj* tumultuōsus,
turbidus.

tumultuously *adv* tumultuōsē.

tumulus *n* tumulus *m*.

tun *n* dolium *nt*.

tune *n* modī *mpl*, carmen *nt*; **keep
in ~** concentum servāre; **out of ~**
absonus, dissonus; (*strings*)
incontentus ♦ *vt* (*strings*)
intendere.

tuneful *adj* canōrus.

tunefully *adv* numerōsē.

tunic *n* tunica *f*; **wearing a ~**
tunicātus.

tunnel *n* cunīculus *m*.

tunny *n* thunnus *m*.

turban *n* mitra *f*, mitella *f*.

turbid *adj* turbidus.

turbot *n* rhombus *m*.

turbulence *n* tumultus *m*.

turbulent *adj* turbulentus,
turbidus.

turbulently *adv* turbulentē,
turbidē.

turf *n* caespes *m*.

turgid *adj* turgidus, īnflātus.

turgidity *n* (*RHET*) ampullae *fpl*.

turgidly *adv* īnflātē.

turmoil *n* turba *f*, tumultus *m*;
(*mind*) perturbātiō *f*.

turn *n* (*motion*) conversiō *f*; (*bend*)
flexus *m*, ānfractus *m*; (*change*)
commūtātiō *f*, vicissitūdō *f*; (*walk*)
spatium *nt*; (*of mind*) adfectus *m*;
(*of language*) sententia *f*,
cōnfōrmātiō *f*; **~ of events** mutātiō
rērum *f*; **bad ~** iniūria *f*; **good ~**
beneficium *nt*; **~ of the scale**
mōmentum *nt*; **take a ~ for the
worse** in pēiōrem partem vertī; **in
~s** invicem, vicissim, alternī; **in
one's ~** locō ōrdine ♦ *vt* vertere,
convertere, flectere; (*change*)
vertere, mūtāre; (*direct*)
intendere, dīrigere; (*translate*)
vertere, reddere; (*on a lathe*)
tornāre; **~ the edge of** retundere;
~ the head mentem exturbāre; **~
the laugh against** rīsum
convertere in (*acc*); **~ the scale**
(*fig*) mōmentum habēre; **~ the
stomach** nauseam facere; **~ to
account** ūtī (*abl*), in rem suam
convertere ♦ *vi* versārī,
circumagī; (*change*) vertere,
mūtārī; (*crisis*) pendēre; (*direction*)
convertī; (*scale*) prōpendēre; **~
king's/queen's evidence** indicium
profitērī; **~ against** *vt* aliēnāre ab
♦ *vi* dēscīscere ab; **~ around** (*se*)
circumvertere; **~ aside** *vt*
dēflectere, dēclīnāre ♦ *vi*
dēvertere, sē dēclīnāre; **~ away**
vt āvertere, dēpellere ♦ *vi*

āversārī, discēdere; ~ **back** *vi*
revertī; ~ **down** *vt* invertere;
(*proposal*) rēicere; ~ **into** *vi*
vertere in (*acc*), mūtārī in (*acc*); ~
out *vt* ēicere, expellere ♦ *vi*
cadere, ēvenīre, ēvādere; ~
outside in excutere; ~ **over** *vt*
ēvertere; (*book*) ēvolvere; (*in
mind*) volūtāre, agitāre; ~ **round**
vt circumagere ♦ *vi* convertī; ~
up *vt* retorquēre; (*earth*) versāre;
(*nose*) corrūgāre ♦ *vi* adesse,
intervenīre; ~ **upside down**
invertere.

turncoat *n* trānsfuga *m*.

turning *n* flexus *m*, ānfrāctus *m*.

turning point *n* discrīmen *nt*, mēta
f.

turnip *n* rāpum *nt*.

turpitude *n* turpitūdō *f.*

turquoise *n* callais *f* ♦ *adj*
callainus.

turret *n* turris *f.*

turreted *adj* turrītus.

turtle *n* testūdō *f*; **turn** ~ invertī.

turtle dove *n* turtur *m.*

tusk *n* dēns *m.*

tussle *n* luctātiō *f* ♦ *vi* luctārī

tutelage *n* tūtēla *f.*

tutelary *adj* praeses.

tutor *n* praeceptor *m*, magister *m*
♦ *vt* docēre, praecipere (*dat*).

tutorship *n* tūtēla *f.*

twaddle *n* nūgae *fpl.*

twang *n* sonus *m* ♦ *vi* increpāre.

tweak *vi* vellicāre.

tweezers *n* forceps *m/f*, volsella *f.*

twelfth *adj* duodecimus ♦ *n*
duodecima pars *f*, ūncia *f*; **eleven
~s** deūnx *m*; **five ~** quīncūnx *m*;
seven ~s septūnx *m.*

twelve *num* duodecim; ~ **each**
duodēnī; ~ **times** duodeciēns.

twelvemonth *n* annus *m.*

twentieth *adj* vīcēsimus ♦ *n*
vīcēsima pars *f*; (*tax*) vīcēsima *f.*

twenty *num* vīgintī; ~ **each** vīcēnī;

~ **times** vīciēns.

twice *adv* bis; ~ **as much** duplus,
bis tantō; ~ **a day** bis diē, bis in
diē.

twig *n* virga *f*, rāmulus *m.*

twilight *n* (*morning*) dīlūculum *nt*;
(*evening*) crepusculum *nt.*

twin *adj* gemīnus ♦ *n* geminus *m*,
gemina *f.*

twine *n* resticula *f* ♦ *vt* nectere,
implicāre, contexere ♦ *vi* sē
implicāre; ~ **round** complectī.

twinge *n* dolor *m.*

twinkle *vi* micāre.

twirl *vt* intorquēre, contorquēre
♦ *vi* circumagī.

twist *vt* torquēre, intorquēre ♦ *vi*
torquērī.

twit *vt* obicere (*dat*).

twitch *vt* vellicāre ♦ *vi* micāre.

twitter *vi* pīpilāre.

two *num* duo; ~ **each** bīnī; ~ **days**
bidum *nt*; ~ **years** biennium *nt*; ~
years old bīmus; ~ **by** ~ bīnī; ~
feet long bipedālis; **in ~ parts**
bifāriam, bipartītō.

two-coloured *adj* bicolor.

two-edged *adj* anceps.

twofold *adj* duplex, anceps.

two-footed *adj* bipēs.

two-headed *adj* biceps.

two-horned *adj* bicornis.

two hundred *num* ducentī; ~ **each**
ducēnī; ~ **times** ducentiēns.

two hundredth *adj* ducentēsimus.

two-oared *adj* birēmis.

two-pronged *adj* bidēns, bifurcus.

two-way *adj* bivius.

type *n* (*pattern*) exemplar *nt*; (*kind*)
genus *nt.*

typhoon *n* turbō *m.*

typical *adj* proprius, solitus.

typically *adv* dē mōre, ut mōs est.

typify *vt* exprimere.

tyrannical *adj* superbus, crūdēlis.

tyrannically *adv* superbē,
crūdēliter.

tyrannize vi dominārī, rēgnāre.
tyrannous adj see **tyrannical**
tyrannously adv see **tyrannically**.
tyranny n dominātiō f, rēgnum nt.
tyrant n rēx m, crūdēlis dominus
    m; (Greek) tyrannus m.
tyro n tīrō m, rudis m.

U

ubiquitous adj omnibus locīs
    praesēns.
ubiquity n ūniversa praesentia f.
udder n ūber nt.
ugliness n foedītās f, dēfōrmitās f,
    turpitūdō f.
ugly adj foedus, dēfōrmis, turpis.
ulcer n ulcus nt, vomica f.
ulcerate vi ulcerārī.
ulcerous adj ulcerōsus.
ulterior adj ulterior.
ultimate adj ultimus, extrēmus.
ultimately adv tandem, ad
    ultimum.
umbrage n offēnsiō f; **take ~ at**
    indignē ferre, patī.
umbrageous adj umbrōsus.
umbrella n umbella f.
umpire n arbiter m, disceptātor m.
unabashed adj intrepidus,
    impudēns.
unabated adj integer.
unable adj impotēns; **be ~** nōn
    posse, nequīre.
unacceptable adj ingrātus.
unaccompanied adj sōlus.
unaccomplished adj īnfectus,
    imperfectus; (person) indoctus.
unaccountable adj inexplicābilis.
unaccountably adv sine causā,
    repentē.
unaccustomed adj īnsuētus,
    īnsolitus.
unacquainted adj ignārus (gen),
    imperītus (gen).
unadorned adj inōrnātus,
    incōmptus; (speech) nūdus,

ēnucleātus.
unadulterated adj sincērus,
    integer.
unadvisedly adv imprūdenter,
    incōnsultē.
unaffected adj simplex, candidus.
unaffectedly adv simpliciter.
unaided adj sine auxiliō, nūdus.
unalienable adj proprius.
unalloyed adj pūrus.
unalterable adj immūtābilis.
unaltered adj immūtātus.
unambiguous adj apertus, certus.
unambitious adj humilis,
    modestus.
unanimity n cōnsēnsiō f,
    ūnanimitās f.
unanimous adj concors,
    ūnanimus; **be ~** idem omnēs
    sentīre.
unanimously adv ūnā vōce,
    omnium cōnsēnsū.
unanswerable adj necessārius.
unanswerably adv sine
    contrōversiā.
unappreciative adj ingrātus.
unapproachable adj inaccessus;
    (person) difficilis.
unarmed adj inermis.
unasked adj ultrō, suā sponte.
unassailable adj inexpugnābilis.
unassailed adj intāctus, incolumis.
unassuming adj modestus,
    dēmissus; **~ manners** modestia f.
unassumingly adv modestē.
unattached adj līber.
unattempted adj intentātus; **leave**
    ~ praetermittere.
unattended adj sōlus, sine
    comitibus.
unattractive adj invenustus.
unauthentic adj incertō auctōre.
unavailing adj inūtilis, inānis.
unavenged adj inultus.
unavoidable adj necessārius.
unavoidably adv necessāriō.
unaware adj īnscius, ignārus.

unawares adv inopīnātō, dē imprōvīsō; incautus.

unbalanced adj turbātus.

unbar vt reserāre.

unbearable adj intolerābilis, intolerandus.

unbearably adv intoleranter.

unbeaten adj invictus.

unbecoming adj indecōrus, inhonestus; it is ~ dēdecet.

unbeknown adj ignōtus.

unbelief n diffīdentia f.

unbelievable adj incrēdibilis.

unbelievably adv incrēdibiliter.

unbelieving adj incrēdulus.

unbend vt remittere, laxāre ♦ vi animum remittere, aliquid dē sevēritāte remittere.

unbending adj inexōrābilis, sevērus.

unblassed adj integer, incorruptus, aequus.

unbidden adj ultrō, sponte.

unbind vt solvere, resolvere.

unblemished adj pūrus, integer.

unblushing adj impudēns.

unblushingly adv impudenter.

unbolt vt reserāre.

unborn adj nōndum nātus.

unbosom vt patefacere, effundere.

unbound adj solūtus.

unbounded adj īnfīnītus, immēnsus.

unbridled adj īnfrēnātus; (fig) effrēnātus, indomitus, impotēns.

unbroken adj integer; (animal) intractātus; (friendship) inviolātus; (series) perpetuus, continuus.

unburden vt exonerāre; ~ oneself of aperīre, patefacere.

unburied adj inhumātus, īnsepultus.

unbusinesslike adj iners.

uncalled-for adj supervacāneus.

uncanny adj mīrus, mōnstruōsus.

uncared-for adj neglectus.

unceasing adj perpetuus, adsiduus.

unceasingly adv perpetuō, adsiduē.

unceremonious adj agrestis, inurbānus.

unceremoniously adv inurbānē.

uncertain adj incertus, dubius, anceps; **be ~** dubitāre, pendēre.

uncertainly adv incertē, dubitanter.

uncertainty n incertum nt, (state) dubitātiō f.

unchangeable adj immūtābilis; (person) cōnstāns.

unchanged adj immūtātus, īdem; **remain ~** permanēre.

uncharitable adj inhūmānus, malignus.

uncharitableness n inhūmānitās f.

uncharitably adv inhūmānē, malignē.

unchaste adj impudīcus, libīdinōsus.

unchastely adv impudīcē.

unchastity n incestus m, libīdō f.

unchecked adj līber, indomitus.

uncivil adj inurbānus, importūnus, inhūmānus.

uncivilized adj barbarus, incultus, ferus.

uncivilly adv inurbānē.

uncle n (paternal) patruus m; (maternal) avunculus m.

unclean adj immundus; (fig) impūrus, obscēnus.

uncleanly adv impūrē.

uncleanness n sordēs fpl; (fig) impūritās f, obscēnitās f.

unclose vt aperīre.

unclothe vt nūdāre, vestem dētrahere (dat).

unclothed adj nūdus.

unclouded adj serēnus.

uncoil vt explicāre, ēvolvere.

uncomely adj dēfōrmis, turpis.

uncomfortable adj incommodus,

molestus.

uncomfortably adv incommodē.

uncommitted adj vacuus.

uncommon adj rārus, īnsolitus, inūsitātus; (eminent) ēgregius, singulāris, eximius.

uncommonly adv rārō; ēgregiē, ūnicē.

uncommonness n īnsolentia f.

uncommunicative adj tēctus, taciturnus.

uncomplaining adj patiēns.

uncompleted adj imperfectus.

uncompromising adj dūrus, rigidus.

unconcern n sēcūritās f.

unconcerned adj sēcūrus, ōtiōsus.

unconcernedly adv lentē.

uncondemned adj indemnātus.

unconditional adj absolūtus.

unconditionally adv nūllā condiciōne.

uncongenial adj ingrātus.

unconnected adj sēparātus, disiūnctus; (style) dissolūtus.

unconquerable adj invictus.

unconquered adj invictus.

unconscionable adj improbus.

unconscionably adv improbē.

unconscious adj: ~ of īnscius (gen), ignārus (gen); become ~ sōpīrī, animō linquī.

unconsciousness n sopor m.

unconsecrated adj profānus.

unconsidered adj neglectus.

unconstitutional adj illicitus.

unconstitutionally adv contrā lēgēs, contrā rem pūblicam.

uncontaminated adj pūrus, incorruptus, integer.

uncontrollable adj impotēns, effrēnātus.

uncontrollably adv effrēnātē.

uncontrolled adj līber, solūtus.

unconventional adj īnsolitus, solūtus.

unconvicted adj indemnātus.

unconvincing adj incrēdibilis, nōn vērī similis.

uncooked adj crūdus.

uncorrupted adj incorruptus, integer.

uncouple vt disiungere.

uncouth adj horridus, agrestis, inurbānus.

uncouthly adv inurbānē.

uncouthness n inhūmānitās f, rūsticitās f.

uncover vt dētegere, aperīre, nūdāre.

uncritical adj indoctus, crēdulus.

uncultivated adj incultus; (fig) agrestis, rūsticus, impolītus.

uncultured adj agrestis, rudis.

uncut adj intōnsus.

undamaged adj integer, inviolātus.

undaunted adj intrepidus, fortis.

undecayed adj incorruptus.

undeceive vt errōrem tollere (dat), errōrem ēripere (dat).

undecided adj dubius, anceps; (case) integer.

undecked adj (ship) apertus.

undefended adj indēfēnsus, nūdus.

undefiled adj integer, incontāminātus.

undemonstrative adj taciturnus.

undeniable adj certus.

undeniably adv sine dubiō.

undependable adj inconstāns, mōbilis.

under adv īnfrā, subter ♦ prep sub (abl), īnfrā (acc); (number) intrā (acc); (motion) sub (acc); ~ arms in armīs; ~ colour (pretext of) speciē (gen), per speciem (gen); ~ my leadership mē duce; ~ the circumstances cum haec ita sint; labour ~ labōrāre ex; ~ the eyes of in cōnspectū (+ gen); ~ the leadership of abl + duce.

underage adj impūbēs.

undercurrent *n*: an ~ of lātens.

underestimate *vt* minōris aestimāre.

undergarment *n* subūcula *f*.

undergo *vt* subīre, patī, ferre.

underground *adj* subterrāneus ♦ *adv* sub terrā.

undergrowth *n* virgulta *ntpl*.

underhand *adj* clandestīnus, fūrtīvus ♦ *adv* clam, fūrtim.

underline *vt* subscrībere.

underling *n* minister *m*, satelles *m/f*.

undermine *vt* subruere; (*fig*) labefacere, labefactāre.

undermost *adj* īnfimus.

underneath *adv* īnfrā ♦ *prep* sub (*abl*), īnfrā (*acc*); (*motion*) sub (*acc*).

underprop *vt* fulcīre.

underrate *vt* obtrectāre, extenuāre, minōris aestimāre.

understand *vt* intellegere, comprehendere; (*be told*) accipere, comperīre; (*in a sense*) interpretārī; ~ **Latin** Latīnē scīre.

understandable *adj* crēdibilis.

understanding *adj* sapiēns, perītus ♦ *n* intellegentia *f*; (*faculty*) mēns *f*, intellectus *m*; (*agreement*) cōnsēnsus *m*; (*condition*) condiciō *f*.

undertake *vt* suscipere, sūmere, adīre ad; (*business*) condūcere; (*case*) agere, dēfendere; (*promise*) recipere, spondēre.

undertaker *n* dissignātor *m*.

undertaking *n* inceptum *nt*, inceptiō *f*.

undervalue *vt* minōris aestimāre.

underwood *n* virgulta *ntpl*.

underworld *n* īnferī *mpl*.

undeserved *adj* immeritus, iniūstus.

undeservedly *adv* immeritō, indignē.

undeserving *adj* indignus.

undesigned *adj* fortuītus.

undesignedly *adv* fortuītō, temerē.

undesirable *adj* odiōsus, ingrātus.

undeterred *adj* immōtus.

undeveloped *adj* immātūrus.

undeviating *adj* dīrēctus.

undigested *adj* crūdus.

undignified *adj* levis, inhonestus.

undiminished *adj* integer.

undiscernible *adj* invīsus, obscūrus.

undisciplined *adj* lascīvus, immoderātus; (MIL) inexercitātus.

undiscovered *adj* ignōtus.

undisguised *adj* apertus.

undisguisedly *adv* palam, apertē.

undismayed *adj* impavidus, intrepidus.

undisputed *adj* certus.

undistinguished *adj* ignōbilis, inglōrius.

undisturbed *adj* tranquillus, placidus.

undo *vt* (*knot*) expedīre, resolvere; (*sewing*) dissuere; (*fig*) īnfectum reddere.

undoing *n* ruīna *f*.

undone *adj* īnfectus; (*ruined*) perditus; **be** ~ perīre, disperīre; **hopelessly** ~ dēperditus.

undoubted *adj* certus.

undoubtedly *adv* sine dubiō, plānē.

undress *vt* exuere, vestem dētrahere (*dat*).

undressed *adj* nūdus.

undue *adj* nimius, immoderātus, inīquus.

undulate *vi* fluctuāre.

undulation *n* spīra *f*.

unduly *adv* nimis, plūs aequō.

undutiful *adj* impius.

undutifully *adv* impiē.

undutifulness *n* impietās *f*.

undying *adj* immortālis, aeternus.

unearth *vt* ēruere, dētegere.

unearthly *adj* mōnstruōsus,

dīvīnus, hūmānō māior.

uneasily adv aegrē.

uneasiness n sollicitūdō f, perturbātiō f.

uneasy adj sollicitus, anxius, inquiētus.

uneducated adj illitterātus, indoctus, rudis; **be ~** litterās nescīre.

unemployed adj ōtiōsus.

unemployment n cessātiō f.

unencumbered adj expedītus, līber.

unending adj perpetuus, sempiternus.

unendowed adj indōtātus.

unendurable adj intolerandus, intolerābilis.

unenjoyable adj iniūcundus, molestus.

unenlightened adj rudis, inērudītus.

unenterprising adj iners.

unenviable adj nōn invidendus.

unequal adj impār, dispār.

unequalled adj ūnicus, singulāris.

unequally adv inaequāliter, iniquē.

unequivocal adj apertus, plānus.

unerring adj certus.

unerringly adv certē.

unessential adj adventīcius, supervacāneus.

uneven adj impār; (surface) asper, inīquus, inaequābilis.

unevenly adv inīquē, inaequāliter.

unevenness n inīquitās f, asperitās f.

unexamined adj (case) incognitus.

unexampled adj inaudītus, ūnicus, singulāris.

unexceptionable adj ēmendātus; (authority) certissimus.

unexpected adj imprōvīsus, inopīnātus, īnsperātus.

unexpectedly adv dē imprōvīsō, ex īnspērātō, inopīnātō, necopīnātō.

unexplored adj inexplōrātus.

unfading adj perennis, vīvus.

unfailing adj perennis, certus, perpetuus.

unfailingly adv semper.

unfair adj inīquus, iniūstus.

unfairly adv inīquē, iniūstē.

unfairness n inīquitās f, iniūstitia f.

unfaithful adj īnfidēlis, īnfīdus, perfidus.

unfaithfully adv īnfidēliter.

unfaithfulness n īnfidēlitās f.

unfamiliar adj novus, ignōtus, īnsolēns; (sight) invīsitātus.

unfamiliarity n īnsolentia f.

unfashionable adj obsolētus.

unfasten vt solvere, refīgere.

unfathomable adj īnfīnītus, profundus.

unfavourable adj inīquus, adversus, importūnus.

unfavourably adv inīquē, male; **be ~ disposed** āversō animō esse.

unfed adj iēiūnus.

unfeeling adj dūrus, crūdēlis, ferreus.

unfeelingly adv crūdēliter.

unfeigned adj sincērus, vērus, simplex.

unfeignedly adv sincērē, vērē.

unfilial adj impius.

unfinished adj īnfectus, imperfectus.

unfit adj inūtilis, incommodus, aliēnus.

unfix vt refīgere.

unflinching adj impavidus, firmus.

unfold vt explicāre, ēvolvere; (story) expōnere, ēnārrāre.

unfolding n explicātiō f.

unforeseen adj imprōvīsus.

unforgettable adj memorābilis.

unforgiving adj implācābilis.

unformed adj īnfōrmis.

unfortified adj immūnītus, nūdus.

unfortunate adj īnfēlīx, īnfortūnātus.

unfortunately adv īnfēlīciter, male; ~ **you did not come** male accidit quod nōn vēnistī.

unfounded adj inānis, vānus.

unfrequented adj dēsertus.

unfriendliness n inimīcitia f.

unfriendly adj inimicus, malevolus; **in an ~ manner** inimīcē.

unfruitful adj sterilis; (fig) inānis, vānus.

unfruitfulness n sterilitās f.

unfulfilled adj īnfectus, inritus.

unfurl vt explicāre, pandere.

unfurnished adj nūdus.

ungainly adj agrestis, rūsticus.

ungallant adj inurbānus, parum cōmis.

ungenerous adj illīberālis; ~ **conduct** illīberālitās f.

ungentlemanly adj illīberālis.

ungirt adj discinctus.

ungodliness n impietās f.

ungodly adj impius.

ungovernable adj impotēns, indomitus.

ungovernableness n impotentia f.

ungraceful adj inconcinnus, inēlegāns.

ungracefully adv inēleganter.

ungracious adj inhūmānus, petulāns, importūnus.

ungraciously adv acerbē.

ungrammatical adj barbarus; **be ~** soloecismum facere.

ungrateful adj ingrātus.

ungrudging adj largus, nōn invītus.

ungrudgingly adv sine invidiā.

unguarded adj intūtus; (word) incautus, incōnsultus.

unguardedly adv temerē, incōnsultē.

unguent n unguentum nt.

unhallowed adj profānus, impius.

unhand vt mittere.

unhandy adj inhabilis.

unhappily adv īnfēlīciter, miserē.

unhappiness n miseria f, tristitia f, maestitia f.

unhappy adj īnfēlix, miser, tristis.

unharmed adj incolumis, integer, salvus.

unharness vt disiungere.

unhealthiness n valētūdō f; (climate) gravitās f.

unhealthy adj invalidus, aeger; (climate) gravis, pestilens.

unheard adj inaudītus; (law) indictā causā.

unheard-of adj inaudītus.

unheeded adj neglectus.

unheeding adj immemor, sēcūrus.

unhelpful adj difficilis, invītus.

unhesitating adj audāx, prōmptus.

unhesitatingly adv sine dubitātiōne.

unhewn adj rudis.

unhindered adj expedītus.

unhinged adj mente captus.

unhistorical adj fictus, commentīcius.

unholiness n impietās f.

unholy adj impius.

unhonoured adj inhonōrātus.

unhoped-for adj īnspērātus.

unhorse vt excutere, equō dēicere.

unhurt adj integer, incolumis.

unicorn n monocerōs m.

uniform adj aequābilis, aequālis ♦ n īnsignia ntpl; (MIL) sagum nt; **in ~** sagātus; **put on ~** saga sūmere.

uniformity n aequābilitās f, cōnstantia f.

uniformly adv aequābiliter, ūnō tenōre.

unify vt coniungere.

unimaginative adj hebes, stolidus.

unimpaired adj integer, incolumis, illībātus.

unimpeachable adj (character) integer; (style) ēmendātus.

unimportant adj levis, nullīus mōmentī.

uninformed *adj* indoctus, ignārus.
uninhabitable *adj* inhabitābilis.
uninhabited *adj* dēsertus.
uninitiated *adj* profānus; (*fig*)
  rudis.
uninjured *adj* integer, incolumis.
unintelligent *adj* īnsipiēns, tardus,
  excors.
unintelligible *adj* obscūrus.
unintelligibly *adv* obscūrē.
unintentionally *adv* imprūdēns,
  temerē.
uninteresting *adj* frīgidus, āridus.
uninterrupted *adj* continuus,
  perpetuus.
uninterruptedly *adv* continenter,
  sine ūllā intermissiōne.
uninvited *adj* invocātus; ~ **guest**
  umbra *f*.
uninviting *adj* iniūcundus,
  invenustus.
union *n* coniūnctiō *f*; (*social*)
  cōnsociātiō *f*, societās *f*; (*POL*)
  foederātae cīvitātēs *fpl*;
  (*agreement*) concordia *f*, cōnsēnsus
  m; (*marriage*) coniugium *nt*.
unique *adj* ūnicus, ēgregius,
  singulāris.
unison *n* concentus *m*; (*fig*)
  concordia *f*, cōnsēnsus *m*.
unit *n* ūniō *f*.
unite *vt* coniungere, cōnsociāre,
  cōpulāre ♦ *vi* coīre; cōnsentīre,
  cōnspīrāre; (*rivers*) cōnfluere.
unity *n* (*concord*) concordia *f*,
  cōnsēnsus *m*.
universal *adj* ūniversus,
  commūnis.
universally *adv* ūniversus, omnis;
  (*place*) ubīque.
universe *n* mundus *m*, rērum
  nātūra *f*.
university *n* acadēmia *f*.
unjust *adj* iniūstus, inīquus.
unjustifiable *adj* indignus,
  inexcūsābilis.
unjustly *adv* iniūstē, iniūriā.

unkempt *adj* horridus.
unkind *adj* inhūmānus, inīquus.
unkindly *adv* inhūmānē, asperē.
unkindness *n* inhūmānitās *f*.
unknowingly *adv* imprūdēns,
  īnscius.
unknown *adj* ignōtus, incognitus;
  (*fame*) obscūrus.
unlawful *adj* vetitus, iniūriōsus.
unlawfully *adv* iniūriōsē, iniūriā.
unlearn *vt* dēdiscere.
unlearned *adj* indoctus,
  inērudītus.
unless *conj* nisī.
unlettered *adj* illitterātus.
unlike *adj* dissimilis (+ *gen or dat*),
  dispār.
unlikely *adj* nōn vērīsimilis.
unlimited *adj* īnfīnītus, immēnsus.
unload *vt* exonerāre, deonerāre;
  (*from ship*) expōnere.
unlock *vt* reserāre, reclūdere.
unlooked-for *adj* īnspērātus,
  inexpectātus.
unloose *vt* solvere, exsolvere.
unlovely *adj* invenustus.
unluckily *adv* īnfēlīciter.
unlucky *adj* īnfēlīx, īnfortūnātus;
  (*day*) āter.
unmake *vt* īnfectum reddere.
unman *vt* mollīre, frangere,
  dēbilitāre.
unmanageable *adj* inhabilis.
unmanly *adj* mollis, ēnervātus,
  muliebris.
unmanneriness *n* importūnitās *f*,
  inhūmānitās *f*.
unmannerly *adj* importūnus,
  inhūmānus.
unmarried *adj* (*man*) caelebs;
  (*woman*) vidua.
unmask *vt* nūdāre, dētegere.
unmatched *adj* ūnicus, singulāris.
unmeaning *adj* inānis.
unmeasured *adj* īnfīnītus,
  immoderātus.
unmeet *adj* parum idōneus.

unmelodious *adj* absonus, absurdus.

unmentionable *adj* īnfandus.

unmentioned *adj* indictus; **leave ~** ōmittere.

unmerciful *adj* immisericors, inclēmēns.

unmercifully *adv* inclēmenter.

unmerited *adj* immeritus, indignus.

unmindful *adj* immemor.

unmistakable *adj* certus, manifestus.

unmistakably *adv* sine dubiō, certē.

unmitigated *adj* merus.

unmixed *adj* pūrus.

unmolested *adj* intāctus.

unmoor *vt* solvere.

unmoved *adj* immōtus.

unmusical *adj* absonus, absurdus.

unmutilated *adj* integer.

unnatural *adj* (event) mōnstruōsus; (feelings) impius, inhūmānus; (style) arcessītus, pūtidus.

unnaturally *adv* contrā nātūram; impiē, inhūmānē; pūtidē.

unnavigable *adj* innāvigābilis.

unnecessarily *adv* nimis.

unnecessary *adj* inūtilis, supervacāneus.

unnerve *vt* dēbilitāre, frangere.

unnoticed *adj*: **be ~** latēre, fallere.

unnumbered *adj* innumerus.

unobjectionable *adj* honestus, culpae expers.

unobservant *adj* tardus.

unobserved *adj*: **be ~** latēre, fallere.

unobstructed *adj* apertus, pūrus.

unobtrusive *adj* verēcundus; **be ~** fallere.

unobtrusiveness *n* verēcundia *f*.

unoccupied *adj* vacuus, ōtiōsus.

unoffending *adj* innocēns.

unofficial *adj* prīvātus.

unorthodox *adj* abnōrmis.

unostentatious *adj* modestus, verēcundus.

unostentatiously *adv* nullā iactātiōne.

unpaid *adj* (services) grātuītus; (money) dēbitus.

unpalatable *adj* amārus; (fig) iniūcundus, īnsuāvis.

unparalleled *adj* ūnicus, inaudītus.

unpardonable *adj* inexcūsābilis.

unpatriotic *adj* impius.

unpitying *adj* immisericors, ferreus.

unpleasant *adj* iniūcundus, ingrātus, īnsuāvis, gravis, molestus.

unpleasantly *adv* iniūcundē, ingrātē, graviter.

unpleasantness *n* iniūcunditās *f*, molestia *f*.

unpleasing *adj* ingrātus, invenustus.

unploughed *adj* inarātus.

unpoetical *adj* pedester.

unpolished *adj* impolītus; (person) incultus, agrestis, inurbānus; (style) incondītus, rudis.

unpopular *adj* invidiōsus, invīsus.

unpopularity *n* invidia *f*, odium *nt*.

unpractised *adj* inexercitātus, imperītus.

unprecedented *adj* īnsolēns, novus, inaudītus.

unprejudiced *adj* integer, aequus.

unpremeditated *adj* repentīnus, subitus.

unprepared *adj* imparātus.

unprepossessing *adj* invenustus, illepidus.

unpretentious *adj* modestus, verēcundus.

unprincipled *adj* improbus, levis, prāvus.

unproductive *adj* īnfēcundus, sterilis.

unprofitable *adj* inūtilis, vānus.

unprofitably *adv* frustrā, ab rē.

unpropitious adj īnfēlīx, adversus.

unpropitiously adv malīs ōminibus.

unprotected adj indēfēnsus, intūtus, nūdus.

unprovoked adj ultrō (adv).

unpunished adj impūnītus ♦ adv impūne.

unqualified adj nōn idōneus; (unrestricted) absolūtus.

unquestionable adj certus.

unquestionably adv facile, certē.

unquestioning adj crēdulus.

unravel vt retexere; (fig) ēnōdāre, explicāre.

unready adj imparātus.

unreal adj falsus, vānus.

unreality n vānitās f.

unreasonable adj inīquus, importūnus.

unreasonableness n inīquitās f.

unreasonably adv inīquē.

unreasoning adj stolidus, temerārius.

unreclaimed adj (land) incultus.

unrefined adj impolītus, inurbānus, rudis.

unregistered adj incēnsus.

unrelated adj aliēnus.

unrelenting adj implācābilis, inexōrābilis.

unreliable adj incertus, levis.

unreliably adv leviter.

unrelieved adj perpetuus, adsiduus.

unremitting adj adsiduus.

unrequited adj inultus, inānis.

unreservedly adv apertē, sine ullā exceptiōne.

unresponsive adj hebes.

unrest n inquiēs f, sollicitūdō f.

unrestrained adj līber, impotēns, effrēnātus, immoderātus.

unrestricted adj līber, absolūtus.

unrevenged adj inultus.

unrewarded adj inhonōrātus.

unrewarding adj ingrātus, vānus.

unrighteous adj iniūstus, impius.

unrighteously adv iniūstē, impiē.

unrighteousness n impietās f.

unripe adj immātūrus, crūdus.

unrivalled adj ēgregius, singulāris, ūnicus.

unroll vt ēvolvere, explicāre.

unromantic adj pedester.

unruffled adj immōtus, tranquillus.

unruliness n licentia f, impotentia f.

unruly adj effrēnātus, impotēns, immoderātus.

unsafe adj perīculōsus, dubius; (structure) īnstābilis.

unsaid adj indictus.

unsatisfactorily adv nōn ex sententiā, male.

unsatisfactory adj parum idōneus, malus.

unsatisfied adj parum contentus.

unsavoury adj īnsuāvis, taeter.

unscathed adj incolumis, integer.

unschooled adj indoctus, inērudītus.

unscrupulous adj improbus, impudēns.

unscrupulously adv improbē, impudenter.

unscrupulousness n improbitās f, impudentia f.

unseal vt resignāre, solvere.

unseasonable adj intempestīvus, importūnus.

unseasonableness n incommoditās f.

unseasonably adv intempestīvē, importūnē.

unseasoned adj (food) nōn condītus; (wood) viridis.

unseat vt (rider) excutere.

unseaworthy adj īnfīrmus.

unseeing adj caecus.

unseemly adj indecōrus.

unseen adj invīsus; (ever before) invīsitātus.

unselfish adj innocēns, probus,

līberālis.
unselfishly adv līberāliter.
unselfishness n innocentia f,
līberālitās f.
unserviceable adj inūtilis.
unsettle vt ad incertum revocāre,
turbāre, sollicitāre.
unsettled adj incertus, dubius;
(mind) sollicitus, suspēnsus;
(times) turbidus.
unsew vt dissuere.
unshackle vt expedīre, solvere.
unshaken adj immōtus, firmus,
stabilis.
unshapely adj dēfōrmis.
unshaven adj intōnsus.
unsheathe vt dēstringere,
stringere.
unshod adj nūdis pedibus.
unshorn adj intōnsus.
unsightliness n dēfōrmitās f,
turpitūdō f.
unsightly adj foedus, dēfōrmis.
unskilful adj indoctus, īnscītus,
incallidus.
unskilfully adv indoctē, īnscītē,
incallidē.
unskilfulness n īnscītia f,
imperītia f.
unskilled adj imperītus, indoctus;
~ **in** imperītus (+ gen).
unslaked adj (lime) vīvus; (thirst)
inexplētus.
unsociable adj īnsociābilis,
difficilis.
unsoiled adj integer, pūrus.
unsolicited adj voluntārius ♦ adv
ultrō.
unsophisticated adj simplex,
ingenuus.
unsound adj īnfirmus; (mind)
īnsānus; (opinion) falsus,
perversus.
unsoundness n īnfirmitās f;
īnsānitās f; prāvitās f.
unsparing adj inclēmēns,
immisericors; (lavish) prōdigus.

unsparingly adv inclēmenter;
prōdigē.
unspeakable adj īnfandus,
incrēdibilis.
unspeakably adv incrēdibiliter.
unspoilt adj integer.
unspoken adj indictus, tacitus.
unspotted adj integer, pūrus.
unstable adj īnstabilis; (fig)
incōnstāns, levis.
unstained adj pūrus, incorruptus,
integer.
unstatesmanlike adj illīberālis.
unsteadily adv incōnstanter; **walk**
~ titubāre.
unsteadiness n (fig) incōnstantia f.
unsteady adj īnstabilis; (fig)
incōnstāns.
unstitch vt dissuere.
unstring vt retendere.
unstudied adj simplex.
unsubdued adj invictus.
unsubstantial adj levis, inānis.
unsuccessful adj īnfēlīx; (effort)
irritus; **be** ~ offendere; **I am** ~
mihī nōn succēdit.
unsuccessfully adv īnfēlīciter, rē
īnfectā.
unsuitable adj incommodus,
aliēnus, importūnus; **it is** ~
dēdecet.
unsuitableness n incommoditās f.
unsuitably adv incommodē,
ineptē.
unsuited adj parum idōneus.
unsullied adj pūrus, incorruptus.
unsure adj incertus, dubius.
unsurpassable adj
inexsuperābilis.
unsurpassed adj ūnicus,
singulāris.
unsuspected adj latēns, nōn
suspectus; **be** ~ latēre, in
suspiciōnem nōn venīre.
unsuspecting adj imprōvidus,
imprūdēns.
unsuspicious adj nōn suspicāx,

crēdulus.
unswerving *adj* cōnstāns.
unsworn *adj* iniūrātus.
unsymmetrical *adj* inaequālis.
untainted *adj* incorruptus, integer.
untamable *adj* indomitus.
untamed *adj* indomitus, ferus.
untaught *adj* indoctus, rudis.
unteach *vt* dēdocēre.
unteachable *adj* indocilis.
untenable *adj* inānis, īnfirmus.
unthankful *adj* ingrātus.
unthankfully *adv* ingrātē.
unthankfulness *n* ingrātus animus *m*.
unthinkable *adj* incrēdibilis.
unthinking *adj* incōnsīderātus, imprōvisus.
unthriftily *adv* prōdigē.
unthrifty *adj* prōdigus, profūsus.
untidily *adv* neglegenter.
untidiness *n* neglegentia *f*.
untidy *adj* neglegēns, inconcinnus, squālidus.
untie *vt* solvere.
until *conj* dum, dōnec ♦ *prep* usque ad (*acc*), in (*acc*); ~ **now** adhūc.
untilled *adj* incultus.
untimely *adj* intempestīvus, immātūrus, importūnus.
untiring *adj* impiger; (*effort*) adsiduus.
unto *prep* ad (*acc*), in (*acc*).
untold *adj* innumerus.
untouched *adj* intāctus, integer.
untoward *adj* adversus, malus.
untrained *adj* inexercitātus, imperītus, rudis.
untried *adj* intemptātus, inexpertus; (*trial*) incognitus.
untrodden *adj* āvius.
untroubled *adj* tranquillus, placidus, quiētus; (*mind*) sēcūrus.
untrue *adj* falsus, fictus; (*disloyal*) īnfīdus, īnfidēlis.
untrustworthy *adj* īnfīdus, mōbilis.

untruth *n* mendācium *nt*, falsum *nt*.
untruthful *adj* mendāx, falsus.
untruthfully *adv* falsō, falsē.
untuneful *adj* absonus.
unturned *adj*: **leave no stone ~** nihil intemptātum relinquere, omnia experīrī.
untutored *adj* indoctus, incultus.
unused *adj* (*person*) īnsuētus, īnsolitus; (*thing*) integer.
unusual *adj* īnsolitus, inūsitātus, īnsolēns, novus.
unusually *adv* īnsolenter, praeter cōnsuētūdinem.
unusualness *n* īnsolentia *f*, novitās *f*.
unutterable *adj* īnfandus, inēnārrābilis.
unvarnished *adj* (*fig*) simplex, nūdus.
unveil *vt* (*fig*) aperīre, patefacere.
unversed *adj* ignārus (*gen*), imperītus (*gen*).
unwanted *adj* supervacāneus.
unwarily *adv* imprūdenter, incautē, incōnsultē.
unwariness *n* imprūdentia *f*.
unwarlike *adj* imbellis.
unwarrantable *adj* inīquus, iniūstus.
unwarrantably *adv* iniūriā.
unwary *adj* imprūdēns, incautus, incōnsultus.
unwavering *adj* stabilis, immōtus.
unwearied, unwearying *adj* indēfessus, adsiduus.
unweave *vt* retexere.
unwedded *adj* (*man*) caelebs; (*woman*) vidua.
unwelcome *adj* ingrātus.
unwell *adj* aeger, aegrōtus.
unwept *adj* indēflētus.
unwholesome *adj* pestilēns, gravis.
unwieldy *adj* inhabilis.
unwilling *adj* invītus; **be ~** nolle.

unwillingly *adv* invītus.

unwind *vt* ēvolvere, retexere.

unwise *adj* stultus, īnsipiēns, imprūdēns.

unwisely *adv* īnsipienter, imprūdenter.

unwittingly *adv* imprūdēns, īnsciēns.

unwonted *adj* īnsolitus, inūsitātus.

unworthily *adv* indignē.

unworthiness *n* indignitās *f*.

unworthy *adj* indignus (+ *abl*).

unwounded *adj* intāctus, integer.

unwrap *vt* ēvolvere, explicāre.

unwritten *adj* nōn scrīptus; ~ **law** mōs *m*.

unwrought *adj* īnfectus, rudis.

unyielding *adj* dūrus, firmus, inexōrābilis.

unyoke *vt* disiungere.

up *adv* sūrsum; ~ **and down** sūrsum deōrsum; ~ **to** usque ad (*acc*), tenus (*abl*, *after noun*); **bring** ~ (*child*) ēducāre; **climb** ~ ēscendere, **come** ~ **to** aequāre; **lift** ~ ērigere, sublevāre; **from childhood** ~ ā puerō; **it is all** ~ **with** āctum est dē; **well** ~ **in** gnārus (*gen*), perītus (*gen*); **what is he** ~ **to?** quid struit? ♦ *prep* (*motion*) in (*acc*) ♦ *n*: ~**s and downs** (*fig*) vicissitūdinēs *fpl*.

upbraid *vt* exprobrāre (*dat pers*, *acc charge*); obicere (*dat and acc*), increpāre, castīgāre.

upbringing *n* ēducātiō *f*.

upheaval *n* ēversiō *f*.

upheave *vt* ēvertere.

uphill *adj* acclīvis ♦ *adv* adversō colle, in adversum collem.

uphold *vt* sustinēre, tuērī, servāre.

upholstery *n* supellex *f*.

upkeep *n* impēnsa *f*.

upland *adj* montānus.

uplift *vt* extollere, sublevāre.

upon *prep* in (*abl*), super (*abl*); (*motion*) in (*acc*), super (*acc*);

(*dependence*) ex (*abl*); ~ **this** quō factō.

upper *adj* superior; **gain the** ~ **hand** superāre, vincere.

uppermost *adj* suprēmus, summus.

uppish *adj* superbus.

upright *adj* rēctus, ērēctus; (*character*) integer, probus, honestus.

uprightly *adv* rēctē; integrē.

uprightness *n* integritās *f*.

upriver *adj*, *adv* adversō flūmine.

uproar *n* tumultus *m*; clāmor *m*.

uproarious *adj* tumultuōsus.

uproariously *adv* tumultuōsē.

uproot *vt* ērādīcāre, exstirpāre, ēruere.

upset *vt* ēvertere, invertere, subvertere; ~ **the apple cart** plaustrum percellere ♦ *adj* (*fig*) perturbātus.

upshot *n* ēventus *m*.

upside-down *adv*: **turn** ~ ēvertere, invertere; (*fig*) miscēre.

upstart *n* novus homō *m* ♦ *adj* repentīnus.

upstream *adj*, *adv* adversō flūmine.

upward(s) *adv* sūrsum; ~ **of** (*number*) amplius.

urban *adj* urbānus, oppidānus.

urbane *adj* urbānus, cōmis.

urbanely *adv* urbānē, cōmiter.

urbanity *n* urbānitās *f*.

urchin *n* (*boy*) puerulus *m*; (*animal*) ēchīnus *m*.

urge *vt* urgēre, impellere; (*speech*) hortārī, incitāre; (*advice*) suādēre; (*request*) sollicitāre; ~ **on** incitāre ♦ *n* impulsus *m*; dēsīderium *nt*.

urgency *n* necessitās *f*.

urgent *adj* praesēns, gravis; **be** ~ īnstāre.

urgently *adv* graviter.

urn *n* urna *f*.

usage *n* mōs *m*, īnstitūtum *nt*, ūsus *m*.

use *n* ūsus *m*; (*custom*) mōs *m*,
cōnsuētūdō *f*; **be of ~** ūsuī esse,
prōdesse, condūcere; **out of ~**
dēsuētus; **go out of ~** exolēscere;
in common ~ ūsitātus; **it's no ~**
agis, nīl agimus ♦ *vt* ūtī (*abl*);
(*improperly*) abūtī; (*for a purpose*)
adhibēre; (*word*) ūsurpāre; **~ up**
cōnsūmere, exhaurīre; **~d to**
adsuētus (*dat*); solēre (+ *infin*); **I ~d**
to do faciēbam.
useful *adj* ūtilis; **be ~** ūsuī esse.
usefully *adv* ūtiliter.
usefulness *n* ūtilitās *f*.
useless *adj* inūtilis; (*thing*) inānis,
inritus; **be ~** nihil valēre.
uselessly *adv* inūtiliter, frustrā.
uselessness *n* inānitās *f*.
usher *n* (*court*) appāritor *m*;
(*theatre*) dēsignātor *m* ♦ *vt*: **~ in**
indūcere, intrōdūcere.
usual *adj* ūsitātus, solitus; **as ~** ut
adsolet, ut fert cōnsuētūdō, ex
cōnsuētūdine; **out of the ~**
īnsolitus, extrā ōrdinem.
usually *adv* ferē, plērumque; **he ~**
comes venīre solet.
usufruct *n* ūsus et frūctus *m*.
usurer *n* faenerātor *m*.
usurp *vt* occupāre, invādere in
(*acc*), ūsurpāre.
usurpation *n* occupātiō *f*.
usury *n* faenerātiō *f*, ūsūra *f*;
practise ~ faenerārī.
utensil *n* īnstrūmentum *nt*, vās *nt*.
utility *n* ūtilitās *f*, commodum *nt*.
utilize *vt* ūtī (*abl*); (*for a purpose*)
adhibēre.
utmost *adj* extrēmus, summus; **at**
the ~ summum; **do one's ~**
omnibus vīribus contendere.
utter *adj* tōtus, extrēmus, summus
♦ *vt* ēmittere, ēdere, ēloquī,
prōnūntiāre.
utterance *n* dictum *nt*; (*process*)
prōnūntiātiō *f*.
utterly *adv* funditus, omnīnō,

penitus.
uttermost *adj* extrēmus, ultimus.

V

vacancy *n* inānitās *f*; (*office*)
vacuitās *f*; **there is a ~** locus
vacat; **elect to fill a ~** sufficere.
vacant *adj* inānis, vacuus; **be ~**
vacāre.
vacate *vt* vacuum facere.
vacation *n* fēriae *fpl*.
vacillate *vi* vacillāre, dubitāre.
vacillation *n* dubitātiō *f*.
vacuity *n* inānitās *f*.
vacuous *adj* vacuus.
vacuum *n* ināne *nt*.
vagabond *n* grassātor *m* ♦ *adj*
vagus.
vagary *n* libīdō *f*.
vagrancy *n* errātiō *f*.
vagrant *n* grassātor *m*, vagus *m*.
vague *adj* incertus, dubius.
vaguely *adv* incertē.
vain *adj* vānus, inānis, inritus;
(*person*) glōriōsus; **in ~** frustrā.
vainglorious *adj* glōriōsus.
vainglory *n* glōria *f*, iactantia *f*.
vainly *adv* frustrā, nēquīquam.
vale *n* vallis *f*.
valet *n* cubiculārius *m*.
valiant *adj* fortis, ācer.
valiantly *adv* fortiter, ācriter.
valid *adj* ratus; (*argument*) gravis,
firmus.
validity *n* vīs *f*, auctōritās *f*.
valley *n* vallis *f*.
valorous *adj* fortis.
valour *n* virtūs *f*.
valuable *adj* pretiōsus.
valuation *n* aestimātiō *f*.
value *n* pretium *nt*; (*fig*) vīs *f*, honor
m ♦ *vt* aestimāre; (*esteem*) dīligere; **~ highly** māgnī aestimāre; **~**
little parvī aestimāre, parvī
facere.
valueless *adj* vīlis, minimī pretī.

valuer n aestimātor m.

van n (in battle) prīma aciēs f; (on march) prīmum agmen nt.

vanguard n prīmum agmen nt.

vanish vi diffugere, ēvānēscere, dīlābī.

vanity n (unreality) vānitās f; (conceit) glōria f.

vanquish vt vincere, superāre, dēvincere.

vanquisher n victor m.

vantage n (ground) locus superior m.

vapid adj vapidus, īnsulsus.

vapidly adv īnsulsē.

vaporous adj nebulōsus.

vapour n vapor m, nebula f; (from earth) exhālātiō f.

variable adj varius, mūtābilis.

variableness n mūtābilitās f, incōnstantia f.

variance n discordia f, dissēnsiō f, discrepantia f; **at ~** discors; **be at ~** dissidēre, inter sē discrepāre; **set at ~** aliēnāre.

variant adj varius.

variation n varietās f, vicissitūdō f.

variegate vt variāre.

variegated adj varius.

variety n varietās f; (number) multitūdō f; (kind) genus nt; **a ~ of** dīversī.

various adj varius, dīversus.

variously adv variē.

varlet n verberō m.

varnish n pigmentum nt; (fig) fūcus m.

varnished adj (fig) fūcātus.

vary vt variāre, mūtāre; (decorate) distinguere ♦ vi mūtārī.

vase n vās nt.

vassal n ambāctus m; (fig) cliēns m.

vast adj vastus, immānis, ingēns, immēnsus.

vastly adv valdē.

vastness n māgnitūdō f,

immēnsitās f.

vat n cūpa f.

vault n (ARCH) fornix f; (jump) saltus m ♦ vi salīre.

vaulted adj fornicātus.

vaunt vt iactāre, ostentāre ♦ vi sē iactāre, glōriārī.

vaunting n ostentātiō f, glōria f ♦ adj glōriōsus.

veal n vitulīna f.

vedette n excursor m.

veer vi sē vertere, flectī.

vegetable n holus nt.

vehemence n vīs f, violentia f; (passion) ārdor m, impetus m.

vehement adj vehemēns, violentus, ācer.

vehemently adv vehementer, ācriter.

vehicle n vehiculum nt.

Veii n Veiī, Veiōrum mpl.

veil n rīca f; (bridal) flammeum nt; (fig) integumentum nt ♦ vt vēlāre, tegere.

vein n vēna f.

vellum n membrāna f.

velocity n celeritās f, vēlōcitās f.

venal adj vēnālis.

vend vt vēndere.

vendetta n simultās f.

vendor n caupō m.

veneer n (fig) speciēs f, fūcus m.

venerable adj gravis, augustus.

venerate vt colere, venerārī.

veneration n venerātiō f, cultus m.

venerator n cultor m.

vengeance n ultiō f, poena f; **take ~ on** ulcīscī, vindicāre in (acc); **take ~ for** ulcīscī, vindicāre.

vengeful adj ultor.

venial adj ignōscendus.

venison n dāma f, ferīna f.

venom n venēnum nt; (fig) vīrus nt.

venomous adj venēnātus.

vent n spīrāculum nt; (outlet) exitus m; **give ~ to** profundere, ēmittere; **emittere** (feelings _on_) profundere in (_acc_), ērumpere in (_acc_).

ventilate _vt_ perflāre; (_opinion_) in medium prōferre, vulgāre.

ventilation _n_ perflāre.

venture _n_ perīculum _nt_; (_gamble_) ālea _f_; **at a ~** temerē ♦ _vi_ audēre ♦ _vt_ perīclitārī, in āleam dare.

venturesome _adj_ audāx, temerārius.

venturesomeness _n_ audācia _f_, temeritās _f_.

veracious _adj_ vērāx, vēridicus.

veracity _n_ vēritās _f_, fidēs _f_.

verb _n_ verbum _nt_.

verbally _adv_ per colloquia; (_translate_) ad verbum, verbum prō verbo.

verbatim _adv_ ad verbum, totidem verbīs.

verbiage _n_ verba _ntpl_.

verbose _adj_ verbōsus.

verbosity _n_ loquendī prōfluentia _f_.

verdant _adj_ viridis.

verdict _n_ sententia _f_, iūdicium _nt_; **deliver a ~** sententiam prōnūntiāre; **give a ~ in favour of** causam adiūdicāre (_dat_).

verdigris _n_ aerūgō _f_.

verdure _n_ viriditās _f_.

verge _n_ ōra _f_; **the ~ of** extrēmus; **on the ~ of** (_fig_) prope (_acc_) ♦ _vi_ vergere.

verification _n_ cōnfirmātiō _f_.

verify _vt_ cōnfirmāre, comprobāre.

verily _adv_ profectō, certē.

verisimilitude _n_ vērī similitūdō _f_.

veritable _adj_ vērus.

veritably _adv_ vērē.

verity _n_ vēritās _f_.

vermilion _n_ sandīx _f_.

vermin _n_ bestiolae _fpl_.

vernacular _adj_ patrius ♦ _n_ patrius sermō _m_.

vernal _adj_ vērnus.

versatile _adj_ versūtus, varius.

versatility _n_ versātile ingenium _nt_.

verse _n_ (_line_) versus _m_; (_poetry_) versus _mpl_, carmina _ntpl_.

versed _adj_ īnstructus, perītus, exercitātus.

versification _n_ ars versūs faciendī.

versify _vt_ versū inclūdere ♦ _vi_ versūs facere.

version _n_ (_of story_) fōrma _f_; **give a Latin ~ of** Latīnē reddere.

vertex _n_ vertex _m_, fastīgium _nt_.

vertical _adj_ rēctus, dīrēctus.

vertically _adv_ ad līneam, rēctā līneā, ad perpendiculum.

vertigo _n_ vertīgō _f_.

vervain _n_ verbēna _f_.

verve _n_ ācrimōnia _f_.

very _adj_ ipse ♦ _adv_ admodum, valdē, vehementer ♦ _superl_: **at that ~ moment** tum māximē; **not ~** nōn ita.

vessel _n_ (_receptacle_) vās _nt_; (_ship_) nāvigium _nt_.

vest _n_ subūcula _f_ ♦ _vt_: **~ power in** imperium dēferre (_dat_); **~ed interests** nummī locātī _mpl_.

vestal _adj_ vestālis ♦ _n_ virgō vestālis _f_.

vestibule _n_ vestibulum _nt_.

vestige _n_ vestīgium _nt_, indicium _nt_.

vestment _n_ vestīmentum _nt_.

vesture _n_ vestis _f_.

vetch _n_ vicia _f_.

veteran _adj_ veterānus ♦ _n_ (MIL) veterānus _m_; (_fig_) veterātor _m_.

veto _n_ interdictum _nt_; (_tribune's_) intercessiō _f_ ♦ _vt_ interdīcere (_dat_); (_tribune_) intercēdere (_dat_).

vex _vt_ vexāre, sollicitāre, stomachum movēre (_dat_); **be ~ed** aegrē ferre, stomachārī.

vexation _n_ (_caused_) molestia _f_; (_felt_) dolor _m_, stomachus _m_.

vexatious _adj_ odiōsus, molestus.

vexatiously _adv_ molestē.

vexed _adj_ īrātus; (_question_) anceps.

via _prep per_ (_acc_).

viaduct _n_ pōns _m_.

viands n cibus m.

vibrate vi vibrāre, tremere.

vibration n tremor m.

vicarious adj vicārius.

vice n (general) prāvitās f, perditī mōrēs mpl; (particular) vitium nt, flāgitium nt; (clamp) fībula f.

viceroy n prōcūrātor m.

vicinity n vīcīnia f, vīcīnitās f.

vioious adj prāvus, vitiōsus, flāgitiōsus; (temper) contumāx.

viciously adv flāgitiōsē; contumāciter.

vicissitude n vicissitūdō f; **~s** pl vicēs fpl.

victim n victima f, hostia f; (fig) piāculum nt; (exploited) praeda f; **be the ~ of** labōrāre ex; **fall a ~ to** morī (abl); (trickery) circumvenīrī (abl).

victimize vt nocēre (dat), circumvenīre.

victor n victor m.

victorious adj victor, victrīx f; **be ~** vincere.

victory n victōria f; **win a ~** victōriam reportāre; **win a ~ over** vincere, superāre.

victory message n laureātae litterae fpl.

victory parade n triumphus m.

victual vt rem frūmentāriam suppeditāre (dat).

victualler n caupō m; (MIL) frūmentārius m.

victuals n cibus m; (MIL) frūmentum nt, commeātus m.

vie vi certāre, contendere; **~ with** aemulārī.

view n cōnspectus m; (from far) prōspectus m; (from high) dēspectus m; (opinion) sententia f; **exposed to ~** in mediō; **entertain a ~** sentīre; **in ~ of** propter (acc); **in my ~** meā sententiā, meō iūdiciō; **end in ~** prōpositum m; **have in ~** spectāre; **point of ~** iūdicium nt;

with a ~ to eō cōnsiliō ut ♦ vt īnspicere, spectāre, intuērī.

vigil n pervigilium nt; **keep a ~** vigilāre.

vigilance n vigilantia f, dīligentia f.

vigilant adj vigilāns, dīligēns.

vigilantly adv vigilanter, dīligenter.

vigorous adj ācer, vegetus, integer; (style) nervōsus.

vigorously adv ācriter, strēnuē.

vigour n vīs f, nervī mpl, integritās f.

vile adj turpis, impūrus, abiectus.

vilely adv turpiter, impūrē.

vileness n turpitūdō f, impūritās f.

vilification n obtrectātiō f, calumnia f.

vilify vt obtrectāre, calumniārī, maledīcere (dat).

villa n vīlla f.

village n pāgus m, vīcus m; **in every ~** pāgātim.

villager n pāgānus m, vīcānus m.

villain n furcifer m, scelerātus m.

villainous adj scelestus, scelerātus, nēquam.

villainously adv scelestē.

villainy n scelus nt, nēquitia f.

vindicate vt (right) vindicāre; (action) pūrgāre; (belief) arguere; (person) dēfendere, prōpugnāre prō (abl).

vindication n dēfēnsiō f, pūrgātiō f.

vindicator n dēfēnsor m, prōpugnātor m.

vindictive adj ultor, ulcīscendī cupidus.

vine n vītis f; **wild ~** labrusca f.

vinedresser n vīnitor m.

vinegar n acētum nt.

vineyard n vīnea f, vīnētum nt.

vintage n vindēmia f.

vintner n vīnārius m.

violate vt violāre.

violation n violātiō f.

violator n violātor m.

violence n violentia f, vīs f, iniūria f; **do ~ to** violāre; **offer ~ to** vim īnferre (dat).

violent adj violentus, vehemēns; (passion) ācer, impotēns; **~ death** nex f.

violently adv vehementer, per vim.

violet n viola f.

viper n vīpera f.

viperous adj (fig) malignus.

virgin n virgō f ♦ adj virginālis.

virginity n virginitās f.

virile adj virīlis.

virility n virtūs f.

virtually adv rē vērā, ferē.

virtue n virtūs f, honestum nt; (woman's) pudīcitia f; (power) vīs f, potestās f; **by ~ of** ex (abl).

virtuous adj honestus, probus, integer.

virtuously adv honestē.

virulence n vīs f, vīrus nt.

virulent adj acerbus.

virus n vīrus nt.

visage n ōs n, faciēs f.

vis-à-vis prep exadversus (acc).

viscosity n lentor m.

viscous adj lentus, tenāx.

visible adj ēvidēns, cōnspicuus, manifestus; **be ~** appārēre.

visibly adv manifestō.

vision n (sense) vīsus m; (power) aspectus m; (apparition) vīsum nt, vīsiō f; (whim) somnium nt.

visionary adj vānus ♦ n somniāns m.

visit n adventus m; (formal) salūtātiō f; (long) commorātiō f; **pay a ~ to** invīsere ♦ vt vīsere; **~ occasionally** intervīsere; **go to ~** invīsere.

visitation n (to inspect) recēnsiō f; (to punish) animadversiō f.

visitor n hospes m, hospita f; (formal) salūtātor m.

visor n buccula f.

vista n prōspectus m.

visual adj oculōrum.

visualize vt animō cernere, ante oculōs pōnere.

visually adv oculīs.

vital adj (of life) vītālis; (essential) necessārius, māximī mōmentī.

vitality n vīs f; (style) sanguis m.

vitally adv praecipuē, imprīmīs.

vitals n viscera ntpl.

vitiate vt corrumpere, vitiāre.

vitreous adj vitreus.

vitrify vt in vitrum excoquere.

vituperate vt vituperāre, obiūrgāre.

vituperation n vituperātiō f, maledicta ntpl.

vituperative adj maledicus.

vivacious adj alacer, vegetus, hilaris.

vivaciously adv hilare.

vivacity n alacritās f, hilaritās f.

vivid adj vīvidus, ācer.

vividly adv ācriter.

vivify vt animāre.

vixen n vulpēs f.

vocabulary n verbōrum cōpia f.

vocal adj: **~ music** vōcis cantus m.

vocation n officium nt, mūnus nt.

vociferate vt, vi vōciferārī, clāmāre.

vociferation n vōciferātiō f, clāmor m.

vociferous adj vōciferāns.

vociferously adv māgnīs clāmōribus.

vogue n mōs m; **be in ~** flōrēre, in honōre esse.

voice n vōx f ♦ vt exprimere, ēloquī.

void adj inānis, vacuus; **~ of** expers (gen); **null and ~** inritus ♦ n ināne nt ♦ vt ēvomere, ēmittere.

volatile adj levis, mōbilis.

volatility n levitās f.

volition n voluntās f.

volley n imber m.

volubility n volūbilitās f.

voluble adj volūbilis.

volume n (book) liber m; (mass) mōlēs f; (of sound) māgnitūdō f.

voluminous adj cōpiōsus.

voluntarily adv ultrō, suā sponte.

voluntary adj voluntārius; (unpaid) grātuītus.

volunteer n (MIL) ēvocātus m ♦ vt ultrō offerre ♦ vi (MIL) nōmen dare.

voluptuary n dēlicātus m, homō voluptārius m.

voluptuous adj voluptārius, mollis, dēlicātus, luxuriōsus.

voluptuously adv molliter, dēlicātē, luxuriōsē.

voluptuousness n luxuria f, libīdō f.

vomit vt vomere, ēvomere; ~ **up** ēvomere.

voracious adj vorāx, edāx.

voraciously adv avidē.

voracity n edācitās f, gula f.

vortex n vertex m, turbō m.

votary n cultor m.

vote n suffrāgium nt; (opinion) sententia f; ~ **for** (candidate) suffrāgārī (dat); (senator's motion) discēdere in sententiam (gen) ♦ vi (election) suffrāgium ferre; (judge) sententiam ferre; (senator) cēnsēre; **take a ~** (senate) discessiōnem facere ♦ vt (senate) dēcernere; ~ **against** (bill) antīquāre.

voter n suffrāgātor m.

votive adj vōtīvus.

vouch vi spondēre; ~ **for** prae-stāre, testificārī.

voucher n (person) auctor m; (document) auctōritās f.

vouchsafe vt concēdere.

vow n vōtum nt; (promise) fidēs f ♦ vt vovēre; (promise) spondēre.

vowel n vōcālis f.

voyage n nāvigātiō f, cursus m

♦ vi nāvigāre.

vulgar adj (common) vulgāris; (low) plēbēius, sordidus, īnsulsus.

vulgarity n sordēs fpl, īnsulsitās f.

vulgarly adv vulgō; īnsulsē.

vulnerable adj nūdus; (fig) obnoxius; **be ~** vulnerārī posse.

vulture n vultur m; (fig) vulturius m.

W

wad n massa f.

wade vi per vada īre; ~ **across** vadō trānsīre.

waft vt ferre, vehere.

wag n facētus homō m, ioculātor m ♦ vt movēre, mōtāre, agitāre ♦ vi movērī, agitārī.

wage n mercēs f; (pl) mercēs f, manūpretium nt; (fig) pretium nt, praemium nt ♦ vt gerere; ~ **war on** bellum īnferre (dat)/gerere.

wager n spōnsiō f ♦ vi spōnsiōnem facere ♦ vt dēpōnere, oppōnere.

waggery n facētiae fpl.

waggish adj facētus, rīdiculus.

waggle vt agitāre, mōtāre.

wagon n plaustrum nt, carrus m.

waif n inops m/f.

wail n ēiulātus m ♦ vi ēiulāre, dēplōrāre, lāmentārī.

wailing n plōrātus m, lāmentātiō f.

waist n medium corpus nt; **hold by the ~** medium tenēre.

wait n: **have a long ~** diū exspectāre; **lie in ~** īnsidiārī ♦ vi manēre, opperīrī, exspectāre; ~ **for** exspectāre; ~ **upon** (accompany) adsectārī, dēdūcere; (serve) famulārī (dat); (visit) salūtāre.

waiter n famulus m, minister m.

waive vt dēpōnere, remittere.

wake vt excitāre, suscitāre ♦ vi expergīscī.

wake n vestīgia ntpl; **in the ~** pōne,

ā tergō; **follow in the ~ of** vestīgiīs
īnstāre (*gen*).
wakeful *adj* vigil.
wakefulness *n* vigilantia *f*.
waken *vt* excitāre ♦ *vi* expergīscī.
walk *n* (*act*) ambulātiō *f*,
deambulātiō *f*; (*gait*) incessus *m*;
(*place*) ambulātiō *f*, xystus *m*; **~ of
life** status *m*; **go for a ~** spatiārī,
deambulāre ♦ *vi* ambulāre, īre,
gradī; (*with dignity*) incēdere; **~
about** inambulāre; **~ out** ēgredī.
wall *n* mūrus *m*; (*indoors*) pariēs
m; (*afield*) māceria *f*; **~s** *pl* (*of
town*) moenia *ntpl* ♦ *vt* mūnīre,
saepīre; **~ up** inaedificāre.
wallet *n* pēra *f*.
wallow *vi* volūtārī.
walnut *n* iūglāns *f*.
wan *adj* pallidus.
wand *n* virga *f*.
wander *vi* errāre, vagārī; (*in mind*)
ālūcinārī; **~ over** pervagārī.
wanderer *n* errō *m*, vagus *m*.
wandering *adj* errābundus, vagus
♦ *n* errātiō *f*, error *m*.
wane *vi* dēcrēscere, senēscere.
want *n* inopia *f*, indigentia *f*,
egestās *f*, pēnūria *f* (*craving*)
dēsīderium *nt*; **in ~** inops; **be in ~**
egēre ♦ *vt* (*lack*) carēre (*abl*),
egēre (*abl*), indigēre (*abl*); (*miss*)
dēsīderāre; (*wish*) velle.
wanting *adj* (*missing*) absēns;
(*defective*) vitiōsus, parum
idōneus; **be ~** deesse, dēficere
♦ *prep* sine (*abl*).
wanton *adj* lascīvus, libīdinōsus
♦ *vi* lascīvīre.
wantonly *adv* lascīvē, libīdinōsē.
war *n* bellum *nt*; **regular ~** iūstum
bellum; **fortunes of ~** fortūna
bellī; **outbreak of ~** exortum
bellum; **be at ~ with** bellum
gerere cum; **declare ~** bellum
indīcere; **discontinue ~** bellum
dēpōnere; **end ~** (*by agreement*)

compōnere; (*by victory*) cōnficere;
enter ~ bellum suscipere; **give the
command of a ~** bellum mandāre;
make ~ bellum īnferre; **prolong a
~** bellum trahere; **provoke ~**
bellum movēre; **wage ~** bellum
gerere; **wage ~ on** bellum īnferre
(*dat*) ♦ *vi* bellāre.
warble *vi* canere, cantāre.
warbling *adj* garrulus, canōrus ♦ *n*
cantus *m*.
war cry *n* clāmor *m*.
ward *n* custōdia *f*; (*person*) pupillus
m, pupilla *f*; (*of town*) regiō *f* ♦ *vt*:
~ off arcēre, dēfendere,
prōpulsāre.
warden *n* praefectus *m*.
warder *n* custōs *m*.
wardrobe *n* vestiārium *nt*.
wardship *n* tūtēla *f*.
warehouse *n* apothēca *f*.
wares *n* merx *f*, merces *fpl*.
warfare *n* bellum *nt*.
warily *adv* prōvidenter, cautē.
wariness *n* circumspectiō *f*, cautiō
f.
warlike *adj* ferōx, bellicōsus.
warm *adj* calidus; (*fig*) ācer,
studiōsus; **be ~** calēre; **become ~**
calefierī, incalēscere; **keep ~**
fovēre; **~ baths** thermae *fpl* ♦ *vt*
calefacere, tepefacere, fovēre
♦ *vi* calefierī.
warmly *adv* (*fig*) ferventer,
studiōsē.
warmth *n* calor *m*.
warn *vt* monēre, admonēre.
warning *n* (*act*) monitiō *f*;
(*particular*) monitum *nt*; (*lesson*)
documentum *nt*, exemplum *nt*.
warp *n* stāmina *ntpl* ♦ *vt*
dēprāvāre, īnflectere.
warped *adj* (*fig*) prāvus.
warrant *n* auctōritās *f* ♦ *vt*
praestāre.
warranty *n* cautiō *f*.
warrior *n* bellātor *m*, bellātrīx *f*,

míles *m.*

warship *n* nāvis longa *f.*

wart *n* verrūca *f.*

wary *adj* prōvidus, cautus, prūdēns.

wash *vt* lavāre; (*of rivers, sea*) adluere; **~ away** dīluere; **~ clean** abluere; **~ out** (*fig*) ēluere ♦ *vi* lavārī.

washbasin *n* aquālis *m.*

washing *n* lavātiō *f.*

wasp *n* vespa *f.*

waspish *adj* acerbus, stomachōsus.

waste *n* dētrīmentum *nt*, intertrīmentum *nt*; (*extravagance*) effūsiō *f*; (*of time*) iactūra *f*; (*land*) sōlitūdō *f*, vastitās *f* ♦ *adj* dēsertus, vastus; **lay ~** vastāre, populārī ♦ *vt* cōnsūmere, perdere, dissipāre; (*time*) terere, absūmere; (*with disease*) absūmere ♦ *vi*: **~ away** tābēscere, intābēscere.

wasteful *adj* prōdigus, profūsus; (*destructive*) damnōsus, perniciōsus.

wastefully *adv* prōdigē.

wasting *n* tābēs *f.*

wastrel *n* nebulō *m.*

watch *n* (*being awake*) vigilia *f*; (*sentry*) statiō *f*, excubiae *fpl*; **keep ~** excubāre; **keep ~ on, over** custōdīre, invigilāre (*dat*); **set ~** vigiliās dispōnere; **at the third ~** ad tertiam būcinam ♦ *vt* (*guard*) custōdīre; (*observe*) intuērī, observāre, spectāre ad (*+ acc*); **~ for** observāre, exspectāre; (*enemy*) īnsidiārī (*dat*); **~ closely** adservāre.

watcher *n* custōs *m.*

watchful *adj* vigilāns.

watchfully *adv* vigilanter.

watchfulness *n* vigilantia *f.*

watchman *n* custōs *m*, vigil *m.*

watchtower *n* specula *f.*

watchword *n* tessera *f*, signum *nt.*

water *n* aqua *f*; **deep ~** gurges *m*; **fresh ~** aqua dulcis; **high ~** māximus aestus; **running ~** aqua prōfluēns; **still ~** stagnum *nt*; **fetch ~** aquārī; **fetching ~** aquātiō *f*; **cold ~** frīgida *f*; **hot ~** calida *f*; **troubled ~s** (*fig*) turbidae rēs ♦ *vt* (*land*) inrigāre; (*animal*) adaquāre.

water carrier *n* aquātor *m*; (*Zodiac*) Aquārius *m.*

water clock *n* clepsydra *f.*

waterfall *n* cataracta *f.*

watering *n* aquātiō *f*; **~ place** *n* (*spa*) aquae *fpl.*

water pipe *n* fistula *f.*

watershed *n* aquārum dīvortium *nt.*

water snake *n* hydrus *m.*

water spout *n* prēstēr *m.*

watery *adj* aquōsus, ūmidus.

wattle *n* crātēs *f.*

wave *n* unda *f*, fluctus *m* ♦ *vt* agitāre, iactāre ♦ *vi* fluctuāre.

waver *vi* dubitāre, fluctuārī, nūtāre, vacillāre, labāre, inclināre.

wavering *adj* dubius, incōnstāns ♦ *n* dubitātiō *f*, fluctuātiō *f.*

wavy *adj* undātus; (*hair*) crispus.

wax *n* cēra *f* ♦ *vt* cērāre ♦ *vi* crēscere.

waxen *adj* cēreus.

waxy *adj* cērōsus.

way *n* via *f*; (*route*) iter *nt*; (*method*) modus *m*, ratiō *f*; (*habit*) mōs *m*; (*ship's*) impetus *m*; **all the ~ to, from** usque ad, ab; **by the ~** (*parenthesis*) etenim; **get in the ~ of** intervenīre (*dat*), impedīre; **get under ~** nāvem solvere; **give ~** (*structure*) labāre, (*MIL*) cēdere; **give ~ to** indulgēre (*dat*); **go out of one's ~** to **~ to do** ultrō facere; **have one's ~** imperāre; **in a ~** quōdam modō; **in this ~** ad hunc modum; **it is not my ~ to** nōn meum est

(*infin*); **lose one's ~** deerrāre;
**make ~ dē viā dēcēdere; make ~
for** cēdere (*dat*); **make one's ~ into**
sē īnsinuāre in (*acc*); **on the ~**
inter viam, in itinere; **out of the ~**
āvius, dēvius; (*fig*) recondītus;
pave the ~ for praeparāre; **put out
of the ~** tollere; **right of ~** iter;
stand in the ~ of obstāre (*dat*); **that
~ illāc; this ~** hāc; **~s and means**
opēs *fpl*, reditūs *mpl*.
wayfarer n viātor m.
waylay vt īnsidiārī (*dat*).
wayward adj protervus,
incōnstāns, levis.
waywardness n libīdō f, levitās f.
we pron nōs.
weak adj dēbilis, īnfirmus,
imbēcillus; (*health*) invalidus;
(*argument*) levis, tenuis; (*senses*)
hebes.
weaken vt dēbilitāre, īnfirmāre;
(*resistance*) frangere, labefactāre
♦ vi imminuī, labāre.
weakling n imbēcillus m.
weakly adj invalidus, aeger ♦ adv
īnfirmē.
weak-minded adj mollis.
weakness n dēbilitās f, īnfirmitās
f; (*of argument*) levitās f; (*of mind*)
mollitia f, imbēcillitās f; (*flaw*)
vitium nt; **have a ~ for** dēlectārī
(*abl*).
weal n salūs f, rēs f; (*mark of blow*)
vībex f; **the common ~** rēs pūblica
f.
wealth n dīvitiae *fpl*, opēs *fpl*; **a ~
of** cōpia f, abundantia f.
wealthy adj dīves, opulentus,
locuplēs, beātus; **make ~**
locuplētāre, dītāre; **very ~**
praedīves.
wean vt lacte dēpellere; (*fig*)
dēdocēre.
weapon n tēlum nt.
wear n (*dress*) habitus m; **~ and
tear** intertrīmentum nt ♦ vt

gerere, gestāre; (*rub*) terere,
conterere; **~ out** cōnficere ♦ vi
dūrāre; **~ off** minuī.
wearily adv cum lassitūdine,
languidē.
weariness n fatīgātiō f, lassitūdō f;
(*of*) taedium nt.
wearisome adj molestus,
operōsus, labōriōsus.
weary adj lassus, fessus, dēfessus,
fatīgātus ♦ vt fatīgāre; **I am weary
of** me taedet (+ *gen*).
weasel n mustēla f.
weather n tempestās f, caelum nt;
fine ~ serēnitās f ♦ vt superāre.
weather-beaten adj tempestāte
dūrātus.
weave vt texere.
weaver n textor m, textrīx f.
web n (*on loom*) tēla f; (*spider's*)
arāneum nt.
wed vt (*a wife*) dūcere; (*a husband*)
nūbere (*dat*).
wedding n nūptiae *fpl*.
wedge n cuneus m ♦ vt cuneāre.
wedlock n mātrimōnium nt.
weed n inūtilis herba f ♦ vt
runcāre.
weedy adj exīlis.
week n hebdomas f.
ween vt arbitrārī, putāre.
weep vi flēre, lacrimārī; **~ for**
dēflēre, dēplōrāre.
weeping n flētus m ♦ lacrimae *fpl*.
weevil n curculiō m.
weft n subtēmen nt; (*web*) tēla f.
weigh vt pendere, exāmināre;
(*anchor*) tollere; (*thought*)
ponderāre; **~ down** dēgravāre,
opprimere; **~ out** expendere ♦ vi
pendere.
weight n pondus nt; (*influence*)
auctōritās f, mōmentum nt;
(*burden*) onus nt; **have great ~** (*fig*)
multum valēre; **he is worth his ~
in gold** aurō contrā cōnstat.
weightily adv graviter.

weightiness n gravitās f.

weighty adj gravis.

weir n mōlēs f.

weird adj mōnstruōsus ♦ n fātum nt.

welcome adj grātus, exspectātus, acceptus ♦ n salūtatiō f ♦ vt excipere, salvēre iubēre ♦ interj salvē, salvēte.

welfare n salūs f.

well n puteus m; (spring) fōns m ♦ vi scatēre ♦ adj salvus, sānus, valēns; **be ~** valēre ♦ adv bene, probē; (transition) age ♦ interj (concession) estō; (surprise) heia; **~ and good** estō; **~ begun is half done** dimidium factī quī coepit habet; **~ done!** probē!; **~ met** opportūnē venis; **~ on in years** aetāte prōvectus; **all is ~** bene habet; **as ~** etiam; **as ~ as** cum ... tum, et ... et; **let ~ alone** quiēta nōn movēre; **take ~** in bonam partem accipere; **wish ~** favēre (dat); **you may ~ say** iūre dīcis; **you might as ~ say** illud potius dīcās.

well-advised adj prūdēns.

well-behaved adj modestus.

wellbeing n salūs f.

well-bred adj generōsus, līberālis.

well-disposed adj benevolus, amīcus.

well-informed adj ērudītus.

well-judged adj ēlegāns.

well-knit adj dēnsus.

well-known adj nōtus, nōbilis; (saying) trītus.

well-nigh adv paene.

well-off adj beātus, fortūnātus; **you are ~** bene est tibī.

well-read adj litterātus.

well-timed adj opportūnus.

well-to-do adj beātus, dīves.

well-tried adj probātus.

well-turned adj rotundus.

well-versed adj perītus, expertus.

well-wisher n amīcus m, benevolēns m.

well-worn adj trītus.

welter n turba f ♦ vi miscērī, turbārī; (wallow) volūtārī.

wench n muliercula f.

wend vt: **~ one's way** īre, sē ferre.

west n occidēns m, sōlis occāsus m ♦ adj occidentālis.

westerly, western adj occidentālis.

westwards adv ad occidentem.

west wind n Favōnius m.

wet adj ūmidus, madidus; **be ~** madēre; **~ weather** pluvia f ♦ vt madefacere.

wether n vervēx m.

wet nurse n nūtrīx f.

whack n ictus m, plāga f ♦ vt pulsāre, verberāre.

whale n bālaena f.

wharf n crepīdō f.

what pron (interrog) quid; (adj) quī; (relat) id quod, ea quae; **~ kind of?** quālis.

whatever, whatsoever pron quidquid, quodcumque; (adj) quīcumque.

wheat n trīticum nt.

wheaten adj trīticeus.

wheedle vt blandīrī, pellicere.

wheedling adj blandus ♦ n blanditiae fpl.

wheel n rota f ♦ vt flectere, circumagere ♦ vi sē flectere, circumagī.

wheelbarrow n pabō m.

wheeze vi anhēlāre.

whelm vt obruere.

whelp n catulus m.

when adv (interrog) quandō, quō tempore ♦ conj (time) cum (+ subj), ubī (+ indic).

whence adv unde.

whenever conj quotiēns, utcumque, quandocumque, cum (+ perf/pluperf indic); (as soon as) simul āc.

where adv ubī; (to) quō; ~ .. **from unde**; ~ **to** quo (interrog and relat).

whereabouts n locus m; **your** ~ quō in locō sīs.

whereas conj quŏniam; (contrast) not expressed.

whereby adv quō pāctŏ, quō.

wherefore adv (interrog) quārē, cūr; (relat) quamobrem, quāpropter.

wherein adv in quō, in quā.

whereof adv cūius, cūius reī.

whereon adv in quō, in quā.

whereupon adv quō factŏ.

wherever conj ubiubī, quācumque.

wherewith adv quī, cum quō.

wherry n linter f.

whet vt acuere; (fig) exacuere.

whether conj (interrog) utrum; (single question) num; (condition) sīve, seu; ~ .. **or** utrum .. an (in indir question); (in cond clauses) seu (sive) .. seu (sive); ~ .. **not** utrum .. necne (in indir question).

whetstone n cōs f.

whey n serum nt.

which pron (interrog) quis; (of two) uter; (relat) quī ♦ adj quī; (of two) uter.

whichever pron quisquis, quīcumque; (of two) utercumque.

whiff n odor m.

while n spatium nt, tempus nt; **for a** ~ parumper; **a little** ~ paulisper; **a long** ~ diū; **it is worth** ~ expedit, operae pretium est; **once in a** ~ interdum ♦ conj dum + pres indic (= during the time that); + imperf indic (= all the time that) ♦ vt: ~ **away** dēgere, fallere.

whilst conj dum.

whim n libīdŏ f, arbitrium nt.

whimper n vāgītus m ♦ vi vāgīre.

whimsical adj facētus, īnsolēns.

whimsically adv facētē.

whimsy n dēliciae fpl, facētiae fpl.

whine n quīritātiŏ f ♦ vi quīritāre.

whinny n hinnītus m ♦ vi hinnīre.

whip n flagellum nt, flagrum nt ♦ vt flagellāre, verberāre.

whirl n turbō m ♦ vt intorquēre contorquēre ♦ vi contorquērī.

whirlpool n vertex m, vŏragŏ f.

whirlwind n turbō m.

whisper n susurrus m ♦ vt, vi susurrāre, īnsusurrāre; ~ **to** ad aurem admonēre, in aurem dīcere.

whistle n (instrument) fistula f; (sound) sībilus m ♦ vi sībilāre.

white adj albus; (shining) candidus; (complexion) pallidus; (hair) cānus; **turn** ~ exalbēscere ♦ n album nt; (egg) albūmen nt.

white-hot adj: **to be** ~ excandēscere.

whiten vt dealbāre ♦ vi albēscere.

whiteness n candor m.

whitewash n albārium nt ♦ vt dealbāre.

whither adv quō; ~**soever** quōcumque.

whitish adj albulus.

whizz n strīdor m ♦ vi strīdere, increpāre.

who pron quis; (relat) quī.

whoever pron quisquis, quīcumque.

whole adj tōtus, cūnctus; (unhurt) integer, incolumis; (healthy) sānus ♦ n tōtum nt, summa f, ūniversitās f; **on the** ~ plērumque.

wholehearted adj studiŏsissimus.

wholeheartedly adv ex animō.

wholesale adj māgnus, cŏpiŏsus; ~ **business** negōtiātiŏ f; ~ **dealer** mercātor m, negōtiātor m.

wholesome adj salūtāris, salūbris.

wholesomeness n salūbritās f.

wholly adv omnīnŏ, tōtus.

whoop n ululātus m ♦ vi ululāre.

whose pron cūius.

why adv cūr, quārē, quamobrem

qua de causa.

wick n mergulus m.

wicked adj improbus, scelestus; (to gods, kin, country) impius.

wickedly adv improbē, scelestē, impiē.

wickedness n improbitās f, scelus nt, impietās f.

wicker adj vīmineus ♦ n vīmen nt.

wide adj lātus, amplus; **be ~ of** aberrāre ab ♦ adv lātē; **far and ~** longē lātēque.

widely adv lātē; (among people) vulgō.

widen vt laxāre, dīlātāre.

widespread adj effūsus, vulgātus.

widow n vidua f.

widowed adj viduus, orbus.

widower n viduus m.

widowhood n viduitās f.

width n lātitūdō f, amplitūdō f.

wield vt tractāre, gestāre, ūtī (abl).

wife n uxor f.

wifely adj uxōrius.

wig n capillāmentum nt.

wild adj ferus, indomitus, saevus; (plant) agrestis; (land) incultus; (temper) furibundus, impotens, āmēns; (shot) temerārius; **~ state** feritās f.

wild beast n fera f.

wilderness n sōlitūdō f, loca dēserta ntpl.

wildly adv saevē.

wildness n feritās f.

wile n dolus m, ars f, fraus f.

wilful adj pervicāx, contumāx; (action) cōnsultus.

wilfully adv contumāciter, cōnsultō.

wilfulness n pervicācia f, libīdō f.

wilily adv astūtē, vafrē.

wiliness n astūtia f.

will n (faculty) voluntās f, animus m; (intent) cōnsilium nt; (decision) arbitrium nt; (of gods) nūtus m; (document) testāmentum nt; **~ and**

pleasure libīdō f; **against one's ~** invītus; **at ~** ad libīdinem suam; **good ~** studium nt; **ill ~** invidia f; **with a ~** summō studiō; **without making a ~** intestātō ♦ vt velle, fut; (legacy) lēgāre; **as you ~** ut libet.

willing adj libēns, parātus; **be ~** velle; **not be ~** nōlle.

willingly adv libenter.

willingness n voluntās f.

willow n salix f ♦ adj salignus.

willowy adj gracilis.

wilt vi flaccēscere.

wily adj astūtus, vafer, callidus.

wimple n mitra f.

win vt ferre, obtinēre, adipisci; (after effort) auferre; (victory) reportāre; (fame) cōnsequī, adsequī; (friends) sibī conciliāre; **~ the day** vincere; **~ over** dēlēnīre, conciliāre ♦ vi vincere.

wince vi resilīre.

winch n māchina f, sucula f.

wind n ventus m; (north) aquilō m; (south) auster m; (east) eurus m; (west) favōnius m; **I get ~ of** subolet mihī; **run before the ~** vento sē dare; **take the ~ out of one's sails** suō sibī gladiō iugulāre; **there is something in the ~** nescioquid olet; **which way the ~ blows** quōmodo sē rēs habeat.

wind vt torquēre; **~ round** intorquēre ♦ vi flectī, sinuāre; **~ up** (speech) perōrāre.

windbag n verbōsus m.

winded adj anhēlāns.

windfall n repentīnum bonum nt.

winding adj flexuōsus, tortuōsus ♦ n flexiō f, flexus m; **~s** pl (speech) ambāgēs fpl.

windlass n māchina f, sucula f.

window n fenestra f.

windpipe n aspera artēria f.

windward adj ad ventum conversus ♦ adv: **to ~** ventum

versus.

windy adj ventōsus.

wine n vīnum nt; (new) mustum nt; (undiluted) merum nt.

winebibber n vīnōsus m.

wine cellar n apothēca f.

wine merchant n vīnārius m.

wine press n prēlum nt.

wing n āla f; (MIL) cornū nt, āla f; (of bird) penna f; **take ~** ēvolāre; **take under one's ~** patrōnus fierī (gen), clientem habēre, in custōdiam recipere.

winged adj ālātus, pennātus, volucer.

wink n nictus m ♦ vi nictāre; **~ at** cōnīvēre (dat).

winner n victor m.

winning adj blandus, iūcundus.

winningly adv blandē, iūcundē.

winning post n mēta f.

winnings n lucra ntpl.

winnow vt ventilāre; (fig) excutere.

winnowing-fan n vannus f.

winsome adj blandus, suāvis.

winter n hiems f; (cold) brūma f ♦ adj hiemālis, hībernus ♦ vi hībernāre.

winter quarters n hīberna ntpl.

wintry adj hiemālis, hībernus.

wipe vt dētergēre; **~ away** abstergēre; **~ dry** siccāre; **~ off** dētergēre; **~ out** dēlēre; **~ the nose** ēmungere.

wire n fīlum aēneum nt.

wiry adj nervōsus.

wisdom n sapientia f; (in action) prūdentia f; (in judgment) cōnsilium nt.

wise adj sapiēns, prūdēns.

wisely adv sapienter, prūdenter.

wish n optātum nt, vōtum nt; (for something missing) dēsīderium nt; **~es** pl (greeting) salūs f ♦ vt optāre, cupere, velle; **~ for** exoptāre, expetere, dēsīderāre; **~**

good-day salvēre iubēre; **as you ~** ut libet; **I ~ I could** utinam possim.

wishful adj cupidus.

wishing n optātiō f.

wisp n manipulus m.

wistful adj dēsīderī plenus.

wistfully adv cum dēsīderiō.

wistfulness n dēsīderium nt.

wit n (humour) facētiae fpl, salēs mpl; (intellect) argūtiae fpl, ingenium nt; (caustic ~ dicācitās f; **be at one's wits' end** valdē haerēre; **be out of one's ~s** dēlīrāre; **have one's ~s about one** prūdens esse; **to ~** nempe, dīcō.

witch n sāga f, strīga f.

witchcraft n veneficium nt, magicae artēs fpl.

with prep (person) cum (abl); (thing) abl; (in company) apud (acc); (fight) cum (abl), contrā (acc); **be angry ~** īrāscī (dat); **begin ~** incipere ab; **rest ~** esse penes (acc); **end ~** dēsinere in (acc); **what do you want ~ me?** quid mē vis?

withdraw vt dēdūcere, dētrahere; (fig) āvocāre; (words) retractāre ♦ vi discēdere, abscēdere, sē recipere, sē subdūcere.

withdrawal n (MIL) receptus m.

wither vt torrēre ♦ vi dēflōrēscere.

withered adj marcidus.

withhold vt abstinēre, retinēre, supprimere.

within adv intus, intrā; (motion) intrō ♦ prep intrā (acc), in (abl).

without adv extrā, forīs; **from ~** extrīnsecus; **be ~** vacāre (abl), carēre (abl) ♦ prep sine (abl), expers (gen); **I admire ~ fearing** ita laudō ut nōn timeam; **~ breaking the law** salvīs lēgibus; **you cannot see ~ admiring** vidēre nōn potes quīn laudēs; **you cannot appreciate ~ seeing for yourself** aestimāre nōn potes nisi ipse

vīderis; ~ **doubt** sine dubiō; ~ **the
order of** iniūssū (gen); ~ **striking a
blow** rē integrā.

withstand vt resistere (dat),
obsistere (dat); (attack) ferre,
sustinēre.

withy n vīmen nt.

witless adj excors, ineptus, stultus.

witness n (person) testis m/f; (to a
document) obsignātor m;
(spectator) arbiter m; (evidence)
testimōnium nt; **call as ~**
antestārī; **bear ~** testificārī; **call to
~ testārī ♦** vt testificārī; (see)
vidēre, intuērī.

witnessing n testificātiō f.

witticism n dictum nt; ~**s** pl
facētiae fpl.

wittily adv facētē, salsē.

wittingly adv sciēns.

witty adj facētus, argūtus, salsus;
(caustic) dicāx.

wizard n magus m, venēficus m.

wizardry n magicae artēs fpl.

wizened adj marcidus.

woad n vitrum nt.

wobble vi titubāre; (structure)
labāre.

woe n luctus m, dolor m, aerumna
f; ~**s** pl mala ntpl, calamitātēs fpl;
~ **to** vae (dat).

woeful adj tristis, maestus,
aerumnōsus.

woefully adv triste, miserē.

wolf n lupus m, lupa f; ~**'s** lupīnus.

woman n fēmina f, mulier f; **old ~**
anus f; **married ~** mātrōna f; ~**'s**
muliebris.

womanish adj muliebris,
effēminātus.

womanly adj muliebris.

womb n uterus m.

wonder n admīrātiō f; (of a thing)
admīrābilitās f; (thing) mīrāculum
nt, mīrum nt, portentum nt ♦ vi
mīrārī; ~ **at** admīrārī, dēmīrārī.

wonderful adj mīrus, mīrābilis,

vīderis; ~ **to relate** mīrābile
dictū.

wonderfully adv mīrē, mīrābiliter,
mīrum quantum.

wonderfulness n admīrābilitās f.

wondering adj mīrābundus.

wonderment n admīrātiō f.

wondrous adj mīrus, mīrābilis.

wont n mōs m, cōnsuētūdō f.

wonted adj solitus.

woo vt petere.

wood n silva f, nemus nt; (material)
lignum nt; **gather ~** lignārī; **touch
~!** absit verbō invidia ♦ adj
ligneus.

woodcutter n lignātor m.

wooded adj silvestris, saltuōsus.

wooden adj ligneus.

woodland n silvae fpl ♦ adj
silvestris.

woodman n lignātor m.

wood nymph n dryas f.

woodpecker n pīcus m.

wood pigeon n palumbēs m/f.

woodwork n tigna ntpl.

woodworker n faber tignārius m.

woody adj silvestris, silvōsus.

wooer n procus m.

woof n subtēmen nt.

wool n lāna f.

woollen adj lāneus.

woolly adj lānātus.

word n verbum nt; (spoken) vōx f;
(message) nūntius m; (promise)
fidēs f; (term) vocābulum nt; ~ **for
~** ad verbum, verbum ē verbō; **a ~
with you!** paucīs tē volō!; **break
one's ~** fidem fallere; **bring back
~** renūntiāre; **by ~ of mouth** ōre;
fair ~ blanditiae fpl; **give one's ~**
fidem dare; **have a ~ with** colloquī
cum; **have ~s with** iūrgāre cum;
have a good ~ for laudāre; **in a ~**
ūnō verbō, dēnique; **keep one's ~**
fidem praestāre; **of few ~s**
taciturnus; **take at one's ~**
crēdere (dat).

wording n verba ntpl.
wordy adj verbōsus.
work n (energy) labor m, opera f; (task) opus nt; (thing done) opus nt; (book) liber m; (trouble) negōtium nt; **-s** (MIL) opera ntpl; (mechanism) māchinātiō f; (place) officīna f ♦ vi labōrāre ♦ vt (men) exercēre; (metal) fabricārī; (soil) subigere; (results) efficere; **~ at** ēlabōrāre; **~ in** admiscēre; **~ off** exhaurīre; **~ out** ēlabōrāre; **~ up** (emotion) efferre; **~ one's way up** prōficere ♦ vi gerī.
workaday adj cottīdiānus.
workhouse n ergastulum nt.
working n (mechanism) māchinātiō f; (soil) cultus m.
workman n (unskilled) operārius m; (skilled) opifex m, faber m; **workmen** operae fpl.
workmanship n ars f, artificium nt.
workshop n fabrica f, officīna f.
world n (universe) mundus m; (earth) orbis terrārum m; (nature) rērum nātūra f; (mankind) hominēs mpl; (masses) vulgus nt; **of the ~** mundānus; **man of the ~** homō urbānus; **best in the ~** rērum optimus; **where in the ~** ubī gentium.
worldliness n quaestūs studium nt.
worldly adj quaestuī dēditus.
worm n vermis m ♦ vi: **~ one's way** sē īnsinuāre.
worm-eaten adj vermiculōsus.
wormwood n absinthium nt.
worn adj trītus.
worried adj sollicitus, anxius.
worry n cūra f, sollicitūdō f ♦ vi sollicitārī ♦ vt vexāre, sollicitāre; (of dogs) lacerāre.
worse adj pēior, dēterior; **grow ~** ingravēscere; **make matters ~** rem exasperāre ♦ adv pēius, dēterius.
worsen vi ingravēscere, dēterior

fierī.
worship n venerātiō f, deōrum cultus m; (rite) sacra ntpl, rēs dīvīnae fpl ♦ vt adōrāre, venerārī, colere.
worst adj pessimus, dēterrimus; **~ enemy** inimīcissimus m; **endure the ~** ultima patī; vincere.
worsted n lāna f.
worth n (value) pretium nt; (moral) dignitās f, frūgālitās f, virtūs f; (prestige) auctōritās f ♦ adj dignus; **for all one's ~** prō virīlī parte; **how much is it ~?** quantī vēnit?; **it is ~ a lot** multum valet; **it is ~ doing** operae pretium est.
worthily adv dignē, meritō.
worthiness n dignitās f.
worthless adj (person) nēquam; (thing) vīlis, inānis.
worthlessness n levitās f, nēquitia f; vīlitās f.
worthy adj dignus; (person) frūgī, honestus; **~ of** dignus (abl).
wound n vulnus nt ♦ vt vulnerāre; (feelings) offendere.
wounded adj saucius.
wrangle n iūrgium nt, rixa f ♦ vi iūrgāre, rixārī, altercārī.
wrap vt involvere, obvolvere; **~ round** intorquēre; **~ up** involvere.
wrapper n involūcrum n.
wrapping n integumentum nt.
wrath n īra f, īrācundia f.
wrathful adj īrātus.
wrathfully adv īrācundē.
wreak vt: **~ vengeance on** saevīre in (acc), ulcīscī.
wreath n corōna f, sertum nt.
wreathe vt (garland) torquēre; (object) corōnāre.
wreck n naufragium nt ♦ vt frangere, (fig) perdere; **be ~ed** naufragium facere.
wreckage n fragmenta ntpl.
wrecked adj (person) naufragus; (ship) frāctus.

wrecker n perditor m.

wren n rēgulus m.

wrench vt intorquēre, extorquēre;
~ **away** ēripere; ~ **open**
effringere.

wrest vt extorquēre.

wrestle vi luctārī.

wrestler n luctātor m, athlēta m.

wrestling n luctātiō f.

wretch n scelerātus m, nēquam
homō m; **poor** ~ miser homō m;
(pitiful) flēbilis.

wretched adj īnfēlīx, miser;
(pitiful) flēbilis.

wretchedly adv miserē.

wretchedness n miseria f;
maestitia f.

wriggle vi sē torquēre.

wriggling adj sinuōsus.

wright n faber m.

wring vt torquēre; ~ **from**
extorquēre.

wrinkle n rūga f ♦ vt corrūgāre.

wrinkled adj rūgōsus.

wrist n prīma palmae pars f.

writ n (legal) auctōritās f.

write vt scrībere; (book)
cōnscrībere; ~ **off** indūcere; ~ **on**
īnscrībere (dat); ~ **out** exscrībere,
dēscrībere; ~ **out in full**
perscrībere.

writer n (lit) scrīptor m, auctor m;
(clerk) scrība m.

writhe vi torquērī.

writing n (act) scrīptiō f; (result)
scrīptum nt.

wrong adj falsus, perversus,
prāvus; (unjust) iniūstus, inīquus;
be ~, **go** ~ errāre ♦ n iniūria f,
culpa f, noxa f, malum nt; **do** ~
peccāre, dēlinquere; **right and** ~
(moral) honesta ac turpia ntpl ♦ vt
laedere, nocēre (dat); (by deceit)
fraudāre.

wrongdoer n maleficus m,
scelerātus m.

wrongdoing n scelus nt.

wrongful adj iniūstus, iniūriōsus,

inīquus.

wrongfully adv iniūriā, iniūstē,
inīquē.

wrong-headed adj perversus.

wrong-headedness n perversitās
f.

wrongly adv falsō, dēprāvātē,
male, perperam.

wroth adj īrātus.

wrought adj factus.

wry adj dētortus; **make a** ~ **face** ōs
dūcere.

wryness n prāvitās f.

Y

yacht n phasēlus m.

yard n (court) ārea f; (measure) trēs
pedēs.

yardarm n antenna f.

yarn n fīlum nt; (story) fābula f.

yawn n hiātus m ♦ vi hiāre,
ōscitāre; (chasm) dehīscere.

ye pron vōs.

yean vt parere.

year n annus m; **every** ~ quotannīs;
for a ~ in annum; **half** ~ sēmēstre
spatium nt; **this** ~'s hōrnus; **twice**
a ~ bis annō; **two** ~**s** biennium f;
three ~**s** triennium nt; **four** ~**s**
quadriennium nt; **five** ~**s**
quīnquennium nt.

yearly adj annuus, anniversārius
♦ adv quotannīs.

yearn vi: ~ **for** dēsīderāre,
exoptāre.

yearning n dēsīderium nt.

yeast n fermentum nt.

yell n clāmor m; (of pain) ēiulātiō f
♦ vi clāmāre, ēiulāre.

yellow adj flāvus; (pale) gilvus;
(deep) fulvus; (gold) lūteus;
(saffron) croceus.

yelp n gannītus m ♦ vi gannīre.

yeoman n colōnus m.

yes adv ita vērō (est), māximē;
(correcting) immō.

yesterday adv herī ♦ n hesternus diēs m; **~'s** hesternus; **the day before ~** nudius tertius.

yet adv (contrast) tamen, nihilōminus, attamen; (time) adhūc, etiam; (with compar) etiam; **and ~** atquī, quamquam; **as ~** adhūc; **not ~** nōndum.

yew n taxus f.

yield n fructus m ♦ vt (crops) ferre, efferre; (pleasure) adferre; (concession) dare, concēdere; (surrender) dēdere ♦ vi cēdere; (surrender) sē dēdere, sē trādere; **~ to the wishes of** mōrem gerere (dat), obsequī (dat).

yielding adj (person) facilis, obsequēns; (thing) mollis ♦ n cessio f; dēditiō f.

yoke n iugum nt ♦ vt iungere, coniungere.

yokel n agrestis m.

yolk n vitellus m.

yonder adv illīc ♦ adj ille, iste.

yore n: **of ~** quondam, ōlim.

you pron tū, vōs.

young adj iuvenis, adulēscēns; (child) parvus; **~er** iūnior, nātū minor; **~est** nātū minimus ♦ n fētus m, pullus m, catulus m.

young man n iuvenis m; adulēscēns m.

youngster n puer m.

your adj tuus, vester.

yourself pron ipse.

youth n (age) iuventūs f, adulescentia f; (person) iuvenis m, adulēscēns m; (collective) iuventūs f.

youthful adj iuvenīlis, puerīlis.

youthfully adv iuvenīliter.

Z

zeal n studium nt, ārdor m.

zealot n studiōsus m, fautor m.

zealous adj studiōsus, ārdēns.

zealously adv studiōsē, ārdenter.

zenith n vertex m.

zephyr n Favōnius m.

zero n nihil nt.

zest n (taste) sapor m; (fig) gustātus m, impetus m.

zigzag n ānfrāctus m ♦ adj tortuōsus.

zither n cithara f.

zodiac n signifer orbis m.

zone n cingulus m.

ROMAN CULTURE

KEY DATES IN ROMAN HISTORY

B.C.

753	Traditional date of the founding of Rome.
510	Expulsion of the kings.
450	Twelve Tables codifying Roman Law.
390	Capture of Rome by Gaul.
338	Final subjugation of the Latin League.
281–272	War with Tarentum and Pyrrhus.
264	First Punic war – the beginning of the long struggle against Carthage.
216	Battle of Cannae.
202	Battle of Zama.
197	Romans defeat Macedonians at Cynoscephalae.
146	Destruction of Carthage.
133	Tribunate of Tiberius Gracchus.
107–100	Marius consul.
82–79	Sulla dictator.
70	First consulate of Pompey and Crassus.
63	Catiline conspiracy during consulship of Cicero.
60	"First Triumvirate" – Caesar, Pompey and Crassus.
58–51	Caesar's campaigns in Gaul.
48	Caesar defeats Pompey at Pharsalus.
44	Assassination of Caesar.
43	"Second Triumvirate – Octavian, Antony and Lepidus.
42	Battle of Philippi.
31	Battle of Actium.
27	Octavian takes the title "Augustus".

A.D.

43–45	Roman annexation of Britain.
96	The Roman Empire reaches its widest extent under the Emperor Trajan.
285	Empire divided into two parts by Diocletian.
313	Constantine legalizes Christianity.

THE SEVEN KINGS OF ANCIENT ROME

1	Romulus	4	Ancus Marcius
2	Numa Pompilius	5	Tarquinius Priscus
3	Tullus Hostilius	6	Servius Tullius
	7	Tarquinius Superbus	

NUMERALS

	Cardinal		Ordinal	
1	ūnus	I	prīmus	1st
2	duo	II	secundus, alter	2nd
3	trēs	III	tertius	3rd
4	quattuor	IV	quārtus	4th
5	quīnque	V	quīntus	5th
6	sex	VI	sextus	6th
7	septem	VII	septimus	7th
8	octō	VIII	octāvus	8th
9	novem	IX	nōnus	9th
10	decem	X	decimus	10th
11	undecim	XI	undecimus	11th
12	duodecim	XII	duodecimus	12th
13	tredecim	XIII	tertius decimus	13th
14	quattuordecim	XIV	quārtus decimus	14th
15	quīndecim	XV	quīntus decimus	15th
16	sēdecim	XVI	sextus decimus	16th
17	septendecim	XVII	septimus decimus	17th
18	duodēvīgintī	XVIII	duodēvīcēsimus	18th
19	ūndēvīgintī	XIX	ūndēvīcēsimus	19th
20	vīgintī	XX	vīcēsimus	20th
21	vīgintī ūnus	XXI	vīcēsimus prīmus	21st
28	duodētrīgintā	XXVIII	duodētrīcēsimus	28th
29	ūndētrīgintā	XXIX	ūndētrīcēsimus	29th
30	trīgintā	XXX	trīcēsimus	30th
40	quadrāgintā	XL	quadrāgēsimus	40th
50	quīnquāgintā	L	quīnquāgēsimus	50th
60	sexāgintā	LX	sexāgēsimus	60th
70	septuāgintā	LXX	septuāgēsimus	70th

80	octōgintā	LXXX	octōgēsimus	80th
90	nōnāgintā	XC	nōnāgēsimus	90th
100	centum	C	centēsimus	100th
101	centum et ūnus	CI	centēsimus prīmus	101st
122	centum vīgintī duo	CXXII	centēsimus vīcēsimus alter	122nd
200	ducentī	CC	ducentēsimus	200th
300	trecentī	CCC	trecentēsimus	300th
400	quadringentī	CCCC	quadringentēsimus	400th
500	quīngentī	D	quīngentēsimus	500th
600	sēscentī	DC	sēscentēsimus	600th
700	septingentī	DCC	septingentēsimus	700th
800	octingentī	DCCC	octingentēsimus	800th
900	nōngentī	DCCCC	nōngentēsimus	900th
1000	mīlle	M	mīllēsimus	1000th
1001	mīlle et ūnus	MI	mīllēsimus prīmus	1001st
1102	mīlle centum duo	MCII	mīllēsimus centēsimus alter	1102nd
3000	tria mīlia	MMM	ter mīllēsimus	3000th
5000	quīnque mīlia	IↃↃ	quīnquiēs mīllēsimus	5000th
10,000	decem mīlia	CCIↃↃ	deciēs mīllēsimus	10,000th
100,000	centum mīlia	CCCIↃↃↃ	centiēs mīllēsimus	100,000th
1,000,000	deciēs centēna mīlia	CCCCIↃↃↃↃ	deciēs centiēs mīllēsimus	1,000,000th

NUMERALS

	Distributive		Adverb	
1	singulī	I	semel	1st
2	bīnī	II	bis	2nd
3	ternī (trīnī)	III	ter	3rd
4	quaternī	IV	quater	4th
5	quīnī	V	quīnquiēs	5th
6	sēnī	VI	sexiēs	6th
7	septēnī	VII	septiēs	7th
8	octōnī	VIII	octiēs	8th
9	novēnī	IX	noviēs	9th
10	dēnī	X	deciēs	10th
11	undēnī	XI	undeciēs	11th
12	duodēnī	XII	duodeciēs	12th
13	ternī dēnī	XIII	ter deciēs	13th
14	quaternī dēnī	XIV	quattuordeciēs	14th
15	quīnī dēnī	XV	quīndeciēs	15th
16	sēnī dēnī	XVI	sēdeciēs	16th
17	septēnī dēnī	XVII	septiēs deciēs	17th
18	duodēvīcēnī	XVIII	duodēvīciēs	18th
19	ūndēvīcēnī	XIX	ūndēvīciēs	19th
20	vīcēnī	XX	vīciēs	20th
21	vīcēnī singulī	XXI	semel et vīciēs	21st
28	duodētrīcēnī	XXVIII	duodētrīciēs	28th
29	ūndētrīcēnī	XXIX	ūndētrīciēs	29th
30	trīcēnī	XXX	trīciēs	30th
40	quadrāgēnī	XL	quadrāgiēs	40th
50	quīnquāgēnī	L	quīnquāgiēs	50th
60	sexāgēnī	LX	sexāgiēs	60th
70	septuāgēnī	LXX	septuāgiēs	70th
80	octōgēnī	LXXX	octōgiēs	80th
90	nōnāgēnī	XC	nōnāgiēs	90th
100	centēnī	C	centiēs	100th
101	centēnī singulī	CI	semel et centiēs	101st
122	centēnī vīcēnī bīnī	CXXII	centiēs vīciēs bis	122nd

200	ducēnī	CC	ducentiēs	200th
300	trecēnī	CCC	trecentiēs	300th
400	quadringēnī	CCCC	quadringentiēs	400th
500	quīngēnī	D	quīngentiēs	500th
600	sexcēnī	DC	sexcentiēs	600th
700	septingēnī	DCC	septingentiēs	700th
800	octingēnī	DCCC	octingentiēs	800th
900	nōngēnī	DCCCC	nōngentiēs	900th
1000	singula mīlia	M	mīlliēs	1000th
1001	singula mīlia singulī	MI	semel et mīlliēs	1001st
1102	singula mīlia centēnī bīnī	MCII	mīlliēs centiēs bis	1102nd
3000	trīna mīlia	MMM	ter mīlliēs	3000th
5000	quīna mīlia	IƆƆ	quīnquiēs mīlliēs	5000th
10,000	dēna mīlia	CCIƆƆ	deciēs mīlliēs	10,000th
100,000	centēna mīlia	CCCIƆƆƆ	centiēs mīlliēs	100,000th
1,000,000	deciēs centēna mīlia	CCCCIƆƆƆƆ	mīlliēs mīlliēs	1,000,000th

DATES

MONTHS

Three days of the month have special names:

Kalendae the 1st.

Nōnae the 5th of most months, but the 7th of March, May, July and October.

> "In March, July, October, May,
> The Nones are on the 7th day."

Idūs the 13th of most months, but the 15th of March, May, July and October.

If the date is one of these three days, it is expressed in the ablative, with the adjective of the month in agreement, *e.g.*

1st January, **Kalendīs Iānuāriīs**, usually abbreviated **Kal. Ian.**

The day immediately before any of these three is expressed by **prīdiē** with the accusative, *e.g.*

4th February, **prīdiē Nōnās Februāriās**, usually abbreviated **prid. Non. Feb.**

All other dates are expressed as so many days before the next named day, and in reckoning the interval both the date and the named day are counted, *e.g.* the 11th is the 5th day before the 15th. The formula is all in the accusative, begining with the words **ante diem**, *e.g.* 11th March, **ante diem quīntum Idūs Martiās**, usually abbreviated **a.d. V Id. Mar.**

The selection of dates opposite for April and May should be a sufficient guide to the dates of any month in the year:—

APRIL		**MAY**
Kal. Apr.	1	Kal. Mai.
a.d IV Non. Apr.	2	a.d. VI Non. Mai.
a.d. III Non. Apr.	3	a.d. V Non. Mai.
prid. Non. Apr.	4	a.d. IV Non. Mai.
Non. Apr.	5	a.d. III Non. Mai.
a.d. VIII Id. Apr.	6	prid. Non. Mai.
a.d. VII Id. Apr.	7	Non. Mai.
a.d. VI Id. Apr.	8	a.d. VIII Id. Mai.
a.d. V Id. Apr.	9	a.d. VII Id. Mai.
a.d. IV Id. Apr.	10	a.d. VI Id. Mai.
a.d. III Id. Apr.	11	a.d. V Id. Mai.
prid. Id. Apr.	12	a.d. IV Id. Mai.
Id. Apr.	13	a.d. III Id. Mai.
a.d. XVIII Kal. Mai.	14	prid. Id. Mai.
a.d. XVII Kal. Mai.	15	Id. Mai.
a.d. XVI Kal. Mai.	16	a.d. XVII Kal. Iun.
a.d. XV Kal. Mai.	17	a.d. XVI Kal. Iun.
a.d. XII Kal. Mai.	20	a.d. XIII Kal. Iun.
a.d. VII Kal. Mai.	25	a.d. VIII Kal. Iun.
prid. Kal. Mai.	30	a.d. III Kal. Iun.
—	31	prid. Kal. Iun.

YEARS

A year is denoted either by giving the names of the consuls or by reckoning the number of years from the traditional date of the foundation of Rome, 753 B.C. (A date B.C. should be subtracted from 754, a date A.D. should be added to 753.)

E.g. "In the year 218 B.C.," *either* P. Cornelio Scipione Ti. Sempronio Longo coss. *or* a. u. c. DXXXVI.

MEASURES

Length

12 ūnciae	=	1 pēs
5 pedēs	=	1 passus
125 passūs	=	1 stadium
8 stadia	=	mīlle passūs

The Roman mile was about 1.48 km.

Area

100 pedēs quadrātī	=	1 scrīpulum
144 scrīpula	=	1 āctus quadrātus
2 āctūs quadrātī	=	1 iugerum
2 iugera	=	1 hērēdium
100 hērēdia	=	1 centuria

The **iugerum** was about 2529.28 square metres.

Capacity

	4 cochleāria	=	1 cyathus
	12 cyathī	=	1 sextārius
(*liquid*)	6 sextāriī	=	1 congius
	8 congiī	=	1 amphora
	20 amphorae	=	1 culleus
(*dry*)	8 sextāriī	=	1 sēmodius
	2 sēmodiī	=	1 modius

The **sextārius** was about half a litre, the **modius** about 9 litres.

Weight

4 scrīpula	=	1 sextula
6 sextulae	=	1 ūncia
12 ūnciae	=	1 lībra

The Roman lb. was about 326 gr, and the **ūncia** was therefore about 27 gr.

The twelfths of the **lībra** have the following names, which are also used to denote fractions generally, *e.g.* **hērēs ex triente**, heir to a third of an estate.

¹⁄₁₂ ūncia	⁵⁄₁₂ quīncūnx	¾ dōdrāns
⅙ sextāns	½ sēmis	⅚ dextāns
¼ quadrāns	⁷⁄₁₂ septūnx	¹¹⁄₁₂ deūnx
⅓ triēns	⅔ bēs	

MONEY

Roman

2½ assēs	=	1 sēstertius (*or* nummus)
4 sēstertii	=	1 dēnārius
25 dēnārii	=	1 aureus

The sesterce is represented by a symbol for 2½, properly II S(ēmis), *usually standardized in the form HS*. The *ntpl* **sēstertia** with the distributive numeral denotes thousands of sesterces, and the numeral adverb with the *gen pl* **sēstertium** (understanding **centēna mīlia**) means hundred thousands, *e.g.*

10,000 sesterces	=	dēna sēstertia	=	HS X̄
1,000,000 "	=	deciēs sēstertium	=	HS IX̄I

Greek

100 drachumae	=	1 mina
60 minae	=	1 talentum

GEOGRAPHICAL NAMES

The following list of geographical names and their adjectives includes both ancient and medieval Latin forms. The former are printed in Roman type, the latter in Italics. Medieval place names tend to have a variety of Latin forms, but only one has been selected in each case; occasionally both the ancient and the medieval forms have been given. Modern names which have a ready-made Latin form (*e.g.* America) have been omitted, and many names not included in this selection can be easily Latinized on the analogy of those which do appear.

Aachen	*Aquīsgrānum* nt	adj	*Aquīsgrānēnsis*
Aberdeen	*Aberdōnia* f	adj	*Aberdōnēnsis*
Abergavenny	Gobannium nt		
Aberystwith	*Aberistyvium* nt		
Adige, *River*	Athesis m		
Adriatic	Mare superum nt	adj	Hadriāticus
Aegean	Mare Aegaeum nt	adj	Aegaeus
Afghanistan	Ariāna f	adj	Ariānus
Africa	Libya f,	adj	Libycus,
	Africa f		Africānus
Agrigento	Agrigentum nt	adj	Agrigentīnus
Aisne, *River*	Axona m		
Aix-en-Provence	Aquae Sextiae fpl	adj	*Aquēnsis*
Aix-la-Chapelle	*Aquīsgrānum* nt	adj	*Aquisgrānēnsis*
Aix-Les-Bains	Aquae Grātiānae fpl		
Ajaccio	*Adiacium* nt	adj	*Adiacēnsis*
Aldborough	Isurium (nt) Brigantum		
Alexandria	Alexandrēa,		
	Alexandrīa f	adj	Alexandrīnus
Algiers	*Algerium* nt	adj	*Algerīnus*
Alps	Alpēs fpl	adj	Alpīnus
Alsace	*Alsatia* f		
Amalfi	*Amalphis* f	adj	*Amalphītānus*
Ambleside	*Galava* f		
Amiens	*Ambiānum* nt	adj	*Ambiānēnsis*

Amsterdam	*Amstelodamum* nt	adj	*Amsteloda-mēnsis*
Ancaster	Causennae *fpl*		
Angers	*Andegāvum* nt	adj	Andegāvēnsis
Anglesey	Mona *f*		
Aniene, *River*	Aniō *m*	adj	Aniēnus
Anjou	Andegāvēnsis ager *m*		
Ankara	Ancyra *f*	adj	Ancyrānus
Antibes	Antipolis *f*	adj	Antipolitānus
Antioch	Antiochīa *f*	adj	Antiochēnus
Antwerp	*Antwerpium* nt	adj	*Antwerpiēnsis*
Anzio	Antium *nt*	adj	Antiās, Antiānus
Aosta	Augusta Praetōria *f*		
Apennines	Mōns Apennīnus *m*		
Aragon	*Aragōnia f*		
Archangel	*Archangelopolis f*		
Ardennes	Arduenna *f*		
Arezzo	Ārētium *nt*	adj	Ārētīnus
Argenteuil	*Argentōlium nt*		
Argyll	*Argadia f*		
Arles	Arelās *f*	adj	Arelātēnsis
Armagh	Armācha *f*	adj	Armāchānus
Arno, *River*	Arnus *m*	adj	Arniēnsis
Arras	Atrebatēs *mpl*	adj	Atrebatēnsis
Artois	Atrebatēs *mpl*		
Assisi	Assīsium *nt*	adj	Assīsiēnsis
Athens	Athēnae *fpl*	adj	Athēniēnsis
Atlantic	Mare Atlanticum *nt*		
Augsburg	Augusta (*f*) Vindelicōrum	adj	Augustānus
Autun	Augustodūnum *nt*	adj	Augustodūnēnsis
Auvergne	Arvernī *mpl*	adj	Arvernus
Aventine	Aventīnus *m*		
Avignon	Aveniō *f*	adj	Aveniōnēnsis
Avon, *River*	Auvona *m*		
Babylon	Babylōn *f*	adj	Babylōnius
Baden-Baden	Aquae Aurēliae *fpl*		
Balearic Islands	Baliārēs Insulae *fpl*	adj	Baliāricus

742

Balkh	Bactra *ntpl*	*adj*	Bactriānus
Baltic	*Balticum Mare nt*		
Bangor	*Bangertium nt*	*adj*	*Bangertiēnsis*
Barcelona	Barcinō f	*adj*	Barcinōnēnsis
Bari	Bārium *nt*	*adj*	*Bārēnsis*
Basle	Basilēa f	*adj*	Basilēēnsis
Basques	Vasconēs *mpl*	*adj*	Vasconicus
Bath	Aquae *(fpl)* Sulis		
Bayeux	*Augustodūrum nt*		
Bayreuth	*Barūthum nt*		
Beauvais	Bellovacī *mpl*	*adj*	*Bellovacēnsis*
Beirut	Bērȳtus f	*adj*	Bērȳtius
Belgium	Belgae *mpl*	*adj*	Belgicus
Bergen	*Bergae fpl*		
Berlin	Berolīnum *nt*	*adj*	*Berolīnēnsis*
Berne	Vērona f		
Berwick	*Barvīcum nt*		
Besançon	Vesontiō m	*adj*	*Bisuntīnus*
Black Sea	Pontus (Euxīnus) *m*	*adj*	Ponticus
Bobblo	*Bobbium nt*	*adj*	*Bobbiēnsis*
Bohemia	Boiohaemī *mpl*		
Bologna	Bonōnia f	*adj*	Bonōniēnsis
Bonn	*Bonna f*		
Bordeaux	Burdigala f	*adj*	*Burdigalēnsis*
Boulogne	Bonōnia f	*adj*	Bonōniēnsis
Bourges	Avāricum *nt*	*adj*	Avāricēnsis
Brabant	*Brabantia f*		
Braganza	Brigantia f	*adj*	*Brigantiēnsis*
Brancaster	*Branodūnum nt*		
Brandenburg	Brandenburgia f	*adj*	*Brandenburgēnsis*
Bremen	Brēma f	*adj*	*Brēmēnsis*
Breslau	Bratislavia f	*adj*	*Bratislaviēnsis*
Brindisi	Brundisium *nt*	*adj.*	Brundisīnus
Bristol	Bristolium *nt*	*adj*	*Bristoliēnsis*
Britain	Britannia f	*adj*	Britannicus
Brittany	Armoricae *fpl*		
Bruges	Brugae *fpl*	*adj*	*Brugēnsis*
Brunswick	Brunsvīcum *nt*	*adj*	*Brunsvīcēnsis*

743

Brussels	*Bruxellae fpl*	*adj*	*Bruxellēnsis*
Bucharest	*Bucarestum nt*	*adj*	*Bucarestiēnsis*
Burgos	*Burgī mpl*	*adj*	*Burgitānus*
Burgundy	Burgundiōnēs *mpl*		
Cadiz	*Gādēs fpl*	*adj*	Gāditānus
Caen	*Cadomum nt*	*adj*	*Cadomēnsis*
Caerleon	Isca *f*		
Caermarthen	Maridūnum *nt*		
Caernarvon	Segontium *nt*		
Caerwent	Venta (*f*) Silurum		
Cagliari	Caralis *f*	*adj*	Caralītānus
Cairo	*Cairus f*		
Calais	*Calētum nt*	*adj*	*Calētanus*
Cambrai	*Camerācum nt*	*adj*	*Camerācēnsis*
Cambridge	*Cantabrigia f*	*adj*	*Cantabrigiēnsis*
Campagna	Campānia *f*	*adj*	Campānus
Cannes	*Canoē f*		
Canterbury	Durovernum *nt*,	*adj*	*Cantuāriēnsis*
	Cantuāria f		
Capri	*Capreae fpl*	*adj*	*Capreēnsis*
Cardigan	Ceretica *f*		
Carlisle	Luguvallium *nt*		
Cartagena	Carthāgō Nova *f*		
Carthage	*Carthāgō f*	*adj*	*Carthāginiēnsis*
Caspian Sea	Mare Caspium *nt*		
Cevennes	Gebenna *f*	*adj*	Gebennicus
Ceylon	Tāprobanē *f*		
Champagne	*Campānia f*	*adj*	*Campānicus*
Chartres	Carnūtēs *mpl*	*adj*	Carnōtēnus
Chelmsford	Caesaromagus *m*		
Cherbourg	*Caesaris burgus m*		
Chester	Deva *f*		
Chichester	Rēgnum *nt*		
China	Sēres *mpl*	*adj*	Sēricus
Cirencester	Corinium (*nt*) Dobunōrum		
Clairvaux	*Clāra Vallis f*	*adj*	*Clāravallēnsis*
Clermont	Nemossus *f*		

744

Cluny	Clīniacum *nt*	*adj*	Clīniacēnsis
Clyde, *River*	Clōta *f*		
Colchester	Camulodūnum *nt*		
Cologne	Colōnia Agrippīna *f*	*adj*	Colōniēnsis
Como, *Lake*	Lārius *m*	*adj*	Lārius
Constance, *Lake*	Lacus Brigantīnus *m*		
Copenhagen	Hafnia *f*		
Corbridge	Corstopitum *nt*		
Cordoba	Corduba *f*	*adj*	Cordubēnsis
Corfu	Corcȳra *f*	*adj*	Corcȳraeus
Corinth	Corinthus *f*	*ndj*	Corinthius
Cork	Corcagia *f*	*adj*	Corcagiēnsis
Cornwall	Cornubia *f*		
Cracow	Cracovia *f*	*adj*	Cracoviēnsis
Crete	Crēta *f*	*adj*	Crētēnsis, Crēticus
Cumberland	Cumbria *f*		
Cyprus	Cyprus *f*	*adj*	Cyprius
Cyrene	Cȳrēnae *fpl*	*adj*	Cȳrēnaicus
Damascus	Damascus *f*	*adj*	Damascēnus
Danube, *River*	*(lower)* Ister *m*, *(upper)* Dānuvius *m*		
Dardanelles	Hellēspontus *m*	*adj*	Hellēspontius
Dee, *River*	Dēva *f*		
Denmark	Dānia *f*	*adj*	Dānicus
Derby	Derventiō *m*		
Devon	Devōnia *f*		
Dijon	Diviō *f*	*adj*	Diviōnēnsis
Dneiper, *River*	Borysthenēs *m*		
Dneister, *River*	Danaster *m*		
Don, *River* (Russian)	Tanais *m*		
Doncaster	Dānum *nt*		
Dorchester	Durnovāria *f*		
Douro, *River*	Durius *m*		
Dover	Dubrī *mpl*		
Dover, *Straits of*	Fretum Gallicum *nt*		
Dresden	Dresda *f*	*adj*	Dresdēnsis
Dublin	Dublīnum *nt*	*adj*	Dublīnēnsis

Dumbarton	*Britannodūnum* nt		
Dundee	*Taodūnum* nt		
Dunstable	*Durocobrīvae* fpl		
Durham	*Dunelmum* nt	adj	*Dunelmēnsis*
Ebro, *River*	Hibērus m		
Eden, *River*	Itūna f		
Edinburgh	*Edinburgum* nt	adj	*Edinburgēnsis*
Egypt	Aegyptus f	adj	Aegyptius
Elba	Ilva f		
Elbe, *River*	Albis m		
England	Anglia f	adj	Anglicus
Etna	Aetna f	adj	Aetnaeus
Europe	Eurōpa f	adj	Eurōpaeus
Exeter	Isca (f) Dumnoniōrum		
Fiesole	*Faesulae* fpl	adj	*Faesulānus*
Flanders	Menapiī mpl		
Florence	Flōrentia f	adj	Flōrentīnus
Fontainebleau	*Bellofontānum* nt		
Forth, *River*	Bodotria f		
France	Gallia f	adj	Gallicus
Frankfurt	*Francofurtum* nt		
Frejus	Forum (nt) Iūliī	adj	Foroiūliēnsis
Friesland	Frīsiī mpl	adj	Frīsius
Gallipoli	Callipolis f	adj	Callipolitānus
Galloway	*Gallovidia* f		
Ganges	Gangēs m	adj	Gangēticus
Garda, *Lake*	Bēnācus m		
Garonne, *River*	Garumna f		
Gaul	Gallia f	adj	Gallicus
Gdansk	*Gedānum* m		
Geneva	Genāva f	adj	Genāvēnsis
Geneva, *Lake*	Lemannus lacus m		
Genoa	Genua f	adj	Genuēnsis
Germany	Germānia f	adj	Germānicus
Ghent	*Gandavum* nt	adj	*Gandavēnsis*
Gibraltar	Calpē f	adj	Calpētānus
Gibraltar, *Straits of*	Fretum Gāditānum nt		
Glasgow	*Glasgua* f	adj	*Glasguēnsis*

Gloucester	Glevum *nt*		
Gothenburg	*Gothoburgum nt*		
Graz	*Graecium nt*		
Greece	Graecia f	*adj*	Graecus
Greenwich	*Grenovīcum nt*		
Grenoble	Grātiānopolis f		
Groningen	*Groninga f*		
Guadalquivir, *River*	Baetis m		
Guadiana, *River*	Anas m		
Guernsey	Sarnia f		
Hague, *The*	Haga (f) Comitis		
Halle	Halla f	*adj*	*Hallēnsis*
Hamadān	Ecbatana *ntpl*		
Hamburg	*Hamburgum nt*	*adj*	*Hamburgēn-sis*
Hanover	*Hannovera f*		
Harwich	*Harvīcum nt*		
Havre	Grātiae Portus m		
Hebrides	Ebūdae Insulae *fpl*		
Hexham	Axelodūnum *nt*		
Holland	Batāvī *mpl*	*adj*	Batāvus
Ibiza	Ebusus f	*adj*	Ebusitānus
Ilkley	Olicāna f		
Inn, *River*	Aenus m		
Ipswich	*Gippevīcum nt*		
Ireland	Hibernia f	*adj*	Hibernicus
Isar, *River*	Isara f		
Istanbul	Bȳzantium *nt*	*adj*	Bȳzantīnus
Italy	Italia f	*adj*	Italicus
Jersey	Caesarea f		
Jerusalem	Hierosolyma *ntpl*	*adj*	Hierosoly-mītānus
Jutland	Chersonnēsus Cimbrica f		
Karlsbad	*Aquae Carolīnae fpl*		
Kent	Cantium *nt*		
Kiel	*Chilonium nt*		
Koblenz	Cōnfluentēs *mpl*		
Lancaster	*Lancastria f*		

Lanchester	Longovicium *nt*		
Land's End	Bolerium Prōmunturium *nt*		
Lausanne	Lausōnium *nt*	*adj*	Lausōniēnsis
Lebanon	Libanus *m*		
Leeds	Ledesia *f*		
Leicester	Ratae *(fpl)* Coritānōrum		
Leiden	Lugdūnum *(nt)* Batāvōrum		
Leipsig	Lipsia *f*	*adj*	Lipsiēnsis
Lērida	Ilerda *f*	*adj*	Ilerdēnsis
Lichfield	Etocētum *nt*		
Limoges	Augustorītum *nt*		
Lincoln	Lindum *nt*		
Lisbon	Olisīpō *m*	*adj*	Olisīpōnēnsis
Lizard Point	Damnonium Prōmunturium *nt*		
Loire, *River*	Liger *m*	*adj*	Ligericus
Lombardy	Langobardia *f*		
London	Londinium *nt*	*adj*	Londiniēnsis
Lorraine	Lōthāringia *f*		
Lucerne	Lūceria *f*	*adj*	Lūcernēnsis
Lund	Londinium *(nt)* Gothōrum		
Lyons	Lugdūnum *nt*	*adj*	Lugdūnēnsis
Madrid	Matrītum *nt*	*adj*	Matrītēnsis
Maggiore, *Lake*	Verbannus *m*		
Main, *River*	Moenus *m*		
Mainz	Mogontiacum *nt*		
Majorca	Baliāris Māior *f*		
Malta	Melita *f*		
Man, *Isle of*	Monapia *f*		
Manchester	Mancunium *nt*		
Marmara, *Sea of*	Propontis *f*		
Marne, *River*	Māterna *f*		
Marseilles	Massilia *f*	*adj*	Massiliēnsis
Matapan	Taenarum *nt*	*adj*	Taenarius
Mediterranean	Mare internum *nt*		
Melun	Melodūnum *nt*		

Mérida	Ēmerita *f*	*adj*	Ēmeritēnsis
Messina	Messāna *f*	*adj*	Messānius
Metz	Dīvodūrum *nt*		
Meuse, *River*	Mosa *f*		
Milan	Mediōlānum *nt*	*adj*	Mediōlānēnsis
Minorca	Baliāris Minor *f*		
Modena	Mutina *f*	*adj*	Mutinēnsis
Mons	Montēs *mpl*		
Monte Cassino	Casīnum *nt*	*adj*	Casīnās
Moray	Moravia *f*		
Morocco	Maurētānia *f*	*adj*	Maurus
Moscow	Moscovia *f*		
Moselle, *River*	Mosella *f*		
Munich	Monacum *nt*	*adj*	Monacēnsis
Nantes	Namnētēs *mpl*		
Naples	Neāpolis *f*	*adj*	Neāpolītānus
Neckar, *River*	Nīcer *m*		
Newcastle	Pōns (*m*) Aeliī,	*adj*	Novocastrēnsis
	Novum Castrum *nt*		
Nice	Nīcaea *f*	*adj*	Nicaeēnsis
Nile, *River*	Nīlus *m*	*adj*	Nīlōticus
Nîmes	Nemausus *f*	*adj*	Nemausēnsis
Norway	Norvēgia *f*	*adj*	Norvēgiānus
Norwich	Nordovīcum *nt*		
Oder, *River*	Viadrus *m*		
Oporto	Portus Calēnsis *m*		
Orange	Arausiō *f*		
Orkneys	Orcades *fpl*		
Orléans	Aurēliānum *nt*	*adj*	Aurēliānēnsis
Oudenarde	Aldenarda *f*		
Oxford	Oxonia *f*	*adj*	Oxoniēnsis
Padua	Patavium *nt*	*adj*	Patavīnus
Palermo	Panormus *m*	*adj*	Panormitānus
Paris	Lutetia *f*, Parīsiī *mpl*	*adj*	Parīsiēnsis
Patras	Patrae *fpl*	*adj*	Patrēnsis
Persian Gulf	Mare Rubrum *nt*		
Piacenza	Placentia *f*	*adj*	Placentīnus
Po, *River*	Padus *m*	*adj*	Padānus

749

Poitiers	Limōnum *nt*		
Poland	Polōnia *f*		
Portsmouth	Māgnus Portus *m*		
Portugal	Lūsitānia *f*		
Pozzuoli	Puteolī *mpl*	*adj*	Puteolānus
Prague	Prāga *f*	*adj*	Prāgēnsis
Provence	Prōvincia *f*		
Pyrenees	Pȳrēnaeī montēs *mpl*		
Red Sea	Sinus Arābicus *m*		
Rheims	Dūrocortorum *nt*		
Rhine, *River*	Rhēnus *m*	*adj*	Rhēnānus
Rhodes	Rhodos *f*	*adj*	Rhodius
Rhône, *River*	Rhodanus *m*		
Richborough	Rutupiae *fpl*	*adj*	Rutupīnus
Rimini	Arīminum	*adj*	Arīminēnsis
Rochester	Dūrobrīvae *fpl*		
Rome	Rōma *f*	*adj*	Rōmānus
Rotterdam	Roterodamum *nt*	*adj*	Roterodamēnsis
Rouen	Rothomagus *f*	*adj*	Rothomagēnsis
Saar, *River*	Sangona *f*		
Salisbury	Sarisberia *f*		
Salzburg	Iuvāvum *nt*	*adj*	Salisburgēnsis
Saône, *River*	Arar *m*		
Savoy	Sabaudia *f*		
Scheldt, *River*	Scaldis *m*		
Schleswig	Slesvīcum *nt*		
Scilly Isles	Cassiterides *fpl*		
Scotland	Calēdonia *f*	*adj*	Calēdonius
Seine, *River*	Sēquana *f*		
Severn, *River*	Sabrīna *f*		
Seville	Hīspalis *f*	*adj*	Hispalēnsis
Shrewsbury	Salōpia *f*		
Sicily	Sicilia *f*	*adj*	Siculus
Sidra, *Gulf of*	Syrtis (māior) *f*		
Silchester	Callēva (*f*) Atrebatum		
Soissons	Augusta (*f*) Suessiōnum		
Solway Firth	Itūna (*f*) aestuārium		

750

Somme, *River*	Samara *f*		
Spain	Hispānia *f*	*adj*	Hispānus
St. Albans	Verulamium *nt*		
St. Andrews	Andreopolis *f*		
St. Bernard	(*Great*) Mōns Pennīnus *m*, (*Little*) Alpis Grāia *f*		
St. Gallen	*Sangallēnse coenobium nt*	*adj*	*Sangallēnsis*
St. Gotthard	Alpēs summae *fpl*		
St. Moritz	*Agaunum nt*	*adj*	Agaunēnsis
Strasbourg	Argentorātus *f*	*adj*	Argentorātēnsis
Swabia	Suēvia *f*	*adj*	Suēvicus
Sweden	Suēcia *f*	*adj*	Suēcicus
Switzerland	Helvētia *f*	*adj*	Helvēticus
Syracuse	Syrācūsae *fpl*	*adj*	Syrācūsānus
Tangier	Tingī *f*	*adj*	Tingitānus
Taranto	Tarentum *nt*	*adj*	Tarentīnus
Tarragona	Tarracō *f*	*adj*	Tarracōnēnsis
Tay, *River*	*Taus m*		
Thames, *River*	Tamesis *m*		
Thebes	Thēbae *fpl*	*adj*	Thēbānus
Tiber, *River*	Tiberis *m*	*adj*	Tiberīnus
Tivoli	Tībur *nt*	*adj*	Tīburtīnus
Toledo	Tolētum *nt*	*adj*	Tolētānus
Toulon	*Tolōna f*	*adj*	*Tolōnēnsis*
Toulouse	Tolōsa *f*	*adj*	Tolōsānus
Tours	Caesarodūnum *nt*		
Trèves, Trier	Augusta (*f*) Treverōrum		
Trieste	Tergeste *nt*	*adj*	Tergestīnus
Tripoli	Tripolis *f*	*adj*	Tripolitānus
Tunis	Tūnēs *f*	*adj*	Tūnetānus
Turin	Augusta (*f*) Taurīnōrum	*adj*	Taurīnus
Tuscany	Etrūria *f*	*adj*	Etrūscus
Tyrrhenian Sea	Mare īnferum *nt*		
Utrecht	*Ultrāiectum nt*	*adj*	*Ultrāiectēnsis*

751

Vardar, *River*	Axius *m*		
Venice	Venetī *mpl*,		
	Venetiae *fpl*	*adj*	Venetus
Verdun	Virodūnum *nt*	*adj*	*Virodūnēnsis*
Versailles	Versāliae *fpl*	*adj*	*Versāliēnsis*
Vichy	Aquae (*fpl*) Sōlis		
Vienna	Vindobona *f*	*adj*	*Vindobenēnsis*
Vosges	Vosegus *m*		
Wales	Cambria *f*		
Wallsend	Segedūnum *nt*		
Warsaw	Varsavia *f*	*adj*	*Varsaviēnsis*
Wash, The	Metaris (*m*) aestuārium		
Wear, *River*	Vedra *f*		
Weser, *River*	Visurgis *m*		
Westminster	*Westmonastērium nt*	*adj*	*Westmonastēriēnsis*
Wiesbaden	Mattiacum *nt*	*adj*	Mattiacus
Wight, *Isle of*	Vectis *f*		
Winchester	Venta (*f*) Belgārum		
Worcester	Vigornia *f*		
Worms	Vormatia *f*		
Wroxeter	Viroconium *nt*		
York	Eburācum *nt*	*adj*	Eburācēnsis
Zuider Zee	Flēvō *m*		
Zurich	*Turicum nt*	*adj*	Tigurīnus